OECD International Direct Investment Statistics 2020

OECD
BETTER POLICIES FOR BETTER LIVES

Please cite this publication as:
OECD (2021), *OECD International Direct Investment Statistics 2020*, OECD Publishing, Paris, *https://doi.org/10.1787/e6696186-en*.

ISBN 978-92-64-28288-9 (print)
ISBN 978-92-64-81407-3 (pdf)

OECD International Direct Investment Statistics
ISSN 2307-4361 (print)
ISSN 2307-437X (online)

Corrigenda to publications may be found on line at: *www.oecd.org/about/publishing/corrigenda.htm*.

Table of contents

Turkey

United Kingdom

United States

Conventional signs and abbreviations

Data in this publication are current up to 21 December 2018.

FDI flows and FDI positions are converted using average exchange rates and end of period exchange rates, respectively. Data in national currencies are available and can be accessed at: *http:/dx.doi.org/10.1787/idi-data-en.*

Signs and abbreviations

..	Not available
.	Decimal point
|	Break in series
c	Confidential data
d	Secondary confidentiality
-	Nil

Reporting and partner countries

OECD-Total	The OECD aggregate corresponds to the member country composition of the reporting period. 2010-2015: 34 member countries 2016-2017: 35 member countries, including Latvia 2018: 36 member countries, aggregate data will include Lithuania
European Union	EU27 for 2007 to 2012 and EU28 as from 2013.
ASEAN countries	Association of South-East Asian Nations. Brunei Darussalam, Indonesia, Cambodia, Lao People's Democratic Republic, Myanmar, Malaysia, Philippines, Singapore, Thailand, Viet Nam

Colombia was not an OECD Member at the time of preparation of this publication. Accordingly, Colombia does not appear in the list of OECD Members and is not included in the zone aggregates.

International comparisons

INTERNATIONAL COMPARISONS

Table 1. Foreign direct investment inflows, US dollars

Million US dollars

	2010	2011	2012	2013	2014	2015	2016	2017	2018	2019
Australia[1]	36 442	58 907	59 540	56 273	58 505	29 584	48 291	45 300	68 033	36 151
Austria[2]	2 728	10 820	4 003	5 813	4 800	1 295	-8 401	14 926	5 409	846
Belgium	132 604	241 730	-26 383	-68 019	-41 191	-70 573	59 185	-706	30 801	2 886
Canada	28 399	39 667	43 118	69 371	59 008	43 853	36 062	22 764	38 232	47 829
Chile[2]	16 020	25 565	31 662	22 020	22 793	20 508	12 249	6 129	7 736	12 499
Czech Republic[1]	6 147	2 323	8 000	3 641	5 492	465	9 814	9 518	11 010	10 109
Denmark[2]	-9 179	11 457	644	1 045	4 680	3 617	235	3 771	1 199	3 587
Estonia	1 509	1 006	1 566	771	684	36	1 058	1 938	1 497	3 091
Finland[1]	7 359	2 552	4 156	-106 |	18 548	2 110	8 576	2 858	-2 170	13 455
France[1]	13 891	31 671	16 069	34 264	2 669	45 355	23 055	24 780	38 162	33 964
Germany[1]	65 646	67 573	28 190	12 771 |	-3 200	30 534	15 618	48 538	62 034	54 061
Greece[1]	330	1 144	1 741	2 817	2 683	1 268	2 762	3 477	3 971	5 019
Hungary[2]	2 355	6 553	14 625	3 587	7 967	-14 545	-5 439	3 514	6 410	3 885
Iceland[2]	245	1 107	1 025	397	447	709	-427	-41	-382	-301
Ireland	42 807	23 566	48 901 |	50 585	48 186	217 820	39 377	52 722	232 723	81 102
Israel[1]	6 985	8 653	9 018	11 842	6 049	11 336	11 988	16 893	21 515	19 047
Italy[1]	9 179	34 355	93	24 267 |	23 224	19 631	28 441	23 996	37 659	18 145
Japan	-1 252	-1 757	1 732	2 303	10 622	-2 251	19 357	9 354	9 255	14 548
Korea	8 117	10 247	11 117	6 083 |	-917	3 076	7 415	12 699	13 299	9 634
Latvia[1]	420	1 469	1 113	901	896	739	254	708	968	875
Lithuania	1 020	1 801	802	574	-133	1 055	302	1 019	976	1 169
Luxembourg[2]	35 661	13 302	19 997 |	24 097	19 778	31 408	81 378	-23 157	-76 414	14 791
Mexico[2]	27 141	25 574	21 741	48 216	30 462	35 436	31 069	34 200	33 730	34 097
Netherlands[2]	-5 717	25 041	14 465	46 689	53 487	191 560	65 276	40 990	120 238	42 238
New Zealand[1]	-61	4 229	3 502	1 860	2 437	-309	2 844	2 429	2 397	4 278
Norway	17 043	20 608	16 655	-5 916 |	19 504	-2 515	-3 900	-5 922	226	6 698
Poland	12 800	15 953	12 441	3 626	17 612	13 063	16 596	9 537	16 376	10 991
Portugal[2]	1 517	5 997	8 157	8 216	4 560	9 180	5 684	6 912	7 175	11 979
Slovak Republic[1]	1 770	2 146	2 826	-604	-512	106	805	4 008	1 643	2 449
Slovenia[1]	106	1 088	339	-151	1 050	1 675	1 245	896	1 383	1 227
Spain	40 331	32 412	24 667	28 342	22 571	8 557	31 538	41 877	53 462	8 514
Sweden	141	12 946	16 349	4 125	4 032	8 449	19 153	15 903	4 218	10 115
Switzerland	28 750	25 857	28 969	646	9 352 |	84 327	150 512	110 722	-68 312	-79 075
Turkey[1]	9 086	16 136	13 743	13 565	12 973	18 978	13 653	10 962	12 846	9 290
United Kingdom	58 180	42 196	55 626	51 673	24 704	39 189	258 570	96 401	65 285	45 445
United States[1]	210 544	242 155	211 467	217 274	211 985	483 849	480 016	314 977	243 424	282 053
OECD total	**815 492**	**1 080 691**	**726 715**	**699 067**	**681 977**	**1 280 295**	**1 478 061**	**978 728**	**1 017 546**	**791 007**
European Union[3]	**466 970**	**641 684**	**335 277**	**272 314**	**282 731**	**581 157**	**674 889**	**409 042**	**632 759**	**420 805**
G20	**904 178**	**1 067 755**	**890 940**	**1 013 427**	**866 367**	**1 133 821**	**1 288 499**	**978 082**	**1 014 600**	**960 694**
of which:										
Non-OECD G20 countries	**438 805**	**501 032**	**428 504**	**477 367**	**436 332**	**386 589**	**326 953**	**334 110**	**392 643**	**375 475**
Argentina	11 333	10 840	15 324	9 822	5 065	11 759	3 260	11 517	11 873	6 663
Brazil	77 687	97 422	82 060	59 089	63 846	49 961	53 700	66 585	59 802	65 386
China	243 703	280 072	241 214	290 928	268 097	242 489	174 750	166 084	235 365	187 170
India	27 397	36 497	23 995	28 153	34 577	44 009	44 459	39 966	42 117	50 610
Indonesia	13 771	19 241	19 138	18 817	21 811	16 641	3 921	20 579	20 563	23 883
Russian Federation	31 668	36 868	30 188	53 397	29 152	11 858	37 176	25 954	13 228	32 076
Saudi Arabia	29 233	16 308	12 182	8 865	8 012	8 141	7 453	1 419	4 247	4 563
South Africa	4 015	3 785	4 403	8 296	5 772	1 729	2 235	2 007	5 447	5 125
World	**1 589 621**	**1 951 808**	**1 553 454**	**1 516 785**	**1 524 660**	**2 111 438**	**2 183 758**	**1 714 941**	**1 745 198**	**1 530 492**

| Break in series

Note: Detailed metadata at: *http://stats.oecd.org/OECDStat_Metadata/ShowMetadata.ashx?Dataset=FDI_AGGR_SUMM.*

1. Resident Special Purpose Entities (SPEs) are not present or not significant.
2. Data excludes Special Purpose Entities (SPEs).
3. EU27 for 2007 to 2012 and EU28 as from 2013.

Source: *OECD International Direct Investment Statistics (database): https://doi.org/10.1787/idi-data-en*

Table 2. Foreign direct investment outflows, US dollars

Million US dollars

	2010	2011	2012	2013	2014	2015	2016	2017	2018	2019
Australia[1]	19 803	1 716	7 889	1 441	18 184	-9 340	2 266	5 932	6 361	5 397
Austria[2]	9 548	22 004	13 060	15 598	-665	6 915	-1 323	10 679	5 680	11 041
Belgium	60 335	54 135	79 719	26 217	26 189	57 563	36 337	29 634	39 474	1 581
Canada	34 721	52 144	55 875	57 364	60 273	67 467	69 518	76 179	57 405	78 886
Chile[2]	9 461	20 252	21 225	9 315	10 847	15 171	8 070	3 558	1 940	9 904
Czech Republic[1]	1 168	-328	1 794	4 021	1 620	2 488	2 182	7 557	8 663	4 128
Denmark[2]	1 368	11 278	7 349	7 162	8 249	9 424	10 112	10 025	-370	11 404
Estonia	167	-1 455	1 054	516	42	182	486	879	58	1 987
Finland[1]	10 189	5 016	7 546	-2 307 |	1 743	-16 080	24 252	-575	11 448	4 865
France[1]	48 158	51 462	35 453	20 365	49 785	53 206	64 785	35 908	105 570	38 663
Germany[1]	125 453	78 002	62 188	39 512 |	83 968	99 003	63 599	86 333	86 190	139 274
Greece[1]	1 558	1 774	678	-785	3 015	1 578	-1 665	168	477	642
Hungary[2]	1 234	4 804	11 802	1 943	3 854	-16 118	-8 272	1 220	3 022	2 849
Iceland[2]	-2 368	18	-3 205	460	-257	-31	-1 147	-208	76	465
Ireland	22 350	-1 166	22 557 |	29 164	41 182	168 443	30 055	-2 043	9 613	-16 634
Israel[1]	7 944	7 401	2 276	3 858	4 526	10 969	14 579	7 624	6 087	8 598
Italy[1]	32 657	53 677	7 992	25 130 |	26 327	21 640	16 165	24 478	32 797	19 786
Japan	56 276	107 550	122 514	135 745	129 157	128 698	155 923	164 563	143 075	226 573
Korea	26 821	26 989	27 355	31 488 |	19 994	18 490	30 508	51 044	45 232	35 239
Latvia[1]	20	61	193	413	541	70	159	133	205	-104
Lithuania	42	750	541	132	59	377	43	80	704	143
Luxembourg[2]	20 842	9 052	805 |	45 748	41 379	59 766	27 304	10 987	-7 238	34 471
Mexico[2]	14 560	13 311	22 313	15 459	7 507	10 672	193	3 988	8 365	10 985
Netherlands[2]	69 830	35 682	515	65 284	62 419	261 283	190 570	43 484	-12 828	74 869
New Zealand[1]	716	2 682	-433	530	472	-59	196	227	426	-172
Norway	23 238	19 901	19 791	6 213 |	32 939	30 947	3 092	-7 415	11 405	4 035
Poland	6 149	1 028	2 905	-451	4 701	3 172	12 389	1 908	1 239	1 404
Portugal[2]	-10 064	13 627	-8 474	769	-3 260	4 810	879	-928	1 374	3 720
Slovak Republic[1]	946	491	-73	-313	43	6	95	1 323	291	153
Slovenia[1]	-19	200	-258	-214	275	267	290	338	281	389
Spain	38 393	45 248	-2 479	14 294	36 743	41 917	43 902	55 926	37 710	19 671
Sweden	20 364	29 912	28 977	30 279	9 162	13 045	4 703	27 367	17 839	15 553
Switzerland	85 718	48 098	43 572	38 568	-47 |	91 551	166 901	19 522	43 491	-43 722
Turkey[1]	1 469	2 330	4 106	3 536	6 681	4 813	2 953	2 625	3 602	2 971
United Kingdom	48 075	95 578	20 767	40 483	-151 368	-66 827	-37 587	142 443	41 415	-6 080
United States[1]	296 334	415 271	338 363	321 937	347 658	274 486	305 441	353 356	-169 354	118 893
OECD total	**1 088 939**	**1 236 917**	**955 642**	**996 525**	**887 836**	**1 354 182**	**1 242 470**	**1 172 009**	**546 851**	**825 047**
European Union[3]	**544 390**	**554 155**	**360 873**	**384 409**	**306 899**	**744 795**	**479 673**	**492 323**	**367 576**	**379 927**
G20	**848 876**	**1 031 158**	**812 092**	**856 529**	**815 989**	**817 607**	**919 268**	**1 167 303**	**567 769**	**883 637**
of which:										
Non-OECD G20 countries	**144 550**	**133 127**	**107 278**	**164 068**	**217 823**	**215 298**	**245 504**	**220 454**	**207 110**	**212 691**
Argentina	965	1 488	1 055	890	1 921	875	1 787	1 156	1 802	1 539
Brazil	22 060	11 062	-8 425	-478	-3 261	-11 643	-5 901	19 040	-16 336	19 031
China	57 954	48 421	64 963	72 971	123 130	174 391	216 424	138 293	143 027	136 910
India	15 968	12 608	8 553	1 765	11 686	7 514	5 047	11 090	11 418	13 141
Indonesia	2 664	7 713	5 422	6 647	7 077	5 937	-12 215	2 077	8 053	3 352
Russian Federation	41 116	48 635	28 423	70 685	64 203	27 090	26 951	34 153	35 820	22 024
Saudi Arabia	3 907	3 430	4 402	4 943	5 396	5 390	8 936	7 280	19 252	13 547
South Africa	-84	-229	2 886	6 646	7 671	5 744	4 474	7 366	4 074	3 147
World	**1 460 700**	**1 613 679**	**1 313 910**	**1 384 878**	**1 434 291**	**1 786 953**	**1 662 897**	**1 618 212**	**880 557**	**1 183 521**

| Break in series

Note: Detailed metadata at: *http://stats.oecd.org/OECDStat_Metadata/ShowMetadata.ashx?Dataset=FDI_AGGR_SUMM.*

1. Resident Special Purpose Entities (SPEs) are not present or not significant.
2. Data excludes Special Purpose Entities (SPEs).
3. EU27 for 2007 to 2012 and EU28 as from 2013.

Source: *OECD International Direct Investment Statistics (database): https://doi.org/10.1787/idi-data-en*

Table 3. Foreign direct investment inflows as a percentage of GDP

Per cent

	2010	2011	2012	2013	2014	2015	2016	2017	2018	2019
Australia[1]	2.8	3.8	3.7	3.6	4.0	2.4	3.7	3.2	4.7	2.6
Austria[2]	0.7	2.5	1.0	1.4	1.1	0.3	-2.1	3.6	1.2	0.2
Belgium	27.5	46.2	-5.3	-13.0	-7.7	-15.3	12.4	-0.1	5.7	0.5
Canada	1.8	2.2	2.4	3.8	3.3	2.8	2.4	1.4	2.2	2.7
Chile[2]	7.3	10.1	11.9	7.9	8.7	8.4	4.9	2.2	2.6	4.4
Czech Republic[1]	2.9	1.0	3.8	1.7	2.6	0.2	5.0	4.4	4.4	4.0
Denmark[2]	-2.9	3.3	0.2	0.3	1.3	1.2	0.1	1.1	0.3	1.0
Estonia	7.7	4.3	6.8	3.0	2.6	0.2	4.4	7.2	4.9	9.8
Finland[1]	3.0	0.9	1.6	0.0 |	6.7	0.9	3.6	1.1	-0.8	5.0
France[1]	0.5	1.1	0.6	1.2	0.1	1.9	0.9	1.0	1.4	1.3
Germany[1]	1.9	1.8	0.8	0.3 |	-0.1	0.9	0.5	1.3	1.6	1.4
Greece[1]	0.1	0.4	0.7	1.2	1.1	0.6	1.4	1.7	1.9	2.4
Hungary[2]	1.8	4.6	11.4	2.6	5.7	-11.6	-4.2	2.5	4.0	2.4
Iceland[2]	1.8	7.3	6.9	2.5	2.5	4.0	-2.1	-0.2	-1.5	-1.2
Ireland	19.3	9.9	21.7 |	21.2	18.6	74.7	13.1	15.5	60.3	20.3
Israel[1]	3.0	3.3	3.5	4.0	2.0	3.8	3.8	4.8	5.8	4.8
Italy[1]	0.4	1.5	0.0	1.1 |	1.1	1.1	1.5	1.2	1.8	0.9
Japan	0.0	0.0	0.0	0.0	0.2	-0.1	0.4	0.2	0.2	0.3
Korea	0.7	0.8	0.9	0.4 |	-0.1	0.2	0.5	0.8	0.8	0.6
Latvia[1]	1.8	5.1	3.9	3.0	2.9	2.7	0.9	2.3	2.8	2.6
Lithuania	2.7	4.1	1.9	1.2	-0.3	2.5	0.7	2.1	1.8	2.1
Luxembourg[2]	67.0	22.1	35.3 |	39.0	29.9	54.4	134.0	-36.1	-107.7	20.8
Mexico[2]	2.6	2.2	1.8	3.8	2.3	3.0	2.9	3.0	2.8	2.7
Netherlands[2]	-0.7	2.8	1.7	5.3	6.0	25.0	8.3	4.9	13.2	4.7
New Zealand[1]	0.0	2.5	2.0	1.0	1.2	-0.2	1.5	1.2	1.1	2.0
Norway	4.0	4.1	3.3	-1.1 |	3.9	-0.7	-1.1	-1.5	0.1	1.7
Poland	2.7	3.0	2.5	0.7	3.2	2.7	3.5	1.8	2.8	1.8
Portugal[2]	0.6	2.4	3.8	3.6	2.0	4.6	2.8	3.1	3.0	5.0
Slovak Republic[1]	2.0	2.2	3.0	-0.6	-0.5	0.1	0.9	4.2	1.6	2.3
Slovenia[1]	0.2	2.1	0.7	-0.3	2.1	3.9	2.8	1.8	2.6	2.3
Spain	2.8	2.2	1.9	2.1	1.6	0.7	2.6	3.2	3.8	0.6
Sweden	0.0	2.3	3.0	0.7	0.7	1.7	3.7	2.9	0.8	1.9
Switzerland	4.8	3.6	4.2	0.1	1.3 |	12.0	21.6	15.7	-9.3	-10.8
Turkey[1]	1.2	1.9	1.6	1.4	1.4	2.2	1.6	1.3	1.7	1.2
United Kingdom	2.3	1.6	2.1	1.9	0.8	1.3	9.6	3.6	2.3	1.6
United States[1]	1.4	1.6	1.3	1.3	1.2	2.7	2.6	1.6	1.2	1.3
OECD total	**1.8**	**2.2**	**1.5**	**1.4**	**1.4**	**2.7**	**3.1**	**1.9**	**1.9**	**1.5**
European Union[3]	**2.8**	**3.5**	**1.9**	**1.5**	**1.5**	**3.5**	**4.1**	**2.3**	**3.4**	**2.3**
G20	**1.8**	**1.9**	**1.5**	**1.7**	**1.4**	**1.9**	**2.2**	**1.5**	**1.5**	**1.4**
of which:										
Non-OECD G20 countries	**3.2**	**3.0**	**2.4**	**2.5**	**2.2**	**2.1**	**1.7**	**1.6**	**1.7**	**1.6**
Argentina	2.7	2.0	2.6	1.6	0.9	1.8	0.6	1.8	2.3	1.5
Brazil	3.5	3.7	3.3	2.4	2.6	2.8	3.0	3.2	3.1	3.6
China	4.0	3.7	2.8	3.0	2.6	2.2	1.6	1.3	1.7	1.3
India	1.6	2.0	1.3	1.5	1.7	2.1	1.9	1.5	1.6	1.8
Indonesia	1.8	2.2	2.1	2.1	2.4	1.9	0.4	2.0	2.0	2.1
Russian Federation	1.9	1.8	1.4	2.3	1.4	0.9	2.9	1.6	0.8	1.9
Saudi Arabia	5.5	2.4	1.7	1.2	1.1	1.2	1.2	0.2	0.5	0.6
South Africa	1.1	0.9	1.1	2.3	1.6	0.5	0.8	0.6	1.5	1.5

| Break in series

Note: Detailed metadata at: *http://stats.oecd.org/OECDStat_Metadata/ShowMetadata.ashx?Dataset=FDI_AGGR_SUMM.*

1. Resident Special Purpose Entities (SPEs) are not present or not significant.
2. Data excludes Special Purpose Entities (SPEs).
3. EU27 for 2007 to 2012 and EU28 as from 2013.

Source: OECD *International Direct Investment Statistics (database): https://doi.org/10.1787/idi-data-en*

Table 4. Foreign direct investment outflows as a percentage of GDP

Per cent

	2010	2011	2012	2013	2014	2015	2016	2017	2018	2019
Australia[1]	1.5	0.1	0.5	0.1	1.2	-0.7	0.2	0.4	0.4	0.4
Austria[2]	2.4	5.1	3.2	3.6	-0.2	1.8	-0.3	2.6	1.2	2.5
Belgium	12.5	10.3	16.1	5.0	4.9	12.5	7.6	5.9	7.3	0.3
Canada	2.1	2.9	3.1	3.1	3.3	4.3	4.5	4.6	3.3	4.5
Chile[2]	4.3	8.0	7.9	3.3	4.2	6.2	3.2	1.3	0.7	3.5
Czech Republic[1]	0.6	-0.1	0.9	1.9	0.8	1.3	1.1	3.5	3.5	1.6
Denmark[2]	0.4	3.3	2.2	2.1	2.3	3.1	3.2	3.0	-0.1	3.3
Estonia	0.8	-6.2	4.5	2.0	0.2	0.8	2.0	3.3	0.2	6.3
Finland[1]	4.1	1.8	2.9	-0.9 |	0.6	-6.9	10.1	-0.2	4.1	1.8
France[1]	1.8	1.8	1.3	0.7	1.7	2.2	2.6	1.4	3.8	1.4
Germany[1]	3.7	2.1	1.8	1.1 |	2.2	2.9	1.8	2.3	2.2	3.6
Greece[1]	0.5	0.6	0.3	-0.3	1.3	0.8	-0.9	0.1	0.2	0.3
Hungary[2]	0.9	3.4	9.2	1.4	2.7	-12.9	-6.4	0.9	1.9	1.7
Iceland[2]	-17.2	0.1	-21.7	2.9	-1.4	-0.2	-5.5	-0.8	0.3	1.9
Ireland	10.1	-0.5	10.0 |	12.2	15.9	57.8	10.0	-0.6	2.5	-4.2
Israel[1]	3.4	2.8	0.9	1.3	1.5	3.7	4.6	2.2	1.6	2.2
Italy[1]	1.5	2.3	0.4	1.2 |	1.2	1.2	0.9	1.2	1.6	1.0
Japan	1.0	1.7	2.0	2.6	2.7	2.9	3.2	3.4	2.9	4.5
Korea	2.3	2.2	2.1	2.3 |	1.3	1.3	2.0	3.1	2.6	2.1
Latvia[1]	0.1	0.2	0.7	1.4	1.7	0.3	0.6	0.4	0.6	-0.3
Lithuania	0.1	1.7	1.3	0.3	0.1	0.9	0.1	0.2	1.3	0.3
Luxembourg[2]	39.1	15.1	1.4 |	74.1	62.5	103.5	45.0	17.1	-10.2	48.5
Mexico[2]	1.4	1.1	1.9	1.2	0.6	0.9	0.0	0.3	0.7	0.9
Netherlands[2]	8.2	3.9	0.1	7.4	7.0	34.1	24.3	5.2	-1.4	8.3
New Zealand[1]	0.5	1.6	-0.2	0.3	0.2	0.0	0.1	0.1	0.2	-0.1
Norway	5.4	4.0	3.9	1.2 |	6.6	8.0	0.8	-1.9	2.6	1.0
Poland	1.3	0.2	0.6	-0.1	0.9	0.7	2.6	0.4	0.2	0.2
Portugal[2]	-4.2	5.6	-3.9	0.3	-1.4	2.4	0.4	-0.4	0.6	1.6
Slovak Republic[1]	1.0	0.5	-0.1	-0.3	0.0	0.0	0.1	1.4	0.3	0.1
Slovenia[1]	0.0	0.4	-0.6	-0.4	0.6	0.6	0.6	0.7	0.5	0.7
Spain	2.7	3.1	-0.2	1.1	2.7	3.5	3.6	4.3	2.7	1.4
Sweden	4.1	5.2	5.2	5.2	1.6	2.6	0.9	5.1	3.2	2.9
Switzerland	14.2	6.7	6.3	5.4	0.0 |	13.0	24.0	2.8	5.9	-6.0
Turkey[1]	0.2	0.3	0.5	0.4	0.7	0.6	0.3	0.3	0.5	0.4
United Kingdom	1.9	3.6	0.8	1.5	-4.9	-2.3	-1.4	5.3	1.4	-0.2
United States[1]	2.0	2.7	2.1	1.9	2.0	1.5	1.6	1.8	-0.8	0.6
OECD total	**2.4**	**2.5**	**2.0**	**2.0**	**1.8**	**2.9**	**2.6**	**2.3**	**1.0**	**1.5**
European Union[3]	**3.2**	**3.0**	**2.1**	**2.1**	**1.6**	**4.5**	**2.9**	**2.8**	**2.0**	**2.1**
G20	**1.7**	**1.8**	**1.4**	**1.4**	**1.3**	**1.4**	**1.5**	**1.8**	**0.8**	**1.3**
of which:										
Non-OECD G20 countries	**1.1**	**0.8**	**0.6**	**0.9**	**1.1**	**1.1**	**1.3**	**1.0**	**0.9**	**0.9**
Argentina	0.2	0.3	0.2	0.1	0.3	0.1	0.3	0.2	0.3	0.3
Brazil	1.0	0.4	-0.3	0.0	-0.1	-0.6	-0.3	0.9	-0.9	1.0
China	1.0	0.6	0.8	0.8	1.2	1.6	1.9	1.1	1.0	1.0
India	0.9	0.7	0.5	0.1	0.6	0.4	0.2	0.4	0.4	0.5
Indonesia	0.4	0.9	0.6	0.7	0.8	0.7	-1.3	0.2	0.8	0.3
Russian Federation	2.5	2.4	1.3	3.1	3.1	2.0	2.1	2.2	2.1	1.3
Saudi Arabia	0.7	0.5	0.6	0.7	0.7	0.8	1.4	1.1	2.4	1.7
South Africa	0.0	-0.1	0.7	1.8	2.2	1.8	1.5	2.1	1.1	0.9

| Break in series

Note: Detailed metadata at: *http://stats.oecd.org/OECDStat_Metadata/ShowMetadata.ashx?Dataset=FDI_AGGR_SUMM*.

1. Resident Special Purpose Entities (SPEs) are not present or not significant.
2. Data excludes Special Purpose Entities (SPEs).
3. EU27 for 2007 to 2012 and EU28 as from 2013.

Source: *OECD International Direct Investment Statistics (database)*: *https://doi.org/10.1787/idi-data-en*

Table 5. Foreign direct investment inward positions (stocks), US dollars

At year end

Million US dollars

	2010	2011	2012	2013	2014	2015	2016	2017	2018	2019
Australia[1]	527 096	554 931	615 116	568 855	582 540	566 437	611 062	699 544	701 809	714 274
Austria[2]	166 478	158 863	171 697	186 591	182 785	165 845	156 671	198 302	195 464	203 137
Belgium[2]	..	..	..	557 245	496 519	520 992	517 401	580 190	491 008	489 054
Canada	983 889	862 698	953 503	982 529	994 712	806 298	903 454	940 279	844 786	1 062 726
Chile[2]	..	..	207 298	216 519	224 928	231 213	247 684	270 773	266 028	265 763
Czech Republic[1]	128 505	120 569	136 494	134 085	121 512	116 628	121 855	155 994	164 225	171 334
Denmark[2]	96 984	98 423	98 320	74 943	95 766	91 979	99 403	115 887	116 251	121 482
Estonia	15 551	16 349	.. d	21 780	.. d	18 447	19 119	23 297	24 358	27 212
Finland[1]	..	..	..	..	..	..	..	87 215	69 534	83 269
France[1]	630 692	698 832	680 337	761 383	700 027	687 394	694 881	819 328	820 535	868 642
Germany[1]	959 200	988 551	863 410 |	955 173	862 229	795 471	805 991	996 954	967 780	1 026 802
Greece[1]	35 025	29 058	24 763	25 850	24 567	26 951	24 615	33 404	35 737	45 151
Hungary[2]	91 020	85 615	104 401	109 150	100 411	86 254	82 701	92 556	92 001	93 258
Iceland[2]	11 784	12 656	10 367	7 367	7 889	7 851	9 841	10 130	8 751	8 350
Ireland	285 572	290 479	383 164 |	414 747	429 823	890 126	840 646	1 058 012	1 048 602	1 152 313
Israel[1]	60 086	64 842	75 805	86 531	89 619	99 313	107 483	127 161	143 971	164 838
Italy[1]	328 055	355 108	363 586	364 965 |	352 482	340 477	352 626	424 743	433 366	444 485
Japan	214 890	225 785	205 754	170 713	171 664	174 146	196 614	202 441	204 524	220 785
Korea[2]	..	..	..	166 375	168 827	168 923	174 979	210 864	213 966	..
Latvia[1]	10 869	12 062	13 488	15 905	15 120	14 732	14 326	17 618	17 474	17 889
Lithuania	15 455	16 146	17 725	19 526	16 888	16 047	16 171	19 622	19 418	20 853
Luxembourg[2]	..	..	166 774	180 065	196 069	222 100	269 904	245 786	164 747	160 185
Mexico[2]	355 512	336 179	426 101	469 236	456 569	430 576	432 742	495 953	515 015	567 747
Netherlands[2]	636 049	651 352	668 530	836 716	..	1 546 194	1 565 339	1 825 814	1 824 828	1 985 951
New Zealand[1]	57 364	64 433	71 579	75 344	76 622	66 479	69 960	75 292	75 967	81 238
Norway[2]	..	..	..	190 836	173 127	147 487	147 524	145 488	153 178	161 469
Poland[2]	187 602	164 424	198 953	229 167	211 951	183 869	186 735	238 990	231 603	236 469
Portugal[2]	90 878	92 308	105 726	132 122	123 728	123 513	122 726	152 168	147 826	158 109
Slovak Republic[1]	50 327	51 978	55 118	58 022	49 738	46 016	47 592	59 510	59 857	60 951
Slovenia[1]	10 667	11 490	12 202	12 269	12 385	12 642	13 672	16 739	17 465	17 982
Spain[2]	..	..	..	638 731	587 426	553 237	554 200	676 444	706 664	724 882
Sweden[2]	..	..	..	359 801	293 526	291 338	293 910	339 860	316 601	315 807
Switzerland[2]	..	..	..	..	720 433	822 116	1 030 857	1 165 992	1 112 810	1 153 180
Turkey[1]	187 147	136 606	190 125	151 832	183 679	159 435	149 366	196 759	145 419	161 751
United Kingdom	1 068 143	1 157 485	1 440 525	1 512 648	1 581 494	1 530 652	1 460 578	1 881 501	1 930 435	2 045 078
United States[1]	3 422 293	3 498 726	3 915 804	4 948 418	5 456 888	5 731 383	6 502 750	7 756 732	7 333 453	9 398 404
OECD total	**13 298 070**	**13 561 649**	**14 873 917**	**16 530 267**	**17 150 499**	**17 920 880**	**19 087 368**	**22 536 906**	**21 804 751**	**24 850 499**
European Union[3]	**6 954 172**	**7 228 927**	**7 784 008**	**8 471 101**	**8 456 436**	**9 100 050**	**9 086 415**	**10 939 569**	**10 740 189**	**11 350 046**
G20	**12 288 373**	**12 738 372**	**13 873 082**	**15 388 334**	**15 929 595**	**15 715 732**	**17 007 643**	**19 488 052**	**18 969 678**	**21 833 605**
of which:										
Non-OECD G20 countries	**3 482 033**	**3 794 597**	**4 068 272**	**4 336 208**	**4 418 485**	**4 324 540**	**4 722 599**	**4 862 954**	**4 858 590**	**5 108 945**
Argentina	85 591	92 295	98 706	88 338	89 716	79 773	74 868	80 700	72 573	70 458
Brazil	640 330	649 126	664 208	627 789	601 490	429 843	563 539	623 021	568 741	705 031
China	1 569 604	1 906 908	2 068 000	2 331 238	2 599 102	2 696 344	2 755 147	2 725 662	2 827 064	2 796 396
India	205 603	206 373	224 987	226 549	265 838	282 617	318 320	377 287	386 172	426 940
Indonesia	160 735	184 804	211 635	230 799	217 487	222 410	249 859	231 492	225 720	235 348
Russian Federation	464 228	408 942	438 195	471 475	290 039	262 748	393 910	441 123	408 097	493 156
Saudi Arabia	176 378	186 758	199 032	207 897	215 909	224 050	231 502	227 566	231 814	236 370
South Africa	179 564	159 391	163 509	152 123	138 904	126 755	135 453	156 103	138 410	145 247
World	**20 389 259**	**21 285 226**	**23 455 362**	**25 750 263**	**26 797 315**	**27 649 446**	**29 497 867**	**34 019 073**	**33 490 659**	**37 009 197**

.. Not available; d Secondary Confidentiality; | Break in series

Note: Detailed metadata at: *http://stats.oecd.org/OECDStat_Metadata/ShowMetadata.ashx?Dataset=FDI_AGGR_SUMM*.

1. Resident Special Purpose Entities (SPEs) are not present or not significant.
2. Data excludes Special Purpose Entities (SPEs).
3. EU27 for 2007 to 2012 and EU28 as from 2013.

Source: *OECD International Direct Investment Statistics (database): https://doi.org/10.1787/idi-data-en*

Table 6. Foreign direct investment outward positions (stocks), US dollars
At year end

Million US dollars

	2010	2011	2012	2013	2014	2015	2016	2017	2018	2019
Australia[1]	449 768	418 814	476 541	456 977	467 173	416 606	435 767	503 204	497 022	579 278
Austria[2]	187 857	199 307	215 786	238 357	224 039	210 510	202 757	240 856	234 497	241 536
Belgium[2]	..	..	..	565 311	554 624	582 582	599 380	707 828	531 899	612 188
Canada	998 466	891 619	972 042	1 131 177	1 125 917	1 156 042	1 290 015	1 532 829	1 379 872	1 720 413
Chile[2]	..	..	97 193	102 396	107 027	107 589	121 419	126 478	126 343	137 601
Czech Republic[1]	14 922	13 214	17 368	20 627	18 235	18 591	19 426	32 364	41 003	45 135
Denmark[2]	165 375	176 065	183 987	157 753	167 395	164 758	169 708	205 107	209 111	217 685
Estonia	5 545	4 805	.. d	.. d	.. d	5 607	5 843	7 224	7 347	9 329
Finland[1]	..	..	..	..	..	..	..	124 607	128 744	146 329
France[1]	1 172 979	1 247 922	1 272 327	1 325 443	1 294 151	1 268 228	1 284 859	1 440 434	1 499 081	1 532 740
Germany[1]	1 383 601	1 432 696	1 344 222 |	1 448 428	1 388 804	1 362 440	1 380 580	1 671 520	1 632 912	1 773 608
Greece[1]	42 623	48 041	44 960	36 300	32 431	27 288	18 006	20 104	19 498	19 235
Hungary[2]	23 613	27 557	39 165	39 929	40 533	35 537	25 019	29 293	28 551	31 478
Iceland[2]	11 466	11 521	12 305	9 503	8 415	7 637	6 058	5 269	5 229	5 420
Ireland	340 110	330 793	412 011 |	534 765	618 800	909 668	856 582	986 846	967 868	1 085 869
Israel[1]	67 893	72 177	72 565	77 745	79 011	84 696	94 633	101 540	104 879	112 256
Italy[1]	489 654	519 660	534 980	533 906 |	477 456	456 619	456 380	547 578	554 876	557 002
Japan	831 110	955 854	1 037 700	1 118 009	1 152 007	1 228 767	1 315 221	1 497 525	1 568 766	1 769 193
Korea[2]	..	..	..	237 932	242 792	276 100	296 641	343 089	383 983	..
Latvia[1]	894	864	1 113	1 600	1 805	1 838	1 933	2 243	2 338	2 183
Lithuania	2 647	3 284	3 898	4 063	3 659	3 670	3 714	4 330	4 836	4 796
Luxembourg[2]	..	..	145 116	197 131	220 212	251 682	275 132	321 727	280 342	358 942
Mexico[2]	119 967	117 592	154 746	145 921	152 103	143 720	149 645	180 077	159 328	172 419
Netherlands[2]	1 016 108	1 036 720	1 041 826	1 186 661	..	2 183 870	2 368 469	2 694 742	2 546 526	2 806 445
New Zealand[1]	16 053	19 100	19 130	18 385	17 996	17 026	16 888	17 800	17 279	17 045
Norway[2]	..	..	..	181 736	162 028	172 432	192 013	200 887	200 999	204 930
Poland[2]	16 407	18 928	26 102	27 725	21 797	22 281	25 388	28 478	26 424	26 415
Portugal[2]	52 495	63 082	57 941	71 462	56 919	58 878	57 777	62 673	52 523	56 066
Slovak Republic[1]	3 456	4 021	4 765	4 830	2 820	2 462	2 631	4 590	4 589	4 727
Slovenia[1]	8 147	7 826	7 533	7 142	6 477	5 997	6 052	7 159	6 993	7 455
Spain[2]	..	..	..	572 343	519 308	505 765	496 605	585 615	564 600	591 381
Sweden[2]	..	..	..	414 533	377 441	338 754	.. d	372 465	382 260	397 878
Switzerland[2]	..	..	..	..	943 605	1 039 201	1 175 877	1 257 545	1 329 205	1 335 894
Turkey[1]	22 506	27 652	30 936	33 318	39 458	35 546	38 453	45 585	44 557	49 059
United Kingdom	1 686 191	1 728 556	1 693 955	1 796 164	1 681 283	1 605 446	1 567 989	1 849 781	1 788 180	1 965 930
United States[1]	4 809 587	4 514 327	5 222 874	6 254 171	6 320 124	6 059 272	6 395 424	7 865 018	6 375 672	7 649 975
OECD total	**17 023 558**	**17 088 316**	**18 331 060**	**20 233 178**	**20 358 627**	**20 908 784**	**21 851 258**	**25 679 915**	**23 768 769**	**26 695 666**
European Union[3]	**8 692 496**	**8 969 166**	**9 150 499**	**9 856 519**	**10 020 689**	**10 646 855**	**10 794 271**	**12 546 232**	**12 074 593**	**13 064 396**
G20	**13 175 620**	**13 219 879**	**14 340 313**	**16 103 602**	**16 191 740**	**16 063 869**	**17 073 310**	**20 572 305**	**19 078 021**	**21 687 200**
of which:										
Non-OECD G20 countries	**1 068 662**	**1 193 694**	**1 398 205**	**1 622 156**	**1 850 473**	**2 055 083**	**2 462 335**	**3 095 666**	**3 193 771**	**3 533 599**
Argentina	30 328	31 891	32 919	34 517	36 180	37 843	39 735	40 930	42 228	42 671
Brazil	149 333	159 809	203 897	203 799	209 993	184 909	203 186	242 964	213 261	247 605
China	339 286	443 521	551 941	691 346	922 481	1 156 046	1 423 737	1 844 990	2 001 548	2 236 641
India	96 911	109 519	118 072	119 838	132 741	139 038	144 086	155 176	166 594	179 734
Indonesia	6 672	6 204	12 401	19 350	25 396	29 351	59 134	65 928	72 765	80 727
Russian Federation	336 355	315 742	332 836	385 322	332 961	290 092	342 849	388 693	346 593	407 318
Saudi Arabia	26 528	29 958	34 359	39 303	44 699	63 121	73 973	84 437	104 613	123 904
South Africa	83 248	97 051	111 779	128 681	146 023	154 683	175 635	272 548	246 170	214 999
World	**20 257 991**	**20 673 427**	**22 478 832**	**24 816 440**	**25 494 986**	**26 445 399**	**27 975 194**	**33 013 658**	**31 209 188**	**34 552 311**

.. Not available; d Secondary Confidentiality; | Break in series

Note: Detailed metadata at: *http://stats.oecd.org/OECDStat_Metadata/ShowMetadata.ashx?Dataset=FDI_AGGR_SUMM*.

1. Resident Special Purpose Entities (SPEs) are not present or not significant.
2. Data excludes Special Purpose Entities (SPEs).
3. EU27 for 2007 to 2012 and EU28 as from 2013.

Source: OECD *International Direct Investment Statistics (database)*: *https://doi.org/10.1787/idi-data-en*

Table 7. Foreign direct investment inward positions (stocks), as a percentage of GDP

At year end

Per cent

	2010	2011	2012	2013	2014	2015	2016	2017	2018	2019
Australia[1]	40.6	35.9	38.7	36.9	39.8	45.4	46.6	49.4	48.1	51.8
Austria[2]	42.4	36.8	41.9	43.4	41.3	43.4	39.6	47.5	43.0	45.6
Belgium[2]	..	..	..	106.8	92.7	112.7	108.7	115.4	90.3	91.7
Canada	60.8	48.1	52.2	53.2	55.1	51.8	59.1	57.0	49.1	61.0
Chile[2]	..	..	77.6	77.8	86.3	94.8	98.9	97.7	89.2	94.1
Czech Republic[1]	61.5	52.5	65.4	63.3	58.0	62.0	62.1	71.4	66.0	68.3
Denmark[2]	30.1	28.6	30.1	21.8	27.1	30.4	31.7	34.9	32.6	34.7
Estonia	79.0	69.8	.. d	86.2	.. d	80.0	78.8	86.4	79.5	86.5
Finland[1]	..	..	..	..	..	..	..	34.1	25.2	31.0
France[1]	23.8	24.4	25.4	27.1	24.5	28.2	28.1	31.6	29.4	32.0
Germany[1]	28.2	26.4	24.5 |	25.6	22.2	23.7	23.2	27.1	24.4	26.6
Greece[1]	11.8	10.3	10.2	10.8	10.4	13.8	12.8	16.7	16.8	22.0
Hungary[2]	69.0	60.4	81.3	80.6	71.3	69.0	64.4	64.7	57.4	57.0
Iceland[2]	85.7	83.1	70.3	45.7	44.2	44.8	47.3	41.0	33.4	33.9
Ireland	128.5	122.1	170.3 |	173.9	165.8	305.2	280.4	311.8	271.5	289.1
Israel[1]	25.7	24.8	29.5	29.6	28.9	33.1	33.7	36.1	38.9	41.8
Italy[1]	15.4	15.5	17.4	17.0 |	16.3	18.5	18.8	21.7	20.7	22.2
Japan	3.8	3.7	3.3	3.3	3.5	4.0	4.0	4.2	4.1	4.3
Korea[2]	..	..	..	12.1	11.4	11.5	11.7	13.0	12.4	..
Latvia[1]	45.5	42.1	47.6	52.3	48.2	54.1	51.0	57.8	50.8	52.5
Lithuania	41.6	37.0	41.3	42.0	34.8	38.7	37.6	41.1	36.1	38.2
Luxembourg[2]	..	..	294.3	291.6	296.2	384.5	444.4	383.0	232.3	225.3
Mexico[2]	33.6	28.5	35.5	36.8	34.7	36.7	40.1	42.8	42.1	44.7
Netherlands[2]	75.1	72.0	79.7	95.4	..	202.0	199.6	219.0	199.6	218.9
New Zealand[1]	39.2	38.3	40.6	39.5	38.1	37.3	37.0	36.4	35.8	38.3
Norway[2]	..	..	..	36.5	34.7	38.2	40.0	36.5	35.1	39.8
Poland[2]	39.1	31.1	39.9	44.0	39.1	38.5	39.5	45.4	39.4	39.7
Portugal[2]	38.2	37.7	48.9	58.3	53.8	61.9	59.5	68.7	61.0	66.0
Slovak Republic[1]	55.7	52.4	58.3	58.7	49.1	52.0	53.0	62.3	56.6	58.0
Slovenia[1]	22.1	22.3	26.2	25.3	24.8	29.3	30.5	34.5	32.2	33.2
Spain[2]	..	..	..	47.1	42.8	46.3	45.0	51.5	49.7	52.0
Sweden[2]	..	..	..	61.3	50.4	57.7	57.0	62.8	57.0	59.4
Switzerland[2]	..	..	..	..	98.1	117.1	148.2	165.5	151.2	157.7
Turkey[1]	24.1	16.3	21.6	15.9	19.6	18.4	17.2	22.9	18.7	21.2
United Kingdom	43.0	43.5	53.3	54.3	51.6	52.2	54.2	70.7	67.6	72.2
United States[1]	22.8	22.5	24.2	29.5	31.1	31.4	34.7	39.7	35.6	43.8
OECD total	**29.4**	**27.9**	**30.7**	**33.7**	**34.2**	**37.9**	**39.5**	**44.7**	**40.9**	**46.2**
European Union[3]	**41.0**	**39.4**	**45.0**	**46.9**	**45.2**	**55.2**	**54.8**	**62.8**	**57.1**	**61.5**
G20	**24.1**	**22.6**	**24.0**	**26.0**	**26.1**	**27.0**	**28.6**	**30.8**	**28.3**	**32.0**
of which:										
Non-OECD G20 countries	**25.4**	**22.9**	**23.0**	**23.0**	**22.5**	**23.0**	**24.8**	**22.8**	**21.2**	**21.8**
Argentina	20.1	17.4	17.0	14.4	15.8	12.4	13.4	12.6	14.0	15.7
Brazil	29.0	24.8	26.9	25.4	24.5	23.9	31.4	30.2	29.7	38.3
China	25.8	25.3	24.2	24.4	24.8	24.4	24.5	22.1	20.3	19.5
India	12.0	11.3	12.3	12.2	13.0	13.4	13.9	14.2	14.2	14.9
Indonesia	21.3	20.7	23.1	25.3	24.4	25.8	26.8	22.8	21.7	21.0
Russian Federation	28.3	20.0	19.8	20.6	14.1	19.3	30.9	28.0	24.4	29.0
Saudi Arabia	33.4	27.8	27.0	27.8	28.5	34.2	35.9	33.0	29.5	29.8
South Africa	47.8	38.3	41.3	41.5	39.6	39.9	45.7	44.7	37.6	41.3

.. Not available; d Secondary Confidentiality; | Break in series

Note: Detailed metadata at: *http://stats.oecd.org/OECDStat_Metadata/ShowMetadata.ashx?Dataset=FDI_AGGR_SUMM.*

1. Resident Special Purpose Entities (SPEs) are not present or not significant.
2. Data excludes Special Purpose Entities (SPEs).
3. EU27 for 2007 to 2012 and EU28 as from 2013.

Source: OECD *International Direct Investment Statistics (database): https://doi.org/10.1787/idi-data-en*

Table 8. Foreign direct investment outward positions (stocks), as a percentage of GDP

At year end

Per cent

	2010	2011	2012	2013	2014	2015	2016	2017	2018	2019
Australia[1]	34.6	27.1	30.0	29.6	31.9	33.4	33.3	35.5	34.1	42.0
Austria[2]	47.9	46.2	52.7	55.4	50.6	55.1	51.2	57.7	51.5	54.3
Belgium[2]	..	..	..	108.3	103.6	126.0	125.9	140.8	97.8	114.8
Canada	61.7	49.7	53.2	61.3	62.4	74.3	84.4	92.9	80.1	98.8
Chile[2]	..	..	36.4	36.8	41.1	44.1	48.5	45.7	42.4	48.7
Czech Republic[1]	7.1	5.8	8.3	9.7	8.7	9.9	9.9	14.8	16.5	18.0
Denmark[2]	51.4	51.2	56.2	45.9	47.4	54.4	54.2	61.8	58.6	62.2
Estonia	28.2	20.5	.. d	.. d	.. d	24.3	24.1	26.8	24.0	29.6
Finland[1]	..	..	..	..	..	..	..	48.7	46.6	54.4
France[1]	44.3	43.6	47.4	47.1	45.3	52.0	52.0	55.5	53.8	56.4
Germany[1]	40.7	38.2	38.1 |	38.8	35.7	40.6	39.8	45.4	41.2	45.9
Greece[1]	14.3	17.0	18.6	15.2	13.8	14.0	9.3	10.0	9.2	9.4
Hungary[2]	17.9	19.4	30.5	29.5	28.8	28.4	19.5	20.5	17.8	19.3
Iceland[2]	83.4	75.7	83.4	58.9	47.1	43.6	29.1	21.3	20.0	22.0
Ireland	153.0	139.0	183.1 |	224.2	238.7	311.9	285.8	290.8	250.6	272.4
Israel[1]	29.0	27.7	28.2	26.6	25.5	28.2	29.7	28.8	28.3	28.4
Italy[1]	22.9	22.6	25.6	24.9 |	22.1	24.9	24.3	27.9	26.5	27.8
Japan	14.6	15.5	16.7	21.7	23.8	28.0	26.7	30.8	31.7	34.8
Korea[2]	..	..	..	17.4	16.4	18.8	19.8	21.1	22.3	..
Latvia[1]	3.7	3.0	3.9	5.3	5.8	6.7	6.9	7.4	6.8	6.4
Lithuania	7.1	7.5	9.1	8.7	7.5	8.9	8.6	9.1	9.0	8.8
Luxembourg[2]	..	..	256.1	319.2	332.7	435.7	453.0	501.3	395.3	504.8
Mexico[2]	11.3	10.0	12.9	11.4	11.6	12.3	13.9	15.5	13.0	13.6
Netherlands[2]	119.9	114.5	124.2	135.3	..	285.3	302.1	323.2	278.6	309.4
New Zealand[1]	11.0	11.3	10.9	9.6	8.9	9.6	8.9	8.6	8.1	8.0
Norway[2]	..	..	..	34.8	32.5	44.7	52.1	50.4	46.0	50.5
Poland[2]	3.4	3.6	5.2	5.3	4.0	4.7	5.4	5.4	4.5	4.4
Portugal[2]	22.0	25.7	26.8	31.6	24.8	29.5	28.0	28.3	21.7	23.4
Slovak Republic[1]	3.8	4.1	5.0	4.9	2.8	2.8	2.9	4.8	4.3	4.5
Slovenia[1]	16.9	15.2	16.2	14.8	13.0	13.9	13.5	14.7	12.9	13.8
Spain[2]	..	..	..	42.2	37.9	42.3	40.3	44.6	39.7	42.4
Sweden[2]	..	..	..	70.6	64.9	67.1	.. d	68.8	68.8	74.9
Switzerland[2]	..	..	..	..	128.5	148.0	169.0	178.5	180.6	182.6
Turkey[1]	2.9	3.3	3.5	3.5	4.2	4.1	4.4	5.3	5.7	6.4
United Kingdom	67.9	65.0	62.6	64.5	54.8	54.7	58.2	69.5	62.6	69.4
United States[1]	32.1	29.0	32.2	37.3	36.1	33.2	34.1	40.2	30.9	35.7
OECD total	**37.6**	**35.1**	**37.8**	**41.2**	**40.6**	**44.3**	**45.2**	**50.9**	**44.6**	**49.7**
European Union[3]	**51.2**	**48.9**	**52.9**	**54.5**	**53.5**	**64.6**	**65.1**	**72.0**	**64.1**	**70.8**
G20	**25.8**	**23.4**	**24.8**	**27.2**	**26.6**	**27.5**	**28.7**	**32.5**	**28.4**	**31.8**
of which:										
Non-OECD G20 countries	**7.8**	**7.2**	**7.9**	**8.6**	**9.4**	**10.9**	**12.9**	**14.5**	**13.9**	**15.1**
Argentina	7.1	6.0	5.7	5.6	6.4	5.9	7.1	6.4	8.1	9.5
Brazil	6.8	6.1	8.3	8.2	8.6	10.3	11.3	11.8	11.1	13.5
China	5.6	5.9	6.5	7.2	8.8	10.5	12.7	15.0	14.4	15.6
India	5.7	6.0	6.5	6.5	6.5	6.6	6.3	5.8	6.1	6.3
Indonesia	0.9	0.7	1.4	2.1	2.9	3.4	6.3	6.5	7.0	7.2
Russian Federation	20.5	15.4	15.1	16.8	16.2	21.3	26.9	24.7	20.8	24.0
Saudi Arabia	5.0	4.5	4.7	5.3	5.9	9.6	11.5	12.3	13.3	15.6
South Africa	22.2	23.3	28.2	35.1	41.6	48.7	59.3	78.0	66.8	61.2

.. Not available; d Secondary Confidentiality; | Break in series

Note: Detailed metadata at: *http://stats.oecd.org/OECDStat_Metadata/ShowMetadata.ashx?Dataset=FDI_AGGR_SUMM.*

1. Resident Special Purpose Entities (SPEs) are not present or not significant.
2. Data excludes Special Purpose Entities (SPEs).
3. EU27 for 2007 to 2012 and EU28 as from 2013.

Source: *OECD International Direct Investment Statistics (database): https://doi.org/10.1787/idi-data-en*

Table 9. Income on inward Foreign Direct Investment, US dollars

At year end

Million US dollars

	2010	2011	2012	2013	2014	2015	2016	2017	2018	2019
Australia[1]	39 894	45 666	35 683	33 996	29 806	23 884	27 454	37 311	44 029	43 575
Austria[2]	9 127	12 151	11 598	9 505	9 459	9 845	12 146	15 987	16 271	13 114
Belgium	32 634	24 464	27 461	26 890	34 389	28 819	33 268	28 057	38 348	36 579
Canada	40 075	45 524	48 209	47 319	47 786	34 640	31 001	37 274	41 599	42 323
Chile[2]	..	..	18 890	18 899	15 058	10 741	10 982	14 744	17 037	15 160
Czech Republic[1]	15 395	15 278	15 115	15 441	16 098	14 474	15 344	19 127	19 260	20 343
Denmark[2]	..	..	..	6 395	5 452	4 620	5 481	6 134	6 363	7 043
Estonia	1 639		2 053	1 818	1 846	1 916	1 385	1 591	1 737	1 921	1 955
Finland[1]	5 331	6 772	6 267	5 536		6 597	4 632	6 492	8 426	7 765	8 323
France[1]	29 143	19 745	30 551		26 824	24 900	26 923	29 484	36 341	37 510	36 509
Germany[1]	43 208	41 092	40 166	32 635		41 345	28 784	37 942	45 450	43 217	36 853
Greece[1]	-867	-2 139	-3 481	-332	522	1 157	1 150	1 452	1 552	1 868
Hungary[2]	6 714	7 955	7 530	6 828	9 484	8 855	7 682	10 335	10 574	9 340
Iceland[2]	-249	116	751		-47		-47	31	-29	40	-42	-264
Ireland	49 849	59 083	50 379		49 514	52 055	71 582	61 829	75 987	88 205	97 130
Israel[1]	4 177	3 644	6 425	5 362	3 949	5 808	5 846	5 586	6 311	7 292
Italy[1]	16 725	20 810	12 486	10 059		11 199	11 685	14 147	19 621	20 410	17 824
Japan[1]	5 771	11 013	15 278	13 031	26 287		23 858	34 242	33 302	34 221	34 800
Korea[1]	..	..	..	7 580	-1 142	2 261	4 031	3 633	4 447	12 483
Latvia[1]	188	633	1 004	1 077	1 043	1 155	1 190	1 390	1 861	1 590
Lithuania[1]	516	1 558	1 245	1 186	684	1 642	1 678	1 944	2 193	2 297
Luxembourg[2]	..	..	8 364	22 091	11 981	10 622	13 247	11 778	10 146	11 313
Mexico[2]	10 043	14 441	19 360	30 448	22 640	18 457	17 325	18 887	23 155	24 967
Netherlands[2]	190 627	208 738	181 992	202 878	246 260	203 789	212 932	200 625	250 654	239 857
New Zealand[1]	4 722	5 819	6 185	6 758	7 330	5 849	5 534	7 207	7 001	5 891
Norway	13 477	16 400	17 688	15 179		7 757	6 038	7 061	10 943	13 012	12 320
Poland[1]	16 907	17 505	16 000	18 620	21 426	18 178	20 939	21 419	23 500	22 822
Portugal[2]	7 215	2 371	4 774	3 211	4 035	4 842	5 699	6 223	8 397	7 245
Slovak Republic[1]	5 102	6 279	4 079	3 297		3 949	4 421	4 411	4 330	4 553	4 655
Slovenia[1]	301	422	265	-1	-49	1 078	1 252	1 255	1 566	1 601
Spain	31 122	30 540	22 199	28 313	24 010	22 030	23 653	28 808	31 281	26 860
Sweden	23 256	21 430	19 443	21 065	23 603	22 053	21 836	22 166	25 396	23 848
Switzerland	35 947	36 212	40 637	33 750	73 369		61 255	72 638	96 041	119 225	98 933
Turkey[1]	2 871	2 931	2 655	3 678	2 363	3 589	3 137	3 279	3 201	3 501
United Kingdom	61 503	72 858	72 338	79 526	79 045	73 586	67 864	74 333	96 727	55 925
United States[1]	157 583	178 262	172 761	184 116	187 547	166 149	162 199	193 923	226 546	228 781
OECD total	**906 552**	**979 174**	**947 386**	**986 162**	**1 063 758**	**943 936**	**987 391**	**1 112 703**	**1 298 256**	**1 224 351**
European Union[3]	..	..	..	..	..	..	..	..	..	..
G20	..	..	..	..	..	..	..	..	..	..
of which:										
Non-OECD G20 countries	..	..	..	..	..	..	..	..	..	..
Argentina	..	..	..	..	..	..	..	..	..	..
Brazil	65 373	62 427	46 366	23 326	27 980	13 915	30 359	41 474	45 740	54 051
China	..	..	..	..	..	..	..	..	..	..
India	..	..	..	..	..	..	..	..	..	..
Indonesia	..	..	..	..	..	..	..	..	..	..
Russian Federation	..	..	..	..	..	..	..	..	..	..
Saudi Arabia	..	..	..	..	..	..	..	..	..	..
South Africa	..	..	..	..	..	..	..	..	..	..
World	..	..	..	..	..	..	..	..	..	..

.. Not available; | Break in series

Note: Detailed metadata at: *http://stats.oecd.org/OECDStat_Metadata/ShowMetadata.ashx?Dataset=FDI_AGGR_SUMM*.

1. Resident Special Purpose Entities (SPEs) are not present or not significant.
2. Data excludes Special Purpose Entities (SPEs).
3. EU27 for 2007 to 2012 and EU28 as from 2013.

Source: *OECD International Direct Investment Statistics (database): https://doi.org/10.1787/idi-data-en*

INTERNATIONAL COMPARISONS

Table 10. Income on outward Foreign Direct Investment, US dollars

At year end

Million US dollars

	2010	2011	2012	2013	2014	2015	2016	2017	2018	2019
Australia[1]	16 397	19 810	20 772	19 746	19 180	13 785	13 315	14 218	16 748	16 860
Austria[2]	12 644	15 127	13 963	14 106	11 648	10 823	15 536	15 260	15 239	15 622
Belgium	25 024	9 436	23 559	26 157	34 250	29 336	33 352	28 221	37 635	36 009
Canada	37 481	44 448	45 094	44 446	47 130	41 825	40 774	54 143	62 401	64 146
Chile[2]	..	..	4 163	4 400	5 397	3 824	3 388	4 119	4 043	5 302
Czech Republic[1]	1 093	1 187	2 251	1 320	1 589	1 861	2 015	4 665	4 194	5 619
Denmark[2]	..	..	..	12 430	13 709	12 126	12 027	13 256	15 120	15 622
Estonia	403 |	535	440	652	595	364	492	485	698	691
Finland[1]	10 946	10 698	10 144	7 865 |	10 942	7 373	7 890	8 836	10 202	13 653
France[1]	77 095	76 027	78 845 |	78 541	78 586	70 308	69 441	77 145	94 515	89 877
Germany[1]	83 489	101 941	81 156	89 600 |	89 541	84 972	98 391	94 299	128 763	121 627
Greece[1]	1 047	438	1 169	795	3 114	1 801	627	1 099	694	935
Hungary[2]	992	1 273	1 710	1 437	1 687	988	1 823	2 058	1 898	2 123
Iceland[2]	-27	572	-268 |	300 |	164	283	436	302	364	314
Ireland	18 989	21 295	13 905 |	16 389	17 675	11 765	14 640	17 470	19 562	16 360
Israel[1]	3 720	4 517	4 194	4 239	5 188	6 575	6 453	7 202	7 740	6 925
Italy[1]	28 200	33 669	26 239	22 849 |	26 374	12 049	17 895	24 782	29 994	28 628
Japan[1]	38 261	58 880	68 079	68 225	100 236 |	96 359	110 503	120 205	128 407	132 230
Korea[1]	..	..	..	9 924	6 305	-124	9 055	10 259	9 631	16 721
Latvia[1]	-29	58	82	97	54	153	116	218	157	113
Lithuania[1]	60	56	100	165	120	136	146	166	303	228
Luxembourg[2]	..	..	7 192	7 974	7 795	8 094	8 295	10 458	8 825	7 163
Mexico[2]	6 567	6 904	6 779	8 076	7 332	3 430	3 014	4 764	5 227	6 262
Netherlands[2]	236 895	267 543	238 781	244 829	273 875	236 455	238 478	246 192	299 704	282 743
New Zealand[1]	594	342	679	572	707	511	741	523	373	605
Norway	10 944	8 263	11 065	8 667 |	13 770	9 078	6 772	8 408	12 160	5 383
Poland[1]	528	-262	1 332	406	1 641	719	977	2 288	2 205	2 042
Portugal[2]	3 928	2 510	2 355	2 542	2 045	2 008	2 517	3 694	4 418	2 771
Slovak Republic[1]	495	441	216	273 |	811	350	206	391	424	366
Slovenia[1]	-318	-54	-388	-552	-87	55	176	220	357	374
Spain	38 740	41 158	33 934	38 884	35 392	31 694	33 709	36 232	41 982	35 978
Sweden	34 394	33 851	32 720	34 882	36 148	26 830	25 633	30 744	34 933	34 739
Switzerland	72 271	49 358	64 148	61 238	90 614 |	85 935	86 094	100 162	104 657	91 709
Turkey[1]	681	220	98	273	314	224	202	299	957	813
United Kingdom	135 386	158 549	127 585	123 000	112 807	87 381	69 270	113 394	125 452	117 344
United States[1]	436 161	466 938	458 257	467 395	471 765	443 462	451 921	544 229	569 017	558 063
OECD total	**1 361 037**	**1 467 549**	**1 409 944**	**1 424 949**	**1 531 598**	**1 346 371**	**1 390 052**	**1 604 337**	**1 802 984**	**1 740 560**
European Union[3]	..	..	..	..	..	..	..	..	..	..
G20	..	..	..	..	..	..	..	..	..	..
of which:										
Non-OECD G20 countries	..	..	..	..	..	..	..	..	..	..
Argentina	..	..	..	..	..	..	..	..	..	..
Brazil	10 773	13 613	2 457	7 447	2 526	-2 398	7 878	17 332	4 835	16 071
China	..	..	..	..	..	..	..	..	..	..
India	..	..	..	..	..	..	..	..	..	..
Indonesia	..	..	..	..	..	..	..	..	..	..
Russian Federation	..	..	..	..	..	..	..	..	..	..
Saudi Arabia	..	..	..	..	..	..	..	..	..	..
South Africa	..	..	..	..	..	..	..	..	..	..
World	..	..	..	..	..	..	..	..	..	..

.. Not available; | Break in series

Note: Detailed metadata at: *http://stats.oecd.org/OECDStat_Metadata/ShowMetadata.ashx?Dataset=FDI_AGGR_SUMM.*

1. Resident Special Purpose Entities (SPEs) are not present or not significant.
2. Data excludes Special Purpose Entities (SPEs).
3. EU27 for 2007 to 2012 and EU28 as from 2013.

Source: *OECD International Direct Investment Statistics (database): https://doi.org/10.1787/idi-data-en*

Table 11. Income on inward Foreign Direct Investment as a percentage of GDP

At year end

Per cent

	2010	2011	2012	2013	2014	2015	2016	2017	2018	2019
Australia[1]	3.1	3.0	2.2	2.2	2.0	1.9	2.1	2.6	3.0	3.2
Austria[2]	2.3	2.8	2.8	2.2	2.1	2.6	3.1	3.8	3.6	2.9
Belgium	6.8	4.7	5.5	5.2	6.4	6.2	7.0	5.6	7.1	6.9
Canada	2.5	2.5	2.6	2.6	2.6	2.2	2.0	2.3	2.4	2.4
Chile[2]	..	..	7.1	6.8	5.8	4.4	4.4	5.3	5.7	5.4
Czech Republic[1]	7.4	6.7	7.2	7.3	7.7	7.7	7.8	8.7	7.7	8.1
Denmark[2]	..	..	..	1.9	1.5	1.5	1.8	1.8	1.8	2.0
Estonia	8.3 |	8.8	7.8	7.3	7.1	6.0	6.6	6.4	6.3	6.2
Finland[1]	2.1	2.5	2.4	2.0 |	2.4	2.0	2.7	3.3	2.8	3.1
France[1]	1.1	0.7	1.1 |	1.0	0.9	1.1	1.2	1.4	1.3	1.3
Germany[1]	1.3	1.1	1.1	0.9 |	1.1	0.9	1.1	1.2	1.1	1.0
Greece[1]	-0.3	-0.8	-1.4	-0.1	0.2	0.6	0.6	0.7	0.7	0.9
Hungary[2]	5.1	5.6	5.9	5.0	6.7	7.1	6.0	7.2	6.6	5.7
Iceland[2]	-1.8	0.8	5.1 |	-0.3 |	-0.3	0.2	-0.1	0.2	-0.2	-1.1
Ireland	22.4	24.8	22.4 |	20.8	20.1	24.5	20.6	22.4	22.8	24.4
Israel[1]	1.8	1.4	2.5	1.8	1.3	1.9	1.8	1.6	1.7	1.8
Italy[1]	0.8	0.9	0.6	0.5 |	0.5	0.6	0.8	1.0	1.0	0.9
Japan[1]	0.1	0.2	0.2	0.3	0.5 |	0.5	0.7	0.7	0.7	0.7
Korea[1]	..	..	..	0.6	-0.1	0.2	0.3	0.2	0.3	0.8
Latvia[1]	0.8	2.2	3.5	3.5	3.3	4.2	4.2	4.6	5.4	4.7
Lithuania[1]	1.4	3.6	2.9	2.5	1.4	4.0	3.9	4.1	4.1	4.2
Luxembourg[2]	..	..	14.8	35.8	18.1	18.4	21.8	18.4	14.3	15.9
Mexico[2]	0.9	1.2	1.6	2.4	1.7	1.6	1.6	1.6	1.9	2.0
Netherlands[2]	22.5	23.1	21.7	23.1	27.6	26.6	27.2	24.1	27.4	26.4
New Zealand[1]	3.2	3.5	3.5	3.5	3.6	3.3	2.9	3.5	3.3	2.8
Norway	3.1	3.3	3.5	2.9 |	1.6	1.6	1.9	2.7	3.0	3.0
Poland[1]	3.5	3.3	3.2	3.6	3.9	3.8	4.4	4.1	4.0	3.8
Portugal[2]	3.0	1.0	2.2	1.4	1.8	2.4	2.8	2.8	3.5	3.0
Slovak Republic[1]	5.6	6.3	4.3	3.3 |	3.9	5.0	4.9	4.5	4.3	4.4
Slovenia[1]	0.6	0.8	0.6	0.0	-0.1	2.5	2.8	2.6	2.9	3.0
Spain	2.2	2.1	1.7	2.1	1.8	1.8	1.9	2.2	2.2	1.9
Sweden	4.7	3.7	3.5	3.6	4.1	4.4	4.2	4.1	4.6	4.5
Switzerland	6.0	5.0	5.9	4.7	10.0 |	8.7	10.4	13.6	16.2	13.5
Turkey[1]	0.4	0.3	0.3	0.4	0.3	0.4	0.4	0.4	0.4	0.5
United Kingdom	2.5	2.7	2.7	2.9	2.6	2.5	2.5	2.8	3.4	2.0
United States[1]	1.1	1.1	1.1	1.1	1.1	0.9	0.9	1.0	1.1	1.1
OECD total	**2.0**	**2.0**	**2.0**	**2.0**	**2.1**	**2.0**	**2.0**	**2.2**	**2.4**	**2.3**
European Union[3]	..	..	..	..	..	..	..	..	..	..
G20	..	..	..	..	..	..	..	..	..	..
of which:										
Non-OECD G20 countries	..	..	..	..	..	..	..	..	..	..
Argentina	..	..	..	..	..	..	..	..	..	..
Brazil	3.0	2.4	1.9	0.9	1.1	0.8	1.7	2.0	2.4	2.9
China	..	..	..	..	..	..	..	..	..	..
India	..	..	..	..	..	..	..	..	..	..
Indonesia	..	..	..	..	..	..	..	..	..	..
Russian Federation	..	..	..	..	..	..	..	..	..	..
Saudi Arabia	..	..	..	..	..	..	..	..	..	..
South Africa	..	..	..	..	..	..	..	..	..	..

.. Not available; | Break in series

Note: Detailed metadata at: *http://stats.oecd.org/OECDStat_Metadata/ShowMetadata.ashx?Dataset=FDI_AGGR_SUMM.*

1. Resident Special Purpose Entities (SPEs) are not present or not significant.
2. Data excludes Special Purpose Entities (SPEs).
3. EU27 for 2007 to 2012 and EU28 as from 2013.

Source: OECD *International Direct Investment Statistics (database): https://doi.org/10.1787/idi-data-en*

Table 12. Income on outward Foreign Direct Investment as a percentage of GDP

At year end

Per cent

	2010	2011	2012	2013	2014	2015	2016	2017	2018	2019
Australia[1]	1.3	1.3	1.3	1.3	1.3	1.1	1.0	1.0	1.1	1.2
Austria[2]	3.2	3.5	3.4	3.3	2.6	2.8	3.9	3.7	3.3	3.5
Belgium	5.2	1.8	4.7	5.0	6.4	6.3	7.0	5.6	6.9	6.8
Canada	2.3	2.5	2.5	2.4	2.6	2.7	2.7	3.3	3.6	3.7
Chile[2]	..	..	1.6	1.6	2.1	1.6	1.4	1.5	1.4	1.9
Czech Republic[1]	0.5	0.5	1.1	0.6	0.8	1.0	1.0	2.1	1.7	2.2
Denmark[2]	..	..	..	3.6	3.9	4.0	3.8	4.0	4.2	4.5
Estonia	2.0 |	2.3	1.9	2.6	2.2	1.6	2.0	1.8	2.3	2.2
Finland[1]	4.4	3.9	3.9	2.9 |	4.0	3.1	3.3	3.5	3.7	5.1
France[1]	2.9	2.7	2.9 |	2.8	2.8	2.9	2.8	3.0	3.4	3.3
Germany[1]	2.5	2.7	2.3	2.4 |	2.3	2.5	2.8	2.6	3.2	3.2
Greece[1]	0.4	0.2	0.5	0.3	1.3	0.9	0.3	0.5	0.3	0.5
Hungary[2]	0.8	0.9	1.3	1.1	1.2	0.8	1.4	1.4	1.2	1.3
Iceland[2]	-0.2	3.8	-1.8 |	1.9 |	0.9	1.6	2.1	1.2	1.4	1.3
Ireland	8.5	8.9	6.2 |	6.9	6.8	4.0	4.9	5.1	5.1	4.1
Israel[1]	1.6	1.7	1.6	1.4	1.7	2.2	2.0	2.0	2.1	1.8
Italy[1]	1.3	1.5	1.3	1.1 |	1.2	0.7	1.0	1.3	1.4	1.4
Japan[1]	0.7	1.0	1.1	1.3	2.1 |	2.2	2.2	2.5	2.6	2.6
Korea[1]	..	..	..	0.7	0.4	0.0	0.6	0.6	0.6	1.0
Latvia[1]	-0.1	0.2	0.3	0.3	0.2	0.6	0.4	0.7	0.5	0.3
Lithuania[1]	0.2	0.1	0.2	0.4	0.2	0.3	0.3	0.3	0.6	0.4
Luxembourg[2]	..	..	12.7	12.9	11.8	14.0	13.7	16.3	12.4	10.1
Mexico[2]	0.6	0.6	0.6	0.6	0.6	0.3	0.3	0.4	0.4	0.5
Netherlands[2]	28.0	29.6	28.5	27.9	30.7	30.9	30.4	29.5	32.8	31.2
New Zealand[1]	0.4	0.2	0.4	0.3	0.4	0.3	0.4	0.3	0.2	0.3
Norway	2.6	1.7	2.2	1.7 |	2.8	2.4	1.8	2.1	2.8	1.3
Poland[1]	0.1	0.0	0.3	0.1	0.3	0.2	0.2	0.4	0.4	0.3
Portugal[2]	1.6	1.0	1.1	1.1	0.9	1.0	1.2	1.7	1.8	1.2
Slovak Republic[1]	0.5	0.4	0.2	0.3 |	0.8	0.4	0.2	0.4	0.4	0.3
Slovenia[1]	-0.7	-0.1	-0.8	-1.1	-0.2	0.1	0.4	0.5	0.7	0.7
Spain	2.7	2.8	2.6	2.9	2.6	2.7	2.7	2.8	3.0	2.6
Sweden	6.9	5.9	5.9	5.9	6.2	5.3	5.0	5.7	6.3	6.5
Switzerland	12.0	6.8	9.3	8.6	12.3 |	12.2	12.4	14.2	14.2	12.5
Turkey[1]	0.1	0.0	0.0	0.0	0.0	0.0	0.0	0.0	0.1	0.1
United Kingdom	5.5	6.0	4.7	4.4	3.7	3.0	2.6	4.3	4.4	4.1
United States[1]	2.9	3.0	2.8	2.8	2.7	2.4	2.4	2.8	2.8	2.6
OECD total	**3.0**	**3.0**	**2.9**	**2.9**	**3.1**	**2.9**	**2.9**	**3.2**	**3.4**	**3.2**
European Union[3]	..	..	..	..	..	..	..	..	..	..
G20	..	..	..	..	..	..	..	..	..	..
of which:										
Non-OECD G20 countries	..	..	..	..	..	..	..	..	..	..
Argentina	..	..	..	..	..	..	..	..	..	..
Brazil	0.5	0.5	0.1	0.3	0.1	-0.1	0.4	0.8	0.3	0.9
China	..	..	..	..	..	..	..	..	..	..
India	..	..	..	..	..	..	..	..	..	..
Indonesia	..	..	..	..	..	..	..	..	..	..
Russian Federation	..	..	..	..	..	..	..	..	..	..
Saudi Arabia	..	..	..	..	..	..	..	..	..	..
South Africa	..	..	..	..	..	..	..	..	..	..

.. Not available; | Break in series

Note: Detailed metadata at: *http://stats.oecd.org/OECDStat_Metadata/ShowMetadata.ashx?Dataset=FDI_AGGR_SUMM.*

1. Resident Special Purpose Entities (SPEs) are not present or not significant.
2. Data excludes Special Purpose Entities (SPEs).
3. EU27 for 2007 to 2012 and EU28 as from 2013.

Source: *OECD International Direct Investment Statistics (database): https://doi.org/10.1787/idi-data-en*

Country tables

AUSTRALIA

Table 1. Foreign direct investment flows by country

Million US dollars

	Inward					Outward				
	2015	2016	2017	2018	2019	2015	2016	2017	2018	2019
WORLD	**29 583.7**	**48 291.1**	**45 300.0**	**68 033.2**	**36 151.4**	**-9 339.5**	**2 265.7**	**5 932.3**	**6 361.4**	**5 396.5**
OECD COUNTRIES	**21 060.9**	**38 536.4**	**32 815.5**	**52 769.9**	**27 818.2**	**-6 961.5**	**10 727.7**	**12 610.9**	**15 852.7**	**14 981.6**
Australia	-	-	-	-	-	-	-	-	-	-
Austria	.. c	.. c	.. c	.. c	177.2	.. c	.. c	.. c	.. c	1.4
Belgium	-671.7	98.1	-135.6	316.7	-73.0	.. c	-3.7	.. c	.. c	.. c
Canada	1 758.2	1 296.4	2 481.4	5 243.9	4 527.7	-530.5	199.2	875.2	5 138.6	1 479.8
Chile	.. c	.. c	.. c	.. c	.. c	136.0	37.9	95.0	109.8	41.0
Czech Republic	0.8	-2.2	-0.8	.. c	.. c	3.0	.. c	.. c	7.5	.. c
Denmark	.. c	.. c	.. c	85.2	.. c	.. c	.. c	.. c	.. c	.. c
Estonia	.. c	.. c	-	-	-	.. c	.. c	.. c	.. c	.. c
Finland	.. c	.. c	.. c	133.7	.. c	.. c	3.0	.. c	-	.. c
France	314.1	37.9	286.6	15 587.5	-10 254.4	93.9	406.6	11.5	469.1	-326.7
Germany	586.1	579.1	1 225.4	1 547.8	688.8	.. c	507.7	570.9	632.7	319.0
Greece	.. c	.. c	.. c	.. c	.. c	.. c	.. c	.. c	.. c	13.2
Hungary	1.5	-0.7	.. c	.. c	0.7	.. c	.. c	.. c	.. c	.. c
Iceland	-	.. c	-	-	-	-	-	-	-	.. c
Ireland	2 356.3	-15.6	-1 612.4	404.1	289.2	-98.4	5.9	-223.0	-4.5	.. c
Israel	9.0	.. c	.. c	3.0	.. c	-	-	.. c	.. c	.. c
Italy	.. c	-91.4	25.3	-100.1	-36.8	.. c	1.5	.. c	3.7	.. c
Japan	10 058.6	7 047.5	4 949.8	7 031.4	8 319.3	33.1	.. c	.. c	216.6	.. c
Korea	8.3	959.6	.. c	1 257.2	1 129.5	20.3	.. c	.. c	221.1	29.2
Latvia	-	-	-	-	-	-	-	-	-	-
Lithuania	-	.. c	.. c	.. c	-	-	-	-	-	-
Luxembourg	-220.9	2 732.5	2 544.3	-826.2	331.5	.. c	.. c	.. c	91.9	.. c
Mexico	0.8	-	.. c	.. c	-1.4	61.6	.. c	.. c	-68.7	.. c
Netherlands	2 494.6	2 100.6	3 019.4	-3 997.2	3 038.2	.. c	.. c	.. c	492.3	.. c
New Zealand	369.7	681.6	-39.9	611.8	-526.9	-232.9	893.5	885.9	-648.4	2 448.0
Norway	-0.8	.. c	-90.4	-56.0	.. c	.. c	.. c	.. c	.. c	.. c
Poland	-	.. c	.. c	-1.5	1.4	.. c	.. c	.. c	.. c	.. c
Portugal	.. c	-	.. c	.. c	.. c	.. c	.. c	.. c	.. c	.. c
Slovak Republic	-	.. c	.. c	-	-	.. c	.. c	.. c	.. c	.. c
Slovenia	.. c	-	-	-	-	.. c	.. c	.. c	.. c	.. c
Spain	2.3	-4.5	-1.5	2.2	.. c	.. c	.. c	.. c	8.2	55.6
Sweden	200.6	85.5	50.6	274.9	125.1	.. c	.. c	2.3	-20.9	.. c
Switzerland	1 100.8	709.9	421.5	776.1	-551.2	.. c	.. c	.. c	.. c	219.6
Turkey	-	-	.. c	.. c	.. c	.. c	.. c	.. c	-0.7	.. c
United Kingdom	-12 248.1	12 557.1	11 924.3	6 197.1	20 111.2	4 970.3	859.3	2 690.6	9 528.6	8 458.3
United States	14 826.1	9 814.2	7 013.6	18 046.6	397.6	-5 294.2	6 785.1	4 684.7	1 799.5	1 940.6
EUROPE	..	..	..	..	..	..	..	..	..	..
Bulgaria	.. c	.. c	.. c	.. c	.. c	.. c	.. c	.. c	.. c	.. c
Croatia	.. c	.. c	.. c	.. c	-	.. c	.. c	.. c	.. c	.. c
Cyprus	.. c	.. c	-	-	-	.. c	.. c	-	.. c	.. c
Malta	.. c	.. c	-	-	-	-	.. c	.. c	.. c	.. c
Romania	.. c	.. c	-	-	-	.. c	0.7	.. c	.. c	.. c
Russian Federation	.. c	.. c	.. c	.. c	.. c	-0.8	10.4	.. c	20.2	.. c
Ukraine	-	-	-	-	-	.. c	.. c	.. c	.. c	.. c
AFRICA	..	..	..	..	..	..	..	..	..	..
Northern Africa	..	..	..	..	..	..	..	..	..	..
Algeria	.. c	.. c	.. c	.. c	-	-	-	-	-	.. c
Egypt	.. c	.. c	.. c	.. c	.. c	.. c	.. c	.. c	.. c	.. c
Libya	-	-	-	-	-	.. c	.. c	.. c	.. c	-
Morocco	.. c	.. c	.. c	-	-	.. c	.. c	.. c	-	.. c
Tunisia	.. c	.. c	.. c	.. c	-	-	-	-	-	-
Other African countries	..	..	..	..	..	..	..	..	..	..
Nigeria	.. c	.. c	.. c	.. c	.. c	.. c	.. c	.. c	.. c	.. c
South Africa	268.2	.. c	121.1	220.4	-22.9	54.1	-26.0	39.9	-162.1	13.9
AMERICA	..	..	..	..	..	..	..	..	..	..
Northern America	16 584.3	11 110.5	9 495.0	23 290.5	4 925.3	-5 824.6	6 984.3	5 559.8	6 938.1	3 420.4
Central America and Caribbean countries	..	..	..	..	..	..	..	..	..	..
Bahamas	-11.3	.. c	.. c	.. c	.. c	.. c	.. c	.. c	.. c	.. c
Bermuda	.. c	540.4	3 034.7	2 616.0	.. c	.. c	-356.1	.. c	278.6	.. c
Cayman Islands	.. c	.. c	49.0	-1 054.8	.. c	.. c	.. c	.. c	-895.6	.. c
Costa Rica	.. c	.. c	-	-	.. c	.. c	.. c	.. c	.. c	.. c
El Salvador	-	-	-	-	-	.. c	.. c	.. c	.. c	.. c
Guatemala	-	-	-	-	-	.. c	.. c	.. c	.. c	.. c
Honduras	-	-	-	-	-	-	.. c	.. c	.. c	.. c
Nicaragua	-	-	-	-	-	.. c	-	.. c	.. c	.. c
Panama	-	.. c	.. c	.. c	-	.. c	.. c	.. c	.. c	.. c
Virgin Islands, U.S.	-	-	.. c	.. c	-	-	-	-	-	-
South America	..	..	..	..	..	..	..	..	..	..
Argentina	.. c	.. c	-2.3	.. c	.. c	-48.1	.. c	.. c	0.7	.. c
Bolivia	-	-	-	-	-	.. c	.. c	.. c	.. c	.. c
Brazil	.. c	.. c	.. c	.. c	29.9	450.1	124.1	333.4	-171.8	-37.5
Colombia	.. c	.. c	.. c	.. c	.. c	12.0	-12.6	.. c	-39.6	.. c
Ecuador	-	-	-	-	-	.. c	.. c	29.1	.. c	.. c
Paraguay	-	-	-	-	-	-	-	-	-	-
Peru	.. c	.. c	.. c	.. c	.. c	21.8	.. c	.. c	5.2	.. c
Uruguay	-	-	-	-	-	.. c	.. c	.. c	.. c	.. c
Venezuela	.. c	.. c	.. c	.. c	.. c	.. c	.. c	.. c	.. c	.. c

Table 1. Foreign direct investment flows by country *(cont.)*

Million US dollars

	Inward					Outward				
	2015	2016	2017	2018	2019	2015	2016	2017	2018	2019
ASIA	..	..	..	..	..	..	..	..	..	..
Near and Middle East	..	..	..	..	..	..	..	..	..	..
Gulf Arabian countries	..	..	..	..	..	..	..	..	..	..
Kuwait	1 973.1	.. c	.. c	.. c	.. c	.. c	.. c	.. c	.. c	.. c
Qatar	.. c	.. c	.. c	.. c	.. c	.. c	.. c	-	.. c	.. c
Saudi Arabia	-6.8	-89.9	.. c	.. c	.. c	.. c	.. c	.. c	4.5	.. c
United Arab Emirates	-3 606.6	-136.0	95.0	60.5	.. c	-335.1	19.3	.. c	.. c	12.5
Other Near and Middle East	..	..	..	..	..	..	..	..	..	..
Jordan	.. c	.. c	.. c	.. c	.. c	.. c	-	-	.. c	-
Other Asian countries	..	..	..	..	..	..	..	..	..	..
China	2 202.3	1 266.6	705.0	3 244.9	3 017.3	457.6	-266.9	-1 526.6	816.5	198.1
Hong Kong, China	2 423.2	1 102.4	1 917.4	1 824.9	672.8	-171.3	-487.6	237.6	38.1	-380.2
India	-82.7	44.6	26.8	-17.2	287.1	81.1	50.5	98.1	38.1	79.2
Indonesia	-16.5	7.4	.. c	1.5	.. c	-37.6	56.5	136.4	.. c	269.0
Iran, Islamic Republic of	.. c	.. c	.. c	.. c	.. c	-	-	-	-	-
Malaysia	740.1	142.7	1 102.0	162.8	221.0	240.4	176.2	68.2	103.8	.. c
Philippines	.. c	0.7	-4.6	-44.8	-11.1	43.6	61.0	71.3	-85.9	28.5
Singapore	355.4	-3 491.4	2 827.8	4 180.9	2 976.3	1 828.8	159.8	118.0	265.2	787.5
Chinese Taipei	15.0	-3.0	39.9	32.9	.. c	.. c	-7.4	.. c	.. c	.. c
Thailand	.. c	.. c	508.1	-59.0	-198.8	.. c	6.7	91.2	-3.0	-52.8
Viet Nam	-4.5	3.0	-1.5	3.7	-2.1	23.3	6.7	28.4	.. c	63.3
AUSTRALIA, OCEANIA AND POLAR REGIONS	..	..	..	..	..	..	..	..	..	..
WORLD unallocated and confidential	**2 343.5**	**10 414.0**	**3 764.3**	**3 067.2**	**790.3**	**-11 190.2**	**-6 669.1**	**-3 387.2**	**-11 068.2**	**-10 325.3**
European Union (EU28)	**-6 802.2**	**17 142.6**	**17 144.6**	**19 870.8**	**14 502.7**	**4 944.8**	**2 843.2**	**2 671.5**	**11 292.3**	**8 526.4**
G20 countries excl. European Union	**.. d**	**.. d**	**.. d**	**.. d**	**.. d**	**.. d**	**.. d**	**.. d**	**.. d**	**.. d**
G20 OECD countries	**.. d**	**32 200.3**	**.. d**	**.. d**	**.. d**	**.. d**	**.. d**	**.. d**	**17 940.5**	**.. d**
G20 Non-OECD countries	**.. d**	**.. d**	**.. d**	**.. d**	**.. d**	**.. d**	**.. d**	**.. d**	**.. d**	**.. d**
MENA countries	**.. d**	**.. d**	**.. d**	**.. d**	**.. d**	**.. d**	**.. d**	**.. d**	**.. d**	**.. d**
ASEAN countries	**1 475.7**	**-4 058.6**	**4 428.7**	**4 248.9**	**2 992.3**	**2 587.7**	**596.9**	**875.9**	**-3 070.1**	**1 106.6**

- Nil; .. Not available; c Confidential data; d Secondary Confidentiality

Note: Detailed metadata at: *http://stats.oecd.org/OECDStat_Metadata/ShowMetadata.ashx?Dataset=FDI_CTRY_IND_SUMM.*

Source: *OECD International Direct Investment Statistics (database): https://doi.org/10.1787/idi-data-en*

AUSTRALIA

Table 2. Foreign direct investment positions by country

At year end

Million US dollars

	Inward					Outward				
	2015	2016	2017	2018	2019	2015	2016	2017	2018	2019
WORLD	**566 436.8**	**611 062.2**	**699 543.7**	**701 809.0**	**714 273.8**	**416 605.5**	**435 767.0**	**503 204.1**	**497 022.2**	**579 278.4**
OECD COUNTRIES	**346 614.3**	**375 223.6**	**426 988.5**	**436 587.4**	**441 921.1**	**217 905.3**	**227 866.9**	**267 834.0**	**272 452.7**	**333 515.0**
Australia	-	-	-	-	-	-	-	-	-	-
Austria	.. c	.. c	.. c	.. c	.. c	.. c	.. c	.. c	.. c	.. c
Belgium	1 862.4	1 818.4	1 737.8	2 783.7	2 482.3	.. c	.. c	.. c	.. c	2 972.7
Canada	18 109.2	20 142.5	25 415.3	28 521.3	33 008.5	5 768.2	5 883.5	8 180.3	23 772.6	24 589.1
Chile	.. c	.. c	.. c	.. c	.. c	.. c	1 159.2	1 259.7	1 279.6	1 436.3
Czech Republic	3.7	1.4	.. c	.. c	.. c	.. c	.. c	.. c	.. c	.. c
Denmark	.. c	.. c	.. c	723.5	751.8	3.7	.. c	.. c	.. c	.. c
Estonia	.. c	-	-	-	-	.. c	.. c	.. c	.. c	.. c
Finland	.. c	.. c	.. c	253.4	234.0	.. c	3.6	3.9	.. c	6.3
France	4 670.1	4 428.4	4 892.0	19 408.5	8 854.5	1 596.4	1 895.8	1 880.5	2 227.6	2 696.0
Germany	12 417.6	14 141.1	18 724.0	17 154.2	15 436.1	.. c	.. c	.. c	.. c	.. c
Greece	.. c	.. c	.. c	.. c	-	.. c	.. c	.. c	32.5	.. c
Hungary	.. c	.. c	.. c	.. c	.. c	.. c	.. c	.. c	.. c	.. c
Iceland	-	-	-	-	-	-	-	-	-	.. c
Ireland	3 016.0	2 925.5	1 514.7	1 487.9	1 623.3	.. c	.. c	.. c	.. c	536.7
Israel	.. c	.. c	.. c	.. c	.. c	-	-	.. c	.. c	.. c
Italy	.. c	433.4	542.1	382.6	372.0	101.6	112.9	178.6	.. c	100.9
Japan	67 160.8	70 806.8	76 388.0	77 025.7	81 343.8	.. c	.. c	691.1	926.7	1 158.1
Korea	2 346.0	3 324.2	4 239.1	4 789.7	5 250.5	.. c	589.7	669.2	765.1	861.8
Latvia	-	-	-	-	-	-	-	-	-	-
Lithuania	-	.. c	-	-	-	-	-	-	-	-
Luxembourg	2 045.0	4 592.6	7 355.9	5 943.0	5 650.5	1 296.1	1 191.8	1 783.0	.. c	.. c
Mexico	0.7	-	1.6	.. c	.. c	895.0	1 041.2	723.0	600.6	765.1
Netherlands	35 093.2	37 278.6	43 626.9	36 699.6	38 385.8	5 552.7	5 845.9	5 343.6	5 424.2	3 730.8
New Zealand	4 087.8	4 280.8	4 469.2	4 473.5	3 917.2	43 427.3	48 034.0	48 760.6	40 024.0	58 577.7
Norway	678.7	619.4	627.1	452.4	449.1	.. c	.. c	.. c	.. c	.. c
Poland	.. c	0.7	3.1	1.4	2.8	.. c	.. c	33.5	31.8	37.1
Portugal	.. c	.. c	-	.. c	.. c	2.9	8.7	9.4	7.1	9.8
Slovak Republic	-	.. c	-	-	-	.. c	.. c	.. c	.. c	.. c
Slovenia	-	-	-	-	-	.. c	.. c	.. c	.. c	.. c
Spain	.. c	.. c	.. c	.. c	.. c	.. c	31.8	28.1	33.9	91.8
Sweden	1 500.0	1 516.6	1 625.5	1 651.6	1 647.9	212.6	266.3	290.9	.. c	334.9
Switzerland	6 983.3	7 255.4	7 575.1	7 949.6	7 388.8	.. c	.. c	.. c	257.6	505.9
Turkey	.. c	.. c	.. c	.. c	.. c	.. c	91.2	.. c	.. c	.. c
United Kingdom	47 044.6	54 824.9	69 744.2	69 767.1	89 064.0	62 810.0	57 693.9	70 470.3	83 219.2	100 512.2
United States	136 024.7	143 942.8	155 360.7	154 894.1	143 742.0	80 235.3	89 867.6	104 398.3	91 698.9	102 163.5
EUROPE	..	..	..	..	..	..	..	..	..	..
Bulgaria	.. c	.. c	.. c	.. c	.. c	.. c	.. c	.. c	.. c	.. c
Croatia	.. c	-	.. c	-	-	.. c	.. c	.. c	.. c	.. c
Cyprus	.. c	-	-	-	-	.. c	.. c	.. c	.. c	.. c
Malta	.. c	-	-	-	-	.. c	.. c	.. c	.. c	.. c
Romania	.. c	.. c	.. c	.. c	.. c	.. c	.. c	.. c	.. c	4.2
Russian Federation	.. c	.. c	.. c	.. c	.. c	.. c	36.2	.. c	179.3	.. c
Ukraine	-	-	-	-	-	.. c	.. c	.. c	.. c	.. c
AFRICA	..	..	..	..	..	..	..	..	..	..
Northern Africa	..	..	..	..	..	..	..	..	..	..
Algeria	.. c	.. c	.. c	.. c	.. c	-	-	-	-	.. c
Egypt	.. c	.. c	.. c	.. c	.. c	.. c	5.8	.. c	.. c	2.1
Libya	-	-	-	-	-	.. c	.. c	.. c	.. c	.. c
Morocco	.. c	.. c	-	-	-	.. c	-	.. c	.. c	.. c
Tunisia	.. c	.. c	.. c	-	-	.. c	.. c	.. c	.. c	.. c
Other African countries	..	..	..	..	..	..	..	..	..	..
Nigeria	.. c	.. c	.. c	.. c	.. c	.. c	.. c	.. c	.. c	.. c
South Africa	2 134.9	2 556.4	2 309.5	2 151.3	2 067.5	853.4	875.5	2 131.7	758.8	634.1
AMERICA	..	..	..	..	..	..	..	..	..	..
Northern America	154 133.9	164 085.4	180 776.1	183 415.4	176 750.5	86 003.5	95 751.1	112 578.6	115 471.5	126 752.6
Central America and Caribbean countries	..	..	..	..	..	..	..	..	..	..
Bahamas	.. c	1 424.0	1 511.6	.. c	.. c	.. c	.. c	.. c	.. c	.. c
Bermuda	26 912.4	27 295.2	32 931.1	31 415.9	29 164.2	24 097.3	24 045.6	.. c	.. c	.. c
Cayman Islands	1 869.7	4 119.4	4 391.2	2 901.6	3 131.1	.. c	.. c	.. c	.. c	.. c
Costa Rica	.. c	-	-	-	-	.. c	.. c	.. c	.. c	18.2
El Salvador	-	-	-	-	-	.. c	.. c	.. c	.. c	25.2
Guatemala	-	-	-	-	-	.. c	.. c	.. c	.. c	.. c
Honduras	-	-	-	-	-	-	.. c	.. c	.. c	.. c
Nicaragua	-	-	-	-	-	-	-	.. c	.. c	.. c
Panama	-	-	.. c	-	-	.. c	.. c	.. c	.. c	.. c
Virgin Islands, U.S.	-	-	.. c	-	-	-	-	-	-	-
South America	..	..	..	..	..	..	..	..	..	..
Argentina	.. c	.. c	.. c	.. c	.. c	174.6	170.8	287.8	.. c	316.7
Bolivia	-	-	-	-	-	.. c	.. c	.. c	.. c	.. c
Brazil	.. c	.. c	.. c	.. c	.. c	3 023.3	3 217.8	.. c	3 099.9	3 138.8
Colombia	.. c	.. c	.. c	.. c	.. c	.. c	91.9	157.6	150.3	149.2
Ecuador	-	-	-	-	-	.. c	.. c	103.0	.. c	43.4
Paraguay	-	-	-	-	-	-	-	-	-	-
Peru	.. c	.. c	.. c	.. c	.. c	157.8	200.4	230.9	226.6	255.0
Uruguay	-	-	-	-	-	.. c	4.3	.. c	.. c	.. c
Venezuela	.. c	.. c	.. c	.. c	-	.. c	.. c	.. c	.. c	.. c

Table 2. Foreign direct investment positions by country *(cont.)*

At year end

Million US dollars

	Inward					Outward				
	2015	2016	2017	2018	2019	2015	2016	2017	2018	2019
ASIA	..	..	..	..	..	..	..	..	..	..
Near and Middle East	..	..	..	..	..	..	..	..	..	..
Gulf Arabian countries	..	..	..	..	..	..	..	..	..	..
Kuwait	3 453.6	.. c	.. c	.. c	.. c	.. c	.. c	.. c	.. c	.. c
Qatar	.. c	.. c	.. c	.. c	.. c	.. c	-2.9	.. c	.. c	.. c
Saudi Arabia	.. c	646.9	713.7	662.8	381.8	633.4	.. c	.. c	.. c	.. c
United Arab Emirates	1 325.3	1 186.0	1 708.9	1 197.8	1 860.9	.. c	.. c	.. c	.. c	.. c
Other Near and Middle East	..	..	..	..	..	..	..	..	..	..
Jordan	.. c	.. c	.. c	.. c	.. c	.. c	.. c	.. c	-	-
Other Asian countries	..	..	..	..	..	..	..	..	..	..
China	26 100.7	27 997.8	29 941.5	29 493.9	32 223.1	10 150.5	9 672.9	10 492.2	9 812.3	10 867.4
Hong Kong, China	9 171.5	9 895.8	12 418.7	12 646.8	11 293.4	3 630.5	3 230.1	3 350.8	4 047.1	5 346.5
India	655.4	670.8	701.2	612.6	781.9	1 176.3	1 270.6	1 442.9	1 144.8	1 353.6
Indonesia	.. c	-	.. c	-	11.9	4 057.1	4 515.9	5 886.4	1 610.7	2 484.4
Iran, Islamic Republic of	.. c	.. c	-	.. c	-	-	-	-	-	-
Malaysia	7 925.8	8 890.7	10 502.3	9 935.8	10 305.5	4 021.3	4 036.9	4 619.0	4 203.8	4 441.3
Philippines	2.9	3.6	.. c	.. c	.. c	571.3	695.4	753.5	554.8	641.8
Singapore	21 305.6	17 081.0	21 588.8	23 111.9	25 268.0	13 677.9	14 549.9	15 749.2	17 852.2	19 695.9
Chinese Taipei	85.5	80.3	120.9	131.3	401.5	.. c	.. c	.. c	.. c	946.5
Thailand	4 105.4	3 372.6	4 260.2	4 141.7	4 123.2	1 088.6	1 265.6	1 363.4	979.0	1 095.8
Viet Nam	.. c	.. c	.. c	.. c	.. c	995.1	1 120.8	1 576.3	.. c	1 849.6
AUSTRALIA, OCEANIA AND POLAR REGIONS	..	..	..	..	..	..	..	..	..	..
WORLD unallocated and confidential	**100 325.1**	**115 487.7**	**133 970.0**	**130 304.2**	**132 972.0**	**145 376.6**	**140 559.3**	**196 991.7**	**191 292.3**	**223 713.3**
European Union (EU28)	**111 993.1**	**124 833.6**	**152 881.2**	**158 473.3**	**166 804.5**	**85 100.5**	**80 604.2**	**96 903.5**	**112 143.6**	**142 551.7**
G20 countries excl. European Union	.. d	.. d	.. d	.. d	.. d	.. d	.. d	.. d	.. d	.. d
G20 OECD countries	.. d	.. d	.. d	.. d	.. d	.. d	.. d	.. d	.. d	.. d
G20 Non-OECD countries	.. d	.. d	.. d	.. d	.. d	.. d	.. d	.. d	.. d	.. d
MENA countries	.. d	.. d	.. d	.. d	.. d	.. d	.. d	.. d	.. d	.. d
ASEAN countries	**33 330.2**	**29 348.0**	**36 346.6**	**37 151.3**	**39 652.5**	**25 581.9**	**27 463.1**	**31 541.2**	**28 377.3**	**31 841.9**

- Nil; .. Not available; c Confidential data; d Secondary Confidentiality

Note: Detailed metadata at: *http://stats.oecd.org/OECDStat_Metadata/ShowMetadata.ashx?Dataset=FDI_CTRY_IND_SUMM.*

Source: OECD *International Direct Investment Statistics (database): https://doi.org/10.1787/idi-data-en*

AUSTRALIA

Table 3. Foreign direct investment income by country

Million US dollars

	Inward					Outward				
	2015	2016	2017	2018	2019	2015	2016	2017	2018	2019
WORLD	**23 883.8**	**27 454.1**	**37 310.9**	**44 029.3**	**43 575.5**	**13 784.7**	**13 315.2**	**14 217.9**	**16 748.3**	**16 859.7**
OECD COUNTRIES	**14 068.7**	**15 566.8**	**23 427.8**	**28 555.3**	**29 568.4**	**7 361.2**	**7 112.2**	**7 936.2**	**9 686.3**	**9 758.8**
Australia	-	-	-	-	-	-	-	-	-	-
Austria	.. c	.. c	.. c	.. c	.. c	.. c	.. c	.. c	.. c	.. c
Belgium	.. c	19.3	111.1	218.9	177.9	.. c	-	.. c	.. c	.. c
Canada	399.7	304.8	671.3	632.0	1 007.2	.. c	.. c	58.2	316.0	.. c
Chile	.. c	-	-	-	-	.. c	.. c	92.7	.. c	.. c
Czech Republic	-	-	-	-	-	.. c	.. c	.. c	.. c	.. c
Denmark	.. c	.. c	.. c	.. c	89.0	1.5	.. c	.. c	.. c	.. c
Estonia	-	-	-	-	-	.. c	.. c	.. c	.. c	.. c
Finland	.. c	.. c	.. c	.. c	.. c	.. c	.. c	.. c	.. c	.. c
France	365.9	557.5	505.8	783.6	793.8	.. c	.. c	101.9	.. c	.. c
Germany	.. c	.. c	.. c	1 110.8	.. c	.. c	.. c	.. c	.. c	.. c
Greece	-	-	-	-	-	.. c	.. c	.. c	.. c	.. c
Hungary	-	-	-	-	-	.. c	.. c	.. c	.. c	.. c
Iceland	-	-	-	-	-	-	-	-	-	-
Ireland	182.6	263.1	.. c	.. c	193.2	.. c	.. c	.. c	.. c	.. c
Israel	.. c	.. c	.. c	.. c	.. c	-	-	-	-	-
Italy	.. c	.. c	.. c	.. c	.. c	.. c	.. c	.. c	.. c	.. c
Japan	3 246.7	4 103.2	5 257.9	6 382.3	6 993.1	.. c	98.9	.. c	.. c	79.9
Korea	.. c	123.4	.. c	404.1	.. c	.. c	.. c	5.4	12.0	5.6
Latvia	-	-	-	-	-	-	-	-	-	-
Lithuania	-	-	-	-	-	-	-	-	-	-
Luxembourg	.. c	180.6	239.9	82.9	79.2	.. c	.. c	.. c	.. c	.. c
Mexico	-	-	-	-	-	.. c	.. c	99.6	.. c	.. c
Netherlands	741.6	726.2	1 273.7	1 862.3	1 788.4	406.5	.. c	.. c	.. c	.. c
New Zealand	116.5	459.4	474.4	273.4	.. c	3 526.9	3 301.9	3 635.5	3 598.3	2 849.8
Norway	.. c	.. c	.. c	.. c	.. c	.. c	.. c	.. c	.. c	.. c
Poland	-	-	-	-	-	.. c	.. c	.. c	.. c	.. c
Portugal	-	-	-	-	-	.. c	.. c	.. c	.. c	.. c
Slovak Republic	-	-	-	-	-	.. c	.. c	.. c	.. c	.. c
Slovenia	-	-	-	-	-	.. c	.. c	.. c	.. c	.. c
Spain	-	-	-	.. c	.. c	10.5	.. c	.. c	.. c	2.8
Sweden	122.5	96.6	.. c	130.7	.. c	.. c	.. c	.. c	.. c	.. c
Switzerland	39.8	.. c	.. c	722.3	.. c	.. c	.. c	.. c	5.2	.. c
Turkey	-	-	-	-	-	.. c	.. c	.. c	.. c	.. c
United Kingdom	1 380.3	991.6	4 152.8	5 691.3	5 759.4	1 442.6	1 436.9	1 117.3	1 398.4	2 122.8
United States	6 105.6	6 226.1	8 125.5	9 723.6	9 509.3	711.5	903.9	1 564.9	2 849.0	3 013.8
EUROPE	..	..	..	..	..	..	..	..	..	..
Bulgaria	-	-	-	-	-	.. c	.. c	.. c	.. c	.. c
Croatia	-	-	-	-	-	.. c	.. c	.. c	.. c	.. c
Cyprus	-	-	-	-	-	-	.. c	-	.. c	.. c
Malta	.. c	.. c	-	-	-	-	-	.. c	-	-
Romania	-	-	-	-	-	.. c	-	.. c	.. c	.. c
Russian Federation	.. c	.. c	.. c	-	-	.. c	.. c	1.5	.. c	.. c
Ukraine	-	-	-	-	-	.. c	.. c	.. c	.. c	.. c
AFRICA	..	..	..	..	..	..	..	..	..	..
Northern Africa	..	..	..	..	..	..	..	..	..	..
Algeria	-	-	-	-	-	-	-	-	-	-
Egypt	-	-	-	-	-	.. c	.. c	.. c	.. c	.. c
Libya	-	-	-	-	-	.. c	.. c	.. c	-	-
Morocco	-	-	-	-	-	-	-	-	-	.. c
Tunisia	-	-	-	-	-	-	-	-	-	-
Other African countries	..	..	..	..	..	..	..	..	..	..
Nigeria	-	-	-	-	-	.. c	.. c	.. c	-	-
South Africa	.. c	168.7	105.8	125.5	189.8	11.3	14.1	.. c	.. c	.. c
AMERICA	..	..	..	..	..	..	..	..	..	..
Northern America	6 505.4	6 530.9	8 796.8	10 355.6	10 516.4	..	..	1 623.1	3 165.0	..
Central America and Caribbean countries	..	..	..	..	..	..	..	..	..	..
Bahamas	.. c	.. c	.. c	.. c	.. c	-	.. c	-	-	-
Bermuda	846.0	1 549.1	1 906.7	2 913.3	1 716.8	.. c	.. c	.. c	.. c	.. c
Cayman Islands	130.7	.. c	216.9	228.6	241.2	168.3	.. c	.. c	.. c	.. c
Costa Rica	-	-	-	-	-	.. c	.. c	.. c	.. c	.. c
El Salvador	-	-	-	-	-	.. c	.. c	.. c	.. c	.. c
Guatemala	-	-	-	-	-	.. c	.. c	.. c	.. c	.. c
Honduras	-	-	-	-	-	-	.. c	.. c	.. c	.. c
Nicaragua	-	-	-	-	-	-	-	.. c	.. c	.. c
Panama	-	.. c	-	-	-	.. c	.. c	.. c	.. c	.. c
Virgin Islands, U.S.	-	-	-	-	-	-	-	-	-	-
South America	..	..	..	..	..	..	..	..	..	..
Argentina	.. c	.. c	.. c	.. c	.. c	.. c	.. c	.. c	.. c	.. c
Bolivia	-	-	-	-	-	.. c	.. c	.. c	.. c	.. c
Brazil	.. c	.. c	.. c	.. c	.. c	118.0	.. c	98.9	.. c	.. c
Colombia	-	-	-	-	-	.. c	.. c	.. c	.. c	.. c
Ecuador	-	-	-	-	-	.. c	.. c	.. c	.. c	-
Paraguay	-	-	-	-	-	-	-	-	-	-
Peru	-	-	-	-	-	.. c	.. c	.. c	.. c	.. c
Uruguay	-	-	-	-	-	.. c	.. c	.. c	.. c	.. c
Venezuela	-	-	-	-	-	.. c	.. c	.. c	.. c	.. c

AUSTRALIA

Table 3. Foreign direct investment income by country *(cont.)*

Million US dollars

	Inward					Outward				
	2015	2016	2017	2018	2019	2015	2016	2017	2018	2019
ASIA	..	..	..	..	..	..	..	..	..	..
Near and Middle East	..	..	..	..	..	..	..	..	..	..
Gulf Arabian countries	..	..	..	..	..	..	..	..	..	..
Kuwait	.. c	.. c	11.5	.. c	.. c	.. c	.. c	.. c	-	-
Qatar	.. c	.. c	.. c	.. c	.. c	.. c	.. c	-	-	-
Saudi Arabia	.. c	.. c	.. c	.. c	.. c	0.8	.. c	.. c	.. c	.. c
United Arab Emirates	112.0	94.4	158.6	76.2	7.6	20.3	2.2	.. c	9.0	.. c
Other Near and Middle East	..	..	..	..	..	..	..	..	..	..
Jordan	.. c	.. c	.. c	.. c	.. c	-	-	-	-	-
Other Asian countries	..	..	..	..	..	..	..	..	..	..
China	28.6	136.0	456.7	1 306.5	1 547.9	287.0	492.8	174.7	239.0	155.7
Hong Kong, China	818.2	813.2	888.2	1 053.3	.. c	319.3	208.9	201.5	242.0	.. c
India	.. c	40.1	.. c	.. c	.. c	.. c	65.4	70.5	.. c	.. c
Indonesia	.. c	-	-	-	-	69.1	61.7	162.5	268.2	.. c
Iran, Islamic Republic of	-	-	-	-	-	-	-	-	-	-
Malaysia	.. c	84.7	.. c	.. c	.. c	.. c	.. c	219.2	184.5	209.9
Philippines	-	-	-	-	-	53.3	54.3	.. c	.. c	29.2
Singapore	777.7	.. c	799.3	735.0	1 378.3	976.0	396.2	.. c	673.0	980.7
Chinese Taipei	.. c	3.0	11.5	.. c	.. c	.. c	.. c	.. c	.. c	.. c
Thailand	.. c	.. c	.. c	.. c	.. c	.. c	29.0	38.3	17.9	.. c
Viet Nam	-	-	-	-	-	.. c	10.4	.. c	44.1	.. c
AUSTRALIA, OCEANIA AND POLAR REGIONS	..	..	..	..	..	..	..	..	..	..
WORLD unallocated and confidential	**7 221.4**	**10 337.5**	**10 436.0**	**8 417.1**	**12 103.3**	**4 950.8**	**5 910.2**	**6 463.3**	**6 534.7**	**6 933.3**
European Union (EU28)	**4 156.6**	**3 887.6**	**7 942.4**	**10 378.0**	**10 612.4**	**2 877.0**	**2 659.6**	**2 351.9**	**2 788.5**	**3 539.3**
G20 countries excl. European Union	**.. d**	**.. d**	**.. d**	**.. d**	**.. d**	**.. d**	**.. d**	**.. d**	**.. d**	**.. d**
G20 OECD countries	**.. d**	**.. d**	**.. d**	**.. d**	**.. d**	**.. d**	**.. d**	**.. d**	**.. d**	**.. d**
G20 Non-OECD countries	**.. d**	**.. d**	**.. d**	**.. d**	**.. d**	**.. d**	**.. d**	**.. d**	**.. d**	**.. d**
MENA countries	**.. d**	**.. d**	**.. d**	**.. d**	**.. d**	**.. d**	**.. d**	**.. d**	**.. d**	**.. d**
ASEAN countries	**1 133.8**	**1 233.2**	**964.1**	**880.7**	**1 527.8**	**1 639.5**	**849.6**	**1 412.4**	**1 410.3**	**1 627.9**

- Nil; .. Not available; c Confidential data; d Secondary Confidentiality

Note: Detailed metadata at: *http://stats.oecd.org/OECDStat_Metadata/ShowMetadata.ashx?Dataset=FDI_CTRY_IND_SUMM.*

Source: *OECD International Direct Investment Statistics (database): https://doi.org/10.1787/idi-data-en*

AUSTRALIA

Table 4. Foreign direct investment flows by industrial sector

Million US dollars

	Inward					Outward				
	2015	2016	2017	2018	2019	2015	2016	2017	2018	2019
All FDI activities	**29 583.7**	**48 291.1**	**45 300.0**	**68 033.2**	**36 151.4**	**-9 339.5**	**2 265.7**	**5 932.3**	**6 361.4**	**5 396.5**
Agriculture, forestry and fishing	**.. c**	**.. c**	**308.8**	**-366.8**	**.. c**	**.. c**	**.. c**	**.. c**	**.. c**	**.. c**
Mining and quarrying	**.. c**	**23 351.7**	**14 658.6**	**13 385.4**	**3 270.3**	**-13 542.7**	**300.3**	**-465.2**	**3 232.2**	**5 330.5**
Extraction activities	..	..	..	..	..	..	..	..	..	..
Manufacturing	**2 587.7**	**3 785.0**	**5 859.5**	**7 909.9**	**15 500.1**	**6 006.5**	**3 306.3**	**4 728.3**	**4 728.5**	**7 764.6**
of which:										
Food products, beverages and tobacco	..	..	..	..	..	..	..	..	..	..
Textiles, wood and paper products; printing	..	..	..	..	..	..	..	..	..	..
Chemical, rubber, plastic, non-metallic mineral products	..	..	..	..	..	..	..	..	..	..
Metal and machinery products, except electrical equipment	..	..	..	..	..	..	..	..	..	..
Motor vehicles, trailers, semi-trailers, other transport equipment	..	..	..	..	..	..	..	..	..	..
Other manufacturing	..	..	..	..	..	..	..	..	..	..
Electricity, gas, steam and air conditioning supply	**2 235.3**	**-762.7**	**2 889.9**	**1 111.5**	**.. c**	**.. c**	**20.8**	**388.5**	**462.4**	**.. c**
Water supply; sewerage, waste management and remediation activities	..	..	..	..	..	..	..	..	..	..
Construction	**-811.5**	**102.6**	**951.8**	**570.7**	**1 378.3**	**-544.0**	**127.1**	**460.6**	**685.7**	**.. c**
Services	**14 891.4**	**25 740.7**	**22 041.5**	**43 594.5**	**9 036.6**	**10 516.9**	**5 933.2**	**8 812.2**	**7 208.5**	**-5 498.0**
Wholesale and retail trade; repair of motor vehicles and motorcycles	-2 097.1	2 192.8	2 031.6	4 546.9	1 593.8	916.7	997.5	-296.6	2 813.9	209.2
Transportation and storage	5 677.4	3 710.0	630.7	860.5	1 085.0	151.8	-198.5	-216.1	47.1	59.8
Accommodation and food service activities	-823.5	-25.3	269.8	1 764.4	966.8	.. c	3.7	90.4	.. c	.. c
Information and communication	783.7	-305.5	1 378.7	2 711.6	2 562.7	.. c	-427.4	477.4	258.5	.. c
Financial and insurance activities	3 790.7	5 360.1	9 221.4	24 995.1	476.8	5 603.7	4 919.3	6 818.9	3 581.1	-5 435.5
Activities of holding companies	..	..	..	..	..	..	..	..	..	..
Real estate activities	.. c	.. c	.. c	5 505.3	519.2	.. c	-334.5	2 401.7	374.2	-2 098.4
Professional, scientific and technical activities	307.3	842.2	968.7	833.6	770.1	60.1	.. c	-264.4	-150.1	.. c
Administrative and support service activities	-250.2	.. c	360.2	.. c	510.2	.. c	599.1	611.5	130.7	253.0
Public administration; activities of households and of extraterritorial organisations	.. c	.. c	.. c	148.7	.. c	.. c	-	-	-	-
Education	.. c	.. c	.. c	-485.5	.. c	.. c	.. c	.. c	.. c	.. c
Human health and social work activities	-825.0	1 449.5	482.8	-72.5	-409.4	-204.4	503.2	.. c	307.8	1 389.4
Arts, entertainment and recreation	.. c	.. c	.. c	.. c	.. c	.. c	.. c	.. c	.. c	43.8
Other services	.. c	.. c	.. c	.. c	38.2	-	-	-	.. c	.. c
Not allocated and confidential	**.. c**	**.. c**	**-1 410.1**	**1 827.9**	**.. c**	**.. c**	**.. c**	**.. c**	**.. c**	**.. c**
Private real estate activities	..	..	..	..	..	..	..	..	..	..

- Nil; .. Not available; c Confidential data

Note: Detailed metadata at: *http://stats.oecd.org/OECDStat_Metadata/ShowMetadata.ashx?Dataset=FDI_CTRY_IND_SUMM.*

Source: *OECD International Direct Investment Statistics (database): https://doi.org/10.1787/idi-data-en*

AUSTRALIA

Table 5. Foreign direct investment positions by industrial sector

At year end

Million US dollars

	Inward					Outward				
	2015	2016	2017	2018	2019	2015	2016	2017	2018	2019
All FDI activities	**566 436.8**	**611 062.2**	**699 543.7**	**701 809.0**	**714 273.8**	**416 605.5**	**435 767.0**	**503 204.1**	**497 022.2**	**579 278.4**
Agriculture, forestry and fishing	**2 344.6**	**2 372.6**	**2 783.7**	**2 232.5**	**2 370.2**	**.. c**	**.. c**	**.. c**	**.. c**	**.. c**
Mining and quarrying	**229 975.9**	**245 386.4**	**271 293.2**	**263 284.9**	**252 264.4**	**84 094.4**	**92 374.8**	**102 974.0**	**108 060.4**	**121 657.7**
Extraction activities	..	..	..	..	..	..	..	..	..	..
Manufacturing	**66 139.4**	**68 764.8**	**79 385.4**	**78 193.8**	**92 090.0**	**70 271.8**	**68 969.6**	**88 580.5**	**99 330.2**	**138 332.5**
of which:										
Food products, beverages and tobacco	..	..	..	..	..	..	..	..	..	..
Textiles, wood and paper products; printing	..	..	..	..	..	..	..	..	..	..
Chemical, rubber, plastic, non-metallic mineral products	..	..	..	..	..	..	..	..	..	..
Metal and machinery products, except electrical equipment	..	..	..	..	..	..	..	..	..	..
Motor vehicles, trailers, semi-trailers, other transport equipment	..	..	..	..	..	..	..	..	..	..
Other manufacturing	..	..	..	..	..	..	..	..	..	..
Electricity, gas, steam and air conditioning supply	**11 635.9**	**11 457.3**	**15 913.0**	**15 638.8**	**15 228.8**	**3 509.2**	**3 374.1**	**3 906.1**	**4 211.6**	**4 389.4**
Water supply; sewerage, waste management and remediation activities	..	..	..	..	..	..	..	..	..	..
Construction	**12 793.9**	**14 157.7**	**18 064.9**	**14 323.1**	**12 650.5**	**6 426.5**	**6 360.3**	**7 564.2**	**5 480.7**	**6 231.3**
Services	**174 000.9**	**198 319.8**	**232 652.7**	**252 951.0**	**259 466.1**	**154 253.7**	**158 719.2**	**177 943.2**	**161 785.7**	**174 956.2**
Wholesale and retail trade; repair of motor vehicles and motorcycles	38 611.1	39 201.9	44 242.3	42 800.7	42 258.1	4 493.3	5 324.9	4 633.0	6 730.7	6 672.0
Transportation and storage	15 468.0	18 687.4	17 174.9	16 257.1	16 357.5	2 987.5	2 919.7	2 864.1	2 947.5	3 043.5
Accommodation and food service activities	5 291.2	5 045.6	5 336.6	6 282.5	6 548.7	62.8	58.6	128.7	57.2	156.9
Information and communication	19 313.9	18 188.9	19 856.5	19 565.2	21 365.5	2 333.6	1 360.3	2 176.9	2 204.3	2 017.1
Financial and insurance activities	46 528.1	49 826.3	61 665.2	80 555.5	79 286.8	121 368.5	125 790.9	141 538.9	124 203.8	135 143.3
Activities of holding companies	..	..	..	..	..	..	..	..	..	..
Real estate activities	42 448.3	54 721.4	71 255.8	72 900.9	77 704.1	11 741.8	11 984.1	14 897.4	14 176.3	13 374.9
Professional, scientific and technical activities	3 301.7	3 909.6	5 234.4	5 186.3	5 628.1	2 121.7	2 069.5	2 183.9	2 025.0	2 802.5
Administrative and support service activities	1 136.1	2 730.1	3 176.8	5 246.3	5 563.7	.. c	2 343.7	3 382.0	3 377.3	3 927.7
Public administration; activities of households and of extraterritorial organisations	.. c	.. c	.. c	.. c	.. c	-	-	-	-	-
Education	.. c	.. c	.. c	.. c	.. c	.. c	.. c	.. c	.. c	.. c
Human health and social work activities	1 299.8	2 553.5	3 107.4	2 722.3	2 360.4	4 287.3	4 591.9	4 682.2	4 743.1	6 956.5
Arts, entertainment and recreation	.. c	.. c	.. c	.. c	.. c	.. c	.. c	.. c	.. c	.. c
Other services	.. c	219.2	.. c	.. c	.. c	-	-	-	.. c	-
Not allocated and confidential	**69 546.3**	**70 603.5**	**79 450.9**	**75 184.9**	**80 203.9**	**.. c**	**.. c**	**.. c**	**.. c**	**.. c**
Private real estate activities	..	..	..	..	..	..	..	..	..	..

- Nil; .. Not available; c Confidential data

Note: Detailed metadata at: *http://stats.oecd.org/OECDStat_Metadata/ShowMetadata.ashx?Dataset=FDI_CTRY_IND_SUMM.*

Source: *OECD International Direct Investment Statistics (database): https://doi.org/10.1787/idi-data-en*

Table 6. Foreign direct investment income by industrial sector

Million US dollars

	Inward					Outward				
	2015	2016	2017	2018	2019	2015	2016	2017	2018	2019
All FDI activities	**23 883.8**	**27 454.1**	**37 310.9**	**44 029.3**	**43 575.5**	**13 784.7**	**13 315.2**	**14 217.9**	**16 748.3**	**16 859.7**
Agriculture, forestry and fishing	**48.8**	**107.8**	**105.8**	**.. c**	**16.0**	**-**	**-**	**-**	**.. c**	**.. c**
Mining and quarrying	**4 992.1**	**4 842.8**	**12 388.7**	**17 431.8**	**18 523.0**	**-81.9**	**-164.3**	**2 207.8**	**2 296.3**	**2 818.5**
Extraction activities	..	..	..	..	..	..	..	..	..	..
Manufacturing	**3 850.0**	**4 677.8**	**4 493.8**	**4 815.1**	**3 492.0**	**2 993.5**	**2 993.4**	**3 321.3**	**3 743.9**	**3 904.9**
of which:										
Food products, beverages and tobacco	..	..	..	..	..	..	..	..	..	..
Textiles, wood and paper products; printing	..	..	..	..	..	..	..	..	..	..
Chemical, rubber, plastic, non-metallic mineral products	..	..	..	..	..	..	..	..	..	..
Metal and machinery products, except electrical equipment	..	..	..	..	..	..	..	..	..	..
Motor vehicles, trailers, semi-trailers, other transport equipment	..	..	..	..	..	..	..	..	..	..
Other manufacturing	..	..	..	..	..	..	..	..	..	..
Electricity, gas, steam and air conditioning supply	**507.9**	**815.4**	**.. c**	**1 175.8**	**1 295.6**	**193.9**	**.. c**	**.. c**	**.. c**	**.. c**
Water supply; sewerage, waste management and remediation activities	..	..	..	..	..	..	..	..	..	..
Construction	**.. c**	**.. c**	**1 160.2**	**1 249.7**	**.. c**	**.. c**	**.. c**	**422.3**	**.. c**	**.. c**
Services	**11 650.0**	**14 249.6**	**15 772.9**	**17 266.0**	**16 790.2**	**7 549.8**	**6 985.1**	**4 928.3**	**6 643.0**	**6 151.4**
Wholesale and retail trade; repair of motor vehicles and motorcycles	2 194.0	2 583.1	1 969.5	3 563.2	3 373.9	616.9	197.0	-87.4	162.8	.. c
Transportation and storage	337.4	767.1	627.6	904.6	674.2	121.7	20.1	108.1	147.9	182.1
Accommodation and food service activities	571.0	799.8	784.0	660.3	745.1	.. c	.. c	.. c	.. c	.. c
Information and communication	822.8	1 064.4	1 246.8	1 054.8	809.1	87.9	82.5	-76.6	-52.3	73.7
Financial and insurance activities	3 413.5	3 734.5	4 831.8	4 995.9	5 122.0	5 462.5	5 491.0	3 827.9	5 051.9	4 528.4
Activities of holding companies	..	..	..	..	..	..	..	..	..	..
Real estate activities	.. c	.. c	.. c	.. c	.. c	540.2	.. c	.. c	.. c	491.4
Professional, scientific and technical activities	139.8	161.3	-1.5	132.2	230.1	.. c	.. c	.. c	.. c	.. c
Administrative and support service activities	107.4	139.7	153.3	106.1	.. c	.. c	.. c	.. c	.. c	.. c
Public administration; activities of households and of extraterritorial organisations	72.1	.. c	.. c	.. c	.. c	.. c	-	-	.. c	-
Education	-	.. c	.. c	.. c	43.8	.. c	.. c	.. c	.. c	-
Human health and social work activities	212.6	191.0	187.8	115.0	2.1	436.5	.. c	.. c	.. c	.. c
Arts, entertainment and recreation	.. c	.. c	.. c	.. c	1.4	.. c	.. c	.. c	.. c	.. c
Other services	.. c	.. c	.. c	.. c	52.8	-	-	-	-	-
Not allocated and confidential	**.. c**	**.. c**	**.. c**	**.. c**	**.. c**	**.. c**	**.. c**	**.. c**	**.. c**	**.. c**
Private real estate activities	..	..	..	..	..	..	..	..	..	..

- Nil; .. Not available; c Confidential data

Note: Detailed metadata at: *http://stats.oecd.org/OECDStat_Metadata/ShowMetadata.ashx?Dataset=FDI_CTRY_IND_SUMM.*

Source: *OECD International Direct Investment Statistics (database): https://doi.org/10.1787/idi-data-en*

AUSTRIA

Table 1. Foreign direct investment flows by country

Million US dollars

	Inward					Outward				
	2015	2016	2017	2018	2019	2015	2016	2017	2018	2019
WORLD	**1 487.5**	**-8 500.5**	**14 921.7**	**5 283.8**	**967.2**	**7 027.2**	**-2 031.4**	**10 228.8**	**5 608.4**	**10 894.4**
OECD COUNTRIES	**3 124.8**	**-8 340.2**	**7 038.7**	**8 234.4**	**-178.0**	**4 321.7**	**8 929.6**	**6 060.2**	**1 645.2**	**5 513.3**
Australia	54.4	-11.1	-55.2	-70.8	25.7	175.3	119.4	86.8	345.8	394.0
Austria	-	-	-	-	-	-	-	-	-	-
Belgium	410.4	14.4	665.1	-1 352.5	1 982.5	257.3	454.5	-273.9	-291.5	70.5
Canada	-44.4	25.4	230.0	-41.3	-293.3	-117.6	-184.7	-391.2	-275.0	-217.2
Chile	-149.8	-2.2	-3.4	-15.3	-1.1	-1.1	17.7	-	31.9	32.5
Czech Republic	66.6	28.8	3.4	184.1	-59.3	676.7	-1 019.6	554.6	584.2	351.5
Denmark	-119.8	-426.8	-	7.1	22.4	43.3	12.2	-78.9	5.9	16.8
Estonia	-	-3.3	-	-	-1.1	83.2	18.8	-77.8	113.3	-11.2
Finland	25.5	44.2	57.5	-10.6	-25.7	44.4	91.8	113.9	129.8	-4.5
France	1 090.4	-315.2	7.9	-186.5	206.0	-55.5	19.9	310.0	101.5	73.9
Germany	-1 559.6	938.8	4 137.1	6 553.8	-876.5	602.3	1 282.8	1 889.3	-2 334.5	1 865.0
Greece	299.5	38.7	48.5	-355.2	182.5	49.9	85.1	3.4	-334.0	5.6
Hungary	219.6	-8.8	-80.0	-4.7	47.0	733.2	-832.7	335.9	738.8	-378.4
Iceland	-1.1	1.1	13.5	-	-	-	-	-	-4.7	-
Ireland	-1 013.9	696.7	-811.6	1 628.7	181.4	31.1	86.3	31.6	-296.2	31.3
Israel	-8.9	-10.0	-1.1	-2.4	5.6	-8.9	-2.2	4.5	-1.2	59.3
Italy	1 279.0	-7 566.1	666.2	112.1	-779.1	563.5	811.7	-168.0	669.2	7.8
Japan	-68.8	80.7	287.5	-77.9	-47.0	46.6	31.0	-9.0	38.9	39.2
Korea	11.1	364.9	319.0	1 308.9	179.1	10.0	-43.1	-10.1	86.2	71.6
Latvia	..	..	..	-	..	..	..	..	..	..
Lithuania	..	..	-	-	-	..	..	..	..	..
Luxembourg	1 558.5	2 051.3	110.5	1 279.4	-1 043.3	-215.2	800.6	-232.2	172.3	-7 943.6
Mexico	-16.6	-33.2	196.1	-11.8	-	155.3	174.7	131.9	142.8	208.2
Netherlands	1 232.4	-2 337.7	355.1	-5 645.0	-661.6	-1 009.4	6 886.0	5 024.2	-1 865.9	9 777.2
New Zealand	2.2	-	-1.1	-5.9	-2.2	-287.3	-31.0	-34.9	570.0	-256.4
Norway	18.9	-33.2	19.2	-10.6	6.7	185.2	191.3	-804.9	-666.8	-186.9
Poland	83.2	-5.5	144.3	-216.0	-14.6	82.1	558.4	1 079.9	-9.4	326.9
Portugal	-5.5	18.8	7.9	7.1	-31.3	10.0	-1.1	32.7	-59.0	75.0
Slovak Republic	-93.2	-36.5	-379.9	428.4	2.2	287.3	5.5	-479.1	231.3	9.0
Slovenia	56.6	-117.2	-62.0	-27.1	21.3	183.0	-81.8	320.1	211.3	71.6
Spain	-46.6	-97.3	-11.3	291.5	-24.6	94.3	194.6	280.7	577.1	-79.5
Sweden	54.4	70.8	157.8	240.8	-148.9	208.5	21.0	411.5	126.3	-133.2
Switzerland	-516.9	1 237.4	951.4	643.2	582.1	653.4	1 237.4	-799.2	1 311.2	745.6
Turkey	218.5	180.3	231.1	164.1	129.9	211.9	-2 687.2	-1 252.4	354.1	-45.9
United Kingdom	98.7	-808.4	857.9	1 413.9	-131.0	-16.6	826.1	-210.8	-293.9	-31.3
United States	-10.0	-2 326.7	-1 028.1	2 007.6	386.2	646.7	-213.4	248.0	1 524.8	592.2
EUROPE	**3 269.0**	**-6 914.7**	**13 042.5**	**2 974.2**	**726.5**	**5 748.2**	**4 073.9**	**7 960.8**	**849.8**	**4 955.8**
Bulgaria	-85.4	195.7	30.4	-9.4	-97.4	345.0	-1 933.0	-308.9	-119.2	53.7
Croatia	-25.5	16.6	-94.7	53.1	-3.4	-211.9	-1 803.6	58.6	74.4	-77.2
Cyprus	..	..	..	..	..	..	..	..	..	..
Malta	..	..	..	..	..	..	..	..	..	..
Romania	13.3	-10.0	-	-20.1	-148.9	1 325.6	-1 015.2	756.4	1 207.4	324.6
Russian Federation	-164.2	-25.4	6 417.5	-2 747.6	1 619.8	434.8	-517.5	1 364.0	594.8	162.3
Ukraine	119.8	14.4	-7.9	7.1	-25.7	541.3	-222.3	-13.5	110.9	-72.8
AFRICA	**-855.2**	**276.5**	**1 288.5**	**16.5**	**41.4**	**-108.7**	**-35.4**	**144.3**	**-61.4**	**72.8**
Northern Africa	3.3	-3.3	-24.8	-	4.5	31.1	-54.2	28.2	7.1	32.5
Algeria	..	..	-	-	-	..	..	-	..	-
Egypt	..	..	..	-	..	..	..	..	..	-
Libya	-	-	-	-	-	..	..	-	-	..
Morocco	..	..	..	..	..	..	..	..	..	..
Tunisia	..	..	..	..	..	..	..	..	-	..
Other African countries	..	..	..	..	..	..	..	..	..	..
Nigeria	..	..	..	..	-	..	..	..	-	-
South Africa	..	..	..	..	..	..	..	..	..	..
AMERICA	**-379.4**	**-2 345.5**	**-77.8**	**1 583.9**	**433.2**	**359.4**	**-7 431.2**	**351.7**	**1 038.6**	**673.9**
Northern America	-54.4	-2 301.2	-798.1	1 965.1	92.9	529.1	-398.1	-143.2	1 249.9	375.0
Central America and Caribbean countries	71.0	174.7	1 403.4	376.5	398.5	-306.2	-7 227.7	441.9	-467.4	279.9
Bahamas	..	-	-	..	-	..	..	-	-	-
Bermuda	..	..	..	..	..	..	..	..	..	..
Cayman Islands	..	..	..	..	..	..	..	..	..	..
Costa Rica	..	..	-	-	-	..	..	..	-	..
El Salvador	-	-	-	-	-	-	-	-	-	-
Guatemala	-	..	-	-	-	..	..	-	-	-
Honduras	-	-	-	-	-	..	..	..	..	..
Nicaragua	-	-	-	-	-	..	..	-	..	..
Panama	..	..	..	..	..	..	..	..	-	..
Virgin Islands, U.S.	..	..	..	..	..	-	-	-	-	-
South America	-396.0	-219.0	-684.3	-758.9	-58.2	136.4	194.6	53.0	256.1	19.0
Argentina	3.3	-1.1	7.9	17.7	29.1	12.2	121.6	18.0	18.9	5.6
Bolivia	-	-	-	-	-	..	..	-	..	..
Brazil	-244.0	-105.1	-688.8	-744.7	-64.9	117.6	-39.8	47.3	128.6	-11.2
Colombia	..	..	..	..	..	..	..	..	..	..
Ecuador	-	-	-	-	-	..	..	-	-	-
Paraguay	-	-	-	-	-	..	..	..	-	-
Peru	..	..	..	..	-	..	..	-	..	..
Uruguay	..	..	-	-	..	..	..	..	..	..
Venezuela	..	..	-	-	-	..	..	..	-	-

Table 1. Foreign direct investment flows by country *(cont.)*

Million US dollars

	Inward					Outward				
	2015	2016	2017	2018	2019	2015	2016	2017	2018	2019
ASIA	**-556.9**	**492.1**	**724.8**	**781.3**	**-257.5**	**1 132.6**	**1 255.1**	**1 720.2**	**2 865.6**	**5 055.4**
Near and Middle East	-391.6	-152.6	86.8	-363.5	-556.4	448.1	548.5	45.1	1 921.4	2 703.5
Gulf Arabian countries	-383.8	-139.3	86.8	-361.1	-559.7	453.7	528.6	55.2	1 921.4	2 636.3
Kuwait	..	..	..	..	..	-	-	-	..	-
Qatar	-	..	..	..	..	..	..	..	..	..
Saudi Arabia	..	..	..	..	-	..	..	..	..	..
United Arab Emirates	..	..	..	..	..	..	..	..	..	..
Other Near and Middle East	-6.7	-13.3	-	-2.4	4.5	-4.4	19.9	-10.1	-	67.2
Jordan	..	..	..	-	..	..	..	..	..	..
Other Asian countries	-165.3	644.7	638.0	1 144.8	298.9	684.4	706.6	1 675.1	944.2	2 352.0
China	62.1	2.2	22.5	139.3	36.9	140.9	268.7	592.9	434.3	288.8
Hong Kong, China	-99.8	147.1	-134.1	87.3	-86.2	108.7	206.8	242.4	276.2	399.6
India	8.9	-1.1	-	-16.5	-10.1	49.9	86.3	39.5	114.5	126.5
Indonesia	-1.1	-3.3	3.4	-1.2	-	-16.6	21.0	-5.6	20.1	61.6
Iran, Islamic Republic of	..	..	-	-	-	..	..	..	..	..
Malaysia	..	..	..	..	..	..	..	..	..	..
Philippines	-	-2.2	-	-	-	6.7	8.8	9.0	5.9	17.9
Singapore	48.8	-5.5	-19.2	7.1	-124.3	72.1	7.7	1 030.3	-118.0	269.8
Chinese Taipei	..	..	..	..	..	..	..	..	..	..
Thailand	-126.5	-88.5	-23.7	-421.3	241.8	306.2	28.8	-232.2	34.2	73.9
Viet Nam	..	..	-	-	-	..	..	..	..	..
AUSTRALIA, OCEANIA AND POLAR REGIONS	**56.6**	**-11.1**	**-56.4**	**-77.9**	**23.5**	**-117.6**	**87.4**	**51.9**	**915.9**	**136.6**
WORLD unallocated and confidential	**-46.6**	**2.2**	**-**	**5.9**	**-**	**13.3**	**18.8**	**-**	**-**	**-**
European Union (EU28)	**3 452.0**	**-8 227.4**	**5 451.5**	**4 882.6**	**-1 737.4**	**4 066.6**	**6 032.3**	**9 428.5**	**-1 083.4**	**4 134.1**
G20 countries excl. European Union	**-143.1**	**-9 319.9**	**12 939.9**	**7 883.9**	**457.9**	**3 046.0**	**127.2**	**2 748.3**	**1 624.0**	**3 674.0**
G20 OECD countries	**1 051.6**	**-9 470.3**	**5 849.4**	**11 169.6**	**-1 201.2**	**2 220.7**	**136.0**	**624.5**	**360.0**	**2 957.6**
G20 Non-OECD countries	**-1 194.7**	**150.4**	**7 090.5**	**-3 286.9**	**1 659.0**	**826.4**	**-8.8**	**2 123.8**	**1 264.0**	**716.4**
MENA countries	**-379.4**	**-146.0**	**62.0**	**-361.1**	**-557.5**	**484.7**	**473.3**	**69.9**	**1 927.3**	**2 674.4**
ASEAN countries	**-76.5**	**-45.3**	**-3.4**	**-347.0**	**221.7**	**369.4**	**103.9**	**789.1**	**18.9**	**1 409.4**

- Nil; .. Not available

Note: Data excludes resident Special Purpose Entities (SPEs). Detailed metadata at: *http://stats.oecd.org/OECDStat_Metadata/ShowMetadata.ashx?Dataset=FDI_CTRY_IND_SUMM.*

Source: *OECD International Direct Investment Statistics (database): https://doi.org/10.1787/idi-data-en*

AUSTRIA

Table 2. Foreign direct investment positions by country

At year end

Million US dollars

	Inward					Outward				
	2015	2016	2017	2018	2019	2015	2016	2017	2018	2019
WORLD	**159 723.5**	**150 648.3**	**191 442.8**	**188 795.5**	**196 716.5**	**205 235.7**	**196 996.9**	**233 762.3**	**227 984.9**	**234 977.5**
OECD COUNTRIES	**122 621.7**	**113 170.7**	**137 211.6**	**140 628.6**	**145 672.9**	**148 300.5**	**152 926.1**	**181 758.2**	**173 488.7**	**174 297.9**
Australia	54.4	67.5	87.6	80.1	91.0	2 064.2	2 130.3	2 551.0	3 020.4	3 402.6
Austria	2 423.5	2 342.2	5 155.9	5 863.3	5 614.5	-	-	-	-	-
Belgium	823.1	765.3	891.1	794.6	745.9	1 653.8	2 004.8	1 921.3	1 576.6	1 614.2
Canada	2 920.0	3 706.1	4 439.9	6 040.8	5 624.6	1 260.8	986.6	512.1	152.3	268.5
Chile	1.1	1.1	1.2	1.1	1.1	141.5	159.2	167.9	176.3	198.8
Czech Republic	197.1	254.0	206.3	416.8	342.6	14 398.5	11 573.7	14 570.6	14 618.7	15 071.9
Denmark	201.4	179.2	218.3	226.7	206.7	154.6	176.0	277.0	266.8	325.8
Estonia	-	-8.4	1.2	1.1	2.2	254.8	246.7	203.9	271.4	255.0
Finland	731.6	728.4	838.3	640.0	535.8	544.4	615.6	804.7	891.9	871.7
France	4 604.2	3 677.7	5 865.9	4 915.3	5 124.7	4 148.1	4 177.3	4 940.0	3 927.2	2 135.5
Germany	45 058.2	44 714.9	56 338.5	60 221.0	59 269.8	26 271.1	28 231.3	36 575.9	33 133.7	35 446.0
Greece	664.1	758.9	899.5	476.3	627.9	335.3	376.3	417.4	138.5	141.5
Hungary	155.7	190.8	207.5	221.0	246.0	7 952.1	6 870.5	8 163.8	8 229.9	7 817.3
Iceland	-	-	-	-	-	4.4	4.2	6.0	2.3	2.2
Ireland	341.9	662.0	722.0	700.7	889.7	179.6	179.2	251.9	89.3	120.2
Israel	18.5	160.2	266.3	425.9	308.9	7.6	5.3	9.6	3.4	66.3
Italy	18 500.8	10 314.1	11 662.3	11 270.9	11 153.7	2 469.2	3 163.3	3 788.7	4 485.9	4 761.9
Japan	2 102.3	2 142.9	4 072.9	4 001.6	5 845.9	133.9	175.0	171.5	296.5	338.1
Korea	189.4	227.7	255.5	1 632.7	1 760.3	1 196.5	1 105.7	1 166.9	1 205.6	1 240.2
Latvia	..	..	..	..	..	..	..	..	..	..
Lithuania	..	..	-	-	-	..	..	..	..	..
Luxembourg	2 394.1	3 321.4	3 328.1	2 951.7	3 716.0	11 665.8	12 643.6	14 292.4	13 891.7	5 658.3
Mexico	1 779.0	1 660.2	2 729.7	2 200.6	2 564.6	675.0	717.8	889.9	1 076.3	1 322.2
Netherlands	8 135.0	4 421.8	-399.4	542.7	5 684.1	20 751.2	25 500.2	36 103.4	33 697.0	41 143.6
New Zealand	-	-	-	-	-	124.1	97.0	62.4	612.5	355.0
Norway	235.2	248.8	310.6	128.2	138.2	2 572.7	2 792.2	2 203.2	1 462.1	1 267.1
Poland	9.8	16.9	25.2	17.2	16.9	4 849.2	5 051.1	7 031.7	5 920.5	6 218.8
Portugal	68.6	85.4	88.8	90.5	73.0	261.3	227.7	297.4	258.8	328.0
Slovak Republic	25.0	24.2	28.8	26.3	21.3	6 541.1	6 250.7	7 266.7	7 202.9	6 372.7
Slovenia	167.7	122.3	154.7	20.6	18.0	3 358.7	2 843.9	3 642.4	3 711.9	3 713.8
Spain	1 020.1	1 242.8	1 452.4	731.6	702.1	1 071.3	1 183.7	1 560.3	1 957.9	1 838.9
Sweden	793.7	918.1	1 036.2	1 221.7	1 250.3	1 552.5	1 535.8	1 772.6	1 678.5	1 621.0
Switzerland	7 989.1	9 112.5	13 261.0	12 744.4	13 175.7	8 315.7	9 551.0	8 546.4	8 513.9	9 305.8
Turkey	206.9	218.2	247.1	243.9	352.7	4 881.9	3 580.7	1 790.6	1 386.5	1 277.2
United Kingdom	5 259.7	5 716.2	6 682.7	5 992.7	5 807.7	7 618.9	8 187.0	7 778.8	6 123.2	5 756.0
United States	15 551.4	15 170.2	16 128.6	15 775.1	13 752.0	10 890.6	10 451.1	11 849.4	13 234.5	13 799.1
EUROPE	**124 238.4**	**113 256.0**	**142 347.1**	**139 855.7**	**146 482.8**	**167 276.0**	**166 382.4**	**198 366.5**	**187 723.8**	**188 115.0**
Bulgaria	4.4	278.3	317.8	295.4	204.4	4 593.4	3 152.7	3 238.2	2 973.4	2 971.2
Croatia	-	1.1	3.6	-2.3	-2.2	5 264.0	3 959.1	4 552.7	4 704.6	4 492.2
Cyprus	..	..	..	..	..	..	..	..	..	..
Malta	..	..	..	..	..	..	..	..	..	..
Romania	56.6	55.9	68.4	60.7	-16.9	9 527.5	8 282.9	10 100.7	10 266.8	10 089.9
Russian Federation	21 389.2	20 206.6	30 197.9	25 330.9	27 582.6	5 693.0	4 966.8	6 103.4	6 861.7	8 015.1
Ukraine	18.5	42.2	45.6	52.7	53.9	997.3	331.0	488.1	603.4	621.2
AFRICA	**1 948.8**	**1 924.7**	**3 004.3**	**2 875.0**	**2 861.2**	**887.3**	**820.1**	**993.0**	**1 033.9**	**1 108.7**
Northern Africa	-	-	-	-	-	234.1	172.9	293.8	360.7	393.2
Algeria	-	-	-	-	-	..	..	..	..	..
Egypt	..	-	-	-	-	..	..	..	..	..
Libya	-	-	-	-	-	..	..	..	..	..
Morocco	-	-	-	-	-	..	..	..	..	..
Tunisia	-	-	-	-	-	..	..	..	..	..
Other African countries	..	..	..	..	..	..	..	..	..	..
Nigeria	-	..	-	-	-	..	..	..	..	..
South Africa	..	..	..	..	..	..	..	..	..	..
AMERICA	**21 442.6**	**21 840.4**	**26 765.4**	**26 778.1**	**26 427.8**	**23 296.7**	**15 143.9**	**16 569.9**	**17 841.8**	**18 753.1**
Northern America	18 471.4	18 877.4	20 568.5	21 815.9	19 375.4	12 151.3	11 437.8	12 361.5	13 386.8	14 067.6
Central America and Caribbean countries	1 793.1	1 666.5	2 581.0	2 679.2	3 045.4	9 623.3	1 933.2	2 360.3	2 458.2	2 773.5
Bahamas	..	-	-	-	-	..	..	-	-	-
Bermuda	..	..	..	-	..	..	..	..	-	..
Cayman Islands	..	-	-	-	..	..	..	..	..	..
Costa Rica	..	-	-	-	-	..	..	..	..	..
El Salvador	-	-	-	-	-	-	-	-	-	-
Guatemala	-	-	-	-	-	..	..	..	-	-
Honduras	-	-	-	-	-	..	..	..	..	..
Nicaragua	-	-	-	-	-	..	..	..	..	..
Panama	..	..	..	..	..	..	..	..	..	..
Virgin Islands, U.S.	..	-	-	-	-	-	-	-	-	-
South America	1 176.9	1 296.5	3 617.2	2 284.2	4 005.8	1 522.0	1 773.0	1 848.2	1 995.6	1 911.9
Argentina	50.1	49.5	62.4	708.7	702.1	98.0	92.8	106.7	130.5	97.7
Bolivia	-	-	-	-	-	..	..	..	..	..
Brazil	1 118.1	1 239.6	3 552.4	1 574.3	3 303.8	1 077.8	1 173.2	1 334.9	1 356.8	1 299.7
Colombia	-	-	-	-	-	..	..	..	..	..
Ecuador	-	-	-	-	-	..	..	..	..	..
Paraguay	-	-	-	-	-	..	..	-	-	-
Peru	-	-	-	-	-	..	..	..	..	..
Uruguay	-	-	-	-	-	..	..	..	..	..
Venezuela	..	..	-	-	-	..	..	-	..	..

Table 2. Foreign direct investment positions by country *(cont.)*

At year end

Million US dollars

	Inward					Outward				
	2015	2016	2017	2018	2019	2015	2016	2017	2018	2019
ASIA	**11 746.3**	**13 276.1**	**18 914.6**	**18 898.6**	**20 550.4**	**11 573.2**	**12 422.3**	**15 217.1**	**17 751.3**	**23 243.1**
Near and Middle East	5 549.3	6 269.6	8 725.1	7 213.2	7 175.9	4 559.6	4 986.8	5 805.9	7 618.5	10 795.3
Gulf Arabian countries	5 527.5	6 108.4	8 457.7	6 787.3	6 865.9	4 498.6	4 921.5	5 724.4	7 554.4	10 661.6
Kuwait	..	..	..	..	..	-	-	-	-	-
Qatar	-	-	-	-	-	..	..	..	..	..
Saudi Arabia	..	..	..	..	..	..	..	..	..	..
United Arab Emirates	..	..	..	..	..	..	..	..	..	..
Other Near and Middle East	20.7	162.3	267.5	425.9	310.0	61.0	65.4	81.6	64.1	133.7
Jordan	..	..	..	-	-	..	..	..	..	..
Other Asian countries	6 198.1	7 005.4	10 189.5	11 685.4	13 374.5	7 013.6	7 435.4	9 411.1	10 132.8	12 447.8
China	484.5	375.3	903.1	1 353.3	1 231.2	2 481.2	2 615.2	3 445.7	3 764.6	3 999.1
Hong Kong, China	2 802.4	3 301.4	3 500.8	3 145.2	2 976.9	679.4	877.0	1 232.9	1 551.4	1 923.2
India	138.3	123.3	328.6	311.4	334.8	427.9	450.1	645.2	717.9	830.2
Indonesia	-	-	-	-	-	211.2	226.6	226.7	240.4	307.8
Iran, Islamic Republic of	..	-	-	..	..	..	..	..	..	..
Malaysia	..	..	..	..	..	..	..	..	..	..
Philippines	1.1	-	-	-	-	74.0	79.1	79.2	73.3	94.4
Singapore	457.3	610.3	568.5	603.4	549.3	1 281.4	1 290.2	1 805.0	1 702.5	2 031.0
Chinese Taipei	..	..	..	..	..	..	..	..	..	..
Thailand	-	-	16.8	5.7	4.5	310.3	331.0	249.5	139.7	226.9
Viet Nam	-	-	-	-	-	..	..	..	..	..
AUSTRALIA, OCEANIA AND POLAR REGIONS	**54.4**	**67.5**	**87.6**	**80.1**	**91.0**	**2 189.4**	**2 228.3**	**2 615.7**	**3 634.1**	**3 757.6**
WORLD unallocated and confidential	**292.9**	**283.5**	**323.8**	**308.0**	**303.3**	**13.1**	**-**	**-**	**-**	**-**
European Union (EU28)	**93 426.2**	**82 307.4**	**97 519.8**	**100 073.3**	**103 736.2**	**137 523.1**	**139 249.5**	**172 073.6**	**161 935.0**	**160 441.5**
G20 countries excl. European Union	**121 521.0**	**111 744.5**	**146 831.4**	**144 779.0**	**147 619.6**	**72 022.9**	**72 912.4**	**84 441.1**	**81 648.7**	**84 918.0**
G20 OECD countries	**96 225.4**	**87 616.7**	**108 510.4**	**112 375.8**	**111 345.8**	**61 611.3**	**62 907.1**	**72 017.3**	**68 043.3**	**69 748.4**
G20 Non-OECD countries	**25 294.5**	**24 127.8**	**38 320.9**	**32 403.3**	**36 272.7**	**10 411.5**	**10 005.3**	**12 425.0**	**13 605.5**	**15 169.6**
MENA countries	**5 528.6**	**6 108.4**	**8 457.7**	**6 787.3**	**6 865.9**	**4 759.9**	**5 118.6**	**6 054.2**	**7 954.0**	**11 100.9**
ASEAN countries	**462.7**	**689.4**	**716.0**	**883.9**	**839.1**	**2 063.1**	**2 139.8**	**2 642.1**	**2 512.0**	**4 017.1**

- Nil; .. Not available

Note: Data excludes resident Special Purpose Entities (SPEs). Detailed metadata at: *http://stats.oecd.org/OECDStat_Metadata/ShowMetadata.ashx?Dataset=FDI_CTRY_IND_SUMM.*

1. Inward FDI positions are allocated according to the ultimate investing country. Detailed metadata at: *http://stats.oecd.org/OECDStat_Metadata/ShowMetadata.ashx?Dataset=FDI_CTRY_IND_SUMM.*

Source: *OECD International Direct Investment Statistics (database): https://doi.org/10.1787/idi-data-en*

AUSTRIA

Table 3. Foreign direct investment income by country

Million US dollars

	Inward					Outward				
	2015	2016	2017	2018	2019	2015	2016	2017	2018	2019
WORLD	**9 651.7**	**11 956.2**	**15 794.2**	**16 065.1**	**12 920.6**	**10 661.1**	**15 376.5**	**15 095.3**	**15 065.5**	**15 458.4**
OECD COUNTRIES	**9 462.0**	**10 632.5**	**13 050.4**	**13 112.2**	**10 313.4**	**6 815.3**	**9 847.4**	**9 533.3**	**8 484.6**	**9 179.4**
Australia	7.8	10.0	11.3	11.8	12.3	129.8	123.9	147.7	36.6	333.6
Austria	-	-	-	-	-	-	-	-	-	-
Belgium	30.0	130.5	73.3	69.6	88.4	83.2	129.4	137.5	125.1	67.2
Canada	16.6	16.6	-6.8	9.4	16.8	147.5	224.5	-143.2	-393.0	9.0
Chile	-	-	-	-11.8	-	-6.7	13.3	-3.4	31.9	14.6
Czech Republic	6.7	4.4	22.5	64.9	43.7	1 846.9	1 712.9	1 924.2	2 079.5	1 673.6
Denmark	-56.6	27.6	28.2	34.2	24.6	4.4	21.0	10.1	16.5	10.1
Estonia	-	-3.3	-	-	-	11.1	14.4	20.3	28.3	-
Finland	64.3	63.0	55.2	94.4	40.3	26.6	54.2	77.8	138.1	32.5
France	287.3	253.2	200.7	123.9	295.5	187.5	94.0	-128.5	118.0	72.8
Germany	2 794.2	3 680.2	4 781.9	6 770.9	4 122.9	1 134.8	954.3	2 409.0	2 261.3	1 648.9
Greece	-48.8	38.7	47.3	24.8	24.6	-23.3	-3.3	-5.6	-4.7	3.4
Hungary	63.2	44.2	44.0	23.6	14.6	1 122.6	680.1	1 050.6	1 154.3	87.3
Iceland	-	-	-	-	-	-	-	-	-	-
Ireland	16.6	34.3	-21.4	-157.0	11.2	33.3	27.6	28.2	-5.9	-14.6
Israel	-	-	-	-	-	-3.3	-	-1.1	-3.5	10.1
Italy	474.8	412.5	812.8	594.8	560.8	62.1	76.3	11.3	-131.0	133.2
Japan	1.1	50.9	49.6	35.4	45.9	10.0	2.2	6.8	38.9	34.7
Korea	-5.5	-10.0	3.4	38.9	96.3	105.4	189.1	99.2	135.7	163.4
Latvia	..	..	-	-	..	..	..	..	..	-
Lithuania	..	..	-	-	-	..	..	..	..	..
Luxembourg	311.7	1 402.2	12.4	985.5	1 183.3	-470.3	732.1	-307.7	-1 017.3	695.2
Mexico	7.8	7.7	10.1	7.1	9.0	134.2	152.6	121.7	122.7	126.5
Netherlands	3 088.2	2 069.0	4 775.1	2 568.2	1 999.3	-786.5	1 091.5	383.3	511.0	1 285.1
New Zealand	-	-	-	-	-	-144.2	58.6	48.5	30.7	36.9
Norway	13.3	-16.6	-13.5	-1.2	12.3	-219.6	19.9	19.2	257.3	109.7
Poland	-4.4	-2.2	-12.4	-22.4	-16.8	471.4	329.5	455.4	411.9	396.3
Portugal	7.8	28.8	15.8	14.2	6.7	23.3	14.4	-	-33.0	5.6
Slovak Republic	16.6	-	3.4	-22.4	4.5	641.2	755.3	695.5	731.7	603.4
Slovenia	-	-	2.3	-	1.1	286.2	305.2	402.4	407.2	193.7
Spain	92.1	81.8	87.9	47.2	53.7	144.2	232.2	151.1	283.3	56.0
Sweden	186.4	191.3	158.9	245.5	90.7	142.0	160.3	220.9	109.8	38.1
Switzerland	688.9	1 406.6	1 084.4	827.3	912.3	713.3	901.3	98.1	234.9	658.2
Turkey	156.4	194.6	193.9	158.1	79.5	251.8	170.3	170.2	138.1	16.8
United Kingdom	560.2	362.7	423.9	385.9	310.1	93.2	-69.7	742.9	5.9	13.4
United States	684.4	150.4	206.3	192.4	266.4	662.2	660.2	664.0	627.9	660.5
EUROPE	**8 824.2**	**10 810.6**	**13 110.1**	**13 297.5**	**11 507.9**	**7 862.5**	**12 057.9**	**11 928.8**	**11 974.5**	**10 398.5**
Bulgaria	-1.1	110.6	22.5	4.7	16.8	526.9	291.9	143.2	133.4	228.4
Croatia	-10.0	-11.1	-10.1	-10.6	-4.5	-231.8	334.0	223.2	407.2	339.2
Cyprus	..	..	..	..	..	..	..	..	..	..
Malta	..	..	..	..	..	..	..	..	..	..
Romania	-3.3	-4.4	-2.3	-2.4	-9.0	531.3	525.3	860.1	1 370.2	920.2
Russian Federation	-52.1	-102.8	87.9	152.2	1 447.4	902.9	927.8	1 197.2	1 147.2	557.5
Ukraine	-33.3	-42.0	-22.5	-2.4	-	-106.5	112.8	152.2	237.2	26.9
AFRICA	**-225.2**	**43.1**	**478.0**	**28.3**	**99.6**	**-26.6**	**-43.1**	**59.7**	**64.9**	**47.0**
Northern Africa	-1.1	-1.1	-1.1	-2.4	-2.2	6.7	-58.6	-3.4	-1.2	16.8
Algeria	-	..	-	-	-	..	..	..	..	-
Egypt	..	..	-	-	-	..	..	-	-	-
Libya	-	..	-	-	-	..	..	-	-	..
Morocco	-	..	..	..	..	..	..	..	-	..
Tunisia	..	..	..	-	-	..	..	..	..	..
Other African countries	..	..	..	..	..	..	..	..	..	..
Nigeria	-	..	-	-	-	..	..	..	-	-
South Africa	..	..	..	..	..	..	..	..	..	..
AMERICA	**758.7**	**-171.4**	**846.6**	**1 357.3**	**586.6**	**1 171.4**	**1 427.6**	**824.0**	**721.1**	**1 084.7**
Northern America	701.1	167.0	199.5	201.8	283.2	809.8	884.7	520.8	233.7	670.5
Central America and Caribbean countries	153.1	139.3	231.1	102.7	134.3	311.7	457.8	264.9	358.8	274.3
Bahamas	-	..	..	-	-	..	..	-	-	-
Bermuda	-	..	..	..	..	..	..	..	-	-
Cayman Islands	..	..	..	..	..	..	..	..	-	..
Costa Rica	-	..	-	-	-	..	..	..	-	..
El Salvador	-	..	-	-	-	-	..	-	-	-
Guatemala	-	..	-	-	-	..	..	-	-	-
Honduras	-	..	-	-	-	..	..	..	-	..
Nicaragua	-	..	-	-	-	..	..	..	..	..
Panama	..	..	..	..	..	..	..	..	..	..
Virgin Islands, U.S.	..	..	..	..	..	-	..	-	-	-
South America	-95.4	-477.7	416.0	1 052.8	169.0	49.9	85.1	37.2	127.5	141.1
Argentina	-	-	37.2	24.8	25.7	25.5	18.8	7.9	1.2	9.0
Bolivia	-	..	-	-	-	-	..	-	..	..
Brazil	-95.4	-477.7	378.8	1 039.8	143.3	33.3	15.5	15.8	41.3	89.6
Colombia	-	..	-	-	-	..	..	..	..	..
Ecuador	-	..	-	-	-	..	..	-	-	-
Paraguay	-	..	-	-	-	..	..	-	-	-
Peru	-	..	-	-	-	..	..	-	..	..
Uruguay	-	..	-	-	-	..	..	..	..	..
Venezuela	-	..	-	-	-	..	..	-	-	-

AUSTRIA

Table 3. Foreign direct investment income by country *(cont.)*

Million US dollars

	Inward					Outward				
	2015	2016	2017	2018	2019	2015	2016	2017	2018	2019
ASIA	**331.7**	**1 261.7**	**1 341.5**	**1 367.9**	**713.1**	**1 692.7**	**1 764.9**	**2 097.8**	**2 244.8**	**3 563.2**
Near and Middle East	55.5	875.8	939.0	781.3	384.0	868.6	834.9	762.0	858.0	1 731.8
Gulf Arabian countries	64.3	888.0	945.8	782.5	384.0	864.1	831.6	768.8	862.7	1 710.5
Kuwait	..	..	..	..	..	-	..	-	-	-
Qatar	-	..	..	..	..	..	..	..	..	..
Saudi Arabia	..	..	..	..	..	..	..	..	..	..
United Arab Emirates	..	..	..	..	..	..	..	..	..	..
Other Near and Middle East	-8.9	-12.2	-6.8	-	-	4.4	2.2	-6.8	-4.7	21.3
Jordan	..	..	..	-	-	..	..	..	..	..
Other Asian countries	276.2	385.9	402.4	585.4	329.1	825.3	930.0	1 335.8	1 385.6	1 831.4
China	-1.1	-1.1	-7.9	5.9	4.5	545.8	504.3	1 148.7	986.7	978.4
Hong Kong, China	275.1	289.7	322.4	433.1	160.1	48.8	23.2	99.2	208.9	154.5
India	-	-	-	-	-	26.6	24.3	38.3	36.6	70.5
Indonesia	-	-	-	-	-	3.3	17.7	14.7	4.7	22.4
Iran, Islamic Republic of	..	..	-	-	-	..	..	..	..	..
Malaysia	..	..	..	..	..	..	..	..	..	..
Philippines	-	-1.1	-	-	-	13.3	16.6	14.7	14.2	12.3
Singapore	8.9	3.3	-4.5	5.9	-2.2	82.1	79.6	-131.9	-135.7	235.1
Chinese Taipei	..	..	..	..	..	..	..	..	..	..
Thailand	-4.4	-4.4	-2.3	-2.4	-2.2	33.3	29.9	18.0	16.5	21.3
Viet Nam	-	..	-	-	-	..	..	..	..	..
AUSTRALIA, OCEANIA AND POLAR REGIONS	**7.8**	**8.8**	**11.3**	**11.8**	**12.3**	**-14.4**	**183.6**	**196.1**	**67.3**	**370.5**
WORLD unallocated and confidential	**-45.5**	**3.3**	**6.8**	**2.4**	**1.1**	**-24.4**	**-14.4**	**-11.3**	**-7.1**	**-5.6**
European Union (EU28)	**8 061.0**	**9 182.8**	**11 635.7**	**12 105.5**	**8 974.6**	**5 885.7**	**9 210.4**	**9 705.8**	**9 372.1**	**8 520.1**
G20 countries excl. European Union	**4 612.3**	**4 596.9**	**7 659.8**	**9 575.1**	**7 545.1**	**4 480.3**	**4 102.6**	**6 523.5**	**5 181.2**	**4 990.5**
G20 OECD countries	**4 986.1**	**5 128.8**	**6 687.0**	**8 328.8**	**5 816.6**	**2 918.5**	**2 578.8**	**4 102.1**	**2 962.4**	**3 213.9**
G20 Non-OECD countries	**-372.7**	**-533.0**	**972.8**	**1 246.3**	**1 728.4**	**1 561.8**	**1 523.8**	**2 421.4**	**2 218.8**	**1 777.7**
MENA countries	**55.5**	**875.8**	**937.9**	**778.9**	**381.7**	**869.7**	**773.0**	**762.0**	**859.2**	**1 732.9**
ASEAN countries	**6.7**	**54.2**	**30.4**	**62.6**	**6.7**	**124.2**	**174.7**	**-68.8**	**-24.8**	**417.6**

- Nil; .. Not available

Note: Data excludes resident Special Purpose Entities (SPEs). Detailed metadata at: *http://stats.oecd.org/OECDStat_Metadata/ShowMetadata.ashx?Dataset=FDI_CTRY_IND_SUMM.*

Source: *OECD International Direct Investment Statistics (database): https://doi.org/10.1787/idi-data-en*

AUSTRIA

Table 4. Foreign direct investment flows by industrial sector

Million US dollars

	Inward					Outward				
	2015	2016	2017	2018	2019	2015	2016	2017	2018	2019
All FDI activities	**1 487.5**	**-8 500.5**	**14 921.7**	**5 283.8**	**967.2**	**7 027.2**	**-2 031.4**	**10 228.8**	**5 608.4**	**10 894.4**
Agriculture, forestry and fishing	**-1.1**	**-1.1**	**-1.1**	**-1.2**	**1.1**	**-2.2**	**110.6**	**14.7**	**-61.4**	**24.6**
Mining and quarrying	**76.5**	**64.1**	**-189.4**	**166.4**	**115.3**	**-572.4**	**-796.2**	**-1 209.6**	**1 725.5**	**2 868.0**
Extraction activities	..	..	..	..	..	..	..	..	..	..
Manufacturing	**619.0**	**483.2**	**354.0**	**1 303.0**	**1 573.9**	**2 881.9**	**2 566.6**	**2 431.5**	**4 445.9**	**862.0**
of which:										
Food products, beverages and tobacco	-53.2	360.5	-80.0	-16.5	-246.3	109.8	68.6	92.4	-118.0	-62.7
Textiles, wood and paper products; printing	-106.5	-22.1	-	159.3	-117.5	303.9	831.6	1 481.2	1 307.7	331.4
Chemical, rubber, plastic, non-metallic mineral products	-178.6	-19.9	157.8	-139.3	166.8	695.5	57.5	-370.9	1 023.3	479.1
Metal and machinery products, except electrical equipment	563.5	-7.7	325.8	863.9	745.6	1 083.7	-230.0	301.0	1 396.2	-191.4
Motor vehicles, trailers, semi-trailers, other transport equipment	-203.0	434.6	-120.6	361.1	663.8	558.0	1 006.3	800.4	374.1	307.8
Other manufacturing	596.8	-262.1	69.9	74.4	361.6	132.0	833.8	128.5	462.6	-1.1
Electricity, gas, steam and air conditioning supply	**113.1**	**-8.8**	**102.6**	**49.6**	**77.2**	**-142.0**	**52.0**	**-1 778.8**	**218.3**	**113.1**
Water supply; sewerage, waste management and remediation activities	**4.4**	**2.2**	**-**	**4.7**	**-11.2**	**58.8**	**58.6**	**-25.9**	**29.5**	**19.0**
Construction	**-2.2**	**34.3**	**200.7**	**298.6**	**166.8**	**-331.7**	**-786.2**	**-206.3**	**-208.9**	**179.1**
Services	**676.7**	**-9 216.0**	**14 453.8**	**3 462.8**	**-956.0**	**5 124.8**	**-3 909.1**	**10 766.5**	**-723.5**	**5 849.1**
Wholesale and retail trade; repair of motor vehicles and motorcycles	-1 930.1	2 502.5	2 988.4	341.1	307.8	1 941.2	1 668.7	1 698.8	-388.3	-947.1
Transportation and storage	-237.4	409.2	41.7	-22.4	245.2	1.1	110.6	225.5	-72.0	-368.3
Accommodation and food service activities	-21.1	-87.4	14.7	-10.6	-24.6	179.7	-66.4	-199.5	29.5	69.4
Information and communication	-718.8	1 016.3	-720.3	-2 159.8	50.4	378.3	-110.6	590.7	-141.6	298.9
Financial and insurance activities	3 455.4	-8 222.9	-1 357.2	444.9	-2 075.5	3 407.7	-8 549.2	889.4	3 196.0	-5 571.5
Activities of holding companies	1 748.2	-311.8	-1 379.8	11.8	-2 466.1	-51.0	-2 634.1	-7.9	2 428.9	-5 796.5
Real estate activities	485.9	-682.3	2 198.2	-225.4	2 684.4	-307.3	-253.2	567.0	-1 874.2	119.8
Professional, scientific and technical activities	-464.8	-4 017.5	10 990.9	4 369.2	-2 022.8	-631.2	2 961.4	7 134.5	-1 961.5	11 739.6
Administrative and support service activities	112.0	-106.2	273.9	782.5	-216.1	108.7	275.4	-390.0	310.4	245.2
Public administration; activities of households and of extraterritorial organisations	-	-	-	-	-	-1.1	-1.1	5.6	82.6	7.8
Education	..	..	..	..	..	..	..	-	-	..
Human health and social work activities	..	..	..	..	..	..	..	..	..	..
Arts, entertainment and recreation	2.2	-31.0	22.5	-43.7	59.3	10.0	59.7	245.7	112.1	229.5
Other services	-7.8	-1.1	-5.6	-	1.1	28.8	-42.0	7.9	-10.6	1.1
Not allocated and confidential	**1.1**	**141.5**	**1.1**	**-**	**-**	**10.0**	**672.3**	**236.7**	**182.9**	**979.5**
Private real estate activities	**-**	**..**	**-**	**-**	**-**	**-**	**..**	**-**	**-**	**-**

- Nil; .. Not available

Note: Data excludes resident Special Purpose Entities (SPEs). Detailed metadata at: *http://stats.oecd.org/OECDStat_Metadata/ShowMetadata.ashx?Dataset=FDI_CTRY_IND_SUMM.*

Source: OECD *International Direct Investment Statistics (database): https://doi.org/10.1787/idi-data-en*

Table 5. Foreign direct investment positions by industrial sector
At year end

Million US dollars

	Inward					Outward				
	2015	2016	2017	2018	2019	2015	2016	2017	2018	2019
All FDI activities	**159 723.5**	**150 648.3**	**191 442.8**	**188 795.5**	**196 716.5**	**205 235.7**	**196 996.9**	**233 762.3**	**227 984.9**	**234 977.5**
Agriculture, forestry and fishing	**17.4**	**21.1**	**22.8**	**20.6**	**21.3**	**101.3**	**83.3**	**189.5**	**174.0**	**193.2**
Mining and quarrying	**280.9**	**403.7**	**266.3**	**361.8**	**462.8**	**7 995.6**	**6 124.2**	**4 882.5**	**6 852.5**	**9 684.3**
Extraction activities	..	..	..	..	..	..	..	..	..	..
Manufacturing	**14 734.9**	**14 262.7**	**17 458.6**	**18 548.2**	**19 906.8**	**38 175.3**	**39 284.3**	**46 703.0**	**49 252.3**	**50 812.2**
of which:										
Food products, beverages and tobacco	1 371.8	1 696.0	1 745.0	1 893.7	1 603.0	1 199.8	1 559.0	1 953.7	1 836.5	1 736.7
Textiles, wood and paper products; printing	816.5	919.2	2 287.1	2 157.1	2 040.0	4 632.6	5 516.0	7 232.0	7 971.1	8 313.9
Chemical, rubber, plastic, non-metallic mineral products	4 592.3	4 047.6	4 454.3	4 416.1	4 497.9	14 196.0	13 321.4	14 671.4	14 542.0	15 205.6
Metal and machinery products, except electrical equipment	3 644.0	3 324.5	4 365.6	5 290.8	5 940.2	8 653.2	8 363.0	10 202.7	11 049.9	10 998.7
Motor vehicles, trailers, semi-trailers, other transport equipment	2 438.8	2 492.9	2 764.5	3 078.8	3 678.9	2 911.3	3 760.9	5 030.0	5 132.8	5 650.4
Other manufacturing	1 871.5	1 781.4	1 842.2	1 711.7	2 146.7	6 582.5	6 765.0	7 613.3	8 721.1	8 905.9
Electricity, gas, steam and air conditioning supply	**776.3**	**807.4**	**1 262.9**	**1 098.0**	**1 421.0**	**4 531.3**	**4 305.9**	**2 299.1**	**1 970.5**	**2 138.8**
Water supply; sewerage, waste management and remediation activities	**74.0**	**78.0**	**91.1**	**97.3**	**84.3**	**700.1**	**710.4**	**885.1**	**970.9**	**984.0**
Construction	**136.1**	**387.9**	**466.5**	**679.0**	**752.6**	**3 437.1**	**2 706.9**	**3 197.4**	**4 380.6**	**4 746.1**
Services	**143 703.9**	**134 557.8**	**171 874.5**	**167 989.5**	**174 066.5**	**150 301.6**	**142 510.8**	**175 605.7**	**164 385.2**	**166 303.1**
Wholesale and retail trade; repair of motor vehicles and motorcycles	15 906.4	18 748.8	25 600.9	24 734.4	26 109.9	27 506.8	28 932.2	33 926.6	31 496.5	29 156.4
Transportation and storage	1 024.5	1 531.6	2 223.6	2 213.2	2 421.9	1 176.9	1 292.3	1 634.7	1 706.0	1 519.9
Accommodation and food service activities	354.9	303.6	442.6	413.3	380.8	607.5	595.6	379.0	409.9	495.4
Information and communication	2 792.6	3 649.2	3 112.3	2 675.8	2 708.4	3 323.9	3 100.0	3 451.7	3 347.8	3 683.4
Financial and insurance activities	31 829.1	22 282.1	26 037.4	29 901.5	27 067.0	74 683.7	64 026.6	77 059.2	73 858.5	68 794.7
Activities of holding companies	6 565.1	6 343.4	8 737.1	13 992.4	11 053.7	34 315.7	32 799.6	38 105.1	38 402.8	32 916.2
Real estate activities	4 065.3	3 869.5	7 615.7	6 629.3	9 528.2	5 345.7	6 417.2	7 449.0	7 154.8	7 448.9
Professional, scientific and technical activities	83 415.4	81 512.6	103 522.4	96 741.5	101 409.8	33 511.2	33 278.2	45 436.6	39 862.6	48 298.1
Administrative and support service activities	4 180.7	2 530.8	3 157.8	4 561.5	4 228.3	3 061.5	3 754.6	3 649.6	2 846.3	3 031.9
Public administration; activities of households and of extraterritorial organisations	-	-	-	-	-	17.4	17.9	21.6	81.3	82.0
Education	..	..	..	..	..	..	..	-	..	..
Human health and social work activities	..	..	..	..	..	..	..	..	..	..
Arts, entertainment and recreation	95.8	91.7	122.3	85.9	143.8	856.8	878.0	1 162.1	1 506.8	1 558.1
Other services	16.3	14.8	9.6	8.0	7.9	137.2	99.1	113.9	87.0	109.0
Not allocated and confidential	-	**129.7**	..	**1.1**	..	**-6.5**	**-5.3**	-	**-1.1**	**115.7**
Private real estate activities	-	..	-	-	-	-	..	-	-	-

- Nil; .. Not available

Note: Data excludes resident Special Purpose Entities (SPEs). Detailed metadata at: *http://stats.oecd.org/OECDStat_Metadata/ShowMetadata.ashx?Dataset=FDI_CTRY_IND_SUMM.*

Source: OECD *International Direct Investment Statistics (database): https://doi.org/10.1787/idi-data-en*

Table 6. Foreign direct investment income by industrial sector

Million US dollars

	Inward					Outward				
	2015	2016	2017	2018	2019	2015	2016	2017	2018	2019
All FDI activities	**9 651.7**	**11 956.2**	**15 794.2**	**16 065.1**	**12 920.6**	**10 661.1**	**15 376.5**	**15 095.3**	**15 065.5**	**15 458.4**
Agriculture, forestry and fishing	**-1.1**	**-1.1**	**-1.1**	**-1.2**	**1.1**	**-5.5**	**1.1**	**-**	**2.4**	**13.4**
Mining and quarrying	**6.7**	**67.5**	**87.9**	**90.9**	**61.6**	**-1 139.2**	**-748.6**	**259.3**	**383.6**	**868.7**
Extraction activities	..	..	..	..	..	..	..	..	..	..
Manufacturing	**1 817.0**	**2 001.5**	**1 869.0**	**2 205.8**	**2 627.3**	**4 288.4**	**5 229.5**	**4 709.7**	**5 725.2**	**4 416.2**
of which:										
Food products, beverages and tobacco	359.4	382.6	361.9	555.9	236.2	146.4	165.9	180.4	126.3	99.6
Textiles, wood and paper products; printing	122.0	108.4	139.8	174.7	148.9	907.4	1 271.7	1 370.8	1 742.0	998.5
Chemical, rubber, plastic, non-metallic mineral products	342.8	527.5	417.1	429.6	527.3	1 878.0	2 191.8	1 790.1	1 776.2	1 825.8
Metal and machinery products, except electrical equipment	617.9	666.8	783.5	867.5	977.3	732.1	764.1	553.5	1 066.9	708.6
Motor vehicles, trailers, semi-trailers, other transport equipment	-16.6	270.9	9.0	-26.0	388.4	110.9	238.9	281.8	342.3	309.0
Other manufacturing	391.6	45.3	157.8	204.2	348.1	513.6	597.1	533.2	671.5	473.5
Electricity, gas, steam and air conditioning supply	**36.6**	**27.6**	**136.4**	**75.5**	**42.5**	**107.6**	**13.3**	**86.8**	**135.7**	**126.5**
Water supply; sewerage, waste management and remediation activities	**6.7**	**11.1**	**25.9**	**16.5**	**3.4**	**72.1**	**38.7**	**65.4**	**64.9**	**49.3**
Construction	**1.1**	**-2.2**	**18.0**	**21.2**	**54.9**	**313.9**	**267.6**	**128.5**	**253.7**	**240.7**
Services	**7 784.8**	**9 851.8**	**13 656.9**	**13 656.3**	**10 129.9**	**7 023.8**	**10 573.9**	**9 844.4**	**8 498.8**	**9 739.2**
Wholesale and retail trade; repair of motor vehicles and motorcycles	2 490.3	2 177.4	3 261.2	3 659.9	2 174.0	2 757.6	2 730.3	3 670.4	2 505.6	2 133.7
Transportation and storage	143.1	168.1	139.8	-40.1	157.8	130.9	133.8	162.3	192.4	76.1
Accommodation and food service activities	-4.4	29.9	12.4	10.6	1.1	31.1	66.4	24.8	11.8	16.8
Information and communication	351.6	482.1	411.5	276.2	295.5	281.8	90.7	111.6	131.0	207.1
Financial and insurance activities	854.1	1 604.6	2 356.0	2 412.4	1 362.4	4 364.9	5 180.8	4 793.1	4 087.1	4 951.3
Activities of holding companies	615.6	1 130.2	1 289.6	1 537.8	613.5	664.4	2 119.9	496.0	-83.8	2 156.1
Real estate activities	232.9	143.8	214.2	316.3	335.8	-97.6	186.9	343.8	126.3	297.8
Professional, scientific and technical activities	3 458.7	4 859.0	7 079.2	6 857.1	5 681.2	-778.7	1 861.1	1 101.3	1 088.2	1 687.0
Administrative and support service activities	251.8	385.9	178.1	151.1	118.7	307.3	291.9	-375.4	308.0	150.0
Public administration; activities of households and of extraterritorial organisations	-	-	-	-	-	-1.1	-1.1	-1.1	-1.2	2.2
Education	..	..	..	..	-	..	..	-	-	-
Human health and social work activities	..	..	..	..	..	..	..	..	..	..
Arts, entertainment and recreation	5.5	-2.2	4.5	2.4	-	35.5	50.9	12.4	57.8	90.7
Other services	-1.1	-1.1	-4.5	2.4	1.1	-3.3	-11.1	9.0	-9.4	5.6
Not allocated and confidential	**-**	**-**	**1.1**	**-**	**-**	**-**	**1.1**	**1.1**	**1.2**	**4.5**
Private real estate activities	**-**	**..**	**-**	**-**	**-**	**-**	**..**	**-**	**-**	**-**

- Nil; .. Not available

Note: Data excludes resident Special Purpose Entities (SPEs). Detailed metadata at: *http://stats.oecd.org/OECDStat_Metadata/ShowMetadata.ashx?Dataset=FDI_CTRY_IND_SUMM.*

Source: *OECD International Direct Investment Statistics (database): https://doi.org/10.1787/idi-data-en*

BELGIUM

Table 1. Foreign direct investment flows by country

Million US dollars

	Inward					Outward				
	2015	2016	2017	2018	2019	2015	2016	2017	2018	2019
WORLD	..	**68 178.7**	**-3 058.3**	**23 941.9**	**-8 651.1**	..	**40 165.9**	**29 563.7**	**41 319.5**	**-6 924.9**
OECD COUNTRIES	..	**65 172.0**	**-2 678.4**	**26 625.8**	**-7 780.1**	..	**41 489.6**	**25 016.3**	**38 154.1**	**-9 853.4**
Australia	..	-259.9	978.5	158.1	.. c	..	8.8	.. c	-664.5	.. c
Austria	..	404.7	-387.8	-54.3	-487.0	..	17.7	-361.9	.. c	.. c
Belgium	..	-	-	-	-	..	-	-	-	-
Canada	..	325.1	461.1	23.6	-237.3	..	317.4	.. c	240.8	.. c
Chile	..	-12.2	45.1	.. c	85.1	..	-84.0	.. c	.. c	.. c
Czech Republic	..	.. c	.. c	329.3	-451.1	..	722.1	665.1	335.2	.. c
Denmark	..	-151.5	-77.8	.. c	.. c	..	27.6	171.3	167.6	493.7
Estonia	..	8.8	.. c	.. c	2.2	..	11.1	6.8	4.7	4.5
Finland	..	-96.2	-940.1	1 637.0	-1 193.3	..	37.6	68.8	466.2	.. c
France	..	11 004.1	-146.5	6 739.1	-5 561.4	..	5 402.0	3 379.6	7 394.1	540.7
Germany	..	-1 407.7	-11 309.9	.. c	10 846.3	..	-1 307.1	.. c	.. c	.. c
Greece	..	-8.8	36.1	-9.4	.. c	..	.. c	98.1	.. c	.. c
Hungary	..	1 403.3	-2 199.3	.. c	.. c	..	76.3	.. c	.. c	-142.2
Iceland	..	.. c	.. c	.. c	.. c	..	.. c	.. c	.. c	.. c
Ireland	..	3 518.7	.. c	9 332.0	10 184.7	..	-353.9	148.8	.. c	.. c
Israel	..	-76.3	.. c	-34.2	-25.7	..	12.2	30.4	.. c	.. c
Italy	..	907.9	346.1	152.2	-912.3	..	745.3	.. c	1 666.5	1 529.2
Japan	..	2 961.4	.. c	.. c	1 456.4	..	447.9	-347.2	-129.8	.. c
Korea	..	137.1	173.6	123.9	.. c	..	25.4	168.0	164.1	63.8
Latvia	..	.. c	.. c	.. c	11.2	..	-14.4	12.4	10.6	10.1
Lithuania	..	.. c	.. c	.. c	.. c	..	1.1	1.1	-	2.2
Luxembourg	..	14 935.3	6 442.3	.. c	-14 858.4	..	12 966.9	.. c	325.7	.. c
Mexico	..	-63.0	.. c	-118.0	-78.4	..	-21 045.0	.. c	.. c	.. c
Netherlands	..	-19 941.4	-976.2	13 797.9	-7 552.9	..	6 772.1	.. c	-3 126.4	.. c
New Zealand	..	115.0	-41.7	-23.6	9.0	..	-64.1	140.9	16.5	17.9
Norway	..	-8 077.0	-1 323.4	.. c	294.4	..	307.4	-21.4	-55.5	.. c
Poland	..	116.1	390.0	153.4	58.2	..	179.1	.. c	768.3	500.4
Portugal	..	226.7	.. c	-13.0	9.0	..	335.1	.. c	.. c	.. c
Slovak Republic	..	147.1	.. c	.. c	.. c	..	-44.2	135.3	134.5	80.6
Slovenia	..	-15.5	.. c	16.5	.. c	..	98.4	10.1	7.1	12.3
Spain	..	2 707.1	-545.6	1 299.4	-123.1	..	822.7	326.9	876.9	944.8
Sweden	..	4 525.0	-3 593.7	-10 669.2	1 200.0	..	61.9	1 270.4	16.5	.. c
Switzerland	..	1 842.3	2 314.3	-2 980.1	-9 797.4	..	-122.7	.. c	6 407.4	174.6
Turkey	..	10.0	.. c	.. c	164.6	..	1 300.5	-102.6	.. c	270.9
United Kingdom	..	6 184.9	862.4	3 231.4	595.5	..	.. c	.. c	-6 842.9	.. c
United States	..	43 172.6	2 108.0	14 959.3	5 905.1	..	-60 143.8	.. c	30 152.2	12 373.2
EUROPE	..	**19 181.7**	**-5 966.6**	**8 915.4**	**-15 336.4**	..	**122 805.5**	**20 518.5**	**7 771.7**	**-23 440.1**
Bulgaria	..	31.0	.. c	.. c	.. c	..	89.6	732.7	89.7	51.5
Croatia	..	5.5	.. c	.. c	.. c	..	21.0	7.9	14.2	-3.4
Cyprus	..	174.7	-57.5	.. c	.. c	..	303.0	1 016.8	.. c	17.9
Malta	..	39.8	639.2	.. c	.. c	..	21.0	12.4	-7.1	7.8
Romania	..	-4.4	80.0	-34.2	11.2	..	140.4	69.9	.. c	.. c
Russian Federation	..	128.3	-314.5	-136.9	.. c	..	211.2	-206.3	574.8	-274.3
Ukraine	..	6.6	.. c	-10.6	.. c	..	-3.3	6.8	17.7	-11.2
AFRICA	..	**-598.3**	**463.3**	**-54.3**	**.. c**	..	**294.2**	**550.1**	**-315.1**	**-155.6**
Northern Africa	..	-22.1	50.7	.. c	-53.7	..	394.8	.. c	-23.6	.. c
Algeria	..	.. c	.. c	.. c	.. c	..	-1.1	-1.1	.. c	.. c
Egypt	..	-7.7	45.1	.. c	.. c	..	362.7	.. c	.. c	.. c
Libya	..	.. c	.. c	.. c	.. c	..	.. c	.. c	.. c	.. c
Morocco	..	.. c	.. c	-3.5	.. c	..	33.2	31.6	-24.8	12.3
Tunisia	..	.. c	.. c	.. c	.. c	..	-	.. c	5.9	4.5
Other African countries	..	-577.2	412.6	.. c	.. c	..	-100.6	.. c	.. c	-174.6
Nigeria	..	.. c	.. c	.. c	.. c	..	32.1	11.3	-2.4	-1.1
South Africa	..	66.4	230.0	.. c	.. c	..	28.8	.. c	.. c	.. c
AMERICA	..	**43 824.0**	**1 811.5**	**14 709.1**	**5 024.1**	..	**-80 869.2**	**.. c**	**30 940.6**	**13 567.7**
Northern America	..	43 496.6	2 570.2	14 982.9	5 667.7	..	-59 826.4	578.3	30 393.0	12 890.4
Central America and Caribbean countries	..	-59.7	-227.7	-953.6	-335.8	..	-21 046.1	.. c	-86.2	49.3
Bahamas	..	.. c	.. c	.. c	.. c	..	.. c	-	-	-
Bermuda	..	.. c	.. c	.. c	.. c	..	-4.4	.. c	.. c	.. c
Cayman Islands	..	-77.4	-23.7	.. c	.. c	..	-17.7	.. c	.. c	.. c
Costa Rica	..	.. c	.. c	7.1	.. c	..	-1.1	.. c	.. c	.. c
El Salvador	..	.. c	.. c	.. c	.. c	..	.. c	.. c	.. c	.. c
Guatemala	..	.. c	.. c	.. c	-	..	.. c	.. c	-	.. c
Honduras	..	-	.. c	-	-	..	.. c	.. c	.. c	.. c
Nicaragua	..	.. c	.. c	-	.. c	..	.. c	.. c	.. c	.. c
Panama	..	5.5	.. c	.. c	.. c	..	.. c	.. c	.. c	.. c
Virgin Islands, U.S.	..	-	.. c	.. c	.. c	..	-	-	-	-
South America	..	387.0	-529.8	678.6	-307.8	..	3.3	570.4	633.8	628.0
Argentina	..	.. c	-136.4	.. c	.. c	..	52.0	.. c	.. c	.. c
Bolivia	..	-	.. c	-	.. c	..	-	-	.. c	.. c
Brazil	..	677.9	-445.3	538.2	.. c	..	-60.8	440.8	237.2	.. c
Colombia	..	-3.3	.. c	.. c	.. c	..	29.9	.. c	.. c	.. c
Ecuador	..	-6.6	-	2.4	.. c	..	.. c	.. c	5.9	25.7
Paraguay	..	-1.1	.. c	-	.. c	..	.. c	.. c	.. c	.. c
Peru	..	.. c	.. c	.. c	.. c	..	.. c	.. c	.. c	.. c
Uruguay	..	.. c	.. c	.. c	.. c	..	3.3	.. c	.. c	.. c
Venezuela	..	.. c	34.9	.. c	.. c	..	-77.4	.. c	.. c	.. c

Table 1. Foreign direct investment flows by country *(cont.)*

Million US dollars

	Inward					Outward				
	2015	2016	2017	2018	2019	2015	2016	2017	2018	2019
ASIA	..	**5 912.9**	**-302.1**	**270.3**	**1 344.5**	..	**-2 014.8**	**1 455.3**	**2 652.0**	**2 930.7**
Near and Middle East	..	-298.6	19.2	-474.4	-61.6	..	147.1	.. c	.. c	.. c
Gulf Arabian countries	..	-16.6	45.1	-427.2	-31.3	..	148.2	263.8	109.8	.. c
Kuwait	..	.. c	.. c	.. c	.. c	..	-	-	-	-
Qatar	..	6.6	.. c	.. c	.. c	..	-10.0	.. c	.. c	-7.8
Saudi Arabia	..	-28.8	13.5	-15.3	9.0	..	60.8	5.6	.. c	.. c
United Arab Emirates	..	2.2	-101.5	-434.3	-30.2	..	97.3	278.4	40.1	36.9
Other Near and Middle East	..	.. c	.. c	-47.2	-30.2	..	-1.1	.. c	.. c	.. c
Jordan	..	.. c	.. c	.. c	.. c	..	.. c	.. c	.. c	.. c
Other Asian countries	..	6 211.4	-321.3	745.9	1 406.0	..	-2 161.9	.. c	2 509.1	2 371.0
China	..	319.6	153.3	948.9	206.0	..	-46.4	.. c	.. c	.. c
Hong Kong, China	..	1 872.2	-431.7	-3 600.9	-250.8	..	-2 960.3	.. c	.. c	.. c
India	..	-42.0	.. c	.. c	.. c	..	278.7	264.9	-160.5	438.8
Indonesia	..	-23.2	.. c	1.2	.. c	..	164.8	237.9	.. c	.. c
Iran, Islamic Republic of	..	.. c	.. c	.. c	.. c	..	.. c	.. c	4.7	.. c
Malaysia	..	.. c	.. c	.. c	.. c	..	67.5	208.5	-186.5	5.6
Philippines	..	.. c	.. c	.. c	.. c	..	19.9	4.5	3.5	5.6
Singapore	..	457.8	.. c	466.2	-86.2	..	-353.9	629.0	.. c	.. c
Chinese Taipei	..	39.8	37.2	-36.6	.. c	..	-6.6	-11.3	-8.3	.. c
Thailand	..	.. c	.. c	.. c	.. c	..	61.9	13.5	7.1	-13.4
Viet Nam	..	-1.1	.. c	.. c	.. c	..	6.6	.. c	.. c	35.8
AUSTRALIA, OCEANIA AND POLAR REGIONS	..	**-139.3**	**933.4**	**122.7**	**368.3**	..	**-49.8**	**1 320.0**	**.. c**	**.. c**
WORLD unallocated and confidential	..	**-2.2**	**2.3**	**-21.2**	**.. d**	..	**-**	**- d**	**- d**	**- d**
European Union (EU28)	..	**25 383.2**	**-6 513.4**	**9 424.1**	**-6 018.1**	..	**121 102.5**	**20 984.1**	**312.8**	**-23 698.6**
G20 countries excl. European Union	..	**63 831.7**	**-7 176.2**	**18 882.3**	**12 540.0**	..	**20 416.9**	**-3 150.7**	**32 986.0**	**12 338.5**
G20 OECD countries	..	**62 971.4**	**-6 706.1**	**17 356.3**	**12 557.9**	..	**19 726.9**	**-4 025.5**	**32 803.0**	**10 882.1**
G20 Non-OECD countries	..	**860.3**	**-470.1**	**1 526.0**	**-17.9**	..	**690.0**	**874.8**	**181.8**	**1 456.4**
MENA countries	..	**-38.7**	**95.8**	**-417.8**	**-89.6**	..	**505.4**	**545.6**	**.. c**	**.. c**
ASEAN countries	..	**931.1**	**-219.8**	**551.2**	**-82.8**	..	**-2.2**	**1 356.1**	**2 901.0**	**.. c**

- Nil; .. Not available; c Confidential data; d Secondary Confidentiality

Note: Data excludes resident Special Purpose Entities (SPEs). Detailed metadata at: *http://stats.oecd.org/OECDStat_Metadata/ShowMetadata.ashx?Dataset=FDI_CTRY_IND_SUMM.*

Source: *OECD International Direct Investment Statistics (database): https://doi.org/10.1787/idi-data-en*

Table 2. Foreign direct investment positions by country
At year end

Million US dollars

	Inward					Outward				
	2015	2016	2017	2018	2019	2015	2016	2017	2018	2019
WORLD	**520 992.9**	**517 401.7**	**580 190.7**	**491 008.7**	**489 054.1**	**582 582.5**	**599 379.2**	**707 828.0**	**531 899.5**	**612 188.3**
OECD COUNTRIES	**.. d**	**507 827.6**	**569 778.1**	**485 724.8**	**484 570.9**	**.. d**	**573 158.0**	**675 578.1**	**510 993.8**	**585 941.4**
Australia	-797.0	-1 033.0	-20.4	-103.0	353.9	2 035.9	2 224.1	2 973.1	1 104.9	1 646.8
Austria	1 200.9	1 412.5	1 183.7	859.9	731.3	696.8	635.6	259.1	233.6	1 097.5
Belgium	-	-	-	-	-	-	-	-	-	-
Canada	-312.5	-144.4	127.1	683.5	392.0	1 008.2	1 540.0	2 190.0	1 889.2	2 008.5
Chile	8.7	24.2	-307.0	-263.3	.. c	1 004.9	1 019.3	1 255.7	1 181.6	996.4
Czech Republic	.. d	3 388.8	5 169.1	1 156.4	568.4	4 707.7	6 267.5	6 527.9	6 038.5	6 280.6
Denmark	1 327.2	748.4	832.3	1 711.7	2 284.9	688.1	561.8	916.3	751.1	988.5
Estonia	.. d	9.5	6.0	-2.3	-50.6	15.2	7.4	31.2	35.5	12.4
Finland	1 399.0	1 345.0	833.5	2 066.6	1 499.7	634.7	598.7	485.7	989.2	403.3
France	115 236.8	127 166.6	134 665.4	85 050.4	85 151.7	36 172.0	41 659.1	44 699.0	46 577.7	54 722.5
Germany	15 651.6	10 587.1	395.8	5 069.8	16 662.5	.. d	9 343.3	12 020.9	10 614.8	12 435.4
Greece	603.2	599.8	893.5	748.8	2 601.7	.. d	774.7	1 596.3	1 109.5	1 333.4
Hungary	3 051.7	4 297.5	2 058.0	-63.0	37.1	1 822.5	1 852.0	2 936.0	2 251.0	2 097.3
Iceland	.. d	-	3.6	1.1	1.1	28.3	112.8	145.1	119.1	116.8
Ireland	-2 297.2	1 769.8	5 397.0	16 866.3	14 760.7	7 073.5	6 589.0	6 657.5	4 325.6	3 242.0
Israel	.. d	-71.7	-84.0	61.8	35.9	44.6	64.3	36.0	50.4	61.8
Italy	-1 050.6	1 411.4	2 126.4	1 440.3	613.3	9 442.6	9 295.9	11 009.8	10 139.7	11 590.7
Japan	13 285.8	15 879.6	18 331.7	19 684.0	21 096.4	1 932.5	2 631.0	2 421.4	1 257.2	1 434.5
Korea	966.8	1 054.1	1 397.2	470.6	521.2	292.9	336.3	615.3	1 008.7	2 327.6
Latvia	-12.0	.. c	-2.4	-4.6	-	31.6	10.5	37.2	57.2	42.7
Lithuania	.. d	-8.4	1.2	6.9	7.9	10.9	6.3	7.2	-3.4	1.1
Luxembourg	143 213.9	127 452.3	155 106.7	107 138.8	97 776.9	169 294.5	140 822.2	203 565.6	147 943.7	148 959.8
Mexico	-704.4	-660.9	-714.8	-435.1	-64.0	.. d	-4 890.9	-	-106.5	704.3
Netherlands	185 607.0	156 584.8	176 560.3	134 532.9	137 903.8	216 541.1	228 930.1	247 303.9	201 308.7	209 928.1
New Zealand	-128.5	-6.3	-38.4	-36.6	-25.8	10.9	-14.8	122.3	139.7	126.9
Norway	3 572.1	-4 635.8	-4 587.4	-322.9	-38.2	513.9	756.8	621.3	337.8	396.5
Poland	-3 002.7	-2 209.3	-2 088.0	-52.7	131.4	.. d	2 777.5	3 658.0	3 512.7	3 875.5
Portugal	-443.1	-163.4	-143.9	-9.2	-157.3	2 541.1	2 709.0	3 157.8	366.4	428.0
Slovak Republic	.. d	266.7	284.2	-24.0	35.9	1 368.5	1 322.9	1 623.9	1 694.5	1 561.4
Slovenia	.. d	-21.1	-24.0	.. c	.. c	680.5	675.7	756.8	156.9	174.1
Spain	-3 514.4	-375.3	181.1	2 775.4	2 657.8	3 909.6	4 341.7	4 926.8	5 243.9	6 221.1
Sweden	7 923.8	11 575.8	8 120.7	4 829.4	4 145.1	732.7	748.4	967.9	809.5	1 721.0
Switzerland	44 021.8	43 837.9	53 512.8	57 411.3	43 161.1	2 151.3	1 569.5	3 986.6	3 545.9	3 415.0
Turkey	-42.5	-14.8	-51.6	200.4	15.7	2 616.2	3 767.3	3 653.2	3 003.2	2 961.1
United Kingdom	-3 011.4	4 119.3	5 367.0	15 128.2	19 199.1	34 476.9	142 859.7	135 060.0	60 531.3	95 854.9
United States	-9 404.5	3 629.2	5 286.6	29 129.8	32 730.8	22 250.4	-38 736.2	-30 638.0	-7 224.6	6 777.1
EUROPE	**513 532.9**	**490 791.6**	**548 100.3**	**436 785.0**	**430 056.2**	**514 788.2**	**614 905.7**	**705 694.4**	**516 410.6**	**575 979.6**
Bulgaria	68.6	95.9	125.9	6.9	-6.7	377.8	474.3	1 577.1	1 373.9	1 480.6
Croatia	-10.9	-6.3	-1.2	1.1	-	545.5	470.1	668.0	828.9	1 480.6
Cyprus	774.1	845.4	927.1	483.2	676.3	.. d	2 246.2	3 476.9	-573.6	135.9
Malta	.. d	781.1	1 554.3	-49.2	-179.7	.. d	32.7	49.2	45.8	80.9
Romania	-28.3	-42.2	-51.6	-114.5	-92.1	837.2	1 425.1	1 352.8	1 032.7	1 319.9
Russian Federation	-59.9	44.3	-261.5	49.2	4.5	.. d	1 203.8	1 408.0	1 061.4	1 397.4
Ukraine	-9.8	-5.3	-3.6	-14.9	-10.1	.. d	-2.1	-1.2	8.0	14.6
AFRICA	**-233.0**	**-796.9**	**-191.9**	**20.6**	**31.5**	**2 202.5**	**2 049.1**	**2 640.9**	**910.2**	**884.1**
Northern Africa	14.2	-3.2	.. c	.. c	28.1	452.9	645.1	1 261.7	171.7	165.1
Algeria	.. d	2.1	3.6	2.3	-	16.3	15.8	22.8	11.5	6.7
Egypt	.. d	-34.8	8.4	34.3	6.7	215.6	446.9	792.8	29.8	30.3
Libya	.. d	4.2	1.2	2.3	2.2	3.3	3.2	3.6	3.4	-
Morocco	26.1	21.1	38.4	.. c	7.9	185.1	151.8	407.8	100.8	97.7
Tunisia	.. d	.. c	.. c	12.6	11.2	32.7	27.4	34.8	26.3	30.3
Other African countries	-248.2	-793.7	-251.9	-67.6	4.5	1 749.6	1 404.0	1 379.2	738.5	721.2
Nigeria	.. d	.. c	.. c	.. c	.. c	432.2	73.8	78.0	75.6	67.4
South Africa	.. d	-431.1	-225.5	-21.8	.. c	235.2	320.4	305.8	-26.3	66.3
AMERICA	**-10 009.8**	**4 536.7**	**5 542.1**	**29 116.1**	**32 016.4**	**44 118.7**	**-37 018.0**	**-22 230.8**	**-2 680.3**	**12 482.6**
Northern America	-9 716.9	3 485.8	5 413.8	29 812.2	33 124.0	23 258.6	-37 196.2	-28 448.1	-5 336.6	8 785.7
Central America and Caribbean countries	2 695.7	3 413.1	3 729.9	-706.4	-649.3	.. d	-4 766.5	36.0	-292.0	774.0
Bahamas	-	7.4	7.2	-1.1	-1.1	2.2	2.1	-	-	-
Bermuda	.. d	3 106.4	3 374.9	-1 204.5	-713.3	.. d	85.4	142.7	-	-
Cayman Islands	167.7	1 191.1	1 283.3	1 068.2	176.4	32.7	8.4	2.4	3.4	11.2
Costa Rica	.. d	.. c	.. c	143.1	1.1	- d	-	-1.2	-	30.3
El Salvador	-	-	-	-	-	4.4	5.3	6.0	6.9	5.6
Guatemala	.. d	1.1	1.2	-	-	1.1	1.1	1.2	1.1	1.1
Honduras	-	-	-	-	-	3.3	4.2	-129.5	-216.4	1.1
Nicaragua	-	-	-	-	-	-	11.6	13.2	18.3	14.6
Panama	-113.2	-95.9	-116.3	.. c	-16.9	-3.3	1.1	-6.0	-1.1	1.1
Virgin Islands, U.S.	-	-	1.2	-	-1.1	-	-	-	-	-
South America	-2 988.6	-2 362.2	-3 601.6	10.3	-458.3	4 572.7	4 944.7	6 182.5	2 948.2	2 922.9
Argentina	486.7	239.3	-513.3	142.0	-195.5	.. d	1 634.9	1 741.4	127.1	150.5
Bolivia	-	-	-2.4	-2.3	-2.2	2.2	1.1	1.2	1.1	1.1
Brazil	-3 416.4	-2 540.3	-2 720.1	98.5	-65.2	.. d	1 562.1	2 313.5	1 944.1	2 272.5
Colombia	.. d	-40.1	-61.2	.. c	-11.2	19.6	128.6	253.1	281.7	110.1
Ecuador	-14.2	-13.7	-8.4	-8.0	-	14.2	7.4	12.0	14.9	38.2
Paraguay	-	-	-	-	-	-	33.7	60.0	77.9	55.0
Peru	.. d	-10.5	.. c	-1.1	-7.9	.. d	600.8	621.3	628.6	605.5
Uruguay	.. d	-6.3	1.2	1.1	-1.1	15.2	10.5	9.6	8.0	6.7
Venezuela	.. d	-22.1	12.0	52.7	11.2	68.6	-53.8	-86.4	-1 316.7	-1 313.2

Table 2. Foreign direct investment positions by country *(cont.)*

At year end

Million US dollars

	Inward					Outward				
	2015	2016	2017	2018	2019	2015	2016	2017	2018	2019
ASIA	**18 290.7**	**23 561.7**	**26 427.2**	**24 890.1**	**26 288.5**	**19 420.8**	**17 215.1**	**18 279.0**	**15 186.6**	**20 662.8**
Near and Middle East	148.1	91.7	214.7	8.0	-171.9	.. d	2 257.8	1 914.1	1 165.6	1 697.4
Gulf Arabian countries	-98.0	75.9	179.9	-163.7	-316.8	.. d	1 432.5	1 168.1	1 099.2	1 621.0
Kuwait	.. d	-23.2	1.2	-1.1	-1.1	-	-	-	-	-
Qatar	.. d	3.2	70.8	5.7	-1.1	66.4	56.9	54.0	125.9	6.7
Saudi Arabia	.. d	-40.1	-20.4	-17.2	-10.1	.. d	71.7	73.2	83.6	561.7
United Arab Emirates	.. d	186.6	159.5	-154.6	-306.7	1 193.3	1 295.5	1 024.2	887.3	1 034.6
Other Near and Middle East	.. d	15.8	34.8	171.7	144.9	786.1	825.3	746.0	66.4	76.4
Jordan	-	-	3.6	2.3	2.2	734.9	745.2	684.8	-5.7	-4.5
Other Asian countries	18 142.6	23 470.0	26 211.3	24 884.4	26 464.8	17 309.7	14 957.3	16 364.8	14 022.2	18 966.5
China	-1 020.1	-412.1	-295.0	184.3	411.1	2 406.1	2 094.4	2 529.4	1 795.3	2 244.4
Hong Kong, China	5 470.9	6 592.2	6 617.9	2 420.4	3 948.6	6 559.6	3 639.7	3 346.1	2 856.7	2 845.4
India	155.7	52.7	178.7	392.7	364.0	.. d	1 303.9	1 499.2	835.8	1 209.8
Indonesia	.. d	25.3	34.8	35.5	-25.8	238.4	495.4	761.6	693.8	619.0
Iran, Islamic Republic of	- d	-	4.8	2.3	-1.1	10.9	-	14.4	13.7	18.0
Malaysia	136.1	163.4	125.9	55.0	55.0	.. d	472.2	735.2	554.2	579.6
Philippines	12.0	.. c	.. c	-19.5	-30.3	35.9	311.0	64.8	67.6	65.2
Singapore	-204.7	313.1	-171.5	1 535.4	-5.6	3 363.1	2 779.6	3 486.4	4 307.3	7 102.9
Chinese Taipei	33.8	72.7	115.1	89.3	71.9	68.6	76.9	57.6	30.9	-112.3
Thailand	-710.9	-302.5	-172.7	13.7	27.0	515.0	353.1	393.4	424.8	417.9
Viet Nam	-4.4	-4.2	-2.4	-6.9	-1.1	49.0	21.1	289.0	14.9	57.3
AUSTRALIA, OCEANIA AND POLAR REGIONS	**-589.0**	**-693.6**	**287.8**	**193.5**	**670.6**	**2 052.3**	**2 227.3**	**3 444.5**	**2 071.2**	**2 178.2**
WORLD unallocated and confidential	**1.1**	**2.1**	**25.2**	**3.4**	**-9.0**	**-**	**-**	**-**	**1.1**	**1.1**
European Union (EU28)	**466 027.2**	**451 644.4**	**499 491.5**	**379 578.7**	**386 978.2**	**508 222.1**	**607 433.3**	**695 350.2**	**507 477.7**	**567 510.7**
G20 countries excl. European Union	**125 515.5**	**158 933.3**	**163 088.3**	**157 182.3**	**.. d**	**145 368.5**	**178 715.1**	**194 636.6**	**135 310.3**	**200 985.2**
G20 OECD countries	**129 820.4**	**161 996.4**	**166 910.5**	**156 319.0**	**176 672.7**	**137 067.0**	**170 028.5**	**184 004.6**	**128 795.5**	**192 463.5**
G20 Non-OECD countries	**-4 304.8**	**-3 063.1**	**-3 822.3**	**863.3**	**.. d**	**8 301.6**	**8 686.6**	**10 632.0**	**6 514.8**	**8 521.7**
MENA countries	**4.4**	**162.3**	**.. d**	**.. d**	**-180.9**	**2 517.1**	**2 824.9**	**3 117.1**	**1 267.5**	**.. d**
ASEAN countries	**-794.8**	**201.3**	**-176.3**	**1 620.1**	**20.2**	**4 710.9**	**4 551.5**	**5 817.9**	**6 098.0**	**8 878.9**

- Nil; .. Not available; c Confidential data; d Secondary Confidentiality

Note: Data excludes resident Special Purpose Entities (SPEs). Detailed metadata at: *http://stats.oecd.org/OECDStat_Metadata/ShowMetadata.ashx?Dataset=FDI_CTRY_IND_SUMM.*

Source: *OECD International Direct Investment Statistics (database): https://doi.org/10.1787/idi-data-en*

BELGIUM

Table 3. Foreign direct investment income by country

Million US dollars

	Inward					Outward				
	2015	2016	2017	2018	2019	2015	2016	2017	2018	2019
WORLD	..	**31 450.8**	..	..	..	..	**32 119.9**	..	..	..
OECD COUNTRIES	..	**31 321.5**	..	..	..	..	**30 771.9**	..	..	..
Australia	..	-24.3	..	..	..	..	4.4	..	..	..
Austria	..	118.3	..	..	..	..	52.0	..	..	..
Belgium	..	-	..	..	..	..	-	..	..	..
Canada	..	60.8	..	..	..	..	78.5	..	..	..
Chile	..	-16.6	..	..	..	..	28.8	..	..	..
Czech Republic	..	3.3	..	..	..	..	799.5	..	..	..
Denmark	..	67.5	..	..	..	..	27.6	..	..	..
Estonia	..	-	..	..	..	..	3.3	..	..	..
Finland	..	2.2	..	..	..	..	96.2	..	..	..
France	..	7 862.4	..	..	..	..	3 345.1	..	..	..
Germany	..	1 607.9	..	..	..	..	290.8	..	..	..
Greece	..	-2.2	..	..	..	..	-10.0	..	..	..
Hungary	..	46.4	..	..	..	..	214.5	..	..	..
Iceland	..	.. c	..	..	..	..	3.3	..	..	..
Ireland	..	222.3	..	..	..	..	395.9	..	..	..
Israel	..	-8.8	..	..	..	..	18.8	..	..	..
Italy	..	-73.0	..	..	..	..	662.4	..	..	..
Japan	..	822.7	..	..	..	..	113.9	..	..	..
Korea	..	57.5	..	..	..	..	57.5	..	..	..
Latvia	..	-	..	..	..	..	3.3	..	..	..
Lithuania	..	.. c	..	..	..	..	1.1	..	..	..
Luxembourg	..	9 896.1	..	..	..	..	1 073.8	..	..	..
Mexico	..	-19.9	..	..	..	..	822.7	..	..	..
Netherlands	..	8 477.3	..	..	..	..	11 435.4	..	..	..
New Zealand	..	-2.2	..	..	..	..	66.4	..	..	..
Norway	..	-56.4	..	..	..	..	35.4	..	..	..
Poland	..	-73.0	..	..	..	..	320.7	..	..	..
Portugal	..	42.0	..	..	..	..	499.8	..	..	..
Slovak Republic	..	-1.1	..	..	..	..	123.9	..	..	..
Slovenia	..	-	..	..	..	..	118.3	..	..	..
Spain	..	120.5	..	..	..	..	494.3	..	..	..
Sweden	..	749.8	..	..	..	..	84.0	..	..	..
Switzerland	..	754.2	..	..	..	..	-245.5	..	..	..
Turkey	..	4.4	..	..	..	..	217.8	..	..	..
United Kingdom	..	230.0	..	..	..	..	10 470.0	..	..	..
United States	..	457.8	..	..	..	..	-928.9	..	..	..
EUROPE	..	**30 000.0**	..	..	..	..	**31 049.4**	..	..	..
Bulgaria	..	-1.1	..	..	..	..	26.5	..	..	..
Croatia	..	-	..	..	..	..	34.3	..	..	..
Cyprus	..	58.6	..	..	..	..	193.5	..	..	..
Malta	..	-19.9	..	..	..	..	8.8	..	..	..
Romania	..	-3.3	..	..	..	..	95.1	..	..	..
Russian Federation	..	-25.4	..	..	..	..	174.7	..	..	..
Ukraine	..	.. c	..	..	..	..	-6.6	..	..	..
AFRICA	..	**-22.1**	..	..	..	..	**-277.6**	..	..	..
Northern Africa	..	2.2	..	..	..	..	-32.1	..	..	..
Algeria	..	-	..	..	..	..	3.3	..	..	..
Egypt	..	-1.1	..	..	..	..	-153.7	..	..	..
Libya	..	-	..	..	..	..	-	..	..	..
Morocco	..	.. c	..	..	..	..	105.1	..	..	..
Tunisia	..	-	..	..	..	..	12.2	..	..	..
Other African countries	..	-24.3	..	..	..	..	-245.5	..	..	..
Nigeria	..	.. c	..	..	..	..	13.3	..	..	..
South Africa	..	-8.8	..	..	..	..	29.9	..	..	..
AMERICA	..	**347.2**	..	..	..	..	**301.9**	..	..	..
Northern America	..	518.6	..	..	..	..	-849.3	..	..	..
Central America and Caribbean countries	..	32.1	..	..	..	..	828.3	..	..	..
Bahamas	..	-	..	..	..	..	-	..	..	..
Bermuda	..	.. c	..	..	..	..	3.3	..	..	..
Cayman Islands	..	14.4	..	..	..	..	-	..	..	..
Costa Rica	..	.. c	..	..	..	..	-1.1	..	..	..
El Salvador	..	-	..	..	..	..	1.1	..	..	..
Guatemala	..	.. c	..	..	..	..	-	..	..	..
Honduras	..	-	..	..	..	..	-	..	..	..
Nicaragua	..	-	..	..	..	..	1.1	..	..	..
Panama	..	-	..	..	..	..	.. c	..	..	..
Virgin Islands, U.S.	..	-	..	..	..	..	-	..	..	..
South America	..	-203.5	..	..	..	..	324.0	..	..	..
Argentina	..	-	..	..	..	..	40.9	..	..	..
Bolivia	..	-	..	..	..	..	-	..	..	..
Brazil	..	-184.7	..	..	..	..	94.0	..	..	..
Colombia	..	-1.1	..	..	..	..	16.6	..	..	..
Ecuador	..	-	..	..	..	..	1.1	..	..	..
Paraguay	..	-	..	..	..	..	1.1	..	..	..
Peru	..	.. c	..	..	..	..	.. c	..	..	..
Uruguay	..	.. c	..	..	..	..	5.5	..	..	..
Venezuela	..	-	..	..	..	..	-52.0	..	..	..

Table 3. Foreign direct investment income by country *(cont.)*

Million US dollars

	Inward					Outward				
	2015	2016	2017	2018	2019	2015	2016	2017	2018	2019
ASIA	..	**1 152.3**	..	..	..	..	**968.7**	..	..	..
Near and Middle East	..	4.4	..	..	..	..	170.3	..	..	..
Gulf Arabian countries	..	13.3	..	..	..	..	110.6	..	..	..
Kuwait	..	-	..	..	..	..	-	..	..	..
Qatar	..	.. c	..	..	..	..	-6.6	..	..	..
Saudi Arabia	..	.. c	..	..	..	..	17.7	..	..	..
United Arab Emirates	..	14.4	..	..	..	..	99.5	..	..	..
Other Near and Middle East	..	-8.8	..	..	..	..	59.7	..	..	..
Jordan	..	-	..	..	..	..	32.1	..	..	..
Other Asian countries	..	1 147.8	..	..	..	..	798.4	..	..	..
China	..	241.1	..	..	..	..	14.4	..	..	..
Hong Kong, China	..	86.3	..	..	..	..	310.7	..	..	..
India	..	-19.9	..	..	..	..	103.9	..	..	..
Indonesia	..	-1.1	..	..	..	..	28.8	..	..	..
Iran, Islamic Republic of	..	-	..	..	..	..	4.4	..	..	..
Malaysia	..	-2.2	..	..	..	..	59.7	..	..	..
Philippines	..	-	..	..	..	..	11.1	..	..	..
Singapore	..	-24.3	..	..	..	..	-16.6	..	..	..
Chinese Taipei	..	2.2	..	..	..	..	8.8	..	..	..
Thailand	..	-14.4	..	..	..	..	46.4	..	..	..
Viet Nam	..	-	..	..	..	..	-	..	..	..
AUSTRALIA, OCEANIA AND POLAR REGIONS	..	**-26.5**	..	..	..	..	**76.3**	..	..	..
WORLD unallocated and confidential	..	**-**	..	..	..	..	**1.1**	..	..	..
European Union (EU28)	..	**29 329.9**	..	..	..	..	**30 859.2**	..	..	..
G20 countries excl. European Union	..	**10 985.3**	..	..	..	..	**15 639.7**	..	..	..
G20 OECD countries	..	**10 985.3**	..	..	..	..	**15 134.4**	..	..	..
G20 Non-OECD countries	..	**1.1**	..	..	..	..	**505.4**	..	..	..
MENA countries	..	**16.6**	..	..	..	..	**118.3**	..	..	..
ASEAN countries	..	**-42.0**	..	..	..	..	**140.4**	..	..	..

- Nil; .. Not available; c Confidential data

Note: Data excludes resident Special Purpose Entities (SPEs). Detailed metadata at: *http://stats.oecd.org/OECDStat_Metadata/ShowMetadata.ashx?Dataset=FDI_CTRY_IND_SUMM*.

Source: *OECD International Direct Investment Statistics (database): https://doi.org/10.1787/idi-data-en*

BELGIUM

Table 4. Foreign direct investment flows by industrial sector

Million US dollars

	Inward					Outward				
	2015	2016	2017	2018	2019	2015	2016	2017	2018	2019
All FDI activities	..	**68 178.7**	**-3 058.3**	**23 941.9**	**-8 651.1**	..	**40 165.9**	**29 563.7**	**41 319.5**	**-6 924.9**
Agriculture, forestry and fishing	..	**2.2**	**.. c**	**.. c**	**-**	..	**-5.5**	**1.1**	**1.2**	**-2.2**
Mining and quarrying	..	**-**	**.. c**	**-**	**-**	..	**-497.6**	**53.0**	**-334.0**	**-273.1**
Extraction activities	..	-	-	-	-	..	-	-	-	-
Manufacturing	..	**11 350.2**	**-7 497.5**	**131.0**	**-335.8**	..	**3 827.3**	**1 953.6**	**-7 079.0**	**3 975.1**
of which:										
Food products, beverages and tobacco	..	2 281.3	-354.0	270.3	-1 408.3	..	2 085.6	435.1	-946.5	-361.6
Textiles, wood and paper products; printing	..	101.7	189.4	-614.9	.. c	..	236.6	.. c	.. c	785.9
Chemical, rubber, plastic, non-metallic mineral products	..	5 607.7	-8 187.4	-4 589.9	2 734.8	..	288.6	199.5	-1 262.8	3 288.9
Metal and machinery products, except electrical equipment	..	74.1	1 096.8	5 302.7	-2 222.1	..	938.8	657.2	-4 406.9	1 066.8
Motor vehicles, trailers, semi-trailers, other transport equipment	..	1 623.4	93.6	-187.7	160.1	..	520.8	112.7	.. c	-61.6
Other manufacturing	..	1 662.1	-334.8	-48.4	-534.0	..	-243.3	217.6	-1 091.7	-742.2
Electricity, gas, steam and air conditioning supply	..	**-4 599.1**	**3 727.9**	**.. c**	**.. c**	..	**1 056.1**	**2 918.5**	**.. c**	**.. c**
Water supply; sewerage, waste management and remediation activities	..	**-112.8**	**.. c**	**-313.9**	**.. c**	..	**-18.8**	**-39.5**	**-18.9**	**.. c**
Construction	..	**-382.6**	**339.3**	**-210.1**	**268.7**	..	**-95.1**	**490.4**	**175.9**	**167.9**
Services	..	**62 415.1**	**1 432.8**	**19 924.5**	**1 477.7**	..	**35 780.2**	**26 024.1**	**36 318.9**	**-712.0**
Wholesale and retail trade; repair of motor vehicles and motorcycles	..	7 904.5	-5 789.7	.. c	.. c	..	533.0	1 376.4	-7 287.9	.. c
Transportation and storage	..	254.3	-213.1	.. c	.. c	..	455.6	.. c	-246.7	-565.3
Accommodation and food service activities	..	37.6	.. c	167.6	-86.2	..	95.1	216.4	.. c	80.6
Information and communication	..	3 822.8	696.7	.. c	.. c	..	338.4	1 229.9	.. c	.. c
Financial and insurance activities	..	10 456.7	5 407.5	10 537.0	-4 343.4	..	-13 526.5	30 395.7	43 794.4	3 628.1
Activities of holding companies	..	-13 570.7	-1 685.3	-806.1	-6 948.4	..	-30 043.1	11 857.7	16 032.1	175.8
Real estate activities	..	1 332.5	-92.4	-2 617.7	1 301.9	..	899.0	-158.9	-236.0	1 008.6
Professional, scientific and technical activities	..	41 210.9	1 172.4	5 831.5	3 876.6	..	48 179.8	-6 105.3	998.5	1 093.7
Administrative and support service activities	..	-2 416.2	160.1	.. c	-1 020.9	..	-1 081.5	993.1	.. c	531.7
Public administration; activities of households and of extraterritorial organisations	..	-	-	-	-	..	1.1	.. c	-	-
Education	..	-	-	-	-	..	1.1	.. c	.. c	.. c
Human health and social work activities	..	-	.. c	.. c	-	..	-	.. c	.. c	-
Arts, entertainment and recreation	..	-25.4	-25.9	73.2	17.9	..	-	.. c	.. c	.. c
Other services	..	-163.7	-71.0	.. c	.. c	..	-115.0	-444.1	26.0	10.1
Not allocated and confidential	..	**-14.4**	**.. c**	**.. c**	**.. c**	..	**119.4**	**-1 837.4**	**.. c**	**.. c**
Private real estate activities	..	**-479.9**	**.. c**	**.. c**	**.. c**	..	-	-	-	-

- Nil; .. Not available; c Confidential data

Note: Data excludes resident Special Purpose Entities (SPEs). Detailed metadata at: *http://stats.oecd.org/OECDStat_Metadata/ShowMetadata.ashx?Dataset=FDI_CTRY_IND_SUMM.*

Source: *OECD International Direct Investment Statistics (database): https://doi.org/10.1787/idi-data-en*

BELGIUM

Table 5. Foreign direct investment positions by industrial sector

At year end

Million US dollars

	Inward					Outward				
	2015	2016	2017	2018	2019	2015	2016	2017	2018	2019
All FDI activities	**520 992.9**	**517 401.7**	**580 190.7**	**491 008.7**	**489 054.1**	**582 582.5**	**599 379.2**	**707 828.0**	**531 899.5**	**612 188.3**
Agriculture, forestry and fishing	**145.9**	**.. d**	**109.1**	**112.2**	**..**	**35.9**	**5.3**	**6.0**	**5.7**	**..**
Mining and quarrying	**300.5**	**250.9**	**268.7**	**628.6**	**..**	**5 265.1**	**4 550.4**	**4 544.3**	**4 921.0**	**..**
Extraction activities	-	-	-	-	..	-	-	-	-	..
Manufacturing	**148 903.6**	**142 889.2**	**158 937.4**	**163 929.5**	**..**	**112 978.8**	**119 590.0**	**141 909.3**	**147 229.2**	**..**
of which:										
Food products, beverages and tobacco	9 297.8	8 780.4	10 467.7	12 623.1	..	16 881.9	26 508.9	33 335.3	41 354.5	..
Textiles, wood and paper products; printing	4 458.4	4 208.9	4 816.5	4 127.5	..	2 252.6	2 363.2	2 913.2	2 923.1	..
Chemical, rubber, plastic, non-metallic mineral products	117 469.8	110 265.6	119 929.2	120 353.8	..	69 504.6	63 177.0	70 122.3	70 380.1	..
Metal and machinery products, except electrical equipment	11 040.8	11 550.5	14 947.2	18 723.4	..	16 805.7	19 568.9	26 560.3	25 014.9	..
Motor vehicles, trailers, semi-trailers, other transport equipment	928.7	1 620.1	2 120.4	1 952.1	..	394.1	979.2	1 621.5	1 702.5	..
Other manufacturing	5 708.2	6 464.6	6 655.1	6 150.7	..	7 138.8	6 993.8	7 356.7	5 855.3	..
Electricity, gas, steam and air conditioning supply	**32 155.7**	**14 817.1**	**18 481.7**	**19 340.5**	**..**	**32 501.9**	**20 636.7**	**30 477.3**	**30 998.4**	**..**
Water supply; sewerage, waste management and remediation activities	**1 632.0**	**1 419.8**	**1 713.8**	**1 031.6**	**..**	**523.7**	**597.7**	**544.5**	**201.5**	**..**
Construction	**3 253.1**	**2 583.5**	**3 713.1**	**3 002.1**	**..**	**1 984.8**	**1 997.5**	**2 759.7**	**3 237.9**	**..**
Services	**316 591.2**	**322 023.8**	**378 251.4**	**285 510.6**	**..**	**416 545.5**	**436 127.3**	**514 180.9**	**332 726.1**	**..**
Wholesale and retail trade; repair of motor vehicles and motorcycles	37 419.7	42 686.8	51 069.8	43 382.2	..	29 968.4	31 281.8	36 072.2	23 418.8	..
Transportation and storage	3 725.6	3 602.8	4 202.4	5 984.7	..	3 402.3	3 177.0	7 950.3	4 139.0	..
Accommodation and food service activities	2 524.8	2 654.2	2 808.8	2 325.4	..	1 022.3	1 029.8	1 779.8	841.5	..
Information and communication	4 156.8	8 008.9	10 161.9	10 168.3	..	10 478.0	11 070.9	12 528.2	12 642.5	..
Financial and insurance activities	128 049.0	125 992.4	153 926.6	129 388.6	..	100 215.6	79 222.1	108 631.6	101 489.6	..
Activities of holding companies	70 659.8	69 405.5	70 684.8	56 179.3	..	63 162.8	36 950.6	49 890.9	39 858.0	..
Real estate activities	6 047.9	7 845.5	8 314.9	5 154.6	..	4 568.3	2 980.9	3 635.2	4 694.3	..
Professional, scientific and technical activities	117 679.9	114 280.6	131 084.2	75 541.6	..	254 009.8	297 704.2	336 712.6	180 872.5	..
Administrative and support service activities	16 376.7	16 215.9	15 068.4	12 281.9	..	5 348.9	1 757.1	5 919.9	4 227.2	..
Public administration; activities of households and of extraterritorial organisations	-	-	-	-	..	6 929.8	7 487.1	26.4	-	..
Education	87.1	84.3	95.9	114.5	..	.. d	.. d	6.0	6.9	..
Human health and social work activities	26.1	326.8	403.0	411.0	..	1.1	.. d	33.6	51.5	..
Arts, entertainment and recreation	230.8	253.0	292.6	327.5	..	175.3	181.3	211.1	201.5	..
Other services	266.7	72.7	822.7	429.4	..	421.3	200.3	674.0	140.8	..
Not allocated and confidential	**-209.0**	**.. d**	**638.0**	**1 702.5**	**489 054.1**	**719.7**	**-650.4**	**-121.1**	**-506.1**	**612 188.3**
Private real estate activities	**18 219.9**	**17 768.5**	**18 077.5**	**15 751.1**	**..**	**12 027.2**	**11 728.7**	**13 527.2**	**13 085.6**	**..**

- Nil; .. Not available; d Secondary Confidentiality

Note: Data excludes resident Special Purpose Entities (SPEs). Detailed metadata at: *http://stats.oecd.org/OECDStat_Metadata/ShowMetadata.ashx?Dataset=FDI_CTRY_IND_SUMM.*

Source: *OECD International Direct Investment Statistics (database): https://doi.org/10.1787/idi-data-en*

BELGIUM

Table 6. Foreign direct investment income by industrial sector

Million US dollars

	Inward					Outward				
	2015	2016	2017	2018	2019	2015	2016	2017	2018	2019
All FDI activities	..	**31 450.8**	..	..	..	..	**32 119.9**	..	..	..
Agriculture, forestry and fishing	..	**-13.3**	..	..	..	..	**-17.7**	..	..	..
Mining and quarrying	..	**-64.1**	..	..	..	..	**85.1**	..	..	..
Extraction activities	..	-	..	..	..	..	-	..	..	..
Manufacturing	..	**11 927.5**	..	..	..	..	**8 360.1**	..	..	..
of which:										
Food products, beverages and tobacco	..	644.7	..	..	..	..	263.2	..	..	..
Textiles, wood and paper products; printing	..	216.7	..	..	..	..	147.1	..	..	..
Chemical, rubber, plastic, non-metallic mineral products	..	9 062.3	..	..	..	..	6 170.5	..	..	..
Metal and machinery products, except electrical equipment	..	1 373.4	..	..	..	..	1 155.6	..	..	..
Motor vehicles, trailers, semi-trailers, other transport equipment	..	266.5	..	..	..	..	82.9	..	..	..
Other manufacturing	..	362.7	..	..	..	..	540.8	..	..	..
Electricity, gas, steam and air conditioning supply	..	**658.0**	..	..	..	..	**-141.5**	..	..	..
Water supply; sewerage, waste management and remediation activities	..	**88.5**	..	..	..	..	**5.5**	..	..	..
Construction	..	**10.0**	..	..	..	..	**-144.9**	..	..	..
Services	..	**16 930.2**	..	..	..	..	**22 231.6**	..	..	..
Wholesale and retail trade; repair of motor vehicles and motorcycles	..	4 093.8	..	..	..	..	1 836.8	..	..	..
Transportation and storage	..	171.4	..	..	..	..	128.3	..	..	..
Accommodation and food service activities	..	68.6	..	..	..	..	-17.7	..	..	..
Information and communication	..	376.0	..	..	..	..	499.8	..	..	..
Financial and insurance activities	..	7 905.6	..	..	..	..	6 929.1	..	..	..
Activities of holding companies	..	1 167.8	..	..	..	..	3 248.9	..	..	..
Real estate activities	..	-420.2	..	..	..	..	113.9	..	..	..
Professional, scientific and technical activities	..	3 072.0	..	..	..	..	10 903.5	..	..	..
Administrative and support service activities	..	1 612.3	..	..	..	..	802.8	..	..	..
Public administration; activities of households and of extraterritorial organisations	..	-	..	..	..	..	1 015.2	..	..	..
Education	..	6.6	..	..	..	..	3.3	..	..	..
Human health and social work activities	..	-4.4	..	..	..	..	4.4	..	..	..
Arts, entertainment and recreation	..	36.5	..	..	..	..	10.0	..	..	..
Other services	..	11.1	..	..	..	..	3.3	..	..	..
Not allocated and confidential	..	**1 914.2**	..	..	..	..	**1 741.7**	..	..	..
Private real estate activities	..	-	..	..	..	..	-	..	..	..

- Nil; .. Not available

Note: Data excludes resident Special Purpose Entities (SPEs). Detailed metadata at: *http://stats.oecd.org/OECDStat_Metadata/ShowMetadata.ashx?Dataset=FDI_CTRY_IND_SUMM*.

Source: *OECD International Direct Investment Statistics (database): https://doi.org/10.1787/idi-data-en*

Table 1. Foreign direct investment flows by country

Million US dollars

	Inward					Outward				
	2015	2016	2017	2018	2019	2015	2016	2017	2018	2019
WORLD	**43 852.8**	**36 061.9**	**26 518.3**	**43 449.7**	**50 612.6**	**67 466.2**	**69 518.2**	**78 338.3**	**49 868.7**	**76 553.9**
OECD COUNTRIES	..	..	..	..	..	..	..	..	..	..
Australia	3 649.4	-498.5	316.5	1 992.6	1 746.2	1 944.0	1 469.4	337.1	3 033.5	-753.7
Austria	..	..	..	..	..	..	..	..	..	..
Belgium	..	..	..	..	..	..	..	..	..	..
Canada	-	-	-	-	-	-	-	-	-	-
Chile	..	..	..	..	..	..	..	..	..	..
Czech Republic	..	..	..	..	..	..	..	..	..	..
Denmark	..	..	..	..	..	..	..	..	..	..
Estonia	..	..	..	..	..	..	..	..	..	..
Finland	..	..	..	..	..	..	..	..	..	..
France	929.4	427.4	846.3	2 776.1	1 417.5	352.0	-98.4	192.3	894.4	1 330.3
Germany	300.4	370.7	514.6	401.3	298.9	1 177.3	1 381.9	-286.9	893.2	744.7
Greece	..	..	..	..	..	..	..	..	..	..
Hungary	..	..	..	..	..	..	..	..	..	..
Iceland	..	..	..	..	..	..	..	..	..	..
Ireland	..	..	..	..	..	..	..	..	..	..
Israel	..	..	..	..	..	..	..	..	..	..
Italy	..	..	..	..	..	..	..	..	..	..
Japan	499.1	1 009.7	772.2	447.6	57.9	-687.6	-131.6	1 021.7	280.7	-46.7
Korea	..	..	..	..	..	..	..	..	..	..
Latvia	..	..	..	..	..	..	..	..	..	..
Lithuania	..	..	..	..	..	..	..	..	..	..
Luxembourg	2 106.7	1 617.1	2 592.5	665.0	2 361.8	-991.2	-2 124.5	-2 545.4	4 005.5	5 109.4
Mexico	-100.1	-50.8	192.4	23.9	-9.9	927.8	1 458.4	905.6	854.8	1 212.6
Netherlands	17 207.2	4 824.4	441.3	3 078.2	4 070.8	896.5	1 039.2	1 020.5	210.2	1 380.9
New Zealand	..	..	..	..	..	..	..	..	..	..
Norway	..	..	..	..	..	..	..	..	..	..
Poland	..	..	..	..	..	..	..	..	..	..
Portugal	..	..	..	..	..	..	..	..	..	..
Slovak Republic	..	..	..	..	..	..	..	..	..	..
Slovenia	..	..	..	..	..	..	..	..	..	..
Spain	..	..	..	..	..	..	..	..	..	..
Sweden	..	..	..	..	..	..	..	..	..	..
Switzerland	-8 985.4	9 600.3	-3 185.8	2 907.7	5 844.6	-424.8	-455.7	1 435.9	1 543.1	5 002.0
Turkey	..	..	..	..	..	..	..	..	..	..
United Kingdom	-7 502.2	-1 773.1	3 062.6	2 119.8	1 934.9	13 918.5	8 183.6	3 358.9	7 079.5	5 748.9
United States	32 375.8	18 669.4	14 584.1	18 295.2	24 110.0	47 122.7	55 928.3	67 638.9	25 864.4	27 710.9
EUROPE	..	..	..	..	..	..	..	..	..	..
Bulgaria	..	..	..	..	..	..	..	..	..	..
Croatia	..	..	..	..	..	..	..	..	..	..
Cyprus	..	..	..	..	..	..	..	..	..	..
Malta	..	..	..	..	..	..	..	..	..	..
Romania	..	..	..	..	..	..	..	..	..	..
Russian Federation	..	..	..	..	..	..	..	..	..	..
Ukraine	..	..	..	..	..	..	..	..	..	..
AFRICA	..	..	..	..	..	..	..	..	..	..
Northern Africa	..	..	..	..	..	..	..	..	..	..
Algeria	..	..	..	..	..	..	..	..	..	..
Egypt	..	..	..	..	..	..	..	..	..	..
Libya	..	..	..	..	..	..	..	..	..	..
Morocco	..	..	..	..	..	..	..	..	..	..
Tunisia	..	..	..	..	..	..	..	..	..	..
Other African countries	..	..	..	..	..	..	..	..	..	..
Nigeria	..	..	..	..	..	..	..	..	..	..
South Africa	..	..	..	..	..	..	..	..	..	..
AMERICA	..	..	..	..	..	..	..	..	..	..
Northern America	..	..	..	..	..	..	..	..	..	..
Central America and Caribbean countries	..	..	..	..	..	..	..	..	..	..
Bahamas	..	..	..	..	..	..	..	..	..	..
Bermuda	..	..	..	..	..	..	..	..	..	..
Cayman Islands	-723.6	245.5	176.5	1 542.3	3 064.4	5 246.0	2 615.7	1 780.2	-3 178.5	2 302.6
Costa Rica	..	..	..	..	..	..	..	..	..	..
El Salvador	..	..	..	..	..	..	..	..	..	..
Guatemala	..	..	..	..	..	..	..	..	..	..
Honduras	..	..	..	..	..	..	..	..	..	..
Nicaragua	..	..	..	..	..	..	..	..	..	..
Panama	..	..	..	..	..	..	..	..	..	..
Virgin Islands, U.S.	..	..	..	..	..	..	..	..	..	..
South America	..	..	..	..	..	..	..	..	..	..
Argentina	..	..	..	..	..	..	..	..	..	..
Bolivia	..	..	..	..	..	..	..	..	..	..
Brazil	1 092.9	443.6	1 098.5	1 171.2	1 115.9	453.7	-90.6	32.4	323.5	196.1
Colombia	..	..	..	..	..	..	..	..	..	..
Ecuador	..	..	..	..	..	..	..	..	..	..
Paraguay	..	..	..	..	..	..	..	..	..	..
Peru	..	..	..	..	..	..	..	..	..	..
Uruguay	..	..	..	..	..	..	..	..	..	..
Venezuela	..	..	..	..	..	..	..	..	..	..

CANADA

Table 1. Foreign direct investment flows by country *(cont.)*

Million US dollars

	Inward					Outward				
	2015	2016	2017	2018	2019	2015	2016	2017	2018	2019
ASIA	..	..	..	..	..	..	..	..	..	..
Near and Middle East	..	..	..	..	..	..	..	..	..	..
Gulf Arabian countries	..	..	..	..	..	..	..	..	..	..
Kuwait	..	..	..	..	..	..	..	..	..	..
Qatar	..	..	..	..	..	..	..	..	..	..
Saudi Arabia	..	..	..	..	..	..	..	..	..	..
United Arab Emirates	..	..	..	..	..	..	..	..	..	..
Other Near and Middle East	..	..	..	..	..	..	..	..	..	..
Jordan	..	..	..	..	..	..	..	..	..	..
Other Asian countries	..	..	..	..	..	..	..	..	..	..
China	-4 807.2	5 693.4	1 959.4	2 560.1	882.0	2 303.8	968.8	1 324.9	667.6	458.7
Hong Kong, China	77.4	1 188.8	-209.8	1 439.1	-519.3	1 105.4	666.9	1 824.2	608.6	1 062.6
India	..	..	..	..	..	..	..	..	..	..
Indonesia	..	..	..	..	..	..	..	..	..	..
Iran, Islamic Republic of	..	..	..	..	..	..	..	..	..	..
Malaysia	..	..	..	..	..	..	..	..	..	..
Philippines	..	..	..	..	..	..	..	..	..	..
Singapore	..	..	..	..	..	..	..	..	..	..
Chinese Taipei	..	..	..	..	..	..	..	..	..	..
Thailand	..	..	..	..	..	..	..	..	..	..
Viet Nam	..	..	..	..	..	..	..	..	..	..
AUSTRALIA, OCEANIA AND POLAR REGIONS	..	..	..	..	..	..	..	..	..	..
WORLD unallocated and confidential	**7 323.8**	**-5 987.4**	**2 948.3**	**3 573.6**	**3 935.5**	**-2 154.4**	**-6 017.7**	**4 999.8**	**4 659.1**	**23 525.3**
European Union (EU28)	..	..	..	..	..	..	..	..	..	..
G20 countries excl. European Union	..	..	..	..	..	..	..	..	..	..
G20 OECD countries	..	..	..	..	..	..	..	..	..	..
G20 Non-OECD countries	..	..	..	..	..	..	..	..	..	..
MENA countries	..	..	..	..	..	..	..	..	..	..
ASEAN countries	..	..	..	..	..	..	..	..	..	..

- Nil; .. Not available

Note: Detailed metadata at: *http://stats.oecd.org/OECDStat_Metadata/ShowMetadata.ashx?Dataset=FDI_CTRY_IND_SUMM.*

Source: *OECD International Direct Investment Statistics (database): https://doi.org/10.1787/idi-data-en*

CANADA

Table 2. Foreign direct investment positions by country

At year end

Million US dollars

	Inward					Outward				
	2015	2016	2017	2018	2019	2015	2016	2017	2018	2019
WORLD	**565 687.9**	**603 759.6**	**658 556.6**	**663 183.1**	..	**754 206.6**	**823 099.0**	**938 918.8**	**994 673.4**	**1 065 361.8**
OECD COUNTRIES	..	**510 685.4**	**554 670.2**	**564 562.3**	..	**551 341.5**	**611 580.4**	**707 399.9**	**760 505.8**	**801 827.9**
Australia	5 172.0	7 319.9	6 649.4	6 503.3	..	18 649.9	21 327.9	28 290.4	29 234.7	28 953.2
Austria	285.4	1 455.2	1 392.7	1 494.3	..	906.1	1 575.2	2 228.3	1 947.8	1 922.8
Belgium	1 685.7	1 664.1	2 051.0	2 152.7	..	627.5	1 043.4	1 078.8	1 715.4	1 091.2
Canada	5 321.5	6 439.6	9 977.3	12 699.0	..	-	-	-	-	-
Chile	279.6	530.6	243.7	176.0	..	11 355.2	13 129.5	15 403.6	18 285.3	17 234.9
Czech Republic	..	..	..	..	..	36.7	456.5	9.5	396.6	413.5
Denmark	425.6	706.3	731.8	776.9	..	288.9	592.1	548.1	1 472.8	1 445.0
Estonia	..	..	..	..	..	33.0	96.1	133.5	63.0	73.5
Finland	603.3	420.8	833.4	640.8	..	1 042.6	1 120.9	1 275.8	1 196.4	1 161.7
France	8 338.2	11 681.5	14 076.0	16 912.7	..	4 130.8	4 681.6	8 682.1	7 226.0	7 938.6
Germany	16 653.2	18 610.6	21 256.3	20 018.6	..	7 654.0	8 619.9	7 278.4	8 345.4	8 846.8
Greece	..	..	..	..	..	18.8	201.8	235.9	239.7	91.9
Hungary	..	..	..	..	..	4 350.0	3 633.0	3 995.9	16.9	235.1
Iceland	..	..	..	..	..	82.9	-	138.2	-	0.8
Ireland	2 742.8	4 445.1	8 056.6	5 969.8	..	11 224.6	8 295.2	6 989.2	7 003.2	7 257.1
Israel	324.4	846.2	992.7	1 289.9	..	801.7	601.8	908.0	-151.7	-292.5
Italy	3 887.3	3 602.0	5 136.1	1 590.6	..	350.0	414.8	827.8	305.0	355.3
Japan	27 344.7	28 801.6	30 856.5	32 181.3	..	3 281.2	3 627.0	5 026.2	6 423.3	6 419.3
Korea	1 379.3	2 262.9	2 895.2	3 433.8	..	1 020.9	1 190.9	1 468.9	1 812.2	1 647.9
Latvia	..	..	..	..	..	2.2	5.2	2.4	2.2	2.3
Lithuania	..	..	..	..	..	331.7	344.8	388.5	360.7	371.4
Luxembourg	11 355.5	14 640.5	18 175.1	17 618.7	..	51 572.0	58 760.7	63 221.3	75 148.5	77 505.2
Mexico	1 375.0	2 255.7	2 258.0	1 866.8	..	12 129.7	13 110.9	16 311.6	19 505.2	21 389.8
Netherlands	25 450.9	20 498.1	15 874.0	15 162.3	..	22 771.8	24 983.2	27 059.1	26 762.0	27 517.4
New Zealand	..	..	..	..	..	491.0	440.9	328.1	975.0	1 023.8
Norway	6 226.9	5 644.6	4 955.9	5 746.9	..	1 025.5	1 194.6	1 456.1	1 416.3	1 121.1
Poland	1 369.9	2 018.0	2 422.0	2 180.3	..	813.8	192.2	233.6	257.3	261.1
Portugal	..	..	..	..	..	170.3	35.0	46.9	128.3	359.1
Slovak Republic	..	..	..	..	..	3.9	-13.4	1.6	-1.5	-
Slovenia	..	..	..	..	..	..	-	0.8	-	-
Spain	3 775.3	3 900.4	4 007.1	7 178.6	..	3 048.4	4 082.8	4 092.0	5 863.9	5 825.1
Sweden	2 083.8	1 747.5	1 894.2	2 105.1	..	4 186.6	3 151.1	3 377.0	3 133.2	2 831.0
Switzerland	15 638.0	20 058.1	23 425.4	23 307.5	..	-175.7	-43.9	3 429.5	7 089.7	12 263.6
Turkey	..	..	..	..	..	699.4	804.3	1 184.5	947.1	997.8
United Kingdom	34 830.9	38 114.8	36 759.1	35 587.2	..	66 803.7	69 159.2	80 122.3	74 194.0	81 927.4
United States	294 034.0	312 802.9	338 727.1	346 923.7	..	322 967.0	365 109.9	422 014.6	459 192.1	483 635.8
EUROPE	**139 817.9**	**152 762.2**	**166 229.8**	**164 130.1**	..	**196 129.3**	**206 281.4**	**232 646.2**	**238 464.2**	**269 330.0**
Bulgaria	..	..	..	..	..	6.2	-	22.2	77.7	91.1
Croatia	..	..	..	..	..	-1.0	-	-	-0.7	-0.8
Cyprus	2 246.4	1 384.7	1 967.9	2 017.8	..	3 321.5	3 320.9	2 789.2	1 428.8	2 023.9
Malta	..	..	..	..	..	448.6	569.0	1 010.5	2 101.8	3 327.2
Romania	..	..	..	..	..	142.0	408.9	539.4	683.2	693.8
Russian Federation	1 813.6	1 988.1	2 719.6	3 120.0	..	1 253.6	928.0	1 220.2	748.5	1 029.2
Ukraine	..	..	..	..	..	399.2	234.6	540.2	4.4	32.9
AFRICA	**2 437.9**	**1 385.5**	**1 450.2**	**934.5**	..	**3 180.6**	**4 864.8**	**7 113.1**	**7 185.7**	**8 208.9**
Northern Africa	..	..	..	..	..	..	93.1	54.0	25.7	-40.6
Algeria	..	..	..	..	..	11.5	7.4	7.9	-27.9	-85.8
Egypt	..	..	..	..	..	0.4	-6.0	-25.4	4.4	4.6
Libya	..	..	..	..	..	..	-	-	-	-
Morocco	..	..	..	..	..	-2.8	5.2	13.5	-	-3.1
Tunisia	..	..	..	..	..	122.1	86.4	58.0	49.1	43.6
Other African countries	..	..	..	..	..	..	4 772.5	7 058.3	7 158.6	8 248.7
Nigeria	..	..	..	..	..	315.7	404.4	398.0	285.9	298.6
South Africa	1 040.5	564.9	503.0	812.4	..	1 407.0	1 471.7	1 621.4	630.5	657.8
AMERICA	**327 026.0**	**346 476.1**	**375 883.1**	**383 476.7**	..	..	**552 763.8**	**626 374.3**	**670 162.0**	**705 985.1**
Northern America	..	..	..	..	..	322 994.5	365 109.9	422 014.6	459 192.1	483 635.8
Central America and Caribbean countries	..	..	..	..	..	..	147 596.6	158 195.1	163 100.2	174 429.9
Bahamas	..	..	..	..	..	14 188.7	16 873.5	19 170.6	19 261.1	20 112.6
Bermuda	774.6	596.3	722.5	1 301.6	..	31 393.3	31 658.6	36 352.9	42 578.3	48 627.0
Cayman Islands	1 187.1	1 143.0	917.2	978.7	..	28 834.3	30 575.7	32 423.7	30 656.1	32 684.7
Costa Rica	..	..	..	..	..	26.8	3.0	128.7	252.9	265.0
El Salvador	..	..	..	..	..	697.5	586.1	498.9	480.9	199.9
Guatemala	..	..	..	..	..	19.9	9.7	-2.4	64.5	59.0
Honduras	..	..	..	..	..	230.3	66.3	352.7	546.9	541.4
Nicaragua	..	..	..	..	..	251.4	353.0	278.0	524.2	526.1
Panama	..	..	..	..	..	3 521.6	3 498.9	3 832.2	2 809.9	2 823.3
Virgin Islands, U.S.	..	..	..	..	..	-	-	-	-	-
South America	..	..	..	..	..	..	38 812.8	45 023.8	46 552.3	46 788.4
Argentina	..	..	..	..	..	2 380.1	2 478.6	1 688.9	2 010.1	1 254.3
Bolivia	..	..	..	..	..	114.9	102.8	107.2	104.1	109.5
Brazil	23 541.9	22 035.7	22 041.4	19 296.7	..	8 564.9	8 987.1	11 538.0	9 176.7	9 379.0
Colombia	..	..	..	..	..	2 656.3	2 967.9	3 449.3	4 197.6	4 557.0
Ecuador	..	..	..	..	..	705.5	1 055.3	965.2	1 767.5	1 913.6
Paraguay	..	..	..	..	..	..	-	31.8	-	-
Peru	..	..	..	..	..	9 665.8	9 615.7	10 804.7	9 924.5	11 227.5
Uruguay	..	..	..	..	..	546.3	334.4	779.3	766.8	774.2
Venezuela	..	..	..	..	..	329.4	-35.7	136.6	-0.7	0.8

Table 2. Foreign direct investment positions by country *(cont.)*

At year end

Million US dollars

	Inward					Outward				
	2015	2016	2017	2018	2019	2015	2016	2017	2018	2019
ASIA	..	..	..	..	..	..	**36 945.0**	**43 848.9**	**47 960.6**	**51 209.9**
Near and Middle East	..	..	..	..	..	..	886.3	797.6	-79.2	-214.4
Gulf Arabian countries	..	..	..	..	..	..	285.2	-110.4	72.6	78.9
Kuwait	1 659.7	1 483.8	1 732.1	1 563.4	..	0.0	-	-	-	13.0
Qatar	..	..	..	..	..	0.6	-	-	-5.1	-5.4
Saudi Arabia	..	..	..	..	..	96.1	14.2	81.8	1.5	-7.7
United Arab Emirates	8 357.7	7 672.5	7 104.4	6 699.1	..	-193.0	257.7	-211.3	54.2	85.8
Other Near and Middle East	..	..	..	..	..	..	601.0	908.0	-151.7	-293.3
Jordan	..	..	..	..	..	-	-	-	-	-
Other Asian countries	..	..	..	..	..	..	35 947.7	42 879.7	48 044.1	51 428.1
China	17 449.4	18 662.4	21 359.3	18 358.1	..	7 407.6	7 610.0	10 398.0	9 962.6	10 254.2
Hong Kong, China	7 794.8	8 544.3	9 619.4	9 436.7	..	5 298.4	6 338.7	6 871.6	7 896.8	8 967.0
India	3 139.5	3 931.8	4 706.7	2 812.4	..	920.1	1 112.7	1 314.0	1 788.0	1 920.5
Indonesia	308.5	295.9	306.5	673.5	..	2 340.1	2 211.2	2 313.3	2 317.3	2 945.1
Iran, Islamic Republic of	..	..	..	..	..	..	-	-	-	-
Malaysia	6 342.5	7 346.8	7 122.8	5 553.5	..	682.4	719.4	882.6	27.1	9.2
Philippines	..	..	..	..	..	1 268.7	1 510.4	1 615.8	2 258.6	2 398.3
Singapore	631.5	389.1	393.1	415.4	..	3 087.6	3 349.2	4 335.9	6 984.8	7 136.8
Chinese Taipei	..	..	..	..	..	83.3	84.2	70.7	425.2	425.8
Thailand	..	..	..	..	..	103.3	115.4	139.0	191.3	231.3
Viet Nam	..	..	..	..	..	-55.0	72.2	525.1	156.9	170.0
AUSTRALIA, OCEANIA AND POLAR REGIONS	..	..	..	..	..	..	**22 244.0**	**28 936.3**	**30 900.2**	**30 627.9**
WORLD unallocated and confidential	**96 406.1**	..	..	..	..	**906.5**	-	-	**0.7**	-
European Union (EU28)	..	**102 512.0**	**117 286.5**	**114 963.8**	..	**184 284.9**	**195 730.2**	**216 190.0**	**220 067.4**	**233 567.7**
G20 countries excl. European Union	..	..	..	..	..	**462 056.2**	**512 859.9**	**601 382.3**	**633 820.1**	**669 544.4**
G20 OECD countries	..	..	..	..	..	**437 686.6**	**488 046.5**	**571 206.7**	**607 185.0**	**642 112.0**
G20 Non-OECD countries	..	..	..	..	..	**24 369.5**	**24 813.4**	**30 175.6**	**26 635.1**	**27 432.4**
MENA countries	..	..	..	..	..	..	**378.3**	**-56.4**	**98.2**	**38.3**
ASEAN countries	..	..	..	..	..	..	**8 088.2**	**9 992.9**	**12 216.8**	**13 427.5**

- Nil; .. Not available

Note: Inward FDI positions are allocated according to the ultimate investing country. Inward FDI positions by immediate counterpart country are available for the most recent year in the *OECD FDI database according to BMD4*. Detailed metadata at: *http://stats.oecd.org/OECDStat_Metadata/ShowMetadata.ashx?Dataset=FDI_CTRY_IND_SUMM.*

Source: *OECD International Direct Investment Statistics (database): https://doi.org/10.1787/idi-data-en*

Table 3. Foreign direct investment income by country

Million US dollars

	Inward					Outward				
	2015	2016	2017	2018	2019	2015	2016	2017	2018	2019
WORLD	**34 466.1**	**31 001.1**	**37 795.4**	**41 472.2**	**42 435.2**	**40 014.9**	**40 774.1**	**54 572.7**	**60 286.9**	**64 052.0**
OECD COUNTRIES	..	..	..	..	..	..	..	..	..	..
Australia	..	..	..	..	..	..	..	..	..	..
Austria	..	..	..	..	..	..	..	..	..	..
Belgium	..	..	..	..	..	..	..	..	..	..
Canada	-	-	-	-	-	-	-	-	-	-
Chile	..	..	..	..	..	..	..	..	..	..
Czech Republic	..	..	..	..	..	..	..	..	..	..
Denmark	..	..	..	..	..	..	..	..	..	..
Estonia	..	..	..	..	..	..	..	..	..	..
Finland	..	..	..	..	..	..	..	..	..	..
France	..	..	..	..	..	..	..	..	..	..
Germany	..	..	..	..	..	..	..	..	..	..
Greece	..	..	..	..	..	..	..	..	..	..
Hungary	..	..	..	..	..	..	..	..	..	..
Iceland	..	..	..	..	..	..	..	..	..	..
Ireland	..	..	..	..	..	..	..	..	..	..
Israel	..	..	..	..	..	..	..	..	..	..
Italy	..	..	..	..	..	..	..	..	..	..
Japan	451.4	565.9	591.9	998.8	1 416.7	-36.0	-123.8	1 010.0	151.4	98.0
Korea	..	..	..	..	..	..	..	..	..	..
Latvia	..	..	..	..	..	..	..	..	..	..
Lithuania	..	..	..	..	..	..	..	..	..	..
Luxembourg	..	..	..	..	..	..	..	..	..	..
Mexico	..	..	..	..	..	..	..	..	..	..
Netherlands	..	..	..	..	..	..	..	..	..	..
New Zealand	..	..	..	..	..	..	..	..	..	..
Norway	..	..	..	..	..	..	..	..	..	..
Poland	..	..	..	..	..	..	..	..	..	..
Portugal	..	..	..	..	..	..	..	..	..	..
Slovak Republic	..	..	..	..	..	..	..	..	..	..
Slovenia	..	..	..	..	..	..	..	..	..	..
Spain	..	..	..	..	..	..	..	..	..	..
Sweden	..	..	..	..	..	..	..	..	..	..
Switzerland	..	..	..	..	..	..	..	..	..	..
Turkey	..	..	..	..	..	..	..	..	..	..
United Kingdom	2 238.9	3 035.8	2 942.5	2 511.5	2 243.6	5 558.2	6 768.6	4 027.1	5 566.9	5 397.4
United States	22 184.2	15 744.4	16 553.1	18 826.2	18 046.0	19 047.2	13 734.5	23 359.8	25 550.6	25 392.0
EUROPE	..	..	..	..	..	..	..	..	..	..
Bulgaria	..	..	..	..	..	..	..	..	..	..
Croatia	..	..	..	..	..	..	..	..	..	..
Cyprus	..	..	..	..	..	..	..	..	..	..
Malta	..	..	..	..	..	..	..	..	..	..
Romania	..	..	..	..	..	..	..	..	..	..
Russian Federation	..	..	..	..	..	..	..	..	..	..
Ukraine	..	..	..	..	..	..	..	..	..	..
AFRICA	..	..	..	..	..	..	..	..	..	..
Northern Africa	..	..	..	..	..	..	..	..	..	..
Algeria	..	..	..	..	..	..	..	..	..	..
Egypt	..	..	..	..	..	..	..	..	..	..
Libya	..	..	..	..	..	..	..	..	..	..
Morocco	..	..	..	..	..	..	..	..	..	..
Tunisia	..	..	..	..	..	..	..	..	..	..
Other African countries	..	..	..	..	..	..	..	..	..	..
Nigeria	..	..	..	..	..	..	..	..	..	..
South Africa	..	..	..	..	..	..	..	..	..	..
AMERICA	..	..	..	..	..	..	..	..	..	..
Northern America	..	..	..	..	..	..	..	..	..	..
Central America and Caribbean countries	..	..	..	..	..	..	..	..	..	..
Bahamas	..	..	..	..	..	..	..	..	..	..
Bermuda	..	..	..	..	..	..	..	..	..	..
Cayman Islands	..	..	..	..	..	..	..	..	..	..
Costa Rica	..	..	..	..	..	..	..	..	..	..
El Salvador	..	..	..	..	..	..	..	..	..	..
Guatemala	..	..	..	..	..	..	..	..	..	..
Honduras	..	..	..	..	..	..	..	..	..	..
Nicaragua	..	..	..	..	..	..	..	..	..	..
Panama	..	..	..	..	..	..	..	..	..	..
Virgin Islands, U.S.	..	..	..	..	..	..	..	..	..	..
South America	..	..	..	..	..	..	..	..	..	..
Argentina	..	..	..	..	..	..	..	..	..	..
Bolivia	..	..	..	..	..	..	..	..	..	..
Brazil	..	..	..	..	..	..	..	..	..	..
Colombia	..	..	..	..	..	..	..	..	..	..
Ecuador	..	..	..	..	..	..	..	..	..	..
Paraguay	..	..	..	..	..	..	..	..	..	..
Peru	..	..	..	..	..	..	..	..	..	..
Uruguay	..	..	..	..	..	..	..	..	..	..
Venezuela	..	..	..	..	..	..	..	..	..	..

CANADA

Table 3. Foreign direct investment income by country *(cont.)*

Million US dollars

	Inward					Outward				
	2015	2016	2017	2018	2019	2015	2016	2017	2018	2019
ASIA	..	..	..	..	..	..	..	..	..	..
Near and Middle East	..	..	..	..	..	..	..	..	..	..
Gulf Arabian countries	..	..	..	..	..	..	..	..	..	..
Kuwait	..	..	..	..	..	..	..	..	..	..
Qatar	..	..	..	..	..	..	..	..	..	..
Saudi Arabia	..	..	..	..	..	..	..	..	..	..
United Arab Emirates	..	..	..	..	..	..	..	..	..	..
Other Near and Middle East	..	..	..	..	..	..	..	..	..	..
Jordan	..	..	..	..	..	..	..	..	..	..
Other Asian countries	..	..	..	..	..	..	..	..	..	..
China	..	..	..	..	..	..	..	..	..	..
Hong Kong, China	..	..	..	..	..	..	..	..	..	..
India	..	..	..	..	..	..	..	..	..	..
Indonesia	..	..	..	..	..	..	..	..	..	..
Iran, Islamic Republic of	..	..	..	..	..	..	..	..	..	..
Malaysia	..	..	..	..	..	..	..	..	..	..
Philippines	..	..	..	..	..	..	..	..	..	..
Singapore	..	..	..	..	..	..	..	..	..	..
Chinese Taipei	..	..	..	..	..	..	..	..	..	..
Thailand	..	..	..	..	..	..	..	..	..	..
Viet Nam	..	..	..	..	..	..	..	..	..	..
AUSTRALIA, OCEANIA AND POLAR REGIONS	..	..	..	..	..	..	..	..	..	..
WORLD unallocated and confidential	**9 591.6**	**11 655.1**	**17 707.9**	**19 135.6**	**20 728.9**	**15 444.7**	**20 394.8**	**26 175.9**	**29 018.0**	**33 164.7**
European Union (EU28)	..	..	..	..	..	..	..	..	..	..
G20 countries excl. European Union	..	..	..	..	..	..	..	..	..	..
G20 OECD countries	..	..	..	..	..	..	..	..	..	..
G20 Non-OECD countries	..	..	..	..	..	..	..	..	..	..
MENA countries	..	..	..	..	..	..	..	..	..	..
ASEAN countries	..	..	..	..	..	..	..	..	..	..

- Nil; .. Not available

Note: Detailed metadata at: *http://stats.oecd.org/OECDStat_Metadata/ShowMetadata.ashx?Dataset=FDI_CTRY_IND_SUMM.*

Source: *OECD International Direct Investment Statistics (database): https://doi.org/10.1787/idi-data-en*

CANADA

Table 4. Foreign direct investment flows by industrial sector

Million US dollars

	Inward					Outward				
	2015	2016	2017	2018	2019	2015	2016	2017	2018	2019
All FDI activities	**43 852.8**	**36 061.9**	**26 518.3**	**43 449.7**	**50 612.6**	**67 466.2**	**69 518.2**	**78 338.3**	**49 868.7**	**76 553.9**
Agriculture, forestry and fishing	..	..	..	..	..	..	..	..	..	..
Mining and quarrying	**2 370.1**	**8 148.0**	**-3 795.7**	**4 900.6**	**14 627.9**	**-13 580.8**	**12 721.0**	**-1 725.9**	**10 219.0**	**15 060.5**
Extraction activities	..	..	..	..	..	..	..	..	..	..
Manufacturing	**2 724.1**	**3 285.9**	**9 934.4**	**14 157.0**	**13 747.2**	**19 593.2**	**4 524.6**	**-1 698.8**	**4 973.7**	**2 782.8**
of which:										
Food products, beverages and tobacco	..	..	..	..	..	..	..	..	..	..
Textiles, wood and paper products; printing	..	..	..	..	..	..	..	..	..	..
Chemical, rubber, plastic, non-metallic mineral products	..	..	..	..	..	..	..	..	..	..
Metal and machinery products, except electrical equipment	..	..	..	..	..	..	..	..	..	..
Motor vehicles, trailers, semi-trailers, other transport equipment	..	..	..	..	..	..	..	..	..	..
Other manufacturing	..	..	..	..	..	..	..	..	..	..
Electricity, gas, steam and air conditioning supply	..	..	..	..	..	..	..	..	..	..
Water supply; sewerage, waste management and remediation activities	..	..	..	..	..	..	..	..	..	..
Construction	..	..	..	..	..	..	..	..	..	..
Services	..	..	..	..	..	..	..	..	..	..
Wholesale and retail trade; repair of motor vehicles and motorcycles	..	..	..	..	..	..	..	..	..	..
Transportation and storage	7 220.1	8 787.9	10 310.4	7 333.6	1 988.3	1 314.0	17 115.3	44 592.0	14 758.0	10 212.2
Accommodation and food service activities	..	..	..	..	..	..	..	..	..	..
Information and communication	..	..	..	..	..	..	..	..	..	..
Financial and insurance activities	171.5	6 928.6	3 465.5	3 719.2	6 872.3	42 447.8	17 922.0	21 047.3	17 311.3	22 360.5
Activities of holding companies	..	..	..	..	..	..	..	..	..	..
Real estate activities	..	..	..	..	..	..	..	..	..	..
Professional, scientific and technical activities	10 930.0	3 837.9	1 038.2	1 293.6	7 110.2	9 687.5	-1 204.4	5 793.0	5 532.7	23 151.8
Administrative and support service activities	..	..	..	..	..	..	..	..	..	..
Public administration; activities of households and of extraterritorial organisations	..	..	..	..	..	..	..	..	..	..
Education	..	..	..	..	..	..	..	..	..	..
Human health and social work activities	..	..	..	..	..	..	..	..	..	..
Arts, entertainment and recreation	..	..	..	..	..	..	..	..	..	..
Other services	..	..	..	..	..	..	..	..	..	..
Not allocated and confidential	**20 437.5**	**5 073.6**	**5 565.6**	**12 045.7**	**6 266.7**	**8 004.0**	**18 439.6**	**10 330.7**	**-2 926.0**	**2 986.2**
Private real estate activities	..	..	..	..	..	..	..	..	..	..

.. Not available

Note: Detailed metadata at: *http://stats.oecd.org/OECDStat_Metadata/ShowMetadata.ashx?Dataset=FDI_CTRY_IND_SUMM.*

Source: *OECD International Direct Investment Statistics (database): https://doi.org/10.1787/idi-data-en*

CANADA

Table 5. Foreign direct investment positions by industrial sector

At year end

Million US dollars

	Inward					Outward				
	2015	2016	2017	2018	2019	2015	2016	2017	2018	2019
All FDI activities	**565 687.9**	**603 759.6**	**658 556.6**	**663 183.1**	..	**754 206.6**	**823 099.0**	**938 918.8**	**994 673.4**	**1 065 361.8**
Agriculture, forestry and fishing	**307.1**	**107.2**	**144.6**	**197.2**	**565.1**	**1 919.8**	**2 432.4**	**1 236.9**	**1 427.3**	**1 585.9**
Mining and quarrying	**121 970.4**	**128 794.2**	**137 229.9**	**123 801.8**	**144 168.0**	**135 925.6**	**139 518.1**	**144 041.2**	**121 103.3**	**135 662.0**
Extraction activities	106 750.7	110 904.9	117 823.3	105 451.9	111 509.3	76 402.5	76 560.7	77 378.5	62 057.8	67 370.4
Manufacturing	**130 824.4**	**135 076.3**	**141 055.8**	**139 131.3**	**159 129.3**	**59 023.1**	**67 044.8**	**73 464.4**	**79 036.0**	**80 465.6**
of which:										
Food products, beverages and tobacco	20 377.9	20 252.5	20 165.2	23 256.4	29 748.8	12 462.4	11 257.2	13 439.0	16 479.7	17 992.2
Textiles, wood and paper products; printing	7 843.9	9 324.5	9 021.3	7 823.5	7 588.6	2 356.2	5 154.5	5 931.8	7 625.5	9 016.8
Chemical, rubber, plastic, non-metallic mineral products	60 877.9	69 323.8	71 748.5	69 805.0	79 918.1	11 437.9	11 788.2	12 477.0	13 751.2	11 742.1
Metal and machinery products, except electrical equipment	21 432.8	12 814.5	13 717.0	15 813.4	16 901.0	12 518.1	13 876.5	11 178.9	9 252.3	10 237.4
Motor vehicles, trailers, semi-trailers, other transport equipment	13 422.7	14 454.5	16 178.1	13 855.3	15 351.9	11 720.4	14 796.3	16 599.9	18 830.7	18 541.2
Other manufacturing	6 869.9	8 767.4	9 934.1	8 357.2	9 372.8	8 527.5	10 171.3	13 783.8	13 000.5	12 813.4
Electricity, gas, steam and air conditioning supply	**1 794.8**	**1 557.3**	**1 263.1**	**7 270.7**	**7 476.1**	**19 913.3**	**23 957.7**	**30 637.9**	**49 603.4**	**50 614.9**
Water supply; sewerage, waste management and remediation activities	..	..	..	..	..	..	..	..	..	..
Construction	**3 174.1**	**2 422.7**	**2 948.8**	**3 780.5**	**4 122.1**	**619.9**	**926.5**	**2 568.3**	**3 422.0**	**2 905.3**
Services	**303 605.5 e**	**331 108.2 e**	**369 780.7 e**	**379 429.7 e**	**420 114.9 e**	**518 263.7 e**	**570 010.4 e**	**669 448.7 e**	**725 855.9 e**	**780 203.7 e**
Wholesale and retail trade; repair of motor vehicles and motorcycles	67 195.1	76 746.9	85 603.0	85 963.6	92 710.8	21 244.9	28 031.6	28 607.4	27 122.6	28 722.7
Transportation and storage	6 343.2	7 906.5	10 888.1	10 012.5	10 803.3	24 583.8	35 114.3	53 816.3	73 834.0	82 131.9
Accommodation and food service activities	2 560.7	3 009.6	3 139.5	4 009.2	4 011.8	3 057.1	2 044.4	3 008.4	2 317.3	2 465.7
Information and communication	4 215.3	4 874.5	4 895.1	9 354.2	10 956.4	29 538.3	34 336.0	35 806.3	35 337.6	38 918.0
Financial and insurance activities	83 708.8	215 556.7	240 722.9	245 006.2	274 708.6	274 206.6	404 099.2	469 118.2	488 723.0	529 866.8
Activities of holding companies	..	121 448.6	136 620.6	154 813.4	172 875.4	..	105 888.9	126 549.9	132 324.6	154 299.7
Real estate activities	7 338.9	8 783.0	9 747.4	10 964.7	11 879.9	45 101.9	46 784.8	58 827.5	62 943.3	62 727.6
Professional, scientific and technical activities	132 243.5	14 231.0	14 784.7	14 119.2	15 044.0	120 531.1	19 600.1	20 264.5	35 578.0	35 371.0
Administrative and support service activities	..	..	..	..	..	..	..	..	..	..
Public administration; activities of households and of extraterritorial organisations	..	..	..	..	..	..	..	..	..	..
Education	..	..	..	..	..	..	..	..	..	..
Human health and social work activities	..	..	..	..	..	..	..	..	..	..
Arts, entertainment and recreation	..	..	..	..	..	..	..	..	..	..
Other services	..	..	..	..	..	..	..	..	..	..
Not allocated and confidential	..	**4 693.5 e**	**6 133.6 e**	**9 571.9 e**	**10 185.3 e**	..	**19 209.1 e**	**17 521.4 e**	**14 225.5 e**	**13 924.5 e**
Private real estate activities	..	..	..	..	..	..	..	..	..	..

.. Not available; e Estimated value

Note: Detailed metadata at: *http://stats.oecd.org/OECDStat_Metadata/ShowMetadata.ashx?Dataset=FDI_CTRY_IND_SUMM.*

Source: OECD *International Direct Investment Statistics (database): https://doi.org/10.1787/idi-data-en*

CANADA

Table 6. Foreign direct investment income by industrial sector

Million US dollars

	Inward					Outward				
	2015	2016	2017	2018	2019	2015	2016	2017	2018	2019
All FDI activities	**34 466.1**	**31 001.1**	**37 795.4**	**41 472.2**	**42 435.2**	**40 014.9**	**40 774.1**	**54 572.7**	**60 286.9**	**64 052.0**
Agriculture, forestry and fishing	..	..	..	..	..	..	..	..	..	..
Mining and quarrying	..	..	..	..	..	..	..	..	..	..
Extraction activities	..	..	..	..	..	..	..	..	..	..
Manufacturing	..	..	..	..	..	..	..	..	..	..
of which:										
Food products, beverages and tobacco	..	..	..	..	..	..	..	..	..	..
Textiles, wood and paper products; printing	..	..	..	..	..	..	..	..	..	..
Chemical, rubber, plastic, non-metallic mineral products	..	..	..	..	..	..	..	..	..	..
Metal and machinery products, except electrical equipment	..	..	..	..	..	..	..	..	..	..
Motor vehicles, trailers, semi-trailers, other transport equipment	..	..	..	..	..	..	..	..	..	..
Other manufacturing	..	..	..	..	..	..	..	..	..	..
Electricity, gas, steam and air conditioning supply	..	..	..	..	..	..	..	..	..	..
Water supply; sewerage, waste management and remediation activities	..	..	..	..	..	..	..	..	..	..
Construction	..	..	..	..	..	..	..	..	..	..
Services	..	..	..	..	..	..	..	..	..	..
Wholesale and retail trade; repair of motor vehicles and motorcycles	..	..	..	..	..	..	..	..	..	..
Transportation and storage	..	..	..	..	..	..	..	..	..	..
Accommodation and food service activities	..	..	..	..	..	..	..	..	..	..
Information and communication	..	..	..	..	..	..	..	..	..	..
Financial and insurance activities	..	..	..	..	..	..	..	..	..	..
Activities of holding companies	..	..	..	..	..	..	..	..	..	..
Real estate activities	..	..	..	..	..	..	..	..	..	..
Professional, scientific and technical activities	..	..	..	..	..	..	..	..	..	..
Administrative and support service activities	..	..	..	..	..	..	..	..	..	..
Public administration; activities of households and of extraterritorial organisations	..	..	..	..	..	..	..	..	..	..
Education	..	..	..	..	..	..	..	..	..	..
Human health and social work activities	..	..	..	..	..	..	..	..	..	..
Arts, entertainment and recreation	..	..	..	..	..	..	..	..	..	..
Other services	..	..	..	..	..	..	..	..	..	..
Not allocated and confidential	..	..	..	..	..	..	..	..	..	..
Private real estate activities	..	..	..	..	..	..	..	..	..	..

.. Not available

Note: Detailed metadata at: *http://stats.oecd.org/OECDStat_Metadata/ShowMetadata.ashx?Dataset=FDI_CTRY_IND_SUMM.*

Source: *OECD International Direct Investment Statistics (database): https://doi.org/10.1787/idi-data-en*

CZECH REPUBLIC

Table 1. Foreign direct investment flows by country

Million US dollars

	Inward					Outward				
	2015	2016	2017	2018	2019	2015	2016	2017	2018	2019
WORLD	**465.2**	**9 814.5**	**9 517.9**	**11 010.4**	**7 576.9**	**2 488.1**	**2 181.7**	**7 557.0**	**8 662.6**	**4 918.2**
OECD COUNTRIES	**264.4**	**.. c**	**.. c**	**11 773.8**	**6 604.5**	**1 943.3**	**.. c**	**3 372.3**	**9 873.9**	**5 052.5**
Australia	-20.7	31.3	23.3	-17.7	15.7	-31.8	.. c	.. c	.. c	-0.4
Austria	-115.8	-188.5	861.0	650.0	785.1	4.0	5.5	17.1	10.5	-134.2
Belgium	-237.0	-484.9	-739.0	2 913.9	-647.0	7.7	-17.2	0.6	28.2	3.7
Canada	25.4	-53.1	8.3	32.7	4.1	-7.3	-3.0	7.3	-0.3	-3.0
Chile	0.6	0.0	0.0	0.8	-0.1	0.0	0.1	.. c	.. c	6.9
Czech Republic	-	-	-	-	-	-	-	-	-	-
Denmark	149.6	73.0	6.7	-135.4	-41.6	-0.3	0.4	2.0	-1.7	0.4
Estonia	-0.7	4.0	2.3	1.1	3.4	1.8	-1.5	0.6	-1.9	0.7
Finland	-12.9	13.1	57.6	30.3	14.6	.. c	20.5	2.2	5.7	9.0
France	221.1	707.3	416.4	784.0	531.1	64.8	42.5	8.0	-47.3	-51.1
Germany	1 003.5	2 535.1	4 553.2	2 406.4	1 158.4	276.2	-227.7	234.5	108.2	54.3
Greece	2.8	-4.4	-10.5	4.5	0.2	23.4	0.2	-937.4	0.5	-0.8
Hungary	-77.6	20.0	126.4	-123.8	62.7	-7.2	-29.8	175.5	247.2	164.4
Iceland	1.7	.. c	.. c	.. c	-0.3	0.0	0.0	0.0	0.0	0.0
Ireland	138.8	41.3	-184.2	163.9	22.9	145.1	-294.8	-368.3	-94.3	1.7
Israel	20.3	52.2	-0.5	42.5	8.2	-	-	.. c	.. c	.. c
Italy	134.2	739.9	325.4	313.6	337.5	13.6	-89.2	151.3	27.9	-30.0
Japan	92.9	97.1	122.1	171.3	-1.8	-0.1	0.1	.. c	-3.5	-3.3
Korea	479.6	167.6	478.2	67.6	-14.6	.. c	-0.5	.. c	.. c	-
Latvia	-0.7	9.1	4.4	2.0	7.2	1.1	3.7	11.2	-4.4	-3.3
Lithuania	4.3	-6.1	4.5	-10.5	-0.8	-1.6	-0.2	5.5	-9.0	-0.4
Luxembourg	1 208.6	1 015.7	2 493.6	2 631.0	1 199.2	848.7	379.0	2 785.0	894.0	1 568.8
Mexico	-66.8	-19.5	-44.4	36.5	31.1	1.0	-6.0	2.3	0.2	-5.4
Netherlands	-2 272.3	2 044.1	-2 043.9	459.4	1 784.6	89.5	464.0	2 330.7	3 324.3	1 632.1
New Zealand	3.3	-1.7	0.6	1.3	-0.6	-	-	-	-	-0.1
Norway	-5.4	99.9	-13.9	46.7	9.2	.. c	50.6	7.8	-84.0	10.7
Poland	427.3	450.9	997.5	-305.8	302.5	145.4	-67.5	240.6	572.3	122.5
Portugal	25.3	-27.6	11.2	-10.4	-14.2	0.1	0.2	-0.2	-0.1	0.0
Slovak Republic	-164.5	361.2	-232.3	404.1	216.3	387.5	607.2	-1 148.4	1 169.8	919.3
Slovenia	-32.9	1.1	-0.5	73.1	39.2	-94.7	233.9	-9.9	-69.6	9.8
Spain	-159.0	215.0	77.3	210.0	58.2	6.7	-1.1	15.1	30.5	1.5
Sweden	-125.1	246.2	261.8	332.6	157.6	-0.7	3.7	4.8	-2.7	-21.5
Switzerland	-650.0	426.1	1 190.3	315.5	336.0	44.6	-45.5	-19.0	1 347.2	146.1
Turkey	7.3	2.8	-9.6	16.2	27.2	-30.8	-44.0	56.4	76.9	0.6
United Kingdom	1 157.7	-620.1	-583.0	34.0	27.2	-11.9	8.6	-283.2	1 840.2	424.6
United States	-895.0	81.4	-303.0	232.4	186.0	67.9	-29.2	48.1	550.8	228.8
EUROPE	**.. c**	**8 666.3**	**9 273.3**	**10 729.7**	**6 722.2**	**2 497.0**	**2 182.8**	**7 331.9**	**7 889.4**	**4 684.1**
Bulgaria	-12.0	6.0	4.2	-4.9	-4.6	-78.2	77.6	48.8	3.9	151.3
Croatia	8.5	3.4	3.3	5.3	12.9	-210.5	-63.2	103.0	131.6	157.9
Cyprus	-403.5	1 099.5	1 657.7	-550.4	322.3	594.9	693.2	3 667.1	-1 953.1	193.5
Malta	99.0	-194.5	16.4	-18.0	27.5	-4.8	28.3	23.2	-0.9	33.2
Romania	-9.4	20.5	-14.7	-9.2	32.3	229.9	348.5	150.9	296.1	-770.1
Russian Federation	110.4	-1.3	-123.8	103.2	-49.6	-9.4	33.4	51.3	-8.7	84.9
Ukraine	13.4	35.4	13.0	5.2	4.9	-16.3	-1.4	3.8	9.6	7.9
AFRICA	**.. c**	**.. c**	**.. c**	**-32.4**	**22.9**	**.. c**	**.. c**	**.. c**	**66.7**	**89.9**
Northern Africa	.. c	.. c	.. c	-9.1	23.6	.. c	.. c	.. c	.. c	66.4
Algeria	.. c	.. c	.. c	-	.. c	-	-	-	-	-
Egypt	-0.6	3.8	-3.8	2.0	0.0	.. c	.. c	.. c	.. c	64.9
Libya	-	-	-	-	-	-	-	-	-	-
Morocco	-1.2	-0.9	-2.7	-11.2	27.9	-	-	-	-	.. c
Tunisia	-2.8	0.1	0.4	0.2	-4.4	0.4	-0.1	-0.9	1.0	.. c
Other African countries	1.0	-0.6	11.9	-23.4	-0.6	-1.0	5.6	23.9	21.3	23.5
Nigeria	.. c	.. c	-2.4	-4.5	.. c	-	-0.2	0.0	-	-
South Africa	-5.4	2.2	16.7	-15.8	0.8	0.0	5.6	23.9	21.3	23.5
AMERICA	**.. c**	**.. c**	**-405.1**	**216.5**	**902.2**	**46.5**	**-38.0**	**91.7**	**523.7**	**233.2**
Northern America	-869.6	28.3	-294.7	265.1	190.1	60.6	-32.2	55.4	550.5	225.8
Central America and Caribbean countries	141.8	-29.3	-112.3	-53.0	583.0	-8.8	-7.1	3.4	18.9	-5.3
Bahamas	62.3	28.8	27.1	8.8	2.7	-	-	-	-	-
Bermuda	18.0	-0.6	-24.6	0.2	1.1	-	-	-	-	-
Cayman Islands	1.1	-4.3	0.6	-7.2	1.5	-	-	-	-	-
Costa Rica	.. c	.. c	.. c	.. c	.. c	0.0	-0.1	0.0	-	-
El Salvador	.. c	-	.. c	.. c	.. c	-	-	-	-	-
Guatemala	-	-	0.0	-1.0	0.0	-	-	-	-	-
Honduras	.. c	.. c	.. c	.. c	-	-	-	-	-	-
Nicaragua	.. c	.. c	.. c	.. c	.. c	-	-	-	-	-
Panama	-0.8	10.2	-11.4	21.6	4.4	-	-	-	-	0.0
Virgin Islands, U.S.	-	-	-	-	-	-	-	-	-	-
South America	.. c	.. c	1.8	4.4	129.1	-5.3	1.2	32.9	-45.6	12.8
Argentina	7.9	0.5	2.7	1.6	0.7	.. c	.. c	.. c	.. c	4.5
Bolivia	-	-	-	-	.. c	-	-	-	-	-
Brazil	-1.5	5.3	0.3	0.1	129.2	-2.5	-1.0	0.2	-7.4	-0.2
Colombia	0.3	0.3	-0.9	0.4	0.0	-	0.5	-0.3	0.5	0.0
Ecuador	.. c	.. c	.. c	.. c	-0.1	-	-	-	-	-
Paraguay	-	-	-	-	-0.1	-	-	-	-	-
Peru	0.2	-0.2	.. c	.. c	-0.1	-	0.4	-0.1	0.1	0.0
Uruguay	-	-	-	-	.. c	-	-	-	-	-
Venezuela	-	-	-	.. c	-	-	-	-	-	-

Table 1. Foreign direct investment flows by country *(cont.)*

Million US dollars

	Inward					Outward				
	2015	2016	2017	2018	2019	2015	2016	2017	2018	2019
ASIA	**695.9**	**.. c**	**.. c**	**106.9**	**-111.6**	**.. c**	**55.8**	**131.5**	**190.1**	**-88.4**
Near and Middle East	-78.0	.. c	.. c	27.6	31.7	.. c	78.3	151.7	64.2	36.3
Gulf Arabian countries	-45.9	0.9	-8.9	-14.8	20.8	.. c	-2.4	.. c	-1.9	2.8
Kuwait	.. c	.. c	.. c	0.4	-	-	-	-	-	-
Qatar	-0.1	.. c	.. c	.. c	-1.1	-	-	-	-	-
Saudi Arabia	1.5	2.5	-5.1	2.8	8.1	.. c	-	-	-	0.2
United Arab Emirates	15.5	-7.8	-4.6	-8.9	14.6	-0.2	-2.4	2.3	-1.9	2.6
Other Near and Middle East	-32.1	.. c	.. c	42.5	10.9	-13.6	80.7	.. c	.. c	.. c
Jordan	-	-1.2	1.3	0.0	.. c	-	-	-	-	-
Other Asian countries	773.9	1 108.1	508.5	79.3	-143.3	-3.4	-22.5	-20.2	126.0	-124.7
China	277.1	512.0	-59.6	-55.0	76.6	0.1	-45.4	-32.8	14.0	9.5
Hong Kong, China	-59.4	46.2	-9.0	-11.2	38.2	.. c	0.3	0.1	-0.1	14.6
India	-14.7	-108.9	-23.2	-1.7	-6.6	-0.1	21.2	8.4	118.4	-138.4
Indonesia	0.2	-0.4	-0.4	-2.0	-0.6	-	-0.3	-0.1	-	0.0
Iran, Islamic Republic of	-0.3	0.3	-	-	.. c	-	-	-	-	-
Malaysia	-4.3	10.9	1.3	-0.7	0.6	-	-	-	-	.. c
Philippines	-0.5	0.0	1.7	2.7	0.3	-	-	-	0.2	-
Singapore	53.9	121.5	-9.0	104.8	-44.4	.. c	.. c	.. c	.. c	0.8
Chinese Taipei	-31.2	209.3	-7.5	-198.6	-192.7	-	-	0.4	-0.1	-0.5
Thailand	-24.9	-11.5	12.0	1.9	3.9	0.0	0.1	0.0	.. c	14.5
Viet Nam	-1.8	-1.2	2.8	-0.9	-0.8	-1.0	0.8	6.7	-1.4	-0.3
AUSTRALIA, OCEANIA AND POLAR REGIONS	**-17.4**	**31.3**	**117.5**	**-6.3**	**20.4**	**-31.8**	**.. c**	**.. c**	**-5.1**	**-0.4**
WORLD unallocated and confidential	**.. d**	**.. d**	**.. d**	**-3.9**	**20.8**	**.. d**	**.. d**	**.. d**	**-2.3**	**-0.2**
European Union (EU28)	**957.1**	**8 080.3**	**8 072.5**	**10 250.9**	**6 394.5**	**.. c**	**2 124.8**	**7 230.3**	**6 506.1**	**4 437.2**
G20 countries excl. European Union	**2 514.8**	**4 081.5**	**4 794.5**	**4 110.2**	**2 460.4**	**.. c**	**-334.5**	**.. c**	**2 682.3**	**599.1**
G20 OECD countries	**2 139.2**	**3 669.9**	**4 986.9**	**4 077.0**	**2 301.9**	**.. c**	**.. c**	**224.2**	**2 545.5**	**615.1**
G20 Non-OECD countries	**375.6**	**411.7**	**-192.4**	**33.3**	**158.5**	**-12.1**	**.. c**	**.. c**	**136.8**	**-16.0**
MENA countries	**-50.4**	**4.2**	**-13.9**	**-23.1**	**43.9**	**-5.7**	**.. c**	**-26.4**	**43.6**	**69.2**
ASEAN countries	**22.9**	**.. c**	**8.6**	**100.6**	**-40.9**	**.. c**	**.. c**	**.. c**	**-1.6**	**15.5**

- Nil; .. Not available; c Confidential data; d Secondary Confidentiality

Note: Detailed metadata at: *http://stats.oecd.org/OECDStat_Metadata/ShowMetadata.ashx?Dataset=FDI_CTRY_IND_SUMM.*

Source: *OECD International Direct Investment Statistics (database): https://doi.org/10.1787/idi-data-en*

CZECH REPUBLIC

Table 2. Foreign direct investment positions by country

At year end

Million US dollars

	Inward					Outward				
	2015	2016	2017	2018	2019	2015	2016	2017	2018	2019
WORLD	**116 627.8**	**121 854.6**	**155 994.1**	**164 224.5**	**170 182.1**	**18 591.4**	**19 426.3**	**32 364.1**	**41 003.4**	**44 112.9**
OECD COUNTRIES	**109 917.7**	**113 133.7**	**145 348.9**	**153 452.7**	**157 874.2**	**14 588.6**	**14 557.3**	**22 431.2**	**32 851.7**	**35 995.8**
Australia	89.5	88.1	103.2	101.2	90.7	.. c	-	.. c	.. c	.. c
Austria	11 904.1	11 581.3	13 659.9	13 675.2	14 703.4	37.6	41.1	72.7	73.9	51.3
Belgium	5 006.7	4 974.1	5 314.4	5 524.2	5 782.0	211.4	184.5	212.5	225.4	100.5
Canada	393.3	390.3	488.6	570.2	596.2	25.1	.. c	28.3	26.2	28.5
Chile	1.5	1.3	1.6	1.6	1.5	-	-0.2	.. c	.. c	.. c
Czech Republic	9 132.4	9 482.4	22 133.1	23 397.5	25 639.6	-	-	-	-	-
Denmark	717.6	869.2	927.5	823.0	834.3	0.3	5.8	8.6	6.6	-0.4
Estonia	-	.. c	3.3	7.0	7.0	0.8	0.7	2.6	0.2	0.5
Finland	266.8	356.8	489.6	480.0	453.9	.. c	5.0	7.0	8.5	20.2
France	8 957.7	10 620.3	12 579.8	11 780.4	11 694.3	202.5	233.8	286.8	233.1	136.9
Germany	27 595.1	26 097.5	31 225.7	34 730.2	32 694.0	1 004.1	492.8	857.5	721.6	721.7
Greece	61.7	.. c	4.6	.. c	.. c	910.3	881.3	3.8	4.2	4.7
Hungary	193.4	244.8	382.7	393.8	369.8	138.9	132.0	430.8	403.8	507.7
Iceland	17.4	.. c	.. c	.. c	.. c	0.0	0.0	0.0	0.0	0.0
Ireland	289.4	576.9	586.5	379.0	403.8	873.2	511.2	188.8	89.1	36.2
Israel	228.4	607.5	733.3	693.7	640.5	-	-	.. c	.. c	.. c
Italy	5 612.5	5 676.6	6 222.4	6 239.7	6 502.9	55.2	-37.2	119.7	164.8	137.7
Japan	2 676.8	2 519.3	3 284.3	3 328.8	3 457.2	0.0	.. c	.. c	0.0	0.5
Korea	2 056.6	2 294.0	3 174.2	2 892.5	3 161.0	.. c	.. c	.. c	.. c	.. c
Latvia	.. c	15.2	25.3	22.8	25.9	8.3	8.3	26.5	14.5	9.6
Lithuania	.. c	.. c	2.8	.. c	.. c	1.4	1.4	7.3	-1.5	1.1
Luxembourg	3 259.8	1 838.7	1 978.9	2 286.3	5 389.5	660.2	952.7	6 180.9	9 690.6	10 197.2
Mexico	.. c	293.2	.. c	.. c	.. c	11.0	4.6	7.0	7.0	7.1
Netherlands	6 399.4	8 392.4	10 505.4	12 092.7	12 003.6	6 349.8	6 581.6	9 636.3	11 967.4	13 838.1
New Zealand	.. c	-	-	2.3	1.2	-	-	-	-	-
Norway	82.2	120.7	147.6	151.4	155.1	.. c	.. c	131.7	67.8	67.4
Poland	1 693.4	2 038.8	3 869.4	4 200.0	4 321.8	368.2	645.1	794.8	1 138.3	1 166.7
Portugal	40.0	49.3	67.0	32.2	31.8	4.2	4.3	4.7	4.4	4.8
Slovak Republic	3 051.2	2 766.9	1 986.1	2 779.2	2 765.1	3 131.3	3 085.1	2 888.4	3 633.7	3 875.1
Slovenia	42.2	34.9	34.6	48.3	42.1	-1.3	211.1	218.9	103.6	116.7
Spain	1 016.5	1 102.0	1 325.8	1 276.1	1 310.0	30.7	28.6	48.6	82.5	107.0
Sweden	1 037.4	946.2	1 307.3	1 615.4	1 758.0	19.1	22.4	29.8	19.6	-11.9
Switzerland	3 242.4	4 657.7	6 157.6	6 758.2	5 694.0	44.7	1.0	-19.6	1 274.3	1 280.9
Turkey	2.4	.. c	2.6	7.6	7.6	109.6	44.1	83.3	-74.2	-176.4
United Kingdom	5 350.9	5 604.1	5 949.8	5 562.8	5 844.7	304.0	314.1	58.0	2 283.4	3 146.5
United States	9 278.4	8 867.5	10 321.0	11 251.4	11 134.8	97.7	69.7	85.2	685.8	628.3
EUROPE	**99 618.3**	**.. c**	**133 052.4**	**140 584.1**	**146 265.3**	**18 043.6**	**.. c**	**31 190.6**	**39 215.8**	**42 441.7**
Bulgaria	9.2	10.4	9.0	12.2	9.2	438.7	482.7	742.0	583.1	616.9
Croatia	.. c	17.1	37.8	35.8	36.9	65.0	1.9	114.5	555.3	557.3
Cyprus	3 338.1	4 096.8	4 424.5	4 638.4	5 108.6	1 539.2	1 923.5	5 890.9	3 568.5	3 417.1
Malta	363.7	363.1	440.8	440.7	468.5	13.5	42.8	53.6	16.6	6.8
Romania	2.7	3.8	3.3	4.0	3.8	670.4	1 039.0	1 211.2	1 473.3	1 483.4
Russian Federation	656.5	799.6	955.7	793.2	835.9	162.4	192.7	272.5	262.1	440.3
Ukraine	62.8	89.6	117.0	118.8	131.3	-0.6	4.2	9.7	12.9	13.9
AFRICA	**.. c**	**43.2**	**.. c**	**78.1**	**92.2**	**.. c**	**.. c**	**.. c**	**137.8**	**35.4**
Northern Africa	.. c	5.7	.. c	.. c	.. c	.. c	.. c	.. c	.. c	.. c
Algeria	-	-	-	-	-	-	-	-	-	-
Egypt	.. c	.. c	.. c	.. c	.. c	.. c	.. c	.. c	.. c	.. c
Libya	-	-	-	-	-	-	-	-	-	-
Morocco	-	-	-	-	-	-	-	-	-	-
Tunisia	-	.. c	-	-	-	0.9	0.8	-0.4	0.7	0.7
Other African countries	168.1	37.5	14.6	73.5	87.9	0.0	2.7	28.0	49.3	-45.5
Nigeria	-	-	-	-	-	-	-0.3	-	-	-
South Africa	168.7	.. c	-	.. c	46.6	0.0	3.1	28.0	49.3	-46.6
AMERICA	**.. c**	**.. c**	**12 143.3**	**12 978.6**	**12 875.6**	**165.2**	**.. c**	**180.6**	**764.3**	**692.8**
Northern America	9 671.7	9 257.8	10 809.7	11 821.5	11 731.0	122.8	.. c	113.5	712.1	656.8
Central America and Caribbean countries	711.7	1 042.3	1 329.7	1 151.2	1 138.9	33.4	4.5	24.5	50.0	33.1
Bahamas	168.2	191.9	.. c	.. c	.. c	-	-	-	-	-
Bermuda	27.5	65.3	68.9	66.0	71.9	-	-	-	-	-
Cayman Islands	77.7	290.4	448.9	219.2	227.3	-	-	-	-	-
Costa Rica	-	-	.. c	-	-	1.5	-0.1	-	-	-
El Salvador	-	-	-	-	-	-	-	-	-	-
Guatemala	-	-	-	-	-	-	-	-	-	-
Honduras	-	-	-	-	-	-	-	-	-	-
Nicaragua	-	-	-	-	-	-	-	-	-	-
Panama	-7.0	-53.3	-65.1	-59.6	-98.6	-	-	-	-	0.4
Virgin Islands, U.S.	-	-	-	-	-	-	-	-	-	-
South America	.. c	.. c	4.0	5.9	5.8	9.0	9.7	42.6	2.2	2.9
Argentina	-	-	-	-	-	.. c	.. c	.. c	.. c	.. c
Bolivia	-	-	-	-	-	-	-	-	-	-
Brazil	.. c	1.8	2.3	2.8	2.8	0.0	0.1	-0.3	0.0	0.0
Colombia	-	-	-	-	-	-	0.4	-	0.4	-
Ecuador	-	.. c	-	-	-	-	-	-	-	-
Paraguay	-	-	-	-	-	-	-	-	-	-
Peru	-	-	-	-	-	-	0.0	-	0.1	-
Uruguay	-	-	-	-	-	-	-	-	-	-
Venezuela	-	-	-	1.5	1.5	-	-	-	-	-

Table 2. Foreign direct investment positions by country *(cont.)*

At year end

Million US dollars

	Inward					Outward				
	2015	2016	2017	2018	2019	2015	2016	2017	2018	2019
ASIA	**6 124.1**	**7 656.0**	**10 526.7**	**10 335.8**	**10 705.3**	**240.3**	**.. c**	**858.8**	**852.2**	**911.8**
Near and Middle East	283.3	.. c	.. c	824.2	766.3	88.1	.. c	713.9	321.6	318.6
Gulf Arabian countries	44.1	.. c	100.7	71.7	67.0	1.2	.. c	.. c	1.5	7.6
Kuwait	.. c	6.9	6.3	.. c	.. c	-	-	-	-	-
Qatar	-	-	-	-	-	-	-	-	-	-
Saudi Arabia	.. c	7.2	.. c	-0.8	-3.7	-	-	-	-	.. c
United Arab Emirates	38.1	66.2	81.4	58.5	56.4	1.2	.. c	1.3	.. c	.. c
Other Near and Middle East	239.2	632.3	.. c	752.5	699.2	86.9	186.9	.. c	.. c	311.0
Jordan	1.2	-	1.5	1.4	1.4	-	-	-	-	-
Other Asian countries	5 840.8	.. c	.. c	9 511.6	9 939.0	152.2	153.4	144.9	530.6	593.2
China	370.7	794.3	1 100.9	1 012.0	1 031.9	85.3	64.0	39.2	424.4	397.1
Hong Kong, China	-17.6	191.7	244.8	243.8	252.5	.. c	5.2	5.2	6.0	6.0
India	190.9	97.1	91.6	126.0	147.6	48.7	68.7	80.7	196.7	284.3
Indonesia	-	-	-	-	-	-	0.2	-	-	-
Iran, Islamic Republic of	-	-	-	-	-	-	-	-	-	-
Malaysia	.. c	.. c	.. c	.. c	15.5	-	-	-	-	-
Philippines	-	-	-	-	-	-	-	-	0.2	-
Singapore	.. c	392.7	824.7	911.6	905.4	.. c	.. c	.. c	.. c	.. c
Chinese Taipei	421.4	554.6	833.7	798.3	765.9	-	-	0.4	0.4	0.4
Thailand	.. c	-	-	92.9	112.1	0.0	0.0	-	.. c	.. c
Viet Nam	5.1	5.1	6.4	-	-	10.7	11.5	18.1	16.7	16.5
AUSTRALIA, OCEANIA AND POLAR REGIONS	**.. c**	**95.9**	**.. c**	**117.0**	**105.4**	**.. c**	**-**	**.. c**	**-4.3**	**-6.2**
WORLD unallocated and confidential	**.. d**	**.. d**	**.. d**	**130.9**	**138.4**	**.. d**	**.. d**	**.. d**	**37.6**	**37.4**
European Union (EU28)	**95 350.3**	**97 761.2**	**125 497.2**	**132 489.8**	**138 219.1**	**.. c**	**17 795.8**	**30 097.5**	**37 064.6**	**40 249.5**
G20 countries excl. European Union	**.. c**	**64 159.4**	**75 830.8**	**78 741.4**	**77 556.0**	**.. c**	**.. c**	**.. c**	**4 974.9**	**5 705.0**
G20 OECD countries	**.. c**	**.. c**	**.. c**	**76 771.5**	**75 494.9**	**1 809.1**	**1 142.0**	**1 525.0**	**4 041.1**	**4 622.8**
G20 Non-OECD countries	**1 457.7**	**.. c**	**.. c**	**1 969.9**	**2 061.1**	**.. c**	**.. c**	**.. c**	**933.8**	**1 082.2**
MENA countries	**47.3**	**94.9**	**108.6**	**79.8**	**74.3**	**.. c**	**86.2**	**67.5**	**90.0**	**88.5**
ASEAN countries	**112.6**	**.. c**	**.. c**	**1 019.2**	**1 032.9**	**.. c**	**.. c**	**.. c**	**-98.2**	**-98.7**

- Nil; .. Not available; c Confidential data; d Secondary Confidentiality

Note: Inward FDI positions are allocated according to the ultimate investing country. Detailed metadata at: *http://stats.oecd.org/OECDStat_Metadata/ShowMetadata.ashx?Dataset=FDI_CTRY_IND_SUMM*.

Source: *OECD International Direct Investment Statistics (database): https://doi.org/10.1787/idi-data-en*

Table 3. Foreign direct investment income by country

Million US dollars

	Inward					Outward				
	2015	2016	2017	2018	2019	2015	2016	2017	2018	2019
WORLD	**14 473.5**	**15 343.8**	**19 127.2**	**19 259.5**	**20 753.0**	**1 860.9**	**2 014.9**	**4 665.4**	**4 194.2**	**4 607.6**
OECD COUNTRIES	**13 878.2**	**.. c**	**.. c**	**18 890.1**	**20 269.1**	**1 622.0**	**1 585.0**	**3 715.0**	**3 754.0**	**3 544.1**
Australia	1.6	2.6	2.9	4.6	4.1	0.0	-	.. c	.. c	.. c
Austria	1 945.5	1 982.7	2 029.7	2 292.9	2 040.4	-0.7	2.2	3.0	12.5	2.9
Belgium	977.6	1 003.2	804.4	1 148.6	929.8	3.6	2.8	3.3	-0.1	2.6
Canada	6.1	7.7	6.9	14.0	7.6	.. c	.. c	-2.2	-0.2	-0.9
Chile	-	-	-	-	-	-	0.1	-	.. c	.. c
Czech Republic	-	-	-	-	-	-	-	-	-	-
Denmark	88.7	99.5	92.0	109.0	81.3	0.1	0.7	1.0	0.8	1.3
Estonia	.. c	-1.3	1.9	0.5	2.0	0.3	-1.4	0.5	-0.1	0.5
Finland	44.9	54.6	45.6	52.7	31.0	0.0	4.4	2.0	-7.9	-0.3
France	1 060.4	1 187.1	1 316.2	1 386.7	1 178.8	11.6	10.7	11.2	21.0	6.2
Germany	2 163.2	2 666.0	2 984.8	3 450.1	4 092.2	333.3	34.3	286.9	-74.5	171.8
Greece	.. c	-0.4	.. c	.. c	.. c	-	-	0.1	0.1	-0.6
Hungary	-5.7	102.6	-5.1	23.7	106.5	7.9	-1.0	60.8	51.7	93.6
Iceland	0.0	-	-	-	-	0.0	0.0	0.0	0.0	0.0
Ireland	29.7	0.7	-8.9	5.8	25.1	8.2	-1.3	2.0	3.5	2.9
Israel	1.1	4.6	3.2	4.9	3.5	-	-	.. c	-	.. c
Italy	134.4	373.8	493.2	553.0	756.6	8.4	-0.1	1.8	24.7	7.4
Japan	149.7	151.9	117.0	91.8	136.3	.. c	.. c	.. c	-0.2	0.0
Korea	300.3	413.9	351.8	351.7	316.5	-	-0.5	-0.6	-	-
Latvia	.. c	3.4	4.6	.. c	5.4	4.8	1.3	13.3	9.5	5.6
Lithuania	.. c	.. c	1.7	3.9	1.4	0.1	-0.2	-0.3	-2.7	-0.1
Luxembourg	1 946.6	1 786.1	4 721.1	2 958.1	4 398.4	-17.8	3.9	1 342.0	1 409.1	1 550.7
Mexico	.. c	-2.4	-3.4	-3.4	10.6	0.7	1.2	1.1	0.6	0.2
Netherlands	2 915.5	2 982.4	3 518.3	3 365.1	3 769.7	656.9	1 314.7	1 620.3	1 621.8	960.1
New Zealand	.. c	-	-	-	0.3	-	-	-	-	-
Norway	15.1	30.3	20.9	29.7	28.9	-	1.9	.. c	-8.7	10.6
Poland	279.7	286.7	209.3	676.2	303.1	-70.6	-21.4	66.9	104.9	82.9
Portugal	0.6	-19.1	-13.4	-3.8	-6.2	-	.. c	0.0	-0.1	0.0
Slovak Republic	396.8	300.5	325.8	431.6	397.9	670.8	213.5	221.5	267.6	556.6
Slovenia	5.4	11.3	8.3	12.8	12.9	13.4	16.5	20.4	6.7	16.6
Spain	112.7	96.2	106.7	111.9	164.6	2.5	2.3	2.2	4.1	4.1
Sweden	218.4	224.5	203.8	366.1	243.7	.. c	.. c	-0.1	-2.4	-1.4
Switzerland	470.0	483.3	670.7	759.0	629.8	0.1	0.1	0.7	254.2	63.0
Turkey	1.3	.. c	1.1	0.8	0.6	-28.8	-26.7	25.8	-68.6	-47.0
United Kingdom	506.8	297.9	315.6	512.6	407.8	5.0	1.5	2.0	112.1	25.0
United States	113.8	191.0	190.9	175.0	188.5	14.8	7.2	12.7	14.6	29.6
EUROPE	**13 966.3**	**.. c**	**18 552.8**	**18 827.8**	**20 162.2**	**.. c**	**1 928.8**	**4 637.3**	**4 095.6**	**4 535.4**
Bulgaria	-	-1.3	.. c	.. c	0.3	27.3	26.1	44.8	41.7	28.3
Croatia	2.3	2.0	1.0	2.5	4.9	-0.2	-0.7	1.5	45.8	84.0
Cyprus	664.6	572.2	710.2	677.4	618.2	267.4	307.4	683.2	23.3	659.0
Malta	-1.8	28.3	52.4	24.8	46.6	12.9	25.9	.. c	.. c	52.3
Romania	-0.2	0.3	-0.4	0.0	7.9	-106.9	-50.7	95.0	161.3	107.9
Russian Federation	-3.5	7.8	8.1	-86.0	-92.5	-32.2	-10.7	44.7	25.6	66.4
Ukraine	-2.3	-0.3	-0.3	-3.2	2.8	-3.2	1.2	1.1	3.3	6.1
AFRICA	**.. c**	**.. c**	**-3.8**	**-5.1**	**27.5**	**.. c**	**.. c**	**.. c**	**17.8**	**18.6**
Northern Africa	.. c	0.1	0.3	0.7	31.1	.. c	.. c	.. c	.. c	18.8
Algeria	-	-	-	-	-	-	-	-	-	-
Egypt	.. c	.. c	.. c	.. c	.. c	.. c	.. c	.. c	.. c	.. c
Libya	-	-	-	-	-	-	-	-	-	-
Morocco	-	-	.. c	.. c	.. c	-	-	-	-	-
Tunisia	0.0	.. c	-	-	-	0.0	0.0	0.0	0.0	.. c
Other African countries	-3.3	.. c	-4.1	-5.8	-3.7	0.0	2.6	1.1	-1.8	-0.3
Nigeria	-	-	-	-	-	-	-0.2	-	-	-
South Africa	-	-	-	-	-	0.0	2.6	1.2	-1.8	-0.3
AMERICA	**.. c**	**200.8**	**.. c**	**177.3**	**198.7**	**.. c**	**.. c**	**13.0**	**33.0**	**34.3**
Northern America	119.9	198.7	197.8	189.0	196.2	.. c	.. c	10.5	14.4	28.7
Central America and Caribbean countries	-11.9	2.2	3.5	-11.6	2.2	2.7	1.1	1.4	19.1	0.2
Bahamas	2.1	11.1	8.0	9.1	2.7	-	-	-	-	-
Bermuda	1.6	0.6	0.7	2.2	1.0	-	-	-	-	-
Cayman Islands	0.6	1.4	1.1	2.4	1.5	-	-	-	-	-
Costa Rica	-	-	-	-	-	0.0	-0.1	-	-	-
El Salvador	-	-	-	-	-	-	-	-	-	-
Guatemala	-	-	-	-	-	-	-	-	-	-
Honduras	-	-	-	-	-	-	-	-	-	-
Nicaragua	.. c	.. c	.. c	.. c	.. c	-	-	-	-	-
Panama	-5.4	-8.2	1.1	-2.8	1.8	-	-	-	-	-
Virgin Islands, U.S.	-	-	-	-	-	-	-	-	-	-
South America	.. c	0.0	.. c	.. c	0.4	-0.9	-1.0	1.2	-0.4	5.4
Argentina	-	-	-	-	.. c	.. c	.. c	-	0.0	4.4
Bolivia	-	-	-	-	-	-	-	-	-	-
Brazil	.. c	.. c	.. c	.. c	.. c	-1.3	-1.3	-0.9	-0.4	-0.5
Colombia	-	-	-	-	-	-	0.2	-	0.0	0.0
Ecuador	-	.. c	-	-	-	-	-	-	-	-
Paraguay	-	-	-	-	-	-	-	-	-	-
Peru	-	-	-	-	-	-	0.3	-	0.0	0.0
Uruguay	-	-	-	-	-	-	-	-	-	-
Venezuela	-	-	-	-	-	-	-	-	-	-

Table 3. Foreign direct investment income by country *(cont.)*

Million US dollars

	Inward					Outward				
	2015	2016	2017	2018	2019	2015	2016	2017	2018	2019
ASIA	**401.9**	**.. c**	**.. c**	**254.8**	**360.3**	**-0.4**	**.. c**	**2.4**	**47.5**	**19.2**
Near and Middle East	.. c	.. c	.. c	9.0	7.0	3.2	.. c	30.9	40.7	33.5
Gulf Arabian countries	.. c	2.1	.. c	0.5	2.0	0.1	.. c	.. c	-0.1	0.0
Kuwait	-	-	-	-	-	-	-	-	-	-
Qatar	-	-	-	-	-	-	-	-	-	-
Saudi Arabia	-	.. c	-	.. c	0.3	-	-	-	-	-
United Arab Emirates	0.6	2.1	-0.9	0.5	1.8	0.1	.. c	0.0	.. c	0.0
Other Near and Middle East	1.1	.. c	4.7	8.6	5.0	3.1	66.5	.. c	40.8	.. c
Jordan	-	-	-	-	-	-	-	-	-	-
Other Asian countries	.. c	572.8	370.7	245.8	353.2	-3.6	-11.9	-28.5	6.8	-14.3
China	-4.4	-17.9	-111.8	-252.5	-150.6	-6.7	-11.9	-31.7	3.9	0.1
Hong Kong, China	-53.9	3.9	5.8	1.7	7.6	.. c	.. c	.. c	0.3	1.8
India	-14.5	1.0	-0.8	-0.4	0.8	3.6	1.2	4.1	3.3	-12.9
Indonesia	-	-	-	-	-	-	-0.4	-	-	-
Iran, Islamic Republic of	-	-	-	-	-	-	-	-	-	-
Malaysia	.. c	.. c	.. c	.. c	.. c	-	-	-	-	-
Philippines	.. c	.. c	.. c	.. c	.. c	-	-	-	-	-
Singapore	13.9	9.6	2.6	22.8	19.4	.. c	.. c	.. c	.. c	.. c
Chinese Taipei	8.4	9.1	3.7	29.3	20.8	-	-	-0.2	-0.2	-0.3
Thailand	-	0.8	1.0	1.3	0.8	-	0.1	-	.. c	.. c
Viet Nam	-	-	-	-	-	-	-	0.3	-0.3	-0.2
AUSTRALIA, OCEANIA AND POLAR REGIONS	**.. c**	**.. c**	**2.5**	**4.7**	**4.3**	**0.0**	**-**	**.. c**	**0.3**	**0.1**
WORLD unallocated and confidential	**.. d**	**.. d**	**.. d**	**0.0**	**0.0**	**- d**	**.. d**	**- d**	**-**	**0.0**
European Union (EU28)	**13 485.3**	**.. c**	**17 918.9**	**18 166.6**	**19 620.1**	**.. c**	**1 891.9**	**.. c**	**3 844.6**	**4 419.9**
G20 countries excl. European Union	**4 414.1**	**.. c**	**.. c**	**6 197.9**	**6 857.9**	**.. c**	**.. c**	**356.1**	**60.3**	**249.7**
G20 OECD countries	**.. c**	**.. c**	**5 776.9**	**6 537.0**	**7 099.6**	**347.0**	**45.2**	**338.7**	**29.7**	**192.4**
G20 Non-OECD countries	**.. c**	**-9.1**	**.. c**	**-339.1**	**-241.7**	**.. c**	**.. c**	**17.4**	**30.6**	**57.2**
MENA countries	**0.1**	**2.2**	**-0.7**	**1.1**	**33.1**	**.. c**	**3.6**	**11.5**	**19.5**	**18.8**
ASEAN countries	**14.6**	**11.5**	**4.5**	**24.6**	**21.0**	**.. c**	**.. c**	**.. c**	**-0.4**	**-0.3**

- Nil; .. Not available; c Confidential data; d Secondary Confidentiality

Note: Detailed metadata at: *http://stats.oecd.org/OECDStat_Metadata/ShowMetadata.ashx?Dataset=FDI_CTRY_IND_SUMM.*

Source: *OECD International Direct Investment Statistics (database): https://doi.org/10.1787/idi-data-en*

CZECH REPUBLIC

Table 4. Foreign direct investment flows by industrial sector

Million US dollars

	Inward					Outward				
	2015	2016	2017	2018	2019	2015	2016	2017	2018	2019
All FDI activities	**465.2**	**9 814.5**	**9 517.9**	**11 010.4**	**7 576.9**	**2 488.1**	**2 181.7**	**7 557.0**	**8 662.6**	**4 918.2**
Agriculture, forestry and fishing	**.. c**	**26.6**	**-19.1**	**25.9**	**16.1**	**.. c**	**10.7**	**0.5**	**-11.1**	**.. c**
Mining and quarrying	**.. c**	**.. c**	**.. c**	**-8.5**	**46.9**	**-0.4**	**4.9**	**1.6**	**10.6**	**0.8**
Extraction activities	-50.6	3.9	12.9	-7.0	-20.8	-	-	-	-	-
Manufacturing	**2 006.8**	**2 310.9**	**1 595.5**	**3 734.1**	**-200.0**	**-344.8**	**260.1**	**444.3**	**170.4**	**554.7**
of which:										
Food products, beverages and tobacco	.. c	393.5	-5.3	-512.4	50.7	.. c	.. c	.. c	1.0	334.7
Textiles, wood and paper products; printing	.. c	308.2	.. c	267.8	66.0	-0.5	-29.0	29.0	73.7	25.1
Chemical, rubber, plastic, non-metallic mineral products	518.6	305.0	355.0	-73.4	459.2	.. c	.. c	177.5	-56.1	117.7
Metal and machinery products, except electrical equipment	756.0	284.7	210.8	348.2	-167.4	.. c	.. c	-38.1	14.4	420.9
Motor vehicles, trailers, semi-trailers, other transport equipment	326.3	732.7	.. c	3 033.6	-835.3	-42.4	.. c	.. c	273.8	-300.9
Other manufacturing	137.9	.. c	.. c	670.2	226.8	.. c	.. c	302.7	-136.3	-42.7
Electricity, gas, steam and air conditioning supply	**78.4**	**540.2**	**309.5**	**460.9**	**368.0**	**-373.8**	**.. c**	**.. c**	**907.2**	**141.1**
Water supply; sewerage, waste management and remediation activities	**.. c**	**.. c**	**.. c**	**-204.5**	**63.0**	**0.0**	**0.2**	**-0.2**	**-0.3**	**8.8**
Construction	**.. c**	**.. c**	**450.2**	**319.2**	**71.8**	**262.4**	**543.9**	**233.9**	**66.4**	**53.8**
Services	**-325.6**	**6 869.8**	**6 917.1**	**6 086.9**	**7 268.5**	**2 915.4**	**1 071.5**	**6 954.9**	**7 549.1**	**4 154.6**
Wholesale and retail trade; repair of motor vehicles and motorcycles	-376.7	419.1	.. c	377.4	364.3	-31.1	38.3	.. c	440.3	-182.3
Transportation and storage	46.1	-240.2	.. c	-58.4	115.7	-409.7	.. c	80.6	-14.8	8.0
Accommodation and food service activities	177.3	.. c	.. c	35.3	24.6	-1.3	3.2	-0.3	.. c	.. c
Information and communication	-1 897.8	.. c	.. c	30.6	483.5	.. c	-955.5	398.0	94.0	-165.4
Financial and insurance activities	1 390.9	2 068.7	.. c	6 107.6	4 527.5	.. c	.. c	5 931.1	3 970.5	3 980.8
Activities of holding companies	622.0	.. c	.. c	3 229.5	2 823.6	3 960.6	1 780.9	.. c	1 639.4	3 802.0
Real estate activities	.. c	.. c	1 507.2	-854.1	753.8	225.7	-48.4	131.3	1 545.1	208.9
Professional, scientific and technical activities	133.7	1 011.5	.. c	911.0	854.1	-711.8	-0.8	341.3	1 593.6	285.4
Administrative and support service activities	.. c	.. c	267.4	-502.7	117.8	49.6	-13.5	.. c	-68.3	11.6
Public administration; activities of households and of extraterritorial organisations	-	-	-	-	-	-	-	-	-	-
Education	.. c	-3.1	2.0	8.0	2.6	-	-	-	-	0.5
Human health and social work activities	-7.5	9.1	.. c	38.1	-16.3	0.3	-	-	-	-0.1
Arts, entertainment and recreation	96.6	-0.1	33.3	-9.6	20.1	2.8	0.1	5.1	4.9	7.8
Other services	.. c	.. c	.. c	3.8	20.7	8.7	-4.3	.. c	.. c	.. c
Not allocated and confidential	**.. c**	**.. c**	**.. c**	**0.4**	**4.0**	**.. c**	**.. c**	**.. c**	**-22.1**	**.. c**
Private real estate activities	**-245.3**	**299.0**	**139.9**	**596.0**	**-61.4**	**6.4**	**-3.3**	**27.3**	**-7.7**	**-2.4**

- Nil; c Confidential data

Note: Detailed metadata at: *http://stats.oecd.org/OECDStat_Metadata/ShowMetadata.ashx?Dataset=FDI_CTRY_IND_SUMM.*

Source: *OECD International Direct Investment Statistics (database): https://doi.org/10.1787/idi-data-en*

CZECH REPUBLIC

Table 5. Foreign direct investment positions by industrial sector

At year end

Million US dollars

	Inward					Outward				
	2015	2016	2017	2018	2019	2015	2016	2017	2018	2019
All FDI activities	**116 627.8**	**121 854.6**	**155 994.1**	**164 224.5**	**170 182.1**	**18 591.4**	**19 426.3**	**32 364.1**	**41 003.4**	**44 112.9**
Agriculture, forestry and fishing	**.. c**	**319.4**	**.. c**	**370.7**	**336.8**	**53.9**	**61.7**	**69.8**	**58.8**	**57.6**
Mining and quarrying	**.. c**	**.. c**	**672.9**	**637.2**	**582.5**	**7.4**	**14.9**	**14.7**	**32.3**	**18.0**
Extraction activities	283.6	265.4	353.7	340.5	322.2	-	-	-	-	-
Manufacturing	**38 352.3**	**38 458.9**	**45 505.7**	**46 661.3**	**46 830.7**	**1 450.5**	**1 581.3**	**2 421.3**	**3 143.4**	**3 358.4**
of which:										
Food products, beverages and tobacco	4 122.0	.. c	5 032.5	4 467.1	4 453.2	214.8	.. c	.. c	611.7	602.3
Textiles, wood and paper products; printing	2 388.4	2 689.1	3 237.8	3 224.9	3 418.1	126.8	98.2	200.9	236.3	150.9
Chemical, rubber, plastic, non-metallic mineral products	5 343.1	5 724.8	.. c	6 357.6	6 361.2	.. c	.. c	955.0	866.6	1 136.4
Metal and machinery products, except electrical equipment	9 665.7	.. c	11 892.9	11 764.3	11 935.9	.. c	.. c	276.6	218.3	169.1
Motor vehicles, trailers, semi-trailers, other transport equipment	10 312.9	9 627.7	.. c	12 684.7	12 302.6	.. c	.. c	.. c	934.9	985.4
Other manufacturing	.. c	6 469.6	7 976.8	8 162.8	8 359.5	.. c	85.8	.. c	275.7	314.3
Electricity, gas, steam and air conditioning supply	**3 560.7**	**3 859.4**	**4 747.7**	**4 973.3**	**5 403.1**	**.. c**	**.. c**	**779.2**	**1 667.7**	**1 748.0**
Water supply; sewerage, waste management and remediation activities	**.. c**	**935.9**	**.. c**	**690.6**	**672.6**	**0.8**	**1.9**	**2.1**	**1.7**	**1.5**
Construction	**.. c**	**1 733.0**	**2 551.9**	**2 390.4**	**2 645.0**	**409.4**	**832.5**	**1 382.4**	**995.6**	**965.5**
Services	**69 047.3**	**73 030.0**	**97 525.3**	**104 435.0**	**109 688.5**	**15 219.9**	**15 146.9**	**26 560.5**	**34 223.1**	**37 089.2**
Wholesale and retail trade; repair of motor vehicles and motorcycles	.. c	.. c	13 789.2	14 916.5	15 508.7	629.4	.. c	867.6	1 217.8	1 056.8
Transportation and storage	1 927.3	.. c	.. c	1 466.7	1 558.6	.. c	.. c	275.1	169.1	162.1
Accommodation and food service activities	.. c	.. c	.. c	689.3	578.6	-28.5	-22.8	32.4	.. c	.. c
Information and communication	.. c	7 109.2	8 686.1	8 642.0	8 579.9	197.7	.. c	-626.9	-539.4	-469.3
Financial and insurance activities	31 828.9	32 849.8	.. c	51 185.4	55 449.2	.. c	14 545.4	.. c	29 314.9	31 654.4
Activities of holding companies	5 896.9	7 123.5	15 236.4	19 523.4	22 212.5	12 095.1	12 799.5	.. c	25 661.8	28 052.8
Real estate activities	.. c	.. c	.. c	13 668.0	15 424.2	0.2	-41.1	141.1	1 566.3	2 207.3
Professional, scientific and technical activities	5 927.4	6 730.1	.. c	11 684.9	10 041.7	312.4	478.6	.. c	2 360.7	2 423.9
Administrative and support service activities	1 363.1	1 211.0	1 838.4	1 502.0	1 897.1	16.2	-6.9	.. c	14.5	-78.6
Public administration; activities of households and of extraterritorial organisations	-	-	-	-	-	-	-	-	-	-
Education	21.0	33.0	42.9	42.3	41.9	-	-	-	-	-
Human health and social work activities	.. c	217.6	.. c	255.6	230.0	-	-	-	0.0	0.0
Arts, entertainment and recreation	.. c	76.7	.. c	210.4	214.9	74.6	70.4	83.7	69.5	85.1
Other services	.. c	.. c	.. c	172.0	163.7	35.8	30.6	.. c	19.7	19.5
Not allocated and confidential	**.. c**	**.. c**	**.. c**	**-2.1**	**-2.1**	**.. c**	**.. c**	**651.9**	**423.9**	**421.0**
Private real estate activities	**2 563.5**	**2 822.1**	**3 618.3**	**4 068.3**	**4 025.0**	**413.4**	**400.2**	**481.9**	**456.7**	**453.6**

\- Nil; c Confidential data

Note: Detailed metadata at: *http://stats.oecd.org/OECDStat_Metadata/ShowMetadata.ashx?Dataset=FDI_CTRY_IND_SUMM.*

Source: *OECD International Direct Investment Statistics (database): https://doi.org/10.1787/idi-data-en*

Table 6. Foreign direct investment income by industrial sector

Million US dollars

	Inward					Outward				
	2015	2016	2017	2018	2019	2015	2016	2017	2018	2019
All FDI activities	**14 473.5**	**15 343.8**	**19 127.2**	**19 259.5**	**20 753.0**	**1 860.9**	**2 014.9**	**4 665.4**	**4 194.2**	**4 607.6**
Agriculture, forestry and fishing	**4.6**	**8.5**	**.. c**	**8.3**	**5.3**	**-**	**2.9**	**2.1**	**-1.2**	**.. c**
Mining and quarrying	**-156.3**	**-171.3**	**.. c**	**96.3**	**85.3**	**.. c**	**0.5**	**0.7**	**1.5**	**1.2**
Extraction activities	37.1	.. c	1.7	-7.2	-11.8	-	-	-	-	-
Manufacturing	**7 005.8**	**7 025.9**	**6 923.6**	**6 476.7**	**6 252.2**	**37.4**	**140.8**	**170.5**	**45.7**	**250.0**
of which:										
Food products, beverages and tobacco	495.4	.. c	.. c	363.5	442.2	.. c	.. c	.. c	-22.1	90.0
Textiles, wood and paper products; printing	347.9	461.7	433.5	469.0	467.4	2.5	5.8	29.2	48.3	52.8
Chemical, rubber, plastic, non-metallic mineral products	1 320.2	1 536.9	1 263.4	1 156.9	1 239.2	.. c	.. c	50.7	-64.8	18.2
Metal and machinery products, except electrical equipment	1 087.4	942.3	1 096.2	876.4	794.9	5.1	31.4	.. c	18.8	18.1
Motor vehicles, trailers, semi-trailers, other transport equipment	2 712.9	2 484.4	2 612.8	2 487.9	2 365.0	-21.8	.. c	.. c	27.9	34.2
Other manufacturing	.. c	1 075.4	.. c	1 123.1	943.5	51.3	.. c	10.1	37.6	36.6
Electricity, gas, steam and air conditioning supply	**.. c**	**641.1**	**510.0**	**561.8**	**789.3**	**31.6**	**.. c**	**48.4**	**-0.5**	**-23.4**
Water supply; sewerage, waste management and remediation activities	**.. c**	**137.3**	**161.9**	**114.3**	**142.6**	**-**	**0.7**	**0.9**	**0.7**	**4.0**
Construction	**.. c**	**191.8**	**.. c**	**352.4**	**120.9**	**.. c**	**-23.1**	**92.0**	**72.0**	**15.7**
Services	**7 291.6**	**7 506.3**	**11 054.3**	**11 649.3**	**13 355.2**	**.. c**	**1 671.5**	**4 342.0**	**4 052.5**	**4 357.5**
Wholesale and retail trade; repair of motor vehicles and motorcycles	.. c	1 709.0	.. c	2 100.5	1 449.0	141.6	-10.8	.. c	74.8	130.6
Transportation and storage	193.3	278.7	.. c	244.0	199.2	.. c	.. c	.. c	31.7	21.5
Accommodation and food service activities	98.5	.. c	.. c	72.3	82.3	-	0.8	0.6	.. c	.. c
Information and communication	683.5	879.5	944.8	1 288.2	1 307.5	114.1	.. c	61.1	79.0	55.0
Financial and insurance activities	.. c	.. c	6 428.6	6 264.7	6 855.6	1 520.2	1 402.7	.. c	3 594.7	3 985.3
Activities of holding companies	739.1	.. c	3 350.4	2 260.8	3 257.0	1 502.9	1 349.1	.. c	3 021.1	3 813.1
Real estate activities	338.6	.. c	.. c	281.3	1 178.9	0.2	28.4	.. c	110.9	41.3
Professional, scientific and technical activities	824.1	332.4	757.9	1 195.3	2 051.7	13.3	63.4	.. c	135.1	109.1
Administrative and support service activities	.. c	97.8	139.9	150.2	162.2	-0.1	27.5	.. c	4.6	-3.8
Public administration; activities of households and of extraterritorial organisations	-	-	-	-	-	-	-	-	-	-
Education	.. c	2.1	4.5	1.7	0.8	-	-	-	-	0.2
Human health and social work activities	-30.6	21.8	.. c	15.1	25.2	0.5	-	-	-	-0.1
Arts, entertainment and recreation	5.5	29.3	.. c	14.2	22.1	2.0	15.7	20.5	21.8	18.1
Other services	10.9	.. c	.. c	21.8	20.7	-	0.7	3.8	-0.7	.. c
Not allocated and confidential	**.. c**	**4.3**	**.. c**	**0.4**	**1.0**	**.. c**	**.. c**	**8.7**	**23.5**	**.. c**
Private real estate activities	**-**	**-**	**-**	**-**	**1.4**	**-**	**-**	**-**	**-**	**0.2**

- Nil; c Confidential data

Note: Detailed metadata at: *http://stats.oecd.org/OECDStat_Metadata/ShowMetadata.ashx?Dataset=FDI_CTRY_IND_SUMM.*

Source: *OECD International Direct Investment Statistics (database): https://doi.org/10.1787/idi-data-en*

DENMARK

Table 1. Foreign direct investment flows by country

Million US dollars

	Inward					Outward				
	2015	2016	2017	2018	2019	2015	2016	2017	2018	2019
WORLD	**2 995.2**	**235.0**	**3 771.2**	**1 198.7**	**3 586.9**	**8 707.7**	**10 111.9**	**10 024.8**	**-369.5**	**11 404.2**
OECD COUNTRIES	**2 880.7**	**188.7**	**3 963.0**	**399.6**	**3 307.6**	**7 503.2**	**7 635.1**	**9 134.0**	**-4 133.7**	**8 361.1**
Australia	2.1	-3.4	-11.8	2.2	-15.6	-60.2	-56.9	-113.3	-505.0	-222.4
Austria	16.2	0.1	-2.4	-17.1	4.3	-35.4	14.7	-53.6	-23.4	57.7
Belgium	4.5	17.2	218.7	93.0	83.8	138.7	341.0	-294.5	-210.5	114.7
Canada	1.6	-5.5	-1.2	0.5	-0.9	46.2	89.0	154.8	107.5	-75.3
Chile	0.7	-1.5	-0.2	-	-	-11.4	69.2	35.4	44.5	35.8
Czech Republic	4.8	-7.6	0.8	1.4	-0.3	171.9	5.8	68.3	-78.6	34.6
Denmark	-	-	-	-	-	-	-	-	-	-
Estonia	1.2	-28.2	88.8	-49.6	106.9	12.3	59.4	-169.7	2.7	-32.5
Finland	712.1	1 270.3	-3 111.0	367.6	291.9	518.9	-337.6	-2 858.5	-475.2	-100.8
France	302.4	-316.9	7 802.6	-1 965.9	-1 538.1	397.0	340.5	312.8	467.9	431.1
Germany	245.6	-280.8	9.2	-88.7	211.3	2 630.8	746.9	5 328.9	-1 673.7	-4 181.5
Greece	0.9	-3.0	-0.3	-	-	-16.1	8.0	10.8	31.2	5.8
Hungary	11.7	87.1	54.1	-17.4	16.6	32.4	235.8	128.6	202.4	-25.8
Iceland	3.0	-2.1	-20.1	-36.9	-	7.6	10.4	91.8	60.0	5.5
Ireland	-465.5	38.8	-40.6	917.2	1 051.3	4.0	227.9	-45.7	-561.7	-69.3
Israel	0.3	-1.3	-0.2	-	-	59.0	-2.7	44.4	-23.4	-42.1
Italy	57.7	22.4	172.4	-59.2	130.6	-3.3	218.5	199.8	75.7	-97.2
Japan	31.4	-109.1	-50.6	88.9	1 077.0	54.3	82.0	-119.5	85.7	-283.2
Korea	1.9	-5.9	-1.8	-2.4	14.1	32.6	20.8	56.8	101.7	-63.9
Latvia	1.5	-2.4	24.1	-0.8	-0.2	13.2	-20.4	-55.4	23.3	7.2
Lithuania	1.9	-3.3	0.2	-1.0	3.4	19.0	67.5	-58.3	38.3	41.5
Luxembourg	940.6	-3 052.2	-4 001.8	-4 203.7	-562.9	-46.5	275.0	-57.7	436.8	91.3
Mexico	9.1	10.8	17.4	-6.2	-8.5	113.3	142.2	46.4	63.2	42.4
Netherlands	-1 532.8	-743.2	2 763.2	1 264.6	191.9	330.4	732.8	91.6	-1 615.4	1 142.0
New Zealand	-0.7	-2.4	3.2	3.2	-3.4	3.7	15.2	2.9	-3.5	-4.0
Norway	1 043.2	504.2	236.0	4 721.0	314.1	82.8	-136.4	783.4	-4 202.3	790.9
Poland	9.7	-22.3	-5.6	31.8	-7.2	187.2	493.1	31.7	154.0	212.6
Portugal	1.2	-2.2	2.6	-5.1	0.9	-49.1	18.4	26.7	269.6	-18.9
Slovak Republic	1.3	-1.3	-0.2	-0.3	0.5	42.5	-13.7	14.7	-8.4	3.0
Slovenia	0.4	-0.1	0.9	-1.7	0.3	-	-2.1	-1.1	1.1	-0.9
Spain	129.4	61.1	447.9	401.0	-564.7	167.9	701.8	218.7	576.1	-213.8
Sweden	1 686.7	-1 303.9	-862.0	85.7	330.0	474.3	-504.8	165.3	3 151.3	775.8
Switzerland	-547.0	106.8	-365.1	-702.1	2 581.6	1 201.6	-664.7	392.5	-168.7	3 730.7
Turkey	3.3	-6.7	1.5	-11.6	-15.9	81.9	11.9	-37.6	74.8	143.3
United Kingdom	273.3	2 795.1	604.1	334.8	526.6	1 727.8	4 227.7	3 963.6	-1 934.6	2 474.1
United States	-69.3	1 175.9	-9.7	-743.6	-912.0	-793.9	286.4	770.9	1 383.1	3 652.2
EUROPE	**2 839.1**	**-728.3**	**3 582.8**	**1 276.3**	**3 217.6**	**8 275.8**	**6 730.0**	**9 133.0**	**-5 778.9**	**5 678.3**
Bulgaria	0.4	-0.9	-0.2	-	-	-14.4	-10.8	27.6	71.4	71.4
Croatia	-	-	-	-	-	14.0	6.7	18.0	30.7	5.1
Cyprus	-40.1	9.5	-29.5	10.6	14.8	-17.4	14.3	27.3	-18.1	4.2
Malta	-38.5	133.1	-327.6	-4.0	0.3	-96.8	-	0.2	2.4	0.5
Romania	1.0	-2.1	-	-	-	12.3	2.5	307.0	-120.1	65.7
Russian Federation	16.2	11.7	-77.4	8.7	31.5	-196.7	-239.8	321.1	302.8	162.7
Ukraine	0.6	-1.6	-0.2	-	-	4.3	18.1	87.9	28.7	-2.1
AFRICA	**2.7**	**-4.2**	**91.8**	**-60.7**	**47.1**	**197.3**	**17.4**	**-163.6**	**499.6**	**99.6**
Northern Africa	0.7	-3.7	-0.5	-	-	-77.3	101.2	-238.9	461.7	133.9
Algeria	0.1	-1.0	-0.2	-	-	-35.5	43.1	-232.8	217.8	151.9
Egypt	0.3	-1.9	-0.2	-	-	-43.9	66.6	-95.0	4.0	-63.1
Libya	-	-	-	-	-	-	-	-	-	-
Morocco	0.3	-0.7	-	-	-	2.2	-8.3	89.2	232.5	45.1
Tunisia	-	-	-0.2	-	-	-0.3	-0.1	-0.3	7.4	-
Other African countries	1.9	-0.4	92.2	-60.7	47.1	274.5	-83.9	75.3	37.9	-34.3
Nigeria	1.3	-1.2	-0.2	-	-	44.0	-4.5	-42.9	44.7	-58.5
South Africa	0.4	-2.2	92.4	-60.7	47.1	13.7	43.2	254.8	43.9	98.7
AMERICA	**-37.5**	**1 162.9**	**20.1**	**-818.6**	**-923.3**	**-142.7**	**1 863.8**	**750.7**	**1 939.3**	**4 003.0**
Northern America	-40.1	1 162.1	2.4	-770.4	-920.2	-744.2	323.0	929.4	1 456.6	3 601.2
Central America and Caribbean countries	26.5	9.1	15.1	4.9	9.3	598.3	1 727.7	-294.2	267.8	191.6
Bahamas	13.2	-13.8	-19.1	0.3	11.1	-0.3	-	-	-0.6	0.3
Bermuda	3.9	11.9	16.4	10.1	6.4	-66.5	-5.6	14.2	11.6	-0.9
Cayman Islands	0.4	-0.1	0.2	0.2	-	455.1	-36.1	44.2	-138.3	20.4
Costa Rica	-	-	-	-	-	99.2	282.4	211.3	276.4	92.2
El Salvador	-	-	-	-	-	-	-	-	-	-
Guatemala	-	-	-	-	-	-0.9	0.7	0.8	-1.4	2.1
Honduras	-	-	-	-	-	-8.0	-5.6	10.6	3.0	-4.5
Nicaragua	-	-	-	-	-	-1.9	-0.3	-1.2	-0.5	-1.8
Panama	-	0.3	0.3	0.3	0.3	-88.6	-57.1	2.9	33.4	-16.3
Virgin Islands, U.S.	-	-	-	-	-	-0.6	-	-0.2	-	0.2
South America	-23.6	-8.5	2.7	-53.1	-12.6	3.1	-187.1	115.6	214.9	210.2
Argentina	-21.6	-1.5	5.0	-24.9	-34.3	-54.7	-63.9	-51.4	36.1	-4.5
Bolivia	-	-	-	-	-	-	-0.1	-1.1	-1.7	-2.8
Brazil	-3.7	-3.7	-2.1	-28.2	21.7	59.5	-161.5	-27.6	129.9	141.7
Colombia	0.4	-0.7	-	-	-	0.1	-8.5	5.0	-5.7	39.6
Ecuador	-	-	-	-	-	0.3	-	167.7	5.7	0.2
Paraguay	-	-	-	-	-	-	-	-	-	-
Peru	0.3	-0.1	-	-	-	-	-12.9	-3.3	15.2	15.0
Uruguay	0.3	-0.9	-	-	-	-3.4	0.1	-7.6	4.6	-14.5
Venezuela	-	-	-	-	-	12.8	-9.5	-2.0	-13.5	-

Table 1. Foreign direct investment flows by country *(cont.)*

Million US dollars

	Inward					Outward				
	2015	2016	2017	2018	2019	2015	2016	2017	2018	2019
ASIA	**92.5**	**-280.2**	**-47.7**	**657.0**	**1 133.1**	**390.6**	**1 684.5**	**510.0**	**3 541.9**	**1 841.8**
Near and Middle East	4.5	-13.4	-1.7	-6.2	11.1	-84.3	31.2	-742.7	21.1	62.4
Gulf Arabian countries	3.9	-10.4	-1.5	-6.2	11.1	-135.9	34.9	-788.0	34.5	153.1
Kuwait	0.7	-0.4	-0.2	0.3	-0.2	0.6	1.6	0.8	7.3	9.6
Qatar	1.0	-0.9	-0.2	-	-	-164.7	19.3	-689.5	7.8	-22.9
Saudi Arabia	1.0	-4.9	-0.9	-	-	23.9	14.1	6.5	45.6	9.4
United Arab Emirates	0.9	-3.3	-	-6.5	11.2	0.6	16.9	-88.6	-24.2	94.2
Other Near and Middle East	0.6	-3.1	-0.2	-	-	51.4	-3.7	45.3	-13.5	-90.7
Jordan	0.1	-0.7	-	-	-	1.2	1.5	-3.2	6.3	-6.6
Other Asian countries	88.0	-266.7	-46.0	663.2	1 122.0	474.8	1 653.4	1 252.7	3 520.9	1 779.4
China	34.3	-29.9	-4.2	-6.7	24.1	79.1	347.7	334.0	374.4	296.1
Hong Kong, China	25.6	-6.1	-0.3	630.4	2.1	-348.8	24.1	-38.2	70.5	41.5
India	2.2	-3.3	-0.6	-0.5	0.5	-25.9	93.5	98.3	262.3	195.1
Indonesia	0.7	-1.2	-0.2	-	-	21.7	-6.8	8.5	15.5	34.5
Iran, Islamic Republic of	0.1	-1.3	-0.2	-	-	4.5	55.7	30.7	8.4	-53.1
Malaysia	4.6	-1.5	-0.9	-1.3	7.0	24.8	72.7	50.9	82.4	60.6
Philippines	0.1	-1.0	-	-	-	20.2	-24.8	-8.8	-9.3	4.3
Singapore	-18.1	-84.8	22.4	-33.6	-3.7	784.6	1 107.3	824.9	1 744.5	922.4
Chinese Taipei	1.3	-2.5	-0.8	-1.9	7.3	4.9	9.8	31.2	112.6	192.7
Thailand	1.2	-16.9	-8.2	-9.8	-6.4	-212.3	-121.4	-153.0	165.7	85.8
Viet Nam	1.2	-2.8	-0.3	-	-	4.6	-17.2	17.3	42.8	4.9
AUSTRALIA, OCEANIA AND POLAR REGIONS	**1.3**	**-5.8**	**-8.8**	**5.4**	**-19.0**	**72.1**	**-192.5**	**-190.9**	**-539.8**	**-213.5**
WORLD unallocated and confidential	**97.1**	**90.6**	**133.0**	**139.2**	**131.5**	**-85.3**	**8.8**	**-14.4**	**-31.7**	**-4.9**
European Union (EU28)	**2 327.6**	**-1 334.9**	**3 808.4**	**-2 906.6**	**-**	**6 615.5**	**7 848.5**	**7 347.1**	**-1 184.4**	**797.8**
G20 countries excl. European Union	**888.9**	**3 241.1**	**8 544.0**	**-2 563.4**	**-440.8**	**4 147.1**	**6 135.5**	**11 507.8**	**-543.1**	**2 753.4**
G20 OECD countries	**859.1**	**3 276.0**	**8 532.1**	**-2 451.3**	**-531.4**	**4 226.5**	**6 109.1**	**10 563.5**	**-1 753.7**	**1 819.7**
G20 Non-OECD countries	**29.7**	**-34.9**	**12.0**	**-112.1**	**90.6**	**-79.4**	**26.4**	**944.3**	**1 210.6**	**933.7**
MENA countries	**4.9**	**-15.6**	**-1.8**	**-6.2**	**11.1**	**-210.0**	**139.5**	**-1 029.6**	**501.3**	**284.4**
ASEAN countries	**-10.3**	**-108.0**	**12.7**	**-44.7**	**-3.0**	**671.5**	**1 028.6**	**867.3**	**2 525.4**	**1 423.4**

- Nil

Note: Data excludes resident Special Purpose Entities (SPEs). Detailed metadata at: *http://stats.oecd.org/OECDStat_Metadata/ShowMetadata.ashx?Dataset=FDI_CTRY_IND_SUMM.*

Source: *OECD International Direct Investment Statistics (database): https://doi.org/10.1787/idi-data-en*

DENMARK

Table 2. Foreign direct investment positions by country

At year end

Million US dollars

	Inward					Outward				
	2015	2016	2017	2018	2019	2015	2016	2017	2018	2019
WORLD	**91 978.8**	**99 403.4**	**115 887.4**	**116 251.5**	**121 482.3**	**164 757.8**	**169 708.2**	**205 106.7**	**209 111.4**	**217 684.5**
OECD COUNTRIES	**86 914.3**	**93 622.7**	**109 363.4**	**108 738.2**	**113 860.5**	**131 524.2**	**134 466.7**	**168 343.0**	**170 552.5**	**174 782.4**
Australia	14.5	9.2	1.0	10.7	-7.0	2 095.9	2 000.3	2 189.1	1 709.7	1 422.9
Austria	309.5	236.5	215.1	253.6	228.3	206.0	219.3	317.0	325.5	355.0
Belgium	756.4	822.1	1 289.2	1 409.5	1 408.3	1 095.6	974.1	753.9	696.5	838.5
Canada	139.5	30.1	70.4	68.4	44.0	1 314.1	1 095.6	1 195.9	1 590.5	1 514.9
Chile	1.5	0.1	0.5	164.9	173.5	319.6	346.5	381.9	269.7	286.9
Czech Republic	30.2	38.6	24.8	14.7	63.1	886.1	997.8	1 113.5	1 078.8	1 111.0
Denmark	-	-	-	-	-	-	-	-	-	-
Estonia	5.6	-17.2	65.9	57.4	123.3	243.8	272.1	262.9	375.2	329.1
Finland	3 484.3	4 690.6	2 591.1	7 929.9	6 155.1	6 473.1	6 248.4	3 228.9	3 028.0	2 648.5
France	3 969.0	3 805.2	7 334.6	6 060.2	4 338.3	5 901.3	6 111.3	7 192.8	7 670.3	7 528.6
Germany	4 670.1	5 145.8	6 090.2	6 594.3	7 048.8	14 553.4	15 171.4	26 470.4	26 963.1	23 604.3
Greece	-3.5	-7.5	-4.2	5.4	5.1	234.1	219.6	191.7	190.2	197.3
Hungary	-60.0	5.5	97.6	73.6	88.1	649.8	852.4	1 117.0	1 187.4	1 000.0
Iceland	62.5	66.9	60.4	30.4	30.3	951.1	871.6	1 042.9	1 279.0	1 930.4
Ireland	1 385.8	1 555.6	1 574.0	2 822.5	3 911.2	1 222.0	1 358.9	1 537.6	1 236.3	1 063.7
Israel	21.5	28.1	33.0	16.1	20.7	105.7	114.1	144.3	123.9	98.7
Italy	465.6	483.2	804.8	626.0	788.2	1 091.7	1 352.8	1 527.6	1 532.7	1 373.3
Japan	382.4	470.7	468.6	634.6	1 807.2	896.0	992.7	770.2	944.1	689.5
Korea	-5.0	-9.8	33.2	39.0	52.0	362.2	268.4	272.7	351.0	260.6
Latvia	11.0	9.9	153.0	72.7	19.5	354.3	279.6	310.4	597.0	582.8
Lithuania	12.2	15.5	9.5	2.5	6.4	545.5	577.6	629.4	919.6	1 028.3
Luxembourg	11 449.9	14 934.5	13 139.0	12 889.2	12 975.8	881.4	995.3	1 188.5	1 561.3	1 707.5
Mexico	100.6	105.3	139.0	-14.7	-22.6	656.7	689.2	912.4	1 085.5	1 181.3
Netherlands	10 530.2	10 385.5	16 798.8	17 553.1	15 566.9	10 044.9	11 616.5	14 675.8	11 755.2	12 401.8
New Zealand	-4.5	43.4	60.9	51.2	42.4	112.2	167.7	122.3	243.7	343.5
Norway	9 623.4	10 008.9	12 381.6	13 096.0	14 303.5	6 304.7	6 282.0	9 095.5	7 425.1	7 856.0
Poland	58.7	61.1	28.8	191.7	138.6	3 115.4	3 839.0	4 379.4	4 710.4	4 867.7
Portugal	6.6	15.9	-1.0	2.5	-1.8	238.8	350.5	492.8	591.2	576.4
Slovak Republic	6.9	21.1	15.5	16.7	12.0	538.7	548.4	635.0	854.2	808.1
Slovenia	7.8	7.4	1.1	-0.3	0.4	39.4	36.3	71.0	102.0	85.5
Spain	1 618.4	1 149.0	734.2	1 359.3	662.8	3 043.5	3 605.7	4 423.2	5 573.4	4 967.4
Sweden	22 250.1	20 240.3	23 444.1	17 654.1	21 218.9	27 177.3	25 608.3	28 915.9	30 173.5	31 151.0
Switzerland	2 421.5	3 557.7	3 356.8	2 975.0	5 985.0	5 062.1	3 922.3	4 445.3	4 142.7	4 086.2
Turkey	13.8	9.5	-6.6	-22.1	-36.4	546.3	525.5	654.8	826.9	1 004.5
United Kingdom	7 371.6	9 431.7	11 806.9	11 274.4	12 270.7	20 838.8	21 918.4	30 084.6	27 815.8	31 043.6
United States	5 829.6	6 287.6	6 560.6	4 825.6	4 440.0	14 323.0	14 613.8	18 225.8	21 623.6	24 836.8
EUROPE	**81 616.0**	**88 774.2**	**104 024.7**	**105 118.4**	**109 498.2**	**114 538.5**	**117 257.5**	**148 825.0**	**146 234.3**	**148 221.5**
Bulgaria	1.5	0.7	0.3	1.4	2.1	96.9	84.1	121.0	218.4	282.1
Croatia	-	-	-	-	0.3	147.9	162.5	262.7	287.1	274.4
Cyprus	254.5	396.6	229.7	430.9	445.6	131.8	117.4	134.7	168.7	232.8
Malta	592.5	435.7	142.7	23.5	22.0	83.7	64.5	92.0	67.6	69.5
Romania	1.0	7.7	1.0	2.9	0.6	380.4	298.7	741.5	1 038.0	1 097.2
Russian Federation	96.5	1 020.7	1 056.6	1 010.1	988.2	481.8	277.8	788.5	1 165.8	1 375.8
Ukraine	-0.6	-0.4	0.2	1.7	0.4	151.5	192.5	255.3	311.2	364.1
AFRICA	**-3.5**	**-6.8**	**79.4**	**198.9**	**210.5**	**1 725.8**	**1 851.0**	**2 020.9**	**2 681.2**	**2 738.8**
Northern Africa	-10.7	-9.6	-1.3	19.5	1.2	1 032.4	1 087.2	784.7	1 189.7	1 358.9
Algeria	-2.8	-3.8	-0.3	-	-	637.9	687.5	486.2	582.9	741.8
Egypt	-4.8	-3.1	-0.6	18.1	-0.2	348.0	369.5	153.5	171.3	113.4
Libya	-	-	-	-	-	0.1	0.1	0.2	0.5	-
Morocco	-3.1	-2.7	-0.2	0.9	0.9	38.1	21.3	129.8	409.1	467.4
Tunisia	-	-	-	0.5	0.4	8.2	8.8	14.8	26.1	36.5
Other African countries	7.2	2.8	80.7	179.5	209.3	693.3	763.8	1 236.4	1 491.5	1 379.9
Nigeria	12.3	4.5	1.1	-	-	37.8	45.2	77.3	153.8	90.6
South Africa	-6.4	-4.8	6.9	-30.1	20.5	297.4	348.4	704.9	737.5	817.7
AMERICA	**6 556.8**	**7 095.2**	**7 477.8**	**5 752.5**	**5 316.1**	**20 047.1**	**21 295.2**	**25 624.6**	**30 016.1**	**33 897.6**
Northern America	6 275.1	6 609.9	6 968.9	5 198.9	4 788.9	15 829.1	15 832.3	19 556.5	23 273.8	26 410.4
Central America and Caribbean countries	263.4	478.3	520.6	440.2	418.1	2 235.0	3 699.5	3 866.2	4 525.9	4 780.3
Bahamas	174.1	172.0	159.2	168.0	178.4	16.4	9.5	9.5	21.6	24.3
Bermuda	73.1	86.2	131.0	133.8	135.4	110.5	85.8	107.0	112.0	108.9
Cayman Islands	-93.7	-78.8	-82.5	-47.9	-43.0	770.0	600.5	139.5	456.9	475.0
Costa Rica	-	-	-	-	-	124.7	403.1	612.8	886.7	985.9
El Salvador	-	-	-	-	-	2.1	1.1	1.1	0.8	0.9
Guatemala	-	-	-	-	-	0.3	0.7	1.0	0.2	1.9
Honduras	-	-	-	-	-	30.3	26.8	105.8	35.4	32.1
Nicaragua	-	-	-	-	-	13.3	14.5	15.6	26.2	30.4
Panama	4.7	167.6	153.7	151.9	146.5	54.6	-21.0	-28.4	18.9	21.6
Virgin Islands, U.S.	-	-	-	-	-	1.9	-	1.5	1.4	1.5
South America	18.3	7.1	-11.9	113.4	108.9	1 983.0	1 763.6	2 202.1	2 216.5	2 706.9
Argentina	7.9	5.7	-24.5	-58.9	-91.5	175.0	116.3	452.7	498.2	496.3
Bolivia	-	-	-	-	-	1.5	1.4	3.7	5.2	-
Brazil	6.3	4.0	12.1	7.5	27.1	1 284.6	1 048.4	1 010.5	1 096.7	1 193.5
Colombia	1.6	-2.8	-0.3	-0.2	-0.2	55.2	78.7	103.1	80.7	455.2
Ecuador	-	-	-	-	-	2.8	2.1	93.4	100.0	99.0
Paraguay	-	-	-	-	-	1.6	2.0	2.7	2.5	0.2
Peru	3.4	3.3	0.5	-	-	84.8	73.3	78.5	125.0	138.9
Uruguay	-2.9	-3.3	-0.3	-	-	50.2	54.4	28.8	32.5	31.8
Venezuela	0.4	-	-	-	-	7.5	40.4	46.7	6.1	4.9

Table 2. Foreign direct investment positions by country *(cont.)*

At year end

Million US dollars

	Inward					Outward				
	2015	2016	2017	2018	2019	2015	2016	2017	2018	2019
ASIA	**1 739.7**	**1 402.8**	**1 706.6**	**2 701.0**	**4 061.8**	**25 262.1**	**26 292.0**	**25 489.6**	**27 427.2**	**30 258.5**
Near and Middle East	12.9	24.8	73.5	120.7	352.8	1 245.4	1 371.8	773.7	1 039.1	1 176.9
Gulf Arabian countries	-3.5	3.0	41.7	102.2	331.8	1 077.3	1 211.0	599.6	883.8	1 095.0
Kuwait	7.8	6.5	7.2	7.2	6.7	9.4	10.9	13.2	21.5	27.0
Qatar	8.6	5.0	1.1	-	-	576.6	597.1	94.1	73.5	48.7
Saudi Arabia	-12.7	-15.0	41.1	42.8	41.8	169.7	197.8	193.5	254.0	260.0
United Arab Emirates	-5.0	9.5	-7.2	51.8	283.1	245.8	348.4	274.3	397.1	553.5
Other Near and Middle East	16.4	21.8	31.7	18.6	21.0	168.1	160.6	174.1	155.2	82.1
Jordan	-2.1	-2.7	-0.2	-	-	16.5	18.0	4.8	14.9	8.2
Other Asian countries	1 726.8	1 378.0	1 633.3	2 580.5	3 709.0	24 016.7	24 920.2	24 715.9	26 388.2	29 081.6
China	179.2	310.5	259.2	136.7	144.0	4 154.5	4 362.4	4 329.9	5 502.5	4 822.1
Hong Kong, China	958.7	237.6	410.3	1 132.0	1 009.8	3 255.6	3 068.3	2 712.1	2 648.4	2 909.6
India	22.0	61.7	5.3	7.4	5.8	744.5	820.8	1 061.4	1 424.8	1 332.6
Indonesia	5.1	3.8	1.0	4.9	1.9	143.2	142.9	118.9	140.5	181.2
Iran, Islamic Republic of	-2.8	-5.0	-0.5	0.3	-	44.8	101.1	118.4	117.2	68.0
Malaysia	16.0	30.8	28.0	101.7	102.6	777.2	922.3	988.5	1 201.0	1 740.3
Philippines	-2.6	-3.8	-0.3	0.2	-0.2	146.0	161.4	136.9	136.2	121.6
Singapore	101.2	100.8	194.3	272.6	342.9	12 458.9	13 205.5	13 370.0	12 887.7	15 416.3
Chinese Taipei	33.7	36.9	110.3	95.4	106.1	59.3	47.9	42.9	118.9	308.0
Thailand	7.8	143.1	145.6	143.7	134.2	703.2	569.7	419.3	519.1	619.8
Viet Nam	4.1	1.1	0.8	8.7	0.3	120.4	118.8	115.0	215.5	223.8
AUSTRALIA, OCEANIA AND POLAR REGIONS	**10.2**	**52.9**	**67.5**	**68.9**	**40.6**	**2 317.4**	**2 124.0**	**2 202.9**	**1 833.6**	**1 659.1**
WORLD unallocated and confidential	**2 059.6**	**2 085.0**	**2 531.4**	**2 411.7**	**2 355.2**	**866.9**	**888.4**	**943.7**	**919.0**	**908.9**
European Union (EU28)	**69 185.2**	**73 871.1**	**86 592.9**	**87 322.0**	**87 498.8**	**100 215.4**	**103 881.4**	**130 870.9**	**130 716.8**	**131 226.1**
G20 countries excl. European Union	**23 249.5**	**27 155.0**	**34 660.3**	**31 216.7**	**31 861.0**	**70 030.0**	**72 054.1**	**98 156.6**	**102 933.1**	**104 939.6**
G20 OECD countries	**22 951.7**	**25 768.5**	**33 302.7**	**30 096.3**	**30 723.2**	**62 579.4**	**64 739.4**	**89 496.3**	**92 113.1**	**94 460.2**
G20 Non-OECD countries	**297.8**	**1 386.5**	**1 357.7**	**1 120.3**	**1 137.8**	**7 450.7**	**7 314.7**	**8 660.4**	**10 820.0**	**10 479.3**
MENA countries	**-19.5**	**-12.8**	**39.3**	**124.1**	**332.8**	**2 165.4**	**2 346.0**	**1 412.6**	**2 099.0**	**2 475.9**
ASEAN countries	**131.5**	**252.9**	**343.6**	**532.0**	**582.1**	**14 497.8**	**15 280.0**	**15 359.6**	**15 216.7**	**18 578.6**

- Nil

Note: Data excludes resident Special Purpose Entities (SPEs). Detailed metadata at: *http://stats.oecd.org/OECDStat_Metadata/ShowMetadata.ashx?Dataset=FDI_CTRY_IND_SUMM.*

Source: *OECD International Direct Investment Statistics (database): https://doi.org/10.1787/idi-data-en*

DENMARK

Table 3. Foreign direct investment income by country

Million US dollars

	Inward					Outward				
	2015	2016	2017	2018	2019	2015	2016	2017	2018	2019
WORLD	**4 606.0**	**5 481.4**	**6 133.9**	**6 363.3**	**7 043.1**	**12 131.8**	**12 061.1**	**13 256.1**	**15 120.5**	**15 622.1**
OECD COUNTRIES	**4 450.7**	**5 340.7**	**5 999.3**	**6 224.0**	**6 812.1**	**10 213.1**	**9 531.7**	**11 169.1**	**12 217.2**	**12 313.6**
Australia	3.3	3.3	3.0	2.4	2.1	97.4	104.1	28.8	75.1	84.3
Austria	24.5	15.2	4.7	10.5	18.1	29.7	23.8	28.0	40.7	26.1
Belgium	25.1	36.5	72.1	103.9	32.2	62.2	69.8	112.4	112.8	104.2
Canada	11.4	4.2	5.5	4.3	5.2	122.2	75.2	102.1	87.6	91.2
Chile	-	-	-	10.8	10.8	47.6	79.6	24.4	25.5	47.2
Czech Republic	0.1	0.7	0.9	1.0	1.3	69.0	87.8	68.2	118.0	74.4
Denmark	-	-	-	-	-	-	-	-	-	-
Estonia	-	0.1	0.2	2.7	1.3	15.5	39.4	61.5	63.5	31.2
Finland	156.4	99.7	217.7	484.7	448.6	483.2	385.8	365.2	318.5	188.6
France	249.9	240.4	549.2	544.4	570.4	532.3	394.2	635.1	514.0	542.2
Germany	393.3	559.4	392.2	583.5	574.9	626.3	444.5	1 050.3	1 150.7	899.5
Greece	-	-	-	0.5	0.5	-10.9	23.6	18.2	25.5	21.6
Hungary	-	-	-	-	-	58.9	76.8	130.0	111.3	67.5
Iceland	4.5	4.2	3.5	2.7	2.2	9.5	12.2	18.6	20.7	16.5
Ireland	68.5	168.3	166.0	156.6	124.5	99.2	83.6	272.8	230.0	165.1
Israel	..	..	..	..	..	..	..	..	..	..
Italy	46.7	23.8	35.4	23.4	38.8	81.3	77.1	133.6	164.7	4.3
Japan	-5.8	-78.4	-28.0	7.8	-	77.9	94.2	83.2	90.1	60.7
Korea	0.4	-	0.5	1.0	1.1	24.1	32.1	23.2	46.4	26.2
Latvia	-	0.1	24.2	2.9	2.2	17.4	23.5	17.6	42.1	32.2
Lithuania	0.3	0.4	0.6	0.3	0.3	17.7	56.0	70.9	153.5	181.4
Luxembourg	256.0	497.3	388.2	260.9	360.5	48.2	94.6	60.0	90.3	84.4
Mexico	8.2	14.3	16.4	-	-	65.3	63.9	104.1	80.5	75.4
Netherlands	-313.0	282.6	457.9	470.1	375.9	104.2	383.6	392.0	412.5	424.2
New Zealand	-	-0.9	5.6	6.2	3.1	14.3	21.7	6.7	2.2	16.5
Norway	608.9	573.6	858.3	1 099.1	921.0	646.2	588.6	737.1	686.8	904.9
Poland	14.9	-3.1	0.5	40.4	39.6	251.4	291.1	255.7	324.7	348.3
Portugal	0.3	0.6	2.1	0.6	0.5	30.9	21.7	45.6	56.4	56.5
Slovak Republic	-	0.9	0.9	1.0	0.9	46.1	45.8	53.0	69.7	59.2
Slovenia	-	-	0.2	0.2	0.2	19.3	20.9	13.0	10.5	14.1
Spain	157.9	61.2	306.9	258.0	240.2	217.4	-11.1	198.1	124.5	106.5
Sweden	1 413.0	1 332.1	946.3	840.6	1 096.5	978.2	1 142.8	1 256.9	1 730.6	1 923.2
Switzerland	206.5	232.4	249.6	145.6	96.3	2 776.6	2 341.2	2 120.9	1 842.4	2 101.8
Turkey	-	0.1	0.2	0.3	0.3	88.3	43.5	19.8	54.5	48.4
United Kingdom	484.3	706.2	664.1	629.6	1 117.7	1 326.6	1 547.1	1 481.9	1 501.1	1 432.6
United States	633.3	564.3	653.5	527.6	723.3	1 172.4	805.7	1 246.5	1 835.9	2 050.2
EUROPE	**3 836.8**	**4 986.8**	**5 417.0**	**5 760.0**	**6 152.3**	**8 819.7**	**8 579.7**	**9 944.0**	**10 499.7**	**10 184.9**
Bulgaria	-	-	-	-	0.2	5.8	2.8	4.8	9.0	14.5
Croatia	-	-	-	-	-	21.6	21.1	25.0	27.2	13.5
Cyprus	18.0	33.1	43.5	40.9	41.4	29.3	19.9	12.9	26.1	33.6
Malta	14.3	88.8	8.6	3.5	3.1	1.6	4.9	4.7	4.1	3.7
Romania	-	0.3	0.2	0.2	0.2	28.7	14.6	42.3	86.0	71.2
Russian Federation	1.2	32.1	10.1	21.4	17.4	61.7	30.0	50.7	117.5	146.5
Ukraine	..	..	..	..	..	..	..	..	..	..
AFRICA	**-**	**0.6**	**1.2**	**4.6**	**4.5**	**146.0**	**112.3**	**269.3**	**305.5**	**468.3**
Northern Africa	-	0.1	0.2	1.1	0.5	132.6	119.9	168.7	214.1	398.8
Algeria	..	..	..	..	..	..	..	..	..	..
Egypt	-	0.1	0.2	1.0	0.5	17.5	28.4	18.8	5.4	3.6
Libya	..	..	..	..	..	..	..	..	..	..
Morocco	-	-	-	-	-	1.5	0.1	3.6	4.6	12.7
Tunisia	..	..	..	..	..	..	..	..	..	..
Other African countries	-	0.4	1.1	3.6	4.0	13.4	-7.4	100.4	91.4	69.4
Nigeria	-	-	-	-	-	1.3	5.8	8.5	0.6	3.3
South Africa	-	0.3	0.3	1.0	1.6	18.6	15.9	50.1	45.6	44.1
AMERICA	**692.2**	**602.6**	**688.3**	**565.9**	**777.9**	**1 437.7**	**1 050.1**	**1 645.6**	**2 189.6**	**2 616.4**
Northern America	658.7	576.5	664.5	533.6	740.1	1 301.0	872.7	1 356.6	1 902.9	2 177.6
Central America and Caribbean countries	39.7	22.0	23.8	22.0	27.0	59.9	49.9	180.3	126.6	237.5
Bahamas	..	..	..	..	..	..	..	..	..	..
Bermuda	..	..	..	..	..	..	..	..	..	..
Cayman Islands	..	..	..	..	..	..	..	..	..	..
Costa Rica	..	..	..	..	..	..	..	..	..	..
El Salvador	..	..	..	..	..	..	..	..	..	..
Guatemala	..	..	..	..	..	..	..	..	..	..
Honduras	..	..	..	..	..	..	..	..	..	..
Nicaragua	..	..	..	..	..	..	..	..	..	..
Panama	..	..	..	..	..	..	..	..	..	..
Virgin Islands, U.S.	..	..	..	..	..	..	..	..	..	..
South America	-6.1	4.2	-	10.5	10.8	76.7	127.3	108.8	160.0	201.2
Argentina	-	-	-0.2	-	-0.2	-4.0	2.2	-17.6	49.7	37.0
Bolivia	..	..	..	..	..	..	..	..	..	..
Brazil	-6.1	4.3	-0.2	-0.3	-	10.7	52.3	107.2	62.6	71.2
Colombia	..	..	..	..	..	..	..	..	..	..
Ecuador	..	..	..	..	..	..	..	..	..	..
Paraguay	..	..	..	..	..	..	..	..	..	..
Peru	..	..	..	..	..	..	..	..	..	..
Uruguay	-	-	-	-	-	-5.1	-8.2	-5.0	1.9	3.4
Venezuela	-	-	-	-	-	-1.0	0.7	-0.2	-1.4	1.2

Table 3. Foreign direct investment income by country *(cont.)*

Million US dollars

	Inward					Outward				
	2015	2016	2017	2018	2019	2015	2016	2017	2018	2019
ASIA	**73.6**	**-111.0**	**18.6**	**23.8**	**103.2**	**1 614.5**	**2 191.6**	**1 358.0**	**2 054.0**	**2 246.4**
Near and Middle East	1.8	2.5	3.9	5.4	25.3	282.4	208.9	32.0	75.7	116.5
Gulf Arabian countries	-	0.9	2.0	4.0	23.7	276.1	202.2	25.0	69.7	112.6
Kuwait	..	..	..	..	..	..	..	..	..	..
Qatar	..	..	..	..	..	..	..	..	..	..
Saudi Arabia	..	..	..	..	..	..	..	..	..	..
United Arab Emirates	..	..	..	..	..	..	..	..	..	..
Other Near and Middle East	1.8	1.8	2.0	1.4	1.5	6.2	6.7	7.1	6.0	3.9
Jordan	..	..	..	..	..	..	..	..	..	..
Other Asian countries	72.0	-113.5	14.7	18.5	77.8	1 332.1	1 982.8	1 325.9	1 978.3	2 129.9
China	17.1	4.2	3.9	5.1	4.5	350.3	538.7	403.8	626.4	536.3
Hong Kong, China	26.8	3.6	5.3	9.3	4.8	147.2	239.3	70.3	153.0	112.2
India	0.7	1.0	2.4	0.6	13.3	45.6	44.6	29.1	83.2	127.3
Indonesia	-	-	-	0.3	0.2	21.9	11.3	24.8	30.7	17.2
Iran, Islamic Republic of	..	..	..	..	..	..	..	..	..	..
Malaysia	43.0	1.5	1.2	5.9	36.3	69.7	104.3	88.0	103.7	77.4
Philippines	-	-	-	-	-	7.1	1.2	5.8	1.3	4.3
Singapore	-12.8	-51.1	19.4	-16.8	11.8	432.7	610.5	281.3	518.3	937.9
Chinese Taipei	1.8	1.9	6.5	7.3	7.0	10.7	-6.2	2.7	37.5	14.4
Thailand	-	3.9	3.5	-2.1	-1.6	37.9	205.6	143.7	145.1	107.4
Viet Nam	..	..	..	..	..	..	..	..	..	..
AUSTRALIA, OCEANIA AND POLAR REGIONS	**3.3**	**2.4**	**8.8**	**8.9**	**5.4**	**111.8**	**126.1**	**36.2**	**78.1**	**101.4**
WORLD unallocated and confidential	**0.1**	**-**	**-**	**0.2**	**-0.2**	**2.1**	**1.3**	**3.0**	**-6.5**	**4.8**
European Union (EU28)	**3 011.0**	**4 144.7**	**4 282.3**	**4 460.1**	**5 090.1**	**5 190.6**	**5 385.7**	**6 809.4**	**7 518.3**	**6 924.1**
G20 countries excl. European Union	**..**	**..**	**..**	**..**	**..**	**..**	**..**	**..**	**..**	**..**
G20 OECD countries	**1 825.0**	**2 037.4**	**2 291.8**	**2 324.2**	**3 033.8**	**4 214.2**	**3 681.6**	**4 908.5**	**5 600.5**	**5 315.0**
G20 Non-OECD countries	**..**	**..**	**..**	**..**	**..**	**..**	**..**	**..**	**..**	**..**
MENA countries	**..**	**..**	**..**	**..**	**..**	**..**	**..**	**..**	**..**	**..**
ASEAN countries	**30.2**	**-45.8**	**24.2**	**-12.7**	**46.9**	**648.7**	**1 034.8**	**691.8**	**930.5**	**1 232.7**

- Nil; .. Not available

Note: Data excludes resident Special Purpose Entities (SPEs). Detailed metadata at: *http://stats.oecd.org/OECDStat_Metadata/ShowMetadata.ashx?Dataset=FDI_CTRY_IND_SUMM.*

Source: *OECD International Direct Investment Statistics (database): https://doi.org/10.1787/idi-data-en*

Table 4. Foreign direct investment flows by industrial sector

Million US dollars

	Inward					Outward				
	2015	2016	2017	2018	2019	2015	2016	2017	2018	2019
All FDI activities	**2 995.2**	**235.0**	**3 771.2**	**1 198.7**	**3 586.9**	**8 707.7**	**10 111.9**	**10 024.8**	**-369.5**	**11 404.2**
Agriculture, forestry and fishing	**-**	**-**	**-**	**-**	**-**	**17.0**	**13.5**	**17.0**	**59.4**	**34.5**
Mining and quarrying	**-698.1**	**463.2**	**7 374.1**	**-2 598.1**	**-1 742.6**	**585.7**	**1 905.4**	**-316.1**	**-3 088.8**	**-1 380.4**
Extraction activities	-711.5	456.3	7 374.8	-2 598.1	-1 742.2	585.1	1 905.4	-316.1	-3 088.8	-1 380.4
Manufacturing	**3 001.3**	**-648.7**	**959.4**	**431.6**	**649.6**	**927.2**	**-642.1**	**1 214.5**	**1 920.5**	**4 675.1**
of which:										
Food products, beverages and tobacco	226.0	-16.3	-0.8	469.8	-69.4	260.7	1 400.6	1 067.4	746.8	461.2
Textiles, wood and paper products; printing	-6.8	-0.4	-7.0	-7.8	-10.2	90.4	154.4	60.6	-32.2	35.4
Chemical, rubber, plastic, non-metallic mineral products	1 639.5	-62.3	-171.5	-301.1	231.2	501.7	-1 698.8	-225.4	1 521.8	3 313.0
Metal and machinery products, except electrical equipment	1 158.1	-613.2	993.7	274.0	681.6	-381.5	-390.3	303.7	-398.4	586.6
Motor vehicles, trailers, semi-trailers, other transport equipment	-2.7	9.7	-1.4	65.4	-5.7	22.0	14.0	9.4	27.7	15.1
Other manufacturing	-12.6	34.2	146.2	-68.9	-177.8	434.2	-122.0	-1.2	54.5	263.8
Electricity, gas, steam and air conditioning supply	**-179.6**	**-708.8**	**-1 026.4**	**-56.5**	**454.9**	**300.1**	**588.6**	**1 601.5**	**-331.2**	**4 185.2**
Water supply; sewerage, waste management and remediation activities	**-**	**-5.8**	**6.7**	**0.5**	**-25.8**	**-0.6**	**-0.6**	**-**	**0.3**	**-**
Construction	**8.0**	**34.9**	**13.9**	**-30.4**	**-34.8**	**126.5**	**-33.1**	**-20.4**	**-32.2**	**45.7**
Services	**369.0**	**1 028.6**	**-3 257.3**	**4 118.8**	**4 440.9**	**6 147.3**	**8 079.7**	**7 566.7**	**1 114.4**	**4 053.6**
Wholesale and retail trade; repair of motor vehicles and motorcycles	489.6	79.5	57.1	333.1	110.1	-1 565.6	620.1	474.6	109.6	383.4
Transportation and storage	710.3	-136.8	-37.3	10.0	-109.2	1 433.5	403.8	4 022.5	81.3	-4 122.4
Accommodation and food service activities	0.7	-13.5	-39.5	-3.8	5.4	-	-	-	-	-
Information and communication	-179.6	-349.9	-140.0	563.4	1 187.4	-85.3	-353.2	-104.1	-2 915.2	149.5
Financial and insurance activities	835.6	2 906.3	-3 886.7	-328.8	60.7	5 373.4	4 602.0	1 040.2	1 036.5	1 848.0
Activities of holding companies	..	..	..	..	..	..	..	..	..	..
Real estate activities	67.5	40.9	65.3	187.9	33.6	99.8	165.4	393.5	327.9	188.8
Professional, scientific and technical activities	-1 251.7	-431.4	555.2	371.0	2 611.0	545.5	2 484.3	1 326.0	2 229.7	5 134.2
Administrative and support service activities	-149.3	-1 105.1	138.6	2 940.0	531.8	297.1	194.0	283.4	234.1	394.7
Public administration; activities of households and of extraterritorial organisations	-167.3	23.6	-	-	-	6.5	-83.9	55.0	-8.9	44.1
Education	-	-	-	-	-	-	-	-	-	-
Human health and social work activities	-8.5	-20.4	-11.2	35.6	-	35.1	47.2	75.6	20.1	34.2
Arts, entertainment and recreation	-0.6	10.3	18.3	-18.8	4.5	7.3	-	-	-	-
Other services	22.3	25.0	22.7	29.3	5.7	-	-	-	-0.5	-0.8
Not allocated and confidential	**398.0**	**-23.5**	**-432.3**	**-806.4**	**-287.0**	**1 026.0**	**239.3**	**38.3**	**68.1**	**-133.6**
Private real estate activities	**96.5**	**95.1**	**133.1**	**139.2**	**131.8**	**-421.4**	**-38.9**	**-76.6**	**-80.1**	**-75.9**

\- Nil; .. Not available

Note: Data excludes resident Special Purpose Entities (SPEs). Detailed metadata at: *http://stats.oecd.org/OECDStat_Metadata/ShowMetadata.ashx?Dataset=FDI_CTRY_IND_SUMM.*

Source: *OECD International Direct Investment Statistics (database): https://doi.org/10.1787/idi-data-en*

Table 5. Foreign direct investment positions by industrial sector

At year end

Million US dollars

	Inward					Outward				
	2015	2016	2017	2018	2019	2015	2016	2017	2018	2019
All FDI activities	**91 978.8**	**99 403.4**	**115 887.4**	**116 251.5**	**121 482.3**	**164 757.8**	**169 708.2**	**205 106.7**	**209 111.4**	**217 684.5**
Agriculture, forestry and fishing	**102.8**	**64.4**	**114.2**	**108.9**	**102.6**	**302.6**	**299.5**	**335.7**	**556.2**	**531.3**
Mining and quarrying	**1 911.4**	**2 101.0**	**3 950.4**	**2 364.3**	**978.7**	**3 217.3**	**14 901.3**	**15 228.0**	**11 916.1**	**9 179.6**
Extraction activities	1 877.2	2 062.4	3 913.8	2 325.2	952.2	3 176.4	14 865.0	15 191.6	11 822.1	9 087.8
Manufacturing	**10 288.7**	**9 980.7**	**11 633.5**	**11 364.5**	**11 560.8**	**41 480.8**	**40 865.8**	**47 836.9**	**46 523.5**	**48 248.9**
of which:										
Food products, beverages and tobacco	2 709.4	2 650.9	2 977.9	3 314.7	3 172.0	23 099.4	23 407.7	27 324.6	25 515.1	25 542.8
Textiles, wood and paper products; printing	303.4	306.5	405.9	354.6	348.7	720.5	841.8	981.4	1 078.9	929.2
Chemical, rubber, plastic, non-metallic mineral products	3 507.2	3 364.3	3 874.7	3 568.7	3 758.4	8 164.7	7 354.1	8 501.5	8 512.1	10 962.6
Metal and machinery products, except electrical equipment	2 381.4	2 112.4	2 611.6	2 615.7	3 407.0	8 269.4	8 118.2	9 787.8	8 958.3	8 218.2
Motor vehicles, trailers, semi-trailers, other transport equipment	30.9	37.4	49.3	40.5	36.0	139.4	200.2	197.8	180.8	193.5
Other manufacturing	1 356.4	1 509.2	1 714.3	1 470.1	838.5	1 087.3	943.9	1 043.9	2 278.1	2 402.5
Electricity, gas, steam and air conditioning supply	**2 068.7**	**2 783.3**	**912.4**	**827.1**	**1 480.7**	**8 163.0**	**7 771.0**	**10 667.1**	**13 413.2**	**18 158.2**
Water supply; sewerage, waste management and remediation activities	**147.1**	**162.6**	**195.4**	**193.7**	**158.9**	**8.3**	**13.0**	**13.0**	**25.8**	**30.6**
Construction	**150.5**	**203.7**	**348.1**	**358.9**	**408.9**	**310.0**	**222.3**	**238.9**	**176.1**	**321.3**
Services	**72 113.5**	**80 469.2**	**93 684.9**	**96 226.0**	**101 838.4**	**103 801.9**	**98 500.3**	**122 755.6**	**128 077.1**	**133 232.2**
Wholesale and retail trade; repair of motor vehicles and motorcycles	12 133.1	12 705.3	13 929.5	12 751.9	10 099.3	11 095.3	12 283.2	13 656.6	13 422.9	12 637.8
Transportation and storage	3 216.0	2 927.6	2 532.5	2 719.7	2 768.0	20 169.0	10 093.7	15 116.7	16 746.5	13 349.4
Accommodation and food service activities	155.9	175.3	273.7	328.3	388.4	33.1	33.3	62.7	130.4	133.6
Information and communication	5 625.2	5 076.4	6 251.8	5 859.0	7 355.7	2 455.8	2 040.3	2 092.4	857.1	1 104.4
Financial and insurance activities	41 118.6	46 764.1	52 818.0	52 952.6	54 842.0	44 642.2	44 971.6	55 601.1	53 443.7	57 681.5
Activities of holding companies	..	..	..	..	..	..	..	..	..	..
Real estate activities	2 207.8	2 359.6	3 762.1	5 233.9	6 367.1	2 381.3	2 525.2	3 160.8	3 599.1	3 839.8
Professional, scientific and technical activities	4 439.8	4 603.4	6 622.9	9 349.5	12 803.8	18 643.8	22 034.4	24 731.4	30 941.7	30 822.5
Administrative and support service activities	3 181.3	5 815.3	7 386.8	6 829.6	6 996.2	2 546.9	2 721.6	6 217.9	6 910.9	11 698.2
Public administration; activities of households and of extraterritorial organisations	-0.4	-1.0	-1.0	-	-	943.6	821.2	1 008.1	972.9	922.4
Education	0.7	-9.4	-3.7	20.6	20.1	10.4	21.3	19.5	25.6	24.7
Human health and social work activities	-11.0	-8.8	21.4	55.1	69.1	774.4	818.1	946.7	937.0	928.3
Arts, entertainment and recreation	-18.2	-2.3	14.7	29.0	26.4	61.1	58.0	69.9	8.3	30.3
Other services	64.6	63.5	76.2	97.1	102.2	45.1	78.1	71.8	80.8	59.3
Not allocated and confidential	**3 129.0**	**1 537.1**	**2 515.6**	**2 396.2**	**2 598.0**	**3 732.1**	**3 402.6**	**3 726.0**	**4 323.9**	**3 978.9**
Private real estate activities	**2 067.1**	**2 101.3**	**2 532.8**	**2 411.7**	**2 355.2**	**3 741.9**	**3 732.4**	**4 305.5**	**4 099.6**	**4 003.5**

- Nil; .. Not available

Note: Data excludes resident Special Purpose Entities (SPEs). Detailed metadata at: *http://stats.oecd.org/OECDStat_Metadata/ShowMetadata.ashx?Dataset=FDI_CTRY_IND_SUMM.*

Source: *OECD International Direct Investment Statistics (database): https://doi.org/10.1787/idi-data-en*

Table 6. Foreign direct investment income by industrial sector

Million US dollars

	Inward					Outward				
	2015	2016	2017	2018	2019	2015	2016	2017	2018	2019
All FDI activities	**4 606.0**	**5 481.4**	**6 133.9**	**6 363.3**	**7 043.1**	**12 131.8**	**12 061.1**	**13 256.1**	**15 120.5**	**15 622.1**
Agriculture, forestry and fishing	**17.7**	**12.8**	**15.1**	**8.9**	..	**21.7**	**22.3**	**25.3**	**38.8**	..
Mining and quarrying	**-337.2**	**-234.0**	**-59.2**	**66.8**	..	**437.7**	**429.4**	**717.1**	**437.6**	..
Extraction activities	-349.7	-253.3	-72.7	63.4	..	435.4	426.5	714.4	432.2	..
Manufacturing	**1 050.3**	**1 127.4**	**1 255.1**	**1 211.2**	..	**4 651.3**	**4 672.0**	**4 617.5**	**4 999.9**	..
of which:										
Food products, beverages and tobacco	318.3	275.0	249.3	269.3	..	706.6	1 021.9	1 045.6	1 226.1	..
Textiles, wood and paper products; printing	14.1	22.7	16.2	8.2	..	73.5	70.7	69.5	69.1	..
Chemical, rubber, plastic, non-metallic mineral products	328.6	391.5	404.9	268.8	..	2 902.6	2 705.5	2 734.0	2 835.0	..
Metal and machinery products, except electrical equipment	115.5	204.0	302.8	547.9	..	812.7	769.7	612.0	702.1	..
Motor vehicles, trailers, semi-trailers, other transport equipment	4.3	3.9	7.3	11.2	..	20.5	16.2	19.4	15.2	..
Other manufacturing	269.7	230.1	274.8	105.8	..	135.6	88.0	137.1	152.4	..
Electricity, gas, steam and air conditioning supply	**-30.3**	**69.5**	**53.5**	**73.0**	..	**280.6**	**296.7**	**382.8**	**605.7**	..
Water supply; sewerage, waste management and remediation activities	**18.9**	**-4.0**	**5.8**	**2.7**	..	**-0.1**	-	**0.9**	**1.6**	..
Construction	**77.5**	**72.4**	**63.3**	**53.5**	..	**5.1**	**2.7**	**6.8**	**12.8**	..
Services	**3 564.2**	**4 316.1**	**4 748.9**	**4 890.2**	..	**6 630.2**	**6 570.5**	**7 447.4**	**8 911.2**	..
Wholesale and retail trade; repair of motor vehicles and motorcycles	673.4	944.2	1 122.1	1 243.5	..	883.1	1 006.0	1 136.2	1 220.9	..
Transportation and storage	90.1	-192.5	-1.8	-125.9	..	448.7	465.0	424.4	1 056.2	..
Accommodation and food service activities	15.9	19.5	0.8	32.2	..	2.2	1.9	4.2	6.7	..
Information and communication	153.9	115.7	-43.3	104.7	..	149.9	125.5	211.6	149.7	..
Financial and insurance activities	2 019.1	2 718.5	2 781.4	2 546.8	..	3 102.1	3 060.7	3 480.0	3 943.3	..
Activities of holding companies	..	..	..	..	..	..	..	..	..	..
Real estate activities	65.0	119.0	178.7	282.6	..	81.5	108.6	126.2	159.3	..
Professional, scientific and technical activities	211.4	334.0	267.8	319.3	..	1 603.3	1 549.0	1 650.2	1 793.9	..
Administrative and support service activities	312.8	251.5	431.1	452.7	..	272.8	209.0	339.8	572.4	..
Public administration; activities of households and of extraterritorial organisations	-	-	-	-	..	6.5	-24.5	1.4	-45.0	..
Education	-	0.3	0.9	1.4	..	1.0	0.9	1.4	1.1	..
Human health and social work activities	-0.7	-19.8	-12.9	0.8	..	76.1	61.8	64.2	47.8	..
Arts, entertainment and recreation	0.6	0.6	0.8	2.5	..	0.4	3.6	3.9	0.5	..
Other services	22.6	25.3	23.3	29.9	..	2.4	3.0	4.1	4.6	..
Not allocated and confidential	**244.9**	**121.2**	**51.5**	**57.0**	**7 043.1**	**105.3**	**67.6**	**58.3**	**112.8**	**15 622.1**
Private real estate activities	-	-	-	-	..	-	-	-	-	..

- Nil; .. Not available

Note: Data excludes resident Special Purpose Entities (SPEs). Detailed metadata at: *http://stats.oecd.org/OECDStat_Metadata/ShowMetadata.ashx?Dataset=FDI_CTRY_IND_SUMM.*

Source: *OECD International Direct Investment Statistics (database): https://doi.org/10.1787/idi-data-en*

ESTONIA

Table 1. Foreign direct investment flows by country

Million US dollars

	Inward					Outward				
	2015	2016	2017	2018	2019	2015	2016	2017	2018	2019
WORLD	**35.5**	**1 058.4**	**1 938.3**	**1 496.8**	**3 091.2**	**182.1**	**486.5**	**879.1**	**58.0**	**1 987.2**
OECD COUNTRIES	**-45.0**	**860.3**	**1 570.3**	**1 186.3**	**2 946.9**	**274.8**	**415.1**	**885.4**	**.. d**	**1 948.5**
Australia	-0.2	1.2	-4.2	0.4	6.7	2.5	0.7	-0.6	0.4	0.6
Austria	118.0	16.0	-54.5	67.4	7.2	1.6	-0.4	0.0	0.2	0.4
Belgium	25.9	17.3	11.5	13.5	-19.8	0.2	5.6	3.0	-0.2	0.5
Canada	-2.7	-0.7	-6.8	18.5	-0.1	0.0	0.0	0.1	0.1	0.1
Chile	0.0	0.0	0.0	0.0	-0.1	.. c	.. c	.. c	.. c	0.0
Czech Republic	3.6	4.3	8.3	0.2	1.6	3.8	4.5	2.9	0.3	-1.7
Denmark	-106.0	76.0	0.9	34.6	-102.0	43.0	7.3	-48.3	2.1	1.1
Estonia	-	-	-	-	-	-	-	-	-	-
Finland	192.0	381.0	141.3	336.4	375.6	44.7	64.2	808.9	129.4	155.2
France	93.6	42.8	49.1	23.3	92.3	3.3	6.3	6.3	21.4	2.3
Germany	-62.2	8.0	126.1	175.7	79.6	2.6	17.7	2.0	-7.4	1.4
Greece	0.0	0.4	0.8	1.4	2.1	0.0	0.2	0.0	.. c	0.2
Hungary	-0.3	1.4	-0.4	6.9	5.6	2.4	1.0	-0.2	0.7	0.2
Iceland	16.9	4.6	5.7	6.8	8.3	0.0	0.0	0.0	10.1	.. c
Ireland	21.2	-4.5	-108.8	178.3	81.5	4.0	-10.1	-3.2	-0.7	0.2
Israel	0.7	0.3	1.4	4.7	7.2	0.3	-0.1	0.8	-0.2	0.1
Italy	9.1	19.9	-6.7	-10.4	9.7	3.0	11.9	-0.3	1.8	2.9
Japan	0.0	10.6	5.1	20.1	34.0	.. c	-	-	.. c	-
Korea	0.0	0.2	-1.1	0.0	1.5	-	-	.. c	.. c	.. c
Latvia	-12.5	117.4	46.0	57.1	91.2	135.3	106.6	14.8	222.5	707.7
Lithuania	52.5	26.2	100.7	-2.8	259.1	112.4	-69.7	131.9	23.1	983.2
Luxembourg	217.1	-17.4	109.6	1 086.7	62.0	-0.4	0.9	-0.2	49.9	8.2
Mexico	0.0	0.0	-0.4	-3.0	-3.6	.. c	0.2	.. c	.. c	-1.2
Netherlands	-79.1	15.1	-107.2	-646.5	77.7	109.8	6.9	8.0	-652.2	22.0
New Zealand	0.0	1.7	0.3	0.0	1.4	.. c	.. c	.. c	.. c	.. c
Norway	-204.2	-250.2	37.3	-279.7	35.1	41.1	2.3	14.8	8.1	2.1
Poland	6.7	29.0	3.5	57.7	4.6	-19.8	79.2	11.0	16.3	37.4
Portugal	-11.2	5.1	9.4	-0.1	-0.7	0.0	22.5	-12.9	3.4	-1.1
Slovak Republic	0.3	0.3	3.3	3.6	-17.9	1.2	0.5	-0.6	0.5	2.2
Slovenia	-0.2	0.1	0.1	0.3	0.0	0.0	-	-0.2	0.8	.. c
Spain	3.9	1.5	-4.0	16.7	-2.7	15.0	22.8	21.2	18.5	10.7
Sweden	-322.7	293.9	713.4	-166.5	1 586.3	35.6	30.5	-14.2	25.2	-16.3
Switzerland	-4.8	20.5	38.4	67.0	42.8	1.3	-0.4	-0.8	5.6	-28.1
Turkey	1.6	-2.6	2.7	6.2	3.6	0.2	0.2	0.0	0.6	0.5
United Kingdom	10.5	36.4	547.1	69.9	216.2	0.7	28.1	66.0	25.0	22.8
United States	27.3	30.9	3.1	42.2	0.8	-21.5	5.8	0.3	32.3	35.0
EUROPE	**92.3**	**958.1**	**1 765.5**	**1 362.3**	**3 086.2**	**196.9**	**458.5**	**817.1**	**-15.5**	**1 938.1**
Bulgaria	-0.3	0.8	0.0	1.8	2.7	-2.4	-	4.9	3.4	5.4
Croatia	-0.5	1.1	-0.1	-0.2	1.5	0.1	0.4	1.5	2.1	5.3
Cyprus	93.5	-51.8	-64.4	119.1	42.7	-166.1	32.6	-182.8	-37.3	6.6
Malta	5.7	27.1	12.4	4.0	22.7	-5.0	11.4	6.3	-7.7	3.5
Romania	-0.3	1.5	2.3	-0.2	2.1	-8.5	15.0	-5.0	10.8	-11.2
Russian Federation	-31.9	74.8	54.6	51.4	62.1	4.8	47.0	21.5	10.8	-1.8
Ukraine	25.1	44.6	68.2	51.4	46.4	-4.5	-15.8	-18.3	69.2	-6.8
AFRICA	**-0.4**	**-7.4**	**9.1**	**2.4**	**1.2**	**-0.3**	**-0.9**	**-1.9**	**11.7**	**6.6**
Northern Africa	-0.1	0.0	0.4	1.2	1.3	.. c	.. c	0.3	1.6	1.7
Algeria	.. c	.. c	0.0	0.2	0.2	-	-	-	-	-
Egypt	0.0	0.0	0.3	0.7	0.7	-	-	0.1	0.5	0.3
Libya	-	-	-	.. c	.. c	-	-	-	-	-
Morocco	-	-	0.0	0.3	0.2	.. c	.. c	.. c	.. c	.. c
Tunisia	-0.1	0.0	0.0	0.0	0.1	-	-	-	-	-
Other African countries	-0.3	-7.5	8.7	1.2	-0.1	.. c	-1.0	-2.1	10.1	4.9
Nigeria	.. c	.. c	0.0	0.0	0.0	-	-	.. c	.. c	.. c
South Africa	0.0	0.2	0.0	-0.1	-0.5	-	.. c	.. c	2.5	4.1
AMERICA	**-66.4**	**57.9**	**-87.4**	**38.4**	**-22.5**	**-20.9**	**5.9**	**1.4**	**33.6**	**32.9**
Northern America	24.6	30.2	-3.7	60.7	0.7	-21.5	5.8	0.4	32.4	35.1
Central America and Caribbean countries	-92.1	26.4	-84.6	-23.1	-23.6	0.3	0.0	0.4	0.7	-1.2
Bahamas	0.0	0.4	-0.2	0.0	0.0	-	.. c	-	-	-
Bermuda	.. c	-	.. c	-	-	-	-	-	-	-
Cayman Islands	11.3	-5.2	-10.7	4.1	-5.9	0.3	-	-	-	-
Costa Rica	.. c	0.1	-0.1	0.5	0.4	-	-	-	-	-
El Salvador	-	-	.. c	.. c	0.0	-	-	-	-	-
Guatemala	-	-	-	-	-	-	-	-	-	-
Honduras	-	-	.. c	.. c	.. c	-	-	-	-	-
Nicaragua	-	-	.. c	.. c	-	-	-	-	-	-
Panama	-1.8	8.2	1.6	-1.1	-1.8	0.2	-0.1	0.1	0.1	0.0
Virgin Islands, U.S.	-	-	.. c	.. c	-	-	-	-	-	-
South America	1.1	1.2	1.0	0.8	0.5	0.4	0.1	0.6	0.5	-1.0
Argentina	0.0	-	0.0	0.0	0.0	-	.. c	-	.. c	-
Bolivia	.. c	0.3	.. c	.. c	0.0	-	-	-	-	-
Brazil	0.9	0.8	0.7	0.6	0.2	0.7	0.3	0.2	0.6	-1.0
Colombia	0.0	0.1	0.0	0.0	0.1	-	-	-	-	-
Ecuador	-	0.1	0.0	0.1	0.0	0.0	-	-	.. c	-
Paraguay	-	-	.. c	-	.. c	-	-	-	-	-
Peru	.. c	0.1	0.1	0.1	0.1	-	-	-	-	-
Uruguay	0.0	-	0.0	0.0	0.0	.. c	.. c	.. c	.. c	-
Venezuela	0.0	-	-	0.0	0.0	-	-	-	-	-

Table 1. Foreign direct investment flows by country *(cont.)*

Million US dollars

	Inward					Outward				
	2015	2016	2017	2018	2019	2015	2016	2017	2018	2019
ASIA	**7.0**	**10.3**	**251.6**	**89.4**	**16.8**	**3.7**	**22.3**	**62.9**	**27.8**	**8.5**
Near and Middle East	3.7	1.2	209.8	17.8	-5.4	4.1	16.0	59.3	29.4	4.8
Gulf Arabian countries	0.5	0.3	206.0	5.8	-15.7	-6.8	-0.4	2.4	6.0	6.9
Kuwait	-	.. c	0.0	0.0	0.0	-	-	-	-	-
Qatar	0.1	.. c	0.0	0.0	0.0	-	-	-	-	-
Saudi Arabia	0.0	0.0	0.0	0.0	0.4	-	-	-	-	-
United Arab Emirates	0.1	0.8	206.0	5.6	-16.3	-8.3	2.7	3.1	4.3	4.3
Other Near and Middle East	3.3	0.9	3.8	12.0	10.3	10.9	16.4	56.9	23.3	-2.1
Jordan	.. c	.. c	0.1	0.0	0.0	.. c	.. c	.. c	.. c	.. c
Other Asian countries	3.3	9.2	41.7	71.5	22.2	-0.4	6.2	3.6	-1.6	3.7
China	-7.2	-8.6	5.6	10.1	-1.9	1.3	0.1	0.1	0.7	0.4
Hong Kong, China	2.0	12.6	8.6	10.3	6.1	.. c	4.8	-4.7	0.4	0.1
India	3.6	-0.9	1.7	-0.3	2.9	-0.3	.. c	2.6	.. c	-0.3
Indonesia	0.0	0.0	0.0	-	-0.1	-	-	0.2	0.1	0.8
Iran, Islamic Republic of	0.0	0.1	0.1	0.1	0.1	-	-	-	-	-
Malaysia	0.1	0.2	0.3	0.1	0.0	-	-	.. c	-	.. c
Philippines	0.1	0.1	0.3	-0.1	0.1	-	-	0.1	-	0.0
Singapore	2.1	-4.5	17.8	18.4	-22.4	-1.2	-0.1	-2.8	-1.5	0.7
Chinese Taipei	0.0	0.2	0.6	0.9	-0.4	.. c	.. c	-	-	-
Thailand	-	-0.8	-2.0	3.6	0.8	0.4	0.6	0.3	-0.2	.. c
Viet Nam	0.0	0.1	0.0	0.0	0.0	.. c	.. c	-	-	-
AUSTRALIA, OCEANIA AND POLAR REGIONS	**1.1**	**38.9**	**-1.5**	**1.5**	**8.3**	**2.6**	**0.6**	**-0.4**	**0.5**	**1.3**
WORLD unallocated and confidential	**1.8**	**0.7**	**1.0**	**2.9**	**1.2**	**-**	**0.0**	**-**	**0.0**	**0.0**
European Union (EU28)	**258.5**	**1 048.8**	**1 539.7**	**1 438.5**	**2 881.0**	**316.5**	**396.1**	**820.7**	**-148.1**	**1 949.1**
G20 countries excl. European Union	**42.4**	**213.0**	**776.6**	**404.4**	**503.9**	**-2.5**	**119.6**	**105.5**	**89.2**	**66.6**
G20 OECD countries	**77.0**	**146.7**	**714.0**	**342.7**	**440.8**	**-9.1**	**71.1**	**80.4**	**75.0**	**64.4**
G20 Non-OECD countries	**-34.6**	**66.3**	**62.6**	**61.6**	**63.1**	**6.6**	**48.5**	**25.1**	**14.2**	**2.1**
MENA countries	**0.5**	**0.0**	**206.3**	**7.0**	**-14.4**	**-6.1**	**-0.4**	**41.4**	**11.4**	**13.3**
ASEAN countries	**2.4**	**-4.9**	**16.3**	**22.0**	**-21.5**	**-0.3**	**0.4**	**-2.0**	**-1.7**	**1.6**

- Nil; .. Not available; c Confidential data; d Secondary Confidentiality

Note: Detailed metadata at: *http://stats.oecd.org/OECDStat_Metadata/ShowMetadata.ashx?Dataset=FDI_CTRY_IND_SUMM.*

Source: *OECD International Direct Investment Statistics (database): https://doi.org/10.1787/idi-data-en*

Table 2. Foreign direct investment positions by country
At year end

Million US dollars

	Inward					Outward				
	2015	2016	2017	2018	2019	2015	2016	2017	2018	2019
WORLD	**18 956.5**	**19 658.5**	**24 022.6**	**25 095.9**	**27 924.2**	**6 038.9**	**6 298.5**	**7 805.1**	**7 962.7**	**10 012.8**
OECD COUNTRIES	**15 469.8**	**16 366.1**	**20 008.7**	**22 253.1**	**23 592.0**	**1 476.8**	**2 775.7**	**3 672.6**	**.. d**	**7 591.5**
Australia	22.6	20.0	39.7	40.9	41.7	2.5	3.1	2.9	4.7	5.2
Austria	396.0	281.8	355.7	322.3	395.8	4.0	3.5	3.9	4.8	5.1
Belgium	74.9	79.8	98.9	126.9	138.7	2.7	45.8	4.0	3.7	3.2
Canada	50.2	113.3	68.2	323.8	420.4	0.5	0.4	0.6	0.7	0.8
Chile	.. c	0.0	0.0	0.0	0.1	0.1	0.1	0.2	0.2	0.2
Czech Republic	10.7	12.7	13.8	20.1	17.4	7.0	11.2	16.5	21.2	19.0
Denmark	490.1	528.3	670.9	661.4	528.6	47.6	53.4	10.1	11.6	15.5
Estonia	1 285.5	1 390.4	1 572.1	1 272.6	1 025.0	-	-	-	-	-
Finland	4 180.0	4 421.6	5 356.1	5 936.0	6 557.2	443.7	462.0	919.1	735.1	831.4
France	379.7	451.1	561.1	578.8	636.7	42.0	46.2	54.9	71.7	72.7
Germany	575.1	596.6	716.0	740.8	846.6	59.8	71.3	60.6	49.8	49.4
Greece	26.1	29.1	31.9	4.4	6.1	2.3	2.4	2.7	2.5	2.7
Hungary	4.7	5.9	9.1	11.2	9.4	3.1	4.1	4.5	4.9	5.0
Iceland	40.5	27.2	74.1	98.8	84.8	0.0	0.0	0.0	.. c	.. c
Ireland	59.9	56.6	49.3	58.5	71.1	15.8	5.7	2.2	1.4	1.7
Israel	10.3	11.0	12.0	13.5	13.3	1.0	2.3	3.5	3.1	3.1
Italy	131.6	182.2	187.0	177.3	186.0	108.3	119.6	92.4	89.3	90.1
Japan	130.5	141.5	171.5	273.2	330.9	0.2	0.2	0.2	0.2	0.2
Korea	0.0	0.1	0.2	0.4	0.5	0.1	0.0	6.7	11.5	11.5
Latvia	316.0	530.8	535.5	606.0	566.8	1 060.4	1 102.6	1 379.9	1 634.4	2 336.4
Lithuania	691.1	742.0	1 008.7	1 135.6	1 076.4	1 281.4	1 210.1	1 606.1	1 589.9	2 859.8
Luxembourg	452.4	536.0	687.4	1 117.1	1 357.4	10.6	21.2	24.0	61.6	30.2
Mexico	0.1	0.0	0.1	-1.1	0.4	0.3	0.5	1.0	1.6	0.4
Netherlands	509.6	561.6	674.0	526.3	617.6	239.8	232.4	266.2	277.6	297.9
New Zealand	0.6	1.9	1.9	1.9	3.1	0.1	0.0	4.5	4.4	4.8
Norway	905.6	602.8	1 157.2	440.5	459.3	84.7	44.8	69.6	72.0	73.4
Poland	46.3	94.4	120.6	130.9	164.6	51.3	124.8	152.6	161.2	193.4
Portugal	2.0	0.5	6.6	7.7	12.0	3.2	24.6	14.4	17.0	14.8
Slovak Republic	18.2	21.0	22.3	31.0	30.3	24.2	22.7	25.2	12.3	14.5
Slovenia	-0.1	-0.1	0.2	0.2	0.2	0.1	0.1	-0.2	0.5	0.5
Spain	7.4	33.5	43.0	43.6	47.2	74.1	83.5	122.9	132.0	142.8
Sweden	4 304.5	4 328.0	5 285.8	5 764.8	6 049.4	87.8	109.5	145.1	175.7	157.3
Switzerland	228.6	271.3	298.4	366.6	337.0	30.3	28.9	31.4	52.6	7.5
Turkey	5.2	6.0	9.4	15.5	19.0	2.3	2.4	2.7	3.2	3.6
United Kingdom	399.8	380.6	526.1	719.3	770.8	32.3	47.2	131.6	136.2	138.9
United States	721.3	648.6	652.6	686.4	770.3	95.0	99.0	116.9	145.4	189.8
EUROPE	**17 053.1**	**17 858.7**	**21 841.5**	**22 841.9**	**25 188.8**	**5 843.3**	**6 077.2**	**7 450.4**	**7 572.6**	**9 576.5**
Bulgaria	1.0	2.5	3.3	5.8	6.0	37.7	33.9	42.0	44.6	50.2
Croatia	0.3	0.4	0.7	0.7	1.1	25.1	24.9	28.4	28.5	29.3
Cyprus	355.0	346.7	405.8	387.9	352.3	1 401.9	1 403.8	1 395.0	1 275.1	1 264.2
Malta	23.1	50.9	48.1	50.7	64.1	22.5	33.3	52.9	44.4	50.4
Romania	1.2	2.3	4.8	4.0	5.7	25.5	38.1	37.3	37.7	22.0
Russian Federation	738.7	759.0	708.9	804.8	1 017.3	222.1	250.4	330.3	307.2	275.5
Ukraine	171.5	218.0	280.3	337.8	387.9	248.6	251.8	265.6	321.7	310.9
AFRICA	**9.2**	**18.2**	**42.9**	**30.4**	**27.1**	**15.2**	**15.3**	**15.5**	**29.5**	**36.1**
Northern Africa	0.3	0.8	2.1	3.3	4.9	13.3	13.4	15.5	16.4	17.4
Algeria	-	0.0	0.1	0.3	0.4	-	-	-	-	-
Egypt	0.2	0.7	1.9	2.6	3.6	0.7	0.7	0.8	1.3	1.4
Libya	0.1	0.0	0.1	0.1	0.1	-	-	-	-	-
Morocco	0.0	0.0	0.0	0.3	0.6	12.6	12.7	14.6	15.0	16.0
Tunisia	-	.. c	0.0	0.1	0.2	0.0	0.0	0.1	0.1	0.1
Other African countries	9.0	17.4	40.8	27.1	22.2	1.9	1.9	-0.1	13.1	18.7
Nigeria	0.5	0.6	0.7	0.7	0.7	-	-	.. c	.. c	.. c
South Africa	1.0	1.8	1.1	3.4	1.0	0.1	0.2	0.6	2.9	7.9
AMERICA	**1 023.6**	**1 179.1**	**1 111.3**	**1 296.1**	**1 418.3**	**114.0**	**115.2**	**136.4**	**165.4**	**206.3**
Northern America	771.5	761.9	720.8	1 010.2	1 190.7	95.5	99.5	117.5	146.1	190.5
Central America and Caribbean countries	250.2	413.7	385.9	276.7	213.9	4.4	1.7	2.3	2.8	1.6
Bahamas	1.3	1.7	2.0	1.8	0.8	-	0.0	0.0	0.0	0.0
Bermuda	0.4	0.3	0.5	0.5	0.7	-	-	-	-	-
Cayman Islands	.. c	.. c	.. c	.. c	-0.1	0.3	0.2	0.3	0.3	0.3
Costa Rica	.. c	0.0	0.0	0.7	1.2	0.0	0.0	0.0	0.0	0.0
El Salvador	0.0	0.4	0.8	1.2	2.1	-	-	-	-	-
Guatemala	-	-	-	-	-	-	-	-	-	-
Honduras	-	-	-	-0.1	-0.2	-	-	-	-	-
Nicaragua	-	-	.. c	0.0	0.0	-	-	-	-	-
Panama	16.8	32.3	21.7	18.6	8.6	0.4	0.2	0.2	0.1	0.2
Virgin Islands, U.S.	-	-	.. c	.. c	.. c	-	-	-	-	-
South America	1.9	3.4	4.7	9.2	13.6	14.1	14.1	16.6	16.5	14.3
Argentina	0.5	0.5	0.5	0.6	0.6	0.1	0.1	0.1	0.2	0.1
Bolivia	0.3	0.3	0.3	0.2	0.1	-	-	-	-	-
Brazil	0.4	0.6	0.7	1.0	1.5	13.8	14.0	16.1	16.0	14.0
Colombia	0.1	0.1	0.2	1.9	1.1	-	-	-	-	-
Ecuador	0.5	1.6	2.4	4.5	9.1	0.0	0.0	0.0	0.1	0.1
Paraguay	-	-	.. c	.. c	0.0	-	-	-	-	-
Peru	-	.. c	.. c	0.5	0.6	0.1	-	-	-	-
Uruguay	0.0	0.0	0.0	0.0	0.0	.. c	.. c	.. c	-	-
Venezuela	0.0	-	-	0.2	0.2	.. c	.. c	.. c	.. c	.. c

Table 2. Foreign direct investment positions by country *(cont.)*

At year end

Million US dollars

	Inward					Outward				
	2015	2016	2017	2018	2019	2015	2016	2017	2018	2019
ASIA	**323.8**	**339.4**	**698.0**	**538.1**	**810.0**	**63.7**	**87.6**	**195.4**	**186.1**	**183.7**
Near and Middle East	20.4	22.1	252.2	50.2	223.7	14.6	34.6	103.8	130.7	126.4
Gulf Arabian countries	6.4	7.0	227.4	13.7	187.0	-8.0	-7.3	-6.3	-0.4	7.3
Kuwait	0.1	0.2	0.2	0.2	0.2	-	-	-	-	-
Qatar	0.6	0.6	0.8	1.1	1.3	-	-	-	-	-
Saudi Arabia	1.1	1.5	1.4	1.9	1.5	-	-	-	-	-
United Arab Emirates	2.8	3.4	223.5	8.7	182.1	-11.5	-8.5	-6.5	-2.3	2.1
Other Near and Middle East	14.1	15.1	24.8	36.5	36.7	22.7	41.9	110.1	131.1	119.1
Jordan	.. c	0.0	0.0	0.5	0.1	.. c	.. c	.. c	.. c	.. c
Other Asian countries	303.4	317.3	445.8	487.8	586.3	49.0	53.0	91.5	55.4	57.2
China	5.8	13.3	14.2	19.1	49.8	4.6	4.5	5.2	6.3	6.7
Hong Kong, China	37.2	46.6	48.3	23.5	23.1	0.5	5.0	24.6	13.1	11.5
India	0.2	0.9	1.7	3.7	4.6	0.4	1.4	4.2	3.3	2.4
Indonesia	0.1	0.1	0.2	0.2	0.1	0.3	0.3	0.6	0.6	1.4
Iran, Islamic Republic of	0.2	0.3	0.5	0.4	0.8	-	-	-	-	-
Malaysia	5.6	0.5	0.7	0.7	0.7	-	-	0.1	0.1	0.2
Philippines	0.1	0.4	0.8	1.2	0.7	0.0	0.0	0.2	0.2	0.2
Singapore	109.1	94.1	162.4	117.4	120.3	2.1	1.6	2.5	1.4	3.6
Chinese Taipei	0.0	0.3	0.9	1.6	1.3	0.1	0.1	0.1	0.0	0.0
Thailand	0.2	0.1	0.4	1.8	2.5	5.4	5.7	6.8	6.3	6.2
Viet Nam	.. c	.. c	0.0	0.1	0.1	.. c	.. c	.. c	-	-
AUSTRALIA, OCEANIA AND POLAR REGIONS	**-1.7**	**39.5**	**59.6**	**61.5**	**56.6**	**2.6**	**3.2**	**7.4**	**9.1**	**10.2**
WORLD unallocated and confidential	**548.4**	**223.5**	**269.2**	**327.9**	**423.4**	**-**	**0.0**	**-**	**-**	**0.0**
European Union (EU28)	**14 741.9**	**15 667.3**	**18 994.7**	**20 447.1**	**21 543.1**	**5 114.0**	**5 337.9**	**6 594.2**	**6 624.6**	**8 698.2**
G20 countries excl. European Union	**3 163.7**	**3 317.6**	**3 660.5**	**4 389.8**	**5 099.8**	**584.6**	**660.9**	**827.5**	**850.9**	**870.5**
G20 OECD countries	**2 416.0**	**2 539.9**	**2 931.9**	**3 555.2**	**4 023.4**	**343.2**	**390.0**	**470.5**	**514.3**	**562.5**
G20 Non-OECD countries	**747.7**	**777.6**	**728.7**	**834.6**	**1 076.4**	**241.4**	**270.8**	**357.0**	**336.6**	**308.1**
MENA countries	**7.4**	**12.9**	**236.5**	**26.8**	**198.2**	**5.5**	**6.1**	**46.3**	**60.0**	**72.8**
ASEAN countries	**115.0**	**95.2**	**164.6**	**121.5**	**124.5**	**8.3**	**8.1**	**10.6**	**8.8**	**11.9**

- Nil; .. Not available; c Confidential data; d Secondary Confidentiality

Note: Inward FDI positions are allocated according to the ultimate investing country. Detailed metadata at: *http://stats.oecd.org/OECDStat_Metadata/ShowMetadata.ashx?Dataset=FDI_CTRY_IND_SUMM.*

Source: *OECD International Direct Investment Statistics (database): https://doi.org/10.1787/idi-data-en*

ESTONIA

Table 3. Foreign direct investment income by country

Million US dollars

	Inward					Outward				
	2015	2016	2017	2018	2019	2015	2016	2017	2018	2019
WORLD	**1 385.0**	**1 591.0**	**1 736.6**	**1 920.8**	**1 954.6**	**364.5**	**492.4**	**485.4**	**698.3**	**690.8**
OECD COUNTRIES	**1 171.6**	**1 348.1**	**1 420.6**	**.. d**	**1 752.2**	**12.6**	**190.0**	**222.9**	**468.0**	**540.1**
Australia	0.5	1.3	0.1	-0.5	-0.5	0.6	0.2	0.0	0.1	0.1
Austria	19.2	13.9	28.9	32.9	21.0	0.1	0.1	0.0	0.1	0.2
Belgium	6.3	7.3	14.8	14.0	10.1	0.1	0.6	0.5	2.6	0.0
Canada	0.2	1.7	-0.2	2.9	2.7	0.0	0.0	0.0	0.0	0.0
Chile	-	.. c	-	.. c	0.0	0.0	0.0	0.0	0.0	0.0
Czech Republic	2.0	4.0	9.2	4.6	4.4	0.2	0.5	0.3	1.1	0.7
Denmark	43.3	33.5	34.6	28.6	27.2	1.7	4.3	4.0	-0.1	-0.4
Estonia	-	-	-	-	-	-	-	-	-	-
Finland	307.2	383.1	385.2	394.4	348.9	-13.5	5.2	71.4	131.3	164.4
France	18.1	25.4	31.6	42.3	41.8	1.4	0.9	1.6	1.2	1.7
Germany	34.3	27.8	48.0	59.0	64.5	0.4	1.7	0.5	-10.7	-5.5
Greece	0.0	0.2	0.8	1.8	2.0	0.0	1.4	0.0	0.0	0.0
Hungary	0.2	0.4	1.5	2.5	2.5	0.1	0.2	0.2	0.6	0.4
Iceland	11.7	9.5	7.9	9.8	8.6	0.0	-	-	-	-
Ireland	1.2	0.4	-1.2	7.3	3.2	0.7	0.5	0.2	-0.1	0.0
Israel	1.1	1.8	1.6	0.8	0.9	0.0	0.0	0.0	0.0	0.0
Italy	4.3	4.7	6.0	11.7	11.6	-0.2	-0.4	-0.7	1.6	1.3
Japan	0.2	0.4	0.3	5.5	11.2	0.0	0.0	0.0	0.0	0.0
Korea	-	.. c	-	0.2	0.2	0.0	-	-	-	.. c
Latvia	35.8	31.5	57.5	33.5	23.7	91.0	115.7	107.7	120.6	151.3
Lithuania	59.7	41.9	78.8	47.1	67.8	133.3	105.5	126.7	164.9	200.1
Luxembourg	26.9	18.2	30.3	5.4	76.4	0.9	3.3	4.2	2.9	-4.0
Mexico	0.0	0.0	0.0	-2.8	-1.3	0.0	0.0	0.0	0.0	0.0
Netherlands	123.7	133.3	82.8	119.4	136.0	26.2	39.8	0.5	0.1	4.8
New Zealand	0.0	0.0	0.0	0.0	0.0	0.0	0.0	0.1	0.1	0.1
Norway	56.1	30.6	35.6	42.4	46.2	-4.0	0.8	1.0	0.7	2.9
Poland	9.9	16.8	12.0	7.5	10.9	0.8	-0.1	0.8	5.2	-3.3
Portugal	0.4	2.8	5.7	-1.9	3.3	0.0	0.0	0.1	0.9	0.5
Slovak Republic	0.1	0.3	3.2	3.6	3.1	0.0	0.5	0.7	1.6	-0.7
Slovenia	.. c	0.0	0.3	0.0	0.2	0.0	0.0	-	0.4	0.0
Spain	7.9	4.5	5.0	7.7	7.2	5.1	6.1	4.9	6.2	4.4
Sweden	413.7	536.9	541.7	522.4	650.1	9.0	8.4	13.8	15.3	10.2
Switzerland	19.8	19.7	19.1	25.9	23.3	0.2	0.6	7.9	17.6	5.2
Turkey	1.7	-2.1	0.1	-1.0	0.0	0.1	0.1	0.1	0.1	0.1
United Kingdom	40.6	32.7	53.5	122.1	128.0	-3.9	-0.2	3.1	4.3	3.6
United States	20.9	7.4	4.8	33.1	17.4	-13.7	-0.3	-0.1	-0.8	1.9
EUROPE	**1 339.6**	**1 547.5**	**1 691.7**	**1 809.8**	**1 946.6**	**375.6**	**488.1**	**482.9**	**687.5**	**676.1**
Bulgaria	0.0	0.3	0.4	0.9	1.2	3.1	0.9	1.0	1.9	5.9
Croatia	0.2	0.3	0.3	0.5	0.4	0.1	0.4	0.0	0.2	0.3
Cyprus	25.8	34.2	35.3	137.8	80.7	93.6	107.6	96.6	92.6	67.6
Malta	0.3	14.0	4.5	7.0	20.1	4.8	6.5	3.8	15.8	10.3
Romania	0.0	1.6	2.0	0.3	0.2	0.7	0.1	7.4	1.4	0.3
Russian Federation	23.1	80.6	75.8	53.4	42.6	10.7	29.5	6.0	12.8	20.3
Ukraine	20.2	30.1	62.3	49.7	50.7	2.1	3.5	3.7	78.9	14.0
AFRICA	**0.2**	**-0.4**	**-1.9**	**2.2**	**1.9**	**-0.3**	**0.6**	**0.2**	**1.3**	**1.8**
Northern Africa	0.0	0.1	0.3	1.2	1.3	0.7	0.6	0.2	1.2	1.6
Algeria	.. c	0.0	0.0	0.2	0.2	-	-	-	-	-
Egypt	0.0	0.0	0.3	0.8	0.8	0.0	0.0	0.0	0.0	0.2
Libya	0.0	0.0	0.0	0.0	0.0	-	-	-	-	-
Morocco	-	-	0.0	0.3	0.3	0.7	0.5	0.2	1.2	1.4
Tunisia	-	-	-	0.0	0.0	0.0	0.0	0.0	0.0	0.0
Other African countries	0.2	-0.5	-2.3	1.0	0.6	-1.0	0.0	0.0	0.1	0.2
Nigeria	0.0	0.0	0.0	0.0	0.0	-	-	-	.. c	.. c
South Africa	0.0	0.1	-0.1	0.2	0.2	0.0	0.0	0.0	0.0	0.1
AMERICA	**33.0**	**31.2**	**11.2**	**59.5**	**19.7**	**-11.5**	**1.3**	**0.1**	**-0.5**	**2.9**
Northern America	21.1	9.1	4.6	36.0	20.1	-13.6	-0.3	-0.1	-0.8	1.9
Central America and Caribbean countries	11.6	21.6	6.3	22.9	-1.0	1.7	1.1	0.0	0.0	0.0
Bahamas	-0.1	0.0	-0.2	.. c	.. c	-	-	0.0	0.0	0.0
Bermuda	0.1	0.0	0.0	0.0	0.0	-	-	-	-	-
Cayman Islands	13.9	9.0	7.6	.. c	.. c	0.0	0.0	0.0	0.0	0.0
Costa Rica	.. c	-	.. c	0.5	0.5	0.0	0.0	0.0	0.0	0.0
El Salvador	-	0.0	0.0	0.0	0.0	-	-	-	-	-
Guatemala	-	-	-	-	-	-	-	-	-	-
Honduras	-	-	-	-	-	-	-	-	-	-
Nicaragua	-	-	-	-	-	-	-	-	-	-
Panama	2.1	11.5	3.1	-1.0	-0.3	0.0	0.0	0.0	0.0	0.0
Virgin Islands, U.S.	-	-	-	-	-	-	-	-	-	-
South America	0.2	0.5	0.3	0.5	0.6	0.4	0.5	0.1	0.3	1.0
Argentina	0.0	0.0	-	0.0	0.0	0.0	0.0	0.0	0.0	0.0
Bolivia	0.1	0.4	0.3	0.2	0.2	-	-	-	-	-
Brazil	0.0	0.0	-0.1	0.2	0.1	0.4	0.5	0.1	0.3	1.0
Colombia	0.0	0.0	0.0	0.0	0.0	-	-	-	-	-
Ecuador	0.0	0.0	0.0	0.1	0.1	-	0.0	0.0	0.0	0.0
Paraguay	-	-	-	-	-	-	-	-	-	-
Peru	.. c	.. c	.. c	0.1	0.1	0.0	-	-	-	-
Uruguay	-	-	0.0	0.0	.. c	-	-	-	-	-
Venezuela	-	-	-	-	0.0	-	-	-	-	-

Table 3. Foreign direct investment income by country *(cont.)*

Million US dollars

	Inward					Outward				
	2015	2016	2017	2018	2019	2015	2016	2017	2018	2019
ASIA	**7.8**	**8.7**	**32.0**	**45.5**	**-16.7**	**0.0**	**2.2**	**2.2**	**9.7**	**9.6**
Near and Middle East	3.2	3.9	7.8	11.5	6.3	0.5	1.6	1.2	8.2	8.2
Gulf Arabian countries	0.3	0.5	3.9	5.2	2.2	-0.6	0.0	-1.1	0.6	-0.1
Kuwait	0.0	0.0	0.0	0.0	0.0	-	-	-	-	-
Qatar	0.0	0.0	0.0	0.0	0.0	-	-	-	-	-
Saudi Arabia	0.0	0.0	0.0	0.0	0.0	-	-	-	-	-
United Arab Emirates	0.2	0.4	3.8	5.1	2.2	-0.2	-0.3	-0.4	-0.1	-0.8
Other Near and Middle East	2.9	3.4	3.9	6.3	4.0	1.1	1.6	2.3	7.6	8.3
Jordan	.. c	.. c	.. c	-	-	-	-	-	-	-
Other Asian countries	4.6	4.8	24.2	34.0	-23.0	-0.5	0.6	1.0	1.5	1.4
China	0.3	0.2	0.8	3.8	2.1	0.0	-0.1	0.0	0.0	-0.1
Hong Kong, China	-5.3	1.6	0.5	-18.5	-28.3	0.0	0.2	0.5	0.2	0.0
India	0.7	0.1	0.4	0.6	0.2	-0.2	0.0	0.3	0.0	0.0
Indonesia	.. c	0.0	0.0	-0.1	-0.1	0.0	0.0	0.0	0.0	0.0
Iran, Islamic Republic of	0.0	0.1	0.0	0.0	0.0	-	-	-	-	-
Malaysia	0.0	0.0	0.1	0.1	0.1	-	-	-	-	-
Philippines	0.1	-	0.3	0.0	0.0	0.0	0.0	0.0	0.0	0.0
Singapore	6.1	6.6	15.7	32.9	-10.3	0.0	-0.1	0.0	0.1	0.1
Chinese Taipei	-	-0.1	-0.3	0.8	-0.4	0.0	0.0	0.0	0.0	0.0
Thailand	0.0	0.1	0.1	0.6	0.6	0.2	0.2	0.2	0.2	0.2
Viet Nam	.. c	.. c	.. c	.. c	.. c	.. c	-	-	-	-
AUSTRALIA, OCEANIA AND POLAR REGIONS	**2.5**	**2.3**	**2.3**	**1.0**	**0.0**	**0.6**	**0.2**	**0.1**	**0.2**	**0.4**
WORLD unallocated and confidential	**2.0**	**1.6**	**1.3**	**2.8**	**3.2**	**0.0**	**0.0**	**0.0**	**0.0**	**-**
European Union (EU28)	**1 181.1**	**1 370.1**	**1 472.5**	**1 612.3**	**1 746.4**	**355.8**	**409.5**	**449.4**	**562.1**	**614.2**
G20 countries excl. European Union	**145.0**	**180.3**	**221.1**	**330.6**	**320.5**	**-4.2**	**32.0**	**11.0**	**8.9**	**24.5**
G20 OECD countries	**120.8**	**99.2**	**144.3**	**272.4**	**275.4**	**-15.2**	**2.0**	**4.6**	**-4.2**	**3.2**
G20 Non-OECD countries	**24.2**	**81.1**	**76.8**	**58.1**	**45.2**	**11.0**	**29.9**	**6.4**	**13.1**	**21.4**
MENA countries	**0.3**	**0.7**	**4.4**	**6.6**	**3.6**	**0.1**	**0.5**	**-0.9**	**1.8**	**1.5**
ASEAN countries	**6.2**	**6.7**	**16.2**	**33.5**	**-9.7**	**0.2**	**0.1**	**0.1**	**0.3**	**0.4**

- Nil; .. Not available; c Confidential data; d Secondary Confidentiality

Note: Detailed metadata at: *http://stats.oecd.org/OECDStat_Metadata/ShowMetadata.ashx?Dataset=FDI_CTRY_IND_SUMM.*

Source: *OECD International Direct Investment Statistics (database): https://doi.org/10.1787/idi-data-en*

ESTONIA

Table 4. Foreign direct investment flows by industrial sector

Million US dollars

	Inward					Outward				
	2015	2016	2017	2018	2019	2015	2016	2017	2018	2019
All FDI activities	**35.5**	**1 058.4**	**1 938.3**	**1 496.8**	**3 091.2**	**182.1**	**486.5**	**879.1**	**58.0**	**1 987.2**
Agriculture, forestry and fishing	**26.0**	**28.1**	**31.5**	**31.7**	**30.4**	**-0.4**	**4.2**	**2.9**	**21.0**	**3.1**
Mining and quarrying	**-4.3**	**-3.4**	**-3.2**	**4.1**	**4.8**	**-150.0**	**29.6**	**-51.3**	**1.5**	**-0.2**
Extraction activities	0.0	0.4	0.1	0.1	0.1	-150.1	29.6	-49.9	1.6	.. c
Manufacturing	**167.1**	**215.6**	**858.6**	**241.2**	**254.2**	**217.1**	**164.5**	**586.6**	**224.4**	**103.6**
of which:										
Food products, beverages and tobacco	59.3	11.3	62.5	59.8	-13.5	46.5	8.2	-35.7	1.2	-14.6
Textiles, wood and paper products; printing	22.4	96.0	28.1	123.9	39.9	148.9	5.3	-31.8	76.8	22.2
Chemical, rubber, plastic, non-metallic mineral products	26.9	-77.6	-15.1	40.3	30.4	-7.6	2.5	-2.4	18.0	-0.3
Metal and machinery products, except electrical equipment	-13.3	-0.5	72.3	2.7	135.0	6.9	10.2	1.5	20.3	-5.8
Motor vehicles, trailers, semi-trailers, other transport equipment	30.9	88.5	705.5	23.6	43.2	12.2	112.0	649.5	50.8	37.8
Other manufacturing	41.1	97.8	5.2	-9.2	19.1	10.3	26.2	5.5	57.4	64.3
Electricity, gas, steam and air conditioning supply	**-51.6**	**-28.4**	**5.0**	**9.5**	**6.6**	**22.0**	**38.1**	**10.9**	**9.4**	**136.4**
Water supply; sewerage, waste management and remediation activities	**-11.3**	**-2.0**	**19.0**	**5.7**	**-0.4**	**.. c**	**.. c**	**.. c**	**.. c**	**0.8**
Construction	**17.6**	**45.2**	**-3.6**	**-58.0**	**59.5**	**14.8**	**-54.7**	**31.9**	**32.2**	**20.9**
Services	**-108.1**	**803.3**	**1 031.0**	**1 262.7**	**2 736.3**	**78.0**	**281.2**	**272.8**	**-264.9**	**1 701.2**
Wholesale and retail trade; repair of motor vehicles and motorcycles	194.3	182.3	345.7	211.1	354.0	23.0	39.8	40.0	136.9	6.1
Transportation and storage	26.7	2.0	-2.2	158.5	72.1	43.6	11.2	-53.6	29.6	8.0
Accommodation and food service activities	1.6	9.0	2.6	0.1	7.8	-1.8	-1.8	25.5	9.5	4.0
Information and communication	22.3	70.5	143.2	-18.8	212.3	3.7	-15.0	32.6	43.8	-220.5
Financial and insurance activities	-427.4	427.6	353.1	1 171.8	1 684.4	-109.2	15.4	290.3	111.9	1 731.5
Activities of holding companies	5.4	82.5	-10.7	447.3	36.8	-59.7	-16.1	104.5	-2.0	31.1
Real estate activities	24.9	14.9	-24.9	-30.4	186.4	109.0	93.5	72.4	4.9	181.6
Professional, scientific and technical activities	-34.1	-12.7	64.2	399.6	122.7	24.1	37.6	-6.5	-607.2	2.4
Administrative and support service activities	72.8	104.9	140.2	-637.1	78.7	-56.6	56.5	-114.5	-25.0	-10.9
Public administration; activities of households and of extraterritorial organisations	-	-	-	-	-	-	-	.. c	.. c	.. c
Education	1.1	1.7	1.5	0.3	5.4	0.1	.. c	0.9	.. c	1.6
Human health and social work activities	-1.3	-2.9	-0.1	-0.9	2.4	3.4	-0.1	-0.3	.. c	0.4
Arts, entertainment and recreation	5.4	2.2	4.9	5.8	6.9	34.0	20.6	6.1	19.5	-3.6
Other services	5.5	3.7	2.8	2.7	3.2	4.7	23.5	-19.6	12.3	0.7
Not allocated and confidential	**0.0**	**0.0**	**0.0**	**0.0**	**0.0**	**.. c**	**.. c**	**.. c**	**.. c**	**21.4**
Private real estate activities	-	-	-	-	-	-	-	-	-	-

- Nil; c Confidential data

Note: Detailed metadata at: *http://stats.oecd.org/OECDStat_Metadata/ShowMetadata.ashx?Dataset=FDI_CTRY_IND_SUMM.*

Source: *OECD International Direct Investment Statistics (database): https://doi.org/10.1787/idi-data-en*

Table 5. Foreign direct investment positions by industrial sector
At year end

Million US dollars

	Inward					Outward				
	2015	2016	2017	2018	2019	2015	2016	2017	2018	2019
All FDI activities	**18 956.5**	**19 658.5**	**24 022.6**	**25 095.9**	**27 924.2**	**6 038.9**	**6 298.5**	**7 805.1**	**7 962.7**	**10 012.8**
Agriculture, forestry and fishing	**381.5**	**367.2**	**427.4**	**523.2**	**587.2**	**14.2**	**21.6**	**36.8**	**53.3**	**60.7**
Mining and quarrying	**81.6**	**76.6**	**80.9**	**88.7**	**86.8**	**76.1**	**101.6**	**109.5**	**105.7**	**102.5**
Extraction activities	0.1	0.5	0.5	0.6	1.0	69.9	97.2	105.9	102.4	99.2
Manufacturing	**2 599.9**	**2 662.1**	**3 149.8**	**3 196.7**	**3 439.9**	**830.0**	**1 009.0**	**1 217.3**	**1 380.5**	**1 441.2**
of which:										
Food products, beverages and tobacco	584.7	572.9	690.9	719.4	706.4	88.1	111.9	102.3	93.1	88.9
Textiles, wood and paper products; printing	656.8	688.8	812.6	869.6	950.0	303.5	296.3	305.9	365.4	370.9
Chemical, rubber, plastic, non-metallic mineral products	381.2	287.1	331.6	352.7	336.7	103.6	110.3	111.3	119.4	113.0
Metal and machinery products, except electrical equipment	332.6	305.9	396.6	353.2	473.2	57.0	89.5	59.2	87.7	84.5
Motor vehicles, trailers, semi-trailers, other transport equipment	115.1	195.2	230.1	241.0	279.3	226.8	328.1	556.9	413.2	449.0
Other manufacturing	529.5	612.3	687.9	660.8	694.2	50.9	72.9	81.7	301.7	334.9
Electricity, gas, steam and air conditioning supply	**210.7**	**167.2**	**181.4**	**190.0**	**192.7**	**118.1**	**172.2**	**168.7**	**165.8**	**310.6**
Water supply; sewerage, waste management and remediation activities	**141.6**	**134.9**	**140.2**	**126.1**	**122.1**	**.. c**	**.. c**	**.. c**	**3.0**	**.. c**
Construction	**173.3**	**202.8**	**305.8**	**239.1**	**277.4**	**289.5**	**258.6**	**379.6**	**424.5**	**446.9**
Services	**14 858.1**	**15 526.1**	**19 141.3**	**20 000.3**	**22 531.0**	**4 237.9**	**4 231.9**	**5 332.9**	**5 209.9**	**7 029.9**
Wholesale and retail trade; repair of motor vehicles and motorcycles	2 596.9	2 498.6	3 018.3	2 910.3	3 119.4	485.2	504.1	663.5	747.6	768.9
Transportation and storage	991.9	927.4	989.8	1 098.6	961.4	264.5	238.9	201.2	200.6	201.8
Accommodation and food service activities	111.0	108.9	134.5	119.4	125.7	85.6	91.5	84.7	86.7	91.8
Information and communication	670.2	689.9	971.8	1 257.7	1 403.1	76.1	87.5	111.8	145.5	188.9
Financial and insurance activities	4 900.6	5 427.3	6 939.8	7 769.0	9 551.3	947.8	845.8	1 425.1	1 167.4	2 777.3
Activities of holding companies	638.6	1 058.9	1 072.3	1 075.0	1 341.6	169.5	137.3	261.1	177.4	265.9
Real estate activities	3 417.7	3 514.1	4 315.0	4 517.7	5 166.4	774.2	868.2	1 206.6	1 313.8	1 505.6
Professional, scientific and technical activities	1 430.4	1 614.2	1 779.7	1 597.5	1 461.8	116.2	149.9	142.6	110.7	98.3
Administrative and support service activities	666.7	674.1	890.6	638.8	632.4	1 326.4	1 332.8	1 383.1	1 296.7	1 258.7
Public administration; activities of households and of extraterritorial organisations	-	-	-	-	-	-	-	.. c	.. c	.. c
Education	2.0	3.5	6.2	4.2	9.2	0.3	0.3	1.8	.. c	3.9
Human health and social work activities	29.5	28.9	33.8	32.4	30.8	.. c	.. c	.. c	.. c	.. c
Arts, entertainment and recreation	25.3	25.5	44.1	43.1	51.2	153.9	78.0	94.5	112.4	106.4
Other services	15.8	13.7	17.6	11.5	18.3	5.9	30.9	13.6	24.0	24.8
Not allocated and confidential	**470.9**	**521.6**	**595.8**	**731.7**	**704.2**	**.. c**	**.. c**	**.. c**	**620.0**	**.. c**
Private real estate activities	-	-	-	-	-	-	-	-	-	-

- Nil; c Confidential data

Note: Detailed metadata at: *http://stats.oecd.org/OECDStat_Metadata/ShowMetadata.ashx?Dataset=FDI_CTRY_IND_SUMM.*

Source: *OECD International Direct Investment Statistics (database)*: *https://doi.org/10.1787/idi-data-en*

ESTONIA

Table 6. Foreign direct investment income by industrial sector

Million US dollars

	Inward					Outward				
	2015	2016	2017	2018	2019	2015	2016	2017	2018	2019
All FDI activities	**1 385.0**	**1 591.0**	**1 736.6**	**1 920.8**	**1 954.6**	**364.5**	**492.4**	**485.4**	**698.3**	**690.8**
Agriculture, forestry and fishing	**22.5**	**9.3**	**13.3**	**27.9**	**33.2**	**-0.3**	**0.3**	**-0.5**	**2.5**	**2.1**
Mining and quarrying	**3.3**	**3.6**	**6.9**	**9.0**	**5.4**	**.. c**	**29.7**	**1.4**	**0.1**	**.. c**
Extraction activities	0.0	0.5	0.1	0.1	0.1	.. c	.. c	1.2	0.2	.. c
Manufacturing	**255.3**	**298.2**	**315.7**	**308.4**	**230.2**	**16.3**	**49.3**	**73.9**	**133.0**	**142.0**
of which:										
Food products, beverages and tobacco	38.2	44.0	56.3	54.4	49.4	0.6	1.8	2.7	2.9	-4.2
Textiles, wood and paper products; printing	70.4	80.5	69.6	78.8	41.7	10.4	26.8	23.3	19.4	25.8
Chemical, rubber, plastic, non-metallic mineral products	28.9	42.8	31.0	47.2	13.6	-16.9	-2.8	-3.9	-0.4	-2.9
Metal and machinery products, except electrical equipment	35.1	43.2	50.7	38.8	43.5	1.7	-1.0	1.1	7.8	0.1
Motor vehicles, trailers, semi-trailers, other transport equipment	28.4	15.2	47.9	23.7	24.0	16.7	13.9	41.4	47.7	14.1
Other manufacturing	54.4	72.4	60.1	65.5	58.0	3.8	10.5	9.2	55.6	109.1
Electricity, gas, steam and air conditioning supply	**8.4**	**17.6**	**14.3**	**16.6**	**10.8**	**12.0**	**10.0**	**9.7**	**15.7**	**32.3**
Water supply; sewerage, waste management and remediation activities	**8.1**	**13.7**	**15.4**	**11.0**	**6.2**	**.. c**	**.. c**	**.. c**	**.. c**	**1.1**
Construction	**-1.9**	**32.4**	**-3.1**	**4.3**	**15.9**	**31.6**	**18.5**	**16.8**	**15.2**	**22.5**
Services	**1 089.3**	**1 216.3**	**1 374.2**	**1 543.6**	**1 653.0**	**288.1**	**357.8**	**363.5**	**508.6**	**463.5**
Wholesale and retail trade; repair of motor vehicles and motorcycles	234.4	284.8	331.2	328.3	333.1	29.1	61.6	43.2	113.5	44.5
Transportation and storage	83.3	59.5	52.9	78.2	100.4	-23.8	-19.8	-5.8	2.3	-0.3
Accommodation and food service activities	10.8	14.3	16.4	16.1	13.9	-1.4	-3.6	-3.0	-0.2	-0.8
Information and communication	111.5	79.6	101.3	101.7	39.7	2.2	2.3	11.7	13.3	10.3
Financial and insurance activities	360.6	522.2	502.6	627.8	757.3	101.8	113.5	112.6	168.7	232.1
Activities of holding companies	35.6	79.0	35.4	82.5	136.4	2.2	29.3	4.6	9.4	4.1
Real estate activities	160.3	140.7	147.6	165.7	184.6	32.0	38.0	64.4	79.3	64.2
Professional, scientific and technical activities	74.6	47.5	124.5	115.3	113.4	13.3	13.9	18.3	1.4	9.2
Administrative and support service activities	50.3	60.0	90.2	104.6	90.8	92.7	106.0	94.8	100.6	73.4
Public administration; activities of households and of extraterritorial organisations	-	-	-	-	-	-	-	.. c	.. c	.. c
Education	0.3	1.1	1.4	0.1	0.4	.. c	.. c	.. c	.. c	0.1
Human health and social work activities	2.1	3.8	3.4	5.7	6.8	.. c	.. c	.. c	.. c	.. c
Arts, entertainment and recreation	-4.2	-1.7	-1.9	-1.5	9.8	42.5	45.5	27.4	29.4	30.3
Other services	5.2	4.5	4.4	1.6	2.8	0.0	0.0	0.1	0.0	.. c
Not allocated and confidential	**-**	**0.0**	**0.0**	**0.0**	**0.0**	**.. c**	**.. c**	**.. c**	**.. c**	**.. c**
Private real estate activities	**-**	**-**	**-**	**-**	**-**	**-**	**-**	**-**	**-**	**-**

- Nil; c Confidential data

Note: Detailed metadata at: *http://stats.oecd.org/OECDStat_Metadata/ShowMetadata.ashx?Dataset=FDI_CTRY_IND_SUMM.*

Source: *OECD International Direct Investment Statistics (database): https://doi.org/10.1787/idi-data-en*

FINLAND

Table 1. Foreign direct investment flows by country

Million US dollars

	Inward					Outward				
	2015	2016	2017	2018	2019	2015	2016	2017	2018	2019
WORLD	**2 108.7**	**8 573.5**	**2 857.6**	**-2 170.4**	**13 612.4**	**-16 079.9**	**24 251.9**	**-572.7**	**12 035.9**	**4 864.0**
OECD COUNTRIES	**2 396.0**	**8 751.5**	**2 567.9**	**-3 982.1**	**8 663.4**	**-13 594.0**	**22 307.9**	**-3 970.2**	**11 716.0**	**3 158.0**
Australia	-1.1	-	-4.5	11.8	1.1	179.7	-88.5	-137.5	147.5	120.9
Austria	-259.6	112.8	-16.9	246.7	414.2	42.2	-4.4	-65.4	145.2	76.1
Belgium	158.6	149.3	-209.7	165.2	-223.9	-2 326.1	778.5	-3 038.0	.. d	-181.4
Canada	.. d	-1 132.4	-14.7	-33.0	.. d	-1 023.8	134.9	-359.6	1 026.8	120.9
Chile	-3.3	-	-21.4	20.1	-3.4	.. d	4.4	-11.3	128.6	23.5
Czech Republic	-3.3	17.7	20.3	-10.6	-4.5	-4.4	25.4	58.6	73.2	-4.5
Denmark	-871.9	42.0	418.2	500.4	-117.5	97.6	974.2	440.8	-132.2	-433.2
Estonia	-14.4	.. d	684.3	100.3	-38.1	33.3	665.7	822.9	565.3	245.2
Finland	-	-	-	-	-	-	-	-	-	-
France	-3.3	.. d	243.5	.. d	568.7	213.0	13 415.9	-11 932.1	-1 037.4	-776.9
Germany	897.4	556.2	372.0	260.8	413.1	790.9	-768.6	-466.7	-154.6	-99.6
Greece	-	-	1.1	-1.2	.. d	2.2	-3.3	55.2	-4.7	-9.0
Hungary	-	5.5	4.5	-20.1	-22.4	-28.8	1.1	10.1	11.8	-43.7
Iceland	12.2	.. d	-	.. d	.. d	-5.5	-1.1	-	-1.2	-
Ireland	230.7	-23.2	85.7	-439.0	.. d	-195.2	-1 257.3	582.8	1 811.6	996.3
Israel	298.4	6.6	40.6	-53.1	.. d	.. c	3.3	25.9	24.8	.. d
Italy	55.5	.. d	21.4	.. d	60.5	494.7	52.0	-450.9	516.9	38.1
Japan	309.5	-3 132.8	-5.6	416.6	-24.6	-15.5	.. d	329.2	-82.6	268.7
Korea	12.2	-	7.9	.. d	-2.2	26.6	-19.9	-27.1	21.2	.. d
Latvia	-1.1	-24.3	7.9	11.8	1.1	-10.0	7.7	18.0	33.0	47.0
Lithuania	-2.2	-6.6	-3.4	-2.4	3.4	10.0	61.9	119.5	49.6	-16.8
Luxembourg	-3 101.5	8 525.9	2 944.4	-180.6	2 303.8	457.0	1 306.0	-240.1	67.3	312.3
Mexico	.. d	-7.7	2.3	-1.2	-1.1	-1.1	-87.4	108.2	.. d	-202.6
Netherlands	867.4	639.2	1 940.0	-2 133.8	366.1	-12 035.5	4 202.1	14 293.8	-237.2	53.7
New Zealand	.. c	-	3.4	-3.5	-	-	8.8	-48.5	24.8	26.9
Norway	479.2	398.1	175.9	420.2	3 445.7	2 970.6	-71.9	-262.7	548.8	1 400.4
Poland	17.7	55.3	-4.5	5.9	-24.6	-82.1	140.4	102.6	-113.3	-14.6
Portugal	-	6.6	-5.6	-1.2	-32.5	7.8	3.3	-5.6	72.0	-19.0
Slovak Republic	.. c	47.6	6.8	-49.6	3.4	20.0	6.6	-15.8	-29.5	31.3
Slovenia	-	-	-	-	.. d	-1.1	-4.4	7.9	2.4	1.1
Spain	-2.2	15.5	-30.4	47.2	22.4	13.3	.. d	237.9	24.8	47.0
Sweden	2 361.6	656.9	-2 561.2	-3 461.6	3 192.7	-5 355.5	3 347.3	385.5	2 744.0	1 635.5
Switzerland	-46.6	607.1	-268.3	400.1	-11.2	-2 619.0	.. d	-51.9	51.9	106.3
Turkey	24.4	-	2.3	8.3	-19.0	3 161.4	.. d	80.0	.. d	.. d
United Kingdom	261.8	400.3	-66.5	-770.7	645.9	487.0	-765.2	588.4	138.1	448.9
United States	274.0	755.3	-1 206.2	436.7	.. d	1 062.7	1 539.3	-5 009.6	2 939.9	-1 568.3
EUROPE	**489.2**	**12 383.1**	**3 990.5**	**-3 396.7**	**9 553.3**	**-13 874.7**	**21 212.0**	**1 680.8**	**7 115.5**	**3 782.6**
Bulgaria	-	-	-	-	-	1.1	-1.1	2.3	.. d	5.6
Croatia	-	-	-	-	-	.. d	-2.2	1.1	5.9	-6.7
Cyprus	-102.1	12.2	22.5	1 345.5	494.8	17.7	4.4	1.1	1.2	2.2
Malta	.. c	.. d	-3.4	11.8	.. d	.. c	.. d	16.9	-2.4	-23.5
Romania	-3.3	.. d	-1.1	-2.4	2.2	-10.0	2.2	-32.7	24.8	30.2
Russian Federation	-520.2	376.0	219.8	74.4	.. d	126.5	176.9	237.9	112.1	-85.1
Ukraine	-	-	-	1.2	-	-13.3	-36.5	9.0	.. d	.. d
AFRICA	**10.0**	**35.4**	**-41.7**	**-3.5**	**.. d**	**16.6**	**-6.6**	**110.5**	**36.6**	**190.3**
Northern Africa	-	-	-	-2.4	-1.1	1.1	-2.2	34.9	21.2	105.2
Algeria	-	-	-	-	-	-	-	-	-	-2.2
Egypt	-	-	-	-3.5	1.1	-1.1	-	.. d	16.5	.. d
Libya	-	-	-	-	-	-	-	-	-	-
Morocco	-	-	-	-	-1.1	2.2	-2.2	3.4	9.4	.. d
Tunisia	-	-	-	-	-	-	-	.. d	-2.4	3.4
Other African countries	10.0	35.4	-40.6	-1.2	.. d	14.4	-4.4	74.4	13.0	84.0
Nigeria	-	-	-	-	-	-1.1	-1.1	3.4	22.4	10.1
South Africa	.. d	1.1	-1.1	-2.4	-6.7	-	2.2	54.1	1.2	52.6
AMERICA	**920.7**	**-629.2**	**-1 136.3**	**732.9**	**.. d**	**-2 585.7**	**3 133.9**	**-3 520.5**	**4 357.4**	**-1 201.2**
Northern America	722.1	-377.1	.. d	403.6	-330.2	37.7	1 674.2	-5 368.1	3 966.7	-1 447.4
Central America and Caribbean countries	210.8	-247.7	.. d	310.4	-265.3	-2 567.9	1 618.9	1 720.2	376.5	-195.9
Bahamas	-	-	.. d	24.8	23.5	.. d	-	-	-	-
Bermuda	.. c	.. d	.. d	.. d	.. d	.. c	.. d	.. d	2.4	-1.1
Cayman Islands	.. c	.. d	.. d	.. d	.. d	-	-	-	-	-
Costa Rica	-	-	-	-	-	-	-	2.3	-1.2	-1.1
El Salvador	-	-	-	-	-	-	-	-1.1	-	-
Guatemala	-	-	-	-	-	-	-	-3.4	-1.2	2.2
Honduras	-	-	-	-	-	3.3	4.4	1.1	.. d	-
Nicaragua	-	-	-	-	-	-	-	-	-	-
Panama	-	-	-	-	-	1.1	-4.4	-2.3	-	4.5
Virgin Islands, U.S.	-	-	-	-	-	-	-	-	-	-
South America	-11.1	-4.4	-13.5	20.1	3.4	-55.5	-159.2	126.3	16.5	439.9
Argentina	.. d	-10.0	9.0	-1.2	-	-2.2	-3.3	18.0	-2.4	-10.1
Bolivia	-	-	-	-	-	-	-	1.1	-	-1.1
Brazil	-8.9	-	3.4	-	2.2	-112.0	-282.0	98.1	100.3	209.3
Colombia	-	-	-	-	-1.1	-	-	19.2	72.0	-33.6
Ecuador	-	-	-	-	-	.. c	.. d	-5.6	-1.2	11.2
Paraguay	-	-	-	-	-	-	-	2.3	-	-
Peru	.. d	-	-1.1	-1.2	2.2	5.5	-2.2	-6.8	20.1	-14.6
Uruguay	-	4.4	-3.4	1.2	3.4	26.6	133.8	14.7	-304.5	254.1
Venezuela	-	-	-	-	-	-	-	-	-1.2	-

Table 1. Foreign direct investment flows by country *(cont.)*

Million US dollars

	Inward					Outward				
	2015	2016	2017	2018	2019	2015	2016	2017	2018	2019
ASIA	**651.1**	**-3 157.1**	**48.5**	**491.0**	**4 621.1**	**184.1**	**-7.7**	**1 342.6**	**350.5**	**1 944.5**
Near and Middle East	294.0	-46.4	50.7	-15.3	.. d	232.9	146.0	136.4	33.0	4.5
Gulf Arabian countries	-4.4	-53.1	9.0	36.6	5.6	215.2	134.9	118.4	7.1	-29.1
Kuwait	-	-	-	1.2	-	-	-	-2.3	-1.2	-2.2
Qatar	-	-	-2.3	3.5	-	2.2	3.3	13.5	3.5	-22.4
Saudi Arabia	-4.4	-54.2	21.4	30.7	-	25.5	27.6	87.9	-77.9	-39.2
United Arab Emirates	-1.1	1.1	-9.0	3.5	5.6	159.7	14.4	-82.3	63.7	-67.2
Other Near and Middle East	298.4	6.6	40.6	-53.1	.. d	17.7	10.0	18.0	24.8	34.7
Jordan	-	-	-	-	-	-	-	-	-2.4	2.2
Other Asian countries	358.3	-3 109.6	-2.3	507.5	.. d	-49.9	-153.7	1 207.3	319.8	1 937.8
China	21.1	8.8	-46.2	5.9	.. d	-539.1	109.5	213.1	68.5	26.9
Hong Kong, China	.. c	4.4	.. d	28.3	403.0	112.0	-131.6	10.1	-51.9	470.2
India	3.3	13.3	11.3	-10.6	.. d	88.7	-2.2	381.0	62.6	-73.9
Indonesia	-	-	-1.1	-10.6	-	43.3	40.9	-15.8	115.7	-73.9
Iran, Islamic Republic of	-	-	-	-	-	.. c	.. d	19.2	-38.9	14.6
Malaysia	-	1.1	-2.3	-1.2	2.2	6.7	-22.1	32.7	4.7	39.2
Philippines	-	-	-1.1	-	-	3.3	-8.8	.. d	1.2	-5.6
Singapore	-3.3	-10.0	-13.5	47.2	-31.3	206.3	-19.9	174.7	2.4	1 120.6
Chinese Taipei	.. d	-1.1	1.1	-3.5	1.1	.. c	-36.5	7.9	-3.5	-5.6
Thailand	-	-	-2.3	1.2	-2.2	14.4	-	95.8	236.0	-206.0
Viet Nam	-	-	-	-	-	-	-4.4	.. d	4.7	-9.0
AUSTRALIA, OCEANIA AND POLAR REGIONS	**-4.4**	**-**	**-2.3**	**8.3**	**1.1**	**180.8**	**-77.4**	**-187.1**	**175.9**	**148.9**
WORLD unallocated and confidential	**42.2**	**-58.6**	**-1.1**	**-2.4**	**.. d**	**-1.1**	**-2.2**	**1.1**	**-**	**-1.1**
European Union (EU28)	**553.5**	**11 098.1**	**3 865.4**	**-4 286.6**	**6 176.0**	**-17 492.0**	**22 458.3**	**1 501.5**	**6 609.2**	**2 343.0**
G20 countries excl. European Union	**1 768.2**	**-2 085.6**	**-430.6**	**540.5**	**5 610.7**	**5 005.0**	**13 578.5**	**-16 203.4**	**4 206.3**	**-1 147.4**
G20 OECD countries	**2 276.2**	**-2 422.9**	**-645.9**	**454.4**	**1 312.0**	**5 375.5**	**13 508.8**	**-17 277.6**	**3 825.1**	**-1 154.1**
G20 Non-OECD countries	**-508.0**	**336.2**	**216.4**	**86.2**	**4 300.9**	**-369.4**	**70.8**	**1 074.3**	**380.0**	**6.7**
MENA countries	**-4.4**	**-53.1**	**9.0**	**34.2**	**4.5**	**218.5**	**134.9**	**147.7**	**28.3**	**79.5**
ASEAN countries	**-3.3**	**-8.8**	**-19.2**	**36.6**	**-31.3**	**272.9**	**-17.7**	**297.6**	**363.5**	**862.0**

- Nil; .. Not available; c Confidential data; d Secondary Confidentiality

Note: Detailed metadata at: *http://stats.oecd.org/OECDStat_Metadata/ShowMetadata.ashx?Dataset=FDI_CTRY_IND_SUMM.*

Source: *OECD International Direct Investment Statistics (database): https://doi.org/10.1787/idi-data-en*

Table 2. Foreign direct investment positions by country

At year end

Million US dollars

	Inward					Outward				
	2015	2016	2017	2018	2019	2015	2016	2017	2018	2019
WORLD	**81 660.3**	**79 930.4**	**89 986.8**	**72 068.9**	**85 816.7**	**94 610.8**	**108 938.5**	**124 908.9**	**128 845.9**	**146 462.6**
OECD COUNTRIES	**77 404.5**	**68 168.0**	**76 454.8**	**60 545.0**	**68 179.1**	**92 311.4**	**104 142.5**	**115 754.4**	**119 009.6**	**134 262.0**
Australia	.. c	.. c	.. c	.. d	.. c	423.5	431.1	411.4	454.5	569.5
Austria	-66.4	-50.6	-80.4	40.1	-9.0	98.0	121.2	-32.4	3.4	120.2
Belgium	100.2	170.8	155.9	131.7	434.7	3 240.1	3 350.9	1 650.3	3 284.9	1 929.9
Canada	2 536.7	1 085.7	1 256.9	2 545.2	2 500.6	1 413.2	1 634.9	1 129.8	1 625.8	1 849.0
Chile	-	-	-	-	-	144.8	148.6	217.1	282.8	247.1
Czech Republic	-	.. c	.. c	.. c	.. c	176.4	161.3	241.1	301.1	313.4
Denmark	4 782.8	5 656.2	6 622.7	3 666.1	3 605.9	1 502.5	2 076.5	3 087.1	7 410.1	7 390.5
Estonia	19.6	27.4	115.1	87.0	269.6	2 081.7	2 638.3	3 403.7	4 593.5	4 159.7
Finland	6 561.8	4 711.7	3 192.6	-1 260.6	2 288.3	-	-	-	-	-
France	1 641.8	1 687.6	2 094.0	2 326.5	3 225.1	1 702.8	14 709.6	3 811.5	2 608.2	1 636.7
Germany	3 051.7	2 997.8	7 569.0	8 115.4	7 902.7	2 086.0	2 151.4	2 367.5	2 779.9	2 660.1
Greece	-	-	-	-	-	.. d	9.5	52.8	46.9	33.7
Hungary	-	-	-	-	-	31.6	36.9	33.6	43.5	-10.1
Iceland	.. c	.. c	.. c	.. c	.. c	.. c	.. d	2.4	6.9	2.2
Ireland	184.0	1 373.5	1 737.8	2 066.6	1 858.0	12 131.7	9 971.5	12 187.6	12 812.0	23 588.0
Israel	.. c	.. c	.. c	.. c	.. c	.. c	.. c	166.7	179.8	68.5
Italy	634.7	937.1	1 077.0	1 199.9	1 189.6	292.9	332.0	-10.8	414.5	606.6
Japan	2 059.9	1 467.3	2 019.7	950.3	1 159.3	-37.0	-43.2	311.8	224.4	492.0
Korea	-	-	.. c	.. c	.. c	130.6	109.6	195.5	158.0	561.7
Latvia	-	-	.. c	-	-	186.2	258.2	221.9	148.8	217.9
Lithuania	-	-	-	-	-	385.4	286.7	458.1	454.5	474.1
Luxembourg	2 732.7	2 330.6	2 807.6	2 593.3	2 808.4	1 623.3	2 687.9	2 369.9	2 325.4	2 345.5
Mexico	-	-	-	-	-	83.8	74.8	181.1	458.0	150.5
Netherlands	9 304.3	8 122.7	4 317.6	4 222.6	3 298.1	13 921.6	19 254.8	37 856.8	33 524.2	35 577.4
New Zealand	.. d	-	.. c	.. c	-	17.4	.. d	-21.6	27.5	50.6
Norway	1 354.4	971.9	1 314.5	1 483.9	5 257.2	2 409.4	2 452.8	2 203.2	5 518.7	7 393.8
Poland	.. c	.. c	.. c	.. c	.. c	1 387.0	1 098.3	1 593.9	1 384.2	1 390.7
Portugal	.. c	.. c	.. c	.. c	.. c	17.4	40.1	19.2	90.5	50.6
Slovak Republic	-	-	-	-	-	180.7	165.5	103.1	38.9	204.4
Slovenia	-	-	-	-	-	9.8	6.3	14.4	37.8	40.4
Spain	424.6	308.8	381.4	420.2	426.9	906.9	940.2	1 290.5	1 229.7	1 239.0
Sweden	33 199.8	29 237.9	27 312.3	17 534.9	17 697.1	31 497.0	29 774.4	32 377.1	25 269.1	28 840.7
Switzerland	1 168.2	879.1	1 156.2	967.5	1 222.2	1 436.0	-483.8	596.1	486.6	694.2
Turkey	.. d	.. c	.. c	.. c	-	2 798.0	1 997.5	2 432.2	1 835.4	1 342.4
United Kingdom	740.3	746.3	1 101.0	2 576.1	2 490.5	2 154.6	818.0	3 334.1	3 740.6	4 162.0
United States	6 792.6	5 332.6	10 308.2	9 466.5	9 165.4	8 310.3	7 051.8	1 958.5	5 210.7	3 868.8
EUROPE	**68 972.2**	**58 389.4**	**60 094.7**	**50 221.0**	**57 274.8**	**85 146.4**	**98 504.3**	**115 503.7**	**114 029.1**	**130 730.2**
Bulgaria	-	-	-	-	-	15.2	6.3	9.6	17.2	22.5
Croatia	-	-	-	-	-	.. d	-	2.4	8.0	1.1
Cyprus	13.1	.. c	.. c	33.2	.. c	-1.1	1.1	7.2	8.0	9.0
Malta	.. c	.. c	.. c	.. c	-	344.0	360.5	427.0	405.3	386.4
Romania	-	-	-	-	-	84.9	83.3	58.8	58.4	89.9
Russian Federation	1 408.8	.. d	1 713.8	1 598.4	1 594.0	2 297.2	2 886.1	2 852.0	2 852.1	3 511.6
Ukraine	-	-	-	-	-	76.2	150.7	194.3	63.0	60.7
AFRICA	**178.6**	**.. c**	**.. d**	**71.0**	**.. d**	**149.2**	**160.2**	**386.2**	**415.6**	**571.8**
Northern Africa	-	-	-	-	-	3.3	5.3	42.0	74.4	129.2
Algeria	-	-	-	-	-	-	-	1.2	11.5	10.1
Egypt	-	-	-	-	-	-	-	26.4	42.4	94.4
Libya	-	-	-	-	-	-	-	-	-	-
Morocco	-	-	-	-	-	3.3	5.3	12.0	19.5	20.2
Tunisia	-	-	-	-	-	-	-	2.4	2.3	5.6
Other African countries	178.6	.. c	115.1	71.0	137.0	147.0	154.9	343.0	340.1	442.6
Nigeria	-	-	-	-	-	-1.1	-1.1	10.8	32.1	40.4
South Africa	178.6	.. c	.. c	.. c	.. c	72.9	69.6	203.9	185.5	255.0
AMERICA	**9 560.2**	**6 740.8**	**14 173.7**	**13 813.8**	**14 098.0**	**6 840.5**	**7 618.8**	**3 749.1**	**8 668.4**	**7 400.6**
Northern America	9 329.3	6 418.3	11 566.3	12 010.5	11 665.9	9 723.5	8 686.6	3 088.3	6 836.5	5 717.8
Central America and Caribbean countries	230.8	322.5	2 607.3	1 803.3	2 432.0	-3 436.0	-1 961.6	-466.5	514.1	203.3
Bahamas	-	-	-	.. c	.. c	.. c	2.1	.. c	-	-
Bermuda	.. d	.. d	104.3	.. c	.. c	.. c	-2 085.0	-689.6	35.5	.. c
Cayman Islands	.. c	.. c	2 503.0	1 670.5	1 612.0	-	-	-	-	-
Costa Rica	-	-	-	-	-	-	-	1.2	-1.1	-2.2
El Salvador	-	-	-	-	-	-	-	-1.2	-	-
Guatemala	-	-	-	-	-	-	-	-3.6	-4.6	-1.1
Honduras	-	-	-	-	-	.. c	.. c	.. c	.. c	.. c
Nicaragua	-	-	-	-	-	-	-	-	-	-
Panama	-	-	-	-	-	.. d	4.2	21.6	9.2	14.6
Virgin Islands, U.S.	-	-	-	-	-	-	-	-	-	-
South America	-	-	-	-	-	552.0	894.9	1 127.4	1 317.8	1 478.3
Argentina	-	-	-	-	-	16.3	12.6	36.0	29.8	19.1
Bolivia	-	-	-	-	-	-	-	1.2	1.1	-1.1
Brazil	-	-	-	-	-	348.4	455.4	681.2	863.3	787.5
Colombia	-	-	-	-	-	-	.. c	32.4	96.2	61.8
Ecuador	-	-	-	-	-	25.0	16.9	16.8	20.6	31.5
Paraguay	-	-	-	-	-	-	-	1.2	-	-
Peru	-	-	-	-	-	45.7	44.3	64.8	85.9	68.5
Uruguay	-	-	-	-	-	-27.2	214.0	78.0	-64.1	259.5
Venezuela	-	-	-	-	-	-	.. d	1.2	-1.1	-

FINLAND

Table 2. Foreign direct investment positions by country *(cont.)*

At year end

Million US dollars

	Inward					Outward				
	2015	2016	2017	2018	2019	2015	2016	2017	2018	2019
ASIA	**2 921.1**	**9 828.2**	**12 374.7**	**9 195.1**	**12 004.0**	**2 028.3**	**2 187.2**	**4 870.5**	**5 239.3**	**7 125.4**
Near and Middle East	548.7	558.7	2 395.1	1 788.4	1 817.6	362.5	540.7	766.4	746.5	608.9
Gulf Arabian countries	.. d	.. d	.. d	.. d	.. d	227.5	395.3	591.3	556.4	529.1
Kuwait	-	-	-	-	-	-	-	-2.4	-3.4	-5.6
Qatar	-	-	-	-	-	5.4	9.5	26.4	26.3	2.2
Saudi Arabia	-	-	-	-	-	149.2	187.6	353.8	264.5	217.9
United Arab Emirates	532.4	539.7	734.0	701.9	596.5	56.6	94.9	64.8	108.8	51.7
Other Near and Middle East	.. c	.. c	.. c	.. c	.. c	133.9	145.5	176.3	190.1	79.8
Jordan	-	-	-	-	-	-	-	-	-2.3	-
Other Asian countries	2 372.3	9 269.5	9 979.6	7 405.5	10 186.5	1 666.8	1 646.5	4 104.1	4 492.8	6 516.5
China	-	7 790.7	.. d	.. d	.. d	-328.8	-318.3	190.7	330.9	621.2
Hong Kong, China	-	-	.. c	24.0	4 599.0	-213.4	-296.2	-279.4	-246.2	-11.2
India	-	-	.. c	.. d	.. d	121.9	188.7	435.4	490.0	468.4
Indonesia	-	-	-	-	-	67.5	104.4	189.5	288.5	240.4
Iran, Islamic Republic of	-	-	-	-	-	.. c	.. c	-21.6	-59.5	-44.9
Malaysia	-	-	-	-	-	68.6	47.4	130.7	119.1	150.5
Philippines	-	-	-	-	-	8.7	1.1	.. d	2.3	1.1
Singapore	.. c	.. c	.. c	99.6	19.1	1 667.9	1 653.8	2 425.0	2 513.2	3 589.1
Chinese Taipei	301.6	-	-	.. c	-	.. d	5.3	42.0	32.1	22.5
Thailand	-	-	-	-	-	202.5	178.1	334.6	559.9	348.2
Viet Nam	-	-	-	-	-	3.3	33.7	55.2	26.3	14.6
AUSTRALIA, OCEANIA AND POLAR REGIONS	**28.3**	**.. c**	**.. c**	**28.6**	**.. c**	**446.4**	**468.0**	**399.4**	**493.5**	**634.7**
WORLD unallocated and confidential	**-**	**.. d**	**.. d**	**-1 260.6**	**.. d**	**-**	**-**	**-**	**-**	**-**
European Union (EU28)	**63 883.5**	**58 834.2**	**58 967.4**	**44 223.7**	**47 618.5**	**76 051.2**	**91 340.8**	**106 934.5**	**103 036.4**	**117 481.5**
G20 countries excl. European Union	**19 092.0**	**23 765.2**	**35 154.7**	**35 216.4**	**33 675.6**	**22 103.4**	**32 853.4**	**21 079.4**	**24 814.5**	**24 021.6**
G20 OECD countries	**17 505.7**	**14 303.8**	**25 561.3**	**27 299.1**	**27 665.7**	**19 358.7**	**29 266.4**	**16 138.2**	**19 510.0**	**17 899.3**
G20 Non-OECD countries	**1 586.3**	**9 461.4**	**9 592.2**	**7 917.3**	**6 009.9**	**2 744.7**	**3 587.0**	**4 941.2**	**5 304.6**	**6 122.2**
MENA countries	**532.4**	**539.7**	**734.0**	**701.9**	**596.5**	**241.7**	**413.2**	**640.4**	**636.6**	**666.1**
ASEAN countries	**.. c**	**.. c**	**.. c**	**99.6**	**19.1**	**2 019.6**	**2 018.6**	**3 153.0**	**3 521.9**	**4 353.0**

- Nil; .. Not available; c Confidential data; d Secondary Confidentiality

Note: Inward FDI positions are allocated according to the ultimate investing country. Detailed metadata at: *http://stats.oecd.org/OECDStat_Metadata/ShowMetadata.ashx?Dataset=FDI_CTRY_IND_SUMM.*

Source: *OECD International Direct Investment Statistics (database): https://doi.org/10.1787/idi-data-en*

FINLAND

Table 3. Foreign direct investment income by country

Million US dollars

	Inward					Outward				
	2015	2016	2017	2018	2019	2015	2016	2017	2018	2019
WORLD	**4 631.2**	**6 491.2**	**8 425.2**	**7 764.7**	**8 324.2**	**7 373.3**	**7 889.0**	**8 835.5**	**10 201.8**	**13 652.7**
OECD COUNTRIES	**4 554.6**	**6 489.0**	**8 303.5**	**7 676.1**	**8 400.3**	**6 566.8**	**7 260.9**	**7 702.6**	**9 529.1**	**11 876.2**
Australia	-	-	-1.1	-	9.0	23.3	-17.7	40.6	60.2	-4.5
Austria	-	64.1	92.4	109.8	103.0	33.3	50.9	64.3	121.6	118.7
Belgium	38.8	42.0	29.3	-14.2	38.1	122.0	98.4	347.2	-20.1	97.4
Canada	-362.7	5.5	16.9	5.9	9.0	-32.2	85.1	102.6	98.0	150.0
Chile	-	-	-	-	-	33.3	26.5	16.9	20.1	20.2
Czech Republic	-	4.4	2.3	-1.2	-4.5	31.1	38.7	56.4	44.8	61.6
Denmark	457.0	332.9	520.8	640.9	298.9	221.9	237.8	629.0	315.1	418.7
Estonia	-17.7	-40.9	9.0	-20.1	22.4	255.1	193.5	294.2	322.2	281.0
Finland	-	-	-	-	-	-	-	-	-	-
France	48.8	89.6	85.7	125.1	120.9	91.0	-3.3	42.8	66.1	-1.1
Germany	490.3	321.8	342.7	269.1	87.3	106.5	-261.0	-157.8	-8.3	509.3
Greece	-	-	-	-	-	3.3	4.4	11.3	5.9	12.3
Hungary	-	1.1	-	1.2	1.1	-1.1	2.2	13.5	15.3	12.3
Iceland	15.5	-	-	-5.9	-6.7	3.3	3.3	-	2.4	-
Ireland	15.5	13.3	12.4	-5.9	63.8	64.3	122.7	120.6	92.1	288.8
Israel	7.8	6.6	40.6	9.4	4.5	7.8	11.1	11.3	10.6	4.5
Italy	102.1	121.6	147.7	165.2	150.0	15.5	34.3	-50.7	72.0	77.2
Japan	350.5	180.3	162.3	182.9	60.5	1.1	-	-31.6	16.5	7.8
Korea	-	-	4.5	4.7	-	16.6	7.7	11.3	15.3	26.9
Latvia	-	-	-	2.4	-1.1	11.1	22.1	40.6	31.9	20.2
Lithuania	-	-	-	-	-	42.2	26.5	36.1	66.1	79.5
Luxembourg	-2 313.9	779.6	710.2	257.3	1 172.1	186.4	105.1	102.6	67.3	443.3
Mexico	-	-	-	-	-	18.9	-68.6	12.4	47.2	16.8
Netherlands	1 891.3	520.8	1 485.7	1 576.8	1 460.9	1 812.5	2 552.3	1 789.0	1 364.3	2 669.9
New Zealand	-	-	-	-	-	-	1.1	-	5.9	2.2
Norway	129.8	148.2	112.7	211.3	136.6	44.4	226.7	46.2	328.1	717.6
Poland	-8.9	2.2	3.4	3.5	-	119.8	125.0	202.9	172.3	206.0
Portugal	-	-	-	-	-	-	6.6	7.9	9.4	14.6
Slovak Republic	2.2	6.6	7.9	2.4	2.2	11.1	7.7	9.0	13.0	16.8
Slovenia	-	-	-	-	-	3.3	2.2	2.3	9.4	3.4
Spain	12.2	6.6	4.5	9.4	-1.1	36.6	74.1	30.4	54.3	45.9
Sweden	3 232.4	3 435.8	3 948.8	3 541.8	4 260.6	3 109.3	3 079.7	3 181.2	4 766.9	4 448.7
Switzerland	133.1	216.7	168.0	178.2	174.6	88.7	97.3	93.6	88.5	97.4
Turkey	2.2	1.1	1.1	1.2	1.1	325.0	118.3	184.9	110.9	122.0
United Kingdom	230.7	146.0	312.3	301.0	154.5	275.1	121.6	130.8	299.8	339.2
United States	99.8	87.4	84.5	125.1	84.0	-461.5	154.8	346.1	846.2	551.9
EUROPE	**4 498.1**	**6 179.4**	**8 047.6**	**7 463.7**	**8 241.4**	**7 325.6**	**7 379.2**	**7 689.1**	**8 871.7**	**11 567.2**
Bulgaria	-	-	-	-	-	5.5	-	1.1	-7.1	1.1
Croatia	-	-	-	-	-	-	-	-	-	-
Cyprus	23.3	18.8	25.9	42.5	30.2	2.2	1.1	2.3	2.4	5.6
Malta	8.9	17.7	14.7	29.5	10.1	32.2	29.9	10.1	-2.4	-12.3
Romania	-	-	-	-	-	-6.7	2.2	5.6	4.7	12.3
Russian Federation	7.8	-65.2	4.5	61.4	6.7	301.7	231.1	425.0	453.2	431.0
Ukraine	-	-	-	-	-	-21.1	23.2	19.2	8.3	17.9
AFRICA	**-**	**-**	**1.1**	**1.2**	**9.0**	**11.1**	**4.4**	**10.1**	**4.7**	**10.1**
Northern Africa	-	-	-	-	-	-1.1	-	4.5	-4.7	4.5
Algeria	-	-	-	-	-	-	-	-	-1.2	-
Egypt	-	-	-	-	-	-1.1	-	2.3	-2.4	2.2
Libya	-	-	-	-	-	-	-	-	-	-
Morocco	-	-	-	-	-	-	-	2.3	1.2	-
Tunisia	-	-	-	-	-	-	-	-1.1	-2.4	2.2
Other African countries	-	-	1.1	1.2	9.0	11.1	4.4	5.6	9.4	6.7
Nigeria	-	-	-	-	-	-	-	-	1.2	1.1
South Africa	-	-	-	-	-	1.1	4.4	2.3	2.4	6.7
AMERICA	**-236.3**	**120.5**	**170.2**	**107.4**	**176.9**	**-535.8**	**-220.1**	**587.3**	**887.5**	**886.6**
Northern America	-261.8	91.8	101.5	131.0	91.8	-493.6	240.0	448.7	944.2	700.8
Central America and Caribbean countries	26.6	28.8	68.8	-23.6	84.0	36.6	-57.5	23.7	53.1	21.3
Bahamas	-	-	48.5	24.8	23.5	8.9	-	-	-	-
Bermuda	7.8	8.8	1.1	1.2	-	2.2	3.3	1.1	1.2	-
Cayman Islands	17.7	19.9	16.9	14.2	6.7	-	-	-	-	-
Costa Rica	-	-	-	-	-	-	-	-	-	-
El Salvador	-	-	-	-	-	-	-	-	-	-
Guatemala	-	-	-	-	-	-	-	-	-	-
Honduras	-	-	-	-	-	3.3	4.4	1.1	1.2	-
Nicaragua	-	-	-	-	-	-	-	-	-	-
Panama	-	-	-	-	-	1.1	-1.1	7.9	-	2.2
Virgin Islands, U.S.	-	-	-	-	-	-	-	-	-	-
South America	-	-	-	-	-	-78.8	-402.5	115.0	-109.8	164.6
Argentina	-	-	-	-	-	2.2	4.4	4.5	-3.5	-5.6
Bolivia	-	-	-	-	-	-	-	-	-	-
Brazil	-	-	-	-	-	-125.3	-319.6	28.2	-7.1	-15.7
Colombia	-	-	-	-	-	-	-	1.1	-	-1.1
Ecuador	-	-	-	-	-	7.8	-8.8	-1.1	-2.4	4.5
Paraguay	-	-	-	-	-	-	-	-	-	-
Peru	-	-	-	-	-	7.8	10.0	6.8	9.4	5.6
Uruguay	-	-	-	-	-	-4.4	-113.9	59.7	-127.5	156.7
Venezuela	-	-	-	-	-	-	-	-	-	-

FINLAND

Table 3. Foreign direct investment income by country *(cont.)*

Million US dollars

	Inward					Outward				
	2015	2016	2017	2018	2019	2015	2016	2017	2018	2019
ASIA	**368.3**	**190.2**	**207.4**	**193.6**	**-111.9**	**549.1**	**743.1**	**508.4**	**370.6**	**1 190.0**
Near and Middle East	7.8	6.6	40.6	9.4	4.5	92.1	98.4	58.6	27.1	-9.0
Gulf Arabian countries	-	-	-	-	-	85.4	87.4	51.9	18.9	-21.3
Kuwait	-	-	-	-	-	-	-	-	-	-
Qatar	-	-	-	-	-	2.2	6.6	6.8	-5.9	-3.4
Saudi Arabia	-	-	-	-	-	43.3	52.0	28.2	23.6	-33.6
United Arab Emirates	-	-	-	-	-	31.1	22.1	11.3	-1.2	6.7
Other Near and Middle East	7.8	6.6	40.6	9.4	4.5	5.5	12.2	7.9	9.4	12.3
Jordan	-	-	-	-	-	-	-	-	-2.4	2.2
Other Asian countries	360.5	184.7	166.8	184.1	-117.5	458.1	643.6	449.8	343.4	1 200.0
China	-	-	-	-	84.0	37.7	127.2	-181.5	-62.6	-202.6
Hong Kong, China	-	-	1.1	-10.6	-270.9	148.6	-36.5	-37.2	-81.4	244.0
India	6.7	-	-7.9	-11.8	-2.2	14.4	-15.5	56.4	24.8	5.6
Indonesia	-	-	-	-	-	-	15.5	-7.9	16.5	6.7
Iran, Islamic Republic of	-	-	-	-	-	-1.1	-3.3	-4.5	-11.8	1.1
Malaysia	-	-	-	-	-	4.4	11.1	-14.7	-3.5	6.7
Philippines	-	-	-	-	-	2.2	1.1	2.3	-	-
Singapore	3.3	4.4	7.9	20.1	11.2	226.3	561.8	645.9	429.6	1 094.8
Chinese Taipei	-	-	-	-	-	1.1	-33.2	2.3	-	1.1
Thailand	-	-	-	-	-	2.2	3.3	6.8	16.5	-4.5
Viet Nam	-	-	-	-	-	-	-4.4	1.1	2.4	3.4
AUSTRALIA, OCEANIA AND POLAR REGIONS	**-**	**-**	**-1.1**	**-**	**9.0**	**23.3**	**-16.6**	**41.7**	**66.1**	**-2.2**
WORLD unallocated and confidential	**1.1**	**1.1**	**-**	**-1.2**	**-**	**-**	**-1.1**	**-1.1**	**1.2**	**1.1**
European Union (EU28)	**4 226.3**	**5 881.9**	**7 754.5**	**7 035.3**	**7 969.3**	**6 586.8**	**6 677.0**	**6 922.6**	**7 878.0**	**10 169.0**
G20 countries excl. European Union	**977.3**	**886.9**	**1 153.2**	**1 228.6**	**764.6**	**655.6**	**268.7**	**988.6**	**2 071.3**	**1 985.9**
G20 OECD countries	**961.7**	**952.1**	**1 156.6**	**1 180.2**	**676.1**	**380.5**	**170.3**	**633.5**	**1 622.8**	**1 793.4**
G20 Non-OECD countries	**14.4**	**-65.2**	**-3.4**	**48.4**	**88.4**	**275.1**	**98.4**	**355.1**	**448.5**	**192.5**
MENA countries	**-**	**-**	**-**	**-**	**-**	**83.2**	**87.4**	**51.9**	**10.6**	**-13.4**
ASEAN countries	**3.3**	**4.4**	**7.9**	**20.1**	**11.2**	**234.1**	**588.3**	**632.4**	**461.5**	**1 107.1**

- Nil

Note: Detailed metadata at: *http://stats.oecd.org/OECDStat_Metadata/ShowMetadata.ashx?Dataset=FDI_CTRY_IND_SUMM.*

Source: OECD *International Direct Investment Statistics (database): https://doi.org/10.1787/idi-data-en*

FINLAND

Table 4. Foreign direct investment flows by industrial sector

Million US dollars

	Inward					Outward				
	2015	2016	2017	2018	2019	2015	2016	2017	2018	2019
All FDI activities	**2 108.7**	**8 573.5**	**2 857.6**	**-2 170.4**	**13 612.4**	**-16 079.9**	**24 251.9**	**-572.7**	**12 035.9**	**4 864.0**
Agriculture, forestry and fishing	**-**	**-**	**-**	**.. d**	**-**	**1.1**	**-2.2**	**.. d**	**.. d**	**51.5**
Mining and quarrying	**254.0**	**-1 301.6**	**-124.0**	**.. d**	**57.1**	**18.9**	**168.1**	**.. d**	**.. d**	**145.5**
Extraction activities	254.0	-1 301.6	-124.0	93.2	57.1	18.9	168.1	-3.4	60.2	145.5
Manufacturing	**-1 907.9**	**2 754.6**	**2 059.5**	**-2 126.8**	**-157.8**	**-11 460.9**	**19 691.5**	**-2 345.8**	**5 177.6**	**2 028.4**
of which:										
Food products, beverages and tobacco	7.8	-116.1	160.1	128.6	59.3	64.3	-285.3	207.4	343.4	-85.1
Textiles, wood and paper products; printing	-3.3	173.6	-18.0	-1 712.5	-40.3	392.7	426.8	184.9	-692.8	1 874.0
Chemical, rubber, plastic, non-metallic mineral products	1 129.2	882.5	366.4	-514.6	569.8	-74.3	846.0	206.3	505.1	522.8
Metal and machinery products, except electrical equipment	-3 219.1	1 291.6	1 595.1	-180.6	-792.6	-11 691.6	18 452.9	-2 672.8	4 076.5	518.3
Motor vehicles, trailers, semi-trailers, other transport equipment	-120.9	367.1	-62.0	68.5	-22.4	-23.3	2.2	16.9	31.9	12.3
Other manufacturing	299.5	158.1	15.8	82.6	68.3	-128.7	248.8	-288.6	914.7	-815.0
Electricity, gas, steam and air conditioning supply	**.. c**	**210.1**	**195.0**	**79.1**	**373.9**	**-8 153.1**	**.. d**	**928.9**	**3 619.7**	**9.0**
Water supply; sewerage, waste management and remediation activities	**.. d**	**-3.3**	**-3.4**	**.. d**	**21.3**	**-54.4**	**-137.1**	**184.9**	**.. d**	**3.4**
Construction	**58.8**	**-297.5**	**-127.4**	**-161.7**	**153.4**	**-203.0**	**-196.8**	**-74.4**	**616.1**	**895.6**
Services	**3 575.2**	**7 212.2**	**528.7**	**-220.7**	**12 971.0**	**3 771.5**	**3 088.6**	**446.4**	**2 148.0**	**1 656.8**
Wholesale and retail trade; repair of motor vehicles and motorcycles	-1 414.3	-380.4	1 677.4	-175.9	-170.2	65.4	228.9	-232.2	29.5	1 134.0
Transportation and storage	20.0	283.1	134.1	249.0	139.9	140.9	15.5	-45.1	49.6	-38.1
Accommodation and food service activities	17.7	.. d	80.0	16.5	113.1	.. c	-	-	-	-32.5
Information and communication	-505.8	9 871.7	-1 737.1	243.1	-1 608.6	-1 815.9	43.1	-1 281.7	-707.0	-508.2
Financial and insurance activities	4 784.2	-2 866.3	-2 558.9	-717.6	9 252.2	1 235.7	2 236.0	1 614.2	1 412.7	1 814.6
Activities of holding companies	734.3	.. d	.. d	-225.4	4 425.2	85.4	211.2	326.9	85.0	71.6
Real estate activities	235.2	263.2	2 371.8	552.3	1 025.4	3 098.2	12.2	-58.6	.. d	-740.0
Professional, scientific and technical activities	631.2	27.6	84.5	-31.9	1 711.6	604.5	289.7	-75.5	136.9	186.9
Administrative and support service activities	-224.1	-63.0	343.8	-245.5	536.2	12.2	136.0	-10.1	354.1	-189.2
Public administration; activities of households and of extraterritorial organisations	-	-	-	-	-	412.6	127.2	546.7	280.9	10.1
Education	-	-	-	-	-	-	-	-	-	-
Human health and social work activities	37.7	.. d	.. d	-105.0	1 968.0	-	.. d	2.3	-	-2.2
Arts, entertainment and recreation	-6.7	.. d	.. d	-3.5	-4.5	.. c	.. d	-16.9	.. d	-
Other services	-	-	-	-	5.6	1.1	19.9	2.3	21.2	21.3
Not allocated and confidential	**128.7**	**-1.1**	**-1.1**	**.. d**	**4.5**	**-**	**.. d**	**.. d**	**.. d**	**-1.1**
Private real estate activities	**-**	**-**	**330.3**	**.. d**	**189.2**	**-**	**.. d**	**285.2**	**.. d**	**75.0**

- Nil; .. Not available; c Confidential data; d Secondary Confidentiality

Note: Detailed metadata at: *http://stats.oecd.org/OECDStat_Metadata/ShowMetadata.ashx?Dataset=FDI_CTRY_IND_SUMM.*

Source: *OECD International Direct Investment Statistics (database): https://doi.org/10.1787/idi-data-en*

FINLAND

Table 5. Foreign direct investment positions by industrial sector

At year end

Million US dollars

	Inward					Outward				
	2015	2016	2017	2018	2019	2015	2016	2017	2018	2019
All FDI activities	**81 660.3**	**79 930.4**	**89 986.8**	**72 068.9**	**85 816.7**	**94 610.8**	**108 938.5**	**124 908.9**	**128 845.9**	**146 462.6**
Agriculture, forestry and fishing	-	-	-	.. c	.. c	.. c	.. c	.. c	.. c	.. c
Mining and quarrying	**2 456.2**	**1 853.1**	**2 401.1**	.. d	.. d	.. d	.. d	.. d	.. d	.. d
Extraction activities	2 456.2	1 853.1	2 401.1	2 413.6	2 478.1	505.2	436.4	458.1	585.1	554.9
Manufacturing	**21 722.4**	**23 635.5**	**34 032.1**	**25 588.5**	**26 133.5**	**40 485.6**	**57 161.4**	**64 925.6**	**62 412.4**	**64 067.6**
of which:										
Food products, beverages and tobacco	1 986.9	1 256.5	1 527.9	1 623.5	1 530.0	2 878.6	1 639.1	2 079.6	2 226.9	1 792.9
Textiles, wood and paper products; printing	2 348.4	3 492.1	4 108.9	2 139.9	2 260.2	11 865.0	12 492.9	13 474.5	12 639.1	15 233.7
Chemical, rubber, plastic, non-metallic mineral products	8 019.6	7 982.5	9 425.5	8 717.7	9 706.8	6 509.5	7 279.4	8 732.3	8 448.6	9 339.5
Metal and machinery products, except electrical equipment	6 824.2	9 202.1	16 392.4	10 459.1	9 987.6	17 371.8	34 582.1	38 118.3	35 029.8	34 769.7
Motor vehicles, trailers, semi-trailers, other transport equipment	119.8	306.7	435.4	373.3	141.5	-33.8	5.3	197.9	211.8	5.6
Other manufacturing	2 423.5	1 394.5	2 140.8	2 276.2	2 507.3	1 894.4	1 162.6	2 323.1	3 856.2	2 924.1
Electricity, gas, steam and air conditioning supply	**3 119.2**	**3.2**	**1 283.3**	**1 227.4**	**1 965.9**	**11 488.3**	**11 238.5**	**14 346.4**	**16 289.2**	**32 429.8**
Water supply; sewerage, waste management and remediation activities	**19.6**	**16.9**	**16.8**	**26.3**	**47.2**	**450.7**	**63.2**	**239.9**	**247.3**	**95.5**
Construction	**731.6**	**659.9**	**899.5**	**841.5**	**1 258.1**	**419.2**	**322.5**	**321.4**	**997.3**	**1 983.8**
Services	**52 462.7**	**52 648.9**	**49 737.3**	**40 263.3**	**52 068.1**	**38 949.4**	**36 933.7**	**41 141.8**	**44 611.9**	**43 621.7**
Wholesale and retail trade; repair of motor vehicles and motorcycles	4 351.7	3 593.3	6 110.6	5 374.4	5 290.9	2 916.7	2 422.3	2 619.3	2 829.2	3 820.5
Transportation and storage	553.1	874.9	1 113.0	1 187.3	1 234.6	875.3	441.7	435.4	385.8	533.6
Accommodation and food service activities	455.1	381.6	549.3	572.5	689.7	.. c	.. c	-	-	85.4
Information and communication	8 859.0	14 733.8	14 074.1	12 944.8	11 324.4	10 639.1	7 353.2	6 874.6	6 014.4	4 798.9
Financial and insurance activities	28 289.6	25 317.8	14 137.7	6 867.4	15 468.4	5 464.3	21 625.4	25 770.0	28 708.5	28 641.9
Activities of holding companies	1 463.3	.. d	199.1	147.7	4 730.4	491.0	1 065.7	1 379.2	1 448.4	1 285.1
Real estate activities	4 264.6	3 540.6	8 728.7	8 202.4	8 035.3	1 780.1	1 414.6	1 212.5	1 795.3	1 095.3
Professional, scientific and technical activities	3 488.3	1 848.8	2 356.7	2 040.3	3 455.4	14 622.8	1 196.4	1 279.7	1 130.1	1 245.8
Administrative and support service activities	1 892.2	1 473.6	2 122.8	1 898.3	2 452.3	1 725.6	1 408.2	1 674.3	2 091.8	1 647.9
Public administration; activities of households and of extraterritorial organisations	-	-	-	-	-	458.4	626.1	1 147.8	1 353.3	1 391.8
Education	-	-	-	-	-	-	-	-	-	-
Human health and social work activities	273.3	874.9	526.5	1 161.0	3 945.2	.. c	325.7	-	158.0	205.6
Arts, entertainment and recreation	35.9	9.5	16.8	14.9	3.4	.. d	.. d	34.8	24.0	32.6
Other services	-	-	-	-	168.5	64.2	82.2	92.3	121.4	121.3
Not allocated and confidential	-	**1.1**	-	.. c	.. c	**647.8**	.. c	.. c	.. c	.. c
Private real estate activities	**1 148.6**	**1 112.0**	**1 616.7**	**1 679.6**	**1 837.8**	**2 169.8**	**2 634.1**	**3 300.6**	**3 493.2**	**3 502.6**

- Nil; .. Not available; c Confidential data; d Secondary Confidentiality

Note: Detailed metadata at: *http://stats.oecd.org/OECDStat_Metadata/ShowMetadata.ashx?Dataset=FDI_CTRY_IND_SUMM.*

Source: *OECD International Direct Investment Statistics (database): https://doi.org/10.1787/idi-data-en*

FINLAND

Table 6. Foreign direct investment income by industrial sector

Million US dollars

	Inward					Outward				
	2015	2016	2017	2018	2019	2015	2016	2017	2018	2019
All FDI activities	**4 631.2**	**6 491.2**	**8 425.2**	**7 764.7**	**8 324.2**	**7 373.3**	**7 889.0**	**8 835.5**	**10 201.8**	**13 652.7**
Agriculture, forestry and fishing	**-**	**-**	**-**	**1.2**	**1.1**	**1.1**	**-2.2**	**1.1**	**36.6**	**49.3**
Mining and quarrying	**-392.7**	**-63.0**	**36.1**	**116.8**	**133.2**	**22.2**	**21.0**	**13.5**	**33.0**	**-28.0**
Extraction activities	-392.7	-63.0	36.1	116.8	133.2	22.2	21.0	13.5	33.0	-28.0
Manufacturing	**931.8**	**1 819.1**	**3 048.1**	**3 095.7**	**2 311.7**	**2 387.1**	**2 466.0**	**4 566.6**	**4 529.7**	**6 442.4**
of which:										
Food products, beverages and tobacco	181.9	125.0	217.6	310.4	190.3	246.3	128.3	175.9	131.0	142.2
Textiles, wood and paper products; printing	147.5	188.0	267.2	231.3	167.9	610.1	1 200.9	1 400.1	1 069.3	2 226.6
Chemical, rubber, plastic, non-metallic mineral products	1 247.9	1 033.9	1 057.4	1 307.7	1 106.0	686.6	1 153.4	820.7	1 022.1	1 348.9
Metal and machinery products, except electrical equipment	-1 382.1	204.6	1 203.9	735.3	391.8	764.3	-269.8	2 179.0	2 111.4	2 705.7
Motor vehicles, trailers, semi-trailers, other transport equipment	-21.1	-85.1	7.9	57.8	22.4	-1.1	-1.1	2.3	5.9	9.0
Other manufacturing	757.6	352.8	293.1	453.2	431.0	79.9	254.3	-11.3	190.0	11.2
Electricity, gas, steam and air conditioning supply	**-115.4**	**-55.3**	**293.1**	**134.5**	**658.2**	**658.9**	**374.9**	**560.3**	**794.3**	**857.5**
Water supply; sewerage, waste management and remediation activities	**-3.3**	**-5.5**	**2.3**	**1.2**	**-**	**-35.5**	**10.0**	**2.3**	**1.2**	**-4.5**
Construction	**126.5**	**-18.8**	**47.3**	**69.6**	**73.9**	**686.6**	**559.5**	**280.7**	**279.7**	**588.8**
Services	**4 083.2**	**4 813.7**	**4 998.3**	**4 345.6**	**5 145.0**	**3 651.7**	**4 460.9**	**3 411.1**	**4 526.1**	**5 746.1**
Wholesale and retail trade; repair of motor vehicles and motorcycles	454.8	613.7	617.7	636.1	584.4	203.0	310.7	227.7	102.7	497.0
Transportation and storage	43.3	82.9	121.7	139.3	150.0	10.0	49.8	-9.0	8.3	13.4
Accommodation and food service activities	13.3	32.1	39.5	17.7	52.6	12.2	-	-	-	3.4
Information and communication	325.0	860.3	1 098.0	922.9	2 229.9	612.3	1 387.8	392.3	311.6	391.8
Financial and insurance activities	2 961.7	2 855.2	2 360.5	1 690.1	1 069.1	768.7	2 376.4	2 456.3	3 703.5	4 642.3
Activities of holding companies	656.7	504.3	25.9	-56.7	-226.1	51.0	49.8	80.0	206.5	123.1
Real estate activities	138.7	170.3	387.8	504.0	935.9	76.5	103.9	90.2	31.9	-82.8
Professional, scientific and technical activities	74.3	66.4	116.1	164.1	-155.6	1 848.0	96.2	18.0	116.8	24.6
Administrative and support service activities	116.5	112.8	162.3	253.7	119.8	89.9	100.6	195.0	219.5	173.5
Public administration; activities of households and of extraterritorial organisations	-	-	-	-	-	22.2	35.4	36.1	26.0	76.1
Education	-	-	-	-	-	-	-	-	-	-
Human health and social work activities	-44.4	26.5	100.3	24.8	145.5	-	-	-	-	3.4
Arts, entertainment and recreation	1.1	-5.5	-5.6	-7.1	-4.5	-	-3.3	-7.9	-4.7	-5.6
Other services	-	-	-	-	17.9	6.7	4.4	11.3	11.8	9.0
Not allocated and confidential	**1.1**	**1.1**	**-**	**-**	**1.1**	**1.1**	**-1.1**	**-**	**1.2**	**1.1**
Private real estate activities	**-**	**-**	**-**	**-**	**-**	**-**	**-**	**-**	**-**	**-**

- Nil

Note: Detailed metadata at: *http://stats.oecd.org/OECDStat_Metadata/ShowMetadata.ashx?Dataset=FDI_CTRY_IND_SUMM.*

Source: *OECD International Direct Investment Statistics (database): https://doi.org/10.1787/idi-data-en*

FRANCE

Table 1. Foreign direct investment flows by country

Million US dollars

	Inward					Outward				
	2015	2016	2017	2018	2019	2015	2016	2017	2018	2019
WORLD	**45 354.4**	**23 054.3**	**24 779.6**	**38 162.4**	**33 964.0**	**53 205.8**	**64 784.9**	**35 908.0**	**105 569.5**	**38 662.3**
OECD COUNTRIES	**38 489.2**	**22 293.5**	**23 757.2**	**38 145.9**	**33 810.6**	**44 911.8**	**55 650.8**	**33 573.4**	**105 518.7**	**38 707.0**
Australia	174.2	497.6	-518.5	-174.7	-85.1	78.8	-742.0	1 748.4	8 547.2	-2 449.3
Austria	-393.8	142.7	121.7	-1 317.1	-315.7	1 134.8	181.4	354.0	1 334.8	45.9
Belgium	4 128.7	-5 049.2	-822.9	508.7	1 565.0	-1 919.0	8 497.2	-20 665.1	5 087.9	834.0
Canada	-556.9	320.7	954.8	1 758.5	-526.1	230.7	369.3	1 834.1	-2 148.0	21.3
Chile	120.9	74.1	11.3	..	1.1	402.7	-94.0	1 769.8	383.6	29.1
Czech Republic	-221.9	102.8	-137.5	-159.3	131.0	188.6	421.3	414.8	804.9	319.0
Denmark	429.3	320.7	484.7	1 398.6	34.7	1 453.1	424.6	622.3	4 070.6	-5 715.9
Estonia	..	..	..	..	..	..	..	..	..	..
Finland	-176.4	13 714.5	-11 199.4	-2 530.4	-115.3	248.5	34.3	1 424.9	-673.9	1 195.6
France	-	-	-	-	-	-	-	-	-	-
Germany	5 961.2	5 461.7	11 767.6	3 769.6	1 398.2	3 456.5	10 055.3	9 023.8	-26 935.0	1 448.6
Greece	..	-70.8	233.3	-258.5	-48.1	201.9	77.4	-200.7	-89.7	28.0
Hungary	18.9	10.0	15.8	332.8	-304.5	105.4	-209.0	-261.5	1 214.4	91.8
Iceland	..	..	..	..	..	..	..	..	..	..
Ireland	-1 812.5	-750.9	1 376.4	-2 686.2	774.7	2 940.7	-2 332.2	2 664.9	2 443.1	-4 742.0
Israel	-7.8	59.7	53.0	95.6	20.2	179.7	243.3	-170.2	241.9	136.6
Italy	1 368.8	3 314.2	727.1	3 125.2	765.7	7 401.0	13 788.6	3 496.8	30 902.9	3 108.7
Japan	129.8	1 006.3	1 334.7	898.1	957.1	37.7	1 712.9	2 730.2	567.7	1 511.3
Korea	309.5	237.8	83.4	604.3	565.3	241.8	-531.9	649.3	872.2	-29.1
Latvia	-1.1	..	..	..	..	39.9	..	..	..	..
Lithuania	..	..	..	..	..	-1 048.3	-32.1	32.7	61.4	129.9
Luxembourg	2 434.8	13 760.9	-7 702.6	22 788.9	225.0	3 783.7	-3 212.4	11 172.4	4 735.0	6 909.2
Mexico	-313.9	161.5	-74.4	-583.0	..	-577.9	127.2	1 273.8	265.5	328.0
Netherlands	-6 681.1	-4 129.2	4 066.1	15 868.1	2 349.7	3 947.9	4 009.7	3 121.4	46 559.7	6 224.1
New Zealand	..	78.5	-5.6	-59.0	6.7	92.1	36.5	-10.1	16.5	263.1
Norway	292.8	76.3	251.4	575.9	1 430.7	-7.8	-412.5	-1 794.6	-501.6	97.4
Poland	-754.3	-806.1	962.7	278.5	1 446.3	1 432.1	1 184.3	-443.0	1 629.9	50.4
Portugal	323.9	123.9	224.3	90.9	-63.8	949.5	-614.8	307.7	1 003.2	227.2
Slovak Republic	..	-18.8	..	63.7	-26.9	-76.5	131.6	39.5	432.0	-111.9
Slovenia	..	..	..	..	..	-51.0	34.3	115.0	2.4	..
Spain	2 126.5	-241.1	2 792.2	1 070.5	3 355.0	3 673.9	4 780.5	1 961.4	2 001.7	-2 845.6
Sweden	1 180.3	802.8	75.5	-161.7	-292.2	-127.6	834.9	3 627.6	260.8	138.8
Switzerland	22 381.6	2 109.9	-2 199.3	3 106.3	4 963.6	-513.6	3 236.8	169.1	3 332.9	-1 803.4
Turkey	217.4	-105.1	-94.7	13.0	11.2	603.4	-474.4	369.7	279.7	345.9
United Kingdom	14 600.1	-972.0	21 544.4	-1 933.2	8 205.5	7 351.1	-1 291.6	12 058.4	581.8	8 501.1
United States	-6 761.0	-7 935.4	-615.5	-8 088.0	6 160.3	8 012.2	15 409.7	-3 848.5	-745.9	9 773.9
EUROPE	**46 619.0**	**27 703.2**	**21 898.3**	**45 142.2**	**25 646.5**	**36 703.3**	**43 957.8**	**29 230.1**	**80 216.0**	**14 942.3**
Bulgaria	..	..	..	49.6	4.5	67.7	207.9	-72.1	133.4	-645.9
Croatia	..	..	..	..	..	42.2	28.8	-473.5	-68.5	9.0
Cyprus	644.5	-149.3	224.3	60.2	-28.0	1 296.7	653.5	-48.5	768.3	281.0
Malta	495.8	179.1	-653.8	546.4	-16.8	45.5	71.9	-36.1	47.2	-307.8
Romania	..	..	..	..	156.7	234.1	89.6	264.9	531.1	338.1
Russian Federation	139.8	-94.0	341.6	-103.9	-108.6	890.7	3 626.0	1 636.8	118.0	1 506.8
Ukraine	..	..	..	..	..	-2.2	170.3	60.9	342.3	164.6
AFRICA	**-249.6**	**-631.4**	**319.0**	**-1 408.0**	**470.2**	**7 671.7**	**303.0**	**-1 580.4**	**697.5**	**5 478.6**
Northern Africa	1.1	-371.6	-25.9	77.9	64.9	904.0	820.5	-171.3	141.6	105.2
Algeria	125.3	-328.4	45.1	-34.2	44.8	245.1	70.8	205.2	283.3	91.8
Egypt	-14.4	-8.8	-77.8	-85.0	148.9	-239.6	160.3	-649.3	155.8	119.8
Libya	1.1	8.8	6.8	10.6	6.7	-128.7	14.4	..	-313.9	28.0
Morocco	-51.0	-43.1	-20.3	128.6	-48.1	834.2	505.4	443.0	29.5	-190.3
Tunisia	..	1.1	20.3	56.7	-87.3	193.0	69.7	178.1	-14.2	54.9
Other African countries	-250.7	-259.9	344.9	-1 485.9	406.4	6 767.6	-517.5	-1 409.1	557.1	5 374.5
Nigeria	..	..	..	..	..	-278.4	235.5	-30.4	-768.3	481.4
South Africa	..	150.4	-217.6	26.0	63.8	754.3	181.4	273.9	113.3	186.9
AMERICA	**-7 181.4**	**-8 503.8**	**382.1**	**-6 321.3**	**4 609.9**	**3 317.8**	**22 464.9**	**6 046.7**	**12 786.5**	**14 551.7**
Northern America	-7 317.8	-7 614.7	340.4	-6 329.5	5 634.2	8 242.9	15 779.1	-2 014.4	-2 895.1	9 795.1
Central America and Caribbean countries	-118.7	-940.0	-22.5	351.7	-1 170.9	149.8	3 250.0	2 119.3	13 697.6	2 902.7
Bahamas	..	..	..	..	..	631.2	-53.1	31.6	1.2	1.1
Bermuda	..	-140.4	5.6	125.1	-52.6	-110.9	1 093.7	108.2	16 105.3	2 653.1
Cayman Islands	-112.0	-38.7	15.8	217.2	..	43.3	2 190.6	-36.1	-2 873.8	7.8
Costa Rica	..	..	..	..	..	..	..	..	..	..
El Salvador	..	..	..	..	..	..	..	..	..	..
Guatemala	..	..	..	..	..	..	..	..	..	..
Honduras	..	..	..	..	..	..	..	..	..	..
Nicaragua	..	..	..	..	..	..	..	..	..	..
Panama	23.3	-	29.3	-7.1	-5.6	221.9	-282.0	166.8	114.5	-77.2
Virgin Islands, U.S.	-	-	-	-	..	..	..	..	..	..
South America	254.0	50.9	65.4	-343.4	146.6	-5 074.9	3 435.8	5 943.0	1 983.9	1 853.8
Argentina	..	..	..	..	..	431.5	-66.4	467.8	36.6	-554.1
Bolivia	..	..	..	..	..	-401.6	-23.2	421.6	-40.1	-15.7
Brazil	122.0	-31.0	172.5	108.6	49.3	-5 851.4	2 239.3	2 899.3	1 664.1	2 625.1
Colombia	..	..	..	..	..	203.0	68.6	-19.2	-41.3	12.3
Ecuador	..	-	..	..	..	..	..	..	..	17.9
Paraguay	..	..	..	..	..	..	..	..	..	..
Peru	..	..	..	..	..	17.7	1 427.6	491.5	21.2	-322.4
Uruguay	..	..	..	..	..	-24.4	5.5	-107.1	-15.3	1.1
Venezuela	..	..	..	..	..	240.7	-96.2	36.1	-175.9	7.8

Table 1. Foreign direct investment flows by country *(cont.)*

Million US dollars

	Inward					Outward				
	2015	2016	2017	2018	2019	2015	2016	2017	2018	2019
ASIA	**4 846.4**	**3 891.4**	**2 799.0**	**537.0**	**3 526.3**	**4 939.5**	**-1 118.0**	**-1 380.9**	**3 185.4**	**5 902.8**
Near and Middle East	2 776.5	612.6	1 592.8	-540.5	339.2	-1 468.7	1 089.2	-774.4	586.6	329.1
Gulf Arabian countries	1 697.2	801.7	438.5	-672.7	119.8	-2 067.7	884.7	-738.4	-375.3	-219.4
Kuwait	..	..	..	181.8	48.1	..	5.5	..	81.4	..
Qatar	787.6	1 425.4	864.6	-889.9	62.7	-397.1	353.9	-1 479.0	115.7	-126.5
Saudi Arabia	237.4	38.7	-96.9	-1.2	-5.6	989.5	278.7	-815.0	170.0	-1 003.0
United Arab Emirates	738.8	-557.3	-308.9	55.5	-60.5	-536.9	257.7	1 534.2	-206.5	141.1
Other Near and Middle East	1 079.3	-189.1	1 155.5	132.2	219.4	599.0	204.6	-36.1	961.9	548.5
Jordan	..	..	..	..	..	25.5	-7.7	-5.6	437.9	-12.3
Other Asian countries	2 069.9	3 277.7	1 205.1	1 076.4	3 187.1	6 408.2	-2 207.2	-605.3	2 598.8	5 573.7
China	620.1	226.7	130.8	-572.4	287.7	826.4	593.8	851.1	774.2	157.8
Hong Kong, China	17.7	1 612.3	899.6	234.9	737.7	1 802.6	-2 101.1	-412.6	129.8	-1 441.8
India	91.0	-86.3	-36.1	..	226.1	1 096.0	-246.6	463.3	644.4	328.0
Indonesia	..	173.6	436.3	304.5	-125.4	-518.0	-632.5	-1 137.4	574.8	472.4
Iran, Islamic Republic of	-480.3	-54.2	166.8	-207.7	4.5	-136.4	-73.0	747.4	-736.5	-23.5
Malaysia	-	-1.1	11.3	-9.4	13.4	-164.2	-39.8	36.1	160.5	263.1
Philippines	1 251.2	-8.8	..	..	..	-49.9	-869.2	25.9	2.4	-17.9
Singapore	339.4	94.0	-459.9	109.8	461.2	611.2	178.0	-2 138.4	375.3	4 295.3
Chinese Taipei	-4.4	39.8	21.4	-4.7	-3.4	62.1	36.5	119.5	118.0	-71.6
Thailand	..	42.0	-67.6	-2.4	15.7	-1 192.5	200.2	-546.7	-82.6	223.9
Viet Nam	..	..	..	-	24.6	-127.6	-75.2	136.4	41.3	80.6
AUSTRALIA, OCEANIA AND POLAR REGIONS	**156.4**	**597.1**	**-621.1**	**-122.7**	**-87.3**	**567.9**	**-800.6**	**3 591.5**	**8 680.5**	**-1 991.5**
WORLD unallocated and confidential	**1 163.6**	**-2.2**	**2.3**	**335.2**	**-201.5**	**5.5**	**-22.1**	**1.1**	**3.5**	**-221.7**
European Union (EU28)	**23 719.4**	**25 597.7**	**23 974.7**	**40 834.4**	**19 120.1**	**36 809.8**	**37 707.6**	**28 519.9**	**76 924.3**	**15 125.9**
G20 countries excl. European Union	**16 402.7**	**2 365.4**	**35 866.3**	**-1 134.2**	**17 502.5**	**25 454.2**	**44 397.9**	**33 974.7**	**16 282.3**	**26 277.8**
G20 OECD countries	**15 128.1**	**1 986.1**	**35 109.9**	**-610.2**	**17 118.5**	**26 835.3**	**38 424.2**	**29 336.0**	**12 186.9**	**22 559.1**
G20 Non-OECD countries	**1 274.5**	**379.3**	**756.4**	**-522.8**	**384.0**	**-1 379.9**	**5 973.7**	**4 638.7**	**4 095.4**	**3 719.9**
MENA countries	**2 766.5**	**165.9**	**1 481.2**	**-502.8**	**385.1**	**-1 110.4**	**1 747.2**	**-800.4**	**277.4**	**-29.1**
ASEAN countries	**1 386.6**	**291.9**	**-1 402.3**	**410.7**	**413.1**	**604.5**	**-1 198.7**	**-5 600.3**	**741.2**	**5 345.3**

- Nil; .. Not available

Note: Detailed metadata at: *http://stats.oecd.org/OECDStat_Metadata/ShowMetadata.ashx?Dataset=FDI_CTRY_IND_SUMM.*

Source: *OECD International Direct Investment Statistics (database): https://doi.org/10.1787/idi-data-en*

FRANCE

Table 2. Foreign direct investment positions by country

At year end

Million US dollars

	Inward					Outward				
	2015	2016	2017	2018	2019	2015	2016	2017	2018	2019
WORLD	**687 394.7**	**694 881.4**	**819 327.2**	**820 534.7**	**868 641.9**	**1 268 227.5**	**1 284 859.3**	**1 440 434.2**	**1 499 081.7**	**1 532 739.8**
OECD COUNTRIES	**635 455.6**	**635 961.8**	**744 135.3**	**820 534.7**	**868 641.9**	**1 061 566.7**	**1 069 930.4**	**1 204 348.8**	**1 499 031.4**	**1 532 736.5**
Australia	4 105.6	3 484.8	3 157.8	3 992.4	4 638.3	12 640.2	12 319.0	11 922.5	17 844.1	15 266.2
Austria	1 437.1	1 744.5	1 724.6	1 654.5	1 649.1	2 783.9	2 853.4	3 187.8	4 175.6	4 137.3
Belgium	40 031.6	46 226.4	44 391.9	48 287.2	57 317.5	166 371.3	165 440.1	170 187.1	161 238.8	159 469.8
Canada	6 797.0	7 132.9	11 829.0	15 069.8	13 574.5	9 781.2	12 018.6	12 535.4	11 648.7	12 265.8
Chile	474.7	765.3	906.7	493.5	146.0	1 820.4	1 767.7	3 830.7	3 948.9	3 582.3
Czech Republic	..	183.4	182.3	227.8	334.8	9 421.9	8 511.6	9 847.7	10 762.5	10 681.9
Denmark	5 315.2	4 775.0	5 911.5	5 758.0	5 799.8	7 407.7	7 817.0	9 521.5	18 660.4	12 615.1
Estonia	..	..	..	..	..	..	..	..	..	..
Finland	1 651.6	20 905.5	12 363.9	9 335.9	9 226.0	1 192.2	1 092.0	2 812.4	2 057.5	3 193.7
France	46 694.6	42 307.4	60 788.0	22 688.3	..	-	-	-	-	-
Germany	80 557.4	72 064.9	90 006.0	90 918.3	95 661.6	61 591.7	62 205.1	87 449.0	72 305.9	74 171.0
Greece	..	246.7	298.6	301.1	307.8	1 479.6	1 610.6	1 731.8	1 368.2	1 342.4
Hungary	..	120.2	322.6	499.2	522.4	3 411.0	3 210.7	3 600.4	3 816.1	3 739.6
Iceland	192.7	154.9	170.3	..	..	..	..	..	..	..
Ireland	6 720.7	5 303.0	6 235.3	6 404.9	6 280.6	23 325.0	19 622.6	25 185.9	37 354.0	31 773.8
Israel	680.5	953.9	1 219.7	1 297.2	1 279.5	2 995.1	3 138.0	3 261.0	3 218.5	3 574.5
Italy	22 089.3	24 305.9	30 323.8	31 182.7	29 422.6	57 632.0	65 369.5	77 132.4	96 171.3	96 464.8
Japan	19 314.1	16 865.2	19 702.6	18 698.2	18 741.9	28 202.5	27 856.0	29 297.2	26 269.8	23 612.7
Korea	1 129.0	331.0	280.6	594.2	453.8	4 689.2	4 202.6	5 087.6	4 783.6	4 591.1
Latvia	129.6	..	..	..	..	236.3	..	..	..	..
Lithuania	..	..	..	..	..	206.9	157.1	262.7	286.2	410.0
Luxembourg	24 682.6	33 639.7	42 169.6	81 523.9	103 662.1	50 607.5	46 858.9	59 832.1	57 090.7	63 046.5
Mexico	1 082.2	1 424.1	1 333.7	1 517.1	1 426.6	2 646.7	2 569.8	4 051.3	4 735.5	5 237.0
Netherlands	50 586.8	46 167.4	38 517.6	34 350.8	43 000.4	130 150.2	134 564.1	155 648.8	196 194.2	203 416.1
New Zealand	123.0	129.7	184.7	224.4	235.9	408.3	428.0	362.2	445.4	707.7
Norway	3 048.4	2 187.2	3 698.7	3 107.4	3 650.9	7 242.2	6 882.0	5 441.4	4 740.1	4 824.8
Poland	-1 220.5	-1 538.9	-1 182.5	-871.3	-258.4	16 775.2	17 193.0	19 641.4	19 764.1	20 294.3
Portugal	1 035.4	1 704.4	2 336.3	2 388.4	2 512.9	4 280.9	3 742.0	4 712.2	5 333.2	5 388.7
Slovak Republic	..	..	..	..	..	341.9	450.1	548.1	1 040.8	911.0
Slovenia	..	..	..	..	..	518.2	635.6	632.0	392.7	..
Spain	12 675.0	15 922.8	21 730.6	22 105.6	26 378.3	45 978.2	49 303.3	60 416.2	57 577.3	54 057.5
Sweden	7 143.2	6 407.7	9 198.8	8 499.0	8 160.0	4 666.3	5 598.2	9 399.1	9 087.5	8 992.4
Switzerland	82 888.4	85 522.3	94 039.3	94 274.1	110 900.9	42 635.8	44 511.4	49 269.6	49 057.7	48 044.3
Turkey	277.6	269.8	261.5	415.6	447.1	4 228.6	3 788.3	3 789.9	3 330.7	3 329.6
United Kingdom	84 679.4	74 732.8	98 854.6	92 744.4	92 765.7	129 384.9	116 238.0	136 754.6	131 443.8	144 682.1
United States	130 959.2	121 413.5	143 063.1	161 286.9	166 682.8	226 904.7	238 007.8	237 090.4	232 727.3	243 554.3
EUROPE	**477 213.9**	**486 007.2**	**564 768.5**	**559 360.0**	**601 450.2**	**792 676.1**	**796 403.5**	**928 930.2**	**976 993.4**	**993 658.7**
Bulgaria	..	..	..	..	..	733.8	994.0	1 079.4	1 043.1	376.3
Croatia	..	..	..	..	..	770.8	748.4	211.1	158.0	164.0
Cyprus	859.0	319.4	359.8	321.7	378.6	1 494.8	1 408.2	1 427.2	2 127.3	2 364.6
Malta	272.2	967.6	370.6	966.3	1 104.2	666.3	657.7	794.0	859.9	537.0
Romania	..	183.4	237.5	267.9	277.5	4 699.0	4 519.9	5 219.5	5 351.5	5 895.3
Russian Federation	2 256.9	1 073.0	977.5	983.5	989.7	10 071.9	17 820.2	19 896.9	20 447.7	25 774.0
Ukraine	..	..	..	..	..	426.8	570.3	766.4	1 118.6	1 426.6
AFRICA	**4 695.7**	**9 495.1**	**11 404.4**	**10 627.4**	**11 155.9**	**62 084.9**	**60 422.7**	**62 233.1**	**61 321.3**	**64 552.9**
Northern Africa	1 518.8	3 072.6	3 590.8	3 714.2	3 759.8	18 289.6	16 715.5	18 714.3	18 787.5	18 885.6
Algeria	830.7	496.5	584.1	705.3	615.6	2 449.6	2 855.5	2 798.0	2 895.6	2 961.1
Egypt	..	183.4	250.7	215.3	231.4	3 650.5	1 988.0	1 609.5	2 520.0	2 916.2
Libya	..	..	..	..	..	751.2	421.6	..	-203.8	-180.9
Morocco	476.9	1 853.1	2 113.2	2 136.5	2 231.0	10 496.5	10 591.3	13 154.2	12 683.8	12 170.3
Tunisia	..	461.7	546.9	559.9	579.6	941.8	857.0	1 108.2	891.9	1 018.9
Other African countries	3 173.7	6 422.5	7 813.6	6 913.2	7 396.1	43 795.3	43 707.2	43 518.8	42 533.8	45 667.3
Nigeria	..	..	..	..	..	9 927.1	11 545.3	11 444.0	10 594.2	10 913.3
South Africa	2 259.1	2 579.3	3 173.4	2 035.7	1 679.4	2 303.8	2 588.8	2 798.0	3 195.6	3 431.8
AMERICA	**143 683.2**	**135 828.0**	**163 649.6**	**184 601.6**	**188 663.2**	**275 976.0**	**296 572.2**	**307 705.7**	**315 408.7**	**329 262.0**
Northern America	137 760.5	128 544.3	154 892.1	176 354.5	180 256.1	236 685.9	250 026.4	249 625.8	244 376.0	255 821.2
Central America and Caribbean countries	5 320.6	5 524.4	6 603.5	6 553.7	7 110.8	9 417.5	11 229.1	14 297.2	30 167.2	32 948.8
Bahamas	..	..	..	..	..	488.8	440.6	488.1	444.2	442.6
Bermuda	2 307.0	2 346.4	3 692.7	3 341.0	3 554.3	2 812.2	3 757.8	5 124.7	20 649.2	23 085.8
Cayman Islands	655.4	591.3	190.7	..	376.3	581.4	1 940.6	1 733.0	510.6	513.4
Costa Rica	..	..	..	..	..	..	..	..	..	..
El Salvador	..	..	..	..	..	..	..	..	..	..
Guatemala	..	..	..	..	..	..	..	..	..	..
Honduras	..	..	..	..	..	..	..	..	..	..
Nicaragua	..	..	..	..	..	..	..	..	..	..
Panama	373.4	307.8	380.2	122.5	133.7	839.4	687.3	677.6	782.0	698.7
Virgin Islands, U.S.	..	..	..	..	..	..	..	..	..	..
South America	602.1	1 759.2	2 154.0	1 693.4	1 296.3	29 872.6	35 316.7	43 783.9	40 865.6	40 492.0
Argentina	..	123.3	141.5	146.6	151.7	3 465.4	3 032.6	3 586.0	1 732.3	879.6
Bolivia	..	..	..	..	..	414.8	806.4	831.1	791.2	771.7
Brazil	..	528.1	761.6	794.6	702.1	20 078.4	25 305.2	30 149.9	29 453.9	31 102.0
Colombia	..	..	..	..	118.0	1 203.0	904.4	909.1	1 398.0	1 381.7
Ecuador	..	131.8	..	..	..	..	..	..	..	115.7
Paraguay	..	..	..	..	..	..	..	..	..	..
Peru	..	..	..	..	..	140.4	1 247.0	1 120.2	1 079.7	751.5
Uruguay	..	..	..	..	..	283.1	288.8	203.9	171.7	152.8
Venezuela	..	..	..	..	..	2 311.4	1 813.0	3 024.7	2 014.0	1 532.2

FRANCE

Table 2. Foreign direct investment positions by country *(cont.)*

At year end

Million US dollars

	Inward					Outward				
	2015	2016	2017	2018	2019	2015	2016	2017	2018	2019
ASIA	**42 967.9**	**45 882.8**	**57 786.0**	**55 271.4**	**59 046.3**	**123 546.0**	**118 080.5**	**126 623.9**	**124 187.1**	**126 384.0**
Near and Middle East	10 371.3	12 174.6	14 179.7	14 834.0	15 768.4	12 261.3	12 576.2	13 747.9	13 375.3	14 159.7
Gulf Arabian countries	8 737.1	10 120.2	9 696.6	9 949.6	10 711.1	7 762.7	7 861.3	8 740.7	7 951.7	8 006.1
Kuwait	..	139.1	229.1	578.2	596.5	..	108.6	..	117.9	..
Qatar	4 214.5	5 328.3	6 324.1	6 237.7	6 578.3	3 154.1	3 296.1	2 308.7	2 006.0	1 894.0
Saudi Arabia	1 035.4	527.0	626.0	606.8	636.9	5 592.8	5 382.1	4 685.8	4 875.2	4 188.9
United Arab Emirates	3 323.9	3 990.7	2 373.5	2 368.9	2 732.0	-953.7	-797.9	1 693.5	1 668.2	1 758.0
Other Near and Middle East	1 634.2	2 055.4	4 483.1	4 885.5	5 057.3	4 498.6	4 714.9	5 007.2	5 423.6	6 153.7
Jordan	..	..	..	..	..	227.5	261.4	278.2	459.1	413.4
Other Asian countries	32 595.5	33 708.2	43 606.4	40 436.2	43 276.8	111 284.7	105 504.4	112 877.2	110 811.8	112 224.2
China	5 456.7	7 131.9	12 088.0	9 929.0	12 222.0	24 859.0	24 350.2	29 357.2	32 204.0	32 335.4
Hong Kong, China	3 342.4	4 148.8	5 163.1	5 237.0	6 326.7	12 172.0	10 327.8	10 948.7	11 400.3	9 979.8
India	372.3	527.0	516.9	338.9	..	5 762.7	5 762.6	6 543.5	6 436.9	6 595.1
Indonesia	..	870.7	782.0	972.1	926.8	2 684.8	2 711.1	1 190.9	1 396.8	1 928.8
Iran, Islamic Republic of	247.1	237.2	303.4	293.1	295.4	719.7	728.4	1 544.7	858.7	800.9
Malaysia	139.4	338.4	370.6	393.9	407.8	865.5	744.2	1 091.4	1 238.8	1 503.0
Philippines	..	..	..	..	..	1 176.9	402.7	352.6	288.5	278.6
Singapore	1 363.1	1 513.7	2 417.8	2 011.7	1 798.5	12 054.4	10 478.6	11 928.5	11 016.7	15 408.9
Chinese Taipei	162.2	153.9	275.8	304.6	286.5	642.4	585.0	759.2	889.6	847.0
Thailand	631.5	1 082.5	1 116.6	1 070.5	1 139.1	1 909.6	2 011.2	1 718.6	1 660.2	2 032.1
Viet Nam	..	148.6	190.7	191.2	201.1	717.5	593.4	730.4	717.9	796.5
AUSTRALIA, OCEANIA AND POLAR REGIONS	**4 458.4**	**3 766.2**	**3 568.0**	**4 448.1**	**5 094.4**	**13 953.2**	**13 409.9**	**14 973.6**	**21 199.9**	**19 084.5**
WORLD unallocated and confidential	**14 375.6**	**13 902.2**	**18 150.6**	**6 226.2**	**3 231.9**	**-8.7**	**-29.5**	**-32.4**	**-28.6**	**-202.2**
European Union (EU28)	**385 971.7**	**396 907.3**	**465 383.8**	**459 828.3**	**484 775.3**	**726 168.8**	**720 838.0**	**847 351.9**	**895 823.2**	**908 280.2**
G20 countries excl. European Union	**409 228.1**	**377 689.5**	**478 667.5**	**454 914.1**	**441 179.5**	**612 520.4**	**631 527.4**	**703 318.5**	**701 003.0**	**729 411.4**
G20 OECD countries	**397 685.4**	**364 331.2**	**459 600.6**	**439 106.9**	**423 805.9**	**537 702.8**	**544 575.7**	**605 111.5**	**601 260.6**	**623 174.6**
G20 Non-OECD countries	**11 542.7**	**13 358.3**	**19 066.9**	**15 806.0**	**17 373.6**	**74 817.6**	**86 951.6**	**98 208.2**	**99 742.4**	**106 235.7**
MENA countries	**11 206.3**	**14 362.8**	**16 602.3**	**17 302.5**	**18 302.6**	**26 979.9**	**25 685.7**	**28 702.3**	**28 100.5**	**28 300.4**
ASEAN countries	**2 387.6**	**4 188.9**	**5 141.5**	**4 907.3**	**4 749.5**	**22 243.9**	**19 810.3**	**17 890.4**	**16 927.0**	**22 584.8**

- Nil; .. Not available

Note: Inward FDI positions are allocated according to the ultimate investing country. Detailed metadata at: *http://stats.oecd.org/OECDStat_Metadata/ShowMetadata.ashx?Dataset=FDI_CTRY_IND_SUMM.*

Source: *OECD International Direct Investment Statistics (database): https://doi.org/10.1787/idi-data-en*

FRANCE

Table 3. Foreign direct investment income by country

Million US dollars

	Inward					Outward				
	2015	2016	2017	2018	2019	2015	2016	2017	2018	2019
WORLD	**26 922.9**	**29 483.6**	**36 340.9**	**37 501.5**	**36 506.2**	**70 308.4**	**69 441.6**	**77 144.6**	**94 514.3**	**89 876.9**
OECD COUNTRIES	..	..	..	..	..	..	..	..	..	..
Australia	..	..	..	..	..	..	..	..	..	..
Austria	..	..	..	..	..	..	..	..	..	..
Belgium	3 088.2	3 294.3	3 110.1	2 948.2	2 588.2	6 552.4	7 248.7	5 726.5	10 830.9	8 927.6
Canada	61.0	54.2	-315.6	69.6	87.3	321.7	1 036.2	-604.2	532.3	823.9
Chile	..	..	..	..	..	..	..	..	..	..
Czech Republic	16.6	16.6	-18.0	14.2	10.1	1 159.2	974.2	1 050.6	1 097.6	1 007.5
Denmark	..	..	..	..	..	..	..	..	..	..
Estonia	..	..	..	..	..	..	..	..	..	..
Finland	..	..	..	..	..	..	..	..	..	..
France	-	-	-	-	-	-	-	-	-	-
Germany	2 261.8	2 247.0	4 191.2	2 918.7	2 917.3	4 190.8	5 174.2	7 534.7	5 456.2	5 771.9
Greece	..	..	..	..	..	..	..	..	..	..
Hungary	..	..	..	..	..	..	..	..	..	..
Iceland	..	..	..	..	..	..	..	..	..	..
Ireland	215.2	126.1	95.8	70.8	105.2	2 021.1	1 541.5	1 464.3	4 238.2	2 988.9
Israel	..	..	..	..	..	..	..	..	..	..
Italy	629.0	994.1	579.4	926.5	1 113.8	2 303.9	3 731.1	4 101.0	4 628.8	4 131.9
Japan	572.4	535.2	737.2	672.7	632.5	1 986.7	3 550.8	3 788.8	2 918.7	2 851.2
Korea	..	..	..	..	..	..	..	..	..	..
Latvia	..	..	..	..	..	..	..	..	..	..
Lithuania	..	..	..	..	..	..	..	..	..	..
Luxembourg	3 825.8	4 075.0	5 334.2	5 084.4	4 564.0	2 109.8	2 599.8	2 386.4	2 783.0	2 930.7
Mexico	..	..	..	..	..	..	..	..	..	..
Netherlands	5 880.2	6 679.2	8 007.0	11 750.3	10 045.9	6 665.6	6 190.4	5 424.4	11 246.3	9 817.5
New Zealand	..	..	..	..	..	..	..	..	..	..
Norway	177.5	118.3	190.5	241.9	223.9	814.2	637.0	445.3	638.5	737.7
Poland	-85.4	-107.3	-137.5	-123.9	-59.3	1 250.1	954.3	1 366.3	1 683.0	1 371.3
Portugal	88.7	103.9	56.4	66.1	45.9	607.9	464.4	529.8	978.4	987.4
Slovak Republic	..	..	..	..	..	..	..	..	..	..
Slovenia	..	..	..	..	..	..	..	..	..	..
Spain	1 002.8	1 071.5	1 340.3	1 838.8	1 712.8	2 587.9	3 060.9	4 513.6	3 662.2	3 415.4
Sweden	307.3	391.5	714.7	531.1	563.1	216.3	408.1	560.3	482.7	492.6
Switzerland	2 409.3	2 654.0	1 518.4	3 598.5	4 390.5	4 532.4	5 463.9	6 428.8	1 889.5	3 412.1
Turkey	2.2	3.3	1.1	3.5	25.7	367.2	263.2	441.9	421.3	353.7
United Kingdom	2 650.0	4 122.5	4 213.7	3 166.5	4 040.1	5 554.1	6 108.6	6 157.1	7 331.5	7 046.9
United States	2 941.8	2 073.4	3 416.8	1 649.9	1 692.6	9 131.4	5 539.1	5 383.8	9 892.6	9 086.5
EUROPE	..	..	..	..	..	..	..	..	..	..
Bulgaria	..	..	..	..	..	..	..	..	..	..
Croatia	..	..	..	..	..	..	..	..	..	..
Cyprus	..	..	..	..	..	..	..	..	..	..
Malta	..	..	..	..	..	..	..	..	..	..
Romania	-	-1.1	-2.3	-2.4	1.1	416.0	538.5	724.8	723.5	622.4
Russian Federation	22.2	1.1	31.6	36.6	47.0	52.1	1 119.1	1 289.6	457.9	464.6
Ukraine	..	..	..	..	..	..	..	..	..	..
AFRICA	..	..	..	..	..	..	..	..	..	..
Northern Africa	..	..	..	..	..	..	..	..	..	..
Algeria	..	..	..	..	..	..	..	..	..	..
Egypt	..	..	..	..	..	..	..	..	..	..
Libya	..	..	..	..	..	..	..	..	..	..
Morocco	18.9	17.7	1.1	7.1	12.3	637.8	404.7	559.1	668.0	609.0
Tunisia	..	..	..	..	..	..	..	..	..	..
Other African countries	..	..	..	..	..	..	..	..	..	..
Nigeria	..	..	..	..	..	..	..	..	..	..
South Africa	..	..	..	..	..	..	..	..	..	..
AMERICA	..	..	..	..	..	..	..	..	..	..
Northern America	..	..	..	..	..	..	..	..	..	..
Central America and Caribbean countries	..	..	..	..	..	..	..	..	..	..
Bahamas	..	..	..	..	..	..	..	..	..	..
Bermuda	..	..	..	..	..	..	..	..	..	..
Cayman Islands	..	..	..	..	..	..	..	..	..	..
Costa Rica	..	..	..	..	..	..	..	..	..	..
El Salvador	..	..	..	..	..	..	..	..	..	..
Guatemala	..	..	..	..	..	..	..	..	..	..
Honduras	..	..	..	..	..	..	..	..	..	..
Nicaragua	..	..	..	..	..	..	..	..	..	..
Panama	..	..	..	..	..	..	..	..	..	..
Virgin Islands, U.S.	..	..	..	..	..	..	..	..	..	..
South America	..	..	..	..	..	..	..	..	..	..
Argentina	..	..	..	..	..	..	..	..	..	..
Bolivia	..	..	..	..	..	..	..	..	..	..
Brazil	-1.1	-5.5	-1.1	-2.4	-3.4	252.9	938.8	874.8	629.1	901.2
Colombia	..	..	..	..	..	..	..	..	..	..
Ecuador	..	..	..	..	..	..	..	..	..	..
Paraguay	-	..	..	..	..	..	..	..	..	..
Peru	..	..	..	..	..	..	..	..	..	..
Uruguay	..	..	..	..	..	..	..	..	..	..
Venezuela	..	..	..	..	..	..	..	..	..	..

Table 3. Foreign direct investment income by country *(cont.)*

Million US dollars

	Inward					Outward				
	2015	2016	2017	2018	2019	2015	2016	2017	2018	2019
ASIA	..	..	..	..	..	..	..	..	..	..
Near and Middle East	..	..	..	..	..	..	..	..	..	..
Gulf Arabian countries	..	..	..	..	..	..	..	..	..	..
Kuwait	..	..	..	..	..	..	..	..	..	..
Qatar	..	..	..	..	..	..	..	..	..	..
Saudi Arabia	..	..	..	..	..	..	..	..	..	..
United Arab Emirates	..	..	..	..	..	..	..	..	..	..
Other Near and Middle East	..	..	..	..	..	..	..	..	..	..
Jordan	..	..	..	..	..	..	..	..	..	..
Other Asian countries	..	..	..	..	..	..	..	..	..	..
China	-13.3	1.1	11.3	10.6	89.6	2 796.5	988.6	1 636.8	2 050.0	2 016.1
Hong Kong, China	92.1	144.9	276.2	101.5	100.8	1 469.8	1 071.5	1 643.6	2 176.3	2 477.3
India	-4.4	-3.3	-7.9	-2.4	1.1	399.3	275.4	289.7	437.9	334.7
Indonesia	-	-64.1	54.1	49.6	31.3	544.6	374.9	471.2	140.4	211.6
Iran, Islamic Republic of	..	..	..	..	..	..	..	..	..	..
Malaysia	..	..	..	..	..	..	..	..	..	..
Philippines	..	..	..	..	..	..	..	..	..	..
Singapore	-54.4	23.2	16.9	24.8	20.2	1 517.5	270.9	1 463.2	2 449.0	2 409.0
Chinese Taipei	..	..	..	..	..	..	..	..	..	..
Thailand	..	..	..	..	..	..	..	..	..	..
Viet Nam	..	..	..	..	..	..	..	..	..	..
AUSTRALIA, OCEANIA AND POLAR REGIONS	..	..	..	..	..	..	..	..	..	..
WORLD unallocated and confidential	..	..	..	..	..	..	..	..	..	..
European Union (EU28)	**20 565.7**	**24 236.4**	**28 337.3**	**30 134.5**	**28 512.3**	**38 546.9**	**41 311.5**	**44 010.8**	**58 582.6**	**52 724.7**
G20 countries excl. European Union	..	..	..	..	..	..	..	..	..	..
G20 OECD countries	..	..	..	..	..	..	..	..	..	..
G20 Non-OECD countries	..	..	..	..	..	..	..	..	..	..
MENA countries	..	..	..	..	..	..	..	..	..	..
ASEAN countries	..	..	..	..	..	..	..	..	..	..

- Nil; .. Not available

Note: Detailed metadata at: *http://stats.oecd.org/OECDStat_Metadata/ShowMetadata.ashx?Dataset=FDI_CTRY_IND_SUMM.*

Source: *OECD International Direct Investment Statistics (database): https://doi.org/10.1787/idi-data-en*

FRANCE

Table 4. Foreign direct investment flows by industrial sector

Million US dollars

	Inward					Outward				
	2015	2016	2017	2018	2019	2015	2016	2017	2018	2019
All FDI activities	**45 354.4**	**23 054.3**	**24 779.6**	**38 162.4**	**33 964.0**	**53 205.8**	**64 784.9**	**35 908.0**	**105 569.5**	**38 662.3**
Agriculture, forestry and fishing	**26.6**	**113.9**	**60.9**	**96.8**	**211.6**	**155.3**	**-131.6**	**81.2**	**-35.4**	**67.2**
Mining and quarrying	**-288.4**	**-134.9**	**-3.4**	**898.1**	**-78.4**	**12 299.5**	**4 397.9**	**-4 293.8**	**5 091.5**	**6 547.6**
Extraction activities	-296.2	-136.0	470.1	643.2	-206.0	12 294.0	4 399.0	-4 296.0	5 090.3	6 547.6
Manufacturing	**-4 221.9**	**8 033.8**	**99.2**	**17 532.2**	**-2 758.3**	**-4 329.5**	**16 377.3**	**10 104.8**	**43 905.3**	**-4 609.9**
of which:										
Food products, beverages and tobacco	-593.5	-3 915.7	2 968.1	-440.2	-2 330.7	2 478.1	3 229.0	12 788.9	-901.7	-1 907.5
Textiles, wood and paper products; printing	26.6	513.1	-64.3	-140.4	3 136.7	-216.3	915.6	-2 191.4	951.3	-1 810.1
Chemical, rubber, plastic, non-metallic mineral products	3 263.5	984.2	8 918.9	-4 205.1	3 140.0	117.6	6 261.2	-2 232.0	11 743.2	-12 126.9
Metal and machinery products, except electrical equipment	2 285.1	12 446.1	-8 000.2	-317.5	-2 140.4	-2 463.7	8 010.6	-5 372.6	721.1	6 162.5
Motor vehicles, trailers, semi-trailers, other transport equipment	-1 044.9	-393.7	-740.6	-3 007.2	-6 160.3	3 808.1	-263.2	8 317.0	715.2	-623.5
Other manufacturing	-8 158.6	-1 600.1	-2 982.8	25 642.6	1 596.3	-8 054.4	-1 776.0	-1 205.1	30 676.3	5 695.7
Electricity, gas, steam and air conditioning supply	**829.7**	**1 255.1**	**-2 509.3**	**157.0**	**1 305.3**	**1 797.0**	**803.9**	**-2 885.8**	**3 317.6**	**-2 665.4**
Water supply; sewerage, waste management and remediation activities	**24.4**	**49.8**	**-302.1**	**77.9**	**29.1**	**1 198.0**	**2.2**	**-58.6**	**972.5**	**-2 321.7**
Construction	**16 924.0**	**1 359.1**	**-4 831.5**	**-2 757.0**	**-578.8**	**-1 026.1**	**-764.1**	**-5 233.9**	**2 978.9**	**949.3**
Services	**25 407.7**	**-2 208.3**	**30 207.4**	**32 269.6**	**32 074.3**	**44 645.6**	**40 132.7**	**37 348.7**	**49 099.5**	**16 765.9**
Wholesale and retail trade; repair of motor vehicles and motorcycles	2 376.0	212.3	6 160.5	3 240.9	1 665.7	4 411.5	4 821.4	-1 790.1	6 550.2	-2 273.6
Transportation and storage	2 134.2	1 351.3	3 233.0	534.6	434.3	1 812.5	-360.5	-983.0	722.3	2 871.4
Accommodation and food service activities	-549.1	2 440.6	175.9	-1 278.2	2 209.8	173.0	2 612.0	8 212.2	-3 993.9	-301.1
Information and communication	2 072.1	557.3	3 414.5	3 315.2	3 358.3	2 978.4	116.1	983.0	11 744.4	6 168.1
Financial and insurance activities	13 513.0	-11 714.0	13 628.7	26 296.5	17 076.0	12 863.0	26 855.0	10 899.6	7 056.5	579.9
Activities of holding companies	4 495.8	-5 298.0	4 306.2	9 005.1	3 885.6	2 794.2	819.4	1 029.2	979.6	4 349.0
Real estate activities	8 722.1	-2 011.5	-564.8	259.6	1 376.9	13 164.7	3 758.7	2 248.9	24 547.4	4 070.3
Professional, scientific and technical activities	-1 724.9	3 773.1	3 514.8	140.4	5 869.2	4 169.7	1 586.9	11 917.5	2 236.5	1 756.4
Administrative and support service activities	-56.6	2 275.8	-1 508.3	-1 450.5	-1 141.8	4 022.2	560.7	4 954.3	73.2	3 352.7
Public administration; activities of households and of extraterritorial organisations	-	..	..	..	-	..	201.3	224.3	-13.0	117.5
Education	-6.7	266.5	437.4	-135.7	10.1	..	..	..	..	..
Human health and social work activities	-748.8	512.0	912.0	560.6	258.6	1 213.5	-84.0	579.4	67.3	-106.3
Arts, entertainment and recreation	-320.6	130.5	756.4	732.9	385.1	..	..	-2.3	..	..
Other services	..	..	47.3	61.4	570.9	23.3	50.9	104.8	108.6	538.5
Not allocated and confidential	**6 652.2**	**14 585.9**	**2 058.4**	**-10 112.1**	**3 759.1**	**-1 534.1**	**3 966.6**	**845.5**	**239.6**	**23 929.3**
Private real estate activities	-	-	-	-	-	-	-	-	-	-

- Nil; .. Not available

Note: Detailed metadata at: *http://stats.oecd.org/OECDStat_Metadata/ShowMetadata.ashx?Dataset=FDI_CTRY_IND_SUMM.*

Source: *OECD International Direct Investment Statistics (database): https://doi.org/10.1787/idi-data-en*

Table 5. Foreign direct investment positions by industrial sector
At year end

Million US dollars

	Inward					Outward				
	2015	2016	2017	2018	2019	2015	2016	2017	2018	2019
All FDI activities	**687 394.7**	**694 881.4**	**819 327.2**	**820 534.7**	**868 641.9**	**1 268 227.5**	**1 284 859.3**	**1 440 434.2**	**1 499 081.7**	**1 532 739.8**
Agriculture, forestry and fishing	**496.5**	**678.8**	**847.9**	**849.6**	**1 053.7**	**499.7**	**393.2**	**407.8**	**437.4**	**508.9**
Mining and quarrying	**4 272.2**	**4 899.3**	**3 903.8**	**4 431.0**	**3 976.6**	**103 472.0**	**113 755.7**	**114 652.2**	**123 695.9**	**131 455.9**
Extraction activities	4 058.8	4 707.5	3 945.8	4 213.4	3 725.0	103 462.2	113 755.7	114 543.1	123 611.2	131 369.4
Manufacturing	**166 421.3**	**179 479.3**	**250 229.1**	**253 291.7**	**263 191.4**	**373 918.3**	**380 503.8**	**424 525.1**	**474 905.0**	**474 275.4**
of which:										
Food products, beverages and tobacco	32 898.2	26 577.4	34 992.8	35 565.6	32 479.2	60 243.9	61 354.5	91 396.0	87 091.8	86 977.1
Textiles, wood and paper products; printing	7 163.9	7 447.0	13 992.6	13 726.8	16 058.2	15 648.3	15 642.5	15 067.2	15 298.8	13 522.8
Chemical, rubber, plastic, non-metallic mineral products	71 850.8	75 444.3	111 517.2	108 274.6	121 428.9	135 303.2	137 969.9	155 922.3	183 607.7	175 238.1
Metal and machinery products, except electrical equipment	17 823.6	36 895.8	43 413.3	38 900.8	36 570.4	27 742.0	41 073.0	36 492.0	38 342.1	45 777.4
Motor vehicles, trailers, semi-trailers, other transport equipment	16 751.2	14 685.4	24 424.3	18 331.8	13 002.7	67 343.5	62 618.3	69 664.2	63 831.0	59 940.5
Other manufacturing	19 932.5	18 427.3	21 887.7	38 492.1	43 653.1	67 637.5	61 845.7	55 983.4	86 733.5	92 820.7
Electricity, gas, steam and air conditioning supply	**3 713.7**	**4 382.8**	**5 323.8**	**6 772.4**	**7 195.0**	**89 245.5**	**85 793.2**	**88 933.8**	**86 466.7**	**84 505.7**
Water supply; sewerage, waste management and remediation activities	**621.7**	**719.9**	**714.8**	**792.3**	**795.3**	**5 516.6**	**4 973.1**	**5 159.5**	**6 327.0**	**4 382.2**
Construction	**22 391.9**	**22 863.9**	**22 698.5**	**17 741.0**	**15 951.5**	**27 436.0**	**22 586.7**	**19 678.6**	**19 869.5**	**22 084.9**
Services	**475 276.0**	**454 420.8**	**507 705.7**	**519 847.7**	**562 387.1**	**641 045.2**	**647 115.0**	**755 963.1**	**757 351.7**	**785 203.3**
Wholesale and retail trade; repair of motor vehicles and motorcycles	51 325.0	46 885.2	80 057.6	82 593.3	82 908.3	91 222.6	95 101.7	106 775.0	124 956.5	125 377.4
Transportation and storage	9 737.6	9 967.3	18 323.3	17 611.6	17 560.1	8 999.5	8 656.1	11 310.9	13 196.7	16 276.1
Accommodation and food service activities	5 684.3	7 609.4	12 461.0	11 991.1	14 815.8	12 861.2	12 998.8	23 490.0	16 856.0	16 539.0
Information and communication	16 681.5	18 234.4	31 699.4	32 119.3	35 009.0	79 499.2	75 413.7	84 315.2	90 310.3	100 293.2
Financial and insurance activities	189 669.0	172 687.9	126 715.0	142 239.5	153 810.4	311 113.8	322 707.9	353 574.0	316 954.4	333 211.6
Activities of holding companies	75 523.1	74 580.0	12 072.4	18 058.2	18 465.5	35 098.5	34 721.2	32 918.0	12 119.3	19 918.0
Real estate activities	152 710.9	143 840.0	179 183.3	178 550.5	188 650.9	76 129.6	74 232.1	75 231.5	94 787.0	108 570.0
Professional, scientific and technical activities	35 528.6	39 808.2	36 422.4	33 193.3	37 671.3	52 194.9	48 424.2	56 524.3	54 742.4	56 468.2
Administrative and support service activities	8 761.0	9 265.3	11 709.0	9 782.5	18 872.2	5 457.8	5 912.3	39 611.4	40 476.3	22 823.0
Public administration; activities of households and of extraterritorial organisations	..	..	..	..	..	..	256.1	530.1	494.6	603.2
Education	1 087.6	1 368.2	2 169.6	2 047.2	2 016.4	..	..	..	..	..
Human health and social work activities	3 193.3	3 723.0	6 199.3	5 511.8	5 965.0	2 938.5	2 757.5	3 943.4	3 952.4	3 849.7
Arts, entertainment and recreation	726.2	904.4	2 290.7	3 561.9	3 855.3	..	..	130.7	..	..
Other services	..	..	381.4	564.5	1 171.6	512.8	546.0	447.3	446.5	1 067.2
Not allocated and confidential	**14 201.4**	**27 436.5**	**27 903.6**	**16 809.0**	**14 091.2**	**27 094.2**	**29 738.6**	**31 114.2**	**30 028.6**	**30 323.5**
Private real estate activities	-	-	-	-	-	-	-	-	-	-

- Nil; .. Not available

Note: Detailed metadata at: *http://stats.oecd.org/OECDStat_Metadata/ShowMetadata.ashx?Dataset=FDI_CTRY_IND_SUMM.*

Source: *OECD International Direct Investment Statistics (database): https://doi.org/10.1787/idi-data-en*

FRANCE

Table 6. Foreign direct investment income by industrial sector

Million US dollars

	Inward					Outward				
	2015	2016	2017	2018	2019	2015	2016	2017	2018	2019
All FDI activities	**26 922.9**	**29 483.6**	**36 340.9**	**37 501.5**	**36 506.2**	**70 308.4**	**69 441.6**	**77 144.6**	**94 514.3**	**89 876.9**
Agriculture, forestry and fishing	..	..	..	..	-	..	..	..	..	-
Mining and quarrying	..	..	..	..	..	..	..	..	..	..
Extraction activities	..	..	..	..	..	..	..	..	..	..
Manufacturing	..	..	..	..	..	..	..	..	..	..
of which:										
Food products, beverages and tobacco	..	..	..	..	..	..	..	..	..	..
Textiles, wood and paper products; printing	..	..	..	..	..	..	..	..	..	..
Chemical, rubber, plastic, non-metallic mineral products	..	..	..	..	..	..	..	..	..	..
Metal and machinery products, except electrical equipment	..	..	..	..	..	..	..	..	..	..
Motor vehicles, trailers, semi-trailers, other transport equipment	..	..	..	..	..	..	..	..	..	..
Other manufacturing	..	..	..	..	..	..	..	..	..	..
Electricity, gas, steam and air conditioning supply	..	..	..	..	..	..	..	..	..	..
Water supply; sewerage, waste management and remediation activities	..	..	..	..	..	..	..	..	..	..
Construction	..	..	..	..	..	..	..	..	..	..
Services	..	..	..	..	..	..	..	..	..	..
Wholesale and retail trade; repair of motor vehicles and motorcycles	..	..	..	..	..	..	..	..	..	..
Transportation and storage	..	..	..	..	..	..	..	..	..	..
Accommodation and food service activities	..	..	..	..	..	..	..	..	..	..
Information and communication	..	..	..	..	..	..	..	..	..	..
Financial and insurance activities	..	..	..	..	..	..	..	..	..	..
Activities of holding companies	..	..	..	..	..	..	..	..	..	..
Real estate activities	..	..	..	..	..	..	..	..	..	..
Professional, scientific and technical activities	..	..	..	..	..	..	..	..	..	..
Administrative and support service activities	..	..	..	..	..	..	..	..	..	..
Public administration; activities of households and of extraterritorial organisations	-	-	-	-	-	-	-	..	..	..
Education	..	..	..	..	..	..	..	..	..	-
Human health and social work activities	..	..	..	..	..	..	..	..	..	..
Arts, entertainment and recreation	..	..	..	..	..	..	..	..	..	..
Other services	..	..	..	..	..	..	..	..	..	..
Not allocated and confidential	..	..	..	..	..	..	..	..	..	..
Private real estate activities	-	-	-	-	-	-	-	-	-	-

- Nil; .. Not available

Note: Detailed metadata at: *http://stats.oecd.org/OECDStat_Metadata/ShowMetadata.ashx?Dataset=FDI_CTRY_IND_SUMM.*

Source: *OECD International Direct Investment Statistics (database): https://doi.org/10.1787/idi-data-en*

GERMANY

Table 1. Foreign direct investment flows by country

Million US dollars

	Inward					Outward				
	2015	2016	2017	2018	2019	2015	2016	2017	2018	2019
WORLD	**30 534.1**	**15 617.9**	**60 225.2**	**73 523.6**	**57 793.5**	**99 003.2**	**63 599.0**	**103 865.1**	**78 763.9**	**120 133.5**
OECD COUNTRIES	**39 848.9**	**16 871.5**	**58 973.7**	**73 247.0**	**59 179.7**	**82 634.8**	**53 929.1**	**86 864.8**	**60 983.2**	**113 208.1**
Australia	-116.0	-159.0	953.8	438.5	785.2	801.3	209.9	2 101.4	2 176.6	-540.3
Austria	3 036.4	-338.5	2 481.4	3 133.7	2 233.8	-1 147.0	11 292.7	4 307.1	708.3	3 499.8
Belgium	-5 721.5	316.1	-8 510.0	-4 374.0	-5 736.0	8 723.2	-4 667.6	-14 325.3	-2 512.5	13 268.0
Canada	-367.4	2 436.0	650.8	285.1	2 865.1	614.7	994.4	633.7	1 429.9	903.0
Chile	2.7	9.5	265.8	-175.8	76.4	668.4	-83.7	157.8	-39.5	121.6
Czech Republic	-88.5	1 234.9	-43.1	-557.5	328.5	284.8	2 185.1	2 591.5	2 031.4	1 015.5
Denmark	1 799.3	-1 176.1	5 487.5	-522.9	704.2	-449.1	-165.6	933.1	1 032.0	910.6
Estonia	-10.7	23.5	11.6	-19.4	7.5	-104.0	21.9	112.5	72.9	22.5
Finland	248.6	-248.3	-762.1	-347.6	-878.0	593.0	-347.3	780.2	525.5	772.6
France	-187.0	5 034.5	7 880.4	-20 101.4	2 733.9	-639.3	-402.6	10 520.0	7 910.3	3 015.9
Germany	-	-	-	-	-	-	-	-	-	-
Greece	-113.8	-10.0	32.7	-40.7	52.7	63.1	244.6	869.4	652.0	267.3
Hungary	-119.0	-27.1	-241.1	96.5	1 798.5	228.3	1 432.7	-2 119.3	-461.1	1 959.4
Iceland	8.5	-9.7	0.5	0.8	5.0	18.3	26.6	48.7	74.3	12.8
Ireland	1 961.1	-3 128.6	116.2	46 303.9	3 847.0	198.6	-3 038.3	298.2	14 514.3	-4 670.7
Israel	163.6	113.4	58.6	171.3	138.3	131.3	288.3	237.3	-12.0	223.3
Italy	-479.7	644.9	-1 315.3	1 136.2	-799.9	964.1	3 275.7	421.8	2 672.6	8 020.3
Japan	2 474.4	1 872.4	2 787.8	2 109.7	4 892.8	-2 816.9	1 715.0	613.4	669.9	732.9
Korea	162.4	712.8	117.6	-8.1	1 110.9	684.2	467.1	1 052.8	-18.6	1 208.0
Latvia	-2.6	3.0	-31.0	8.6	-1.4	2.5	23.6	35.4	73.6	324.9
Lithuania	-10.9	-12.4	-22.7	-41.0	63.0	65.4	150.9	-21.5	35.7	292.0
Luxembourg	14 628.0	356.8	7 144.3	6 990.1	32 734.9	12 182.8	11 634.0	25 541.2	11 915.3	31 778.7
Mexico	-281.9	91.5	-101.5	176.5	84.2	1 764.3	1 382.7	3 238.5	2 048.2	679.5
Netherlands	10 580.5	2 378.8	13 096.9	37 091.7	-10 242.4	27 708.0	3 411.0	-177.4	-9 495.8	16 905.2
New Zealand	-53.9	-10.1	5.4	-10.1	-18.3	28.8	-2.7	-19.7	182.0	124.4
Norway	-150.4	-968.6	734.1	155.3	350.4	1 375.4	-746.8	1 037.6	-553.2	926.4
Poland	190.5	-305.4	-203.9	357.4	-419.5	2 435.5	2 931.4	2 645.5	1 931.7	1 666.0
Portugal	-15.1	58.8	-31.5	-54.5	-9.1	-46.0	824.6	201.2	197.4	204.7
Slovak Republic	383.6	181.7	-223.7	-127.6	-10.3	-120.5	71.2	842.3	-56.6	713.1
Slovenia	-3.3	-3.4	16.2	4.6	-21.5	202.8	25.3	44.4	225.0	124.2
Spain	921.2	1 845.0	-1 439.1	534.2	-363.6	717.6	2 558.2	5 767.5	8 815.3	3 219.1
Sweden	-452.2	-1 034.5	8 817.2	-5 991.4	2 230.3	7 575.0	1 064.8	-693.5	2 243.5	-673.3
Switzerland	6 687.4	6 133.6	3 584.6	10 352.0	-2 108.6	690.3	3 701.1	3 134.3	526.5	1 057.4
Turkey	208.7	-56.6	220.2	-445.5	355.3	1 083.8	602.3	1 606.3	2 169.5	1 135.9
United Kingdom	2 760.2	866.4	-6 083.1	657.6	11 661.5	-1 866.8	616.1	4 793.1	-451.7	-11 073.3
United States	1 792.1	33.9	23 495.3	-3 938.9	10 728.9	20 086.9	12 383.5	29 633.8	9 750.4	35 061.0
EUROPE	**33 888.2**	**8 473.1**	**30 379.6**	**74 940.4**	**41 536.7**	**63 758.1**	**35 830.4**	**53 209.7**	**49 009.9**	**72 017.0**
Bulgaria	38.7	103.4	23.6	51.6	-5.7	184.4	219.7	240.4	226.8	-153.9
Croatia	6.5	34.0	-40.0	10.8	4.7	36.5	135.5	282.6	275.3	43.2
Cyprus	98.7	213.5	312.0	1 467.3	156.1	308.4	79.9	-722.6	-1 639.6	-4 877.0
Malta	55.8	58.2	90.5	6.6	2 825.8	1 207.3	-4 755.1	346.2	-1 042.2	66.2
Romania	10.5	25.6	50.9	-5.3	-77.2	483.2	1 058.4	-36.3	872.8	631.4
Russian Federation	542.2	-231.6	-995.0	-524.3	-418.1	517.2	1 643.0	2 436.8	4 117.8	1 826.5
Ukraine	-50.3	-48.0	-6.9	6.1	104.9	-106.3	35.2	235.0	-52.6	-224.6
AFRICA	**-19.4**	**-65.6**	**299.1**	**44.4**	**150.7**	**692.5**	**1 940.2**	**1 491.3**	**2 489.3**	**1 417.1**
Northern Africa	-17.2	-6.4	76.0	-45.0	34.2	269.2	1 201.1	667.4	1 548.7	457.6
Algeria	-1.1	1.2	6.0	-6.0	1.1	276.4	328.4	325.3	319.6	-91.0
Egypt	-7.6	-12.6	54.6	-26.3	64.2	298.3	689.4	-69.8	-416.2	102.3
Libya	0.1	-16.6	-1.3	18.9	0.0	-304.1	-213.4	356.1	173.4	304.9
Morocco	-3.1	13.0	-5.2	2.5	-2.4	10.3	385.8	10.9	1 407.8	85.3
Tunisia	-5.5	8.5	21.9	-34.1	-28.7	-11.6	10.9	44.8	64.0	56.2
Other African countries	-2.2	-59.2	223.1	89.4	116.5	423.3	739.1	823.9	940.6	959.4
Nigeria	7.8	39.6	-15.6	11.8	-20.2	57.0	42.5	62.9	124.1	-12.1
South Africa	-0.1	-99.6	267.3	116.7	73.9	348.1	712.3	486.2	671.4	718.3
AMERICA	**-5 698.8**	**2 624.0**	**26 591.4**	**-5 077.9**	**8 764.8**	**26 423.8**	**13 379.7**	**34 235.3**	**14 132.5**	**36 812.8**
Northern America	1 424.7	2 469.9	24 146.1	-3 653.8	13 594.0	20 701.6	13 377.9	30 267.5	11 180.3	35 963.9
Central America and Caribbean countries	-7 064.0	66.0	2 078.4	-1 083.0	-4 879.5	2 095.0	518.8	2 004.4	1 266.5	-159.8
Bahamas	173.1	5.8	58.1	-2 077.2	-891.9	7.6	4.3	12.3	19.6	17.9
Bermuda	-5 141.0	-1 084.3	22.7	-284.5	1 748.6	14.2	115.0	-134.9	266.9	-542.5
Cayman Islands	-1 478.6	-77.1	531.6	-2 427.5	-1 250.3	411.0	-987.5	-1 086.6	-671.8	21.0
Costa Rica	6.6	-0.3	-1.1	-1.1	-6.0	2.9	16.2	-38.0	23.2	-47.2
El Salvador	-	-	-1.1	-3.5	-1.1	3.3	-5.5	-1.4	-22.1	-3.5
Guatemala	-	2.2	1.2	-2.0	-4.4	3.8	-12.9	5.8	-3.8	-8.6
Honduras	2.2	2.2	1.1	-3.5	1.1	8.8	-7.5	-13.6	-3.4	11.2
Nicaragua	-10.0	-	-	-	-	8.9	0.5	-22.9	6.9	-1.6
Panama	-56.8	-3.3	33.4	-18.4	-8.8	84.4	-27.8	119.9	38.9	-15.8
Virgin Islands, U.S.	-	-	-496.5	-67.2	-	-	-	-	-	-
South America	-59.6	88.1	367.0	-341.1	50.3	3 627.2	-517.0	1 963.4	1 685.8	1 008.7
Argentina	-65.0	42.7	31.6	-23.9	-7.1	458.3	204.1	725.2	309.1	915.7
Bolivia	1.1	0.0	0.0	1.2	0.0	7.3	-91.3	1.1	6.6	16.2
Brazil	43.4	35.7	41.2	-115.4	-21.8	1 904.9	-991.9	1 156.6	85.1	-607.6
Colombia	-6.6	-12.6	3.1	-32.2	8.9	114.6	174.1	132.2	122.5	130.3
Ecuador	-1.8	1.8	-2.2	4.6	-1.1	53.9	21.1	27.8	26.4	48.0
Paraguay	-0.5	9.2	0.8	-2.3	-0.3	0.1	0.7	15.4	25.2	29.0
Peru	-2.2	0.4	-5.6	-11.8	-0.4	82.7	72.1	25.0	72.6	124.9
Uruguay	-8.7	-11.0	2.0	-7.0	-3.4	251.4	-4.2	153.2	1 224.0	166.7
Venezuela	-22.0	12.3	29.7	21.6	-0.8	52.4	159.1	-442.8	-136.7	61.9

GERMANY

Table 1. Foreign direct investment flows by country (*cont.*)

Million US dollars

	Inward					Outward				
	2015	2016	2017	2018	2019	2015	2016	2017	2018	2019
ASIA	**2 534.0**	**4 770.2**	**2 258.4**	**3 367.3**	**6 793.0**	**7 302.0**	**12 237.2**	**12 848.2**	**10 768.9**	**10 302.4**
Near and Middle East	-155.1	190.3	611.3	-55.2	-389.0	851.6	947.2	964.3	276.9	882.2
Gulf Arabian countries	-324.6	59.1	545.8	-232.0	-527.9	756.6	613.4	815.5	286.5	680.4
Kuwait	11.9	11.6	-13.5	-8.5	1.3	-8.5	85.0	88.9	13.3	28.6
Qatar	-301.1	124.3	554.9	-209.4	-498.2	101.6	126.3	28.5	-301.4	50.2
Saudi Arabia	52.8	-132.2	-123.7	19.5	35.2	64.8	356.3	0.0	-286.8	-90.4
United Arab Emirates	-97.5	71.1	140.7	-15.9	-51.0	631.8	-74.7	659.6	910.1	656.1
Other Near and Middle East	169.5	131.2	65.5	176.8	138.9	95.0	333.8	148.7	-9.6	201.8
Jordan	-6.2	7.7	2.3	1.2	-0.1	-1.7	0.6	-17.4	-25.6	-25.8
Other Asian countries	2 689.1	4 579.9	1 647.2	3 422.5	7 182.0	6 450.4	11 290.0	11 883.9	10 492.0	9 420.2
China	101.9	527.1	13.1	15.8	1 446.3	6 079.7	8 429.1	7 019.5	4 068.6	3 774.8
Hong Kong, China	26.8	1 109.9	-705.4	1 263.1	445.5	271.6	363.6	622.9	609.5	2 152.8
India	-22.5	-48.5	-53.2	-142.3	-117.9	1 789.3	1 501.2	1 217.5	1 705.6	1 289.8
Indonesia	25.3	22.2	-38.4	14.4	-17.7	13.2	98.8	167.1	304.7	207.2
Iran, Islamic Republic of	-5.4	14.8	31.1	97.4	40.3	25.5	264.6	-553.0	135.7	-41.5
Malaysia	131.1	67.4	-209.0	-13.0	-41.0	205.7	580.5	561.0	335.4	165.0
Philippines	-5.6	4.5	2.8	-11.8	0.1	59.3	-362.8	181.5	201.4	224.0
Singapore	-220.0	171.3	-536.1	-4.3	-410.9	166.1	-2 685.1	-8.6	1 151.8	-311.1
Chinese Taipei	59.5	72.0	21.1	46.8	-22.4	53.1	130.7	171.6	754.0	-67.4
Thailand	-27.7	-109.6	3.7	80.0	-71.2	-281.3	389.0	533.7	190.7	-16.5
Viet Nam	3.6	4.2	10.1	-16.1	2.4	80.2	107.2	91.1	11.0	57.9
AUSTRALIA, OCEANIA AND POLAR REGIONS	**-169.8**	**-183.7**	**696.6**	**239.9**	**557.3**	**826.7**	**211.6**	**2 080.6**	**2 363.4**	**-415.8**
WORLD unallocated and confidential	**0.0**	**0.0**	**-**	**9.4**	**-9.0**	**-**	**0.0**	**-**	**-**	**-**
European Union (EU28)	**29 515.5**	**7 094.9**	**26 614.8**	**65 667.4**	**42 817.8**	**59 791.8**	**29 880.7**	**43 477.7**	**41 272.2**	**67 272.4**
G20 countries excl. European Union	**6 643.9**	**11 592.5**	**27 749.0**	**-20 330.0**	**35 390.6**	**31 851.8**	**33 197.0**	**67 823.7**	**39 332.8**	**47 177.1**
G20 OECD countries	**5 965.9**	**11 476.7**	**28 606.1**	**-19 690.5**	**34 417.8**	**20 676.2**	**21 244.1**	**54 614.8**	**28 357.2**	**39 142.7**
G20 Non-OECD countries	**678.0**	**115.9**	**-857.1**	**-639.5**	**972.8**	**11 175.5**	**11 952.9**	**13 208.9**	**10 975.6**	**8 034.3**
MENA countries	**-345.5**	**70.3**	**630.6**	**-274.0**	**-494.2**	**981.4**	**1 817.0**	**1 472.1**	**1 812.3**	**1 088.2**
ASEAN countries	**-82.0**	**154.5**	**-771.3**	**48.0**	**-541.4**	**254.6**	**-1 866.9**	**1 528.8**	**2 163.7**	**367.2**

- Nil

Note: Detailed metadata at: *http://stats.oecd.org/OECDStat_Metadata/ShowMetadata.ashx?Dataset=FDI_CTRY_IND_SUMM*.

Source: *OECD International Direct Investment Statistics (database)*: *https://doi.org/10.1787/idi-data-en*

GERMANY

Table 2. Foreign direct investment positions by country
At year end

Million US dollars

	Inward					Outward				
	2015	2016	2017	2018	2019	2015	2016	2017	2018	2019
WORLD	**781 743.1**	**794 510.4**	**963 121.9**	**934 402.3**	..	**1 369 209.6**	**1 367 630.4**	**1 650 292.6**	**1 651 416.3**	**1 754 495.6**
OECD COUNTRIES	**734 250.4**	**740 795.8**	**894 279.2**	**870 929.7**	..	**1 143 407.7**	**1 135 030.0**	**1 372 342.3**	**1 383 611.2**	**1 474 083.4**
Australia	3 246.6	4 354.4	4 985.6	4 993.1	..	11 603.7	11 963.7	14 618.6	13 369.6	14 447.3
Austria	24 989.7	23 894.8	30 129.5	26 609.8	..	44 631.5	50 981.3	67 678.1	68 091.4	69 304.7
Belgium	11 479.6	10 011.6	12 332.7	11 306.4	..	40 618.4	35 196.6	23 258.6	20 827.8	35 823.4
Canada	.. d	.. d	.. d	.. d	..	13 905.3	14 705.4	16 977.7	16 732.3	18 156.6
Chile	620.6	1 499.9	563.7	522.1	..	1 984.8	.. d	.. d	.. d	.. d
Czech Republic	808.9	855.9	990.6	1 033.9	..	18 904.7	20 343.6	27 824.4	21 829.6	22 229.8
Denmark	7 646.2	8 241.8	9 631.8	8 363.9	..	5 242.2	6 134.7	7 669.7	7 547.5	8 136.4
Estonia	3.3	5.3	.. c	.. c	..	4.4	23.2	135.5	223.3	302.2
Finland	3 071.3	2 875.5	4 096.9	8 081.1	..	3 078.9	2 937.7	3 693.9	3 739.4	4 677.6
France	54 028.3	53 257.1	71 321.7	67 486.8	..	72 999.5	70 393.2	101 458.4	98 793.2	101 510.9
Germany	62 546.5	71 940.6	92 616.9	69 856.9	..	..	-	-	-	-
Greece	67.5	76.9	52.8	48.1	..	4 497.6	5 065.9	7 118.0	7 149.1	8 431.8
Hungary	66.4	99.1	122.3	108.8	..	13 728.9	13 877.9	18 726.3	16 556.0	17 779.2
Iceland	397.4	16.9	18.0	20.6	..	57.7	.. d	.. d	.. d	.. d
Ireland	7 584.1	5 347.3	5 403.0	43 063.9	..	10 260.2	10 209.8	12 131.2	25 859.9	20 565.0
Israel	5 585.2	5 062.7	6 658.7	6 313.3	..	1 094.2	1 197.4	1 432.0	1 258.3	1 571.6
Italy	35 062.6	33 599.7	35 820.3	33 491.0	..	31 816.0	32 880.8	39 486.7	38 715.4	44 111.4
Japan	36 272.2	37 322.7	42 010.1	46 012.1	..	6 525.9	8 340.9	10 455.7	10 224.4	10 820.0
Korea	4 536.7	5 755.2	6 801.4	6 076.3	..	9 208.5	8 271.3	10 551.7	10 224.4	11 203.1
Latvia	9.8	.. c	14.4	14.9	..	769.7	649.3	819.1	771.7	1 134.6
Lithuania	2.2	.. c	.. c	.. c	..	724.0	953.9	1 002.6	880.5	1 102.0
Luxembourg	54 835.1	53 514.3	59 018.9	64 758.4	..	139 543.8	136 757.7	179 161.7	182 680.3	213 170.1
Mexico	.. d	.. d	.. d	.. d	..	8 260.2	9 058.7	12 890.4	14 185.9	16 104.2
Netherlands	51 801.9	46 522.6	56 352.8	55 098.5	..	120 076.2	133 641.8	160 338.2	173 764.6	201 172.8
New Zealand	55.5	.. d	.. d	.. d	..	508.4	663.0	1 590.3	1 653.3	1 827.7
Norway	2 155.7	2 241.0	3 022.3	2 499.4	..	7 277.1	6 929.5	6 646.7	5 895.4	6 996.2
Poland	432.2	716.8	946.3	753.4	..	29 566.7	29 132.5	38 969.8	37 691.8	40 069.6
Portugal	445.3	416.4	405.4	413.3	..	3 166.0	3 359.3	4 188.1	4 437.8	5 058.4
Slovak Republic	1.1	1.1	1.2	2.3	..	3 881.3	3 158.0	4 368.0	3 975.3	5 137.0
Slovenia	84.9	76.9	67.2	68.7	..	1 198.7	1 135.2	1 492.0	1 494.2	1 577.2
Spain	25 955.4	24 900.4	29 051.3	25 034.3	..	49 805.1	48 540.1	66 265.3	67 325.4	70 043.8
Sweden	15 486.1	14 714.9	20 596.1	18 887.1	..	25 171.5	23 485.8	25 335.8	24 164.2	21 953.5
Switzerland	54 352.7	59 685.9	68 648.4	66 154.1	..	34 801.3	38 921.7	45 225.5	42 149.1	38 878.9
Turkey	1 585.2	1 612.7	2 002.9	1 762.1	..	9 992.4	9 351.7	10 593.7	9 624.5	9 527.1
United Kingdom	89 879.2	92 148.2	102 553.4	82 912.8	..	151 477.4	140 717.8	158 648.4	144 977.1	140 303.3
United States	171 474.1	171 626.4	217 855.6	209 477.9	..	268 515.0	254 632.7	289 576.6	304 196.2	310 956.0
EUROPE	**520 013.1**	**527 565.1**	**628 361.7**	**609 726.4**	..	**873 252.0**	**873 344.6**	**1 079 400.3**	**1 073 739.4**	**1 151 995.1**
Bulgaria	.. c	.. c	.. c	53.8	..	1 734.3	1 926.8	2 168.4	1 979.6	2 008.5
Croatia	.. c	.. c	-	.. c	..	2 164.4	2 160.9	2 547.4	2 441.0	2 767.9
Cyprus	1 475.2	1 300.7	1 760.6	1 946.4	..	1 694.1	215.0	-1 079.4	-2 591.0	-6 057.1
Malta	370.2	721.0	369.4	338.9	..	13 850.8	9 407.6	21 597.5	20 848.4	18 057.7
Romania	6.5	6.3	.. c	.. c	..	7 060.4	7 802.3	9 087.3	9 436.7	9 530.4
Russian Federation	7 914.0	8 730.9	11 671.9	10 472.9	..	14 918.9	18 945.9	22 066.4	20 509.5	23 901.4
Ukraine	135.0	.. c	.. c	.. c	..	2 880.8	2 679.5	2 844.8	3 273.4	4 003.6
AFRICA	**1 699.5**	**1 514.7**	**1 800.2**	**2 265.9**	..	**8 916.7**	**10 170.8**	**11 134.6**	**10 928.6**	**14 265.3**
Northern Africa	236.3	198.2	104.3	144.3	..	2 403.9	2 624.6	2 422.6	2 340.3	4 483.3
Algeria	3.3	3.2	3.6	3.4	..	389.8	533.4	663.2	546.1	797.6
Egypt	.. c	56.9	.. d	123.7	..	1 367.4	1 573.7	973.9	601.1	1 246.9
Libya	167.7	134.9	.. c	.. c	..	-57.7	-255.1	-26.4	-41.2	924.5
Morocco	.. c	.. c	.. c	.. c	..	411.5	536.5	581.7	973.2	1 168.3
Tunisia	1.1	.. d	1.2	2.3	..	292.9	237.2	230.3	261.0	346.0
Other African countries	1 463.3	1 316.5	1 694.7	2 121.6	..	6 513.9	7 546.1	8 713.1	8 588.3	9 782.1
Nigeria	.. c	.. c	.. c	.. c	..	381.1	374.2	315.4	563.3	698.7
South Africa	1 464.3	1 308.1	.. d	.. d	..	4 843.8	5 764.7	6 751.0	6 430.0	7 052.3
AMERICA	**185 536.2**	**185 547.6**	**233 380.9**	**224 921.0**	..	**321 532.9**	**310 884.4**	**352 379.5**	**363 661.6**	**370 771.7**
Northern America	178 657.6	179 464.5	227 303.9	218 607.7	..	282 420.3	269 338.0	306 554.3	320 928.6	329 112.6
Central America and Caribbean countries	5 210.7	2 931.4	4 084.9	4 555.8	..	16 474.7	16 394.0	19 362.0	18 860.8	19 627.1
Bahamas	.. c	.. c	6.0	5.7	..	103.4	106.5	136.7	140.8	155.0
Bermuda	1 457.8	1 368.2	1 911.7	2 490.3	..	2 112.1	1 794.0	1 838.6	2 230.4	1 672.7
Cayman Islands	1 730.0	-546.0	-582.9	-600.0	..	1 921.6	1 418.8	887.5	-755.7	-797.6
Costa Rica	-	-	-	1.1	..	127.4	190.8	145.1	142.0	24.7
El Salvador	-	-	-	-	..	119.8	117.0	36.0	61.8	59.5
Guatemala	-	4.2	4.8	5.7	..	105.6	98.0	100.7	99.6	91.0
Honduras	-	-	-	-	..	79.5	84.3	116.3	108.8	38.2
Nicaragua	-	-	-	-	..	67.5	.. d	42.0	38.9	33.7
Panama	.. c	.. c	.. c	.. c	..	2 669.6	2 534.0	2 465.8	1 916.6	1 960.2
Virgin Islands, U.S.	1.1	1.1	1.2	2.3	..	.. c	.. c	.. c	.. c	.. c
South America	1 666.8	3 150.6	1 992.1	1 757.5	..	22 636.9	25 152.3	26 464.4	23 872.2	22 032.1
Argentina	2.2	2.1	2.4	3.4	..	2 499.7	2 286.3	2 597.7	2 387.2	2 718.5
Bolivia	-	-	-	-	..	168.8	84.3	84.0	83.6	98.9
Brazil	1 028.9	1 620.1	1 390.0	1 195.3	..	13 490.5	14 884.6	15 774.8	13 985.6	13 106.0
Colombia	3.3	3.2	3.6	3.4	..	1 127.9	1 342.9	1 573.5	1 584.6	1 732.2
Ecuador	-	-	1.2	1.1	..	324.4	326.8	367.0	396.2	378.6
Paraguay	-	-	-	-	..	156.8	173.9	.. d	.. d	.. d
Peru	2.2	3.2	3.6	3.4	..	627.1	714.7	704.0	770.6	938.0
Uruguay	.. c	13.7	18.0	19.5	..	687.0	770.5	827.5	786.6	1 076.2
Venezuela	7.6	8.4	9.6	9.2	..	1 558.0	2 297.9	1 498.0	1 243.4	-587.5

Table 2. Foreign direct investment positions by country *(cont.)*
At year end

Million US dollars

	Inward					Outward				
	2015	2016	2017	2018	2019	2015	2016	2017	2018	2019
ASIA	**71 192.2**	**75 274.6**	**94 770.9**	**92 474.2**	..	**153 341.3**	**160 563.9**	**191 111.8**	**188 002.1**	**201 342.4**
Near and Middle East	17 895.5	16 689.2	19 673.8	17 887.6	..	7 609.1	8 090.0	10 865.9	10 925.1	12 665.7
Gulf Arabian countries	12 252.6	11 551.6	12 940.8	11 502.2	..	5 587.4	5 991.4	8 801.9	8 781.8	10 159.5
Kuwait	327.7	322.5	430.6	455.7	..	163.3	220.3	263.9	243.9	253.9
Qatar	6 874.3	6 660.7	8 334.1	7 854.4	..	271.1	300.4	319.0	309.1	374.1
Saudi Arabia	365.8	378.4	428.2	297.7	..	1 476.3	1 613.8	1 498.0	1 912.1	1 392.9
United Arab Emirates	2 780.6	2 343.2	2 257.1	1 495.3	..	3 574.3	3 462.6	6 430.8	6 125.5	7 934.2
Other Near and Middle East	5 642.9	5 136.5	6 734.2	6 384.2	..	2 021.8	2 098.7	2 064.0	2 143.3	2 506.2
Jordan	3.3	5.3	.. c	.. c	..	167.7	158.1	134.3	129.4	104.5
Other Asian countries	53 296.7	58 585.4	75 097.1	74 587.8	..	145 731.1	152 473.9	180 247.1	177 078.1	188 676.7
China	4 935.2	7 611.5	16 408.0	12 644.8	..	72 182.9	77 044.4	92 397.5	91 009.8	93 525.1
Hong Kong, China	853.6	1 265.9	1 917.7	2 528.1	..	5 930.3	5 402.1	6 351.6	4 863.8	9 210.3
India	.. d	2 874.5	3 271.8	2 589.9	..	24 132.8	25 177.6	28 169.8	26 328.1	27 174.8
Indonesia	.. c	3.2	.. c	.. c	..	2 573.8	2 743.8	3 010.3	2 792.5	3 300.4
Iran, Islamic Republic of	1 673.4	1 710.8	2 140.8	2 312.8	..	248.2	406.9	410.2	448.8	407.8
Malaysia	755.6	770.5	911.5	837.0	..	3 924.9	4 412.4	5 441.4	5 728.2	6 148.1
Philippines	-	-	.. c	.. c	..	1 032.1	1 022.5	1 303.7	1 473.6	1 725.5
Singapore	386.5	341.5	472.5	488.9	..	13 846.5	12 935.6	14 070.5	15 517.5	16 117.7
Chinese Taipei	542.2	609.3	912.7	845.0	..	1 935.8	1 922.6	2 312.3	2 262.4	2 505.1
Thailand	52.3	186.6	56.4	67.6	..	2 554.2	2 996.7	3 763.5	4 000.5	4 223.8
Viet Nam	.. c	.. c	.. c	.. c	..	636.9	708.3	828.7	893.1	913.3
AUSTRALIA, OCEANIA AND POLAR REGIONS	**3 303.2**	**4 609.5**	**4 808.1**	**5 013.7**	..	**12 167.7**	**12 666.8**	**16 265.3**	**15 085.9**	**16 333.4**
WORLD unallocated and confidential	**-1.1**	**-1.1**	**-**	**1.1**	..	**-1.1**	**-**	**1.2**	**-1.1**	**-212.3**
European Union (EU28)	**448 199.2**	**445 338.9**	**533 794.7**	**519 782.5**	..	**797 669.0**	**791 088.9**	**984 093.3**	**983 612.3**	**1 059 904.5**
G20 countries excl. European Union	**485 193.3**	**502 493.9**	**620 960.7**	**561 021.3**	..	**720 423.5**	**708 777.3**	**837 523.4**	**826 399.1**	**849 311.4**
G20 OECD countries	**466 323.4**	**479 965.2**	**586 121.4**	**531 730.0**	..	**584 305.9**	**560 316.2**	**665 257.9**	**661 043.1**	**677 140.0**
G20 Non-OECD countries	**18 869.9**	**22 528.7**	**34 838.1**	**29 291.3**	..	**136 117.6**	**148 461.1**	**172 265.5**	**165 356.1**	**172 171.4**
MENA countries	**12 521.5**	**11 805.6**	**13 099.1**	**11 700.3**	..	**8 372.3**	**8 992.3**	**11 597.5**	**11 480.4**	**14 923.6**
ASEAN countries	**1 302.1**	**1 332.4**	**1 516.0**	**1 462.1**	..	**24 587.9**	**24 840.3**	**28 446.9**	**30 433.9**	**32 438.8**

- Nil; .. Not available; c Confidential data; d Secondary Confidentiality

Note: Inward FDI positions are allocated according to the ultimate investing country. Detailed metadata at: *http://stats.oecd.org/OECDStat_Metadata/ShowMetadata.ashx?Dataset=FDI_CTRY_IND_SUMM.*

Source: *OECD International Direct Investment Statistics (database): https://doi.org/10.1787/idi-data-en*

GERMANY

Table 3. Foreign direct investment income by country

Million US dollars

	Inward					Outward				
	2015	2016	2017	2018	2019	2015	2016	2017	2018	2019
WORLD	**34 566.9**	**37 941.7**	**54 730.7**	**54 599.5**	**53 051.9**	**74 861.3**	**98 391.1**	**108 764.4**	**121 926.2**	**121 902.5**
OECD COUNTRIES	**31 583.1**	**37 472.1**	**53 643.0**	**53 275.8**	**51 856.1**	**50 712.9**	**74 706.3**	**80 973.2**	**91 308.9**	**91 873.5**
Australia	-120.1	70.8	770.4	756.9	686.2	577.5	512.3	1 053.9	1 195.4	1 203.1
Austria	2 143.9	1 941.1	3 942.8	4 012.3	3 593.7	2 906.0	4 100.8	4 540.3	5 000.8	5 189.2
Belgium	1 355.6	984.8	1 243.9	1 136.8	1 120.5	2 514.4	1 744.5	2 051.7	2 330.0	2 254.7
Canada	48.5	91.1	392.8	393.1	354.4	739.0	884.9	635.0	776.7	743.6
Chile	0.0	-19.7	-19.1	-33.6	-21.8	-11.7	127.5	103.9	93.0	97.6
Czech Republic	131.6	1 458.7	73.0	76.0	53.7	1 805.5	2 269.4	2 555.7	2 874.6	4 014.0
Denmark	1 779.0	738.9	561.0	582.6	563.8	163.6	544.4	757.4	833.6	815.9
Estonia	0.1	0.2	0.1	4.8	0.0	14.9	18.4	26.2	34.0	31.5
Finland	89.3	119.1	-243.9	-268.3	-201.8	340.6	351.9	321.2	372.6	369.8
France	4 362.3	5 865.7	7 640.9	7 654.7	7 894.2	1 690.5	2 975.1	6 926.2	7 426.5	7 471.9
Germany	-	-	-	-	-	-	-	-	-	-
Greece	10.9	1.2	23.6	16.0	7.3	270.1	187.9	447.7	407.9	390.9
Hungary	39.3	40.0	34.2	36.0	44.1	976.4	951.7	1 757.3	1 885.6	1 802.1
Iceland	1.8	1.1	1.8	1.7	2.1	-4.0	0.0	1.6	3.0	4.1
Ireland	714.8	869.7	718.8	744.1	760.0	654.9	687.6	819.8	958.7	997.5
Israel	64.0	67.9	92.8	91.8	83.6	36.7	78.6	70.1	74.0	74.7
Italy	2 323.0	2 054.0	3 937.1	4 031.3	4 065.3	1 518.0	2 097.3	2 402.9	2 566.5	2 508.1
Japan	246.2	233.6	1 072.7	1 058.8	979.4	1 313.2	1 172.2	1 526.7	1 716.5	1 689.8
Korea	103.9	206.7	181.4	175.3	157.1	1 030.2	1 097.0	1 472.4	1 646.3	1 588.6
Latvia	0.2	0.7	0.1	-0.7	-1.2	45.7	38.3	55.1	63.1	64.3
Lithuania	2.7	2.5	3.5	1.5	2.1	88.4	31.1	82.9	68.7	66.8
Luxembourg	4 164.0	855.5	6 271.2	6 242.2	6 587.8	4 206.9	7 997.8	7 365.5	8 321.7	9 304.0
Mexico	-29.0	-9.1	-52.4	-33.2	-31.3	527.6	916.5	932.9	1 080.7	1 086.7
Netherlands	4 901.2	8 349.7	10 562.0	10 687.9	9 483.3	4 645.6	8 497.8	11 503.7	14 248.1	13 529.4
New Zealand	1.9	0.8	2.1	2.1	1.8	76.9	113.6	140.6	153.6	148.2
Norway	144.4	30.7	348.8	350.2	427.7	461.6	355.3	630.9	678.1	658.4
Poland	169.3	254.1	205.2	253.6	199.1	2 701.0	2 544.6	2 798.2	3 203.6	3 086.2
Portugal	6.4	-15.9	4.8	5.7	4.6	444.9	414.6	494.6	554.2	534.2
Slovak Republic	2.6	8.8	10.9	12.4	15.9	376.4	600.9	612.4	692.6	661.6
Slovenia	13.9	30.1	27.0	28.1	35.5	101.7	152.1	164.0	183.9	177.4
Spain	1 480.7	2 165.7	-189.9	-213.9	-184.8	1 589.5	2 404.4	3 420.6	3 814.0	3 654.6
Sweden	1 391.3	-560.5	1 212.2	1 093.7	1 066.6	1 228.4	4 856.9	843.3	912.6	987.1
Switzerland	2 976.0	6 880.6	4 216.3	4 163.3	4 018.4	3 675.0	5 513.5	4 911.2	5 413.6	5 329.1
Turkey	70.6	49.8	98.7	98.0	95.3	931.1	863.4	1 346.5	1 380.2	1 383.9
United Kingdom	308.9	1 858.4	4 377.3	4 264.1	4 516.2	3 610.8	4 808.0	3 925.1	4 118.4	4 427.3
United States	2 686.9	2 847.6	6 124.2	5 850.6	5 477.5	9 599.7	14 827.0	14 358.4	16 226.2	15 527.1
EUROPE	**30 307.3**	**33 652.4**	**45 930.6**	**45 888.2**	**44 988.4**	**41 016.2**	**60 331.6**	**67 252.1**	**75 456.4**	**76 569.8**
Bulgaria	17.5	12.4	13.4	10.3	6.4	71.8	152.3	182.5	202.9	197.3
Croatia	-3.6	11.1	5.9	11.9	12.1	130.8	235.8	188.8	254.4	245.6
Cyprus	545.0	90.4	334.7	327.6	296.9	50.2	143.7	13.5	11.9	7.9
Malta	61.0	49.9	88.0	77.2	101.0	1 086.0	410.8	634.3	702.7	661.0
Romania	5.4	15.1	19.4	21.2	17.8	589.7	987.2	983.8	1 105.9	1 065.2
Russian Federation	682.3	-100.0	506.3	499.9	441.5	1 952.3	3 041.3	3 538.2	3 740.4	3 624.4
Ukraine	4.2	1.2	-3.6	-4.7	-4.9	-176.9	22.1	-17.9	-6.1	-7.3
AFRICA	**89.8**	**197.3**	**166.7**	**168.6**	**153.1**	**736.5**	**1 270.2**	**1 051.9**	**1 363.3**	**1 292.3**
Northern Africa	6.2	17.7	13.2	14.2	12.1	99.6	387.9	329.5	556.2	378.7
Algeria	4.7	0.2	0.1	0.2	0.3	60.1	210.2	91.6	117.9	126.8
Egypt	1.8	16.6	12.3	13.3	11.9	86.3	251.7	38.3	192.5	40.8
Libya	-0.9	0.0	0.0	0.0	-	-126.3	-140.4	174.9	199.9	167.3
Morocco	-	0.1	0.2	0.2	0.1	48.9	50.4	-6.6	10.8	9.7
Tunisia	0.5	0.8	0.7	0.5	-0.2	30.6	16.0	31.4	35.2	34.0
Other African countries	83.7	179.6	153.4	154.4	141.1	636.8	882.3	722.3	807.1	913.7
Nigeria	19.7	-5.1	1.3	0.8	-1.2	18.9	-13.8	16.9	19.6	19.3
South Africa	53.2	190.1	136.9	139.0	132.8	537.4	826.1	646.2	727.2	840.1
AMERICA	**3 511.9**	**3 492.7**	**7 154.5**	**7 038.1**	**6 517.8**	**12 859.3**	**16 170.5**	**15 362.7**	**17 376.2**	**16 704.9**
Northern America	2 735.4	2 938.8	6 516.9	6 243.6	5 831.9	10 338.7	15 711.8	14 993.4	17 002.9	16 270.8
Central America and Caribbean countries	759.8	570.8	649.7	816.5	704.3	2 663.6	188.8	437.1	521.2	544.6
Bahamas	136.4	3.3	21.4	21.8	19.2	3.6	1.3	13.9	15.7	14.9
Bermuda	391.8	272.9	370.6	388.6	410.2	276.3	257.3	188.6	211.2	194.4
Cayman Islands	190.7	194.5	180.4	132.3	123.1	1 645.2	-1 053.8	-440.9	-496.5	-475.1
Costa Rica	0.1	-0.3	0.2	0.2	0.1	-4.6	-11.2	-26.2	-29.6	-28.1
El Salvador	-	-	-	-	-	2.8	-1.1	0.6	1.8	1.4
Guatemala	0.4	-	-	0.0	-	4.3	-3.0	7.0	6.8	5.8
Honduras	0.0	0.2	0.2	0.2	-	10.2	18.3	19.2	21.5	20.6
Nicaragua	-	-	-	-	-	1.7	3.0	1.6	1.5	6.0
Panama	-6.3	-4.5	-1.8	-1.6	-1.9	159.2	53.0	30.7	35.5	35.3
Virgin Islands, U.S.	-	-	0.0	-	-	-	-	-	-	-
South America	16.7	-16.8	-12.1	-22.0	-18.4	-143.0	269.8	-67.9	-147.9	-110.5
Argentina	0.1	-4.4	-3.3	-2.4	-1.8	85.8	242.3	202.8	243.8	245.2
Bolivia	0.0	0.0	0.0	-	-	13.1	4.5	8.9	9.5	8.6
Brazil	15.6	8.9	9.9	13.1	5.9	-195.4	-825.8	-709.3	-875.7	-819.6
Colombia	0.2	0.0	-0.1	0.3	-0.2	38.0	36.8	78.8	86.6	81.9
Ecuador	-	0.1	0.0	0.1	0.0	19.2	17.7	24.3	26.1	27.0
Paraguay	-0.1	-0.6	-0.3	-0.2	-0.3	4.0	-2.0	2.1	3.5	4.0
Peru	0.1	0.6	0.6	0.6	0.0	61.8	90.4	58.9	66.7	66.2
Uruguay	0.8	-2.3	-0.4	-0.1	-0.1	28.0	26.1	38.5	47.5	45.7
Venezuela	0.0	0.6	0.6	0.4	0.0	-181.5	560.0	125.4	153.6	135.3

GERMANY

Table 3. Foreign direct investment income by country *(cont.)*

Million US dollars

	Inward					Outward				
	2015	2016	2017	2018	2019	2015	2016	2017	2018	2019
ASIA	**775.8**	**543.0**	**925.4**	**960.6**	**900.5**	**19 591.9**	**20 000.6**	**23 909.9**	**26 386.5**	**25 989.3**
Near and Middle East	186.4	192.7	237.1	263.2	253.1	879.8	1 007.5	610.5	567.1	536.0
Gulf Arabian countries	120.2	121.2	137.6	166.7	169.0	764.3	840.8	462.8	442.2	394.2
Kuwait	8.9	16.0	18.1	16.0	13.5	37.9	51.5	84.6	47.4	45.2
Qatar	107.4	118.7	85.4	114.3	130.1	25.3	29.1	38.2	39.1	33.5
Saudi Arabia	-5.6	-19.2	28.8	29.0	24.8	374.4	292.8	95.0	65.1	20.1
United Arab Emirates	11.8	8.0	3.3	5.9	1.5	312.4	381.3	208.1	248.3	254.6
Other Near and Middle East	66.3	71.5	99.5	96.5	84.1	115.5	166.8	147.7	124.9	141.8
Jordan	0.0	0.7	0.3	1.1	0.0	8.5	32.4	21.2	2.8	7.9
Other Asian countries	589.3	350.3	688.3	697.4	647.4	18 712.1	18 993.1	23 299.4	25 819.4	25 453.3
China	128.0	11.2	-83.2	-67.7	-52.5	11 431.1	11 920.5	14 311.4	15 867.8	15 769.6
Hong Kong, China	12.7	-143.6	-383.1	-377.4	-345.2	1 432.7	1 074.6	1 514.0	1 658.2	1 587.2
India	-37.2	-26.5	-32.7	-33.5	-31.2	780.6	915.4	1 321.5	1 587.1	1 486.5
Indonesia	-1.9	0.8	-0.3	-1.3	-1.2	401.9	366.5	371.9	414.1	395.7
Iran, Islamic Republic of	50.0	64.8	27.1	26.9	25.0	273.9	73.5	121.8	76.8	45.2
Malaysia	25.7	45.9	19.0	16.8	14.7	302.9	583.7	518.8	576.3	590.1
Philippines	0.3	0.9	1.0	0.9	0.3	62.0	8.8	175.1	204.4	195.4
Singapore	47.5	-60.8	-141.2	-127.3	-112.3	1 000.9	708.5	930.8	1 037.7	1 011.1
Chinese Taipei	7.8	8.8	16.7	15.8	13.7	180.8	183.7	199.9	226.8	217.0
Thailand	8.6	10.6	9.4	9.2	2.2	319.0	533.5	518.8	579.6	557.8
Viet Nam	-3.4	-2.5	0.5	0.2	-0.3	43.1	179.5	94.3	86.3	129.0
AUSTRALIA, OCEANIA AND POLAR REGIONS	**-118.0**	**56.2**	**553.5**	**544.1**	**492.0**	**657.4**	**627.1**	**1 197.0**	**1 353.4**	**1 355.5**
WORLD unallocated and confidential	**-**	**0.1**	**0.1**	**0.0**	**0.1**	**0.0**	**-8.9**	**-9.1**	**-9.6**	**-9.4**
European Union (EU28)	**26 016.1**	**27 201.4**	**40 877.4**	**40 849.0**	**40 060.0**	**33 822.6**	**50 205.3**	**55 874.9**	**63 149.4**	**64 515.6**
G20 countries excl. European Union	**10 835.9**	**13 329.5**	**25 105.6**	**24 825.6**	**24 712.5**	**36 905.8**	**46 932.9**	**54 357.5**	**59 903.0**	**59 192.3**
G20 OECD countries	**10 001.3**	**13 268.8**	**24 543.1**	**24 249.5**	**24 194.2**	**21 537.7**	**30 153.8**	**34 579.9**	**38 133.2**	**37 630.1**
G20 Non-OECD countries	**834.6**	**60.8**	**562.4**	**576.1**	**518.3**	**15 368.2**	**16 779.1**	**19 777.6**	**21 769.8**	**21 562.2**
MENA countries	**128.0**	**140.9**	**155.7**	**183.6**	**181.2**	**839.3**	**1 270.4**	**826.0**	**1 012.1**	**797.9**
ASEAN countries	**78.4**	**-4.2**	**-111.2**	**-101.0**	**-96.3**	**2 138.0**	**2 391.3**	**2 721.5**	**2 910.0**	**2 891.0**

- Nil

Note: Detailed metadata at: *http://stats.oecd.org/OECDStat_Metadata/ShowMetadata.ashx?Dataset=FDI_CTRY_IND_SUMM.*

Source: *OECD International Direct Investment Statistics (database): https://doi.org/10.1787/idi-data-en*

Table 4. Foreign direct investment flows by industrial sector

Million US dollars

	Inward					Outward				
	2015	2016	2017	2018	2019	2015	2016	2017	2018	2019
All FDI activities	**30 534.1**	**15 617.9**	**60 225.2**	**73 523.6**	**57 793.5**	**99 003.2**	**63 599.0**	**103 865.1**	**78 763.9**	**120 133.5**
Agriculture, forestry and fishing	**37.7**	**3.9**	**30.4**	**37.6**	..	**29.9**	**-25.1**	**-59.1**	**-53.5**	..
Mining and quarrying	**-36.1**	**124.4**	**-89.0**	**51.3**	..	**581.2**	**1 085.8**	**1 999.7**	**337.8**	..
Extraction activities	105.4	10.4	-95.3	49.2	..	-479.9	93.9	1 476.9	318.1	..
Manufacturing	**4 521.1**	**-946.5**	**8 636.9**	**4 998.0**	..	**26 260.2**	**2 254.5**	**3 944.1**	**-30 616.9**	..
of which:										
Food products, beverages and tobacco	267.8	1 002.7	-388.2	326.9	..	-137.4	-299.9	-188.7	2 267.3	..
Textiles, wood and paper products; printing	135.7	-65.0	-121.8	-60.2	..	31.7	-12.7	204.4	147.8	..
Chemical, rubber, plastic, non-metallic mineral products	1 956.7	-2 783.6	4 698.6	4 427.6	..	6 197.5	-402.1	1 156.1	3 714.8	..
Metal and machinery products, except electrical equipment	526.6	-1 023.1	1 376.6	-116.5	..	5 821.1	2 818.5	-3 879.6	2 320.6	..
Motor vehicles, trailers, semi-trailers, other transport equipment	1 250.2	592.9	1 155.8	1 767.3	..	17 052.7	3 352.5	4 053.5	-22 975.2	..
Other manufacturing	384.0	1 329.5	1 915.9	-1 347.1	..	-2 705.3	-3 201.9	2 598.3	-16 092.2	..
Electricity, gas, steam and air conditioning supply	**5 352.9**	**-6 861.0**	**-256.5**	**2 618.0**	..	**-2 681.7**	**-7 335.9**	**208.1**	**563.6**	..
Water supply; sewerage, waste management and remediation activities	**59.2**	**35.0**	**15.0**	**-155.3**	..	**216.9**	**111.1**	**29.6**	**1 095.4**	..
Construction	**386.2**	**-239.4**	**278.7**	**300.9**	..	**281.7**	**39.3**	**62.4**	**187.7**	..
Services	**13 586.6**	**7 303.8**	**40 250.1**	**38 815.9**	..	**45 110.7**	**25 124.1**	**55 121.8**	**59 669.0**	..
Wholesale and retail trade; repair of motor vehicles and motorcycles	-2 325.4	1 253.2	3 111.5	3 929.1	..	-846.3	3 452.1	7 371.4	-8 455.2	..
Transportation and storage	243.4	564.1	3 956.7	-1 626.9	..	1 295.0	-3 048.7	641.7	735.0	..
Accommodation and food service activities	-80.3	.. d	546.0	-21.8	..	62.9	70.3	.. d	116.6	..
Information and communication	1 553.5	-2 332.6	-1 988.2	-678.4	..	5 737.1	-5 190.8	-1 660.2	-2 427.2	..
Financial and insurance activities	4 918.9	-1 432.5	-9 052.0	-6 668.1	..	17 461.8	18 767.8	15 677.2	23 088.2	..
Activities of holding companies	2 840.5	-4 015.0	-2 638.6	-9 627.9	..	5 307.3	12 759.5	3 660.5	2 976.7	..
Real estate activities	1 503.8	64.3	6 332.3	-431.8	..	392.1	-224.6	436.1	-7.9	..
Professional, scientific and technical activities	6 717.2	8 204.3	37 564.5	42 814.9	..	22 977.7	9 455.2	34 198.9	46 102.1	..
Administrative and support service activities	900.2	860.2	-412.1	1 207.7	..	-1 260.9	1 752.0	-1 318.8	839.6	..
Public administration; activities of households and of extraterritorial organisations	.. c	.. c	.. c	6.9	..	-723.2	.. d	-259.3	-373.9	..
Education	5.5	19.0	5.3	-0.6	..	.. d	-9.2	0.4	12.3	..
Human health and social work activities	5.3	18.8	50.3	320.7	..	.. c	.. c	.. c	1.1	..
Arts, entertainment and recreation	143.3	33.3	123.2	1.6	..	4.3	79.8	-10.6	29.7	..
Other services	.. d	30.6	.. d	-37.6	..	-2.9	-0.6	-7.0	8.6	..
Not allocated and confidential	**5 506.4**	**15 016.0**	**10 263.8**	**25 596.8**	**57 793.5**	**30 350.8**	**41 810.2**	**40 567.0**	**45 080.4**	**120 133.5**
Private real estate activities	**1 120.1**	**1 181.7**	**1 095.8**	**1 260.5**	..	**-1 146.6**	**535.0**	**1 991.6**	**2 500.3**	..

.. Not available; c Confidential data; d Secondary Confidentiality

Note: Detailed metadata at: *http://stats.oecd.org/OECDStat_Metadata/ShowMetadata.ashx?Dataset=FDI_CTRY_IND_SUMM.*

Source: *OECD International Direct Investment Statistics (database): https://doi.org/10.1787/idi-data-en*

Table 5. Foreign direct investment positions by industrial sector

At year end

Million US dollars

	Inward					Outward				
	2015	2016	2017	2018	2019	2015	2016	2017	2018	2019
All FDI activities	**781 743.1**	**794 510.4**	**963 121.9**	**934 402.3**	..	**1 369 209.6**	**1 367 630.4**	**1 650 292.6**	**1 651 416.3**	**1 754 495.6**
Agriculture, forestry and fishing	**181.8**	**335.2**	**317.8**	**295.4**	..	**2 640.2**	**2 718.5**	**3 446.9**	**3 420.0**	..
Mining and quarrying	**153.5**	**2 109.2**	**756.8**	**493.5**	..	**8 209.0**	**7 578.8**	**6 292.9**	**5 936.6**	..
Extraction activities	-19.6	1 834.1	467.7	311.4	..	7 929.2	7 142.4	5 674.0	5 374.4	..
Manufacturing	**42 703.3**	**40 651.4**	**61 803.8**	**60 547.3**	..	**195 268.4**	**207 732.7**	**252 445.4**	**253 271.1**	..
of which:										
Food products, beverages and tobacco	4 213.4	3 687.2	5 164.3	5 906.8	..	5 960.8	6 068.3	6 851.8	7 339.1	..
Textiles, wood and paper products; printing	3 009.3	4 339.6	5 170.3	4 765.3	..	5 330.4	5 025.8	6 114.2	5 871.3	..
Chemical, rubber, plastic, non-metallic mineral products	16 707.7	16 038.8	23 623.2	21 472.4	..	44 548.7	47 308.9	58 905.0	62 773.1	..
Metal and machinery products, except electrical equipment	14 317.9	14 714.9	14 385.9	14 120.7	..	52 372.3	55 578.2	62 529.4	65 780.9	..
Motor vehicles, trailers, semi-trailers, other transport equipment	-566.1	-2 861.8	5 397.0	7 654.0	..	48 897.1	52 905.0	71 795.4	66 878.9	..
Other manufacturing	5 020.1	4 732.8	8 063.1	6 627.0	..	38 157.9	40 846.4	46 250.9	44 627.9	..
Electricity, gas, steam and air conditioning supply	**8 231.9**	**7 424.9**	**7 964.7**	**6 843.4**	..	**18 329.9**	**13 382.5**	**16 228.1**	**15 525.5**	..
Water supply; sewerage, waste management and remediation activities	**420.3**	**416.4**	**448.5**	**423.6**	..	**1 488.3**	**1 545.3**	**1 842.2**	**1 768.9**	..
Construction	**1 644.0**	**792.7**	**2 481.4**	**2 357.5**	..	**1 609.1**	**2 079.7**	**2 293.1**	**2 468.5**	..
Services	**703 984.8**	**717 454.4**	**858 397.7**	**831 660.2**	..	**963 449.1**	**957 855.0**	**1 162 030.5**	**1 162 174.3**	..
Wholesale and retail trade; repair of motor vehicles and motorcycles	42 561.8	43 973.9	57 640.9	48 445.2	..	107 732.2	113 203.3	140 154.7	126 566.3	..
Transportation and storage	6 561.8	8 046.8	9 555.0	9 518.0	..	6 814.4	7 031.7	11 362.4	11 972.8	..
Accommodation and food service activities	1 428.4	1 534.7	2 091.6	2 264.7	..	1 814.9	1 760.3	2 197.2	2 275.0	..
Information and communication	35 860.6	36 232.7	35 265.1	27 397.5	..	20 088.2	21 608.5	28 622.0	28 343.3	..
Financial and insurance activities	285 777.9	284 748.6	333 929.0	327 695.2	..	582 034.8	507 963.5	604 655.8	589 996.6	..
Activities of holding companies	226 884.0	221 776.1	257 343.5	244 676.0	..	517 573.2	454 265.8	559 715.8	596 944.1	..
Real estate activities	24 980.9	23 540.6	25 747.2	29 632.5	..	27 331.5	27 663.1	34 245.6	31 943.0	..
Professional, scientific and technical activities	305 542.7	317 975.1	391 577.1	382 401.0	..	197 033.2	257 246.8	316 247.3	342 288.8	..
Administrative and support service activities	538.9	567.1	1 638.3	3 393.6	..	12 080.6	12 629.9	14 358.4	16 747.2	..
Public administration; activities of households and of extraterritorial organisations	.. c	.. c	.. c	.. c	..	.. c	.. c	.. c	67.6	..
Education	-2.2	20.0	32.4	32.1	..	34.8	32.7	55.2	52.7	..
Human health and social work activities	251.5	265.6	345.4	360.7	..	8 093.6	8 298.7	9 624.6	11 423.2	..
Arts, entertainment and recreation	301.6	348.9	418.6	348.1	..	126.3	150.7	177.5	201.5	..
Other services	.. d	.. d	.. d	.. d	..	.. d	.. d	.. d	296.5	..
Not allocated and confidential	**-2.2**	**-**	**-2.4**	**-1.1**	**1 023 306.0**	**-2.2**	**-**	**-**	**-**	**1 754 495.6**
Private real estate activities	**24 425.7**	**25 326.2**	**30 953.5**	**31 782.7**	..	**178 217.7**	**174 738.1**	**205 713.6**	**206 851.4**	..

- Nil; .. Not available; c Confidential data; d Secondary Confidentiality

Note: Detailed metadata at: *http://stats.oecd.org/OECDStat_Metadata/ShowMetadata.ashx?Dataset=FDI_CTRY_IND_SUMM.*

Source: *OECD International Direct Investment Statistics (database): https://doi.org/10.1787/idi-data-en*

Table 6. Foreign direct investment income by industrial sector

Million US dollars

	Inward					Outward				
	2015	2016	2017	2018	2019	2015	2016	2017	2018	2019
All FDI activities	**34 566.9**	**37 941.7**	**54 730.7**	**54 599.5**	**53 051.9**	**74 861.3**	**98 391.1**	**108 764.4**	**121 926.2**	**121 902.5**
Agriculture, forestry and fishing	**4.3**	**4.0**	**4.1**	**7.4**	..	**20.0**	**6.3**	**17.3**	**3.9**	..
Mining and quarrying	**3.7**	**4.8**	**-2.2**	**-0.6**	..	**572.9**	**624.3**	**194.8**	**174.3**	..
Extraction activities	0.8	0.8	-4.7	-1.3	..	546.1	606.9	174.9	148.6	..
Manufacturing	**3 098.9**	**2 645.4**	**3 824.7**	**4 372.8**	..	**12 792.9**	**16 594.8**	**21 596.7**	**25 554.5**	..
of which:										
Food products, beverages and tobacco	736.5	302.5	603.0	622.4	..	437.1	327.9	508.0	659.3	..
Textiles, wood and paper products; printing	167.0	195.6	142.3	321.4	..	248.3	210.1	262.6	233.5	..
Chemical, rubber, plastic, non-metallic mineral products	464.3	507.4	1 495.9	1 554.5	..	2 894.3	2 243.5	2 705.0	2 682.5	..
Metal and machinery products, except electrical equipment	1 303.2	1 412.7	1 271.4	1 422.5	..	2 804.7	3 546.9	3 537.3	3 449.7	..
Motor vehicles, trailers, semi-trailers, other transport equipment	137.3	-16.3	9.2	118.7	..	3 821.6	7 869.3	11 993.9	16 338.5	..
Other manufacturing	290.6	243.6	302.9	333.3	..	2 586.8	2 397.1	2 590.0	2 191.0	..
Electricity, gas, steam and air conditioning supply	**736.1**	**354.9**	**1 026.5**	**1 212.3**	..	**680.4**	**341.6**	**-31.1**	**60.6**	..
Water supply; sewerage, waste management and remediation activities	**12.0**	**12.0**	**12.9**	**14.7**	..	**9.7**	**15.7**	**10.5**	**14.0**	..
Construction	**1 055.4**	**864.2**	**674.3**	**798.7**	..	**234.8**	**299.5**	**227.5**	**202.3**	..
Services	**20 954.0**	**26 775.4**	**23 114.1**	**21 709.8**	..	**36 919.6**	**35 207.9**	**42 054.6**	**47 094.1**	..
Wholesale and retail trade; repair of motor vehicles and motorcycles	2 230.4	2 142.9	2 033.5	1 898.1	..	1 318.3	1 541.1	1 078.4	1 753.0	..
Transportation and storage	138.7	206.9	271.6	363.1	..	682.3	510.7	1 514.2	817.7	..
Accommodation and food service activities	60.0	98.1	23.4	29.3	..	2.1	3.3	.. d	.. d	..
Information and communication	330.8	561.2	1 049.7	904.6	..	-133.9	44.2	179.2	43.1	..
Financial and insurance activities	2 607.2	5 736.7	8 660.7	7 807.5	..	10 694.5	19 997.9	28 141.3	29 592.6	..
Activities of holding companies	963.3	3 452.3	7 644.3	5 527.7	..	1 992.5	13 470.7	20 070.8	20 840.9	..
Real estate activities	495.0	450.1	805.9	496.1	..	214.2	253.2	120.5	298.7	..
Professional, scientific and technical activities	14 795.5	17 238.7	10 059.9	9 957.2	..	23 841.5	12 575.5	10 820.6	14 351.2	..
Administrative and support service activities	210.8	205.1	100.3	118.2	..	195.5	127.8	53.4	101.1	..
Public administration; activities of households and of extraterritorial organisations	75.0	88.9	94.0	114.8	..	106.0	152.9	119.8	98.3	..
Education	0.0	.. c	.. c	0.2	..	-18.1	-16.6	-12.1	-0.7	..
Human health and social work activities	4.2	.. d	.. c	6.3	..	1.6	0.0	.. c	.. c	..
Arts, entertainment and recreation	5.8	7.5	14.3	12.5	..	14.6	16.1	25.7	30.6	..
Other services	0.4	39.0	.. c	2.0	..	1.0	1.9	10.0	5.2	..
Not allocated and confidential	**7 013.7**	**5 497.6**	**24 365.9**	**24 483.1**	**53 051.9**	**19 665.0**	**41 322.3**	**40 009.6**	**44 487.4**	**121 902.5**
Private real estate activities	**1 688.8**	**1 783.4**	**1 710.4**	**2 001.3**	..	**3 966.0**	**3 978.6**	**4 684.4**	**4 335.1**	..

.. Not available; c Confidential data; d Secondary Confidentiality

Note: Detailed metadata at: *http://stats.oecd.org/OECDStat_Metadata/ShowMetadata.ashx?Dataset=FDI_CTRY_IND_SUMM.*

Source: *OECD International Direct Investment Statistics (database): https://doi.org/10.1787/idi-data-en*

GREECE

Table 1. Foreign direct investment flows by country

Million US dollars

	Inward					Outward				
	2015	2016	2017	2018	2019	2015	2016	2017	2018	2019
WORLD	**1 267.8**	**2 762.4**	**3 477.4**	**3 970.8**	**5 019.2**	**1 577.9**	**-1 665.4**	**168.0**	**476.6**	**641.6**
OECD COUNTRIES	**1 003.5**	**1 925.6**	**2 864.7**	**2 371.6**	**3 409.7**	**537.6**	**-2 404.6**	**302.6**	**86.2**	**-73.6**
Australia	2.6	5.4	7.9	16.3	18.6	0.9	-0.2	-0.3	-2.0	-0.7
Austria	-30.2	7.3	-1.7	2.5	56.1	3.4	-7.2	-7.2	-2.3	-2.3
Belgium	15.0	-18.1	37.0	163.0	38.4	1.2	-1.0	-0.6	-0.3	2.9
Canada	710.9	205.6	183.8	176.7	246.1	0.0	0.0	-0.1	0.1	0.0
Chile	-	-	-	-	0.1	-	-	-	-	-
Czech Republic	-5.3	6.5	5.2	18.6	4.4	-7.1	-6.9	-7.7	-7.1	1.0
Denmark	4.9	-3.8	-3.1	-18.1	1.6	0.1	-	-1.0	-1.9	-1.6
Estonia	0.1	0.6	0.6	0.6	2.1	-	-	-	-	-
Finland	0.2	-2.1	4.8	-15.1	7.2	-	-	-0.6	-0.7	-0.6
France	-130.6	144.2	-46.2	-28.9	154.0	-0.2	-3.0	8.2	-10.9	6.4
Germany	123.6	242.3	715.4	541.6	509.0	7.8	12.4	12.5	5.1	2.2
Greece	-	-	-	-	-	-	-	-	-	-
Hungary	-0.1	0.6	0.3	8.8	6.0	-1.3	0.6	0.6	0.2	0.4
Iceland	0.0	0.0	-0.3	-1.0	-0.8	-	-	-	-	-
Ireland	9.2	-15.4	26.2	-66.4	-62.0	-0.1	11.0	-	-	-
Israel	2.5	3.2	32.1	28.3	79.1	0.0	0.7	-	0.9	0.6
Italy	102.0	84.0	133.4	341.5	72.8	13.7	-2.7	13.1	-44.8	-5.2
Japan	-0.7	-0.6	-4.7	-3.8	-1.7	-0.5	-0.3	-0.3	-0.4	0.5
Korea	1.3	1.3	-0.6	-0.2	1.3	-	-	-	-	0.0
Latvia	1.1	1.6	1.1	2.3	1.2	-	-	-	-	-
Lithuania	0.0	0.0	0.1	0.8	1.1	-	-	-	-	-
Luxembourg	-151.3	810.7	111.8	406.7	491.5	18.7	55.1	95.5	55.6	48.1
Mexico	0.1	0.0	0.5	1.9	0.1	-	-	0.0	-	-
Netherlands	317.3	99.5	489.9	-91.7	1 107.6	135.6	-38.3	29.4	-61.7	-69.0
New Zealand	-	0.0	0.5	1.5	1.1	-	-	-	-	-
Norway	10.9	-0.3	1.8	4.9	37.7	-	0.0	-0.4	-0.8	-0.5
Poland	0.1	1.7	5.1	2.9	9.7	5.2	5.9	4.8	-7.8	45.1
Portugal	0.1	0.0	6.5	-2.3	2.0	0.2	0.6	0.5	-0.4	1.3
Slovak Republic	0.1	0.4	0.7	1.9	4.0	-0.3	-0.3	-0.3	-0.3	-0.3
Slovenia	-0.1	0.7	0.6	-1.4	-0.1	0.2	1.3	2.6	3.0	2.4
Spain	138.4	109.3	47.0	30.7	259.3	4.3	11.6	0.3	0.2	6.4
Sweden	-4.2	4.5	1.6	18.9	26.7	0.2	0.7	-5.4	-3.6	-3.1
Switzerland	-66.9	152.3	849.3	552.8	220.0	-16.8	-0.8	22.6	5.3	-6.4
Turkey	-1.4	5.8	44.7	35.6	15.6	791.6	-2 467.4	58.0	57.0	27.8
United Kingdom	79.7	14.6	175.2	159.3	10.3	-437.9	-118.1	8.5	31.0	-58.0
United States	-124.5	63.5	38.4	82.3	89.6	18.7	141.8	70.3	72.6	-70.9
EUROPE	**513.1**	**1 990.1**	**3 082.9**	**3 070.2**	**3 702.2**	**1 464.6**	**-2 084.1**	**-3.2**	**365.6**	**626.2**
Bulgaria	-4.1	35.7	24.0	33.3	41.6	553.6	259.6	-545.7	42.7	67.6
Croatia	0.0	0.2	0.1	-0.1	-2.1	0.0	2.6	0.5	0.5	0.4
Cyprus	91.2	285.2	413.8	810.2	585.6	436.3	51.6	391.3	811.6	489.7
Malta	1.8	4.6	11.1	24.8	5.5	90.9	2.8	-0.1	-0.2	-0.1
Romania	1.1	2.2	-0.5	6.7	12.4	-104.5	52.6	-0.8	-354.3	41.7
Russian Federation	22.4	14.8	18.9	11.8	28.0	38.9	38.6	39.1	42.7	0.0
Ukraine	0.1	0.3	0.0	0.2	-0.2	-36.4	-3.7	-2.8	-2.2	-3.6
AFRICA	**-12.1**	**-11.4**	**-4.9**	**-13.2**	**-1.0**	**-2.6**	**12.9**	**0.9**	**-12.2**	**-0.6**
Northern Africa	1.0	2.6	7.3	8.7	9.9	0.5	0.1	0.5	0.0	-0.1
Algeria	-	-	-	-	-	-	-	0.1	-	0.0
Egypt	0.9	2.0	7.3	8.7	9.8	0.5	0.3	0.4	0.2	0.0
Libya	-	-	-	-	-	0.0	-0.2	0.0	-0.3	-0.1
Morocco	-	0.3	-	-	0.1	-	-	-	-	-
Tunisia	0.1	0.3	-	-	0.0	0.0	0.0	-	-	-
Other African countries	-13.1	-14.0	-12.2	-22.0	-10.9	-3.0	12.8	0.5	-12.1	-0.6
Nigeria	-	-	-	0.9	0.4	-	-	-	-	-
South Africa	0.0	0.0	0.5	0.8	1.1	-3.0	-	0.2	-11.9	-
AMERICA	**640.4**	**364.1**	**229.7**	**141.7**	**382.8**	**-71.1**	**107.3**	**21.7**	**-92.5**	**-100.9**
Northern America	586.4	269.1	222.3	259.0	335.7	18.7	141.8	70.2	72.7	-70.9
Central America and Caribbean countries	54.1	94.9	7.3	-118.9	46.6	-89.9	-34.8	-48.4	-164.7	-29.8
Bahamas	0.3	1.6	3.8	2.5	0.1	0.2	-	-	-	-
Bermuda	64.6	106.3	17.6	7.0	0.3	-	-	-13.9	-	-
Cayman Islands	2.4	-0.4	0.1	-0.3	41.7	-68.4	-2.4	-30.5	-31.8	-30.1
Costa Rica	-	-	-	-	-	-	-	-	-	-
El Salvador	-	-	-	-	-	-	-	-	-	-
Guatemala	-	-	-	0.0	-	-	-	-	-0.1	-0.1
Honduras	0.1	-	-	-	-	-	-	-	-	-
Nicaragua	-	-	-	-	-	-	-	-	-	-
Panama	-0.2	0.5	-0.8	0.1	-1.8	-	-0.1	-	-	-
Virgin Islands, U.S.	-	-	-	-	-	-	-	-	-	-
South America	0.0	0.1	0.2	1.7	0.5	0.1	0.3	0.0	-0.5	-0.2
Argentina	-	-	-	0.5	-	-	-	-	-	-
Bolivia	-	-	-	-	-	-	-	-	-	-
Brazil	0.0	-	0.2	0.4	0.4	0.1	0.3	-0.1	-0.6	-0.2
Colombia	-	-	-	-	-	-	0.1	0.1	0.1	-
Ecuador	-	-	-	-	-	-	-	-	-	-
Paraguay	-	-	-	-	-	-	-	-	-	-
Peru	-	-	-	0.4	-	-	-	-	-	-
Uruguay	-	0.1	-	0.3	-	-	-	-	-	-
Venezuela	-	-	-	-	-	-	-	-	-	-

Table 1. Foreign direct investment flows by country *(cont.)*

Million US dollars

	Inward					Outward				
	2015	2016	2017	2018	2019	2015	2016	2017	2018	2019
ASIA	**130.6**	**420.0**	**169.7**	**755.3**	**918.4**	**185.7**	**298.8**	**149.0**	**217.7**	**117.6**
Near and Middle East	73.4	33.1	85.8	96.1	144.8	-33.8	13.2	45.1	42.7	13.3
Gulf Arabian countries	59.3	18.4	25.7	31.5	32.3	-32.8	17.2	45.6	44.4	13.2
Kuwait	1.1	1.0	4.9	1.4	2.5	0.2	-	-	-	-
Qatar	31.8	9.2	2.5	1.9	-3.1	0.8	16.7	44.9	36.6	8.9
Saudi Arabia	10.8	2.4	1.1	3.9	2.4	-	-0.1	-	-	0.0
United Arab Emirates	13.3	2.9	13.6	20.7	29.0	-33.7	0.6	0.9	7.8	4.2
Other Near and Middle East	14.1	14.7	60.1	64.6	112.5	-1.0	-4.0	-0.6	-1.7	0.1
Jordan	1.1	2.9	4.6	4.5	2.8	-	-	-	-2.3	-
Other Asian countries	57.2	386.9	84.0	659.2	773.6	219.5	285.5	104.0	175.0	104.4
China	20.7	32.4	53.7	254.2	205.7	0.2	0.4	0.7	10.9	0.2
Hong Kong, China	35.1	350.6	29.2	370.5	484.9	219.9	285.5	103.6	164.4	100.9
India	0.1	0.3	0.0	1.3	3.2	0.0	0.0	0.0	0.0	0.5
Indonesia	-	0.0	-	-	-	-	-	-	-	-
Iran, Islamic Republic of	-	0.0	1.5	2.8	0.7	-	-	-	-	-
Malaysia	-	0.2	0.2	0.3	0.5	-	-	-	-	-
Philippines	-	-	-	-	-	-	-	-	-	-
Singapore	0.0	1.3	2.9	28.1	74.3	-	-	-	-	-
Chinese Taipei	-	0.1	-	3.0	1.6	-	-	-	-	-
Thailand	0.1	0.0	0.2	-	-0.3	-	-	-	-	-
Viet Nam	-	-	-	0.3	0.7	-	-	-	-	-
AUSTRALIA, OCEANIA AND POLAR REGIONS	**-4.4**	**-0.9**	**-0.6**	**13.8**	**14.6**	**0.9**	**-0.2**	**-0.5**	**-2.0**	**-0.7**
WORLD unallocated and confidential	**0.2**	**0.5**	**0.5**	**3.0**	**2.2**	**0.4**	**0.0**	**0.0**	**0.0**	**-0.1**
European Union (EU28)	**560.0**	**1 817.0**	**2 159.8**	**2 351.1**	**3 346.0**	**719.9**	**290.8**	**-1.8**	**453.9**	**575.3**
G20 countries excl. European Union	**816.9**	**816.1**	**1 322.3**	**1 595.3**	**1 356.4**	**430.2**	**-2 398.3**	**209.6**	**149.0**	**-97.4**
G20 OECD countries	**763.0**	**766.2**	**1 247.8**	**1 322.4**	**1 115.7**	**394.1**	**-2 437.4**	**169.8**	**107.9**	**-97.9**
G20 Non-OECD countries	**53.9**	**49.8**	**74.4**	**272.9**	**240.7**	**36.1**	**39.1**	**39.9**	**41.1**	**0.5**
MENA countries	**70.7**	**31.9**	**60.4**	**73.2**	**72.4**	**-33.1**	**13.0**	**45.8**	**42.0**	**12.8**
ASEAN countries	**0.1**	**1.5**	**3.4**	**28.8**	**74.6**	-	-	-	-	**2.3**

\- Nil

Note: Detailed metadata at: *http://stats.oecd.org/OECDStat_Metadata/ShowMetadata.ashx?Dataset=FDI_CTRY_IND_SUMM.*

Source: *OECD International Direct Investment Statistics (database): https://doi.org/10.1787/idi-data-en*

Table 2. Foreign direct investment positions by country
At year end

Million US dollars

	Inward					Outward				
	2015	2016	2017	2018	2019	2015	2016	2017	2018	2019
WORLD	**24 082.0**	**24 614.9**	**33 404.1**	**35 736.7**	**45 151.2**	**24 419.0**	**18 005.9**	**20 104.3**	**19 497.9**	**19 234.9**
OECD COUNTRIES	**25 225.0**	**24 961.0**	**33 380.5**	**33 761.7**	**40 909.6**	**8 194.0**	**4 570.0**	**5 863.0**	**6 243.4**	**7 240.9**
Australia	-5.0	-4.5	9.8	19.6	33.8	2.0	1.9	11.7	9.2	8.9
Austria	255.2	351.7	507.5	291.6	278.9	688.6	625.6	722.2	416.6	243.2
Belgium	1 415.9	1 450.0	801.5	1 296.8	2 707.9	4.5	47.9	153.1	148.6	153.5
Canada	748.9	591.1	876.3	722.0	1 315.3	2.3	-	17.4	15.7	13.9
Chile	0.0	0.0	0.0	0.0	0.1	-	-	0.2	0.2	0.2
Czech Republic	-0.1	-0.3	13.6	21.9	335.9	0.1	-0.4	0.2	-0.7	-0.7
Denmark	89.7	86.6	194.2	204.5	212.6	7.1	5.0	2.0	-1.8	-5.5
Estonia	0.0	0.0	5.3	5.6	7.2	-	-	0.1	0.1	0.1
Finland	2.7	12.0	50.1	52.5	39.7	-	-	1.1	0.6	0.7
France	2 060.0	1 464.2	1 743.3	1 523.3	1 723.5	18.0	26.0	69.0	64.6	66.2
Germany	5 559.1	5 226.2	7 721.0	7 963.9	9 246.9	185.9	232.4	366.7	368.1	374.5
Greece	-	-	-	-	-	-	-	-	-	-
Hungary	60.5	39.0	44.8	14.9	18.8	-0.8	0.4	1.9	2.0	2.2
Iceland	1.1	1.1	1.7	1.7	1.7	-	-	-	-	-
Ireland	376.2	410.6	474.4	448.5	387.0	11.5	11.4	13.8	13.3	13.1
Israel	36.1	34.9	46.5	64.0	112.4	0.0	-	0.5	3.6	3.7
Italy	920.0	1 024.3	1 241.4	1 527.5	1 729.7	533.8	339.7	568.5	560.5	569.2
Japan	46.8	44.7	47.1	42.0	39.4	11.3	-0.6	12.9	12.3	12.1
Korea	4.9	8.2	20.2	12.4	11.1	-6.1	-12.5	-14.9	-14.2	-14.0
Latvia	0.0	0.0	12.8	13.9	15.0	-	-	0.3	0.3	0.3
Lithuania	0.0	0.0	3.5	3.9	4.9	-	-	0.1	0.1	0.1
Luxembourg	4 766.5	5 634.6	7 731.4	7 495.4	9 000.2	406.9	-192.6	-383.6	-368.6	-113.1
Mexico	-25.8	-25.0	-27.9	-25.6	-24.9	-	-	-	-	-
Netherlands	4 980.6	5 014.6	5 763.3	5 734.8	7 156.6	2 137.1	2 034.0	2 185.0	2 023.9	1 773.3
New Zealand	-0.1	-0.1	0.8	1.6	2.4	-	-	0.7	0.7	0.7
Norway	52.5	59.4	37.3	24.1	52.8	29.9	29.0	6.8	7.1	7.4
Poland	-4.6	5.1	15.2	10.9	18.5	-125.6	51.7	44.5	50.9	41.7
Portugal	1.4	0.6	1.5	2.5	3.5	5.5	4.7	5.4	4.9	4.8
Slovak Republic	-2.9	-5.8	-5.4	-3.8	-3.7	-7.1	-6.6	-6.5	-4.8	-4.7
Slovenia	7.8	5.7	6.9	22.2	21.6	13.6	11.9	20.0	20.9	21.4
Spain	835.5	818.6	865.6	785.2	789.4	118.2	125.9	154.0	110.7	81.7
Sweden	107.0	101.2	143.3	122.5	147.4	4.2	3.9	10.0	8.4	7.7
Switzerland	1 781.4	1 928.8	3 408.4	3 556.3	3 560.2	-32.6	0.6	92.9	98.8	102.0
Turkey	13.4	6.7	42.6	59.8	71.0	3 589.7	143.5	153.5	273.2	264.3
United Kingdom	342.2	106.5	549.3	785.7	649.3	-1 547.9	-1 253.0	-784.3	-85.7	48.2
United States	798.1	570.3	1 036.7	959.5	1 243.6	2 143.9	2 340.3	2 438.0	2 504.0	3 563.5
EUROPE	**21 225.6**	**21 772.7**	**29 790.5**	**32 077.4**	**39 725.3**	**19 318.6**	**12 646.7**	**13 554.8**	**13 249.9**	**12 402.9**
Bulgaria	1.9	-8.0	4.9	71.6	92.7	1 766.4	1 328.0	1 474.7	1 354.3	1 226.5
Croatia	-1.4	0.0	0.4	0.0	0.2	56.3	62.7	6.9	5.8	5.9
Cyprus	-2 484.2	-2 040.2	-1 728.8	-112.7	1 189.8	5 435.7	4 500.8	4 971.6	5 043.1	5 196.4
Malta	1.2	1.4	-38.9	-41.6	5.8	561.2	-4.7	-0.8	-2.3	-2.2
Romania	-6.3	-3.2	5.7	10.1	17.0	2 828.9	2 486.5	1 792.6	1 767.9	1 402.6
Russian Federation	36.3	27.3	102.7	110.6	119.7	89.0	86.1	77.6	11.3	12.4
Ukraine	-1.9	-0.2	2.4	2.3	2.1	53.4	37.8	46.8	44.3	44.7
AFRICA	**72.2**	**62.9**	**64.5**	**45.8**	**69.3**	**518.2**	**91.1**	**302.3**	**340.0**	**53.1**
Northern Africa	-0.2	-0.2	8.6	13.6	20.8	439.1	18.5	279.7	334.0	46.9
Algeria	0.0	0.0	0.0	0.0	0.0	-	-	-	-	-
Egypt	0.0	-0.1	8.3	13.1	20.2	438.7	12.9	278.9	333.4	16.0
Libya	-	-	-	-	-	0.5	0.3	0.3	0.0	30.4
Morocco	0.0	0.0	0.2	0.2	0.3	0.0	5.4	0.2	0.2	0.2
Tunisia	-0.2	-0.2	0.2	0.3	0.4	-0.1	-0.1	0.3	0.3	0.3
Other African countries	72.4	63.2	55.8	32.2	48.5	79.0	72.6	22.5	6.0	6.2
Nigeria	0.0	0.0	0.0	0.5	0.8	26.0	25.2	0.3	0.3	0.3
South Africa	-0.2	-0.1	0.7	1.5	2.1	24.6	19.8	16.5	2.7	2.8
AMERICA	**2 102.7**	**1 837.9**	**2 239.4**	**2 095.3**	**2 961.0**	**3 256.2**	**3 383.2**	**3 802.5**	**3 574.6**	**4 481.5**
Northern America	1 547.0	1 161.4	1 913.0	1 681.5	2 558.9	2 146.3	2 340.3	2 455.4	2 519.7	3 577.4
Central America and Caribbean countries	556.5	679.0	299.7	414.6	402.9	1 109.7	1 042.8	1 193.1	915.2	901.2
Bahamas	-	-	0.9	1.0	1.1	-	-	1.0	1.0	1.0
Bermuda	295.7	500.3	1.0	1.5	1.6	-	-	-	-	-
Cayman Islands	118.1	23.2	13.2	13.9	65.0	504.5	490.9	131.5	125.6	123.3
Costa Rica	-	-	-	-	-	-	-	0.1	0.1	0.1
El Salvador	-	-	-	-	-	-	-	-	-	-
Guatemala	0.0	0.0	-0.1	0.0	0.0	-	-	-	0.3	0.5
Honduras	-0.3	-0.3	-0.3	-0.3	-0.3	-	-	-	-	-
Nicaragua	-	-	-	-	-	-	-	-	-	-
Panama	81.7	91.4	147.2	141.8	140.4	9.8	9.5	12.3	1.5	1.5
Virgin Islands, U.S.	-	-	-	-	-	-	-	-	-	-
South America	-0.8	-2.5	26.8	-0.8	-0.8	0.2	-	154.0	139.7	2.9
Argentina	0.4	-0.7	-0.8	-0.5	-0.5	-	-	0.5	0.5	0.5
Bolivia	-	-	-	-	-	-	-	0.0	0.0	0.0
Brazil	-1.1	-1.6	27.6	-0.4	-0.5	0.2	-	151.9	137.5	0.7
Colombia	-0.1	-0.2	-0.2	-0.2	-0.2	-	-	1.0	1.0	1.0
Ecuador	-	-	0.0	-	-	-	-	0.1	0.1	0.1
Paraguay	-	-	-	-	-	-	-	-	-	-
Peru	-	-	0.0	0.0	0.0	-	-	0.1	0.1	0.1
Uruguay	-	0.0	0.1	0.2	0.3	-	-	0.3	0.3	0.3
Venezuela	-	-	0.0	0.0	0.0	-	-	-	-	-

Table 2. Foreign direct investment positions by country *(cont.)*

At year end

Million US dollars

	Inward					Outward				
	2015	2016	2017	2018	2019	2015	2016	2017	2018	2019
ASIA	**636.1**	**909.5**	**1 246.0**	**1 441.1**	**2 328.4**	**1 324.1**	**1 883.0**	**2 391.5**	**2 283.0**	**2 246.8**
Near and Middle East	156.9	217.4	235.4	277.8	561.1	-19.3	33.4	48.0	48.4	50.2
Gulf Arabian countries	113.4	177.9	98.7	108.9	320.6	-27.5	25.5	35.0	28.9	38.1
Kuwait	-	-	4.0	4.8	6.7	-	-	-	-	-
Qatar	22.7	33.4	63.0	62.3	59.6	-	0.0	0.2	0.3	14.2
Saudi Arabia	0.0	-0.4	10.8	12.8	15.2	-	-	0.0	0.0	-3.5
United Arab Emirates	90.8	144.9	14.5	20.7	229.2	-37.2	14.9	20.5	21.3	18.9
Other Near and Middle East	43.4	39.5	136.7	168.9	240.5	8.2	7.9	13.0	19.5	12.1
Jordan	0.2	1.0	8.1	10.3	12.6	-	-	0.9	4.8	0.9
Other Asian countries	479.2	692.0	1 010.6	1 163.3	1 767.3	1 343.4	1 849.6	2 343.5	2 234.5	2 196.6
China	6.4	10.1	128.8	256.0	400.4	39.2	24.1	22.3	21.4	21.2
Hong Kong, China	361.6	574.9	744.3	764.4	1 174.9	1 280.0	1 823.5	2 316.4	2 208.0	2 167.0
India	0.8	0.4	0.8	0.8	1.5	12.8	12.4	0.0	0.0	0.4
Indonesia	0.0	0.0	0.1	0.1	0.1	8.9	8.6	0.3	0.3	0.3
Iran, Islamic Republic of	53.0	48.6	56.7	56.6	56.6	-	-	-	-	-
Malaysia	0.1	0.3	0.7	0.9	1.3	-1.0	-1.1	-1.1	-1.1	-1.0
Philippines	0.0	0.0	-	-	-	0.0	0.0	0.1	0.1	0.1
Singapore	2.1	1.6	4.3	19.4	67.2	-0.4	-0.8	2.4	2.4	2.5
Chinese Taipei	0.2	0.1	0.1	1.8	2.9	-0.7	-1.9	-2.1	-2.0	-1.9
Thailand	0.5	0.5	0.7	0.7	0.5	-2.1	-2.5	-1.4	-1.3	-1.2
Viet Nam	-	0.0	0.0	0.2	0.6	-	-	-	-	-
AUSTRALIA, OCEANIA AND POLAR REGIONS	**45.3**	**31.8**	**47.7**	**61.2**	**49.7**	**2.0**	**1.9**	**13.4**	**10.8**	**10.5**
WORLD unallocated and confidential	**0.0**	**-**	**16.0**	**15.9**	**17.4**	**0.0**	**0.0**	**39.9**	**39.6**	**40.0**
European Union (EU28)	**19 283.8**	**19 695.3**	**26 127.9**	**28 251.8**	**35 796.2**	**13 102.1**	**10 441.2**	**11 388.2**	**11 501.6**	**11 107.3**
G20 countries excl. European Union	**10 505.1**	**9 047.7**	**13 530.6**	**13 970.8**	**16 576.7**	**5 107.7**	**1 968.7**	**3 107.6**	**3 881.4**	**4 941.7**
G20 OECD countries	**10 462.5**	**9 012.7**	**13 259.9**	**13 590.1**	**16 038.6**	**4 933.0**	**1 817.7**	**2 838.6**	**3 707.7**	**4 906.9**
G20 Non-OECD countries	**42.6**	**35.0**	**270.7**	**380.7**	**538.1**	**174.7**	**151.0**	**269.0**	**173.7**	**34.8**
MENA countries	**116.4**	**181.6**	**196.1**	**224.1**	**463.9**	**417.4**	**49.6**	**317.7**	**369.4**	**87.6**
ASEAN countries	**2.7**	**2.3**	**5.9**	**21.4**	**70.0**	**5.3**	**4.2**	**8.2**	**8.4**	**11.2**

- Nil

Note: Detailed metadata at: *http://stats.oecd.org/OECDStat_Metadata/ShowMetadata.ashx?Dataset=FDI_CTRY_IND_SUMM.*

Source: *OECD International Direct Investment Statistics (database): https://doi.org/10.1787/idi-data-en*

GREECE

Table 3. Foreign direct investment income by country

Million US dollars

	Inward					Outward				
	2015	2016	2017	2018	2019	2015	2016	2017	2018	2019
WORLD	**1 156.8**	**1 149.8**	**1 451.9**	**1 551.9**	**1 868.3**	**1 801.5**	**627.5**	**1 098.5**	**694.2**	**934.7**
OECD COUNTRIES	**1 017.5**	**922.0**	**1 325.3**	**1 426.1**	**1 681.8**	**719.6**	**200.7**	**360.7**	**472.2**	**469.3**
Australia	0.1	0.1	0.1	0.1	5.0	0.1	0.1	0.2	0.2	0.3
Austria	-29.0	-10.2	-9.1	-9.2	-3.1	36.5	-6.0	-7.4	-2.2	-2.3
Belgium	-26.7	-11.9	61.2	63.3	46.7	0.8	3.2	1.1	3.8	4.8
Canada	146.8	192.4	179.8	172.5	258.8	2.7	2.8	2.5	3.8	3.7
Chile	0.0	0.0	0.0	0.0	0.0	0.0	0.0	0.0	0.0	0.0
Czech Republic	40.3	1.1	-0.1	0.2	0.8	-6.1	-6.4	-5.8	-5.4	1.1
Denmark	5.1	4.8	5.9	6.6	6.2	0.0	0.0	-0.3	0.4	-1.6
Estonia	0.0	0.0	0.0	0.0	0.0	0.9	1.3	1.3	2.6	1.0
Finland	0.7	-2.2	4.2	11.5	8.7	-	-	-0.6	-0.7	-0.6
France	17.6	14.9	27.3	66.5	189.2	3.3	2.5	7.5	1.5	6.2
Germany	238.6	207.0	291.9	231.0	448.8	19.9	32.9	52.1	44.0	44.8
Greece	-	-	-	-	-	-	-	-	-	-
Hungary	-	0.0	0.0	0.0	0.0	-1.3	0.6	0.6	0.3	0.2
Iceland	0.0	0.0	0.0	-0.1	-0.1	0.0	0.0	0.0	0.0	0.0
Ireland	7.4	-13.7	20.6	4.9	-62.0	0.0	0.1	0.2	1.4	2.7
Israel	1.0	0.9	1.1	0.5	0.9	0.3	0.3	0.3	1.0	1.4
Italy	133.6	104.7	45.8	59.1	-0.7	11.8	15.6	27.1	36.1	36.4
Japan	-0.7	-0.3	-4.4	-4.0	-2.7	-0.3	-0.3	-0.3	-0.3	-0.3
Korea	0.0	0.0	-0.6	7.0	2.2	0.0	-	-	0.0	3.2
Latvia	0.0	0.0	0.0	0.0	0.0	0.2	0.1	0.1	0.1	0.1
Lithuania	-	-	0.0	0.0	0.0	0.0	-	-	-	-
Luxembourg	-142.9	116.3	180.0	458.1	113.7	30.5	56.9	65.7	42.3	51.8
Mexico	0.0	-	0.0	-	0.0	0.0	-	-	-	0.0
Netherlands	265.0	-18.6	223.8	212.6	407.0	131.0	-70.3	-14.0	43.8	142.6
New Zealand	-	-	0.0	0.0	-	0.0	0.0	0.0	0.0	0.0
Norway	10.0	-1.3	-0.2	0.4	2.6	0.2	0.1	-0.7	-0.4	-0.2
Poland	0.2	0.0	0.3	0.3	0.3	4.4	5.9	3.4	2.9	3.3
Portugal	0.0	0.0	0.1	1.0	0.0	0.2	0.9	0.5	-0.4	1.3
Slovak Republic	0.2	0.1	0.1	0.1	0.2	-0.2	-0.2	-0.2	-0.1	-0.2
Slovenia	0.3	-0.1	-0.1	-1.4	0.0	0.2	1.9	3.1	3.1	2.4
Spain	155.3	110.1	73.4	78.9	-3.0	4.2	3.3	2.5	7.2	7.7
Sweden	4.3	5.6	2.8	12.4	15.6	0.3	0.3	-3.8	-2.9	-3.0
Switzerland	7.4	-28.0	83.0	115.9	113.1	52.1	47.0	77.9	88.6	82.1
Turkey	-3.8	-1.8	-2.1	-2.2	-2.1	800.5	47.4	61.6	53.6	50.7
United Kingdom	169.2	212.5	115.3	-88.3	90.5	-401.9	-100.7	14.0	66.4	-37.9
United States	17.7	39.4	25.3	28.5	45.0	29.4	161.4	72.3	81.5	67.4
EUROPE	**1 003.6**	**925.7**	**1 303.6**	**1 386.3**	**1 602.8**	**1 671.2**	**206.7**	**947.7**	**527.3**	**767.8**
Bulgaria	-1.0	-0.7	-0.5	-0.3	-0.8	539.4	124.0	330.7	-1.5	138.8
Croatia	0.0	0.0	0.0	0.0	0.0	0.0	0.4	0.4	0.4	0.4
Cyprus	170.2	249.9	201.8	190.1	265.5	436.2	-77.1	254.4	172.4	174.2
Malta	0.0	0.0	-6.4	-6.7	-17.9	91.9	12.5	0.1	7.6	0.1
Romania	0.1	0.2	0.4	0.2	0.4	-101.5	17.6	-34.9	-63.0	7.7
Russian Federation	1.2	-2.6	-6.7	-6.3	-1.4	39.3	41.9	40.2	44.0	1.7
Ukraine	0.0	0.0	-	0.0	0.0	-36.1	-3.1	-1.9	-1.2	-3.2
AFRICA	**-12.6**	**-12.9**	**-15.8**	**-25.5**	**-19.8**	**-0.8**	**2.1**	**3.1**	**1.4**	**2.2**
Northern Africa	0.0	0.0	0.0	0.0	0.1	0.5	0.1	2.1	-0.1	0.1
Algeria	-	-	-	-	-	0.0	0.0	0.0	0.0	0.0
Egypt	0.0	0.0	0.0	0.0	0.1	0.4	0.3	0.4	0.2	0.2
Libya	-	0.0	0.0	0.0	-	0.0	-0.2	0.0	-0.3	-0.1
Morocco	-	-	-	0.0	-	0.1	-	1.7	-	-
Tunisia	-	-	0.0	-	0.0	0.0	0.0	-	-	-
Other African countries	-12.6	-12.9	-15.8	-25.5	-19.9	-1.3	1.9	1.0	1.5	2.1
Nigeria	0.0	-	-	-	-	-	-	-	-	-
South Africa	0.0	0.0	0.0	0.0	0.8	-3.0	0.0	0.1	0.0	0.6
AMERICA	**153.6**	**215.2**	**188.2**	**184.4**	**310.6**	**-56.9**	**132.2**	**41.9**	**53.1**	**49.5**
Northern America	164.5	231.9	205.0	201.0	303.8	32.1	164.2	74.8	85.2	71.2
Central America and Caribbean countries	-11.2	-16.8	-17.1	-17.3	6.2	-89.0	-32.0	-33.0	-32.7	-23.2
Bahamas	0.0	-	-	-	-	1.0	2.6	1.2	2.8	1.2
Bermuda	-0.1	-0.1	0.0	-0.2	-0.1	0.0	0.0	0.0	0.0	0.0
Cayman Islands	2.4	-0.4	-0.3	-0.3	3.5	-68.4	-2.4	-30.4	-31.5	-29.7
Costa Rica	0.0	0.0	0.0	0.0	0.0	0.0	0.0	0.0	0.0	0.0
El Salvador	-	-	-	-	-	0.0	0.0	0.0	0.0	0.0
Guatemala	0.0	0.0	0.0	0.0	0.0	0.0	0.0	0.0	-0.1	-0.1
Honduras	0.0	0.0	0.0	0.0	0.0	-	-	-	-	-
Nicaragua	0.0	0.0	-	0.0	0.0	0.0	-	-	-	-
Panama	-0.7	-3.7	-2.7	-2.9	-3.0	0.3	0.1	0.3	0.2	0.1
Virgin Islands, U.S.	-	-	-	-	-	-	-	-	-	4.9
South America	0.3	0.1	0.2	0.7	0.6	0.0	0.0	0.1	0.5	1.6
Argentina	0.0	0.0	0.0	0.0	0.0	0.0	-	-	0.0	-
Bolivia	0.0	0.0	0.0	0.0	-	0.0	0.0	0.0	0.0	0.0
Brazil	0.2	0.1	0.2	0.7	0.6	0.0	0.0	-0.3	-1.0	-0.2
Colombia	0.0	-	-	-	-	0.0	-	-	-	-
Ecuador	-	-	-	-	-	0.0	0.0	0.0	0.0	0.0
Paraguay	0.0	0.0	0.0	0.0	0.0	0.0	0.0	0.0	0.0	0.0
Peru	-	0.0	-	-	-	0.0	0.0	0.5	1.5	1.8
Uruguay	0.1	-	-	-	-	0.0	-	-	-	-
Venezuela	-	-	0.0	0.0	-	-	-	-	-	-

GREECE

Table 3. Foreign direct investment income by country *(cont.)*

Million US dollars

	Inward					Outward				
	2015	2016	2017	2018	2019	2015	2016	2017	2018	2019
ASIA	**19.0**	**28.3**	**-13.8**	**16.0**	**-27.3**	**187.0**	**285.7**	**105.1**	**110.0**	**112.2**
Near and Middle East	-7.2	-6.0	-5.9	-10.9	-34.0	-33.5	0.6	4.1	4.0	4.1
Gulf Arabian countries	-8.9	-7.0	-7.0	-11.5	-34.9	-33.2	1.3	2.4	3.2	2.8
Kuwait	-	-	-	0.0	-	-	-	-	-	-
Qatar	-12.5	-0.5	-0.4	-2.6	-9.0	0.0	-	0.0	0.8	0.0
Saudi Arabia	0.0	0.0	0.0	0.0	1.1	0.1	0.0	-	-	-
United Arab Emirates	3.6	-6.6	-6.8	-9.0	-27.0	-33.3	1.3	2.4	2.4	2.8
Other Near and Middle East	1.7	1.0	1.2	0.6	0.9	-0.3	-0.7	1.7	0.8	1.4
Jordan	-	0.0	0.0	0.0	0.0	0.0	0.0	0.0	0.0	0.0
Other Asian countries	26.2	34.3	-8.0	26.9	6.7	220.5	285.1	101.1	106.0	108.1
China	0.4	1.8	0.2	20.3	0.2	0.1	0.1	0.1	0.3	0.4
Hong Kong, China	26.4	32.7	-3.1	3.5	6.4	220.1	284.7	100.0	105.0	102.8
India	-	-	-	0.0	-	0.0	0.0	0.3	0.1	0.5
Indonesia	-	-	-	-	-	0.0	0.0	0.0	0.0	0.0
Iran, Islamic Republic of	-	-	0.0	0.0	0.0	-	0.0	-	-	-
Malaysia	0.0	0.0	0.0	0.0	0.0	0.0	-	0.1	0.1	0.1
Philippines	-	-	-	-	-	-	-	-	0.1	-
Singapore	0.1	0.0	-	0.0	0.0	0.5	0.5	0.7	0.3	1.2
Chinese Taipei	-	-	-	0.0	-	0.0	0.0	0.2	0.4	0.2
Thailand	-	-	-	-	-	0.0	-	-	0.0	-
Viet Nam	0.0	-	-	0.0	-	0.0	0.0	0.0	0.0	0.0
AUSTRALIA, OCEANIA AND POLAR REGIONS	**-6.8**	**-6.3**	**-10.2**	**-11.2**	**0.5**	**0.6**	**0.6**	**0.2**	**1.0**	**1.6**
WORLD unallocated and confidential	**0.0**	**0.0**	**-0.1**	**2.0**	**1.5**	**0.5**	**0.2**	**0.4**	**1.5**	**1.4**
European Union (EU28)	**1 008.5**	**969.9**	**1 238.7**	**1 290.9**	**1 506.1**	**800.7**	**19.3**	**697.6**	**360.1**	**582.1**
G20 countries excl. European Union	**720.9**	**768.3**	**672.0**	**485.0**	**1 035.5**	**502.1**	**203.7**	**277.3**	**330.0**	**177.5**
G20 OECD countries	**719.1**	**769.0**	**678.3**	**470.3**	**1 034.2**	**465.6**	**161.7**	**236.9**	**286.6**	**174.6**
G20 Non-OECD countries	**1.8**	**-0.7**	**-6.3**	**14.7**	**1.3**	**36.5**	**42.1**	**40.4**	**43.4**	**2.9**
MENA countries	**-8.9**	**-7.0**	**-7.0**	**-11.4**	**-34.7**	**-33.1**	**0.7**	**6.1**	**3.1**	**2.8**
ASEAN countries	**0.2**	**0.0**	**0.0**	**0.0**	**0.0**	**0.5**	**0.5**	**0.8**	**0.6**	**1.3**

\- Nil

Note: Detailed metadata at: *http://stats.oecd.org/OECDStat_Metadata/ShowMetadata.ashx?Dataset=FDI_CTRY_IND_SUMM.*

Source: *OECD International Direct Investment Statistics (database): https://doi.org/10.1787/idi-data-en*

GREECE

Table 4. Foreign direct investment flows by industrial sector

Million US dollars

	Inward					Outward				
	2015	2016	2017	2018	2019	2015	2016	2017	2018	2019
All FDI activities	**1 267.8**	**2 762.4**	**3 477.4**	**3 970.8**	**5 019.2**	**1 577.9**	**-1 665.4**	**168.0**	**476.6**	**641.6**
Agriculture, forestry and fishing	**1.7**	**5.2**	**10.3**	**17.2**	**-35.1**	**-5.0**	**-0.3**	**7.5**	**0.3**	**1.5**
Mining and quarrying	**156.8**	**128.6**	**128.0**	**37.9**	**-90.4**	**-1.8**	**35.3**	**10.2**	**1.2**	**14.0**
Extraction activities	9.0	-6.1	20.8	26.9	-44.3	0.1	0.1	10.1	6.8	13.7
Manufacturing	**8.0**	**50.1**	**311.6**	**364.9**	**375.9**	**-6.3**	**188.3**	**126.6**	**74.6**	**-114.7**
of which:										
Food products, beverages and tobacco	22.4	54.7	68.2	-5.5	190.8	5.1	28.7	41.8	35.8	9.5
Textiles, wood and paper products; printing	1.4	3.3	-6.2	5.9	7.8	-4.1	1.3	2.3	5.1	-3.0
Chemical, rubber, plastic, non-metallic mineral products	0.4	20.3	179.5	350.8	258.3	-8.2	22.3	4.8	5.5	-12.1
Metal and machinery products, except electrical equipment	-3.5	-3.1	29.0	19.0	-18.2	-22.5	-21.8	31.7	-1.0	34.2
Motor vehicles, trailers, semi-trailers, other transport equipment	4.5	4.5	0.7	0.2	-0.2	-	-	0.8	-	-
Other manufacturing	-17.1	-29.6	40.5	-5.6	-62.6	23.5	157.8	45.0	29.1	-143.2
Electricity, gas, steam and air conditioning supply	**-35.7**	**19.6**	**465.4**	**85.6**	**55.2**	**9.4**	**7.5**	**27.3**	**47.7**	**13.2**
Water supply; sewerage, waste management and remediation activities	**0.9**	**0.0**	**1.0**	**1.0**	**1.2**	**5.2**	**4.1**	**0.8**	**-1.6**	**0.0**
Construction	**22.4**	**39.1**	**-15.6**	**-77.0**	**40.9**	**17.7**	**100.2**	**116.5**	**78.5**	**150.8**
Services	**947.3**	**2 308.8**	**2 200.3**	**2 756.4**	**3 832.6**	**1 579.0**	**-2 030.8**	**-125.2**	**272.4**	**575.0**
Wholesale and retail trade; repair of motor vehicles and motorcycles	94.7	97.2	100.7	133.1	83.2	312.0	402.6	150.5	301.2	54.5
Transportation and storage	107.0	600.6	1 455.9	870.4	278.0	44.0	6.5	8.7	-50.9	7.8
Accommodation and food service activities	15.6	488.6	123.1	137.2	124.6	0.2	6.6	1.0	-0.8	35.4
Information and communication	-119.0	-165.5	-132.9	301.6	104.6	-60.0	-189.4	-144.5	-147.4	-145.7
Financial and insurance activities	650.3	886.6	516.4	721.9	764.0	1 292.6	-2 305.7	-334.3	47.9	273.0
Activities of holding companies	102.3	153.8	49.7	300.2	27.0	278.2	-240.5	365.1	291.7	133.2
Real estate activities	135.0	162.6	78.3	844.3	1 989.2	-42.4	-7.1	138.6	102.0	207.4
Professional, scientific and technical activities	-28.7	10.1	24.0	-123.1	296.1	30.8	-22.0	-2.8	9.3	-33.3
Administrative and support service activities	59.0	50.6	52.8	56.2	46.3	5.2	-36.8	53.1	5.7	13.7
Public administration; activities of households and of extraterritorial organisations	-	-	-	-	-	-	-	-	-	-
Education	0.1	4.2	-0.1	0.0	0.1	-	-	-0.1	-	-
Human health and social work activities	-5.6	30.9	20.6	-89.3	194.6	-3.3	-6.2	-3.8	-4.3	-4.4
Arts, entertainment and recreation	35.0	131.9	-35.7	-100.1	-62.4	-0.1	151.7	8.7	9.7	166.1
Other services	3.9	11.0	-2.8	4.2	14.3	0.0	-31.0	-0.2	0.0	0.4
Not allocated and confidential	**34.6**	**45.8**	**6.8**	**11.6**	**-0.4**	**-6.9**	**31.6**	**0.0**	**-1.3**	**0.1**
Private real estate activities	**131.7**	**165.4**	**369.5**	**773.3**	**839.3**	**-13.4**	**-1.2**	**4.2**	**4.7**	**1.8**

- Nil

Note: Detailed metadata at: *http://stats.oecd.org/OECDStat_Metadata/ShowMetadata.ashx?Dataset=FDI_CTRY_IND_SUMM.*

Source: OECD *International Direct Investment Statistics (database): https://doi.org/10.1787/idi-data-en*

Table 5. Foreign direct investment positions by industrial sector

At year end

Million US dollars

	Inward					Outward				
	2015	2016	2017	2018	2019	2015	2016	2017	2018	2019
All FDI activities	**24 082.0**	**24 614.9**	**33 404.1**	**35 736.7**	**45 151.2**	**24 419.0**	**18 005.9**	**20 104.3**	**19 497.9**	**19 234.9**
Agriculture, forestry and fishing	**286.2**	**260.7**	**327.6**	**82.0**	**234.0**	**60.5**	**56.1**	**63.0**	**60.1**	**6.5**
Mining and quarrying	**387.5**	**1 222.2**	**1 403.1**	**1 578.6**	**1 731.5**	**24.0**	**22.4**	**32.5**	**18.2**	**17.8**
Extraction activities	209.2	101.2	111.6	314.9	244.3	11.2	10.8	19.3	5.6	5.5
Manufacturing	**7 579.7**	**8 005.2**	**9 072.8**	**9 187.1**	**11 222.8**	**3 220.5**	**2 956.4**	**3 455.2**	**3 726.8**	**4 013.1**
of which:										
Food products, beverages and tobacco	1 858.0	1 867.2	2 097.2	2 565.6	2 864.5	258.8	207.1	278.1	279.0	266.7
Textiles, wood and paper products; printing	133.5	119.0	132.2	124.1	192.6	46.4	39.4	63.8	60.3	59.2
Chemical, rubber, plastic, non-metallic mineral products	2 940.7	3 009.9	4 339.3	3 947.6	4 331.0	77.9	136.7	150.1	217.5	230.5
Metal and machinery products, except electrical equipment	1 485.5	1 526.1	848.1	1 090.3	1 479.7	517.2	483.9	372.0	260.7	281.5
Motor vehicles, trailers, semi-trailers, other transport equipment	11.8	11.4	11.3	1.2	11.0	-	-	5.3	-	-
Other manufacturing	1 150.3	1 471.7	1 644.6	1 458.4	2 344.1	2 320.2	2 089.3	2 585.9	2 909.4	3 175.2
Electricity, gas, steam and air conditioning supply	**2 983.0**	**2 529.6**	**3 103.2**	**2 673.3**	**2 479.6**	**181.4**	**174.8**	**220.8**	**245.6**	**296.4**
Water supply; sewerage, waste management and remediation activities	**34.6**	**37.0**	**35.4**	**40.0**	**42.7**	**23.1**	**22.4**	**25.5**	**25.3**	**25.0**
Construction	**425.1**	**241.4**	**337.2**	**493.2**	**719.0**	**59.2**	**98.3**	**116.8**	**137.2**	**256.8**
Services	**12 313.1**	**12 237.3**	**17 180.0**	**18 999.8**	**24 526.9**	**20 780.2**	**14 607.9**	**15 190.6**	**14 244.8**	**13 247.9**
Wholesale and retail trade; repair of motor vehicles and motorcycles	5 432.4	5 447.0	5 782.3	5 707.9	6 627.8	3 157.9	3 683.9	4 910.7	4 419.0	4 243.3
Transportation and storage	875.8	1 769.0	3 552.6	4 082.2	4 214.8	203.4	187.1	212.7	199.1	195.2
Accommodation and food service activities	812.1	874.9	1 039.1	1 021.3	1 099.8	47.4	41.8	39.7	31.3	161.0
Information and communication	4 378.0	4 137.7	5 926.0	5 969.6	6 756.8	2 295.2	1 768.8	1 420.3	1 571.4	622.2
Financial and insurance activities	-4 537.5	-4 369.9	-4 743.9	-2 935.7	-882.5	14 540.8	8 013.3	7 469.1	6 890.9	6 487.1
Activities of holding companies	799.8	716.9	644.8	1 775.5	2 612.0	4 817.1	4 864.3	4 096.5	3 789.7	3 726.8
Real estate activities	2 588.1	2 103.9	2 316.0	2 151.9	2 609.9	185.3	382.6	367.4	383.4	767.4
Professional, scientific and technical activities	692.7	273.6	333.7	413.1	316.8	-32.9	189.4	389.3	327.0	210.2
Administrative and support service activities	661.1	711.4	1 050.0	988.8	1 176.5	177.8	136.9	157.6	134.2	152.0
Public administration; activities of households and of extraterritorial organisations	-	1.7	2.0	1.9	1.8	-	-	-	-	-
Education	0.6	0.9	1.0	0.9	0.9	-	-	-	-	-
Human health and social work activities	137.9	84.1	298.9	368.8	560.2	16.2	15.7	17.4	15.3	15.1
Arts, entertainment and recreation	1 262.5	1 194.0	1 612.0	1 213.1	2 027.2	173.3	167.8	191.0	260.1	385.4
Other services	9.4	9.0	10.3	16.2	16.9	15.7	20.7	15.5	13.0	8.9
Not allocated and confidential	**72.8**	**81.4**	**105.6**	**106.7**	**401.5**	**70.0**	**67.7**	**-421.4**	**-363.4**	**-59.9**
Private real estate activities	**-**	**-**	**1 839.2**	**2 576.1**	**3 793.1**	**-**	**-**	**1 421.2**	**1 403.2**	**1 431.2**

- Nil

Note: Detailed metadata at: *http://stats.oecd.org/OECDStat_Metadata/ShowMetadata.ashx?Dataset=FDI_CTRY_IND_SUMM.*

Source: *OECD International Direct Investment Statistics (database): https://doi.org/10.1787/idi-data-en*

Table 6. Foreign direct investment income by industrial sector

Million US dollars

	Inward					Outward				
	2015	2016	2017	2018	2019	2015	2016	2017	2018	2019
All FDI activities	**1 156.8**	**1 149.8**	**1 451.9**	**1 551.9**	**1 868.3**	**1 801.5**	**627.5**	**1 098.5**	**694.2**	**934.7**
Agriculture, forestry and fishing	**1.5**	**1.6**	**2.7**	**3.4**	**-45.5**	**-1.5**	**0.1**	**0.2**	**0.1**	**2.0**
Mining and quarrying	**1.1**	**-6.1**	**74.0**	**10.2**	**-128.5**	**4.1**	**1.8**	**12.8**	**5.4**	**10.8**
Extraction activities	0.6	27.6	108.0	46.4	-34.6	1.4	0.9	3.7	4.6	1.7
Manufacturing	**174.4**	**103.9**	**332.8**	**593.3**	**664.5**	**23.4**	**142.1**	**142.1**	**175.3**	**203.2**
of which:										
Food products, beverages and tobacco	127.5	65.2	85.3	136.4	235.7	5.8	6.4	44.7	50.0	115.9
Textiles, wood and paper products; printing	12.3	-1.3	-14.1	-7.8	-13.8	38.2	1.2	1.9	2.6	2.9
Chemical, rubber, plastic, non-metallic mineral products	46.6	73.1	233.6	443.7	469.8	-11.0	4.3	3.9	11.1	14.0
Metal and machinery products, except electrical equipment	-4.0	-9.5	26.5	3.7	-33.4	-33.2	-22.3	-9.9	-9.3	4.6
Motor vehicles, trailers, semi-trailers, other transport equipment	4.3	7.0	0.0	-0.3	0.3	-	-	-	0.1	0.2
Other manufacturing	-12.4	-30.6	1.5	17.5	5.9	23.6	152.4	101.4	120.9	65.5
Electricity, gas, steam and air conditioning supply	**2.7**	**34.2**	**109.9**	**-21.9**	**40.7**	**7.7**	**12.8**	**2.9**	**-8.2**	**3.9**
Water supply; sewerage, waste management and remediation activities	**0.2**	**0.0**	**1.0**	**1.0**	**1.8**	**0.8**	**0.8**	**0.8**	**0.0**	**0.3**
Construction	**0.6**	**17.2**	**34.7**	**34.6**	**40.8**	**6.9**	**50.7**	**59.4**	**76.5**	**40.1**
Services	**877.3**	**931.5**	**841.3**	**858.8**	**1 236.0**	**1 670.8**	**301.0**	**789.5**	**351.1**	**571.0**
Wholesale and retail trade; repair of motor vehicles and motorcycles	126.8	206.3	180.4	265.2	301.0	285.2	354.5	165.0	175.3	121.4
Transportation and storage	181.6	174.0	136.9	176.3	197.1	57.7	89.6	129.7	190.7	150.2
Accommodation and food service activities	-15.7	-14.9	-15.4	-10.6	-5.0	2.0	1.9	4.4	5.2	9.6
Information and communication	-17.9	-64.1	27.7	138.4	188.5	-36.6	-187.7	-152.2	-147.6	-144.4
Financial and insurance activities	424.1	448.8	364.5	332.2	325.3	1 353.6	37.5	207.3	48.6	342.5
Activities of holding companies	87.5	145.8	18.4	98.8	97.2	297.9	-86.4	-183.2	-50.2	151.3
Real estate activities	32.2	58.1	28.5	42.8	165.5	-55.3	5.3	39.5	21.8	47.8
Professional, scientific and technical activities	-20.3	-8.6	26.1	30.6	30.9	34.0	-20.8	-2.4	16.1	-43.1
Administrative and support service activities	17.4	19.0	31.7	37.5	55.0	4.9	6.7	391.7	17.4	44.5
Public administration; activities of households and of extraterritorial organisations	-	-	-	-	-	-	-	-	-	-
Education	0.1	-0.1	-0.1	5.8	1.0	-	-	-	-	0.1
Human health and social work activities	-3.4	29.0	-23.0	-26.4	37.2	-2.3	-2.8	-2.9	-3.1	-3.1
Arts, entertainment and recreation	151.7	69.2	82.7	-145.9	-66.1	27.7	16.8	9.4	26.9	45.4
Other services	0.6	14.9	1.3	12.8	5.7	0.0	0.1	0.1	-0.1	0.2
Not allocated and confidential	**98.7**	**67.2**	**55.2**	**69.7**	**58.0**	**81.7**	**103.5**	**76.1**	**72.0**	**71.9**
Private real estate activities	**0.3**	**0.4**	**0.3**	**2.9**	**0.4**	**7.6**	**14.7**	**14.7**	**21.8**	**31.5**

- Nil

Note: Detailed metadata at: *http://stats.oecd.org/OECDStat_Metadata/ShowMetadata.ashx?Dataset=FDI_CTRY_IND_SUMM.*

Source: *OECD International Direct Investment Statistics (database): https://doi.org/10.1787/idi-data-en*

HUNGARY

Table 1. Foreign direct investment flows by country

Million US dollars

	Inward					Outward				
	2015	2016	2017	2018	2019	2015	2016	2017	2018	2019
WORLD	**-14 544.6**	**-5 438.6**	**3 527.5**	**8 401.4**	**1 164.6**	**-16 117.7**	**-8 272.2**	**1 221.6**	**5 159.1**	**1 285.0**
OECD COUNTRIES	**-7 902.9**	**-6 730.6**	**1 662.5**	**8 315.8**	**530.4**	**-16 476.6**	**1 277.8**	**-947.9**	**3 986.9**	**-213.3**
Australia	10.0	13.6	-47.1	11.1	-4.0	-12.0	9.7	-18.8	10.3	5.5
Austria	1 145.8	-186.2	264.2	478.7	677.5	-23.2	23.8	9.2	32.1	-24.3
Belgium	-408.3	299.5	-278.1	1 817.4	-936.1	50.4	77.9	-2 841.3	0.2	-0.5
Canada	28.3	8.6	-69.4	-98.5	4.4	.. c	9.4	13.0	11.5	.. c
Chile	-0.2	3.5	2.0	1.2	-0.7	.. c	.. c	.. c	.. c	-
Czech Republic	42.4	131.8	186.2	93.2	113.1	-34.6	-3.3	297.9	84.0	180.6
Denmark	50.1	147.1	148.3	231.6	70.7	.. c	.. c	.. c	.. c	.. c
Estonia	0.0	-0.1	0.3	0.3	0.0	-0.6	-0.3	0.5	0.0	-1.3
Finland	-22.0	1.3	8.5	11.3	11.1	-0.3	0.1	0.0	0.0	-1.3
France	-1 545.4	1 912.5	381.4	601.9	257.1	-20.6	3.9	23.4	14.2	9.3
Germany	-2 189.9	3 707.4	-1 772.3	-807.9	1 198.0	49.2	115.2	21.2	-1.7	-0.7
Greece	-4.4	50.7	1.4	-4.2	3.8	0.0	0.1	0.4	-0.2	-0.2
Hungary	-	-	-	-	-	-	-	-	-	-
Iceland	-1.5	-1.1	-3.7	1.8	-0.6	-	-	.. c	.. c	.. c
Ireland	5 757.4	-4 021.9	59.9	830.5	-4 733.3	10.7	1.2	440.4	1 361.6	-1 114.4
Israel	863.1	-25.2	-2 104.0	-34.6	-108.8	546.1	317.2	330.3	162.9	-157.0
Italy	308.9	1 387.8	7.9	-188.8	256.8	-24.3	371.1	5.1	63.2	-26.3
Japan	-467.1	118.2	173.1	223.1	250.7	-0.5	3.1	1.0	1.4	1.9
Korea	169.6	185.8	264.3	1 086.9	648.4	22.6	16.5	11.5	-0.3	-14.9
Latvia	-0.2	-4.6	-1.3	-0.4	-1.2	1.5	-0.3	0.3	-0.1	1.5
Lithuania	-1.6	3.5	1.9	-2.2	8.5	1.0	1.3	0.7	0.7	-0.6
Luxembourg	-13 183.7	-164.3	468.8	1 063.3	1 354.8	-2 200.1	215.6	-239.8	-149.7	-165.8
Mexico	-414.9	74.1	-30.5	-68.7	-44.4	229.5	85.5	18.4	18.9	-3.4
Netherlands	5 066.5	-9 255.4	2 038.7	622.4	-573.7	52.1	-62.3	183.2	1 669.1	-93.0
New Zealand	-0.9	-9.9	2.2	-4.9	0.8	-	-	-	-	-
Norway	-19.5	-14.2	10.5	-416.6	-16.0	.. c	.. c	.. c	.. c	.. c
Poland	100.9	124.2	764.7	20.5	107.7	51.3	51.0	395.8	116.9	306.8
Portugal	-43.3	-9.5	18.7	-0.8	7.2	-40.2	-4.5	-0.3	0.2	0.1
Slovak Republic	-42.9	-3.9	-15.5	-9.7	5.7	277.8	162.4	21.2	-181.6	147.6
Slovenia	5.6	5.3	-1.8	3.1	4.1	-72.5	1.3	4.2	38.9	392.4
Spain	-15.6	37.4	3.0	187.6	-174.1	83.8	118.3	164.1	154.3	136.5
Sweden	73.6	33.9	-35.1	-20.8	128.0	-0.5	0.5	.. c	1.5	137.5
Switzerland	-1 116.2	134.7	2 256.6	-49.4	597.3	-15 532.0	17.4	252.1	-466.9	-296.3
Turkey	-2.0	11.4	11.6	-7.8	8.8	1.5	-23.8	-1.6	-3.8	-2.4
United Kingdom	995.4	-882.4	-1 398.2	-915.4	1 882.3	18.8	21.0	40.9	17.4	98.9
United States	-3 042.8	-540.6	347.3	3 660.6	-473.7	62.0	-249.9	-80.8	1 030.5	267.8
EUROPE	**-4 716.1**	**-5 978.5**	**3 607.2**	**3 802.3**	**359.0**	**-16 988.9**	**1 799.7**	**281.3**	**4 285.2**	**1 209.2**
Bulgaria	-11.3	3.7	3.0	11.8	8.8	17.5	-42.8	-25.3	737.2	306.0
Croatia	-221.7	-4.8	-18.7	17.2	-8.4	7.2	163.7	725.4	191.6	60.7
Cyprus	-59.2	0.4	20.2	37.3	-420.2	38.7	354.1	192.5	210.7	117.5
Malta	349.0	-117.8	48.5	-479.7	24.6	23.1	-22.0	120.7	64.0	59.7
Romania	-26.4	23.2	28.0	7.4	62.2	170.3	-21.7	189.6	128.6	264.2
Russian Federation	-25.8	154.1	63.5	165.8	152.3	-32.1	71.7	199.4	33.5	107.0
Ukraine	99.2	57.8	51.7	8.0	-79.1	121.4	191.5	61.3	65.8	98.2
AFRICA	**274.6**	**311.7**	**306.1**	**166.1**	**94.6**	**43.1**	**10.5**	**1.9**	**-6.4**	**-4.2**
Northern Africa	-8.3	5.6	4.7	3.7	-22.6	.. c	-0.4	-0.5	-2.7	0.2
Algeria	-0.2	0.1	0.6	0.1	-2.3	-	-	-	-	-
Egypt	-2.3	1.7	5.3	1.9	0.6	.. c	.. c	.. c	.. c	.. c
Libya	-	-	-	-	.. c	-	-	-	-	-
Morocco	-5.2	3.4	-2.2	1.6	2.2	-	-	.. c	.. c	.. c
Tunisia	-0.4	0.4	1.1	0.2	-23.1	-	-	-	-	-
Other African countries	282.9	306.1	301.4	162.4	117.2	43.2	.. c	.. c	.. c	-4.3
Nigeria	-0.2	-0.3	0.3	0.1	-0.1	-	-	-	-	-
South Africa	7.1	-2.7	-2.8	0.7	4.1	.. c	.. c	.. c	.. c	.. c
AMERICA	**-10 743.2**	**-374.1**	**1 598.6**	**2 534.3**	**-324.7**	**276.2**	**-10 421.6**	**559.6**	**671.9**	**382.3**
Northern America	-3 014.5	-532.0	277.9	3 562.1	-469.4	90.0	-240.5	-67.8	1 042.0	271.2
Central America and Caribbean countries	-7 743.7	145.7	1 314.1	-917.0	142.8	132.9	-10 260.9	566.4	-427.8	1.4
Bahamas	0.6	.. c	6.1	-20.9	-0.8	-	-	-	-	-
Bermuda	0.5	-1.3	1.5	0.9	-4.5	-	-	-	-	.. c
Cayman Islands	99.6	230.0	252.2	60.2	370.7	-	-	.. c	.. c	-
Costa Rica	0.0	0.0	-0.1	0.0	0.0	-	-	-	-	-
El Salvador	.. c	.. c	-	.. c	-	-	-	-	.. c	.. c
Guatemala	.. c	.. c	.. c	0.0	0.0	-	-	-	.. c	.. c
Honduras	0.4	-0.5	0.0	0.1	0.1	-	-	-	-	-
Nicaragua	-	-	-	-	-	-	-	-	-	-
Panama	15.9	-26.5	-2.1	5.7	-4.8	.. c	.. c	.. c	-	-
Virgin Islands, U.S.	-	-	-	-	-	-	-	-	-	-
South America	15.0	12.1	6.6	-110.7	1.9	53.3	79.7	60.9	57.8	109.7
Argentina	-0.7	0.6	0.5	1.5	0.4	.. c	.. c	.. c	.. c	.. c
Bolivia	-	.. c	-	-	-	-	-	-	-	-
Brazil	8.6	5.0	-4.1	0.7	9.8	37.0	70.4	76.5	57.3	107.1
Colombia	0.3	0.4	-0.3	-113.3	-6.9	.. c	.. c	.. c	.. c	.. c
Ecuador	-0.1	0.2	-0.1	0.2	0.0	-	.. c	-	-	-
Paraguay	.. c	.. c	.. c	.. c	.. c	-	-	-	-	-
Peru	-1.6	1.9	0.2	-1.1	-0.8	.. c	.. c	.. c	-	-
Uruguay	-0.3	0.3	0.3	0.2	0.0	.. c	-	.. c	.. c	.. c
Venezuela	9.2	0.1	8.1	0.0	0.1	-	-	-	-	-

HUNGARY

Table 1. Foreign direct investment flows by country *(cont.)*

Million US dollars

	Inward					Outward				
	2015	2016	2017	2018	2019	2015	2016	2017	2018	2019
ASIA	**524.3**	**470.8**	**-2 070.7**	**1 568.4**	**615.6**	**563.2**	**329.0**	**397.2**	**197.5**	**-307.6**
Near and Middle East	886.0	117.4	-2 165.6	-33.2	-308.4	552.6	337.4	353.6	179.0	-148.8
Gulf Arabian countries	28.3	146.2	-58.6	-3.0	-200.4	6.0	20.1	23.3	15.8	7.6
Kuwait	.. c	0.0	.. c	0.0	0.0	-	.. c	-	-	-
Qatar	-2.8	-0.5	-0.7	-3.0	-2.4	-	-	-	-	-
Saudi Arabia	0.9	1.2	0.5	0.3	-0.2	-	-	-	-	-
United Arab Emirates	30.9	147.6	-59.2	-2.2	-198.0	.. c	.. c	.. c	.. c	10.0
Other Near and Middle East	857.6	-28.8	-2 107.0	-30.2	-107.9	546.7	317.3	330.2	163.2	-156.4
Jordan	.. c	0.0	.. c	.. c	0.0	-	-	-	-	-
Other Asian countries	-361.6	353.5	95.0	1 601.6	923.9	10.5	-8.4	43.7	18.5	-158.8
China	22.8	80.9	8.7	58.5	150.9	-3.4	7.9	3.3	-2.3	-1.6
Hong Kong, China	-9.9	9.5	-275.9	310.9	-229.2	-8.6	28.8	20.1	-67.2	-25.5
India	-141.9	-64.9	-0.5	7.6	10.3	0.0	-1.1	0.6	-0.7	-1.0
Indonesia	-3.1	-3.5	4.7	0.7	-1.0	-	-	-	-	-
Iran, Islamic Republic of	-	.. c	.. c	.. c	.. c	-	-	-	-	-
Malaysia	31.1	-22.1	3.3	24.7	2.1	.. c	.. c	-	-	-
Philippines	2.4	-0.8	23.5	-41.7	33.1	-	.. c	.. c	-	.. c
Singapore	55.7	13.6	-63.3	-19.4	7.8	-9.5	-71.2	-0.3	48.9	-119.0
Chinese Taipei	-29.1	40.8	-54.8	-51.3	50.8	.. c	.. c	.. c	.. c	0.6
Thailand	-0.3	-1.2	-3.1	8.5	-2.4	-	-	-	-	-
Viet Nam	-0.9	-0.2	0.7	-3.4	0.9	.. c	-	-	-	-
AUSTRALIA, OCEANIA AND POLAR REGIONS	**5.3**	**3.8**	**-44.9**	**168.6**	**111.2**	**-12.0**	**9.7**	**-18.8**	**10.3**	**5.5**
WORLD unallocated and confidential	**110.4**	**127.7**	**131.0**	**161.7**	**309.0**	**0.7**	**0.5**	**0.3**	**0.5**	**-0.3**
European Union (EU28)	**-3 880.4**	**-6 781.3**	**932.5**	**3 605.6**	**-665.0**	**-1 563.2**	**1 525.0**	**-270.1**	**4 553.3**	**791.0**
G20 countries excl. European Union	**-6 282.0**	**6 167.3**	**-2 061.3**	**3 732.4**	**4 311.0**	**415.2**	**530.6**	**298.4**	**1 245.2**	**547.6**
G20 OECD countries	**-6 149.9**	**5 996.4**	**-2 131.8**	**3 496.6**	**3 984.4**	**354.3**	**361.8**	**33.2**	**1 161.7**	**339.1**
G20 Non-OECD countries	**-132.1**	**170.9**	**70.5**	**235.8**	**326.6**	**60.9**	**168.8**	**265.3**	**83.5**	**208.4**
MENA countries	**14.6**	**151.8**	**-57.2**	**3.5**	**-223.2**	**5.8**	**19.7**	**22.8**	**13.1**	**7.8**
ASEAN countries	**84.9**	**-14.1**	**-34.4**	**-30.5**	**40.5**	**-9.7**	**-71.2**	**-0.3**	**48.9**	**-119.0**

- Nil; c Confidential data

Note: Data excludes resident Special Purpose Entities (SPEs). Detailed metadata at: *http://stats.oecd.org/OECDStat_Metadata/ShowMetadata.ashx?Dataset=FDI_CTRY_IND_SUMM.*

Source: *OECD International Direct Investment Statistics (database): https://doi.org/10.1787/idi-data-en*

Table 2. Foreign direct investment positions by country

At year end

Million US dollars

	Inward					Outward				
	2015	2016	2017	2018	2019	2015	2016	2017	2018	2019
WORLD	**86 253.7**	**82 701.0**	**93 537.1**	**95 797.4**	**97 979.2**	**35 536.9**	**25 018.8**	**29 846.5**	**31 099.5**	**37 249.9**
OECD COUNTRIES	**75 892.9**	**70 880.2**	**78 905.2**	**79 622.5**	..	**15 709.4**	**14 722.5**	**16 436.5**	**17 120.0**	**21 393.4**
Australia	25.2	28.9	6.6	4.6	..	1.6	33.6	31.9	8.1	16.4
Austria	5 969.9	6 608.4	8 205.0	8 041.7	..	78.2	93.7	104.4	125.5	77.5
Belgium	1 295.4	1 499.5	1 632.5	1 701.9	..	3 521.7	3 469.1	2 081.7	8.3	4.5
Canada	381.4	352.3	1 960.0	1 774.6	..	53.1	18.6	4.3	-17.5	1 454.4
Chile	-	-	-	-	..	.. c	.. c	.. c	.. c	.. c
Czech Republic	336.1	384.8	545.5	1 131.9	..	374.8	329.9	737.5	759.2	956.7
Denmark	709.4	781.3	995.1	947.5	..	.. c	.. c	.. c	.. c	.. c
Estonia	-	-	10.3	17.4	..	0.6	0.3	0.8	0.8	-0.4
Finland	80.0	74.2	103.9	97.3	..	0.5	1.1	1.3	1.2	0.2
France	4 522.2	4 711.2	5 830.0	5 718.4	..	40.8	41.9	48.5	73.5	61.3
Germany	24 172.2	24 020.3	22 322.3	20 133.4	..	154.7	199.7	225.8	218.7	227.7
Greece	3.2	3.1	3.5	3.4	..	0.2	0.2	0.7	0.5	0.0
Hungary	394.2	322.9	738.8	834.5	..	-	-	-	-	-
Iceland	2.1	-	-	-	..	-	-	.. c	.. c	.. c
Ireland	246.0	275.4	370.9	613.3	..	140.0	137.5	592.3	1 282.0	244.7
Israel	11 205.0	931.1	1 287.5	1 329.9	..	4 548.9	3 177.7	2 983.8	2 455.4	2 553.6
Italy	2 944.4	3 209.0	3 896.3	3 519.2	..	5.3	397.3	449.0	764.6	564.1
Japan	2 282.8	2 563.0	3 186.7	3 248.8	..	2.5	5.7	6.7	8.0	9.6
Korea	1 241.8	1 438.1	3 423.0	4 074.9	..	512.5	551.0	645.9	575.2	541.0
Latvia	-	-	-	-	..	1.8	0.8	2.7	2.5	3.7
Lithuania	3.0	3.5	3.6	4.3	..	3.9	4.3	6.9	7.7	7.0
Luxembourg	1 273.7	1 366.1	1 522.2	1 626.9	..	1 048.8	1 230.6	1 375.6	1 271.6	958.8
Mexico	148.6	162.8	182.9	161.4	..	234.5	136.7	164.2	153.7	137.4
Netherlands	2 299.1	2 285.3	2 722.4	2 744.4	..	3.7	-167.0	364.9	2 285.0	5 329.0
New Zealand	51.4	36.7	41.6	36.6	..	-	-	-	-	-
Norway	548.4	514.4	586.3	145.8	..	.. c	.. c	.. c	.. c	.. c
Poland	263.5	237.9	411.8	407.9	..	376.5	429.4	1 396.5	1 393.7	1 475.4
Portugal	88.1	76.2	99.1	90.1	..	0.7	-3.8	-4.1	-3.9	-3.7
Slovak Republic	53.8	81.2	100.3	142.6	..	2 142.7	2 445.7	2 779.1	2 623.3	2 811.2
Slovenia	-1.2	4.9	10.1	9.3	..	15.5	16.5	24.4	60.7	438.6
Spain	706.2	701.9	700.8	615.1	..	882.3	994.6	1 337.2	1 405.6	1 500.8
Sweden	368.6	463.3	605.8	729.6	..	0.1	0.2	.. c	6.4	14.2
Switzerland	1 798.1	1 855.0	2 342.6	2 528.6	..	509.0	285.9	335.9	-224.0	-324.6
Turkey	53.5	53.5	63.1	45.5	..	58.3	27.1	23.2	12.7	13.9
United Kingdom	3 617.1	3 046.9	3 842.4	3 851.7	..	65.8	70.2	120.8	146.9	281.1
United States	8 812.6	12 790.4	11 156.0	13 290.1	..	935.6	796.8	596.7	1 708.7	2 034.5
EUROPE	**54 680.3**	**56 534.3**	**62 547.6**	**60 705.3**	..	**18 430.5**	**19 513.7**	**23 990.1**	**24 999.6**	**29 281.8**
Bulgaria	-0.8	9.8	16.5	12.2	..	974.3	897.9	1 031.8	1 671.1	1 896.4
Croatia	11.8	12.6	27.3	25.6	..	2 939.6	2 952.7	4 284.9	4 273.7	4 237.4
Cyprus	816.2	973.0	887.5	976.7	..	2 665.2	3 008.0	3 060.5	3 274.4	3 384.5
Malta	258.1	402.9	222.3	200.7	..	138.0	128.5	199.6	273.4	347.0
Romania	131.8	146.0	259.4	318.9	..	1 226.4	1 181.9	1 554.3	1 460.0	1 858.4
Russian Federation	465.3	640.6	856.0	1 024.5	..	330.3	463.8	783.0	627.4	779.6
Ukraine	491.8	456.3	554.6	562.2	..	-52.8	116.2	157.3	218.2	351.9
AFRICA	**239.7**	**274.7**	**283.5**	**169.9**	..	**56.6**	**6.0**	**6.3**	**7.6**	**6.6**
Northern Africa	0.5	0.1	0.1	0.1	..	4.6	2.7	2.6	-0.3	2.1
Algeria	-	-	-	-	..	-	-	-	-	-
Egypt	0.5	0.1	0.1	0.1	..	.. c	.. c	2.2	.. c	.. c
Libya	-	-	-	-	..	.. c	.. c	.. c	.. c	.. c
Morocco	-	-	-	-	..	-	-	.. c	.. c	.. c
Tunisia	-	-	-	-	..	-	-	-	-	-
Other African countries	239.2	274.6	283.4	169.8	..	52.0	.. c	.. c	.. c	4.4
Nigeria	-	-	-	-	..	-	-	-	-	-
South Africa	24.9	48.6	65.7	43.2	..	.. c	.. c	.. c	.. c	.. c
AMERICA	**9 374.8**	**13 345.5**	**13 545.1**	**15 479.2**	..	**11 365.1**	**1 100.9**	**1 496.2**	**2 299.7**	**4 181.5**
Northern America	9 193.9	13 142.7	13 116.0	15 064.8	..	988.7	815.4	601.0	1 691.2	3 488.9
Central America and Caribbean countries	172.8	193.1	418.5	405.7	..	10 301.1	144.1	690.5	187.6	182.1
Bahamas	2.0	1.9	6.8	30.6	..	-	-	-	-	-
Bermuda	-0.1	2.6	0.6	-	..	-	-	-	-	-
Cayman Islands	43.4	39.3	34.5	32.6	..	-	-	.. c	.. c	-
Costa Rica	-	-	-	-	..	-	-	-	-	-
El Salvador	-	-	-	-	..	-	-	-	.. c	.. c
Guatemala	-	-	-	-	..	-	-	-	.. c	.. c
Honduras	-	-	-	-	..	-	-	-	-	-
Nicaragua	-	-	-	-	..	-	-	-	-	-
Panama	-21.1	13.6	13.2	1.0	..	.. c	.. c	-	-	-
Virgin Islands, U.S.	-	-	-	-	..	-	-	-	-	-
South America	8.1	9.7	10.6	8.7	..	75.4	141.4	204.7	421.0	510.5
Argentina	5.8	5.6	6.3	6.1	..	.. c	.. c	.. c	.. c	.. c
Bolivia	-	-	-	-	..	-	-	-	-	-
Brazil	-	1.8	1.5	-	..	44.0	109.6	194.1	414.5	502.9
Colombia	-	-	-	-	..	.. c	.. c	.. c	.. c	.. c
Ecuador	-	-	-	-	..	-	.. c	-	-	-
Paraguay	-	-	-	-	..	-	-	-	-	-
Peru	-	-	-	-	..	.. c	.. c	-	-	-
Uruguay	2.4	2.3	2.8	2.5	..	.. c	.. c	.. c	.. c	-
Venezuela	-	-	-	-	..	-	-	-	-	-

Table 2. Foreign direct investment positions by country *(cont.)*

At year end

Million US dollars

	Inward					Outward				
	2015	2016	2017	2018	2019	2015	2016	2017	2018	2019
ASIA	**19 276.5**	**10 009.1**	**14 163.1**	**16 019.9**	..	**5 668.4**	**4 351.1**	**4 308.6**	**3 773.5**	**3 754.4**
Near and Middle East	11 415.6	1 345.0	1 676.5	1 585.7	..	4 833.2	3 481.0	3 315.1	2 766.6	2 871.6
Gulf Arabian countries	208.1	411.6	386.4	250.6	..	275.3	294.5	322.6	302.2	308.5
Kuwait	-	-	-	-	..	-	-	-	-	-
Qatar	-7.0	-8.0	-9.5	-12.1	..	-	-	-	-	-
Saudi Arabia	10.2	6.3	7.0	8.4	..	-	-	-	-	-
United Arab Emirates	204.9	413.3	388.8	254.3	..	4.4	.. c	90.0	82.7	93.4
Other Near and Middle East	11 207.5	933.4	1 290.2	1 335.1	..	4 558.0	3 186.5	2 992.6	2 464.4	2 563.1
Jordan	-	-	-	-	..	-	-	-	-	-
Other Asian countries	7 860.9	8 664.1	12 486.5	14 434.2	..	835.2	870.0	993.4	1 006.9	882.8
China	1 951.7	1 933.8	1 989.3	2 504.0	..	30.4	35.8	40.8	38.5	37.5
Hong Kong, China	144.3	177.6	231.1	289.1	..	-35.2	-19.9	-2.0	-22.6	-49.1
India	1 798.0	2 200.4	2 676.1	3 182.7	..	24.3	23.1	25.4	23.7	22.3
Indonesia	-	-	-	-	..	-	-	-	-	-
Iran, Islamic Republic of	-	-	-	-	..	-	-	-	-	-
Malaysia	25.0	26.0	30.7	36.9	..	.. c	.. c	.. c	.. c	.. c
Philippines	-	-	-	119.5	..	-	.. c	-	-	.. c
Singapore	158.7	22.9	-56.1	-238.0	..	290.2	254.8	245.9	327.3	253.7
Chinese Taipei	207.9	299.7	978.7	1 195.8	..	.. c	.. c	.. c	.. c	1.4
Thailand	53.3	5.1	9.1	8.6	..	-	-	-	-	-
Viet Nam	-	-	-	-	..	.. c	.. c	.. c	.. c	.. c
AUSTRALIA, OCEANIA AND POLAR REGIONS	**78.5**	**65.7**	**48.2**	**41.1**	..	**1.6**	**33.6**	**31.9**	**8.1**	**16.4**
WORLD unallocated and confidential	**2 603.8**	**2 471.8**	**2 949.6**	**3 382.1**	**97 979.2**	**14.7**	**13.6**	**13.3**	**11.0**	**9.2**
European Union (EU28)	**50 562.2**	**51 701.8**	**56 085.6**	**54 515.9**	..	**16 802.7**	**17 862.4**	**21 777.2**	**23 387.1**	**26 676.8**
G20 countries excl. European Union	**52 457.5**	**57 213.3**	**61 471.2**	**62 591.5**	..	**2 570.0**	**2 943.6**	**3 372.5**	**4 761.2**	**6 684.1**
G20 OECD countries	**48 201.5**	**52 376.2**	**55 869.3**	**55 822.6**	..	**2 064.5**	**2 278.5**	**2 317.0**	**3 652.5**	**5 341.5**
G20 Non-OECD countries	**4 255.9**	**4 837.1**	**5 601.9**	**6 769.0**	..	**505.5**	**665.1**	**1 055.5**	**1 108.7**	**1 342.6**
MENA countries	**211.1**	**414.0**	**389.1**	**255.9**	..	**279.9**	**297.2**	**325.2**	**301.9**	**310.7**
ASEAN countries	**237.1**	**54.1**	**-16.4**	**-73.0**	..	**282.8**	**247.7**	**237.3**	**319.2**	**256.8**

- Nil; .. Not available; c Confidential data

Note: Data excludes resident Special Purpose Entities (SPEs). Detailed metadata at: *http://stats.oecd.org/OECDStat_Metadata/ShowMetadata.ashx?Dataset=FDI_CTRY_IND_SUMM.*

1. Data excludes resident Special Purpose Entities (SPEs). Inward FDI positions are allocated according to the ultimate investing country. Inward FDI positions by immediate counterpart country are available for the most recent year in the *OECD FDI database according to BMD4*. Detailed metadata at: *http://stats.oecd.org/OECDStat_Metadata/ShowMetadata.ashx?Dataset=FDI_CTRY_IND_SUMM.*

Source: *OECD International Direct Investment Statistics (database): https://doi.org/10.1787/idi-data-en*

HUNGARY

Table 3. Foreign direct investment income by country

Million US dollars

	Inward					Outward				
	2015	2016	2017	2018	2019	2015	2016	2017	2018	2019
WORLD	**8 855.2**	**7 682.1**	**10 474.0**	**10 564.4**	**9 403.6**	**988.0**	**1 822.6**	**2 149.5**	**1 970.8**	**2 083.3**
OECD COUNTRIES	**7 742.7**	**6 183.6**	**8 876.2**	**8 989.9**	**7 966.6**	**653.7**	**1 019.5**	**1 143.5**	**875.4**	**908.5**
Australia	-1.1	21.3	1.1	-0.2	1.0	.. c	.. c	0.8	9.2	.. c
Austria	1 667.6	855.8	981.2	1 176.4	1 212.6	22.9	-0.5	9.9	20.8	18.9
Belgium	18.2	17.0	137.4	192.8	175.0	59.7	52.3	1.5	1.5	1.0
Canada	32.7	29.9	38.6	9.3	-0.2	.. c	.. c	.. c	.. c	.. c
Chile	.. c	.. c	.. c	.. c	-	-	-	.. c	.. c	-
Czech Republic	-13.3	45.6	42.8	52.3	90.3	66.1	24.2	23.9	-20.9	48.0
Denmark	66.6	118.2	155.7	212.6	120.5	.. c	.. c	.. c	.. c	.. c
Estonia	-	-	-	-	-	-0.2	-0.3	0.0	-0.1	-0.1
Finland	5.3	7.7	17.5	27.8	30.8	0.1	0.0	0.1	-0.1	-0.2
France	386.5	535.1	597.1	519.0	440.0	5.4	5.6	12.4	12.5	11.4
Germany	1 294.8	1 229.8	1 889.2	2 052.5	1 551.0	17.2	9.7	23.1	12.9	16.0
Greece	-1.0	-0.9	-	0.0	0.0	-	0.0	0.0	-0.4	-0.2
Hungary	-	-	-	-	-	-	-	-	-	-
Iceland	.. c	-	-	-	-	-	-	.. c	.. c	.. c
Ireland	100.7	188.6	158.5	324.2	51.0	14.8	1.4	-1.7	140.9	2.7
Israel	-15.2	8.3	7.1	-63.1	-72.6	287.0	320.6	267.3	142.0	176.2
Italy	93.2	287.7	183.8	155.5	207.7	-67.3	-7.6	-6.9	23.6	3.8
Japan	82.3	98.5	122.0	123.3	86.1	0.9	3.0	1.5	1.8	2.0
Korea	173.0	158.3	178.9	155.5	151.4	107.7	108.2	102.1	71.8	82.5
Latvia	-	-	-	-	-	0.2	-1.1	-1.5	-2.3	-2.0
Lithuania	3.8	5.0	3.2	6.6	7.0	-1.8	-3.1	-4.1	-5.3	-6.4
Luxembourg	507.5	348.1	845.9	979.1	854.5	89.9	79.3	85.4	41.0	109.0
Mexico	-14.0	-24.2	-17.2	-18.7	-20.2	15.0	82.6	14.3	14.0	-7.2
Netherlands	2 155.9	1 250.1	1 625.2	1 664.8	1 724.3	-314.5	-21.0	173.9	123.8	384.5
New Zealand	.. c	.. c	.. c	.. c	.. c	-	-	-	-	-
Norway	89.8	96.5	117.5	1.1	1.6	.. c	-	-	-	-
Poland	31.5	45.5	45.4	20.6	162.6	28.4	32.6	76.5	46.4	23.3
Portugal	60.2	58.4	62.8	62.0	66.7	2.3	3.0	0.1	0.1	0.1
Slovak Republic	13.1	29.2	19.2	34.6	27.5	324.3	275.8	212.1	199.8	88.3
Slovenia	3.3	5.3	6.2	7.6	7.6	11.6	7.4	11.4	9.6	63.2
Spain	127.7	165.4	230.7	173.9	79.9	0.3	-0.4	19.5	5.4	-4.2
Sweden	65.0	68.9	73.0	96.2	63.3	-0.3	.. c	.. c	0.5	2.7
Switzerland	270.9	164.5	834.4	589.4	396.5	-62.0	58.4	127.3	84.7	-44.5
Turkey	5.0	7.1	6.2	8.1	0.1	.. c	-7.2	-2.8	-3.1	-1.1
United Kingdom	364.3	410.7	516.7	354.2	418.8	15.4	14.3	22.7	31.8	-1.2
United States	173.2	-31.9	-1.4	78.4	133.7	26.4	-26.7	-35.2	-90.7	-70.7
EUROPE	**7 661.0**	**6 518.4**	**9 208.6**	**9 477.8**	**8 210.3**	**580.8**	**1 189.7**	**1 703.0**	**1 763.6**	**1 830.7**
Bulgaria	-1.0	-1.2	-0.7	0.0	0.0	183.7	154.7	136.8	169.8	218.6
Croatia	5.8	-3.2	3.6	12.2	3.1	-31.1	84.9	171.6	153.5	205.2
Cyprus	75.3	112.5	329.2	296.8	-1.5	154.6	277.0	266.8	468.1	248.1
Malta	41.1	132.2	38.6	43.4	25.6	23.1	23.8	120.1	64.9	59.7
Romania	15.0	15.0	5.4	-7.7	-20.3	25.5	47.4	68.8	40.5	70.2
Russian Federation	-2.0	8.8	14.2	-6.7	113.3	-37.6	39.7	48.3	59.5	88.1
Ukraine	1.5	-0.5	0.1	0.3	1.7	-30.0	5.4	61.3	53.8	100.1
AFRICA	**275.2**	**319.4**	**281.3**	**157.9**	**161.0**	**.. c**	**13.4**	**3.7**	**-7.0**	**-5.1**
Northern Africa	.. c	0.0	0.0	0.0	0.0	.. c	-0.5	-0.6	-2.8	0.0
Algeria	-	-	-	-	-	-	-	-	-	-
Egypt	-	-	-	-	-	.. c	.. c	.. c	.. c	.. c
Libya	-	-	-	-	-	-	-	-	-	-
Morocco	-	-	-	-	-	-	-	.. c	.. c	.. c
Tunisia	.. c	.. c	.. c	.. c	.. c	-	-	-	-	-
Other African countries	275.7	319.4	281.4	158.0	161.1	.. c	.. c	.. c	.. c	.. c
Nigeria	-	-	-	-	-	-	-	-	-	-
South Africa	.. c	.. c	.. c	.. c	.. c	-	.. c	.. c	.. c	.. c
AMERICA	**305.0**	**207.5**	**195.3**	**177.2**	**145.1**	**-21.2**	**138.0**	**41.6**	**-28.0**	**-49.1**
Northern America	205.8	-2.0	37.2	87.6	133.4	26.5	-21.2	-30.1	-86.8	-67.3
Central America and Caribbean countries	99.1	209.6	157.8	89.8	21.6	-86.7	83.0	18.4	15.8	-5.0
Bahamas	.. c	.. c	1.4	1.4	0.0	-	-	-	-	-
Bermuda	-0.1	.. c	.. c	.. c	.. c	-	-	-	-	.. c
Cayman Islands	113.5	206.9	96.3	62.6	8.5	-	-	-	-	-
Costa Rica	-	-	-	-	-	-	-	-	-	-
El Salvador	-	-	-	-	-	-	-	-	.. c	.. c
Guatemala	-	-	-	-	-	-	-	-	.. c	.. c
Honduras	-	-	-	-	-	-	-	-	-	-
Nicaragua	-	-	-	-	-	-	-	-	-	-
Panama	-5.2	4.2	10.3	5.7	-1.2	.. c	.. c	-	-	-
Virgin Islands, U.S.	-	-	-	-	-	-	-	-	-	-
South America	0.1	-0.1	0.2	-0.3	-9.9	39.1	76.2	53.3	43.0	23.2
Argentina	-	-	-	-	-	.. c	.. c	.. c	.. c	.. c
Bolivia	-	-	-	-	-	-	-	-	-	-
Brazil	.. c	.. c	.. c	.. c	.. c	32.7	73.2	50.6	45.9	24.2
Colombia	-	-	-	.. c	.. c	.. c	.. c	.. c	.. c	.. c
Ecuador	-	-	-	-	-	-	-	-	-	-
Paraguay	-	-	-	-	-	-	-	-	-	-
Peru	-	-	-	-	-	-	-	-	-	-
Uruguay	.. c	.. c	.. c	.. c	.. c	.. c	-	-	-	-
Venezuela	-	-	-	-	-	-	-	-	-	-

Table 3. Foreign direct investment income by country *(cont.)*

Million US dollars

	Inward					Outward				
	2015	2016	2017	2018	2019	2015	2016	2017	2018	2019
ASIA	**274.2**	**344.5**	**414.2**	**384.7**	**333.6**	**425.6**	**481.1**	**400.2**	**232.1**	**297.6**
Near and Middle East	-16.0	10.3	-15.9	-45.5	-47.0	299.2	360.0	291.6	169.8	207.4
Gulf Arabian countries	-0.8	2.1	-22.9	17.6	23.5	12.0	39.2	24.8	28.6	32.0
Kuwait	-	-	-	-	-	-	.. c	-	-	-
Qatar	.. c	.. c	.. c	.. c	.. c	-	-	-	-	-
Saudi Arabia	-	-	.. c	-	-	-	-	-	-	-
United Arab Emirates	3.8	5.3	-18.6	25.1	32.6	.. c	.. c	.. c	.. c	.. c
Other Near and Middle East	-15.2	8.2	7.0	-63.1	-70.5	287.2	320.8	266.8	141.2	175.4
Jordan	-	-	-	-	-	-	-	-	-	-
Other Asian countries	290.2	334.2	430.0	430.2	380.6	126.4	121.1	108.6	62.3	90.2
China	10.9	46.4	55.3	71.6	44.2	2.4	3.3	-2.5	0.8	2.4
Hong Kong, China	-5.2	6.9	23.2	90.2	46.0	.. c	.. c	-2.5	-46.9	.. c
India	1.2	1.9	5.6	5.8	.. c	1.0	0.6	1.3	1.7	1.0
Indonesia	-	-	-	-	-	-	-	-	-	-
Iran, Islamic Republic of	-	-	-	-	-	-	-	-	-	-
Malaysia	1.7	1.8	0.8	.. c	.. c	.. c	.. c	-	-	-
Philippines	.. c	.. c	.. c	.. c	.. c	-	-	-	-	-
Singapore	24.7	19.7	26.2	27.2	26.8	3.6	3.7	7.0	30.5	-4.1
Chinese Taipei	-	-	.. c	.. c	.. c	.. c	.. c	.. c	.. c	.. c
Thailand	.. c	.. c	.. c	.. c	.. c	-	-	-	-	-
Viet Nam	-	-	-	-	-	.. c	-	-	-	-
AUSTRALIA, OCEANIA AND POLAR REGIONS	**-2.5**	**10.7**	**1.8**	**-5.7**	**4.4**	**.. c**	**.. c**	**0.8**	**9.2**	**.. c**
WORLD unallocated and confidential	**342.2**	**281.7**	**372.9**	**372.5**	**549.2**	**.. d**	**.. d**	**0.3**	**0.9**	**.. d**
European Union (EU28)	**7 087.4**	**5 926.4**	**7 967.7**	**8 457.3**	**7 298.0**	**630.1**	**1 059.6**	**1 422.8**	**1 538.4**	**1 560.3**
G20 countries excl. European Union	**2 599.3**	**2 779.1**	**3 590.0**	**3 507.4**	**3 128.7**	**127.9**	**320.9**	**242.0**	**190.4**	**159.6**
G20 OECD countries	**2 589.8**	**2 722.2**	**3 515.0**	**3 436.9**	**2 969.3**	**123.0**	**187.4**	**137.2**	**87.6**	**47.7**
G20 Non-OECD countries	**9.4**	**56.9**	**75.0**	**70.6**	**159.4**	**4.9**	**133.5**	**104.9**	**102.9**	**111.8**
MENA countries	**-1.3**	**2.0**	**-22.9**	**17.7**	**23.5**	**11.5**	**38.8**	**24.2**	**25.8**	**32.0**
ASEAN countries	**27.9**	**23.7**	**50.9**	**-9.9**	**52.1**	**3.4**	**3.6**	**7.0**	**30.5**	**-4.1**

- Nil; .. Not available; c Confidential data; d Secondary Confidentiality

Note: Data excludes resident Special Purpose Entities (SPEs). Detailed metadata at: *http://stats.oecd.org/OECDStat_Metadata/ShowMetadata.ashx?Dataset=FDI_CTRY_IND_SUMM.*

Source: *OECD International Direct Investment Statistics (database): https://doi.org/10.1787/idi-data-en*

HUNGARY

Table 4. Foreign direct investment flows by industrial sector

Million US dollars

	Inward					Outward				
	2015	2016	2017	2018	2019	2015	2016	2017	2018	2019
All FDI activities	**-14 544.6**	**-5 438.6**	**3 527.5**	**8 401.4**	**1 164.6**	**-16 117.7**	**-8 272.2**	**1 221.6**	**5 159.1**	**1 285.0**
Agriculture, forestry and fishing	**45.3**	**10.5**	**43.6**	**-31.1**	**14.6**	**0.1**	**-0.1**	**-0.7**	**9.8**	**11.8**
Mining and quarrying	**-9.6**	**-19.0**	**0.7**	**86.4**	**-29.5**	**-192.6**	**22.6**	**143.4**	**-185.2**	**516.8**
Extraction activities	..	..	..	..	..	..	..	..	..	..
Manufacturing	**-13 886.7**	**16 552.9**	**1 262.3**	**3 316.2**	**3 313.4**	**1 323.9**	**1 478.4**	**1 229.9**	**243.7**	**894.1**
of which:										
Food products, beverages and tobacco	109.0	151.4	47.4	-506.3	108.4	13.7	5.6	7.7	29.4	4.4
Textiles, wood and paper products; printing	198.9	524.3	91.6	-18.3	259.1	-17.8	5.1	5.2	76.2	47.2
Chemical, rubber, plastic, non-metallic mineral products	-324.5	964.6	1 269.4	1 315.2	315.5	544.7	825.6	189.4	184.0	-65.9
Metal and machinery products, except electrical equipment	-14 774.4	14 054.3	2 617.0	1 688.5	1 543.2	212.8	501.1	854.5	-88.1	761.0
Motor vehicles, trailers, semi-trailers, other transport equipment	577.4	548.2	-2 717.1	277.2	682.9	555.3	87.0	117.1	16.1	188.8
Other manufacturing	326.8	310.1	-46.0	559.9	404.2	15.1	54.0	56.2	26.1	-41.5
Electricity, gas, steam and air conditioning supply	**97.2**	**-243.1**	**-455.5**	**-523.0**	**-289.6**	**12.1**	**-18.0**	**23.9**	**-30.2**	**-30.5**
Water supply; sewerage, waste management and remediation activities	**-13.8**	**2.3**	**9.0**	**-3.5**	**1.6**	**0.8**	**0.6**	**1.6**	**1.3**	**2.3**
Construction	**6.7**	**121.7**	**-53.3**	**132.5**	**22.1**	**-39.1**	**24.7**	**-4.4**	**3.2**	**8.6**
Services	**-1 037.7**	**-22 150.2**	**2 373.5**	**5 067.1**	**-2 181.9**	**-17 461.6**	**-10 141.4**	**-608.8**	**4 538.4**	**-592.2**
Wholesale and retail trade; repair of motor vehicles and motorcycles	441.9	-166.6	676.3	1 520.0	466.2	-15 813.4	-153.8	206.8	186.4	104.0
Transportation and storage	246.8	630.9	327.6	-117.7	994.8	16.6	30.9	13.4	81.1	5.9
Accommodation and food service activities	49.0	60.5	64.4	-10.8	47.3	-0.5	-17.5	-71.1	-0.8	11.1
Information and communication	698.5	-340.0	-404.7	8.8	198.9	227.0	53.4	-50.1	-50.9	376.1
Financial and insurance activities	473.8	-9 860.4	27.1	3 130.8	-1 822.4	864.9	596.2	-826.8	1 834.0	-456.9
Activities of holding companies	618.0	-10 430.7	-64.5	2 980.0	-1 629.9	226.4	155.0	405.3	1 427.7	-1 340.2
Real estate activities	0.0	-97.5	135.5	254.5	-751.1	39.8	6.8	-1.6	33.7	294.0
Professional, scientific and technical activities	-2 557.4	-3 715.1	78.7	966.8	-29.4	-2 616.9	221.6	57.1	-75.3	100.7
Administrative and support service activities	-371.9	-8 754.4	1 390.5	-705.8	-1 329.4	-186.5	-10 887.7	58.8	2 532.5	-1 025.5
Public administration; activities of households and of extraterritorial organisations	-	-	0.0	-	0.2	-	-	-	-	-
Education	-0.8	-0.4	3.3	12.2	9.7	-	1.2	0.1	0.7	0.0
Human health and social work activities	8.1	9.8	9.1	3.5	31.9	-0.2	2.0	1.0	0.7	1.3
Arts, entertainment and recreation	-9.3	5.3	54.3	1.1	0.0	4.6	2.8	2.6	-0.2	-0.8
Other services	-16.4	77.8	11.5	3.7	1.4	3.1	2.7	1.0	-3.5	-2.1
Not allocated and confidential	**0.0**	**0.0**	**0.0**	**-**	**0.0**	**4.5**	**0.0**	**0.0**	**0.4**	**0.0**
Private real estate activities	**254.0**	**286.2**	**347.3**	**356.7**	**313.8**	**234.2**	**361.1**	**436.5**	**577.7**	**474.2**

- Nil; .. Not available

Note: Data excludes resident Special Purpose Entities (SPEs). Detailed metadata at: *http://stats.oecd.org/OECDStat_Metadata/ShowMetadata.ashx?Dataset=FDI_CTRY_IND_SUMM.*

Source: OECD *International Direct Investment Statistics (database): https://doi.org/10.1787/idi-data-en*

Table 5. Foreign direct investment positions by industrial sector

At year end

Million US dollars

	Inward					Outward				
	2015	2016	2017	2018	2019	2015	2016	2017	2018	2019
All FDI activities	**86 253.7**	**82 701.0**	**93 537.1**	**95 797.4**	**97 979.2**	**35 536.9**	**25 018.8**	**29 846.5**	**31 099.5**	**37 249.9**
Agriculture, forestry and fishing	**554.5**	**547.3**	**672.9**	**593.0**	**586.8**	**3.5**	**3.3**	**3.1**	**9.1**	**20.5**
Mining and quarrying	**203.3**	**229.0**	**377.9**	**418.4**	**372.6**	**3 037.0**	**2 887.1**	**3 273.1**	**2 896.5**	**3 377.7**
Extraction activities	..	..	..	..	..	..	..	..	..	..
Manufacturing	**9 329.4**	**24 494.8**	**39 236.7**	**37 770.5**	**39 348.5**	**8 269.3**	**7 846.0**	**9 979.7**	**9 723.9**	**10 473.9**
of which:										
Food products, beverages and tobacco	2 185.6	2 301.3	2 714.6	2 232.9	2 251.0	40.2	42.2	67.8	70.5	108.9
Textiles, wood and paper products; printing	1 342.5	1 805.7	2 198.9	1 962.3	2 019.6	72.4	70.0	83.2	150.9	192.7
Chemical, rubber, plastic, non-metallic mineral products	5 958.4	6 561.9	8 736.9	9 569.3	9 262.2	6 236.1	5 631.0	5 728.7	5 335.3	5 506.8
Metal and machinery products, except electrical equipment	-8 926.8	4 686.8	7 689.3	8 772.5	9 919.5	940.0	1 391.7	2 611.5	2 817.6	3 037.5
Motor vehicles, trailers, semi-trailers, other transport equipment	4 794.9	5 089.6	13 404.9	10 810.6	11 108.8	594.7	295.3	992.7	858.2	1 172.6
Other manufacturing	3 974.8	4 049.6	4 492.1	4 422.8	4 787.3	386.0	415.8	495.7	491.3	455.4
Electricity, gas, steam and air conditioning supply	**2 707.7**	**2 392.4**	**2 275.4**	**1 474.9**	**1 284.9**	**58.7**	**23.5**	**41.6**	**10.4**	**8.5**
Water supply; sewerage, waste management and remediation activities	**54.1**	**62.7**	**88.1**	**75.6**	**75.9**	**17.5**	**16.6**	**17.9**	**15.9**	**16.3**
Construction	**766.5**	**931.3**	**1 100.6**	**1 174.7**	**1 124.9**	**2.5**	**15.2**	**25.6**	**28.8**	**79.3**
Services	**69 822.3**	**50 688.9**	**45 108.4**	**48 957.1**	**49 377.0**	**20 169.3**	**9 904.0**	**11 410.1**	**12 906.4**	**17 372.1**
Wholesale and retail trade; repair of motor vehicles and motorcycles	8 685.1	8 074.2	9 842.2	10 539.3	10 322.4	1 709.9	1 544.0	1 861.0	1 950.9	2 046.0
Transportation and storage	1 482.3	1 925.3	2 597.1	2 092.1	2 863.9	60.3	64.1	85.6	96.8	119.6
Accommodation and food service activities	574.5	695.1	902.6	912.8	988.1	163.4	137.6	77.3	76.0	93.8
Information and communication	5 543.6	5 117.6	4 951.7	4 588.7	4 819.5	447.7	470.9	256.9	218.6	564.5
Financial and insurance activities	15 326.4	6 459.3	7 901.6	10 621.3	12 571.4	6 666.8	7 065.1	8 292.9	7 479.4	12 500.7
Activities of holding companies	10 041.2	118.4	4.3	2 956.3	4 912.1	1 231.0	1 397.4	2 360.9	3 913.3	7 404.0
Real estate activities	5 673.7	5 743.4	6 967.5	8 188.7	7 582.1	103.7	98.4	141.4	161.3	223.7
Professional, scientific and technical activities	19 739.4	15 887.2	6 206.1	6 660.6	7 115.0	324.7	401.6	525.9	473.0	467.1
Administrative and support service activities	12 602.0	6 631.1	5 483.1	5 144.4	2 856.6	10 655.3	78.9	114.8	2 401.5	1 312.3
Public administration; activities of households and of extraterritorial organisations	-	-	0.2	-	0.7	-	-	-	-	-
Education	23.2	23.5	31.4	44.8	46.3	-	1.2	1.4	2.1	-0.6
Human health and social work activities	54.6	61.2	81.0	76.1	96.7	3.4	4.4	7.1	7.4	8.5
Arts, entertainment and recreation	73.2	28.1	88.3	32.1	62.7	17.0	19.9	23.8	22.4	21.8
Other services	44.2	42.7	55.7	56.0	51.6	17.3	17.8	22.0	17.0	14.8
Not allocated and confidential	**-**	**0.0**	**0.0**	**0.0**	**0.0**	**0.3**	**0.3**	**0.4**	**0.4**	**0.0**
Private real estate activities	**2 815.9**	**3 354.5**	**4 677.0**	**5 333.2**	**5 808.7**	**3 978.7**	**4 322.7**	**5 095.0**	**5 508.1**	**5 901.7**

- Nil; .. Not available

Note: Data excludes resident Special Purpose Entities (SPEs). Detailed metadata at: *http://stats.oecd.org/OECDStat_Metadata/ShowMetadata.ashx?Dataset=FDI_CTRY_IND_SUMM*.

Source: *OECD International Direct Investment Statistics (database): https://doi.org/10.1787/idi-data-en*

Table 6. Foreign direct investment income by industrial sector

Million US dollars

	Inward					Outward				
	2015	2016	2017	2018	2019	2015	2016	2017	2018	2019
All FDI activities	**8 855.2**	**7 682.1**	**10 474.0**	**10 564.4**	**9 403.6**	**988.0**	**1 822.6**	**2 149.5**	**1 970.8**	**2 083.3**
Agriculture, forestry and fishing	**35.0**	**38.9**	**56.2**	**52.7**	**64.2**	**0.0**	**0.0**	**0.0**	**0.1**	**0.0**
Mining and quarrying	**7.0**	**4.6**	**30.3**	**52.0**	**29.8**	**-182.5**	**33.3**	**229.2**	**140.4**	**133.0**
Extraction activities	..	..	..	..	..	..	..	..	..	..
Manufacturing	**3 515.0**	**3 784.6**	**5 024.4**	**4 741.8**	**3 904.0**	**764.7**	**868.9**	**958.5**	**542.3**	**462.6**
of which:										
Food products, beverages and tobacco	205.2	336.8	249.9	280.0	263.8	6.6	1.8	15.1	-6.9	5.9
Textiles, wood and paper products; printing	134.1	171.8	155.5	180.8	199.2	9.7	10.1	12.2	3.3	11.1
Chemical, rubber, plastic, non-metallic mineral products	1 252.0	1 325.0	1 991.7	1 708.1	1 312.6	549.1	607.0	585.4	307.8	248.7
Metal and machinery products, except electrical equipment	791.0	712.9	1 037.8	1 086.2	818.2	158.5	188.0	259.9	247.5	167.9
Motor vehicles, trailers, semi-trailers, other transport equipment	711.0	749.0	1 045.5	888.9	842.7	21.4	27.9	31.2	-42.5	2.8
Other manufacturing	421.8	489.1	543.9	597.7	467.5	19.4	34.1	54.7	33.1	26.1
Electricity, gas, steam and air conditioning supply	**112.1**	**156.7**	**116.1**	**111.4**	**150.5**	**-2.7**	**-16.5**	**-7.1**	**0.5**	**0.6**
Water supply; sewerage, waste management and remediation activities	**3.1**	**7.5**	**11.0**	**9.9**	**12.0**	**1.7**	**2.6**	**3.2**	**1.4**	**1.0**
Construction	**110.5**	**127.8**	**113.7**	**123.4**	**308.5**	**-21.9**	**26.8**	**4.5**	**4.9**	**6.0**
Services	**5 072.6**	**3 562.0**	**5 122.2**	**5 473.1**	**4 934.6**	**205.4**	**669.7**	**748.8**	**965.1**	**1 205.2**
Wholesale and retail trade; repair of motor vehicles and motorcycles	976.1	1 068.2	1 372.0	1 517.7	1 584.9	222.9	224.9	205.8	248.1	264.7
Transportation and storage	358.1	496.6	455.4	592.5	583.2	-4.4	-12.9	-16.9	-16.0	-29.4
Accommodation and food service activities	48.1	58.4	88.8	96.3	187.4	6.7	7.7	4.8	-0.7	2.9
Information and communication	561.1	531.6	511.3	645.8	687.7	45.8	16.7	11.4	3.5	46.2
Financial and insurance activities	448.7	560.9	1 077.4	1 126.3	925.4	-15.5	379.9	502.7	625.6	911.2
Activities of holding companies	-97.8	6.7	230.8	189.8	173.0	-146.5	112.7	206.7	329.1	325.3
Real estate activities	120.4	148.7	427.9	319.7	254.0	18.8	1.9	1.6	10.3	19.7
Professional, scientific and technical activities	617.2	285.5	275.3	492.5	479.0	31.8	6.8	61.7	9.2	24.1
Administrative and support service activities	1 874.1	369.6	880.1	657.3	204.7	-109.8	38.9	-26.5	86.9	-32.7
Public administration; activities of households and of extraterritorial organisations	-	-	0.0	-	0.2	-	-	-	-	-
Education	1.6	1.7	5.0	7.8	5.3	-	-0.1	0.1	0.7	-0.2
Human health and social work activities	11.6	9.3	11.0	7.9	10.0	0.8	0.9	1.0	0.7	1.3
Arts, entertainment and recreation	19.1	28.8	12.8	4.4	9.9	5.1	2.9	2.6	-0.2	-0.8
Other services	36.6	2.7	5.1	4.9	3.1	3.1	1.9	0.4	-3.0	-1.9
Not allocated and confidential	**-**	**0.0**	**0.0**	**0.0**	**0.0**	**0.0**	**0.0**	**0.0**	**0.0**	**0.0**
Private real estate activities	**-**	**-**	**-**	**-**	**-**	**223.3**	**237.8**	**212.4**	**316.1**	**274.8**

- Nil; .. Not available

Note: Data excludes resident Special Purpose Entities (SPEs). Detailed metadata at: *http://stats.oecd.org/OECDStat_Metadata/ShowMetadata.ashx?Dataset=FDI_CTRY_IND_SUMM.*

Source: *OECD International Direct Investment Statistics (database): https://doi.org/10.1787/idi-data-en*

ICELAND

Table 1. Foreign direct investment flows by country

Million US dollars

	Inward					Outward				
	2015	2016	2017	2018	2019	2015	2016	2017	2018	2019
WORLD	**708.7**	**-427.2**	**-41.4**	**-381.6**	**-252.5**	**-31.3**	**-1 147.3**	**-208.3**	**76.0**	**524.6**
OECD COUNTRIES	**597.6**	**-679.8**	**154.3**	**-432.6**	**-430.9**	**-280.9**	**-1 171.4**	**-291.8**	**51.2**	**400.8**
Australia	7.7	-5.2	87.2	-0.8	-0.2	274.6	-3.8	-6.6	0.9	6.6
Austria	7.4	1.8	-4.3	-6.4	8.0	-	-	-	-	-
Belgium	-10.6	36.7	-1.4	0.0	0.0	0.2	0.3	0.1	0.0	0.1
Canada	106.3	-134.7	44.9	0.3	-0.2	1.2	-44.5	-29.5	4.2	6.2
Chile	1.5	-	-	-	-	2.2	4.6	6.1	-10.7	1.4
Czech Republic	-0.6	5.2	-3.9	-3.0	0.6	0.0	0.0	0.0	0.0	16.8
Denmark	10.3	30.7	174.3	46.5	12.4	11.7	5.7	-3.5	-5.6	6.8
Estonia	-	-	-	-	-	2.1	4.9	4.1	-15.0	3.7
Finland	2.5	5.8	21.5	3.1	2.3	-60.1	-25.3	-2.1	-3.9	-18.7
France	8.0	25.7	-75.8	0.0	0.0	5.0	0.0	-47.9	-6.0	-8.5
Germany	71.3	-12.3	27.8	41.9	47.4	13.1	21.2	8.0	24.5	11.4
Greece	1.8	12.8	-12.3	-	-	0.0	0.0	0.0	0.0	0.0
Hungary	1.7	1.4	-2.5	0.0	0.0	-0.1	-0.2	-1.9	0.1	-0.5
Iceland	-	-	-	-	-	-	-	-	-	-
Ireland	32.7	69.1	-135.5	-69.8	-86.3	0.5	0.9	0.9	18.2	1.2
Israel	-	-0.4	-0.3	0.3	1.2	-	-	-	-	-
Italy	9.0	-26.5	-3.9	-10.0	-3.0	0.0	0.0	0.0	0.0	0.0
Japan	-	-	-	-	-	1.9	0.0	-	-	-
Korea	0.3	-	-	204.3	-	-	0.0	0.0	-0.8	-0.7
Latvia	1.0	0.9	2.1	9.3	9.4	-22.7	1.3	15.8	-23.3	0.9
Lithuania	1.0	0.7	0.1	-	-	-4.4	0.8	1.0	0.8	1.3
Luxembourg	-478.9	-444.7	-553.2	-386.5	-276.6	-9.5	-3.9	25.3	30.9	17.8
Mexico	-3.6	-2.8	7.4	-	-	0.4	-0.3	0.3	-0.2	0.0
Netherlands	515.3	-506.8	-841.9	80.2	-8.7	-192.1	20.7	-45.6	-127.0	230.0
New Zealand	-	-	-	-	-	-0.1	0.4	0.3	0.7	0.2
Norway	36.7	85.5	-14.6	33.6	-21.7	-314.5	-41.1	-3.9	-80.5	19.5
Poland	-	-	0.2	-0.4	0.2	0.0	0.1	0.3	0.3	-0.2
Portugal	-	-	-	-	-	0.0	0.0	-	0.2	3.7
Slovak Republic	-0.2	2.8	-	-	-	0.6	0.3	-0.3	-0.6	-0.4
Slovenia	-	-	-	-	-	-	-	-	-	-
Spain	0.9	-1.8	-2.2	3.1	-2.8	27.4	-207.7	-8.6	59.1	2.6
Sweden	-1.8	-4.5	-80.3	-44.8	-47.6	-89.1	-132.7	-160.8	42.0	-4.2
Switzerland	5.8	151.9	-1 275.8	-301.6	28.3	-43.6	-6.5	-10.4	179.5	-124.9
Turkey	-5.6	9.1	-0.1	0.8	-	-4.2	3.0	0.1	0.2	0.1
United Kingdom	255.3	116.6	-144.2	27.7	-70.7	94.5	-771.2	-45.7	-66.7	35.0
United States	24.2	-96.4	2 941.3	-60.5	-22.9	-2.9	2.3	13.7	30.2	193.4
EUROPE	**528.4**	**-211.4**	**-3 138.8**	**-560.9**	**-242.6**	**-310.4**	**-1 095.6**	**-246.4**	**9.5**	**216.8**
Bulgaria	-0.5	-5.0	-6.6	-1.2	-0.3	-	-	-	-	-
Croatia	-	-0.1	2.6	-1.9	0.2	-	-	0.1	-	-
Cyprus	-0.4	-3.2	-6.5	1.2	-2.4	274.3	-38.9	11.4	13.2	-9.0
Malta	74.0	278.9	-207.5	-2.9	170.3	-	0.1	-	-	-
Romania	1.0	-1.1	0.5	-0.8	1.8	0.1	0.0	0.0	-0.1	-
Russian Federation	-1.0	0.0	-1.2	19.2	-	-2.6	-2.0	-2.5	-1.8	3.2
Ukraine	0.0	5.7	-	-	-	-	-	-	0.2	0.2
AFRICA	**-**	**0.1**	**1.5**	**0.2**	**0.2**	**-0.2**	**-0.2**	**0.1**	**-0.3**	**3.2**
Northern Africa	-	-	-	-	-	0.0	-	-	-	-
Algeria	-	-	-	-	-	-	-	-	-	-
Egypt	-	-	-	-	-	-	-	-	-	-
Libya	-	-	-	-	-	-	-	-	-	-
Morocco	-	-	-	-	-	0.0	-	-	-	-
Tunisia	-	-	-	-	-	-	-	-	-	-
Other African countries	-	0.1	1.5	0.2	0.2	-0.2	-0.2	0.1	-0.3	3.2
Nigeria	-	-	-	-	-	-	-	-	-	-
South Africa	-	0.1	0.4	0.2	0.2	-0.2	-0.2	0.0	0.2	0.2
AMERICA	**132.6**	**-223.1**	**2 998.5**	**-60.8**	**-23.7**	**0.6**	**-68.8**	**-10.4**	**17.4**	**201.1**
Northern America	130.5	-231.1	2 986.2	-60.3	-23.2	-1.5	-42.1	-15.8	34.5	199.6
Central America and Caribbean countries	10.5	-2.3	6.5	-0.5	-0.5	0.2	-30.9	-0.4	-6.8	-0.5
Bahamas	12.6	-	-	-	-	-	-	-	-	-
Bermuda	0.6	-0.7	1.3	-	-	-	0.7	-2.0	-3.0	0.0
Cayman Islands	-	-	-2.5	-0.1	-0.1	-0.2	-31.2	0.9	-3.9	-0.7
Costa Rica	-	-	-	-	-	-	-	-	-	-
El Salvador	-	-	-	-	-	-	-	-	-	-
Guatemala	-	-	-	-	-	-	-	-	-	-
Honduras	-	-	-	-	-	-	-	-	-	-
Nicaragua	-	-	-	-	-	-	-	-	-	-
Panama	-	-	-	-	-	-	-	-	-	-
Virgin Islands, U.S.	-	-	-	-	-	-	-	-	-	-
South America	-8.4	10.2	5.8	0.0	-	1.9	4.3	5.8	-10.2	2.0
Argentina	-	-	-	-	-	-	-	-	-	-
Bolivia	-	-	-	-	-	-	-	-	-	-
Brazil	-9.9	10.2	5.8	0.0	-	0.0	-0.2	-0.1	0.6	0.6
Colombia	-	-	-	-	-	-	-	-	0.0	-
Ecuador	-	-	-	-	-	-	-	-	-	-
Paraguay	-	-	-	-	-	-	-	-	-	-
Peru	-	-	-	-	-	-	-	-	-	-
Uruguay	-	-	-	-	-	-0.3	-0.1	-0.1	-0.1	0.0
Venezuela	-	-	-	-	-	-	-	-	-	-

Table 1. Foreign direct investment flows by country *(cont.)*

Million US dollars

	Inward					Outward				
	2015	2016	2017	2018	2019	2015	2016	2017	2018	2019
ASIA	**17.2**	**-1.5**	**6.4**	**243.3**	**12.9**	**4.2**	**5.8**	**6.7**	**2.8**	**51.8**
Near and Middle East	1.6	-3.6	6.4	0.3	1.2	0.0	0.1	0.0	0.3	0.0
Gulf Arabian countries	1.6	-3.3	6.7	-	-	0.0	0.0	0.0	0.3	0.0
Kuwait	-	-	-	-	-	-	-	-	-	-
Qatar	-	-	-	-	-	-	-	-	-	-
Saudi Arabia	-	-	1.9	-	-	-	-	-	-	-
United Arab Emirates	1.6	-3.3	4.9	-	-	0.0	0.0	0.0	0.3	0.0
Other Near and Middle East	-	-0.4	-0.3	0.3	1.2	-	0.1	0.0	-	-
Jordan	-	-	-	-	-	-	-	-	-	-
Other Asian countries	15.6	2.1	0.0	243.0	11.7	4.2	5.7	6.7	2.5	51.8
China	13.8	-2.0	-0.7	-1.2	-0.9	1.9	3.1	6.1	2.8	52.4
Hong Kong, China	0.0	-6.4	-6.3	22.1	-1.1	0.2	2.3	0.2	0.2	0.2
India	0.0	0.0	-	-	-0.7	-0.1	0.0	-	-	-
Indonesia	-	0.1	-	-	-	-	-	-	-	-
Iran, Islamic Republic of	-	-	-	-	-	-	-	-	-	-
Malaysia	-	-0.1	0.1	-	14.8	-	-	0.1	-0.1	0.1
Philippines	-	-	-	-	-	-	-	-	-	0.0
Singapore	-2.9	3.0	4.5	17.6	-0.7	0.0	0.1	0.0	-0.3	0.0
Chinese Taipei	-	-	0.0	-	-	-	-	-	-	-
Thailand	4.4	7.5	2.3	0.3	0.3	0.2	0.2	0.2	0.2	0.0
Viet Nam	-	-	-	-	-	-	-	0.0	0.4	-0.2
AUSTRALIA, OCEANIA AND POLAR REGIONS	**7.7**	**-5.2**	**87.2**	**-0.8**	**-0.2**	**274.5**	**-3.4**	**-6.3**	**1.5**	**6.9**
WORLD unallocated and confidential	**22.6**	**13.8**	**3.9**	**-2.5**	**0.9**	**0.0**	**14.9**	**48.1**	**45.0**	**44.8**
European Union (EU28)	**500.3**	**-416.7**	**-1 853.1**	**-314.8**	**-245.8**	**51.4**	**-1 123.6**	**-249.2**	**-59.0**	**289.9**
G20 countries excl. European Union	**475.9**	**-117.9**	**2 890.7**	**221.9**	**-50.9**	**382.7**	**-792.4**	**-104.2**	**-12.0**	**300.0**
G20 OECD countries	**473.0**	**-126.3**	**2 884.5**	**203.7**	**-49.5**	**383.6**	**-793.1**	**-107.7**	**-13.9**	**243.7**
G20 Non-OECD countries	**2.9**	**8.5**	**6.2**	**18.1**	**-1.4**	**-1.0**	**0.7**	**3.5**	**1.8**	**56.3**
MENA countries	**1.6**	**-3.3**	**6.7**	**-**	**-**	**0.0**	**0.0**	**0.0**	**0.3**	**0.0**
ASEAN countries	**1.5**	**10.5**	**6.9**	**17.9**	**14.4**	**0.1**	**0.3**	**0.4**	**0.3**	**-0.2**

- Nil

Note: Data excludes resident Special Purpose Entities (SPEs). Detailed metadata at: *http://stats.oecd.org/OECDStat_Metadata/ShowMetadata.ashx?Dataset=FDI_CTRY_IND_SUMM.*

Source: *OECD International Direct Investment Statistics (database): https://doi.org/10.1787/idi-data-en*

ICELAND

Table 2. Foreign direct investment positions by country

At year end

Million US dollars

	Inward					Outward				
	2015	2016	2017	2018	2019	2015	2016	2017	2018	2019
WORLD	**7 851.0**	**9 841.0**	**10 129.9**	**8 750.7**	**8 380.7**	**7 636.6**	**6 058.2**	**5 268.6**	**5 229.4**	**5 501.3**
OECD COUNTRIES	**7 152.8**	**9 091.9**	**9 500.3**	**8 088.6**	**7 730.1**	**6 177.3**	**5 022.9**	**4 684.5**	**4 647.7**	**4 801.7**
Australia	-	-	-	0.0	0.0	239.9	240.1	-162.7	13.3	20.0
Austria	26.6	16.0	16.7	1.6	9.5	-	-	-	-	-
Belgium	4.3	4.9	5.3	4.8	4.6	0.0	0.1	17.1	16.4	16.2
Canada	157.7	195.4	190.2	196.4	5.2	102.5	35.6	12.0	15.4	22.1
Chile	1.1	-	-	-	-	29.5	32.6	39.2	41.7	43.2
Czech Republic	-	-	-	-	-	0.1	0.2	0.2	0.2	17.0
Denmark	451.7	424.6	467.8	475.1	469.8	70.5	84.8	109.1	62.1	67.8
Estonia	-	-	-	-	-	22.4	30.8	38.9	29.7	32.5
Finland	0.8	2.6	9.8	2.3	2.4	120.3	81.3	83.2	80.8	62.0
France	8.5	15.1	18.9	13.7	15.4	1.8	8.2	82.7	73.1	62.4
Germany	104.8	83.4	97.7	110.6	214.0	107.0	128.5	137.1	149.5	146.7
Greece	-	-	-	-	-	0.3	0.2	0.2	0.2	0.1
Hungary	-	-	-	-	-	1.0	1.5	1.0	3.2	2.6
Iceland	62.7	116.3	69.4	48.5	44.5	-	-	-	-	-
Ireland	39.1	57.7	63.2	58.1	57.7	9.1	9.1	12.4	19.7	20.5
Israel	1.3	2 788.6	2 789.5	2 328.0	2 099.9	-	-	-	-	-
Italy	4.3	6.0	5.6	4.9	5.7	0.0	0.0	0.0	0.0	0.0
Japan	-	-	-	-	-	14.8	5.6	5.8	6.0	6.1
Korea	-	-	-	188.4	188.4	-	8.2	8.2	8.0	7.3
Latvia	-9.5	48.8	64.2	69.4	77.6	53.9	51.7	69.8	17.5	18.1
Lithuania	-	-	-	-	-	23.2	17.8	29.0	28.6	29.3
Luxembourg	136.3	568.5	329.2	226.2	197.1	690.1	290.2	158.1	158.1	-85.4
Mexico	-	-	-	-	-	0.4	0.1	0.3	0.1	0.1
Netherlands	118.3	162.6	265.6	184.9	198.1	2 513.5	2 532.7	3 033.8	2 772.3	2 946.2
New Zealand	-	-	-	-	-	1.8	2.1	2.6	3.2	3.4
Norway	109.9	239.5	282.1	247.6	223.5	120.6	124.5	186.2	82.2	102.6
Poland	-	-	-	-	-	0.2	0.1	0.5	0.7	0.5
Portugal	-	-	-	-	-	0.0	-	-	0.5	4.1
Slovak Republic	-	-	-	-	-	6.1	6.2	-0.4	-1.0	-1.4
Slovenia	-	-	-	-	-	-	-	-	-	-
Spain	84.7	10.3	-1.7	0.8	-0.2	91.4	47.1	45.8	51.1	52.8
Sweden	42.7	31.1	32.6	70.7	92.4	371.7	207.0	62.7	146.1	156.7
Switzerland	32.8	68.1	118.0	89.4	92.0	-0.7	-7.0	-59.0	111.3	-17.6
Turkey	-	-	-	-	-	7.1	4.9	11.3	11.0	10.9
United Kingdom	744.4	1 648.7	2 016.0	1 576.0	1 493.3	1 636.1	1 076.3	752.0	651.2	763.7
United States	5 020.9	2 603.7	2 660.1	2 191.3	2 239.2	20.1	20.4	36.4	95.7	291.4
EUROPE	**2 126.3**	**3 664.8**	**3 977.5**	**3 299.5**	**3 311.4**	**6 528.8**	**5 449.8**	**5 093.0**	**4 788.2**	**4 756.1**
Bulgaria	-	-	-	-	-	-	-	-	-	-
Croatia	-	-	-	-	-	-	-	0.1	0.1	0.1
Cyprus	56.6	76.2	29.9	40.5	43.1	556.1	526.1	109.6	85.9	81.8
Malta	41.8	53.1	54.6	44.9	39.5	-	0.1	0.1	0.1	0.1
Romania	-	-	-	-	-	0.5	0.5	0.6	-	-
Russian Federation	0.3	0.3	0.4	0.3	0.3	30.6	32.0	36.1	37.7	40.3
Ukraine	-	-	-	-	-	-	-	-	0.9	1.1
AFRICA	**-**	**-**	**2.4**	**2.6**	**2.7**	**1.3**	**1.0**	**1.7**	**0.4**	**0.0**
Northern Africa	-	-	-	-	-	0.4	-	-	-	-
Algeria	-	-	-	-	-	-	-	-	-	-
Egypt	-	-	-	-	-	-	-	-	-	-
Libya	-	-	-	-	-	-	-	-	-	-
Morocco	-	-	-	-	-	0.4	-	-	-	-
Tunisia	-	-	-	-	-	-	-	-	-	-
Other African countries	-	-	2.4	2.6	2.7	0.9	1.0	1.7	0.4	0.0
Nigeria	-	-	-	-	-	-	-	-	-	-
South Africa	-	-	1.3	1.6	1.7	0.9	1.0	1.0	0.9	1.2
AMERICA	**5 259.6**	**2 884.2**	**2 887.9**	**2 422.1**	**2 276.9**	**438.0**	**102.8**	**102.5**	**160.4**	**363.8**
Northern America	5 178.6	2 799.1	2 850.2	2 388.5	2 245.0	123.0	56.0	48.4	111.1	313.5
Central America and Caribbean countries	79.9	85.1	37.6	33.6	31.9	285.0	14.1	15.0	7.2	6.1
Bahamas	4.8	-	-	-	-	-	-	-	-	-
Bermuda	2.7	3.1	3.4	3.0	2.9	4.8	5.9	7.3	4.2	4.2
Cayman Islands	71.1	81.7	34.0	30.4	29.1	31.2	8.0	6.9	2.2	1.0
Costa Rica	-	-	-	-	-	-	-	-	-	-
El Salvador	-	-	-	-	-	-	-	-	-	-
Guatemala	-	-	-	-	-	-	-	-	-	-
Honduras	-	-	-	-	-	-	-	-	-	-
Nicaragua	-	-	-	-	-	-	-	-	-	-
Panama	0.2	0.2	0.2	0.2	0.2	-	-	-	-	-
Virgin Islands, U.S.	-	-	-	-	-	-	-	-	-	-
South America	1.1	-	-	-	-	30.0	32.7	39.1	42.1	44.2
Argentina	-	-	-	-	-	-	-	-	-	-
Bolivia	-	-	-	-	-	-	-	-	-	-
Brazil	-	-	-	-	-	0.2	0.0	-0.1	0.4	1.0
Colombia	-	-	-	-	-	-	-	-	-	-
Ecuador	-	-	-	-	-	-	-	-	-	-
Paraguay	-	-	-	-	-	-	-	-	-	-
Peru	-	-	-	-	-	-	-	-	-	-
Uruguay	-	-	-	-	-	0.3	0.1	0.0	0.0	0.0
Venezuela	-	-	-	-	-	-	-	-	-	-

Table 2. Foreign direct investment positions by country *(cont.)*
At year end

Million US dollars

	Inward					Outward				
	2015	2016	2017	2018	2019	2015	2016	2017	2018	2019
ASIA	**183.4**	**2 981.1**	**2 965.5**	**2 760.1**	**2 533.8**	**63.3**	**74.5**	**83.8**	**80.6**	**130.6**
Near and Middle East	1.3	2 788.6	2 791.4	2 329.7	2 101.5	0.9	0.8	0.0	0.3	0.3
Gulf Arabian countries	-	-	1.9	1.7	1.6	0.9	0.7	0.0	0.3	0.3
Kuwait	-	-	-	-	-	-	-	-	-	-
Qatar	-	-	-	-	-	-	-	-	-	-
Saudi Arabia	-	-	1.9	1.7	1.6	-	-	-	-	-
United Arab Emirates	-	-	-	-	-	0.9	0.7	0.0	0.3	0.3
Other Near and Middle East	1.3	2 788.6	2 789.5	2 328.0	2 099.9	-	0.1	0.0	-	-
Jordan	-	-	-	-	-	-	-	-	-	-
Other Asian countries	182.1	192.5	174.1	430.3	432.3	62.4	73.6	83.7	80.4	130.3
China	125.7	143.8	124.0	150.5	141.1	43.7	58.2	67.0	63.2	113.6
Hong Kong, China	24.3	29.4	23.7	33.7	30.8	0.6	0.7	0.9	1.2	1.4
India	-	-	-	-	-	0.0	0.0	-	-	-
Indonesia	-	-	-	-	-	-	-	-	-	-
Iran, Islamic Republic of	-	-	-	-	-	-	-	-	-	-
Malaysia	-	-	-	-	15.0	-	-	0.2	0.1	0.2
Philippines	-	-	-	-	-	-	-	-	-	0.0
Singapore	32.0	19.3	26.3	57.7	57.0	2.6	0.0	0.3	0.0	0.0
Chinese Taipei	-	-	-	-	-	-	-	-	-	-
Thailand	-	-	-	-	-	0.8	1.0	1.3	1.5	1.6
Viet Nam	-	-	-	-	-	-	-	0.0	0.4	0.1
AUSTRALIA, OCEANIA AND POLAR REGIONS	**-**	**-**	**-**	**0.0**	**0.0**	**241.7**	**242.2**	**-160.2**	**16.5**	**23.3**
WORLD unallocated and confidential	**281.7**	**310.9**	**296.7**	**266.4**	**255.9**	**363.5**	**188.0**	**147.7**	**183.4**	**227.5**
European Union (EU28)	**1 855.4**	**3 209.5**	**3 475.5**	**2 884.4**	**2 920.1**	**6 275.2**	**5 100.5**	**4 743.5**	**4 345.9**	**4 394.3**
G20 countries excl. European Union	**6 166.6**	**4 696.4**	**5 116.1**	**4 435.5**	**4 306.0**	**2 205.0**	**1 619.0**	**987.1**	**1 125.4**	**1 486.7**
G20 OECD countries	**6 040.5**	**4 552.3**	**4 988.5**	**4 281.3**	**4 161.2**	**2 129.6**	**1 527.9**	**883.2**	**1 023.2**	**1 330.7**
G20 Non-OECD countries	**126.0**	**144.2**	**127.6**	**154.1**	**144.8**	**75.4**	**91.1**	**104.0**	**102.2**	**156.1**
MENA countries	**-**	**-**	**1.9**	**1.7**	**1.6**	**1.3**	**0.7**	**0.0**	**0.3**	**0.3**
ASEAN countries	**32.0**	**19.3**	**26.3**	**57.7**	**72.1**	**3.4**	**1.0**	**1.8**	**2.0**	**2.0**

- Nil

Note: Data excludes resident Special Purpose Entities (SPEs). Detailed metadata at: *http://stats.oecd.org/OECDStat_Metadata/ShowMetadata.ashx?Dataset=FDI_CTRY_IND_SUMM.*

1. Inward FDI positions are allocated according to the ultimate investing country. Detailed metadata at: *http://stats.oecd.org/OECDStat_Metadata/ShowMetadata.ashx?Dataset=FDI_CTRY_IND_SUMM.*

Source: OECD *International Direct Investment Statistics (database): https://doi.org/10.1787/idi-data-en*

Table 3. Foreign direct investment income by country

Million US dollars

	Inward					Outward				
	2015	2016	2017	2018	2019	2015	2016	2017	2018	2019
WORLD	**31.2**	**-29.2**	**40.4**	**-42.4**	**-219.2**	**283.4**	**435.8**	**302.1**	**363.9**	**347.5**
OECD COUNTRIES	**58.4**	**-18.5**	**49.1**	**-25.5**	**-216.6**	**260.1**	**390.9**	**270.0**	**320.6**	**309.3**
Australia	-6.4	-4.1	-1.7	-	-	-2.9	-5.3	-0.2	0.8	2.1
Austria	-2.8	3.1	6.1	9.1	8.0	-	-	-	-	-
Belgium	-1.2	-0.1	0.3	0.3	0.3	0.2	0.3	0.1	0.1	0.1
Canada	-0.8	-1.9	0.0	0.2	-0.4	1.3	5.3	0.7	0.4	0.6
Chile	-	-	-	-	-	-5.4	5.5	6.3	2.9	1.8
Czech Republic	0.0	-0.2	0.0	-	-	-	-	-	-	0.0
Denmark	10.2	13.1	12.1	4.7	18.8	24.6	24.4	22.4	16.9	16.1
Estonia	-	-	-	-	-	2.0	4.9	4.3	4.3	3.9
Finland	3.7	9.0	9.2	11.8	10.4	0.1	-0.8	0.9	1.1	3.0
France	0.1	-0.1	-0.1	0.0	0.0	0.6	0.1	2.2	2.0	1.6
Germany	-4.1	0.6	-1.1	7.1	-7.3	22.6	16.1	7.7	24.4	13.0
Greece	0.0	0.0	-	-	-	0.0	0.0	0.0	0.0	0.0
Hungary	-0.1	0.0	0.0	-	-	0.5	-0.5	-1.2	-0.6	-0.5
Iceland	-	-	-	-	-	-	-	-	-	-
Ireland	0.2	7.0	12.6	9.3	5.4	0.5	0.6	0.7	1.4	1.2
Israel	-	-	-	-	-	-	-	-	-	-
Italy	-4.5	0.9	-3.1	-5.9	-5.4	-	-	-	-	-
Japan	-	-	-	-	-	0.2	0.0	-	-	-
Korea	-	-	-	-0.7	-	-	0.0	0.0	-0.8	-0.7
Latvia	1.0	3.2	2.9	10.6	9.4	4.1	7.4	11.2	1.1	0.9
Lithuania	-0.1	-0.1	0.0	-	-	2.2	1.1	1.5	1.4	1.2
Luxembourg	99.4	134.6	-25.2	-50.9	-105.9	20.0	16.9	24.3	30.9	17.8
Mexico	-0.3	-0.5	-0.5	-	-	-	-	-	-	-
Netherlands	70.2	65.1	97.8	52.1	-11.8	62.9	117.5	112.6	153.9	160.3
New Zealand	-	-	-	-	-	0.1	0.0	0.1	0.2	0.1
Norway	21.7	-0.5	7.9	9.5	-16.0	2.6	3.5	31.9	16.5	4.7
Poland	-	-	-	-	-	-	0.0	0.0	0.0	0.0
Portugal	-	-	-	-	-	-	-	-	0.2	0.2
Slovak Republic	-0.1	-0.1	-	-	-	0.5	0.4	-	-	-
Slovenia	-	-	-	-	-	-	-	-	-	-
Spain	0.4	-1.8	-3.8	-1.5	-1.3	24.2	3.5	3.1	3.8	3.2
Sweden	-4.9	-17.4	-49.7	-31.4	6.5	4.1	2.0	-1.7	10.0	16.7
Switzerland	4.5	-25.8	94.6	-11.9	-54.0	-0.1	0.1	0.2	1.2	1.9
Turkey	-0.8	-0.9	-0.1	-0.2	-	-4.2	3.0	0.1	0.2	0.1
United Kingdom	-11.5	39.8	2.7	-5.8	5.2	105.1	181.5	37.1	46.7	51.8
United States	-114.4	-241.5	-112.0	-32.0	-78.4	0.5	4.6	7.3	1.6	8.0
EUROPE	**157.5**	**216.2**	**157.2**	**-5.1**	**-138.2**	**287.2**	**418.0**	**278.5**	**354.8**	**336.4**
Bulgaria	-	-	-	-	-	-	-	-	-	-
Croatia	-	-	-	-	-	-	-	-	-	-
Cyprus	0.4	-1.5	-6.5	-7.7	1.2	5.0	11.0	-2.8	5.2	4.8
Malta	-14.8	-7.2	-1.0	-3.0	-2.7	-	-	-	-	-
Romania	-	-	-	-	-	0.1	0.1	0.1	-0.1	-
Russian Federation	-3.5	-2.5	-2.6	-0.6	-	-3.7	-2.0	-2.5	-0.2	3.4
Ukraine	-0.3	-0.2	-	-	-	-	-	-	0.2	0.2
AFRICA	**-**	**-**	**-0.3**	**0.2**	**0.2**	**0.3**	**-0.1**	**0.1**	**-0.5**	**-4.4**
Northern Africa	-	-	-	-	-	-	-	-	-	-
Algeria	-	-	-	-	-	-	-	-	-	-
Egypt	-	-	-	-	-	-	-	-	-	-
Libya	-	-	-	-	-	-	-	-	-	-
Morocco	-	-	-	-	-	-	-	-	-	-
Tunisia	-	-	-	-	-	-	-	-	-	-
Other African countries	-	-	-0.3	0.2	0.2	0.3	-0.1	0.1	-0.5	-4.4
Nigeria	-	-	-	-	-	-	-	-	-	-
South Africa	-	-	-0.3	0.2	0.2	0.3	-0.1	0.1	0.2	0.2
AMERICA	**-123.4**	**-247.2**	**-115.5**	**-32.5**	**-79.4**	**-3.2**	**16.9**	**20.3**	**5.9**	**10.8**
Northern America	-115.2	-243.4	-112.0	-32.0	-79.0	2.0	9.8	8.0	2.0	8.6
Central America and Caribbean countries	-6.1	-1.9	-2.8	-0.5	-0.4	0.1	1.6	6.0	1.0	0.4
Bahamas	-5.8	-	-	-	-	-	-	-	-	-
Bermuda	-	-1.4	0.4	-	-	-	0.7	0.5	0.0	0.0
Cayman Islands	-	-	-2.5	-0.1	-0.1	0.1	0.9	5.4	0.7	0.1
Costa Rica	-	-	-	-	-	-	-	-	-	-
El Salvador	-	-	-	-	-	-	-	-	-	-
Guatemala	-	-	-	-	-	-	-	-	-	-
Honduras	-	-	-	-	-	-	-	-	-	-
Nicaragua	-	-	-	-	-	-	-	-	-	-
Panama	0.0	0.0	0.0	0.0	0.0	-	-	-	-	-
Virgin Islands, U.S.	-	-	-	-	-	-	-	-	-	-
South America	-2.1	-2.0	-0.7	-	-	-5.4	5.5	6.3	2.9	1.8
Argentina	-	-	-	-	-	-	-	-	-	-
Bolivia	-	-	-	-	-	-	-	-	-	-
Brazil	-2.1	-2.0	-0.7	-	-	-	-	-	-	-
Colombia	-	-	-	-	-	-	-	-	-	-
Ecuador	-	-	-	-	-	-	-	-	-	-
Paraguay	-	-	-	-	-	-	-	-	-	-
Peru	-	-	-	-	-	-	-	-	-	-
Uruguay	-	-	-	-	-	-	-	-	-	-
Venezuela	-	-	-	-	-	-	-	-	-	-

Table 3. Foreign direct investment income by country *(cont.)*

Million US dollars

	Inward					Outward				
	2015	2016	2017	2018	2019	2015	2016	2017	2018	2019
ASIA	**0.4**	**-2.7**	**0.8**	**-5.0**	**-1.7**	**2.0**	**3.5**	**1.6**	**2.8**	**2.4**
Near and Middle East	-0.3	-0.1	-0.1	-	-	0.0	0.0	0.0	0.0	0.0
Gulf Arabian countries	-0.3	-0.1	-0.1	-	-	0.0	0.0	0.0	0.0	0.0
Kuwait	-	-	-	-	-	-	-	-	-	-
Qatar	-	-	-	-	-	-	-	-	-	-
Saudi Arabia	-	-	-	-	-	-	-	-	-	-
United Arab Emirates	-0.3	-0.1	-0.1	-	-	0.0	0.0	0.0	0.0	0.0
Other Near and Middle East	-	-	-	-	-	-	0.0	0.0	-	-
Jordan	-	-	-	-	-	-	-	-	-	-
Other Asian countries	0.6	-2.6	0.9	-5.0	-1.7	2.0	3.5	1.6	2.8	2.4
China	-0.2	-2.0	-0.7	-1.2	-1.1	1.4	3.0	1.2	3.1	2.7
Hong Kong, China	0.5	0.4	-1.1	-3.3	-0.9	0.2	0.2	0.2	0.2	0.2
India	-	-	-	-	-	-0.1	-	-	-	-
Indonesia	-	-	-	-	-	-	-	-	-	-
Iran, Islamic Republic of	-	-	-	-	-	-	-	-	-	-
Malaysia	-	0.0	0.0	-	-	-	-	0.0	0.1	0.1
Philippines	-	-	-	-	-	-	-	-	-	-
Singapore	0.2	-1.2	2.4	-0.1	-0.1	0.1	0.1	0.0	0.0	0.0
Chinese Taipei	-	-	-	-	-	-	-	-	-	-
Thailand	0.1	0.2	0.3	0.3	0.3	0.2	0.1	0.2	0.1	0.1
Viet Nam	-	-	-	-	-	-	-	-	-	-
AUSTRALIA, OCEANIA AND POLAR REGIONS	**-6.4**	**-4.1**	**-1.7**	**-**	**-**	**-2.8**	**-5.3**	**-0.1**	**1.0**	**2.2**
WORLD unallocated and confidential	**3.1**	**8.7**	**-0.1**	**0.0**	**0.0**	**0.0**	**2.8**	**1.7**	**0.0**	**0.0**
European Union (EU28)	**141.5**	**247.9**	**53.5**	**-1.3**	**-69.3**	**279.1**	**386.3**	**222.5**	**302.7**	**295.4**
G20 countries excl. European Union	**-148.5**	**-214.1**	**-120.1**	**-38.9**	**-87.3**	**121.1**	**206.1**	**53.6**	**78.3**	**82.8**
G20 OECD countries	**-142.8**	**-207.6**	**-115.8**	**-37.3**	**-86.4**	**123.3**	**205.2**	**54.8**	**75.3**	**76.5**
G20 Non-OECD countries	**-5.7**	**-6.5**	**-4.2**	**-1.6**	**-0.9**	**-2.1**	**1.0**	**-1.2**	**3.0**	**6.3**
MENA countries	**-0.3**	**-0.1**	**-0.1**	**-**	**-**	**0.0**	**0.0**	**0.0**	**0.0**	**0.0**
ASEAN countries	**0.3**	**-1.0**	**2.6**	**0.2**	**0.2**	**0.3**	**0.2**	**0.2**	**0.2**	**0.2**

- Nil

Note: Data excludes resident Special Purpose Entities (SPEs). Detailed metadata at: *http://stats.oecd.org/OECDStat_Metadata/ShowMetadata.ashx?Dataset=FDI_CTRY_IND_SUMM.*

Source: *OECD International Direct Investment Statistics (database): https://doi.org/10.1787/idi-data-en*

Table 4. Foreign direct investment flows by industrial sector

Million US dollars

	Inward					Outward				
	2015	2016	2017	2018	2019	2015	2016	2017	2018	2019
All FDI activities	**708.7**	**-427.2**	**-41.4**	**-381.6**	**-252.5**	**-31.3**	**-1 147.3**	**-208.3**	**76.0**	**524.6**
Agriculture, forestry and fishing	**1.3**	**40.4**	**10.1**	**13.5**	**-5.8**	**21.0**	**-22.3**	**34.7**	**47.3**	**23.8**
Mining and quarrying	**30.9**	**2.7**	**-0.9**	**46.0**	**47.9**	**-**	**-**	**-**	**-**	**-**
Extraction activities	30.9	0.3	-0.9	42.5	47.9	-	-	-	-	-
Manufacturing	**-82.7**	**-96.3**	**98.3**	**175.7**	**-107.4**	**133.4**	**97.5**	**3.3**	**119.4**	**316.4**
of which:										
Food products, beverages and tobacco	-2.6	-3.6	14.4	3.7	0.7	-220.5	-26.6	1.3	-29.0	5.0
Textiles, wood and paper products; printing	-	-	-	-	-	0.4	77.5	23.1	79.9	23.7
Chemical, rubber, plastic, non-metallic mineral products	-19.5	-20.8	0.4	154.1	-107.2	298.1	10.9	-6.6	2.8	4.5
Metal and machinery products, except electrical equipment	-114.8	-95.4	-18.1	74.1	-13.2	59.8	39.8	79.4	61.0	217.5
Motor vehicles, trailers, semi-trailers, other transport equipment	-	-	-	-	-	-0.1	-0.7	-	-	-
Other manufacturing	54.2	23.5	101.7	-56.2	12.2	-4.4	-3.4	-93.9	4.8	65.6
Electricity, gas, steam and air conditioning supply	**13.5**	**1.8**	**-60.9**	**10.5**	**-37.2**	**1.1**	**0.4**	**0.8**	**3.1**	**2.7**
Water supply; sewerage, waste management and remediation activities	**0.0**	**0.1**	**0.8**	**-23.6**	**-**	**-**	**-**	**-**	**-**	**-**
Construction	**1.6**	**15.1**	**8.6**	**-23.9**	**-9.6**	**54.5**	**-409.5**	**4.9**	**-1.7**	**2.1**
Services	**740.0**	**-391.1**	**-98.0**	**-579.7**	**-135.7**	**-241.3**	**-825.8**	**-260.8**	**-95.0**	**176.5**
Wholesale and retail trade; repair of motor vehicles and motorcycles	-2 218.0	681.0	3 217.0	-279.7	240.7	52.8	40.2	7.8	39.4	17.8
Transportation and storage	-1.3	1.6	-2.5	3.3	1.6	9.7	35.3	47.4	-34.2	36.4
Accommodation and food service activities	-	29.6	-3.4	34.7	21.6	-4.4	-1.7	-17.8	-	-
Information and communication	38.8	18.7	136.7	78.6	5.4	0.4	-1.6	-33.9	-44.7	-8.6
Financial and insurance activities	2 880.5	-1 176.1	-3 460.0	-508.9	-402.7	-155.0	-411.0	-247.0	-87.7	44.2
Activities of holding companies	2 883.4	-841.0	-3 446.5	-571.9	-91.9	-82.0	-407.2	-244.9	-86.9	42.6
Real estate activities	23.8	15.3	8.1	-1.5	-7.2	-45.9	-96.7	-5.3	37.8	35.3
Professional, scientific and technical activities	21.8	35.3	11.3	76.7	-0.2	-87.3	-236.0	-4.0	5.1	50.3
Administrative and support service activities	-5.6	3.9	-4.9	17.1	5.0	-12.6	-14.9	-8.5	-11.1	0.7
Public administration; activities of households and of extraterritorial organisations	-	-	-	-	-	-	-	-	-	-
Education	-	-0.5	-0.3	-	-	-	-	-	-	-
Human health and social work activities	-	-	-	-	-	1.2	-139.4	-	-	-
Arts, entertainment and recreation	-	-	0.0	-	-	-	-	0.4	0.5	0.4
Other services	-	-	-	-	-	-	-	-	-	-
Not allocated and confidential	**4.0**	**0.0**	**0.6**	**-0.2**	**-4.7**	**0.2**	**12.3**	**8.9**	**2.9**	**3.0**
Private real estate activities	**-**	**-**	**-**	**-**	**-**	**-**	**-**	**-**	**-**	**-**

- Nil

Note: Data excludes resident Special Purpose Entities (SPEs). Detailed metadata at: *http://stats.oecd.org/OECDStat_Metadata/ShowMetadata.ashx?Dataset=FDI_CTRY_IND_SUMM*.

Source: *OECD International Direct Investment Statistics (database): https://doi.org/10.1787/idi-data-en*

Table 5. Foreign direct investment positions by industrial sector

At year end

Million US dollars

	Inward					Outward				
	2015	2016	2017	2018	2019	2015	2016	2017	2018	2019
All FDI activities	**7 851.0**	**9 841.0**	**10 129.9**	**8 750.7**	**8 380.7**	**7 636.6**	**6 058.2**	**5 268.6**	**5 229.4**	**5 501.3**
Agriculture, forestry and fishing	**67.4**	**147.8**	**189.8**	**168.3**	**158.3**	**126.8**	**124.4**	**173.6**	**158.5**	**218.5**
Mining and quarrying	**36.2**	**39.8**	**39.8**	**67.7**	**133.4**	**-**	**-**	**-**	**-**	**-**
Extraction activities	36.2	27.4	39.8	55.0	133.4	-	-	-	-	-
Manufacturing	**1 362.1**	**1 238.4**	**1 243.8**	**1 311.9**	**1 267.2**	**1 585.7**	**1 573.7**	**821.0**	**1 091.2**	**1 376.2**
of which:										
Food products, beverages and tobacco	92.6	97.9	120.4	105.9	105.0	73.1	13.2	14.5	18.5	21.4
Textiles, wood and paper products; printing	-	-	-	-	-	101.7	144.7	156.5	225.2	243.7
Chemical, rubber, plastic, non-metallic mineral products	118.6	108.3	88.8	194.2	155.1	680.6	669.7	-150.0	64.0	67.4
Metal and machinery products, except electrical equipment	778.1	648.3	618.2	602.0	589.6	559.5	583.9	729.5	733.7	940.1
Motor vehicles, trailers, semi-trailers, other transport equipment	-	-	-	-	-	0.4	-	-	-	-
Other manufacturing	372.7	383.9	416.2	409.8	417.6	170.4	162.2	70.6	49.8	103.6
Electricity, gas, steam and air conditioning supply	**182.0**	**184.8**	**183.6**	**190.9**	**193.8**	**43.6**	**53.0**	**57.1**	**56.8**	**59.0**
Water supply; sewerage, waste management and remediation activities	**19.2**	**22.1**	**24.5**	**-**	**-**	**-**	**-**	**-**	**-**	**-**
Construction	**4.1**	**37.4**	**46.2**	**29.7**	**19.6**	**159.2**	**19.1**	**17.4**	**16.9**	**19.0**
Services	**6 021.7**	**7 991.8**	**8 193.8**	**6 848.9**	**6 480.5**	**5 357.3**	**4 054.0**	**3 999.0**	**3 756.1**	**3 676.0**
Wholesale and retail trade; repair of motor vehicles and motorcycles	145.5	734.3	1 419.8	1 086.9	962.0	605.4	673.6	666.4	638.0	665.9
Transportation and storage	34.0	31.3	35.0	36.0	39.5	244.5	263.5	303.5	290.6	320.8
Accommodation and food service activities	2.2	4.3	14.8	8.2	26.5	19.2	0.3	0.3	0.3	0.3
Information and communication	158.5	207.6	334.8	174.4	171.4	27.8	32.8	10.9	23.2	12.9
Financial and insurance activities	5 192.3	6 405.2	5 709.3	4 917.4	4 679.4	3 752.1	2 872.9	2 846.9	2 595.8	2 386.6
Activities of holding companies	5 160.9	6 046.8	5 004.5	4 219.6	3 721.8	3 707.9	2 834.2	2 804.3	2 556.0	2 345.4
Real estate activities	285.8	318.5	353.2	308.8	289.3	215.4	119.9	132.4	162.0	195.9
Professional, scientific and technical activities	80.4	151.9	179.0	232.9	226.3	314.1	59.7	6.2	13.0	59.8
Administrative and support service activities	122.9	133.6	142.9	80.0	81.9	65.4	31.2	30.9	31.4	31.7
Public administration; activities of households and of extraterritorial organisations	-	-	-	-	-	-	-	-	-	-
Education	-	5.0	5.1	4.4	4.2	-	-	-	-	-
Human health and social work activities	-	-	-	-	-	113.3	-	-	-	-
Arts, entertainment and recreation	-	-	0.0	0.0	0.0	-	-	1.4	1.8	2.1
Other services	-	-	-	-	-	-	-	-	-	-
Not allocated and confidential	**158.3**	**178.9**	**208.4**	**133.3**	**127.9**	**363.9**	**234.1**	**200.5**	**149.9**	**152.7**
Private real estate activities	**-**	**-**	**-**	**-**	**-**	**-**	**-**	**-**	**-**	**-**

- Nil

Note: Data excludes resident Special Purpose Entities (SPEs). Detailed metadata at: *http://stats.oecd.org/OECDStat_Metadata/ShowMetadata.ashx?Dataset=FDI_CTRY_IND_SUMM.*

Source: *OECD International Direct Investment Statistics (database): https://doi.org/10.1787/idi-data-en*

Table 6. Foreign direct investment income by industrial sector

Million US dollars

	Inward					Outward				
	2015	2016	2017	2018	2019	2015	2016	2017	2018	2019
All FDI activities	**31.2**	**-29.2**	**40.4**	**-42.4**	**-219.2**	**283.4**	**435.8**	**302.1**	**363.9**	**347.5**
Agriculture, forestry and fishing	**-0.3**	**-0.4**	**-3.3**	**-14.9**	**-4.6**	**21.4**	**27.5**	**20.5**	**38.6**	**39.3**
Mining and quarrying	**0.0**	**-0.2**	**-0.9**	**5.6**	**-8.7**	**-**	**-**	**-**	**-**	**-**
Extraction activities	0.0	-0.2	-0.9	5.4	-8.7	-	-	-	-	-
Manufacturing	**-29.7**	**-46.3**	**-73.5**	**-126.1**	**-189.5**	**75.0**	**121.0**	**129.4**	**181.1**	**152.9**
of which:										
Food products, beverages and tobacco	-2.8	-1.3	2.8	-4.5	1.7	1.7	1.4	1.3	2.3	1.2
Textiles, wood and paper products; printing	-	-	-	-	-	1.5	14.4	19.5	27.6	24.4
Chemical, rubber, plastic, non-metallic mineral products	-53.3	-36.5	-92.8	-107.7	-103.3	-7.2	10.9	-0.4	2.8	4.5
Metal and machinery products, except electrical equipment	13.2	-33.1	-4.1	-29.6	-104.6	70.5	76.9	111.0	147.9	119.8
Motor vehicles, trailers, semi-trailers, other transport equipment	-	-	-	-	-	-0.1	-	-	-	-
Other manufacturing	13.1	24.5	20.6	15.8	16.8	8.7	17.3	-2.0	0.6	2.9
Electricity, gas, steam and air conditioning supply	**16.5**	**1.8**	**4.1**	**10.5**	**1.0**	**1.1**	**0.4**	**0.8**	**3.1**	**2.7**
Water supply; sewerage, waste management and remediation activities	**0.0**	**0.1**	**0.8**	**-**	**-**	**-**	**-**	**-**	**-**	**-**
Construction	**0.2**	**1.1**	**-14.3**	**-17.9**	**-7.1**	**48.9**	**123.1**	**4.8**	**3.2**	**2.9**
Services	**44.5**	**14.7**	**130.2**	**100.6**	**-10.1**	**136.9**	**161.5**	**144.0**	**135.0**	**147.3**
Wholesale and retail trade; repair of motor vehicles and motorcycles	-45.1	-103.0	-119.1	12.8	13.5	38.3	31.3	26.5	32.2	36.4
Transportation and storage	-1.2	1.1	-0.4	0.3	1.6	22.8	35.3	25.0	39.7	29.4
Accommodation and food service activities	0.0	-0.1	2.3	4.0	3.6	0.3	-2.0	-	-	-
Information and communication	4.0	13.5	8.5	2.5	5.8	3.4	3.3	4.5	-10.3	-8.7
Financial and insurance activities	55.1	76.5	209.6	75.6	-44.5	59.9	92.0	90.4	80.6	87.0
Activities of holding companies	59.2	74.6	191.1	62.2	-43.7	56.3	90.8	85.5	79.1	84.3
Real estate activities	4.2	6.2	7.3	-0.6	-0.6	8.0	9.1	2.0	1.4	1.2
Professional, scientific and technical activities	3.0	4.7	11.4	4.5	3.0	9.9	1.8	0.4	-0.1	0.9
Administrative and support service activities	24.5	16.2	10.8	1.5	7.5	-10.1	-14.1	-5.1	-9.0	0.5
Public administration; activities of households and of extraterritorial organisations	-	-	-	-	-	-	-	-	-	-
Education	-	-0.5	-0.3	-	-	-	-	-	-	-
Human health and social work activities	-	-	-	-	-	4.3	4.8	-	-	-
Arts, entertainment and recreation	-	-	-	-	-	-	-	0.4	0.4	0.4
Other services	-	-	-	-	-	-	-	-	-	-
Not allocated and confidential	**0.0**	**0.0**	**-2.7**	**-0.2**	**-0.2**	**0.2**	**2.3**	**2.4**	**2.9**	**2.5**
Private real estate activities	**-**	**-**	**-**	**-**	**-**	**-**	**-**	**-**	**-**	**-**

- Nil

Note: Data excludes resident Special Purpose Entities (SPEs). Detailed metadata at: *http://stats.oecd.org/OECDStat_Metadata/ShowMetadata.ashx?Dataset=FDI_CTRY_IND_SUMM.*

Source: *OECD International Direct Investment Statistics (database): https://doi.org/10.1787/idi-data-en*

IRELAND

Table 1. Foreign direct investment flows by country

Million US dollars

	Inward					Outward				
	2015	2016	2017	2018	2019	2015	2016	2017	2018	2019
WORLD	**217 818.1**	**39 375.2**	**52 722.4**	**-16 086.4**	**81 101.5**	**168 442.6**	**30 056.4**	**-2 043.7**	**9 614.1**	**-16 632.7**
OECD COUNTRIES	**141 354.4**	**-51 120.2**	**37 331.8**	**.. c**	**-113 948.3**	**155 159.2**	**11 446.4**	**-32 593.8**	**-53 330.6**	**.. c**
Australia	-806.4	-1 280.5	790.2	-368.2	425.4	326.1	-358.3	39.5	194.7	142.2
Austria	-170.8	129.4	69.9	-99.1	33.6	-8.9	-225.6	-126.3	247.8	-12.3
Belgium	6 319.5	4 772.8	-1 586.1	13 176.0	6 021.5	392.7	-709.9	565.9	902.9	659.4
Canada	-1 074.9	-1 058.3	-1 867.9	-717.6	-1 648.9	579.0	118.3	326.9	-354.1	241.8
Chile	-81.0	-57.5	-78.9	5.9	28.0	.. c	10.0	9.0	.. c	17.9
Czech Republic	.. c	-157.0	10.1	43.7	43.7	37.7	.. c	22.5	.. c	-4.5
Denmark	-35.5	-531.9	-466.7	-70.8	-257.5	67.7	.. c	101.5	341.1	108.6
Estonia	.. c	1.1	-	1.2	1.1	-	-	-	.. c	.. c
Finland	761.0	-142.7	40.6	-63.7	692.9	.. c	.. c	-76.7	.. c	68.3
France	4 184.1	1 866.6	2 790.0	5 614.3	1 403.8	196.3	418.0	1 406.8	-677.4	2 780.7
Germany	-1 896.8	2 813.2	-886.0	2 019.4	-2 273.6	-62.1	-1 073.8	-423.9	-846.2	923.5
Greece	.. c	.. c	-158.9	129.8	.. c	-6.7	7.7	.. c	-7.1	.. c
Hungary	30.0	.. c	.. c	.. c	.. c	106.5	807.3	.. c	.. c	.. c
Iceland	.. c	.. c	.. c	.. c	.. c	.. c	.. c	.. c	.. c	.. c
Ireland	.. c	-	.. c	-	-	-	-154.8	-	-	-
Israel	569.1	14.4	33.8	64.9	12.3	.. c	119.4	158.9	-94.4	159.0
Italy	2 337.2	2 306.8	1 856.6	1 634.6	2 157.2	-117.6	-629.2	98.1	331.6	52.6
Japan	-1 236.8	586.1	-2 614.1	4 559.2	2 709.1	3 943.4	428.0	-1 650.3	-279.7	64.9
Korea	.. c	.. c	164.6	-437.9	.. c	.. c	321.8	-6.8	.. c	75.0
Latvia	-	.. c	3.4	.. c	-10.1	-	.. c	.. c	.. c	-
Lithuania	.. c	.. c	.. c	.. c	-47.0	.. c	19.9	.. c	24.8	.. c
Luxembourg	.. c	-61 160.0	64 617.3	.. c	-116 793.9	63 727.1	-8 409.8	-91 038.2	31 717.2	19 772.8
Mexico	-16.6	-424.6	.. c	.. c	159.0	-99.8	-125.0	189.4	41.3	-
Netherlands	8 790.9	7 410.2	26 319.5	.. c	90 767.9	5 254.6	4 833.6	31 481.2	-85 876.3	-37 790.2
New Zealand	-122.0	.. c	64.3	-100.3	39.2	21.1	6.6	-1.1	3.5	3.4
Norway	25.5	186.9	20.3	478.0	753.4	66.6	.. c	-38.3	-364.7	.. c
Poland	15.5	112.8	-32.7	64.9	-9.0	5.5	28.8	33.8	-48.4	5.6
Portugal	143.1	183.6	251.4	4.7	64.9	-18.9	-49.8	30.4	-77.9	-19.0
Slovak Republic	-26.6	-55.3	-18.0	.. c	79.5	6.7	.. c	-18.0	.. c	-23.5
Slovenia	.. c	.. c	.. c	.. c	-	-	-	-	.. c	.. c
Spain	-1 196.9	-759.7	1 821.7	2 559.9	2 862.4	116.5	67.5	-209.7	-200.6	-304.5
Sweden	215.2	1 087.0	-426.1	-1 205.0	109.7	.. c	471.1	.. c	-72.0	104.1
Switzerland	4 823.1	42 488.1	626.8	8 247.4	-6 401.0	6 256.2	-3 384.9	1 821.7	.. c	.. c
Turkey	46.6	-95.1	-147.7	.. c	-68.3	.. c	-163.7	151.1	-119.2	409.7
United Kingdom	-1 592.9	-17 207.8	5 254.2	-27 215.9	-10 997.4	2 157.5	12 006.0	2 265.8	4 680.8	7 176.8
United States	84 810.9	-61 299.3	-59 817.4	88 201.3	-79 701.1	69 739.3	7 802.7	4 073.9	-5 443.2	20 488.1
EUROPE	**88 714.4**	**106 699.1**	**114 122.4**	**-186 761.5**	**-9 269.0**	**82 472.5**	**591.6**	**-28 036.3**	**-11 667.7**	**-28 822.3**
Bulgaria	-3.3	.. c	-3.4	3.5	3.4	.. c	1.1	.. c	3.5	.. c
Croatia	-4.4	-16.6	.. c	.. c	.. c	.. c	.. c	.. c	.. c	.. c
Cyprus	-205.2	.. c	.. c	.. c	.. c	.. c	.. c	6.8	4.7	.. c
Malta	-74.3	-165.9	.. c	-118.0	48.1	.. c	.. c	.. c	.. c	.. c
Romania	-4.4	14.4	9.0	23.6	-68.3	81.0	-70.8	13.5	74.4	12.3
Russian Federation	583.5	1 090.3	127.4	177.0	-659.4	13.3	182.5	7.9	-272.6	.. c
Ukraine	.. c	11.1	2.3	.. c	.. c	.. c	.. c	.. c	.. c	.. c
AFRICA	**.. c**	**-96.2**	**121.7**	**107.4**	**14.6**	**21.1**	**.. c**	**45.1**	**.. c**	**.. c**
Northern Africa	.. c	.. c	68.8	-2.4	29.1	.. c	.. c	-2.3	.. c	-4.5
Algeria	-	.. c	.. c	.. c	-1.1	-	-	.. c	-	.. c
Egypt	43.3	60.8	40.6	.. c	2.2	.. c	.. c	.. c	.. c	-4.5
Libya	.. c	.. c	.. c	.. c	.. c	-	-	-	-	-
Morocco	.. c	.. c	.. c	-13.0	15.7	.. c	.. c	.. c	2.4	.. c
Tunisia	.. c	.. c	-2.3	.. c	.. c	-	.. c	.. c	.. c	.. c
Other African countries	.. c	.. c	53.0	108.6	-13.4	.. c	.. c	47.3	.. c	.. c
Nigeria	.. c	45.3	11.3	2.4	10.1	-	.. c	-	.. c	.. c
South Africa	332.8	380.4	89.1	62.6	.. c	-13.3	-22.1	40.6	46.0	36.9
AMERICA	**94 538.0**	**-55 142.1**	**-35 596.9**	**130 203.0**	**104 298.7**	**72 220.7**	**19 726.9**	**-5 317.3**	**-711.7**	**14 137.5**
Northern America	83 736.0	-62 357.6	-61 685.3	87 482.6	-81 348.9	70 316.1	7 921.0	4 400.9	-5 798.4	20 729.9
Central America and Caribbean countries	11 032.7	7 215.5	26 099.7	.. c	185 619.6	.. c	11 437.6	.. c	4 798.8	-6 777.1
Bahamas	.. c	206.8	.. c	624.3	.. c	-	-	-	-	-
Bermuda	4 214.1	6 736.7	1 420.4	49 150.2	133 603.5	3 089.3	.. c	-4 191.2	.. c	-6 111.0
Cayman Islands	3 881.3	1 781.5	.. c	-2 817.2	14 211.4	-1 365.5	588.3	-5 755.8	.. c	-773.5
Costa Rica	.. c	.. c	38.3	.. c	56.0	1.1	.. c	37.2	.. c	-4.5
El Salvador	-	.. c	.. c	.. c	-	-	-	-	-	-
Guatemala	-	.. c	-	-	-1.1	-	-	-	-	-
Honduras	-	.. c	-	.. c	.. c	-	-	-	-	-
Nicaragua	-	.. c	.. c	-	-	-	-	-	-	-
Panama	42.2	103.9	36.1	.. c	-53.7	-	-4.4	36.1	56.7	.. c
Virgin Islands, U.S.	-	-	.. c	-	.. c	-	-	-	-	-
South America	-230.7	1.1	-13.5	.. c	28.0	.. c	367.1	.. c	286.8	184.7
Argentina	-55.5	23.2	-21.4	23.6	-7.8	24.4	29.9	31.6	51.9	-
Bolivia	-	.. c	.. c	.. c	-	-	-	-	-	-
Brazil	-99.8	171.4	81.2	-201.8	.. c	175.3	-86.3	-330.3	34.2	95.2
Colombia	.. c	-182.5	-16.9	-132.2	-49.3	-	.. c	.. c	.. c	.. c
Ecuador	17.7	.. c	6.8	.. c	4.5	-	.. c	-	-	.. c
Paraguay	.. c	.. c	.. c	-	.. c	-	-	-	-	-
Peru	1.1	-33.2	10.1	-79.1	.. c	3.3	.. c	.. c	.. c	-
Uruguay	-2.2	-5.5	-	.. c	2.2	-	-	-	-	.. c
Venezuela	-	.. c	7.9	68.5	.. c	.. c	.. c	-	.. c	.. c

Table 1. Foreign direct investment flows by country *(cont.)*

Million US dollars

	Inward					Outward				
	2015	2016	2017	2018	2019	2015	2016	2017	2018	2019
ASIA	**8 543.5**	**-12 911.6**	**-1 615.4**	**22 820.7**	**-8 184.3**	**10 320.6**	**-2 007.1**	**.. c**	**5 254.3**	**1 169.8**
Near and Middle East	629.0	-1 333.6	-395.7	-173.5	-555.2	485.9	-59.7	137.5	830.9	.. c
Gulf Arabian countries	100.9	-909.0	-418.2	-247.8	-569.8	.. c	-179.1	-19.2	.. c	.. c
Kuwait	.. c	.. c	3.4	.. c	.. c	-	.. c	-	-	.. c
Qatar	.. c	.. c	.. c	-17.7	.. c	.. c	.. c	.. c	-	.. c
Saudi Arabia	.. c	-161.5	.. c	-439.0	-831.7	.. c	.. c	.. c	.. c	.. c
United Arab Emirates	363.8	-538.5	-248.0	210.1	222.8	15.5	202.4	11.3	.. c	.. c
Other Near and Middle East	525.8	-423.5	24.8	74.4	14.6	.. c	118.3	157.8	.. c	156.7
Jordan	.. c	.. c	.. c	.. c	.. c	.. c	.. c	.. c	.. c	.. c
Other Asian countries	7 915.7	-11 576.9	-1 220.8	22 994.2	-7 629.0	9 834.7	-1 948.5	.. c	4 423.5	.. c
China	1 474.2	2 097.8	120.6	-15.3	1 996.0	-22.2	.. c	.. c	.. c	.. c
Hong Kong, China	-384.9	268.7	266.0	5.9	490.3	.. c	-479.9	.. c	.. c	-105.2
India	-715.5	-217.8	31.6	192.4	176.9	44.4	-10.0	9.0	15.3	-38.1
Indonesia	73.2	.. c	.. c	.. c	-1.1	.. c	.. c	.. c	.. c	.. c
Iran, Islamic Republic of	-	.. c	-	-	-	106.5	-	-	-	-
Malaysia	-6.7	6.6	11.3	17.7	-12.3	.. c	.. c	1.1	.. c	-14.6
Philippines	14.4	-61.9	-45.1	34.2	11.2	.. c	.. c	.. c	.. c	1.1
Singapore	7 982.3	-14 155.7	962.7	.. c	.. c	1 611.8	248.8	.. c	-181.8	.. c
Chinese Taipei	100.9	2.2	-87.9	-152.2	.. c	.. c	25.4	31.6	.. c	142.2
Thailand	8.9	.. c	-18.0	.. c	-12.3	.. c	.. c	-6.8	.. c	3.4
Viet Nam	.. c	.. c	.. c	-1.2	-	8.9	16.6	.. c	-13.0	4.5
AUSTRALIA, OCEANIA AND POLAR REGIONS	**-929.6**	**.. c**	**859.0**	**-474.4**	**466.8**	**348.3**	**-350.5**	**38.3**	**199.5**	**144.4**
WORLD unallocated and confidential	**26 580.1**	**.. d**	**-25 168.5**	**18 018.4**	**-6 225.2**	**3 059.3**	**.. d**	**32 711.1**	**16 491.2**	**-3 294.5**
European Union (EU28)	**54 290.6**	**-28 657.5**	**98 602.2**	**-202 819.5**	**-29 944.0**	**73 949.0**	**7 187.9**	**-51 835.2**	**-58 662.8**	**-16 579.0**
G20 countries excl. European Union	**..**	**.. d**	**.. d**	**.. d**	**.. d**	**..**	**.. d**	**.. d**	**.. d**	**.. d**
G20 OECD countries	**..**	**.. d**	**.. d**	**.. d**	**.. d**	**..**	**18 744.9**	**6 470.5**	**.. d**	**32 355.3**
G20 Non-OECD countries	**..**	**.. d**	**.. d**	**.. d**	**.. d**	**..**	**.. d**	**.. d**	**.. d**	**.. d**
MENA countries	**..**	**.. d**	**.. d**	**.. d**	**.. d**	**..**	**.. d**	**.. d**	**.. d**	**.. d**
ASEAN countries	**8 051.0**	**-14 402.3**	**.. c**	**18 861.1**	**.. c**	**1 679.4**	**-372.7**	**.. c**	**793.1**	**.. c**

- Nil; .. Not available; c Confidential data; d Secondary Confidentiality

Note: Detailed metadata at: *http://stats.oecd.org/OECDStat_Metadata/ShowMetadata.ashx?Dataset=FDI_CTRY_IND_SUMM.*

Source: *OECD International Direct Investment Statistics (database): https://doi.org/10.1787/idi-data-en*

Table 2. Foreign direct investment positions by country

At year end

Million US dollars

	Inward					Outward				
	2015	2016	2017	2018	2019	2015	2016	2017	2018	2019
WORLD	**890 125.2**	**840 646.1**	**1 058 012.7**	**1 048 602.0**	**1 152 313.0**	**909 667.9**	**856 581.6**	**986 845.8**	**967 868.1**	**1 085 869.5**
OECD COUNTRIES	**765 318.5**	**639 685.9**	**870 374.2**	**764 862.6**	**677 835.3**	**797 432.8**	**711 684.4**	**798 833.1**	**723 865.4**	**848 612.7**
Australia	480.1	-731.5	403.0	443.1	889.7	1 829.1	.. c	1 364.8	614.8	1 035.7
Austria	299.4	448.0	480.9	389.3	324.6	136.1	.. c	-217.1	-49.2	-42.7
Belgium	10 843.8	9 638.5	7 419.0	24 984.0	-3 627.3	7 787.7	.. c	1 686.3	1 703.7	3 657.6
Canada	1 973.9	2 496.0	425.8	11 657.9	11 151.4	2 350.6	2 463.4	2 500.6	2 665.4	2 898.2
Chile	-98.0	-161.3	-136.7	-121.4	-70.8	.. c	31.6	40.8	.. c	485.3
Czech Republic	17.4	-132.8	12.0	74.4	130.3	497.6	.. c	-67.2	279.4	278.6
Denmark	1 434.9	506.0	130.7	-99.6	-335.9	167.7	.. c	-116.3	207.2	283.1
Estonia	.. c	1.1	1.2	1.1	2.2	.. c	.. c	.. c	.. c	.. c
Finland	-203.6	-183.4	-101.9	-137.4	551.6	1 253.1	-763.2	-847.9	-87.0	-28.1
France	20 562.9	20 509.1	23 816.3	24 112.7	25 380.8	2 971.1	3 319.3	5 361.0	4 339.4	1 723.2
Germany	3 928.1	4 759.1	7 140.8	7 272.7	5 973.9	5 248.8	3 725.1	3 871.4	3 810.4	4 902.3
Greece	40.3	.. c	.. c	229.0	249.4	.. c	100.1	-217.1	76.7	41.6
Hungary	.. c	.. c	.. c	.. c	-812.2	25 814.9	.. c	.. c	.. c	-257.2
Iceland	.. c	.. c	.. c	.. c	.. c	.. c	.. c	.. c	.. c	.. c
Ireland	-	-	.. c	-	-	96.9	.. c	.. c	-	.. c
Israel	123.0	128.6	151.1	-82.4	-70.8	.. c	.. c	.. c	.. c	1 473.8
Italy	8 373.4	8 216.5	10 142.7	9 976.0	8 876.7	1 234.6	549.2	682.4	82.4	15.7
Japan	1 907.5	2 539.3	421.0	4 906.1	.. c	5 797.5	6 232.7	3 882.2	3 612.3	3 549.8
Korea	.. c	4 837.1	5 111.5	648.0	34.8	460.5	.. c	758.0	976.6	978.4
Latvia	.. c	.. c	.. c	5.7	.. c	-	.. c	.. c	.. c	.. c
Lithuania	15.2	40.1	34.8	6.9	-48.3	-5.4	.. c	25.2	46.9	51.7
Luxembourg	152 394.1	.. c	268 463.7	200 456.8	77 773.5	462 149.2	423 202.3	339 971.2	377 783.4	472 393.8
Mexico	101.3	-321.5	.. c	-405.3	-205.6	926.5	695.7	941.5	943.4	962.7
Netherlands	100 641.3	89 640.6	110 159.5	-14 634.8	101 012.1	56 332.1	57 785.4	181 039.8	82 735.3	66 425.5
New Zealand	45.7	80.1	139.1	33.2	62.9	.. c	.. c	353.8	.. c	.. c
Norway	386.5	591.3	813.1	1 683.1	2 475.8	6.5	.. c	.. c	113.4	.. c
Poland	-94.7	24.2	-24.0	99.6	18.0	302.7	.. c	375.4	659.5	648.2
Portugal	427.9	629.3	952.3	613.7	757.1	.. c	.. c	.. c	.. c	.. c
Slovak Republic	7.6	-47.4	-72.0	.. c	37.1	.. c	959.2	961.9	.. c	.. c
Slovenia	.. c	.. c	-6.0	-8.0	-9.0	.. c	.. c	.. c	14.9	14.6
Spain	12 201.4	8 403.1	11 107.0	12 542.9	15 031.5	.. c	.. c	.. c	7 980.3	.. c
Sweden	2 476.9	3 085.3	2 655.3	1 505.6	1 382.8	1 882.4	.. c	6 608.3	6 464.4	5 224.7
Switzerland	13 802.9	60 657.7	86 613.1	79 882.1	98 350.9	-6 112.1	-18 538.0	-15 808.3	4 751.5	16 033.5
Turkey	.. c	.. c	.. c	-113.4	-200.0	1 920.5	.. c	.. c	1 210.2	1 592.9
United Kingdom	56 807.8	78 050.0	70 197.9	57 715.8	46 124.5	98 851.4	99 266.4	106 291.7	100 275.9	108 386.9
United States	375 156.2	235 690.9	233 552.4	338 338.7	248 875.5	112 705.5	92 687.9	111 362.4	107 867.0	140 069.6
EUROPE	**396 315.7**	**497 426.0**	**729 005.8**	**525 721.3**	**533 855.3**	**693 740.9**	**630 141.2**	**708 088.3**	**666 134.6**	**737 581.4**
Bulgaria	18.5	-	-4.8	-1.1	3.4	.. c	.. c	.. c	.. c	203.3
Croatia	.. c	.. c	-4.8	.. c	10.1	.. c	.. c	.. c	.. c	.. c
Cyprus	343.0	.. c	.. c	.. c	.. c	344.0	.. c	844.3	869.0	861.6
Malta	1 986.9	.. c	467.7	330.9	258.4	.. c	.. c	.. c	.. c	.. c
Romania	-22.9	-8.4	2.4	29.8	-40.4	285.2	.. c	225.5	75.6	.. c
Russian Federation	1 495.9	2 422.3	2 680.5	2 641.4	1 950.1	403.9	.. c	604.5	337.8	319.0
Ukraine	.. c	-15.8	.. c	.. c	.. c	.. c	.. c	.. c	.. c	.. c
AFRICA	**81.7**	**4.2**	**.. c**	**.. c**	**278.6**	**390.9**	**.. c**	**-227.9**	**-474.0**	**69.6**
Northern Africa	.. c	.. c	-4.8	-53.8	-9.0	311.4	.. c	.. c	92.7	.. c
Algeria	.. c	-	.. c	-4.6	.. c	-	-	.. c	.. c	.. c
Egypt	-24.0	44.3	-46.8	-29.8	-10.1	214.5	-	.. c	.. c	-3.4
Libya	.. c	.. c	.. c	.. c	.. c	-	-	-	-	-
Morocco	.. c	.. c	54.0	-6.9	5.6	96.9	83.3	93.5	92.7	92.1
Tunisia	-	-	.. c	.. c	-2.2	-	.. c	.. c	-	-
Other African countries	.. c	.. c	.. c	.. c	286.5	79.5	.. c	.. c	-566.8	.. c
Nigeria	-6.5	24.2	-10.8	-9.2	21.3	.. c	.. c	.. c	.. c	.. c
South Africa	9.8	418.5	61.2	142.0	43.8	32.7	5.3	51.6	95.0	123.6
AMERICA	**453 350.0**	**308 094.2**	**320 768.8**	**477 773.1**	**558 818.2**	**165 850.8**	**170 419.5**	**181 131.0**	**181 351.0**	**217 684.8**
Northern America	377 131.2	238 187.0	233 977.0	349 996.6	260 027.0	115 056.1	95 151.3	113 863.0	110 531.3	142 969.0
Central America and Caribbean countries	76 844.9	70 498.6	86 959.7	128 241.4	299 149.6	50 141.5	74 008.6	66 319.3	69 660.0	73 434.1
Bahamas	.. c	.. c	.. c	11 920.1	48 898.0	-	-	-	-	-
Bermuda	54 299.4	48 187.0	29 124.5	74 603.8	197 845.4	29 632.0	53 506.9	50 314.2	54 484.8	52 290.5
Cayman Islands	11 024.5	12 142.9	45 767.6	41 228.5	51 327.8	19 175.8	.. c	.. c	13 442.9	.. c
Costa Rica	.. c	.. c	-70.8	-26.3	50.6	.. c	.. c	105.5	16.0	12.4
El Salvador	.. c	.. c	-	.. c	.. c	-	-	-	-	-
Guatemala	-	-2.1	-2.4	-2.3	.. c	-	-	-	-	-
Honduras	-	.. c	.. c	.. c	.. c	-	-	-	-	-
Nicaragua	-	.. c	-	-	-	-	-	-	-	-
Panama	.. c	.. c	.. c	132.8	.. c	.. c	.. c	54.0	106.5	92.1
Virgin Islands, U.S.	-	-	.. c	.. c	.. c	-	-	-	-	-
South America	-626.0	-591.3	-167.9	-463.7	-358.3	653.2	1 260.7	948.7	1 159.8	1 280.6
Argentina	-61.0	-47.4	-67.2	-38.9	-14.6	116.5	.. c	.. c	213.0	204.4
Bolivia	-	.. c	.. c	-	-	-	-	-	-	-
Brazil	-263.5	-131.8	-133.1	-327.5	-250.5	572.7	744.2	398.2	400.7	475.2
Colombia	-38.1	.. c	254.3	113.4	64.0	.. c	.. c	.. c	.. c	104.5
Ecuador	.. c	.. c	-	-8.0	.. c	-	.. c	.. c	.. c	.. c
Paraguay	-	.. c	.. c	.. c	.. c	-	-	-	-	-
Peru	.. c	.. c	-10.8	.. c	-61.8	.. c	.. c	.. c	.. c	.. c
Uruguay	.. c	.. c	-8.4	-5.7	.. c	-	-	-	-	.. c
Venezuela	-164.4	.. c	-63.6	17.2	.. c	.. c	.. c	.. c	.. c	.. c

Table 2. Foreign direct investment positions by country *(cont.)*
At year end

Million US dollars

	Inward					Outward				
	2015	2016	2017	2018	2019	2015	2016	2017	2018	2019
ASIA	**13 510.1**	**.. c**	**6 856.6**	**26 392.3**	**46 163.8**	**23 483.9**	**21 248.0**	**69 186.9**	**72 712.4**	**76 970.3**
Near and Middle East	-1 145.3	.. c	-2 326.7	-1 347.6	-1 819.8	1 563.4	1 414.6	1 602.3	1 790.7	2 277.0
Gulf Arabian countries	-1 267.3	-2 174.6	-2 485.0	-1 282.3	-1 777.1	.. c	.. c	.. c	.. c	797.6
Kuwait	-2.2	.. c	.. c	.. c	.. c	-	.. c	-	-	.. c
Qatar	.. c	.. c	.. c	.. c	.. c	.. c	.. c	.. c	.. c	.. c
Saudi Arabia	.. c	.. c	.. c	.. c	.. c	-1.1	.. c	7.2	57.2	.. c
United Arab Emirates	80.6	-462.7	-630.8	999.5	1 300.8	.. c	.. c	110.3	794.6	697.6
Other Near and Middle East	121.9	.. c	158.3	-65.3	-42.7	.. c	.. c	.. c	.. c	1 479.4
Jordan	.. c	.. c	.. c	.. c	.. c	-	-	.. c	.. c	.. c
Other Asian countries	14 655.4	5 633.0	9 183.3	27 739.9	47 983.6	21 921.6	19 833.5	67 584.6	70 921.7	74 693.3
China	.. c	.. c	.. c	7 263.6	9 014.8	.. c	.. c	.. c	.. c	.. c
Hong Kong, China	313.6	634.6	855.1	808.3	1 204.2	.. c	5 621.4	.. c	.. c	.. c
India	-252.6	-470.1	-796.4	-553.0	-349.4	72.9	44.3	50.4	113.4	-27.0
Indonesia	5.4	.. c	7.2	-2.3	-5.6	.. c	.. c	.. c	.. c	.. c
Iran, Islamic Republic of	.. c	-	-	-	-	-	-	-	-	-
Malaysia	-22.9	3.2	-39.6	-20.6	-31.5	56.6	.. c	.. c	17.2	4.5
Philippines	20.7	-41.1	8.4	41.2	55.0	-	.. c	.. c	10.3	5.6
Singapore	.. c	-4 653.7	-4 852.5	.. c	-1 006.5	984.2	1 219.6	.. c	.. c	.. c
Chinese Taipei	310.3	315.2	209.9	49.2	405.5	52.3	.. c	97.1	690.4	1 509.8
Thailand	-26.1	-44.3	-	-95.0	-105.6	.. c	.. c	.. c	4.6	7.9
Viet Nam	-	.. c	-	-	1.1	8.7	.. c	13.2	17.2	20.2
AUSTRALIA, OCEANIA AND POLAR REGIONS	**525.9**	**-653.5**	**544.5**	**475.2**	**951.5**	**2 176.4**	**.. c**	**1 718.6**	**1 127.8**	**1 824.3**
WORLD unallocated and confidential	**26 341.9**	**.. d**	**724.4**	**17 962.0**	**12 245.6**	**24 025.0**	**.. d**	**26 948.9**	**47 016.3**	**51 738.9**
European Union (EU28)	**374 145.9**	**339 587.9**	**544 762.5**	**333 133.7**	**283 805.9**	**682 620.6**	**630 117.0**	**683 589.6**	**605 162.6**	**681 976.0**
G20 countries excl. European Union	**..**	**.. d**	**.. d**	**.. d**	**.. d**	**..**	**.. d**	**.. d**	**.. d**	**.. d**
G20 OECD countries	**..**	**.. d**	**.. d**	**454 552.3**	**.. d**	**234 296.1**	**.. d**	**.. d**	**226 398.0**	**266 115.5**
G20 Non-OECD countries	**..**	**.. d**	**.. d**	**.. d**	**.. d**	**..**	**.. d**	**.. d**	**.. d**	**.. d**
MENA countries	**..**	**.. d**	**.. d**	**.. d**	**.. d**	**..**	**.. d**	**.. d**	**.. d**	**.. d**
ASEAN countries	**9 568.9**	**.. c**	**.. c**	**13 610.0**	**-1 091.9**	**1 102.9**	**688.3**	**.. c**	**.. c**	**.. c**

- Nil; .. Not available; c Confidential data; d Secondary Confidentiality

Note: Detailed metadata at: *http://stats.oecd.org/OECDStat_Metadata/ShowMetadata.ashx?Dataset=FDI_CTRY_IND_SUMM.*

Source: *OECD International Direct Investment Statistics (database): https://doi.org/10.1787/idi-data-en*

IRELAND

Table 3. Foreign direct investment income by country

Million US dollars

	Inward					Outward				
	2015	2016	2017	2018	2019	2015	2016	2017	2018	2019
WORLD	**71 584.0**	**61 827.9**	**75 764.9**	**93 908.9**	**102 748.2**	**11 762.6**	**14 638.9**	**17 361.1**	**25 320.4**	**23 183.7**
OECD COUNTRIES	**36 967.3**	**38 457.4**	**49 354.1**	**68 338.3**	**73 492.7**	**14 581.3**	**15 449.5**	**15 750.2**	**24 807.0**	**.. c**
Australia	.. c	.. c	22.5	-2.4	24.6	42.2	91.8	-12.4	-9.4	22.4
Austria	.. c	12.2	4.5	5.9	7.8	4.4	15.5	-1.1	13.0	-1.1
Belgium	1 620.6	1 217.5	2 008.8	4 311.3	2 908.3	17.7	79.6	39.5	115.7	91.8
Canada	14.4	35.4	-48.5	7.1	-22.4	34.4	-25.4	4.5	69.6	90.7
Chile	.. c	-2.2	.. c	-	-	-	-	-	-	.. c
Czech Republic	-	-	-	-	-	16.6	.. c	-11.3	.. c	-36.9
Denmark	166.4	89.6	74.4	.. c	247.4	.. c	11.1	6.8	27.1	36.9
Estonia	-	-	-	-	-	-	-	-	-	-
Finland	.. c	13.3	11.3	9.4	9.0	2.2	-	.. c	.. c	9.0
France	2 399.3	2 255.9	2 437.2	2 814.8	2 774.0	48.8	142.7	140.9	80.3	305.6
Germany	881.9	758.6	352.8	961.9	1 035.5	255.1	268.7	165.7	-108.6	131.0
Greece	-	-	.. c	.. c	.. c	.. c	.. c	.. c	.. c	.. c
Hungary	4.4	.. c	.. c	.. c	.. c	.. c	.. c	.. c	.. c	.. c
Iceland	.. c	-	.. c	.. c	.. c	.. c	-	-	-	-
Ireland	.. c	-	-	-	-	-	-	.. c	-	-
Israel	-	-	-	-	-	.. c	.. c	.. c	108.6	.. c
Italy	1 978.9	1 659.8	1 652.6	1 651.1	2 011.6	-73.2	67.5	16.9	59.0	35.8
Japan	13.3	419.1	406.9	593.7	3 212.8	4.4	-11.1	-20.3	.. c	.. c
Korea	.. c	85.1	67.6	5.9	16.8	.. c	.. c	.. c	.. c	.. c
Latvia	-	-	-	-	-	-	-	.. c	-	-
Lithuania	-	-	-	-	-	-	-	-	-	.. c
Luxembourg	4 657.8	4 598.0	11 272.7	15 353.5	17 355.9	8 481.4	10 401.4	9 696.8	11 845.9	12 535.5
Mexico	-	-1.1	-4.5	-	1.1	.. c	45.3	.. c	.. c	.. c
Netherlands	13 148.1	12 987.9	7 436.6	9 446.5	8 210.0	2 142.0	2 981.3	4 123.5	8 315.8	6 800.6
New Zealand	-	-	4.5	1.2	-	.. c	.. c	.. c	.. c	.. c
Norway	.. c	.. c	-301.0	-10.6	90.7	.. c	1.1	4.5	5.9	-1.1
Poland	-	-	-	1.2	2.2	8.9	1.1	19.2	8.3	11.2
Portugal	112.0	71.9	32.7	36.6	.. c	.. c	.. c	-6.8	.. c	.. c
Slovak Republic	-	-	-	-1.2	-	.. c	.. c	.. c	.. c	.. c
Slovenia	-	-	-	-	-	-	-	-	-	-
Spain	168.6	246.6	558.0	546.4	436.6	-10.0	45.3	-6.8	2.4	-61.6
Sweden	168.6	188.0	181.5	234.9	165.7	14.4	96.2	50.7	56.7	68.3
Switzerland	6 703.3	8 283.8	9 189.5	14 483.7	17 378.3	-397.1	-1 003.0	.. c	18.9	.. c
Turkey	-	-	.. c	.. c	.. c	.. c	26.5	.. c	.. c	.. c
United Kingdom	4 266.2	4 133.6	4 438.1	4 746.8	4 420.7	604.5	424.6	2 207.2	3 093.4	1 940.0
United States	411.5	684.5	8 332.8	12 716.9	13 086.3	1 859.1	498.7	-1 226.5	462.6	1 680.3
EUROPE	**54 418.2**	**42 523.5**	**51 193.8**	**65 324.0**	**70 182.5**	**13 742.7**	**16 078.7**	**18 749.9**	**25 183.5**	**23 240.8**
Bulgaria	-	-	-	-	-	.. c	-	.. c	.. c	-
Croatia	-	-	-	-	.. c	-	-	-	-	-
Cyprus	.. c	.. c	.. c	.. c	.. c	-	.. c	.. c	.. c	.. c
Malta	33.3	29.9	32.7	36.6	.. c	.. c	.. c	.. c	.. c	.. c
Romania	-	-	-	-	-	.. c	18.8	10.1	3.5	7.8
Russian Federation	-	.. c	.. c	18.9	-22.4	.. c	.. c	.. c	-24.8	.. c
Ukraine	-	-	-	-	-	.. c	.. c	.. c	.. c	.. c
AFRICA	**11.1**	**12.2**	**.. c**	**13.0**	**40.3**	**.. c**	**.. c**	**.. c**	**.. c**	**.. c**
Northern Africa	-	-	-	.. c	-	.. c	-	.. c	-	-
Algeria	-	-	-	-	-	-	-	-	-	-
Egypt	-	-	-	-	-	.. c	-	-	-	-
Libya	-	-	-	-	-	-	-	-	-	-
Morocco	-	-	-	-	-	-	-	-	-	-
Tunisia	-	-	-	.. c	-	-	-	.. c	-	-
Other African countries	11.1	12.2	.. c	.. c	40.3	-	.. c	-	.. c	.. c
Nigeria	-	-	-	-	-1.1	-	.. c	.. c	-	-
South Africa	.. c	11.1	.. c	13.0	.. c	-	-	-	-	-
AMERICA	**16 677.8**	**18 402.1**	**22 968.1**	**26 340.1**	**27 612.2**	**3 740.4**	**3 290.9**	**2 165.5**	**3 866.4**	**3 225.1**
Northern America	424.8	721.0	8 283.2	12 721.6	13 065.0	1 894.6	473.3	-1 222.0	532.3	1 771.0
Central America and Caribbean countries	16 252.9	17 685.5	14 686.1	.. c	.. c	1 770.4	2 729.2	3 270.2	.. c	1 378.0
Bahamas	.. c	.. c	.. c	.. c	700.8	-	-	.. c	2.4	4.5
Bermuda	12 073.2	13 110.7	8 614.6	7 682.0	9 108.9	888.5	1 272.8	1 749.5	1 259.3	-39.2
Cayman Islands	4 400.4	4 472.0	5 631.8	4 844.8	4 550.5	859.7	1 405.5	.. c	1 891.9	1 341.1
Costa Rica	-	.. c	.. c	-	-	.. c	4.4	.. c	-	-
El Salvador	-	-	-	-	-	-	-	-	-	-
Guatemala	-	-	-	-	-	-	-	-	-	-
Honduras	-	-	-	-	-	-	-	-	-	-
Nicaragua	-	-	-	-	-	-	-	-	-	-
Panama	.. c	-11.1	-1.1	13.0	5.6	-	-	-	.. c	.. c
Virgin Islands, U.S.	-	-	-	-	-	-	-	-	-	-
South America	-	-4.4	-1.1	.. c	.. c	76.5	88.5	117.2	.. c	77.2
Argentina	-	-	-	-	.. c	33.3	32.1	.. c	.. c	17.9
Bolivia	-	-	-	-	-	-	-	-	-	-
Brazil	-	.. c	-	.. c	-	.. c	54.2	.. c	.. c	.. c
Colombia	-	-	-	-	-	-	-	-	-	.. c
Ecuador	-	-	-	-	-	-	-	-	-	-
Paraguay	.. c	-	.. c	-	-	-	-	-	-	-
Peru	-	-	-	-	-	.. c	-	.. c	-	1.1
Uruguay	-	-	-	-	-	-	-	-	-	-
Venezuela	-	-	-	-	-	-	-	.. c	-	-

Table 3. Foreign direct investment income by country *(cont.)*

Million US dollars

	Inward					Outward				
	2015	2016	2017	2018	2019	2015	2016	2017	2018	2019
ASIA	**391.6**	**677.9**	**1 139.7**	**1 823.4**	**4 471.1**	**.. c**	**.. c**	**.. c**	**.. c**	**.. c**
Near and Middle East	8.9	7.7	7.9	-21.2	.. c	10.0	.. c	.. c	182.9	167.9
Gulf Arabian countries	.. c	7.7	6.8	-23.6	.. c	.. c	.. c	.. c	.. c	.. c
Kuwait	-	-	-	-	-	-	-	-	-	-
Qatar	-	-	-	-	-	-	-	-	-	-
Saudi Arabia	-	-	-	-	-	-	.. c	-	.. c	.. c
United Arab Emirates	.. c	7.7	6.8	.. c	.. c	.. c	-	.. c	.. c	.. c
Other Near and Middle East	.. c	-	-	-	1.1	.. c	.. c	.. c	.. c	.. c
Jordan	.. c	-	-	-	-	-	-	-	.. c	-
Other Asian countries	381.6	670.1	1 132.9	1 844.7	.. c	.. c	.. c	.. c	.. c	.. c
China	.. c	.. c	.. c	.. c	.. c	.. c	.. c	.. c	.. c	.. c
Hong Kong, China	.. c	.. c	.. c	.. c	.. c	4.4	2.2	-11.3	8.3	.. c
India	-	.. c	.. c	-	-	.. c	18.8	15.8	.. c	.. c
Indonesia	-	-	-	-	-	-	-	-	-	-
Iran, Islamic Republic of	-	-	-	-	-	.. c	-	-	-	-
Malaysia	-	-	-	-	.. c	-	-	-	-	.. c
Philippines	-	-	-	-	-	-	-	-	-	-
Singapore	89.9	99.5	138.7	.. c	.. c	.. c	.. c	11.3	8.3	.. c
Chinese Taipei	-	-	-	-	.. c	.. c	.. c	.. c	.. c	-
Thailand	-	-	-	-	-	-	-	-	-	2.2
Viet Nam	-	-	-	-	-	-	-	-	-	-
AUSTRALIA, OCEANIA AND POLAR REGIONS	**.. c**	**.. c**	**23.7**	**-**	**25.7**	**48.8**	**99.5**	**-7.9**	**-15.3**	**22.4**
WORLD unallocated and confidential	**85.4**	**.. d**	**439.6**	**408.4**	**416.4**	**-5 788.1**	**.. d**	**-3 541.9**	**-3 973.8**	**-3 474.8**
European Union (EU28)	**29 638.4**	**28 608.9**	**31 754.0**	**40 482.7**	**39 620.5**	**13 379.9**	**16 209.2**	**18 116.3**	**24 364.5**	**22 964.3**
G20 countries excl. European Union	**..**	**.. d**	**.. d**	**.. d**	**.. d**	**..**	**.. d**	**.. d**	**.. d**	**.. d**
G20 OECD countries	**..**	**.. d**	**.. d**	**.. d**	**.. d**	**..**	**.. d**	**.. d**	**.. d**	**.. d**
G20 Non-OECD countries	**..**	**.. d**	**.. d**	**.. d**	**.. d**	**..**	**.. d**	**.. d**	**.. d**	**.. d**
MENA countries	**..**	**7.7**	**6.8**	**.. d**	**.. d**	**..**	**.. d**	**.. d**	**.. d**	**.. d**
ASEAN countries	**89.9**	**102.8**	**138.7**	**.. c**	**.. c**	**.. c**	**15.5**	**.. c**	**10.6**	**4.5**

- Nil; .. Not available; c Confidential data; d Secondary Confidentiality

Note: Detailed metadata at: *http://stats.oecd.org/OECDStat_Metadata/ShowMetadata.ashx?Dataset=FDI_CTRY_IND_SUMM.*

Source: *OECD International Direct Investment Statistics (database): https://doi.org/10.1787/idi-data-en*

IRELAND

Table 4. Foreign direct investment flows by industrial sector

Million US dollars

	Inward					Outward				
	2015	2016	2017	2018	2019	2015	2016	2017	2018	2019
All FDI activities	**217 818.1**	**39 375.2**	**52 722.4**	**-16 086.4**	**81 101.5**	**168 442.6**	**30 056.4**	**-2 043.7**	**9 614.1**	**-16 632.7**
Agriculture, forestry and fishing	.. c	.. c	.. c	.. c	.. c	-	-	-	-	-
Mining and quarrying	.. c	-	.. c	.. c	.. c	.. c	.. c	.. c	.. c	.. c
Extraction activities	-	-	-	-	-	-	-	-	-	-
Manufacturing	**23 021.6**	**-3 059.8**	**-40 928.9**	**60 965.4**	**26 125.6**	**4 891.8**	**4 749.5**	**3 760.6**	**16 994.0**	**314.6**
of which:										
Food products, beverages and tobacco	89.9	-410.3	-109.3	.. c	13 122.1	-66.6	358.3	.. c	626.7	3 545.3
Textiles, wood and paper products; printing	.. c	.. c	-	-	.. c	.. c	.. c	.. c	.. c	.. c
Chemical, rubber, plastic, non-metallic mineral products	7 018.3	12 029.2	-8 361.0	20 689.2	.. c	.. c	.. c	.. c	.. c	.. c
Metal and machinery products, except electrical equipment	.. c	.. c	.. c	.. c	.. c	170.8	.. c	.. c	.. c	-1 893.0
Motor vehicles, trailers, semi-trailers, other transport equipment	.. c	.. c	.. c	.. c	-	.. c	.. c	.. c	.. c	.. c
Other manufacturing	1 985.6	1 066.0	1 938.9	3 851.1	1 390.4	442.6	-97.3	16.9	1 863.6	.. c
Electricity, gas, steam and air conditioning supply	.. c	.. c	.. c	.. c	.. c	.. c	.. c	.. c	.. c	.. c
Water supply; sewerage, waste management and remediation activities	-	-	-	-	-	-	-	-	-	-
Construction	-	-	-	-	-	-	-	-	-	-
Services	**194 743.2**	**42 325.6**	**93 448.3**	**-77 925.2**	**54 958.0**	**160 920.7**	**23 942.3**	**-8 973.1**	**-9 180.9**	**-18 474.2**
Wholesale and retail trade; repair of motor vehicles and motorcycles	3 237.9	.. c	31 392.2	12 246.0	1 997.1	1 975.6	1 925.2	-1 792.4	644.4	-802.6
Transportation and storage	.. c	.. c	.. c	.. c	.. c	.. c	.. c	.. c	.. c	.. c
Accommodation and food service activities	-	-	-	-	-	-	-	-	-	-
Information and communication	9 404.3	7 806.0	90 701.2	-62 834.9	29 985.4	2 991.7	-1 297.1	.. c	.. c	.. c
Financial and insurance activities	104 400.4	6 564.2	5 056.9	-20 616.1	13 413.2	.. c	14 734.0	8 090.4	-12 159.8	1 400.4
Activities of holding companies	3 130.3	-1 812.5	1 630.0	-2 783.0	-2 759.4	175.3	-754.2	2 427.0	.. c	34.7
Real estate activities	-	-	-	.. c	.. c	-	-	-	-	-
Professional, scientific and technical activities	51 088.2	18 794.6	.. c	-3 289.3	-1 840.4	80 381.6	2 079.0	-59 940.3	55 711.1	11 239.2
Administrative and support service activities	.. c	1 533.8	-3 125.9	-4 221.6	10 473.5	.. c	797.3	.. c	3 596.1	1 303.0
Public administration; activities of households and of extraterritorial organisations	-	-	-	-	-	-	-	-	-	-
Education	-	-	-	-	-	-	-	-	-	-
Human health and social work activities	-	-	-	-	-	-	-	-	-	-
Arts, entertainment and recreation	-	-	-	-	.. c	.. c	.. c	.. c	.. c	.. c
Other services	-	-	-	-	-	-	-	-	-	-
Not allocated and confidential	.. c	.. c	.. c	.. c	.. c	.. c	.. c	.. c	.. c	.. c
Private real estate activities	-	-	-	-	-	-	-	-	-	-

- Nil; c Confidential data

Note: Detailed metadata at: *http://stats.oecd.org/OECDStat_Metadata/ShowMetadata.ashx?Dataset=FDI_CTRY_IND_SUMM.*

Source: *OECD International Direct Investment Statistics (database): https://doi.org/10.1787/idi-data-en*

Table 5. Foreign direct investment positions by industrial sector

At year end

Million US dollars

	Inward					Outward				
	2015	2016	2017	2018	2019	2015	2016	2017	2018	2019
All FDI activities	**890 125.2**	**840 646.1**	**1 058 012.7**	**1 048 602.0**	**1 152 313.0**	**909 667.9**	**856 581.6**	**986 845.8**	**967 868.1**	**1 085 869.5**
Agriculture, forestry and fishing	**.. c**	**.. c**	**.. c**	**.. c**	**.. c**	-	-	-	-	-
Mining and quarrying	**.. c**	**.. c**	**.. c**	**.. c**	**.. c**	**.. c**	**.. c**	**.. c**	**.. c**	**.. c**
Extraction activities	-	-	-	-	-	-	-	-	-	-
Manufacturing	**346 463.8**	**338 813.1**	**323 992.6**	**423 967.3**	**448 955.3**	**61 224.8**	**66 143.1**	**87 474.2**	**133 867.6**	**149 049.7**
of which:										
Food products, beverages and tobacco	6 550.9	5 640.4	5 044.4	.. c	.. c	22 185.1	20 756.8	.. c	37 648.3	.. c
Textiles, wood and paper products; printing	.. c	-	-	-	.. c	.. c	.. c	.. c	.. c	.. c
Chemical, rubber, plastic, non-metallic mineral products	68 160.0	75 389.5	88 749.1	122 857.8	165 938.0	.. c	.. c	.. c	.. c	.. c
Metal and machinery products, except electrical equipment	.. c	.. c	.. c	.. c	.. c	.. c	.. c	.. c	.. c	.. c
Motor vehicles, trailers, semi-trailers, other transport equipment	.. c	.. c	.. c	.. c	-	.. c	.. c	.. c	.. c	.. c
Other manufacturing	17 171.5	15 863.8	20 788.0	18 025.0	15 312.3	10 055.5	.. c	10 560.1	12 150.2	10 785.2
Electricity, gas, steam and air conditioning supply	**1 289.1**	**.. c**	**.. c**	**.. c**	**.. c**	**.. c**	**.. c**	**.. c**	**.. c**	**.. c**
Water supply; sewerage, waste management and remediation activities	-	-	-	-	-	-	-	-	-	-
Construction	-	-	-	-	-	-	-	-	-	-
Services	**542 177.5**	**500 819.0**	**732 762.1**	**623 480.7**	**702 213.0**	**820 501.9**	**758 951.2**	**865 181.1**	**807 978.0**	**900 244.9**
Wholesale and retail trade; repair of motor vehicles and motorcycles	17 702.8	18 194.4	52 753.7	54 469.9	54 641.7	15 996.7	16 775.6	19 342.8	13 770.3	14 794.4
Transportation and storage	.. c	.. c	.. c	.. c	.. c	.. c	.. c	.. c	.. c	.. c
Accommodation and food service activities	-	-	-	-	-	-	-	-	-	-
Information and communication	20 554.2	20 304.6	198 402.5	139 240.9	168 734.0	4 987.5	3 578.6	.. c	.. c	.. c
Financial and insurance activities	275 921.6	255 443.2	.. c	.. c	281 417.7	93 710.4	96 473.1	105 693.2	104 103.5	105 392.0
Activities of holding companies	23 430.6	22 537.2	24 346.4	24 569.5	21 452.5	9 313.0	7 573.5	9 648.6	9 532.9	9 888.8
Real estate activities	.. c	.. c	.. c	.. c	.. c	.. c	.. c	.. c	.. c	.. c
Professional, scientific and technical activities	118 391.9	137 960.4	121 421.2	84 113.8	112 673.6	609 615.7	555 569.7	507 453.8	536 020.2	658 397.0
Administrative and support service activities	107 810.6	67 058.1	75 790.4	69 151.6	79 073.2	55 463.3	43 842.1	42 764.5	28 568.8	29 829.3
Public administration; activities of households and of extraterritorial organisations	-	-	-	-	-	-	-	-	-	-
Education	-	-	-	-	-	-	-	-	-	-
Human health and social work activities	-	-	-	-	-	-	-	-	-	-
Arts, entertainment and recreation	-	-	-	-	.. c	.. c	.. c	.. c	.. c	.. c
Other services	-	-	-	-	-	-	-	-	-	-
Not allocated and confidential	**.. c**	**.. c**	**.. c**	**.. c**	**.. c**	**.. c**	**.. c**	**.. c**	**.. c**	**.. c**
Private real estate activities	-	-	-	-	-	-	-	-	-	-

- Nil; c Confidential data

Note: Detailed metadata at: *http://stats.oecd.org/OECDStat_Metadata/ShowMetadata.ashx?Dataset=FDI_CTRY_IND_SUMM.*

Source: *OECD International Direct Investment Statistics (database): https://doi.org/10.1787/idi-data-en*

IRELAND

Table 6. Foreign direct investment income by industrial sector

Million US dollars

	Inward					Outward				
	2015	2016	2017	2018	2019	2015	2016	2017	2018	2019
All FDI activities	**71 584.0**	**61 827.9**	**75 764.9**	**93 908.9**	**102 748.2**	**11 762.6**	**14 638.9**	**17 361.1**	**25 320.4**	**23 183.7**
Agriculture, forestry and fishing	**.. c**	**.. c**	**.. c**	**.. c**	**.. c**	**-**	**-**	**-**	**-**	**-**
Mining and quarrying	**.. c**	**.. c**	**.. c**	**.. c**	**.. c**	**.. c**	**.. c**	**.. c**	**.. c**	**.. c**
Extraction activities	-	-	-	-	-	-	-	-	-	-
Manufacturing	**46 930.7**	**35 241.6**	**42 271.4**	**53 986.8**	**57 208.1**	**-3 803.7**	**-3 473.4**	**-2 141.8**	**-2 127.9**	**-2 217.6**
of which:										
Food products, beverages and tobacco	6 719.9	6 375.1	3 587.0	5 633.2	5 666.6	519.1	529.7	.. c	402.5	314.6
Textiles, wood and paper products; printing	.. c	.. c	-	.. c	.. c	556.9	.. c	.. c	.. c	.. c
Chemical, rubber, plastic, non-metallic mineral products	15 142.5	16 080.9	21 823.9	32 562.3	33 218.4	.. c	.. c	-39.5	.. c	.. c
Metal and machinery products, except electrical equipment	.. c	8 734.9	12 636.7	12 760.5	14 222.5	.. c	.. c	.. c	.. c	.. c
Motor vehicles, trailers, semi-trailers, other transport equipment	.. c	.. c	.. c	.. c	-	-	.. c	.. c	.. c	.. c
Other manufacturing	4 524.7	4 035.2	.. c	3 008.4	.. c	119.8	-	-234.5	-20.1	.. c
Electricity, gas, steam and air conditioning supply	**53.2**	**.. c**	**.. c**	**.. c**	**.. c**	**39.9**	**.. c**	**-83.4**	**.. c**	**.. c**
Water supply; sewerage, waste management and remediation activities	**-**	**-**	**-**	**-**	**-**	**-**	**-**	**-**	**-**	**-**
Construction	**-**	**-**	**-**	**-**	**-**	**-**	**-**	**-**	**-**	**-**
Services	**24 584.6**	**24 096.0**	**33 309.7**	**33 985.6**	**39 770.5**	**14 745.4**	**17 443.3**	**17 939.4**	**19 735.6**	**18 160.8**
Wholesale and retail trade; repair of motor vehicles and motorcycles	.. c	829.4	.. c	.. c	.. c	48.8	97.3	428.4	-60.2	16.8
Transportation and storage	.. c	.. c	.. c	.. c	.. c	.. c	-	.. c	.. c	.. c
Accommodation and food service activities	-	-	-	-	-	-	-	-	-	-
Information and communication	9 163.6	8 431.9	12 257.9	14 851.9	17 385.0	-345.0	-360.5	-130.8	-500.4	-1 051.2
Financial and insurance activities	6 939.5	7 267.5	7 559.5	6 009.7	5 532.3	827.5	893.5	1 122.8	434.3	-933.6
Activities of holding companies	600.1	914.5	1 105.9	394.2	172.4	437.0	686.7	976.2	312.8	30.2
Real estate activities	-	-	-	-	-	-	-	-	-	-
Professional, scientific and technical activities	2 143.1	3 626.0	2 839.6	3 577.2	6 359.6	14 154.2	16 497.8	15 956.5	19 369.8	20 021.3
Administrative and support service activities	4 881.9	4 021.9	7 782.7	8 258.0	8 995.9	-16.6	274.2	273.9	250.2	-88.4
Public administration; activities of households and of extraterritorial organisations	-	-	-	-	-	-	-	-	-	-
Education	-	-	-	-	-	-	-	-	-	-
Human health and social work activities	-	-	-	-	-	-	-	-	-	-
Arts, entertainment and recreation	-	-	-	-	-	.. c	.. c	.. c	.. c	.. c
Other services	-	-	-	-	-	-	-	-	-	-
Not allocated and confidential	**.. c**	**120.5**	**.. c**	**.. c**	**.. c**	**.. c**	**1 352.4**	**.. c**	**.. c**	**.. c**
Private real estate activities	**-**	**-**	**-**	**-**	**-**	**-**	**-**	**-**	**-**	**-**

- Nil; c Confidential data

Note: Detailed metadata at: *http://stats.oecd.org/OECDStat_Metadata/ShowMetadata.ashx?Dataset=FDI_CTRY_IND_SUMM.*

Source: *OECD International Direct Investment Statistics (database): https://doi.org/10.1787/idi-data-en*

ISRAEL

Table 1. Foreign direct investment flows by country

Million US dollars

	Inward					Outward				
	2015	2016	2017	2018	2019	2015	2016	2017	2018	2019
WORLD	**11 337.0**	**11 988.0**	**16 893.0**	**21 515.0**	**19 047.0**	**10 969.0**	**14 579.0**	**7 624.0**	**6 087.0**	**8 598.0**
OECD COUNTRIES	**3 668.0**	**6 374.0**	**7 630.0**	**10 537.0**	**6 754.0**	**8 088.0**	**11 850.0**	**4 640.0**	**3 949.0**	**3 505.0**
Australia	.. c	-	.. c	.. c	.. c	96.0	79.0	76.0	41.0	.. d
Austria	-	-	..	..	..	-	-	..	..	..
Belgium	63.0	-22.0	.. d	-7.0	.. c	-591.0	-	4.0	7.0	.. c
Canada	102.0	61.0	.. c	.. d	298.0	-71.0	125.0	327.0	108.0	108.0
Chile	-	-	..	..	..	.. c	-	.. c	-	..
Czech Republic	-	-	..	..	..	9.0	-3.0	-1.0	.. d	4.0
Denmark	-	-	.. c	.. c	..	.. c	.. c	.. c	.. c	.. c
Estonia	-	-	..	..	..	-	-	..	..	..
Finland	-	-	..	..	..	.. c	10.0	.. c	.. c	.. c
France	372.0	114.0	.. d	-77.0	48.0	2.0	-20.0	-17.0	95.0	87.0
Germany	25.0	-5.0	30.0	27.0	1 159.0	134.0	115.0	266.0	.. d	.. d
Greece	-	-	..	..	..	1.0	2.0	-5.0	-1.0	1.0
Hungary	.. c	.. c	.. c	.. c	.. c	-88.0	-15.0	.. c	.. c	.. c
Iceland	.. c	.. c	.. c	.. c	.. c	-	-	.. c	..	..
Ireland	.. c	.. c	.. c	.. c	.. c	-	-	.. c	.. c	.. c
Israel	-	-	..	..	..	-	-	..	..	..
Italy	.. c	.. c	.. c	.. c	.. c	3.0	-8.0	13.0	19.0	.. d
Japan	12.0	137.0	573.0	152.0	.. c	162.0	96.0	.. d	1 369.0	.. c
Korea	-	-	..	..	..	21.0	19.0	19.0	17.0	.. c
Latvia	-	-	..	..	..	.. c	.. c	..	..	..
Lithuania	-	-	..	..	..	-	-	.. c	.. c	.. c
Luxembourg	-33.0	672.0	-293.0	-344.0	417.0	242.0	178.0	76.0	34.0	.. c
Mexico	.. c	34.0	.. c	1 595.0	.. d	4.0	-6.0	.. d	3.0	1.0
Netherlands	480.0	1 746.0	160.0	-94.0	1 767.0	7 756.0	9 875.0	3 427.0	2 239.0	1 829.0
New Zealand	-	-	..	..	..	.. c	-	..	..	..
Norway	.. c	-	..	..	..	.. c	.. c	.. c	.. c	.. c
Poland	.. c	.. c	.. c	.. c	.. c	111.0	15.0	-34.0	.. d	8.0
Portugal	-	-	..	..	..	-	-	..	..	..
Slovak Republic	-	-	..	..	..	-	-	..	..	..
Slovenia	-	-	..	..	..	-	-	..	..	..
Spain	.. c	-	..	..	..	-34.0	-47.0	8.0	92.0	27.0
Sweden	176.0	65.0	-39.0	.. d	18.0	1.0	-5.0	.. c	.. c	.. c
Switzerland	113.0	26.0	-142.0	13.0	-93.0	165.0	85.0	51.0	-295.0	.. c
Turkey	.. c	.. c	.. c	.. c	.. c	5.0	6.0	12.0	8.0	7.0
United Kingdom	72.0	260.0	608.0	-190.0	162.0	631.0	-79.0	172.0	.. d	76.0
United States	1 596.0	2 818.0	.. d	.. d	2 630.0	-807.0	1 407.0	144.0	707.0	1 135.0
EUROPE	**1 800.0**	**3 371.0**	**7 124.0**	**-7.0**	**3 869.0**	**8 913.0**	**10 213.0**	**4 670.0**	**1 820.0**	**2 433.0**
Bulgaria	-	-	..	..	..	30.0	26.0	21.0	.. c	.. c
Croatia	-	-	..	..	..	.. c	-	..	..	..
Cyprus	-	-	.. c	.. c	.. c	-288.0	-140.0	79.0	-9.0	5.0
Malta	-	-	..	..	..	-	-	..	..	..
Romania	-	-	..	..	..	13.0	-11.0	5.0	13.0	.. c
Russian Federation	.. c	-	..	..	..	75.0	70.0	46.0	26.0	.. d
Ukraine	-	-	..	..	..	61.0	55.0	47.0	.. c	.. c
AFRICA	**-**	**-**	**-**	**-**	**-**	**-5.0**	**-23.0**	**-1.0**	**6.0**	**198.0**
Northern Africa	-	-	-	-	-	-	-	-	-	-
Algeria	-	-	..	..	..	-	-	..	..	..
Egypt	-	-	..	..	..	-	-	..	..	..
Libya	-	-	..	..	..	-	-	..	..	..
Morocco	-	-	..	..	..	-	-	..	..	..
Tunisia	-	-	..	..	..	-	-	..	..	..
Other African countries	-	-	-	-	-	-3.0	-15.0	-1.0	6.0	198.0
Nigeria	-	-	..	..	..	.. c	-	.. c	.. c	.. c
South Africa	-	-	..	..	..	4.0	2.0	5.0	.. d	.. c
AMERICA	**1 425.0**	**2 726.0**	**2 109.0**	**12 219.0**	**5 272.0**	**-529.0**	**1 973.0**	**656.0**	**1 146.0**	**1 496.0**
Northern America	1 698.0	2 879.0	844.0	9 207.0	2 928.0	-878.0	1 532.0	471.0	815.0	1 243.0
Central America and Caribbean countries	-398.0	-159.0	1 255.0	3 002.0	2 334.0	322.0	333.0	174.0	158.0	206.0
Bahamas	-	-	..	..	..	-	-	..	..	..
Bermuda	-37.0	15.0	.. c	.. c	.. c	.. c	.. c	..	..	..
Cayman Islands	-364.0	-209.0	1 260.0	1 195.0	2 276.0	319.0	256.0	.. c	.. c	.. c
Costa Rica	-	-	..	..	..	.. c	.. c	.. c	.. c	.. c
El Salvador	-	-	..	..	..	-	-	..	..	..
Guatemala	-	-	..	..	..	-	-	..	..	..
Honduras	-	-	..	..	..	-	-	..	..	..
Nicaragua	-	-	..	..	..	-	-	..	..	..
Panama	3.0	1.0	.. c	.. d	.. c	.. c	-	.. c	-	.. c
Virgin Islands, U.S.	.. c	-	.. c	..	..	-1.0	75.0	.. c	.. c	.. c
South America	-	-	11.0	9.0	10.0	22.0	17.0	11.0	173.0	47.0
Argentina	-	-	..	..	..	.. c	-1.0	.. c	.. c	.. c
Bolivia	-	-	..	..	..	-	-	..	..	..
Brazil	-	-	..	..	..	22.0	18.0	14.0	174.0	.. d
Colombia	-	-	..	..	..	.. c	-	1.0	.. c	..
Ecuador	-	-	..	..	..	.. c	-	.. c	.. c	..
Paraguay	-	-	..	..	..	-	-	..	..	..
Peru	-	-	..	..	..	.. c	-	.. c	.. c	-
Uruguay	.. c	.. c	.. c	.. c	.. c	-	-	..	..	..
Venezuela	-	-	..	..	..	-	-	..	..	..

ISRAEL

Table 1. Foreign direct investment flows by country *(cont.)*

Million US dollars

	Inward					Outward				
	2015	2016	2017	2018	2019	2015	2016	2017	2018	2019
ASIA	**2 144.0**	**674.0**	**886.0**	**721.0**	**359.0**	**518.0**	**297.0**	**185.0**	**1 492.0**	**309.0**
Near and Middle East	-	-	-	-	25.0	-	-1.0	-	-	-
Gulf Arabian countries	-	-	-	-	25.0	-	-	-	-	-
Kuwait	-	-	..	..	..	-	-	..	..	..
Qatar	-	-	..	..	..	-	-	..	..	..
Saudi Arabia	-	-	..	..	.. c	-	-	..	..	..
United Arab Emirates	-	-	..	..	..	-	-	..	..	..
Other Near and Middle East	-	-	-	-	-	-	-1.0	-	-	-
Jordan	-	-	..	..	..	-	-	..	..	..
Other Asian countries	2 144.0	674.0	886.0	721.0	334.0	482.0	298.0	185.0	1 492.0	309.0
China	107.0	161.0	.. d	.. d	.. c	85.0	-2.0	.. d	.. d	116.0
Hong Kong, China	7.0	2.0	.. c	.. c	.. c	-7.0	14.0	.. d	.. c	-1.0
India	.. c	-	.. c	.. c	.. c	135.0	108.0	55.0	55.0	44.0
Indonesia	-	-	..	..	..	.. c	-	-	-	..
Iran, Islamic Republic of	-	-	..	..	..	-	-	..	..	..
Malaysia	-	-	..	..	..	.. c	-	.. c	.. c	.. c
Philippines	-	-	..	..	..	.. c	-	.. c	.. c	.. c
Singapore	2 018.0	374.0	204.0	33.0	23.0	-2.0	1.0	7.0	3.0	.. c
Chinese Taipei	-	-	..	..	.. c	-	24.0	.. c	.. c	.. c
Thailand	-	-	..	..	..	88.0	1.0	.. d	.. d	.. c
Viet Nam	-	-	..	..	..	.. c	12.0	.. c	.. c	12.0
AUSTRALIA, OCEANIA AND POLAR REGIONS	**-**	**-29.0**	**-10.0**	**-**	**-10.0**	**96.0**	**81.0**	**76.0**	**41.0**	**61.0**
WORLD unallocated and confidential	**5 968.0**	**5 246.0**	**6 784.0**	**8 582.0**	**9 557.0**	**1 976.0**	**2 038.0**	**2 038.0**	**1 582.0**	**4 101.0**
European Union (EU28)	**.. c**	**3 339.0**	**6 403.0**	**-91.0**	**3 883.0**	**.. c**	**9 921.0**	**4 037.0**	**1 993.0**	**2 034.0**
G20 countries excl. European Union	**.. c**	**3 645.0**	**2 121.0**	**11 195.0**	**4 558.0**	**.. c**	**1 929.0**	**1 179.0**	**2 030.0**	**1 694.0**
G20 OECD countries	**2 190.0**	**3 484.0**	**2 035.0**	**10 661.0**	**4 373.0**	**180.0**	**1 734.0**	**1 056.0**	**1 746.0**	**1 463.0**
G20 Non-OECD countries	**.. c**	**161.0**	**86.0**	**533.0**	**185.0**	**.. c**	**195.0**	**123.0**	**284.0**	**231.0**
MENA countries	**-**	**-**	**-**	**-**	**25.0**	**-**	**-**	**-**	**-**	**-**
ASEAN countries	**2 018.0**	**374.0**	**204.0**	**33.0**	**23.0**	**.. c**	**14.0**	**15.0**	**29.0**	**16.0**

- Nil; .. Not available; c Confidential data; d Secondary Confidentiality

Note: Detailed metadata at: *http://stats.oecd.org/OECDStat_Metadata/ShowMetadata.ashx?Dataset=FDI_CTRY_IND_SUMM.*

Source: OECD *International Direct Investment Statistics (database): https://doi.org/10.1787/idi-data-en*

Table 2. Foreign direct investment positions by country

At year end

Million US dollars

	Inward					Outward				
	2015	2016	2017	2018	2019	2015	2016	2017	2018	2019
WORLD	**99 313.0**	**107 483.0**	**127 161.0**	**143 971.0**	**164 838.0**	**84 696.0**	**94 633.0**	**101 540.0**	**104 879.0**	**112 256.0**
OECD COUNTRIES	**46 415.0**	**50 293.0**	**59 903.0**	**66 676.0**	**73 808.0**	**63 195.0**	**68 899.0**	**76 436.0**	**76 803.0**	**77 976.0**
Australia	.. c	-	.. c	.. c	.. c	805.0	822.0	849.0	.. d	.. d
Austria	-	-	..	..	..	-	-	..	..	.. c
Belgium	324.0	384.0	158.0	149.0	119.0	157.0	151.0	177.0	175.0	176.0
Canada	3 959.0	3 835.0	.. c	3 373.0	5 275.0	2 197.0	2 461.0	2 664.0	1 809.0	2 253.0
Chile	-	-	..	..	..	.. c	-	.. c	.. c	.. c
Czech Republic	-	-	..	..	..	36.0	32.0	.. c	.. c	.. c
Denmark	-	-	.. c	.. c	.. c	.. c	.. c	.. c	.. c	.. c
Estonia	-	-	..	..	..	-	-	..	..	..
Finland	-	-	..	..	..	.. c	.. c	.. c	.. c	.. c
France	829.0	853.0	824.0	707.0	722.0	138.0	46.0	23.0	185.0	114.0
Germany	468.0	489.0	535.0	554.0	594.0	1 433.0	1 583.0	1 992.0	1 295.0	1 291.0
Greece	-	-	..	..	..	15.0	16.0	14.0	12.0	8.0
Hungary	.. c	.. c	.. c	.. c	.. c	95.0	73.0	.. c	.. c	.. c
Iceland	.. c	.. c	.. c	.. c	.. c	-	-	.. c	..	..
Ireland	.. c	.. c	.. c	.. c	.. c	-	.. c	.. c	.. c	.. c
Israel	-	-	..	..	..	-	-	..	..	..
Italy	.. c	.. c	.. c	.. c	.. c	125.0	115.0	139.0	101.0	99.0
Japan	-	359.0	1 409.0	1 517.0	1 515.0	1 807.0	1 763.0	1 759.0	3 028.0	3 032.0
Korea	-	-	..	..	..	243.0	237.0	239.0	209.0	208.0
Latvia	-	-	..	..	..	.. c	.. c	..	..	..
Lithuania	-	-	..	..	..	-	-	.. c	.. c	.. c
Luxembourg	2 854.0	3 522.0	3 343.0	3 270.0	3 824.0	1 055.0	1 349.0	1 727.0	1 461.0	1 292.0
Mexico	.. c	321.0	.. c	1 833.0	1 858.0	34.0	26.0	28.0	.. d	.. d
Netherlands	10 332.0	12 375.0	12 032.0	11 445.0	12 850.0	37 708.0	45 089.0	48 863.0	48 473.0	48 903.0
New Zealand	-	-	..	..	..	-	-	..	.. c	.. c
Norway	.. c	-	..	..	..	.. c	.. c	.. c	.. c	.. c
Poland	.. c	.. c	.. c	.. c	.. c	200.0	250.0	305.0	280.0	303.0
Portugal	-	-	..	..	..	-	-	..	.. c	.. c
Slovak Republic	-	-	..	..	..	-	-	..	..	..
Slovenia	-	-	..	..	..	-	-	..	..	..
Spain	.. c	-	..	..	..	31.0	-10.0	-3.0	109.0	84.0
Sweden	1 054.0	1 081.0	951.0	452.0	522.0	10.0	6.0	.. c	.. c	.. c
Switzerland	1 696.0	1 740.0	1 733.0	1 694.0	1 839.0	1 731.0	2 244.0	2 348.0	3 219.0	3 177.0
Turkey	.. c	.. c	.. c	.. c	.. c	784.0	711.0	864.0	584.0	667.0
United Kingdom	2 264.0	2 442.0	2 640.0	2 203.0	2 759.0	2 909.0	2 239.0	2 176.0	2 079.0	2 149.0
United States	16 853.0	18 680.0	.. d	29 734.0	31 881.0	10 776.0	10 517.0	11 133.0	12 017.0	12 911.0
EUROPE	**25 997.0**	**27 767.0**	**34 174.0**	**32 120.0**	**35 357.0**	**51 397.0**	**55 871.0**	**63 682.0**	**62 404.0**	**62 666.0**
Bulgaria	-	-	..	..	..	254.0	253.0	247.0	216.0	.. c
Croatia	-	-	..	..	..	.. c	-	..	..	..
Cyprus	-	-	-	.. c	.. c	387.0	230.0	367.0	293.0	218.0
Malta	-	-	..	..	..	-	-	..	..	..
Romania	-	-	..	..	..	73.0	75.0	71.0	.. c	84.0
Russian Federation	.. c	-	..	..	..	562.0	606.0	596.0	525.0	592.0
Ukraine	-	-	..	..	..	488.0	504.0	519.0	447.0	447.0
AFRICA	**-**	**-**	**-**	**-**	**-**	**-21.0**	**-125.0**	**-129.0**	**-186.0**	**-19.0**
Northern Africa	-	-	-	-	-	-	-	-	-	-
Algeria	-	-	..	..	..	-	-	..	..	..
Egypt	-	-	..	..	..	-	-	..	..	..
Libya	-	-	..	..	..	-	-	..	..	..
Morocco	-	-	..	..	..	-	-	..	..	..
Tunisia	-	-	..	..	..	-	-	..	..	..
Other African countries	-	-	-	-	-	28.0	-37.0	-129.0	-186.0	-19.0
Nigeria	-	-	..	..	..	.. c	5.0	.. c	.. c	.. c
South Africa	-	-	..	..	..	12.0	13.0	19.0	19.0	21.0
AMERICA	**28 200.0**	**30 493.0**	**35 164.0**	**45 703.0**	**52 323.0**	**15 717.0**	**16 976.0**	**17 147.0**	**16 764.0**	**18 316.0**
Northern America	20 812.0	22 515.0	25 546.0	33 107.0	37 156.0	12 973.0	12 978.0	13 797.0	13 826.0	15 165.0
Central America and Caribbean countries	6 732.0	7 949.0	9 391.0	12 433.0	14 937.0	1 565.0	2 399.0	3 227.0	2 847.0	3 014.0
Bahamas	-	-	..	..	..	-	-	..	..	..
Bermuda	351.0	518.0	.. c	.. c	.. c	.. c	.. c	..	..	-
Cayman Islands	6 337.0	7 067.0	8 486.0	9 801.0	12 302.0	1 264.0	1 471.0	.. c	.. c	.. c
Costa Rica	-	-	..	..	..	.. c	.. c	.. c	.. c	.. c
El Salvador	-	-	..	..	..	-	-	..	..	..
Guatemala	-	-	..	..	..	-	-	..	..	..
Honduras	-	-	..	..	..	-	-	..	..	..
Nicaragua	-	-	..	..	..	-	-	..	..	..
Panama	44.0	37.0	.. c	.. c	.. c	.. c	-	.. c	.. c	.. c
Virgin Islands, U.S.	.. c	6.0	..	..	..	267.0	369.0	.. c	.. c	.. c
South America	-	-	228.0	164.0	231.0	81.0	104.0	123.0	91.0	138.0
Argentina	-	-	..	..	..	.. c	-3.0	.. d	.. d	.. d
Bolivia	-	-	..	..	..	-	-	..	..	..
Brazil	-	-	..	..	..	81.0	107.0	108.0	91.0	132.0
Colombia	-	-	..	..	..	.. c	-	..	.. c	.. c
Ecuador	-	-	..	..	..	.. c	.. c	.. c	.. c	.. c
Paraguay	-	-	..	..	..	-	-	..	..	..
Peru	-	-	..	..	..	.. c	.. c	.. c	.. c	.. c
Uruguay	.. c	.. c	.. c	.. c	.. c	-	-	..	..	..
Venezuela	-	-	..	..	..	-	-	..	..	..

Table 2. Foreign direct investment positions by country *(cont.)*

At year end

Million US dollars

	Inward					Outward				
	2015	2016	2017	2018	2019	2015	2016	2017	2018	2019
ASIA	**5 171.0**	**5 860.0**	**7 926.0**	**8 638.0**	**9 292.0**	**4 159.0**	**4 228.0**	**4 199.0**	**5 914.0**	**6 829.0**
Near and Middle East	-	-	-	-	39.0	-	21.0	21.0	19.0	18.0
Gulf Arabian countries	-	-	-	-	39.0	-	-	-	-	-
Kuwait	-	-	..	..	..	-	-	..	..	..
Qatar	-	-	..	..	..	-	-	..	..	..
Saudi Arabia	-	-	-	-	.. c	-	-	..	..	..
United Arab Emirates	-	-	..	..	..	-	-	..	..	..
Other Near and Middle East	-	-	-	-	-	-	21.0	21.0	19.0	18.0
Jordan	-	-	..	..	..	-	-	..	..	..
Other Asian countries	5 155.0	5 852.0	7 926.0	8 638.0	9 254.0	3 905.0	3 720.0	4 178.0	5 895.0	6 811.0
China	77.0	373.0	.. d	.. d	.. d	469.0	218.0	228.0	848.0	931.0
Hong Kong, China	270.0	30.0	.. c	.. c	.. c	296.0	308.0	333.0	306.0	309.0
India	.. c	-	.. c	.. c	.. c	1 047.0	1 130.0	1 053.0	989.0	991.0
Indonesia	-	-	..	..	..	.. c	-	.. c	.. c	.. c
Iran, Islamic Republic of	-	-	..	..	..	-	-	..	..	..
Malaysia	-	-	..	..	..	.. c	-	.. c	.. c	.. c
Philippines	-	-	..	..	..	.. c	.. c	.. c	.. c	.. c
Singapore	4 808.0	5 090.0	2 891.0	2 809.0	3 210.0	29.0	30.0	39.0	41.0	854.0
Chinese Taipei	-	-	-	-	.. c	-	.. c	.. c	.. c	.. c
Thailand	-	-	..	..	..	14.0	15.0	21.0	5.0	7.0
Viet Nam	-	-	..	..	..	.. c	19.0	.. c	.. c	.. c
AUSTRALIA, OCEANIA AND POLAR REGIONS	**-**	**-**	**64.0**	**52.0**	**44.0**	**805.0**	**826.0**	**849.0**	**760.0**	**792.0**
WORLD unallocated and confidential	**39 945.0**	**43 363.0**	**49 833.0**	**57 458.0**	**67 822.0**	**12 639.0**	**16 857.0**	**15 792.0**	**19 223.0**	**23 672.0**
European Union (EU28)	**.. c**	**25 227.0**	**30 676.0**	**28 757.0**	**31 662.0**	**.. c**	**50 792.0**	**57 548.0**	**55 794.0**	**55 462.0**
G20 countries excl. European Union	**.. c**	**27 732.0**	**35 286.0**	**44 490.0**	**49 280.0**	**.. c**	**22 591.0**	**23 867.0**	**24 564.0**	**26 213.0**
G20 OECD countries	**24 956.0**	**27 351.0**	**31 705.0**	**40 224.0**	**44 846.0**	**21 251.0**	**20 520.0**	**21 865.0**	**22 094.0**	**23 544.0**
G20 Non-OECD countries	**.. c**	**381.0**	**3 582.0**	**4 266.0**	**4 434.0**	**.. c**	**2 071.0**	**2 002.0**	**2 469.0**	**2 669.0**
MENA countries	**-**	**-**	**-**	**-**	**39.0**	**-**	**-**	**-**	**-**	**-**
ASEAN countries	**4 808.0**	**5 090.0**	**2 891.0**	**2 809.0**	**3 210.0**	**.. c**	**69.0**	**85.0**	**96.0**	**922.0**

- Nil; .. Not available; c Confidential data; d Secondary Confidentiality

Note: Detailed metadata at: *http://stats.oecd.org/OECDStat_Metadata/ShowMetadata.ashx?Dataset=FDI_CTRY_IND_SUMM.*

Source: *OECD International Direct Investment Statistics (database): https://doi.org/10.1787/idi-data-en*

ISRAEL

Table 4. Foreign direct investment flows by industrial sector

Million US dollars

	Inward					Outward				
	2015	2016	2017	2018	2019	2015	2016	2017	2018	2019
All FDI activities	**11 337.0**	**11 988.0**	**16 893.0**	**21 515.0**	**19 047.0**	**10 969.0**	**14 579.0**	**7 624.0**	**6 087.0**	**8 598.0**
Agriculture, forestry and fishing	**-**	**-1.0**	**36.0**	**.. d**	**38.0**	**-**	**15.0**	**1.0**	**27.0**	**22.0**
Mining and quarrying	**-**	**-194.0**	**310.0**	**680.0**	**226.0**	**-**	**-200.0**	**.. d**	**.. d**	**29.0**
Extraction activities	-	-194.0	310.0	680.0	226.0	-	-200.0	10.0	9.0	27.0
Manufacturing	**1 695.0**	**2 870.0**	**2 189.0**	**5 059.0**	**3 548.0**	**9 958.0**	**12 136.0**	**4 295.0**	**3 385.0**	**2 813.0**
of which:										
Food products, beverages and tobacco	144.0	24.0	-8.0	22.0	-9.0	-2.0	1.0	220.0	29.0	298.0
Textiles, wood and paper products; printing	204.0	27.0	64.0	21.0	3.0	85.0	147.0	66.0	203.0	216.0
Chemical, rubber, plastic, non-metallic mineral products	410.0	566.0	181.0	3 225.0	-168.0	9 454.0	11 403.0	3 689.0	3 300.0	2 135.0
Metal and machinery products, except electrical equipment	899.0	1 495.0	2 151.0	1 735.0	3 758.0	265.0	556.0	314.0	-158.0	128.0
Motor vehicles, trailers, semi-trailers, other transport equipment	27.0	33.0	7.0	24.0	-77.0	34.0	9.0	-31.0	-3.0	9.0
Other manufacturing	11.0	725.0	-206.0	32.0	41.0	122.0	20.0	37.0	14.0	27.0
Electricity, gas, steam and air conditioning supply	**846.0**	**46.0**	**.. d**	**.. d**	**.. c**	**122.0**	**56.0**	**-69.0**	**13.0**	**2.0**
Water supply; sewerage, waste management and remediation activities	**2.0**	**3.0**	**.. d**	**-43.0**	**.. d**	**6.0**	**-3.0**	**.. c**	**.. d**	**2.0**
Construction	**-1.0**	**115.0**	**20.0**	**30.0**	**7.0**	**-34.0**	**-101.0**	**62.0**	**80.0**	**108.0**
Services	**5 630.0**	**6 319.0**	**11 276.0**	**16 149.0**	**12 307.0**	**-782.0**	**1 299.0**	**3 778.0**	**4 846.0**	**4 596.0**
Wholesale and retail trade; repair of motor vehicles and motorcycles	110.0	284.0	138.0	79.0	128.0	-597.0	51.0	568.0	64.0	47.0
Transportation and storage	-24.0	-23.0	11.0	59.0	91.0	-75.0	-12.0	34.0	.. d	51.0
Accommodation and food service activities	16.0	27.0	37.0	44.0	30.0	12.0	36.0	323.0	.. d	43.0
Information and communication	1 984.0	2 847.0	2 362.0	3 605.0	7 328.0	125.0	71.0	75.0	151.0	103.0
Financial and insurance activities	1 611.0	1 132.0	680.0	8 642.0	2 376.0	-200.0	1 019.0	2 144.0	3 606.0	2 950.0
Activities of holding companies	..	..	1 004.0	8 702.0	2 283.0	..	..	591.0	906.0	454.0
Real estate activities	293.0	168.0	401.0	535.0	531.0	-122.0	125.0	509.0	726.0	1 064.0
Professional, scientific and technical activities	1 362.0	1 837.0	1 498.0	2 943.0	1 665.0	94.0	-11.0	85.0	223.0	350.0
Administrative and support service activities	264.0	-	.. d	199.0	106.0	-20.0	-16.0	.. d	-13.0	-18.0
Public administration; activities of households and of extraterritorial organisations	-	-	-	-	-	-	-	-	-	.. c
Education	5.0	2.0	.. d	14.0	23.0	1.0	11.0	4.0	1.0	6.0
Human health and social work activities	-34.0	35.0	17.0	6.0	11.0	5.0	15.0	36.0	35.0	9.0
Arts, entertainment and recreation	36.0	4.0	..	22.0	16.0	1.0	8.0	.. d	2.0	.. d
Other services	7.0	6.0	3.0	1.0	2.0	-6.0	2.0	1.0	7.0	1.0
Not allocated and confidential	**3 165.0**	**2 830.0**	**.. d**	**.. d**	**.. c**	**1 699.0**	**1 377.0**	**.. c**	**.. d**	**1 026.0**
Private real estate activities	**-**	**-**	**..**	**..**	**..**	**-**	**-**	**..**	**..**	**..**

- Nil; .. Not available; c Confidential data; d Secondary Confidentiality

Note: The statistical data for Israel are supplied by and under the responsibility of the relevant Israeli authorities. The use of such data by the OECD is without prejudice to the status of the Golan Heights, East Jerusalem and Israeli settlements in the West Bank under the terms of international law.

Note: Detailed metadata at: *http://stats.oecd.org/OECDStat_Metadata/ShowMetadata.ashx?Dataset=FDI_CTRY_IND_SUMM.*

Source: *OECD International Direct Investment Statistics (database): https://doi.org/10.1787/idi-data-en*

Table 5. Foreign direct investment positions by industrial sector

At year end

Million US dollars

	Inward					Outward				
	2015	2016	2017	2018	2019	2015	2016	2017	2018	2019
All FDI activities	**99 313.0**	**107 483.0**	**127 161.0**	**143 971.0**	**164 838.0**	**84 696.0**	**94 633.0**	**101 540.0**	**104 879.0**	**112 256.0**
Agriculture, forestry and fishing	-	**260.0**	**308.0**	**286.0**	**332.0**	-	**25.0**	**96.0**	**119.0**	**143.0**
Mining and quarrying	-	**1 552.0**	**1 862.0**	**2 598.0**	**2 823.0**	-	**1 126.0**	**1 016.0**	**896.0**	**926.0**
Extraction activities	-	1 552.0	1 860.0	2 595.0	2 820.0	-	1 126.0	15.0	35.0	63.0
Manufacturing	**30 233.0**	**30 944.0**	**32 753.0**	**37 169.0**	**40 031.0**	**53 723.0**	**60 386.0**	**64 304.0**	**65 965.0**	**66 627.0**
of which:										
Food products, beverages and tobacco	125.0	1 611.0	1 671.0	1 625.0	1 736.0	803.0	749.0	1 503.0	1 199.0	1 498.0
Textiles, wood and paper products; printing	2 477.0	855.0	990.0	821.0	877.0	803.0	894.0	954.0	1 100.0	1 140.0
Chemical, rubber, plastic, non-metallic mineral products	6 765.0	5 540.0	5 599.0	8 546.0	7 276.0	44 658.0	52 970.0	56 203.0	58 055.0	58 336.0
Metal and machinery products, except electrical equipment	18 602.0	20 106.0	22 898.0	23 866.0	27 825.0	6 587.0	4 887.0	4 538.0	4 542.0	4 656.0
Motor vehicles, trailers, semi-trailers, other transport equipment	416.0	449.0	443.0	467.0	405.0	183.0	185.0	355.0	306.0	213.0
Other manufacturing	1 848.0	2 383.0	1 152.0	1 844.0	1 912.0	689.0	701.0	751.0	763.0	784.0
Electricity, gas, steam and air conditioning supply	**964.0**	**1 027.0**	**1 054.0**	**1 052.0**	**1 066.0**	**871.0**	**934.0**	**139.0**	**131.0**	**134.0**
Water supply; sewerage, waste management and remediation activities	**24.0**	**28.0**	**33.0**	**-11.0**	**-9.0**	**20.0**	**18.0**	**20.0**	**26.0**	**29.0**
Construction	**815.0**	**868.0**	**812.0**	**849.0**	**982.0**	**898.0**	**910.0**	**916.0**	**978.0**	**1 098.0**
Services	**56 515.0**	**62 242.0**	**76 830.0**	**88 946.0**	**102 751.0**	**17 952.0**	**19 906.0**	**24 914.0**	**26 800.0**	**31 849.0**
Wholesale and retail trade; repair of motor vehicles and motorcycles	2 011.0	2 939.0	2 285.0	2 409.0	2 488.0	181.0	310.0	393.0	480.0	512.0
Transportation and storage	222.0	151.0	179.0	289.0	409.0	-88.0	-117.0	-91.0	-112.0	-66.0
Accommodation and food service activities	283.0	466.0	595.0	723.0	825.0	144.0	259.0	637.0	301.0	346.0
Information and communication	22 174.0	22 952.0	26 798.0	29 490.0	36 855.0	1 381.0	1 338.0	2 084.0	2 221.0	3 146.0
Financial and insurance activities	11 209.0	12 544.0	14 219.0	21 531.0	22 998.0	12 190.0	13 821.0	16 875.0	18 153.0	20 545.0
Activities of holding companies	..	..	10 743.0	18 172.0	19 448.0	..	..	13 097.0	11 636.0	11 597.0
Real estate activities	4 209.0	4 365.0	5 432.0	4 680.0	6 786.0	3 751.0	3 862.0	4 623.0	5 111.0	6 398.0
Professional, scientific and technical activities	14 885.0	16 971.0	19 635.0	21 865.0	24 275.0	253.0	292.0	320.0	523.0	873.0
Administrative and support service activities	1 115.0	1 471.0	7 267.0	7 509.0	7 613.0	5.0	-31.0	-18.0	-30.0	-48.0
Public administration; activities of households and of extraterritorial organisations	-	-	.. c	.. c	.. c	-	-	.. c	.. c	..
Education	48.0	82.0	.. d	.. d	.. d	2.0	16.0	.. d	.. d	24.0
Human health and social work activities	130.0	164.0	177.0	181.0	189.0	-6.0	7.0	34.0	70.0	79.0
Arts, entertainment and recreation	164.0	64.0	78.0	89.0	108.0	33.0	46.0	40.0	58.0	31.0
Other services	65.0	73.0	70.0	70.0	72.0	106.0	103.0	1.0	8.0	9.0
Not allocated and confidential	**10 762.0**	**10 562.0**	**13 509.0**	**13 082.0**	**16 862.0**	**11 232.0**	**11 328.0**	**10 135.0**	**9 964.0**	**11 450.0**
Private real estate activities	-	-	..	..	..	-	-	..	..	..

- Nil; .. Not available; c Confidential data; d Secondary Confidentiality

Note: The statistical data for Israel are supplied by and under the responsibility of the relevant Israeli authorities. The use of such data by the OECD is without prejudice to the status of the Golan Heights, East Jerusalem and Israeli settlements in the West Bank under the terms of international law.

Note: Detailed metadata at: *http://stats.oecd.org/OECDStat_Metadata/ShowMetadata.ashx?Dataset=FDI_CTRY_IND_SUMM.*

Source: *OECD International Direct Investment Statistics (database): https://doi.org/10.1787/idi-data-en*

ITALY

Table 1. Foreign direct investment flows by country

Million US dollars

	Inward					Outward				
	2015	2016	2017	2018	2019	2015	2016	2017	2018	2019
WORLD	**19 630.8**	**28 440.8**	**23 995.9**	**37 658.7**	**18 152.1**	**21 639.9**	**16 164.8**	**24 478.4**	**32 797.4**	**19 586.5**
OECD COUNTRIES	**17 185.7**	**28 509.7**	**23 571.6**	**35 916.8**	**17 429.3**	**10 636.9**	**4 114.4**	**13 985.5**	**18 725.6**	**9 119.6**
Australia	17.1	66.2	34.4	89.3	65.0	121.3	45.8	177.4	202.6	-85.1
Austria	-335.0	321.5	105.2	184.5	101.7	173.7	-9 176.9	709.2	317.9	852.5
Belgium	-4 390.8	-2 813.9	1 102.5	115.9	-1 188.3	1 572.7	2 926.1	-3 876.6	-2 311.7	2 444.1
Canada	-24.9	-56.1	261.8	70.1	51.3	255.0	75.0	390.8	595.6	945.1
Chile	-42.5	7.0	-246.8	-5.4	4.8	69.9	-12.3	9 808.8	166.1	3 055.2
Czech Republic	22.0	55.2	75.9	-0.9	92.6	12.6	3 459.4	10.5	-212.0	254.3
Denmark	300.4	-764.2	44.6	-104.6	222.3	482.4	456.6	-181.0	-82.3	106.1
Estonia	-0.4	-29.2	-6.5	-49.0	-1.9	2.2	-5.3	15.8	-2.4	0.5
Finland	-139.0	62.8	146.4	-320.5	301.5	-31.4	152.7	1.8	-202.4	-25.0
France	6 802.2	18 029.3	-1 577.7	35 774.6	1 074.2	1 668.8	1 009.7	1 107.6	2 600.6	1 379.4
Germany	1 575.3	4 884.2	2 714.2	3 055.0	5 988.4	-190.4	-15.3	-2 132.3	2 459.6	206.4
Greece	-40.4	76.5	-140.6	-29.9	49.0	177.3	150.3	80.9	506.2	206.6
Hungary	-585.9	200.7	17.0	116.0	4.8	559.2	142.4	-35.8	164.4	242.9
Iceland	-46.1	18.6	28.3	0.2	0.2	65.4	-11.2	-66.6	-10.7	-13.0
Ireland	-232.1	70.0	1 940.2	78.2	-1 998.1	3 950.9	-336.2	-50.9	917.2	306.5
Israel	-64.0	41.1	59.0	-21.9	44.8	194.9	292.4	414.6	178.2	183.8
Italy	-	-	-	-	-	-	-	-	-	-
Japan	1 120.8	278.8	163.4	176.6	-63.0	116.3	293.1	42.0	54.5	-93.5
Korea	-188.0	-112.9	134.6	519.8	-290.0	-65.3	133.5	36.7	278.3	105.4
Latvia	6.4	7.1	4.2	-1.8	-29.3	-1.0	48.2	3.2	2.8	-18.3
Lithuania	0.3	0.0	-1.3	3.6	-0.1	11.6	-14.4	-1.9	0.0	0.0
Luxembourg	4 114.8	-3 325.6	8 131.6	-9 968.8	10 310.1	733.8	6 909.7	12 629.1	445.8	1 782.2
Mexico	219.1	98.9	-84.7	51.1	-2.2	226.7	121.4	337.1	429.1	486.7
Netherlands	2 677.9	528.0	4 287.1	844.0	1 835.0	-5 639.7	-4 234.1	340.1	-459.8	-12 614.7
New Zealand	1.2	0.6	-2.2	-2.2	2.1	6.6	34.7	14.1	12.2	15.1
Norway	-371.4	403.7	121.2	384.8	126.0	110.1	1 420.1	180.8	283.7	319.7
Poland	31.0	-14.6	-91.5	114.2	173.0	1 071.6	-207.2	-2 207.3	-11.1	1 344.6
Portugal	23.0	52.1	60.4	12.3	105.4	34.5	124.3	163.6	208.7	161.3
Slovak Republic	-76.2	-17.0	-22.0	27.7	-4.7	26.1	-3 449.1	826.3	-87.7	-65.6
Slovenia	40.4	46.2	28.6	4.8	-0.1	42.1	332.2	12.4	127.3	203.1
Spain	1 235.1	820.2	601.5	444.1	935.3	1 293.0	-387.1	-7 105.1	8 173.7	2 710.9
Sweden	-72.7	478.4	730.1	186.9	1 666.2	332.3	87.4	-45.1	179.0	147.6
Switzerland	2 238.8	259.8	3 453.9	890.6	2 978.0	712.8	-939.2	222.7	-427.7	2 398.8
Turkey	47.9	-317.2	-0.1	23.7	106.1	777.4	3 545.3	652.7	548.1	-29.5
United Kingdom	3 863.5	7 443.1	1 714.2	4 050.2	-4 472.5	-269.3	1 960.5	992.8	-285.9	461.1
United States	-535.3	1 710.5	-216.5	-796.2	-758.0	2 043.5	-832.5	515.3	3 967.8	1 744.2
EUROPE	**17 600.8**	**25 794.9**	**24 274.1**	**35 293.0**	**18 845.3**	**10 226.4**	**10 867.8**	**5 199.9**	**16 804.2**	**7 821.9**
Bulgaria	0.1	23.6	-5.1	6.5	5.4	141.7	1 141.2	1 240.3	168.9	210.6
Croatia	11.8	39.5	24.9	35.5	24.1	102.9	2 081.0	104.1	268.0	104.4
Cyprus	29.6	223.4	-245.3	-671.9	657.9	-8.3	-3.0	7.1	-2.9	0.6
Malta	497.6	-617.6	314.2	120.6	-20.1	-57.4	35.2	-42.0	-68.1	25.2
Romania	38.6	-26.9	103.8	-96.6	61.1	274.3	788.5	501.8	3 340.9	379.0
Russian Federation	139.4	-437.2	415.2	-63.6	-322.8	1 025.5	2 424.6	938.8	660.3	1 762.4
Ukraine	28.1	-8.6	6.4	-6.5	15.8	33.9	-26.9	-206.7	-302.8	34.2
AFRICA	**-39.4**	**320.4**	**74.2**	**-42.8**	**90.9**	**4 344.2**	**2 687.1**	**2 711.1**	**3 350.7**	**1 540.1**
Northern Africa	-8.3	100.7	29.8	22.5	-66.1	3 780.0	1 279.7	2 130.5	1 955.4	1 510.1
Algeria	39.8	64.1	16.2	68.1	46.6	1 835.6	920.0	981.0	1 060.0	807.8
Egypt	-15.2	28.2	-6.1	7.6	8.0	1 654.9	236.1	794.3	291.1	716.1
Libya	1.5	-13.6	10.0	-52.7	-114.2	1.3	-44.1	17.7	30.1	-43.6
Morocco	-28.8	13.3	9.8	14.2	-9.1	118.5	14.8	72.0	202.6	46.3
Tunisia	-5.5	8.7	0.0	-14.7	2.5	169.7	153.0	265.4	371.5	-16.4
Other African countries	-31.1	219.7	44.4	-65.3	157.1	564.2	1 407.4	580.6	1 395.4	30.0
Nigeria	1.9	27.6	0.1	-0.3	0.4	88.0	346.5	279.5	671.0	-58.5
South Africa	-64.0	177.0	25.7	14.5	54.3	396.9	485.3	231.4	101.2	-178.3
AMERICA	**-271.2**	**1 899.3**	**-537.1**	**241.3**	**-933.2**	**3 834.1**	**127.4**	**12 295.5**	**6 061.5**	**7 180.8**
Northern America	-560.2	1 654.4	45.3	-726.1	-706.7	2 298.5	-757.5	906.1	4 563.4	2 689.4
Central America and Caribbean countries	219.1	21.7	-460.5	494.4	-82.9	602.4	677.8	1 380.3	321.6	746.1
Bahamas	0.0	0.0	0.0	0.0	6.4	0.5	0.5	0.3	0.2	0.0
Bermuda	-12.0	-0.3	-10.7	9.7	0.7	-10.4	-27.2	135.4	-6.1	4.7
Cayman Islands	249.0	-241.7	-16.7	-15.0	-25.9	2.4	1.0	-23.5	-14.0	-45.5
Costa Rica	4.5	2.3	2.4	2.3	2.2	1.0	19.6	11.9	112.7	-184.0
El Salvador	0.0	0.0	0.0	29.9	0.0	-0.3	1.0	-0.9	-0.2	0.0
Guatemala	41.7	0.5	0.4	0.5	0.5	6.9	22.3	-42.9	5.2	-15.1
Honduras	0.0	0.0	0.0	0.0	0.0	5.6	-4.3	-0.8	-2.3	1.8
Nicaragua	0.0	0.0	0.0	0.0	0.0	-0.5	0.0	0.1	0.0	0.3
Panama	-59.7	-8.2	0.3	2.3	1.4	-84.7	-34.6	109.5	-562.0	338.0
Virgin Islands, U.S.	-	-	-	-	-	-0.1	-	-	-	-2.9
South America	69.9	223.2	-121.9	473.1	-143.6	933.2	207.0	10 009.1	1 176.6	3 745.3
Argentina	3.4	129.9	81.8	121.1	57.0	245.5	-1 171.1	271.2	62.2	-28.4
Bolivia	1.7	2.7	4.4	3.1	3.0	-1.4	2.9	3.1	4.2	0.4
Brazil	245.3	55.7	45.0	70.8	-118.9	481.2	1 552.3	273.8	863.3	545.6
Colombia	0.1	21.1	5.7	-0.9	4.2	37.7	81.0	90.7	36.0	6.6
Ecuador	10.4	1.5	3.9	1.9	1.7	-40.1	-11.2	5.5	4.0	-0.4
Paraguay	0.3	0.1	-0.3	0.2	0.7	0.9	0.2	0.3	0.3	-1.5
Peru	-1.9	24.5	9.3	10.4	0.4	43.7	44.8	45.3	176.1	110.1
Uruguay	-147.7	88.5	-118.2	262.5	-96.1	11.7	-1.8	4.4	-9.9	27.5
Venezuela	0.9	-107.6	93.3	9.5	-0.3	83.9	-262.2	-528.0	-156.1	2.6

ITALY

Table 1. Foreign direct investment flows by country *(cont.)*

Million US dollars

	Inward					Outward				
	2015	2016	2017	2018	2019	2015	2016	2017	2018	2019
ASIA	**1 931.6**	**290.8**	**-64.4**	**2 128.3**	**4.9**	**3 134.4**	**2 450.9**	**3 914.4**	**6 364.7**	**3 217.0**
Near and Middle East	307.6	78.8	126.2	86.8	35.8	9.4	2 621.3	1 364.0	1 826.9	2 548.4
Gulf Arabian countries	372.4	37.6	67.3	105.2	-12.6	-462.9	2 211.8	724.0	1 238.8	2 064.3
Kuwait	852.5	-1.3	1.7	-9.3	0.6	-808.5	123.1	828.8	262.4	100.6
Qatar	-48.4	-26.1	27.6	16.2	-16.7	-763.2	107.9	283.6	-118.4	466.2
Saudi Arabia	9.0	6.9	72.3	2.7	3.4	552.9	-148.3	-487.8	-359.3	252.6
United Arab Emirates	-420.0	51.7	-33.7	114.8	1.9	317.4	1 831.4	309.0	1 154.6	974.5
Other Near and Middle East	-64.8	41.2	58.9	-18.4	48.4	472.3	409.5	639.9	588.1	484.1
Jordan	0.4	0.4	-0.3	1.0	0.4	129.7	44.5	74.1	-132.8	-67.8
Other Asian countries	1 624.0	212.0	-190.6	2 041.4	-30.9	3 125.0	-170.4	2 550.4	4 537.8	668.6
China	59.8	-124.6	-400.7	1 303.4	70.4	538.5	357.3	686.4	1 866.8	25.2
Hong Kong, China	296.0	57.4	-239.2	-31.5	48.2	113.0	-1 523.1	86.9	-56.2	-91.6
India	115.8	-47.7	20.2	15.4	30.4	1 151.2	-18.3	291.5	189.2	-506.6
Indonesia	-2.2	1.1	-1.2	1.0	9.5	16.5	57.7	537.5	71.5	82.5
Iran, Islamic Republic of	-0.3	34.9	1.0	2.6	0.8	252.0	-123.9	-43.6	-177.9	150.1
Malaysia	-14.8	6.4	16.9	-1.1	-3.3	244.7	223.7	722.9	436.9	179.2
Philippines	1.9	-0.1	0.7	2.3	1.2	6.5	3.2	9.3	473.2	239.0
Singapore	-1.5	-10.7	118.6	-119.3	175.7	225.5	103.1	101.4	366.1	114.9
Chinese Taipei	122.3	-79.6	-55.0	82.6	-66.6	21.0	-13.7	4.1	0.5	9.3
Thailand	41.2	11.3	-5.1	6.7	0.4	-39.7	-42.4	59.4	171.8	13.4
Viet Nam	0.1	-0.6	-1.6	-3.2	-4.3	105.4	93.8	132.3	256.6	-18.3
AUSTRALIA, OCEANIA AND POLAR REGIONS	**18.5**	**67.1**	**32.3**	**86.8**	**67.2**	**140.7**	**40.5**	**355.5**	**216.2**	**51.3**
WORLD unallocated and confidential	**390.5**	**68.2**	**216.7**	**-47.8**	**77.0**	**-40.0**	**-8.9**	**2.0**	**0.0**	**-224.6**
European Union (EU28)	**15 397.6**	**25 752.7**	**20 056.6**	**33 930.3**	**15 892.7**	**6 466.1**	**3 976.9**	**3 068.7**	**16 154.7**	**806.5**
G20 countries excl. European Union	**13 404.4**	**31 785.9**	**3 401.9**	**44 479.5**	**1 482.7**	**9 092.1**	**9 875.9**	**4 862.7**	**14 305.5**	**7 075.1**
G20 OECD countries	**12 897.8**	**32 024.7**	**3 143.6**	**43 014.2**	**1 699.3**	**4 683.9**	**6 336.5**	**2 120.0**	**10 850.2**	**5 120.2**
G20 Non-OECD countries	**506.6**	**-238.8**	**258.3**	**1 465.3**	**-216.6**	**4 408.2**	**3 539.4**	**2 742.7**	**3 455.2**	**1 954.9**
MENA countries	**364.2**	**139.2**	**97.2**	**129.7**	**-75.7**	**3 438.2**	**3 556.1**	**2 886.7**	**2 964.8**	**3 507.7**
ASEAN countries	**38.5**	**66.0**	**141.8**	**-107.6**	**180.0**	**585.9**	**443.6**	**1 563.3**	**1 788.7**	**639.1**

- Nil

Note: Detailed metadata at: *http://stats.oecd.org/OECDStat_Metadata/ShowMetadata.ashx?Dataset=FDI_CTRY_IND_SUMM.*

Source: *OECD International Direct Investment Statistics (database): https://doi.org/10.1787/idi-data-en*

ITALY

Table 2. Foreign direct investment positions by country

At year end

Million US dollars

	Inward					Outward				
	2015	2016	2017	2018	2019	2015	2016	2017	2018	2019
WORLD	**340 477.1**	**352 626.2**	**424 743.1**	**433 366.3**	**445 174.6**	**456 619.5**	**456 380.4**	**547 577.5**	**554 876.3**	**554 940.5**
OECD COUNTRIES	**258 838.7**	**282 861.8**	**336 621.5**	**343 652.7**	**348 767.0**	**354 248.8**	**338 716.9**	**405 727.5**	**407 889.6**	**398 190.9**
Australia	218.1	587.2	3.9	7.0	27.8	2 141.9	2 246.0	2 844.8	2 693.9	2 581.2
Austria	4 737.4	3 960.9	4 163.6	4 243.6	4 180.6	27 311.3	18 268.5	20 986.6	20 029.4	19 889.2
Belgium	2 668.5	4 047.3	3 656.4	2 295.4	2 741.1	13 202.1	14 468.4	10 672.5	7 954.6	10 179.0
Canada	777.0	1 040.3	1 605.3	1 817.8	1 925.4	1 743.7	2 068.5	2 723.9	3 198.7	4 151.9
Chile	283.3	266.1	0.2	-115.9	-128.0	1 956.4	1 794.0	13 467.1	11 077.7	13 095.1
Czech Republic	219.6	585.9	775.5	149.9	167.0	879.3	3 696.9	4 361.7	4 045.6	4 118.4
Denmark	3 142.6	2 661.3	2 560.0	2 062.7	2 380.8	1 711.0	1 971.0	2 104.7	2 158.7	2 228.5
Estonia	82.1	59.1	-	-	-	35.8	32.2	56.5	88.3	129.6
Finland	184.2	247.1	560.4	255.5	270.2	1 959.2	1 862.4	1 820.6	1 763.0	1 830.9
France	51 578.5	58 481.4	63 308.5	69 221.7	72 758.3	25 724.3	26 415.8	32 418.1	35 318.4	35 918.1
Germany	22 366.9	33 032.3	39 738.7	36 021.3	37 385.3	38 260.1	37 048.3	42 944.3	43 765.3	41 703.3
Greece	-	-	0.0	-	-	2 840.9	2 957.5	3 739.8	3 993.0	4 129.2
Hungary	10.9	111.7	151.3	275.4	271.7	1 407.0	2 572.0	1 593.8	2 824.1	2 782.2
Iceland	-	-	-	-	-	44.1	33.8	-31.4	-3.4	20.9
Ireland	683.5	1 387.5	3 557.0	2 051.8	1 678.8	13 181.9	9 351.2	9 745.4	8 833.2	8 633.4
Israel	103.7	156.5	252.5	217.2	132.4	859.9	1 602.2	2 279.4	1 772.1	1 849.2
Italy	32 732.4	33 128.2	32 382.3	41 280.6	46 852.8	-	-	-	-	-
Japan	7 104.1	4 646.9	11 113.6	8 600.8	8 682.9	1 245.3	1 507.7	1 859.9	2 134.8	2 092.1
Korea	545.6	596.3	1 225.2	1 500.3	1 155.3	1 088.1	1 183.0	1 444.7	1 717.2	1 787.8
Latvia	-	-	-	-	-	24.8	76.6	96.0	94.3	69.0
Lithuania	-	-	0.0	-	-	25.4	33.8	38.9	43.0	46.5
Luxembourg	19 495.6	25 704.5	25 893.6	24 855.9	26 621.7	20 494.5	25 480.2	46 329.0	44 690.4	35 877.4
Mexico	-	177.6	176.9	52.7	-82.9	1 441.3	1 784.7	2 183.3	2 445.6	3 136.9
Netherlands	16 483.1	19 368.6	17 535.7	12 803.3	13 734.8	66 185.9	59 628.1	64 437.8	64 231.1	50 083.6
New Zealand	-	-	782.4	281.3	298.8	33.5	44.4	64.1	51.1	64.0
Norway	-599.4	532.0	616.8	477.9	493.1	819.1	978.0	1 224.8	1 433.7	1 683.9
Poland	120.1	101.0	-10.4	127.4	120.2	11 342.7	9 623.9	8 313.8	8 000.9	8 979.4
Portugal	323.5	307.0	330.0	318.4	281.6	1 733.1	2 098.3	2 526.4	2 803.7	2 878.9
Slovak Republic	-	-	0.0	-	-	3 659.5	646.6	1 586.8	1 374.4	1 244.5
Slovenia	-	51.8	0.7	1.1	1.2	1 139.5	1 303.8	1 268.3	1 420.3	1 588.8
Spain	6 271.4	4 967.1	5 289.2	5 355.2	5 684.5	37 973.9	33 982.5	35 783.5	41 466.6	45 641.1
Sweden	2 206.8	1 004.1	2 988.7	2 371.8	3 250.0	1 783.7	1 603.1	1 796.3	1 687.5	1 869.7
Switzerland	19 707.5	18 533.4	25 084.4	31 183.1	26 198.5	10 917.4	9 941.7	11 709.6	9 660.3	12 451.9
Turkey	288.3	-	1.3	13.3	49.4	5 341.1	8 283.1	8 527.9	7 705.2	5 990.2
United Kingdom	32 016.8	32 979.6	46 767.8	45 481.0	43 461.6	24 295.9	19 503.1	26 403.5	25 291.1	25 501.3
United States	35 086.6	34 139.1	46 109.7	50 445.1	48 172.0	31 495.4	34 659.3	38 444.0	42 125.8	43 964.2
EUROPE	**219 094.8**	**243 847.4**	**279 230.2**	**284 942.8**	**292 673.1**	**337 118.6**	**323 587.4**	**376 763.5**	**377 521.7**	**367 416.8**
Bulgaria	64.7	-	0.0	-	-	1 094.4	2 261.3	2 926.0	2 520.6	2 838.5
Croatia	0.4	-	-	-	-	883.5	3 138.5	3 353.8	3 695.1	3 839.1
Cyprus	199.2	517.2	344.9	253.9	240.1	141.5	141.5	160.2	148.1	146.1
Malta	-	-	7.5	143.2	96.2	460.5	530.6	568.7	426.2	501.8
Romania	-1.0	-1.3	-8.4	55.3	69.8	4 833.2	6 556.0	7 288.2	9 663.4	9 917.5
Russian Federation	2 393.3	478.3	2 219.6	1 694.9	1 872.2	9 078.6	11 514.0	13 238.5	12 162.9	13 992.1
Ukraine	827.2	-	592.1	582.1	806.8	745.9	684.6	586.0	315.6	431.0
AFRICA	**212.1**	**157.4**	**964.2**	**528.6**	**123.6**	**21 412.1**	**22 576.5**	**27 942.1**	**29 491.4**	**30 773.9**
Northern Africa	190.4	151.1	183.5	110.1	225.9	18 602.4	18 780.7	23 400.9	24 200.6	25 158.4
Algeria	-	-	-	-	-	8 389.1	9 016.2	11 176.6	11 544.3	12 161.0
Egypt	-	-	-	-	-	7 760.3	7 380.2	9 155.9	8 968.9	9 406.6
Libya	185.0	146.2	177.9	104.5	220.4	310.1	263.6	317.5	331.9	357.0
Morocco	5.4	5.0	5.6	5.5	5.5	607.2	524.0	677.3	996.4	965.2
Tunisia	-	-	-	-	-	1 535.8	1 596.8	2 073.7	2 359.1	2 268.7
Other African countries	21.6	6.3	780.7	418.5	-102.3	2 809.6	3 795.8	4 541.2	5 290.8	5 615.4
Nigeria	-	-	-	-	-	503.6	837.8	1 239.0	1 815.4	1 716.1
South Africa	21.6	6.3	780.7	418.5	-102.3	1 335.6	1 634.1	2 014.9	2 036.1	2 210.0
AMERICA	**46 168.2**	**45 224.3**	**60 165.5**	**65 313.4**	**80 599.5**	**49 505.5**	**57 647.6**	**77 918.9**	**80 173.1**	**86 353.5**
Northern America	35 863.6	35 179.4	47 714.9	52 262.9	50 097.4	33 239.0	36 727.9	41 167.8	45 324.5	48 116.1
Central America and Caribbean countries	9 617.6	9 346.0	12 393.1	12 881.1	30 309.8	3 193.0	4 272.9	6 027.4	6 102.8	7 170.7
Bahamas	-	-	-	-	-	4.4	4.7	5.6	5.6	5.5
Bermuda	586.9	-	83.1	188.1	146.1	6.6	3.0	135.8	122.4	127.1
Cayman Islands	8 137.9	8 962.0	10 611.6	11 190.1	28 807.8	3.2	4.0	-20.5	-33.1	-78.2
Costa Rica	-	-	-	-	-	231.9	362.9	240.3	379.4	176.6
El Salvador	-	-	-	-	-	0.3	7.8	7.0	6.8	6.8
Guatemala	-	-	-	-	-	195.9	162.5	484.2	489.5	489.4
Honduras	-	-	-	-	-	29.7	15.1	9.1	6.4	12.4
Nicaragua	-	-	-	-	-	0.7	0.6	0.8	0.7	1.0
Panama	11.5	8.7	65.5	21.3	-42.4	227.7	414.3	534.6	-16.5	516.0
Virgin Islands, U.S.	-	-	-	-	-	-	-	-	-	-2.9
South America	687.0	698.9	57.5	169.3	192.3	13 073.5	16 646.8	30 723.6	28 745.8	31 066.6
Argentina	-153.0	92.3	49.6	28.1	27.6	1 488.2	1 223.5	1 563.5	1 593.6	1 544.6
Bolivia	-	-	-	-	-	28.9	30.9	29.3	39.9	39.8
Brazil	220.9	337.2	3.0	253.6	289.2	6 878.0	10 969.9	13 269.7	13 249.2	13 394.2
Colombia	-	-	0.2	-	-	283.3	570.1	434.6	455.4	568.4
Ecuador	-	-	-	-	-	63.9	35.9	44.0	49.5	46.0
Paraguay	-	-	0.1	-	-	7.6	8.0	8.9	10.5	8.7
Peru	-	-	0.2	-	-	341.2	374.8	537.9	683.6	766.3
Uruguay	335.8	3.2	4.2	3.6	3.5	52.0	48.5	59.5	53.6	83.3
Venezuela	-	-	-	-	-	1 981.8	1 612.9	1 297.5	1 493.2	1 455.0

Table 2. Foreign direct investment positions by country *(cont.)*
At year end

Million US dollars

	Inward					Outward				
	2015	2016	2017	2018	2019	2015	2016	2017	2018	2019
ASIA	**11 613.3**	**13 249.1**	**25 274.1**	**22 547.8**	**21 443.7**	**45 855.7**	**50 028.5**	**61 585.3**	**64 506.4**	**67 427.5**
Near and Middle East	2 646.4	2 427.1	3 465.2	2 841.9	2 629.8	21 383.7	23 986.0	27 916.5	28 014.3	30 284.8
Gulf Arabian countries	2 537.0	2 270.6	2 965.7	2 643.4	2 324.8	18 597.5	20 413.9	23 154.0	23 484.5	25 342.5
Kuwait	1 644.4	455.7	537.8	681.8	519.3	1 634.1	1 699.5	2 503.1	2 648.3	2 688.1
Qatar	539.9	1 373.0	2 136.2	1 448.7	1 423.7	821.9	950.9	1 204.0	1 084.7	1 612.5
Saudi Arabia	286.1	145.8	238.5	453.1	236.9	6 027.6	5 831.4	5 810.2	5 299.7	5 518.5
United Arab Emirates	66.7	296.1	53.2	59.8	144.9	8 955.9	10 421.0	12 093.0	12 683.9	13 515.6
Other Near and Middle East	109.4	156.5	499.5	198.5	305.0	2 786.1	3 572.1	4 762.5	4 529.8	4 942.2
Jordan	-	-	-	-	-	966.5	981.1	1 191.9	1 013.7	981.8
Other Asian countries	8 966.9	10 822.0	21 809.0	19 705.9	18 813.8	24 472.0	26 042.5	33 668.8	36 492.1	37 142.7
China	623.8	3 556.6	5 791.0	5 551.5	5 302.9	8 592.7	8 480.6	10 858.2	11 719.5	11 662.7
Hong Kong, China	45.0	692.8	-56.5	13.3	4.5	2 398.0	2 842.6	4 067.4	4 284.5	4 082.2
India	177.2	364.4	909.2	863.6	805.3	5 726.2	6 106.2	7 373.6	6 958.8	6 829.7
Indonesia	-	-	-	-	-	173.8	262.9	808.1	854.7	923.5
Iran, Islamic Republic of	25.8	58.0	68.0	65.7	65.0	1 519.2	1 316.6	1 594.3	1 595.0	1 739.4
Malaysia	-14.6	57.2	-	-	-	824.6	1 059.3	1 987.0	2 298.1	2 421.0
Philippines	-	-	-	-	-	59.9	64.0	72.4	536.9	765.7
Singapore	204.4	190.7	1 646.6	1 638.7	1 613.4	558.0	689.1	745.8	940.1	1 097.6
Chinese Taipei	254.3	334.4	432.3	868.5	834.6	67.9	80.3	69.2	76.0	89.9
Thailand	1.3	1.3	33.5	-	-	360.9	317.0	346.8	455.3	445.8
Viet Nam	-	-	0.0	-	-	451.8	553.6	749.0	776.7	792.2
AUSTRALIA, OCEANIA AND POLAR REGIONS	**218.1**	**587.2**	**786.3**	**288.3**	**326.6**	**2 190.9**	**2 266.1**	**3 056.0**	**2 886.8**	**2 906.0**
WORLD unallocated and confidential	**63 170.7**	**49 560.8**	**58 322.7**	**59 745.5**	**50 008.1**	**536.6**	**274.3**	**311.6**	**296.9**	**62.8**
European Union (EU28)	**195 587.2**	**222 702.3**	**249 993.2**	**249 624.7**	**262 248.3**	**302 584.8**	**285 252.1**	**333 321.1**	**338 330.3**	**322 564.7**
G20 countries excl. European Union	**186 284.2**	**203 789.7**	**252 424.9**	**263 704.8**	**268 819.6**	**172 077.7**	**180 722.1**	**214 731.2**	**220 270.4**	**222 902.3**
G20 OECD countries	**182 714.3**	**198 808.7**	**242 433.2**	**254 441.5**	**260 387.8**	**132 777.1**	**134 699.6**	**159 794.5**	**166 396.0**	**166 826.9**
G20 Non-OECD countries	**3 569.9**	**4 981.0**	**9 991.7**	**9 263.3**	**8 431.8**	**39 300.7**	**46 022.5**	**54 936.7**	**53 874.4**	**56 075.3**
MENA countries	**2 733.2**	**2 421.8**	**3 396.1**	**2 734.7**	**2 723.4**	**38 643.4**	**40 662.5**	**48 263.8**	**49 108.4**	**51 886.1**
ASEAN countries	**191.1**	**440.1**	**2 173.7**	**2 130.3**	**1 879.0**	**2 569.1**	**3 085.9**	**4 868.9**	**6 026.6**	**6 636.0**

- Nil

Note: Inward FDI positions are allocated according to the ultimate investing country. Detailed metadata at: *http://stats.oecd.org/OECDStat_Metadata/ShowMetadata.ashx?Dataset=FDI_CTRY_IND_SUMM*.

Source: *OECD International Direct Investment Statistics (database): https://doi.org/10.1787/idi-data-en*

Table 3. Foreign direct investment income by country

Million US dollars

	Inward					Outward				
	2015	2016	2017	2018	2019	2015	2016	2017	2018	2019
WORLD	**11 685.3**	**14 146.7**	**19 620.5**	**20 409.6**	**17 823.5**	**12 048.9**	**17 894.9**	**24 781.8**	**29 994.4**	**28 627.9**
OECD COUNTRIES	**11 788.9**	**14 015.2**	**19 607.3**	**20 383.7**	**17 613.2**	**10 457.2**	**15 165.6**	**20 785.8**	**25 314.9**	**23 525.7**
Australia	9.7	9.7	18.7	36.2	21.2	26.5	80.6	155.6	108.1	101.8
Austria	-26.1	281.6	213.3	264.5	291.3	741.6	874.8	926.8	938.9	1 085.5
Belgium	574.4	66.4	728.2	112.1	399.6	192.5	298.5	437.3	388.0	279.4
Canada	-12.4	4.6	23.5	42.4	50.5	60.8	150.6	125.4	173.1	111.9
Chile	6.4	5.6	6.1	-0.1	-0.2	5.9	12.9	524.9	734.1	1 621.0
Czech Republic	32.0	28.4	49.6	47.2	194.6	113.3	770.7	381.2	347.5	505.0
Denmark	279.7	237.1	274.0	51.7	275.9	-3.3	-11.6	9.2	15.4	8.1
Estonia	-0.9	-30.6	-2.3	-1.8	-3.8	0.9	1.3	0.9	1.6	1.2
Finland	5.3	11.6	-1.8	-0.4	20.2	121.4	170.8	170.4	73.2	78.8
France	3 357.0	2 873.2	3 337.7	4 340.4	800.3	309.1	1 606.3	1 294.6	1 626.0	1 528.3
Germany	1 897.7	1 773.7	2 181.4	1 425.3	1 209.9	2 045.9	1 826.5	2 047.3	2 621.4	3 177.0
Greece	6.1	6.5	9.3	13.5	8.0	90.3	67.0	91.8	78.7	42.1
Hungary	-118.6	30.0	-32.4	11.5	11.4	76.6	85.6	83.6	150.1	278.1
Iceland	-	-1.1	-0.7	-	-	-2.4	-41.8	1.3	0.3	-13.0
Ireland	12.9	6.9	87.6	62.3	73.1	1 656.0	1 245.0	1 482.7	1 676.6	1 505.1
Israel	-0.7	-0.5	1.8	4.2	0.1	42.2	130.5	98.8	211.6	197.1
Italy	-	-	-	-	-	-	-	-	-	-
Japan	170.1	248.4	356.9	224.7	139.5	-8.5	47.7	66.1	60.2	121.1
Korea	71.9	86.3	149.8	97.1	85.7	-0.4	13.6	26.0	8.6	-29.6
Latvia	-0.2	-0.1	0.0	0.1	0.0	-0.1	0.4	3.3	4.3	4.1
Lithuania	0.0	0.0	0.0	-0.1	0.0	0.0	1.5	1.4	1.7	0.7
Luxembourg	1 250.4	1 273.0	3 378.2	3 221.1	1 348.7	2 436.2	1 625.9	1 308.1	1 725.0	2 226.9
Mexico	-7.3	-2.6	-0.5	-3.0	-1.2	68.5	108.6	26.1	-38.2	100.9
Netherlands	2 538.2	4 379.8	4 197.2	6 244.2	8 474.7	-2 109.1	1 874.7	4 085.7	7 844.9	4 349.8
New Zealand	0.1	0.2	0.1	0.0	-0.1	4.4	10.5	8.9	4.7	5.6
Norway	-5.6	-15.9	-61.8	11.4	54.3	74.5	-13.7	44.1	18.5	36.9
Poland	0.4	1.1	0.7	-2.0	0.3	995.5	1 134.0	795.3	590.6	612.9
Portugal	25.8	56.6	13.6	65.3	93.7	93.7	-11.0	113.7	128.4	202.9
Slovak Republic	2.6	0.9	0.5	-0.1	0.4	99.3	95.0	117.7	174.3	73.6
Slovenia	39.2	50.8	0.1	1.0	0.9	76.6	94.3	116.3	140.0	108.2
Spain	715.4	425.1	827.1	379.8	174.2	1 423.4	1 093.8	2 679.2	2 892.6	2 993.5
Sweden	209.9	188.1	144.5	292.8	244.8	203.1	120.5	64.7	107.2	163.3
Switzerland	709.8	615.9	1 619.3	1 033.9	1 121.8	135.5	290.0	235.1	616.6	481.3
Turkey	3.7	5.5	-2.3	-2.5	-2.2	342.1	471.5	667.7	473.7	145.2
United Kingdom	-181.3	1 007.8	1 545.7	2 100.7	2 339.1	394.2	1 120.2	1 677.0	695.4	745.3
United States	223.2	391.3	543.9	310.1	186.5	750.7	-178.2	918.9	721.9	675.7
EUROPE	**11 448.6**	**13 385.7**	**18 490.0**	**19 863.7**	**17 192.7**	**10 370.5**	**16 041.7**	**20 709.4**	**25 254.3**	**22 558.5**
Bulgaria	1.0	10.3	0.3	0.6	-0.1	224.0	225.2	237.0	252.4	323.5
Croatia	-0.5	-0.5	-0.1	0.6	0.1	20.8	92.9	236.9	242.6	248.8
Cyprus	-18.7	-1.0	3.3	5.2	10.3	-1.3	-0.8	-0.6	0.5	-0.5
Malta	18.1	28.3	-8.1	10.4	-10.0	-49.1	-10.4	-25.9	-40.0	-34.7
Romania	-1.1	-1.9	2.5	14.9	28.2	175.9	270.5	420.2	358.4	433.9
Russian Federation	47.1	7.6	-12.3	129.5	48.3	208.0	475.6	811.4	914.0	781.3
Ukraine	-0.5	0.1	-0.2	-0.1	-0.3	-14.3	11.8	-8.4	0.7	23.3
AFRICA	**-14.5**	**-14.7**	**-4.2**	**-31.4**	**-42.9**	**504.0**	**495.5**	**736.8**	**905.9**	**767.9**
Northern Africa	-9.7	-3.6	0.6	-30.1	-40.2	145.3	236.4	324.3	335.9	450.4
Algeria	-0.6	-0.6	-0.1	-0.8	-0.1	-75.3	36.2	95.9	39.0	58.2
Egypt	-9.6	-0.4	0.4	0.1	0.1	195.1	119.6	104.0	101.4	228.0
Libya	0.4	-1.8	0.8	-15.6	-28.2	-2.7	-0.3	-2.6	81.0	-1.2
Morocco	0.1	-0.7	-0.5	-0.4	0.0	5.7	42.8	73.6	50.6	80.2
Tunisia	0.0	-0.2	-0.1	-13.4	-12.0	22.5	38.2	53.3	63.9	85.2
Other African countries	-4.8	-11.1	-4.8	-1.4	-2.7	358.7	259.1	412.6	570.0	317.5
Nigeria	-0.9	-0.5	0.0	1.0	0.9	19.7	-37.1	33.4	22.4	48.8
South Africa	-5.0	-6.7	-3.2	-2.9	-2.8	118.9	70.0	67.2	21.8	75.0
AMERICA	**218.5**	**383.9**	**564.2**	**210.1**	**413.7**	**54.8**	**-690.1**	**1 063.7**	**1 565.2**	**3 267.9**
Northern America	210.7	395.9	567.3	352.5	237.0	811.5	-27.6	1 044.3	895.0	787.6
Central America and Caribbean countries	-0.4	-26.7	-25.5	-45.2	-23.7	-42.8	64.3	111.0	28.8	148.9
Bahamas	0.0	-	-	-	-	-	-	-	-	-
Bermuda	0.4	-23.2	0.1	-0.3	0.0	-0.2	-23.4	0.9	7.3	0.0
Cayman Islands	-0.6	5.5	-22.3	-32.4	-27.1	-	-	-	-0.7	-0.8
Costa Rica	-0.1	0.0	0.0	-	0.0	5.6	18.8	1.1	2.0	-6.4
El Salvador	-	-	-	-	-	0.0	0.0	0.0	0.0	0.0
Guatemala	-0.9	-	-	-	-	11.2	31.9	18.6	23.7	15.5
Honduras	-	-	-	-	-	1.6	1.0	0.1	-5.8	0.1
Nicaragua	-	-	-	-	-	0.0	0.0	-	0.0	-
Panama	2.0	0.2	0.0	0.0	0.0	-135.1	-96.4	33.4	29.1	11.9
Virgin Islands, U.S.	-	-	-	-	-	0.0	-	-	-	-
South America	8.1	14.7	22.3	-97.2	200.4	-713.9	-726.8	-91.6	641.4	2 331.5
Argentina	-1.8	-2.8	-2.6	-2.5	-0.8	143.5	179.1	119.7	93.9	119.6
Bolivia	0.0	0.0	-0.1	0.0	-	9.2	3.4	0.1	0.0	-0.2
Brazil	9.2	20.3	28.5	-84.9	203.4	-731.6	-714.0	-330.5	-3.1	484.7
Colombia	-0.4	-0.4	-0.1	0.0	-0.1	-10.4	60.3	-8.8	-19.3	68.4
Ecuador	-0.2	0.0	0.0	0.0	0.0	0.9	5.2	0.1	1.5	-0.6
Paraguay	-	-	0.0	0.0	0.0	-1.8	-0.5	0.3	-0.2	-1.8
Peru	-0.4	-0.5	0.0	0.1	0.2	3.4	-7.9	-1.2	33.5	35.2
Uruguay	-4.3	-7.3	-5.4	-9.6	-2.0	0.0	-1.3	-3.3	-10.1	-2.8
Venezuela	-0.3	-0.1	-4.1	-0.4	0.0	-134.6	-263.6	-392.0	-188.9	8.0

Table 3. Foreign direct investment income by country *(cont.)*

Million US dollars

	Inward					Outward				
	2015	2016	2017	2018	2019	2015	2016	2017	2018	2019
ASIA	**24.2**	**383.5**	**553.0**	**330.9**	**238.7**	**1 088.6**	**1 956.7**	**2 108.4**	**2 155.3**	**1 923.2**
Near and Middle East	-215.9	10.6	7.6	11.2	8.8	200.7	318.7	487.2	323.2	275.0
Gulf Arabian countries	-215.3	11.1	5.9	7.1	8.7	152.6	187.1	397.9	47.5	65.5
Kuwait	-19.3	0.0	0.0	1.6	1.1	0.4	0.1	294.4	1.9	30.7
Qatar	7.4	7.0	6.8	8.0	7.1	20.9	12.0	-19.4	-46.6	-45.0
Saudi Arabia	-0.3	-0.2	-0.2	0.0	-0.1	84.2	137.9	53.4	31.4	43.1
United Arab Emirates	-203.4	4.4	-0.7	-2.5	1.1	46.7	37.5	41.6	60.7	29.7
Other Near and Middle East	-0.6	-0.5	1.8	4.1	0.1	48.1	131.6	89.3	275.7	209.5
Jordan	-	-	-	0.0	0.0	2.1	-0.2	-1.1	31.4	-2.0
Other Asian countries	240.1	372.9	545.3	319.7	229.9	888.0	1 638.0	1 621.1	1 832.1	1 648.2
China	-1.6	2.7	-20.8	-12.3	-7.5	463.3	809.5	1 010.9	962.2	899.4
Hong Kong, China	-4.6	8.5	10.5	6.9	5.4	-0.9	154.0	135.5	250.7	200.1
India	-5.4	-1.9	-2.9	-2.8	-0.5	122.2	221.5	209.2	237.6	175.4
Indonesia	0.1	-0.1	0.0	-0.1	-0.1	3.1	27.8	11.4	10.3	5.2
Iran, Islamic Republic of	0.1	0.4	0.3	1.6	0.5	1.4	12.3	-93.5	-87.3	-15.3
Malaysia	-0.3	-0.5	-0.6	-0.1	-0.1	58.7	84.2	42.5	7.9	-7.2
Philippines	0.0	0.0	-0.1	-0.1	-0.1	1.4	0.3	2.4	2.4	2.7
Singapore	11.4	12.2	45.5	1.1	-3.4	42.4	72.2	26.9	49.1	-12.2
Chinese Taipei	-0.2	2.0	1.3	-0.8	2.1	3.7	3.5	-0.8	1.4	7.3
Thailand	-0.7	0.4	0.1	-0.2	0.6	15.7	23.6	76.6	54.3	30.8
Viet Nam	-0.1	-0.1	-0.1	-0.2	-0.2	95.2	121.1	53.1	83.7	38.1
AUSTRALIA, OCEANIA AND POLAR REGIONS	**9.9**	**9.8**	**18.9**	**36.3**	**21.1**	**31.0**	**91.1**	**163.5**	**112.8**	**107.4**
WORLD unallocated and confidential	**-1.2**	**-1.6**	**-1.3**	**0.0**	**0.2**	**0.1**	**0.1**	**0.1**	**0.9**	**3.0**
European Union (EU28)	**10 618.6**	**12 703.0**	**16 950.4**	**18 660.8**	**15 985.8**	**9 327.4**	**14 661.6**	**18 756.0**	**23 035.6**	**20 940.8**
G20 countries excl. European Union	**5 574.5**	**6 416.8**	**8 141.3**	**8 595.7**	**5 069.0**	**4 400.5**	**6 454.8**	**8 957.4**	**8 718.5**	**9 261.2**
G20 OECD countries	**5 532.3**	**6 397.8**	**8 154.8**	**8 571.6**	**4 829.2**	**3 988.9**	**5 247.4**	**7 004.6**	**6 450.2**	**6 677.6**
G20 Non-OECD countries	**42.1**	**19.0**	**-13.6**	**24.0**	**239.8**	**411.5**	**1 207.4**	**1 952.8**	**2 268.2**	**2 583.6**
MENA countries	**-225.0**	**7.5**	**6.4**	**-23.0**	**-31.5**	**304.6**	**425.1**	**722.2**	**429.4**	**513.4**
ASEAN countries	**10.1**	**12.0**	**46.5**	**2.6**	**-1.5**	**216.5**	**329.3**	**213.0**	**207.8**	**57.4**

- Nil

Note: Detailed metadata at: *http://stats.oecd.org/OECDStat_Metadata/ShowMetadata.ashx?Dataset=FDI_CTRY_IND_SUMM.*

Source: *OECD International Direct Investment Statistics (database): https://doi.org/10.1787/idi-data-en*

ITALY

Table 4. Foreign direct investment flows by industrial sector

Million US dollars

	Inward					Outward				
	2015	2016	2017	2018	2019	2015	2016	2017	2018	2019
All FDI activities	**19 630.8**	**28 440.8**	**23 995.9**	**37 658.7**	**18 152.1**	**21 639.9**	**16 164.8**	**24 478.4**	**32 797.4**	**19 586.5**
Agriculture, forestry and fishing	**-334.4**	**448.3**	**408.0**	**67.9**	**289.0**	**3.5**	**50.6**	**-73.7**	**59.8**	**-294.8**
Mining and quarrying	**459.4**	**-372.5**	**2 196.2**	**-148.2**	**157.0**	**-3 491.1**	**-3 407.4**	**2 068.5**	**-240.2**	**278.7**
Extraction activities	472.5	-372.5	2 198.1	-148.2	157.0	-3 712.2	-3 380.1	2 068.1	-238.4	285.4
Manufacturing	**1 606.9**	**5 184.9**	**9 130.0**	**8 480.8**	**2 695.2**	**12 894.0**	**10 408.6**	**7 250.6**	**12 290.5**	**5 066.6**
of which:										
Food products, beverages and tobacco	183.7	1 721.0	-76.2	-315.4	-708.7	1 109.6	339.8	831.6	524.1	624.9
Textiles, wood and paper products; printing	1 811.0	-1 313.9	346.6	-469.3	-56.7	942.2	-993.1	298.2	425.6	299.2
Chemical, rubber, plastic, non-metallic mineral products	1 368.8	305.6	3 882.9	-167.8	-691.6	273.6	631.4	1 092.6	3 620.7	560.2
Metal and machinery products, except electrical equipment	-163.1	277.6	2 351.7	5 906.0	1 908.0	8 661.7	4 827.0	5 549.7	4 889.0	3 579.6
Motor vehicles, trailers, semi-trailers, other transport equipment	-2 208.7	-1 448.8	179.1	2 767.5	-1 969.9	397.6	4 811.2	-200.2	738.4	688.7
Other manufacturing	615.2	5 643.4	2 445.8	759.8	4 214.1	1 509.3	792.4	-321.3	2 092.7	-686.0
Electricity, gas, steam and air conditioning supply	**599.0**	**-983.3**	**-45.7**	**886.8**	**-121.8**	**206.9**	**-3 158.1**	**1 551.2**	**3 104.9**	**341.9**
Water supply; sewerage, waste management and remediation activities	**-707.5**	**-120.8**	**-20.8**	**-36.5**	**-21.8**	**9.7**	**-3.3**	**29.5**	**-30.6**	**0.8**
Construction	**-327.2**	**-847.8**	**137.9**	**111.4**	**-264.2**	**582.7**	**2 636.5**	**3 765.0**	**8 623.1**	**4 039.6**
Services	**16 485.8**	**23 288.9**	**10 311.5**	**26 329.4**	**13 545.0**	**11 143.2**	**10 257.5**	**10 110.3**	**9 131.1**	**10 511.3**
Wholesale and retail trade; repair of motor vehicles and motorcycles	1 339.3	3 673.6	3 717.7	-1 435.3	2 023.3	-1 231.2	2 075.6	110.4	3 835.6	3 098.5
Transportation and storage	1 190.6	225.0	-769.7	1 304.8	2 487.6	248.9	-293.0	807.3	-790.6	177.4
Accommodation and food service activities	-66.1	657.5	-330.8	179.8	-463.4	8.2	-30.7	-356.4	183.3	-660.6
Information and communication	10 835.8	509.6	182.4	-7.0	11 365.7	-314.9	-849.3	393.9	2 619.2	1 373.8
Financial and insurance activities	7 734.5	9 882.5	4 731.8	4 367.0	-6 550.7	11 478.5	9 897.5	6 914.3	-3 714.3	-2 100.4
Activities of holding companies	85.3	-4 279.2	284.0	4 778.1	-312.4	-3 348.5	3 014.9	325.5	-128.9	-4 125.8
Real estate activities	-2 424.5	945.1	1 126.0	-391.7	1 248.8	631.1	-241.0	254.0	383.7	14.2
Professional, scientific and technical activities	-3 489.4	5 933.2	228.4	19 342.8	5 717.0	-153.4	1 815.2	1 100.2	2 679.2	8 271.4
Administrative and support service activities	1 752.7	1 255.2	680.7	3 142.4	-2 222.2	339.8	-1 946.1	872.3	912.1	385.1
Public administration; activities of households and of extraterritorial organisations	-	-	-	138.8	-0.4	74.3	57.4	-19.8	2 929.4	-297.7
Education	0.0	-0.1	-	-	-	0.8	-2.2	-1.9	-7.3	1.7
Human health and social work activities	-11.5	19.4	18.1	30.0	17.5	17.0	-39.4	-25.9	-72.0	96.7
Arts, entertainment and recreation	-594.3	-118.0	686.4	-471.6	-118.7	32.5	-187.6	55.2	172.7	145.4
Other services	218.7	305.9	40.5	129.5	40.3	11.5	1.3	6.7	0.1	5.9
Not allocated and confidential	**0.0**	**0.0**	**0.0**	**0.0**	**8.0**	**0.0**	**0.0**	**0.0**	**0.0**	**0.0**
Private real estate activities	**1 848.8**	**1 843.1**	**1 878.8**	**1 967.1**	**1 865.8**	**291.0**	**-619.7**	**-222.9**	**-141.1**	**-357.7**

- Nil

Note: Detailed metadata at: *http://stats.oecd.org/OECDStat_Metadata/ShowMetadata.ashx?Dataset=FDI_CTRY_IND_SUMM.*

Source: *OECD International Direct Investment Statistics (database): https://doi.org/10.1787/idi-data-en*

Table 5. Foreign direct investment positions by industrial sector
At year end

Million US dollars

	Inward					Outward				
	2015	2016	2017	2018	2019	2015	2016	2017	2018	2019
All FDI activities	**340 477.1**	**352 626.2**	**424 743.1**	**433 366.3**	**445 174.6**	**456 619.5**	**456 380.4**	**547 577.5**	**554 876.3**	**554 940.5**
Agriculture, forestry and fishing	**1 209.5**	**1 254.4**	**2 164.8**	**1 686.4**	**1 887.0**	**655.0**	**541.8**	**531.2**	**703.0**	**371.1**
Mining and quarrying	**3 288.1**	**2 771.2**	**3 138.5**	**3 489.9**	**3 629.5**	**-1 758.6**	**-3 435.0**	**3 665.2**	**5 888.1**	**10 336.1**
Extraction activities	3 277.0	2 771.2	3 138.5	3 489.9	3 629.5	-2 283.1	-3 599.5	3 635.6	2 656.1	2 748.5
Manufacturing	**83 141.0**	**92 095.8**	**118 455.3**	**110 046.9**	**119 560.8**	**118 515.6**	**125 553.4**	**154 183.5**	**155 568.9**	**159 613.9**
of which:										
Food products, beverages and tobacco	16 657.9	17 642.0	19 755.0	15 718.5	17 729.1	8 694.4	9 274.3	11 370.0	9 711.2	10 508.6
Textiles, wood and paper products; printing	5 754.8	2 337.0	3 644.6	2 878.9	3 588.2	5 423.8	4 137.6	4 694.3	4 731.5	5 126.4
Chemical, rubber, plastic, non-metallic mineral products	23 660.3	23 144.1	30 069.6	24 246.2	25 972.8	15 846.0	18 255.5	20 485.5	22 927.6	23 910.2
Metal and machinery products, except electrical equipment	20 160.8	21 661.9	31 012.2	32 976.4	32 325.6	62 864.3	64 057.4	77 722.6	79 111.2	82 549.4
Motor vehicles, trailers, semi-trailers, other transport equipment	9 423.0	14 758.4	18 019.1	18 780.0	21 523.5	10 925.7	14 893.1	18 215.5	16 034.4	16 156.1
Other manufacturing	7 484.4	12 552.4	15 954.8	15 446.9	18 421.7	14 761.5	14 935.4	21 695.6	23 052.9	21 363.2
Electricity, gas, steam and air conditioning supply	**4 467.9**	**4 444.9**	**6 160.7**	**4 744.1**	**5 635.6**	**5 457.5**	**6 638.7**	**5 790.1**	**7 080.1**	**7 224.6**
Water supply; sewerage, waste management and remediation activities	**517.5**	**413.7**	**453.4**	**452.1**	**372.9**	**144.9**	**157.9**	**83.3**	**66.1**	**49.6**
Construction	**4 111.8**	**3 272.6**	**4 790.3**	**4 038.6**	**2 990.6**	**32 353.9**	**36 078.0**	**43 940.9**	**50 306.4**	**52 690.6**
Services	**220 137.2**	**223 761.4**	**259 574.3**	**278 351.3**	**279 242.6**	**279 211.8**	**269 361.2**	**314 669.1**	**311 367.9**	**299 711.6**
Wholesale and retail trade; repair of motor vehicles and motorcycles	29 318.0	34 988.9	42 779.8	50 174.9	44 774.6	30 140.9	33 006.2	33 939.0	40 516.2	42 209.3
Transportation and storage	11 577.1	11 172.3	13 318.6	12 471.4	15 875.6	5 098.4	4 930.8	6 610.3	6 623.7	7 052.9
Accommodation and food service activities	1 912.5	2 493.1	2 341.2	4 290.1	3 729.4	1 651.2	1 432.5	1 374.3	2 151.0	2 029.3
Information and communication	27 928.7	25 519.3	27 943.1	28 223.5	37 857.1	6 081.8	6 088.7	5 607.9	7 035.0	9 042.1
Financial and insurance activities	56 116.2	40 681.7	45 975.5	44 374.0	46 974.5	209 645.6	203 772.1	240 929.7	226 302.8	164 808.5
Activities of holding companies	24 550.1	4 226.3	3 883.0	8 692.6	8 656.7	128 167.8	125 687.5	125 777.7	122 369.1	78 396.0
Real estate activities	12 033.5	17 142.5	22 241.1	21 734.9	21 407.7	3 536.3	3 653.9	5 273.9	5 429.5	5 490.9
Professional, scientific and technical activities	70 970.6	77 692.3	87 400.4	97 977.2	91 606.2	20 050.6	14 409.8	17 420.2	16 530.3	62 569.9
Administrative and support service activities	9 244.0	12 224.2	14 409.7	15 631.0	13 190.6	1 059.2	-798.9	106.9	1 563.7	1 650.2
Public administration; activities of households and of extraterritorial organisations	-	-	-	135.9	133.3	331.7	425.9	324.4	3 017.6	2 568.6
Education	7.8	-	-	-	-	7.8	-2.5	-1.9	7.5	10.6
Human health and social work activities	194.5	193.5	119.3	181.6	219.9	121.0	92.3	123.8	128.3	261.4
Arts, entertainment and recreation	98.5	539.0	1 427.3	1 389.9	1 790.1	1 427.3	2 255.8	2 752.8	1 727.9	1 764.1
Other services	736.0	1 114.9	1 618.4	1 766.9	1 683.4	60.2	94.7	207.9	334.7	253.8
Not allocated and confidential	**0.0**	**0.0**	**0.0**	**0.0**	**0.0**	**783.7**	**749.6**	**841.2**	**1 140.4**	**2 169.5**
Private real estate activities	**23 604.0**	**24 612.2**	**30 005.9**	**30 556.8**	**31 855.5**	**21 255.6**	**20 734.8**	**23 873.0**	**22 755.4**	**22 773.5**

- Nil

Note: Detailed metadata at: *http://stats.oecd.org/OECDStat_Metadata/ShowMetadata.ashx?Dataset=FDI_CTRY_IND_SUMM.*

Source: *OECD International Direct Investment Statistics (database): https://doi.org/10.1787/idi-data-en*

Table 6. Foreign direct investment income by industrial sector

Million US dollars

	Inward					Outward				
	2015	2016	2017	2018	2019	2015	2016	2017	2018	2019
All FDI activities	**11 685.3**	**14 146.7**	**19 620.5**	**20 409.6**	**17 823.5**	**12 048.9**	**17 894.9**	**24 781.8**	**29 994.4**	**28 627.9**
Agriculture, forestry and fishing	**-99.0**	**-40.3**	**98.7**	**27.1**	**156.6**	**4.8**	**2.8**	**34.6**	**-14.9**	**-23.4**
Mining and quarrying	**183.3**	**-184.7**	**-48.2**	**263.1**	**98.2**	**2 262.8**	**70.1**	**42.9**	**560.2**	**132.8**
Extraction activities	183.1	-184.7	-48.2	263.1	98.2	2 166.0	69.7	42.6	562.6	140.9
Manufacturing	**2 736.6**	**4 037.7**	**7 010.3**	**7 078.6**	**9 076.2**	**5 034.1**	**7 555.1**	**8 295.1**	**8 163.7**	**6 467.9**
of which:										
Food products, beverages and tobacco	639.9	831.5	879.6	1 064.8	523.2	382.1	679.5	805.8	640.0	987.0
Textiles, wood and paper products; printing	169.8	-31.8	-0.2	87.3	16.5	255.7	307.7	232.4	199.4	306.5
Chemical, rubber, plastic, non-metallic mineral products	1 511.9	2 106.2	2 587.1	2 047.2	1 895.8	1 042.5	1 987.7	1 937.5	1 765.0	1 822.2
Metal and machinery products, except electrical equipment	622.8	883.4	1 897.8	1 767.6	2 013.5	1 441.5	2 232.0	2 284.9	2 450.9	1 300.3
Motor vehicles, trailers, semi-trailers, other transport equipment	-1 126.3	-682.3	80.2	-678.1	471.0	1 036.7	1 474.4	1 713.1	1 257.8	843.4
Other manufacturing	918.6	930.7	1 565.8	2 789.7	4 156.1	875.7	873.8	1 321.4	1 850.7	1 208.5
Electricity, gas, steam and air conditioning supply	**286.2**	**-69.0**	**216.4**	**293.3**	**333.9**	**-114.9**	**-252.6**	**75.1**	**27.0**	**121.3**
Water supply; sewerage, waste management and remediation activities	**-5.7**	**-34.8**	**-16.5**	**-50.4**	**10.5**	**-0.1**	**6.0**	**-2.0**	**2.4**	**6.4**
Construction	**54.6**	**38.9**	**24.6**	**-148.8**	**-104.8**	**-827.7**	**-244.1**	**710.1**	**432.7**	**622.0**
Services	**8 529.3**	**10 398.8**	**12 335.2**	**12 946.8**	**8 252.9**	**5 690.0**	**10 757.6**	**15 626.1**	**20 823.2**	**21 300.9**
Wholesale and retail trade; repair of motor vehicles and motorcycles	2 412.6	2 352.1	3 654.4	4 057.7	4 061.8	691.9	1 077.4	1 404.3	1 990.3	2 039.3
Transportation and storage	306.2	843.4	1 031.0	1 384.4	2 332.9	-6.7	273.3	287.0	36.6	231.1
Accommodation and food service activities	100.5	37.1	-74.4	-14.4	58.0	158.9	210.0	215.2	180.8	128.0
Information and communication	345.8	1 491.4	1 078.8	969.3	1 463.3	-923.7	-343.2	192.8	66.1	323.3
Financial and insurance activities	3 952.2	2 885.8	2 731.6	1 386.0	-2 984.9	5 814.6	8 407.7	12 865.0	17 330.3	15 099.0
Activities of holding companies	948.0	210.5	189.2	609.1	326.3	388.9	1 963.1	5 422.2	8 945.3	4 666.9
Real estate activities	-791.9	1 129.1	128.8	1 576.9	883.5	184.5	142.8	370.5	281.8	125.2
Professional, scientific and technical activities	1 213.6	1 069.1	2 996.4	2 796.5	1 573.7	-381.5	861.2	169.8	632.3	3 071.0
Administrative and support service activities	732.4	694.9	844.2	1 096.6	919.0	112.0	80.2	112.5	40.8	90.2
Public administration; activities of households and of extraterritorial organisations	-	-	-	-1.0	1.9	13.9	7.2	8.6	0.4	-6.0
Education	0.2	-	-	-	-	-3.0	0.6	-1.3	0.0	0.0
Human health and social work activities	-8.7	8.7	18.1	5.9	29.8	4.2	-5.2	-9.4	-6.4	-12.5
Arts, entertainment and recreation	-91.1	-141.8	-88.3	-436.3	-176.2	16.5	45.1	9.5	259.7	205.9
Other services	357.5	28.9	14.4	125.1	90.0	8.4	0.6	1.4	10.5	6.5
Not allocated and confidential	**0.0**	**0.0**	**0.0**	**0.0**	**0.0**	**0.0**	**0.0**	**0.0**	**0.0**	**0.0**
Private real estate activities	-	-	-	-	-	-	-	-	-	-

- Nil

Note: Detailed metadata at: *http://stats.oecd.org/OECDStat_Metadata/ShowMetadata.ashx?Dataset=FDI_CTRY_IND_SUMM.*

Source: *OECD International Direct Investment Statistics (database): https://doi.org/10.1787/idi-data-en*

JAPAN

Table 1. Foreign direct investment flows by country

Million US dollars

	Inward					Outward				
	2015	2016	2017	2018	2019	2015	2016	2017	2018	2019
WORLD	**2 976.6**	**17 749.5**	**9 354.2**	**9 254.7**	**14 547.5**	**136 295.5**	**151 287.1**	**164 563.0**	**143 075.3**	**226 572.6**
OECD COUNTRIES	**-864.7**	**10 116.4**	**3 872.9**	**7 212.7**	**8 604.0**	**92 921.6**	**113 752.1**	**111 236.0**	**71 730.2**	**163 542.4**
Australia	371.0	442.2	307.6	96.9	151.8	6 725.2	4 399.5	4 549.6	2 082.3	10 967.9
Austria	7.8	11.5	35.6	7.8	-0.7	15.4	14.3	286.9	-44.7	12.5
Belgium	-29.5	70.7	-136.2	363.3	-1 437.7	923.6	1 918.5	1 200.3	1 762.6	3 319.0
Canada	-38.2	-52.4	61.4	68.6	93.4	1 217.1	676.2	937.5	2 726.9	3 369.8
Chile	2.2	1.5	2.2	3.1	3.1	80.3	-201.7	-57.3	303.7	1 257.8
Czech Republic	-	-	-6.4	1.0	-	343.9	142.2	168.3	184.8	142.8
Denmark	0.1	91.2	11.3	60.5	17.1	-214.4	-162.9	304.1	156.2	-20 697.3
Estonia	-	-	-	2.0	-	-	-	2.0	1.1	3.2
Finland	-1.1	-21.1	35.9	-444.5	-31.0	117.3	-4 089.1	831.3	589.7	-102.0
France	2 190.7	4 719.0	3 353.6	2 399.4	2 876.7	844.4	1 175.9	1 555.7	997.6	1 607.9
Germany	-4 396.8	581.7	-1 127.1	-1 575.0	-1 038.0	2 949.8	1 509.1	2 578.5	2 026.0	11 672.8
Greece	-	-	-	-	0.6	0.1	-0.4	-1.7	-3.7	-1.2
Hungary	4.9	0.4	27.0	-	-174.2	-4.6	125.9	139.9	201.9	272.4
Iceland	-0.9	-	-	1.2	-	-	-	7.3	-75.0	-37.8
Ireland	-1 235.5	511.0	-1 486.0	376.8	-104.9	-782.2	2 572.1	2 070.9	6 534.4	58 937.2
Israel	-28.7	-64.5	35.6	1 245.2	-7.6	31.7	193.5	1 074.6	22.2	2.2
Italy	257.4	24.1	98.1	-63.3	-51.5	687.2	454.7	-156.4	950.6	1 329.4
Japan	-	-	-	-	-	-	-	-	-	-
Korea	904.9	581.8	997.4	1 884.6	808.4	1 562.6	1 631.6	1 625.2	4 464.9	2 435.0
Latvia	-	-	-	-	-	-	0.7	0.4	-	-
Lithuania	-	-	-	-	-	-	-	-	-	-
Luxembourg	-1 065.2	1 004.3	1 398.5	-827.6	-118.6	1 560.3	1 020.6	6 111.6	-462.8	1 099.3
Mexico	-2.7	-	-	2.0	0.7	1 222.4	1 886.6	1 308.7	1 294.4	703.2
Netherlands	-1 233.6	-940.9	-1 363.1	-843.5	-1 435.3	7 268.4	3 585.0	14 266.4	7 961.0	1 091.7
New Zealand	-7.0	-26.3	-17.4	5.4	3.0	123.2	400.0	369.0	347.7	276.0
Norway	-139.3	-151.8	182.3	-152.5	-129.6	-33.0	340.6	-102.4	425.3	654.3
Poland	-	-	0.3	-	-	-69.6	144.6	72.5	18.1	81.6
Portugal	-	-6.2	-67.6	0.9	9.9	8.8	92.6	8.3	14.4	-8.6
Slovak Republic	-	0.9	-	2.0	-	-3.3	48.4	16.6	17.0	-11.7
Slovenia	-	-	-	-	-	26.6	-0.2	-17.7	-39.5	0.1
Spain	38.4	2.0	33.1	-226.4	-46.7	544.4	800.4	317.0	4 323.3	452.3
Sweden	-273.6	-87.4	267.3	192.6	141.5	2 479.2	247.2	1 062.0	1 344.4	1 075.6
Switzerland	-215.8	762.4	-2 499.9	-1 765.8	-3 183.4	-569.2	1 935.7	-1 543.3	-450.6	34 013.5
Turkey	-	0.4	0.8	-	0.4	442.4	509.8	562.3	330.7	636.2
United Kingdom	839.5	-1 296.8	-104.5	1 142.0	2 396.2	16 421.5	41 413.2	25 876.0	17 008.7	5 155.9
United States	3 186.3	3 958.8	3 832.9	5 255.9	9 860.3	49 001.6	50 967.7	45 812.3	16 716.7	43 831.0
EUROPE	**-5 277.3**	**5 422.5**	**-1 338.3**	**-1 327.2**	**-2 148.3**	**33 225.2**	**53 766.4**	**55 919.6**	**45 417.5**	**101 520.7**
Bulgaria	-	-	0.7	-	0.4	-	-63.0	74.8	-1.1	3.6
Croatia	-	-	-	-	-	0.2	-0.1	0.3	0.2	0.0
Cyprus	2.0	-0.4	0.4	2.4	2.5	1.4	3.0	96.7	1.6	47.9
Malta	-	1.1	0.8	0.9	-0.4	-2.1	-26.4	0.1	14.7	56.7
Romania	-	0.4	-	-	-	15.9	22.2	7.4	83.2	2.5
Russian Federation	-0.5	2.7	3.6	1.4	3.6	465.4	108.1	240.6	485.4	393.1
Ukraine	-	-	-	-	-	31.2	28.4	24.7	23.6	17.9
AFRICA	**-4.4**	**34.7**	**6.5**	**4.9**	**573.3**	**1 481.2**	**-555.5**	**1 820.5**	**1 742.6**	**-1 002.8**
Northern Africa	0.4	-	-	-	-	56.1	-15.9	140.5	58.4	117.0
Algeria	-	-	-	-	-	-	-	18.4	36.9	18.0
Egypt	0.4	-	-	-	-	46.9	-21.1	115.3	3.1	29.6
Libya	-	-	-	-	-	-	-	-	2.8	37.4
Morocco	-	-	-	-	-	9.2	5.3	6.8	15.0	32.0
Tunisia	-	-	-	-	-	-	-	-	0.5	-
Other African countries	-4.9	34.7	6.5	4.9	573.3	1 425.1	-539.6	1 680.0	1 684.2	-1 119.8
Nigeria	-	-	-	-	-	9.6	7.3	2.0	5.5	3.3
South Africa	-0.5	0.7	-3.1	-0.6	-0.5	1 037.9	928.2	1 107.4	1 410.1	-1 331.0
AMERICA	**3 454.9**	**4 833.5**	**7 292.4**	**9 273.8**	**12 622.9**	**59 489.2**	**77 855.5**	**58 473.4**	**43 968.7**	**60 643.7**
Northern America	3 148.1	3 906.5	3 894.3	5 324.5	9 953.8	50 218.7	51 643.9	46 749.8	19 443.6	47 200.8
Central America and Caribbean countries	267.5	944.8	3 412.6	3 946.3	2 674.8	9 204.4	25 455.0	12 755.2	21 972.4	8 781.2
Bahamas	2.0	-	2.3	-	1.9	25.1	-281.7	34.9	80.8	21.2
Bermuda	78.7	-18.2	20.7	-78.0	18.4	310.4	-315.2	7 278.9	104.2	-130.1
Cayman Islands	140.9	748.6	3 315.7	3 552.8	2 276.4	7 855.2	20 485.0	4 131.7	17 297.2	2 608.6
Costa Rica	-	-	-	-	-	-	-1.1	1.0	0.3	8.2
El Salvador	-	-	-	-	-	1.9	2.3	0.9	0.2	0.3
Guatemala	-	-	-	-	-	-	-	-	-	-
Honduras	-	-	-	-	-	-	-	-	-	-
Nicaragua	-	-	-	-	-	-	-	-	-	-
Panama	7.0	14.2	7.3	26.6	6.1	-474.0	91.6	-226.5	124.0	390.7
Virgin Islands, U.S.	-	1.8	-3.1	-	8.8	1.4	-2.1	-1.5	1.2	1.6
South America	39.3	-17.8	-14.4	3.0	-5.7	66.0	756.7	-1 031.6	2 552.7	4 661.7
Argentina	-7.0	-19.2	-14.1	-8.3	-8.8	18.5	122.4	583.1	450.6	174.3
Bolivia	-	-	-	-	-	-0.4	-	-	-	-
Brazil	44.6	-	-2.6	8.2	-	-204.7	835.9	-1 618.9	1 724.8	2 565.9
Colombia	-	-	-	-	-	21.5	5.6	29.9	45.8	43.1
Ecuador	-	-	-	-	-	-	-0.7	-	1.2	39.8
Paraguay	-	-	-	-	-	-12.0	-7.4	30.0	-4.2	0.6
Peru	-0.4	-	-	-	-	100.5	94.6	158.8	222.9	596.4
Uruguay	-	-	-	-	-	207.1	35.0	-113.2	-191.9	-8.3
Venezuela	-	-	-	-	-	-144.7	-127.1	-44.0	-0.5	-7.9

Table 1. Foreign direct investment flows by country *(cont.)*

Million US dollars

	Inward					Outward				
	2015	2016	2017	2018	2019	2015	2016	2017	2018	2019
ASIA	**4 426.9**	**7 009.9**	**3 156.1**	**1 220.2**	**3 320.3**	**34 397.8**	**14 223.4**	**41 919.8**	**51 414.2**	**55 081.0**
Near and Middle East	38.6	43.1	112.8	1 401.7	187.4	522.0	682.2	1 959.1	778.5	176.5
Gulf Arabian countries	66.6	107.5	77.1	156.5	195.0	489.3	489.7	884.6	754.3	172.8
Kuwait	-	-	-	0.3	-	10.3	1.8	1.6	1.9	1.8
Qatar	-	-	-	-	-	164.1	40.0	72.5	13.0	16.4
Saudi Arabia	53.0	58.6	55.4	77.0	63.9	482.5	267.4	173.2	406.4	-230.0
United Arab Emirates	13.6	48.9	17.1	76.7	131.1	-168.9	147.6	644.9	407.2	147.6
Other Near and Middle East	-28.0	-64.5	35.6	1 245.2	-7.6	32.7	192.5	1 074.6	24.1	3.7
Jordan	-	-	-	-	-	0.0	-	-	-	-
Other Asian countries	4 388.3	6 966.9	3 043.3	-181.5	3 132.9	33 875.8	13 541.1	39 960.6	50 635.8	54 904.5
China	83.7	278.7	612.7	454.8	375.1	9 454.8	9 811.3	12 023.4	11 650.1	12 831.5
Hong Kong, China	872.3	1 226.8	-164.4	724.7	1 354.0	2 636.2	1 967.3	2 910.8	2 565.2	1 663.6
India	24.7	0.4	5.6	-4.6	3.3	-1 055.2	4 104.3	1 619.8	3 295.3	5 078.6
Indonesia	20.8	38.9	195.8	-2.6	2.3	3 150.4	2 985.4	3 534.9	3 220.7	8 390.2
Iran, Islamic Republic of	-	-	-	-	-	1.4	2.7	-	2.5	-
Malaysia	46.6	15.7	38.1	19.5	73.7	2 970.7	1 458.4	1 140.4	1 145.3	278.5
Philippines	12.1	-4.5	17.7	12.5	36.6	1 529.0	2 288.1	1 111.5	1 109.3	1 776.5
Singapore	1 845.6	2 450.3	484.6	-3 771.6	-655.5	7 007.6	-18 361.5	6 910.5	13 460.4	13 587.7
Chinese Taipei	547.8	2 281.6	788.7	468.5	1 119.2	444.9	1 411.2	1 096.3	1 598.3	1 305.0
Thailand	43.3	102.1	72.9	47.4	23.0	3 760.2	4 085.4	5 455.7	5 561.0	4 109.2
Viet Nam	0.3	1.7	0.1	1.0	1.6	1 445.5	1 658.9	2 022.5	1 944.2	2 508.9
AUSTRALIA, OCEANIA AND POLAR REGIONS	**376.5**	**449.0**	**237.0**	**116.9**	**173.7**	**7 703.4**	**5 998.5**	**5 456.6**	**477.3**	**10 269.9**
WORLD unallocated and confidential	**0.0**	**0.0**	**0.5**	**-33.9**	**5.6**	**-1.3**	**-1.2**	**973.2**	**55.0**	**60.0**
European Union (EU28)	**-4 894.4**	**4 665.4**	**971.8**	**571.5**	**1 005.9**	**33 132.5**	**50 948.3**	**56 872.1**	**43 639.4**	**65 543.8**
G20 countries excl. European Union	**3 530.9**	**9 319.6**	**8 273.6**	**9 736.5**	**15 537.5**	**94 423.8**	**123 787.0**	**102 312.6**	**71 242.3**	**109 581.9**
G20 OECD countries	**3 312.1**	**8 958.8**	**7 420.3**	**9 211.2**	**15 098.5**	**81 074.5**	**104 624.1**	**84 649.3**	**48 598.8**	**81 709.3**
G20 Non-OECD countries	**218.8**	**360.7**	**853.3**	**525.3**	**439.0**	**13 349.4**	**19 162.9**	**17 663.3**	**22 643.5**	**27 872.7**
MENA countries	**67.8**	**107.5**	**77.1**	**156.5**	**195.0**	**545.4**	**473.8**	**1 025.1**	**814.1**	**291.4**
ASEAN countries	**1 967.4**	**2 605.7**	**809.2**	**-3 691.6**	**-515.8**	**20 610.6**	**-5 621.8**	**20 469.8**	**26 904.2**	**31 273.3**

- Nil

Note: Detailed metadata at: *http://stats.oecd.org/OECDStat_Metadata/ShowMetadata.ashx?Dataset=FDI_CTRY_IND_SUMM.*

Source: *OECD International Direct Investment Statistics (database): https://doi.org/10.1787/idi-data-en*

JAPAN

Table 2. Foreign direct investment positions by country
At year end

Million US dollars

	Inward					Outward				
	2015	2016	2017	2018	2019	2015	2016	2017	2018	2019
WORLD	..	..	**202 441.1**	**204 523.6**	**220 784.8**	**1 228 766.5**	**1 315 221.1**	**1 497 525.0**	**1 568 765.7**	**1 769 193.4**
OECD COUNTRIES	..	..	..	..	..	**825 579.1**	**886 155.2**	**1 005 386.9**	**1 032 678.4**	**1 178 506.8**
Australia	..	..	667.9	919.3	926.8	66 927.8	65 442.8	68 041.5	65 321.2	71 051.5
Austria	..	..	..	..	..	..	..	..	..	..
Belgium	..	..	1 311.4	881.6	3 086.9	16 904.9	17 439.5	20 514.5	21 236.0	25 460.5
Canada	..	..	1 378.9	1 386.7	1 560.3	16 075.6	15 840.7	16 439.6	17 070.1	20 665.9
Chile	..	..	..	..	..	..	..	..	..	..
Czech Republic	..	..	..	..	..	..	..	..	..	..
Denmark	..	..	..	..	..	..	..	..	..	..
Estonia	..	..	..	..	..	..	..	..	..	..
Finland	..	..	..	..	..	..	..	..	..	..
France	..	..	39 072.7	44 718.6	45 400.1	12 369.6	12 799.6	15 330.6	15 516.2	16 244.8
Germany	..	..	8 109.0	10 385.3	10 470.0	17 169.5	18 057.7	23 074.2	22 467.0	33 978.7
Greece	..	..	..	..	..	..	..	..	..	..
Hungary	..	..	..	..	..	..	..	..	..	..
Iceland	..	..	..	..	..	..	..	..	..	..
Ireland	..	..	..	..	..	..	..	..	..	..
Israel	..	..	..	..	..	..	..	..	..	..
Italy	..	..	632.4	575.2	755.4	3 466.3	3 621.4	3 395.0	4 140.7	5 361.8
Japan	..	..	..	370.1	373.7	-	..	-	-	-
Korea	..	..	6 243.0	6 771.2	8 830.5	31 428.7	32 028.8	36 771.6	38 372.1	38 869.9
Latvia	..	..	..	..	..	..	..	..	..	..
Lithuania	..	..	..	..	..	..	..	..	..	..
Luxembourg	..	..	4 584.4	4 790.2	4 893.0	10 231.1	9 532.4	15 162.9	12 698.2	13 624.7
Mexico	..	..	234.6	259.8	256.8	7 357.9	8 794.5	10 377.8	11 913.7	13 272.2
Netherlands	..	..	8 130.9	6 573.9	6 483.6	99 814.4	94 713.0	114 317.0	116 814.4	116 189.0
New Zealand	..	..	338.8	342.2	313.7	3 060.7	3 396.2	3 730.2	3 909.9	3 808.0
Norway	..	..	..	..	..	..	..	..	..	..
Poland	..	..	..	..	..	..	..	..	..	..
Portugal	..	..	..	..	..	..	..	..	..	..
Slovak Republic	..	..	..	..	..	..	..	..	..	..
Slovenia	..	..	..	..	..	..	..	..	..	..
Spain	..	..	-182.5	-881.5	-212.7	2 396.2	2 910.4	3 206.4	7 358.4	7 356.6
Sweden	..	..	425.4	495.4	624.7	4 676.6	4 336.6	5 572.4	7 694.0	7 732.8
Switzerland	..	..	9 805.8	10 379.7	10 047.8	6 071.3	8 285.1	8 082.2	5 909.1	33 893.3
Turkey	..	..	..	..	..	..	..	..	..	..
United Kingdom	..	..	6 362.6	2 913.4	-3 385.3	86 153.6	118 135.2	151 633.6	154 551.4	163 593.5
United States	..	..	71 722.9	59 144.4	76 146.2	413 342.0	445 853.6	479 995.3	487 940.2	518 490.4
EUROPE	..	..	**83 039.9**	**87 743.7**	**83 265.0**	**286 386.4**	**312 439.5**	**387 489.8**	**408 444.3**	**515 254.9**
Bulgaria	..	..	..	..	..	..	..	..	..	..
Croatia	..	..	..	..	..	..	..	..	..	..
Cyprus	..	..	..	..	..	..	..	..	..	..
Malta	..	..	..	..	..	..	..	..	..	..
Romania	..	..	..	..	..	..	..	..	..	..
Russian Federation	..	..	51.4	52.7	55.1	1 806.0	1 503.9	1 576.5	1 523.4	2 194.5
Ukraine	..	..	..	..	..	..	..	..	..	..
AFRICA	..	..	**92.7**	**92.7**	**103.3**	**8 898.2**	**10 008.6**	**7 793.2**	**8 921.7**	**6 069.6**
Northern Africa	..	..	..	..	..	..	..	..	..	..
Algeria	..	..	..	..	..	..	..	..	..	..
Egypt	..	..	..	..	..	..	..	..	..	..
Libya	..	..	..	..	..	..	..	..	..	..
Morocco	..	..	..	..	..	..	..	..	..	..
Tunisia	..	..	..	..	..	..	..	..	..	..
Other African countries	..	..	..	..	..	..	..	..	..	..
Nigeria	..	..	..	..	..	..	..	..	..	..
South Africa	..	..	3.8	4.9	5.2	7 154.5	8 229.6	6 199.5	7 103.7	4 437.2
AMERICA	..	..	**78 573.0**	**67 867.3**	**84 321.4**	**499 646.7**	**549 724.5**	**596 208.4**	**618 796.8**	**662 693.2**
Northern America	..	..	73 101.8	60 531.1	77 706.5	429 417.5	461 694.3	496 434.9	505 010.3	539 156.2
Central America and Caribbean countries	..	..	..	..	..	..	..	..	..	..
Bahamas	..	..	..	..	..	..	..	..	..	..
Bermuda	..	..	..	..	..	..	..	..	..	..
Cayman Islands	..	..	5 423.7	9 012.1	7 757.6	15 359.0	31 340.5	35 222.3	46 565.8	45 982.9
Costa Rica	..	..	..	..	..	..	..	..	..	..
El Salvador	..	..	..	..	..	..	..	..	..	..
Guatemala	..	..	..	..	..	..	..	..	..	..
Honduras	..	..	..	..	..	..	..	..	..	..
Nicaragua	..	..	..	..	..	..	..	..	..	..
Panama	..	..	..	..	..	..	..	..	..	..
Virgin Islands, U.S.	..	..	..	..	..	..	..	..	..	..
South America	..	..	..	..	..	..	..	..	..	..
Argentina	..	..	..	..	..	..	..	..	..	..
Bolivia	..	..	..	..	..	..	..	..	..	..
Brazil	..	..	-1 169.7	-3 147.8	-2 799.3	24 763.5	24 467.1	21 659.2	21 265.6	22 906.7
Colombia	..	..	..	..	..	..	..	..	..	..
Ecuador	..	..	..	..	..	..	..	..	..	..
Paraguay	..	..	..	..	..	..	..	..	..	..
Peru	..	..	..	..	..	..	..	..	..	..
Uruguay	..	..	..	..	..	..	..	..	..	..
Venezuela	..	..	..	..	..	..	..	..	..	..

Table 2. Foreign direct investment positions by country *(cont.)*
At year end

Million US dollars

	Inward					Outward				
	2015	2016	2017	2018	2019	2015	2016	2017	2018	2019
ASIA	..	..	**38 398.7**	**47 335.1**	**51 610.3**	**359 992.3**	**369 450.9**	**429 113.7**	**460 081.1**	**507 260.3**
Near and Middle East	..	..	1 290.4	-522.1	-507.1	6 779.5	6 990.5	9 012.6	8 597.7	8 862.5
Gulf Arabian countries	..	..	..	..	..	..	..	..	..	..
Kuwait	..	..	..	..	..	..	..	..	..	..
Qatar	..	..	..	..	..	..	..	..	..	..
Saudi Arabia	..	..	-778.3	-3 159.2	-4 018.1	4 921.6	4 850.9	4 897.0	5 202.8	4 725.4
United Arab Emirates	..	..	1 430.4	563.4	533.4	280.5	563.6	1 445.3	1 976.5	2 135.4
Other Near and Middle East	..	..	..	..	..	..	..	..	..	..
Jordan	..	..	..	..	..	..	..	..	..	..
Other Asian countries	..	..	37 108.3	47 857.3	52 117.5	353 212.8	362 460.4	420 101.1	451 483.4	498 397.8
China	..	..	1 593.8	2 339.1	2 654.9	107 575.6	108 230.4	117 568.0	121 165.3	127 517.2
Hong Kong, China	..	..	6 541.9	7 627.8	9 412.3	23 908.3	27 538.7	29 957.1	31 958.3	33 909.1
India	..	..	164.4	189.2	199.8	14 089.4	17 934.7	22 145.1	24 279.9	27 917.6
Indonesia	..	..	30.2	26.4	42.5	24 414.0	27 001.5	30 343.0	31 155.3	40 228.6
Iran, Islamic Republic of	..	..	..	..	..	6.1	8.8	9.1	11.8	12.0
Malaysia	..	..	292.3	306.5	225.6	13 358.2	12 618.5	14 096.4	16 335.4	16 973.7
Philippines	..	..	64.8	96.8	118.1	12 303.3	13 740.9	15 023.0	14 444.1	15 690.0
Singapore	..	..	13 939.3	21 031.3	20 225.3	48 957.0	39 563.3	59 361.9	71 573.3	81 874.3
Chinese Taipei	..	..	7 967.4	8 813.8	9 647.5	11 307.9	12 359.6	14 382.2	14 678.2	15 656.9
Thailand	..	..	135.0	121.6	175.7	50 019.5	53 797.8	61 409.8	66 729.9	75 138.9
Viet Nam	..	..	1.5	3.9	3.9	13 146.6	14 517.8	15 621.7	16 827.7	19 446.2
AUSTRALIA, OCEANIA AND POLAR REGIONS	..	..	**1 171.9**	**1 453.2**	**1 452.8**	**73 839.9**	**73 593.6**	**76 915.9**	**72 517.7**	**77 911.1**
WORLD unallocated and confidential	..	..	**1 164.8**	**31.6**	**32.1**	**2.9**	**4.0**	**4.1**	**4.2**	**4.2**
European Union (EU28)	..	..	..	..	..	**272 982.7**	**298 349.4**	**373 327.7**	**394 421.8**	**468 524.5**
G20 countries excl. European Union	..	..	..	..	..	..	..	..	..	..
G20 OECD countries	..	..	..	..	..	..	..	..	..	..
G20 Non-OECD countries	..	..	..	..	..	..	..	..	..	..
MENA countries	..	..	..	..	..	..	..	..	..	..
ASEAN countries	..	..	..	..	..	**163 967.2**	**163 435.0**	**198 170.1**	**219 933.6**	**252 971.6**

- Nil; .. Not available

Note: Inward FDI positions are allocated according to the ultimate investing country. Inward FDI positions by immediate counterpart country are available for more geographic details and for 2014 onwards in the *OECD FDI database according to BMD4*. Detailed metadata at: *http://stats.oecd.org/OECDStat_Metadata/ShowMetadata.ashx?Dataset=FDI_CTRY_IND_SUMM.*

Source: *OECD International Direct Investment Statistics (database): https://doi.org/10.1787/idi-data-en*

Table 3. Foreign direct investment income by country

Million US dollars

	Inward					Outward				
	2015	2016	2017	2018	2019	2015	2016	2017	2018	2019
WORLD	**23 857.9**	**32 634.0**	**33 301.9**	**34 220.8**	**34 800.5**	**96 358.7**	**105 867.5**	**120 205.2**	**128 406.9**	**132 230.5**
OECD COUNTRIES	**19 930.5**	**28 694.7**	**28 043.9**	**28 016.5**	**29 131.3**	**53 905.8**	**57 586.0**	**61 302.6**	**65 286.4**	**67 385.6**
Australia	150.4	93.4	106.5	50.7	118.5	1 997.5	3 452.5	7 919.0	8 236.8	9 478.3
Austria	..	..	..	..	..	..	..	..	..	..
Belgium	107.2	89.9	162.1	163.8	194.9	711.8	1 007.3	974.8	1 254.3	1 377.7
Canada	-28.0	12.0	62.3	79.8	80.5	1 138.3	1 097.7	1 651.2	1 500.4	1 559.1
Chile	..	..	..	..	..	..	..	..	..	..
Czech Republic	..	..	..	..	..	..	..	..	..	..
Denmark	..	..	..	..	..	..	..	..	..	..
Estonia	..	..	..	..	..	..	..	..	..	..
Finland	..	..	..	..	..	..	..	..	..	..
France	4 387.7	5 341.1	5 318.0	4 859.8	4 949.9	768.1	605.5	672.8	808.0	822.0
Germany	1 151.1	1 124.8	1 852.4	1 479.1	954.9	964.5	941.5	2 180.2	1 993.8	2 778.8
Greece	..	..	..	..	..	..	..	..	..	..
Hungary	..	..	..	..	..	..	..	..	..	..
Iceland	..	..	..	..	..	..	..	..	..	..
Ireland	..	..	..	..	..	..	..	..	..	..
Israel	..	..	..	..	..	..	..	..	..	..
Italy	8.2	10.8	13.5	27.6	14.3	125.4	131.2	145.4	18.8	29.9
Japan	..	..	-	-	-	..	..	-	-	-
Korea	425.2	492.1	705.5	664.4	667.8	2 428.8	2 639.0	2 738.8	2 781.3	3 428.9
Latvia	..	..	..	..	..	..	..	..	..	..
Lithuania	..	..	..	..	..	..	..	..	..	..
Luxembourg	526.0	980.0	720.3	1 200.3	1 158.6	299.3	384.2	539.7	528.0	533.2
Mexico	0.7	1.2	3.3	0.3	5.7	422.0	592.3	675.1	698.8	721.2
Netherlands	2 750.6	7 945.2	4 729.5	5 652.8	7 878.5	8 943.9	7 745.4	7 635.3	10 290.2	8 899.2
New Zealand	8.2	-2.8	-1.7	21.4	12.5	199.9	218.7	214.8	244.9	199.2
Norway	..	..	..	..	..	..	..	..	..	..
Poland	..	..	..	..	..	..	..	..	..	..
Portugal	..	..	..	..	..	..	..	..	..	..
Slovak Republic	..	..	..	..	..	..	..	..	..	..
Slovenia	..	..	..	..	..	..	..	..	..	..
Spain	11.5	3.3	3.0	6.5	0.8	153.9	186.3	297.7	339.1	317.1
Sweden	73.7	207.3	68.2	26.0	6.9	298.3	349.8	497.5	618.7	553.0
Switzerland	1 095.4	1 485.8	1 724.9	2 187.5	2 020.6	43.9	133.0	-3.7	751.7	1 061.1
Turkey	..	..	..	..	..	..	..	..	..	..
United Kingdom	526.8	1 078.5	855.1	1 012.5	1 137.9	4 575.6	5 201.1	6 197.7	6 469.9	6 678.6
United States	7 752.7	9 373.1	11 431.1	10 406.0	9 820.8	29 948.4	32 054.7	27 212.2	26 911.1	26 721.7
EUROPE	**11 757.1**	**18 785.6**	**15 714.8**	**16 807.5**	**18 509.5**	**18 336.9**	**17 927.9**	**21 306.9**	**25 546.1**	**26 126.3**
Bulgaria	..	..	..	..	..	..	..	..	..	..
Croatia	..	..	..	..	..	..	..	..	..	..
Cyprus	..	..	..	..	..	..	..	..	..	..
Malta	..	..	..	..	..	..	..	..	..	..
Romania	..	..	..	..	..	..	..	..	..	..
Russian Federation	-	1.0	-	0.3	-	100.8	36.4	353.8	524.1	666.0
Ukraine	..	..	..	..	..	..	..	..	..	..
AFRICA	**3.5**	**7.1**	**9.8**	**12.9**	**7.0**	**822.6**	**680.0**	**645.8**	**750.4**	**881.7**
Northern Africa	..	..	..	..	..	..	..	..	..	..
Algeria	..	..	..	..	..	..	..	..	..	..
Egypt	..	..	..	..	..	..	..	..	..	..
Libya	..	..	..	..	..	..	..	..	..	..
Morocco	..	..	..	..	..	..	..	..	..	..
Tunisia	..	..	..	..	..	..	..	..	..	..
Other African countries	..	..	..	..	..	..	..	..	..	..
Nigeria	..	..	..	..	..	..	..	..	..	..
South Africa	-	0.1	0.5	-	-	329.2	183.9	267.9	479.3	498.9
AMERICA	**8 925.7**	**10 324.9**	**12 240.1**	**11 500.1**	**10 461.9**	**35 010.1**	**38 256.8**	**36 834.0**	**37 557.3**	**37 605.6**
Northern America	7 724.7	9 385.1	11 493.4	10 485.9	9 901.3	31 086.7	33 152.4	28 863.5	28 411.5	28 280.8
Central America and Caribbean countries	..	..	..	..	..	..	..	..	..	..
Bahamas	..	..	..	..	..	..	..	..	..	..
Bermuda	..	..	..	..	..	..	..	..	..	..
Cayman Islands	933.3	748.2	474.3	300.5	272.6	2 974.3	3 835.4	4 198.5	4 561.0	4 542.6
Costa Rica	..	..	..	..	..	..	..	..	..	..
El Salvador	..	..	..	..	..	..	..	..	..	..
Guatemala	..	..	..	..	..	..	..	..	..	..
Honduras	..	..	..	..	..	..	..	..	..	..
Nicaragua	..	..	..	..	..	..	..	..	..	..
Panama	..	..	..	..	..	..	..	..	..	..
Virgin Islands, U.S.	..	..	..	..	..	..	..	..	..	..
South America	..	..	..	..	..	..	..	..	..	..
Argentina	..	..	..	..	..	..	..	..	..	..
Bolivia	..	..	..	..	..	..	..	..	..	..
Brazil	1.5	-	-	-	-	-648.7	-213.0	1 672.1	1 687.1	1 690.1
Colombia	..	..	..	..	..	..	..	..	..	..
Ecuador	..	..	..	..	..	..	..	..	..	..
Paraguay	..	..	..	..	..	..	..	..	..	..
Peru	..	..	..	..	..	..	..	..	..	..
Uruguay	..	..	..	..	..	..	..	..	..	..
Venezuela	..	..	..	..	..	..	..	..	..	..

Table 3. Foreign direct investment income by country *(cont.)*

Million US dollars

	Inward					Outward				
	2015	2016	2017	2018	2019	2015	2016	2017	2018	2019
ASIA	**3 010.7**	**3 423.3**	**5 230.9**	**5 827.9**	**5 684.9**	**39 873.3**	**45 107.9**	**53 107.6**	**55 965.4**	**57 833.7**
Near and Middle East	-92.7	-56.0	37.1	3.9	2.7	1 101.5	1 127.4	1 348.4	1 249.8	1 336.2
Gulf Arabian countries	..	..	..	..	..	..	..	..	..	..
Kuwait	..	..	..	..	..	..	..	..	..	..
Qatar	..	..	..	..	..	..	..	..	..	..
Saudi Arabia	-	-	-	-	-	464.7	611.1	697.0	1 039.8	998.7
United Arab Emirates	0.7	0.8	7.1	8.1	0.6	612.2	511.5	761.3	287.8	361.5
Other Near and Middle East	..	..	..	..	..	..	..	..	..	..
Jordan	..	..	..	..	..	..	..	..	..	..
Other Asian countries	3 103.4	3 479.3	5 193.8	5 824.0	5 682.2	38 771.7	43 980.4	51 759.2	54 715.6	56 497.5
China	31.6	41.4	83.0	125.3	62.8	12 669.9	14 757.1	17 983.2	19 344.5	21 308.0
Hong Kong, China	487.0	771.2	950.7	1 029.6	801.9	2 803.0	3 180.8	3 981.0	2 905.5	3 150.8
India	3.9	5.0	16.9	-	0.9	1 057.7	1 421.3	2 152.4	2 366.0	2 261.9
Indonesia	1.8	58.8	6.5	1.9	1.7	1 771.7	2 210.6	3 072.5	2 865.1	2 762.2
Iran, Islamic Republic of	-	-	-	-	-	-	-	-	3.2	-
Malaysia	27.6	13.6	60.4	46.7	18.1	1 548.0	1 527.8	1 555.9	1 748.3	1 687.1
Philippines	1.0	0.4	-	0.0	8.6	1 362.9	1 403.5	1 474.1	1 699.0	1 665.0
Singapore	1 937.5	1 869.2	3 013.8	3 590.3	3 733.6	5 248.6	5 621.3	5 572.4	6 241.1	6 524.9
Chinese Taipei	164.7	188.8	336.2	334.4	354.4	1 945.4	1 770.8	2 366.2	3 253.0	1 813.0
Thailand	14.5	30.6	15.6	28.7	28.4	6 447.6	7 573.6	8 846.4	9 273.2	9 810.9
Viet Nam	0.9	3.1	1.7	2.2	3.6	1 249.0	1 635.4	1 744.9	1 960.5	1 801.6
AUSTRALIA, OCEANIA AND POLAR REGIONS	**161.0**	**93.0**	**106.3**	**72.5**	**137.1**	**2 314.5**	**3 894.9**	**8 310.9**	**8 587.7**	**9 783.3**
WORLD unallocated and confidential	**0.0**	**-**	**0.0**	**0.0**	**0.0**	**1.3**	**0.0**	**0.0**	**-**	**0.0**
European Union (EU28)	**10 641.8**	**17 288.9**	**13 974.7**	**14 599.3**	**16 388.1**	**17 936.8**	**17 705.6**	**20 432.3**	**23 569.2**	**23 655.1**
G20 countries excl. European Union	..	..	..	..	..	..	..	..	..	..
G20 OECD countries	..	..	..	..	..	..	..	..	..	..
G20 Non-OECD countries	..	..	..	..	..	..	..	..	..	..
MENA countries	..	..	..	..	..	..	..	..	..	..
ASEAN countries	**1 986.0**	**1 980.4**	**3 101.3**	**3 669.8**	**3 794.4**	**17 654.6**	**19 978.1**	**22 293.5**	**23 858.0**	**24 341.0**

- Nil; .. Not available

Note: Detailed metadata at: *http://stats.oecd.org/OECDStat_Metadata/ShowMetadata.ashx?Dataset=FDI_CTRY_IND_SUMM.*

Source: *OECD International Direct Investment Statistics (database): https://doi.org/10.1787/idi-data-en*

Table 4. Foreign direct investment flows by industrial sector

Million US dollars

	Inward					Outward				
	2015	2016	2017	2018	2019	2015	2016	2017	2018	2019
All FDI activities	**2 976.6**	**17 749.5**	**9 354.2**	**9 254.7**	**14 547.5**	**136 295.5**	**151 287.1**	**164 563.0**	**143 075.3**	**226 572.6**
Agriculture, forestry and fishing	**10.6**	**0.6**	**12.5**	**51.5**	**15.5**	**281.4**	**53.1**	**-63.9**	**121.1**	**112.1**
Mining and quarrying	**14.5**	**15.9**	**164.6**	**29.9**	**38.6**	**4 813.2**	**4 045.9**	**1 105.5**	**9 130.9**	**9 494.4**
Extraction activities	..	..	..	..	..	..	..	..	..	..
Manufacturing	**2 505.1**	**11 219.7**	**9 062.1**	**10 751.4**	**9 314.1**	**51 038.8**	**52 899.4**	**55 355.3**	**56 468.7**	**106 916.0**
of which:										
Food products, beverages and tobacco	180.4	438.4	257.1	84.1	559.1	3 565.1	2 976.9	10 141.3	655.1	5 461.6
Textiles, wood and paper products; printing	119.0	36.0	24.0	-31.3	45.6	1 418.2	2 757.8	1 215.9	3 203.9	2 217.9
Chemical, rubber, plastic, non-metallic mineral products	..	..	..	..	..	..	..	..	..	..
Metal and machinery products, except electrical equipment	..	..	..	..	..	..	..	..	..	..
Motor vehicles, trailers, semi-trailers, other transport equipment	-1 038.8	3 750.2	3 230.0	1 955.1	3 496.9	12 897.5	12 508.4	8 441.3	10 944.3	20 903.7
Other manufacturing	..	..	..	..	..	..	..	..	..	..
Electricity, gas, steam and air conditioning supply	..	..	..	..	..	..	..	..	..	..
Water supply; sewerage, waste management and remediation activities	..	..	..	..	..	..	..	..	..	..
Construction	**62.5**	**136.0**	**30.6**	**-321.9**	**244.9**	**387.8**	**1 630.1**	**1 547.2**	**2 103.2**	**1 552.9**
Services	**-685.7**	**5 169.0**	**-881.5**	**-2 082.5**	**3 989.2**	**77 273.1**	**89 155.6**	**101 571.0**	**70 090.5**	**103 709.8**
Wholesale and retail trade; repair of motor vehicles and motorcycles	-3 940.6	-2 411.8	-5 345.1	-5 282.0	-4 480.8	13 600.8	18 768.1	28 472.2	13 218.6	54 475.3
Transportation and storage	586.5	1 520.7	767.2	111.4	156.0	8 099.6	2 291.3	1 187.9	2 248.5	2 450.6
Accommodation and food service activities	..	..	..	..	..	..	..	..	..	..
Information and communication	1 015.4	968.7	-667.8	-3 349.1	-1 326.8	11 808.8	16 901.9	23 501.9	39 077.5	3 672.8
Financial and insurance activities	1 516.3	3 313.8	1 525.6	5 668.3	8 139.0	34 621.1	8 502.0	32 908.7	25 011.2	33 239.6
Activities of holding companies	..	..	..	..	..	..	..	..	..	..
Real estate activities	-135.0	308.5	425.8	739.2	319.9	3 716.5	5 119.7	6 463.2	4 179.8	10 902.6
Professional, scientific and technical activities	..	..	..	..	..	..	..	..	..	..
Administrative and support service activities	..	..	..	..	..	..	..	..	..	..
Public administration; activities of households and of extraterritorial organisations	..	..	..	..	..	..	..	..	..	..
Education	..	..	..	..	..	..	..	..	..	..
Human health and social work activities	..	..	..	..	..	..	..	..	..	..
Arts, entertainment and recreation	..	..	..	..	..	..	..	..	..	..
Other services	..	..	..	..	..	..	..	..	..	..
Not allocated and confidential	**1 069.5**	**1 208.4**	**965.8**	**826.3**	**945.3**	**2 501.1**	**3 503.1**	**5 047.9**	**5 160.9**	**4 787.4**
Private real estate activities	..	..	..	..	..	..	..	..	..	..

.. Not available

Note: Detailed metadata at: *http://stats.oecd.org/OECDStat_Metadata/ShowMetadata.ashx?Dataset=FDI_CTRY_IND_SUMM.*

Source: *OECD International Direct Investment Statistics (database): https://doi.org/10.1787/idi-data-en*

Table 5. Foreign direct investment positions by industrial sector

At year end

Million US dollars

	Inward					Outward				
	2015	2016	2017	2018	2019	2015	2016	2017	2018	2019
All FDI activities	..	..	202 441.1	204 523.6	220 784.8	1 228 766.5	1 315 221.1	1 497 525.0	1 568 765.7	1 769 193.4
Agriculture, forestry and fishing	78.4	81.5	80.9	132.7	114.7	3 210.6	3 275.7	2 984.2	2 957.5	3 048.6
Mining and quarrying	59.8	117.6	274.3	160.0	212.2	94 435.8	83 214.4	77 565.0	77 989.6	84 238.0
Extraction activities	..	..	..	..	..	..	..	..	..	..
Manufacturing	73 483.9	81 159.7	88 042.3	79 672.7	90 155.8	535 640.1	554 005.7	617 584.7	625 112.9	733 041.5
of which:										
Food products, beverages and tobacco	2 268.7	2 557.5	2 520.5	2 181.4	2 290.4	74 357.1	72 039.4	83 580.4	83 358.3	81 606.4
Textiles, wood and paper products; printing	398.4	467.2	479.2	453.2	475.7	16 062.8	17 042.1	17 714.1	20 138.0	21 389.9
Chemical, rubber, plastic, non-metallic mineral products	..	..	..	..	..	..	..	..	..	..
Metal and machinery products, except electrical equipment	..	..	..	..	..	..	..	..	..	..
Motor vehicles, trailers, semi-trailers, other transport equipment	22 435.6	26 011.5	29 057.8	31 181.1	32 981.7	108 728.0	114 617.1	125 618.1	127 091.6	144 206.1
Other manufacturing	..	..	..	..	..	..	..	..	..	..
Electricity, gas, steam and air conditioning supply	..	..	..	..	..	..	..	..	..	..
Water supply; sewerage, waste management and remediation activities	..	..	..	..	..	..	..	..	..	..
Construction	270.3	780.1	579.4	161.9	568.6	5 504.6	6 898.9	7 760.8	9 096.2	9 742.8
Services	89 370.8	102 234.8	100 064.8	109 290.1	113 946.6	558 702.1	632 298.9	747 724.3	807 466.7	891 722.7
Wholesale and retail trade; repair of motor vehicles and motorcycles	8 932.6	11 181.4	6 367.8	-179.9	-7 440.0	173 966.9	182 152.0	210 584.8	226 319.3	269 102.0
Transportation and storage	1 580.6	3 693.8	3 563.3	3 949.8	3 738.2	21 302.5	18 025.5	16 791.5	18 247.6	20 316.5
Accommodation and food service activities	..	..	..	..	..	..	..	..	..	..
Information and communication	6 814.4	7 414.3	7 737.9	20 144.4	14 250.2	70 163.4	80 071.0	101 658.3	125 413.4	119 156.8
Financial and insurance activities	61 944.8	66 484.9	66 522.6	69 102.7	87 055.5	241 153.5	260 295.5	304 659.9	329 217.9	369 031.6
Activities of holding companies	..	..	..	..	..	..	..	..	..	..
Real estate activities	3 227.7	3 454.0	3 845.2	4 987.1	4 693.3	19 699.6	24 473.3	30 170.0	32 915.1	43 135.7
Professional, scientific and technical activities	..	..	..	..	..	..	..	..	..	..
Administrative and support service activities	..	..	..	..	..	..	..	..	..	..
Public administration; activities of households and of extraterritorial organisations	..	..	..	..	..	..	..	..	..	..
Education	..	..	..	..	..	..	..	..	..	..
Human health and social work activities	..	..	..	..	..	..	..	..	..	..
Arts, entertainment and recreation	..	..	..	..	..	..	..	..	..	..
Other services	..	..	..	..	..	..	..	..	..	..
Not allocated and confidential	10 882.8	12 240.1	13 399.4	15 106.2	15 786.9	31 273.4	35 527.6	43 906.0	46 142.8	47 399.8
Private real estate activities	..	..	..	..	..	..	..	..	..	..

.. Not available

Note: Detailed metadata at: *http://stats.oecd.org/OECDStat_Metadata/ShowMetadata.ashx?Dataset=FDI_CTRY_IND_SUMM.*

Source: *OECD International Direct Investment Statistics (database): https://doi.org/10.1787/idi-data-en*

Table 6. Foreign direct investment income by industrial sector

Million US dollars

	Inward					Outward				
	2015	2016	2017	2018	2019	2015	2016	2017	2018	2019
All FDI activities	**23 857.9**	**32 634.0**	**33 301.9**	**34 220.8**	**34 800.5**	**96 358.7**	**105 867.5**	**120 205.2**	**128 406.9**	**132 230.5**
Agriculture, forestry and fishing	**8.9**	**0.1**	**8.1**	**29.1**	**7.5**	**46.4**	**55.8**	**109.8**	**196.1**	**167.4**
Mining and quarrying	**3.2**	**4.9**	**31.9**	**15.1**	**12.2**	**1 833.0**	**2 637.9**	**9 063.8**	**10 373.8**	**12 405.6**
Extraction activities	..	..	..	..	..	..	..	..	..	..
Manufacturing	**7 764.5**	**12 640.5**	**11 770.7**	**11 643.1**	**12 884.1**	**48 053.5**	**51 807.8**	**57 379.4**	**60 570.0**	**58 550.0**
of which:										
Food products, beverages and tobacco	926.4	1 162.3	1 016.9	1 051.0	1 069.8	3 879.3	2 768.5	3 995.8	4 779.5	6 001.9
Textiles, wood and paper products; printing	28.0	36.0	43.9	31.0	35.2	843.1	763.5	1 135.0	1 388.4	1 829.5
Chemical, rubber, plastic, non-metallic mineral products	..	..	..	..	..	..	..	..	..	..
Metal and machinery products, except electrical equipment	..	..	..	..	..	..	..	..	..	..
Motor vehicles, trailers, semi-trailers, other transport equipment	3 533.9	4 215.1	3 738.0	3 512.0	3 603.9	15 772.6	16 820.8	16 809.4	16 216.1	16 144.0
Other manufacturing	..	..	..	..	..	..	..	..	..	..
Electricity, gas, steam and air conditioning supply	..	..	..	..	..	..	..	..	..	..
Water supply; sewerage, waste management and remediation activities	..	..	..	..	..	..	..	..	..	..
Construction	**185.0**	**86.4**	**95.6**	**44.6**	**74.7**	**454.4**	**547.2**	**456.1**	**304.3**	**302.3**
Services	**15 071.5**	**18 497.9**	**20 041.2**	**20 969.4**	**20 557.0**	**43 442.6**	**48 240.9**	**50 614.0**	**54 993.0**	**59 087.5**
Wholesale and retail trade; repair of motor vehicles and motorcycles	3 148.5	3 063.8	4 582.5	3 653.3	4 496.4	18 349.0	19 693.9	21 660.4	23 210.9	27 054.9
Transportation and storage	57.4	60.6	2 345.1	201.2	175.8	2 569.4	2 276.2	1 941.4	2 166.4	2 154.1
Accommodation and food service activities	..	..	..	..	..	..	..	..	..	..
Information and communication	1 501.1	4 345.9	3 447.2	1 658.3	1 855.9	901.4	2 942.7	5 496.5	4 736.8	5 392.3
Financial and insurance activities	9 405.9	9 282.3	8 401.3	14 000.1	11 520.7	17 187.3	18 151.0	16 361.9	17 994.1	18 523.6
Activities of holding companies	..	..	..	..	..	..	..	..	..	..
Real estate activities	177.2	274.3	239.8	168.3	231.3	680.4	729.2	1 007.4	1 130.3	1 317.4
Professional, scientific and technical activities	..	..	..	..	..	..	..	..	..	..
Administrative and support service activities	..	..	..	..	..	..	..	..	..	..
Public administration; activities of households and of extraterritorial organisations	..	..	..	..	..	..	..	..	..	..
Education	..	..	..	..	..	..	..	..	..	..
Human health and social work activities	..	..	..	..	..	..	..	..	..	..
Arts, entertainment and recreation	..	..	..	..	..	..	..	..	..	..
Other services	..	..	..	..	..	..	..	..	..	..
Not allocated and confidential	**824.8**	**1 404.2**	**1 354.3**	**1 519.4**	**1 265.0**	**2 528.9**	**2 577.9**	**2 582.1**	**1 969.9**	**1 717.6**
Private real estate activities	..	..	..	..	..	..	..	..	..	..

.. Not available

Note: Detailed metadata at: *http://stats.oecd.org/OECDStat_Metadata/ShowMetadata.ashx?Dataset=FDI_CTRY_IND_SUMM.*

Source: *OECD International Direct Investment Statistics (database): https://doi.org/10.1787/idi-data-en*

KOREA

Table 1. Foreign direct investment flows by country

Million US dollars

	Inward					Outward				
	2015	2016	2017	2018	2019	2015	2016	2017	2018	2019
WORLD	**2 804.7**	**7 263.0**	**11 531.5**	**13 267.2**	**12 589.0**	**18 489.6**	**30 507.5**	**43 463.9**	**45 232.6**	**50 981.1**
OECD COUNTRIES	**972.8**	**4 619.0**	**6 407.4**	**7 131.6**	**8 746.8**	**7 447.0**	**12 486.8**	**20 259.0**	**19 455.3**	**21 501.1**
Australia	5.5	2.0	33.7	2 004.2	54.8	679.9	817.6	-715.4	485.9	233.5
Austria	-166.4	118.0	5.0	-4.0	11.9	.. c	12.3	41.3	1 290.4	13.7
Belgium	-17.3	9.0	63.4	13.5	255.2	101.8	43.2	122.9	262.6	141.2
Canada	191.0	153.0	124.2	-221.0	-48.5	-1 354.6	293.9	-4.7	98.2	773.9
Chile	4.8	9.0	-	0.1	0.2	-11.6	24.5	196.6	104.3	4.0
Czech Republic	-	-	0.2	0.1	0.3	343.0	22.7	436.5	238.4	0.1
Denmark	38.9	-13.0	-7.8	3.7	3.8	.. c	.. c	12.0	2.7	-5.7
Estonia	-	-	13.2	1.1	-7.1	-	-	-	0.0	.. c
Finland	12.3	27.0	12.5	-22.3	8.2	6.9	.. c	36.5	-17.0	0.2
France	2.4	387.0	55.8	635.5	55.8	923.7	-21.0	119.2	490.7	1 386.1
Germany	252.8	-3.0	704.7	-255.1	227.4	153.7	280.1	556.4	503.5	734.0
Greece	-	-	-	-	-	.. c	.. c	0.4	0.5	1.3
Hungary	47.0	27.0	3.7	-	315.4	98.9	125.8	432.0	378.9	784.9
Iceland	1.9	1.0	-0.2	-	1.0	.. c	.. c	0.0	189.3	.. c
Ireland	-245.1	84.0	163.8	500.0	217.3	34.4	.. c	1 509.2	157.1	408.8
Israel	1.9	2.0	1.9	10.8	1.0	.. c	.. c	-0.3	26.1	22.8
Italy	37.6	68.0	60.9	8.4	-16.4	98.0	-1.4	119.0	86.2	257.9
Japan	634.2	1 052.0	1 362.6	1 050.9	1 384.9	1 469.3	181.2	524.1	779.6	656.6
Korea										
Latvia	-	-	-	1.2	0.3	.. c	.. c	0.2	-	0.0
Lithuania	-	-	0.2	0.1	0.1	-	-	-	0.0	.. c
Luxembourg	189.6	92.0	186.5	146.8	112.1	315.5	639.0	879.8	2 634.0	1 931.4
Mexico	29.2	24.0	-	10.1	12.7	220.2	-66.2	516.8	98.0	108.5
Netherlands	-343.0	616.0	1 113.7	133.1	2 306.7	1 157.9	-377.0	35.8	464.4	-181.7
New Zealand	-	1.0	-2.6	-1.3	3.5	-0.7	9.8	-13.4	23.1	-11.1
Norway	-111.2	107.0	46.7	1.1	89.5	.. c	.. c	27.5	2.3	2.9
Poland	-	3.0	-	0.5	-0.3	138.2	-155.9	239.4	438.9	1 356.2
Portugal	3.1	13.0	0.4	-	-	.. c	.. c	48.7	15.6	21.4
Slovak Republic	-	-	0.1	0.1	-	113.4	197.2	-107.6	133.6	337.7
Slovenia	-	-	-	-	-	.. c	.. c	0.6	0.8	.. c
Spain	33.6	45.0	6.8	1 389.7	0.6	52.6	47.9	44.2	92.5	465.7
Sweden	105.7	190.0	2.2	-244.8	-26.2	.. c	.. c	41.0	13.0	-42.1
Switzerland	253.6	401.0	185.8	26.3	201.4	134.2	94.1	65.6	135.9	104.3
Turkey	-	1.0	0.5	5.0	5.2	37.9	580.7	193.0	240.6	360.8
United Kingdom	-810.2	153.0	1 151.8	-149.0	2 044.0	-1 402.1	688.3	1 463.9	2 595.1	1 787.0
United States	821.0	1 050.0	1 118.2	2 087.0	1 532.3	4 263.9	9 100.3	13 437.9	7 490.7	9 832.8
EUROPE	**-98.1**	**2 814.0**	**5 191.0**	**3 567.4**	**6 595.6**	**2 442.1**	**3 348.8**	**7 424.9**	**11 228.4**	**11 611.9**
Bulgaria	-	-	-	-	-	15.3	41.8	-21.7	-6.7	-2.0
Croatia	-	-	-	-	-	-	-	-	-	.. c
Cyprus	-	-	4.1	0.7	-	23.0	.. c	-224.6	-83.5	.. c
Malta	557.5	427.0	1 405.1	1 370.2	782.5	-	-	-	14.2	.. c
Romania	-	-	-	-	0.7	-50.6	.. c	84.5	3.8	-30.5
Russian Federation	-	-	2.0	5.7	4.1	18.0	687.4	513.3	461.6	581.5
Ukraine	-	-	10.1	0.0	-	.. c	.. c	0.3	2.9	6.0
AFRICA	**-**	**-**	**11.2**	**5.5**	**-12.6**	**-539.2**	**-453.8**	**232.2**	**65.3**	**300.6**
Northern Africa	-	-	2.2	1.9	3.1	-9.8	-350.2	69.4	60.6	79.2
Algeria	-	-	-	-	-	2.1	.. c	-0.7	1.8	1.9
Egypt	-	-	1.1	0.8	0.9	-12.6	.. c	36.1	23.1	77.1
Libya	-	-	0.9	0.9	2.1	0.3	.. c	4.8	2.1	2.8
Morocco	-	-	0.2	0.2	0.1	.. c	.. c	25.5	29.6	-3.3
Tunisia	-	-	-	-	-	.. c	.. c	3.7	4.0	.. c
Other African countries	-	-	8.8	3.6	-15.7	-529.4	-103.6	162.8	4.6	221.4
Nigeria	-	-	0.3	0.9	0.4	-12.7	.. c	217.2	37.6	-290.2
South Africa	-	-	0.1	-	-	42.7	23.5	14.8	43.2	68.8
AMERICA	**1 145.9**	**2 103.0**	**2 342.2**	**3 152.1**	**2 545.4**	**4 339.9**	**13 441.6**	**19 126.8**	**13 699.1**	**16 690.7**
Northern America	1 012.0	1 203.0	1 242.3	1 866.0	1 483.8	2 909.3	9 394.2	13 433.2	7 588.9	10 606.7
Central America and Caribbean countries	129.1	891.0	1 098.2	1 285.7	1 061.4	2 473.6	2 471.8	3 755.1	5 005.7	5 801.6
Bahamas	3.5	2.0	14.3	-	-	.. c	-	-	38.2	.. c
Bermuda	299.5	330.0	747.9	133.4	113.7	-5.1	.. c	2.2	-26.6	-106.9
Cayman Islands	-301.0	486.0	174.1	460.4	622.0	2 229.0	2 526.0	3 016.6	4 321.7	4 899.7
Costa Rica	-	-	-	-	-	.. c	.. c	-1.5	2.2	-9.0
El Salvador	-	-	-	-	-	.. c	.. c	-0.6	0.4	10.7
Guatemala	-	-	-	-	-	1.3	.. c	13.9	2.0	2.1
Honduras	-	-	-	-	-	.. c	.. c	-2.1	-6.2	-2.0
Nicaragua	-	-	-	-	-	-2.4	.. c	3.0	9.1	0.3
Panama	9.1	9.0	-4.5	0.7	-	2.3	-168.5	-194.5	18.4	176.3
Virgin Islands, U.S.	87.5	40.0	-	-	-	-	.. c	-	-	.. c
South America	4.8	9.0	1.2	0.4	0.2	-1 043.0	1 575.6	1 938.5	1 104.5	282.4
Argentina	-	-	-	-	-	5.2	-	-1.0	337.1	2.0
Bolivia	-	-	-	-	-	.. c	.. c	51.1	-1.2	2.8
Brazil	-	-	1.1	-	-	-1 314.9	1 308.2	1 571.0	439.0	122.3
Colombia	-	-	-	-	-	4.0	.. c	5.8	-12.8	25.4
Ecuador	-	-	-	-	-	.. c	.. c	6.0	0.0	0.0
Paraguay	-	-	-	0.1	-	.. c	.. c	0.2	0.5	1.2
Peru	-	-	0.1	0.3	-	282.8	182.4	108.8	237.7	124.7
Uruguay	-	-	-	-	-	.. c	.. c	-	-	.. c
Venezuela	-	-	-	-	-	.. c	.. c	0.0	-0.1	.. c

Table 1. Foreign direct investment flows by country *(cont.)*

Million US dollars

	Inward					Outward				
	2015	2016	2017	2018	2019	2015	2016	2017	2018	2019
ASIA	**1 699.9**	**2 291.0**	**3 946.5**	**4 543.5**	**3 399.3**	**11 313.4**	**13 199.5**	**17 362.6**	**19 638.1**	**22 122.8**
Near and Middle East	-6.5	82.0	26.9	99.0	74.7	46.3	396.3	495.0	464.2	316.7
Gulf Arabian countries	-8.4	80.0	22.5	86.0	69.6	16.1	358.8	450.8	374.9	216.8
Kuwait	-	-	-	1.3	-	.. c	.. c	1.3	-	-0.2
Qatar	-	-	0.1	-	-	1.3	0.6	0.2	0.0	1.7
Saudi Arabia	299.4	86.0	-	4.4	25.5	-35.8	373.0	176.8	476.1	216.8
United Arab Emirates	-315.5	-17.0	1.7	0.2	9.6	73.9	-79.3	234.9	-121.7	-3.9
Other Near and Middle East	1.9	2.0	4.3	13.0	5.2	30.3	37.5	44.1	89.3	100.0
Jordan	-	-	0.6	0.3	1.1	.. c	.. c	4.9	2.9	74.5
Other Asian countries	1 706.4	2 209.0	3 919.6	4 444.5	3 324.6	11 267.0	12 803.2	16 867.6	19 173.9	21 806.1
China	106.9	347.0	148.3	758.4	132.9	3 725.9	6 271.3	5 891.8	6 305.2	7 153.9
Hong Kong, China	353.1	313.0	1 194.6	931.5	713.4	1 648.1	-173.9	1 724.3	2 761.6	2 014.5
India	308.2	153.0	0.6	0.5	46.1	664.2	612.1	919.2	1 985.8	1 034.3
Indonesia	0.6	2.0	4.1	0.5	76.6	172.2	633.7	553.1	533.6	1 203.7
Iran, Islamic Republic of	-	-	0.1	1.9	-	.. c	.. c	-12.1	-47.3	-12.8
Malaysia	-58.2	-70.0	142.7	15.2	51.3	147.0	607.9	711.0	217.6	282.0
Philippines	-55.7	-16.0	3.3	0.4	1.0	-13.9	-187.3	486.8	-1 156.1	405.7
Singapore	364.8	425.0	1 020.5	1 441.8	862.6	1 987.0	1 840.8	2 704.7	2 362.4	3 164.8
Chinese Taipei	52.4	3.0	26.1	228.3	13.0	64.1	17.2	104.2	178.4	95.5
Thailand	-	-	5.3	3.1	7.2	244.3	233.4	84.4	345.8	230.0
Viet Nam	-	-	1.1	1.9	19.3	1 126.8	2 295.6	3 339.7	4 353.6	5 030.5
AUSTRALIA, OCEANIA AND POLAR REGIONS	**7.1**	**4.0**	**40.6**	**1 998.7**	**61.9**	**933.5**	**971.5**	**-682.6**	**601.6**	**255.1**
WORLD unallocated and confidential	**49.8**	**51.0**	**0.0**	**0.0**	**-0.6**	**0.0**	**0.0**	**-**	**-**	**0.0**
European Union (EU28)	**-301.7**	**2 243.0**	**4 946.0**	**3 529.3**	**6 292.1**	**2 119.5**	**1 808.5**	**5 869.5**	**9 709.8**	**9 523.0**
G20 countries excl. European Union	**1 878.6**	**3 475.0**	**4 768.3**	**5 945.4**	**5 537.3**	**8 367.3**	**21 759.4**	**25 849.2**	**23 450.2**	**26 514.3**
G20 OECD countries	**1 163.5**	**2 887.0**	**4 612.2**	**5 176.0**	**5 252.1**	**5 089.8**	**11 853.5**	**16 210.2**	**12 868.6**	**16 131.0**
G20 Non-OECD countries	**715.1**	**588.0**	**156.2**	**769.5**	**285.2**	**3 277.5**	**9 906.0**	**9 639.0**	**10 581.6**	**10 383.3**
MENA countries	**-8.4**	**80.0**	**27.1**	**90.2**	**76.9**	**9.1**	**12.5**	**525.1**	**438.4**	**370.5**
ASEAN countries	**251.5**	**341.0**	**1 177.3**	**1 462.9**	**1 018.7**	**3 859.4**	**5 853.5**	**8 286.0**	**7 094.0**	**10 767.4**

- Nil; c Confidential data

Note: Data excludes resident Special Purpose Entities (SPEs). Detailed metadata at: *http://stats.oecd.org/OECDStat_Metadata/ShowMetadata.ashx?Dataset=FDI_CTRY_IND_SUMM.*

Source: OECD *International Direct Investment Statistics (database): https://doi.org/10.1787/idi-data-en*

Table 2. Foreign direct investment positions by country

At year end

Million US dollars

	Inward					Outward				
	2015	2016	2017	2018	2019	2015	2016	2017	2018	2019
WORLD	**168 923.7**	**174 978.0**	**210 863.5**	**213 966.3**	**218 309.7**	**276 100.1**	**296 641.0**	**343 088.5**	**383 982.9**	**433 671.5**
OECD COUNTRIES	**135 470.0**	**135 601.7**	**157 266.9**	**161 400.1**	**165 090.1**	**118 311.7**	**126 418.8**	**148 737.9**	**166 676.3**	**190 948.3**
Australia	776.5	577.8	764.2	1 808.8	1 690.3	10 373.0	11 401.7	11 037.0	11 763.7	11 363.8
Austria	464.7	533.8	649.8	190.0	566.0	209.4	217.4	321.9	315.3	340.4
Belgium	201.1	359.3	602.5	595.0	795.1	1 524.0	1 482.1	1 777.6	1 956.4	2 041.4
Canada	1 500.1	2 201.9	2 344.7	1 842.4	2 652.3	3 935.6	3 735.1	3 883.0	4 135.4	4 891.0
Chile	1.2	24.9	15.7	-7.1	-9.6	195.2	159.7	351.5	589.7	421.9
Czech Republic	-2.5	-2.6	1.1	-33.2	9.2	2 221.1	1 989.3	3 046.0	3 032.1	3 038.4
Denmark	447.3	549.2	223.5	406.9	379.2	28.5	30.8	39.6	35.6	28.0
Estonia	-	-	12.8	25.7	8.0	.. c	.. c	0.1	0.1	.. c
Finland	117.3	177.8	128.2	125.5	565.0	9.5	11.2	53.2	32.6	32.5
France	5 315.6	4 205.1	5 375.6	6 122.5	6 567.4	772.7	626.5	997.6	1 064.7	2 315.2
Germany	6 772.7	6 950.6	8 306.5	9 457.2	8 944.1	3 381.8	3 242.2	4 045.4	4 409.3	5 640.3
Greece	0.5	19.4	5.9	9.9	2.6	.. c	.. c	8.1	8.4	9.7
Hungary	3 790.8	3 589.3	3 582.3	3 759.6	3 669.0	1 074.7	344.3	1 836.2	1 858.3	2 760.3
Iceland	1.3	14.0	38.4	18.4	13.7	.. c	.. c	3.0	192.2	.. c
Ireland	1 262.5	823.6	-53.3	1 989.3	2 224.0	1 193.7	1 202.2	3 008.9	2 991.5	2 529.4
Israel	20.9	14.1	76.1	110.0	229.5	9.6	16.4	6.8	19.0	30.4
Italy	197.9	325.4	567.0	1 024.9	655.5	498.7	628.3	717.1	908.9	1 167.0
Japan	44 596.0	43 315.1	47 519.3	54 761.4	53 944.5	4 812.8	5 090.4	5 612.0	7 089.4	8 748.6
Korea	-	-	-	-	-	-	-	-	-	-
Latvia	-	-	-	1.2	1.5	.. c	.. c	5.8	5.8	0.6
Lithuania	0.0	0.0	0.2	0.3	0.4	.. c	.. c	0.5	0.5	.. c
Luxembourg	1 279.9	1 296.9	1 804.4	1 229.6	1 489.3	3 844.3	3 791.2	4 893.8	6 183.1	7 967.3
Mexico	155.5	152.2	190.3	244.3	291.9	2 968.7	2 504.0	3 196.8	3 047.3	3 018.8
Netherlands	15 359.4	17 549.6	27 591.7	21 609.7	20 234.3	12 444.4	11 694.9	8 572.3	8 398.8	10 434.6
New Zealand	8.9	34.6	55.8	366.5	1 801.3	171.4	200.0	145.0	187.3	200.2
Norway	916.7	738.0	767.2	666.1	1 232.3	.. c	-270.0	11.8	13.2	22.5
Poland	7.4	9.4	9.6	9.1	15.8	1 199.2	828.8	1 209.9	1 677.0	2 819.8
Portugal	166.9	169.9	186.0	218.2	183.6	.. c	.. c	184.7	203.5	226.6
Slovak Republic	0.1	-0.9	-0.7	-18.6	-27.5	2 489.6	2 437.7	2 613.5	2 605.0	2 936.2
Slovenia	5.3	5.4	5.3	13.0	12.6	.. c	.. c	9.0	8.8	.. c
Spain	514.4	510.6	428.8	520.6	535.6	818.3	826.1	987.6	955.3	1 389.0
Sweden	2 158.6	2 307.8	2 099.5	1 847.0	1 846.4	270.5	243.2	416.1	401.1	351.2
Switzerland	3 491.6	3 418.4	5 055.0	3 902.8	3 962.7	940.6	354.4	335.3	443.5	538.5
Turkey	11.0	27.4	34.8	-57.6	25.2	885.6	1 198.6	865.4	1 194.5	1 427.1
United Kingdom	13 003.1	13 952.0	14 941.4	16 209.0	15 481.0	5 352.3	4 888.5	7 627.9	10 352.4	11 700.5
United States	32 927.3	31 751.9	33 937.3	32 431.9	35 097.8	56 038.7	67 395.1	80 918.8	90 626.1	102 371.3
EUROPE	**61 797.5**	**63 544.6**	**82 239.7**	**79 191.3**	**77 751.6**	**44 551.7**	**43 031.6**	**52 276.5**	**57 277.2**	**69 790.9**
Bulgaria	1.1	1.0	1.0	1.0	0.1	231.7	235.3	141.8	135.1	67.6
Croatia	0.0	-	-	0.0	0.1	0.4	.. c	0.4	0.4	.. c
Cyprus	1.2	1.3	1.3	13.0	17.2	338.4	551.0	148.4	53.6	.. c
Malta	6 228.0	5 942.5	9 790.9	9 265.8	8 258.8	.. c	.. c	0.3	-9.7	.. c
Romania	-	-0.6	3.2	-1.5	0.1	71.5	197.4	610.8	113.5	76.4
Russian Federation	48.3	42.9	47.5	-8.8	40.0	1 373.9	2 482.6	2 617.5	3 051.6	3 959.4
Ukraine	1.5	1.3	1.4	1.4	1.5	163.0	158.4	203.4	162.4	168.9
AFRICA	**183.7**	**140.0**	**145.0**	**281.2**	**231.8**	**1 786.0**	**1 431.8**	**2 932.2**	**3 106.8**	**3 075.9**
Northern Africa	17.0	11.0	12.5	15.6	17.2	491.5	272.0	475.0	495.7	591.9
Algeria	-	0.1	0.1	0.1	-1.0	3.8	4.4	2.6	62.5	65.4
Egypt	6.7	5.4	5.7	6.8	8.0	90.3	-128.6	-1.9	-2.6	93.0
Libya	8.9	5.0	6.0	7.2	8.5	387.2	383.0	393.0	369.3	373.3
Morocco	1.4	0.6	0.8	1.5	1.7	5.5	5.5	70.5	54.3	47.2
Tunisia	-	-0.1	0.0	0.0	-	.. c	.. c	10.7	12.2	.. c
Other African countries	165.9	128.8	132.3	265.5	214.6	1 294.5	1 159.9	2 454.5	2 612.8	2 485.8
Nigeria	40.5	7.4	8.3	18.0	17.9	136.7	43.1	450.1	476.2	195.9
South Africa	2.5	-1.7	0.5	1.0	-11.3	172.1	202.9	214.9	223.4	253.2
AMERICA	**37 208.5**	**38 506.1**	**45 533.0**	**40 084.6**	**41 696.6**	**81 340.2**	**97 541.5**	**114 957.7**	**130 672.6**	**148 200.2**
Northern America	34 427.4	33 953.8	36 282.0	34 274.3	37 750.1	59 974.3	71 130.1	84 801.8	94 761.5	107 262.3
Central America and Caribbean countries	2 708.7	4 469.9	9 175.2	5 882.3	3 938.6	16 131.6	18 262.5	21 034.3	25 940.1	31 513.4
Bahamas	40.4	47.0	31.6	52.0	15.0	.. c	.. c	1.9	28.7	.. c
Bermuda	27.3	710.6	1 748.6	480.7	293.6	1 189.3	.. c	824.0	889.6	737.1
Cayman Islands	1 093.2	1 813.6	5 223.2	3 111.5	1 731.0	10 014.0	12 483.8	15 076.3	18 875.1	24 092.9
Costa Rica	0.1	0.1	0.1	0.1	0.0	32.2	34.4	27.4	44.2	35.6
El Salvador	0.0	-	-	-	-	.. c	.. c	46.8	45.6	53.9
Guatemala	2.3	2.3	2.1	2.2	2.9	51.6	45.3	56.1	49.4	54.6
Honduras	-	-	-	-	0.3	20.4	20.8	21.0	14.8	12.8
Nicaragua	-	-	-	-	-	30.6	27.1	32.9	18.0	22.7
Panama	175.9	183.9	210.5	28.9	58.6	1 198.3	1 065.8	891.5	1 408.2	1 624.8
Virgin Islands, U.S.	-	-	-	-	-	.. c	.. c	0.4	0.4	.. c
South America	66.2	73.4	69.7	-76.5	5.2	5 233.6	8 148.6	9 121.5	9 971.1	9 424.5
Argentina	5.0	2.9	4.9	-14.5	4.3	43.4	39.7	40.8	378.1	379.3
Bolivia	0.2	-	-	-	-	9.8	83.1	133.9	12.7	24.8
Brazil	50.5	44.0	47.7	-55.2	2.1	3 025.5	5 656.4	6 141.1	6 274.0	5 811.2
Colombia	0.3	0.1	0.1	-0.5	7.0	221.2	211.9	251.8	222.3	202.4
Ecuador	-	-	-	0.0	0.0	26.2	15.2	36.8	36.8	6.0
Paraguay	3.4	0.8	0.7	0.9	0.8	3.3	.. c	3.8	6.6	7.6
Peru	1.0	0.6	0.4	0.7	0.6	1 698.2	1 970.0	2 132.2	2 421.1	2 544.4
Uruguay	4.6	0.1	0.1	-0.1	-	0.6	.. c	28.0	28.0	.. c
Venezuela	0.0	0.0	0.0	-0.6	0.0	10.2	.. c	1.4	1.8	.. c

KOREA

Table 2. Foreign direct investment positions by country *(cont.)*
At year end

Million US dollars

	Inward					Outward				
	2015	2016	2017	2018	2019	2015	2016	2017	2018	2019
ASIA	**68 758.6**	**71 968.2**	**82 017.6**	**92 143.2**	**95 042.9**	**136 180.1**	**141 198.9**	**159 831.6**	**178 848.4**	**198 873.1**
Near and Middle East	1 806.5	2 193.0	3 155.9	2 398.6	3 001.3	1 753.9	1 590.2	2 476.9	2 600.9	2 357.9
Gulf Arabian countries	1 762.9	2 166.3	3 058.0	2 257.2	2 819.4	1 681.5	1 482.2	2 340.8	2 383.4	2 076.3
Kuwait	12.2	12.5	11.0	12.5	147.0	27.5	22.6	22.8	20.6	20.4
Qatar	0.3	0.1	0.1	0.2	0.4	12.0	12.1	10.3	14.2	24.0
Saudi Arabia	1 528.1	1 667.4	2 617.7	1 840.9	2 212.8	-590.8	-472.2	95.7	210.2	84.7
United Arab Emirates	34.8	309.7	211.2	174.1	218.1	871.0	942.6	1 185.1	1 210.9	1 064.9
Other Near and Middle East	43.5	26.7	97.9	141.4	181.9	72.5	108.0	136.1	217.6	281.6
Jordan	14.5	6.8	12.8	11.6	12.7	12.1	15.0	19.1	17.4	84.7
Other Asian countries	66 945.6	69 771.6	78 858.4	89 740.5	92 037.6	134 426.2	139 604.8	157 350.9	176 243.6	196 511.4
China	4 655.9	5 576.7	5 661.1	8 147.7	8 684.3	67 885.7	69 240.6	77 477.5	77 603.8	79 469.7
Hong Kong, China	5 000.1	6 151.3	6 706.6	7 098.4	8 809.9	13 293.4	12 363.3	13 411.7	15 404.7	18 179.5
India	833.0	1 106.1	650.5	569.9	343.3	4 268.9	5 081.2	5 409.0	12 442.7	9 873.2
Indonesia	64.2	65.8	60.9	63.2	48.9	6 437.1	6 963.7	7 041.3	7 735.4	9 240.7
Iran, Islamic Republic of	74.9	68.6	80.1	80.0	73.5	-4.0	22.4	-19.6	-27.8	-33.6
Malaysia	1 367.5	1 318.0	1 730.7	2 285.9	2 339.2	3 964.9	4 184.0	5 110.6	5 474.4	6 335.0
Philippines	217.3	165.1	691.2	186.4	286.4	2 790.3	2 346.0	2 856.1	1 718.9	2 721.0
Singapore	9 278.9	11 585.3	15 034.3	15 437.3	16 254.6	9 683.1	10 843.1	13 938.5	16 181.9	20 638.9
Chinese Taipei	647.8	339.9	623.2	899.2	1 066.0	873.2	746.6	953.5	1 051.1	1 334.2
Thailand	7.0	-10.3	0.5	25.1	51.4	2 633.3	3 084.4	3 085.3	3 618.7	4 078.3
Viet Nam	2.9	-36.1	-26.6	7.6	-28.5	11 421.2	12 555.8	15 705.7	20 377.0	27 631.4
AUSTRALIA, OCEANIA AND POLAR REGIONS	**958.6**	**803.2**	**911.3**	**2 266.1**	**3 581.9**	**12 242.1**	**13 437.3**	**13 090.6**	**14 078.0**	**13 731.4**
WORLD unallocated and confidential	**16.9**	**16.9**	**16.9**	**0.0**	**4.8**	**0.0**	**-**	**0.0**	**0.0**	**0.0**
European Union (EU28)	**57 293.3**	**59 275.7**	**76 264.6**	**74 590.5**	**72 434.5**	**38 110.0**	**35 616.3**	**43 274.3**	**47 697.3**	**58 089.0**
G20 countries excl. European Union	**112 443.1**	**111 963.4**	**123 071.9**	**134 388.9**	**136 674.5**	**171 635.7**	**189 905.2**	**217 939.0**	**242 510.8**	**261 715.1**
G20 OECD countries	**105 255.6**	**103 459.4**	**113 981.1**	**123 844.7**	**125 350.0**	**89 019.7**	**100 710.4**	**118 901.1**	**134 591.7**	**152 643.6**
G20 Non-OECD countries	**7 187.5**	**8 504.0**	**9 090.8**	**10 544.2**	**11 324.4**	**82 616.0**	**89 194.8**	**99 037.9**	**107 919.1**	**109 071.5**
MENA countries	**1 802.4**	**2 189.7**	**3 092.1**	**2 362.1**	**2 924.6**	**2 193.7**	**1 777.5**	**2 835.6**	**2 904.6**	**2 746.5**
ASEAN countries	**10 959.6**	**13 105.0**	**17 501.5**	**18 023.7**	**18 968.7**	**40 710.4**	**44 390.6**	**52 463.1**	**60 325.3**	**76 546.4**

- Nil; c Confidential data

Note: Data excludes resident Special Purpose Entities (SPEs). Detailed metadata at: *http://stats.oecd.org/OECDStat_Metadata/ShowMetadata.ashx?Dataset=FDI_CTRY_IND_SUMM.*

Source: *OECD International Direct Investment Statistics (database): https://doi.org/10.1787/idi-data-en*

KOREA

Table 3. Foreign direct investment income by country

Million US dollars

	Inward					Outward				
	2015	2016	2017	2018	2019	2015	2016	2017	2018	2019
WORLD	**2 225.8**	**3 997.0**	**3 615.4**	**4 402.0**	**3 443.0**	**-124.1**	**9 054.5**	**10 090.4**	**9 629.2**	**9 062.9**
OECD COUNTRIES	**1 899.9**	**3 098.0**	**3 505.4**	**3 512.6**	**2 986.9**	**-2 776.0**	**46.6**	**1 285.6**	**2 110.9**	**1 783.9**
Australia	-6.3	2.0	-	0.4	0.5	-79.0	-359.5	-1 244.7	383.3	-171.8
Austria	-10.5	86.0	0.1	0.0	9.9	.. c	.. c	8.4	37.1	-15.6
Belgium	-6.6	1.0	8.0	4.2	244.3	61.8	.. c	68.4	36.6	82.8
Canada	32.1	78.0	4.3	-	4.6	-1 803.0	-305.2	-85.0	-210.9	-2.9
Chile	2.5	10.0	-	-	-	-42.0	-12.6	12.2	-0.6	-24.3
Czech Republic	-	-	-	-	-	294.5	406.5	410.7	354.6	356.5
Denmark	-1.7	-1.0	5.6	2.3	0.1	.. c	.. c	1.7	2.2	-2.7
Estonia	-	-	-	-	-	-	-	.. c	-	.. c
Finland	-2.4	15.0	-	-	4.0	.. c	.. c	-0.1	-2.4	-0.8
France	133.6	134.0	97.7	90.2	10.9	127.7	0.2	51.0	32.9	40.5
Germany	169.8	213.0	564.1	705.4	352.5	90.9	197.8	152.7	217.2	117.0
Greece	-	-	-	-	-	.. c	.. c	.. c	0.5	0.7
Hungary	7.0	12.0	8.6	-	3.6	90.5	.. c	419.5	-7.9	48.1
Iceland	0.9	-	-	-	1.0	.. c	.. c	.. c	-0.6	.. c
Ireland	-40.8	66.0	0.0	231.2	80.2	.. c	.. c	-2.7	-3.9	-9.8
Israel	0.0	3.0	0.1	0.0	-0.3	.. c	.. c	-0.3	-6.0	-5.9
Italy	-2.7	10.0	2.5	56.0	-67.3	90.2	55.8	54.4	48.8	57.2
Japan	551.0	643.0	1 041.1	575.3	1 122.3	14.9	64.1	141.3	85.3	-168.3
Korea	-	-	-	-	-	-	-	-	-	-
Latvia	-	-	-	-	-	.. c	.. c	.. c	-	-
Lithuania	-	-	-	-	-	-	-	.. c	-	-
Luxembourg	66.3	83.0	0.1	-	7.3	138.6	-123.5	-13.2	401.9	343.5
Mexico	12.9	21.0	-	1.7	12.7	-801.4	-459.7	-99.0	-58.1	-195.7
Netherlands	-57.5	344.0	253.6	78.4	107.6	48.9	-158.9	89.3	150.1	375.1
New Zealand	-	2.0	2.8	-	-	-11.6	.. c	0.4	16.5	1.8
Norway	5.6	20.0	183.2	5.1	75.4	.. c	.. c	.. c	-4.4	0.4
Poland	-	1.0	-	-	-0.2	115.9	60.5	38.9	-24.4	-225.8
Portugal	1.8	3.0	-	-	-	.. c	.. c	9.8	15.2	15.1
Slovak Republic	-	-	-	-	-	344.2	382.8	367.6	399.5	476.3
Slovenia	-	-	-	-	-	.. c	.. c	.. c	0.2	.. c
Spain	6.7	36.0	-	0.9	1.7	41.5	40.7	59.7	16.1	103.5
Sweden	14.6	104.0	71.4	29.2	249.1	.. c	.. c	29.5	30.8	43.2
Switzerland	216.6	249.0	59.9	30.9	90.8	.. c	.. c	9.5	8.0	1.0
Turkey	-	1.0	0.2	-	-	-113.7	-122.1	86.4	69.2	170.5
United Kingdom	179.3	234.0	759.0	116.3	321.3	-146.1	-31.3	323.9	345.1	183.6
United States	627.7	728.0	443.1	1 585.0	355.1	-1 029.4	464.8	367.9	-220.8	177.3
EUROPE	**898.8**	**1 766.0**	**2 014.1**	**1 352.6**	**1 508.3**	**809.6**	**1 221.5**	**2 472.5**	**2 480.7**	**2 741.9**
Bulgaria	-	-	-	-	-	15.1	48.9	1.4	-3.6	5.8
Croatia	-	-	-	-	-	-	-	.. c	-	.. c
Cyprus	-	-	-	-	-	.. c	.. c	-213.0	-99.5	74.0
Malta	180.2	115.0	-	2.5	13.9	-	-	.. c	-0.5	.. c
Romania	-	-	-	-	-	.. c	.. c	13.9	-10.9	-65.3
Russian Federation	-	-	-	-	0.0	-122.5	583.8	453.6	477.1	546.4
Ukraine	-	-	-	-	-	-	.. c	-	-0.2	-1.6
AFRICA	**-**	**-**	**-**	**-**	**-**	**-667.5**	**-562.4**	**-45.3**	**6.8**	**24.8**
Northern Africa	-	-	-	-	-	-20.7	-367.7	40.7	26.8	45.3
Algeria	-	-	-	-	-	.. c	.. c	-0.7	-0.7	0.4
Egypt	-	-	-	-	-	.. c	.. c	37.4	22.2	44.3
Libya	-	-	-	-	-	.. c	.. c	-1.3	-0.6	-0.5
Morocco	-	-	-	-	-	.. c	.. c	-0.1	-0.8	-3.7
Tunisia	-	-	-	-	-	.. c	.. c	.. c	6.7	.. c
Other African countries	-	-	-	-	-	-646.8	-194.8	-86.0	-20.0	-20.4
Nigeria	-	-	-	-	-	.. c	.. c	-0.7	45.3	18.6
South Africa	-	-	-	-	-	43.7	19.9	15.1	46.6	64.6
AMERICA	**579.9**	**804.0**	**447.7**	**1 598.8**	**500.2**	**-4 217.9**	**730.0**	**1 168.9**	**90.4**	**228.5**
Northern America	659.8	806.0	447.3	1 585.0	359.7	-2 832.4	159.6	282.9	-431.7	174.4
Central America and Caribbean countries	-82.4	-12.0	0.3	13.7	140.6	-600.6	-274.3	-163.0	61.2	-366.8
Bahamas	1.3	2.0	-	-	-	-	-	.. c	15.0	.. c
Bermuda	-3.9	-4.0	0.3	-	78.0	82.7	.. c	48.3	49.4	-58.3
Cayman Islands	-81.8	-46.0	0.0	12.0	0.8	106.9	64.2	-103.7	19.8	-42.1
Costa Rica	-	-	-	-	-	.. c	.. c	-1.6	1.3	3.9
El Salvador	-	-	-	-	-	.. c	.. c	.. c	2.6	5.4
Guatemala	-	-	-	-	-	.. c	.. c	0.1	0.5	0.1
Honduras	-	-	-	-	-	.. c	.. c	-2.1	-7.2	-2.0
Nicaragua	-	-	-	-	-	.. c	.. c	-2.2	-1.6	0.9
Panama	1.3	3.0	-	-	-	-18.3	-40.1	1.7	41.1	34.6
Virgin Islands, U.S.	-12.6	12.0	-	-	-	-	-	.. c	-	.. c
South America	2.5	10.0	-	-	-	-784.9	844.7	1 049.0	461.0	420.9
Argentina	-	-	-	-	-	.. c	.. c	0.3	-46.9	-4.4
Bolivia	-	-	-	-	-	.. c	.. c	1.1	-1.0	0.3
Brazil	-	-	-	-	-	-734.1	859.8	1 040.8	516.2	420.9
Colombia	-	-	-	-	-	1.6	.. c	-1.0	-0.8	26.1
Ecuador	-	-	-	-	-	.. c	.. c	-	-	-
Paraguay	-	-	-	-	-	.. c	.. c	.. c	-0.1	-0.3
Peru	-	-	-	-	-	.. c	.. c	-4.3	-5.8	2.6
Uruguay	-	-	-	-	-	.. c	.. c	.. c	-	.. c
Venezuela	-	-	-	-	-	-	-	.. c	-	.. c

Table 3. Foreign direct investment income by country *(cont.)*

Million US dollars

	Inward					Outward				
	2015	2016	2017	2018	2019	2015	2016	2017	2018	2019
ASIA	**717.3**	**1 389.0**	**1 150.8**	**1 450.2**	**1 434.0**	**4 018.0**	**8 035.5**	**7 709.2**	**6 608.8**	**6 221.9**
Near and Middle East	59.4	72.0	39.5	91.6	69.0	-710.1	-550.3	-103.6	55.0	239.4
Gulf Arabian countries	59.4	69.0	39.4	91.6	67.8	-708.6	-552.6	-105.3	69.3	250.0
Kuwait	-	-	-	-	-	.. c	.. c	-	-	0.0
Qatar	-	-	-	-	-	.. c	.. c	-	-	-
Saudi Arabia	66.7	51.0	-	-	31.0	-709.5	-485.3	-182.1	131.5	268.2
United Arab Emirates	-19.0	8.0	0.1	-	9.4	20.4	-64.1	72.6	-64.4	-29.5
Other Near and Middle East	0.0	3.0	0.1	0.0	1.2	-1.5	2.3	1.8	-14.4	-10.6
Jordan	-	-	-	-	-	.. c	.. c	5.5	-2.2	2.7
Other Asian countries	657.8	1 317.0	1 111.3	1 358.6	1 365.0	4 728.1	8 585.8	7 812.7	6 553.8	5 982.5
China	4.3	136.0	0.8	56.3	-20.0	3 547.7	6 111.4	4 235.5	3 730.7	2 020.4
Hong Kong, China	35.0	249.0	4.6	16.1	21.9	-22.5	-141.5	-726.7	-443.9	-32.4
India	-37.8	64.0	-	-	3.1	502.2	520.4	480.0	972.8	1 103.6
Indonesia	0.1	2.0	-	-	77.8	-267.5	271.6	73.7	218.6	380.1
Iran, Islamic Republic of	-	-	-	-	-	.. c	.. c	-13.8	-47.3	-12.8
Malaysia	61.0	21.0	0.3	-0.9	2.7	128.6	387.2	377.8	349.1	246.5
Philippines	-19.0	-19.0	-	-	-	52.1	-342.0	-95.4	-1 295.7	518.8
Singapore	90.1	189.0	64.6	711.8	138.6	889.5	947.0	1 297.5	1 064.2	1 091.9
Chinese Taipei	-26.9	32.0	-	-	1.5	64.6	15.1	78.9	101.0	81.7
Thailand	-	-	-	-	0.1	186.1	203.8	141.0	173.5	166.7
Viet Nam	-	-	-	-	17.1	-122.9	528.3	1 831.6	1 699.2	649.9
AUSTRALIA, OCEANIA AND POLAR REGIONS	**-6.2**	**4.0**	**2.8**	**0.4**	**0.5**	**-66.3**	**-370.1**	**-1 214.9**	**442.5**	**-154.1**
WORLD unallocated and confidential	**36.0**	**34.0**	**0.0**	**0.0**	**0.0**	**0.0**	**-**	**-**	**-**	**-**
European Union (EU28)	**637.1**	**1 456.0**	**1 770.8**	**1 316.6**	**1 338.8**	**1 102.4**	**875.0**	**1 871.4**	**1 935.8**	**2 003.1**
G20 countries excl. European Union	**1 730.5**	**2 317.0**	**2 912.8**	**3 186.7**	**2 204.4**	**-1 383.7**	**7 383.2**	**5 865.9**	**6 738.4**	**5 007.2**
G20 OECD countries	**1 697.3**	**2 064.0**	**2 912.0**	**3 130.4**	**2 112.5**	**-3 648.9**	**-495.0**	**-251.1**	**691.8**	**207.4**
G20 Non-OECD countries	**33.2**	**253.0**	**0.8**	**56.3**	**91.9**	**2 265.2**	**7 878.2**	**6 117.0**	**6 046.6**	**4 799.9**
MENA countries	**59.4**	**69.0**	**39.4**	**91.6**	**69.3**	**-728.6**	**-918.1**	**-59.2**	**94.0**	**297.9**
ASEAN countries	**132.3**	**193.0**	**64.9**	**710.9**	**236.2**	**829.8**	**1 994.9**	**3 605.3**	**2 147.1**	**2 961.1**

- Nil; c Confidential data

Note: Data excludes resident Special Purpose Entities (SPEs). Detailed metadata at: *http://stats.oecd.org/OECDStat_Metadata/ShowMetadata.ashx?Dataset=FDI_CTRY_IND_SUMM.*

Source: OECD *International Direct Investment Statistics (database): https://doi.org/10.1787/idi-data-en*

Table 4. Foreign direct investment flows by industrial sector

Million US dollars

	Inward					Outward				
	2015	2016	2017	2018	2019	2015	2016	2017	2018	2019
All FDI activities	**2 804.7**	**7 263.0**	**11 531.5**	**13 267.2**	**12 589.0**	**18 489.6**	**30 507.5**	**43 463.9**	**45 232.6**	**50 981.1**
Agriculture, forestry and fishing	**0.7**	**2.0**	**5.0**	**-28.5**	**4.1**	**69.7**	**59.0**	**81.9**	**118.1**	**36.5**
Mining and quarrying	**7.3**	**13.0**	**0.1**	**1.6**	**2.4**	**-3 384.0**	**-1 106.0**	**-1 126.1**	**873.2**	**336.8**
Extraction activities	-	-	0.1	-	2.4	-1 281.6	-1 029.0	-1 102.4	298.5	-511.8
Manufacturing	**1 507.4**	**3 909.0**	**5 180.9**	**5 245.3**	**5 049.5**	**7 794.6**	**11 758.0**	**14 631.2**	**17 421.0**	**19 719.0**
of which:										
Food products, beverages and tobacco	-958.9	154.0	150.3	142.6	524.4	392.0	587.9	570.3	578.5	1 323.9
Textiles, wood and paper products; printing	-61.9	111.0	73.5	30.4	74.9	306.9	489.0	411.4	178.8	459.9
Chemical, rubber, plastic, non-metallic mineral products	2 436.5	2 839.0	2 120.7	2 049.5	3 307.7	1 321.7	1 778.6	1 540.4	1 849.2	3 398.5
Metal and machinery products, except electrical equipment	-189.1	-44.0	1 901.5	964.2	948.6	2 059.6	5 578.1	7 756.9	10 163.9	8 042.7
Motor vehicles, trailers, semi-trailers, other transport equipment	-1 032.3	-139.0	524.3	1 873.1	305.2	2 608.3	2 108.2	3 221.2	2 293.9	2 430.3
Other manufacturing	1 313.1	988.0	410.6	185.4	-111.1	1 106.1	1 216.3	1 131.0	2 356.7	4 063.7
Electricity, gas, steam and air conditioning supply	**7.4**	**50.0**	**-135.9**	**160.0**	**774.3**	**1 805.8**	**781.0**	**1 206.7**	**1 006.0**	**1 468.8**
Water supply; sewerage, waste management and remediation activities	**-5.8**	**10.0**	**149.2**	**1.5**	**3.5**	**12.7**	**3.0**	**174.8**	**442.2**	**14.8**
Construction	**2.6**	**-33.0**	**11.8**	**14.7**	**26.6**	**-105.4**	**778.0**	**638.1**	**885.8**	**502.1**
Services	**1 285.1**	**3 312.0**	**6 320.4**	**7 872.8**	**6 728.7**	**12 296.2**	**18 234.0**	**27 855.9**	**24 486.3**	**28 903.0**
Wholesale and retail trade; repair of motor vehicles and motorcycles	755.3	1 029.0	1 042.4	936.6	1 849.0	2 910.9	4 504.0	11 682.8	5 605.9	4 488.3
Transportation and storage	464.6	315.0	192.6	116.7	89.3	238.2	1 002.0	1 027.2	718.3	687.8
Accommodation and food service activities	625.6	770.0	808.3	281.1	341.5	179.6	401.0	208.9	109.6	427.0
Information and communication	540.4	511.0	756.1	2 821.9	1 522.5	376.7	1 191.0	2 174.6	851.0	309.5
Financial and insurance activities	-749.2	151.0	2 100.2	2 057.5	1 932.9	6 043.7	5 343.0	9 506.9	12 837.0	17 712.8
Activities of holding companies	387.0	580.0	76.4	656.6	482.1	1 226.8	479.3	1 105.3	1 648.6	1 179.3
Real estate activities	-278.7	148.0	912.3	906.9	618.0	1 998.1	4 995.8	2 521.1	3 448.2	3 884.6
Professional, scientific and technical activities	-34.1	309.0	400.6	128.3	249.3	136.0	519.0	458.5	948.7	809.6
Administrative and support service activities	-	-	72.2	377.7	49.5	348.2	176.9	-335.8	-203.7	112.8
Public administration; activities of households and of extraterritorial organisations	-	-	-	-	-	1.0	-	258.0	-	0.1
Education	45.9	21.0	13.7	11.7	62.6	25.0	11.1	125.6	12.8	35.0
Human health and social work activities	-	-	-	-	0.1	44.9	68.9	175.4	181.5	120.0
Arts, entertainment and recreation	-55.3	-14.0	16.0	233.3	30.5	-8.6	9.0	5.4	-26.0	312.0
Other services	-29.4	72.0	5.8	1.1	-16.5	2.5	12.7	47.4	3.0	3.8
Not allocated and confidential	**0.0**	**-**	**0.0**	**0.0**	**0.0**	**0.0**	**0.1**	**1.3**	**0.0**	**0.0**
Private real estate activities	..	-	-	-	-	-	-	-	-	-

- Nil; .. Not available

Note: Data excludes resident Special Purpose Entities (SPEs). Detailed metadata at: *http://stats.oecd.org/OECDStat_Metadata/ShowMetadata.ashx?Dataset=FDI_CTRY_IND_SUMM.*

Source: *OECD International Direct Investment Statistics (database): https://doi.org/10.1787/idi-data-en*

Table 5. Foreign direct investment positions by industrial sector

At year end

Million US dollars

	Inward					Outward				
	2015	2016	2017	2018	2019	2015	2016	2017	2018	2019
All FDI activities	**168 923.7**	**174 978.0**	**210 863.5**	**213 966.3**	**218 309.7**	**276 100.1**	**296 641.0**	**343 088.5**	**383 982.9**	**433 671.5**
Agriculture, forestry and fishing	**153.1**	**200.6**	**235.3**	**203.1**	**105.1**	**855.5**	**842.0**	**910.0**	**1 031.1**	**1 236.4**
Mining and quarrying	**21.5**	**11.1**	**44.8**	**42.8**	**42.7**	**37 533.6**	**35 209.0**	**34 055.1**	**33 676.6**	**34 734.5**
Extraction activities	14.0	3.0	44.8	2.9	2.9	28 624.9	26 806.4	25 601.9	24 678.8	26 666.5
Manufacturing	**62 916.4**	**66 721.2**	**79 861.6**	**82 015.7**	**80 728.3**	**102 207.2**	**110 985.0**	**135 266.9**	**135 519.5**	**162 087.1**
of which:										
Food products, beverages and tobacco	3 166.5	3 296.2	4 817.0	4 134.5	3 841.8	3 279.2	4 319.6	4 152.1	4 414.1	5 967.2
Textiles, wood and paper products; printing	1 375.3	1 606.6	1 359.0	2 538.0	1 785.0	5 205.7	5 729.7	6 424.2	5 536.3	6 413.0
Chemical, rubber, plastic, non-metallic mineral products	25 445.6	27 498.5	37 225.6	33 422.9	34 351.3	12 833.1	13 725.1	15 259.1	17 859.3	21 246.2
Metal and machinery products, except electrical equipment	18 020.9	18 067.2	20 369.9	23 757.8	23 012.2	44 940.0	50 536.8	60 291.8	65 102.0	71 742.6
Motor vehicles, trailers, semi-trailers, other transport equipment	7 060.1	8 216.7	7 099.0	8 347.5	8 252.5	26 545.9	25 735.6	37 816.9	28 616.6	38 267.6
Other manufacturing	7 848.0	8 036.1	8 991.1	9 815.0	9 485.5	9 403.4	10 938.4	11 322.7	13 991.3	18 450.6
Electricity, gas, steam and air conditioning supply	**1 012.6**	**1 002.9**	**1 053.8**	**1 139.1**	**1 071.8**	**4 262.3**	**5 013.0**	**6 391.2**	**7 258.2**	**8 580.8**
Water supply; sewerage, waste management and remediation activities	**92.2**	**146.3**	**194.0**	**245.2**	**123.9**	**30.6**	**18.0**	**166.2**	**612.0**	**803.8**
Construction	**1 310.3**	**1 306.1**	**1 801.4**	**1 635.7**	**1 748.1**	**1 922.7**	**1 813.0**	**2 987.7**	**3 578.6**	**4 566.5**
Services	**103 417.5**	**105 589.9**	**127 672.5**	**128 684.8**	**134 489.8**	**129 287.2**	**142 758.0**	**163 309.9**	**202 305.4**	**221 661.5**
Wholesale and retail trade; repair of motor vehicles and motorcycles	12 813.3	15 313.1	20 940.9	24 163.6	22 996.8	44 506.5	47 874.0	54 164.8	72 349.1	62 546.8
Transportation and storage	3 025.3	3 169.6	3 698.0	2 923.4	3 877.0	2 678.1	4 519.0	4 133.2	5 150.7	5 329.3
Accommodation and food service activities	13 480.6	14 584.0	17 937.6	15 987.5	14 865.7	2 043.3	2 351.0	3 048.4	2 574.5	3 650.4
Information and communication	6 747.2	4 579.9	7 382.6	7 689.8	8 409.2	3 736.8	5 495.0	6 366.3	6 403.3	8 462.5
Financial and insurance activities	52 747.3	54 129.8	61 630.1	60 792.7	66 133.4	57 409.5	54 265.0	68 982.9	84 638.0	105 205.8
Activities of holding companies	0.2	1.4	3 079.2	2 867.6	2 872.6	16 317.3	7 876.2	8 907.4	10 350.3	13 037.3
Real estate activities	7 068.3	6 858.3	8 658.4	10 578.0	11 114.6	11 788.9	15 477.1	17 270.3	21 094.7	24 435.6
Professional, scientific and technical activities	4 312.4	4 737.2	3 491.0	2 599.7	3 373.8	1 472.6	8 205.0	3 845.8	4 625.0	5 007.2
Administrative and support service activities	1 289.8	1 432.9	1 982.3	2 262.8	2 301.0	4 079.7	2 754.5	3 350.1	3 274.1	4 188.0
Public administration; activities of households and of extraterritorial organisations	0.1	-	-	0.1	-	17.7	17.7	17.7	17.7	17.7
Education	222.9	193.8	260.1	249.0	189.9	200.3	204.4	222.4	253.3	465.7
Human health and social work activities	11.3	12.0	12.0	1.9	1.6	193.5	426.7	611.0	674.0	873.4
Arts, entertainment and recreation	1 257.1	454.7	1 398.8	710.3	559.1	875.9	888.0	964.1	927.1	1 179.7
Other services	442.0	124.6	280.6	726.1	667.8	284.3	281.8	332.9	323.9	299.4
Not allocated and confidential	**-0.2**	**0.1**	**0.1**	**0.0**	**0.0**	**1.0**	**2.7**	**1.3**	**1.3**	**1.1**
Private real estate activities	..	-	-	-	-	-	-	-	-	-

- Nil; .. Not available

Note: Data excludes resident Special Purpose Entities (SPEs). Detailed metadata at: *http://stats.oecd.org/OECDStat_Metadata/ShowMetadata.ashx?Dataset=FDI_CTRY_IND_SUMM.*

Source: *OECD International Direct Investment Statistics (database): https://doi.org/10.1787/idi-data-en*

KOREA

Table 6. Foreign direct investment income by industrial sector

Million US dollars

	Inward					Outward				
	2015	2016	2017	2018	2019	2015	2016	2017	2018	2019
All FDI activities	**2 225.8**	**3 997.0**	**3 615.4**	**4 402.0**	**3 443.0**	**-124.1**	**9 054.5**	**10 090.4**	**9 629.2**	**9 062.9**
Agriculture, forestry and fishing	**0.6**	**3.0**	**4.5**	**-**	**3.0**	**-43.0**	**0.3**	**13.6**	**6.9**	**-69.1**
Mining and quarrying	**13.7**	**10.0**	**0.6**	**1.3**	**-**	**-5 337.7**	**-2 267.0**	**-1 637.2**	**-18.3**	**-761.8**
Extraction activities	-	-	0.6	-	-	-3 520.2	-1 951.5	-1 717.3	-347.7	-405.4
Manufacturing	**941.7**	**2 107.0**	**2 869.2**	**3 515.4**	**2 277.6**	**3 949.9**	**8 963.0**	**9 774.4**	**6 177.0**	**5 118.8**
of which:										
Food products, beverages and tobacco	119.0	144.0	147.4	155.3	309.3	20.8	224.1	0.1	8.2	-261.5
Textiles, wood and paper products; printing	-0.6	118.0	22.4	81.8	54.9	96.1	27.4	73.6	-77.0	-127.3
Chemical, rubber, plastic, non-metallic mineral products	345.8	661.0	1 860.1	2 169.2	1 012.2	512.1	834.5	734.4	238.0	473.2
Metal and machinery products, except electrical equipment	50.0	305.0	587.4	732.5	729.8	896.9	5 109.3	6 913.9	5 792.3	2 953.7
Motor vehicles, trailers, semi-trailers, other transport equipment	335.5	760.0	104.4	61.9	116.5	2 194.5	2 204.1	1 544.1	-296.4	1 073.1
Other manufacturing	92.0	119.0	146.8	314.7	54.9	229.4	563.7	508.3	511.9	1 007.7
Electricity, gas, steam and air conditioning supply	**51.2**	**51.0**	**52.4**	**96.3**	**29.5**	**171.7**	**161.3**	**378.2**	**311.4**	**334.0**
Water supply; sewerage, waste management and remediation activities	**-4.4**	**-3.0**	**0.2**	**-**	**0.1**	**0.6**	**13.5**	**11.7**	**19.2**	**4.4**
Construction	**45.3**	**50.0**	**5.5**	**-**	**10.6**	**-897.0**	**-532.0**	**-54.3**	**252.6**	**-95.5**
Services	**1 177.6**	**1 779.0**	**682.9**	**789.1**	**1 122.2**	**2 031.5**	**2 715.5**	**1 604.0**	**2 880.4**	**4 532.2**
Wholesale and retail trade; repair of motor vehicles and motorcycles	157.1	558.0	325.4	205.8	464.5	2 232.3	2 049.6	1 234.6	2 968.4	4 452.6
Transportation and storage	276.6	192.0	211.0	18.5	93.1	192.3	199.2	140.6	168.5	-4.2
Accommodation and food service activities	128.5	172.0	1.7	55.3	-50.4	-64.9	-12.9	-76.2	-181.8	-202.7
Information and communication	316.4	305.0	5.3	2.4	23.0	-250.5	52.8	-9.1	-278.3	-203.3
Financial and insurance activities	188.7	325.0	81.9	475.5	460.0	-452.2	-41.0	180.9	23.9	-158.0
Activities of holding companies	37.2	47.0	44.1	9.6	6.9	-580.8	-31.9	26.2	60.9	-194.3
Real estate activities	22.0	96.0	1.0	25.8	42.7	108.8	211.1	111.5	312.0	690.1
Professional, scientific and technical activities	100.8	129.0	44.5	1.4	72.6	20.8	286.5	6.7	-120.1	-46.2
Administrative and support service activities	-	2.0	11.8	4.2	13.9	320.9	-24.9	124.6	29.1	49.2
Public administration; activities of households and of extraterritorial organisations	-	-	-	-	-	-	-	-	-	-
Education	9.5	5.0	0.3	-	4.7	-4.5	-8.5	-2.3	-19.4	-9.3
Human health and social work activities	-	-	-	-	-	-4.6	19.3	-1.9	68.5	-3.4
Arts, entertainment and recreation	-24.8	-12.0	-	-	-4.0	-66.4	-15.0	-103.7	-86.7	-29.6
Other services	2.8	7.0	-	-	2.0	-0.5	-0.7	-1.7	-3.6	-2.9
Not allocated and confidential	**0.0**	**-**	**0.0**	**0.0**	**0.0**	**0.0**	**0.1**	**0.0**	**0.0**	**-**
Private real estate activities	..	-	-	-	-	-	-	-	-	-

- Nil; .. Not available

Note: Data excludes resident Special Purpose Entities (SPEs). Detailed metadata at: *http://stats.oecd.org/OECDStat_Metadata/ShowMetadata.ashx?Dataset=FDI_CTRY_IND_SUMM.*

Source: *OECD International Direct Investment Statistics (database): https://doi.org/10.1787/idi-data-en*

LATVIA

Table 1. Foreign direct investment flows by country

Million US dollars

	Inward					Outward				
	2015	2016	2017	2018	2019	2015	2016	2017	2018	2019
WORLD	**738.8**	**254.3**	**706.8**	**966.6**	**874.3**	**71.0**	**159.2**	**133.0**	**205.4**	**-105.2**
OECD COUNTRIES	**193.0**	**-69.7**	**409.2**	**574.8**	**684.0**	**-74.3**	**98.4**	**65.4**	**53.1**	**-91.8**
Australia	-	-	-	-	-1.1	-	-	-	-	-
Austria	25.5	108.4	-6.8	13.0	36.9	.. c	.. c	.. c	3.5	-
Belgium	2.2	-7.7	1.1	3.5	5.6	-	-	-	-	-
Canada	5.5	6.6	3.4	-	1.1	.. c	-	-	-	-
Chile	-	-	-	-	-	-	-	-	-	-
Czech Republic	2.2	1.1	-	-	62.7	-	.. c	.. c	-	-
Denmark	5.5	33.2	44.0	-30.7	4.5	.. c	.. c	11.3	13.0	-1.1
Estonia	41.0	79.6	19.2	269.1	808.2	-25.5	43.1	6.8	15.3	36.9
Finland	-3.3	13.3	-25.9	-46.0	-6.7	4.4	-	-6.8	5.9	-1.1
France	4.4	7.7	16.9	15.3	2.2	-4.4	.. c	.. c	3.5	.. c
Germany	16.6	-122.7	-9.0	22.4	401.9	3.3	1.1	-1.1	-9.4	-17.9
Greece	-	-	-	-	-	.. c	.. c	.. c	.. c	-
Hungary	-238.5	-	1.1	-	-	-	-	-	.. c	-
Iceland	2.2	-6.6	22.5	-54.3	-11.2	-	.. c	-	.. c	20.2
Ireland	-1.1	6.6	32.7	-30.7	32.5	-	-	-	-	-
Israel	-2.2	1.1	1.1	4.7	-	-	-	-	1.2	-
Italy	-4.4	44.2	2.3	3.5	3.4	.. c	-	-	-	-
Japan	-	-	-	-	.. c	-	-	-	-	-
Korea	5.5	-7.7	-37.2	-2.4	22.4	-	-	-	-	-
Latvia	-	-	-	-	-	-	-	-	-	-
Lithuania	73.2	61.9	110.5	26.0	87.3	25.5	37.6	53.0	41.3	-126.5
Luxembourg	51.0	210.1	71.0	232.5	-54.9	-1.1	1.1	-10.1	-3.5	19.0
Mexico	-	-	.. c	-1.2	-	-	.. c	.. c	.. c	-
Netherlands	206.3	-8.8	2.3	-148.7	5.6	5.5	-	-	-	-
New Zealand	.. c	-	-	-	-24.6	-	-	-	-	-
Norway	62.1	6.6	-325.8	3.5	-77.2	-	-	-	-	-
Poland	16.6	13.3	36.1	-	23.5	11.1	-15.5	-3.4	7.1	-4.5
Portugal	-	-	-	-	-	.. c	.. c	-	-	-
Slovak Republic	-	-	-1.1	-	-	.. c	.. c	.. c	-33.0	-6.7
Slovenia	-	-	-	-	-	-	-	-	-	-
Spain	-	-1.1	-	233.7	-249.6	3.3	6.6	4.5	1.2	-1.1
Sweden	-82.1	-456.7	597.5	211.3	-317.9	1.1	2.2	16.9	7.1	-4.5
Switzerland	32.2	71.9	-5.6	-4.7	-26.9	-71.0	17.7	-44.0	-24.8	25.7
Turkey	-	1.1	-1.1	3.5	3.4	-	-	-	-	-
United Kingdom	34.4	-60.8	-23.7	-139.3	-38.1	-	1.1	-6.8	-1.2	-11.2
United States	10.0	-3.3	-3.4	-7.1	-9.0	.. c	17.7	42.8	33.0	-16.8
EUROPE	**491.4**	**105.1**	**662.8**	**834.4**	**553.0**	**-6.7**	**109.5**	**71.0**	**112.1**	**-64.9**
Bulgaria	-	1.1	3.4	2.4	-2.2	.. c	.. c	.. c	1.2	.. c
Croatia	-	-	-	-	-	.. c	-	-	-	-
Cyprus	110.9	3.3	-82.3	-115.7	-	73.2	-3.3	-25.9	-34.2	-40.3
Malta	15.5	-68.6	45.1	8.3	-42.5	.. c	.. c	.. c	76.7	-1.1
Romania	-	-	-3.4	4.7	2.2	-	.. c	1.1	.. c	2.2
Russian Federation	106.5	175.8	130.8	354.1	-89.6	12.2	15.5	13.5	2.4	48.1
Ukraine	1.1	17.7	12.4	5.9	9.0	-4.4	-4.4	-4.5	18.9	-3.4
AFRICA	**-**	**7.7**	**5.6**	**1.2**	**-1.1**	**-**	**-**	**-**	**-**	**.. c**
Northern Africa	-	-	-	-	-	-	-	-	-	-
Algeria	-	-	-	-	-	-	-	-	-	-
Egypt	-	-	-	-	-	-	-	-	-	-
Libya	-	-	-	-	-	-	-	-	-	-
Morocco	-	-	-	-	-	-	-	-	-	-
Tunisia	-	-	-	-	-	-	-	-	-	-
Other African countries	-	7.7	5.6	1.2	-1.1	-	-	-	-	.. c
Nigeria	-	-	-	-	-	-	-	-	-	-
South Africa	-	-	-	-	-	-	-	-	-	-
AMERICA	**1.1**	**-23.2**	**-11.3**	**-13.0**	**71.6**	**14.4**	**37.6**	**45.1**	**24.8**	**-13.4**
Northern America	15.5	3.3	-	-7.1	-7.8	13.3	17.7	42.8	33.0	-16.8
Central America and Caribbean countries	-14.4	-26.5	-11.3	-5.9	79.5	1.1	19.9	1.1	-7.1	2.2
Bahamas	-	-	-	-	-	.. c	-	-	-	-
Bermuda	-	-	-	-	-	-	-	-	-	-
Cayman Islands	.. c	.. c	.. c	.. c	-4.5	-	-	-	-	-
Costa Rica	-	-	-	-	-	-	-	-	-	-
El Salvador	-	-	-	-	-	-	-	-	-	-
Guatemala	-	-	-	-	-	-	-	-	-	-
Honduras	-	-	-	-	-	-	-	-	-	-
Nicaragua	-	-	-	-	-	-	-	-	-	-
Panama	-	-2.2	-3.4	-1.2	-	-	-	-	-	.. c
Virgin Islands, U.S.	-	-	-	-	-	-	-	-	-	-
South America	-	-	-	-	-	-	-	-	-	.. c
Argentina	-	-	-	-	-	-	-	-	-	-
Bolivia	-	-	-	-	-	-	-	-	-	-
Brazil	-	-	-	-	-	-	-	-	-	.. c
Colombia	-	-	-	-	-	-	-	-	-	-
Ecuador	-	-	-	-	-	-	-	-	-	-
Paraguay	-	-	-	-	-	-	-	-	-	-
Peru	-	-	-	-	-	-	-	-	-	-
Uruguay	-	-	-	-	-	-	-	-	-	-
Venezuela	-	-	-	-	-	-	-	-	-	-

LATVIA

Table 1. Foreign direct investment flows by country *(cont.)*

Million US dollars

	Inward					Outward				
	2015	2016	2017	2018	2019	2015	2016	2017	2018	2019
ASIA	**35.5**	**48.7**	**-27.1**	**28.3**	**44.8**	**41.0**	**-**	**-12.4**	**11.8**	**-23.5**
Near and Middle East	2.2	29.9	-12.4	2.4	-	41.0	1.1	-13.5	13.0	-24.6
Gulf Arabian countries	-	2.2	-2.3	-1.2	3.4	.. c	.. c	.. c	.. c	.. c
Kuwait	-	-	-	-	-	-	-	-	-	-
Qatar	-	-	-	-	-	-	-	-	-	-
Saudi Arabia	-	-	.. c	-	-	-	-	-	-	-
United Arab Emirates	-	2.2	-1.1	-1.2	3.4	.. c	.. c	.. c	.. c	.. c
Other Near and Middle East	2.2	28.8	-9.0	2.4	-3.4	1.1	10.0	-	2.4	-4.5
Jordan	-	-	-	-	-	-	-	-	-	-
Other Asian countries	32.2	17.7	-14.7	26.0	43.7	1.1	-1.1	1.1	-	1.1
China	7.8	4.4	4.5	10.6	3.4	-	.. c	-	-	-
Hong Kong, China	-	-	-	2.4	2.2	-	-	-	-	-
India	-	-	-	-	5.6	-	-	-	-	-
Indonesia	-	-	-	-	-	-	-	-	-	-
Iran, Islamic Republic of	-	-	-	-	-	-	-	-	-	-
Malaysia	.. c	-	-	-	-	-	.. c	-	-	-
Philippines	-	-	-	-	-	-	-	-	-	-
Singapore	18.9	5.5	4.5	1.2	3.4	-	-	-	-	-
Chinese Taipei	-	-	-	-	-	-	-	-	-	-
Thailand	-	-	-	-	-	-	-	-	-	-
Viet Nam	-	12.2	5.6	5.9	5.6	-	-	-	-	-
AUSTRALIA, OCEANIA AND POLAR REGIONS	**-2.2**	**-**	**-1.1**	**-1.2**	**-25.7**	**-**	**-**	**-**	**-**	**-**
WORLD unallocated and confidential	**213.0**	**116.1**	**77.8**	**116.8**	**231.7**	**22.2**	**12.2**	**29.3**	**56.7**	**.. d**
European Union (EU28)	**282.9**	**-182.5**	**838.7**	**534.6**	**766.8**	**52.1**	**74.1**	**85.7**	**100.3**	**-165.7**
G20 countries excl. European Union	**184.1**	**46.4**	**81.2**	**257.3**	**305.6**	**27.7**	**47.6**	**53.0**	**15.3**	**1.1**
G20 OECD countries	**71.0**	**-133.8**	**-53.0**	**-106.2**	**385.1**	**14.4**	**34.3**	**39.5**	**14.2**	**-48.1**
G20 Non-OECD countries	**114.3**	**180.3**	**134.1**	**364.7**	**-79.5**	**13.3**	**13.3**	**13.5**	**1.2**	**49.3**
MENA countries	**-**	**2.2**	**-2.3**	**-1.2**	**3.4**	**.. c**	**.. c**	**.. c**	**.. c**	**.. c**
ASEAN countries	**17.7**	**17.7**	**10.1**	**7.1**	**10.1**	**-**	**.. c**	**-**	**-**	**-**

- Nil; .. Not available; c Confidential data; d Secondary Confidentiality

Note: Detailed metadata at: *http://stats.oecd.org/OECDStat_Metadata/ShowMetadata.ashx?Dataset=FDI_CTRY_IND_SUMM.*

Source: *OECD International Direct Investment Statistics (database): https://doi.org/10.1787/idi-data-en*

LATVIA

Table 2. Foreign direct investment positions by country

At year end

Million US dollars

	Inward					Outward				
	2015	2016	2017	2018	2019	2015	2016	2017	2018	2019
WORLD	**14 732.7**	**14 325.9**	**17 618.1**	**17 473.1**	**17 889.2**	**1 837.8**	**1 933.2**	**2 241.5**	**2 338.0**	**2 183.8**
OECD COUNTRIES	**9 992.4**	**9 380.2**	**11 565.1**	**12 687.2**	**13 136.4**	**766.5**	**889.6**	**1 069.8**	**1 511.3**	**1 408.7**
Australia	2.2	1.1	-	-	-	-	-	-	-	-
Austria	207.9	215.0	235.1	239.3	276.3	13.1	14.8	16.8	18.3	15.7
Belgium	31.6	53.8	34.8	57.2	85.4	-	-	-	1.1	-
Canada	17.4	12.6	14.4	14.9	14.6	-	-	-	-	-
Chile	-	-	-	-	-	-	-	-	-	-
Czech Republic	15.2	14.8	13.2	20.6	77.5	2.2	8.4	12.0	11.5	11.2
Denmark	622.8	629.3	704.0	651.5	659.4	9.8	20.0	22.8	13.7	13.5
Estonia	1 045.2	1 011.9	1 563.9	1 739.2	2 425.3	184.0	234.0	253.1	230.1	270.7
Finland	436.6	433.2	452.1	471.7	549.3	16.3	14.8	19.2	14.9	20.2
France	87.1	95.9	115.1	169.5	142.7	24.0	22.1	27.6	22.9	27.0
Germany	787.2	643.0	784.4	869.0	1 150.3	22.9	22.1	43.2	55.0	48.3
Greece	-	-	2.4	-	1.1	-	-	13.2	14.9	15.7
Hungary	1.1	1.1	13.2	11.5	7.9	-	-	-	2.3	2.2
Iceland	62.1	102.2	103.1	49.2	49.4	1.1	-	-	1.1	28.1
Ireland	15.2	7.4	54.0	19.5	56.2	4.4	-	-	-	-
Israel	65.3	29.5	37.2	63.0	65.2	-	-	2.4	3.4	1.1
Italy	33.8	101.2	91.1	106.5	83.1	14.2	13.7	15.6	46.9	46.1
Japan	-	1.1	-	-	-	-	-	-	-	-
Korea	50.1	40.1	10.8	8.0	30.3	-	-	-	-	-
Latvia	-	-	-	-	-	-	-	-	-	-
Lithuania	712.0	754.7	1 103.4	1 075.1	1 182.9	314.6	363.7	485.7	565.6	424.6
Luxembourg	474.7	687.3	955.9	1 049.9	957.1	116.5	112.8	117.5	114.5	106.7
Mexico	-	-	1.2	-2.3	-3.4	-	9.5	15.6	-	-
Netherlands	1 335.9	1 274.4	1 464.4	1 246.9	1 271.6	106.7	103.3	117.5	113.4	112.3
New Zealand	27.2	27.4	30.0	25.2	1.1	-	-	-	-	-
Norway	811.1	752.6	644.0	597.7	526.8	10.9	12.6	31.2	18.3	14.6
Poland	66.4	70.6	119.9	116.8	143.8	55.5	65.4	63.6	35.5	34.8
Portugal	-	-	-	-	-	7.6	6.3	7.2	6.9	6.7
Slovak Republic	3.3	2.1	1.2	3.4	1.1	22.9	20.0	67.2	34.3	27.0
Slovenia	-	-	-	-	-	2.2	2.1	3.6	3.4	3.4
Spain	6.5	2.1	9.6	226.7	11.2	5.4	9.5	10.8	12.6	13.5
Sweden	2 854.7	2 254.7	3 030.7	3 050.1	2 728.6	10.9	21.1	27.6	17.2	12.4
Switzerland	197.1	238.2	351.4	277.1	235.9	96.9	111.7	67.2	48.1	68.5
Turkey	24.0	30.6	34.8	16.0	15.7	1.1	-	-	2.3	-
United Kingdom	545.5	442.7	518.1	324.0	235.9	22.9	27.4	30.0	25.2	4.5
United States	166.6	205.5	173.9	188.9	152.8	15.2	36.9	85.2	80.1	77.5
EUROPE	**13 691.9**	**13 299.3**	**16 547.1**	**16 442.6**	**16 703.0**	**1 663.6**	**1 745.5**	**1 981.3**	**2 068.9**	**2 004.0**
Bulgaria	18.5	19.0	24.0	25.2	19.1	147.0	141.2	159.5	161.4	149.4
Croatia	-	-	-	-	-	-	-	-	-	-
Cyprus	1 369.6	1 347.1	1 448.8	1 235.4	1 282.9	175.3	131.8	93.5	87.0	116.8
Malta	334.2	398.4	542.1	512.9	392.0	10.9	7.4	4.8	88.2	91.0
Romania	1.1	-	-3.6	1.1	3.4	5.4	5.3	15.6	9.2	13.5
Russian Federation	1 277.1	1 392.4	1 841.0	1 947.6	1 805.2	117.6	134.9	121.1	115.6	161.8
Ukraine	149.2	150.7	158.3	154.6	162.9	44.6	19.0	20.4	52.7	24.7
AFRICA	**16.3**	**17.9**	**25.2**	**29.8**	**19.1**	**-**	**1.1**	**1.2**	**1.1**	**14.6**
Northern Africa	-	-	-	-	-	-	-	-	-	-
Algeria	-	-	-	-	-	-	-	-	-	-
Egypt	-	-	-	-	-	-	-	-	-	-
Libya	-	-	-	-	-	-	-	-	-	-
Morocco	-	-	-	-	-	-	-	-	-	-
Tunisia	-	-	-	-	-	-	-	-	-	-
Other African countries	16.3	17.9	25.2	28.6	19.1	-	1.1	-	1.1	14.6
Nigeria	-	-	-	-	-	-	-	-	-	-
South Africa	4.4	1.1	-	8.0	-	-	-	-	-	-
AMERICA	**345.1**	**345.7**	**308.2**	**373.3**	**359.5**	**39.2**	**68.5**	**125.9**	**108.8**	**86.5**
Northern America	182.9	218.2	188.3	203.8	167.4	15.2	36.9	85.2	80.1	77.5
Central America and Caribbean countries	162.2	127.5	119.9	168.3	191.0	22.9	30.6	39.6	28.6	7.9
Bahamas	-	-	-	-	-	2.2	1.1	1.2	1.1	1.1
Bermuda	-	17.9	10.8	10.3	13.5	-	-	-	-	-
Cayman Islands	4.4	6.3	10.8	18.3	10.1	-	-	-	-	-
Costa Rica	-	-	-	-	-	-	-	-	-	-
El Salvador	-	-	-	-	-	-	-	-	-	-
Guatemala	-	-	-	-	-	-	-	-	-	-
Honduras	-	-	-	-	-	-	-	-	-	-
Nicaragua	-	-	-	-	-	-	-	-	-	-
Panama	12.0	9.5	4.8	3.4	16.9	-	-	-	-	2.2
Virgin Islands, U.S.	-	-	-	-	-	-	-	-	-	-
South America	-	-	-	1.1	1.1	-	1.1	1.2	-	1.1
Argentina	-	-	-	-	-	-	-	-	-	-
Bolivia	-	-	-	-	-	-	-	-	-	-
Brazil	-	-	-	-	-	-	1.1	1.2	-	1.1
Colombia	-	-	-	-	-	-	-	-	-	-
Ecuador	-	-	-	-	-	-	-	-	-	-
Paraguay	-	-	-	-	-	-	-	-	-	-
Peru	-	-	-	1.1	1.1	-	-	-	-	-
Uruguay	-	-	-	-	-	-	-	-	-	-
Venezuela	-	-	-	-	-	-	-	-	-	-

Table 2. Foreign direct investment positions by country (*cont.*)

At year end

Million US dollars

	Inward					Outward				
	2015	2016	2017	2018	2019	2015	2016	2017	2018	2019
ASIA	**411.5**	**405.8**	**427.0**	**425.9**	**457.2**	**92.5**	**85.4**	**72.0**	**57.2**	**32.6**
Near and Middle East	148.1	121.2	131.9	166.0	169.6	67.5	61.1	55.2	37.8	9.0
Gulf Arabian countries	15.2	2.1	-	12.6	16.9	39.2	29.5	12.0	21.8	-
Kuwait	-	-	-	-	-	-	-	-	-	-
Qatar	-	-	-	-	-	-	-	-	-	-
Saudi Arabia	14.2	-	-2.4	-	-	-	-	-	-	-
United Arab Emirates	-	3.2	2.4	12.6	16.9	39.2	29.5	12.0	21.8	-
Other Near and Middle East	133.9	119.1	131.9	152.3	152.8	28.3	31.6	43.2	17.2	9.0
Jordan	-	-	-	-	-	-	-	-	-	-
Other Asian countries	263.5	283.5	293.8	261.0	287.6	25.0	24.2	16.8	18.3	22.5
China	69.7	69.6	74.4	43.5	30.3	-	-	-	-	-
Hong Kong, China	3.3	1.1	2.4	4.6	14.6	-	-	-	-	-
India	1.1	1.1	3.6	2.3	6.7	-	-	-	-	-
Indonesia	-	-	-	-	-	-	-	-	-	-
Iran, Islamic Republic of	-	-	-	-	-	-	-	-	-	-
Malaysia	-	-	-	-	-	-	1.1	1.2	1.1	1.1
Philippines	-	-	-	-	-	-	-	-	-	-
Singapore	64.2	65.4	79.2	74.4	68.5	-	-	-	-1.1	-1.1
Chinese Taipei	-	-	-	-	-	-	-	-	-	-
Thailand	-	-	-	-	-	-	-	2.4	5.7	3.4
Viet Nam	-	11.6	20.4	25.2	30.3	-	-	-	-	-
AUSTRALIA, OCEANIA AND POLAR REGIONS	**42.5**	**29.5**	**31.2**	**27.5**	**1.1**	**-**	**-**	**-**	**-**	**-**
WORLD unallocated and confidential	**225.4**	**227.7**	**279.4**	**174.0**	**349.4**	**42.5**	**32.7**	**61.2**	**101.9**	**46.1**
European Union (EU28)	**11 081.1**	**10 495.4**	**13 328.1**	**13 273.4**	**13 798.0**	**1 297.8**	**1 371.4**	**1 631.1**	**1 706.0**	**1 591.8**
G20 countries excl. European Union	**3 078.9**	**3 037.8**	**3 662.7**	**3 697.0**	**3 666.6**	**219.9**	**267.7**	**339.4**	**349.2**	**367.3**
G20 OECD countries	**1 712.6**	**1 573.7**	**1 745.0**	**1 695.7**	**1 823.2**	**101.3**	**131.8**	**215.9**	**232.4**	**203.3**
G20 Non-OECD countries	**1 367.4**	**1 464.1**	**1 917.7**	**2 001.4**	**1 843.4**	**118.7**	**136.0**	**123.5**	**115.6**	**164.0**
MENA countries	**15.2**	**2.1**	**-**	**13.7**	**16.9**	**39.2**	**29.5**	**12.0**	**21.8**	**-**
ASEAN countries	**65.3**	**78.0**	**99.5**	**98.5**	**98.9**	**-**	**1.1**	**3.6**	**6.9**	**4.5**

\- Nil

Note: Detailed metadata at: *http://stats.oecd.org/OECDStat_Metadata/ShowMetadata.ashx?Dataset=FDI_CTRY_IND_SUMM.*

Source: *OECD International Direct Investment Statistics (database): https://doi.org/10.1787/idi-data-en*

Table 3. Foreign direct investment income by country

Million US dollars

	Inward					Outward				
	2015	2016	2017	2018	2019	2015	2016	2017	2018	2019
WORLD	**1 154.7**	**1 188.8**	**1 389.9**	**1 861.2**	**1 588.5**	**154.2**	**117.2**	**216.4**	**157.0**	**111.9**
OECD COUNTRIES	**711.0**	**811.7**	**879.3**	**1 115.3**	**1 050.0**	**54.4**	**61.9**	**101.5**	**127.5**	**79.5**
Australia	-	-	-	-	-	-	-	-	-	-
Austria	28.8	18.8	24.8	29.5	30.2	-	.. c	-	-	-
Belgium	-	3.3	.. c	4.7	10.1	-	-	-	-	-
Canada	-1.1	-	1.1	1.2	1.1	-	-	-	-	-
Chile	-	-	-	-	-	-	-	-	-	-
Czech Republic	4.4	6.6	-	9.4	6.7	-	.. c	.. c	-	.. c
Denmark	33.3	54.2	60.9	61.4	52.6	.. c	.. c	.. c	.. c	23.5
Estonia	74.3	89.6	112.7	146.3	170.2	-1.1	-1.1	11.3	10.6	11.2
Finland	21.1	23.2	33.8	46.0	31.3	5.5	6.6	-	1.2	1.1
France	5.5	5.5	7.9	8.3	10.1	-	.. c	.. c	-	.. c
Germany	58.8	47.6	57.5	34.2	44.8	-	-	-1.1	-	-3.4
Greece	-	-	-	-	-	-	-	-	-	-
Hungary	.. c	-	-	-	-	-	-	-	-	-
Iceland	-	10.0	7.9	-	-5.6	-	-	-	-	-
Ireland	-	-	5.6	1.2	1.1	-	-	-	-	-
Israel	-1.1	-1.1	-	-1.2	-	-	-	-	-	-
Italy	3.3	6.6	10.1	7.1	10.1	-	-	-	-	-
Japan	-	-	-	-	-	-	-	-	-	-
Korea	7.8	6.6	.. c	-	-	-	-	-	-	-
Latvia	-	-	-	-	-	-	-	-	-	-
Lithuania	21.1	25.4	57.5	55.5	72.8	39.9	18.8	32.7	30.7	3.4
Luxembourg	41.0	48.7	120.6	81.4	113.1	-6.7	.. c	.. c	-5.9	-6.7
Mexico	-	-	-	-	-	-	-	-	-	-
Netherlands	68.8	54.2	82.3	102.7	113.1	-	-	-	.. c	.. c
New Zealand	.. c	-	-	-	-	-	-	-	-	-
Norway	62.1	91.8	81.2	62.6	51.5	-	-	-	-	-
Poland	2.2	6.6	9.0	15.3	21.3	12.2	26.5	27.1	35.4	-2.2
Portugal	-	-	-	-	-	.. c	-	-	-	-
Slovak Republic	-	-	-	-	-	.. c	.. c	.. c	.. c	1.1
Slovenia	-	-	-	-	-	-	-	-	-	-
Spain	.. c	2.2	1.1	11.8	3.4	.. c	5.5	.. c	-	12.3
Sweden	277.3	291.9	239.0	384.8	288.8	8.9	11.1	11.3	3.5	-
Switzerland	12.2	14.4	10.1	17.7	3.4	23.3	8.8	9.0	.. c	6.7
Turkey	-	-	3.4	4.7	3.4	-	-	-	-	-
United Kingdom	2.2	21.0	3.4	20.1	6.7	-6.7	-3.3	1.1	.. c	6.7
United States	2.2	12.2	4.5	10.6	9.0	-	.. c	.. c	-	-
EUROPE	**925.1**	**1 046.1**	**1 192.7**	**1 480.0**	**1 279.5**	**109.8**	**88.5**	**140.9**	**132.2**	**97.4**
Bulgaria	-	.. c	2.3	1.2	.. c	.. c	-	-	-	-
Croatia	-	-	-	-	-	-	-	-	-	-
Cyprus	76.5	95.1	160.1	194.7	114.2	15.5	16.6	5.6	-1.2	1.1
Malta	65.4	33.2	34.9	34.2	13.4	.. c	.. c	-	-	1.1
Romania	-	-	-	-	-	-	-	-	-	.. c
Russian Federation	48.8	87.4	57.5	135.7	111.9	5.5	-6.6	5.6	3.5	13.4
Ukraine	12.2	12.2	1.1	8.3	3.4	-5.5	-5.5	-5.6	-	1.1
AFRICA	**-**	**-**	**-**	**-**	**-**	**-**	**-**	**-**	**-**	**-**
Northern Africa	-	-	-	-	-	-	-	-	-	-
Algeria	-	-	-	-	-	-	-	-	-	-
Egypt	-	-	-	-	-	-	-	-	-	-
Libya	-	-	-	-	-	-	-	-	-	-
Morocco	-	-	-	-	-	-	-	-	-	-
Tunisia	-	-	-	-	-	-	-	-	-	-
Other African countries	-	-	-	-	-	-	-	-	-	-
Nigeria	-	-	-	-	-	-	-	-	-	-
South Africa	-	-	-	-	-	-	-	-	-	-
AMERICA	**3.3**	**14.4**	**-11.3**	**-30.7**	**-22.4**	**-**	**1.1**	**2.3**	**-**	**-**
Northern America	1.1	12.2	5.6	10.6	10.1	-	.. c	.. c	-	-
Central America and Caribbean countries	2.2	2.2	-15.8	-41.3	-31.3	-	-	-	-	-
Bahamas	-	-	-	-	-	-	-	-	-	-
Bermuda	-	-	-	-	-	-	-	-	-	-
Cayman Islands	.. c	-	-	.. c	.. c	-	-	-	-	-
Costa Rica	-	-	-	-	-	-	-	-	-	-
El Salvador	-	-	-	-	-	-	-	-	-	-
Guatemala	-	-	-	-	-	-	-	-	-	-
Honduras	-	-	-	-	-	-	-	-	-	-
Nicaragua	-	-	-	-	-	-	-	-	-	-
Panama	-	-	-	-	-	-	-	-	-	-
Virgin Islands, U.S.	-	-	-	-	-	-	-	-	-	-
South America	-	-	-	-	-	-	-	-	-	-
Argentina	-	-	-	-	-	-	-	-	-	-
Bolivia	-	-	-	-	-	-	-	-	-	-
Brazil	-	-	-	-	-	-	-	-	-	-
Colombia	-	-	-	-	-	-	-	-	-	-
Ecuador	-	-	-	-	-	-	-	-	-	-
Paraguay	-	-	-	-	-	-	-	-	-	-
Peru	-	-	-	-	-	-	-	-	-	-
Uruguay	-	-	-	-	-	-	-	-	-	-
Venezuela	-	-	-	-	-	-	-	-	-	-

Table 3. Foreign direct investment income by country *(cont.)*

Million US dollars

	Inward					Outward				
	2015	2016	2017	2018	2019	2015	2016	2017	2018	2019
ASIA	**10.0**	**4.4**	**-**	**2.4**	**-**	**25.5**	**11.1**	**21.4**	**1.2**	**1.1**
Near and Middle East	-2.2	-3.3	-3.4	-3.5	-3.4	15.5	13.3	22.5	-	-
Gulf Arabian countries	-	-	1.1	3.5	2.2	-	.. c	.. c	.. c	-
Kuwait	-	-	-	-	-	-	-	-	-	-
Qatar	-	-	-	-	-	-	-	-	-	-
Saudi Arabia	-	-	-	-	-	-	-	-	-	-
United Arab Emirates	-	-	1.1	3.5	2.2	-	.. c	.. c	.. c	-
Other Near and Middle East	-2.2	-3.3	-4.5	-7.1	-5.6	14.4	11.1	21.4	-	-
Jordan	-	-	-	-	-	-	-	-	-	-
Other Asian countries	12.2	7.7	3.4	7.1	3.4	11.1	-2.2	-	1.2	1.1
China	-	-1.1	-	-	-	-	.. c	-	-	-
Hong Kong, China	1.1	-	-	-	-	-	-	-	-	-
India	-	-	-	-	-	-	-	-	-	-
Indonesia	-	-	-	-	-	-	-	-	-	-
Iran, Islamic Republic of	-	-	-	-	-	-	-	-	-	-
Malaysia	-	-	-	-	-	-	-	-	-	-
Philippines	-	-	-	-	-	-	-	-	-	-
Singapore	3.3	3.3	2.3	5.9	4.5	-	-	-	-	.. c
Chinese Taipei	-	-	-	-	-	-	-	-	-	-
Thailand	-	-	-	-	-	-	-	-	-	-
Viet Nam	-	-	-	-	-	-	-	-	-	-
AUSTRALIA, OCEANIA AND POLAR REGIONS	**.. c**	**-**	**-**	**-**	**-**	**-**	**-**	**-**	**-**	**-**
WORLD unallocated and confidential	**.. d**	**123.9**	**208.5**	**409.5**	**331.4**	**18.9**	**16.6**	**51.9**	**23.6**	**13.4**
European Union (EU28)	**788.7**	**831.6**	**1 029.2**	**1 244.0**	**1 112.7**	**84.3**	**88.5**	**128.5**	**119.2**	**73.9**
G20 countries excl. European Union	**126.5**	**184.7**	**145.4**	**220.7**	**197.0**	**-2.2**	**-16.6**	**9.0**	**4.7**	**24.6**
G20 OECD countries	**77.6**	**99.5**	**87.9**	**86.2**	**85.1**	**-6.7**	**-7.7**	**3.4**	**1.2**	**11.2**
G20 Non-OECD countries	**48.8**	**86.3**	**57.5**	**135.7**	**111.9**	**5.5**	**-7.7**	**5.6**	**3.5**	**13.4**
MENA countries	**-**	**-**	**1.1**	**3.5**	**2.2**	**-**	**.. c**	**.. c**	**.. c**	**-**
ASEAN countries	**3.3**	**3.3**	**2.3**	**5.9**	**4.5**	**-**	**-**	**-**	**-**	**.. c**

- Nil; .. Not available; c Confidential data; d Secondary Confidentiality

Note: Detailed metadata at: *http://stats.oecd.org/OECDStat_Metadata/ShowMetadata.ashx?Dataset=FDI_CTRY_IND_SUMM.*

Source: *OECD International Direct Investment Statistics (database): https://doi.org/10.1787/idi-data-en*

Table 4. Foreign direct investment flows by industrial sector

Million US dollars

	Inward					Outward				
	2015	2016	2017	2018	2019	2015	2016	2017	2018	2019
All FDI activities	**738.8**	**254.3**	**706.8**	**966.6**	**874.3**	**71.0**	**159.2**	**133.0**	**205.4**	**-105.2**
Agriculture, forestry and fishing	**13.3**	**14.4**	**45.1**	**15.3**	**11.2**	**-**	**.. c**	**-**	**-**	**-**
Mining and quarrying	**7.8**	**1.1**	**12.4**	**-**	**13.4**	**-**	**-**	**-**	**-**	**-**
Extraction activities	7.8	1.1	12.4	-	13.4	-	-	-	-	-
Manufacturing	**-53.2**	**22.1**	**32.7**	**159.3**	**115.3**	**23.3**	**73.0**	**25.9**	**10.6**	**3.4**
of which:										
Food products, beverages and tobacco	-28.8	-16.6	-37.2	131.0	13.4	-	-	-	-	-
Textiles, wood and paper products; printing	-69.9	22.1	58.6	2.4	30.2	6.7	56.4	9.0	16.5	-10.1
Chemical, rubber, plastic, non-metallic mineral products	-2.2	5.5	-20.3	48.4	4.5	.. c	.. c	-18.0	9.4	4.5
Metal and machinery products, except electrical equipment	25.5	4.4	14.7	11.8	14.6	-1.1	-	-	.. c	-2.2
Motor vehicles, trailers, semi-trailers, other transport equipment	10.0	5.5	22.5	13.0	24.6	-	-	-	-	-
Other manufacturing	12.2	1.1	-6.8	-48.4	28.0	18.9	.. c	.. c	-16.5	.. c
Electricity, gas, steam and air conditioning supply	**-24.4**	**24.3**	**-73.3**	**-24.8**	**1.1**	**.. c**	**-1.1**	**.. c**	**.. c**	**.. c**
Water supply; sewerage, waste management and remediation activities	**1.1**	**-**	**-1.1**	**-1.2**	**-**	**-**	**-**	**-**	**-**	**-**
Construction	**22.2**	**15.5**	**72.1**	**64.9**	**-56.0**	**2.2**	**29.9**	**.. c**	**3.5**	**-31.3**
Services	**485.9**	**87.4**	**485.9**	**546.4**	**509.3**	**17.7**	**39.8**	**83.4**	**119.2**	**-60.5**
Wholesale and retail trade; repair of motor vehicles and motorcycles	61.0	267.6	69.9	310.4	-3.4	8.9	33.2	9.0	85.0	-5.6
Transportation and storage	56.6	66.4	51.9	30.7	11.2	-21.1	-	1.1	2.4	32.5
Accommodation and food service activities	-13.3	4.4	25.9	-22.4	-7.8	.. c	-	-	-	-
Information and communication	6.7	33.2	-45.1	-2.4	31.3	-	4.4	-	8.3	19.0
Financial and insurance activities	352.7	-205.7	310.0	186.5	160.1	24.4	-16.6	67.6	34.2	-97.4
Activities of holding companies	85.4	-6.6	18.0	44.8	10.1	-41.0	-17.7	2.3	11.8	-81.7
Real estate activities	-75.4	-66.4	129.6	182.9	286.6	.. c	8.8	.. c	9.4	1.1
Professional, scientific and technical activities	91.0	-21.0	-78.9	-178.2	39.2	11.1	14.4	5.6	-16.5	-10.1
Administrative and support service activities	-2.2	-	13.5	3.5	-	-	-	-1.1	3.5	1.1
Public administration; activities of households and of extraterritorial organisations	-	-	-	-	-	-	-	-	-	-
Education	-	-	-	3.5	-	-	.. c	-	-	-
Human health and social work activities	-	4.4	-	1.2	2.2	-	-	-	-	-
Arts, entertainment and recreation	10.0	5.5	9.0	29.5	-10.1	1.1	.. c	-	.. c	-
Other services	-	-	-	-	-	-	-	-	-	-
Not allocated and confidential	**.. c**	**.. c**	**.. c**	**.. c**	**.. c**	**.. c**	**.. c**	**.. c**	**.. c**	**.. c**
Private real estate activities	**.. c**	**.. c**	**.. c**	**.. c**	**.. c**	**33.3**	**14.4**	**11.3**	**15.3**	**13.4**

- Nil; c Confidential data

Note: Detailed metadata at: *http://stats.oecd.org/OECDStat_Metadata/ShowMetadata.ashx?Dataset=FDI_CTRY_IND_SUMM.*

Source: *OECD International Direct Investment Statistics (database): https://doi.org/10.1787/idi-data-en*

Table 5. Foreign direct investment positions by industrial sector
At year end

Million US dollars

	Inward					Outward				
	2015	2016	2017	2018	2019	2015	2016	2017	2018	2019
All FDI activities	**14 732.7**	**14 325.9**	**17 618.1**	**17 473.1**	**17 889.2**	**1 837.8**	**1 933.2**	**2 241.5**	**2 338.0**	**2 183.8**
Agriculture, forestry and fishing	**667.4**	**597.7**	**736.4**	**661.8**	**726.8**	**-3.3**	**3.2**	**3.6**	-	-
Mining and quarrying	**124.1**	**121.2**	**148.7**	**167.2**	**140.4**	-	-	-	-	-
Extraction activities	124.1	121.2	148.7	167.2	140.4	-	-	-	-	-
Manufacturing	**1 667.9**	**1 690.7**	**1 978.9**	**2 039.2**	**2 075.9**	**123.0**	**205.5**	**248.3**	**206.1**	**216.8**
of which:										
Food products, beverages and tobacco	229.7	269.8	261.5	317.2	307.8	.. c	1.1	.. c	1.1	.. c
Textiles, wood and paper products; printing	512.8	529.1	629.6	706.4	684.1	58.8	113.8	133.1	140.8	128.1
Chemical, rubber, plastic, non-metallic mineral products	101.3	80.1	88.8	156.9	124.7	27.2	50.6	27.6	37.8	51.7
Metal and machinery products, except electrical equipment	188.4	171.8	244.7	198.1	242.6	2.2	4.2	3.6	5.7	4.5
Motor vehicles, trailers, semi-trailers, other transport equipment	62.1	98.0	124.7	132.8	159.5	-	-	-	-	-
Other manufacturing	573.8	541.8	629.6	527.8	557.2	38.1	35.8	82.8	21.8	31.5
Electricity, gas, steam and air conditioning supply	**548.7**	**521.8**	**686.0**	**636.6**	**596.5**	**10.9**	**10.5**	**9.6**	**22.9**	**12.4**
Water supply; sewerage, waste management and remediation activities	**15.2**	**11.6**	**4.8**	**6.9**	**10.1**	-	-	-	-	-
Construction	**567.2**	**647.2**	**663.2**	**724.8**	**634.7**	**13.1**	**43.2**	**49.2**	**53.8**	**25.8**
Services	**10 157.9**	**9 821.9**	**12 266.7**	**12 190.3**	**12 492.7**	**1 380.5**	**1 372.4**	**1 567.5**	**1 597.2**	**1 533.4**
Wholesale and retail trade; repair of motor vehicles and motorcycles	1 886.8	2 094.4	2 468.2	2 781.1	2 712.9	364.7	337.3	370.6	450.0	413.4
Transportation and storage	550.9	600.8	1 057.8	891.9	900.9	3.3	7.4	7.2	6.9	44.9
Accommodation and food service activities	182.9	148.6	235.1	182.0	251.6	-	-	-	-	-
Information and communication	434.4	457.5	594.9	557.6	607.7	3.3	5.3	6.0	6.9	20.2
Financial and insurance activities	4 214.5	3 730.4	4 218.0	4 194.0	4 253.0	836.1	841.2	940.3	899.9	813.3
Activities of holding companies	746.9	758.9	526.5	654.9	634.7	192.7	206.6	202.7	334.3	247.1
Real estate activities	1 951.0	1 917.4	2 620.5	2 788.0	2 980.2	32.7	40.1	48.0	41.2	50.6
Professional, scientific and technical activities	564.0	548.1	730.4	343.5	356.1	124.1	127.5	175.1	163.7	165.1
Administrative and support service activities	236.3	191.8	176.3	214.1	235.9	8.7	7.4	14.4	27.5	23.6
Public administration; activities of households and of extraterritorial organisations	-	-	-	-	-	-	-	-	-	-
Education	3.3	10.5	7.2	28.6	27.0	-	2.1	1.2	1.1	-
Human health and social work activities	6.5	10.5	7.2	9.2	9.0	-	-	-	-	-
Arts, entertainment and recreation	107.8	108.6	147.5	199.2	159.5	5.4	4.2	4.8	1.1	1.1
Other services	18.5	2.1	3.6	1.1	1.1	-	-	-	-	-
Not allocated and confidential	**226.5**	**183.4**	**247.1**	**176.3**	**344.9**	**6.5**	**-5.3**	**20.4**	**60.7**	**-12.4**
Private real estate activities	**757.8**	**730.5**	**886.3**	**870.2**	**867.2**	**307.0**	**303.6**	**343.0**	**397.3**	**407.8**

- Nil; c Confidential data

Note: Detailed metadata at: *http://stats.oecd.org/OECDStat_Metadata/ShowMetadata.ashx?Dataset=FDI_CTRY_IND_SUMM.*

Source: *OECD International Direct Investment Statistics (database): https://doi.org/10.1787/idi-data-en*

LATVIA

Table 6. Foreign direct investment income by industrial sector

Million US dollars

	Inward					Outward				
	2015	2016	2017	2018	2019	2015	2016	2017	2018	2019
All FDI activities	**1 154.7**	**1 188.8**	**1 389.9**	**1 861.2**	**1 588.5**	**154.2**	**117.2**	**216.4**	**157.0**	**111.9**
Agriculture, forestry and fishing	**7.8**	**-**	**12.4**	**7.1**	**3.4**	**-**	**-**	**-**	**-**	**-**
Mining and quarrying	**11.1**	**12.2**	**16.9**	**14.2**	**17.9**	**-**	**-**	**-**	**-**	**-**
Extraction activities	11.1	12.2	16.9	14.2	17.9	-	-	-	-	-
Manufacturing	**99.8**	**139.3**	**228.8**	**246.7**	**192.5**	**2.2**	**1.1**	**6.8**	**2.4**	**1.1**
of which:										
Food products, beverages and tobacco	-1.1	8.8	30.4	36.6	29.1	-	-	-	-	-
Textiles, wood and paper products; printing	65.4	97.3	143.2	151.1	87.3	-	1.1	1.1	.. c	2.2
Chemical, rubber, plastic, non-metallic mineral products	1.1	1.1	1.1	8.3	4.5	.. c	-	.. c	-	-
Metal and machinery products, except electrical equipment	-	5.5	7.9	11.8	12.3	-	-	-	-	-
Motor vehicles, trailers, semi-trailers, other transport equipment	7.8	13.3	13.5	11.8	10.1	-	-	-	-	-
Other manufacturing	26.6	13.3	32.7	28.3	50.4	-	-	-	-	-
Electricity, gas, steam and air conditioning supply	**38.8**	**54.2**	**39.5**	**31.9**	**28.0**	**.. c**	**.. c**	**.. c**	**-**	**-**
Water supply; sewerage, waste management and remediation activities	**-**	**-**	**-**	**-**	**-**	**-**	**-**	**-**	**-**	**-**
Construction	**4.4**	**-2.2**	**1.1**	**-7.1**	**4.5**	**-**	**-1.1**	**-**	**-**	**-**
Services	**783.1**	**883.6**	**901.8**	**1 172.0**	**1 017.6**	**137.5**	**106.2**	**163.5**	**142.8**	**104.1**
Wholesale and retail trade; repair of motor vehicles and motorcycles	187.5	219.0	250.3	395.4	306.7	45.5	26.5	28.2	18.9	16.8
Transportation and storage	33.3	29.9	55.2	31.9	35.8	1.1	-	1.1	1.2	-
Accommodation and food service activities	1.1	1.1	10.1	-3.5	-3.4	.. c	-	-	-	-
Information and communication	35.5	44.2	83.4	108.6	129.9	.. c	-	-	8.3	10.1
Financial and insurance activities	440.4	503.2	405.8	522.8	460.1	79.9	79.6	128.5	115.7	76.1
Activities of holding companies	72.1	36.5	39.5	66.1	61.6	18.9	2.2	19.2	8.3	15.7
Real estate activities	38.8	31.0	39.5	83.8	58.2	-	-3.3	-	-1.2	-
Professional, scientific and technical activities	11.1	15.5	9.0	-26.0	-29.1	7.8	4.4	4.5	4.7	2.2
Administrative and support service activities	1.1	-1.1	14.7	10.6	14.6	-	-	-	-	-
Public administration; activities of households and of extraterritorial organisations	-	-	-	-	-	-	-	-	-	-
Education	-	-	-	-	-1.1	-	-	-	-	-
Human health and social work activities	-	-	-	-	-	-	-	-	-	-
Arts, entertainment and recreation	33.3	39.8	34.9	48.4	44.8	-	.. c	-	.. c	-
Other services	-	-	-	-	-	-	-	-	-	-
Not allocated and confidential	**209.7**	**101.7**	**189.4**	**396.6**	**324.6**	**.. c**	**.. c**	**.. c**	**11.8**	**6.7**
Private real estate activities	**-**	**-**	**-**	**-**	**-**	**-**	**-**	**-**	**-**	**-**

- Nil; c Confidential data

Note: Detailed metadata at: *http://stats.oecd.org/OECDStat_Metadata/ShowMetadata.ashx?Dataset=FDI_CTRY_IND_SUMM.*

Source: *OECD International Direct Investment Statistics (database)*: *https://doi.org/10.1787/idi-data-en*

LITHUANIA

Table 1. Foreign direct investment flows by country

Million US dollars

	Inward					Outward				
	2015	2016	2017	2018	2019	2015	2016	2017	2018	2019
WORLD	**1 054.8**	**302.3**	**1 018.6**	**976.0**	**1 169.4**	**377.1**	**43.1**	**80.1**	**703.8**	**143.4**
OECD COUNTRIES	**1 175.0**	**-185.1**	**1 082.4**	**583.1**	**753.1**	**206.7**	**-95.4**	**-163.2**	**610.3**	**36.5**
Australia	1.6	-3.3	0.1	8.0	-31.1	-	-	-	.. c	-
Austria	9.0	31.4	-42.5	20.9	-2.7	0.0	.. c	.. d	0.2	-0.1
Belgium	6.3	-47.9	9.3	.. d	7.6	.. d	.. d	.. d	1.5	0.6
Canada	1.2	-0.4	19.1	.. d	-297.6	0.8	.. c	.. d	0.1	.. d
Chile	.. c	.. d	.. d	-	-0.1	-	-	-	-	-
Czech Republic	3.0	-1.7	0.8	-6.3	0.5	1.2	0.6	4.9	0.6	-0.3
Denmark	-36.3	46.2	52.7	59.2	53.1	.. d	-2.1	-1.1	-0.1	0.2
Estonia	90.5	23.5	172.2	128.9	1 261.4	94.8	-34.1	185.3	121.0	77.3
Finland	14.4	68.7	-36.3	-57.9	88.5	0.6	0.4	0.4	-0.4	0.0
France	42.6	19.5	157.7	-77.8	99.5	2.3	1.9	0.3	-1.3	1.6
Germany	111.0	-144.3	15.6	239.3	179.3	-10.5	5.2	4.2	-1.5	39.3
Greece	.. d	1.3	.. d	-0.9	0.0	1.4	1.1	1.0	0.5	0.9
Hungary	0.5	2.9	-4.3	4.8	-1.4	16.6	-1.0	-2.6	-0.2	0.0
Iceland	-7.0	2.0	1.5	-0.7	8.0	-	.. d	.. c	-	-
Ireland	20.7	5.0	20.2	16.8	57.2	.. c	.. d	143.5	-94.3	0.0
Israel	9.9	15.3	13.7	16.9	4.9	-	.. c	-	.. c	-
Italy	-3.8	18.7	4.6	8.9	-1.3	.. d	1.6	1.3	1.4	14.9
Japan	.. d	-0.6	0.3	-0.6	-4.1	.. c	-	-	-	.. c
Korea	.. d	-0.2	-0.1	-0.4	0.6	-	-	-	.. c	.. c
Latvia	17.6	6.4	20.4	5.8	25.4	190.1	53.4	49.7	157.9	97.1
Lithuania	-	-	-	-	-	-	-	-	-	-
Luxembourg	-38.4	-69.0	-23.0	134.3	169.2	.. d	.. c	.. c	11.9	5.6
Mexico	.. d	-0.2	.. d	.. d	1.5	-	-	-	-	.. d
Netherlands	242.1	560.1	154.2	130.5	67.1	46.7	-81.7	-10.6	-31.0	17.7
New Zealand	.. c	.. c	.. d	0.0	-0.2	-	-	-	.. c	.. c
Norway	90.1	90.1	-627.1	55.9	28.7	0.3	-0.1	1.3	-0.7	0.6
Poland	-85.5	287.0	-60.3	101.3	62.0	4.9	4.1	18.7	194.2	-216.0
Portugal	.. d	0.8	0.3	0.4	0.7	0.2	-	.. c	0.2	0.9
Slovak Republic	.. d	.. d	2.2	.. d	.. d	-0.8	1.3	0.1	-0.5	0.2
Slovenia	.. d	-1.4	3.9	-2.3	-4.4	0.1	0.3	-0.1	0.2	-0.3
Spain	30.3	7.7	7.8	20.2	-1.5	.. d	4.1	-1.6	0.4	-3.6
Sweden	284.8	-610.0	1 101.9	163.7	-857.6	33.6	-1.4	-11.4	246.8	6.2
Switzerland	245.9	-276.8	40.6	72.8	87.5	.. c	.. d	.. d	-0.2	0.2
Turkey	.. d	-0.1	-0.2	0.3	.. d	.. c	0.6	.. c	-1.8	.. c
United Kingdom	124.5	-258.7	5.9	-338.4	-259.5	2.6	1.3	-5.3	-4.1	2.8
United States	3.8	41.4	71.7	.. d	13.4	.. d	2.7	0.3	10.9	.. d
EUROPE	**1 028.4**	**-16.1**	**749.2**	**1 160.9**	**1 158.8**	**380.0**	**21.7**	**48.9**	**687.8**	**154.6**
Bulgaria	0.6	1.1	-0.8	2.9	-0.4	23.0	-1.3	-22.4	-4.1	-9.0
Croatia	.. d	.. d	.. d	-0.5	3.2	0.9	0.6	0.4	0.5	0.6
Cyprus	-225.0	228.7	184.4	67.6	-0.2	-61.1	93.3	165.6	98.3	-52.3
Malta	4.3	-28.6	-432.7	340.8	-6.7	-	0.1	.. c	-47.0	44.8
Romania	8.0	1.0	1.2	28.3	3.7	6.7	4.7	7.7	-2.7	-5.5
Russian Federation	40.9	44.1	-15.2	-7.7	18.8	3.9	26.0	-3.6	17.9	21.8
Ukraine	6.5	-7.3	13.8	24.2	22.5	2.1	-19.6	26.9	25.0	91.1
AFRICA	**-0.9**	**-0.5**	**-4.8**	**1.9**	**-14.8**	**.. c**	**.. d**	**.. d**	**0.3**	**0.9**
Northern Africa	0.7	-2.0	-2.7	0.0	-0.1	-	-	-	-	-
Algeria	0.0	-	-	-	.. d	-	-	-	-	-
Egypt	0.7	-2.0	-2.8	-	.. d	-	-	-	-	-
Libya	-	-	0.0	0.1	-	-	-	-	-	-
Morocco	-	-	-	-	.. c	-	-	-	-	-
Tunisia	-	-	-	0.0	-	-	-	-	-	-
Other African countries	-1.6	1.5	-2.0	1.9	-14.7	.. c	.. d	.. d	0.3	0.9
Nigeria	-	.. c	.. c	0.2	-	-	-	.. c	.. c	-
South Africa	.. d	.. d	.. d	-0.7	-0.5	-	-	-	-	-
AMERICA	**-11.9**	**44.1**	**89.5**	**-419.7**	**-313.6**	**.. d**	**2.8**	**-0.8**	**11.3**	**-10.7**
Northern America	5.0	41.1	90.8	-130.1	-284.2	.. d	2.7	0.4	11.0	-10.0
Central America and Caribbean countries	.. d	2.9	-1.6	-289.6	-29.4	-	.. d	.. c	.. d	-0.6
Bahamas	.. c	.. c	-	-	-	-	-	-	-	-
Bermuda	.. c	.. d	.. d	.. c	.. d	-	-	-	-	-
Cayman Islands	.. d	.. d	.. d	-0.7	.. c	-	-	-	-	-
Costa Rica	.. c	.. c	.. c	-	.. c	-	-	-	-	-
El Salvador	0.1	-	-	-	-	-	-	-	-	-
Guatemala	-	-	-	-	-	-	-	-	-	-
Honduras	-	-	-	-	-	-	-	-	-	-
Nicaragua	-	-	-	-	-	-	-	-	-	-
Panama	-1.1	.. d	-5.4	-1.3	-0.3	-	-	-	.. c	.. c
Virgin Islands, U.S.	-	.. c	-	-	-	-	-	-	-	-
South America	.. d	0.1	0.3	0.0	0.1	-	-	.. c	.. c	-
Argentina	.. c	-	-	0.0	.. c	-	-	-	-	-
Bolivia	-	-	-	-	-	-	-	-	-	-
Brazil	0.6	.. d	.. d	.. d	.. d	-	-	-	-	-
Colombia	.. c	.. c	.. c	.. c	-0.1	-	-	-	-	-
Ecuador	-	-	-	0.0	0.0	-	-	-	-	-
Paraguay	-	-	-	-	-	-	-	-	-	-
Peru	.. c	.. c	.. d	-	-	-	-	-	-	-
Uruguay	-	-	-	-	-	-	-	.. c	.. c	-
Venezuela	0.0	0.0	-	-	-	-	-	-	-	-

Table 1. Foreign direct investment flows by country *(cont.)*

Million US dollars

	Inward					Outward				
	2015	2016	2017	2018	2019	2015	2016	2017	2018	2019
ASIA	**.. d**	**.. d**	**171.3**	**174.0**	**364.2**	**-4.3**	**18.7**	**32.4**	**.. d**	**.. d**
Near and Middle East	9.9	17.3	16.3	19.4	65.7	-6.7	2.7	4.7	1.7	5.3
Gulf Arabian countries	0.6	-0.1	1.1	1.6	64.2	.. d	.. d	.. d	1.0	4.4
Kuwait	-	-	-	-	-	-	-	-	-	-
Qatar	.. c	-	-	-	0.0	-	-	-	-	-
Saudi Arabia	.. c	-	-	-	-0.1	-	-	-	-	-
United Arab Emirates	0.2	0.3	0.9	1.6	.. d	.. d	.. d	.. c	-0.4	.. d
Other Near and Middle East	9.3	17.5	15.2	17.8	1.5	.. d	.. d	.. d	0.7	0.9
Jordan	0.1	-	-	-	-	-	-	-	-	-
Other Asian countries	.. d	.. d	155.0	154.6	298.4	2.4	16.1	27.7	.. d	.. d
China	0.5	2.3	2.9	-2.2	2.2	.. d	.. d	20.8	0.9	-9.4
Hong Kong, China	13.3	311.1	144.5	195.3	254.6	-	-	-	.. d	.. c
India	-0.3	0.0	-0.2	-0.6	11.8	-	-	-	-	-
Indonesia	-	-	-	0.0	.. d	.. c	.. c	.. c	.. c	.. c
Iran, Islamic Republic of	.. d	-0.1	0.1	0.0	-	-	-	-	-	-
Malaysia	.. d	.. d	.. c	.. d	.. d	-	-	-	-	-
Philippines	.. c	.. c	-0.1	0.1	-0.1	-	-	-	-	.. c
Singapore	22.0	-2.1	0.6	-28.6	35.3	-	-	0.7	0.1	-
Chinese Taipei	.. d	0.0	0.1	-0.2	0.5	-	-	-	-	-
Thailand	-12.9	-61.1	4.8	.. d	.. d	.. c	.. c	-	.. c	-
Viet Nam	-	0.1	-	-	0.1	-	-	-	-	-
AUSTRALIA, OCEANIA AND POLAR REGIONS	**.. d**	**.. d**	**0.0**	**8.0**	**-31.3**	**-**	**-**	**-**	**.. c**	**.. c**
WORLD unallocated and confidential	**.. d**	**.. d**	**13.4**	**50.9**	**6.2**	**- d**	**- d**	**- d**	**.. d**	**- d**
European Union (EU28)	**633.1**	**149.8**	**1 316.3**	**1 000.4**	**942.7**	**364.6**	**-1.4**	**-14.4**	**648.2**	**23.6**
G20 countries excl. European Union	**325.1**	**-281.9**	**261.7**	**-302.2**	**-264.4**	**2.7**	**55.5**	**21.7**	**23.7**	**61.9**
G20 OECD countries	**283.4**	**-328.2**	**274.4**	**-291.1**	**-300.8**	**-2.2**	**13.3**	**1.0**	**3.9**	**49.3**
G20 Non-OECD countries	**41.7**	**46.4**	**-12.7**	**-11.1**	**36.3**	**4.8**	**42.2**	**20.6**	**19.8**	**12.6**
MENA countries	**.. d**	**-2.4**	**-1.9**	**1.6**	**64.1**	**.. d**	**.. d**	**.. d**	**.. d**	**.. d**
ASEAN countries	**9.1**	**-63.1**	**5.2**	**-36.7**	**33.0**	**.. c**	**.. c**	**3.9**	**0.5**	**0.2**

- Nil; .. Not available; c Confidential data; d Secondary Confidentiality

Note: Detailed metadata at: *http://stats.oecd.org/OECDStat_Metadata/ShowMetadata.ashx?Dataset=FDI_CTRY_IND_SUMM.*

Source: *OECD International Direct Investment Statistics (database): https://doi.org/10.1787/idi-data-en*

Table 2. Foreign direct investment positions by country
At year end

Million US dollars

	Inward					Outward				
	2015	2016	2017	2018	2019	2015	2016	2017	2018	2019
WORLD	**16 046.9**	**16 171.1**	**19 621.7**	**19 417.6**	**20 853.4**	**3 670.0**	**3 713.7**	**4 330.1**	**4 835.7**	**4 795.6**
OECD COUNTRIES	**12 059.8**	**13 645.5**	**15 509.2**	**16 230.8**	**17 275.3**	**2 285.8**	**2 822.2**	**3 077.7**	**3 553.6**	**3 431.8**
Australia	.. d	.. d	.. d	.. d	8.5	-	-	-	.. c	.. c
Austria	167.0	138.7	176.0	175.0	165.4	0.1	0.1	0.7	0.9	0.8
Belgium	222.1	278.2	365.1	278.0	116.6	2.2	1.3	4.5	6.2	6.2
Canada	361.3	.. d	465.5	377.0	152.5	0.8	0.6	0.8	.. d	.. d
Chile	0.0	0.0	0.1	0.0	0.0	-	-	-	-	-
Czech Republic	12.8	12.6	14.5	7.8	14.7	2.7	2.8	7.2	6.1	5.9
Denmark	768.8	808.4	911.9	914.2	902.1	3.1	1.4	2.0	-0.4	1.6
Estonia	706.5	859.7	1 087.3	1 063.1	1 461.0	383.6	406.3	665.0	764.6	805.3
Finland	533.0	570.8	689.4	626.2	676.9	2.9	3.2	5.0	4.5	4.7
France	408.3	441.0	476.0	460.6	530.9	8.4	9.4	11.4	10.0	11.8
Germany	1 064.5	1 090.2	1 324.1	1 299.2	1 605.3	10.6	12.3	22.9	21.5	61.0
Greece	0.6	0.7	1.1	1.1	3.3	5.4	6.3	8.3	8.4	9.5
Hungary	5.1	5.9	5.6	5.4	6.2	21.3	20.0	20.1	21.2	20.9
Iceland	39.8	38.1	44.0	32.9	38.1	-	0.2	0.3	0.3	0.2
Ireland	42.3	43.4	52.8	57.1	68.3	0.7	-49.4	96.5	0.6	0.1
Israel	-37.6	42.8	163.8	-180.5	-166.5	-	.. c	.. c	.. d	-1.4
Italy	39.9	43.6	61.5	63.9	60.8	27.2	9.2	12.2	13.1	29.5
Japan	94.3	23.2	19.8	21.4	10.8	.. c	.. c	.. c	.. c	.. c
Korea	0.2	0.1	0.1	-	0.1	-	-	-	.. c	.. c
Latvia	190.7	204.9	315.7	291.8	462.9	614.4	689.8	876.1	1 001.3	1 057.5
Lithuania	1 641.5	467.7	645.8	1 010.6	886.2	-	-	-	-	-
Luxembourg	176.1	144.9	179.1	189.1	384.8	528.3	511.5	-1.2	10.4	26.2
Mexico	.. d	.. d	.. d	.. d	.. d	-	-	-	-	.. d
Netherlands	538.2	929.5	1 261.3	1 442.0	1 398.2	867.6	766.2	852.9	808.0	815.5
New Zealand	.. d	.. d	.. d	.. d	.. d	-	-	-	.. c	-
Norway	1 103.7	1 047.5	469.4	443.4	472.2	6.6	4.3	7.0	6.0	6.4
Poland	525.6	696.6	873.4	965.5	973.0	325.7	323.2	382.3	549.4	303.1
Portugal	.. d	.. d	.. d	.. d	11.1	0.2	0.2	0.3	0.4	1.3
Slovak Republic	.. d	.. d	11.6	10.0	10.3	7.4	9.4	9.8	8.8	8.9
Slovenia	0.4	0.8	.. d	23.4	13.9	0.7	0.9	0.9	1.1	0.7
Spain	60.3	69.0	82.0	74.3	85.4	4.5	8.3	7.9	8.5	5.0
Sweden	3 683.2	3 124.1	3 360.4	3 368.8	3 477.6	35.5	38.6	36.0	250.8	201.1
Switzerland	310.0	426.9	429.1	439.9	684.5	.. d	0.7	1.1	0.9	1.0
Turkey	0.6	1.0	1.2	0.9	1.1	0.7	2.2	.. c	.. d	.. c
United Kingdom	242.4	1 501.6	1 648.8	1 983.2	1 962.6	34.9	34.6	31.7	26.7	30.9
United States	960.9	716.7	991.0	743.2	781.9	5.1	8.9	13.7	.. d	.. d
EUROPE	**13 926.8**	**14 354.0**	**17 139.4**	**17 510.7**	**19 145.1**	**3 667.3**	**3 692.2**	**4 268.0**	**4 760.7**	**4 727.8**
Bulgaria	.. d	3.9	1.0	1.8	51.8	95.3	89.7	78.2	74.1	63.6
Croatia	0.1	0.1	0.2	0.2	0.3	4.4	4.8	5.9	6.0	6.7
Cyprus	381.8	509.1	470.4	277.8	617.8	338.9	435.2	660.3	748.0	688.5
Malta	19.2	27.0	26.2	32.8	45.1	0.0	0.1	0.1	-45.3	0.5
Romania	0.6	0.8	1.8	2.3	7.1	15.2	19.2	31.8	20.0	14.4
Russian Federation	559.5	392.9	476.1	355.2	439.7	118.3	145.2	146.0	153.2	161.8
Ukraine	248.5	236.7	303.4	273.3	104.8	85.6	54.4	102.1	101.2	192.3
AFRICA	**16.6**	**16.2**	**.. d**	**.. d**	**2.0**	**0.4**	**0.3**	**-0.1**	**0.0**	**1.6**
Northern Africa	3.0	1.0	0.7	0.3	.. d	-	-	-	-	-
Algeria	-	-	-	-	0.0	-	-	-	-	-
Egypt	2.9	1.0	0.7	0.2	.. d	-	-	-	-	-
Libya	-	-	0.0	0.1	0.1	-	-	-	-	-
Morocco	-	-	-	-	-	-	-	-	-	-
Tunisia	0.0	0.0	0.0	-	-	-	-	-	-	-
Other African countries	13.7	15.2	.. d	.. d	.. d	0.4	0.3	-0.1	0.0	1.6
Nigeria	0.0	-	0.0	0.2	.. d	-	-	.. c	.. c	.. c
South Africa	.. d	.. d	.. d	.. d	0.2	-	-	-	-	.. c
AMERICA	**1 760.7**	**1 500.2**	**.. d**	**1 611.9**	**1 450.7**	**6.7**	**10.5**	**16.7**	**27.2**	**16.7**
Northern America	1 322.2	.. d	1 456.5	1 120.2	934.3	5.9	9.5	14.5	25.0	15.0
Central America and Caribbean countries	437.9	423.9	503.3	490.9	515.3	0.8	0.9	.. d	2.2	1.7
Bahamas	0.5	0.5	.. c	.. c	.. c	-	-	-	-	-
Bermuda	.. c	.. c	.. c	.. c	.. c	-	-	-	-	-
Cayman Islands	322.0	331.8	.. c	.. c	.. c	-	-	-	-	-
Costa Rica	-	-	-	-	-	-	-	-	-	-
El Salvador	0.1	0.1	0.1	0.0	0.0	-	-	-	-	-
Guatemala	-	-	-	-	-	-	-	-	-	-
Honduras	0.0	0.0	0.0	0.0	0.0	-	-	-	-	-
Nicaragua	-	-	-	-	-	-	-	-	-	-
Panama	.. d	.. d	.. d	.. d	.. d	.. c	.. c	.. c	.. c	.. c
Virgin Islands, U.S.	-	-	-	-	-	-	-	-	-	-
South America	0.5	.. d	.. d	0.8	1.0	-	-	.. c	-	-
Argentina	0.2	.. d	.. d	.. d	0.1	-	-	-	-	-
Bolivia	-	-	-	-	-	-	-	-	-	-
Brazil	0.1	0.2	0.2	.. d	0.8	-	-	-	-	-
Colombia	0.1	0.1	0.1	0.1	0.1	-	-	-	-	-
Ecuador	-	-	-	-	-	-	-	-	-	-
Paraguay	-	-	-	-	-	-	-	-	-	-
Peru	0.1	0.1	0.1	0.0	0.0	-	-	-	-	-
Uruguay	-	-	-	-	-	-	-	.. c	-	-
Venezuela	0.0	-	-	-	-	-	-	-	-	-

Table 2. Foreign direct investment positions by country *(cont.)*

At year end

Million US dollars

	Inward					Outward				
	2015	2016	2017	2018	2019	2015	2016	2017	2018	2019
ASIA	**254.9**	**205.7**	**379.7**	**155.9**	**145.2**	**-4.4**	**10.8**	**45.6**	**.. d**	**.. d**
Near and Middle East	-27.1	58.9	183.6	-161.3	-143.2	8.6	9.9	15.2	16.1	21.9
Gulf Arabian countries	5.9	7.7	9.2	8.8	.. d	5.4	8.5	12.0	11.6	16.4
Kuwait	-	-	-	-	-	-	-	-	-	-
Qatar	-	-	-	-	-	-	-	-	-	-
Saudi Arabia	.. d	.. d	.. d	.. d	.. d	-	-	-	-	-
United Arab Emirates	.. d	.. d	.. d	5.6	.. d	5.4	8.5	12.0	11.2	.. d
Other Near and Middle East	-33.0	51.1	174.4	-170.1	.. d	3.2	1.4	3.1	4.6	5.5
Jordan	0.1	0.1	0.1	.. d	0.4	-	-	-	-	-
Other Asian countries	282.0	146.9	196.2	317.2	288.4	-13.0	0.9	30.5	.. d	.. d
China	17.8	21.7	40.5	47.3	30.7	12.2	25.9	52.1	50.6	42.9
Hong Kong, China	5.9	8.7	15.4	132.0	161.9	.. c	.. c	.. c	.. d	.. c
India	.. d	.. d	4.2	5.9	5.9	-	-	-	-	-
Indonesia	-	-	.. c	.. c	.. c	.. c	.. c	.. c	.. c	.. c
Iran, Islamic Republic of	.. d	.. d	.. d	.. d	.. d	-	-	-	-	-
Malaysia	.. d	.. d	.. d	0.1	0.0	-	-	-	-	-
Philippines	-	-	-	-	0.0	-	-	-	-	.. c
Singapore	12.1	2.3	5.3	12.9	-15.9	.. c	.. c	-0.1	-0.1	-0.1
Chinese Taipei	0.1	0.1	0.1	.. d	.. d	-	-	-	-	-
Thailand	.. d	77.1	.. d	.. d	.. d	.. c	.. c	-28.4	.. d	.. d
Viet Nam	0.1	0.1	0.2	0.2	0.2	-	-	-	-	-
AUSTRALIA, OCEANIA AND POLAR REGIONS	**11.5**	**5.5**	**4.5**	**.. d**	**8.5**	**-**	**-**	**-**	**.. c**	**.. c**
WORLD unallocated and confidential	**76.4**	**89.5**	**.. d**	**.. d**	**101.9**	**-**	**-**	**-**	**- d**	**- d**
European Union (EU28)	**11 442.8**	**11 982.5**	**14 052.3**	**14 633.7**	**15 999.7**	**3 340.8**	**3 354.3**	**3 828.6**	**4 324.9**	**4 181.4**
G20 countries excl. European Union	**3 781.6**	**4 616.3**	**5 536.6**	**5 405.7**	**5 620.4**	**218.3**	**248.6**	**297.4**	**305.8**	**361.0**
G20 OECD countries	**3 194.5**	**4 193.0**	**5 006.6**	**4 983.6**	**5 129.3**	**87.6**	**77.3**	**95.3**	**97.3**	**151.0**
G20 Non-OECD countries	**587.0**	**423.3**	**530.0**	**422.1**	**491.2**	**130.8**	**171.4**	**202.1**	**208.6**	**210.0**
MENA countries	**10.6**	**10.5**	**12.1**	**12.1**	**16.2**	**5.4**	**8.5**	**12.0**	**11.6**	**16.4**
ASEAN countries	**151.9**	**79.6**	**103.2**	**101.4**	**67.4**	**-27.3**	**-26.1**	**-24.6**	**-23.1**	**-21.9**

- Nil; .. Not available; c Confidential data; d Secondary Confidentiality

Note: Inward FDI positions are allocated according to the ultimate investing country. Detailed metadata at: *http://stats.oecd.org/OECDStat_Metadata/ShowMetadata.ashx?Dataset=FDI_CTRY_IND_SUMM*.

Source: OECD *International Direct Investment Statistics (database): https://doi.org/10.1787/idi-data-en*

LITHUANIA

Table 3. Foreign direct investment income by country

Million US dollars

	Inward					Outward				
	2015	2016	2017	2018	2019	2015	2016	2017	2018	2019
WORLD	**1 642.3**	**1 678.3**	**1 944.2**	**2 193.0**	**2 296.5**	**135.8**	**145.9**	**165.7**	**303.1**	**228.5**
OECD COUNTRIES	**1 491.1**	**1 453.8**	**1 679.9**	**1 796.8**	**1 817.2**	**93.4**	**117.7**	**169.4**	**211.5**	**182.7**
Australia	-	-	0.1	0.1	-3.6	-	-	-	-	-
Austria	6.6	8.0	4.7	7.0	9.2	-	-	-	-	-0.1
Belgium	8.2	6.9	20.8	26.5	.. d	0.6	-1.2	3.9	1.2	1.9
Canada	6.5	4.8	-4.8	6.1	0.7	-	0.0	0.0	-	-
Chile	-	-	-	-	-	-	-	-	-	-
Czech Republic	0.7	0.5	2.7	-2.6	0.7	0.3	0.7	4.6	4.9	0.0
Denmark	57.3	17.0	62.3	70.9	91.1	0.3	0.3	1.8	0.2	0.2
Estonia	111.1	90.2	113.0	161.1	245.4	63.3	70.7	98.1	95.2	61.1
Finland	63.9	59.2	38.2	60.5	117.1	-	0.2	0.1	-0.4	0.2
France	20.7	20.2	58.1	45.1	59.1	2.0	2.3	1.3	1.6	3.4
Germany	67.7	82.6	113.0	130.1	99.3	2.6	1.2	1.1	0.6	1.5
Greece	.. c	-	.. c	.. c	-	0.3	0.3	0.1	0.4	0.0
Hungary	1.0	0.9	1.2	1.4	1.2	3.8	-0.4	-2.5	2.8	0.3
Iceland	2.6	0.8	2.2	1.4	2.4	-	-	0.0	-	-
Ireland	7.7	4.1	4.0	-9.4	12.1	.. c	0.2	-0.2	-0.4	0.1
Israel	0.5	2.7	1.8	.. d	4.4	-	-	-	0.0	.. d
Italy	2.7	3.7	4.6	3.8	3.5	-0.1	0.0	-0.3	-	0.2
Japan	-	-	-	-	-	-	-	-	-	-
Korea	.. c	-	-	-	-	-	-	-	.. c	.. c
Latvia	45.0	51.2	53.0	42.4	38.8	33.0	19.9	27.7	65.0	58.4
Lithuania	-	-	-	-	-	-	-	-	-	-
Luxembourg	55.4	12.4	48.9	71.1	21.7	.. c	.. c	0.0	0.8	6.0
Mexico	-	-	.. c	-	-	-	-	-	-	.. d
Netherlands	168.1	213.4	248.2	260.2	293.0	8.5	19.0	28.4	31.0	8.5
New Zealand	-	-	-	-	-	-	-	-	-	-
Norway	83.5	61.1	93.2	80.1	72.1	0.7	0.4	0.3	-0.2	1.3
Poland	236.7	305.1	288.2	120.6	142.6	-0.5	-6.1	4.6	5.7	33.7
Portugal	.. c	0.5	0.1	0.1	.. d	-	0.0	0.1	-	0.1
Slovak Republic	.. c	.. c	1.3	.. d	.. d	0.1	1.3	1.1	0.4	0.3
Slovenia	.. c	1.9	1.8	-2.5	0.2	0.1	0.1	0.0	0.1	0.3
Spain	-3.4	1.9	0.9	-2.5	9.8	0.4	0.2	-0.5	0.0	-0.3
Sweden	390.8	401.8	396.4	518.8	449.2	0.4	0.8	-0.9	4.2	2.0
Switzerland	107.1	40.2	61.5	123.1	91.6	-	-	-	0.0	0.0
Turkey	-0.3	-0.4	-0.3	-	.. d	.. c	0.6	.. c	-1.6	.. c
United Kingdom	57.0	19.4	26.2	42.3	-8.3	3.1	5.3	0.6	-0.9	1.5
United States	38.7	42.1	38.6	39.0	38.2	0.5	-1.2	-0.5	.. d	.. d
EUROPE	**1 583.7**	**1 560.5**	**1 786.5**	**1 935.0**	**1 963.1**	**139.0**	**147.2**	**165.6**	**301.0**	**223.2**
Bulgaria	0.6	-0.2	0.3	0.2	-0.1	0.3	6.2	0.1	3.6	-9.6
Croatia	.. c	.. c	.. c	.. c	.. c	-0.1	0.1	-	0.0	0.4
Cyprus	48.0	85.7	70.9	94.2	110.9	-1.2	-2.9	3.1	48.8	3.2
Malta	17.0	17.7	11.0	8.6	1.9	-	-	.. c	-0.2	-0.2
Romania	.. c	-	.. c	.. c	0.0	0.8	1.4	-0.4	1.5	1.8
Russian Federation	6.6	16.3	6.3	13.6	20.4	-6.1	14.4	-12.3	8.5	25.0
Ukraine	1.4	3.1	14.5	16.1	2.0	2.8	1.8	-2.7	5.4	8.9
AFRICA	**0.2**	**1.8**	**-1.4**	**2.4**	**1.2**	**-0.2**	**0.1**	**0.1**	**0.4**	**0.8**
Northern Africa	0.3	0.0	0.0	-	-	-	-	-	-	-
Algeria	-	-	-	-	-	-	-	-	-	-
Egypt	0.3	0.0	0.0	-	-	-	-	-	-	-
Libya	-	-	-	-	-	-	-	-	-	-
Morocco	-	-	-	-	-	-	-	-	-	-
Tunisia	-	-	-	-	-	-	-	-	-	-
Other African countries	0.0	1.8	-1.4	2.4	1.2	-0.2	0.1	0.1	0.4	0.8
Nigeria	-	-	-	-	-	-	-	-	-	-
South Africa	.. c	.. c	-	-	-	-	-	-	-	-
AMERICA	**47.1**	**45.4**	**33.4**	**43.6**	**38.5**	**0.5**	**-1.2**	**-1.5**	**0.9**	**1.1**
Northern America	45.2	46.9	33.8	45.1	38.9	0.5	-1.2	-0.5	0.9	1.3
Central America and Caribbean countries	.. d	-1.5	-0.4	-1.5	-0.4	.. c	0.0	.. d	0.1	-0.1
Bahamas	0.0	-0.5	-	-	-	-	-	-	-	-
Bermuda	.. c	.. c	.. c	.. c	.. c	-	-	-	-	-
Cayman Islands	.. c	.. c	.. c	.. c	-	-	-	-	-	-
Costa Rica	-	-	-	-	-	-	-	-	-	-
El Salvador	-	-	-	-	-	-	-	-	-	-
Guatemala	-	-	-	-	-	-	-	-	-	-
Honduras	-	-	-	-	-	-	-	-	-	-
Nicaragua	-	-	-	-	-	-	-	-	-	-
Panama	2.2	0.0	-1.1	-1.3	-0.3	.. c	.. c	.. c	.. c	.. c
Virgin Islands, U.S.	-	-	-	-	-	-	-	-	-	-
South America	.. c	-	-	-	-	-	-	.. c	-	-
Argentina	.. c	-	-	-	-	-	-	-	-	-
Bolivia	-	-	-	-	-	-	-	-	-	-
Brazil	-	-	-	-	-	-	-	-	-	-
Colombia	-	-	-	-	-	-	-	-	-	-
Ecuador	-	-	-	-	-	-	-	-	-	-
Paraguay	-	-	-	-	-	-	-	-	-	-
Peru	-	-	-	-	-	-	-	-	-	-
Uruguay	-	-	-	-	-	-	-	.. c	-	-
Venezuela	-	-	-	-	-	-	-	-	-	-

Table 3. Foreign direct investment income by country *(cont.)*

Million US dollars

	Inward					Outward				
	2015	2016	2017	2018	2019	2015	2016	2017	2018	2019
ASIA	**4.9**	**64.4**	**119.2**	**198.8**	**285.9**	**-3.5**	**-0.2**	**1.5**	**0.7**	**3.3**
Near and Middle East	0.9	2.8	2.5	1.9	5.5	-4.3	0.1	1.1	1.6	2.4
Gulf Arabian countries	0.6	0.3	0.1	-0.1	0.8	-1.9	0.6	1.1	1.8	2.0
Kuwait	-	-	-	-	-	-	-	-	-	-
Qatar	-	-	-	-	-	-	-	-	-	-
Saudi Arabia	.. c	-	-	-	.. c	-	-	-	-	-
United Arab Emirates	0.0	0.3	0.1	.. d	.. d	0.2	0.3	0.4	.. d	.. d
Other Near and Middle East	0.3	2.5	2.4	2.0	4.7	-2.4	-0.4	-	-0.2	0.4
Jordan	-	-	-	-	-	-	-	-	-	-
Other Asian countries	4.0	61.6	116.6	196.9	280.4	0.8	-0.3	0.4	-0.9	0.9
China	0.2	0.4	0.5	-0.5	0.3	0.8	0.1	-0.5	-0.2	1.2
Hong Kong, China	0.2	45.1	102.8	172.0	264.5	-	-	-	-	.. c
India	0.0	-0.6	0.0	0.3	0.3	-	-	-	-	-
Indonesia	-	-	-	-	-	-	-	.. c	.. c	.. c
Iran, Islamic Republic of	0.0	0.0	0.0	0.0	-0.1	-	-	-	-	-
Malaysia	-	-	-	-	.. c	-	-	-	-	-
Philippines	-	-	-	-	-	-	-	-	-	-
Singapore	0.2	-3.8	4.4	-1.0	5.9	.. c	.. c	0.7	0.1	0.0
Chinese Taipei	-	-	-	-	-	-	-	-	-	-
Thailand	4.2	18.0	9.8	26.2	.. d	.. c	.. c	-1.0	.. c	.. d
Viet Nam	-	-	-	-	-	-	-	-	-	-
AUSTRALIA, OCEANIA AND POLAR REGIONS	**0.0**	**0.0**	**0.0**	**0.1**	**-3.7**	**-**	**-**	**-**	**-**	**-**
WORLD unallocated and confidential	**6.4**	**6.1**	**6.6**	**13.0**	**11.6**	**-**	**-**	**0.0**	**-**	**0.0**
European Union (EU28)	**1 363.4**	**1 405.7**	**1 569.9**	**1 645.4**	**1 724.2**	**125.1**	**122.7**	**171.6**	**266.1**	**175.1**
G20 countries excl. European Union	**200.2**	**188.6**	**242.4**	**279.9**	**210.1**	**2.8**	**22.6**	**-10.1**	**9.0**	**35.0**
G20 OECD countries	**192.7**	**172.4**	**235.6**	**266.5**	**188.9**	**8.2**	**8.2**	**2.7**	**0.6**	**8.7**
G20 Non-OECD countries	**7.6**	**16.2**	**6.8**	**13.5**	**21.2**	**-5.3**	**14.5**	**-12.7**	**8.4**	**26.3**
MENA countries	**0.7**	**0.1**	**-0.2**	**-0.2**	**0.8**	**-1.9**	**0.6**	**1.1**	**1.8**	**2.0**
ASEAN countries	**4.4**	**14.2**	**14.3**	**25.2**	**15.8**	**-1.2**	**-1.1**	**-0.5**	**-0.9**	**-1.0**

- Nil; .. Not available; c Confidential data; d Secondary Confidentiality

Note: Detailed metadata at: *http://stats.oecd.org/OECDStat_Metadata/ShowMetadata.ashx?Dataset=FDI_CTRY_IND_SUMM.*

Source: *OECD International Direct Investment Statistics (database): https://doi.org/10.1787/idi-data-en*

Table 4. Foreign direct investment flows by industrial sector

Million US dollars

	Inward					Outward				
	2015	2016	2017	2018	2019	2015	2016	2017	2018	2019
All FDI activities	**1 054.8**	**302.3**	**1 018.6**	**976.0**	**1 169.4**	**377.1**	**43.1**	**80.1**	**703.8**	**143.4**
Agriculture, forestry and fishing	**-6.2**	**65.6**	**61.9**	**-17.2**	**31.7**	**-2.5**	**.. d**	**.. d**	**3.1**	**.. d**
Mining and quarrying	**-6.3**	**-8.3**	**-13.1**	**1.4**	**29.8**	**2.1**	**.. d**	**.. d**	**0.8**	**0.0**
Extraction activities	.. c	.. c	.. c	.. c	.. c	-	-	-	-	-
Manufacturing	**439.9**	**-494.7**	**529.4**	**4.2**	**325.6**	**-0.2**	**-36.7**	**1.2**	**21.2**	**-257.3**
of which:										
Food products, beverages and tobacco	259.0	-102.9	69.1	34.3	41.2	1.0	4.2	6.7	4.5	21.0
Textiles, wood and paper products; printing	16.1	-53.1	82.4	58.9	-26.5	-1.9	0.3	-5.1	-1.7	-0.1
Chemical, rubber, plastic, non-metallic mineral products	91.6	-356.0	266.1	-220.7	138.2	5.2	-51.9	-0.9	16.1	-278.4
Metal and machinery products, except electrical equipment	3.0	35.6	51.1	1.5	33.0	-0.6	5.6	6.9	-0.8	-0.9
Motor vehicles, trailers, semi-trailers, other transport equipment	72.5	-95.0	3.0	119.2	40.1	.. c	.. d	.. c	0.0	0.4
Other manufacturing	-2.3	76.8	57.7	11.0	99.5	.. d	.. d	.. d	3.0	0.7
Electricity, gas, steam and air conditioning supply	**-17.2**	**-7.6**	**11.9**	**.. d**	**.. d**	**.. d**	**.. d**	**.. d**	**.. d**	**.. d**
Water supply; sewerage, waste management and remediation activities	**-8.7**	**-8.5**	**7.5**	**.. d**	**.. d**	**.. d**	**.. d**	**.. d**	**.. d**	**.. d**
Construction	**32.4**	**-19.6**	**24.9**	**-151.8**	**39.1**	**18.4**	**33.0**	**7.3**	**5.9**	**12.4**
Services	**590.1**	**748.4**	**371.0**	**1 083.8**	**546.6**	**353.0**	**50.7**	**75.2**	**658.2**	**368.2**
Wholesale and retail trade; repair of motor vehicles and motorcycles	9.3	208.6	141.7	204.2	129.8	118.6	67.2	74.2	304.2	94.5
Transportation and storage	20.1	24.1	17.3	49.8	65.0	-54.0	7.0	39.1	56.6	15.2
Accommodation and food service activities	1.1	-9.3	14.2	-9.8	5.3	.. d	1.2	-2.5	1.9	-0.4
Information and communication	426.4	51.9	7.7	26.2	65.5	31.2	8.9	-3.7	24.0	36.1
Financial and insurance activities	-42.8	269.5	-100.7	149.5	-42.5	-24.7	29.5	57.0	-201.9	-112.0
Activities of holding companies	-217.0	.. d	-327.8	-45.3	-129.5	-63.1	43.6	-8.0	87.0	-112.3
Real estate activities	173.7	76.8	90.6	100.4	257.9	95.4	-60.0	44.3	21.6	53.8
Professional, scientific and technical activities	-23.2	107.8	191.2	520.3	18.6	163.5	-57.7	-161.7	473.8	237.1
Administrative and support service activities	18.2	15.9	1.0	44.5	48.5	25.8	39.4	26.1	-18.3	42.9
Public administration; activities of households and of extraterritorial organisations	-	-	-	-	-	-	-	-	-	-
Education	0.3	-0.1	-0.2	0.1	.. d	-	.. d	1.6	-3.5	0.9
Human health and social work activities	1.2	-0.5	5.5	3.2	2.7	-0.2	.. d	0.2	0.0	0.2
Arts, entertainment and recreation	4.5	2.7	2.7	-5.3	-4.0	.. c	.. d	0.7	.. d	.. d
Other services	1.2	1.0	-0.1	0.8	0.0	0.2	.. d	.. d	-0.5	-0.5
Not allocated and confidential	**0.0**	**0.0**	**0.0**	**- d**	**.. d**	**.. d**	**- d**	**- d**	**.. d**	**.. d**
Private real estate activities	**30.9**	**27.0**	**25.1**	**47.9**	**53.7**	**6.4**	**2.4**	**3.7**	**-0.1**	**2.3**

- Nil; .. Not available; c Confidential data; d Secondary Confidentiality

Note: Detailed metadata at: *http://stats.oecd.org/OECDStat_Metadata/ShowMetadata.ashx?Dataset=FDI_CTRY_IND_SUMM.*

Source: *OECD International Direct Investment Statistics (database): https://doi.org/10.1787/idi-data-en*

LITHUANIA

Table 5. Foreign direct investment positions by industrial sector
At year end

Million US dollars

	Inward					Outward				
	2015	2016	2017	2018	2019	2015	2016	2017	2018	2019
All FDI activities	**16 046.9**	**16 171.1**	**19 621.7**	**19 417.6**	**20 853.4**	**3 670.0**	**3 713.7**	**4 330.1**	**4 835.7**	**4 795.6**
Agriculture, forestry and fishing	**201.2**	**264.4**	**368.1**	**339.1**	**372.1**	**-4.6**	**28.5**	**32.3**	**34.1**	**36.3**
Mining and quarrying	**78.0**	**65.5**	**63.9**	**60.6**	**88.8**	**6.5**	**0.1**	**0.1**	**0.2**	**0.2**
Extraction activities	.. c	.. c	.. c	.. c	.. c	-	-	-	-	-
Manufacturing	**3 123.0**	**2 599.0**	**3 513.4**	**3 408.1**	**3 757.4**	**514.6**	**426.8**	**462.5**	**468.5**	**207.5**
of which:										
Food products, beverages and tobacco	617.7	520.1	654.3	639.8	710.7	14.4	29.1	27.2	44.6	63.6
Textiles, wood and paper products; printing	437.9	382.4	530.1	572.0	519.7	26.4	20.9	17.6	19.5	23.5
Chemical, rubber, plastic, non-metallic mineral products	1 330.4	980.1	1 377.2	1 086.8	1 209.7	429.7	328.6	358.0	341.0	58.9
Metal and machinery products, except electrical equipment	163.5	188.4	278.2	359.4	390.3	14.7	21.5	29.3	28.9	27.7
Motor vehicles, trailers, semi-trailers, other transport equipment	214.1	107.5	126.3	221.8	234.7	12.6	.. c	9.3	9.0	8.7
Other manufacturing	359.3	420.6	547.2	528.4	692.2	16.9	.. d	21.1	25.6	25.2
Electricity, gas, steam and air conditioning supply	**326.6**	**318.5**	**369.2**	**303.8**	**462.4**	**0.3**	**2.7**	**1.5**	**23.8**	**45.3**
Water supply; sewerage, waste management and remediation activities	**9.8**	**3.9**	**14.0**	**11.4**	**12.8**	**-0.7**	**0.2**	**-2.2**	**-2.5**	**-1.1**
Construction	**403.5**	**405.4**	**520.2**	**336.1**	**378.4**	**44.1**	**79.8**	**86.8**	**87.4**	**89.1**
Services	**11 549.4**	**12 126.5**	**14 288.1**	**14 525.3**	**15 300.4**	**3 015.2**	**3 081.0**	**3 637.6**	**4 118.0**	**4 311.8**
Wholesale and retail trade; repair of motor vehicles and motorcycles	1 639.2	1 981.1	2 366.6	2 325.2	2 489.8	588.6	642.8	833.2	1 088.0	1 073.1
Transportation and storage	369.3	417.0	465.5	459.5	553.4	29.8	32.7	87.5	134.4	132.4
Accommodation and food service activities	76.0	63.0	89.9	143.0	159.2	2.8	4.8	4.6	7.5	21.4
Information and communication	1 236.5	1 141.0	1 294.2	1 339.7	1 481.0	83.7	102.9	96.9	120.4	161.3
Financial and insurance activities	4 361.7	4 754.4	5 748.0	5 445.6	5 415.5	413.1	975.0	1 228.3	953.6	818.4
Activities of holding companies	616.4	1 217.0	1 410.9	1 324.0	1 140.6	244.7	296.3	378.0	435.6	303.3
Real estate activities	2 268.6	2 089.6	2 560.1	2 442.1	2 838.1	264.7	216.5	254.6	260.9	324.2
Professional, scientific and technical activities	1 010.6	1 072.1	1 394.4	1 928.5	1 878.7	1 558.0	966.4	961.1	1 416.0	1 601.6
Administrative and support service activities	535.1	556.6	295.4	378.4	404.6	74.2	120.8	147.1	119.8	159.1
Public administration; activities of households and of extraterritorial organisations	-	-	-	-	-	-	-	-	-	-
Education	1.6	0.8	1.1	1.2	1.4	0.1	14.4	17.8	12.0	14.1
Human health and social work activities	27.3	24.3	44.0	40.5	57.8	0.7	0.5	0.9	0.9	1.2
Arts, entertainment and recreation	20.3	23.0	25.6	18.4	17.5	-1.3	3.7	5.3	4.5	5.0
Other services	3.3	3.5	3.3	3.3	3.4	0.6	0.4	0.4	0.1	0.1
Not allocated and confidential	**-**	**-**	**0.0**	**-**	**-**	**-**	**-**	**-**	**0.0**	**0.0**
Private real estate activities	**355.3**	**387.9**	**484.8**	**433.2**	**481.1**	**94.5**	**94.6**	**111.4**	**106.2**	**106.5**

- Nil; .. Not available; c Confidential data; d Secondary Confidentiality

Note: Detailed metadata at: *http://stats.oecd.org/OECDStat_Metadata/ShowMetadata.ashx?Dataset=FDI_CTRY_IND_SUMM*.

Source: *OECD International Direct Investment Statistics (database): https://doi.org/10.1787/idi-data-en*

Table 6. Foreign direct investment income by industrial sector

Million US dollars

	Inward					Outward				
	2015	2016	2017	2018	2019	2015	2016	2017	2018	2019
All FDI activities	**1 642.3**	**1 678.3**	**1 944.2**	**2 193.0**	**2 296.5**	**135.8**	**145.9**	**165.7**	**303.1**	**228.5**
Agriculture, forestry and fishing	**-5.2**	**5.6**	**16.2**	**-5.5**	**20.9**	**-0.1**	**-0.2**	**-0.1**	**2.5**	**0.2**
Mining and quarrying	**-19.4**	**1.1**	**-6.1**	**8.5**	**4.8**	**-0.1**	**-0.4**	**-0.5**	**0.8**	**0.0**
Extraction activities	.. c	.. c	.. c	.. c	.. c	-	-	-	-	-
Manufacturing	**605.3**	**668.2**	**655.6**	**656.4**	**716.7**	**4.0**	**4.3**	**-7.2**	**16.5**	**7.2**
of which:										
Food products, beverages and tobacco	53.7	43.0	50.4	34.8	45.9	-1.2	1.4	3.7	-1.6	3.9
Textiles, wood and paper products; printing	30.9	33.6	49.6	50.7	53.2	-2.5	1.0	-1.9	-0.6	1.5
Chemical, rubber, plastic, non-metallic mineral products	441.9	495.8	455.3	457.1	515.7	4.0	0.7	-9.0	19.2	-0.7
Metal and machinery products, except electrical equipment	28.9	29.1	33.3	66.0	61.2	2.1	2.4	5.1	1.2	0.8
Motor vehicles, trailers, semi-trailers, other transport equipment	12.3	11.6	16.0	22.6	1.6	.. c	0.0	.. c	-0.1	-0.1
Other manufacturing	37.6	55.1	51.0	25.2	39.2	.. d	-1.3	.. d	-1.6	1.9
Electricity, gas, steam and air conditioning supply	**11.0**	**27.3**	**35.6**	**27.5**	**51.6**	**.. d**	**0.1**	**-0.3**	**-4.9**	**10.0**
Water supply; sewerage, waste management and remediation activities	**0.5**	**0.9**	**3.0**	**1.2**	**1.1**	**.. c**	**1.9**	**1.1**	**0.9**	**0.5**
Construction	**16.2**	**2.4**	**22.2**	**-13.5**	**17.7**	**-0.2**	**7.3**	**1.5**	**6.9**	**15.3**
Services	**1 033.9**	**972.6**	**1 217.8**	**1 518.3**	**1 483.7**	**128.7**	**131.9**	**170.1**	**279.3**	**194.1**
Wholesale and retail trade; repair of motor vehicles and motorcycles	197.2	243.2	266.8	324.7	280.7	43.9	57.3	31.7	84.0	97.5
Transportation and storage	47.1	24.2	71.7	98.9	103.5	-2.8	12.9	20.0	13.2	13.4
Accommodation and food service activities	5.7	8.1	15.1	9.3	15.1	-0.3	-1.1	-2.0	0.1	2.5
Information and communication	168.7	173.2	200.6	214.7	202.4	8.3	21.3	11.6	25.7	6.4
Financial and insurance activities	312.6	279.2	299.4	438.5	418.1	4.2	-4.9	1.9	6.9	-1.7
Activities of holding companies	11.8	-2.0	0.4	26.8	11.1	5.4	3.3	2.9	15.9	9.8
Real estate activities	128.7	123.3	159.0	175.5	218.1	6.5	0.1	21.8	35.7	3.0
Professional, scientific and technical activities	129.8	73.5	160.4	175.5	191.4	70.0	32.8	67.3	106.4	60.5
Administrative and support service activities	37.3	39.4	34.9	66.8	42.4	-0.3	13.7	16.5	8.5	11.5
Public administration; activities of households and of extraterritorial organisations	-	-	-	-	-	-	-	-	-	-
Education	0.3	0.2	0.0	0.1	-0.1	-	.. c	1.6	0.2	0.9
Human health and social work activities	2.7	6.6	7.9	10.7	10.2	-	0.1	0.1	-	0.1
Arts, entertainment and recreation	3.6	0.8	2.0	1.9	1.8	-1.1	-1.1	-0.1	-0.7	0.4
Other services	0.2	1.0	0.1	1.7	0.2	0.2	-0.2	-0.1	-0.6	-0.5
Not allocated and confidential	**-**	**-**	**-**	**-**	**0.0**	**.. c**	**-**	**0.0**	**-**	**0.0**
Private real estate activities	**-**	**-**	**-**	**-**	**-**	**0.8**	**1.0**	**1.2**	**1.1**	**1.2**

- Nil; .. Not available; c Confidential data; d Secondary Confidentiality

Note: Detailed metadata at: *http://stats.oecd.org/OECDStat_Metadata/ShowMetadata.ashx?Dataset=FDI_CTRY_IND_SUMM.*

Source: *OECD International Direct Investment Statistics (database): https://doi.org/10.1787/idi-data-en*

LUXEMBOURG

Table 1. Foreign direct investment flows by country

Million US dollars

	Inward					Outward				
	2015	2016	2017	2018	2019	2015	2016	2017	2018	2019
WORLD	**622 284.0**	**188 439.7**	**69 967.3**	**-404 143.8**	**-137 847.3**	**738 981.7**	**147 117.1**	**209 945.9**	**-396 948.0**	**-159 815.3**
OECD COUNTRIES	**600 038.8**	**62 363.2**	**-247 489.6**	**-215 936.5**	**-77 439.8**	**736 920.7**	**104 740.7**	**176 620.4**	**-371 101.1**	**-186 104.3**
Australia	8 036.6	175.8	483.6	1 360.8	-2 535.5	5 379.9	1 448.6	-997.6	-686.9	-1 071.3
Austria	1 048.3	275.4	913.1	203.0	-8 925.3	1 182.5	1 105.8	1 034.8	3 962.0	978.4
Belgium	-4 278.4	-2 672.8	35 793.0	32 753.5	-20 072.8	-28 177.5	-11 870.0	11 539.8	22 667.3	-14 293.1
Canada	22 738.8	32 494.7	19 785.8	20 187.7	-97 569.7	-1 174.7	11 614.5	4 368.2	14 539.1	-146.6
Chile	-351.6	143.8	-240.1	-77.9	-256.4	-1 129.2	1 235.2	-1 170.1	695.1	578.8
Czech Republic	-42.2	-183.6	-290.8	-1 764.4	3 020.3	1 462.0	1 837.9	5 113.3	-370.6	6 202.8
Denmark	525.8	348.3	66.5	4 986.4	-5 130.4	1 345.5	1 961.7	879.3	2 093.7	2 645.2
Estonia	-256.2	26.5	10.1	-30.7	-14.6	-8.9	26.5	-12.4	407.2	1.1
Finland	1 229.1	377.1	-1 827.3	-322.2	497.0	297.3	9 563.2	2 035.8	2 099.6	816.1
France	7 650.6	-19 997.8	5 968.9	-3 085.1	8 259.3	12 681.1	8 909.7	3 614.0	24 864.9	-1 512.4
Germany	3 832.5	3 556.3	19 587.4	-2 229.4	16 721.1	4 714.4	14 229.8	5 177.5	-1 598.0	31 071.3
Greece	24.4	47.6	-13.5	63.7	29.1	-34.4	5.5	-86.8	515.8	-72.8
Hungary	10 651.1	-13 309.7	-24 126.9	-216.0	5 477.4	-1 222.4	21 391.1	-2 936.5	-28 955.5	4 117.3
Iceland	-3 372.2	3 103.0	-739.5	714.0	75.0	-1 231.3	-3 272.1	273.9	1 079.9	-96.3
Ireland	217 190.2	78 741.6	-49 157.9	-14 012.7	-87 464.5	132 800.9	20 639.2	248 469.2	-70 976.0	-137 077.1
Israel	110.9	121.6	316.8	-560.6	922.4	-260.7	-201.3	126.3	1 287.6	1 679.2
Italy	596.8	28 475.1	8 831.0	-15 417.2	2 842.3	2 638.9	505.4	1 851.0	-5 889.3	10 679.5
Japan	-52.1	359.4	-804.9	695.1	3 647.2	12.2	165.9	170.2	1 439.9	790.3
Korea	-27.7	81.8	332.5	-165.2	2 767.3	379.4	92.9	555.7	51.9	44.8
Latvia	255.1	-40.9	-33.8	21.2	21.3	17.7	91.8	-49.6	11.8	-35.8
Lithuania	13.3	-233.3	1.1	2.4	9.0	45.5	7.7	-93.6	151.1	7.8
Luxembourg	-	-	-	-	-	-	-	-	-	-
Mexico	-1 757.1	-523.1	-1 485.7	296.2	2 114.6	2 158.6	-665.7	778.9	-816.7	-3 224.0
Netherlands	-19 642.8	27 496.4	-46 711.8	-120 021.2	-13 699.8	43 698.3	81 512.8	85 394.0	-70 107.4	-70 657.1
New Zealand	902.9	-269.8	-3 389.7	-828.5	133.2	799.8	-599.4	-242.4	-38.9	126.5
Norway	2 416.0	2 892.8	791.3	-1 343.1	-1 710.5	1 482.0	288.6	225.5	-757.7	283.2
Poland	-1 517.5	-134.9	1 609.7	-1 153.1	-1 942.2	-3 224.6	1 705.2	6 513.4	838.0	3 091.9
Portugal	-819.7	77.4	310.0	-808.5	15.7	6 617.9	-347.2	-25.9	166.4	2 845.6
Slovak Republic	11.1	-561.8	-156.7	-551.2	1 015.3	156.4	-676.8	311.1	-31.9	-151.1
Slovenia	66.6	31.0	117.2	8.3	181.4	198.6	157.0	93.6	567.7	98.5
Spain	2 787.6	2 850.8	-240.1	-4 152.0	5 348.7	-635.6	7 426.7	12 162.1	12 478.5	2 674.4
Sweden	-3 648.4	-1 783.7	-2 180.1	3 125.2	364.9	5 161.4	4 842.4	-1 215.2	-2 849.1	1 804.5
Switzerland	7 070.4	10 513.1	-11 831.8	-22 064.2	-26 710.0	56 506.9	23 354.0	30 824.0	1 494.2	44 650.2
Turkey	-289.5	205.7	-484.7	187.7	-858.6	906.3	-745.3	-1 179.1	-312.8	-1 147.4
United Kingdom	150 982.8	-28 320.2	-26 302.6	-4 847.2	15 431.5	296 257.3	-20 650.2	55 050.2	-107 505.0	-23 327.0
United States	198 221.9	-62 233.8	-172 388.7	-86 892.5	120 553.0	197 182.5	-70 342.8	-292 025.7	-171 614.5	-48 477.6
EUROPE	**392 276.2**	**71 700.8**	**-93 747.0**	**-165 365.3**	**-62 515.4**	**529 054.9**	**145 885.2**	**448 141.1**	**-222 090.2**	**-160 148.9**
Bulgaria	-	47.6	1.1	11.8	16.8	185.2	70.8	47.3	783.7	70.5
Croatia	7.8	-76.3	-1.1	1.2	-6.7	341.7	33.2	402.4	550.0	138.8
Cyprus	-5 757.1	-937.7	-871.4	2 941.1	-1 012.0	-3 080.4	-4 394.6	-22 144.1	-8 588.5	15 043.1
Malta	-3 053.8	3 623.8	1 086.7	-2 550.5	37 632.4	-1 690.5	-67.5	3 075.2	186.5	10 110.8
Romania	-25.5	120.5	13.5	-36.6	-61.6	429.3	295.3	530.9	36.6	-408.6
Russian Federation	21 147.0	-101.7	-3 996.2	10 701.1	7 283.1	360.5	-73.0	-8 078.0	-2 497.3	-7 852.9
Ukraine	37.7	2.2	29.3	-1.2	-12.3	444.8	53.1	168.0	-251.4	183.6
AFRICA	**-1 091.5**	**-1 415.5**	**1 090.1**	**457.9**	**722.0**	**899.6**	**-17 271.9**	**-2 555.5**	**1 698.3**	**-10.1**
Northern Africa	586.8	-21.0	-25.9	92.1	-21.3	140.9	245.5	-2 428.1	69.6	134.3
Algeria	2.2	4.4	5.6	16.5	6.7	-5.5	-6.6	-	-1.2	-1.1
Egypt	535.8	-1.1	-15.8	-10.6	-14.6	61.0	191.3	1 096.8	34.2	119.8
Libya	-	-49.8	-	54.3	-	-	-	-	-	11.2
Morocco	48.8	26.5	-16.9	31.9	-12.3	69.9	67.5	-3 520.5	27.1	1.1
Tunisia	-	-	1.1	-	-	16.6	-6.6	-4.5	9.4	2.2
Other African countries	-1 678.3	-1 394.4	1 117.1	365.9	742.2	757.6	-17 516.3	-126.3	1 628.7	-144.4
Nigeria	2.2	-3.3	-2.3	-18.9	5.6	1.1	8.8	28.2	5.9	44.8
South Africa	-484.7	-35.4	60.9	-1 919.0	801.5	-214.1	-15 922.8	-736.1	2 917.5	-444.4
AMERICA	**217 575.2**	**43 735.5**	**152 492.4**	**-232 780.6**	**-98 365.6**	**208 969.5**	**-44 405.6**	**-310 523.1**	**-111 608.6**	**-86 374.1**
Northern America	220 960.6	-29 737.9	-152 601.7	-66 704.8	22 984.4	196 007.8	-58 728.3	-287 657.5	-157 076.6	-48 624.2
Central America and Caribbean countries	-10 636.7	74 183.3	307 349.8	-173 900.6	-117 894.3	11 383.3	3 807.4	-27 788.3	39 550.3	-35 498.7
Bahamas	-13 419.9	3 641.5	-5 625.1	-292.7	-12 673.2	-615.6	-151.5	-701.2	3 684.6	-5 958.8
Bermuda	-11 758.2	55 650.8	242 090.0	-132 418.3	-163 764.7	18 805.3	-10 309.6	14 790.9	-20 744.7	-30 160.1
Cayman Islands	3 875.8	5 874.2	69 414.9	-37 991.3	4 087.1	-7 617.3	11 651.0	-46 994.7	44 447.1	-4 114.0
Costa Rica	2.2	1.1	-2.3	1.2	-4.5	195.2	286.4	6.8	1 048.0	61.6
El Salvador	6.7	79.6	-87.9	113.3	-97.4	126.5	-2.2	-127.4	-64.9	56.0
Guatemala	-	18.8	5.6	-1.2	-2.2	407.1	-212.3	-381.0	27.1	-6.7
Honduras	-107.6	3.3	-	-	1.1	102.1	-6.6	24.8	-	-6.7
Nicaragua	39.9	-1.1	1.1	2.4	-	3.3	-5.5	68.8	9.4	353.7
Panama	1 162.5	2 473.7	-815.0	37.8	-61.6	221.9	526.4	-1 172.4	-46.0	19.0
Virgin Islands, U.S.	-24.4	-	-2.3	-15.3	14.6	113.1	228.9	263.8	10 034.2	893.3
South America	7 251.2	-709.9	-2 255.7	7 824.9	-3 455.7	1 577.4	10 515.3	4 922.8	5 917.6	-2 251.2
Argentina	-38.8	36.5	-24.8	-29.5	-30.2	297.3	-296.4	382.1	-200.6	-540.7
Bolivia	1.1	7.7	3.4	-10.6	-38.1	18.9	-1.1	-41.7	1.2	-
Brazil	7 879.1	-903.5	-1 703.3	381.2	-1 399.3	-338.3	8 034.9	7 193.1	4 144.9	-511.6
Colombia	64.3	86.3	1 137.4	-131.0	475.8	168.6	-	-	-10.6	-256.4
Ecuador	1.1	1.1	-5.6	-1.2	4.5	11.1	4.4	6.8	406.0	13.4
Paraguay	-3.3	-10.0	-	-1.2	12.3	34.4	4.4	64.3	-129.8	-6.7
Peru	5.5	186.9	224.3	482.7	422.0	1 082.6	1 518.3	-1 265.9	352.9	-320.2
Uruguay	-315.0	-261.0	-1 658.2	7 212.3	-2 653.1	1 394.3	5.5	-289.7	675.1	-1 212.4
Venezuela	10.0	3.3	11.3	-	6.7	38.8	10.0	20.3	-21.2	1.1

Table 1. Foreign direct investment flows by country *(cont.)*

Million US dollars

	Inward					Outward				
	2015	2016	2017	2018	2019	2015	2016	2017	2018	2019
ASIA	**5 311.1**	**74 778.3**	**12 339.1**	**-6 975.1**	**24 275.2**	**-6 128.7**	**62 097.8**	**76 105.3**	**-64 068.2**	**87 655.9**
Near and Middle East	10 736.6	-2 269.2	4 985.9	-1 731.4	32 990.0	146.4	6 610.6	4 964.5	-3 311.7	33 389.7
Gulf Arabian countries	10 399.3	-2 355.4	4 521.5	-1 233.3	32 046.3	280.6	6 307.6	4 385.1	-4 756.3	31 632.2
Kuwait	97.6	-	-	-	-2.2	2.2	-2.2	3.4	-	-
Qatar	9 497.5	-5 175.3	1 022.4	-1 816.4	-969.4	-1.1	-2.2	1.1	-	4.5
Saudi Arabia	203.0	397.0	755.3	448.5	412.0	-59.9	14.4	-76.7	5.9	58.2
United Arab Emirates	132.0	2 355.4	1 250.1	-1 022.1	21 565.0	347.2	6 267.8	4 448.2	-4 774.0	31 563.9
Other Near and Middle East	336.1	86.3	464.4	-498.1	944.8	-134.2	301.9	579.4	1 444.6	1 757.5
Jordan	-	-	-1.1	1.2	-	-61.0	143.8	257.0	-1.2	-1.1
Other Asian countries	-5 424.3	77 047.4	7 353.2	-5 243.7	-8 714.9	-6 275.1	55 487.1	71 140.8	-60 756.5	54 266.2
China	3 199.1	2 251.5	-2 142.9	1 030.3	85.1	-26.6	1 230.8	-32.7	966.6	-2 123.6
Hong Kong, China	-11 121.5	5 355.5	50 954.8	7 933.4	-7 938.0	-5 819.2	13 576.2	17 192.0	-173.5	60 169.0
India	-2 780.9	1 285.0	-154.4	-5.9	10.1	450.4	-775.2	983.0	-3.5	-164.6
Indonesia	-178.6	3 266.6	-53.0	96.8	3.4	87.6	288.6	125.1	67.3	99.6
Iran, Islamic Republic of	1.1	1.1	-	-	-	-11.1	-16.6	-	-	-1 185.5
Malaysia	3 218.0	264.3	73.3	36.6	-1 320.9	-381.6	-1 583.5	214.2	89.7	-1 314.2
Philippines	-17.7	44.2	-6.8	16.5	16.8	-25.5	-32.1	-22.5	-59.0	-32.5
Singapore	2 543.5	63 206.9	-40 346.1	-14 880.2	-5 907.3	-1 454.2	41 653.2	50 701.2	-61 959.2	-2 615.0
Chinese Taipei	-28.8	-33.2	14.7	-47.2	-47.0	39.9	8.8	64.3	46.0	357.1
Thailand	58.8	1 152.3	-390.0	48.4	-6.7	95.4	88.5	311.1	46.0	-69.4
Viet Nam	-	-	-3.4	-10.6	-23.5	36.6	870.3	946.9	-1 275.8	-164.6
AUSTRALIA, OCEANIA AND POLAR REGIONS	**8 213.0**	**-359.4**	**-2 207.2**	**518.1**	**-1 962.4**	**6 186.4**	**811.7**	**-1 222.0**	**-879.3**	**-938.1**
WORLD unallocated and confidential	-	-	-	**1.2**	**-1.1**	-	-	-	-	-
European Union (EU28)	**357 829.2**	**77 843.6**	**-77 604.6**	**-127 079.0**	**-41 445.2**	**472 156.4**	**138 312.5**	**416 730.9**	**-224 490.7**	**-155 138.3**
G20 countries excl. European Union	**418 878.5**	**-39 530.0**	**-153 735.8**	**-79 205.7**	**78 538.0**	**521 692.7**	**-62 936.0**	**-222 876.8**	**-242 126.8**	**-47 800.3**
G20 OECD countries	**389 933.4**	**-45 726.0**	**-146 477.3**	**-89 909.1**	**71 372.4**	**521 135.9**	**-55 437.4**	**-222 636.7**	**-247 527.4**	**-36 320.4**
G20 Non-OECD countries	**28 945.1**	**6 196.0**	**-7 258.5**	**10 703.4**	**7 165.6**	**556.9**	**-7 498.6**	**-240.1**	**5 400.7**	**-11 479.9**
MENA countries	**11 213.5**	**-2 316.7**	**4 548.5**	**-1 115.3**	**32 038.5**	**426.0**	**7 191.2**	**2 423.6**	**-4 397.5**	**31 929.9**
ASEAN countries	**5 622.9**	**67 934.3**	**-40 809.4**	**-14 696.1**	**-7 242.8**	**-1 631.7**	**41 287.2**	**52 289.5**	**-63 096.9**	**-4 099.4**

- Nil

Note: Detailed metadata at: *http://stats.oecd.org/OECDStat_Metadata/ShowMetadata.ashx?Dataset=FDI_CTRY_IND_SUMM.*

Source: *OECD International Direct Investment Statistics (database): https://doi.org/10.1787/idi-data-en*

Table 2. Foreign direct investment positions by country
At year end

Million US dollars

	Inward					Outward				
	2015	2016	2017	2018	2019	2015	2016	2017	2018	2019
WORLD	**3 697 834.5**	**3 775 241.9**	**4 217 697.3**	**3 632 523.5**	**3 495 085.4**	**4 503 887.9**	**4 550 670.4**	**5 078 410.9**	**4 478 133.7**	**4 359 702.3**
OECD COUNTRIES	**2 893 346.8**	**2 874 165.7**	**2 842 259.5**	**2 575 790.0**	**2 529 559.6**	**4 034 168.8**	**4 060 630.3**	**4 479 773.3**	**3 995 645.8**	**3 853 061.1**
Australia	6 526.9	6 755.6	7 546.2	8 235.6	5 641.4	15 291.2	15 865.9	18 396.5	18 229.9	15 494.3
Austria	8 562.9	8 650.8	11 325.3	10 097.3	1 088.5	14 260.2	14 550.4	17 628.9	19 829.4	21 406.4
Belgium	94 437.7	85 918.6	133 979.4	162 302.5	133 955.3	132 597.7	122 230.4	145 645.2	150 105.3	133 890.1
Canada	196 712.0	209 234.7	230 843.1	245 840.4	161 200.9	97 646.2	95 719.4	101 637.1	102 399.8	130 014.6
Chile	178.6	324.7	81.6	8.0	-249.4	1 391.4	2 332.7	675.2	1 344.2	1 758.0
Czech Republic	1 485.0	1 062.5	867.1	-493.5	2 700.5	10 519.3	11 215.3	19 335.6	18 762.3	24 391.1
Denmark	1 627.7	1 424.1	1 259.3	5 316.0	105.6	15 552.5	17 256.2	22 868.8	22 355.2	25 179.7
Estonia	24.0	49.5	64.8	33.2	18.0	148.1	153.9	157.1	540.4	512.2
Finland	1 518.8	1 844.6	151.1	-164.9	303.3	3 375.1	12 342.2	15 245.9	17 339.1	17 178.2
France	17 807.3	-2 516.1	4 543.1	-5 219.8	6 996.2	108 348.4	110 621.9	130 707.6	143 658.1	145 624.6
Germany	74 629.3	78 951.2	111 663.5	108 211.6	131 140.2	117 306.5	126 650.2	154 661.8	148 660.4	183 329.6
Greece	84.9	141.2	166.7	199.2	185.4	4 771.9	3 849.5	4 209.6	4 469.9	4 464.2
Hungary	39 020.1	25 349.4	501.3	406.5	2 200.6	16 279.8	37 702.1	36 486.0	8 410.8	13 689.1
Iceland	-3 075.7	-21.1	-802.4	-79.0	-4.5	6 544.4	2 744.8	3 318.5	4 276.4	4 224.9
Ireland	436 227.5	511 664.4	492 608.5	476 714.0	440 635.8	330 621.7	344 776.0	606 789.4	547 269.3	408 045.4
Israel	-72.9	123.3	430.6	-93.9	1 067.2	2 381.1	2 344.3	1 909.3	3 667.3	5 617.8
Italy	-5 273.8	21 351.3	33 183.0	16 780.4	20 076.4	78 067.5	74 064.5	88 942.2	78 160.1	102 707.3
Japan	3 268.4	3 763.0	3 930.2	3 232.2	6 569.3	5 637.5	5 264.0	5 636.8	6 633.8	8 416.1
Korea	-2 096.9	-2 254.7	-2 118.0	-2 307.1	-1 497.4	867.7	930.7	1 575.9	1 608.7	1 607.5
Latvia	-5.4	-44.3	-86.4	-55.0	-19.1	112.1	211.9	193.1	195.8	201.1
Lithuania	482.3	-12.6	-13.2	-9.2	-1.1	156.8	160.2	88.8	237.0	239.3
Luxembourg	-	-	-	-	-	-	-	-	-	-
Mexico	-5 497.0	-5 489.6	-6 944.1	-6 764.4	-4 806.8	25 403.4	24 503.0	28 078.7	25 910.2	21 518.8
Netherlands	473 131.2	480 306.7	462 771.6	344 966.8	352 099.5	682 132.8	755 495.9	896 278.5	789 246.6	717 026.5
New Zealand	6 067.5	5 337.8	3 165.0	2 702.1	2 793.8	1 211.8	628.2	380.2	293.1	390.9
Norway	9 139.9	11 367.1	13 773.1	11 801.0	3 819.4	13 007.1	13 084.2	14 424.3	13 636.4	13 443.0
Poland	4 292.9	2 200.9	4 065.7	1 983.1	1 118.9	17 047.4	16 678.6	24 036.9	24 157.3	27 302.9
Portugal	2 347.3	2 171.4	2 656.5	1 806.7	1 806.3	21 798.6	20 902.3	24 443.5	24 343.9	27 302.9
Slovak Republic	-290.7	-806.4	-1 633.5	-1 521.6	-630.2	4 501.9	3 556.4	4 334.4	4 074.9	3 836.2
Slovenia	-42.5	-11.6	60.0	83.6	279.7	411.5	523.9	664.4	1 162.1	1 222.2
Spain	-9 213.9	-7 989.9	-9 733.7	-10 622.9	-7 336.6	55 102.9	55 513.9	70 732.8	81 931.5	82 610.6
Sweden	20 984.2	16 421.4	16 025.4	16 629.3	17 603.9	58 520.4	60 597.7	58 334.1	54 227.2	58 794.7
Switzerland	116 427.9	131 998.5	131 486.0	104 080.6	69 640.5	374 832.9	396 531.0	431 542.3	418 361.6	455 714.4
Turkey	-185.1	-37.9	-437.8	-234.7	-1 236.8	10 520.4	8 995.5	11 318.1	5 629.7	3 995.7
United Kingdom	546 347.3	491 017.2	513 326.9	492 225.8	491 504.2	746 456.2	715 626.6	845 608.1	730 819.8	704 501.2
United States	858 246.1	795 907.0	683 540.4	589 702.3	690 792.0	1 061 613.5	987 166.6	693 576.4	523 699.3	487 411.8
EUROPE	**2 155 868.3**	**2 149 562.6**	**2 242 281.1**	**2 029 433.2**	**2 000 405.5**	**3 067 389.2**	**3 152 324.2**	**3 839 472.3**	**3 510 090.5**	**3 356 060.4**
Bulgaria	-61.0	-13.7	-15.6	-4.6	7.9	626.0	669.3	869.5	2 017.4	2 069.2
Croatia	-38.1	-110.7	-128.3	-121.4	-124.7	2 092.5	2 131.3	2 823.2	3 092.5	3 124.0
Cyprus	13 782.3	12 875.5	12 828.0	13 133.7	11 804.1	111 818.2	109 697.5	86 772.6	77 650.6	93 800.3
Malta	10 361.5	12 631.0	14 683.4	12 079.2	48 780.0	13 937.9	14 002.3	17 083.2	15 382.4	27 083.8
Romania	-144.8	26.4	42.0	14.9	-44.9	1 413.2	1 606.4	2 290.7	2 083.8	1 755.8
Russian Federation	-61 850.8	-63 135.9	-63 698.7	-51 743.8	-44 346.2	21 390.3	20 628.2	15 159.5	12 166.2	3 772.2
Ukraine	-46.8	-42.2	-19.2	-18.3	-29.2	617.3	693.6	903.1	652.6	800.9
AFRICA	**1 678.8**	**-1 173.2**	**507.3**	**531.3**	**906.5**	**28 721.8**	**12 001.7**	**13 353.3**	**14 986.3**	**14 241.7**
Northern Africa	328.8	307.8	296.2	430.5	348.2	1 146.4	875.9	1 724.6	1 991.1	2 152.3
Algeria	56.6	62.2	78.0	89.3	94.4	16.3	11.6	10.8	8.0	6.7
Egypt	103.4	113.8	97.1	87.0	80.9	880.8	579.7	1 535.1	1 461.0	1 428.9
Libya	-	-48.5	-55.2	-	-	-	-	-	-	11.2
Morocco	168.8	181.3	176.3	254.2	173.0	222.1	260.4	164.3	502.6	687.5
Tunisia	-1.1	-1.1	-	-	-	28.3	23.2	15.6	19.5	18.0
Other African countries	1 350.0	-1 481.0	211.1	99.6	559.4	27 575.4	11 125.8	11 628.7	12 995.2	12 089.4
Nigeria	-6.5	-9.5	-13.2	-33.2	-27.0	38.1	34.8	64.8	60.7	59.5
South Africa	1 004.9	519.7	933.1	-1 459.8	-921.1	21 288.0	6 346.6	6 087.8	8 300.9	7 761.2
AMERICA	**1 426 503.0**	**1 442 125.0**	**1 766 319.3**	**1 405 274.8**	**1 277 095.0**	**1 333 639.6**	**1 258 388.3**	**1 015 800.0**	**820 640.0**	**772 846.6**
Northern America	1 054 958.1	1 005 141.8	914 383.5	835 542.7	851 991.7	1 159 259.7	1 082 886.1	795 214.7	626 099.2	617 426.4
Central America and Caribbean countries	364 727.3	432 087.1	850 591.3	565 616.0	425 513.4	113 072.4	107 618.8	133 753.9	125 554.2	87 918.4
Bahamas	39 407.7	42 337.9	52 801.6	50 042.4	36 510.9	-1 224.8	-984.5	610.5	3 258.5	-4 058.6
Bermuda	178 954.8	231 852.0	479 866.9	304 811.1	135 734.7	69 958.6	57 205.7	75 399.4	55 909.1	24 173.2
Cayman Islands	94 131.7	94 856.1	242 419.0	140 791.2	129 514.7	11 562.3	18 437.9	16 820.6	16 922.4	12 220.8
Costa Rica	-3.3	-2.1	-3.6	-3.4	-2.2	397.4	389.0	393.4	1 387.7	2 635.4
El Salvador	3.3	79.1	-3.6	105.3	-4.5	154.6	157.1	22.8	-45.8	4.5
Guatemala	-4.4	13.7	19.2	18.3	15.7	455.1	404.8	28.8	53.8	55.0
Honduras	-3.3	-	-	-	-	24.0	25.3	32.4	32.1	32.6
Nicaragua	-2.2	-3.2	-2.4	-	-18.0	7.6	1.1	73.2	83.6	455.0
Panama	2 452.9	5 594.0	5 321.4	4 185.9	4 099.1	1 708.2	2 214.6	984.6	933.1	954.8
Virgin Islands, U.S.	-	-	-2.4	-17.2	-2.2	-	218.2	492.9	9 458.4	10 057.3
South America	6 817.6	4 896.2	1 344.4	4 116.1	-410.0	61 307.6	67 882.4	86 831.4	68 985.6	67 501.7
Argentina	-101.3	-47.4	-82.8	-117.9	-137.0	4 074.0	3 776.7	5 051.6	4 003.9	2 576.9
Bolivia	-1.1	6.3	10.8	12.6	12.4	111.1	99.1	66.0	65.3	61.8
Brazil	8 274.4	6 170.5	3 178.2	-800.3	-2 718.5	48 537.8	53 568.0	73 846.2	57 997.5	58 251.0
Colombia	-62.1	22.1	1 213.7	969.8	707.7	1 276.0	1 190.1	1 337.3	1 560.6	1 571.6
Ecuador	-	-	-6.0	-5.7	-3.4	32.7	36.9	39.6	-760.2	432.5
Paraguay	-4.4	-13.7	-14.4	-14.9	-14.6	168.8	175.0	278.2	92.7	35.9
Peru	-78.4	109.6	349.0	792.3	1 560.3	1 910.7	3 338.3	2 800.4	1 789.6	1 333.4
Uruguay	-1 366.4	-1 657.0	-3 383.3	3 272.3	430.2	3 779.0	3 338.3	2 273.9	2 429.6	1 064.9
Venezuela	-21.8	-17.9	-1.2	-1.1	-1.1	25.0	28.5	50.4	48.1	51.7

Table 2. Foreign direct investment positions by country *(cont.)*

At year end

Million US dollars

	Inward					Outward				
	2015	2016	2017	2018	2019	2015	2016	2017	2018	2019
ASIA	**100 901.5**	**172 388.5**	**197 242.7**	**186 245.7**	**208 093.7**	**57 010.3**	**110 936.0**	**190 350.2**	**113 347.8**	**200 156.1**
Near and Middle East	38 365.8	37 176.1	45 182.3	41 752.9	78 836.2	4 221.0	10 959.2	15 518.1	14 956.5	48 811.5
Gulf Arabian countries	37 725.6	36 427.7	43 951.8	41 040.8	76 989.4	485.6	6 791.4	11 289.3	9 254.6	40 934.6
Kuwait	-	-	-	-	-2.2	2.2	-	3.6	3.4	3.4
Qatar	21 562.3	15 760.5	18 536.8	16 542.2	16 318.8	3.3	2.1	4.8	4.6	10.1
Saudi Arabia	1 550.4	2 633.1	4 258.8	4 159.6	5 885.2	100.2	128.6	131.9	123.7	174.1
United Arab Emirates	13 670.1	16 961.1	18 612.4	16 612.1	39 919.1	-163.3	6 111.5	10 526.5	8 521.9	40 153.9
Other Near and Middle East	641.3	748.4	1 230.5	712.2	1 846.8	3 735.4	4 167.8	4 230.0	5 701.9	7 876.9
Jordan	-	-1.1	-1.2	-1.1	-1.1	3.3	142.3	486.9	416.8	388.7
Other Asian countries	62 535.7	135 213.5	152 059.2	144 492.8	129 257.5	52 789.3	99 976.8	174 832.1	98 390.2	151 344.6
China	4 779.5	6 753.5	6 072.2	9 357.7	9 390.0	8 979.9	9 747.0	9 949.6	11 580.0	8 555.4
Hong Kong, China	32 799.1	33 969.6	89 378.7	92 383.8	81 044.7	4 748.0	10 887.5	31 038.6	25 832.4	86 727.7
India	-1 566.7	-290.9	-417.4	-390.4	-443.7	2 645.6	1 773.0	4 232.4	2 755.9	2 484.8
Indonesia	-3 362.0	-182.4	-241.1	-139.7	-135.9	650.0	894.9	985.8	981.2	1 034.6
Iran, Islamic Republic of	-	-	-	-	-	14.2	-	-	-	-739.2
Malaysia	2 087.1	2 316.9	2 542.6	2 912.8	1 540.1	2 455.1	985.6	1 471.6	1 329.3	3.4
Philippines	-22.9	20.0	13.2	28.6	29.2	174.2	157.1	145.1	119.1	80.9
Singapore	26 209.0	89 792.3	51 513.6	37 887.6	31 435.6	24 623.8	66 739.7	115 281.8	44 441.3	38 380.1
Chinese Taipei	-1.1	-35.8	-26.4	-73.3	-115.7	326.6	323.6	382.6	358.4	693.1
Thailand	326.6	1 432.5	1 199.3	1 205.6	1 170.5	697.9	726.3	1 062.6	1 140.4	1 066.1
Viet Nam	-4.4	-5.3	-8.4	-26.3	-49.4	393.0	1 061.5	2 742.9	1 487.3	1 899.6
AUSTRALIA, OCEANIA AND POLAR REGIONS	**12 881.9**	**12 339.0**	**11 346.8**	**11 038.5**	**8 583.5**	**17 127.9**	**17 020.1**	**19 435.1**	**19 069.2**	**16 397.4**
WORLD unallocated and confidential	**1.1**	**-**	**-**	**-**	**1.1**	**-1.1**	**-**	**-**	**-**	**-**
European Union (EU28)	**1 732 080.6**	**1 742 550.9**	**1 805 159.5**	**1 644 768.7**	**1 656 252.5**	**2 547 973.9**	**2 632 787.0**	**3 277 234.3**	**2 970 180.9**	**2 831 287.4**
G20 countries excl. European Union	**1 639 212.8**	**1 549 101.9**	**1 529 078.9**	**1 408 567.7**	**1 472 952.1**	**2 374 824.2**	**2 262 271.5**	**2 195 584.1**	**1 883 319.2**	**1 889 231.6**
G20 OECD countries	**1 690 484.5**	**1 596 681.8**	**1 579 076.5**	**1 449 702.3**	**1 506 379.5**	**2 267 158.4**	**2 165 408.5**	**2 080 139.1**	**1 785 409.9**	**1 804 621.4**
G20 Non-OECD countries	**-51 271.6**	**-47 579.8**	**-49 997.6**	**-41 134.6**	**-33 427.3**	**107 665.8**	**96 863.1**	**115 445.0**	**97 909.3**	**84 610.2**
MENA countries	**38 771.9**	**37 458.6**	**45 048.0**	**42 247.5**	**78 078.0**	**2 532.4**	**9 197.9**	**14 952.0**	**13 033.0**	**45 123.6**
ASEAN countries	**25 232.4**	**93 372.0**	**55 347.8**	**42 392.9**	**34 415.9**	**29 043.0**	**70 615.6**	**121 753.4**	**49 554.6**	**42 517.4**

- Nil

Note: Detailed metadata at: *http://stats.oecd.org/OECDStat_Metadata/ShowMetadata.ashx?Dataset=FDI_CTRY_IND_SUMM.*

Source: *OECD International Direct Investment Statistics (database): https://doi.org/10.1787/idi-data-en*

Table 3. Foreign direct investment income by country

Million US dollars

	Inward					Outward				
	2015	2016	2017	2018	2019	2015	2016	2017	2018	2019
WORLD	**106 752.1**	**135 529.1**	**128 642.8**	**133 578.4**	**118 318.6**	**127 368.8**	**153 221.3**	**151 447.4**	**157 040.0**	**144 607.6**
OECD COUNTRIES	**76 057.7**	**103 676.9**	**86 760.2**	**90 037.8**	**81 252.7**	**112 867.4**	**136 031.2**	**128 687.9**	**133 489.9**	**124 783.4**
Australia	-33.3	-10.0	-28.2	55.5	-435.5	741.0	332.9	459.9	1 832.9	1 535.9
Austria	-84.3	200.2	-62.0	-2.4	-2.2	582.4	1 106.9	693.3	1 849.4	1 560.5
Belgium	2 968.4	4 569.3	7 325.0	5 943.6	4 980.4	6 971.7	6 729.0	6 234.9	8 654.6	8 091.3
Canada	12 004.4	10 546.3	8 778.0	7 058.9	7 991.7	1 077.1	1 262.9	4 102.1	3 569.0	3 249.7
Chile	3.3	-	-6.8	-1.2	-57.1	54.4	45.3	49.6	38.9	32.5
Czech Republic	14.4	3.3	19.2	-56.7	-85.1	2 003.3	1 790.3	2 888.1	3 081.6	1 191.1
Denmark	-31.1	3.3	34.9	11.8	66.0	765.4	888.0	292.0	452.0	404.1
Estonia	1.1	1.1	2.3	2.4	2.2	10.0	13.3	10.1	9.4	6.7
Finland	346.1	48.7	25.9	-82.6	-60.5	79.9	816.1	611.0	888.7	484.7
France	3 548.5	1 982.7	585.1	2 322.7	1 627.7	3 844.7	3 851.6	5 148.2	5 862.2	5 433.8
Germany	3 518.6	4 587.0	1 954.7	4 707.9	3 970.7	3 530.8	4 282.9	6 513.4	6 905.5	6 413.3
Greece	13.3	13.3	21.4	23.6	22.4	58.8	140.4	220.9	194.7	178.0
Hungary	514.7	1 479.6	524.2	-31.9	-99.6	1 452.0	376.0	83.4	863.9	659.4
Iceland	-58.8	-	-4.5	-10.6	-1.1	143.1	5.5	3.4	44.8	41.4
Ireland	5 202.4	29 000.3	7 567.4	6 448.7	6 282.3	9 868.0	25 373.2	15 338.7	10 406.0	12 073.2
Israel	27.7	17.7	39.5	56.7	33.6	57.7	-201.3	181.5	46.0	42.5
Italy	448.1	656.9	768.8	1 502.4	1 637.7	2 475.9	2 385.3	2 328.9	2 595.3	2 458.3
Japan	41.0	-103.9	-76.7	66.1	-2.2	312.8	422.4	500.5	573.6	772.4
Korea	62.1	-37.6	-157.8	-123.9	-89.6	63.2	107.3	98.1	188.8	239.6
Latvia	-48.8	-1.1	-4.5	-3.5	9.0	2.2	-8.8	12.4	11.8	6.7
Lithuania	4.4	5.5	-	-	-2.2	47.7	14.4	10.1	14.2	17.9
Luxembourg	-	-	-	-	-	-	-	-	-	-
Mexico	-277.3	-305.2	-439.6	-522.8	-	380.5	583.9	714.7	1 387.9	1 240.3
Netherlands	10 175.3	6 417.1	14 721.0	14 403.4	15 692.4	19 442.0	20 017.7	19 842.2	22 427.7	21 132.9
New Zealand	1 081.5	127.2	197.3	66.1	51.5	75.4	76.3	34.9	50.7	43.7
Norway	271.8	31.0	48.5	30.7	-146.6	589.0	200.2	406.9	735.3	538.5
Poland	28.8	-27.6	5.6	100.3	124.3	1 099.3	1 131.3	1 639.0	1 719.6	1 430.7
Portugal	219.6	56.4	48.5	86.2	53.7	629.0	1 130.2	678.6	1 045.7	982.9
Slovak Republic	-13.3	-12.2	-19.2	-34.2	-11.2	545.8	766.3	467.8	834.4	527.3
Slovenia	-3.3	-4.4	-1.1	-1.2	-	41.0	48.7	53.0	68.5	79.5
Spain	-302.8	69.7	609.9	-267.9	424.3	3 089.3	4 302.8	3 677.2	4 539.1	3 377.4
Sweden	209.7	582.8	33.8	817.9	671.7	2 331.7	2 687.2	2 407.8	1 750.3	2 646.4
Switzerland	2 582.4	6 274.5	5 342.1	5 476.2	5 479.7	12 612.3	15 617.6	15 791.9	12 818.4	15 982.3
Turkey	12.2	-	-34.9	-92.1	-176.9	374.9	387.0	521.9	520.5	462.3
United Kingdom	8 299.5	11 371.2	16 322.9	14 624.1	10 003.4	13 059.3	17 482.0	17 969.8	23 032.0	21 846.0
United States	25 266.8	26 139.6	22 619.8	27 463.7	23 295.6	24 505.8	21 881.0	18 711.5	14 476.6	9 600.4
EUROPE	**46 947.3**	**78 884.2**	**70 840.9**	**66 986.9**	**61 020.9**	**93 245.7**	**117 086.1**	**111 591.7**	**118 535.3**	**115 461.8**
Bulgaria	-	-	-1.1	-	-	58.8	78.5	69.9	60.2	50.4
Croatia	-	-25.4	-5.6	-3.5	-3.4	140.9	289.7	316.8	358.8	64.9
Cyprus	865.2	1 690.8	919.9	933.6	884.4	2 488.1	875.8	516.3	-63.7	1 146.3
Malta	448.1	1 219.7	347.2	231.3	161.2	609.0	259.9	383.3	577.1	1 348.9
Romania	-37.7	-3.3	-3.4	-3.5	-4.5	112.0	131.6	117.2	276.2	362.7
Russian Federation	142.0	748.6	197.3	144.0	314.6	54.4	614.8	2 578.1	2 019.4	498.2
Ukraine	-	-	-	-	-	81.0	71.9	87.9	68.5	71.6
AFRICA	**79.9**	**162.6**	**177.0**	**227.8**	**555.2**	**-402.7**	**985.3**	**308.9**	**665.6**	**638.1**
Northern Africa	-76.5	18.8	29.3	34.2	32.5	-241.8	235.5	131.9	401.3	394.0
Algeria	4.4	-	-	-	-	-1.1	2.2	1.1	1.2	1.1
Egypt	-95.4	-1.1	-	-	-	-292.8	184.7	93.6	108.6	98.5
Libya	-	-	-	-3.5	-	-	-	-	-	-
Morocco	14.4	21.0	29.3	37.8	32.5	35.5	42.0	27.1	280.9	284.3
Tunisia	-	-	-	-	-	15.5	6.6	10.1	10.6	10.1
Other African countries	156.4	143.8	147.7	193.6	522.8	-160.8	749.8	177.0	264.4	244.0
Nigeria	-	-	-	-	-	10.0	21.0	19.2	34.2	32.5
South Africa	166.4	140.4	110.5	155.8	164.6	-416.0	597.1	172.5	244.3	220.5
AMERICA	**54 477.0**	**51 178.8**	**51 840.8**	**57 468.4**	**47 509.2**	**30 027.7**	**30 409.2**	**31 436.1**	**28 533.0**	**20 419.8**
Northern America	37 271.2	36 686.9	31 397.8	34 523.8	31 287.4	25 584.0	23 143.9	22 813.7	18 045.6	12 850.1
Central America and Caribbean countries	16 534.7	11 708.5	18 417.3	22 960.0	16 217.4	4 032.2	4 445.4	4 390.7	7 181.6	4 870.7
Bahamas	1 130.3	97.3	780.1	1 680.6	1 450.8	-199.7	-176.9	-171.3	-72.0	-180.2
Bermuda	8 397.1	5 027.1	6 080.5	9 066.4	4 137.5	1 550.7	3 137.2	2 164.4	2 569.3	1 284.0
Cayman Islands	5 666.1	4 410.0	9 014.8	9 448.8	7 646.9	1 513.0	610.4	367.5	1 615.7	1 665.7
Costa Rica	-	-	-	-1.2	1.1	241.8	266.5	254.8	5.9	9.0
El Salvador	-	-	50.7	-	-	8.9	-2.2	5.6	4.7	5.6
Guatemala	-	-	-	1.2	1.1	17.7	-148.2	2.3	-2.4	1.1
Honduras	-	-	-	-	-	-	4.4	3.4	1.2	41.4
Nicaragua	-1.1	-1.1	-	-	-	-	-	-	-	3.4
Panama	17.7	505.4	135.3	480.3	41.4	53.2	1.1	111.6	114.5	92.9
Virgin Islands, U.S.	-	-	-	-	-	-	-	5.6	773.0	15.7
South America	671.1	2 784.5	2 025.7	-14.2	5.6	412.6	2 819.9	4 231.8	3 304.6	2 699.0
Argentina	-1.1	-2.2	-	-7.1	-3.4	225.2	380.4	242.4	581.8	353.7
Bolivia	-	-	-1.1	-	-	35.5	5.5	6.8	7.1	6.7
Brazil	693.3	2 832.0	2 075.3	-181.8	-248.5	-525.8	1 845.6	3 264.6	2 356.9	1 974.7
Colombia	-14.4	-36.5	-41.7	-15.3	-24.6	62.1	61.9	19.2	30.7	69.4
Ecuador	-	-	-	-	-	4.4	-	4.5	5.9	5.6
Paraguay	-	-	-	-	-	4.4	7.7	12.4	13.0	12.3
Peru	-	1.1	-	1.2	7.8	-4.4	-18.8	144.3	147.5	136.6
Uruguay	-8.9	-10.0	-	192.4	334.7	556.9	491.0	458.8	122.7	107.5
Venezuela	-	-	-	-	-3.4	1.1	2.2	-2.3	-2.4	-2.2

Table 3. Foreign direct investment income by country *(cont.)*

Million US dollars

	Inward					Outward				
	2015	2016	2017	2018	2019	2015	2016	2017	2018	2019
ASIA	**4 044.4**	**5 139.9**	**5 206.9**	**8 720.6**	**9 585.8**	**3 799.2**	**4 288.4**	**7 553.8**	**7 368.1**	**6 467.0**
Near and Middle East	1 977.8	2 101.1	1 889.3	1 947.4	2 384.4	239.6	151.5	730.5	730.6	459.0
Gulf Arabian countries	1 892.4	2 030.3	1 812.6	1 844.7	2 306.1	51.0	238.9	317.9	453.2	162.3
Kuwait	-	-	-	-	-	-	-	-	-	-
Qatar	843.0	876.9	833.1	520.5	705.3	-	-	-	-	-
Saudi Arabia	289.5	327.3	344.9	367.0	389.6	6.7	7.7	4.5	-28.3	-31.3
United Arab Emirates	751.0	800.6	558.0	830.9	1 092.6	44.4	224.5	301.0	469.7	182.5
Other Near and Middle East	85.4	69.7	77.8	103.9	78.4	188.6	-88.5	413.7	277.4	295.5
Jordan	-	-	-	-	-	-	-	24.8	24.8	25.7
Other Asian countries	2 066.6	3 038.8	3 317.6	6 773.3	7 201.4	3 560.7	4 136.9	6 822.2	6 637.6	6 008.1
China	108.7	275.4	671.9	64.9	519.4	500.3	525.3	703.4	689.2	475.8
Hong Kong, China	982.8	1 038.4	1 592.8	2 644.9	2 540.0	483.6	568.4	1 397.8	1 901.3	2 082.2
India	-34.4	-40.9	-19.2	-23.6	-56.0	138.7	111.7	55.2	192.4	192.5
Indonesia	-117.6	-102.8	-13.5	-7.1	-4.5	72.1	103.9	145.4	167.6	163.4
Iran, Islamic Republic of	-	-	-	-	-	-2.2	-	-	-	-
Malaysia	41.0	48.7	24.8	147.5	63.8	6.7	127.2	139.8	66.1	60.5
Philippines	-4.4	-4.4	-	-	1.1	-16.6	2.2	23.7	2.4	2.2
Singapore	1 123.7	1 956.2	1 188.1	3 825.1	4 077.0	1 844.7	1 964.0	3 460.7	2 454.9	1 704.9
Chinese Taipei	4.4	-	-2.3	-1.2	-14.6	16.6	35.4	53.0	53.1	39.2
Thailand	1.1	16.6	31.6	27.1	28.0	113.1	66.4	71.0	73.2	72.8
Viet Nam	-	-	-	-	-1.1	18.9	25.4	18.0	112.1	114.2
AUSTRALIA, OCEANIA AND POLAR REGIONS	**1 204.7**	**162.6**	**577.2**	**173.5**	**-352.6**	**698.8**	**452.3**	**555.7**	**1 937.9**	**1 621.0**
WORLD unallocated and confidential	**-1.1**	**1.1**	**-**	**1.2**	**-**	**-**	**-**	**1.1**	**-**	**-**
European Union (EU28)	**36 306.2**	**63 887.0**	**51 745.0**	**51 671.2**	**46 348.4**	**75 341.1**	**96 961.2**	**88 523.3**	**98 413.8**	**93 974.0**
G20 countries excl. European Union	**54 137.5**	**59 004.8**	**53 659.1**	**57 574.6**	**48 898.5**	**50 421.5**	**57 165.8**	**64 235.1**	**67 167.5**	**57 099.5**
G20 OECD countries	**52 890.7**	**54 826.9**	**50 292.0**	**57 062.4**	**47 822.7**	**50 366.1**	**52 979.1**	**57 069.1**	**60 944.2**	**53 252.0**
G20 Non-OECD countries	**1 246.8**	**4 177.8**	**3 367.2**	**512.2**	**1 075.8**	**55.5**	**4 186.7**	**7 166.0**	**6 223.3**	**3 847.5**
MENA countries	**1 873.5**	**2 103.3**	**1 885.9**	**1 926.1**	**2 385.5**	**-65.4**	**608.2**	**697.8**	**1 115.3**	**838.5**
ASEAN countries	**1 044.9**	**1 914.2**	**1 311.0**	**4 149.7**	**4 307.6**	**2 038.8**	**2 291.3**	**3 859.8**	**2 877.4**	**2 119.1**

- Nil

Note: Detailed metadata at: *http://stats.oecd.org/OECDStat_Metadata/ShowMetadata.ashx?Dataset=FDI_CTRY_IND_SUMM.*

Source: *OECD International Direct Investment Statistics (database): https://doi.org/10.1787/idi-data-en*

Table 4. Foreign direct investment flows by industrial sector

Million US dollars

	Inward					Outward				
	2015	2016	2017	2018	2019	2015	2016	2017	2018	2019
All FDI activities	**622 284.0**	**188 439.7**	**69 967.3**	**-404 143.8**	**-137 847.3**	**738 981.7**	**147 117.1**	**209 945.9**	**-396 948.0**	**-159 815.3**
Agriculture, forestry and fishing	-	-	-	-	-	**106.5**	**-60.8**	**-224.3**	**-94.4**	**-115.3**
Mining and quarrying	**1.1**	**2.2**	**2.3**	**2.4**	**3.4**	**-3 970.1**	**-7 305.1**	**-7 684.6**	**813.2**	**2.2**
Extraction activities	-	-	-	-	-	-3 485.3	-5 963.7	-5 208.0	224.2	-36.9
Manufacturing	**-1 203.6**	**2 797.7**	**595.2**	**-193.6**	**1 403.8**	**13 061.6**	**-3 674.7**	**-9 490.5**	**3 558.4**	**2 076.6**
of which:										
Food products, beverages and tobacco	-6.7	-	1.1	-1.2	-	2 057.7	822.7	-7 383.6	649.1	340.3
Textiles, wood and paper products; printing	-1 466.4	639.2	781.2	-512.2	304.5	2 256.2	-1 037.3	36.1	435.5	42.5
Chemical, rubber, plastic, non-metallic mineral products	-100.9	1 335.8	-803.7	-974.9	16.8	3 030.5	3 380.5	-155.6	1 720.8	1 045.6
Metal and machinery products, except electrical equipment	271.8	740.9	573.8	1 267.6	1 057.9	4 107.6	-6 487.9	3 013.2	2 761.7	1 795.6
Motor vehicles, trailers, semi-trailers, other transport equipment	11.1	6.6	33.8	18.9	17.9	494.7	-530.8	-3 990.5	-2 268.4	-1 841.5
Other manufacturing	86.5	74.1	9.0	8.3	7.8	1 115.9	176.9	-1 010.0	258.5	694.1
Electricity, gas, steam and air conditioning supply	**-32.2**	**-88.5**	**56.4**	-	-	**1 393.2**	**-504.3**	**-11.3**	**87.3**	**-137.7**
Water supply; sewerage, waste management and remediation activities	**10.0**	**3.3**	**10.1**	**9.4**	**9.0**	**116.5**	**49.8**	**22.5**	**27.1**	**24.6**
Construction	**-39.9**	**-3.3**	**23.7**	**33.0**	**30.2**	**1 558.5**	**-947.7**	**-413.7**	**-29.5**	**-47.0**
Services	**623 515.3**	**185 729.3**	**69 279.7**	**-403 995.0**	**-139 293.6**	**726 044.4**	**158 655.3**	**226 708.4**	**-402 064.2**	**-162 368.7**
Wholesale and retail trade; repair of motor vehicles and motorcycles	22 545.8	-3 528.7	-6 042.2	-46 506.6	26 725.6	16 602.3	-227.8	-13 846.2	-18 433.8	2 217.6
Transportation and storage	975.0	55.3	-193.9	86.2	-255.2	1 180.3	-435.7	-819.5	918.2	420.9
Accommodation and food service activities	-183.0	142.7	5 571.0	-5 289.7	-166.8	295.1	-434.6	-1 954.7	-134.5	-97.4
Information and communication	-376.0	4 008.6	-10 002.3	22 371.1	-5 635.3	6 838.6	3 744.3	-925.5	481.5	-11 398.2
Financial and insurance activities	599 191.3	192 637.4	84 788.6	-377 632.5	-150 707.5	695 641.7	119 671.6	377 807.5	-330 249.0	-143 820.7
Activities of holding companies	548 053.2	189 958.0	74 439.2	-405 156.4	-182 641.9	692 068.8	124 203.3	376 122.2	-330 024.8	-143 131.1
Real estate activities	1 113.7	261.0	-2 657.0	-158.1	100.8	3 605.1	1 997.1	-3 547.5	473.3	492.6
Professional, scientific and technical activities	824.2	-2 649.6	-12 123.8	4 665.4	-2 598.2	60 427.1	28 394.3	-133 766.2	-52 998.9	-8 993.6
Administrative and support service activities	-549.1	-5 194.1	9 927.9	-1 535.5	-6 762.6	-58 620.1	5 829.9	3 979.3	-2 152.7	-1 218.0
Public administration; activities of households and of extraterritorial organisations	-21.1	-	-	-	-	-	-	-	-	-
Education	-	-	-	-	-	124.2	-42.0	-22.5	-11.8	-13.4
Human health and social work activities	-1.1	-2.2	12.4	5.9	5.6	-28.8	39.8	-13.5	10.6	5.6
Arts, entertainment and recreation	-	-	-	-	-	24.4	118.3	48.5	43.7	43.7
Other services	-4.4	-1.1	-	-	-	-45.5	1.1	-231.1	-9.4	-7.8
Not allocated and confidential	**33.3**	**-1.1**	-	-	-	**23.3**	-	-	-	-
Private real estate activities	-	-	-	-	-	**647.8**	**904.6**	**1 039.3**	**754.2**	**750.0**

- Nil

Note: Detailed metadata at: *http://stats.oecd.org/OECDStat_Metadata/ShowMetadata.ashx?Dataset=FDI_CTRY_IND_SUMM*.

Source: *OECD International Direct Investment Statistics (database): https://doi.org/10.1787/idi-data-en*

Table 5. Foreign direct investment positions by industrial sector

At year end

Million US dollars

	Inward					Outward				
	2015	2016	2017	2018	2019	2015	2016	2017	2018	2019
All FDI activities	**3 697 834.5**	**3 775 241.9**	**4 217 697.3**	**3 632 523.5**	**3 495 085.4**	**4 503 887.9**	**4 550 670.4**	**5 078 410.9**	**4 478 133.7**	**4 359 702.3**
Agriculture, forestry and fishing	-	-	-	-	-	**1 625.5**	**1 624.3**	**1 572.3**	**1 455.2**	**1 379.5**
Mining and quarrying	**5.4**	**5.3**	**7.2**	**8.0**	**9.0**	**22 509.5**	**18 079.5**	**11 283.3**	**11 145.0**	**11 331.2**
Extraction activities	-	-	-	-	-	15 762.7	12 314.7	7 934.8	7 807.4	7 926.3
Manufacturing	**2 493.2**	**4 019.2**	**5 710.0**	**4 816.8**	**4 071.0**	**123 936.9**	**119 094.6**	**119 220.4**	**111 209.1**	**109 387.8**
of which:										
Food products, beverages and tobacco	-41.4	-44.3	-51.6	-52.7	-52.8	15 715.8	16 982.2	10 325.0	9 713.8	9 472.0
Textiles, wood and paper products; printing	273.3	664.1	1 091.4	482.0	329.1	7 242.2	5 968.2	6 357.6	6 104.9	5 851.5
Chemical, rubber, plastic, non-metallic mineral products	2 053.3	3 109.5	4 441.1	4 034.8	3 467.8	38 819.8	39 819.8	43 547.6	41 699.1	41 277.2
Metal and machinery products, except electrical equipment	86.0	162.3	66.0	198.1	178.6	41 233.5	35 316.7	38 255.0	35 256.5	34 925.9
Motor vehicles, trailers, semi-trailers, other transport equipment	9.8	15.8	36.0	34.3	33.7	12 406.1	12 717.4	12 649.3	10 990.4	10 235.9
Other manufacturing	112.1	110.7	127.1	120.2	116.8	8 518.2	8 288.2	8 087.1	7 443.3	7 626.4
Electricity, gas, steam and air conditioning supply	**-30.5**	**-113.8**	**-73.2**	**-74.4**	**-76.4**	**5 701.7**	**5 077.5**	**5 474.9**	**4 823.7**	**4 537.2**
Water supply; sewerage, waste management and remediation activities	**12.0**	**13.7**	**15.6**	**14.9**	**14.6**	**246.1**	**290.9**	**316.6**	**287.4**	**268.5**
Construction	**153.5**	**125.4**	**133.1**	**123.7**	**119.1**	**6 128.5**	**4 917.3**	**4 965.2**	**4 655.4**	**4 511.3**
Services	**3 695 199.8**	**3 771 192.2**	**4 211 905.7**	**3 627 633.4**	**3 490 947.0**	**4 330 692.4**	**4 388 093.2**	**4 919 119.7**	**4 328 114.3**	**4 211 398.6**
Wholesale and retail trade; repair of motor vehicles and motorcycles	70 991.8	68 648.7	66 177.7	17 581.9	42 153.4	101 609.1	105 061.7	96 393.6	68 223.0	67 409.6
Transportation and storage	823.1	834.8	770.0	883.9	823.4	16 935.2	16 086.2	15 887.5	13 923.7	13 772.2
Accommodation and food service activities	212.3	305.7	6 252.1	818.6	585.3	2 104.5	1 663.3	-206.3	-290.8	-305.5
Information and communication	1 701.7	5 835.4	-1 325.3	23 491.0	17 820.7	33 304.3	34 305.9	33 962.6	35 375.5	20 602.1
Financial and insurance activities	3 552 335.3	3 631 807.7	4 080 671.6	3 528 076.5	3 383 555.4	3 644 211.2	3 686 657.5	4 297 488.6	3 823 711.9	3 737 842.1
Activities of holding companies	3 590 650.0	3 677 067.6	4 116 117.8	3 528 997.0	3 355 578.5	3 569 798.6	3 617 644.1	4 219 840.5	3 748 394.8	3 664 868.6
Real estate activities	2 548.7	3 205.4	490.5	338.9	395.4	12 656.5	13 426.8	10 970.3	11 153.0	11 126.7
Professional, scientific and technical activities	34 471.4	32 700.5	22 395.1	24 761.9	19 128.3	494 842.7	500 463.8	428 355.7	344 134.4	330 589.8
Administrative and support service activities	32 026.1	27 763.3	36 367.2	31 575.5	26 376.1	23 653.8	28 987.0	34 881.3	30 539.3	29 017.1
Public administration; activities of households and of extraterritorial organisations	-	-	-	-	-	-	-	-	-	-
Education	-	-	-	-	-	190.5	147.6	154.7	147.7	146.0
Human health and social work activities	63.1	64.3	79.2	80.1	83.1	764.3	776.9	861.1	820.9	805.4
Arts, entertainment and recreation	25.0	24.2	27.6	26.3	25.8	189.4	286.7	345.4	348.1	364.0
Other services	1.1	-	-	-	-	229.7	231.9	26.4	26.3	28.1
Not allocated and confidential	**1.1**	-	**-1.2**	**1.1**	**1.1**	-	**-1.1**	**-1.2**	**-1.1**	**1.1**
Private real estate activities	-	-	-	-	-	**13 047.4**	**13 494.3**	**16 459.6**	**16 444.9**	**16 887.2**

- Nil

Note: Detailed metadata at: *http://stats.oecd.org/OECDStat_Metadata/ShowMetadata.ashx?Dataset=FDI_CTRY_IND_SUMM.*

Source: *OECD International Direct Investment Statistics (database): https://doi.org/10.1787/idi-data-en*

Table 6. Foreign direct investment income by industrial sector

Million US dollars

	Inward					Outward				
	2015	2016	2017	2018	2019	2015	2016	2017	2018	2019
All FDI activities	**106 752.1**	**135 529.1**	**128 642.8**	**133 578.4**	**118 318.6**	**127 368.8**	**153 221.3**	**151 447.4**	**157 040.0**	**144 607.6**
Agriculture, forestry and fishing	-	-	-	-	-	**25.5**	**5.5**	**10.1**	**-27.1**	**-26.9**
Mining and quarrying	**1.1**	**1.1**	**1.1**	**1.2**	**1.1**	**-2 460.3**	**-1 403.3**	**-396.8**	**-262.0**	**-307.8**
Extraction activities	-	-	-	-	-	-2 448.1	-1 123.5	-527.6	-364.7	-357.1
Manufacturing	**366.1**	**1 249.6**	**577.2**	**1 121.2**	**1 417.2**	**5 194.7**	**5 998.0**	**6 602.4**	**7 599.4**	**4 050.2**
of which:										
Food products, beverages and tobacco	-6.7	5.5	3.4	2.4	2.2	411.5	619.3	602.0	617.3	594.4
Textiles, wood and paper products; printing	-46.6	279.8	9.0	98.0	447.8	129.8	457.8	468.9	363.5	312.3
Chemical, rubber, plastic, non-metallic mineral products	317.2	165.9	-163.5	-201.8	-193.7	1 592.9	2 042.5	1 471.1	1 485.9	1 242.6
Metal and machinery products, except electrical equipment	3.3	704.4	689.9	1 138.9	1 080.3	2 092.1	1 572.5	2 889.2	3 689.4	2 476.2
Motor vehicles, trailers, semi-trailers, other transport equipment	14.4	17.7	20.3	64.9	61.6	412.6	609.3	537.7	747.1	-1 220.2
Other manufacturing	84.3	76.3	18.0	18.9	17.9	555.7	695.6	633.5	696.3	644.8
Electricity, gas, steam and air conditioning supply	**4.4**	-	**4.5**	**4.7**	**4.5**	**-102.1**	**2.2**	**116.1**	**90.9**	**82.8**
Water supply; sewerage, waste management and remediation activities	**-2.2**	**4.4**	**12.4**	**13.0**	**12.3**	**128.7**	**45.3**	**94.7**	**46.0**	**44.8**
Construction	**21.1**	**31.0**	**56.4**	**61.4**	**57.1**	**104.3**	**143.8**	**95.8**	**98.0**	**90.7**
Services	**106 348.3**	**134 219.8**	**127 941.6**	**132 303.8**	**116 749.1**	**124 351.6**	**148 277.1**	**144 757.1**	**149 309.6**	**140 488.1**
Wholesale and retail trade; repair of motor vehicles and motorcycles	1 731.6	940.0	2 215.1	1 694.8	1 523.6	5 114.8	6 138.5	7 407.3	6 504.2	4 443.1
Transportation and storage	-137.5	102.8	34.9	67.3	56.0	230.7	648.0	1 309.9	953.6	897.8
Accommodation and food service activities	37.7	46.4	30.4	31.9	31.3	7.8	13.3	-27.1	-29.5	-28.0
Information and communication	-754.3	33.2	-315.6	223.1	203.7	563.5	456.7	290.8	319.8	-103.0
Financial and insurance activities	102 627.8	129 350.9	123 360.4	128 427.9	113 212.8	113 289.0	130 286.4	125 842.6	137 534.5	132 151.6
Activities of holding companies	97 097.1	123 201.4	119 429.6	124 199.2	107 919.0	110 379.4	127 552.8	122 157.6	134 997.0	130 274.3
Real estate activities	22.2	359.4	651.6	9.4	9.0	498.1	706.6	413.7	448.5	422.0
Professional, scientific and technical activities	2 164.2	2 672.8	1 533.1	1 674.7	1 586.3	4 159.7	10 130.5	8 767.9	3 098.1	2 311.7
Administrative and support service activities	647.8	704.4	418.2	159.3	111.9	413.8	-108.4	742.9	468.5	381.7
Public administration; activities of households and of extraterritorial organisations	-	-	-	-	-	-	-	-	-	-
Education	-	-	-	-	-	5.5	-2.2	-7.9	-8.3	-7.8
Human health and social work activities	5.5	6.6	9.0	10.6	10.1	54.4	-1.1	-3.4	-1.2	1.1
Arts, entertainment and recreation	4.4	3.3	4.5	4.7	4.5	12.2	17.7	28.2	28.3	26.9
Other services	-1.1	-1.1	-	-	-	1.1	-7.7	-10.1	-10.6	-10.1
Not allocated and confidential	**13.3**	**23.2**	**49.6**	**73.2**	**77.2**	-	**-1.1**	**2.3**	**1.2**	-
Private real estate activities	-	-	-	-	-	**126.5**	**153.7**	**165.7**	**184.1**	**185.8**

- Nil

Note: Detailed metadata at: *http://stats.oecd.org/OECDStat_Metadata/ShowMetadata.ashx?Dataset=FDI_CTRY_IND_SUMM.*

Source: *OECD International Direct Investment Statistics (database): https://doi.org/10.1787/idi-data-en*

MEXICO

Table 1. Foreign direct investment flows by country

Million US dollars

	Inward					Outward				
	2015	2016	2017	2018	2019	2015	2016	2017	2018	2019
WORLD	**35 436.6**	**31 066.9**	**34 200.2**	**33 740.3**	**34 075.6**	**10 672.1**	**193.3**	**3 987.9**	**8 364.6**	**10 844.9**
OECD COUNTRIES	**33 415.0**	**28 730.3**	**32 919.7**	**31 692.1**	**32 603.4**	..	..	..	..	..
Australia	685.6	97.1	1 378.9	608.4	767.7	..	..	..	..	..
Austria	71.5	50.1	95.5	115.0	173.7	..	..	..	..	..
Belgium	826.9	1 122.6	1 029.4	65.9	1 370.6	..	..	..	..	..
Canada	1 096.7	2 298.8	2 826.4	4 220.6	2 986.6	..	..	..	..	..
Chile	125.6	13.5	34.6	90.4	-30.6	..	..	..	..	..
Czech Republic	0.0	0.3	0.1	1.9	0.1	..	..	..	..	..
Denmark	72.8	56.5	141.0	26.8	190.0	..	..	..	..	..
Estonia	-	-	0.0	0.1	0.2	..	..	..	..	..
Finland	205.2	-98.0	11.8	81.9	71.7	..	..	..	..	..
France	972.0	455.4	558.8	621.9	1 036.5	..	..	..	..	..
Germany	1 234.4	2 765.2	2 636.6	2 923.8	3 430.6	..	..	..	..	..
Greece	-	0.2	-	4.3	-	..	..	..	..	..
Hungary	4.2	4.5	5.4	-0.4	0.2	..	..	..	..	..
Iceland	-	-	0.0	0.0	-	..	..	..	..	..
Ireland	-5.0	51.9	31.5	48.2	50.7	..	..	..	..	..
Israel	-1.6	2 015.2	2.4	1.8	-2.8	..	..	..	..	..
Italy	606.9	806.3	1 864.7	1 530.9	1 498.8	..	..	..	..	..
Japan	2 222.2	1 963.0	2 440.6	2 277.8	1 479.7	..	..	..	..	..
Korea	1 013.2	1 122.8	257.3	702.6	170.7	..	..	..	..	..
Latvia	-	0.0	-	0.1	0.0	..	..	..	..	..
Lithuania	0.0	-	0.0	0.0	0.5	..	..	..	..	..
Luxembourg	118.5	17.3	4.5	310.6	14.5	..	..	..	..	..
Mexico	-	-	-	-	-	..	..	..	..	..
Netherlands	299.6	226.6	-207.5	751.7	909.9	..	..	..	..	..
New Zealand	1.8	1.1	-7.0	0.3	1.1	..	..	..	..	..
Norway	66.7	11.2	45.7	67.4	-2.9	..	..	..	..	..
Poland	0.1	0.4	0.6	-0.5	0.6	..	..	..	..	..
Portugal	0.3	7.3	11.5	26.9	26.3	..	..	..	..	..
Slovak Republic	0.1	0.0	0.9	0.2	0.3	..	..	..	..	..
Slovenia	-	-	0.2	0.1	5.5	..	..	..	..	..
Spain	3 903.3	3 567.3	3 373.2	4 167.3	4 056.0	..	..	..	..	..
Sweden	-33.2	84.8	-40.6	161.7	83.2	..	..	..	..	..
Switzerland	225.7	582.3	300.4	631.1	721.7	..	..	..	..	..
Turkey	0.0	0.0	1.9	0.2	0.3	..	..	..	..	..
United Kingdom	364.7	455.8	500.6	630.1	788.0	..	..	..	..	..
United States	19 336.8	11 050.4	15 620.2	11 623.2	12 804.0	..	..	..	..	..
EUROPE	**8 936.3**	**10 187.0**	**10 395.3**	**12 240.9**	**14 487.6**	..	..	..	..	..
Bulgaria	-	0.0	0.1	1.4	1.9	..	..	..	..	..
Croatia	-	-	0.1	0.1	-	..	..	..	..	..
Cyprus	-	0.0	12.8	9.0	8.6	..	..	..	..	..
Malta	0.1	16.6	0.0	0.1	4.1	..	..	..	..	..
Romania	0.1	0.0	0.4	0.1	0.2	..	..	..	..	..
Russian Federation	0.8	1.9	14.9	63.0	44.7	..	..	..	..	..
Ukraine	0.6	0.3	0.7	0.2	0.7	..	..	..	..	..
AFRICA	**3.1**	**6.3**	**2.4**	**20.0**	**3.5**	..	..	..	..	..
Northern Africa	0.0	0.0	0.1	0.0	0.4	..	..	..	..	..
Algeria	-	-	0.1	-	0.1	..	..	..	..	..
Egypt	-	0.0	-	0.0	0.3	..	..	..	..	..
Libya	-	-	-	-	-	..	..	..	..	..
Morocco	0.0	0.0	-	-	0.0	..	..	..	..	..
Tunisia	0.0	-	-	-	-	..	..	..	..	..
Other African countries	3.1	6.3	2.3	20.0	3.1	..	..	..	..	..
Nigeria	0.0	-	-	0.0	-	..	..	..	..	..
South Africa	3.0	3.4	2.0	19.6	-1.0	..	..	..	..	..
AMERICA	**22 498.0**	**14 862.3**	**18 847.0**	**17 249.0**	**16 804.2**	..	..	..	..	..
Northern America	20 433.5	13 349.3	18 446.6	15 843.8	15 790.6	..	..	..	..	..
Central America and Caribbean countries	82.7	40.1	58.8	86.0	53.0	..	..	..	..	..
Bahamas	-	-	-	-	-	..	..	..	..	..
Bermuda	-0.5	-	-	-	-	..	..	..	..	..
Cayman Islands	-	-	-	-	-	..	..	..	..	..
Costa Rica	0.1	1.5	2.0	-1.4	-9.6	..	..	..	..	..
El Salvador	10.6	35.0	26.6	0.1	10.3	..	..	..	..	..
Guatemala	0.5	0.6	5.5	0.7	7.3	..	..	..	..	..
Honduras	0.7	0.3	0.8	0.5	1.2	..	..	..	..	..
Nicaragua	5.7	-	3.5	0.1	20.5	..	..	..	..	..
Panama	64.3	-1.3	16.6	34.8	21.1	..	..	..	..	..
Virgin Islands, U.S.	-	-	-	-	-	..	..	..	..	..
South America	1 997.9	1 473.0	341.6	1 317.7	960.6	..	..	..	..	..
Argentina	517.9	287.2	349.7	1 085.0	463.5	..	..	..	..	..
Bolivia	0.5	0.1	0.0	0.2	0.7	..	..	..	..	..
Brazil	1 145.3	912.6	-131.0	114.0	299.8	..	..	..	..	..
Colombia	113.9	213.1	73.8	-2.9	223.6	..	..	..	..	..
Ecuador	43.9	2.8	0.1	0.0	3.9	..	..	..	..	..
Paraguay	0.0	0.0	0.3	-	0.1	..	..	..	..	..
Peru	2.9	6.9	8.3	21.3	9.5	..	..	..	..	..
Uruguay	37.3	23.5	-1.2	28.2	26.1	..	..	..	..	..
Venezuela	10.7	13.3	7.1	-18.3	-36.0	..	..	..	..	..

Table 1. Foreign direct investment flows by country *(cont.)*

Million US dollars

	Inward					Outward				
	2015	2016	2017	2018	2019	2015	2016	2017	2018	2019
ASIA	**3 472.3**	**5 388.9**	**3 122.7**	**3 427.7**	**2 010.6**	..	..	..	..	..
Near and Middle East	0.8	2 017.7	2.5	-4.6	-2.8	..	..	..	..	..
Gulf Arabian countries	2.4	2.5	0.1	-6.3	-	..	..	..	..	..
Kuwait	-	-	-	-	-	..	..	..	..	..
Qatar	-	-	-	0.0	-	..	..	..	..	..
Saudi Arabia	-	-	0.1	-6.4	-	..	..	..	..	..
United Arab Emirates	2.4	2.5	-	0.1	-	..	..	..	..	..
Other Near and Middle East	-1.6	2 015.2	2.4	1.8	-2.8	..	..	..	..	..
Jordan	-	-	-	-	0.0	..	..	..	..	..
Other Asian countries	3 471.5	3 371.2	3 120.2	3 432.3	2 013.5	..	..	..	..	..
China	52.9	68.6	203.5	260.5	85.5	..	..	..	..	..
Hong Kong, China	29.7	84.1	73.5	154.5	79.6	..	..	..	..	..
India	23.5	27.2	47.6	23.3	29.2	..	..	..	..	..
Indonesia	10.1	18.0	33.0	37.0	13.8	..	..	..	..	..
Iran, Islamic Republic of	-	-	-	-0.1	-	..	..	..	..	..
Malaysia	-13.0	86.8	81.0	4.0	123.3	..	..	..	..	..
Philippines	-	-131.9	1.8	0.8	0.4	..	..	..	..	..
Singapore	97.9	93.8	13.4	34.9	11.0	..	..	..	..	..
Chinese Taipei	34.5	36.3	-33.0	-64.2	19.0	..	..	..	..	..
Thailand	0.2	-	0.1	0.1	1.4	..	..	..	..	..
Viet Nam	-	2.6	1.2	0.8	-	..	..	..	..	..
AUSTRALIA, OCEANIA AND POLAR REGIONS	**687.4**	**98.3**	**1 371.9**	**608.8**	**768.9**	..	..	..	..	..
WORLD unallocated and confidential	**-160.5**	**524.0**	**460.9**	**193.9**	**0.8**	..	..	..	..	..
European Union (EU28)	**8 642.5**	**9 591.3**	**10 031.6**	**11 479.0**	**13 722.8**	..	..	..	..	..
G20 countries excl. European Union	**29 286.1**	**22 333.8**	**28 605.9**	**26 735.5**	**25 898.3**	..	..	..	..	..
G20 OECD countries	**27 532.6**	**21 014.9**	**28 086.1**	**25 139.6**	**24 962.8**	..	..	..	..	..
G20 Non-OECD countries	**1 753.5**	**1 318.9**	**519.8**	**1 596.0**	**935.5**	..	..	..	..	..
MENA countries	**2.4**	**2.5**	**0.2**	**-6.3**	**0.4**	..	..	..	..	..
ASEAN countries	**95.3**	**69.3**	**130.5**	**77.6**	**149.8**	..	..	..	..	..

- Nil; .. Not available

Note: Data excludes resident Special Purpose Entities (SPEs). Detailed metadata at: *http://stats.oecd.org/OECDStat_Metadata/ShowMetadata.ashx?Dataset=FDI_CTRY_IND_SUMM.*

Source: *OECD International Direct Investment Statistics (database): https://doi.org/10.1787/idi-data-en*

Table 2. Foreign direct investment positions by country
At year end

Million US dollars

	Inward					Outward				
	2015	2016	2017	2018	2019	2015	2016	2017	2018	2019
WORLD	**430 576.5**	**432 742.4**	**495 953.1**	**515 015.0**	**567 746.7**	**143 720.4**	**149 645.1**	**180 076.8**	**159 327.8**	**172 419.3**
OECD COUNTRIES	**418 536.0**	**.. d**	**.. d**	**498 953.9**	**549 749.8**	**.. d**	**.. d**	**.. d**	**.. d**	**.. d**
Australia	450.4	473.2	522.0	614.1	609.7	.. c	.. c	.. c	.. c	.. c
Austria	637.5	651.8	817.1	953.4	1 166.9	.. c	.. c	.. c	.. c	.. c
Belgium	1 405.9	1 378.6	1 477.5	1 688.7	1 867.3	.. c	.. c	.. c	.. c	.. c
Canada	24 157.7	23 892.8	28 306.6	34 410.8	39 025.5	1 004.3	512.7	1 179.6	1 169.0	1 035.2
Chile	1 172.1	1 181.8	1 304.1	1 345.9	1 343.7	3 269.5	2 912.4	3 718.2	3 391.9	2 675.0
Czech Republic	12.3	16.5	21.5	21.6	22.1	.. c	.. c	.. c	.. c	.. c
Denmark	999.7	1 021.8	1 125.5	1 239.5	1 367.9	.. c	.. c	.. c	.. c	.. c
Estonia	0.1	0.1	0.1	0.3	0.5	-	-	-	-	-
Finland	78.8	58.2	59.5	60.1	79.9	-	-	-	-	-
France	4 171.7	3 744.4	4 657.5	5 176.0	6 133.3	.. c	.. c	.. c	-	.. c
Germany	10 764.4	10 750.4	15 184.0	16 442.4	19 465.3	27.2	-30.3	96.8	-127.5	947.1
Greece	1.5	1.5	1.6	1.8	1.8	-	-	-	-	-
Hungary	46.4	31.7	37.6	24.7	16.9	2 124.6	2 214.2	2 112.4	2 183.9	2 134.1
Iceland	5.0	4.9	5.0	5.0	4.9	-	-	-	-	-
Ireland	3 294.8	3 437.4	4 878.5	4 585.3	4 577.5	.. c	.. c	.. c	.. c	.. c
Israel	159.9	111.1	116.7	131.4	143.4	.. c	.. c	.. c	.. c	.. c
Italy	1 426.5	1 578.0	2 016.5	2 948.5	2 487.2	-	-	-	-	-
Japan	7 338.7	7 846.2	9 247.5	9 949.6	10 941.3	.. c	.. c	.. c	.. c	.. c
Korea	3 196.3	2 702.7	3 067.6	3 595.3	3 739.3	-	-	-	-	-
Latvia	.. c	.. c	.. c	0.1	0.2	.. c	.. c	.. c	-	-
Lithuania	0.4	0.3	0.3	0.4	0.9	-	-	-	-	-
Luxembourg	9 480.2	8 882.6	10 060.3	9 872.0	12 583.5	-	-	.. c	.. c	.. c
Mexico	-	-	-	-	-	-	-	-	-	-
Netherlands	75 788.6	74 723.3	105 805.0	102 756.8	115 224.1	30 791.4	30 371.0	31 850.1	26 137.3	25 219.4
New Zealand	187.2	173.1	200.8	217.5	266.2	-	-	-	-	-
Norway	202.7	209.8	217.0	209.5	239.8	-	-	-	-	-
Poland	19.8	19.5	30.9	21.3	22.5	.. c	.. c	.. c	.. c	.. c
Portugal	134.5	149.5	171.6	150.3	210.7	-	-	-	-	-
Slovak Republic	23.9	29.0	37.3	42.2	43.9	.. c	.. c	.. c	.. c	.. c
Slovenia	10.0	13.0	14.5	14.1	12.9	-	-	-	-	-
Spain	62 157.7	61 460.6	68 856.8	86 410.1	96 146.5	7 843.7	8 004.5	9 401.0	11 395.0	13 171.0
Sweden	2 384.1	2 304.9	2 466.0	2 568.3	2 902.0	-	-	-	-	-
Switzerland	12 297.2	12 996.7	14 568.1	13 555.8	14 919.8	416.1	1 080.0	471.8	465.3	1 329.8
Turkey	9.1	15.0	15.9	28.9	30.0	.. c	.. c	.. c	.. c	.. c
United Kingdom	19 101.8	21 609.0	24 358.8	21 643.1	23 647.6	14 985.7	16 809.1	19 619.3	13 371.6	12 729.2
United States	177 419.3	179 967.7	183 890.9	178 269.2	190 504.6	47 321.7	56 161.0	75 879.3	65 555.3	74 854.4
EUROPE	**204 629.1**	**205 321.9**	**257 172.0**	**270 742.8**	**303 572.3**	**59 116.1**	**61 114.7**	**66 287.2**	**55 108.1**	**57 550.7**
Bulgaria	1.7	1.6	1.7	3.1	5.0	-	-	-	-	-
Croatia	0.1	0.1	0.2	0.2	0.3	.. c	-	.. c	.. c	.. c
Cyprus	17.3	25.1	25.5	30.3	33.6	-	-	-	-	-
Malta	43.6	106.5	146.3	172.4	233.6	-	-	-	-	-
Romania	3.0	4.8	5.8	5.3	5.3	-	-	-	-	-
Russian Federation	20.3	16.7	17.4	17.5	18.3	-	-	.. c	.. c	.. c
Ukraine	1.1	1.2	2.0	2.4	3.3	-	-	-	-	-
AFRICA	**46.5**	**22.9**	**37.0**	**28.5**	**47.2**	**7.9**	**7.9**	**-**	**1.3**	**-**
Northern Africa	3.4	2.9	3.3	4.2	4.8	-	-	-	-	-
Algeria	2.7	2.3	2.6	3.0	3.2	-	-	-	-	-
Egypt	0.7	0.7	0.7	0.7	1.0	-	-	-	-	-
Libya	.. c	.. c	.. c	.. c	.. c	-	-	-	-	-
Morocco	.. c	.. c	.. c	0.5	0.6	-	-	-	-	-
Tunisia	0.0	0.0	0.0	.. c	.. c	-	-	-	-	-
Other African countries	32.0	10.4	26.4	14.2	29.5	-	-	-	-	-
Nigeria	0.6	0.5	0.5	0.5	0.5	-	-	-	-	-
South Africa	15.0	8.0	6.8	5.5	5.2	.. c	.. c	-	.. c	-
AMERICA	**210 105.7**	**212 027.9**	**221 120.2**	**224 462.4**	**243 479.5**	**83 160.0**	**87 200.7**	**113 595.5**	**103 253.3**	**113 663.1**
Northern America	201 577.1	203 860.5	212 197.5	212 680.0	229 530.0	48 326.0	56 673.7	77 059.0	66 724.3	75 889.6
Central America and Caribbean countries	3 992.4	3 760.1	4 193.2	4 690.1	5 299.5	13 530.3	11 338.5	4 144.5	4 219.7	5 447.2
Bahamas	260.3	194.4	216.1	231.2	236.1	.. c	.. c	.. c	.. c	.. c
Bermuda	147.2	158.4	145.1	152.3	139.8	.. c	.. c	.. c	.. c	.. c
Cayman Islands	665.7	648.1	477.6	537.9	550.3	-	-	-	.. c	.. c
Costa Rica	66.7	41.9	61.1	66.8	74.7	1 798.1	1 612.6	845.3	794.5	876.2
El Salvador	6.9	8.9	9.2	9.2	9.6	1 130.0	1 189.6	674.0	863.1	927.2
Guatemala	86.9	77.8	101.4	183.0	203.1	1 746.7	1 611.9	811.0	736.1	1 700.4
Honduras	5.3	4.8	5.4	5.8	6.8	942.3	931.4	354.8	336.2	.. c
Nicaragua	35.1	33.2	38.7	43.7	47.4	799.8	781.9	203.2	314.0	852.7
Panama	1 457.0	1 295.4	1 546.9	1 585.2	1 691.3	331.4	345.6	473.0	452.6	318.1
Virgin Islands, U.S.	138.1	131.9	138.3	156.2	163.0	-	-	-	-	-
South America	4 511.0	4 383.1	4 702.7	7 072.3	8 612.4	20 950.4	18 860.8	24 004.5	23 563.0	22 644.8
Argentina	324.4	297.5	386.6	416.7	477.6	-131.7	-766.3	936.5	1 631.4	1 297.7
Bolivia	.. c	.. c	.. c	8.6	.. c	.. c	.. c	.. c	.. c	.. c
Brazil	1 081.0	1 138.1	1 122.9	3 143.0	2 931.0	13 693.8	11 665.0	9 214.7	8 158.5	8 064.4
Colombia	965.5	804.7	937.7	1 057.8	2 885.5	493.7	887.4	4 639.1	4 689.2	5 428.0
Ecuador	53.7	49.0	50.9	53.2	56.8	2 521.2	2 675.0	2 214.3	1 751.7	1 355.7
Paraguay	2.6	2.2	2.7	2.8	3.1	.. c	.. c	.. c	.. c	.. c
Peru	168.0	151.0	160.7	167.5	-58.1	897.3	1 179.4	3 269.6	3 921.1	3 818.3
Uruguay	501.8	538.0	477.4	572.4	636.3	.. c	.. c	.. c	11.3	5.6
Venezuela	217.1	201.6	230.7	255.1	273.0	206.6	307.9	12.0	8.0	.. c

Table 2. Foreign direct investment positions by country *(cont.)*

At year end

Million US dollars

	Inward					Outward				
	2015	2016	2017	2018	2019	2015	2016	2017	2018	2019
ASIA	**13 010.1**	**12 914.3**	**14 998.7**	**16 860.3**	**18 075.4**	**924.2**	**849.5**	**172.9**	**805.2**	**1 080.8**
Near and Middle East	287.8	247.2	303.0	323.6	354.8	-	-	-	-	-
Gulf Arabian countries	126.9	135.3	185.2	191.1	210.2	-	-	-	-	-
Kuwait	.. c	-	-	-	-	-	-	-	-	-
Qatar	.. c	.. c	.. c	.. c	.. c	-	-	-	-	-
Saudi Arabia	6.4	5.4	6.0	4.1	4.4	-	-	-	-	-
United Arab Emirates	120.5	129.8	179.2	186.9	205.8	.. c	.. c	.. c	-	-
Other Near and Middle East	160.9	112.0	117.8	132.5	144.6	-	-	-	-	-
Jordan	0.0	0.0	0.0	0.0	0.0	-	-	-	-	-
Other Asian countries	12 718.5	12 663.4	14 691.6	16 391.6	17 577.1	264.8	213.8	-66.9	134.1	172.4
China	511.7	620.9	698.5	848.7	693.4	59.8	25.5	-66.9	-46.2	-22.9
Hong Kong, China	205.5	211.5	208.9	233.2	221.2	-	-	-	-	-
India	475.4	423.6	500.8	505.7	530.8	205.0	188.3	.. c	180.4	195.3
Indonesia	1.3	0.8	0.7	0.6	0.6	-	-	-	-	.. c
Iran, Islamic Republic of	2.1	1.9	2.0	2.0	2.1	-	-	-	-	-
Malaysia	4.7	3.9	4.1	8.2	14.4	.. c	-	-	-	-
Philippines	1.7	1.6	1.9	2.8	3.4	.. c	.. c	.. c	.. c	.. c
Singapore	669.9	603.6	687.9	974.8	1 084.0	.. c	.. c	.. c	.. c	.. c
Chinese Taipei	296.6	229.3	251.6	245.8	310.3	.. c	.. c	.. c	.. c	.. c
Thailand	9.4	11.0	12.1	15.8	26.6	-	-	-	-	.. c
Viet Nam	0.6	2.9	4.4	5.4	5.8	-	-	-	-	-
AUSTRALIA, OCEANIA AND POLAR REGIONS	**706.4**	**719.6**	**802.4**	**910.4**	**951.9**	**7.9**	**4.3**	**13.9**	**-2.1**	**0.0**
WORLD unallocated and confidential	**2 078.7**	**1 735.8**	**1 822.9**	**2 010.6**	**1 620.4**	**504.4**	**468.1**	**7.4**	**161.9**	**124.8**
European Union (EU28)	**.. d**	**.. d**	**.. d**	**256 832.3**	**288 259.3**	**.. d**	**.. d**	**.. d**	**.. d**	**.. d**
G20 countries excl. European Union	**250 471.5**	**255 090.3**	**274 006.9**	**278 019.8**	**301 245.1**	**.. d**	**.. d**	**.. d**	**.. d**	**.. d**
G20 OECD countries	**248 035.9**	**252 579.3**	**271 267.2**	**273 078.0**	**296 583.8**	**.. d**	**.. d**	**.. d**	**.. d**	**.. d**
G20 Non-OECD countries	**2 435.6**	**2 511.0**	**2 739.6**	**4 941.8**	**4 661.4**	**.. d**	**.. d**	**.. d**	**.. d**	**.. d**
MENA countries	**.. d**	**.. d**	**.. d**	**.. d**	**.. d**	**.. d**	**.. d**	**.. d**	**.. d**	**.. d**
ASEAN countries	**.. d**	**.. d**	**.. d**	**.. d**	**.. d**	**.. d**	**.. d**	**.. d**	**.. d**	**.. d**

- Nil; .. Not available; c Confidential data; d Secondary Confidentiality

Note: Data excludes resident Special Purpose Entities (SPEs). Detailed metadata at: *http://stats.oecd.org/OECDStat_Metadata/ShowMetadata.ashx?Dataset=FDI_CTRY_IND_SUMM.*

Source: *OECD International Direct Investment Statistics (database): https://doi.org/10.1787/idi-data-en*

Table 4. Foreign direct investment flows by industrial sector

Million US dollars

	Inward					Outward				
	2015	2016	2017	2018	2019	2015	2016	2017	2018	2019
All FDI activities	**35 436.6**	**31 066.9**	**34 200.2**	**33 740.3**	**34 075.6**	**10 672.1**	**193.3**	**3 987.9**	**8 364.6**	**10 844.9**
Agriculture, forestry and fishing	**178.3**	**98.3**	**141.1**	**-18.3**	**103.9**	..	..	..	..	..
Mining and quarrying	**1 602.1**	**929.6**	**1 380.2**	**1 655.5**	**1 920.1**	..	..	..	..	..
Extraction activities	1 509.9	231.7	673.0	992.7	1 242.9	..	..	..	..	..
Manufacturing	**17 799.2**	**18 039.9**	**15 522.3**	**15 560.1**	**15 964.4**	..	..	..	..	..
of which:										
Food products, beverages and tobacco	2 791.9	2 659.6	2 015.2	1 082.8	2 524.0	..	..	..	..	..
Textiles, wood and paper products; printing	342.4	821.6	435.6	426.5	250.5	..	..	..	..	..
Chemical, rubber, plastic, non-metallic mineral products	2 007.3	5 259.3	1 561.7	1 827.9	2 706.0	..	..	..	..	..
Metal and machinery products, except electrical equipment	2 585.1	2 789.1	2 526.3	4 210.0	1 413.2	..	..	..	..	..
Motor vehicles, trailers, semi-trailers, other transport equipment	7 058.6	5 482.2	7 848.7	6 595.4	7 405.0	..	..	..	..	..
Other manufacturing	3 013.9	1 028.0	1 134.9	1 417.6	1 665.7	..	..	..	..	..
Electricity, gas, steam and air conditioning supply	**1 088.3**	**1 293.8**	**2 099.7**	**4 971.3**	**1 236.8**	..	..	..	..	..
Water supply; sewerage, waste management and remediation activities	**-10.8**	**8.5**	**10.4**	**-6.1**	**2.1**	..	..	..	..	..
Construction	**2 052.3**	**1 154.2**	**3 032.9**	**1 641.7**	**241.0**	..	..	..	..	..
Services	**12 727.2**	**9 542.7**	**12 013.6**	**9 936.2**	**14 607.1**	..	..	..	..	..
Wholesale and retail trade; repair of motor vehicles and motorcycles	2 648.6	1 919.9	3 116.0	2 898.0	3 244.9	..	..	..	..	..
Transportation and storage	2 926.0	1 869.7	3 374.8	1 330.6	870.5	..	..	..	..	..
Accommodation and food service activities	534.4	623.7	923.1	1 317.7	1 230.3	..	..	..	..	..
Information and communication	2 347.2	981.5	667.0	1 128.8	1 896.8	..	..	..	..	..
Financial and insurance activities	3 236.3	3 390.2	2 562.6	2 364.7	5 381.6	..	..	..	..	..
Activities of holding companies	-	-	-	-	-	..	..	..	..	..
Real estate activities	132.0	322.9	466.6	242.2	238.8	..	..	..	..	..
Professional, scientific and technical activities	557.8	206.8	328.9	328.9	456.2	..	..	..	..	..
Administrative and support service activities	188.5	155.1	349.3	216.3	1 189.2	..	..	..	..	..
Public administration; activities of households and of extraterritorial organisations	-	-	-	-	-	..	..	..	..	..
Education	21.2	0.0	30.2	63.7	-7.0	..	..	..	..	..
Human health and social work activities	16.4	11.9	10.4	6.6	21.2	..	..	..	..	..
Arts, entertainment and recreation	117.3	51.5	166.6	20.3	37.5	..	..	..	..	..
Other services	1.6	9.5	18.2	18.4	47.2	..	..	..	..	..
Not allocated and confidential	**0.0**	**0.0**	**0.0**	**0.0**	**0.0**	**10 672.1**	**193.3**	**3 987.9**	**8 364.6**	**10 844.9**
Private real estate activities	-	-	-	-	-	..	..	..	..	..

- Nil; .. Not available

Note: Data excludes resident Special Purpose Entities (SPEs). Detailed metadata at: *http://stats.oecd.org/OECDStat_Metadata/ShowMetadata.ashx?Dataset=FDI_CTRY_IND_SUMM.*

Source: OECD *International Direct Investment Statistics (database): https://doi.org/10.1787/idi-data-en*

MEXICO

Table 5. Foreign direct investment positions by industrial sector

At year end

Million US dollars

	Inward					Outward				
	2015	2016	2017	2018	2019	2015	2016	2017	2018	2019
All FDI activities	**430 576.5**	**432 742.4**	**495 953.1**	**515 015.0**	**567 746.7**	**143 720.4**	**149 645.1**	**180 076.8**	**159 327.8**	**172 419.3**
Agriculture, forestry and fishing	..	..	..	..	..	..	..	..	..	..
Mining and quarrying	..	..	..	..	..	..	..	..	..	..
Extraction activities	..	..	..	..	..	..	..	..	..	..
Manufacturing	..	..	..	..	..	..	..	..	..	..
of which:										
Food products, beverages and tobacco	..	..	..	..	..	..	..	..	..	..
Textiles, wood and paper products; printing	..	..	..	..	..	..	..	..	..	..
Chemical, rubber, plastic, non-metallic mineral products	..	..	..	..	..	..	..	..	..	..
Metal and machinery products, except electrical equipment	..	..	..	..	..	..	..	..	..	..
Motor vehicles, trailers, semi-trailers, other transport equipment	..	..	..	..	..	..	..	..	..	..
Other manufacturing	..	..	..	..	..	..	..	..	..	..
Electricity, gas, steam and air conditioning supply	..	..	..	..	..	..	..	..	..	..
Water supply; sewerage, waste management and remediation activities	..	..	..	..	..	..	..	..	..	..
Construction	..	..	..	..	..	..	..	..	..	..
Services	..	..	..	..	..	..	..	..	..	..
Wholesale and retail trade; repair of motor vehicles and motorcycles	..	..	..	..	..	..	..	..	..	..
Transportation and storage	..	..	..	..	..	..	..	..	..	..
Accommodation and food service activities	..	..	..	..	..	..	..	..	..	..
Information and communication	..	..	..	..	..	..	..	..	..	..
Financial and insurance activities	..	..	..	..	..	..	..	..	..	..
Activities of holding companies	..	..	..	..	..	..	..	..	..	..
Real estate activities	..	..	..	..	..	..	..	..	..	..
Professional, scientific and technical activities	..	..	..	..	..	..	..	..	..	..
Administrative and support service activities	..	..	..	..	..	..	..	..	..	..
Public administration; activities of households and of extraterritorial organisations	..	..	..	..	..	..	..	..	..	..
Education	..	..	..	..	..	..	..	..	..	..
Human health and social work activities	..	..	..	..	..	..	..	..	..	..
Arts, entertainment and recreation	..	..	..	..	..	..	..	..	..	..
Other services	..	..	..	..	..	..	..	..	..	..
Not allocated and confidential	**430 576.5**	**432 742.4**	**495 953.1**	**515 015.0**	**567 746.7**	**143 720.4**	**149 645.1**	**180 076.8**	**159 327.8**	**172 419.3**
Private real estate activities	..	..	..	..	..	..	..	..	..	..

.. Not available

Note: Data excludes resident Special Purpose Entities (SPEs). Detailed metadata at: *http://stats.oecd.org/OECDStat_Metadata/ShowMetadata.ashx?Dataset=FDI_CTRY_IND_SUMM.*

Source: *OECD International Direct Investment Statistics (database): https://doi.org/10.1787/idi-data-en*

NETHERLANDS

Table 1. Foreign direct investment flows by country

Million US dollars

	Inward					Outward				
	2015	2016	2017	2018	2019	2015	2016	2017	2018	2019
WORLD	**163 853.6**	**59 667.1**	**16 520.1**	**87 630.1**	**48 961.4**	**233 592.9**	**184 985.1**	**19 047.5**	**-45 357.0**	**84 864.2**
OECD COUNTRIES	**126 286.2**	**30 147.1**	**-17 924.7**	**92 744.0**	**67 101.9**	**191 044.9**	**127 409.0**	**-5 015.2**	**-55 424.3**	**86 469.5**
Australia	-74.3	70.8	-66.5	68.5	51.4	6 381.6	3 093.0	1 564.6	7 029.4	-1 031.1
Austria	162.0	5 290.3	2 101.2	1 562.6	396.2	1 993.3	11 205.4	2 545.4	-1 553.2	2 571.3
Belgium	28 340.5	-3 579.6	1 832.9	-1 821.1	9 483.9	3 752.6	-14 228.7	-25 036.6	-7 950.0	-22 638.6
Canada	450.4	445.6	127.4	185.3	-249.6	-420.4	3 895.8	9 853.5	-2 027.6	3 987.5
Chile	2.2	-2.2	56.4	9.4	-1.5	-180.8	-88.5	728.2	-109.8	781.0
Czech Republic	117.6	202.4	22.5	41.3	-170.2	126.5	-287.5	-2 307.5	-217.2	722.0
Denmark	292.8	-159.2	579.4	544.1	-110.8	2 360.5	1 787.0	1 025.8	653.8	-1 706.0
Estonia	2.2	1.1	3.4	3.5	44.8	10.0	-79.6	-56.4	40.1	30.2
Finland	-93.2	-275.4	-60.9	140.4	-698.8	761.0	-763.0	547.9	-825.0	-7.0
France	621.2	2 762.4	16 822.2	18 786.7	5 744.4	-164.2	-7 151.4	19 860.2	1 845.9	3 704.7
Germany	3 423.2	-27 229.9	-10 720.3	-5 960.1	25 232.0	11 086.0	-5 059.2	17 539.2	3 220.8	8 668.7
Greece	-30.0	-3.3	9.0	-3.5	157.2	-54.4	120.5	178.1	40.1	521.0
Hungary	-	-13.3	24.8	21.2	10 843.8	242.9	-321.8	-1 522.9	-249.0	-413.3
Iceland	-248.5	-342.8	365.2	86.2	490.0	-17.7	-13.3	-168.0	-7.1	66.8
Ireland	2 804.2	-6 078.7	1 637.9	12 258.9	8 100.4	-2 695.5	11 707.4	34 432.4	5 563.6	38 628.7
Israel	1 275.7	10 755.3	3 528.4	629.1	1 422.9	-146.4	-1 017.4	1 728.1	454.4	3 105.4
Italy	6 429.3	-7 718.7	5 084.0	3 271.6	1 486.3	14 393.8	5 967.0	-6 271.0	3 318.8	-6 038.6
Japan	928.5	237.8	2 273.7	1 221.5	-1 937.6	-181.9	-1 145.6	-658.3	-34.2	4 343.6
Korea	197.4	-484.4	120.6	38.9	-352.2	1 362.2	-637.0	2 349.2	-653.8	-5 855.3
Latvia	3.3	-3.3	-3.4	-1.2	-4.0	91.0	-119.4	160.1	192.4	28.4
Lithuania	13.3	24.3	-3.4	-34.2	1.1	2.2	15.5	63.1	8.3	-14.6
Luxembourg	58 938.4	45 774.6	-839.8	1 146.0	15 788.7	38 079.9	-11 979.4	-10 890.5	-34 973.4	15 307.3
Mexico	2 154.2	6 377.3	-25.9	1 883.6	-356.7	9 266.8	-1 012.9	2 631.0	3 396.7	317.2
Netherlands	-	-	-	-	-	-	-	-	-	-
New Zealand	-5.5	-6.6	-9.0	69.6	16.4	778.7	-129.4	334.8	817.9	-1 530.7
Norway	930.7	-410.3	3.4	1 781.0	117.6	802.0	674.6	-2 521.7	1 183.8	1 147.5
Poland	110.9	-249.9	301.0	20.1	-298.7	699.9	478.8	857.9	447.3	542.0
Portugal	-17.7	2.2	-46.2	-208.9	-100.4	162.0	581.7	262.7	145.2	510.8
Slovak Republic	-1.1	38.7	-7.9	4.7	28.8	177.5	-120.5	118.4	-288.0	-220.8
Slovenia	-1.1	-	1.1	7.1	-18.1	264.0	94.0	56.4	54.3	-48.3
Spain	398.2	299.7	-250.3	-3 958.5	2 420.5	794.2	1 049.4	62.0	1 817.5	8 449.8
Sweden	418.2	-623.7	2 985.0	773.0	-856.3	1 553.0	5 223.9	962.7	2 936.4	-1 150.8
Switzerland	17 630.6	15 368.8	-34 730.0	18 562.5	-5 628.4	-4 194.1	41 811.3	-56 036.5	52 840.8	2 683.5
Turkey	755.4	285.3	-32.7	-1 488.3	-236.5	921.8	-110.6	767.7	361.1	-151.5
United Kingdom	-31 741.5	-19 167.3	81 049.5	62 210.6	-2 980.3	55 553.0	119 929.2	42 762.9	-88 817.4	18 758.2
United States	32 115.4	8 583.4	-90 060.9	-19 107.8	-723.8	47 577.4	-35 944.9	-40 874.8	-4 087.1	12 400.6
EUROPE	**99 083.7**	**-2 293.5**	**67 155.9**	**109 053.5**	**69 520.3**	**128 828.6**	**171 978.3**	**15 024.2**	**-58 576.7**	**70 920.7**
Bulgaria	2.2	4.4	-	-	8.9	41.0	121.6	152.2	24.8	-12.4
Croatia	-16.6	58.6	3.4	1.2	-32.3	-56.6	268.7	-503.9	100.3	-21.1
Cyprus	3 206.9	-1 753.8	154.4	-1 501.2	736.5	878.5	2 943.7	-447.5	-1 961.5	-1 166.5
Malta	-183.0	-	6.8	5.9	8.8	4.4	2 900.6	169.1	-1 403.3	13.3
Romania	-15.5	224.5	4.5	-3.5	-226.9	322.8	319.6	733.9	631.4	59.7
Russian Federation	-1 757.1	-4 752.8	-1 288.5	986.7	-141.8	1 844.7	713.3	2 300.8	3 309.3	3 167.3
Ukraine	10.0	-5.5	-1.1	1.2	-80.2	87.6	73.0	319.0	416.6	317.2
AFRICA	**773.2**	**32 658.4**	**-2 485.6**	**1 498.9**	**-24 866.7**	**19 892.4**	**-4 954.1**	**-3 798.9**	**-3 034.3**	**-591.5**
Northern Africa	20.0	29 551.0	-60.9	161.7	-37.0	-2 621.2	4 623.5	347.2	1 743.2	-676.2
Algeria	5.5	29 564.3	-112.7	108.6	-14.5	523.6	1 005.2	-391.2	-17.7	125.4
Egypt	13.3	-11.1	47.3	41.3	-24.5	-4 655.6	700.0	1 099.1	981.9	-1 349.9
Libya	-7.8	6.6	4.5	4.7	3.4	1 501.9	2 989.1	-445.3	794.3	528.4
Morocco	8.9	-7.7	-	4.7	-0.3	16.6	21.0	34.9	15.3	-25.0
Tunisia	-	-1.1	-	2.4	-1.0	-7.8	-91.8	49.6	-30.7	44.9
Other African countries	753.2	3 107.4	-2 424.8	1 337.2	-24 829.7	22 513.6	-9 577.6	-4 146.1	-4 777.5	84.7
Nigeria	766.5	-1 965.1	-9.0	13.0	-176.5	1 006.1	-759.7	2 254.5	-20.1	1 816.1
South Africa	5.5	4 843.5	-2 348.1	-114.5	-27 941.9	19 313.4	-11 679.8	1 058.5	-3 172.4	-211.0
AMERICA	**60 346.1**	**17 651.2**	**-57 973.2**	**-30 211.3**	**-12 108.8**	**66 712.1**	**16 772.1**	**-18 870.5**	**4 198.0**	**6 059.8**
Northern America	32 565.7	9 029.1	-89 933.5	-18 922.5	-973.4	47 150.3	-32 469.3	-31 015.7	-6 114.7	16 363.4
Central America and Caribbean countries	26 493.6	15 738.1	21 810.4	-2 770.0	-4 032.1	14 904.0	31 313.7	3 722.2	16 179.6	-11 126.0
Bahamas	-21.1	191.3	-363.0	-1.2	880.6	-1 103.7	837.1	-290.8	8 937.8	222.3
Bermuda	-3 890.2	21 359.1	8 047.6	-7 673.8	-5 855.4	78.8	-1 743.9	-3 510.3	459.1	3 384.5
Cayman Islands	-125.3	-373.8	1 424.9	1 318.3	1 124.4	952.9	6 452.5	1 729.2	1 244.0	1 709.9
Costa Rica	3.3	-3.3	-7.9	28.3	-567.9	-34.4	-53.1	-370.9	-67.3	-1 760.1
El Salvador	-	-	142.0	44.8	82.9	-1.1	-6.6	10.1	-7.1	-6.6
Guatemala	-	-	-	-	-1.5	27.7	458.9	44.0	-113.3	-150.4
Honduras	-1.1	-	-	-	-1.0	-1.1	-11.1	92.4	11.8	52.7
Nicaragua	-	-2.2	9.0	-10.6	28.0	4.4	5.5	46.2	-50.7	-
Panama	15.5	-43.1	-23.7	-	-12.7	3 324.5	-1 846.7	978.5	-82.6	228.0
Virgin Islands, U.S.	-	-	-	-	4.0	-	5.5	-3.4	-50.7	-134.8
South America	1 286.7	-7 116.0	10 149.9	-8 518.8	-7 103.4	4 657.8	17 927.7	8 423.0	-5 866.9	822.3
Argentina	-3.3	1.1	3.4	3.5	59.2	-330.6	795.1	1 559.0	277.4	1 681.3
Bolivia	-	1.1	-	398.9	46.2	25.5	-23.2	2.3	14.2	199.5
Brazil	635.6	-7 197.8	9 414.9	-9 876.1	-7 270.3	3 528.6	17 561.7	4 786.4	-6 313.0	-532.3
Colombia	-1.1	-	125.1	768.3	-13.1	-65.4	-266.5	700.0	16.5	-188.9
Ecuador	1.1	1.1	1.1	-1.2	-23.0	768.7	69.7	-56.4	50.7	-157.3
Paraguay	-	-	-	1.2	4.4	-23.3	-21.0	125.1	-8.3	7.7
Peru	721.0	141.5	-135.3	135.7	192.7	897.4	34.3	747.4	101.5	-379.3
Uruguay	-2.2	-	694.4	-21.2	152.8	134.2	-147.1	124.0	121.6	495.3
Venezuela	-62.1	-59.7	-14.7	55.5	-198.9	-94.3	3.3	-302.1	-23.6	-844.8

Table 1. Foreign direct investment flows by country *(cont.)*

Million US dollars

	Inward					Outward				
	2015	2016	2017	2018	2019	2015	2016	2017	2018	2019
ASIA	**3 587.4**	**11 591.3**	**9 934.6**	**7 141.5**	**16 302.7**	**10 945.1**	**-1 805.8**	**24 767.2**	**4 241.7**	**11 449.9**
Near and Middle East	1 113.7	11 087.0	5 498.8	6 012.0	11 795.9	3 525.2	2 457.1	3 300.6	2 220.0	-458.7
Gulf Arabian countries	-165.3	329.5	1 783.3	5 359.4	10 349.5	3 765.9	3 054.3	1 198.3	1 666.5	-3 533.9
Kuwait	-170.8	2.2	5.6	201.8	305.1	35.5	-301.9	-19.2	29.5	212.2
Qatar	298.4	-14.4	11.3	7.1	4.6	815.3	263.2	196.1	-288.0	-108.5
Saudi Arabia	-335.0	180.3	2 212.8	3 762.5	10 011.7	1 953.4	1 296.0	1 875.8	521.7	-1 829.8
United Arab Emirates	42.2	146.0	-500.5	1 451.7	135.6	-407.1	-309.6	-136.4	849.8	192.7
Other Near and Middle East	1 279.0	10 757.5	3 715.5	652.7	1 446.4	-240.7	-597.1	2 102.4	553.5	3 075.2
Jordan	1.1	1.1	-	1.2	19.3	11.1	7.7	-4.5	37.8	-41.2
Other Asian countries	2 473.7	504.3	4 435.8	1 129.5	4 506.8	7 419.9	-4 263.0	21 466.6	2 021.7	11 908.6
China	556.9	226.7	-188.3	220.7	5 963.2	1 536.3	990.8	909.7	622.0	2 012.7
Hong Kong, China	1 721.6	149.3	2 402.2	138.1	3 287.1	-206.3	-1 094.8	1 724.7	-456.7	11 071.7
India	-123.1	173.6	22.5	3.5	337.2	1 125.9	-251.0	2 050.5	1 759.7	680.8
Indonesia	-44.4	42.0	-10.1	103.9	62.5	756.5	2 991.3	754.1	-545.3	-180.4
Iran, Islamic Republic of	-1.1	2.2	1.1	1.2	1.2	115.4	233.3	-478.0	-3.5	11.3
Malaysia	-693.3	-3.3	-311.1	-631.4	-1 543.5	214.1	416.9	208.5	133.4	-352.4
Philippines	10.0	27.6	-104.8	9.4	441.5	733.2	-144.9	-393.4	107.4	124.7
Singapore	-130.9	102.8	33.8	342.3	-1 598.6	-126.5	-6 369.6	14 672.5	430.8	1 745.2
Chinese Taipei	52.1	-21.0	211.9	-305.7	-22.9	24.4	74.1	444.1	407.2	8.4
Thailand	5.5	-6.6	4.5	-2.4	3.7	72.1	-263.2	124.0	170.0	67.5
Viet Nam	-	-1.1	-2.3	1.2	-100.2	241.8	402.5	179.2	123.9	-403.6
AUSTRALIA, OCEANIA AND POLAR REGIONS	**-79.9**	**64.1**	**-75.5**	**138.1**	**70.5**	**7 209.1**	**2 995.7**	**1 919.7**	**7 813.1**	**-2 594.9**
WORLD unallocated and confidential	**143.1**	**-4.4**	**-36.1**	**9.4**	**43.4**	**5.5**	**-1.1**	**5.6**	**1.2**	**-379.7**
European Union (EU28)	**73 186.9**	**-12 177.4**	**100 695.5**	**87 302.0**	**75 017.4**	**130 372.7**	**124 601.3**	**75 452.6**	**-117 195.8**	**64 952.5**
G20 countries excl. European Union	**14 194.1**	**-42 321.1**	**12 389.8**	**56 200.9**	**6 757.0**	**175 504.2**	**94 240.8**	**64 819.1**	**-79 988.2**	**43 892.3**
G20 OECD countries	**15 259.0**	**-35 837.7**	**4 571.1**	**61 110.6**	**25 677.2**	**145 775.9**	**81 823.5**	**49 524.3**	**-76 447.5**	**39 103.8**
G20 Non-OECD countries	**-1 064.9**	**-6 483.5**	**7 818.7**	**-4 909.7**	**-18 920.2**	**29 728.2**	**12 417.3**	**15 294.8**	**-3 540.7**	**4 788.5**
MENA countries	**-144.2**	**29 882.8**	**1 723.6**	**5 522.2**	**10 341.6**	**1 163.6**	**7 684.4**	**1 545.5**	**3 448.6**	**-4 251.5**
ASEAN countries	**-853.0**	**163.7**	**-388.9**	**-123.9**	**-2 733.0**	**1 934.6**	**-3 070.9**	**15 831.4**	**482.7**	**984.7**

- Nil

Note: Data excludes resident Special Purpose Entities (SPEs). Detailed metadata at: *http://stats.oecd.org/OECDStat_Metadata/ShowMetadata.ashx?Dataset=FDI_CTRY_IND_SUMM.*

Source: *OECD International Direct Investment Statistics (database): https://doi.org/10.1787/idi-data-en*

NETHERLANDS

Table 2. Foreign direct investment positions by country

At year end

Million US dollars

	Inward					Outward				
	2015	2016	2017	2018	2019	2015	2016	2017	2018	2019
WORLD	**1 269 040.8**	**1 328 792.0**	**1 531 807.4**	**1 492 571.6**	**1 491 617.2**	**1 907 339.1**	**2 131 919.5**	**2 400 735.2**	**2 214 260.4**	**2 312 110.3**
OECD COUNTRIES	**1 089 919.4**	**1 149 314.9**	**1 168 037.9**	**1 323 346.7**	**1 290 976.9**	**1 463 163.9**	**1 723 766.2**	**1 917 426.2**	**1 758 462.3**	**1 697 122.7**
Australia	179.6	316.2	695.6	262.2	234.2	28 174.2	43 241.3	45 236.3	50 712.2	41 190.1
Austria	1 493.7	6 102.0	9 723.0	13 939.8	8 120.8	12 080.6	33 136.9	13 422.9	10 330.9	9 250.9
Belgium	73 813.8	70 860.1	86 782.2	74 780.2	55 566.2	95 625.5	88 250.2	90 183.5	87 289.9	51 352.5
Canada	1 943.4	2 243.1	2 128.8	2 243.0	2 906.1	32 394.1	36 799.8	46 436.8	45 191.2	60 584.1
Chile	5.4	4.2	137.9	75.6	-49.6	1 293.4	1 275.4	2 269.1	1 768.9	3 073.3
Czech Republic	90.4	88.5	109.1	164.9	-494.5	5 744.1	7 354.3	7 196.0	6 467.8	6 471.3
Denmark	8 969.0	8 766.7	10 367.0	9 203.1	15 883.3	7 450.2	8 799.4	10 791.6	11 668.2	11 514.6
Estonia	13.1	15.8	20.4	91.6	28.8	168.8	73.8	16.8	58.4	83.9
Finland	3 396.8	2 888.2	2 658.9	2 255.6	1 437.7	5 739.8	4 844.5	6 529.1	4 851.2	3 409.1
France	94 420.3	46 146.3	68 534.4	84 088.6	94 035.4	73 423.0	69 814.5	115 190.7	92 583.0	72 548.1
Germany	138 169.8	117 623.1	124 998.8	143 504.7	157 618.6	98 814.4	90 515.4	134 438.7	127 553.2	124 502.4
Greece	132.8	115.9	169.1	163.7	-16.6	1 393.6	2 159.8	2 724.9	2 657.4	3 597.2
Hungary	110.0	112.8	224.3	246.2	1 169.5	6 918.9	8 052.1	5 919.9	5 491.2	4 675.5
Iceland	875.3	672.5	883.9	660.6	1 488.4	79.5	88.5	3.6	5.7	80.8
Ireland	27 914.0	21 793.0	24 371.6	41 436.9	49 439.4	7 034.3	23 455.3	60 213.5	63 762.3	72 054.6
Israel	27 743.1	34 454.5	53 503.2	55 804.9	39 394.7	1 595.0	10 907.6	11 204.1	10 206.1	24 140.9
Italy	68 471.4	48 198.6	53 288.6	64 413.8	62 650.4	105 849.8	108 110.0	129 377.5	112 391.8	87 724.5
Japan	17 616.8	16 267.5	18 884.6	19 932.4	31 588.6	11 660.3	14 139.3	16 315.7	17 415.8	17 010.9
Korea	1 738.7	1 144.7	1 796.6	945.7	3 343.8	12 750.1	10 729.4	13 583.6	12 694.1	7 315.9
Latvia	9.8	7.4	4.8	22.9	-1.5	105.6	-16.9	160.7	259.9	308.6
Lithuania	47.9	65.4	88.8	45.8	15.0	139.4	154.9	157.1	167.2	150.9
Luxembourg	231 013.6	257 974.1	252 017.3	244 356.5	234 676.1	120 505.2	153 221.3	125 093.5	99 180.2	105 947.7
Mexico	11 240.1	20 951.8	25 068.4	19 649.6	20 632.3	49 603.7	40 253.0	46 634.7	55 117.9	53 475.5
Netherlands	-	-	-	-	-	-	-	-	-	-
New Zealand	15.2	10.5	209.9	96.2	267.4	3 439.3	3 484.8	4 628.2	5 417.9	2 530.9
Norway	11 267.3	8 747.8	1 127.4	1 402.6	1 370.5	5 865.0	7 325.8	6 597.5	6 828.5	7 120.9
Poland	1 034.3	713.6	1 195.7	1 431.2	992.3	8 166.6	9 639.5	12 583.4	13 043.3	13 767.0
Portugal	102.3	1 990.1	2 696.1	2 739.9	1 584.6	3 734.3	5 104.9	6 061.4	6 365.9	7 515.8
Slovak Republic	-12.0	-15.8	-20.4	18.3	-297.9	1 059.3	1 617.0	1 975.3	1 763.2	1 594.9
Slovenia	2.2	3.2	4.8	14.9	47.6	358.2	591.3	738.8	704.1	583.4
Spain	6 357.1	18 189.1	24 683.4	22 398.7	26 825.0	32 970.1	32 810.2	37 481.4	34 523.7	41 252.1
Sweden	10 506.3	9 166.2	13 675.9	13 095.9	15 844.7	7 958.6	14 356.5	19 474.7	18 454.3	21 168.2
Switzerland	69 199.8	90 399.5	112 319.5	123 267.7	84 659.4	179 116.0	221 699.2	210 551.7	237 812.0	186 082.7
Turkey	4 241.7	10 170.8	8 860.6	6 360.2	4 857.0	9 482.9	9 954.7	10 567.3	9 534.0	9 960.4
United Kingdom	109 272.7	97 283.7	193 401.3	175 128.2	159 306.8	215 909.6	303 162.2	368 384.5	265 521.0	294 897.7
United States	168 581.4	255 909.1	73 515.2	199 104.6	215 852.4	316 805.7	358 815.2	355 439.0	340 669.8	350 185.2
EUROPE	**897 258.6**	**847 141.4**	**1 018 630.4**	**1 049 993.1**	**978 406.0**	**1 031 475.2**	**1 239 031.3**	**1 415 814.3**	**1 251 809.0**	**1 176 418.8**
Bulgaria	12.0	15.8	75.6	107.6	19.6	387.6	528.1	676.4	674.4	835.1
Croatia	16.3	9.5	3.6	3.4	-27.1	1 809.5	1 724.5	1 905.7	603.4	591.9
Cyprus	13 016.9	10 884.4	6 982.5	3 456.6	1 341.0	8 381.1	8 540.1	9 013.0	6 423.2	8 124.9
Malta	77.3	15.8	92.3	105.3	24.7	1 225.9	2 507.6	2 987.5	649.2	687.5
Romania	19.6	55.9	129.5	37.8	-57.7	2 957.0	3 845.3	5 026.4	5 492.3	5 719.6
Russian Federation	4 681.5	-119.1	-1 527.9	-58.4	-493.2	12 381.1	13 781.0	16 044.6	14 121.8	17 829.6
Ukraine	25.0	15.8	10.8	163.7	132.5	1 302.1	1 184.8	1 501.6	1 935.0	3 118.3
AFRICA	**3 719.1**	**11 074.1**	**7 627.7**	**3 920.3**	**128 522.4**	**101 702.8**	**57 665.2**	**57 138.4**	**73 161.2**	**66 844.1**
Northern Africa	592.3	512.3	634.4	881.6	307.0	17 269.5	14 918.3	18 432.5	45 728.2	43 371.5
Algeria	446.4	370.0	302.2	458.0	340.7	1 200.9	-422.7	-467.7	-582.8	101.4
Egypt	19.6	2.1	94.7	153.4	-103.3	13 341.3	12 320.0	15 949.9	25 988.1	22 651.2
Libya	112.1	134.9	175.1	192.4	112.3	2 628.2	2 166.1	2 604.9	19 378.3	19 646.1
Morocco	9.8	3.2	45.6	73.3	-48.1	177.5	173.9	231.5	226.7	327.1
Tunisia	4.4	2.1	16.8	4.6	5.4	-78.4	680.9	113.9	717.9	645.7
Other African countries	3 126.8	10 561.8	6 993.3	3 038.7	128 215.4	84 433.3	42 746.9	38 705.9	27 433.0	23 472.6
Nigeria	2 852.5	202.4	91.1	137.4	-56.1	13 693.0	11 911.0	11 740.2	11 456.4	7 033.3
South Africa	67.5	9 897.8	6 271.3	27.5	123 121.2	61 326.1	22 672.1	21 398.4	10 452.3	11 122.7
AMERICA	**298 782.8**	**396 078.8**	**260 929.5**	**327 454.8**	**240 656.7**	**562 248.2**	**627 560.9**	**685 411.4**	**654 639.3**	**587 447.3**
Northern America	170 523.7	258 151.2	75 641.6	201 345.3	218 755.1	349 549.3	395 612.9	401 880.5	385 864.4	410 965.9
Central America and Caribbean countries	140 227.5	157 685.3	198 396.5	161 242.3	50 245.7	114 516.1	136 572.2	159 099.3	156 408.3	87 110.4
Bahamas	258.0	422.7	6.0	12.6	-10 675.0	-1 646.2	324.7	381.4	9 666.8	-407.6
Bermuda	35 073.5	58 286.1	74 989.2	29 863.8	25 037.9	32 094.7	37 198.3	32 318.3	27 062.1	13 136.1
Cayman Islands	7 953.2	5 099.6	6 416.4	7 141.1	-596.1	16 596.6	16 343.4	14 296.0	11 361.3	8 359.2
Costa Rica	28.3	10.5	14.4	50.4	1 895.3	260.2	229.8	-236.3	-329.7	-141.3
El Salvador	-	1.1	248.3	274.8	302.8	57.7	50.6	61.2	46.9	18.6
Guatemala	1.1	1.1	1.2	2.3	11.3	123.0	705.2	705.2	555.3	479.7
Honduras	-	4.2	6.0	1.1	-1.1	169.8	149.7	272.2	265.6	256.2
Nicaragua	1.1	-1.1	18.0	1.1	33.7	5.4	10.5	74.4	12.6	10.1
Panama	33.8	44.3	61.2	58.4	44.0	4 470.3	-365.8	894.7	735.1	911.2
Virgin Islands, U.S.	-	-	-	-	-	39.2	42.2	37.2	-4.6	370.7
South America	-11 968.4	-19 757.6	-13 108.7	-35 132.8	-28 344.1	98 182.9	95 375.8	124 431.5	112 366.6	89 371.0
Argentina	13.1	13.7	115.1	18.3	-100.6	11 076.8	3 251.8	3 896.6	3 887.1	5 464.5
Bolivia	2.2	3.2	4.8	583.9	255.8	70.8	49.5	43.2	57.2	26.7
Brazil	-14 642.4	-22 215.7	-17 527.0	-41 014.4	-34 446.7	77 261.8	83 963.3	110 290.2	99 354.2	72 364.2
Colombia	3.3	2.1	243.5	1 276.6	991.0	851.4	602.9	1 476.4	1 325.9	965.2
Ecuador	10.9	10.5	8.4	9.2	-27.6	1 069.1	1 010.9	1 006.2	1 249.1	280.2
Paraguay	1.1	-	124.7	154.6	0.1	24.0	-3.2	159.5	113.4	115.8
Peru	2 414.8	2 278.9	2 441.8	2 096.4	1 344.8	1 061.5	845.4	1 718.6	1 305.2	1 618.9
Uruguay	3.3	2.1	889.9	996.1	794.2	1 562.3	1 379.8	1 093.8	2 362.0	2 794.9
Venezuela	186.2	111.7	100.7	175.2	100.8	3 866.1	2 952.5	2 408.3	871.3	808.5

Table 2. Foreign direct investment positions by country *(cont.)*
At year end

Million US dollars

	Inward					Outward				
	2015	2016	2017	2018	2019	2015	2016	2017	2018	2019
ASIA	**69 728.9**	**74 173.1**	**106 619.1**	**110 819.8**	**143 461.6**	**180 148.1**	**160 634.6**	**192 229.6**	**178 402.8**	**437 511.3**
Near and Middle East	35 007.1	42 372.7	64 627.0	73 324.9	78 660.1	18 520.4	25 814.3	28 113.5	28 566.5	256 047.3
Gulf Arabian countries	7 240.1	7 891.9	10 800.0	17 105.6	39 072.1	16 255.9	14 256.4	16 447.6	17 852.1	231 064.9
Kuwait	40.3	12.6	39.6	104.2	338.2	763.2	386.8	828.7	929.7	669.6
Qatar	56.6	60.1	145.1	183.2	20.5	1 728.9	69.6	182.3	-72.1	1 338.2
Saudi Arabia	6 315.7	6 846.2	9 821.3	13 882.5	36 675.2	5 236.8	6 401.4	8 034.3	8 274.6	6 346.1
United Arab Emirates	707.7	858.0	545.7	2 753.6	2 007.6	2 620.6	2 403.3	2 034.1	2 789.1	206 854.8
Other Near and Middle East	27 767.0	34 480.9	53 827.1	56 219.4	39 588.0	2 264.6	11 557.9	11 665.9	10 714.4	24 982.3
Jordan	3.3	5.3	13.2	6.9	-9.4	94.7	93.8	113.9	104.2	362.4
Other Asian countries	34 721.8	31 800.4	41 992.1	37 494.8	64 801.5	161 627.7	134 820.3	164 116.1	149 836.3	181 464.1
China	2 039.2	1 577.9	765.2	1 136.9	4 825.9	16 717.5	13 574.4	14 318.8	13 405.1	23 245.3
Hong Kong, China	10 787.2	9 876.7	15 415.0	10 384.7	23 472.5	12 992.9	12 398.0	14 844.1	13 334.1	34 766.6
India	589.0	596.6	87.6	92.7	-610.3	4 529.1	9 129.3	11 482.4	12 592.2	13 595.5
Indonesia	113.2	151.8	160.7	145.4	-93.9	4 721.8	4 376.5	5 500.1	4 921.0	7 022.5
Iran, Islamic Republic of	21.8	24.2	36.0	40.1	112.2	266.7	256.1	314.2	321.7	408.8
Malaysia	648.9	646.1	712.4	49.2	-931.8	1 452.4	1 918.4	2 102.4	2 232.7	4 832.0
Philippines	162.2	173.9	629.6	581.6	145.3	1 945.6	2 098.7	1 639.5	1 670.5	2 425.7
Singapore	361.5	648.3	1 706.6	2 918.5	5 061.9	63 467.6	30 913.9	47 771.6	31 801.0	29 363.1
Chinese Taipei	408.3	378.4	620.1	143.1	-553.6	2 157.9	5 206.1	6 165.7	13 231.1	12 535.6
Thailand	13.1	71.7	693.2	768.3	37.1	1 894.4	4 165.7	4 268.4	1 710.6	2 010.8
Viet Nam	14.2	11.6	38.4	2.3	-1 680.0	2 455.1	2 191.4	2 476.6	2 549.8	1 491.2
AUSTRALIA, OCEANIA AND POLAR REGIONS	**204.7**	**336.3**	**1 009.8**	**391.6**	**498.9**	**31 715.8**	**46 987.5**	**50 066.0**	**56 235.4**	**43 864.4**
WORLD unallocated and confidential	**-653.2**	**-11.6**	**136 990.9**	**-8.0**	**71.6**	**49.0**	**40.1**	**75.6**	**12.6**	**24.4**
European Union (EU28)	**788 470.3**	**719 072.4**	**876 277.3**	**897 246.4**	**885 852.5**	**825 912.9**	**982 353.7**	**1 167 724.9**	**978 936.3**	**950 295.3**
G20 countries excl. European Union	**615 052.8**	**613 004.1**	**569 339.2**	**689 863.8**	**881 903.2**	**1 148 118.7**	**1 242 684.7**	**1 472 570.2**	**1 296 392.3**	**1 276 385.3**
G20 OECD countries	**615 875.9**	**616 254.9**	**571 172.9**	**715 633.2**	**753 025.6**	**954 867.7**	**1 085 534.9**	**1 281 604.7**	**1 129 384.0**	**1 119 394.9**
G20 Non-OECD countries	**-823.1**	**-3 250.8**	**-1 833.8**	**-25 769.4**	**128 877.6**	**193 251.0**	**157 149.8**	**190 965.5**	**167 008.2**	**156 990.4**
MENA countries	**7 844.3**	**8 419.9**	**11 460.8**	**18 012.4**	**39 368.8**	**33 669.0**	**29 327.5**	**35 049.2**	**63 732.5**	**274 938.4**
ASEAN countries	**1 323.9**	**1 716.0**	**3 980.6**	**4 585.5**	**2 547.8**	**77 556.9**	**47 342.7**	**65 531.3**	**46 530.8**	**47 431.0**

- Nil

Note: Data excludes resident Special Purpose Entities (SPEs). Detailed metadata at: *http://stats.oecd.org/OECDStat_Metadata/ShowMetadata.ashx?Dataset=FDI_CTRY_IND_SUMM.*

Source: *OECD International Direct Investment Statistics (database): https://doi.org/10.1787/idi-data-en*

NETHERLANDS

Table 3. Foreign direct investment income by country

Million US dollars

	Inward					Outward				
	2015	2016	2017	2018	2019	2015	2016	2017	2018	2019
WORLD	**72 697.7**	**69 284.5**	**64 179.9**	**86 991.6**	**71 784.6**	**102 674.4**	**87 907.8**	**104 256.6**	**132 951.7**	**110 638.3**
OECD COUNTRIES	**65 666.1**	**66 664.8**	**60 414.8**	**82 276.6**	**71 344.4**	**69 010.5**	**49 882.8**	**66 382.6**	**88 217.9**	**79 296.9**
Australia	8.9	7.7	6.8	5.9	-2.3	854.1	1 379.0	1 858.9	2 998.9	2 098.9
Austria	144.2	45.3	376.5	293.9	195.9	704.4	1 343.6	1 782.2	2 516.2	2 090.0
Belgium	3 505.3	2 435.0	1 137.4	4 491.9	2 841.6	5 652.8	3 464.6	2 823.8	2 984.8	2 956.9
Canada	31.1	131.6	5.6	40.1	-14.5	-2 150.9	40.9	2 465.3	2 463.1	1 632.2
Chile	-	-	2.3	2.4	1.8	65.4	84.0	147.7	1 441.0	43.2
Czech Republic	1.1	2.2	2.3	2.4	-13.2	312.8	631.4	409.2	591.3	336.0
Denmark	112.0	201.3	83.4	106.2	-88.4	1 302.3	162.6	168.0	567.7	187.0
Estonia	-	-	-	-	-	7.8	-48.7	-53.0	5.9	4.5
Finland	-1.1	395.9	400.2	642.0	268.7	1 402.1	133.8	51.9	1 639.3	1 012.0
France	3 455.4	2 013.7	7 545.9	1 847.0	1 872.5	3 527.5	4 128.1	3 937.5	3 900.6	3 154.2
Germany	10 485.9	3 387.2	5 733.3	6 794.5	11 830.0	3 357.7	3 258.9	3 633.2	4 713.8	4 628.6
Greece	3.3	1.1	4.5	10.6	8.7	363.8	52.0	133.0	94.4	59.1
Hungary	2.2	1.1	1.1	-	-1 084.9	113.1	182.5	187.1	384.8	268.5
Iceland	197.4	24.3	255.9	177.0	186.9	5.5	4.4	3.4	51.9	-1.1
Ireland	461.5	635.9	749.6	743.5	2 694.6	1 257.9	1 407.7	2 276.0	2 786.5	1 401.7
Israel	-	-133.8	-11.3	13.0	1 055.7	48.8	31.0	330.3	40.1	21.3
Italy	-2 271.8	522.0	2 811.4	8 110.5	140.1	2 044.4	1 161.1	917.6	2 893.9	4 230.6
Japan	1 982.3	1 887.6	2 271.4	2 575.2	2 113.6	176.4	712.2	636.9	1 288.8	1 915.5
Korea	69.9	48.7	12.4	14.2	91.7	265.1	264.3	358.5	1 162.5	516.0
Latvia	-	-	-	-	1.1	105.4	-44.2	95.8	11.8	12.3
Lithuania	-	-	-	1.2	1.1	4.4	3.3	-	1.2	2.2
Luxembourg	14 322.8	31 675.3	6 551.7	9 281.2	9 960.0	5 071.5	2 163.0	9 205.3	4 461.2	4 227.3
Mexico	936.2	-272.0	1 989.6	2 126.8	820.5	1 774.8	1 094.8	1 812.6	3 093.4	3 099.7
Netherlands	-	-	-	-	-	-	-	-	-	-
New Zealand	2.2	1.1	-	-1.2	-4.7	-57.7	60.8	341.6	452.0	64.7
Norway	133.1	633.6	-56.4	132.2	112.7	92.1	163.7	184.9	108.6	41.0
Poland	11.1	7.7	10.1	10.6	5.0	297.3	613.7	774.4	1 082.3	1 422.2
Portugal	14.4	-23.2	6.8	-8.3	-12.3	183.0	458.9	367.5	469.7	340.3
Slovak Republic	1.1	1.1	-	-	-11.3	67.7	94.0	89.1	152.2	127.5
Slovenia	-	-	-	-	-	3.3	23.2	21.4	47.2	19.0
Spain	1 220.2	1 278.3	2 017.8	7 074.2	807.9	1 428.7	1 014.0	1 560.1	1 298.2	1 573.6
Sweden	441.5	357.2	572.7	1 100.0	-154.6	1 398.8	1 071.5	959.3	2 204.7	455.5
Switzerland	4 286.2	3 976.6	9 646.0	7 874.4	6 589.6	19 987.8	12 378.6	11 789.0	13 276.3	22 196.9
Turkey	84.3	65.2	75.5	-201.8	25.1	318.4	331.7	193.9	262.0	437.1
United Kingdom	10 626.7	11 778.2	13 814.7	21 627.5	8 197.5	10 188.6	8 164.3	10 520.8	14 483.7	12 528.6
United States	15 398.8	5 578.9	4 397.5	7 389.4	22 908.3	8 945.1	3 901.4	6 399.5	14 287.7	6 193.8
EUROPE	**48 606.8**	**60 518.6**	**52 903.8**	**70 816.7**	**44 551.9**	**61 448.7**	**44 836.9**	**54 678.2**	**64 703.2**	**66 521.0**
Bulgaria	1.1	-	1.1	-	1.1	23.3	71.9	63.1	30.7	11.2
Croatia	-	-	-	-	-	7.8	25.4	16.9	35.4	12.3
Cyprus	957.3	495.4	109.3	-35.4	229.3	736.6	415.8	423.9	-337.5	-76.4
Malta	6.7	-	1.1	2.4	2.2	-5.5	12.2	-24.8	11.8	5.6
Romania	-	1.1	-	3.5	2.0	299.5	234.4	241.2	383.6	313.2
Russian Federation	-303.9	-92.9	285.2	-43.7	-80.4	881.9	1 048.3	1 054.0	2 670.8	1 933.5
Ukraine	1.1	1.1	1.1	1.2	1.1	56.6	151.5	325.8	401.3	598.9
AFRICA	**149.8**	**388.1**	**292.0**	**280.9**	**148.9**	**1 396.6**	**3 164.9**	**6 046.7**	**6 643.5**	**2 271.4**
Northern Africa	138.7	101.7	22.5	128.6	-1.1	622.3	948.8	3 071.8	3 190.1	840.7
Algeria	138.7	101.7	22.5	128.6	-	152.0	193.5	99.2	250.2	6.7
Egypt	-	-	-	-	-1.1	482.5	228.9	2 232.0	1 973.3	800.4
Libya	-	-	-	-	-	-	573.9	715.8	973.7	29.1
Morocco	-	-	-	-	-	18.9	6.6	2.3	-3.5	4.5
Tunisia	-	-	-	-	-	-31.1	-54.2	22.5	-3.5	-
Other African countries	11.1	286.4	269.4	152.2	150.0	774.3	2 216.1	2 974.9	3 453.3	1 430.7
Nigeria	5.5	6.6	4.5	4.7	3.4	745.4	1 093.7	2 395.4	1 137.7	878.8
South Africa	2.2	276.5	246.9	108.6	126.5	57.7	85.1	125.1	2 145.6	212.7
AMERICA	**21 056.0**	**5 593.3**	**8 084.8**	**11 965.1**	**22 182.8**	**22 158.6**	**22 876.3**	**24 363.7**	**38 976.8**	**22 829.8**
Northern America	15 429.8	5 710.5	4 403.1	7 429.5	22 893.8	6 780.9	3 934.5	8 862.6	16 750.9	7 826.1
Central America and Caribbean countries	4 325.0	1 632.2	4 737.9	5 162.3	2 018.1	9 411.0	9 704.7	7 964.2	8 802.1	9 545.3
Bahamas	10.0	2.2	-	-	-108.4	-6.7	24.3	18.0	20.1	22.6
Bermuda	675.5	1 095.9	1 038.2	1 773.9	972.2	3 607.3	7 684.4	3 565.6	4 211.0	3 843.6
Cayman Islands	434.8	418.0	1 211.8	331.6	90.1	31.1	128.3	64.3	105.0	-25.2
Costa Rica	-	-	-	1.2	80.4	28.8	24.3	25.9	40.1	-18.1
El Salvador	-	-	2.3	13.0	13.4	8.9	13.3	29.3	7.1	-4.5
Guatemala	-	-	-	-	-	26.6	10.0	33.8	-61.4	20.2
Honduras	-	-	-	-	-	-2.2	3.3	9.0	8.3	7.8
Nicaragua	-	-	-	1.2	1.1	-	2.2	2.3	-1.2	-
Panama	1.1	1.1	1.1	-	0.9	2 881.9	-23.2	14.7	7.1	-1.3
Virgin Islands, U.S.	-	-	-	-	-	-	1.1	-	-	3.4
South America	1 301.2	-1 749.4	-1 056.3	-626.7	-2 729.2	5 966.7	9 237.0	7 536.9	13 423.8	5 458.5
Argentina	-	-	-	2.4	-3.3	-364.9	1.1	391.2	459.1	72.8
Bolivia	-	-	1.1	1.2	17.0	15.5	3.3	16.9	15.3	-5.4
Brazil	1 137.0	-1 751.6	-1 222.0	-725.8	-2 842.2	6 408.2	9 021.3	6 501.0	10 679.8	5 290.5
Colombia	-	-	5.6	49.6	66.5	-53.2	8.8	72.1	151.1	37.4
Ecuador	3.3	-	-	-	1.1	100.9	24.3	62.0	470.9	17.9
Paraguay	-	-	-	-	-	6.7	18.8	33.8	30.7	5.6
Peru	159.7	-	130.8	14.2	2.2	-28.8	-17.7	118.4	83.8	-3.4
Uruguay	-	-	22.5	27.1	23.7	33.3	59.7	63.1	168.8	8.1
Venezuela	-1.1	-	1.1	-	1.8	-230.7	19.9	120.6	-90.9	-12.8

Table 3. Foreign direct investment income by country *(cont.)*

Million US dollars

	Inward					Outward				
	2015	2016	2017	2018	2019	2015	2016	2017	2018	2019
ASIA	**2 888.5**	**2 760.1**	**2 889.2**	**3 921.9**	**4 900.3**	**16 858.6**	**15 583.3**	**16 956.4**	**19 097.1**	**16 817.9**
Near and Middle East	371.6	151.5	458.8	446.1	1 515.5	3 306.7	1 530.5	2 782.1	2 103.2	4 289.5
Gulf Arabian countries	371.6	285.3	467.8	426.1	459.9	3 523.0	988.6	2 060.6	1 995.8	4 264.9
Kuwait	-	-	1.1	1.2	2.2	774.3	219.0	390.0	1 133.0	1 085.9
Qatar	1.1	-15.5	1.1	2.4	1.1	1 141.4	361.6	376.5	42.5	370.5
Saudi Arabia	362.7	291.9	453.2	348.2	446.4	219.6	40.9	128.5	79.1	51.3
United Arab Emirates	5.5	6.6	10.1	70.8	7.8	861.9	131.6	569.3	292.7	1 924.3
Other Near and Middle East	-	-133.8	-9.0	20.1	1 055.7	-216.3	541.9	721.5	107.4	24.6
Jordan	-	-	-	-	-	-25.5	-10.0	2.3	10.6	1.1
Other Asian countries	2 516.9	2 608.6	2 430.4	3 475.7	3 384.7	13 551.9	14 052.9	14 174.3	16 994.0	12 528.4
China	52.1	55.3	62.0	69.6	18.3	1 937.9	1 931.9	1 898.3	2 345.1	1 793.7
Hong Kong, China	307.3	533.0	-12.4	240.8	1 373.4	1 570.7	1 419.9	1 321.2	1 818.7	687.1
India	1.1	-	1.1	1.2	-16.6	195.2	207.9	669.6	170.0	176.0
Indonesia	5.5	4.4	3.4	4.7	1.1	372.7	951.0	542.2	821.4	28.0
Iran, Islamic Republic of	1.1	1.1	1.1	1.2	1.1	285.1	10.0	24.8	29.5	7.8
Malaysia	68.8	31.0	38.3	37.8	47.2	487.0	405.8	135.3	231.3	249.9
Philippines	-	1.1	-	2.4	-31.0	294.0	567.3	341.6	610.2	245.5
Singapore	26.6	32.1	33.8	53.1	-157.1	6 947.3	6 173.8	6 344.3	5 627.3	6 078.2
Chinese Taipei	8.9	8.8	12.4	468.5	3.8	289.5	248.8	354.0	491.0	140.4
Thailand	-	1.1	-1.1	1.2	-1.1	251.8	384.8	319.0	331.6	87.3
Viet Nam	1.1	1.1	1.1	-	-61.9	267.3	339.5	492.6	604.3	-123.5
AUSTRALIA, OCEANIA AND POLAR REGIONS	**11.1**	**7.7**	**6.8**	**5.9**	**-9.2**	**813.1**	**1 457.5**	**2 208.3**	**3 513.5**	**2 173.8**
WORLD unallocated and confidential	**-14.4**	**16.6**	**3.4**	**1.2**	**9.9**	**-1.1**	**-11.1**	**3.4**	**17.7**	**24.4**
European Union (EU28)	**43 500.8**	**55 215.1**	**41 933.3**	**62 103.2**	**37 694.1**	**39 853.6**	**30 201.3**	**40 583.9**	**47 421.2**	**41 304.3**
G20 countries excl. European Union	**42 064.3**	**23 932.3**	**38 494.0**	**50 094.4**	**45 632.3**	**39 009.4**	**37 724.2**	**44 044.6**	**70 919.4**	**49 993.6**
G20 OECD countries	**40 807.5**	**25 148.7**	**38 664.2**	**50 329.3**	**47 982.5**	**29 301.2**	**24 436.6**	**32 734.8**	**51 548.4**	**40 435.2**
G20 Non-OECD countries	**1 256.8**	**-1 216.4**	**-170.2**	**-234.9**	**-2 350.2**	**9 708.3**	**13 287.6**	**11 309.9**	**19 370.9**	**9 558.5**
MENA countries	**510.3**	**387.0**	**490.4**	**554.7**	**458.8**	**4 129.8**	**1 935.2**	**5 140.3**	**5 200.0**	**5 107.8**
ASEAN countries	**103.2**	**71.9**	**76.7**	**99.1**	**-202.8**	**8 642.3**	**8 885.3**	**8 208.8**	**8 255.6**	**6 573.2**

\- Nil

Note: Data excludes resident Special Purpose Entities (SPEs). Detailed metadata at: *http://stats.oecd.org/OECDStat_Metadata/ShowMetadata.ashx?Dataset=FDI_CTRY_IND_SUMM.*

Source: *OECD International Direct Investment Statistics (database): https://doi.org/10.1787/idi-data-en*

NETHERLANDS

Table 4. Foreign direct investment flows by industrial sector

Million US dollars

	Inward					Outward				
	2015	2016	2017	2018	2019	2015	2016	2017	2018	2019
All FDI activities	**163 853.6**	**59 667.1**	**16 520.1**	**87 630.1**	**48 961.4**	**233 592.9**	**184 985.1**	**19 047.5**	**-45 357.0**	**84 864.2**
Agriculture, forestry and fishing	-	-	-	-	..	**-2 959.5**	**-2 657.3**	**-703.4**	**-2.4**	..
Mining and quarrying	**-40 498.1**	**6 925.8**	**116.1**	**-3 069.8**	..	**-38 154.2**	**-148 301.4**	**51 676.2**	**-172 858.5**	..
Extraction activities	-40 498.1	6 925.8	116.1	-3 069.8	..	-38 154.2	-148 301.4	51 676.2	-172 858.5	..
Manufacturing	**74 380.5**	**8 560.2**	**74 662.4**	**-6 147.8**	..	**378 247.4**	**28 921.8**	**-163 565.6**	**450 600.7**	..
of which:										
Food products, beverages and tobacco	10 878.5	-3 337.4	46 330.7	6 014.4	..	40 941.8	-16 410.5	-36 546.0	160 624.3	..
Textiles, wood and paper products; printing	64.3	-11.1	-321.3	207.7	..	34 647.8	2 148.6	6 439.0	99 303.7	..
Chemical, rubber, plastic, non-metallic mineral products	47 139.2	-11 678.6	579.4	-4 710.3	..	-309 708.3	73 755.4	-88 899.8	-118 415.0	..
Metal and machinery products, except electrical equipment	5 665.0	36 306.5	24 070.6	-187.7	..	352 160.8	50 755.3	17 595.5	145 137.5	..
Motor vehicles, trailers, semi-trailers, other transport equipment	10 368.3	-12 863.0	2 634.4	-8 007.8	..	-37 287.9	-59 814.2	-51 849.8	123 427.4	..
Other manufacturing	258.5	147.1	1 368.5	531.1	..	297 506.4	-21 518.3	-10 314.5	40 511.0	..
Electricity, gas, steam and air conditioning supply	**-1 212.4**	**-3.3**	**-16 586.6**	**-1 739.6**	..	**7 590.7**	**-5 400.9**	**-12 729.1**	**11 117.7**	..
Water supply; sewerage, waste management and remediation activities	**339.4**	**-79.6**	**-685.4**	**-48.4**	..	**-44.4**	**-21.0**	**-10.1**	**-105.0**	..
Construction	**1 038.3**	**24.3**	**-51.9**	**-826.2**	..	**753.2**	**911.2**	**-14 530.5**	**-612.5**	..
Services	**129 802.6**	**44 265.2**	**-40 928.9**	**99 455.9**	..	**-131 198.0**	**312 940.4**	**167 136.7**	**-317 548.7**	..
Wholesale and retail trade; repair of motor vehicles and motorcycles	3 927.9	7 695.5	23 324.3	4 252.3	..	92 934.0	46 910.3	44 510.2	-27 900.4	..
Transportation and storage	3 289.0	3 647.0	2 272.6	2 508.0	..	22 921.8	2 247.0	18 616.8	3 515.9	..
Accommodation and food service activities	46.6	-54.2	-73.3	-166.4	..	10 102.1	-2 234.9	1 385.4	4 102.4	..
Information and communication	-13 952.3	1 139.0	313.4	2 119.7	..	692 278.4	132 083.4	-4 385.1	21 371.4	..
Financial and insurance activities	138 677.8	30 199.0	-78 899.8	71 130.7	..	-1 092 136.4	-35 489.3	164 409.9	-198 396.1	..
Activities of holding companies	1 368.8	49.8	-586.2	-449.7	..	-754 396.0	-1 124.6	-33 850.8	-137 718.6	..
Real estate activities	-51.0	-496.5	10 409.2	17 492.0	..	16 584.6	60 464.4	-147 161.5	12 454.9	..
Professional, scientific and technical activities	-3 506.4	1 374.5	-37.2	404.8	..	65 453.1	42 662.8	10 901.8	-126 711.9	..
Administrative and support service activities	1 371.0	760.8	1 761.9	1 714.9	..	-43 218.0	67 938.7	81 365.1	-5 719.3	..
Public administration; activities of households and of extraterritorial organisations	-	-	-	-	..	-181.9	-4.4	-19.2	-34.2	..
Education	-	-	-	-	..	-	-	-	-	..
Human health and social work activities	-	-	-	-	..	569.1	-2 586.5	-846.6	-178.2	..
Arts, entertainment and recreation	-	-	-	-	..	12 066.6	296.4	-2 424.8	-72.0	..
Other services	-	-	-	-	..	91 428.7	652.4	784.6	18.9	..
Not allocated and confidential	**3.3**	**-25.4**	**-5.6**	**5.9**	**48 961.4**	**19 178.0**	**-1 459.7**	**-8 282.0**	**-16 131.2**	**84 864.2**
Private real estate activities	-	-	-	-	..	**179.7**	**52.0**	**55.2**	**182.9**	..

- Nil; .. Not available

Note: Data excludes resident Special Purpose Entities (SPEs). Detailed metadata at: *http://stats.oecd.org/OECDStat_Metadata/ShowMetadata.ashx?Dataset=FDI_CTRY_IND_SUMM.*

Source: *OECD International Direct Investment Statistics (database): https://doi.org/10.1787/idi-data-en*

NETHERLANDS

Table 5. Foreign direct investment positions by industrial sector

At year end

Million US dollars

	Inward					Outward				
	2015	2016	2017	2018	2019	2015	2016	2017	2018	2019
All FDI activities	**1 269 040.8**	**1 328 792.0**	**1 531 807.4**	**1 492 571.6**	**1 491 617.2**	**1 907 339.1**	**2 131 919.5**	**2 400 735.2**	**2 214 260.4**	**2 312 110.3**
Agriculture, forestry and fishing	-	-	-	-	..	**251.5**	**-208.7**	**225.5**	**199.2**	..
Mining and quarrying	**10 636.9**	**13 511.1**	**13 227.4**	**7 713.5**	..	**119 543.8**	**138 952.3**	**161 830.2**	**156 566.3**	..
Extraction activities	10 636.9	13 511.1	13 227.4	7 713.5	..	119 543.8	138 952.3	161 830.2	156 566.3	..
Manufacturing	**348 382.1**	**388 429.4**	**550 852.7**	**417 183.4**	..	**1 017 716.9**	**1 127 740.1**	**1 294 320.0**	**1 193 251.7**	..
of which:										
Food products, beverages and tobacco	92 341.9	83 992.8	132 581.0	97 280.7	..	188 055.5	264 197.3	291 292.9	224 785.9	..
Textiles, wood and paper products; printing	801.3	749.4	1 489.6	1 481.6	..	15 811.6	18 235.5	20 508.5	24 450.4	..
Chemical, rubber, plastic, non-metallic mineral products	191 161.7	213 817.9	295 443.8	251 416.3	..	521 352.2	575 331.5	612 699.7	569 779.0	..
Metal and machinery products, except electrical equipment	47 723.5	80 980.3	109 803.3	57 959.7	..	198 935.2	201 878.4	260 213.5	241 652.2	..
Motor vehicles, trailers, semi-trailers, other transport equipment	11 911.8	4 253.2	5 042.0	3 366.2	..	47 789.9	40 430.1	65 983.4	85 736.2	..
Other manufacturing	4 433.3	4 639.0	6 490.8	5 667.5	..	45 775.7	27 666.3	43 616.0	46 830.8	..
Electricity, gas, steam and air conditioning supply	**12 860.1**	**21 133.1**	**18 969.8**	**12 655.1**	..	**16 174.2**	**22 852.3**	**26 890.1**	**23 184.1**	..
Water supply; sewerage, waste management and remediation activities	**954.8**	**228.7**	**347.8**	**250.7**	..	**-28.3**	**-3.2**	**151.1**	**56.1**	..
Construction	**5 765.9**	**6 140.0**	**5 772.4**	**3 053.6**	..	**10 175.3**	**7 190.9**	**14 796.1**	**13 311.2**	..
Services	**890 912.4**	**899 203.1**	**942 891.6**	**1 052 004.8**	..	**727 917.3**	**819 850.3**	**881 640.7**	**801 904.1**	..
Wholesale and retail trade; repair of motor vehicles and motorcycles	101 551.4	106 813.5	114 293.6	100 851.8	..	207 755.0	235 395.8	182 995.9	151 882.3	..
Transportation and storage	31 415.4	39 356.0	44 826.1	31 613.2	..	29 727.8	31 254.3	46 355.2	42 423.9	..
Accommodation and food service activities	906.9	1 064.6	1 448.8	1 118.6	..	3 257.5	4 729.6	2 181.6	2 302.5	..
Information and communication	33 021.2	29 994.7	29 461.5	26 678.5	..	177 394.7	165 663.5	174 112.5	170 627.4	..
Financial and insurance activities	648 015.2	645 727.8	664 830.9	809 329.1	..	170 837.2	281 854.1	344 816.5	322 241.8	..
Activities of holding companies	-10.9	-45.3	51.6	34.3	..	31 282.5	41 975.3	59 192.9	46 610.9	..
Real estate activities	50 777.4	49 093.5	56 868.6	62 989.5	..	14 422.4	12 203.0	15 873.1	17 604.8	..
Professional, scientific and technical activities	10 598.8	13 497.4	14 176.1	3 646.7	..	28 433.3	43 163.3	35 907.9	40 833.5	..
Administrative and support service activities	14 626.0	13 655.5	16 986.1	15 777.4	..	91 728.9	43 985.5	78 683.1	47 917.3	..
Public administration; activities of households and of extraterritorial organisations	-	-	-	-	..	132.8	107.5	117.5	91.6	..
Education	-	-	-	-	..	-	-	-	-	..
Human health and social work activities	-	-	-	-	..	3 984.8	1 479.9	666.8	5 375.5	..
Arts, entertainment and recreation	-	-	-	-	..	93.6	32.7	-153.5	168.3	..
Other services	-	-	-	-	..	149.2	-19.0	84.0	435.1	..
Not allocated and confidential	**-471.4**	**146.5**	**-254.3**	**-289.7**	**1 491 617.2**	**1 758.3**	**1 331.3**	**3 298.2**	**8 402.8**	**2 312 110.3**
Private real estate activities	-	-	-	-	..	**13 830.2**	**14 214.2**	**17 583.4**	**17 384.9**	..

- Nil; .. Not available

Note: Data excludes resident Special Purpose Entities (SPEs). Detailed metadata at: *http://stats.oecd.org/OECDStat_Metadata/ShowMetadata.ashx?Dataset=FDI_CTRY_IND_SUMM.*

1. National Bank of Netherlands note on the existence of a breaks in series between 2014 and 2015: *http://stats.oecd.org/OECDStat_Metadata/ShowMetadata.ashx?Dataset=FDI_CTRY_IND_SUMM&Lang=en&Coords=[MEASURE].[USD],[ECO_ACT].[FDI_T],[COU].[NLD],[FDI_TYPE].[LE_FA_F],[TIME].[2015],[MEASURE_PRINCIPLE].[DO]*

   Detailed metadata at: *http://stats.oecd.org/OECDStat_Metadata/ShowMetadata.ashx?Dataset=FDI_CTRY_IND_SUMM.*

Source: *OECD International Direct Investment Statistics (database): https://doi.org/10.1787/idi-data-en*

NETHERLANDS

Table 6. Foreign direct investment income by industrial sector

Million US dollars

	Inward					Outward				
	2015	2016	2017	2018	2019	2015	2016	2017	2018	2019
All FDI activities	**72 697.7**	**69 284.5**	**64 179.9**	**86 991.6**	**71 784.6**	**102 674.4**	**87 907.8**	**104 256.6**	**132 951.7**	**110 638.3**
Agriculture, forestry and fishing	**-**	**-**	**-**	**-**	..	**-25.5**	**-23.2**	**11.3**	**15.3**	..
Mining and quarrying	**77.6**	**161.5**	**319.0**	**-971.3**	..	**6 173.0**	**10 853.7**	**6 892.1**	**8 921.3**	..
Extraction activities	77.6	161.5	319.0	-971.3	..	6 173.0	10 853.7	6 892.1	8 921.3	..
Manufacturing	**19 473.1**	**15 051.4**	**19 157.9**	**14 107.2**	..	**48 213.0**	**38 874.3**	**61 174.6**	**81 667.7**	..
of which:										
Food products, beverages and tobacco	6 826.4	3 199.2	6 700.5	3 495.8	..	8 535.8	8 098.0	13 584.7	16 017.9	..
Textiles, wood and paper products; printing	78.8	17.7	27.1	-34.2	..	14.4	-7.7	562.5	986.7	..
Chemical, rubber, plastic, non-metallic mineral products	9 840.3	7 687.7	8 842.3	6 638.7	..	28 376.0	20 044.2	33 322.1	46 532.5	..
Metal and machinery products, except electrical equipment	1 448.7	2 039.1	1 393.3	1 445.8	..	7 352.2	5 021.6	8 315.9	5 995.5	..
Motor vehicles, trailers, semi-trailers, other transport equipment	797.6	1 373.4	798.1	782.5	..	766.5	1 748.3	942.4	7 153.3	..
Other manufacturing	480.3	731.0	1 391.0	1 766.8	..	3 181.4	3 955.5	4 433.5	4 969.9	..
Electricity, gas, steam and air conditioning supply	**1 199.1**	**1 985.0**	**550.1**	**-1 596.8**	..	**950.6**	**927.8**	**1 439.5**	**1 248.7**	..
Water supply; sewerage, waste management and remediation activities	**652.2**	**-69.7**	**-104.8**	**-42.5**	..	**-7.8**	**3.3**	**-2.3**	**-2.4**	..
Construction	**597.9**	**442.3**	**119.5**	**-834.4**	..	**768.7**	**366.0**	**139.8**	**-663.3**	..
Services	**50 692.2**	**51 676.4**	**44 105.5**	**76 304.7**	..	**45 130.3**	**35 375.4**	**32 756.2**	**39 314.3**	..
Wholesale and retail trade; repair of motor vehicles and motorcycles	8 071.0	6 786.5	7 986.7	4 894.4	..	11 516.4	8 750.4	4 387.3	12 027.6	..
Transportation and storage	2 116.5	4 401.2	526.4	2 352.2	..	2 108.7	2 430.6	1 152.1	1 613.4	..
Accommodation and food service activities	47.7	119.4	156.7	185.3	..	63.2	190.2	344.9	-181.8	..
Information and communication	2 184.1	1 684.2	2 016.7	2 787.7	..	5 090.4	5 305.8	3 138.3	3 065.0	..
Financial and insurance activities	31 811.4	32 499.2	23 986.0	57 420.0	..	20 911.8	14 536.1	15 908.0	12 469.0	..
Activities of holding companies	-	-	-	-	..	267.3	-360.5	206.3	-566.5	..
Real estate activities	2 685.5	1 735.0	3 871.0	2 824.3	..	1 385.5	952.1	704.5	892.2	..
Professional, scientific and technical activities	68.8	79.6	116.1	145.2	..	833.1	1 881.0	2 328.9	3 382.5	..
Administrative and support service activities	3 707.2	4 371.3	5 445.8	5 695.7	..	3 200.2	1 287.2	4 846.1	6 123.0	..
Public administration; activities of households and of extraterritorial organisations	-	-	-	-	..	-4.4	-	-	-1.2	..
Education	-	-	-	-	..	-	-	-	-	..
Human health and social work activities	-	-	-	-	..	-	1.1	1.1	3.5	..
Arts, entertainment and recreation	-	-	-	-	..	25.5	40.9	-55.2	-79.1	..
Other services	-	-	-	-	..	-	-	-	-	..
Not allocated and confidential	**5.5**	**37.6**	**32.7**	**24.8**	**71 784.6**	**1 472.0**	**1 530.5**	**1 845.3**	**2 450.1**	**110 638.3**
Private real estate activities	**-**	**-**	**-**	**-**	..	**-**	**-**	**-**	**-**	..

- Nil; .. Not available

Note: Data excludes resident Special Purpose Entities (SPEs). Detailed metadata at: *http://stats.oecd.org/OECDStat_Metadata/ShowMetadata.ashx?Dataset=FDI_CTRY_IND_SUMM.*

Source: *OECD International Direct Investment Statistics (database): https://doi.org/10.1787/idi-data-en*

NEW ZEALAND

Table 1. Foreign direct investment flows by country

Million US dollars

	Inward					Outward				
	2015	2016	2017	2018	2019	2015	2016	2017	2018	2019
WORLD	**-373.7**	**2 910.8**	**2 538.0**	**1 945.2**	**4 277.2**	**99.7**	**62.2**	**-222.5**	**424.9**	**-172.0**
OECD COUNTRIES	**-1 022.4**	**.. c**	**2 320.2**	**811.0**	**2 132.8**	**-756.4**	**.. c**	**-102.4**	**424.7**	**-455.1**
Australia	35.7	2 709.7	1 869.2	-460.0	2 408.8	-1 111.7	7.9	205.2	456.2	303.9
Austria	.. c	.. c	.. c	.. c	.. c	..	..	..	.. c	.. c
Belgium	.. c	.. c	-13.8	.. c	-33.4	.. c	.. c	.. c	.. c	.. c
Canada	456.4	-1 033.0	223.2	-3.7	68.4	-2.9	-33.5	-40.5	43.7	25.3
Chile	.. c	.. c	0.0	..	.. c	.. c	.. c	.. c	.. c	-427.7
Czech Republic	.. c	.. c	.. c	.. c	0.0	..	..	..	..	..
Denmark	.. c	.. c	1.2	.. c	.. c	0.0	..	..	..	..
Estonia	..	..	-	-	0.4	..	..	..	..	..
Finland	-0.1	.. c	1.0	.. c	.. c	-3.8	0.2	-0.1	-7.1	..
France	14.1	35.1	-28.9	31.5	47.6	.. c	8.8	17.8	-34.1	.. c
Germany	-24.2	-49.0	779.8	-53.2	33.8	.. c	20.8	-6.3	.. c	-19.6
Greece	..	..	..	..	.. c	..	..	..	..	..
Hungary	.. c	.. c	.. c	..	.. c	..	..	..	..	..
Iceland	..	..	..	..	..	..	..	..	..	..
Ireland	.. c	-41.1	-30.8	62.0	-15.1	.. c	.. c	1.0	-57.8	.. c
Israel	..	.. c	.. c	.. c	.. c	..	..	..	..	..
Italy	0.0	8.0	-0.2	.. c	0.7	.. c	.. c	.. c	.. c	.. c
Japan	-5.0	280.9	194.9	265.7	87.7	-12.2	6.1	8.3	0.0	-36.4
Korea	16.0	-13.8	5.7	5.3	0.6	5.8	0.2	-27.9	.. c	-0.4
Latvia	..	..	..	..	..	..	..	..	..	..
Lithuania	..	..	..	.. c	..	..	..	..	..	..
Luxembourg	34.7	-13.6	-8.0	177.8	.. c	.. c	.. c	.. c	..	..
Mexico	.. d	-0.1	.. c	.. c	.. c	-1.1	14.4	.. c	.. c	.. c
Netherlands	526.9	28.8	-75.9	156.2	-66.5	44.0	-40.6	-107.0	.. c	.. c
New Zealand	-	-	0.0	-	-	-	-	0.0	-	-
Norway	12.5	.. c	.. c	.. c	.. c	..	..	..	..	..
Poland	.. c	0.0	0.0	.. c	0.3	..	..	..	..	..
Portugal	..	..	..	..	..	..	..	..	..	..
Slovak Republic	.. c	.. c	.. c	.. c	.. c	..	..	..	..	..
Slovenia	..	..	..	-	..	..	..	..	..	..
Spain	.. c	.. c	.. c	.. c	.. c	.. c	.. c	.. c	.. c	.. c
Sweden	11.1	-15.8	.. c	.. c	.. c	.. c	.. c	.. c	.. c	.. c
Switzerland	-67.2	69.2	29.4	16.5	-21.4	0.0	0.0	0.1	..	..
Turkey	.. c	.. c	.. d	.. c	.. c	.. c	.. c	.. c	.. c	.. c
United Kingdom	-596.7	112.0	-485.7	342.0	-1 041.0	56.9	48.4	9.8	-42.4	46.8
United States	-22.9	353.3	-106.4	-227.9	-76.5	367.0	-95.8	-282.6	-331.2	-332.8
EUROPE	**-1 466.5**	**454.6**	**144.6**	**1 245.6**	**-339.5**	**10.9**	**106.8**	**29.1**	**-156.0**	**10.9**
Bulgaria	..	..	..	..	..	..	..	..	..	..
Croatia	-	..	-	0.0	0.0	..	..	..	..	..
Cyprus	..	..	..	..	..	.. c	..	..	..	..
Malta	.. c	.. c	.. c	..	..	..	..	..	..	..
Romania	..	.. c	.. c	.. c	.. c	..	..	..	..	..
Russian Federation	.. c	..	..	..	..	.. c	.. c	.. c	.. c	.. c
Ukraine	..	..	..	..	..	..	..	..	..	..
AFRICA	**-17.5**	**.. c**	**.. c**	**.. c**	**1.2**	**.. c**	**.. c**	**0.6**	**-10.9**	**1.5**
Northern Africa	..	.. c	..	..	..	.. c	..	..	..	..
Algeria	..	..	..	..	..	..	..	..	..	..
Egypt	0.1	.. c	.. c	.. c	.. c	.. c	..	..	..	..
Libya	..	..	..	..	..	..	..	..	..	..
Morocco	..	..	..	..	..	..	..	..	..	..
Tunisia	..	..	..	..	..	..	..	..	..	..
Other African countries	.. c	.. c	..	..	..	.. c	.. c	..	..	..
Nigeria	..	..	..	..	..	..	..	..	..	..
South Africa	.. c	0.1	.. c	.. c	0.7	..	..	.. c	.. c	.. c
AMERICA	**133.8**	**.. c**	**.. d**	**.. d**	**379.2**	**375.4**	**.. c**	**-288.2**	**170.0**	**-120.5**
Northern America	..	..	..	..	..	..	..	..	..	..
Central America and Caribbean countries	.. c	.. c	..	..	..	..	..	..	..	..
Bahamas	.. c	.. c	.. c	.. c	.. c	..	..	..	..	..
Bermuda	-57.5	24.0	52.3	.. c	.. c	4.7	0.5	27.2	13.8	476.9
Cayman Islands	-176.0	25.2	-248.7	-215.8	.. c	..	..	..	.. c	.. c
Costa Rica	..	..	..	..	..	..	..	..	..	..
El Salvador	..	..	..	..	..	..	..	..	..	..
Guatemala	..	..	..	..	..	..	..	..	..	..
Honduras	..	..	..	..	..	..	..	..	..	..
Nicaragua	..	..	..	..	..	..	..	..	..	..
Panama	.. c	..	..	..	..	-0.3	0.2	1.1	..	..
Virgin Islands, U.S.	..	..	..	..	..	..	..	..	..	..
South America	.. c	.. c	..	..	..	.. c	.. c	..	..	..
Argentina	.. c	.. c	-0.1	.. c	0.2	0.6	.. c	.. c	.. c	.. c
Bolivia	..	..	..	..	..	..	..	.. c	.. c	.. c
Brazil	0.1	.. c	0.0	.. c	.. c	.. c	.. c	.. c	3.1	-4.9
Colombia	.. c	.. c	.. c	.. c	.. c	..	..	.. c	.. c	.. c
Ecuador	-	..	..	..	..	..	..	..	..	..
Paraguay	..	..	..	..	..	..	..	..	..	..
Peru	..	..	..	..	..	0.9	2.0	.. c	.. c	.. c
Uruguay	..	..	..	..	..	.. c	.. c	.. c	.. c	.. c
Venezuela	.. c	.. c	.. c	..	..	1.7	-1.1	0.1	-0.2	0.2

Table 1. Foreign direct investment flows by country *(cont.)*

Million US dollars

	Inward					Outward				
	2015	2016	2017	2018	2019	2015	2016	2017	2018	2019
ASIA	**962.0**	**402.4**	**607.4**	**1 056.7**	**1 826.3**	**.. d**	**-23.3**	**-117.3**	**-111.4**	**-374.7**
Near and Middle East	.. c	.. c	..	..	..	.. c	..	..	..	..
Gulf Arabian countries	.. c	.. c	..	..	..	.. c	..	..	..	..
Kuwait	..	..	..	..	..	..	..	..	..	..
Qatar	..	..	..	..	..	..	..	..	..	..
Saudi Arabia	..	..	..	-	..	2.1	-2.9	6.2	-12.8	1.3
United Arab Emirates	.. c	.. c	.. c	.. c	.. c	.. c	-9.4	.. c	-24.4	.. c
Other Near and Middle East	..	.. c	..	..	..	..	..	..	..	..
Jordan	..	-	..	..	..	..	..	..	..	..
Other Asian countries	.. c	.. c	..	..	..	.. c	.. c	..	..	..
China	0.5	33.7	128.9	4.9	28.1	13.0	-68.5	26.7	-21.1	3.3
Hong Kong, China	-14.7	549.4	685.4	1 103.8	293.3	913.8	-22.7	131.6	144.9	-296.9
India	-0.4	0.9	.. d	0.3	.. d	.. c	.. c	.. c	.. c	.. c
Indonesia	0.5	.. c	0.2	0.4	-0.5	.. c	.. c	-21.9	-14.1	7.5
Iran, Islamic Republic of	..	..	..	..	..	..	..	..	..	..
Malaysia	-86.3	.. c	-53.3	-24.9	.. c	.. c	0.3	-0.5	.. c	-24.0
Philippines	1.4	2.2	6.7	.. c	.. c	.. c	.. c	.. c	.. c	.. c
Singapore	1 053.4	-498.5	-338.6	-643.3	1 554.3	-162.7	59.5	-164.7	-13.4	-41.4
Chinese Taipei	0.2	-0.6	0.4	.. c	.. c	-7.1	-4.5	2.5	-0.8	2.4
Thailand	.. c	.. c	3.9	.. c	.. c	.. c	16.6	.. c	6.8	.. c
Viet Nam	.. c	.. c	2.1	.. c	-0.5	.. c	-0.2	..	-6.9	.. c
AUSTRALIA, OCEANIA AND POLAR REGIONS	**36.6**	**2 708.3**	**1 864.0**	**-467.2**	**2 417.2**	**-1 117.5**	**8.3**	**201.0**	**440.8**	**311.6**
WORLD unallocated and confidential	**-22.1**	**-28.3**	**-29.5**	**686.2**	**-7.3**	**78.1**	**77.9**	**-47.8**	**92.5**	**-0.9**
European Union (EU28)	**-1 449.8**	**400.8**	**88.2**	**1 201.7**	**-340.3**	**-26.2**	**164.9**	**21.8**	**-153.5**	**12.5**
G20 countries excl. European Union	**-126.6**	**2 437.0**	**2 582.3**	**-91.5**	**1 560.0**	**-634.8**	**-134.2**	**-83.1**	**38.7**	**-20.3**
G20 OECD countries	**-126.6**	**2 403.0**	**2 451.6**	**-100.5**	**1 530.2**	**-689.4**	**-24.2**	**-102.5**	**77.5**	**-20.5**
G20 Non-OECD countries	**0.1**	**34.0**	**130.7**	**9.0**	**29.8**	**54.6**	**-110.0**	**19.4**	**-38.8**	**0.2**
MENA countries	**.. c**	**-0.3**	**.. c**	**.. d**	**.. c**	**.. c**	**-12.2**	**.. c**	**-37.2**	**.. c**
ASEAN countries	**968.8**	**-448.5**	**-380.6**	**-324.6**	**1 427.2**	**-86.9**	**76.5**	**-212.5**	**-204.7**	**-30.7**

- Nil; .. Not available; c Confidential data; d Secondary Confidentiality

Note: Detailed metadata at: *http://stats.oecd.org/OECDStat_Metadata/ShowMetadata.ashx?Dataset=FDI_CTRY_IND_SUMM.*

Source: *OECD International Direct Investment Statistics (database): https://doi.org/10.1787/idi-data-en*

NEW ZEALAND

Table 2. Foreign direct investment positions by country
At year end

Million US dollars

	Inward					Outward				
	2015	2016	2017	2018	2019	2015	2016	2017	2018	2019
WORLD	**66 837.9**	**70 403.0**	**76 027.5**	**75 158.1**	**81 237.8**	**18 034.8**	**16 740.0**	**17 158.8**	**17 277.6**	**17 045.5**
OECD COUNTRIES	**53 071.1**	**.. c**	**60 092.1**	**58 702.8**	**62 514.4**	**14 012.7**	**.. c**	**13 252.2**	**13 655.4**	**13 067.7**
Australia	34 507.5	37 060.6	40 037.9	37 562.6	39 957.0	8 225.5	8 186.6	8 573.6	8 637.4	8 943.6
Austria	.. c	.. c	.. c	.. c	.. c	..	..	..	.. c	.. c
Belgium	.. c	.. c	427.8	72.8	-16.3	.. c	-6.2	.. c	.. c	.. c
Canada	3 184.1	1 877.4	2 563.8	2 952.4	3 511.4	126.7	112.0	57.2	103.7	133.3
Chile	.. c	.. c	..	..	.. c	.. c	.. c	.. c	435.5	.. c
Czech Republic	..	.. c	..	.. c	.. c	..	..	..	..	..
Denmark	.. c	.. c	1.1	0.7	.. c	..	..	..	..	..
Estonia	..	..	..	..	0.4	..	..	..	..	..
Finland	.. c	.. c	.. c	.. c	.. c	7.2	7.5	7.6	..	..
France	72.5	75.5	75.0	93.3	187.6	.. c	43.6	70.5	.. c	27.7
Germany	-183.9	-184.2	539.4	451.9	514.6	.. c	46.8	44.0	.. c	12.4
Greece	..	..	..	..	.. c	..	..	..	..	..
Hungary	.. c	.. c	.. c	.. c	..	..	..	..	..	..
Iceland	..	..	..	..	..	..	..	..	..	..
Ireland	24.5	-56.0	-81.6	-2.0	-7.7	.. c	.. c	58.8	.. c	.. c
Israel	..	.. c	.. c	.. c	.. c	..	..	..	..	..
Italy	.. c	.. c	.. c	0.4	1.1	.. c	.. c	.. c	.. c	.. c
Japan	3 319.1	3 639.5	3 937.7	3 781.1	3 829.7	-15.2	-10.1	-1.0	73.8	.. c
Korea	.. c	.. c	.. c	.. c	.. c	.. c	.. c	.. c	.. c	.. c
Latvia	..	..	..	..	..	..	..	..	..	..
Lithuania	..	..	..	..	..	..	..	..	..	..
Luxembourg	224.8	226.4	335.8	483.9	445.1	.. c	.. c	.. c	.. c	.. c
Mexico	.. c	..	.. c	.. c	..	-0.9	.. c	18.7	39.5	.. c
Netherlands	2 906.5	2 821.4	2 748.3	2 908.2	2 596.0	333.6	289.1	.. c	.. c	.. c
New Zealand	-	-	0.0	-	-	-	-	0.0	-	-
Norway	.. c	.. c	.. c	.. c	.. c	..	..	..	..	..
Poland	0.0	0.0	0.0	.. c	.. c	..	..	..	..	..
Portugal	..	..	..	..	..	..	..	..	..	..
Slovak Republic	..	.. c	..	.. c	.. c	..	..	..	..	..
Slovenia	..	..	..	..	..	..	..	..	..	..
Spain	.. c	.. c	.. c	.. c	.. c	.. c	.. c	.. c	.. c	.. c
Sweden	36.3	.. c	.. c	.. c	.. c	.. c	.. c	.. c	.. c	.. c
Switzerland	297.2	362.4	443.2	438.0	1 242.9	-0.1	-0.1	..	..	..
Turkey	.. c	.. c	.. c	.. c	.. c	.. c	.. c	.. c	.. c	.. c
United Kingdom	2 881.6	3 735.6	3 334.0	4 311.2	3 262.8	1 038.4	850.3	951.2	885.0	818.6
United States	5 481.1	5 628.2	5 584.6	4 930.5	5 236.0	3 000.4	2 527.5	2 434.8	2 356.6	2 003.1
EUROPE	**7 230.1**	**8 147.4**	**8 624.7**	**10 096.2**	**10 099.5**	**2 697.9**	**1 967.3**	**2 161.9**	**2 005.2**	**1 907.4**
Bulgaria	..	..	..	..	..	..	..	..	..	..
Croatia	..	..	..	0.0	0.0	..	..	..	..	..
Cyprus	..	..	..	..	..	..	..	..	..	..
Malta	.. c	.. c	..	..	..	..	..	..	..	..
Romania	..	.. c	.. c	.. c	.. c	..	..	..	..	..
Russian Federation	..	..	..	..	..	.. c	.. c	.. c	.. c	.. c
Ukraine	..	..	..	..	..	..	..	..	..	..
AFRICA	**.. c**	**.. c**	**.. c**	**.. c**	**-0.1**	**.. c**	**.. c**	**.. c**	**.. c**	**.. c**
Northern Africa	..	.. c	..	..	..	..	..	..	..	..
Algeria	..	..	..	..	..	..	..	..	..	..
Egypt	..	.. c	.. c	.. c	.. c	..	..	..	..	..
Libya	..	..	..	..	..	..	..	..	..	..
Morocco	..	..	..	..	..	..	..	..	..	..
Tunisia	..	..	..	..	..	..	..	..	..	..
Other African countries	.. c	.. c	..	..	..	.. c	.. c	..	..	..
Nigeria	..	..	..	..	..	..	..	..	..	..
South Africa	.. c	-0.7	.. c	.. c	.. c	..	..	.. c	.. c	.. c
AMERICA	**.. d**	**.. c**	**10 511.5**	**.. d**	**12 657.6**	**.. d**	**.. c**	**.. d**	**.. d**	**3 222.4**
Northern America	..	..	..	..	..	..	..	..	..	..
Central America and Caribbean countries	.. c	.. c	..	..	..	..	.. c	..	..	..
Bahamas	.. c	.. c	.. c	.. c	.. c	..	..	..	..	..
Bermuda	.. c	.. c	.. c	.. c	.. c	199.0	203.2	207.7	210.0	.. c
Cayman Islands	723.8	715.5	829.3	897.1	1 686.0	..	..	..	.. c	.. c
Costa Rica	..	..	..	..	..	..	..	..	..	..
El Salvador	..	..	..	..	..	..	..	..	..	..
Guatemala	..	..	..	..	..	..	..	..	..	..
Honduras	..	..	..	..	..	..	..	..	..	..
Nicaragua	..	..	..	..	..	..	..	..	..	..
Panama	..	..	..	..	..	-1.0	-1.0	..	..	..
Virgin Islands, U.S.	..	..	..	..	..	..	..	..	..	..
South America	.. c	.. c	..	..	..	.. c	.. c	..	..	..
Argentina	.. c	.. c	.. c	.. c	.. c	.. c	.. c	.. c	.. c	.. c
Bolivia	..	..	..	..	..	..	..	.. c	.. c	.. c
Brazil	.. c	.. c	.. c	.. c	.. c	.. c	.. c	.. c	16.2	.. c
Colombia	.. c	..	..	.. c	.. c	..	..	.. c	.. c	.. c
Ecuador	..	..	..	..	..	..	..	..	..	..
Paraguay	..	..	..	..	..	..	..	..	..	..
Peru	..	..	..	..	..	5.2	6.1	.. c	.. c	.. c
Uruguay	..	..	..	..	..	.. c	.. c	.. c	.. c	.. c
Venezuela	.. c	.. c	..	..	..	0.5	-0.8	-0.7	-0.8	.. c

Table 2. Foreign direct investment positions by country *(cont.)*

At year end

Million US dollars

	Inward					Outward				
	2015	2016	2017	2018	2019	2015	2016	2017	2018	2019
ASIA	**11 606.7**	**12 296.1**	**13 481.6**	**14 947.4**	**15 859.7**	**3 359.2**	**3 256.0**	**3 259.7**	**3 006.3**	**2 680.8**
Near and Middle East	.. c	.. c	..	..	..	.. c	.. c	..	..	..
Gulf Arabian countries	.. c	.. c	..	..	..	.. c	.. c	..	..	..
Kuwait	..	..	..	..	..	..	..	..	..	..
Qatar	..	..	..	..	..	..	..	..	..	..
Saudi Arabia	..	..	..	..	..	-1.7	.. c	-0.1	27.3	.. c
United Arab Emirates	.. c	.. c	.. c	.. c	.. c	.. c	.. c	.. d	34.4	.. c
Other Near and Middle East	..	.. c	..	..	..	..	..	..	..	..
Jordan	..	..	..	..	..	..	..	..	..	..
Other Asian countries	.. c	.. c	..	..	..	.. c	.. c	..	..	..
China	.. d	.. c	898.8	945.3	945.9	68.4	4.8	32.7	44.7	25.1
Hong Kong, China	3 506.4	3 983.2	5 095.3	7 433.1	6 611.0	1 358.5	1 425.8	1 559.6	1 608.5	.. c
India	.. c	.. c	.. c	.. c	.. c	.. c	.. c	.. c	.. c	.. c
Indonesia	.. c	.. c	.. c	.. c	.. c	.. c	.. c	.. c	.. c	.. c
Iran, Islamic Republic of	..	..	..	..	..	..	..	..	..	..
Malaysia	173.9	.. c	.. c	.. c	.. c	.. c	.. c	.. c	.. c	.. c
Philippines	.. c	.. c	.. c	.. c	.. c	.. c	.. c	0.3	.. c	.. c
Singapore	3 971.2	3 556.9	3 126.4	2 044.4	3 906.0	1 131.9	1 036.8	966.5	556.4	.. c
Chinese Taipei	.. c	-0.4	.. c	.. c	.. c	2.8	-1.3	1.6	10.7	.. c
Thailand	2.9	-0.3	3.6	.. c	.. c	0.5	.. c	-10.1	-0.8	.. c
Viet Nam	.. c	.. c	.. c	.. c	.. c	.. c	..	..	..	..
AUSTRALIA, OCEANIA AND POLAR REGIONS	**34 501.9**	**37 053.1**	**40 025.1**	**37 543.4**	**39 963.0**	**8 274.2**	**8 233.6**	**8 614.2**	**8 662.0**	**8 977.1**
WORLD unallocated and confidential	**2 064.9**	**2 531.7**	**3 384.7**	**2 614.4**	**2 658.1**	**372.6**	**431.4**	**399.9**	**219.3**	**.. d**
European Union (EU28)	**6 105.7**	**7 117.8**	**7 485.3**	**8 978.3**	**8 665.5**	**2 637.1**	**1 969.1**	**2 156.8**	**2 000.2**	**1 904.1**
G20 countries excl. European Union	**49 858.3**	**52 668.0**	**57 071.0**	**55 136.9**	**57 563.5**	**12 631.3**	**11 835.7**	**12 220.7**	**12 298.5**	**12 139.0**
G20 OECD countries	**49 295.1**	**51 858.3**	**56 100.3**	**54 118.5**	**56 542.3**	**12 478.0**	**11 805.6**	**12 170.6**	**12 177.1**	**12 037.4**
G20 Non-OECD countries	**563.2**	**809.6**	**970.7**	**1 018.4**	**1 021.3**	**153.2**	**30.0**	**50.2**	**121.4**	**101.5**
MENA countries	**.. c**	**.. c**	**.. c**	**.. d**	**.. c**	**.. c**	**16.7**	**.. d**	**61.7**	**44.0**
ASEAN countries	**4 149.4**	**3 809.6**	**3 404.1**	**2 637.9**	**4 326.5**	**1 872.7**	**1 784.6**	**1 681.9**	**1 137.8**	**1 205.8**

- Nil; .. Not available; c Confidential data; d Secondary Confidentiality

Note: Detailed metadata at: *http://stats.oecd.org/OECDStat_Metadata/ShowMetadata.ashx?Dataset=FDI_CTRY_IND_SUMM.*

Source: *OECD International Direct Investment Statistics (database): https://doi.org/10.1787/idi-data-en*

Table 3. Foreign direct investment income by country

Million US dollars

	Inward					Outward				
	2015	2016	2017	2018	2019	2015	2016	2017	2018	2019
WORLD	**5 867.8**	**5 437.8**	**7 091.6**	**6 951.9**	**5 891.4**	**491.6**	**741.9**	**522.7**	**372.1**	**604.8**
OECD COUNTRIES	**5 428.0**	**.. c**	**6 571.4**	**6 263.5**	**5 409.6**	**340.1**	**.. c**	**478.3**	**308.4**	**567.4**
Australia	4 469.2	4 201.4	5 062.1	4 918.2	4 273.3	221.5	387.8	265.9	244.3	287.7
Austria	.. c	.. c	.. c	.. c	.. c	..	..	-	..	.. c
Belgium	..	.. c	0.8	.. c	.. c	.. c	0.4	.. c	.. c	.. c
Canada	104.3	136.5	158.6	201.6	226.5	-2.0	-25.8	-19.1	0.7	3.7
Chile	..	..	-	..	..	.. c	.. c	.. c	.. c	.. c
Czech Republic	..	..	..	..	..	..	..	..	..	..
Denmark	..	..	..	..	.. c	..	..	..	..	..
Estonia	..	..	..	..	..	..	..	..	..	..
Finland	.. c	.. c	.. c	.. c	.. c	0.1	0.0	0.0	0.0	..
France	28.7	22.5	30.5	12.2	.. d	.. c	-7.7	-0.7	-7.0	.. c
Germany	.. d	20.4	68.5	9.8	.. d	.. c	-0.8	0.5	.. c	.. c
Greece	..	..	..	..	..	..	..	..	..	..
Hungary	..	..	..	..	..	..	..	..	..	..
Iceland	..	..	..	..	..	..	..	..	..	..
Ireland	.. c	.. c	2.3	3.3	3.8	.. c	.. c	1.0	-0.1	.. c
Israel	..	..	..	..	..	..	..	..	..	..
Italy	..	..	-	..	..	.. c	.. c	.. c	.. c	.. c
Japan	.. d	125.8	174.4	167.1	70.8	.. d	.. c	.. c	.. c	.. c
Korea	.. c	.. c	17.6	17.7	18.1	0.7	4.0	2.5	.. c	.. c
Latvia	..	..	..	..	..	..	..	..	..	..
Lithuania	..	..	..	..	..	..	..	..	..	..
Luxembourg	.. d	-0.8	.. c	21.3	26.7	.. c	.. c	.. c	..	..
Mexico	..	..	-	..	..	.. c	2.8	.. c	.. c	.. c
Netherlands	115.4	167.6	241.6	224.5	177.4	4.0	0.2	.. c	.. c	.. c
New Zealand	-	-	-	-	-	-	-	-	-	-
Norway	.. c	.. c	.. c	.. c	.. c	..	..	-	..	..
Poland	..	..	..	..	..	..	..	..	..	..
Portugal	..	..	..	..	..	..	..	..	..	..
Slovak Republic	..	..	..	..	..	..	..	..	..	..
Slovenia	..	..	..	..	..	..	..	..	..	..
Spain	..	.. c	.. c	.. c	.. c	.. c	.. c	.. c	.. c	.. c
Sweden	.. c	.. c	.. c	.. c	.. c	.. c	.. c	.. c	.. c	.. c
Switzerland	.. c	52.7	.. c	41.7	33.4	..	..	0.0	..	..
Turkey	..	..	-	..	..	.. c	.. c	.. c	.. c	.. c
United Kingdom	189.0	158.8	351.5	363.2	252.0	-16.8	32.7	-18.0	17.1	229.8
United States	341.6	232.9	362.6	238.2	188.9	186.4	51.6	132.0	59.8	12.9
EUROPE	**509.1**	**539.5**	**828.8**	**750.0**	**663.9**	**-85.7**	**150.5**	**96.1**	**16.3**	**260.0**
Bulgaria	..	..	..	..	..	..	..	..	..	..
Croatia	..	..	..	..	..	..	..	..	..	..
Cyprus	..	..	..	..	..	..	..	..	..	..
Malta	..	..	..	..	..	..	..	..	..	..
Romania	..	..	..	..	..	..	..	..	..	..
Russian Federation	..	..	..	..	..	.. c	.. c	.. c	.. c	.. c
Ukraine	..	..	..	..	..	..	..	..	..	..
AFRICA	**.. c**	**.. c**	**.. c**	**.. c**	**..**	**.. c**	**.. c**	**0.8**	**.. c**	**.. c**
Northern Africa	..	..	..	..	..	..	..	..	..	..
Algeria	..	..	..	..	..	..	..	..	..	..
Egypt	..	..	..	..	..	..	..	..	..	..
Libya	..	..	..	..	..	..	..	..	..	..
Morocco	..	..	..	..	..	..	..	..	..	..
Tunisia	..	..	..	..	..	..	..	..	..	..
Other African countries	.. c	.. c	..	..	..	.. c	.. c	..	..	..
Nigeria	..	..	..	..	..	..	..	..	..	..
South Africa	..	..	-	..	..	..	..	.. c	.. c	.. c
AMERICA	**.. d**	**.. c**	**.. d**	**.. d**	**425.9**	**.. d**	**.. c**	**151.6**	**.. d**	**.. d**
Northern America	..	..	..	..	..	..	..	..	..	..
Central America and Caribbean countries	.. c	.. c	..	..	..	.. c	..	..	..	..
Bahamas	.. c	.. c	.. c	.. c	.. c	..	..	-	..	..
Bermuda	28.9	18.9	65.0	88.1	-78.2	31.5	46.9	40.6	14.1	9.3
Cayman Islands	35.5	23.5	.. c	.. c	46.2	..	..	-	.. c	.. c
Costa Rica	..	..	..	..	..	..	..	..	..	..
El Salvador	..	..	..	..	..	..	..	..	..	..
Guatemala	..	..	..	..	..	..	..	..	..	..
Honduras	..	..	..	..	..	..	..	..	..	..
Nicaragua	..	..	..	..	..	..	..	..	..	..
Panama	.. c	..	-	..	..	0.0	0.0	0.0	..	..
Virgin Islands, U.S.	..	..	..	..	..	..	..	..	..	..
South America	..	..	..	..	..	.. c	.. c	..	..	..
Argentina	..	..	-	..	..	.. c	.. c	.. c	.. c	.. c
Bolivia	..	..	-	..	..	..	..	.. c	.. c	..
Brazil	..	..	-	..	..	.. c	.. c	.. c	.. c	-1.0
Colombia	..	..	-	..	..	..	..	.. c	.. c	.. c
Ecuador	..	..	..	..	..	..	..	..	..	..
Paraguay	..	..	..	..	..	..	..	..	..	..
Peru	..	..	-	..	..	..	-0.4	.. c	.. c	.. c
Uruguay	..	..	-	..	..	.. c	.. c	.. c	.. c	.. c
Venezuela	..	..	-	..	..	0.0	0.0	0.0	0.0	0.0

Table 3. Foreign direct investment income by country *(cont.)*

Million US dollars

	Inward					Outward				
	2015	2016	2017	2018	2019	2015	2016	2017	2018	2019
ASIA	**360.5**	**269.7**	**555.9**	**690.7**	**528.3**	**125.9**	**121.0**	**5.7**	**30.7**	**46.3**
Near and Middle East	.. c	.. c	..	..	..	.. c	.. c	..	..	..
Gulf Arabian countries	.. c	.. c	..	..	..	.. c	.. c	..	..	..
Kuwait	..	..	..	..	..	..	..	..	..	..
Qatar	..	..	..	..	..	..	..	..	..	..
Saudi Arabia	..	..	-	..	..	.. d	0.0	-0.1	0.0	0.0
United Arab Emirates	.. c	.. c	.. c	.. c	.. c	.. c	.. c	17.1	.. c	.. c
Other Near and Middle East	..	..	..	..	..	..	..	..	..	..
Jordan	..	..	..	..	..	..	..	..	..	..
Other Asian countries	.. c	.. c	..	..	..	.. c	.. c	..	..	..
China	.. c	.. c	.. d	29.6	.. d	4.7	3.9	4.7	2.9	4.0
Hong Kong, China	158.6	153.3	269.7	288.4	306.7	-8.9	-2.0	15.8	-5.3	-15.5
India	.. c	.. c	.. c	.. c	.. c	.. c	.. c	.. c	.. c	.. c
Indonesia	..	.. c	..	..	..	..	..	..	..	..
Iran, Islamic Republic of	..	..	..	..	..	..	..	..	..	..
Malaysia	.. c	.. c	.. c	.. c	.. c	.. c	.. c	0.4	-1.5	.. c
Philippines	.. c	.. c	.. c	.. c	.. c	.. c	.. c	.. c	.. c	..
Singapore	37.1	-41.3	76.9	189.6	152.0	100.1	85.4	.. c	.. c	45.2
Chinese Taipei	..	..	-	.. c	.. c	.. d	0.4	0.5	.. c	.. c
Thailand	..	..	-	..	..	.. c	.. c	0.3	.. c	.. c
Viet Nam	..	..	..	..	..	..	..	..	..	..
AUSTRALIA, OCEANIA AND POLAR REGIONS	**4 469.2**	**4 201.4**	**5 062.1**	**4 918.2**	**4 273.3**	**231.4**	**391.2**	**268.6**	**248.1**	**290.6**
WORLD unallocated and confidential	**18.7**	**-11.0**	**21.0**	**..**	**-**	**4.1**	**4.3**	**-**	**..**	**.. d**
European Union (EU28)	**428.3**	**458.8**	**748.8**	**671.8**	**595.4**	**-86.8**	**151.5**	**95.5**	**18.3**	**259.4**
G20 countries excl. European Union	**5 283.4**	**4 915.1**	**6 236.6**	**5 958.1**	**5 096.2**	**400.6**	**454.4**	**371.0**	**303.4**	**559.2**
G20 OECD countries	**5 284.6**	**4 913.8**	**6 225.9**	**5 928.0**	**5 085.0**	**395.6**	**447.3**	**365.7**	**299.9**	**556.8**
G20 Non-OECD countries	**-1.2**	**1.3**	**10.7**	**.. d**	**11.1**	**5.0**	**7.1**	**5.3**	**3.5**	**2.4**
MENA countries	**.. c**	**.. c**	**.. c**	**.. c**	**.. c**	**27.7**	**.. c**	**17.0**	**.. c**	**.. c**
ASEAN countries	**45.8**	**-26.9**	**82.9**	**185.5**	**121.8**	**100.8**	**86.6**	**-35.9**	**35.7**	**47.9**

- Nil; .. Not available; c Confidential data; d Secondary Confidentiality

Note: Detailed metadata at: *http://stats.oecd.org/OECDStat_Metadata/ShowMetadata.ashx?Dataset=FDI_CTRY_IND_SUMM.*

Source: *OECD International Direct Investment Statistics (database): https://doi.org/10.1787/idi-data-en*

NEW ZEALAND

Table 4. Foreign direct investment flows by industrial sector

Million US dollars

	Inward					Outward				
	2015	2016	2017	2018	2019	2015	2016	2017	2018	2019
All FDI activities	**-373.7**	**2 910.8**	**2 538.0**	**1 945.2**	**4 277.2**	**99.7**	**62.2**	**-222.5**	**424.9**	**-172.0**
Agriculture, forestry and fishing	..	..	..	..	..	..	..	..	..	..
Mining and quarrying	..	..	..	..	..	..	..	..	..	..
Extraction activities	..	..	..	..	..	..	..	..	..	..
Manufacturing	..	..	..	..	..	..	..	..	..	..
of which:										
Food products, beverages and tobacco	..	..	..	..	..	..	..	..	..	..
Textiles, wood and paper products; printing	..	..	..	..	..	..	..	..	..	..
Chemical, rubber, plastic, non-metallic mineral products	..	..	..	..	..	..	..	..	..	..
Metal and machinery products, except electrical equipment	..	..	..	..	..	..	..	..	..	..
Motor vehicles, trailers, semi-trailers, other transport equipment	..	..	..	..	..	..	..	..	..	..
Other manufacturing	..	..	..	..	..	..	..	..	..	..
Electricity, gas, steam and air conditioning supply	..	..	..	..	..	..	..	..	..	..
Water supply; sewerage, waste management and remediation activities	..	..	..	..	..	..	..	..	..	..
Construction	..	..	..	..	..	..	..	..	..	..
Services	..	..	..	..	..	..	..	..	..	..
Wholesale and retail trade; repair of motor vehicles and motorcycles	..	..	..	..	..	..	..	..	..	..
Transportation and storage	..	..	..	..	..	..	..	..	..	..
Accommodation and food service activities	..	..	..	..	..	..	..	..	..	..
Information and communication	..	..	..	..	..	..	..	..	..	..
Financial and insurance activities	..	..	..	..	..	..	..	..	..	..
Activities of holding companies	..	..	..	..	..	..	..	..	..	..
Real estate activities	..	..	..	..	..	..	..	..	..	..
Professional, scientific and technical activities	..	..	..	..	..	..	..	..	..	..
Administrative and support service activities	..	..	..	..	..	..	..	..	..	..
Public administration; activities of households and of extraterritorial organisations	..	..	..	..	..	..	..	..	..	..
Education	..	..	..	..	..	..	..	..	..	..
Human health and social work activities	..	..	..	..	..	..	..	..	..	..
Arts, entertainment and recreation	..	..	..	..	..	..	..	..	..	..
Other services	..	..	..	..	..	..	..	..	..	..
Not allocated and confidential	..	..	2 538.0	1 945.2	4 277.2	..	..	-222.5	424.9	-172.0
Private real estate activities	..	..	..	..	..	..	..	..	..	..

.. Not available

Note: Detailed metadata at: *http://stats.oecd.org/OECDStat_Metadata/ShowMetadata.ashx?Dataset=FDI_CTRY_IND_SUMM.*

Source: *OECD International Direct Investment Statistics (database): https://doi.org/10.1787/idi-data-en*

NEW ZEALAND

Table 5. Foreign direct investment positions by industrial sector

At year end

Million US dollars

	Inward					Outward				
	2015	2016	2017	2018	2019	2015	2016	2017	2018	2019
All FDI activities	**66 837.9**	**70 403.0**	**76 027.5**	**75 158.1**	**81 237.8**	**18 034.8**	**16 740.0**	**17 158.8**	**17 277.6**	**17 045.5**
Agriculture, forestry and fishing	**4 240.5**	**5 004.1**	**5 802.1**	**6 222.6**	**6 461.4**	**.. c**	**.. c**	**.. c**	**.. c**	**.. c**
Mining and quarrying	**1 039.8**	**504.2**	**380.8**	**1 507.1**	**1 269.5**	**.. c**	**.. c**	**.. c**	**.. c**	**.. c**
Extraction activities	..	..	..	..	..	..	..	..	..	..
Manufacturing	**9 564.9**	**10 848.0**	**10 995.0**	**10 988.6**	**11 358.4**	**7 927.7**	**6 260.4**	**6 543.6**	**6 772.8**	**6 700.0**
of which:										
Food products, beverages and tobacco	..	..	..	..	..	..	..	..	..	..
Textiles, wood and paper products; printing	..	..	..	..	..	..	..	..	..	..
Chemical, rubber, plastic, non-metallic mineral products	..	..	..	..	..	..	..	..	..	..
Metal and machinery products, except electrical equipment	..	..	..	..	..	..	..	..	..	..
Motor vehicles, trailers, semi-trailers, other transport equipment	..	..	..	..	..	..	..	..	..	..
Other manufacturing	..	..	..	..	..	..	..	..	..	..
Electricity, gas, steam and air conditioning supply	**1 773.5**	**1 804.7**	**1 880.9**	**1 793.6**	**1 828.0**	**474.1**	**.. c**	**.. c**	**.. c**	**.. c**
Water supply; sewerage, waste management and remediation activities	..	..	..	..	..	..	..	..	..	..
Construction	**351.4**	**374.9**	**432.8**	**428.0**	**654.8**	**.. c**	**.. c**	**.. c**	**.. c**	**.. c**
Services	**38 721.2**	**40 524.9**	**44 983.5**	**42 788.8**	**48 148.3**	**7 535.2**	**7 807.8**	**7 643.6**	**6 580.8**	**6 247.6**
Wholesale and retail trade; repair of motor vehicles and motorcycles	7 331.3	7 773.9	7 871.9	8 415.1	9 574.0	3 860.3	4 058.2	4 266.8	4 314.9	3 323.9
Transportation and storage	166.1	541.7	466.9	502.1	538.0	854.6	.. c	.. c	.. c	.. c
Accommodation and food service activities	470.9	566.4	801.5	846.6	1 831.3	.. c	.. c	.. c	.. c	.. c
Information and communication	1 840.5	1 657.9	1 605.4	1 462.2	1 479.4	.. c	.. c	.. c	.. c	.. c
Financial and insurance activities	22 899.5	24 833.9	27 777.9	25 933.6	28 909.6	1 503.7	1 743.2	1 269.1	.. c	1 502.9
Activities of holding companies	..	..	..	..	..	..	..	..	..	..
Real estate activities	2 918.0	2 307.9	2 447.5	2 555.9	2 748.7	.. c	.. c	.. c	.. c	.. c
Professional, scientific and technical activities	1 511.5	1 102.8	2 024.5	2 033.4	1 552.2	76.0	51.8	106.9	87.0	105.7
Administrative and support service activities	518.2	702.3	693.1	227.6	245.2	.. c	.. c	.. c	.. c	.. c
Public administration; activities of households and of extraterritorial organisations	101.4	.. c	.. c	.. c	..	..	..	-	..	..
Education	..	..	..	..	..	..	..	..	..	..
Human health and social work activities	782.6	842.6	1 061.4	1 094.9	1 710.7	.. c	.. c	.. c	.. c	.. c
Arts, entertainment and recreation	..	..	-	..	..	350.4	380.4	223.7	380.1	362.9
Other services	91.0	.. c	.. c	.. c	.. c	..	..	-	..	..
Not allocated and confidential	**11 146.5**	**11 537.8**	**11 552.4**	**11 429.3**	**11 517.5**	**2 097.8**	**10 479.6**	**2 971.6**	**.. c**	**.. c**
Private real estate activities	..	..	..	..	..	..	..	..	..	..

- Nil; .. Not available; c Confidential data

Note: Detailed metadata at: *http://stats.oecd.org/OECDStat_Metadata/ShowMetadata.ashx?Dataset=FDI_CTRY_IND_SUMM.*

Source: *OECD International Direct Investment Statistics (database): https://doi.org/10.1787/idi-data-en*

Table 6. Foreign direct investment income by industrial sector

Million US dollars

	Inward					Outward				
	2015	2016	2017	2018	2019	2015	2016	2017	2018	2019
All FDI activities	**5 867.8**	**5 437.8**	**7 091.6**	**6 951.9**	**5 891.4**	**491.6**	**741.9**	**522.7**	**372.1**	**604.8**
Agriculture, forestry and fishing	..	..	..	..	..	..	..	..	..	..
Mining and quarrying	..	..	..	..	..	..	..	..	..	..
Extraction activities	..	..	..	..	..	..	..	..	..	..
Manufacturing	..	..	..	..	..	..	..	..	..	..
of which:										
Food products, beverages and tobacco	..	..	..	..	..	..	..	..	..	..
Textiles, wood and paper products; printing	..	..	..	..	..	..	..	..	..	..
Chemical, rubber, plastic, non-metallic mineral products	..	..	..	..	..	..	..	..	..	..
Metal and machinery products, except electrical equipment	..	..	..	..	..	..	..	..	..	..
Motor vehicles, trailers, semi-trailers, other transport equipment	..	..	..	..	..	..	..	..	..	..
Other manufacturing	..	..	..	..	..	..	..	..	..	..
Electricity, gas, steam and air conditioning supply	..	..	..	..	..	..	..	..	..	..
Water supply; sewerage, waste management and remediation activities	..	..	..	..	..	..	..	..	..	..
Construction	..	..	..	..	..	..	..	..	..	..
Services	..	..	..	..	..	..	..	..	..	..
Wholesale and retail trade; repair of motor vehicles and motorcycles	..	..	..	..	..	..	..	..	..	..
Transportation and storage	..	..	..	..	..	..	..	..	..	..
Accommodation and food service activities	..	..	..	..	..	..	..	..	..	..
Information and communication	..	..	..	..	..	..	..	..	..	..
Financial and insurance activities	..	..	..	..	..	..	..	..	..	..
Activities of holding companies	..	..	..	..	..	..	..	..	..	..
Real estate activities	..	..	..	..	..	..	..	..	..	..
Professional, scientific and technical activities	..	..	..	..	..	..	..	..	..	..
Administrative and support service activities	..	..	..	..	..	..	..	..	..	..
Public administration; activities of households and of extraterritorial organisations	..	..	..	..	..	..	..	..	..	..
Education	..	..	..	..	..	..	..	..	..	..
Human health and social work activities	..	..	..	..	..	..	..	..	..	..
Arts, entertainment and recreation	..	..	..	..	..	..	..	..	..	..
Other services	..	..	..	..	..	..	..	..	..	..
Not allocated and confidential	..	..	**7 091.6**	**6 951.9**	**5 891.4**	..	..	**522.7**	**372.1**	**604.8**
Private real estate activities	..	..	..	..	..	..	..	..	..	..

.. Not available

Note: Detailed metadata at: *http://stats.oecd.org/OECDStat_Metadata/ShowMetadata.ashx?Dataset=FDI_CTRY_IND_SUMM.*

Source: *OECD International Direct Investment Statistics (database): https://doi.org/10.1787/idi-data-en*

NORWAY

Table 1. Foreign direct investment flows by country

Million US dollars

	Inward					Outward				
	2015	2016	2017	2018	2019	2015	2016	2017	2018	2019
WORLD	**-3 070.8**	**-3 979.3**	**-5 758.3**	**-2 141.7**	**9 677.2**	**31 782.4**	**2 329.3**	**-6 865.8**	**9 084.1**	**4 085.2**
OECD COUNTRIES	**..**	**.. d**	**..**	**.. d**	**.. d**	**..**	**.. d**	**..**	**.. d**	**-1 949.6**
Australia	..	..	..	.. d	19.0	..	..	.. d	..	592.3
Austria	..	..	.. d	..	-100.2	..	..	..	..	-29.6
Belgium	..	..	..	..	-2 953.3	..	..	..	..	367.0
Canada	..	..	..	..	.. d	..	..	..	..	608.4
Chile	..	.. d	..	.. d	.. d	..	..	..	.. d	.. d
Czech Republic	..	.. d	..	..	-84.7	.. d	..	..	..	149.1
Denmark	..	..	..	..	-715.3	..	..	..	..	1 346.7
Estonia	..	..	.. d	..	.. d	..	..	..	.. d	.. d
Finland	..	..	..	..	.. d	..	..	..	..	.. d
France	..	..	..	..	-317.6	..	..	..	..	.. d
Germany	..	..	..	..	468.8	..	..	..	..	388.7
Greece	.. d	.. d	.. d	.. d	.. d	..	..	..	..	45.8
Hungary	.. d	..	..	..	.. d	.. d	.. d	..	.. d	-1.4
Iceland	..	..	..	..	-1.4	..	..	..	..	.. d
Ireland	..	..	..	..	-188.3	..	..	..	..	-234.7
Israel	.. d	.. d	.. d	.. d	.. d	.. d	..	..	.. d	0.7
Italy	..	..	..	..	392.8	.. d	.. d	.. d	..	.. d
Japan	..	..	..	.. d	192.3	..	..	..	..	-297.2
Korea	.. d	..	..	..	-9.1	..	..	..	..	344.0
Latvia	..	..	..	..	0.6	..	..	..	.. d	-15.8
Lithuania	..	..	.. d	..	.. d	..	..	..	..	.. d
Luxembourg	..	..	..	..	.. d	..	..	..	..	.. d
Mexico	.. d	..	..	..	-5.2	..	..	..	..	36.0
Netherlands	..	..	..	..	.. d	..	..	..	..	.. d
New Zealand	.. d	..	..	.. d	.. d	.. d	..	..	..	16.3
Norway	..	..	..	..	-	..	..	..	..	-
Poland	..	..	..	..	253.8	..	..	..	..	-53.3
Portugal	.. d	..	..	..	14.7	..	..	..	..	-3.3
Slovak Republic	.. d	.. d	.. d	..	.. d	..	..	..	..	-55.1
Slovenia	.. d	.. d	.. d	- d	-	.. d	.. d	.. d	.. d	.. d
Spain	..	..	..	..	115.0	..	..	..	..	575.7
Sweden	..	..	..	..	.. d	..	..	..	..	-4 301.9
Switzerland	..	..	..	..	.. d	..	..	..	..	-376.1
Turkey	.. d	..	..	..	-5.6	..	..	..	..	110.7
United Kingdom	..	..	..	..	.. d	..	..	..	..	-260.5
United States	..	..	..	..	.. d	..	..	..	..	-2 892.5
EUROPE	**..**	**..**	**..**	**..**	**2 325.1**	**..**	**..**	**..**	**..**	**1 810.7**
Bulgaria	.. d	..	..	- d	.. d	.. d	..	.. d	.. d	.. d
Croatia	.. d	..	.. d	.. d	.. d	..	..	.. d	.. d	.. d
Cyprus	..	..	..	..	.. d	..	..	..	..	.. d
Malta	..	.. d	.. d	.. d	-209.9	..	.. d	.. d	..	1 787.7
Romania	.. d	.. d	.. d	.. d	-1.5	..	.. d	.. d	..	38.3
Russian Federation	..	..	..	..	-51.8	..	..	..	..	249.2
Ukraine	.. d	.. d	..	..	.. d	..	..	.. d	..	0.3
AFRICA	**..**	**..**	**..**	**..**	**.. d**	**..**	**.. d**	**..**	**..**	**926.3**
Northern Africa	..	..	..	..	-1.0	..	..	..	..	.. d
Algeria	.. d	- d	.. d	.. d	.. d	.. d	.. d	.. d	.. d	.. d
Egypt	..	..	..	..	-0.1	..	..	..	..	5.3
Libya	- d	.. d	..	- d	-	.. d	.. d	..	.. d	.. d
Morocco	.. d	.. d	.. d	.. d	-	..	.. d	..	..	.. d
Tunisia	- d	- d	- d	- d	-	.. d	.. d	.. d	.. d	0.1
Other African countries	..	..	..	..	.. d	..	.. d	..	..	.. d
Nigeria	.. d	.. d	..	..	.. d	..	.. d	.. d	.. d	.. d
South Africa	..	..	..	..	-5.9	.. d	.. d	.. d	.. d	.. d
AMERICA	**..**	**..**	**..**	**..**	**6 743.8**	**..**	**..**	**..**	**..**	**-2 417.1**
Northern America	..	..	..	..	.. d	..	..	..	..	-2 291.6
Central America and Caribbean countries	..	..	..	..	.. d	..	..	..	..	.. d
Bahamas	.. d	.. d	.. d	..	.. d	.. d	..	.. d	.. d	.. d
Bermuda	..	..	..	..	.. d	..	.. d	.. d	.. d	.. d
Cayman Islands	.. d	..	..	..	36.5	.. d	.. d	.. d	..	148.9
Costa Rica	..	..	.. d	.. d	.. d	.. d	.. d	.. d	.. d	.. d
El Salvador	..	..	..	..	-	..	..	..	- d	.. d
Guatemala	..	..	..	..	-	.. d	.. d	.. d	.. d	.. d
Honduras	..	..	.. d	.. d	-	.. d	.. d	.. d	.. d	.. d
Nicaragua	..	..	..	..	-	..	.. d	.. d	.. d	.. d
Panama	.. d	.. d	.. d	.. d	.. d	.. d	.. d	.. d	..	.. d
Virgin Islands, U.S.	..	- d	- d	..	-	..	..	..	..	-
South America	..	..	..	..	423.1	..	..	..	..	391.8
Argentina	- d	.. d	..	.. d	1.5	..	..	.. d	.. d	.. d
Bolivia	- d	- d	- d	- d	-0.5	.. d	.. d	.. d	.. d	.. d
Brazil	..	..	..	..	-3.4	..	..	..	..	546.5
Colombia	.. d	.. d	.. d	..	0.8	.. d	.. d	.. d	.. d	16.9
Ecuador	.. d	..	.. d	.. d	.. d	..	.. d	..	.. d	.. d
Paraguay	.. d	.. d	- d	.. d	.. d	..	..	..	..	-
Peru	.. d	.. d	.. d	.. d	.. d	.. d	.. d	.. d	.. d	.. d
Uruguay	.. d	.. d	.. d	.. d	.. d	.. d	.. d	.. d	.. d	1.7
Venezuela	..	.. d	- d	.. d	.. d	.. d	.. d	.. d	.. d	.. d

Table 1. Foreign direct investment flows by country *(cont.)*

Million US dollars

	Inward					Outward				
	2015	2016	2017	2018	2019	2015	2016	2017	2018	2019
ASIA	..	..	..	..	**.. d**	..	..	..	..	**.. d**
Near and Middle East	..	..	..	..	31.1	.. d	..	..	.. d	.. d
Gulf Arabian countries	..	..	..	..	-7.8	..	..	..	..	.. d
Kuwait	- d	.. d	.. d	.. d	.. d	..	.. d	.. d	..	-1.8
Qatar	.. d	.. d	.. d	..	.. d	- d	.. d	..	.. d	0.6
Saudi Arabia	.. d	..	..	..	0.1	..	.. d	.. d	..	-19.0
United Arab Emirates	..	..	..	..	86.2	..	..	..	..	.. d
Other Near and Middle East	.. d	.. d	..	..	.. d	.. d	..	.. d	.. d	.. d
Jordan	- d	..	- d	- d	-	.. d	.. d	.. d	.. d	.. d
Other Asian countries	..	..	..	..	.. d	..	..	..	..	.. d
China	..	..	..	..	502.9	..	..	..	..	164.7
Hong Kong, China	..	..	..	..	.. d	..	..	..	..	-27.8
India	.. d	.. d	..	..	-14.8	..	..	..	..	-18.2
Indonesia	..	.. d	..	..	-11.1	..	..	.. d	..	57.7
Iran, Islamic Republic of	..	..	.. d	- d	-	.. d	.. d	..	..	-0.8
Malaysia	..	..	.. d	.. d	55.2	..	.. d	..	..	40.1
Philippines	..	..	..	..	2.5	..	..	.. d	..	-2.2
Singapore	..	..	..	..	.. d	..	..	..	..	.. d
Chinese Taipei	- d	.. d	.. d	.. d	2.7	..	..	.. d	.. d	3.6
Thailand	.. d	.. d	.. d	..	-2 703.0	.. d	..	..	.. d	512.2
Viet Nam	.. d	..	..	..	4.4	..	.. d	.. d	.. d	.. d
AUSTRALIA, OCEANIA AND POLAR REGIONS	..	..	..	..	**-65.7**	..	..	**.. d**	..	**602.7**
WORLD unallocated and confidential	..	..	..	..	**.. d**	..	**.. d**	**.. d**	..	**.. d**
European Union (EU28)	..	..	..	..	**2 928.4**	..	..	..	..	**1 654.1**
G20 countries excl. European Union	..	..	..	..	**.. d**	..	..	..	..	**3 441.9**
G20 OECD countries	..	..	..	..	**.. d**	..	..	..	..	**2 347.9**
G20 Non-OECD countries	..	..	..	..	**417.5**	..	..	..	..	**1 094.0**
MENA countries	..	..	..	..	**-8.9**	..	..	..	..	**.. d**
ASEAN countries	..	..	..	..	**.. d**	..	..	..	..	**.. d**

- Nil; .. Not available; d Secondary Confidentiality

Note: Data excludes resident Special Purpose Entities (SPEs). Detailed metadata at: *http://stats.oecd.org/OECDStat_Metadata/ShowMetadata.ashx?Dataset=FDI_CTRY_IND_SUMM.*

Source: *OECD International Direct Investment Statistics (database): https://doi.org/10.1787/idi-data-en*

NORWAY

Table 2. Foreign direct investment positions by country

At year end

Million US dollars

	Inward					Outward				
	2015	2016	2017	2018	2019	2015	2016	2017	2018	2019
WORLD	**147 486.5**	**147 524.4**	**145 487.8**	**153 178.3**	**161 469.4**	**172 431.7**	**192 013.0**	**200 887.5**	**200 999.2**	**204 930.2**
OECD COUNTRIES	**123 286.9**	**121 549.8**	**118 490.0**	**..**	**125 627.9**	**132 086.0**	**155 164.8**	**162 795.7**	**..**	**157 894.3**
Australia	220.0	113.9	-78.6	120.3	138.8	1 318.7	942.6	753.0	887.7	1 460.9
Austria	2 694.1	3 144.9	2 405.2	1 552.8	1 435.4	152.2	222.7	211.9	215.1	180.3
Belgium	9 358.9	7 263.2	7 344.3	3 912.1	896.4	8 045.2	5 357.7	-535.9	-386.9	769.4
Canada	750.9	1 191.4	4 717.7	-64.3	332.2	1 224.2	1 172.7	2 013.8	1 281.7	1 965.1
Chile	2.4	-5.7	4.1	.. c	.. c	1 211.5	1 294.0	1 217.1	649.3	687.9
Czech Republic	149.0	190.4	269.4	86.8	1.0	89.4	228.4	218.9	244.8	381.1
Denmark	5 511.0	5 906.3	8 161.4	7 292.6	6 492.3	12 156.6	11 599.2	13 278.0	13 207.3	14 560.4
Estonia	-72.1	.. c	5.0	119.2	41.2	675.9	658.9	486.4	218.8	191.1
Finland	3 332.5	3 279.1	2 451.3	6 307.6	7 935.6	521.1	1 435.4	1 783.9	1 590.1	4 770.6
France	7 326.1	7 331.1	6 638.4	5 226.5	4 857.7	3 406.7	2 750.2	4 606.3	4 905.3	8 239.0
Germany	6 982.2	8 057.8	6 461.5	6 099.7	6 507.2	1 663.2	2 111.8	2 533.3	2 958.5	3 410.5
Greece	.. c	.. c	0.2	-	0.1	45.1	10.7	28.7	35.4	74.7
Hungary	-3.4	2.3	1.9	-1.8	6.4	255.8	416.6	1 461.6	200.1	190.9
Iceland	84.3	50.1	214.4	35.8	33.9	157.7	367.5	412.1	243.8	289.5
Ireland	1.6	-309.5	-59.4	918.6	720.5	1 318.5	2 180.9	2 201.9	2 037.3	2 345.3
Israel	.. c	.. c	.. c	.. c	.. c	-0.5	2.1	-0.6	5.2	5.7
Italy	872.5	740.4	387.3	771.3	1 157.2	-9.6	228.2	229.1	235.7	301.9
Japan	955.4	1 028.1	1 388.7	1 074.9	1 255.7	118.2	112.6	572.8	500.3	517.7
Korea	-119.8	-259.7	-252.1	54.2	44.5	559.6	1 055.8	886.7	805.3	1 139.1
Latvia	-8.6	-6.4	0.5	0.5	1.7	722.1	651.2	588.9	364.9	370.7
Lithuania	-19.8	-20.3	76.6	4.0	8.1	859.9	871.0	465.2	465.6	477.2
Luxembourg	12 193.6	13 070.7	12 330.2	14 122.6	12 464.0	508.5	.. c	.. c	7 535.3	4 891.8
Mexico	.. c	-19.5	-1.6	1.2	-4.0	94.2	65.1	112.5	78.9	111.0
Netherlands	26 861.1	20 664.7	15 704.3	14 676.8	13 712.3	33 311.5	34 458.7	34 517.8	26 073.9	23 095.4
New Zealand	.. c	-22.9	-4.0	.. c	4.6	45.4	6.5	23.6	47.3	62.2
Norway	-	-	-	-	-	-	-	-	-	-
Poland	738.9	488.2	652.4	537.6	787.5	1 178.5	948.1	1 567.4	1 462.5	1 410.5
Portugal	113.2	.. c	.. c	2.8	17.4	18.6	21.3	31.9	73.6	69.4
Slovak Republic	8.3	-1.6	11.2	-0.3	8.4	197.7	170.5	184.5	190.2	148.4
Slovenia	.. c	.. c	.. c	-	0.1	4.5	-6.1	1.8	-9.7	49.7
Spain	363.7	456.0	306.5	640.3	749.4	5 954.7	7 912.1	7 241.8	7 578.5	8 074.0
Sweden	27 732.1	31 404.2	32 143.6	32 542.0	37 623.9	25 913.3	25 640.0	27 733.7	27 229.0	24 073.7
Switzerland	3 095.8	2 932.1	2 713.8	4 303.9	4 449.8	-214.2	456.5	393.9	35.6	-130.8
Turkey	1.5	17.5	6.2	1.5	-4.0	1 193.1	1 811.9	1 168.3	1 068.2	1 073.9
United Kingdom	7 554.8	7 269.5	7 360.4	10 077.3	9 521.6	9 742.5	12 983.9	18 532.3	14 951.8	15 339.3
United States	6 623.8	7 603.2	7 060.5	8 917.7	14 417.2	21 227.9	31 156.4	30 254.9	40 093.4	37 296.8
EUROPE	**120 245.4**	**116 565.9**	**110 452.4**	**114 780.8**	**115 986.3**	**112 592.7**	**123 598.1**	**131 532.9**	**117 669.5**	**120 579.6**
Bulgaria	.. c	-2.2	-2.6	-0.1	0.6	.. c	.. c	.. c	9.0	10.9
Croatia	.. c	-	.. c	-2.2	.. c	114.8	116.5	124.0	90.2	98.2
Cyprus	1 411.9	1 012.9	979.2	832.9	2 828.0	1 354.9	729.8	1 095.4	1 150.4	1 343.2
Malta	206.4	353.4	242.3	544.2	327.0	2 133.8	1 408.9	1 513.3	2 012.2	2 722.6
Romania	-61.1	-216.8	48.2	0.8	-0.7	96.1	110.6	116.8	241.4	274.4
Russian Federation	189.9	177.5	105.1	104.9	51.9	402.6	348.1	404.5	395.6	477.7
Ukraine	-	.. c	4.0	.. c	.. c	13.6	36.7	47.0	34.5	36.6
AFRICA	**113.4**	**-230.7**	**-125.1**	**-39.5**	**269.8**	**7 242.0**	**5 167.5**	**4 448.0**	**3 640.5**	**3 673.0**
Northern Africa	-11.8	-17.1	-13.2	-3.3	-4.4	1 335.5	1 303.9	1 212.7	973.2	908.9
Algeria	.. c	.. c	-	.. c	-0.9	1 165.3	1 118.0	1 014.9	806.3	751.0
Egypt	-8.2	-16.6	-12.8	-3.2	-3.4	50.5	55.9	64.6	65.5	64.8
Libya	.. c	-	-	.. c	-	.. c	.. c	.. c	.. c	.. c
Morocco	.. c	.. c	-0.2	-	-	6.9	11.4	14.0	.. c	10.8
Tunisia	.. c	-0.1	.. c	.. c	-	.. c	.. c	.. c	.. c	.. c
Other African countries	125.2	-213.7	-111.9	-36.0	274.1	5 906.4	3 863.7	3 235.2	2 667.1	2 764.1
Nigeria	.. c	.. c	.. c	.. c	-23.7	-89.0	-1 063.3	.. c	-674.5	-532.6
South Africa	5.4	4.3	-3.5	-4.6	-10.5	52.0	83.6	85.1	135.7	143.3
AMERICA	**16 708.2**	**17 355.1**	**19 010.7**	**14 347.5**	**21 034.5**	**31 305.0**	**40 921.3**	**41 439.2**	**53 165.1**	**50 856.0**
Northern America	7 374.7	8 794.7	11 778.1	8 853.4	14 752.8	22 481.6	32 344.1	32 270.5	41 385.7	39 264.7
Central America and Caribbean countries	9 358.6	8 660.1	6 919.4	5 506.8	5 876.0	4 132.9	2 502.7	1 782.5	2 173.6	1 654.7
Bahamas	39.3	20.5	177.8	-10.8	20.2	27.1	.. c	.. c	34.1	18.8
Bermuda	4 885.4	4 241.5	3 308.9	3 329.5	3 599.0	3 455.5	2 153.2	1 418.3	1 760.4	918.7
Cayman Islands	3 701.1	3 514.6	2 541.5	1 247.2	1 277.7	258.6	222.2	154.8	200.9	349.5
Costa Rica	-	-	.. c	.. c	-	.. c	.. c	16.2	13.9	.. c
El Salvador	-	-	-	-	-	-	-	-	.. c	.. c
Guatemala	-	-	-	-	-	.. c	.. c	.. c	.. c	.. c
Honduras	-	.. c	.. c	.. c	.. c	.. c	.. c	.. c	.. c	.. c
Nicaragua	-	-	-	-	-	-	.. c	.. c	.. c	.. c
Panama	.. c	-0.9	-0.7	-3.6	-2.8	336.2	76.5	59.1	56.2	71.2
Virgin Islands, U.S.	-	.. c	-	-	-	-	-	-	-	-
South America	-25.1	-99.5	313.4	-12.7	405.8	4 690.5	6 074.6	7 386.2	9 605.8	9 936.7
Argentina	-	-0.1	-0.7	0.2	1.7	72.5	149.2	140.4	169.9	210.8
Bolivia	.. c	.. c	.. c	-0.1	-0.6	.. c	.. c	.. c	.. c	.. c
Brazil	-101.0	-118.1	-94.5	-2.8	-6.3	2 936.3	4 176.5	5 660.5	8 310.2	8 762.3
Colombia	-0.3	-0.3	.. c	-0.9	-0.1	.. c	227.5	153.1	191.0	206.7
Ecuador	.. c	-0.2	-2.7	-0.5	-0.2	-	.. c	.. c	.. c	.. c
Paraguay	.. c	.. c	.. c	.. c	.. c	-	-	-	-	-
Peru	.. c	.. c	.. c	.. c	.. c	393.3	216.1	190.1	280.3	72.8
Uruguay	.. c	12.5	8.3	.. c	.. c	.. c	.. c	8.9	-7.3	-5.4
Venezuela	0.1	-	-	.. c	.. c	-5.0	4.5	11.1	.. c	-2.4

NORWAY

Table 2. Foreign direct investment positions by country *(cont.)*

At year end

Million US dollars

	Inward					Outward				
	2015	2016	2017	2018	2019	2015	2016	2017	2018	2019
ASIA	**3 018.3**	**5 349.9**	**6 911.3**	**5 665.2**	**4 819.6**	**15 866.6**	**17 510.2**	**18 018.0**	**17 246.3**	**19 260.0**
Near and Middle East	51.4	-33.9	402.6	489.3	516.4	793.1	1 065.4	1 591.2	1 895.1	1 968.1
Gulf Arabian countries	50.9	-28.3	338.5	442.2	430.5	278.3	727.1	1 049.3	1 053.6	1 074.9
Kuwait	.. c	0.7	.. c	.. c	.. c	0.9	0.7	-0.1	2.2	0.6
Qatar	0.1	-0.2	.. c	13.7	23.3	1.0	5.3	2.2	2.8	3.6
Saudi Arabia	0.7	-1.7	-0.4	-0.9	-0.8	48.2	57.4	56.8	73.3	52.7
United Arab Emirates	51.8	-15.5	20.6	39.5	125.3	137.2	207.9	169.8	195.3	208.4
Other Near and Middle East	0.6	-5.6	64.2	47.0	86.0	514.8	338.3	541.9	841.5	893.2
Jordan	-	-	.. c	-	-	.. c	.. c	.. c	.. c	.. c
Other Asian countries	2 966.9	5 383.8	6 508.8	5 175.9	4 303.1	15 073.6	16 444.8	16 426.8	15 351.1	17 291.9
China	813.5	2 630.6	1 392.6	792.1	1 287.9	-1 327.5	535.6	162.7	966.4	1 123.3
Hong Kong, China	3.3	-12.9	.. c	.. c	448.9	77.4	144.0	152.7	95.9	66.9
India	1.8	-13.7	31.9	30.3	15.1	275.5	189.2	213.6	351.4	384.3
Indonesia	-1.1	0.3	-1.1	-1.6	-12.6	77.4	120.8	158.5	139.4	192.3
Iran, Islamic Republic of	-	-	.. c	.. c	-	-30.3	.. c	.. c	.. c	.. c
Malaysia	210.0	702.8	619.6	37.6	92.8	304.1	223.1	275.8	236.7	282.6
Philippines	0.1	0.6	-1.3	-2.0	0.6	27.7	26.1	33.1	34.9	32.2
Singapore	1 053.8	267.7	124.7	179.2	1 170.5	13 398.6	12 848.0	12 496.0	10 664.6	11 373.8
Chinese Taipei	-	0.3	0.1	-3.7	-1.0	5.8	10.4	16.0	4.3	8.0
Thailand	59.8	.. c	2 824.2	2 692.8	-8.2	836.2	826.2	987.6	1 074.8	1 261.5
Viet Nam	0.6	.. c	36.7	7.9	12.2	80.4	97.9	118.8	85.7	126.1
AUSTRALIA, OCEANIA AND POLAR REGIONS	**589.0**	**471.9**	**492.9**	**303.3**	**234.5**	**1 554.4**	**1 124.5**	**794.2**	**969.9**	**1 552.3**
WORLD unallocated and confidential	**6 812.3**	**8 012.3**	**8 745.6**	**..**	**19 124.6**	**3 870.9**	**3 691.3**	**4 655.2**	**..**	**9 009.2**
European Union (EU28)	**113 247.4**	**110 041.0**	**103 995.3**	**106 264.3**	**108 099.3**	**110 625.1**	**120 184.5**	**128 586.6**	**114 880.2**	**117 864.2**
G20 countries excl. European Union	**32 046.0**	**35 752.8**	**35 117.5**	**33 197.8**	**39 550.6**	**43 075.8**	**60 051.7**	**68 545.3**	**78 308.5**	**82 201.9**
G20 OECD countries	**31 136.9**	**33 073.7**	**33 688.2**	**32 280.2**	**38 224.1**	**40 538.8**	**54 391.3**	**61 663.1**	**67 766.7**	**70 855.2**
G20 Non-OECD countries	**909.1**	**2 679.2**	**1 429.4**	**917.6**	**1 326.4**	**2 537.0**	**5 660.6**	**6 882.2**	**10 541.8**	**11 346.7**
MENA countries	**39.7**	**-45.1**	**325.2**	**438.9**	**426.1**	**1 622.6**	**2 063.5**	**2 293.3**	**2 060.0**	**2 017.3**
ASEAN countries	**1 320.5**	**2 012.2**	**3 602.7**	**2 913.9**	**1 253.6**	**14 727.0**	**14 170.1**	**14 098.7**	**12 267.2**	**13 299.8**

- Nil; .. Not available; c Confidential data

Note: Data excludes resident Special Purpose Entities (SPEs). Detailed metadata at: *http://stats.oecd.org/OECDStat_Metadata/ShowMetadata.ashx?Dataset=FDI_CTRY_IND_SUMM.*

Source: *OECD International Direct Investment Statistics (database): https://doi.org/10.1787/idi-data-en*

NORWAY

Table 3. Foreign direct investment income by country

Million US dollars

	Inward					Outward				
	2015	2016	2017	2018	2019	2015	2016	2017	2018	2019
WORLD	**6 207.2**	**6 312.1**	**11 105.4**	**13 224.2**	**12 450.5**	**9 061.4**	**6 709.1**	**8 328.7**	**12 131.0**	**5 282.2**
OECD COUNTRIES	**6 111.0**	**6 268.1**	**11 101.1**	**..**	**12 757.1**	**8 174.4**	**5 698.7**	**6 079.8**	**..**	**4 672.9**
Australia	1.0	-34.4	-10.4	2.1	0.1	69.7	-34.8	-24.4	-15.2	520.3
Austria	-207.7	33.9	148.1	248.2	145.5	-17.5	-30.5	-28.8	-15.9	19.2
Belgium	286.1	188.6	165.9	115.6	65.9	258.3	261.1	-200.3	21.9	-95.8
Canada	448.3	-139.6	-102.6	36.9	.. c	318.8	153.6	306.4	113.8	95.5
Chile	1.1	.. c	.. c	.. c	-	68.8	-81.5	96.2	157.6	11.7
Czech Republic	16.4	14.2	35.2	.. c	-	7.7	45.8	21.9	20.4	19.0
Denmark	1 098.0	1 218.4	1 531.4	1 798.3	993.5	893.7	236.3	772.8	1 622.7	1 015.4
Estonia	.. c	-9.0	13.9	-1.8	.. c	39.8	35.4	88.4	29.6	61.6
Finland	-29.6	150.1	-27.0	1 000.4	665.7	91.4	77.7	60.9	-103.0	43.5
France	723.3	531.3	922.3	1 041.0	595.9	165.7	114.4	175.2	406.5	149.9
Germany	-346.7	584.7	494.3	333.9	135.7	197.4	952.0	101.1	214.8	208.0
Greece	-	-	-	-	-	20.2	-0.1	0.6	0.4	7.0
Hungary	.. c	-	.. c	-	-	101.3	107.3	12.3	65.3	6.0
Iceland	13.8	4.5	.. c	3.7	2.2	23.8	-2.0	5.9	28.9	-32.3
Ireland	17.5	23.8	76.9	54.0	58.3	-247.1	-15.6	29.5	323.5	85.2
Israel	-	-	.. c	.. c	.. c	.. c	-1.8	.. c	.. c	.. c
Italy	107.9	-4.4	-108.2	8.9	24.4	29.1	1.2	-12.8	6.1	8.1
Japan	.. c	-4.2	34.0	66.1	44.3	29.6	0.4	3.5	3.0	28.1
Korea	-188.6	.. c	48.1	-3.9	.. c	185.9	86.3	32.4	132.9	57.3
Latvia	-0.6	-0.2	.. c	.. c	-	89.8	78.3	132.0	125.0	59.6
Lithuania	.. c	-0.4	-0.2	.. c	.. c	37.2	50.0	53.7	86.3	61.9
Luxembourg	1 035.8	-52.0	534.5	360.7	114.0	-16.7	-11.2	49.2	31.5	4.3
Mexico	.. c	.. c	.. c	.. c	-	38.2	6.1	-7.6	-3.0	-4.5
Netherlands	798.5	452.8	1 519.6	1 349.8	1 544.5	2 040.0	1 813.1	2 081.0	773.6	854.0
New Zealand	.. c	-2.5	.. c	.. c	.. c	6.6	7.4	9.7	16.4	14.5
Norway	-	-	-	-	-	-	-	-	-	-
Poland	-44.3	-27.4	53.4	50.0	61.8	142.2	62.0	13.3	94.7	67.3
Portugal	.. c	.. c	.. c	-0.2	.. c	3.1	0.8	1.1	1.6	0.6
Slovak Republic	.. c	.. c	.. c	-	-	18.0	-3.3	13.1	18.2	-29.9
Slovenia	-	-	-	-	-	1.4	.. c	.. c	-1.7	3.1
Spain	18.7	18.2	78.5	162.5	125.5	51.3	-1.2	7.5	-223.9	-53.0
Sweden	2 999.4	2 951.7	4 732.6	4 006.5	2 522.0	2 404.2	1 779.7	1 437.2	814.2	977.9
Switzerland	-384.4	62.0	376.5	9.6	313.3	51.1	0.2	-18.0	13.0	13.5
Turkey	-	.. c	.. c	.. c	-	30.9	28.8	-159.1	20.9	50.0
United Kingdom	-290.0	26.9	-122.7	1 038.4	1 303.4	818.5	-54.3	512.0	2 895.6	370.4
United States	110.4	396.4	651.2	830.4	.. c	348.6	88.3	566.3	561.5	75.1
EUROPE	**6 136.2**	**6 088.8**	**10 489.5**	**12 287.9**	**8 490.1**	**6 954.6**	**5 734.3**	**5 357.9**	**7 036.7**	**4 337.5**
Bulgaria	-	.. c	-	-	-	.. c	.. c	.. c	.. c	2.2
Croatia	-	-	.. c	-	-	-0.5	3.5	3.6	1.6	1.0
Cyprus	147.4	-13.7	-57.8	-12.7	52.1	-522.3	-58.7	-74.4	-383.8	24.5
Malta	-18.8	24.0	-4.4	.. c	64.3	71.9	160.2	25.0	-23.2	262.8
Romania	0.1	1.7	.. c	-	-	22.4	-0.5	11.6	6.4	18.6
Russian Federation	.. c	2.1	.. c	.. c	.. c	42.7	56.1	50.9	29.1	79.8
Ukraine	-	-	-	-	-	2.6	3.8	0.7	2.0	3.6
AFRICA	**2.1**	**5.7**	**-0.5**	**16.1**	**-3.5**	**-612.8**	**272.6**	**2 142.8**	**3 418.5**	**1 366.9**
Northern Africa	-	-	.. c	-	-	39.4	26.9	235.2	723.9	333.2
Algeria	-	-	-	-	-	42.2	45.8	203.2	618.2	273.8
Egypt	-	-	.. c	-	-	9.7	-11.3	9.6	6.9	2.3
Libya	-	-	-	-	-	-12.3	-5.7	.. c	.. c	.. c
Morocco	-	-	-	-	-	0.4	-1.5	.. c	.. c	-1.5
Tunisia	-	-	-	-	-	.. c	.. c	.. c	.. c	-
Other African countries	2.1	5.7	-0.5	16.1	-3.5	-652.3	245.7	1 907.6	2 694.6	1 033.7
Nigeria	-	.. c	.. c	.. c	-	.. c	.. c	.. c	.. c	-8.4
South Africa	.. c	-	-	-	-	39.3	16.2	-8.3	25.0	2.5
AMERICA	**552.8**	**594.2**	**46.1**	**829.5**	**4 061.2**	**-69.9**	**-80.1**	**900.3**	**1 176.7**	**-1 314.3**
Northern America	558.6	256.8	548.4	867.3	.. c	669.4	240.0	873.1	676.1	171.2
Central America and Caribbean countries	-7.1	344.6	-507.4	-13.0	66.9	79.4	28.2	-7.9	48.7	-706.8
Bahamas	8.6	.. c	-1.9	.. c	.. c	.. c	.. c	.. c	2.3	2.3
Bermuda	58.4	101.9	84.8	-49.2	49.7	10.8	46.3	-11.0	51.5	.. c
Cayman Islands	-111.5	209.8	-613.7	-17.5	-8.5	14.4	-36.8	-0.4	-21.3	13.8
Costa Rica	-	-	-	-	-	.. c	.. c	.. c	1.0	.. c
El Salvador	-	-	-	-	-	-	-	-	.. c	.. c
Guatemala	-	-	-	-	-	.. c	.. c	.. c	.. c	.. c
Honduras	-	-	-	-	-	.. c	.. c	.. c	.. c	.. c
Nicaragua	-	-	-	-	-	-	.. c	.. c	.. c	.. c
Panama	.. c	-	-	.. c	-	19.3	3.8	6.9	7.9	4.7
Virgin Islands, U.S.	-	-	-	-	-	-	-	-	-	-
South America	1.1	-7.3	5.1	-24.7	-0.8	-818.7	-348.4	35.1	451.9	-778.6
Argentina	.. c	.. c	.. c	-	-	13.0	21.1	23.9	18.4	7.8
Bolivia	-	-	.. c	-	-	.. c	.. c	.. c	.. c	.. c
Brazil	-8.3	-13.5	-0.4	1.1	-0.6	-913.5	-280.8	-49.9	285.4	-776.4
Colombia	-	-	.. c	-	-	.. c	-16.2	-40.7	-25.4	-17.6
Ecuador	.. c	-	-	-	-	.. c	.. c	-	.. c	.. c
Paraguay	-	-	-	-	.. c	-	-	-	-	-
Peru	.. c	-	.. c	.. c	-	3.8	1.2	-2.9	19.8	-6.8
Uruguay	.. c	.. c	.. c	.. c	.. c	.. c	.. c	0.1	-11.8	1.9
Venezuela	-	-	-	-	-	.. c	8.2	.. c	.. c	.. c

Table 3. Foreign direct investment income by country *(cont.)*

Million US dollars

	Inward					Outward				
	2015	2016	2017	2018	2019	2015	2016	2017	2018	2019
ASIA	**-441.8**	**-396.4**	**503.4**	**-185.9**	**-115.2**	**2 608.9**	**860.6**	**-85.6**	**497.2**	**354.3**
Near and Middle East	-0.7	-0.7	.. c	52.5	30.0	1 290.9	168.8	214.8	423.5	213.0
Gulf Arabian countries	-0.7	-0.7	.. c	.. c	29.7	57.5	87.9	86.0	56.1	58.8
Kuwait	.. c	-	.. c	.. c	.. c	.. c	-	-	.. c	.. c
Qatar	-	-	.. c	-	.. c	1.2	-1.1	0.4	0.4	-0.3
Saudi Arabia	-	-	-	.. c	-	21.2	.. c	.. c	18.2	21.3
United Arab Emirates	-0.7	-0.7	-3.5	-3.0	.. c	-10.2	49.0	45.5	30.2	8.3
Other Near and Middle East	-	-	.. c	.. c	.. c	.. c	81.0	128.9	367.3	154.2
Jordan	-	-	-	-	-	.. c	.. c	.. c	.. c	.. c
Other Asian countries	-441.1	-395.7	442.5	-238.2	-145.3	1 318.0	691.8	-300.4	73.9	141.3
China	17.6	46.3	47.9	26.8	.. c	208.9	23.6	79.6	258.6	159.3
Hong Kong, China	-30.9	.. c	.. c	.. c	.. c	20.0	73.3	13.9	21.3	10.6
India	-	-	.. c	.. c	-	24.4	19.6	5.9	21.8	28.9
Indonesia	-	.. c	.. c	-	-	-76.0	10.2	21.6	13.0	14.0
Iran, Islamic Republic of	-	-	-	-	-	.. c	-4.6	-0.6	1.0	-0.6
Malaysia	78.2	4.3	.. c	-6.1	.. c	74.0	41.0	-10.5	15.0	-55.8
Philippines	-	.. c	.. c	.. c	-	5.3	2.4	0.7	1.1	2.5
Singapore	-286.7	-375.7	305.3	-373.1	-257.2	396.1	87.5	-823.1	-912.1	-465.1
Chinese Taipei	.. c	.. c	.. c	.. c	-	6.0	.. c	1.6	2.1	2.2
Thailand	.. c	45.6	42.6	40.6	.. c	13.0	15.8	9.4	14.8	76.8
Viet Nam	.. c	.. c	.. c	.. c	.. c	25.0	18.8	24.8	30.5	.. c
AUSTRALIA, OCEANIA AND POLAR REGIONS	**-42.0**	**12.1**	**31.9**	**-31.8**	**-0.1**	**72.4**	**-86.9**	**-14.3**	**1.1**	**534.6**
WORLD unallocated and confidential	**-**	**7.7**	**34.9**	**..**	**18.1**	**108.3**	**8.7**	**27.7**	**..**	**3.2**
European Union (EU28)	**6 280.6**	**6 104.6**	**9 995.2**	**11 646.3**	**8 517.3**	**6 790.9**	**5 701.8**	**5 384.5**	**6 768.9**	**4 152.3**
G20 countries excl. European Union	**535.1**	**1 284.7**	**1 885.3**	**3 421.1**	**6 157.0**	**1 592.3**	**1 233.7**	**1 640.2**	**5 006.4**	**1 095.4**
G20 OECD countries	**522.9**	**1 249.6**	**1 806.1**	**3 353.5**	**6 100.1**	**2 232.3**	**1 341.8**	**1 492.8**	**4 336.9**	**1 558.1**
G20 Non-OECD countries	**12.2**	**35.0**	**79.2**	**67.6**	**56.9**	**-640.0**	**-108.1**	**147.4**	**669.5**	**-462.8**
MENA countries	**-0.7**	**-0.7**	**.. c**	**.. c**	**29.7**	**97.0**	**116.0**	**323.2**	**782.3**	**394.2**
ASEAN countries	**-193.6**	**-326.2**	**302.3**	**-338.9**	**-239.9**	**444.7**	**182.3**	**-774.5**	**-838.1**	**-397.9**

- Nil; .. Not available; c Confidential data

Note: Data excludes resident Special Purpose Entities (SPEs). Detailed metadata at: *http://stats.oecd.org/OECDStat_Metadata/ShowMetadata.ashx?Dataset=FDI_CTRY_IND_SUMM.*

Source: *OECD International Direct Investment Statistics (database): https://doi.org/10.1787/idi-data-en*

NORWAY

Table 4. Foreign direct investment flows by industrial sector

Million US dollars

	Inward					Outward				
	2015	2016	2017	2018	2019	2015	2016	2017	2018	2019
All FDI activities	**-3 070.8**	**-3 979.3**	**-5 758.3**	**-2 141.7**	**9 677.2**	**31 782.4**	**2 329.3**	**-6 865.8**	**9 084.1**	**4 085.2**
Agriculture, forestry and fishing	**.. d**	**.. d**	**..**	**..**	**.. d**	**.. d**	**.. d**	**..**	**.. d**	**297.7**
Mining and quarrying	**..**	**..**	**..**	**..**	**-397.3**	**..**	**..**	**..**	**..**	**-2 895.8**
Extraction activities	..	..	..	..	-397.3	..	..	..	..	-2 895.8
Manufacturing	**..**	**..**	**..**	**..**	**3 490.9**	**..**	**..**	**..**	**..**	**-365.7**
of which:										
Food products, beverages and tobacco	..	..	..	..	1 918.7	..	..	..	..	-187.0
Textiles, wood and paper products; printing	..	..	..	.. d	-113.5	..	..	..	..	662.9
Chemical, rubber, plastic, non-metallic mineral products	..	..	..	..	329.8	..	..	.. d	.. d	.. d
Metal and machinery products, except electrical equipment	..	..	..	..	525.8	..	..	..	..	-943.9
Motor vehicles, trailers, semi-trailers, other transport equipment	..	..	..	..	1 061.8	..	..	..	..	-248.3
Other manufacturing	..	..	..	..	-231.6	..	..	..	..	583.7
Electricity, gas, steam and air conditioning supply	**..**	**..**	**..**	**..**	**264.2**	**..**	**..**	**..**	**..**	**-834.9**
Water supply; sewerage, waste management and remediation activities	**.. d**	**..**	**..**	**.. d**	**-44.3**	**.. d**	**..**	**..**	**.. d**	**.. d**
Construction	**..**	**..**	**..**	**..**	**615.2**	**..**	**..**	**..**	**..**	**107.3**
Services	**..**	**..**	**..**	**..**	**2 500.5**	**..**	**..**	**..**	**..**	**5 668.4**
Wholesale and retail trade; repair of motor vehicles and motorcycles	..	..	..	..	-700.7	..	..	..	..	-443.5
Transportation and storage	..	..	..	..	-682.2	..	..	..	..	1 293.5
Accommodation and food service activities	.. d	.. d	..	.. d	-12.0	..	..	.. d	.. d	.. d
Information and communication	..	..	..	..	537.6	..	..	..	..	4 028.9
Financial and insurance activities	..	..	..	..	1 965.3	..	..	..	..	-2 046.2
Activities of holding companies	.. d	.. d	.. d	.. d	.. d	..	..	..	.. d	-
Real estate activities	..	..	..	..	1 567.1	..	..	..	..	471.7
Professional, scientific and technical activities	..	..	..	..	-70.6	..	..	..	..	1 122.6
Administrative and support service activities	..	..	..	..	149.2	..	..	..	..	866.6
Public administration; activities of households and of extraterritorial organisations	..	.. d	..	..	-	.. d	.. d	.. d	..	312.1
Education	.. d	..	..	.. d	-0.2	.. d	.. d	.. d	.. d	.. d
Human health and social work activities	..	..	..	..	-177.9	..	.. d	..	..	.. d
Arts, entertainment and recreation	.. d	..	.. d	.. d	-3.8	.. d	.. d	.. d	.. d	1.1
Other services	..	..	.. d	.. d	-71.3	.. d	.. d	.. d	.. d	.. d
Not allocated and confidential	**.. d**	**.. d**	**.. d**	**.. d**	**.. d**	**.. d**	**.. d**	**..**	**.. d**	**.. d**
Private real estate activities	**.. d**	**.. d**	**.. d**	**.. d**	**.. d**	**..**	**..**	**..**	**..**	**1 827.9**

- Nil; .. Not available; d Secondary Confidentiality

Note: Data excludes resident Special Purpose Entities (SPEs). Detailed metadata at: *http://stats.oecd.org/OECDStat_Metadata/ShowMetadata.ashx?Dataset=FDI_CTRY_IND_SUMM.*

Source: OECD *International Direct Investment Statistics (database): https://doi.org/10.1787/idi-data-en*

Table 5. Foreign direct investment positions by industrial sector

At year end

Million US dollars

	Inward					Outward				
	2015	2016	2017	2018	2019	2015	2016	2017	2018	2019
All FDI activities	**147 486.5**	**147 524.4**	**145 487.8**	**153 178.3**	**161 469.4**	**172 431.7**	**192 013.0**	**200 887.5**	**200 999.2**	**204 930.2**
Agriculture, forestry and fishing	**651.2**	**155.2**	**256.6**	**-509.4**	**416.1**	**1 999.4**	**2 147.1**	**2 157.7**	**1 180.1**	**1 448.7**
Mining and quarrying	**43 882.2**	**42 126.1**	**40 306.0**	**31 334.4**	**30 645.0**	**44 231.4**	**48 846.6**	**41 749.5**	**48 933.6**	**45 240.8**
Extraction activities	43 882.2	42 126.1	40 306.0	31 334.4	30 645.0	44 231.4	48 846.6	41 749.5	48 933.6	45 240.8
Manufacturing	**21 115.3**	**20 981.3**	**21 158.6**	**19 273.2**	**22 638.8**	**26 799.4**	**27 429.9**	**30 918.6**	**28 785.6**	**28 479.3**
of which:										
Food products, beverages and tobacco	1 293.9	2 892.5	2 879.8	2 272.6	4 169.7	2 432.7	2 625.1	3 050.9	2 772.7	2 627.9
Textiles, wood and paper products; printing	183.7	96.3	193.8	379.1	260.0	1 334.5	1 301.9	1 402.7	1 321.9	1 990.1
Chemical, rubber, plastic, non-metallic mineral products	9 713.8	9 560.1	10 370.8	9 257.2	9 491.3	8 144.0	9 490.4	10 545.2	9 891.5	9 518.5
Metal and machinery products, except electrical equipment	4 481.4	3 848.7	3 903.8	3 581.9	4 137.4	11 188.5	11 372.0	13 317.7	13 353.3	12 596.2
Motor vehicles, trailers, semi-trailers, other transport equipment	3 066.1	2 576.5	1 520.6	1 352.5	2 400.5	2 483.9	1 476.5	1 449.9	603.0	435.1
Other manufacturing	2 376.6	2 007.3	2 289.8	2 429.7	2 180.1	1 215.8	1 164.2	1 152.4	843.2	1 311.5
Electricity, gas, steam and air conditioning supply	**794.6**	**1 052.3**	**1 426.7**	**2 087.5**	**2 331.1**	**5 521.1**	**6 061.1**	**4 304.3**	**4 584.9**	**3 669.8**
Water supply; sewerage, waste management and remediation activities	**145.6**	**138.6**	**164.4**	**186.3**	**140.3**	**3.7**	**0.5**	**.. c**	**.. c**	**.. c**
Construction	**1 597.0**	**1 797.2**	**2 149.2**	**2 413.2**	**3 003.4**	**920.0**	**1 121.3**	**1 231.4**	**1 026.5**	**1 092.9**
Services	**62 762.3**	**69 383.9**	**67 789.4**	**76 518.5**	**78 319.1**	**71 457.1**	**81 890.7**	**93 976.6**	**88 875.6**	**95 555.6**
Wholesale and retail trade; repair of motor vehicles and motorcycles	11 421.9	12 247.8	12 957.1	14 814.7	13 956.2	4 237.5	4 496.2	4 714.4	4 926.0	4 935.2
Transportation and storage	8 775.5	8 922.4	10 352.0	10 966.1	10 172.8	9 776.7	10 227.4	11 244.5	9 047.8	11 357.1
Accommodation and food service activities	511.1	617.1	484.0	1 578.7	1 548.2	252.9	311.0	359.2	347.2	361.7
Information and communication	8 350.5	8 848.0	8 946.9	10 258.6	10 683.3	13 941.5	14 052.4	17 793.8	16 635.0	20 386.4
Financial and insurance activities	15 219.0	17 826.5	12 194.2	14 988.7	16 865.9	17 443.4	16 624.6	17 016.4	16 372.5	14 962.6
Activities of holding companies	.. c	.. c	.. c	.. c	.. c	1 045.6	481.7	.. c	-	-
Real estate activities	8 016.3	9 141.6	11 731.1	11 843.7	13 292.0	8 104.5	7 521.6	8 218.1	8 081.4	8 201.3
Professional, scientific and technical activities	4 500.0	5 653.8	3 889.5	3 376.1	3 287.4	3 467.2	5 620.8	5 838.6	5 896.7	6 983.5
Administrative and support service activities	4 782.2	4 960.9	5 939.8	6 982.6	7 074.9	4 139.2	4 141.5	3 241.0	5 104.4	5 857.3
Public administration; activities of households and of extraterritorial organisations	.. c	-	-	-	-	.. c	.. c	.. c	.. c	22 062.9
Education	.. c	29.4	.. c	12.3	.. c	38.8	15.1	24.5	33.9	34.4
Human health and social work activities	656.9	666.1	810.4	1 098.5	909.0	92.4	116.1	170.3	118.6	88.3
Arts, entertainment and recreation	401.7	326.2	385.4	416.2	408.2	19.5	12.4	.. c	.. c	53.6
Other services	.. c	144.0	72.1	182.4	109.2	.. c	139.2	159.8	.. c	.. c
Not allocated and confidential	**9 335.2**	**3 984.9**	**3 654.0**	**..**	**4 924.3**	**1 995.2**	**3 320.0**	**.. c**	**..**	**.. c**
Private real estate activities	**7 203.1**	**7 904.8**	**8 582.9**	**18 067.4**	**19 051.3**	**19 504.2**	**21 195.7**	**23 200.7**	**27 120.3**	**28 674.0**

- Nil; .. Not available; c Confidential data

Note: Data excludes resident Special Purpose Entities (SPEs). Detailed metadata at: *http://stats.oecd.org/OECDStat_Metadata/ShowMetadata.ashx?Dataset=FDI_CTRY_IND_SUMM.*

Source: *OECD International Direct Investment Statistics (database): https://doi.org/10.1787/idi-data-en*

Table 6. Foreign direct investment income by industrial sector

Million US dollars

	Inward					Outward				
	2015	2016	2017	2018	2019	2015	2016	2017	2018	2019
All FDI activities	**6 207.2**	**6 312.1**	**11 105.4**	**13 224.2**	**12 450.5**	**9 061.4**	**6 709.1**	**8 328.7**	**12 131.0**	**5 282.2**
Agriculture, forestry and fishing	**47.5**	**9.5**	**32.5**	**95.8**	**.. c**	**111.4**	**127.0**	**56.8**	**74.6**	**13.3**
Mining and quarrying	**-293.0**	**945.5**	**4 062.5**	**5 044.5**	**6 752.2**	**-1 407.3**	**143.7**	**2 190.1**	**4 889.4**	**1 009.5**
Extraction activities	2 374.7	945.5	4 062.5	5 044.5	6 752.2	-1 594.6	143.7	2 190.1	4 889.4	1 009.5
Manufacturing	**2 108.9**	**1 110.8**	**683.6**	**1 829.4**	**1 066.3**	**2 595.9**	**2 588.3**	**2 957.7**	**1 735.6**	**1 597.0**
of which:										
Food products, beverages and tobacco	29.6	262.7	223.7	146.4	86.8	457.8	296.1	204.9	127.2	108.9
Textiles, wood and paper products; printing	-84.6	-10.1	11.5	21.8	33.8	-4.2	123.1	36.5	107.4	601.6
Chemical, rubber, plastic, non-metallic mineral products	260.5	1 255.1	1 404.5	1 773.0	909.8	1 840.3	977.5	1 822.5	1 047.7	406.4
Metal and machinery products, except electrical equipment	466.1	-372.7	-159.0	-112.2	69.1	299.8	1 122.1	578.5	559.7	416.0
Motor vehicles, trailers, semi-trailers, other transport equipment	116.6	-365.0	-1 099.7	-99.6	-224.5	-36.8	-10.7	171.4	-189.9	0.5
Other manufacturing	376.0	340.9	302.6	99.9	191.2	62.4	80.4	143.8	83.5	63.5
Electricity, gas, steam and air conditioning supply	**36.5**	**-98.5**	**30.7**	**91.1**	**-9.1**	**191.2**	**217.7**	**-383.6**	**1 881.2**	**-83.2**
Water supply; sewerage, waste management and remediation activities	**.. c**	**9.5**	**14.0**	**-14.5**	**16.0**	**.. c**	**0.8**	**.. c**	**.. c**	**-1.7**
Construction	**181.4**	**127.3**	**127.6**	**-18.9**	**59.6**	**55.1**	**108.6**	**104.7**	**-64.3**	**141.4**
Services	**4 184.0**	**4 144.8**	**6 129.2**	**5 693.3**	**4 402.9**	**7 592.7**	**3 354.9**	**3 416.2**	**3 615.2**	**2 595.2**
Wholesale and retail trade; repair of motor vehicles and motorcycles	960.4	1 441.5	1 679.2	1 157.9	598.7	903.4	326.4	494.4	335.3	449.5
Transportation and storage	-577.6	-377.0	82.2	142.2	152.6	107.8	104.6	142.3	-151.8	-631.5
Accommodation and food service activities	14.8	19.4	30.2	68.5	29.4	-21.6	14.5	64.4	22.4	14.2
Information and communication	741.8	437.6	1 279.0	957.0	828.2	2 533.5	1 673.9	1 378.2	1 598.0	2 148.2
Financial and insurance activities	2 390.8	2 305.7	1 929.2	2 162.2	2 103.2	114.8	479.8	346.5	583.7	100.9
Activities of holding companies	0.2	3.6	7.3	-	-	138.6	26.9	0.5	-	-
Real estate activities	154.6	448.4	1 231.5	733.0	396.7	1 498.2	613.2	668.0	509.9	339.0
Professional, scientific and technical activities	61.8	-266.9	17.9	235.3	185.9	2 208.9	-31.2	161.5	553.1	15.6
Administrative and support service activities	-9.2	94.9	-179.5	170.0	91.9	151.3	155.7	123.2	101.0	18.9
Public administration; activities of households and of extraterritorial organisations	-	-	-	-	-	2.1	10.5	21.6	47.2	120.7
Education	-	2.6	1.8	-	-	3.1	3.0	0.7	7.7	-1.6
Human health and social work activities	14.5	13.8	8.5	32.5	11.5	4.5	5.4	15.0	8.0	2.5
Arts, entertainment and recreation	29.4	16.9	26.0	33.1	5.9	-1.6	-0.7	.. c	.. c	.. c
Other services	12.0	8.0	23.3	2.0	-1.3	0.5	-	-1.7	3.7	12.3
Not allocated and confidential	**1.9**	**63.2**	**25.3**	**..**	**.. c**	**-9.1**	**168.1**	**.. c**	**..**	**10.8**
Private real estate activities	-	-	-	-	-	-	-	-	-	-

- Nil; .. Not available; c Confidential data

Note: Data excludes resident Special Purpose Entities (SPEs). Detailed metadata at: *http://stats.oecd.org/OECDStat_Metadata/ShowMetadata.ashx?Dataset=FDI_CTRY_IND_SUMM.*

Source: *OECD International Direct Investment Statistics (database): https://doi.org/10.1787/idi-data-en*

POLAND

Table 1. Foreign direct investment flows by country

Million US dollars

	Inward					Outward				
	2015	2016	2017	2018	2019	2015	2016	2017	2018	2019
WORLD	**15 268.0**	**15 706.8**	**9 172.4**	**15 997.7**	**10 852.2**	**4 994.6**	**11 598.3**	**2 169.5**	**891.1**	**1 290.2**
OECD COUNTRIES	**14 175.7**	**15 111.8**	**7 065.9**	**13 008.5**	**11 035.8**	**1 909.5**	**12 059.8**	**3 491.4**	**82.2**	**923.6**
Australia	11.4	-1.7	-4.7	6.8	10.3	-10.0	4.0	1.3	-6.9	-2.3
Austria	808.3	1 115.1	1 311.2	1 885.7	319.1	-68.2	7.0	67.7	0.6	-16.8
Belgium	596.0	753.0	-99.6	92.4	797.3	6.2	16.7	31.8	58.7	-1.8
Canada	33.8	-29.8	17.2	-5.5	27.2	611.2	3 150.6	457.9	-1 558.0	146.8
Chile	-0.6	0.9	-0.7	-8.3	7.7	145.7	229.2	159.9	43.2	47.4
Czech Republic	403.3	104.6	754.2	616.9	224.9	98.5	113.8	-172.5	1 219.3	175.8
Denmark	167.1	-99.0	-34.0	170.8	371.3	-68.6	283.1	50.7	-398.9	43.4
Estonia	6.5	3.5	-5.0	-4.6	34.5	-1.5	16.0	-23.3	64.3	-38.8
Finland	-38.8	-40.0	50.4	19.2	236.9	28.0	37.9	-1.3	6.7	86.5
France	-83.1	1 652.8	-913.9	-133.1	171.8	30.8	-28.4	-490.8	-352.0	-261.7
Germany	2 789.0	3 624.3	3 763.9	2 072.7	3 129.1	145.0	295.7	226.8	101.2	298.2
Greece	2.7	8.8	-10.2	8.5	-2.0	0.3	6.3	6.4	0.8	7.0
Hungary	132.2	-89.3	1 000.7	-331.6	481.6	162.0	927.9	173.2	241.6	-79.9
Iceland	0.4	7.1	6.0	-0.3	-6.3	0.0	-0.4	-0.3	0.0	0.2
Ireland	70.4	-577.5	225.5	-410.7	-108.7	46.5	-208.7	55.1	-12.7	108.2
Israel	114.2	77.2	-134.1	52.6	50.6	10.7	8.2	-101.7	2.4	4.9
Italy	121.0	-468.6	-2 184.3	187.4	508.1	35.9	6.1	-67.9	24.5	-1.4
Japan	-109.6	97.5	183.1	122.1	29.6	-7.6	0.5	-4.4	5.3	2.3
Korea	86.1	4.0	184.3	109.0	990.2	-1.7	-8.3	-15.3	3.2	-402.6
Latvia	13.1	12.3	27.0	16.3	44.0	9.6	24.1	24.5	6.2	7.6
Lithuania	15.6	14.9	27.0	142.6	-255.0	59.1	239.8	1.1	61.5	169.8
Luxembourg	2 031.2	2 140.1	2 159.1	1 817.5	1 527.4	-112.1	5 724.4	627.9	1 823.4	-1 446.8
Mexico	2.3	-41.1	-12.7	11.7	1.8	11.9	5.5	-27.2	15.0	-3.5
Netherlands	3 498.4	4 819.8	-1 739.1	9 077.8	2 790.0	236.9	296.4	39.0	-110.2	93.8
New Zealand	-0.2	-0.1	0.5	0.1	0.5	-0.1	0.0	-0.1	-0.3	0.0
Norway	-7.7	201.2	170.0	178.3	169.5	-297.0	-116.2	258.7	206.0	140.3
Poland	-	-	-	-	-	-	-	-	-	-
Portugal	-215.5	79.4	-6.5	226.1	82.2	14.8	1.3	-3.1	39.1	5.1
Slovak Republic	-246.9	-35.1	102.3	164.2	63.3	11.6	83.3	68.3	133.0	94.3
Slovenia	-6.8	-6.6	3.5	-10.2	-8.1	6.8	5.9	1.8	5.8	7.0
Spain	996.7	-203.6	498.1	-2 115.6	-48.9	65.3	80.8	130.3	154.4	284.4
Sweden	769.1	13.2	622.8	-660.3	-300.7	-448.9	984.8	1 927.6	-1 387.9	1 411.4
Switzerland	427.6	909.6	448.1	578.4	86.0	1 133.8	314.6	-55.9	-197.3	-74.8
Turkey	-9.7	33.0	14.8	-7.4	-5.5	24.5	31.9	8.5	-2.2	5.3
United Kingdom	2 636.1	916.4	-63.2	-519.2	-1 015.8	150.4	-218.7	42.4	-24.4	65.0
United States	-809.4	130.3	731.5	-341.9	631.7	-51.6	-15.5	95.5	-83.0	49.3
EUROPE	**15 790.9**	**15 537.7**	**8 046.7**	**15 814.3**	**8 829.1**	**4 354.2**	**8 091.2**	**1 403.2**	**2 601.5**	**1 399.3**
Bulgaria	-7.3	62.3	-31.3	-10.8	-27.3	11.8	139.3	-18.4	70.5	147.3
Croatia	12.0	18.6	-3.0	7.6	2.1	32.8	114.0	54.0	5.8	29.4
Cyprus	1 168.9	437.2	1 601.0	1 043.3	-50.9	2 997.5	-1 616.2	-1 835.5	369.2	-221.0
Malta	-230.1	46.1	290.2	1 693.7	41.6	101.6	182.2	-68.1	64.6	66.7
Romania	6.0	12.7	0.8	-35.1	-31.3	-75.4	132.0	102.6	228.1	171.1
Russian Federation	10.2	11.7	75.1	47.2	-236.6	53.2	17.0	74.5	3.9	35.0
Ukraine	-54.6	-27.0	-7.6	-16.6	-160.3	-24.0	57.3	122.3	139.4	99.8
AFRICA	**-5.1**	**39.2**	**34.2**	**2.2**	**-62.7**	**9.9**	**67.2**	**52.5**	**-139.3**	**4.0**
Northern Africa	-14.1	20.5	14.9	-3.6	-33.9	7.9	4.2	10.9	1.6	-0.1
Algeria	0.0	2.6	0.1	-0.5	0.7	-	0.1	0.0	-	-
Egypt	-5.2	19.2	9.2	6.7	1.2	0.3	2.3	0.7	-0.1	0.9
Libya	0.0	-	-	-	-	0.0	-	0.2	1.2	-0.5
Morocco	-6.7	0.8	2.6	-6.6	-31.8	0.8	2.7	11.7	1.2	0.1
Tunisia	-2.1	-2.1	3.0	-3.2	-4.0	6.8	-0.9	-1.7	-0.7	-0.5
Other African countries	9.0	18.8	19.3	5.6	-28.6	2.0	63.0	41.7	-139.8	4.1
Nigeria	0.5	-0.4	-0.1	-0.1	-0.5	0.3	0.8	1.1	0.4	-0.5
South Africa	0.8	-2.4	-1.6	-3.2	-4.9	0.5	65.4	37.4	-105.2	-2.2
AMERICA	**-758.1**	**14.5**	**785.6**	**-395.4**	**664.1**	**733.3**	**3 449.7**	**743.1**	**-1 535.6**	**312.2**
Northern America	-775.5	100.5	748.7	-347.3	658.9	559.6	3 135.1	553.4	-1 641.0	196.0
Central America and Caribbean countries	10.2	-90.9	35.9	-38.4	6.0	20.7	93.4	8.8	17.3	-35.8
Bahamas	-	-	-0.1	-1.8	1.8	42.2	86.1	47.8	6.8	-31.9
Bermuda	-36.2	-2.0	41.4	17.4	16.5	-	0.0	-	-	-
Cayman Islands	-1.8	25.5	6.7	-48.2	-25.3	-	0.1	-1.0	-	-
Costa Rica	0.5	-0.4	-	-0.4	0.6	-	-	-	-	0.0
El Salvador	-0.1	0.0	0.0	-	-0.1	-	-	-	-	-
Guatemala	-	-0.3	-	0.2	0.1	-	-	-	-	-
Honduras	-	-	-	-	-	-	0.1	-	-	-
Nicaragua	0.1	0.3	0.2	0.2	-1.7	-	-	-	-	-
Panama	2.3	-0.5	0.3	0.7	-0.8	0.3	-0.4	-9.3	-3.9	-0.8
Virgin Islands, U.S.	-	-	-	-	-	-	-	-	-	-
South America	7.3	4.9	1.1	-9.7	-0.8	153.0	221.2	179.3	88.1	152.0
Argentina	-1.2	3.0	-2.6	7.5	-2.7	-0.5	0.3	2.5	0.4	1.1
Bolivia	-	-	0.1	-0.2	-	-0.1	-	-	-	-
Brazil	7.6	3.5	0.6	-3.4	-6.5	8.5	-8.0	17.9	-2.4	5.8
Colombia	-0.3	-1.4	2.1	-2.7	1.2	-0.3	-0.5	-0.4	47.1	96.9
Ecuador	0.1	-	-	-0.1	0.0	-	-	-	-	-
Paraguay	-	-	-	-	0.0	-	-	-	-	-
Peru	1.2	-1.2	0.2	-0.3	-0.1	-0.2	0.1	-0.4	-0.3	0.6
Uruguay	0.6	0.1	1.8	-2.6	-0.4	0.0	0.1	-0.3	0.1	0.2
Venezuela	-0.2	0.1	-0.3	0.3	0.0	-	-	-	-	0.0

Table 1. Foreign direct investment flows by country *(cont.)*

Million US dollars

	Inward					Outward				
	2015	2016	2017	2018	2019	2015	2016	2017	2018	2019
ASIA	**254.0**	**116.8**	**316.2**	**568.0**	**1 413.9**	**-92.6**	**-13.8**	**-30.5**	**-28.3**	**-422.5**
Near and Middle East	123.0	59.0	-108.9	93.5	58.3	5.1	34.5	-77.9	59.0	46.5
Gulf Arabian countries	12.1	-15.2	25.6	40.2	6.3	-5.3	24.9	25.3	53.2	41.9
Kuwait	-0.3	1.2	-0.1	-0.8	4.2	-	-	-	-	0.0
Qatar	0.7	0.2	-0.2	0.4	0.8	0.0	0.0	-	-	-
Saudi Arabia	2.2	-1.8	-1.4	24.1	-5.8	0.1	0.1	-0.4	-1.3	1.7
United Arab Emirates	9.4	4.7	27.2	16.9	7.6	3.8	23.6	25.1	54.5	40.1
Other Near and Middle East	110.9	74.2	-134.5	53.3	52.0	10.3	9.6	-103.2	5.8	4.6
Jordan	0.0	-2.8	2.8	-0.5	0.4	-	-0.1	-	0.1	-
Other Asian countries	131.1	57.8	425.1	474.6	1 355.6	-97.7	-48.4	47.4	-87.3	-469.0
China	-2.2	13.8	56.9	93.4	90.2	-15.7	9.8	-7.2	6.5	-62.8
Hong Kong, China	159.1	-79.6	-25.7	30.7	247.5	-3.3	0.5	7.2	16.2	-16.3
India	6.4	18.9	20.1	-12.7	93.9	-9.4	4.9	22.4	21.9	18.5
Indonesia	0.4	-2.1	-0.2	-1.8	0.7	6.4	-0.6	-0.4	4.0	-1.4
Iran, Islamic Republic of	0.0	0.4	-0.2	-0.1	-	-	-	4.2	2.2	1.0
Malaysia	-14.3	-1.1	0.2	0.4	-2.7	-56.9	-0.3	-4.4	2.0	-0.9
Philippines	0.6	1.0	-82.3	-29.9	-7.5	-1.0	-0.4	0.0	0.3	0.5
Singapore	-11.0	-12.0	54.1	96.7	-71.9	1.2	-1.3	14.3	-137.8	2.9
Chinese Taipei	13.7	-0.9	-1.4	19.9	4.2	0.0	-0.2	0.2	-0.2	-0.3
Thailand	0.1	-3.0	46.3	58.5	0.4	0.3	6.2	-0.1	4.3	-3.9
Viet Nam	2.7	12.4	-11.2	-4.5	-1.3	6.0	-6.5	36.2	-0.8	1.8
AUSTRALIA, OCEANIA AND POLAR REGIONS	**10.3**	**-1.5**	**-8.5**	**1.1**	**13.7**	**-10.1**	**4.1**	**1.3**	**-7.2**	**-2.3**
WORLD unallocated and confidential	**-24.1**	**-**	**-1.7**	**7.5**	**-5.9**	**0.0**	**0.0**	**-0.1**	**0.1**	**-0.5**
European Union (EU28)	**15 415.3**	**14 315.4**	**7 347.4**	**15 011.6**	**8 976.5**	**3 476.6**	**7 646.8**	**950.3**	**2 393.0**	**1 203.9**
G20 countries excl. European Union	**4 692.0**	**5 961.9**	**1 862.7**	**1 653.6**	**4 406.8**	**981.9**	**3 312.2**	**373.4**	**-1 949.3**	**-108.8**
G20 OECD countries	**4 667.9**	**5 917.2**	**1 715.8**	**1 502.5**	**4 478.6**	**938.9**	**3 223.4**	**226.7**	**-1 877.2**	**-104.5**
G20 Non-OECD countries	**24.1**	**44.7**	**146.8**	**151.1**	**-71.8**	**42.9**	**88.8**	**146.7**	**-72.1**	**-4.2**
MENA countries	**-5.1**	**2.6**	**40.4**	**36.6**	**-26.3**	**2.7**	**29.0**	**36.1**	**54.8**	**42.1**
ASEAN countries	**-22.7**	**-2.7**	**6.7**	**117.9**	**-82.5**	**-43.3**	**-3.8**	**42.3**	**-127.6**	**-1.1**

- Nil

Note: Detailed metadata at: *http://stats.oecd.org/OECDStat_Metadata/ShowMetadata.ashx?Dataset=FDI_CTRY_IND_SUMM.*

Source: *OECD International Direct Investment Statistics (database): https://doi.org/10.1787/idi-data-en*

Table 2. Foreign direct investment positions by country

At year end

Million US dollars

	Inward					Outward				
	2015	2016	2017	2018	2019	2015	2016	2017	2018	2019
WORLD	**186 939.8**	**189 750.7**	**241 491.8**	**229 527.0**	**234 925.6**	**27 935.3**	**28 307.2**	**29 615.0**	**24 618.3**	**25 420.3**
OECD COUNTRIES	**181 896.6**	**166 906.9**	**210 833.9**	**201 076.5**	**206 916.9**	**14 439.6**	**19 546.2**	**21 753.3**	**17 761.9**	**16 997.0**
Australia	227.5	341.8	424.4	722.7	938.0	-4.8	7.6	5.4	-0.2	0.7
Austria	6 044.5	5 591.3	7 722.7	8 223.1	7 966.2	234.5	237.3	338.5	344.4	302.5
Belgium	1 869.7	1 810.1	2 961.0	2 999.2	3 016.3	694.1	-45.9	-150.7	-74.2	-61.0
Canada	2 466.5	1 627.5	2 078.3	2 009.3	2 321.1	753.0	1 960.6	1 862.3	-218.3	4.2
Chile	0.7	1.5	0.9	0.8	13.9	147.7	482.3	522.3	566.1	613.8
Czech Republic	1 012.5	917.0	1 279.1	1 428.9	1 289.2	1 823.4	2 038.3	3 495.6	2 788.4	2 996.7
Denmark	3 426.7	2 994.7	3 564.4	3 429.7	3 619.5	-5.2	299.0	414.1	38.8	73.8
Estonia	15.2	11.2	18.4	21.1	43.7	9.4	9.8	-12.2	48.4	9.1
Finland	2 036.8	1 924.5	2 208.7	2 047.5	2 039.2	39.7	97.6	111.9	106.1	193.2
France	24 032.8	19 054.9	23 780.8	23 528.8	24 328.3	-21.2	707.6	307.9	-11.9	49.7
Germany	34 696.4	37 405.8	47 930.0	46 171.0	45 464.3	1 217.0	1 305.8	1 639.5	1 606.9	1 529.7
Greece	605.5	213.9	236.9	228.1	232.4	0.3	7.6	14.3	15.1	16.1
Hungary	188.5	149.9	269.6	294.1	499.4	522.8	1 366.7	1 659.4	2 009.6	1 496.0
Iceland	68.7	22.7	39.2	38.1	35.5	-0.1	-0.4	-0.7	0.1	-0.2
Ireland	607.6	642.2	757.3	945.6	688.4	28.0	-178.9	80.7	11.7	47.4
Israel	841.9	792.8	943.2	1 087.6	1 296.7	178.3	269.8	152.8	137.8	264.6
Italy	10 635.5	7 641.2	4 916.3	5 167.7	5 033.7	112.4	107.1	138.8	152.8	146.7
Japan	3 759.9	4 118.6	6 167.7	5 286.4	6 177.5	-12.1	-3.0	-6.5	-1.0	0.4
Korea	1 949.1	1 208.6	1 747.0	1 853.9	2 273.4	3.9	-7.7	-15.7	-17.8	-421.1
Latvia	78.3	60.1	85.9	103.7	81.3	93.7	109.8	144.5	140.2	144.0
Lithuania	133.2	249.8	292.9	499.4	224.6	869.4	1 057.2	1 074.2	1 110.4	1 237.2
Luxembourg	2 651.8	1 824.6	2 338.2	2 276.4	2 527.3	6 820.8	7 656.0	6 259.6	6 264.1	5 056.0
Mexico	0.4	-5.1	-8.3	14.5	26.9	11.8	16.1	-6.2	6.5	1.7
Netherlands	18 276.2	16 044.0	23 052.9	20 463.8	22 693.9	2 368.8	2 204.6	2 394.2	2 506.1	1 459.0
New Zealand	4.9	3.0	4.1	3.9	3.7	0.4	0.4	0.4	-	0.0
Norway	852.1	832.4	1 669.3	1 673.9	1 841.0	513.9	409.8	553.3	593.9	782.3
Poland	7 269.2	9 691.0	10 769.0	8 782.0	11 764.6	-	-	-	-	-
Portugal	2 361.3	2 236.6	2 949.5	2 844.2	2 457.1	45.6	47.5	60.7	73.3	66.6
Slovak Republic	3.1	264.5	658.9	659.7	751.6	335.3	419.5	562.3	799.9	682.8
Slovenia	78.4	66.9	71.4	74.5	72.3	10.7	15.9	18.6	26.4	22.8
Spain	8 556.2	8 476.1	11 721.2	10 510.2	10 090.6	-63.8	70.8	-37.9	316.8	458.7
Sweden	4 938.4	3 647.5	4 625.5	4 952.5	5 252.0	-5 803.1	-4 684.3	-3 312.8	-4 239.9	-2 568.4
Switzerland	6 384.0	5 045.7	6 308.3	6 183.7	6 538.0	2 279.1	2 558.7	2 376.4	570.8	464.0
Turkey	74.7	85.0	111.7	106.4	119.9	271.6	273.3	271.4	260.9	262.1
United Kingdom	12 323.9	11 723.0	13 863.9	12 031.0	12 053.5	1 096.0	892.6	1 101.9	1 108.7	1 136.7
United States	23 636.0	20 441.6	25 566.4	24 413.1	23 142.0	831.5	894.3	809.1	721.0	529.1
EUROPE	**150 591.4**	**139 486.0**	**176 173.8**	**166 288.8**	**171 169.0**	**24 935.3**	**23 425.6**	**24 822.6**	**21 832.3**	**23 073.5**
Bulgaria	6.5	8.1	21.4	15.2	20.9	57.4	92.4	83.6	147.8	168.8
Croatia	30.4	44.8	59.8	75.3	79.2	105.0	148.4	223.0	218.1	216.5
Cyprus	-	-	-	-	-	9 221.5	3 643.9	1 854.0	1 646.4	3 222.3
Malta	336.7	-	-	-	-	593.3	815.8	822.6	791.2	780.9
Romania	1.7	-3.0	-8.4	-12.8	-17.0	510.1	599.6	803.0	974.2	995.0
Russian Federation	1 048.0	841.4	991.1	775.5	780.8	681.3	720.7	913.1	738.3	821.6
Ukraine	-91.2	-49.4	-230.3	-286.1	-465.4	18.4	15.1	122.5	219.5	352.5
AFRICA	**211.8**	**1 173.4**	**544.7**	**637.8**	**675.2**	**226.0**	**280.9**	**311.6**	**212.9**	**211.1**
Northern Africa	6.7	5.9	10.7	8.2	2.5	30.5	57.2	73.5	73.5	68.5
Algeria	-	-	-	-	-	0.1	0.2	0.2	-	-
Egypt	-	-	-	-	-	-23.3	2.8	1.6	0.7	2.0
Libya	-	-	-	-	-	-0.7	-0.7	-0.6	0.5	0.2
Morocco	6.7	5.9	10.7	8.2	2.5	47.8	49.6	66.7	65.5	65.3
Tunisia	-	-	-	-	-	6.6	5.4	5.6	6.8	1.0
Other African countries	205.1	1 167.5	534.0	629.6	672.7	195.5	223.7	238.1	139.4	142.6
Nigeria	-	-	-	-	-	3.5	4.5	4.9	5.3	4.8
South Africa	133.3	1 167.5	534.0	629.8	670.8	1.5	64.1	117.5	7.7	5.8
AMERICA	**26 197.5**	**22 069.1**	**27 639.1**	**26 442.0**	**25 507.7**	**1 847.9**	**3 537.5**	**3 438.3**	**1 379.3**	**1 534.7**
Northern America	26 102.5	22 069.1	27 644.7	26 422.4	25 463.1	1 584.5	2 854.9	2 671.4	502.7	533.3
Central America and Caribbean countries	91.9	-3.7	-6.7	16.0	28.5	80.8	174.6	198.2	216.8	188.6
Bahamas	-	-	-	-	-	73.6	161.3	214.5	221.4	183.6
Bermuda	56.7	-	-	-	-	-	-	-	-	-
Cayman Islands	-	-	-	-	-	-	0.0	-	-	0.1
Costa Rica	-	-	-	-	-	-	-	-	-	0.0
El Salvador	-	-	-	-	-	-	-	-	-	-
Guatemala	-	-	-	-	-	-	-	-	-	-
Honduras	-	-	-	-	-	-	-	-	-	-
Nicaragua	-	-	-	-	-	-	-	-	-	-
Panama	8.5	-	-	-	-	10.7	10.5	4.2	3.7	3.7
Virgin Islands, U.S.	-	-	-	-	-	-	-	-	-	-
South America	3.1	3.7	1.0	3.6	16.1	182.6	508.0	569.3	659.8	812.7
Argentina	-	-	-	-	-	1.1	0.9	0.7	0.8	1.6
Bolivia	-	-	-	-	-	-0.1	-	-	-	-
Brazil	-	0.0	0.1	-0.7	-0.9	32.3	23.8	45.5	46.4	52.6
Colombia	-	-	-	-	-	-0.7	-1.1	-1.4	45.4	142.8
Ecuador	-	-	-	-	-	-	-	-	-	-
Paraguay	-	-	-	-	-	-	-	-	-	-
Peru	-	-	-	-	-	2.3	1.8	2.2	1.0	1.7
Uruguay	2.4	2.3	-	3.4	3.1	0.1	0.3	-	0.1	0.3
Venezuela	-	-	-	-	-	-	-	-	-	-

Table 2. Foreign direct investment positions by country *(cont.)*

At year end

Million US dollars

	Inward					Outward				
	2015	2016	2017	2018	2019	2015	2016	2017	2018	2019
ASIA	**9 112.8**	**8 323.8**	**11 571.6**	**11 384.5**	**13 440.1**	**930.4**	**1 055.1**	**1 036.7**	**1 194.6**	**601.8**
Near and Middle East	1 125.0	1 027.8	1 198.2	1 218.3	1 402.8	320.7	441.7	356.0	352.4	485.8
Gulf Arabian countries	259.2	213.3	230.7	106.6	94.3	141.0	169.2	201.6	209.0	216.4
Kuwait	49.6	46.5	49.9	43.6	41.2	0.0	0.0	0.0	0.0	-
Qatar	167.8	137.5	169.1	20.7	21.7	-	-	-	-	-
Saudi Arabia	40.6	25.1	1.0	16.8	21.8	0.8	0.9	0.5	0.1	1.9
United Arab Emirates	1.2	4.3	10.7	25.5	9.6	141.5	168.6	200.9	208.8	214.5
Other Near and Middle East	865.8	814.5	967.5	1 111.7	1 308.5	179.7	272.5	154.4	143.3	269.4
Jordan	-	-	-	-	-	-	-0.1	-0.1	-	-
Other Asian countries	7 987.8	7 296.0	10 373.4	10 166.2	12 037.3	609.6	613.4	680.7	842.1	115.9
China	927.5	707.2	847.8	935.4	1 187.9	80.1	87.5	83.9	239.5	182.5
Hong Kong, China	517.8	412.2	454.1	271.7	341.5	5.4	8.7	1.3	17.8	-26.5
India	206.6	251.5	271.8	276.2	315.5	235.1	236.1	250.6	246.6	243.2
Indonesia	-	-	-	-	-	26.3	26.2	22.9	27.0	25.3
Iran, Islamic Republic of	-	5.9	12.6	-	-	-	-	6.0	8.8	9.4
Malaysia	10.7	259.2	246.3	728.0	554.6	27.5	28.2	26.3	33.4	31.9
Philippines	52.8	44.6	51.3	45.5	47.4	7.3	8.2	8.1	8.2	8.5
Singapore	234.8	24.4	235.1	427.3	820.6	97.0	122.7	126.3	118.4	-13.6
Chinese Taipei	295.8	234.4	268.1	282.4	261.1	0.1	-0.1	0.4	0.1	-1.2
Thailand	32.9	26.8	63.8	35.4	38.0	10.6	15.8	17.8	21.8	19.6
Viet Nam	-	2.5	2.2	18.3	19.6	16.4	0.1	44.8	18.9	18.5
AUSTRALIA, OCEANIA AND POLAR REGIONS	**232.4**	**344.8**	**428.5**	**726.4**	**941.3**	**-4.3**	**8.1**	**5.9**	**-0.2**	**0.7**
WORLD unallocated and confidential	**593.8**	**18 353.6**	**25 134.1**	**24 047.7**	**23 192.2**	**0.0**	**-**	**-**	**-0.7**	**-1.4**
European Union (EU28)	**142 217.0**	**132 690.3**	**166 147.5**	**157 759.9**	**162 272.5**	**20 916.0**	**19 041.6**	**20 089.2**	**18 919.8**	**19 878.8**
G20 countries excl. European Union	**116 158.7**	**106 635.5**	**129 224.2**	**123 937.8**	**124 854.3**	**5 317.7**	**7 314.5**	**7 542.9**	**4 913.9**	**4 574.3**
G20 OECD countries	**113 802.8**	**103 643.0**	**126 578.4**	**121 304.8**	**121 878.5**	**4 259.1**	**6 154.3**	**6 108.1**	**3 607.4**	**3 239.8**
G20 Non-OECD countries	**2 355.9**	**2 992.6**	**2 645.8**	**2 633.0**	**2 975.9**	**1 058.5**	**1 160.2**	**1 434.8**	**1 306.4**	**1 334.5**
MENA countries	**289.8**	**235.1**	**257.0**	**129.4**	**98.2**	**171.6**	**226.5**	**275.0**	**282.6**	**284.9**
ASEAN countries	**331.1**	**357.6**	**598.7**	**1 254.5**	**1 480.2**	**185.8**	**201.2**	**242.6**	**228.0**	**90.0**

- Nil

Note: Inward FDI positions are allocated according to the ultimate investing country. Detailed metadata at: *http://stats.oecd.org/OECDStat_Metadata/ShowMetadata.ashx?Dataset=FDI_CTRY_IND_SUMM.*

Source: *OECD International Direct Investment Statistics (database): https://doi.org/10.1787/idi-data-en*

POLAND

Table 3. Foreign direct investment income by country

Million US dollars

	Inward					Outward				
	2015	2016	2017	2018	2019	2015	2016	2017	2018	2019
WORLD	**17 905.4**	**20 777.9**	**21 490.7**	**23 474.4**	**22 805.7**	**814.8**	**1 004.5**	**2 286.9**	**2 182.1**	**2 043.9**
OECD COUNTRIES	**17 773.7**	**20 062.0**	**20 394.5**	**22 780.7**	**22 338.7**	**106.6**	**421.2**	**1 495.3**	**1 492.7**	**1 428.1**
Australia	1.9	2.0	1.9	-1.6	-0.1	-5.7	-2.0	-1.3	0.0	0.0
Austria	707.0	503.1	795.3	637.0	440.4	19.5	6.5	-1.7	-4.2	-6.4
Belgium	442.9	399.8	371.6	339.8	457.2	12.8	7.3	-2.4	-7.1	-5.4
Canada	32.1	29.2	25.3	23.1	26.7	12.0	-1 722.5	552.5	28.7	73.2
Chile	0.0	0.0	-	-	-	-1.5	31.5	39.3	47.5	47.3
Czech Republic	100.8	116.8	94.8	131.4	104.7	110.3	170.1	234.7	224.4	202.8
Denmark	350.9	271.9	307.1	327.5	432.7	18.5	2.7	-1.1	-6.0	30.0
Estonia	2.4	2.2	-8.3	-10.8	1.8	0.8	1.4	0.0	-0.6	-3.8
Finland	185.6	168.4	221.4	290.8	268.3	-0.1	11.1	8.8	4.3	4.7
France	1 730.5	1 672.3	1 991.5	1 859.1	1 879.2	-14.1	6.7	2.9	-22.2	-72.9
Germany	3 635.0	4 030.0	4 479.1	4 723.8	4 870.6	76.0	230.2	156.2	305.0	159.7
Greece	5.5	5.8	2.3	2.2	6.0	-0.1	0.0	-0.5	0.3	0.4
Hungary	28.1	28.1	79.0	38.2	67.8	41.4	58.5	93.7	249.6	183.6
Iceland	1.8	-0.4	1.3	0.6	-0.3	-	-	-	-	-
Ireland	60.5	134.9	129.9	143.7	154.7	-0.8	-0.2	0.3	2.9	72.6
Israel	0.8	4.0	13.9	13.0	33.2	9.3	9.0	1.1	0.4	8.2
Italy	882.7	897.5	731.6	700.8	624.5	-2.8	0.1	-85.5	-21.8	-13.9
Japan	30.2	37.3	193.6	63.4	71.0	-	-	-	-	-
Korea	73.9	59.3	89.4	85.6	153.8	0.7	-0.1	-0.2	-1.3	-0.8
Latvia	16.2	27.3	50.3	48.1	58.5	11.0	9.6	13.0	16.7	18.3
Lithuania	11.5	6.8	17.8	-13.8	35.0	332.3	286.8	323.1	105.2	133.5
Luxembourg	1 958.3	2 812.0	2 351.8	3 336.0	3 174.6	-61.7	1 727.8	128.7	279.4	384.0
Mexico	0.2	0.1	0.4	1.2	0.8	-0.6	-2.8	-0.4	3.3	2.6
Netherlands	4 027.0	4 807.1	4 606.6	6 262.0	5 742.8	-6.7	30.3	84.4	59.4	27.7
New Zealand	-0.1	0.0	-0.1	-0.2	-0.1	-	-	-	-	-
Norway	102.0	14.2	135.2	161.1	138.2	71.1	-10.8	213.9	208.6	120.3
Poland	-	-	-	-	-	-	-	-	-	-
Portugal	138.8	116.0	117.6	139.0	114.6	7.8	6.9	1.1	1.6	2.5
Slovak Republic	24.9	17.2	13.2	27.3	38.3	47.2	58.5	69.0	104.2	128.4
Slovenia	7.8	7.2	7.6	7.1	8.5	2.5	3.0	1.9	1.4	3.1
Spain	710.9	736.7	821.4	812.3	691.5	-18.3	19.0	10.8	18.9	-3.2
Sweden	863.5	661.7	360.1	422.8	470.2	-116.4	-111.4	-82.8	-140.5	-72.3
Switzerland	505.5	676.0	704.0	707.1	699.4	42.9	31.5	78.0	36.4	7.0
Turkey	0.5	0.6	-3.4	-2.6	-2.2	2.0	28.4	4.2	2.0	5.5
United Kingdom	972.4	902.6	1 197.5	1 047.9	978.2	4.8	-190.5	-4.3	0.1	15.2
United States	189.4	920.8	511.8	457.7	598.1	-143.9	11.4	-18.8	-3.8	-23.6
EUROPE	**17 546.8**	**19 706.8**	**20 591.3**	**22 739.7**	**21 787.6**	**924.6**	**2 661.2**	**1 656.8**	**2 021.2**	**1 843.8**
Bulgaria	-0.1	-4.8	-5.4	-4.7	2.9	6.2	3.1	15.7	19.9	152.4
Croatia	4.2	3.2	6.5	7.7	8.8	-0.6	3.0	8.6	14.6	13.8
Cyprus	95.1	588.0	915.2	545.1	478.4	286.3	133.4	57.7	32.7	-83.8
Malta	-15.7	58.6	95.7	51.4	-23.1	44.3	22.4	82.4	224.9	85.9
Romania	-2.1	0.2	1.6	2.2	3.0	-53.2	-30.7	51.6	80.8	160.9
Russian Federation	4.0	24.9	19.4	13.7	5.5	41.0	33.5	57.9	36.5	38.0
Ukraine	-15.9	-14.1	-13.7	-14.6	-157.1	5.3	80.9	93.0	129.0	129.9
AFRICA	**-12.7**	**1.2**	**2.2**	**3.4**	**3.6**	**3.3**	**-5.1**	**8.0**	**6.2**	**5.6**
Northern Africa	-0.3	0.2	0.8	0.6	0.5	3.8	4.6	4.5	2.8	1.1
Algeria	-0.1	-0.1	-	-	-	-	-	-	-	-
Egypt	-	-	-	-	-	0.2	2.3	0.7	0.0	0.5
Libya	-	-	-	-	-	0.1	-0.1	0.1	0.4	-
Morocco	-0.3	0.2	0.8	0.6	0.5	3.6	3.2	5.4	3.1	0.7
Tunisia	-	-	-	-	-	-0.1	-0.8	-1.7	-0.7	-0.1
Other African countries	-12.4	1.0	1.4	2.7	3.1	-0.5	-9.7	3.5	3.5	4.5
Nigeria	-	-	-	-	-	0.1	0.0	0.1	0.2	0.2
South Africa	-	-	-	0.3	-	-0.2	-2.6	1.8	0.2	-0.5
AMERICA	**220.8**	**912.8**	**544.3**	**503.6**	**646.3**	**-128.9**	**-1 681.2**	**570.2**	**81.8**	**116.6**
Northern America	221.6	950.1	537.1	480.8	624.8	-131.9	-1 711.1	533.7	24.9	49.5
Central America and Caribbean countries	-0.3	-37.1	7.3	22.9	21.4	3.8	-2.8	-3.0	10.4	14.3
Bahamas	-	-	1.6	-	-	4.4	0.9	7.4	10.6	12.6
Bermuda	-3.1	-6.5	0.1	17.4	16.0	-	-	-	-	-
Cayman Islands	3.1	-33.5	-3.9	1.2	1.1	-	-	-0.9	-	-
Costa Rica	-	-	-	-	-	-	-	-	-	-
El Salvador	-	-	-	-	-	-	-	-	-	-
Guatemala	-	-	-	-	-	-	-	-	-	-
Honduras	-	-	-	-	-	-	-	-	-	-
Nicaragua	0.1	0.1	0.2	0.2	0.1	-	-	-	-	-
Panama	0.1	0.3	-0.1	-0.1	-0.1	0.2	-0.5	-9.7	-3.5	-0.7
Virgin Islands, U.S.	-	-	-	-	-	-	-	-	-	-
South America	-0.4	-0.2	-	-0.2	0.1	-0.9	32.7	39.5	46.5	52.7
Argentina	-	-	-	-	-	-0.4	0.0	0.2	0.1	0.3
Bolivia	-	-	-	-	-	-	-	-	-	-
Brazil	-	-	-	-	-0.1	1.2	1.3	0.2	-	0.2
Colombia	-	-	-	-	-	-0.1	-0.2	-0.1	-1.1	4.5
Ecuador	-	-	-	-	-	-	-	-	-	-
Paraguay	-	-	-	-	-	-	-	-	-	-
Peru	-	-	-	-	-	-0.1	-0.1	-0.1	-0.1	0.3
Uruguay	-0.5	-0.2	-	-0.2	0.2	0.0	0.1	-0.1	-	-
Venezuela	-	-	-	-	-	-	-	-	-	-

Table 3. Foreign direct investment income by country *(cont.)*

Million US dollars

	Inward					Outward				
	2015	2016	2017	2018	2019	2015	2016	2017	2018	2019
ASIA	**148.7**	**155.0**	**352.9**	**229.7**	**368.5**	**21.4**	**31.6**	**53.4**	**73.1**	**78.0**
Near and Middle East	23.3	16.9	27.9	29.6	46.3	29.7	41.9	25.2	49.0	51.6
Gulf Arabian countries	25.2	12.7	17.0	17.4	13.6	20.5	33.1	24.1	48.5	43.3
Kuwait	1.2	1.0	1.9	0.9	0.9	-	-	-	-	-
Qatar	-	-	-	-	0.3	-	-	-	-	-
Saudi Arabia	-	-0.2	-0.3	-0.1	-0.2	-	-	-0.1	-0.4	-0.2
United Arab Emirates	20.1	11.9	15.4	16.5	12.6	23.4	33.6	24.2	48.9	43.5
Other Near and Middle East	-1.9	4.2	10.9	12.3	32.7	9.2	8.8	1.1	0.4	8.4
Jordan	-	-	-	-	-	-	-	-	-	-
Other Asian countries	125.4	138.1	325.0	200.1	322.2	-8.3	-10.4	28.2	24.1	26.4
China	-2.3	5.2	8.2	17.4	9.4	-4.2	-4.4	-4.4	-5.4	6.8
Hong Kong, China	9.8	0.6	17.9	18.5	19.7	-2.0	-0.6	-5.8	2.9	-0.1
India	10.2	17.3	17.5	13.0	77.0	14.9	14.1	12.8	25.8	29.2
Indonesia	-	-	-	-2.5	-	0.6	-2.0	-1.0	0.6	1.2
Iran, Islamic Republic of	-	0.3	-	-	-	-	-	0.0	0.1	0.3
Malaysia	1.0	0.9	-0.1	-0.4	-	-1.2	-1.0	0.2	-0.7	-0.5
Philippines	-	-0.1	-	0.1	-	-	0.6	0.1	0.0	0.4
Singapore	0.1	5.8	-3.0	3.7	-10.6	8.6	10.5	29.1	9.1	-0.2
Chinese Taipei	0.8	2.2	2.3	-1.6	-0.9	-	0.0	0.0	-	-0.2
Thailand	1.1	-	0.4	4.8	4.3	1.9	2.0	-1.3	0.9	-2.6
Viet Nam	0.6	9.5	-1.1	-2.0	-1.6	-	-	0.2	3.2	2.3
AUSTRALIA, OCEANIA AND POLAR REGIONS	**1.8**	**2.1**	**-0.5**	**-2.5**	**-1.9**	**-5.7**	**-2.0**	**-1.3**	**0.0**	**0.0**
WORLD unallocated and confidential	**0.0**	**-**	**0.5**	**0.6**	**1.6**	**0.0**	**0.0**	**-0.2**	**-0.3**	**-**
European Union (EU28)	**16 944.4**	**18 970.6**	**19 752.6**	**21 873.8**	**21 090.1**	**746.7**	**2 465.7**	**1 166.2**	**1 543.9**	**1 517.7**
G20 countries excl. European Union	**7 560.7**	**8 599.2**	**9 263.2**	**9 000.2**	**9 292.3**	**-18.7**	**-1 601.1**	**672.7**	**347.3**	**219.8**
G20 OECD countries	**7 548.8**	**8 551.9**	**9 218.6**	**8 958.4**	**9 200.6**	**-71.7**	**-1 641.1**	**605.3**	**290.0**	**144.9**
G20 Non-OECD countries	**11.9**	**47.3**	**44.6**	**41.7**	**91.6**	**52.9**	**40.0**	**67.4**	**57.3**	**75.0**
MENA countries	**22.1**	**13.1**	**14.9**	**17.5**	**13.7**	**24.3**	**37.7**	**28.6**	**51.3**	**44.4**
ASEAN countries	**2.8**	**15.9**	**-3.8**	**3.8**	**-7.9**	**9.9**	**10.1**	**24.1**	**13.5**	**0.4**

- Nil

Note: Detailed metadata at: *http://stats.oecd.org/OECDStat_Metadata/ShowMetadata.ashx?Dataset=FDI_CTRY_IND_SUMM.*

Source: *OECD International Direct Investment Statistics (database): https://doi.org/10.1787/idi-data-en*

Table 4. Foreign direct investment flows by industrial sector

Million US dollars

	Inward					Outward				
	2015	2016	2017	2018	2019	2015	2016	2017	2018	2019
All FDI activities	**15 268.0**	**15 706.8**	**9 172.4**	**15 997.7**	**10 852.2**	**4 994.6**	**11 598.3**	**2 169.5**	**891.1**	**1 290.2**
Agriculture, forestry and fishing	**31.4**	**67.6**	**142.5**	**-7.6**	**-27.9**	**-0.6**	**-13.1**	**-8.4**	**16.7**	**3.2**
Mining and quarrying	**-82.2**	**43.1**	**86.8**	**170.6**	**-195.0**	**1 245.1**	**3 287.1**	**918.4**	**-661.6**	**395.5**
Extraction activities	-89.8	-3.4	12.6	112.4	-18.7	89.1	466.0	323.7	208.4	64.2
Manufacturing	**3 155.4**	**3 829.9**	**4 679.8**	**5 634.0**	**5 899.0**	**-280.4**	**52.1**	**96.1**	**2 028.7**	**39.2**
of which:										
Food products, beverages and tobacco	465.0	1 102.8	606.4	493.9	208.5	-97.0	-33.5	54.6	73.3	43.3
Textiles, wood and paper products; printing	586.3	-221.4	640.1	503.5	579.5	54.5	241.6	-44.5	27.1	84.6
Chemical, rubber, plastic, non-metallic mineral products	-257.5	-255.6	802.0	830.0	819.5	-235.7	-238.2	-262.3	1 558.8	151.5
Metal and machinery products, except electrical equipment	528.9	1 222.8	947.6	1 467.9	1 334.8	16.1	283.7	244.7	525.8	165.5
Motor vehicles, trailers, semi-trailers, other transport equipment	1 231.4	1 258.7	1 052.2	933.3	1 351.8	66.2	-274.2	110.9	-214.4	28.9
Other manufacturing	601.3	722.7	631.5	1 405.5	1 604.9	-84.4	72.8	-7.2	58.1	-434.7
Electricity, gas, steam and air conditioning supply	**-71.5**	**-478.1**	**-1 382.1**	**293.4**	**728.0**	**-401.9**	**1.9**	**524.5**	**-226.0**	**726.0**
Water supply; sewerage, waste management and remediation activities	**14.8**	**5.3**	**26.8**	**30.0**	**3.7**	**1.0**	**4.8**	**11.5**	**18.0**	**1.1**
Construction	**338.4**	**889.2**	**953.6**	**1 060.8**	**370.9**	**133.3**	**446.5**	**-12.8**	**51.6**	**66.3**
Services	**11 629.4**	**12 067.6**	**5 310.5**	**7 471.1**	**4 225.1**	**3 714.8**	**7 691.5**	**836.9**	**135.5**	**26.3**
Wholesale and retail trade; repair of motor vehicles and motorcycles	2 883.7	2 369.8	-1 434.0	3 820.0	1 713.3	226.3	1 153.5	515.4	128.0	723.8
Transportation and storage	294.1	-11.1	583.4	690.9	63.5	197.6	114.3	65.5	27.9	105.6
Accommodation and food service activities	39.7	2.1	89.1	227.8	721.0	198.2	154.1	103.6	40.6	102.1
Information and communication	1 737.8	3 330.6	1 875.1	-1 699.7	-542.7	-396.4	1 750.0	1 010.2	66.0	87.7
Financial and insurance activities	1 675.4	1 377.2	2 960.4	795.3	-387.0	4 784.5	-1 055.5	-455.6	432.5	-322.2
Activities of holding companies	1 034.6	854.9	4 159.7	307.6	-721.2	4 165.7	-225.6	-298.8	524.5	-1 103.0
Real estate activities	1 862.6	1 670.1	1 640.5	1 033.1	1 146.6	445.3	840.2	-150.5	-164.0	135.7
Professional, scientific and technical activities	2 874.2	3 118.0	-822.2	2 065.2	1 013.0	-1 635.2	2 816.1	-371.9	-71.8	-544.1
Administrative and support service activities	171.2	106.8	302.8	294.6	172.5	-70.9	2 049.8	124.8	-326.9	-245.8
Public administration; activities of households and of extraterritorial organisations	-1.8	-	-	-	-	-	-	-4.2	-	-
Education	-5.0	8.4	2.0	3.2	6.7	4.9	-17.1	-3.4	0.2	6.7
Human health and social work activities	77.0	51.9	46.9	83.6	218.5	1.3	-0.4	2.4	17.3	6.5
Arts, entertainment and recreation	5.9	36.6	40.7	152.2	81.2	1.4	2.9	2.7	-2.9	-15.9
Other services	14.6	7.0	25.8	5.3	18.5	-42.1	-116.5	-2.1	-11.3	-13.8
Not allocated and confidential	**252.3**	**-717.7**	**-645.5**	**1 345.3**	**-151.6**	**583.5**	**127.6**	**-196.7**	**-471.6**	**32.5**
Private real estate activities	-	-	-	-	-	-	-	-	-	-

- Nil

Note: Detailed metadata at: *http://stats.oecd.org/OECDStat_Metadata/ShowMetadata.ashx?Dataset=FDI_CTRY_IND_SUMM.*

Source: *OECD International Direct Investment Statistics (database): https://doi.org/10.1787/idi-data-en*

Table 5. Foreign direct investment positions by industrial sector

At year end

Million US dollars

	Inward					Outward				
	2015	2016	2017	2018	2019	2015	2016	2017	2018	2019
All FDI activities	**186 939.8**	**189 750.7**	**241 491.8**	**229 527.0**	**234 925.6**	**27 935.3**	**28 307.2**	**29 615.0**	**24 618.3**	**25 420.3**
Agriculture, forestry and fishing	**992.3**	**979.8**	**1 220.4**	**1 101.2**	**1 067.7**	**11.8**	**4.2**	**4.2**	**23.5**	**22.2**
Mining and quarrying	**569.3**	**512.5**	**592.1**	**772.1**	**550.9**	**2 516.1**	**2 903.6**	**2 937.0**	**1 673.4**	**1 874.2**
Extraction activities	224.1	70.4	95.9	224.8	202.9	624.5	1 012.3	1 306.7	1 241.7	1 066.2
Manufacturing	**60 201.9**	**59 236.6**	**77 743.9**	**72 799.0**	**76 469.6**	**3 876.0**	**4 213.9**	**5 382.8**	**5 224.1**	**4 611.7**
of which:										
Food products, beverages and tobacco	11 079.0	11 805.9	15 861.6	13 006.9	13 859.6	734.9	689.8	705.9	768.0	343.1
Textiles, wood and paper products; printing	6 623.1	5 937.7	7 479.9	7 000.7	7 376.9	247.2	366.3	308.8	278.5	358.4
Chemical, rubber, plastic, non-metallic mineral products	10 946.1	9 490.6	12 591.5	11 884.8	11 613.8	1 346.0	1 312.6	2 089.6	1 628.2	1 834.5
Metal and machinery products, except electrical equipment	10 651.0	10 902.1	14 251.4	14 037.4	14 775.2	836.0	1 063.9	1 387.2	1 790.9	1 849.0
Motor vehicles, trailers, semi-trailers, other transport equipment	11 253.6	11 594.5	14 940.1	14 964.5	15 555.8	556.2	497.0	589.3	469.6	389.0
Other manufacturing	9 649.2	9 505.8	12 619.3	11 904.7	13 288.3	155.6	284.4	302.1	289.0	-162.3
Electricity, gas, steam and air conditioning supply	**6 631.3**	**5 438.8**	**5 206.9**	**4 964.7**	**5 624.7**	**-1 496.8**	**-1 329.4**	**-926.1**	**-1 040.0**	**-72.5**
Water supply; sewerage, waste management and remediation activities	**414.0**	**418.0**	**528.9**	**524.8**	**496.0**	**2.6**	**20.2**	**36.2**	**38.0**	**41.9**
Construction	**9 218.0**	**9 028.9**	**12 178.6**	**12 556.1**	**13 172.9**	**-20.3**	**443.8**	**601.3**	**586.2**	**605.3**
Services	**107 959.6**	**114 115.0**	**145 042.2**	**136 932.4**	**134 830.3**	**22 809.3**	**21 557.4**	**21 164.4**	**17 745.5**	**17 851.8**
Wholesale and retail trade; repair of motor vehicles and motorcycles	28 551.3	28 387.8	33 784.8	33 825.1	35 011.5	1 597.9	2 786.1	3 513.9	3 585.5	3 316.7
Transportation and storage	2 619.9	2 184.1	3 097.5	3 891.8	3 326.6	542.5	620.0	724.0	668.7	782.3
Accommodation and food service activities	974.7	968.2	1 438.9	1 701.9	2 480.7	99.2	197.7	346.6	499.5	636.0
Information and communication	10 302.0	12 560.0	15 416.5	12 728.5	12 915.3	-1 933.8	-25.1	640.5	665.4	814.5
Financial and insurance activities	33 638.0	34 432.9	49 361.0	41 991.6	38 474.8	14 161.9	9 756.5	9 075.4	6 250.8	5 462.5
Activities of holding companies	2 759.2	3 631.0	8 155.9	7 530.0	7 649.8	10 488.8	6 729.7	5 511.8	3 478.8	2 356.9
Real estate activities	15 376.2	16 680.8	21 103.9	22 478.5	22 709.1	551.5	787.2	466.7	582.2	907.0
Professional, scientific and technical activities	12 711.7	15 524.7	16 479.5	15 773.9	14 942.2	3 480.0	5 856.4	4 755.8	4 545.8	5 246.1
Administrative and support service activities	2 558.7	2 347.9	3 004.6	3 043.4	3 127.0	3 802.5	1 221.1	1 260.7	603.1	350.7
Public administration; activities of households and of extraterritorial organisations	23.2	-	-	-	-	0.6	0.6	0.7	0.7	0.7
Education	15.7	13.5	12.2	27.2	28.1	30.0	8.0	-3.7	-4.3	2.7
Human health and social work activities	804.5	764.6	970.4	970.0	1 161.7	4.2	4.7	-8.3	19.7	26.5
Arts, entertainment and recreation	265.2	137.9	202.3	348.7	534.1	50.4	37.0	45.2	38.2	20.0
Other services	118.5	112.6	170.7	151.8	119.1	422.4	307.2	346.7	290.2	286.1
Not allocated and confidential	**0.0**	**-968.9**	**-2 130.8**	**-123.2**	**2 713.2**	**236.5**	**493.5**	**415.3**	**367.6**	**485.8**
Private real estate activities	-	-	-	-	-	-	-	-	-	-

- Nil

Note: Detailed metadata at: *http://stats.oecd.org/OECDStat_Metadata/ShowMetadata.ashx?Dataset=FDI_CTRY_IND_SUMM.*

Source: *OECD International Direct Investment Statistics (database): https://doi.org/10.1787/idi-data-en*

POLAND

Table 6. Foreign direct investment income by industrial sector

Million US dollars

	Inward					Outward				
	2015	2016	2017	2018	2019	2015	2016	2017	2018	2019
All FDI activities	**17 905.4**	**20 777.9**	**21 490.7**	**23 474.4**	**22 805.7**	**814.8**	**1 004.5**	**2 286.9**	**2 182.1**	**2 043.9**
Agriculture, forestry and fishing	**82.1**	**85.7**	**35.4**	**51.9**	**34.7**	**0.0**	**0.7**	**0.4**	**1.7**	**-0.1**
Mining and quarrying	**-130.2**	**-69.1**	**-41.4**	**34.4**	**-220.1**	**68.4**	**-1 659.0**	**784.4**	**317.1**	**274.6**
Extraction activities	-134.1	-41.2	-41.3	4.2	8.2	46.5	-20.7	193.0	198.3	103.8
Manufacturing	**7 474.9**	**7 876.9**	**8 380.4**	**9 055.7**	**8 736.2**	**246.3**	**638.2**	**595.3**	**437.9**	**408.3**
of which:										
Food products, beverages and tobacco	1 140.6	1 303.0	1 392.7	1 478.3	1 408.0	8.4	49.1	42.6	28.4	31.3
Textiles, wood and paper products; printing	895.5	792.1	873.0	1 056.9	1 001.1	6.0	103.4	31.3	88.7	51.1
Chemical, rubber, plastic, non-metallic mineral products	1 100.1	1 300.9	1 432.7	1 561.9	1 579.8	167.8	325.8	392.6	117.6	134.4
Metal and machinery products, except electrical equipment	1 558.0	1 733.4	1 640.2	1 870.6	1 615.8	56.9	105.8	76.3	153.6	167.8
Motor vehicles, trailers, semi-trailers, other transport equipment	1 346.2	1 509.4	1 880.7	1 743.8	1 602.1	7.9	46.9	44.8	38.4	8.0
Other manufacturing	1 434.5	1 238.0	1 161.0	1 344.0	1 529.4	-0.7	7.0	7.7	11.2	15.6
Electricity, gas, steam and air conditioning supply	**256.2**	**-59.4**	**376.2**	**474.5**	**503.0**	**-45.4**	**-46.3**	**-20.5**	**-26.9**	**-21.6**
Water supply; sewerage, waste management and remediation activities	**31.4**	**45.6**	**52.5**	**40.3**	**33.7**	**0.0**	**0.9**	**0.4**	**0.4**	**1.4**
Construction	**384.2**	**742.6**	**481.1**	**868.0**	**885.6**	**30.2**	**3.5**	**-38.3**	**18.4**	**92.0**
Services	**9 808.9**	**12 152.5**	**12 205.9**	**12 948.8**	**12 832.4**	**508.9**	**2 059.4**	**960.4**	**1 376.2**	**1 258.4**
Wholesale and retail trade; repair of motor vehicles and motorcycles	2 841.1	3 418.7	4 169.8	4 723.6	4 578.2	206.6	167.6	386.7	495.3	316.5
Transportation and storage	510.9	547.7	652.0	795.1	725.6	5.9	8.5	0.9	51.4	27.6
Accommodation and food service activities	46.8	87.2	96.8	90.9	258.6	18.2	31.7	38.0	63.4	163.6
Information and communication	1 740.3	1 482.2	2 096.5	656.5	893.1	48.5	37.4	43.0	98.5	120.9
Financial and insurance activities	2 591.6	2 514.3	2 435.6	3 162.5	3 351.3	188.5	-93.2	55.6	329.0	388.3
Activities of holding companies	101.0	94.4	283.1	282.5	854.1	84.8	-40.4	-48.6	172.1	180.2
Real estate activities	852.6	1 718.0	962.9	1 682.7	1 499.0	-14.0	82.5	52.9	90.7	205.2
Professional, scientific and technical activities	1 137.7	1 553.4	1 285.1	1 411.6	1 203.4	23.9	2.7	147.4	32.0	-64.9
Administrative and support service activities	40.7	778.0	441.6	330.0	234.7	41.8	1 814.2	191.1	162.2	30.6
Public administration; activities of households and of extraterritorial organisations	2.4	-	-	-	-	-	-	-	-	-
Education	-1.3	5.6	-3.0	-2.3	5.0	2.5	2.4	-0.1	-0.3	-
Human health and social work activities	29.6	35.6	52.8	58.6	54.8	-1.0	-1.1	0.6	1.8	-0.8
Arts, entertainment and recreation	-6.9	-11.7	-4.7	16.7	4.0	-4.7	2.7	1.5	0.0	-0.3
Other services	23.3	23.6	20.7	22.8	24.7	-7.4	3.9	42.9	52.3	71.7
Not allocated and confidential	**-2.1**	**3.1**	**0.6**	**0.8**	**0.1**	**6.3**	**7.1**	**4.9**	**57.3**	**30.9**
Private real estate activities	-	-	-	-	-	-	-	-	-	-

- Nil

Note: Detailed metadata at: *http://stats.oecd.org/OECDStat_Metadata/ShowMetadata.ashx?Dataset=FDI_CTRY_IND_SUMM.*

Source: *OECD International Direct Investment Statistics (database): https://doi.org/10.1787/idi-data-en*

PORTUGAL

Table 1. Foreign direct investment flows by country

Million US dollars

	Inward					Outward				
	2015	2016	2017	2018	2019	2015	2016	2017	2018	2019
WORLD	**9 179.1**	**5 682.8**	**6 913.5**	**7 176.9**	**11 979.2**	**4 809.8**	**878.0**	**-927.7**	**1 373.8**	**3 721.0**
OECD COUNTRIES	..	..	..	..	..	..	..	..	..	..
Australia	4.4	-6.6	4.5	-4.7	-2.2	136.4	102.8	-27.1	-72.0	-13.4
Austria	65.4	-31.0	801.5	233.7	-153.4	-5.5	5.5	-19.2	4.7	-6.7
Belgium	-36.6	36.5	397.9	234.9	134.3	-42.2	47.6	-12.4	-423.7	97.4
Canada	-24.4	10.0	-9.0	-	10.1	3.3	76.3	-5.6	-3.5	4.5
Chile	7.8	-	10.1	14.2	-2.2	5.5	-	192.8	-8.3	209.3
Czech Republic	1.1	3.3	-	-10.6	-14.6	-2.2	-16.6	-21.4	23.6	-
Denmark	-8.9	29.9	111.6	264.4	-26.9	-5.5	-8.8	6.8	5.9	-127.6
Estonia	-	..	-	-	..	..	..	..	-	..
Finland	2.2	12.2	-44.0	10.6	14.6	-35.5	22.1	37.2	-73.2	9.0
France	853.0	109.5	746.3	611.4	1 070.2	-238.5	-96.2	113.9	-88.5	266.4
Germany	-282.9	495.4	-124.0	216.0	253.0	-139.8	-228.9	-73.3	-37.8	-151.1
Greece	-	..	..	..	..	..	-	..	..	..
Hungary	-1.1	-1.1	-1.1	56.7	26.9	-62.1	-12.2	-22.5	69.6	45.9
Iceland	-	-	-	-	-	-	-	-	-	-
Ireland	240.7	-296.4	13.5	-177.0	221.7	2.2	-251.0	-101.5	-4.7	53.7
Israel	..	..	..	..	..	..	..	..	..	..
Italy	244.0	-57.5	196.1	338.7	-15.7	321.7	-12.2	37.2	-93.2	4.5
Japan	1.1	-4.4	103.7	10.6	5.6	16.6	-91.8	-192.8	8.3	1.1
Korea	-2.2	15.5	55.2	27.1	26.9	-	-	-	-1.2	-
Latvia	-	2.2	-	-	2.2	-	-	-	-	-
Lithuania	-	..	..	..	..	-	-	-	-	-
Luxembourg	7 205.8	2 060.2	2 379.7	164.1	2 439.3	-64.3	-1.1	-671.9	177.0	-90.7
Mexico	-11.1	15.5	7.9	-10.6	25.7	189.7	-12.2	7.9	21.2	16.8
Netherlands	-1 077.1	665.7	-51.9	809.6	-476.9	4 033.3	-162.6	-3 429.2	1 103.5	-877.6
New Zealand	3.3	1.1	-	4.7	1.1	-	-	-	-	-
Norway	-17.7	-14.4	4.5	8.3	1.1	-	-	3.4	8.3	5.6
Poland	6.7	13.3	13.5	7.1	11.2	-342.8	-21.0	-23.7	60.2	-9.0
Portugal	-	-	-	-	..	-	-	-	-	..
Slovak Republic	-	-	..	..	..	..	..	..	..	-
Slovenia	-	-	-	-	..	-	-	-	-	-
Spain	-950.6	788.5	210.8	1 982.8	4 804.7	705.5	609.3	1 437.3	566.5	4 140.8
Sweden	42.2	363.8	549.0	-37.8	217.2	7.8	11.1	34.9	-46.0	-53.7
Switzerland	104.3	276.5	414.8	-36.6	248.5	79.9	15.5	38.3	-64.9	144.4
Turkey	16.6	4.4	81.2	-13.0	872.0	-2.2	3.3	11.3	-17.7	-
United Kingdom	1 145.9	-82.9	-12.4	927.7	235.1	402.7	258.8	184.9	125.1	166.8
United States	326.1	71.9	65.4	272.6	242.9	-159.7	3.3	-480.2	-170.0	-324.6
EUROPE	**7 840.3**	**4 562.6**	**5 458.2**	**5 849.2**	**10 104.1**	**4 664.4**	**143.8**	**-2 422.5**	**1 222.7**	**3 590.1**
Bulgaria	-	-	2.3	-2.4	7.8	-	1.1	16.9	-14.2	1.1
Croatia	..	-	-	-	..	-	-	-	-	-
Cyprus	-22.2	55.3	-19.2	72.0	76.1	-	-17.7	11.3	13.0	-3.4
Malta	280.6	-17.7	-245.7	131.0	98.5	61.0	7.7	20.3	26.0	6.7
Romania	-5.5	7.7	-4.5	-4.7	11.2	1.1	-10.0	3.4	-7.1	-19.0
Russian Federation	1.1	8.8	11.3	23.6	17.9	-	-	-45.1	-37.8	-
Ukraine	5.5	3.3	-1.1	18.9	2.2	-2.2	-7.7	-1.1	-	1.1
AFRICA	**391.6**	**-468.9**	**2.3**	**382.4**	**292.2**	**439.3**	**-118.3**	**1 264.8**	**605.5**	**348.1**
Northern Africa	-15.5	16.6	31.6	15.3	57.1	28.8	89.6	308.9	319.8	370.5
Algeria	12.2	8.8	4.5	2.4	10.1	-13.3	-56.4	-23.7	-20.1	39.2
Egypt	..	..	..	..	..	..	..	..	..	..
Libya	-	..	..	..	..	..	-	-	-	..
Morocco	-35.5	8.8	-	8.3	11.2	-18.9	-7.7	-9.0	80.3	13.4
Tunisia	21.1	16.6	19.2	16.5	29.1	4.4	-8.8	7.9	-8.3	-4.5
Other African countries	..	..	..	..	..	..	..	..	..	..
Nigeria	247.4	-215.6	1.1	1.2	2.2	57.7	-57.5	67.6	4.7	9.0
South Africa	-1.1	11.1	-18.0	34.2	72.8	-44.4	24.3	16.9	20.1	-241.8
AMERICA	**-510.3**	**640.3**	**293.1**	**-276.2**	**782.5**	**-535.8**	**765.2**	**558.0**	**-482.7**	**-288.8**
Northern America	301.7	81.8	56.4	272.6	253.0	-156.4	79.6	-485.9	-173.5	-320.2
Central America and Caribbean countries	279.5	325.1	140.9	-27.1	161.2	28.8	232.2	730.5	-500.4	59.3
Bahamas	..	..	..	..	..	..	..	..	-	-
Bermuda	..	..	..	..	-	-	-	..	..	..
Cayman Islands	..	..	..	..	..	..	..	..	..	..
Costa Rica	-	1.1	-	1.2	1.1	-1.1	-	-3.4	-	-
El Salvador	-	-	-	-	-	-	-	-	-	-
Guatemala	-	-	-	-	-	..	-	-	-	-
Honduras	-	-	..	-	-	-	-	-	..	-
Nicaragua	-	-	-	-	-	-	-	-	-	-
Panama	..	..	..	-	..	..	..	..	..	..
Virgin Islands, U.S.	..	-	-	-	-	-	-	-	-	-
South America	-1 092.6	233.3	95.8	-522.8	368.3	-407.1	453.4	313.4	192.4	-28.0
Argentina	-	-1.1	-	1.2	-1.1	-5.5	-1.1	6.8	-2.4	1.1
Bolivia	-	..	-	-	..	..	..	-	..	..
Brazil	-890.7	160.3	86.8	-558.2	380.6	-412.6	276.5	138.7	-86.2	-274.3
Colombia	-1.1	14.4	-2.3	-2.4	-	4.4	1.1	10.1	2.4	7.8
Ecuador	..	..	-	..	-	-	-	-	-	..
Paraguay	-	-	..	..	-	-	..	..	-	..
Peru	-	-	-	..	..	..	..	..	..	..
Uruguay	1.1	-	2.3	3.5	1.1	-1.1	6.6	1.1	-13.0	17.9
Venezuela	-208.5	56.4	-	20.1	-4.5	11.1	165.9	-40.6	136.9	-9.0

PORTUGAL

Table 1. Foreign direct investment flows by country *(cont.)*

Million US dollars

	Inward					Outward				
	2015	2016	2017	2018	2019	2015	2016	2017	2018	2019
ASIA	**1 449.8**	**956.5**	**1 155.5**	**1 220.3**	**779.1**	**105.4**	**-15.5**	**-301.0**	**101.5**	**84.0**
Near and Middle East	..	..	..	..	..	..	..	..	..	..
Gulf Arabian countries	..	..	..	..	..	..	-	..	..	..
Kuwait	22.2	-1.1	7.9	4.7	9.0	-	-	-	22.4	-1.1
Qatar	..	..	..	..	..	..	..	..	..	..
Saudi Arabia	..	..	..	..	..	-	..	..	..	-
United Arab Emirates	51.0	77.4	94.7	151.1	118.7	-2.2	-5.5	-9.0	20.1	40.3
Other Near and Middle East	..	..	..	..	..	..	..	..	..	..
Jordan	..	..	..	..	..	-	..	..	..	..
Other Asian countries	..	..	..	..	..	..	..	..	..	..
China	529.1	561.8	432.9	296.2	114.2	5.5	8.8	-6.8	-	-6.7
Hong Kong, China	736.6	-47.6	210.8	389.5	249.6	..	..	..	..	..
India	-26.6	1.1	39.5	23.6	19.0	-1.1	-11.1	12.4	-1.2	-4.5
Indonesia	..	..	..	..	..	..	..	..	..	..
Iran, Islamic Republic of	..	..	..	..	..	-	-	-	-	-
Malaysia	..	..	..	..	..	..	-	..	..	..
Philippines	..	-	..	..	..	-	-	-	-	-
Singapore	..	..	..	..	..	-	..	..	..	..
Chinese Taipei	-	..	-	..	-	-	-	-	-	-
Thailand	..	..	..	..	..	-	..	..	..	..
Viet Nam	..	..	..	..	..	-	-	..	..	..
AUSTRALIA, OCEANIA AND POLAR REGIONS	**7.8**	**-7.7**	**5.6**	**2.4**	**-**	**136.4**	**102.8**	**-27.1**	**-72.0**	**-12.3**
WORLD unallocated and confidential	**..**	**-**	**-1.1**	**-1.2**	**21.3**	**..**	**-**	**-**	**-1.2**	**-**
European Union (EU28)	**..**	**..**	**..**	**..**	**..**	**..**	**..**	**..**	**..**	**..**
G20 countries excl. European Union	**..**	**..**	**..**	**..**	**..**	**..**	**..**	**..**	**..**	**..**
G20 OECD countries	**..**	**..**	**..**	**..**	**..**	**..**	**..**	**..**	**..**	**..**
G20 Non-OECD countries	**..**	**..**	**..**	**..**	**..**	**..**	**..**	**..**	**..**	**..**
MENA countries	**..**	**..**	**..**	**..**	**..**	**..**	**..**	**..**	**..**	**..**
ASEAN countries	**..**	**..**	**..**	**..**	**..**	**..**	**..**	**..**	**..**	**..**

- Nil; .. Not available

Note: Data excludes resident Special Purpose Entities (SPEs). Detailed metadata at: *http://stats.oecd.org/OECDStat_Metadata/ShowMetadata.ashx?Dataset=FDI_CTRY_IND_SUMM.*

Source: *OECD International Direct Investment Statistics (database): https://doi.org/10.1787/idi-data-en*

PORTUGAL

Table 2. Foreign direct investment positions by country

At year end

Million US dollars

	Inward					Outward				
	2015	2016	2017	2018	2019	2015	2016	2017	2018	2019
WORLD	**123 511.2**	**122 725.8**	**152 169.6**	**147 826.9**	**158 111.7**	**58 877.5**	**57 777.0**	**62 672.1**	**52 522.3**	**56 066.1**
OECD COUNTRIES	..	..	..	..	..	..	..	..	..	..
Australia	17.4	7.4	16.8	11.5	6.7	210.1	..	266.3	194.6	179.7
Austria	638.0	541.8	2 477.8	2 123.9	1 895.1	149.2	..	152.3	147.7	138.2
Belgium	3 089.8	3 126.4	4 053.7	1 861.7	1 986.1	240.6	..	400.6	96.2	207.8
Canada	693.5	682.0	762.8	729.3	731.3	79.5	..	40.8	40.1	43.8
Chile	5.4	6.3	22.8	38.9	30.3	29.4	..	219.5	221.0	424.6
Czech Republic	9.8	11.6	12.0	-3.4	-14.6	28.3	..	57.6	64.1	40.4
Denmark	526.9	540.7	728.0	758.0	723.4	170.9	..	187.1	163.7	182.0
Estonia	..	..	..	..	..	..	..	..	..	..
Finland	80.6	89.6	49.2	83.6	101.1	-17.4	..	36.0	-30.9	-18.0
France	6 540.0	6 867.3	8 683.1	10 038.9	10 952.6	971.1	..	1 384.0	1 049.9	1 413.2
Germany	4 872.1	4 906.7	5 700.4	5 659.5	5 720.1	754.5	..	1 368.4	1 079.7	697.6
Greece	..	..	..	..	..	..	..	..	..	..
Hungary	29.4	27.4	30.0	588.5	29.2	170.9	..	135.5	692.7	98.9
Iceland	..	..	..	..	..	-	-	-	-	-
Ireland	2 263.5	1 853.1	2 169.6	1 788.4	1 871.5	1 430.6	..	1 138.2	893.1	752.6
Israel	..	..	..	..	..	..	..	..	..	..
Italy	1 037.6	845.4	1 162.1	1 473.6	1 280.6	627.1	..	668.0	493.5	563.9
Japan	345.1	326.8	510.9	474.0	485.3	150.2	..	130.7	123.7	126.9
Korea	114.3	122.3	187.1	193.5	205.6	-	..	-1.2	-3.4	-3.4
Latvia	6.5	6.3	7.2	6.9	9.0	1.1	..	-	-	1.1
Lithuania	..	..	..	-	..	-	-	-	-	-
Luxembourg	21 026.7	20 836.9	26 974.1	25 970.9	28 685.7	2 452.9	..	3 249.0	2 439.9	2 444.4
Mexico	-12.0	-2.1	6.0	87.0	110.1	76.2	..	58.8	80.1	125.8
Netherlands	31 325.0	31 140.5	37 041.3	32 080.4	34 406.9	17 856.3	..	14 541.9	10 772.8	12 625.3
New Zealand	6.5	7.4	46.8	49.2	48.3	-	-	-	-	-
Norway	159.0	136.0	190.7	139.7	138.2	10.9	..	16.8	6.9	15.7
Poland	40.3	..	66.0	48.1	61.8	1 465.4	1 263.8	2 074.8	1 986.5	1 392.9
Portugal	-	-	-	-	-	-	-	-	-	-
Slovak Republic	..	..	..	..	..	..	..	..	-	..
Slovenia	..	..	..	..	..	-	-	-	-	-
Spain	20 985.3	22 359.0	26 325.3	27 867.0	31 973.7	11 449.1	..	14 227.6	13 452.0	17 347.8
Sweden	651.1	..	1 776.2	1 740.3	1 890.6	224.3	205.5	160.7	125.9	47.2
Switzerland	2 211.2	2 439.1	3 150.6	3 020.4	3 257.7	194.9	..	109.1	-123.7	-10.1
Turkey	42.5	..	137.9	120.2	203.3	62.1	63.2	63.6	55.0	50.6
United Kingdom	10 467.1	9 980.0	11 219.7	11 585.8	10 515.6	2 742.5	..	2 961.1	2 104.4	1 050.3
United States	1 715.8	..	1 766.6	2 003.7	2 031.0	1 511.2	1 575.8	1 036.2	1 452.9	1 112.1
EUROPE	**108 867.7**	**109 772.3**	**135 317.8**	**130 478.6**	**139 497.9**	**41 800.8**	**..**	**43 872.6**	**36 308.7**	**39 776.5**
Bulgaria	4.4	5.3	8.4	5.7	15.7	27.2	..	48.0	29.8	30.3
Croatia	..	..	..	..	..	-	-	-	-	-
Cyprus	569.4	605.0	665.6	756.8	832.4	20.7	..	16.8	29.8	22.5
Malta	1 231.4	1 267.0	1 321.7	1 407.1	1 535.6	369.1	..	410.2	356.1	341.5
Romania	-6.5	..	-1.2	-11.5	1.1	215.6	194.0	220.7	207.2	173.0
Russian Federation	159.0	..	196.7	211.8	225.8	26.1	31.6	37.2	26.3	28.1
Ukraine	16.3	..	20.4	36.6	39.3	8.7	3.2	3.6	3.4	4.5
AFRICA	**3 063.7**	**1 976.4**	**2 931.2**	**3 059.3**	**3 152.1**	**8 974.4**	**..**	**9 966.4**	**8 392.5**	**8 312.7**
Northern Africa	95.8	109.6	176.3	199.2	257.2	1 174.7	..	1 656.3	2 074.7	2 395.0
Algeria	19.6	27.4	55.2	25.2	34.8	278.7	..	284.2	231.3	269.6
Egypt	..	..	..	..	..	..	..	..	..	..
Libya	..	..	..	..	..	..	..	..	..	..
Morocco	-7.6	2.1	-	2.3	19.1	194.9	..	199.1	266.8	289.8
Tunisia	95.8	..	146.3	159.1	188.7	86.0	69.6	74.4	72.1	69.6
Other African countries	..	..	..	..	..	..	..	..	..	..
Nigeria	221.0	5.3	7.2	8.0	13.5	3.3	..	21.6	18.3	22.5
South Africa	135.0	..	146.3	182.0	246.0	197.1	249.8	287.8	267.9	87.6
AMERICA	**6 294.0**	**5 092.2**	**5 880.3**	**5 669.8**	**6 317.7**	**6 173.1**	**..**	**6 719.8**	**5 969.8**	**6 002.0**
Northern America	2 410.5	2 380.1	2 530.6	2 733.0	2 762.3	1 590.6	..	1 077.0	1 493.0	1 157.0
Central America and Caribbean countries	897.1	-110.7	73.2	219.8	425.7	975.5	..	1 224.5	698.4	751.5
Bahamas	..	..	..	..	..	..	..	..	..	..
Bermuda	..	..	..	..	..	..	..	..	..	..
Cayman Islands	..	..	..	..	..	..	..	..	..	..
Costa Rica	3.3	2.1	2.4	3.4	4.5	6.5	..	6.0	5.7	5.6
El Salvador	-	-	-	-	-	-	..	-	-	-
Guatemala	-	-	..	-	-	..	..	..	..	..
Honduras	-	-	..	..	..	..	..	..	..	..
Nicaragua	-	-	-	-	-	-	-	-	-	-
Panama	..	..	..	..	..	..	..	..	..	..
Virgin Islands, U.S.	..	..	..	..	..	-	-	-	-	-
South America	2 986.4	2 822.8	3 276.6	2 715.8	3 130.8	3 607.0	..	4 418.3	3 778.3	4 093.5
Argentina	-	-1.1	-1.2	-1.1	-3.4	18.5	..	31.2	26.3	25.8
Bolivia	-	..	..	..	..	..	..	..	..	..
Brazil	2 945.0	2 764.8	3 202.2	2 604.8	3 043.1	3 328.3	..	3 749.1	3 150.9	3 212.8
Colombia	-2.2	11.6	1.2	-	-	9.8	..	14.4	14.9	34.8
Ecuador	..	-	-	..	..	..	..	..	..	-
Paraguay	-	..	-	..	..	..	..	..	..	..
Peru	-	..	..	..	..	..	..	..	..	..
Uruguay	3.3	..	6.0	9.2	10.1	18.5	25.3	28.8	18.3	37.1
Venezuela	34.8	..	37.2	55.0	47.2	137.2	294.1	279.4	104.2	78.6

PORTUGAL

Table 2. Foreign direct investment positions by country *(cont.)*

At year end

Million US dollars

	Inward					Outward				
	2015	2016	2017	2018	2019	2015	2016	2017	2018	2019
ASIA	**5 218.3**	..	**7 934.8**	**8 487.5**	**8 998.0**	**1 716.9**	**1 835.1**	**1 837.4**	**1 647.6**	**1 783.9**
Near and Middle East	..	..	..	..	..	..	..	..	..	..
Gulf Arabian countries	..	..	..	..	..	..	..	..	..	..
Kuwait	69.7	64.3	66.0	80.1	87.6	-	-	-	-	-
Qatar	..	..	..	..	..	..	..	..	..	..
Saudi Arabia	..	..	..	..	..	..	..	..	..	..
United Arab Emirates	303.8	366.8	518.1	600.0	772.9	20.7	..	-	-4.6	34.8
Other Near and Middle East	..	..	..	..	..	..	..	..	..	..
Jordan	..	..	..	..	..	-	..	..	..	..
Other Asian countries	..	..	..	..	..	..	..	..	..	..
China	1 356.6	1 849.9	2 569.0	2 730.7	2 798.2	53.3	..	57.6	18.3	18.0
Hong Kong, China	2 496.5	2 224.1	2 764.5	2 845.2	2 865.6	..	..	..	..	..
India	-21.8	-20.0	22.8	35.5	55.0	87.1	..	69.6	58.4	52.8
Indonesia	..	..	..	..	..	..	..	..	..	..
Iran, Islamic Republic of	..	..	..	..	..	..	..	..	..	..
Malaysia	..	..	..	..	..	..	..	..	..	-
Philippines	..	..	..	..	..	-	-	-	-	-
Singapore	..	..	..	..	..	..	..	..	..	..
Chinese Taipei	-	..	-	..	..	..	..	..	..	..
Thailand	..	..	..	..	..	..	..	..	..	..
Viet Nam	..	..	..	..	..	-	-	..	..	..
AUSTRALIA, OCEANIA AND POLAR REGIONS	**43.5**	**32.7**	**82.8**	**111.1**	**102.2**	**210.1**	..	**267.5**	**195.8**	**182.0**
WORLD unallocated and confidential	..	..	**22.8**	**20.6**	**43.8**	..	..	**8.4**	**8.0**	**9.0**
European Union (EU28)	..	..	..	..	..	..	..	..	..	..
G20 countries excl. European Union	..	..	..	..	..	..	..	..	..	..
G20 OECD countries	..	..	..	..	..	..	..	..	..	..
G20 Non-OECD countries	..	..	..	..	..	..	..	..	..	..
MENA countries	..	..	..	..	..	..	..	..	..	..
ASEAN countries	..	..	..	..	..	..	..	..	..	..

- Nil; .. Not available

Note: Data excludes resident Special Purpose Entities (SPEs). Detailed metadata at: *http://stats.oecd.org/OECDStat_Metadata/ShowMetadata.ashx?Dataset=FDI_CTRY_IND_SUMM.*

Source: *OECD International Direct Investment Statistics (database): https://doi.org/10.1787/idi-data-en*

PORTUGAL

Table 3. Foreign direct investment income by country

Million US dollars

	Inward					Outward				
	2015	2016	2017	2018	2019	2015	2016	2017	2018	2019
WORLD	..	**5 700.5**	..	..	..	..	**2 516.9**	..	..	..
OECD COUNTRIES	..	..	..	..	..	..	..	..	..	..
Australia	-	-	..	..	-	..	..	..	..	..
Austria	..	..	..	..	..	..	..	..	..	..
Belgium	..	..	..	..	..	..	..	..	..	..
Canada	..	..	..	..	-	..	..	..	-	..
Chile	-	-	..	..	-	..	..	..	..	..
Czech Republic	-	-	-	..	..	-	..	..	..	..
Denmark	..	..	..	..	..	..	..	..	..	-
Estonia	..	-	..	-	..	..	..	-	-	..
Finland	-	..	..	..	..	-	-	-	-	..
France	..	..	..	..	..	..	..	..	..	..
Germany	..	..	..	..	..	..	..	..	..	..
Greece	-	-	-	..	..	-	-	-	..	..
Hungary	-	..	..	..	..	..	..	..	..	..
Iceland	-	-	-	-	-	-	-	-	-	-
Ireland	..	..	..	..	..	..	..	..	..	..
Israel	-	-	..	..	..	-	-	-	-	..
Italy	..	..	..	..	..	..	..	-	-	..
Japan	..	..	..	..	..	..	..	..	..	..
Korea	..	..	..	..	..	-	-	-	-	-
Latvia	-	-	-	-	-	-	-	-	-	..
Lithuania	-	-	-	-	-	-	-	-	-	-
Luxembourg	..	..	..	..	..	..	..	..	..	..
Mexico	-	-	..	..	..	..	..	..	..	..
Netherlands	..	..	..	..	..	..	..	..	..	..
New Zealand	-	-	-	..	-	-	-	-	-	-
Norway	..	..	..	..	-	..	-	..	..	-
Poland	..	..	-	..	..	..	..	..	..	..
Portugal	-	-	-	-	..	-	-	-	-	..
Slovak Republic	-	-	-	-	..	-	-	-	-	..
Slovenia	-	-	-	-	-	-	-	-	-	-
Spain	..	..	..	..	..	..	..	..	..	..
Sweden	..	..	..	..	..	..	..	..	..	..
Switzerland	..	..	..	..	..	..	..	..	..	..
Turkey	..	..	..	..	..	..	..	..	..	-
United Kingdom	..	..	..	..	..	..	..	..	..	..
United States	..	..	..	..	..	..	..	..	..	..
EUROPE	..	..	..	..	..	..	..	..	..	..
Bulgaria	..	..	-	..	..	-	-	..	..	..
Croatia	-	-	-	-	-	-	-	-	-	-
Cyprus	..	..	..	..	..	..	..	..	..	..
Malta	..	..	..	..	..	..	..	..	..	..
Romania	-	-	-	-	-	..	..	..	..	..
Russian Federation	-	-	-	-	-	-	-	..	-	-
Ukraine	-	-	-	-	-	..	-	-	-	..
AFRICA	..	..	..	..	..	..	..	..	..	..
Northern Africa	..	..	..	..	..	..	..	..	..	..
Algeria	-	-	..	..	-	..	..	..	..	..
Egypt	-	-	-	-	-	..	..	..	..	..
Libya	-	-	-	-	-	..	-	-	-	-
Morocco	..	-	..	..	..	..	..	..	..	..
Tunisia	-	..	..	..	..	..	..	..	..	..
Other African countries	..	..	..	..	..	..	..	..	..	..
Nigeria	..	-	-	-	-	-	..	..	..	..
South Africa	..	..	..	..	..	-	-	..	..	..
AMERICA	..	..	..	..	..	..	..	..	..	..
Northern America	..	..	..	..	..	..	..	..	..	..
Central America and Caribbean countries	..	..	..	..	..	..	..	..	..	..
Bahamas	..	..	..	..	..	..	-	..	-	-
Bermuda	-	-	..	..	-	-	-	-	..	-
Cayman Islands	..	..	-	-	..	..	..	..	..	-
Costa Rica	..	-	-	-	-	..	-	..	-	-
El Salvador	-	-	-	-	-	-	-	-	-	-
Guatemala	-	-	-	-	-	..	-	-	-	-
Honduras	-	-	-	-	-	-	-	-	..	-
Nicaragua	-	-	-	-	-	-	-	-	-	-
Panama	..	..	..	..	..	..	..	..	..	..
Virgin Islands, U.S.	-	-	-	-	-	-	-	-	-	-
South America	..	..	..	..	..	..	..	..	..	..
Argentina	-	-	..	..	-	..	..	..	-	-
Bolivia	-	-	-	-	-	-	-	..	-	-
Brazil	..	..	..	..	..	..	..	..	..	..
Colombia	-	-	-	-	-	-	..	..	..	..
Ecuador	-	-	-	-	-	-	-	..	..	..
Paraguay	-	-	-	-	-	-	-	-	-	..
Peru	-	-	-	-	-	-	..	..	..	..
Uruguay	-	..	-	-	-	..	..	..	..	..
Venezuela	-	-	-	-	-	..	..	..	..	..

Table 3. Foreign direct investment income by country *(cont.)*

Million US dollars

	Inward					Outward				
	2015	2016	2017	2018	2019	2015	2016	2017	2018	2019
ASIA	..	..	..	..	..	..	..	..	..	..
Near and Middle East	..	..	..	..	..	..	..	..	..	..
Gulf Arabian countries	..	..	..	..	..	..	..	..	..	..
Kuwait	..	..	..	..	-	-	-	-	-	-
Qatar	-	-	..	-	..	..	..	..	..	..
Saudi Arabia	..	..	-	-	..	..	..	..	..	..
United Arab Emirates	-	..	..	..	..	..	..	-	..	..
Other Near and Middle East	-	..	..	..	..	..	..	..	..	..
Jordan	-	-	-	-	-	-	-	-	-	-
Other Asian countries	..	..	..	..	..	..	..	..	..	..
China	..	..	..	..	..	..	..	..	..	-
Hong Kong, China	..	..	..	..	..	..	..	..	-	-
India	..	-	-	-	..	..	..	..	..	..
Indonesia	-	-	-	-	-	..	..	-	..	..
Iran, Islamic Republic of	-	-	-	-	-	-	-	-	-	-
Malaysia	-	-	-	-	-	..	-	-	-	-
Philippines	-	-	-	-	-	-	-	-	-	-
Singapore	..	..	..	..	..	..	-	-	..	-
Chinese Taipei	-	-	-	-	-	-	-	-	-	-
Thailand	-	-	-	-	..	-	..	-	-	-
Viet Nam	-	-	-	-	-	-	-	-	-	-
AUSTRALIA, OCEANIA AND POLAR REGIONS	-	..	..	..	..	..	..	..	..	..
WORLD unallocated and confidential	..	..	..	..	..	..	..	..	..	..
European Union (EU28)	..	..	..	..	..	..	..	..	..	..
G20 countries excl. European Union	..	..	..	..	..	..	..	..	..	..
G20 OECD countries	..	..	..	..	..	..	..	..	..	..
G20 Non-OECD countries	..	..	..	..	..	..	..	..	..	..
MENA countries	..	..	..	..	..	..	..	..	..	..
ASEAN countries	..	..	..	..	..	..	..	-	..	..

- Nil; .. Not available

Note: Data excludes resident Special Purpose Entities (SPEs). Detailed metadata at: *http://stats.oecd.org/OECDStat_Metadata/ShowMetadata.ashx?Dataset=FDI_CTRY_IND_SUMM.*

Source: *OECD International Direct Investment Statistics (database): https://doi.org/10.1787/idi-data-en*

PORTUGAL

Table 4. Foreign direct investment flows by industrial sector

Million US dollars

	Inward					Outward				
	2015	2016	2017	2018	2019	2015	2016	2017	2018	2019
All FDI activities	**9 179.1**	**5 682.8**	**6 913.5**	**7 176.9**	**11 979.2**	**4 809.8**	**878.0**	**-927.7**	**1 373.8**	**3 721.0**
Agriculture, forestry and fishing	..	..	..	..	..	..	..	..	-	..
Mining and quarrying	..	..	..	..	..	..	..	..	..	..
Extraction activities	-	-	-	-	-	-	-	-	-	-
Manufacturing	**327.2**	**233.3**	**232.2**	**553.5**	**3 174.7**	**-890.7**	**-158.1**	**423.9**	**-541.7**	**2 896.0**
of which:										
Food products, beverages and tobacco	..	..	..	..	..	..	..	..	..	..
Textiles, wood and paper products; printing	..	..	..	..	..	..	..	..	..	..
Chemical, rubber, plastic, non-metallic mineral products	..	..	..	..	..	..	..	..	..	..
Metal and machinery products, except electrical equipment	..	..	..	..	..	..	..	..	..	..
Motor vehicles, trailers, semi-trailers, other transport equipment	..	..	..	..	..	..	..	..	..	..
Other manufacturing	..	..	..	..	..	..	..	..	..	..
Electricity, gas, steam and air conditioning supply	..	..	..	..	..	..	..	..	..	..
Water supply; sewerage, waste management and remediation activities	..	..	..	..	..	..	..	..	..	..
Construction	**-170.8**	**-328.4**	**284.1**	**-72.0**	**444.4**	**108.7**	**-528.6**	**215.3**	**-62.6**	**-192.5**
Services	**7 202.4**	**3 235.7**	**4 805.5**	**4 152.0**	**5 473.0**	**5 947.9**	**256.6**	**520.8**	**219.5**	**-117.5**
Wholesale and retail trade; repair of motor vehicles and motorcycles	-43.3	566.2	821.8	-34.2	481.4	386.0	544.1	-201.8	-496.9	139.9
Transportation and storage	..	..	..	..	..	..	..	..	..	..
Accommodation and food service activities	..	..	..	..	..	..	..	..	..	..
Information and communication	5 628.4	-91.8	-68.8	-311.6	146.6	27.7	-123.9	-83.4	157.0	24.6
Financial and insurance activities	648.9	1 522.7	1 343.7	1 714.9	757.9	3 702.7	-468.9	-583.9	-480.3	-307.8
Activities of holding companies	..	..	..	..	..	..	..	..	..	..
Real estate activities	936.2	672.3	943.5	1 053.9	2 152.7	1 124.8	807.3	107.1	-87.3	666.1
Professional, scientific and technical activities	-450.4	454.5	926.6	1 137.7	1 342.2	719.9	-496.5	1 145.3	1 293.5	-134.3
Administrative and support service activities	..	..	..	..	..	..	..	..	..	..
Public administration; activities of households and of extraterritorial organisations	-	-	-	-	-	-	-	-	-	-
Education	-	..	..	-	..	..	..	..	..	-
Human health and social work activities	..	..	..	..	..	..	..	..	..	..
Arts, entertainment and recreation	..	..	..	..	..	..	..	..	..	..
Other services	..	..	..	..	-	..	..	..	..	..
Not allocated and confidential	..	..	..	..	..	..	..	..	..	..
Private real estate activities	-	-	..	..	..	-	-	-	-	-

- Nil; .. Not available

Note: Data excludes resident Special Purpose Entities (SPEs). Detailed metadata at: *http://stats.oecd.org/OECDStat_Metadata/ShowMetadata.ashx?Dataset=FDI_CTRY_IND_SUMM.*

Source: *OECD International Direct Investment Statistics (database): https://doi.org/10.1787/idi-data-en*

Table 5. Foreign direct investment positions by industrial sector
At year end

Million US dollars

	Inward					Outward				
	2015	2016	2017	2018	2019	2015	2016	2017	2018	2019
All FDI activities	**123 511.2**	**122 725.8**	**152 169.6**	**147 826.9**	**158 111.7**	**58 877.5**	**57 777.0**	**62 672.1**	**52 522.3**	**56 066.1**
Agriculture, forestry and fishing	..	..	..	..	..	..	..	..	..	..
Mining and quarrying	..	..	..	..	..	..	..	..	..	..
Extraction activities	-	-	-	-	-	-	-	-	-	-
Manufacturing	**8 875.3**	..	**9 338.0**	**9 253.5**	**12 145.6**	**3 022.3**	**3 262.4**	**3 487.6**	**2 681.5**	**5 566.2**
of which:										
Food products, beverages and tobacco	..	..	..	..	..	..	..	..	..	..
Textiles, wood and paper products; printing	..	..	..	..	..	..	..	..	..	..
Chemical, rubber, plastic, non-metallic mineral products	..	..	..	..	..	..	..	..	..	..
Metal and machinery products, except electrical equipment	..	..	..	..	..	..	..	..	..	..
Motor vehicles, trailers, semi-trailers, other transport equipment	..	..	..	..	..	..	..	..	..	..
Other manufacturing	..	..	..	..	..	..	..	..	..	..
Electricity, gas, steam and air conditioning supply	..	..	..	..	..	..	..	..	..	..
Water supply; sewerage, waste management and remediation activities	..	..	..	..	..	..	..	..	..	..
Construction	**3 241.2**	..	**3 370.1**	**2 735.3**	**3 175.7**	**4 258.0**	**3 286.6**	**4 167.7**	**3 113.1**	**2 980.2**
Services	**89 686.4**	..	**110 756.8**	**105 800.3**	**109 722.5**	**51 521.0**	**49 898.8**	**55 653.6**	**45 566.8**	**44 801.2**
Wholesale and retail trade; repair of motor vehicles and motorcycles	10 172.0	..	13 715.5	11 914.4	12 790.4	3 000.5	2 801.7	2 765.7	875.9	933.5
Transportation and storage	..	..	..	..	..	..	..	..	..	..
Accommodation and food service activities	..	..	..	..	..	..	..	..	..	..
Information and communication	7 372.9	..	8 011.5	1 267.5	7 084.9	-128.5	-391.1	-199.1	-494.6	-441.5
Financial and insurance activities	31 536.2	..	36 319.3	45 554.2	36 595.1	23 198.7	19 409.7	21 751.0	23 969.5	21 605.3
Activities of holding companies	..	..	..	..	..	..	..	..	..	..
Real estate activities	7 966.2	..	10 275.8	11 167.9	13 183.6	2 965.7	3 530.1	4 475.9	3 938.6	4 637.2
Professional, scientific and technical activities	23 795.3	..	31 953.7	25 114.5	28 382.4	20 373.4	22 412.8	25 101.9	15 965.2	17 081.6
Administrative and support service activities	..	..	..	..	..	..	..	..	..	..
Public administration; activities of households and of extraterritorial organisations	-	-	-	-	-	..	..	..	..	..
Education	..	..	..	..	..	..	..	..	..	..
Human health and social work activities	..	..	..	..	..	..	..	..	..	..
Arts, entertainment and recreation	..	..	..	..	..	..	..	..	..	..
Other services	..	..	..	..	..	..	..	..	..	..
Not allocated and confidential	..	..	..	..	..	..	..	..	..	..
Private real estate activities	-	-	..	..	..	-	-	..	..	..

- Nil; .. Not available

Note: Data excludes resident Special Purpose Entities (SPEs). Detailed metadata at: *http://stats.oecd.org/OECDStat_Metadata/ShowMetadata.ashx?Dataset=FDI_CTRY_IND_SUMM.*

Source: *OECD International Direct Investment Statistics (database): https://doi.org/10.1787/idi-data-en*

PORTUGAL

Table 6. Foreign direct investment income by industrial sector

Million US dollars

	Inward					Outward				
	2015	2016	2017	2018	2019	2015	2016	2017	2018	2019
All FDI activities	..	**5 700.5**	..	..	..	..	**2 516.9**	..	..	..
Agriculture, forestry and fishing	..	..	..	..	..	..	..	..	-	..
Mining and quarrying	..	..	..	..	..	..	..	..	..	..
Extraction activities	-	-	-	-	-	-	-	-	-	-
Manufacturing	..	..	..	..	..	..	..	..	..	..
of which:										
Food products, beverages and tobacco	..	..	..	..	..	..	..	..	..	..
Textiles, wood and paper products; printing	..	..	..	..	..	..	..	..	..	..
Chemical, rubber, plastic, non-metallic mineral products	..	..	..	..	..	..	..	..	..	..
Metal and machinery products, except electrical equipment	..	..	..	..	..	..	..	..	..	..
Motor vehicles, trailers, semi-trailers, other transport equipment	..	..	..	..	..	..	..	-	..	..
Other manufacturing	..	..	..	..	..	..	..	..	..	..
Electricity, gas, steam and air conditioning supply	..	..	..	..	..	..	..	..	..	..
Water supply; sewerage, waste management and remediation activities	..	..	..	..	..	..	..	..	..	..
Construction	..	..	..	..	..	..	..	..	..	..
Services	..	..	..	..	..	..	..	..	..	..
Wholesale and retail trade; repair of motor vehicles and motorcycles	..	..	..	..	..	..	..	..	..	..
Transportation and storage	..	..	..	..	..	..	..	..	..	..
Accommodation and food service activities	..	..	..	..	..	..	..	..	..	..
Information and communication	..	..	..	..	..	..	..	..	..	..
Financial and insurance activities	..	..	..	..	..	..	..	..	..	..
Activities of holding companies	..	..	..	..	..	..	..	..	..	..
Real estate activities	..	..	..	..	..	..	..	..	..	..
Professional, scientific and technical activities	..	..	..	..	..	..	..	..	..	..
Administrative and support service activities	..	..	..	..	..	..	-	..	..	..
Public administration; activities of households and of extraterritorial organisations	-	-	-	-	..	-	-	-	-	-
Education	..	-	..	-	..	-	-	-	..	-
Human health and social work activities	..	..	..	..	..	..	..	..	..	..
Arts, entertainment and recreation	..	..	..	..	..	..	..	..	..	..
Other services	..	..	..	..	..	..	..	..	..	..
Not allocated and confidential	..	..	..	..	..	..	..	..	..	..
Private real estate activities	-	-	-	-	-	-	-	-	-	-

- Nil; .. Not available

Note: Data excludes resident Special Purpose Entities (SPEs). Detailed metadata at: *http://stats.oecd.org/OECDStat_Metadata/ShowMetadata.ashx?Dataset=FDI_CTRY_IND_SUMM.*

Source: *OECD International Direct Investment Statistics (database): https://doi.org/10.1787/idi-data-en*

SLOVAK REPUBLIC

Table 1. Foreign direct investment flows by country

Million US dollars

	Inward					Outward				
	2015	2016	2017	2018	2019	2015	2016	2017	2018	2019
WORLD	..	**805.1**	**4 008.2**	**1 674.0**	**2 448.6**	..	**95.5**	**1 322.6**	**321.5**	**153.3**
OECD COUNTRIES	..	**1 407.7**	**4 534.0**	**1 707.4**	**3 080.5**	..	**121.3**	**1 252.5**	**306.5**	**117.3**
Australia	..	.. c	1.2	-2.4	13.1	..	.. c	.. c	.. c	.. c
Austria	..	163.0	-152.3	562.9	260.3	..	82.9	1.0	49.3	9.0
Belgium	..	38.4	342.5	280.2	248.3	..	-	-	.. c	.. c
Canada	..	.. c	2.3	3.1	3.5	..	.. c	.. c	.. c	.. c
Chile	..	.. c	-1.7	0.6	-0.7	..	.. c	.. c	.. c	.. c
Czech Republic	..	667.5	1 172.7	486.2	453.1	..	-23.6	1 148.8	-51.1	2.6
Denmark	..	-82.4	76.7	26.3	54.8	..	.. c	.. c	1.0	1.8
Estonia	..	.. c	2.8	3.1	6.6	..	-	-	-	-
Finland	..	.. c	38.3	25.7	28.1	..	.. c	.. c	.. c	.. c
France	..	-76.1	193.4	413.0	-225.7	..	.. c	6.8	1.1	2.1
Germany	..	446.9	901.5	-295.3	1 181.5	..	.. c	-1.5	2.2	12.1
Greece	..	.. c	4.1	-5.8	0.8	..	-	-	-	-
Hungary	..	159.0	-13.4	-261.0	565.7	..	47.1	0.2	15.7	-4.3
Iceland	..	.. c	-0.2	-0.2	-0.2	..	.. c	.. c	.. c	.. c
Ireland	..	.. c	65.8	-109.9	-59.0	..	.. c	-	.. c	.. c
Israel	..	.. c	22.1	11.8	0.7	..	-	-	-	-
Italy	..	-864.4	179.7	154.1	211.0	..	.. c	2.0	0.9	-2.4
Japan	..	.. c	36.6	9.5	-17.2	..	-	-	.. c	.. c
Korea	..	-14.1	48.7	39.2	-37.8	..	.. c	-	.. c	-
Latvia	..	.. c	0.6	19.8	-3.3	..	.. c	.. c	.. c	.. c
Lithuania	..	.. c	0.8	-0.7	-1.1	..	.. c	.. c	.. c	.. c
Luxembourg	..	-408.2	322.9	-117.3	-303.7	..	.. c	-31.8	-15.7	2.1
Mexico	..	.. c	-2.1	-30.5	24.7	..	-	-	-	-0.7
Netherlands	..	1 796.9	-798.9	-312.7	32.5	..	.. c	-98.9	49.0	-65.0
New Zealand	..	-11.4	-12.4	0.1	0.1	..	-	-	-	-
Norway	..	.. c	-20.9	-7.0	31.1	..	.. c	.. c	.. c	.. c
Poland	..	21.4	158.1	16.4	8.9	..	-51.8	109.0	142.8	95.7
Portugal	..	.. c	0.8	-0.2	1.4	..	.. c	.. c	.. c	.. c
Slovak Republic	..	..	-	-	0.2	..	-	-	-	0.2
Slovenia	..	.. c	3.2	-3.7	1.4	..	.. c	-0.6	0.6	-1.7
Spain	..	52.4	145.4	45.1	64.8	..	.. c	.. c	.. c	.. c
Sweden	..	119.0	689.6	79.5	-72.3	..	-	-	-	0.0
Switzerland	..	-75.5	178.5	156.6	72.9	..	.. c	-0.3	-0.9	-4.8
Turkey	..	.. c	20.1	1.3	-2.3	..	.. c	.. c	5.5	-1.0
United Kingdom	..	2.3	705.7	582.9	80.5	..	.. c	70.6	97.0	43.7
United States	..	-413.9	222.4	-63.4	458.0	..	.. c	.. c	-0.2	12.9
EUROPE	..	**1 086.8**	**3 789.3**	**1 689.4**	**2 223.8**	..	**88.6**	**1 275.5**	**304.7**	**125.1**
Bulgaria	..	.. c	-2.7	9.9	-6.9	..	.. c	-0.4	0.7	0.0
Croatia	..	.. c	1.3	7.9	-9.2	..	.. c	2.2	5.2	0.0
Cyprus	..	-182.2	-148.2	-17.9	-63.7	..	-39.1	4.6	6.8	20.3
Malta	..	.. c	31.4	142.4	-13.2	..	.. c	.. c	.. c	.. c
Romania	..	.. c	7.2	-45.9	-1.0	..	-9.2	2.3	-1.7	7.2
Russian Federation	..	.. c	10.8	48.9	-58.3	..	.. c	5.6	1.6	8.1
Ukraine	..	.. c	-1.0	-2.6	2.0	..	-3.1	-6.9	12.5	-12.2
AFRICA	..	**.. c**	**-0.2**	**4.8**	**16.6**	..	**.. c**	**.. c**	**.. c**	**.. c**
Northern Africa	..	.. c	2.4	7.0	18.7	..	.. c	.. c	.. c	.. c
Algeria	..	-	-	-	-	..	-	-	-	-
Egypt	..	.. c	4.4	1.6	11.9	..	-	-	-	-
Libya	..	-	-	-	-	..	-	-	-	-
Morocco	..	.. c	-3.4	3.1	3.8	..	.. c	.. c	.. c	.. c
Tunisia	..	.. c	1.5	2.3	3.0	..	.. c	-	-	-
Other African countries	..	.. c	-2.6	-2.2	-2.0	..	.. c	.. c	.. c	.. c
Nigeria	..	.. c	-0.1	-0.1	-1.1	..	.. c	.. c	.. c	.. c
South Africa	..	.. c	-3.7	2.7	3.6	..	-	-	-	0.0
AMERICA	..	**-332.1**	**242.5**	**-71.3**	**405.0**	..	**3.9**	**9.1**	**1.0**	**14.1**
Northern America	..	-405.6	224.7	-60.3	461.5	..	-2.1	0.4	-0.3	13.8
Central America and Caribbean countries	..	81.4	16.4	-11.2	-12.3	..	-	-	0.5	-0.7
Bahamas	..	.. c	.. c	.. c	.. c	..	-	-	-	-
Bermuda	..	-	.. c	.. c	.. c	..	-	-	-	-
Cayman Islands	..	.. c	24.4	.. c	.. c	..	-	-	-	-
Costa Rica	..	.. c	.. c	-0.1	0.1	..	-	-	-	-
El Salvador	..	.. c	.. c	-	-	..	-	-	-	-
Guatemala	..	-	.. c	.. c	-	..	-	-	-	-
Honduras	..	-	-	-	-	..	-	-	-	-
Nicaragua	..	-	-	-	-	..	-	-	-	-
Panama	..	.. c	-0.2	.. c	-	..	-	-	-	-
Virgin Islands, U.S.	..	-	-	-	-	..	-	-	-	-
South America	..	-8.0	1.3	0.2	-44.2	..	.. c	8.7	0.7	1.0
Argentina	..	0.7	-0.1	2.6	-45.7	..	.. c	.. c	.. c	.. c
Bolivia	..	-	-	-	-	..	-	-	-	-
Brazil	..	.. c	3.0	-2.9	-1.6	..	.. c	.. c	0.3	0.5
Colombia	..	.. c	0.0	0.0	-0.8	..	-	-	-	-
Ecuador	..	.. c	0.0	0.0	-0.1	..	-	-	-	-
Paraguay	..	-	-	-	0.0	..	-	-	-	-
Peru	..	.. c	0.1	-0.1	0.0	..	-	-	-	-
Uruguay	..	.. c	-	.. c	.. c	..	-	-	-	-
Venezuela	..	-	.. c	.. c	.. c	..	-	-	-	-

Table 1. Foreign direct investment flows by country *(cont.)*

Million US dollars

	Inward					Outward				
	2015	2016	2017	2018	2019	2015	2016	2017	2018	2019
ASIA	..	**80.4**	**-12.0**	**52.1**	**-211.0**	..	**.. c**	**37.5**	**15.6**	**12.5**
Near and Middle East	..	.. c	21.9	18.9	-4.2	..	.. c	.. c	.. c	.. c
Gulf Arabian countries	..	.. c	0.1	7.2	-4.7	..	-	-	-	-
Kuwait	..	.. c	.. c	.. c	-	..	-	-	-	-
Qatar	..	.. c	-0.9	0.9	-0.2	..	-	-	-	-
Saudi Arabia	..	.. c	-0.4	0.1	-0.4	..	-	-	-	-
United Arab Emirates	..	.. c	1.4	6.1	-4.1	..	-	-	-	-
Other Near and Middle East	..	.. c	21.9	11.8	0.5	..	.. c	.. c	.. c	.. c
Jordan	..	.. c	-0.1	0.0	0.0	..	-	-	-	-
Other Asian countries	..	78.6	-34.0	33.2	-206.8	..	.. c	37.3	15.4	12.3
China	..	.. c	6.4	-7.6	-2.5	..	.. c	31.4	7.7	13.0
Hong Kong, China	..	.. c	2.6	-14.0	2.6	..	.. c	.. c	.. c	-
India	..	.. c	1.3	-4.7	-1.1	..	.. c	.. c	1.0	-0.4
Indonesia	..	.. c	-4.7	4.8	-2.8	..	-	-	-	-
Iran, Islamic Republic of	..	.. c	.. c	.. c	-	..	-	-	-	-
Malaysia	..	.. c	-8.3	29.7	-55.2	..	-	-	0.0	-
Philippines	..	.. c	-	-0.2	0.7	..	-	-	-	-
Singapore	..	.. c	-65.2	-5.7	-7.7	..	.. c	.. c	.. c	.. c
Chinese Taipei	..	.. c	-67.7	-22.6	10.9	..	-	-	-	-
Thailand	..	.. c	1.9	-0.9	-0.8	..	-	-	-	-
Viet Nam	..	.. c	14.5	4.4	-95.8	..	.. c	.. c	-	-0.5
AUSTRALIA, OCEANIA AND POLAR REGIONS	..	**-24.6**	**-11.3**	**-1.0**	**14.2**	..	**.. c**	**.. c**	**.. c**	**.. c**
WORLD unallocated and confidential	..	**.. d**	**0.0**	**0.0**	**0.0**	..	**- d**	**.. d**	**- d**	**- d**
European Union (EU28)	..	**1 727.9**	**3 929.2**	**1 685.1**	**2 440.6**	..	**72.0**	**1 275.4**	**283.6**	**137.6**
G20 countries excl. European Union	..	**-892.6**	**2 322.2**	**855.4**	**1 580.4**	..	**-8.7**	**128.1**	**118.8**	**90.7**
G20 OECD countries	..	**-858.0**	**2 309.6**	**811.5**	**1 689.2**	..	**-28.2**	**80.1**	**108.2**	**69.5**
G20 Non-OECD countries	..	**-34.7**	**12.6**	**43.9**	**-108.9**	..	**19.5**	**48.0**	**10.6**	**21.2**
MENA countries	..	**2.6**	**2.4**	**14.1**	**13.9**	..	**.. c**	**.. c**	**.. c**	**.. c**
ASEAN countries	..	**31.2**	**-61.8**	**32.2**	**-161.6**	..	**.. c**	**.. c**	**.. c**	**.. c**

- Nil; .. Not available; c Confidential data; d Secondary Confidentiality

Note: Detailed metadata at: *http://stats.oecd.org/OECDStat_Metadata/ShowMetadata.ashx?Dataset=FDI_CTRY_IND_SUMM.*

Source: *OECD International Direct Investment Statistics (database): https://doi.org/10.1787/idi-data-en*

Table 2. Foreign direct investment positions by country
At year end

Million US dollars

	Inward					Outward				
	2015	2016	2017	2018	2019	2015	2016	2017	2018	2019
WORLD	**46 015.8**	**47 591.7**	**59 510.3**	**59 857.3**	**60 951.0**	**2 462.3**	**2 631.0**	**4 589.9**	**4 589.3**	**4 727.1**
OECD COUNTRIES	**44 605.1**	**46 192.4**	**58 505.6**	**58 871.4**	**60 610.9**	**1 948.1**	**2 199.9**	**4 045.3**	**4 050.1**	**4 131.4**
Australia	12.5	-3.4	-2.6	4.1	17.1	.. c	1.3	.. c	.. c	.. c
Austria	7 714.3	6 860.6	7 651.6	7 703.8	7 959.2	50.3	124.1	168.9	205.5	201.1
Belgium	2 165.4	2 340.4	2 995.0	3 113.0	2 908.2	-	-	-	.. c	.. c
Canada	20.0	25.0	33.0	33.7	36.7	.. c	.. c	.. c	.. c	.. c
Chile	-0.8	.. c	-1.6	-0.9	-1.7	.. c	.. c	.. c	.. c	.. c
Czech Republic	4 537.1	5 423.3	7 731.1	8 164.0	8 448.8	948.7	900.1	2 388.7	2 247.9	2 166.7
Denmark	430.8	407.5	521.6	498.1	547.5	.. c	.. c	49.9	49.4	49.6
Estonia	15.6	15.6	16.7	15.5	14.9	-	-	-	-	-
Finland	116.9	107.7	155.7	231.2	252.8	.. c	.. c	.. c	.. c	.. c
France	917.1	881.9	817.5	1 295.7	1 049.3	66.7	64.7	73.4	70.3	70.6
Germany	3 076.0	2 666.1	4 558.9	4 159.3	5 305.9	27.5	40.5	41.4	41.7	51.4
Greece	5.8	-1.1	2.7	-1.2	-0.4	.. c	-	-	-	-
Hungary	2 613.3	2 597.3	2 999.6	2 611.9	3 127.5	83.1	135.1	162.3	168.7	152.6
Iceland	.. c	.. c	0.3	.. c	.. c	.. c	.. c	.. c	.. c	.. c
Ireland	519.7	421.4	547.5	301.1	110.1	.. c	-	-	-	-1.5
Israel	-1.9	-1.0	5.3	16.3	10.3	-	-	-	-	-
Italy	3 399.9	2 311.4	2 791.2	2 907.5	3 152.4	26.1	26.4	31.9	32.0	28.1
Japan	44.2	72.1	127.9	102.8	83.6	-	-	-	.. c	.. c
Korea	3 230.4	3 060.2	3 446.1	3 263.9	3 127.7	.. c	-	-	.. c	.. c
Latvia	5.6	-0.1	-0.7	14.1	13.0	.. c	11.4	14.8	2.1	22.6
Lithuania	-1.0	-2.2	-1.7	-2.3	-3.3	.. c	.. c	.. c	5.2	5.3
Luxembourg	3 872.2	3 303.8	4 018.9	3 909.7	3 529.6	73.3	80.3	77.2	45.2	41.6
Mexico	-62.4	-1.7	-4.8	-77.7	-25.8	.. c	.. c	.. c	.. c	.. c
Netherlands	9 077.4	13 231.4	15 300.2	15 127.1	14 893.1	190.2	253.1	193.5	138.2	185.0
New Zealand	24.1	5.7	-0.1	0.0	0.0	-	-	-	-	-
Norway	150.1	147.6	138.6	137.1	159.9	-	.. c	.. c	.. c	.. c
Poland	316.8	196.3	471.5	591.6	551.8	229.7	156.1	299.5	431.2	496.1
Portugal	4.0	-1.3	-0.8	-2.4	-0.8	.. c	.. c	.. c	.. c	.. c
Slovak Republic	-	..	-	-0.2	-	-	..	-	-0.2	-
Slovenia	15.0	8.8	11.9	6.1	7.5	17.3	17.1	18.9	18.5	14.9
Spain	587.4	650.9	837.8	869.5	863.9	.. c	.. c	.. c	.. c	.. c
Sweden	257.7	351.2	823.1	889.6	788.6	-	-	.. c	.. c	-
Switzerland	718.2	593.7	842.4	887.8	1 088.9	6.1	11.2	12.9	12.1	7.1
Turkey	-3.3	-13.2	5.6	7.8	5.6	149.3	146.1	164.5	159.7	150.4
United Kingdom	492.0	545.6	1 441.6	1 889.5	1 941.9	7.9	138.3	232.8	316.5	350.3
United States	331.5	-11.4	222.6	204.6	647.8	14.9	11.9	10.8	9.4	23.4
EUROPE	**41 801.5**	**43 701.0**	**54 881.7**	**55 537.8**	**56 567.2**	**2 388.2**	**2 517.4**	**4 423.3**	**4 418.9**	**4 525.5**
Bulgaria	12.2	22.7	22.9	31.3	26.4	4.4	4.4	4.9	5.3	5.4
Croatia	4.5	-1.5	-4.2	3.7	-6.3	9.9	12.2	16.0	20.3	13.3
Cyprus	1 383.2	1 809.1	1 795.1	1 763.7	1 708.8	147.4	87.8	95.7	81.9	155.6
Malta	106.2	77.9	150.0	268.6	271.0	.. c	.. c	.. c	.. c	.. c
Romania	6.6	25.4	36.5	-10.0	-8.9	18.8	7.5	11.4	10.1	17.6
Russian Federation	-182.8	-225.4	-243.6	-191.3	-245.5	28.9	35.3	45.9	40.2	52.5
Ukraine	-0.4	-2.6	-3.4	-6.0	-4.0	122.5	113.7	121.6	125.0	97.3
AFRICA	**45.9**	**31.8**	**48.7**	**53.1**	**68.1**	**5.6**	**.. c**	**.. c**	**.. c**	**.. c**
Northern Africa	-1.9	-1.2	-0.5	5.4	23.4	5.6	.. c	.. c	.. c	.. c
Algeria	-	-	-	-	-	-	-	-	-	-
Egypt	-2.0	-4.2	-0.3	0.4	11.1	-	-	-	-	-
Libya	-	-	-	-	-	-	-	-	-	-
Morocco	-0.5	-0.7	-6.0	-2.8	1.7	.. c	.. c	.. c	.. c	.. c
Tunisia	0.8	3.7	5.8	7.8	10.6	.. c	-	-	-	-
Other African countries	47.8	33.0	49.2	47.7	44.7	-	.. c	.. c	.. c	.. c
Nigeria	.. c	0.0	-0.2	.. c	.. c	-	.. c	.. c	.. c	.. c
South Africa	-1.7	-9.8	-15.3	-7.5	-3.8	-	-	-	-	0.0
AMERICA	**546.7**	**322.4**	**671.8**	**487.1**	**890.9**	**28.9**	**52.2**	**66.2**	**64.9**	**77.4**
Northern America	351.6	13.6	255.6	238.3	684.5	15.0	12.2	11.9	10.4	25.5
Central America and Caribbean countries	68.5	123.0	209.7	63.7	73.5	10.9	.. c	.. c	.. c	.. c
Bahamas	27.2	.. c	.. c	.. c	-	-	-	-	-	-
Bermuda	-	-	.. c	.. c	.. c	-	-	-	-	-
Cayman Islands	.. c	.. c	82.5	.. c	.. c	-	-	-	-	-
Costa Rica	0.4	.. c	.. c	-0.2	0.0	-	-	-	-	-
El Salvador	-	.. c	-	-	-	-	-	-	-	-
Guatemala	-	-	.. c	-	-	-	-	-	-	-
Honduras	-	-	-	-	-	-	-	-	-	-
Nicaragua	-	-	-	-	-	-	-	-	-	-
Panama	2.5	1.8	73.1	.. c	.. c	-	-	-	-	-
Virgin Islands, U.S.	-	-	-	-	-	-	-	-	-	-
South America	126.6	185.8	206.4	185.1	132.9	2.9	26.2	38.6	37.3	38.0
Argentina	118.9	182.0	208.0	157.4	104.7	.. c	.. c	.. c	.. c	.. c
Bolivia	-	-	-	-	-	-	-	-	-	-
Brazil	8.6	4.9	1.0	-4.0	-5.0	2.9	8.6	18.1	17.3	17.9
Colombia	-	-0.8	-0.9	-0.8	-1.6	-	-	-	-	-
Ecuador	-0.1	0.0	.. c	.. c	.. c	-	-	-	-	-
Paraguay	-	-	-	-	0.0	-	-	-	-	-
Peru	-	.. c	0.0	.. c	.. c	-	-	-	-	-
Uruguay	.. c	.. c	.. c	.. c	.. c	-	-	-	-	-
Venezuela	.. c	.. c	.. c	-	0.0	-	-	-	-	-

Table 2. Foreign direct investment positions by country *(cont.)*

At year end

Million US dollars

	Inward					Outward				
	2015	2016	2017	2018	2019	2015	2016	2017	2018	2019
ASIA	**3 585.1**	**3 534.1**	**3 910.9**	**3 775.8**	**3 407.0**	**39.6**	**54.7**	**93.1**	**99.6**	**115.8**
Near and Middle East	2.1	4.0	8.6	26.6	-25.3	.. c	.. c	.. c	1.1	1.2
Gulf Arabian countries	1.3	2.4	0.5	7.7	-38.0	-	-	-	.. c	-
Kuwait	-	.. c	.. c	-	-	-	-	-	-	-
Qatar	-	0.0	-1.0	-	-0.2	-	-	-	-	-
Saudi Arabia	12.1	.. c	10.8	10.5	9.9	-	-	-	-	-
United Arab Emirates	-10.9	-9.1	-9.2	-2.7	-47.7	-	-	-	.. c	-
Other Near and Middle East	0.9	1.6	8.0	18.9	12.7	.. c	.. c	.. c	1.1	1.2
Jordan	-0.1	.. c	-0.2	-0.2	-0.2	-	-	-	-	-
Other Asian countries	3 583.0	3 530.1	3 902.3	3 749.1	3 432.3	39.3	54.2	92.3	98.5	114.6
China	15.0	26.7	36.1	25.1	21.0	24.1	23.9	52.6	56.5	75.5
Hong Kong, China	5.8	24.7	30.2	22.3	24.5	.. c	.. c	.. c	.. c	.. c
India	-4.6	-3.4	-2.7	-6.7	-8.4	6.2	9.2	13.7	13.0	12.1
Indonesia	1.0	4.5	0.0	4.7	1.8	-	-	-	-	-
Iran, Islamic Republic of	-	-	-	-	-	-	-	-	-	-
Malaysia	83.1	76.1	77.0	100.5	43.6	.. c	.. c	.. c	-	0.0
Philippines	-	0.3	0.2	0.0	0.8	-	-	-	-	-
Singapore	73.8	103.1	51.2	122.3	115.8	.. c	.. c	.. c	.. c	.. c
Chinese Taipei	74.3	79.6	18.1	-4.8	6.2	-	-	-	-	-
Thailand	2.2	3.0	6.8	6.6	1.7	-	-	-	-	-
Viet Nam	57.9	81.0	112.0	111.8	13.6	.. c	.. c	.. c	.. c	.. c
AUSTRALIA, OCEANIA AND POLAR REGIONS	**36.6**	**2.3**	**-2.8**	**3.6**	**17.8**	**.. c**	**1.3**	**.. c**	**.. c**	**.. c**
WORLD unallocated and confidential	**0.0**	**0.0**	**0.0**	**0.0**	**0.0**	**- d**	**- d**	**.. d**	**.. d**	**- d**
European Union (EU28)	**41 651.8**	**44 250.0**	**55 691.5**	**56 349.8**	**57 452.5**	**1 982.1**	**2 123.2**	**3 975.3**	**3 960.3**	**4 121.7**
G20 countries excl. European Union	**11 424.5**	**9 523.7**	**13 431.5**	**13 779.6**	**15 216.9**	**365.5**	**520.4**	**703.6**	**774.2**	**851.9**
G20 OECD countries	**11 458.0**	**9 532.6**	**13 437.2**	**13 791.4**	**15 342.1**	**303.5**	**443.3**	**573.2**	**647.2**	**693.7**
G20 Non-OECD countries	**-33.5**	**-8.9**	**-5.7**	**-11.9**	**-125.3**	**61.9**	**77.0**	**130.4**	**127.0**	**158.2**
MENA countries	**.. c**	**.. c**	**3.0**	**15.9**	**-12.0**	**.. c**	**.. c**	**.. c**	**.. c**	**.. c**
ASEAN countries	**.. c**	**267.9**	**247.2**	**345.9**	**177.3**	**.. c**	**17.9**	**23.2**	**23.0**	**20.5**

- Nil; .. Not available; c Confidential data; d Secondary Confidentiality

Note: Detailed metadata at: *http://stats.oecd.org/OECDStat_Metadata/ShowMetadata.ashx?Dataset=FDI_CTRY_IND_SUMM.*

Source: *OECD International Direct Investment Statistics (database): https://doi.org/10.1787/idi-data-en*

Table 3. Foreign direct investment income by country

Million US dollars

	Inward					Outward				
	2015	2016	2017	2018	2019	2015	2016	2017	2018	2019
WORLD	..	**4 411.3**	**4 330.4**	**4 553.1**	**4 654.8**	..	**205.8**	**391.1**	**423.6**	**365.8**
OECD COUNTRIES	..	**4 485.3**	**4 421.3**	**4 522.3**	**4 748.2**	..	**167.3**	**354.9**	**377.0**	**324.4**
Australia	..	-	-	.. c	.. c	..	-	-	-	-
Austria	..	744.7	698.1	774.9	741.5	..	19.4	11.9	7.0	14.2
Belgium	..	223.8	211.8	197.8	211.0	..	-	-	.. c	.. c
Canada	..	2.8	.. c	.. c	.. c	..	0.1	0.2	.. c	.. c
Chile	..	-	-	-	-	..	0.4	.. c	.. c	.. c
Czech Republic	..	195.5	314.7	321.9	175.2	..	47.6	229.7	276.6	149.1
Denmark	..	46.0	61.6	56.3	64.8	..	3.0	.. c	2.4	2.8
Estonia	..	0.0	.. c	.. c	.. c	..	-	-	-	-
Finland	..	3.2	6.4	34.3	37.6	..	-	-	-	0.0
France	..	128.3	151.8	92.1	91.0	..	6.9	.. c	0.9	2.1
Germany	..	576.9	524.3	569.1	550.0	..	3.1	14.0	4.3	9.7
Greece	..	-	.. c	.. c	.. c	..	-	-	-	-
Hungary	..	247.1	182.9	155.4	630.4	..	20.7	-1.2	9.7	-3.4
Iceland	..	0.1	-	-	-	..	-	-	-	-
Ireland	..	25.6	22.1	19.5	22.6	..	-	-	-	-
Israel	..	0.2	1.7	1.9	0.7	..	-	-	-	-
Italy	..	349.2	260.3	291.7	89.8	..	0.1	.. c	1.1	2.6
Japan	..	2.7	-19.5	-17.7	-4.2	..	-	-	-	-
Korea	..	398.1	401.4	416.2	146.3	..	-0.8	-	-	-
Latvia	..	-	.. c	.. c	.. c	..	-	-	-	-
Lithuania	..	0.0	.. c	.. c	.. c	..	-	-	-	-
Luxembourg	..	283.3	257.2	367.6	490.5	..	-1.2	.. c	16.1	36.8
Mexico	..	-	-	-	-	..	-	-	-	-0.7
Netherlands	..	946.3	1 056.1	967.3	955.8	..	17.4	24.4	-4.1	13.4
New Zealand	..	0.6	-	-	-	..	-	-	-	-
Norway	..	-1.5	15.3	3.3	-17.0	..	-	-	-	-
Poland	..	29.6	21.5	20.5	5.1	..	4.0	34.8	30.1	83.1
Portugal	..	-	-	-	-	..	-	-	.. c	.. c
Slovak Republic	..	..	-	-	0.2	..	..	-	-	-0.2
Slovenia	..	-0.4	-0.6	0.4	0.3	..	-	-	-	-
Spain	..	77.1	50.8	44.6	43.1	..	-	.. c	.. c	.. c
Sweden	..	24.4	33.0	23.3	48.4	..	-	-	-	-
Switzerland	..	43.6	104.6	43.4	60.1	..	-	-1.3	-1.6	-1.9
Turkey	..	0.8	.. c	.. c	.. c	..	37.3	.. c	2.5	-3.7
United Kingdom	..	139.6	80.5	99.1	158.6	..	9.2	.. c	.. c	.. c
United States	..	-2.6	-21.3	26.9	235.7	..	-	1.6	0.4	2.5
EUROPE	..	**4 006.6**	**4 027.0**	**4 084.5**	**4 319.9**	..	**200.6**	**380.7**	**419.5**	**351.4**
Bulgaria	..	0.4	0.5	.. c	.. c	..	0.1	.. c	0.0	-
Croatia	..	.. c	0.3	.. c	.. c	..	6.3	.. c	1.3	0.0
Cyprus	..	-27.2	29.4	74.2	64.8	..	19.1	19.1	2.8	6.4
Malta	..	4.3	25.4	7.9	7.4	..	1.5	1.9	.. c	.. c
Romania	..	-	.. c	-0.5	0.0	..	0.0	.. c	0.8	0.7
Russian Federation	..	-2.6	-2.8	-2.1	-23.2	..	4.1	5.5	8.8	12.0
Ukraine	..	-0.4	-0.4	-0.6	-0.7	..	0.7	0.4	29.5	4.7
AFRICA	..	**-0.8**	**6.9**	**-0.7**	**-9.1**	..	-	**.. c**	**.. c**	**.. c**
Northern Africa	..	-	-	-	-	..	-	.. c	.. c	-
Algeria	..	-	-	-	-	..	-	-	-	-
Egypt	..	-	-	-	-	..	-	-	-	-
Libya	..	-	-	-	-	..	-	-	-	-
Morocco	..	-	-	-	-	..	-	.. c	.. c	-
Tunisia	..	-	-	-	-	..	-	-	-	-
Other African countries	..	-0.8	6.9	-0.7	-9.1	..	-	-	-	0.0
Nigeria	..	-	-	-	-	..	-	-	-	0.0
South Africa	..	-	.. c	.. c	.. c	..	-	-	-	-
AMERICA	..	**-0.6**	**-21.1**	**27.5**	**202.2**	..	**0.6**	**.. c**	**1.0**	**3.1**
Northern America	..	0.2	-21.6	29.0	238.2	..	0.1	1.8	0.4	2.8
Central America and Caribbean countries	..	-0.1	0.0	-1.7	-14.4	..	-	-	-	-0.7
Bahamas	..	-	-	-	-	..	-	-	-	-
Bermuda	..	-	.. c	.. c	.. c	..	-	-	-	-
Cayman Islands	..	-0.1	-0.1	.. c	.. c	..	-	-	-	-
Costa Rica	..	-	-	-	-	..	-	-	-	-
El Salvador	..	-	-	-	-	..	-	-	-	-
Guatemala	..	-	-	-	-	..	-	-	-	-
Honduras	..	-	-	-	-	..	-	-	-	-
Nicaragua	..	-	-	-	-	..	-	-	-	-
Panama	..	-0.1	-0.1	.. c	-	..	-	-	-	-
Virgin Islands, U.S.	..	-	-	-	-	..	-	-	-	-
South America	..	-0.7	0.6	0.2	-21.6	..	0.5	.. c	0.7	1.0
Argentina	..	0.5	0.5	0.5	-21.2	..	-	-	-	-
Bolivia	..	-	-	-	-	..	-	-	-	-
Brazil	..	-1.2	0.1	-0.3	0.9	..	0.1	0.4	0.2	0.6
Colombia	..	-	-	-	-	..	-	-	-	-
Ecuador	..	-	-	-	-	..	-	-	-	-
Paraguay	..	-	-	-	-	..	-	-	-	-
Peru	..	-	-	-	-	..	-	-	-	-
Uruguay	..	-	-	.. c	.. c	..	-	-	-	-
Venezuela	..	-	-	-	-	..	-	-	-	-

Table 3. Foreign direct investment income by country *(cont.)*

Million US dollars

	Inward					Outward				
	2015	2016	2017	2018	2019	2015	2016	2017	2018	2019
ASIA	..	**405.6**	**317.6**	**440.1**	**140.4**	..	**4.5**	**7.7**	**3.1**	**11.3**
Near and Middle East	..	-0.3	1.3	1.6	-0.3	..	-	-	-	-
Gulf Arabian countries	..	-0.2	.. c	.. c	.. c	..	-	-	-	-
Kuwait	..	-	-	-	-	..	-	-	-	-
Qatar	..	-	-	-	-	..	-	-	-	-
Saudi Arabia	..	-0.2	.. c	.. c	.. c	..	-	-	-	-
United Arab Emirates	..	-	-	-	0.0	..	-	-	-	-
Other Near and Middle East	..	-0.1	1.5	1.7	0.4	..	-	-	-	-
Jordan	..	-	-	-	-	..	-	-	-	-
Other Asian countries	..	405.9	316.3	438.5	140.7	..	4.5	7.7	3.1	11.3
China	..	-0.8	-1.2	0.4	-16.6	..	5.0	8.0	2.2	12.2
Hong Kong, China	..	0.4	.. c	.. c	.. c	..	0.4	.. c	-	-
India	..	-	-	.. c	.. c	..	-	-0.3	1.1	-0.4
Indonesia	..	-	-	-	-	..	-	-	-	-
Iran, Islamic Republic of	..	-	-	-	-	..	-	-	-	-
Malaysia	..	0.2	.. c	.. c	.. c	..	-	-	-	-
Philippines	..	-	-	-	-	..	-	-	-	-
Singapore	..	4.7	-66.2	7.3	-5.3	..	-	-	-	-
Chinese Taipei	..	0.0	.. c	.. c	.. c	..	-	-	-	-
Thailand	..	0.1	.. c	.. c	.. c	..	-	-	-	-
Viet Nam	..	0.6	.. c	.. c	.. c	..	0.0	.. c	-	-0.5
AUSTRALIA, OCEANIA AND POLAR REGIONS	..	**0.6**	**-**	**.. c**	**.. c**	..	**-**	**-**	**-**	**-**
WORLD unallocated and confidential	..	**-**	**0.0**	**.. d**	**.. d**	..	**-**	**.. d**	**- d**	**- d**
European Union (EU28)	..	**4 018.1**	**3 994.8**	**4 126.8**	**4 397.7**	..	**157.5**	**362.0**	**382.2**	**339.3**
G20 countries excl. European Union	..	**1 591.4**	**1 373.8**	**1 479.3**	**1 208.8**	..	**65.1**	**65.4**	**48.0**	**43.6**
G20 OECD countries	..	**1 595.8**	**1 377.4**	**1 480.8**	**1 269.7**	..	**56.0**	**51.8**	**35.7**	**19.2**
G20 Non-OECD countries	..	**-4.4**	**-3.6**	**-1.5**	**-60.9**	..	**9.1**	**13.6**	**12.3**	**24.4**
MENA countries	..	**-0.5**	**.. c**	**.. c**	**.. c**	..	**-**	**.. c**	**.. c**	**-**
ASEAN countries	..	**.. c**	**-64.9**	**38.2**	**15.0**	..	**0.0**	**.. c**	**-**	**-0.5**

- Nil; .. Not available; c Confidential data; d Secondary Confidentiality

Note: Detailed metadata at: *http://stats.oecd.org/OECDStat_Metadata/ShowMetadata.ashx?Dataset=FDI_CTRY_IND_SUMM.*

Source: *OECD International Direct Investment Statistics (database): https://doi.org/10.1787/idi-data-en*

Table 4. Foreign direct investment flows by industrial sector

Million US dollars

	Inward					Outward				
	2015	2016	2017	2018	2019	2015	2016	2017	2018	2019
All FDI activities	..	**805.1**	**4 008.2**	**1 674.0**	**2 448.6**	..	**95.5**	**1 322.6**	**321.5**	**153.3**
Agriculture, forestry and fishing	..	**-40.1**	**14.3**	**-1.1**	..	..	.. c	.. c	.. c	..
Mining and quarrying	..	**-41.0**	**21.9**	**-18.7**	..	..	**0.3**	**243.5**	**167.2**	..
Extraction activities	..	49.5	12.2	-18.1	..	..	.. c	.. c	.. c	..
Manufacturing	..	**845.9**	**1 883.0**	**563.4**	..	..	**78.9**	**74.6**	**16.8**	..
of which:										
Food products, beverages and tobacco	..	-10.7	-13.0	-54.2	..	..	7.8	5.9	-11.3	..
Textiles, wood and paper products; printing	..	93.9	62.7	-31.9	..	..	62.7	8.7	6.5	..
Chemical, rubber, plastic, non-metallic mineral products	..	257.3	132.1	-631.5	..	..	-0.4	8.4	3.9	..
Metal and machinery products, except electrical equipment	..	-124.8	511.4	878.1	..	..	-23.8	6.0	4.9	..
Motor vehicles, trailers, semi-trailers, other transport equipment	..	355.5	788.3	411.6	..	..	8.3	-2.2	2.1	..
Other manufacturing	..	274.7	401.5	-8.6	..	..	24.4	47.8	10.7	..
Electricity, gas, steam and air conditioning supply	..	**12.7**	**-106.1**	**474.9**	..	..	**4.7**	**0.2**	**22.9**	..
Water supply; sewerage, waste management and remediation activities	..	**-2.5**	**17.5**	**16.4**	..	..	.. c	**2.0**	**6.3**	..
Construction	..	**12.5**	**46.8**	**1.8**	..	..	**-103.7**	**23.8**	**32.9**	..
Services	..	**17.6**	**2 130.8**	**637.6**	..	..	**106.4**	**980.1**	**73.0**	..
Wholesale and retail trade; repair of motor vehicles and motorcycles	..	292.9	141.5	199.9	..	..	47.4	44.6	1.0	..
Transportation and storage	..	54.7	83.4	95.1	..	..	54.8	-4.3	1.9	..
Accommodation and food service activities	..	-38.3	-0.6	14.0	..	..	.. c	.. c	.. c	..
Information and communication	..	-202.1	189.3	164.5	..	..	33.0	127.1	56.7	..
Financial and insurance activities	..	701.8	229.4	1 009.9	..	..	1.2	-98.3	34.0	..
Activities of holding companies	..	3.4	-96.0	27.2	..	..	3.7	-53.3	47.0	..
Real estate activities	..	-109.3	507.6	134.5	..	..	1.8	303.8	21.6	..
Professional, scientific and technical activities	..	-132.5	1 173.0	-620.4	..	..	-114.4	137.0	123.1	..
Administrative and support service activities	..	-586.2	-339.8	-33.3	..	..	.. c	6.7	-14.5	..
Public administration; activities of households and of extraterritorial organisations	..	-	-	-	..	..	-	.. c	.. c	..
Education	..	.. c	.. c	.. c	..	..	-	-	-	..
Human health and social work activities	..	-8.5	199.8	-339.9	..	..	.. c	.. c	.. c	..
Arts, entertainment and recreation	..	81.3	-50.1	-4.3	..	..	27.7	.. c	-58.2	..
Other services	..	-36.3	-2.7	.. c	..	..	54.6	.. c	.. c	..
Not allocated and confidential	..	**-**	**0.0**	**-0.2**	**2 448.6**	..	**.. c**	**.. c**	**.. c**	**153.3**
Private real estate activities	..	-	-	-	..	..	-	-	-	..

- Nil; .. Not available; c Confidential data

Note: Detailed metadata at: *http://stats.oecd.org/OECDStat_Metadata/ShowMetadata.ashx?Dataset=FDI_CTRY_IND_SUMM.*

Source: *OECD International Direct Investment Statistics (database): https://doi.org/10.1787/idi-data-en*

Table 5. Foreign direct investment positions by industrial sector

At year end

Million US dollars

	Inward					Outward				
	2015	2016	2017	2018	2019	2015	2016	2017	2018	2019
All FDI activities	**46 015.8**	**47 591.7**	**59 510.3**	**59 857.3**	**60 951.0**	**2 462.3**	**2 631.0**	**4 589.9**	**4 589.3**	**4 727.1**
Agriculture, forestry and fishing	**164.2**	**150.4**	**181.2**	**14.5**	..	**1.7**	**13.2**	**6.2**	**.. c**	..
Mining and quarrying	**111.5**	**94.5**	**76.1**	**-28.1**	..	**.. c**	**70.6**	**413.0**	**595.0**	..
Extraction activities	9.6	.. d	-18.8	-32.3	..	.. c	.. c	.. c	.. c	..
Manufacturing	**15 301.7**	**15 358.3**	**19 091.0**	**15 209.8**	..	**515.8**	**471.8**	**600.4**	**578.9**	..
of which:										
Food products, beverages and tobacco	884.7	637.7	670.5	1 152.3	..	20.4	35.9	48.0	37.4	..
Textiles, wood and paper products; printing	628.1	676.7	809.4	1 123.0	..	76.2	118.3	146.2	132.9	..
Chemical, rubber, plastic, non-metallic mineral products	3 528.0	3 587.1	4 115.7	2 657.8	..	-	61.5	76.6	64.2	..
Metal and machinery products, except electrical equipment	4 845.5	4 830.7	5 673.6	7 179.0	..	80.7	89.3	107.2	103.6	..
Motor vehicles, trailers, semi-trailers, other transport equipment	3 275.4	3 383.9	5 411.5	1 354.9	..	66.6	68.4	70.6	86.0	..
Other manufacturing	2 139.9	2 242.2	2 410.4	1 742.8	..	87.9	98.4	151.8	154.8	..
Electricity, gas, steam and air conditioning supply	**1 948.8**	**3 484.1**	**3 919.6**	**3 008.2**	..	**5.7**	**19.2**	**24.5**	**75.4**	..
Water supply; sewerage, waste management and remediation activities	**126.5**	**121.3**	**154.4**	**175.3**	..	**2.2**	**0.8**	**3.2**	**8.5**	..
Construction	**477.1**	**608.9**	**765.1**	**1 108.1**	..	**87.8**	**54.0**	**86.9**	**69.3**	..
Services	**27 885.9**	**27 774.2**	**35 322.9**	**40 369.5**	..	**1 778.9**	**2 001.4**	**3 455.8**	**3 255.4**	..
Wholesale and retail trade; repair of motor vehicles and motorcycles	4 137.5	4 344.0	5 091.3	7 170.7	..	469.1	485.8	603.8	546.3	..
Transportation and storage	1 856.1	1 833.5	2 149.4	3 318.8	..	65.7	133.1	153.7	113.4	..
Accommodation and food service activities	69.1	124.9	158.6	168.2	..	.. c	.. c	3.9	.. c	..
Information and communication	2 369.6	2 142.0	2 632.1	5 839.8	..	106.5	133.9	290.7	312.6	..
Financial and insurance activities	11 235.6	11 048.2	12 869.9	2 407.8	..	361.1	261.3	214.5	250.9	..
Activities of holding companies	124.0	-120.5	-541.8	-91.0	..	81.5	.. d	80.7	161.0	..
Real estate activities	3 289.5	3 004.2	4 369.4	6 345.8	..	410.3	386.3	754.7	1 125.9	..
Professional, scientific and technical activities	1 598.9	1 636.3	3 315.4	12 877.4	..	146.8	381.6	598.1	678.6	..
Administrative and support service activities	2 882.5	3 158.4	4 019.4	464.4	..	17.9	.. d	23.3	195.7	..
Public administration; activities of households and of extraterritorial organisations	-	-	-	-	..	-	-	.. c	.. c	..
Education	1.5	.. c	.. c	1.0	..	-	-	-	-	..
Human health and social work activities	134.3	126.4	421.8	1 700.7	..	.. c	.. c	.. c	.. c	..
Arts, entertainment and recreation	166.1	252.0	181.2	61.0	..	39.5	49.8	57.7	.. c	..
Other services	145.0	103.3	113.2	14.0	..	14.9	.. c	.. c	.. c	..
Not allocated and confidential	**0.1**	**0.0**	**0.0**	-	**60 951.0**	**.. c**	-	**0.0**	**.. c**	**4 727.1**
Private real estate activities	-	-	-	-	..	-	-	-	-	..

- Nil; .. Not available; c Confidential data; d Secondary Confidentiality

Note: Detailed metadata at: *http://stats.oecd.org/OECDStat_Metadata/ShowMetadata.ashx?Dataset=FDI_CTRY_IND_SUMM.*

Source: *OECD International Direct Investment Statistics (database): https://doi.org/10.1787/idi-data-en*

SLOVAK REPUBLIC

Table 6. Foreign direct investment income by industrial sector

Million US dollars

	Inward					Outward				
	2015	2016	2017	2018	2019	2015	2016	2017	2018	2019
All FDI activities	..	**4 411.3**	**4 330.4**	**4 553.1**	**4 654.8**	..	**205.8**	**391.1**	**423.6**	**365.8**
Agriculture, forestry and fishing	..	**6.6**	**21.1**	**12.9**	..	..	**.. c**	**-3.5**	**.. c**	..
Mining and quarrying	..	**40.7**	**40.2**	**82.5**	..	..	**.. c**	**-44.2**	**154.4**	..
Extraction activities	..	36.7	.. c	77.7	..	..	.. c	.. c	.. c	..
Manufacturing	..	**2 233.4**	**2 049.3**	**2 193.4**	..	..	**29.9**	**28.2**	**32.7**	..
of which:										
Food products, beverages and tobacco	..	89.0	49.1	19.6	..	..	.. c	0.2	0.9	..
Textiles, wood and paper products; printing	..	101.5	85.2	12.8	..	..	16.6	.. c	9.7	..
Chemical, rubber, plastic, non-metallic mineral products	..	616.1	530.5	-99.5	..	..	1.0	.. c	1.9	..
Metal and machinery products, except electrical equipment	..	601.1	505.7	1 670.1	..	..	0.3	5.1	13.4	..
Motor vehicles, trailers, semi-trailers, other transport equipment	..	664.1	688.0	434.8	..	..	3.3	.. c	3.2	..
Other manufacturing	..	161.5	190.7	155.6	..	..	8.2	11.7	3.6	..
Electricity, gas, steam and air conditioning supply	..	**81.0**	**30.1**	**101.7**	..	..	**0.9**	**2.6**	**1.3**	..
Water supply; sewerage, waste management and remediation activities	..	**5.0**	**15.0**	**32.1**	..	..	**0.1**	**0.3**	**1.9**	..
Construction	..	**21.0**	**63.6**	**35.8**	..	..	**3.7**	**25.2**	**4.0**	..
Services	..	**2 023.7**	**2 111.0**	**2 094.8**	..	..	**170.4**	**382.5**	**221.1**	..
Wholesale and retail trade; repair of motor vehicles and motorcycles	..	495.7	627.7	623.1	..	..	53.4	156.8	12.6	..
Transportation and storage	..	116.3	100.1	198.2	..	..	11.1	-5.6	4.2	..
Accommodation and food service activities	..	-16.7	9.6	17.3	..	..	.. c	.. c	.. c	..
Information and communication	..	286.3	335.9	601.0	..	..	10.8	32.1	33.5	..
Financial and insurance activities	..	1 003.3	864.7	531.8	..	..	28.9	34.5	18.6	..
Activities of holding companies	..	-19.9	-30.8	-6.3	..	..	8.6	10.7	6.0	..
Real estate activities	..	105.6	86.1	212.0	..	..	21.6	69.4	78.4	..
Professional, scientific and technical activities	..	74.9	-7.0	-261.9	..	..	33.0	34.0	46.0	..
Administrative and support service activities	..	-8.2	37.4	494.1	..	..	.. c	.. c	19.7	..
Public administration; activities of households and of extraterritorial organisations	..	-	-	-	..	..	-	.. c	.. c	..
Education	..	.. c	0.0	-	..	..	-	-	-	..
Human health and social work activities	..	0.9	-1.5	-327.9	..	..	.. c	.. c	.. c	..
Arts, entertainment and recreation	..	17.4	77.0	3.7	..	..	2.8	.. c	.. c	..
Other services	..	-51.9	.. c	.. c	..	..	.. c	.. c	.. c	..
Not allocated and confidential	..	**0.0**	**0.0**	-	**4 654.8**	..	**.. c**	**0.0**	**.. c**	**365.8**
Private real estate activities	..	-	-	-	..	..	-	-	-	..

- Nil; .. Not available; c Confidential data

Note: Detailed metadata at: *http://stats.oecd.org/OECDStat_Metadata/ShowMetadata.ashx?Dataset=FDI_CTRY_IND_SUMM.*

Source: *OECD International Direct Investment Statistics (database): https://doi.org/10.1787/idi-data-en*

SLOVENIA

Table 1. Foreign direct investment flows by country

Million US dollars

	Inward					Outward				
	2015	2016	2017	2018	2019	2015	2016	2017	2018	2019
WORLD	**1 674.7**	**1 244.7**	**895.8**	**1 383.3**	**1 226.6**	**267.3**	**289.6**	**337.7**	**280.7**	**389.5**
OECD COUNTRIES	**1 491.9**	**1 149.2**	**624.1**	**1 205.2**	**778.1**	**119.7**	**-11.7**	**195.9**	**44.4**	**-9.7**
Australia	-0.7	0.8	1.3	-15.2	-0.8	7.6	2.7	3.1	-4.1	-2.4
Austria	295.9	148.6	435.0	267.0	169.7	3.4	-45.5	-4.6	9.8	-2.1
Belgium	12.7	18.1	18.3	-17.8	-26.9	0.1	-0.3	-0.3	0.4	1.3
Canada	-0.6	-2.0	-1.1	-0.5	-1.1	-0.6	2.4	-0.6	9.3	5.2
Chile	0.0	0.0	0.0	0.0	-3.2	-	1.0	2.3	2.2	-2.2
Czech Republic	92.7	47.3	31.2	4.0	15.1	-3.3	19.7	-7.9	3.7	15.4
Denmark	0.1	-3.5	1.7	0.0	48.3	3.1	-4.9	1.1	3.3	-4.5
Estonia	0.5	-0.2	-0.1	-1.3	2.2	-	-	-	-	-
Finland	1.0	-10.9	3.9	-0.8	-2.4	0.2	-3.5	1.7	4.9	6.2
France	1.4	-22.6	63.1	-29.1	-103.8	-7.3	0.3	-7.4	1.6	-4.0
Germany	151.7	35.4	54.4	190.8	245.3	-42.7	-21.2	129.2	21.2	-22.7
Greece	-1.6	0.4	2.3	1.6	3.2	0.7	2.7	8.8	6.4	-13.4
Hungary	3.7	6.4	9.7	30.7	74.8	-0.8	1.0	2.8	-2.3	4.7
Iceland	0.0	-	0.0	0.0	0.0	-	-	0.0	-	-
Ireland	15.3	31.6	-5.8	-0.7	-6.2	0.2	4.2	0.6	0.1	0.6
Israel	0.3	1.3	2.5	1.6	0.1	-	-	-	-	0.0
Italy	62.3	91.2	-128.2	46.2	66.9	-2.3	13.6	39.0	-3.1	10.3
Japan	25.7	-0.9	-27.4	-28.2	-3.2	0.0	-0.9	-0.4	0.1	0.8
Korea	-1.7	1.0	1.3	-0.5	0.7	0.1	0.1	-0.3	-0.7	-1.2
Latvia	1.0	0.5	0.3	0.3	-0.6	0.0	0.0	0.0	-0.1	-0.1
Lithuania	0.2	0.1	0.1	0.0	-0.1	-0.2	0.0	0.2	-0.2	-0.1
Luxembourg	222.7	469.8	-11.2	452.3	-13.1	-3.2	3.7	-3.4	0.0	-1.2
Mexico	0.2	-0.2	0.0	-0.7	2.7	1.4	-3.7	1.7	-1.1	3.6
Netherlands	325.1	135.8	54.4	91.6	219.4	15.1	17.1	-8.2	27.4	-18.8
New Zealand	0.1	0.0	0.0	-0.1	0.2	-	0.0	0.1	-0.1	0.0
Norway	-0.2	-0.6	1.0	-0.1	2.4	-	-	0.0	-	0.0
Poland	7.9	8.5	-5.6	9.6	12.1	-1.6	2.3	0.5	-3.0	17.8
Portugal	-0.1	0.1	0.6	0.4	0.6	0.9	-0.5	2.6	-1.7	1.9
Slovak Republic	-3.2	3.3	6.3	-1.4	2.7	-2.7	-5.5	-0.1	-3.7	-0.8
Slovenia	-	-	-	-	-	-	-	-	-	-
Spain	0.1	1.9	2.3	-2.5	9.1	2.6	16.9	9.3	1.2	-6.4
Sweden	33.6	81.8	7.8	-17.2	-189.4	10.9	-1.5	7.9	1.1	18.1
Switzerland	182.5	68.5	97.0	123.0	211.2	152.3	-5.6	0.1	-1.3	4.6
Turkey	-3.5	-7.1	14.4	18.6	5.8	-2.5	0.1	15.7	-3.6	1.0
United Kingdom	72.3	43.3	-0.1	16.9	50.3	0.3	-11.5	-15.3	-0.8	-24.1
United States	-4.1	1.8	-5.2	66.6	-14.1	-12.3	5.1	17.9	-22.4	2.7
EUROPE	**1 655.4**	**1 235.5**	**913.3**	**1 375.6**	**1 233.7**	**252.5**	**261.5**	**301.2**	**267.7**	**343.2**
Bulgaria	4.6	1.6	1.9	2.9	0.8	5.4	-0.2	-0.1	-1.3	0.4
Croatia	132.0	-27.2	62.3	35.6	57.9	-15.6	105.6	176.5	139.7	276.0
Cyprus	37.6	15.0	-12.3	69.5	265.6	2.7	10.1	-9.6	1.5	7.9
Malta	1.7	51.6	11.3	6.7	-2.2	0.0	0.0	-0.5	0.4	0.5
Romania	0.5	-1.4	3.3	-4.4	2.4	-6.0	2.2	3.5	-10.8	5.4
Russian Federation	-6.5	6.8	116.8	16.4	22.0	48.7	17.3	28.5	19.7	52.4
Ukraine	5.8	-1.8	-2.2	1.2	4.2	9.7	4.5	7.9	3.4	6.0
AFRICA	**1.6**	**-2.4**	**-0.4**	**1.6**	**-4.0**	**-13.6**	**-11.1**	**-1.2**	**-4.4**	**3.3**
Northern Africa	1.2	0.9	-0.6	2.3	-5.0	1.3	0.7	2.9	0.6	-4.8
Algeria	-0.4	0.6	0.0	0.0	-	-	-	0.0	0.0	0.0
Egypt	1.0	0.0	-0.7	0.9	-7.8	0.0	-	-	-	-
Libya	0.0	0.0	-	-	-	1.4	0.7	2.3	0.5	-4.9
Morocco	0.3	0.3	0.0	1.6	2.7	0.0	0.0	0.6	0.0	0.1
Tunisia	0.2	0.1	0.1	-0.3	0.1	-	-	-	-	-
Other African countries	0.3	-3.3	0.3	-0.7	1.0	-14.9	-11.8	-4.1	-5.0	8.2
Nigeria	0.1	-	-	-	-	-	-	-	-	-
South Africa	0.0	-0.2	0.2	-0.6	1.0	3.3	1.0	-0.7	1.5	3.4
AMERICA	**-4.9**	**3.5**	**-1.1**	**70.5**	**-23.9**	**-11.6**	**5.3**	**23.2**	**-9.5**	**14.1**
Northern America	-4.8	-0.2	-6.3	66.1	-15.2	-12.9	7.5	17.3	-13.1	7.9
Central America and Caribbean countries	-0.1	4.8	5.7	3.6	-4.2	1.4	-3.6	1.7	-1.1	3.6
Bahamas	0.0	0.0	-	-	-	-	-	-	-	-
Bermuda	0.0	-	0.0	0.0	-	-	-	-	-	-
Cayman Islands	0.0	0.0	-	-	-	-	-	-	-	-
Costa Rica	-	-	-0.1	-	-	0.0	-	-	-	-
El Salvador	-	-	-	-	-	-	-	-	-	-
Guatemala	0.0	0.0	0.0	-	-	-	-	-	-	-
Honduras	-	-	-	-	-	-	-	-	-	-
Nicaragua	-	-	-	-	-	-	-	-	-	-
Panama	-0.6	0.1	-2.2	-0.2	-2.6	0.0	0.0	0.0	0.0	-
Virgin Islands, U.S.	-	-	-	-	-	-	-	-	-	-
South America	0.0	-1.1	-0.5	0.7	-4.5	-0.1	1.5	4.1	4.8	2.7
Argentina	-0.3	-0.6	-0.4	-0.1	-0.5	-	-	1.4	2.3	4.7
Bolivia	-	-	0.0	-	-	-	-	-	-	-
Brazil	0.2	-0.5	0.1	0.8	-0.3	0.0	0.9	-1.9	0.3	-0.4
Colombia	0.0	0.0	0.0	0.0	0.0	-	0.4	0.1	-0.2	-0.1
Ecuador	-	-	-	0.0	-	-0.1	-1.1	0.0	0.0	-
Paraguay	-	0.0	-	-	-	-	-	-	-	-
Peru	0.0	-	0.0	0.0	-0.5	-	0.3	2.3	0.3	0.7
Uruguay	-	0.0	0.0	-	-	-	-	-	-	-
Venezuela	0.0	0.0	-0.1	-	-	-	-	-	-	-

Table 1. Foreign direct investment flows by country *(cont.)*

Million US dollars

	Inward					Outward				
	2015	2016	2017	2018	2019	2015	2016	2017	2018	2019
ASIA	**31.1**	**6.4**	**-13.3**	**-8.3**	**20.5**	**14.8**	**14.5**	**-1.9**	**16.0**	**16.4**
Near and Middle East	4.2	13.0	21.0	14.9	2.3	1.4	-0.8	-1.6	1.8	-5.5
Gulf Arabian countries	3.0	11.7	18.7	13.9	1.6	1.3	-0.8	-1.6	1.8	-5.5
Kuwait	0.0	0.0	-0.1	-0.5	0.0	-	-	-	-	-
Qatar	0.0	-0.1	0.1	0.0	-0.1	-	-	-	-	-
Saudi Arabia	1.3	0.4	0.5	0.4	-1.6	-0.2	0.2	-0.1	0.0	-
United Arab Emirates	1.7	11.5	18.2	14.0	3.3	1.6	-1.0	-1.5	1.7	-5.5
Other Near and Middle East	1.2	1.3	2.3	1.0	0.7	0.1	-	0.0	0.0	0.0
Jordan	0.9	0.0	-0.1	-0.5	0.6	0.0	-	-	-	-
Other Asian countries	26.9	-6.7	-34.3	-23.3	18.2	13.4	15.3	-0.3	14.3	21.9
China	4.8	6.2	2.2	0.2	-0.9	9.4	11.8	1.0	14.4	22.6
Hong Kong, China	-3.3	-7.1	-4.4	4.9	8.5	2.1	0.4	1.8	-2.9	-1.9
India	-2.1	2.3	-1.2	-3.3	14.8	-0.5	-0.4	0.2	0.2	0.1
Indonesia	-	-	-	0.0	0.7	-	0.1	-0.1	0.0	0.0
Iran, Islamic Republic of	-	0.0	0.0	0.0	0.0	0.0	-0.1	-0.2	0.1	-
Malaysia	0.0	-0.7	-1.0	2.1	0.0	0.1	0.1	0.1	0.1	0.2
Philippines	-0.1	0.0	0.0	0.0	0.1	-	-	-	-	-
Singapore	4.9	-5.2	-1.6	0.5	-2.1	0.1	0.1	-0.6	0.9	-0.7
Chinese Taipei	-0.1	0.0	0.0	0.0	0.0	-	-	0.0	-	-
Thailand	0.0	0.0	0.0	-0.5	0.7	0.0	-	-0.1	-0.3	-0.1
Viet Nam	0.0	0.0	-	0.0	0.0	-	-	-	-	-
AUSTRALIA, OCEANIA AND POLAR REGIONS	**-0.6**	**0.8**	**1.3**	**-15.3**	**-0.7**	**7.6**	**2.7**	**3.1**	**-4.2**	**-2.4**
WORLD unallocated and confidential	**-7.9**	**0.9**	**-4.0**	**-40.7**	**1.1**	**17.6**	**16.7**	**13.2**	**15.0**	**14.8**
European Union (EU28)	**1 471.5**	**1 126.3**	**606.9**	**1 150.8**	**903.0**	**-40.0**	**105.0**	**326.2**	**195.6**	**268.4**
G20 countries excl. European Union	**300.3**	**155.1**	**90.7**	**278.6**	**283.8**	**2.2**	**17.7**	**211.1**	**34.9**	**52.1**
G20 OECD countries	**302.9**	**140.8**	**-27.5**	**264.9**	**248.7**	**-58.3**	**-13.1**	**182.7**	**-3.5**	**-30.7**
G20 Non-OECD countries	**-2.6**	**14.4**	**118.1**	**13.7**	**35.1**	**60.6**	**30.8**	**28.4**	**38.4**	**82.9**
MENA countries	**5.2**	**12.7**	**17.9**	**15.6**	**-2.8**	**2.7**	**-0.1**	**1.3**	**2.3**	**-10.3**
ASEAN countries	**4.7**	**-6.0**	**-2.6**	**2.1**	**-0.6**	**0.2**	**0.2**	**-0.7**	**0.7**	**-0.5**

- Nil

Note: Detailed metadata at: *http://stats.oecd.org/OECDStat_Metadata/ShowMetadata.ashx?Dataset=FDI_CTRY_IND_SUMM.*

Source: *OECD International Direct Investment Statistics (database): https://doi.org/10.1787/idi-data-en*

SLOVENIA

Table 2. Foreign direct investment positions by country

At year end

Million US dollars

	Inward					Outward				
	2015	2016	2017	2018	2019	2015	2016	2017	2018	2019
WORLD	..	..	**16 738.8**	**17 465.4**	**17 982.2**	**5 997.2**	**6 051.6**	**7 159.3**	**6 992.7**	**7 455.1**
OECD COUNTRIES	..	..	**14 011.5**	**13 711.3**	**14 064.4**	**969.9**	**924.9**	**1 245.2**	**1 248.0**	**1 239.1**
Australia	..	..	-	-	-	17.7	20.5	26.3	20.2	17.8
Austria	..	..	2 539.1	2 354.9	2 556.0	179.6	120.9	129.2	139.9	145.8
Belgium	..	..	142.1	115.2	126.3	2.9	2.7	2.8	3.0	4.3
Canada	..	..	-	-	-	6.1	8.6	8.6	17.0	22.3
Chile	..	..	-	-	-	-	1.0	3.4	5.4	3.1
Czech Republic	..	..	258.0	232.8	231.1	66.9	75.6	82.7	85.0	99.6
Denmark	..	..	-	-	-	15.6	10.5	13.1	15.6	10.9
Estonia	..	..	-	-	-	-	-	-	-	0.2
Finland	..	..	-	-	-	0.8	1.3	3.3	7.9	14.0
France	..	..	815.5	779.9	383.6	15.3	14.3	9.2	9.5	8.0
Germany	..	..	2 526.3	2 612.8	2 556.8	84.0	61.7	209.0	216.0	187.9
Greece	..	..	-	-	-	6.5	9.1	19.4	25.2	11.2
Hungary	..	..	-	-	-	20.5	24.4	25.8	31.9	36.3
Iceland	..	..	-	-	-	-	-	-	-	-
Ireland	..	..	-	-	-	1.2	5.2	6.2	6.0	6.4
Israel	..	..	-	-	-	-	-	-	-	0.0
Italy	..	..	1 568.4	1 512.2	1 690.7	62.0	79.3	127.4	117.8	128.5
Japan	..	..	409.0	392.1	405.9	2.5	1.6	1.3	1.4	2.2
Korea	..	..	-	-	-	4.8	4.8	5.1	4.7	3.4
Latvia	..	..	-	-	-	0.5	0.4	0.4	0.3	0.2
Lithuania	..	..	-	-	-	0.1	0.2	0.4	0.2	0.1
Luxembourg	..	..	313.9	275.0	486.8	2.1	5.6	3.8	3.6	4.3
Mexico	..	..	259.5	237.6	232.0	8.3	5.0	12.3	10.5	14.5
Netherlands	..	..	701.3	595.9	620.4	234.1	243.0	269.0	287.0	211.8
New Zealand	..	..	-	-	-	-	0.0	0.1	0.0	0.0
Norway	..	..	-	-	-	-	-	0.0	0.0	-
Poland	..	..	81.4	33.7	39.0	69.0	70.0	89.7	82.8	101.1
Portugal	..	..	-	-	-	4.6	3.9	7.2	5.2	7.0
Slovak Republic	..	..	-	-	-	16.5	13.9	15.3	11.1	10.9
Slovenia	..	..	314.0	406.7	438.5	-	-	-	-	-
Spain	..	..	-	-	-	29.0	43.0	58.3	56.0	50.3
Sweden	..	..	165.7	181.3	213.4	11.9	9.9	12.9	13.3	31.5
Switzerland	..	..	1 335.1	1 405.2	1 505.8	25.2	20.3	15.7	13.3	21.3
Turkey	..	..	-	-	-	10.3	8.4	24.1	16.2	14.9
United Kingdom	..	..	438.0	877.7	911.1	24.7	14.6	-4.8	-5.8	11.4
United States	..	..	2 144.2	1 698.3	1 667.2	47.8	45.6	68.7	47.9	57.5
EUROPE	..	..	**12 841.8**	**13 197.4**	**13 592.3**	**5 388.9**	**5 524.1**	**6 533.9**	**6 468.2**	**6 867.8**
Bulgaria	..	..	-	-	-	12.1	12.5	13.0	10.7	10.9
Croatia	..	..	744.2	876.4	881.1	1 619.1	1 714.3	2 181.0	2 235.0	2 574.0
Cyprus	..	..	163.8	235.1	261.6	32.5	40.3	37.3	36.8	45.9
Malta	..	..	-	-	-	0.0	0.0	-0.5	-0.1	0.6
Romania	..	..	-	-	-	24.7	27.2	33.2	21.6	26.2
Russian Federation	..	..	599.7	541.1	465.6	332.4	413.2	465.6	408.3	509.1
Ukraine	..	..	-	-	-	30.8	32.4	46.5	49.2	56.9
AFRICA	..	..	-	-	-	**244.3**	**131.3**	**135.2**	**21.8**	**21.8**
Northern Africa	..	..	-	-	-	5.5	5.9	9.5	9.6	1.9
Algeria	..	..	-	-	-	0.1	0.0	0.0	0.0	-
Egypt	..	..	-	-	-	-	-	-	-	-
Libya	..	..	-	-	-	5.4	5.9	8.9	9.0	1.3
Morocco	..	..	-	-	-	0.0	0.0	0.6	0.6	0.7
Tunisia	..	..	-	-	-	-	-	-	-	-
Other African countries	..	..	-	-	-	238.9	125.4	125.7	12.2	19.8
Nigeria	..	..	-	-	-	-	-	-	-	-
South Africa	..	..	-	-	-	22.1	25.9	28.0	27.6	30.6
AMERICA	..	..	**2 403.7**	**1 935.9**	**1 899.2**	**67.5**	**65.2**	**100.3**	**90.7**	**112.0**
Northern America	..	..	2 144.2	1 698.3	1 667.2	53.9	54.3	77.3	64.9	79.8
Central America and Caribbean countries	..	..	259.5	237.6	232.0	11.0	7.6	15.3	13.5	17.4
Bahamas	..	..	-	-	-	-	-	-	-	-
Bermuda	..	..	-	-	-	-	-	-	-	-
Cayman Islands	..	..	-	-	-	-	-	-	-	-
Costa Rica	..	..	-	-	-	-	-	-	-	-
El Salvador	..	..	-	-	-	-	-	-	-	-
Guatemala	..	..	-	-	-	-	-	-	-	-
Honduras	..	..	-	-	-	-	-	-	-	-
Nicaragua	..	..	-	-	-	-	-	-	-	-
Panama	..	..	-	-	-	2.7	2.6	0.8	0.8	0.8
Virgin Islands, U.S.	..	..	-	-	-	-	-	-	-	-
South America	..	..	-	-	-	2.6	3.3	7.7	12.3	14.8
Argentina	..	..	-	-	-	-	-	1.5	3.7	8.4
Bolivia	..	..	-	-	-	-	-	-	-	-
Brazil	..	..	-	-	-	2.4	2.5	0.5	0.7	0.3
Colombia	..	..	-	-	-	-	0.4	0.5	0.3	0.2
Ecuador	..	..	-	-	-	0.2	-0.9	-0.9	-0.9	-0.9
Paraguay	..	..	-	-	-	-	-	-	-	-
Peru	..	..	-	-	-	-	0.3	2.7	3.0	3.7
Uruguay	..	..	-	-	-	-	-	-	-	-
Venezuela	..	..	-	-	-	-	-	-	-	-

Table 2. Foreign direct investment positions by country *(cont.)*

At year end

Million US dollars

	Inward					Outward				
	2015	2016	2017	2018	2019	2015	2016	2017	2018	2019
ASIA	..	..	**411.2**	**800.2**	**771.5**	**63.4**	**75.5**	**82.1**	**92.4**	**112.4**
Near and Middle East	..	..	-	-	-	3.3	3.6	2.3	2.5	1.4
Gulf Arabian countries	..	..	-	-	-	3.3	3.5	2.2	2.5	1.4
Kuwait	..	..	-	-	-	-	-	-	-	-
Qatar	..	..	-	-	-	-	-	-	-	-
Saudi Arabia	..	..	-	-	-	0.0	0.2	0.1	0.1	0.1
United Arab Emirates	..	..	-	-	-	3.2	3.3	2.1	2.3	1.3
Other Near and Middle East	..	..	-	-	-	0.1	0.1	0.1	0.0	0.0
Jordan	..	..	-	-	-	-	-	-	-	-
Other Asian countries	..	..	411.2	800.2	771.5	60.1	72.0	79.8	89.9	111.0
China	..	..	2.2	408.1	365.6	38.3	46.1	53.9	64.0	84.3
Hong Kong, China	..	..	-	-	-	4.5	4.6	6.5	4.0	3.2
India	..	..	-	-	-	-0.1	-0.4	0.5	0.7	0.8
Indonesia	..	..	-	-	-	-	0.1	0.0	0.0	0.0
Iran, Islamic Republic of	..	..	-	-	-	0.0	-0.1	-0.3	-0.2	0.0
Malaysia	..	..	-	-	-	0.5	0.6	1.2	1.2	1.3
Philippines	..	..	-	-	-	-	-	-	-	-
Singapore	..	..	-	-	-	0.0	1.7	1.3	2.2	1.6
Chinese Taipei	..	..	-	-	-	-	-	-	-	0.0
Thailand	..	..	-	-	-	1.3	1.3	0.2	-0.1	0.3
Viet Nam	..	..	-	-	-	-	-	-	-	-
AUSTRALIA, OCEANIA AND POLAR REGIONS	..	..	-	-	-	**17.7**	**20.5**	**26.4**	**20.2**	**17.9**
WORLD unallocated and confidential	..	..	**1 082.1**	**1 531.9**	**1 719.3**	**215.4**	**234.9**	**281.4**	**299.4**	**323.3**
European Union (EU28)	..	..	**10 771.6**	**11 089.5**	**11 396.2**	**2 536.2**	**2 603.7**	**3 344.1**	**3 415.3**	**3 739.5**
G20 countries excl. European Union	..	..	**8 762.8**	**9 059.7**	**8 678.4**	**678.7**	**751.9**	**1 037.4**	**960.7**	**1 102.1**
G20 OECD countries	..	..	**8 160.9**	**8 110.6**	**7 847.2**	**283.5**	**264.3**	**487.2**	**455.5**	**468.5**
G20 Non-OECD countries	..	..	**601.9**	**949.2**	**831.2**	**395.2**	**487.5**	**550.2**	**505.1**	**633.6**
MENA countries	..	..	-	-	-	**8.7**	**9.5**	**11.7**	**12.0**	**3.3**
ASEAN countries	..	..	-	-	-	**1.9**	**3.7**	**2.7**	**3.3**	**3.3**

- Nil; .. Not available

Note: Inward FDI positions are allocated according to the ultimate investing country. Inward FDI positions by immediate counterpart country are available for more years in the *OECD FDI database according to BMD4*. Detailed metadata at: *http://stats.oecd.org/OECDStat_Metadata/ShowMetadata.ashx?Dataset=FDI_CTRY_IND_SUMM*.

Source: *OECD International Direct Investment Statistics (database): https://doi.org/10.1787/idi-data-en*

SLOVENIA

Table 3. Foreign direct investment income by country

Million US dollars

	Inward					Outward				
	2015	2016	2017	2018	2019	2015	2016	2017	2018	2019
WORLD	**1 078.2**	**1 252.3**	**1 254.8**	**1 565.6**	**1 600.7**	**55.2**	**176.5**	**219.7**	**357.3**	**374.2**
OECD COUNTRIES	**1 027.2**	**1 240.3**	**1 310.9**	**1 437.5**	**1 439.6**	**15.3**	**27.0**	**52.6**	**61.4**	**53.9**
Australia	-0.5	0.1	1.2	-0.5	0.8	-1.7	-4.7	-2.4	-1.8	-0.6
Austria	367.6	426.5	458.2	494.5	401.0	2.9	4.7	3.4	4.8	7.0
Belgium	18.7	21.5	18.6	20.1	18.8	-0.6	0.0	0.3	0.3	0.4
Canada	-0.1	-0.1	-	-	-	-0.1	0.0	0.5	-2.5	2.7
Chile	-	-	-	-	-	-	-	0.0	0.0	-
Czech Republic	10.6	16.0	20.6	15.4	12.9	5.1	9.8	7.6	12.4	10.8
Denmark	19.8	20.6	15.4	18.8	14.9	0.5	0.7	0.7	1.3	1.5
Estonia	0.1	0.1	0.0	-	-0.7	-	-	-	-	-
Finland	5.0	4.1	2.4	10.3	3.8	-1.3	0.1	-0.4	0.1	0.3
France	48.3	103.5	105.7	138.0	56.8	-1.3	0.2	-1.5	1.0	-0.1
Germany	172.6	172.6	180.0	172.7	159.2	-1.2	7.3	13.3	2.3	8.8
Greece	0.0	0.9	2.7	3.1	2.5	0.2	0.0	0.3	0.0	-0.6
Hungary	13.2	6.7	11.9	12.3	71.5	0.1	3.7	5.0	4.6	8.1
Iceland	-	-	-	-	-	-	-	-	-	-
Ireland	0.7	-6.9	-0.1	0.6	2.3	0.8	0.7	0.3	0.5	0.9
Israel	0.5	-0.1	0.0	0.2	0.2	-	-	-	-	-
Italy	57.2	96.1	60.9	104.2	100.7	-1.7	0.4	11.6	3.4	0.2
Japan	2.6	4.0	0.2	3.0	3.4	-0.1	-0.5	-0.1	0.0	0.2
Korea	0.4	0.0	-0.3	-0.2	-0.4	0.8	0.8	0.8	-0.3	-1.0
Latvia	0.1	0.1	0.2	0.1	0.1	0.1	0.1	0.1	0.1	0.1
Lithuania	0.1	0.2	-	-	-	0.1	0.2	0.2	0.2	0.2
Luxembourg	45.5	102.9	62.0	6.4	115.5	-0.4	-	0.5	-	-0.6
Mexico	-	-	-	-	0.2	-2.1	-3.0	-1.3	-0.9	-1.7
Netherlands	41.1	56.6	127.2	139.3	175.8	3.5	3.5	3.8	26.2	0.3
New Zealand	0.0	0.0	-	-	-	-	-	-	-	-
Norway	0.5	0.2	1.2	1.0	0.9	-	-	-	0.0	-
Poland	1.3	4.9	3.7	3.3	3.0	7.4	7.0	9.5	10.2	11.8
Portugal	-	-	-	-	-	0.3	0.3	0.3	0.3	0.4
Slovak Republic	2.5	6.2	7.4	-0.6	4.4	0.4	-0.4	-0.7	0.0	0.1
Slovenia	-	-	-	-	-	-	-	-	-	-
Spain	-0.4	0.0	1.7	1.1	1.5	0.9	2.0	1.3	-0.4	1.3
Sweden	8.0	11.5	33.2	33.9	60.2	2.3	0.6	0.9	0.4	1.7
Switzerland	162.9	124.6	137.4	197.1	199.1	-1.7	-3.3	0.0	0.6	4.4
Turkey	-0.7	-0.3	0.5	0.3	-0.6	-0.2	0.3	1.5	2.1	4.0
United Kingdom	37.4	50.3	48.2	39.6	33.8	2.2	-0.1	-0.3	2.6	0.9
United States	12.2	17.8	10.7	23.3	-2.1	0.4	-3.2	-2.1	-6.0	-7.7
EUROPE	**1 064.1**	**1 236.4**	**1 246.7**	**1 523.0**	**1 596.3**	**66.1**	**184.1**	**223.0**	**374.5**	**372.8**
Bulgaria	1.4	1.0	0.1	0.6	0.3	0.5	1.0	-2.1	-0.3	0.7
Croatia	29.7	-29.7	-103.6	60.3	79.8	-21.2	-13.7	35.1	86.1	99.0
Cyprus	20.1	14.7	5.9	4.6	18.3	0.5	9.1	-8.8	0.8	-1.4
Malta	3.9	11.7	11.9	9.2	-16.6	0.0	0.0	-0.5	0.4	0.6
Romania	-0.5	0.1	-	0.2	-0.1	1.5	1.4	1.0	1.3	1.0
Russian Federation	-12.7	-3.5	-3.4	-2.2	1.1	5.0	23.7	23.3	31.0	39.9
Ukraine	-0.3	-0.9	0.2	0.0	0.1	10.3	12.1	4.5	7.9	17.1
AFRICA	**1.5**	**-2.9**	**0.0**	**-0.1**	**-0.1**	**-13.2**	**-11.2**	**-0.3**	**-4.2**	**9.1**
Northern Africa	1.2	0.1	0.0	-0.1	-0.1	1.3	0.7	2.2	0.5	1.2
Algeria	0.0	0.0	-	-	-	-	-	0.0	0.0	0.0
Egypt	1.2	0.0	0.0	-0.1	-0.1	-	-	-	-	-
Libya	0.0	0.0	-	-	-	1.4	0.7	2.3	0.5	1.3
Morocco	0.3	0.3	-	-	-	0.0	0.0	-0.1	0.0	-0.1
Tunisia	-0.3	-0.1	-	-	-	-	-	-	-	-
Other African countries	0.2	-3.0	-	-	-	-14.6	-11.9	-2.5	-4.7	7.9
Nigeria	-	-	-	-	-	-	-	-	-	-
South Africa	-	0.0	-	-	-	3.2	0.8	-0.5	1.5	3.4
AMERICA	**11.4**	**17.9**	**7.4**	**26.5**	**-6.7**	**-2.8**	**-7.4**	**-3.0**	**-9.4**	**-6.6**
Northern America	12.1	17.7	10.7	23.3	-2.1	0.2	-3.3	-1.6	-8.4	-5.0
Central America and Caribbean countries	-0.7	0.2	-3.3	3.1	-4.6	-2.1	-3.0	-1.3	-0.9	-1.7
Bahamas	0.0	0.0	-	-	-	-	-	-	-	-
Bermuda	-	-	-	-	-	-	-	-	-	-
Cayman Islands	0.0	0.0	-	-	-	-	-	-	-	-
Costa Rica	-	-	-	-	-	-	-	-	-	-
El Salvador	-	-	-	-	-	-	-	-	-	-
Guatemala	-	-	-	-	-	-	-	-	-	-
Honduras	-	-	-	-	-	-	-	-	-	-
Nicaragua	-	-	-	-	-	-	-	-	-	-
Panama	0.2	0.1	-2.2	-0.2	-0.7	-	-	-	-	-
Virgin Islands, U.S.	-	-	-	-	-	-	-	-	-	-
South America	0.0	0.0	-	-	-	-0.9	-1.2	-0.1	0.0	0.0
Argentina	0.0	0.0	-	-	-	-	-	0.0	0.0	0.0
Bolivia	-	-	-	-	-	-	-	-	-	-
Brazil	-	-	-	-	-	-0.8	-0.1	-0.1	0.0	-
Colombia	-	-	-	-	-	-	-	-	-	-
Ecuador	-	-	-	-	-	-0.2	-1.0	0.0	-	-
Paraguay	-	-	-	-	-	-	-	-	-	-
Peru	-	-	-	-	-	-	-	0.0	0.0	-
Uruguay	-	-	-	-	-	-	-	-	-	-
Venezuela	-	-	-	-	-	-	-	-	-	-

Table 3. Foreign direct investment income by country *(cont.)*

Million US dollars

	Inward					Outward				
	2015	2016	2017	2018	2019	2015	2016	2017	2018	2019
ASIA	**1.3**	**0.0**	**-0.5**	**16.7**	**10.4**	**6.9**	**15.8**	**2.5**	**-1.8**	**-0.5**
Near and Middle East	1.6	2.8	0.8	14.5	8.3	-0.7	1.3	-1.6	1.0	-1.3
Gulf Arabian countries	1.2	3.0	0.8	14.3	8.1	-0.7	1.3	-1.6	1.0	-1.3
Kuwait	0.0	-0.1	0.0	0.0	0.0	-	-	-	-	-
Qatar	-	-	-	-	-	-	-	-	-	-
Saudi Arabia	0.4	0.4	0.9	0.4	0.4	0.0	-0.1	0.0	-	-
United Arab Emirates	0.8	2.7	-0.1	13.9	7.7	-0.7	1.4	-1.6	1.0	-1.3
Other Near and Middle East	0.5	-0.2	0.0	0.2	0.2	-	-	0.0	0.0	0.0
Jordan	0.0	0.0	-	-	-	-	-	-	-	-
Other Asian countries	-0.3	-2.8	-1.3	2.2	2.1	7.5	14.4	4.1	-2.9	0.8
China	0.1	0.2	-0.1	-0.7	-0.8	6.5	9.1	1.8	-3.6	0.1
Hong Kong, China	-3.6	-6.9	-1.0	0.1	0.0	2.1	4.3	1.3	1.3	0.8
India	0.0	0.0	0.0	0.0	-	-0.2	-0.2	0.1	0.3	0.0
Indonesia	-	-	-	-	0.0	-	-	-	-	-
Iran, Islamic Republic of	-	-	-	-	-	0.0	-0.1	-0.1	-	-
Malaysia	-	-	-	0.0	0.0	-	-	0.0	-	-
Philippines	0.0	0.0	-	-	-	-	-	-	-	-
Singapore	0.3	0.0	0.0	0.1	0.0	0.1	0.0	0.0	0.0	0.0
Chinese Taipei	-0.1	0.0	-	-	-	-	-	-	-	-
Thailand	-	0.0	-	-	-	-	-	-	-0.9	0.2
Viet Nam	-	-	-	-	-	-	-	-	-	-
AUSTRALIA, OCEANIA AND POLAR REGIONS	**-0.4**	**0.1**	**1.2**	**-0.5**	**0.8**	**-1.7**	**-4.7**	**-2.4**	**-1.8**	**-0.6**
WORLD unallocated and confidential	**0.2**	**0.8**	**0.1**	**-**	**0.0**	**-**	**0.0**	**0.0**	**0.0**	**-**
European Union (EU28)	**903.8**	**1 091.9**	**1 074.2**	**1 288.0**	**1 319.6**	**1.6**	**38.6**	**80.7**	**158.3**	**153.3**
G20 countries excl. European Union	**317.3**	**441.1**	**404.4**	**478.0**	**352.4**	**8.7**	**30.9**	**44.4**	**29.1**	**49.1**
G20 OECD countries	**329.5**	**444.0**	**407.1**	**480.5**	**351.7**	**-5.1**	**-2.5**	**19.9**	**-0.1**	**5.7**
G20 Non-OECD countries	**-12.2**	**-3.0**	**-2.7**	**-2.5**	**0.7**	**13.8**	**33.3**	**24.5**	**29.2**	**43.4**
MENA countries	**2.4**	**3.1**	**0.8**	**14.2**	**8.0**	**0.7**	**2.0**	**0.5**	**1.5**	**-0.1**
ASEAN countries	**0.3**	**0.0**	**0.0**	**0.1**	**0.0**	**0.1**	**0.0**	**0.0**	**-0.9**	**0.2**

- Nil

Note: Detailed metadata at: *http://stats.oecd.org/OECDStat_Metadata/ShowMetadata.ashx?Dataset=FDI_CTRY_IND_SUMM.*

Source: OECD *International Direct Investment Statistics (database): https://doi.org/10.1787/idi-data-en*

SLOVENIA

Table 4. Foreign direct investment flows by industrial sector

Million US dollars

	Inward					Outward				
	2015	2016	2017	2018	2019	2015	2016	2017	2018	2019
All FDI activities	**1 674.7**	**1 244.7**	**895.8**	**1 383.3**	**1 226.6**	**267.3**	**289.6**	**337.7**	**280.7**	**389.5**
Agriculture, forestry and fishing	**-0.2**	**3.5**	**0.3**	**-0.1**	**0.6**	**10.0**	**3.7**	**2.4**	**1.1**	**2.6**
Mining and quarrying	**-0.4**	**0.1**	**5.8**	**10.0**	**10.9**	**-0.7**	**5.1**	**16.5**	**3.4**	**5.8**
Extraction activities	0.1	0.6	6.0	-1.6	7.2	-	-	-	-	-
Manufacturing	**809.1**	**508.3**	**254.7**	**817.7**	**352.7**	**108.2**	**120.3**	**244.9**	**53.0**	**143.7**
of which:										
Food products, beverages and tobacco	405.5	207.7	129.8	-1.3	253.3	3.4	6.1	16.5	4.5	19.3
Textiles, wood and paper products; printing	12.7	33.0	59.6	38.8	48.5	-2.2	1.3	0.6	-1.4	6.6
Chemical, rubber, plastic, non-metallic mineral products	159.2	140.6	11.4	125.4	41.6	18.0	41.4	124.7	57.4	66.4
Metal and machinery products, except electrical equipment	106.0	80.4	17.5	95.8	76.8	3.6	55.9	62.6	12.1	30.9
Motor vehicles, trailers, semi-trailers, other transport equipment	20.6	-20.0	-3.9	177.9	-42.9	52.5	4.6	-14.6	0.5	17.9
Other manufacturing	105.2	66.6	40.2	381.1	-24.7	33.0	11.0	55.1	-20.2	2.5
Electricity, gas, steam and air conditioning supply	**14.0**	**-20.7**	**29.8**	**41.5**	**-3.2**	**25.4**	**14.0**	**40.3**	**27.5**	**-0.2**
Water supply; sewerage, waste management and remediation activities	**0.0**	**-0.8**	**1.0**	**3.4**	**11.4**	**-0.1**	**0.0**	**1.1**	**-0.4**	**-2.8**
Construction	**-11.6**	**28.7**	**45.4**	**-11.4**	**-14.3**	**-10.7**	**6.5**	**6.1**	**-6.7**	**0.1**
Services	**844.1**	**715.0**	**557.1**	**498.0**	**858.4**	**95.3**	**81.0**	**-47.5**	**120.8**	**168.9**
Wholesale and retail trade; repair of motor vehicles and motorcycles	67.9	31.6	85.8	220.1	21.6	4.3	68.8	23.1	22.6	102.8
Transportation and storage	40.6	19.9	-6.8	4.4	-34.7	-22.1	-12.8	2.0	9.5	0.2
Accommodation and food service activities	45.5	1.1	-11.5	-9.1	2.9	-7.2	-3.5	6.7	0.0	1.4
Information and communication	211.9	38.2	27.4	55.5	50.3	11.6	13.4	-108.6	-3.3	-36.6
Financial and insurance activities	512.7	445.9	255.2	114.2	693.0	147.6	21.2	25.3	74.4	2.2
Activities of holding companies	105.0	22.8	190.0	-7.2	130.8	0.8	4.6	-20.8	11.6	-13.5
Real estate activities	-57.3	101.0	110.9	64.6	-150.9	4.6	4.9	5.6	4.5	94.2
Professional, scientific and technical activities	3.2	47.1	74.4	30.9	251.3	4.5	-2.9	0.1	7.9	-2.8
Administrative and support service activities	3.4	-15.6	17.8	14.7	10.3	-26.5	-10.0	-6.8	3.4	6.1
Public administration; activities of households and of extraterritorial organisations	0.0	0.0	-	-	-	-	-	-	-	-
Education	-0.3	-0.4	0.2	0.0	0.0	-0.1	0.0	0.0	0.0	0.0
Human health and social work activities	6.2	-0.2	1.1	1.6	12.6	-	-	-	-0.3	-2.3
Arts, entertainment and recreation	8.9	45.6	2.9	1.4	-0.1	-21.7	0.5	1.1	-0.9	-0.4
Other services	1.4	0.9	0.0	-0.3	2.1	0.2	1.4	4.1	2.9	4.1
Not allocated and confidential	**19.6**	**10.7**	**1.7**	**24.2**	**10.0**	**40.0**	**59.0**	**73.9**	**82.0**	**71.3**
Private real estate activities	-	-	-	-	-	-	-	-	-	-

- Nil

Note: Detailed metadata at: *http://stats.oecd.org/OECDStat_Metadata/ShowMetadata.ashx?Dataset=FDI_CTRY_IND_SUMM.*

Source: *OECD International Direct Investment Statistics (database): https://doi.org/10.1787/idi-data-en*

Table 5. Foreign direct investment positions by industrial sector

At year end

Million US dollars

	Inward					Outward				
	2015	2016	2017	2018	2019	2015	2016	2017	2018	2019
All FDI activities	..	..	**16 738.8**	**17 465.4**	**17 982.2**	**5 997.2**	**6 051.6**	**7 159.3**	**6 992.7**	**7 455.1**
Agriculture, forestry and fishing	**17.4**	**19.8**	**26.4**	**26.8**	**29.0**	**29.3**	**40.3**	**49.3**	**30.5**	**34.4**
Mining and quarrying	**46.9**	**46.0**	**61.9**	**68.4**	**61.2**	**18.4**	**26.0**	**42.5**	**45.1**	**49.9**
Extraction activities	32.3	33.7	44.8	41.1	34.7	-	-	-	-	-
Manufacturing	**4 323.9**	**4 446.8**	**5 567.8**	**6 253.7**	**6 340.1**	**1 533.9**	**1 509.5**	**1 903.6**	**1 914.1**	**2 030.6**
of which:										
Food products, beverages and tobacco	577.3	522.0	733.6	704.0	777.2	260.7	216.1	266.9	285.1	297.7
Textiles, wood and paper products; printing	425.1	446.3	552.9	536.8	523.5	8.7	6.5	11.6	10.8	13.7
Chemical, rubber, plastic, non-metallic mineral products	1 508.9	1 602.9	1 904.6	1 943.6	1 978.6	415.2	562.3	754.4	709.3	763.6
Metal and machinery products, except electrical equipment	591.7	639.3	852.3	941.0	987.9	151.6	183.3	324.2	336.2	355.4
Motor vehicles, trailers, semi-trailers, other transport equipment	512.7	393.5	451.6	583.5	642.2	206.6	161.6	81.9	115.1	136.1
Other manufacturing	708.1	842.9	1 073.0	1 544.9	1 430.8	491.1	379.8	464.6	457.7	464.1
Electricity, gas, steam and air conditioning supply	**379.1**	**350.6**	**439.5**	**447.6**	**447.9**	**151.5**	**143.4**	**198.6**	**248.4**	**232.3**
Water supply; sewerage, waste management and remediation activities	**63.5**	**61.3**	**69.9**	**92.5**	**101.4**	**9.9**	**12.4**	**16.2**	**15.0**	**11.0**
Construction	**96.4**	**162.3**	**262.3**	**230.4**	**195.1**	**14.9**	**62.0**	**109.6**	**38.6**	**36.8**
Services	**7 456.3**	**8 307.0**	**9 960.9**	**9 957.2**	**10 395.9**	**3 159.5**	**3 089.2**	**3 385.4**	**3 204.7**	**3 384.2**
Wholesale and retail trade; repair of motor vehicles and motorcycles	2 681.1	2 629.6	2 968.1	3 092.5	3 116.4	1 306.6	1 303.2	1 451.4	1 358.9	1 444.9
Transportation and storage	305.4	307.3	328.3	301.6	233.9	314.6	192.6	192.2	89.5	86.1
Accommodation and food service activities	94.2	102.9	122.7	138.1	154.8	38.9	41.0	53.3	50.7	44.1
Information and communication	774.1	790.1	945.4	976.0	1 011.7	282.2	171.9	213.0	182.5	169.7
Financial and insurance activities	2 241.3	3 080.7	3 682.9	3 379.1	3 904.5	909.7	1 016.0	1 050.8	1 123.9	1 153.5
Activities of holding companies	261.4	264.4	440.9	384.9	515.5	250.1	398.0	308.0	322.1	296.9
Real estate activities	760.1	834.8	1 089.7	1 203.5	1 128.5	140.1	311.8	328.9	316.2	371.4
Professional, scientific and technical activities	430.9	429.5	664.6	661.0	635.6	175.1	52.6	83.8	89.9	96.0
Administrative and support service activities	128.6	77.6	98.7	147.7	143.3	-49.4	-41.2	-17.4	-46.2	-21.2
Public administration; activities of households and of extraterritorial organisations	0.0	0.0	-	-	-	-	-	-	-	-
Education	-0.3	-0.9	-	1.0	1.0	-0.2	-0.2	-0.1	-0.1	0.0
Human health and social work activities	8.0	7.4	10.2	10.5	19.0	2.0	1.9	2.2	1.8	-0.6
Arts, entertainment and recreation	13.1	27.7	27.7	25.5	24.9	11.1	10.4	-3.4	5.2	4.6
Other services	19.9	20.2	22.5	20.8	22.5	28.9	29.2	30.6	32.4	35.8
Not allocated and confidential	**258.9**	**278.0**	**350.0**	**388.8**	**411.6**	**1 080.0**	**1 168.8**	**1 454.0**	**1 496.2**	**1 675.9**
Private real estate activities	-	-	-	-	-	-	-	-	-	-

- Nil; .. Not available

Note: Detailed metadata at: *http://stats.oecd.org/OECDStat_Metadata/ShowMetadata.ashx?Dataset=FDI_CTRY_IND_SUMM.*

Source: *OECD International Direct Investment Statistics (database): https://doi.org/10.1787/idi-data-en*

Table 6. Foreign direct investment income by industrial sector

Million US dollars

	Inward					Outward				
	2015	2016	2017	2018	2019	2015	2016	2017	2018	2019
All FDI activities	**1 078.2**	**1 252.3**	**1 254.8**	**1 565.6**	**1 600.7**	**55.2**	**176.5**	**219.7**	**357.3**	**374.2**
Agriculture, forestry and fishing	**2.6**	**1.1**	**0.7**	**0.6**	**-1.3**	**1.9**	**1.4**	**2.9**	**1.8**	**2.6**
Mining and quarrying	**-1.0**	**0.0**	**-0.9**	**1.5**	**11.2**	**-0.2**	**0.2**	**1.9**	**4.0**	**4.0**
Extraction activities	-1.6	-1.1	-1.4	-1.9	6.9	-	-	-	-	-
Manufacturing	**518.4**	**565.5**	**566.8**	**526.2**	**613.1**	**55.8**	**87.2**	**94.9**	**115.8**	**122.0**
of which:										
Food products, beverages and tobacco	29.3	46.7	59.7	74.8	102.4	16.4	21.6	25.1	29.8	25.5
Textiles, wood and paper products; printing	41.9	45.1	29.2	29.1	44.1	-0.2	-0.4	0.8	0.5	0.2
Chemical, rubber, plastic, non-metallic mineral products	232.3	183.4	194.4	236.6	224.8	21.8	30.6	38.2	48.4	72.4
Metal and machinery products, except electrical equipment	67.8	92.4	42.3	96.4	80.8	5.2	20.9	38.1	32.6	29.5
Motor vehicles, trailers, semi-trailers, other transport equipment	74.1	62.6	90.9	78.6	36.2	-1.8	-1.1	-30.5	-9.5	-14.4
Other manufacturing	73.0	135.3	150.3	10.5	124.8	14.4	15.6	23.2	14.0	8.8
Electricity, gas, steam and air conditioning supply	**7.2**	**-5.7**	**6.7**	**-1.9**	**8.1**	**7.2**	**4.4**	**2.3**	**8.4**	**12.3**
Water supply; sewerage, waste management and remediation activities	**6.4**	**7.2**	**8.1**	**9.7**	**10.2**	**-0.1**	**0.3**	**1.1**	**0.2**	**-2.9**
Construction	**-7.2**	**0.7**	**3.4**	**28.3**	**8.2**	**-3.9**	**1.7**	**0.3**	**-1.7**	**-0.2**
Services	**551.8**	**683.4**	**670.0**	**1 001.2**	**951.1**	**-5.5**	**80.9**	**116.1**	**227.2**	**236.4**
Wholesale and retail trade; repair of motor vehicles and motorcycles	267.4	207.6	127.9	352.8	307.6	45.3	55.0	19.3	64.7	83.3
Transportation and storage	32.5	35.7	27.2	0.8	-14.8	-18.3	-11.5	-2.2	-2.5	7.4
Accommodation and food service activities	-7.6	3.3	4.4	8.3	8.7	-1.2	-0.1	-0.2	1.7	2.1
Information and communication	96.6	64.7	69.2	80.5	72.4	11.7	9.1	10.2	9.6	8.5
Financial and insurance activities	26.1	273.5	276.1	362.8	398.9	-12.2	59.2	97.5	135.6	100.1
Activities of holding companies	4.7	21.4	-2.8	11.9	31.2	-1.8	12.1	-6.7	27.0	2.5
Real estate activities	94.4	65.6	89.5	101.6	124.2	-10.5	-37.1	-12.6	5.2	32.1
Professional, scientific and technical activities	31.5	40.4	60.7	79.0	44.1	4.2	6.4	5.2	8.1	-4.3
Administrative and support service activities	6.8	-18.1	12.5	10.3	7.5	-25.2	-2.6	-5.7	2.0	5.1
Public administration; activities of households and of extraterritorial organisations	-	0.0	-	-	-	-	-	-	-	-
Education	-0.2	-0.4	-	0.0	0.0	-0.1	0.0	0.0	0.0	0.0
Human health and social work activities	1.4	0.7	1.1	1.6	1.4	-	-	-	-0.3	-2.5
Arts, entertainment and recreation	0.2	8.6	-0.7	0.7	-0.9	0.6	1.2	1.3	0.8	0.6
Other services	2.9	1.7	2.2	2.7	2.1	0.2	1.3	3.2	2.4	4.0
Not allocated and confidential	**0.0**	**0.0**	**0.0**	**0.0**	**0.0**	**0.1**	**0.5**	**0.2**	**1.7**	**0.0**
Private real estate activities	-	-	-	-	-	-	-	-	-	-

- Nil

Note: Detailed metadata at: *http://stats.oecd.org/OECDStat_Metadata/ShowMetadata.ashx?Dataset=FDI_CTRY_IND_SUMM.*

Source: *OECD International Direct Investment Statistics (database): https://doi.org/10.1787/idi-data-en*

SPAIN

Table 1. Foreign direct investment flows by country

Million US dollars

	Inward					Outward				
	2015	2016	2017	2018	2019	2015	2016	2017	2018	2019
WORLD	**8 556.9**	**31 538.2**	**41 876.9**	**53 461.6**	**8 514.5**	**41 916.8**	**43 902.5**	**55 926.1**	**37 710.4**	**19 670.9**
OECD COUNTRIES	**3 863.6**	**29 570.9**	**40 210.8**	**49 103.0**	**10 598.9**	**29 547.4**	**31 354.6**	**46 263.1**	**23 840.4**	**13 414.3**
Australia	.. c	.. c	.. d	.. d	.. d	86.5	.. d	574.9	335.2	7.8
Austria	.. c	.. c	125.1	-139.3	66.0	.. d	.. d	688.8	-48.4	111.9
Belgium	1 104.8	-613.7	-812.8	1 124.7	1 309.8	472.5	496.5	1.1	214.8	914.6
Canada	.. d	.. d	48.5	-51.9	108.6	.. c	.. d	.. d	.. d	.. d
Chile	.. c	.. c	22.5	-14.2	70.5	2 327.2	2 945.9	-9 475.8	483.9	1 867.2
Czech Republic	.. c	.. c	81.2	37.8	29.1	.. d	.. d	103.7	.. d	138.8
Denmark	407.1	.. d	-308.9	200.6	-120.9	.. d	.. d	.. d	.. d	.. d
Estonia	.. c	.. c	-6.8	-2.4	-1.1	.. c	.. c	11.3	8.3	3.4
Finland	.. c	.. d	119.5	-11.8	.. d	.. c	.. c	.. d	512.2	-170.2
France	5 733.8	3 236.8	2 427.0	3 151.2	-1 918.7	2 692.2	1 638.8	3 899.2	2 465.5	2 908.3
Germany	455.9	4 997.2	4 912.6	8 322.9	1 645.6	1 487.5	1 946.3	971.7	.. d	-266.4
Greece	.. c	.. c	.. d	40.1	.. c	.. c	.. d	-82.3	-31.9	-586.6
Hungary	-59.9	-327.3	5.6	.. d	35.8	.. c	.. c	90.2	206.5	-1 132.9
Iceland	.. c	.. c	.. d	.. d	.. d	.. c	.. c	-1.1	.. d	.. d
Ireland	-487.0	125.0	5 622.8	-472.1	78.4	905.2	-2 992.4	2 769.7	474.4	4 576.3
Israel	.. c	.. c	.. d	.. d	-	.. c	.. c	22.5	.. c	9.0
Italy	.. c	273.1	-7 963.0	7 950.0	1 423.9	-607.9	1 299.3	1 254.7	-553.5	-619.1
Japan	.. d	.. d	.. d	.. c	.. d	.. c	.. c	24.8	.. d	39.2
Korea	.. d	56.4	.. d	.. d	.. d	.. d	.. d	.. d	.. c	29.1
Latvia	.. c	.. c	.. c	-	-	.. c	.. c	.. c	7.1	.. c
Lithuania	.. c	.. c	-	-	-	.. c	.. c	37.2	3.5	-45.9
Luxembourg	-1 273.4	3 083.0	5 993.7	14 840.1	2 954.2	-555.7	4 707.5	.. d	3 665.8	-68.3
Mexico	.. d	.. d	104.8	-328.1	-263.1	3 667.2	4 497.4	3 151.8	3 584.3	3 637.1
Netherlands	-2 909.6	6 856.1	13 971.4	3 584.3	4 031.1	.. d	-11 090.3	20.3	305.7	7 282.0
New Zealand	.. c	.. c	15.8	-62.6	.. d	.. c	.. c	1.1	.. d	.. c
Norway	.. d	.. d	.. d	63.7	.. d	146.4	.. d	269.4	485.1	237.3
Poland	.. d	.. d	84.5	3 016.6	72.8	621.2	339.5	617.7	846.2	-33.6
Portugal	.. d	498.7	242.4	-172.3	3 384.1	-1 520.8	.. c	918.7	2 478.5	1 903.1
Slovak Republic	.. c	.. c	-3.4	.. d	17.9	.. c	267.6	120.6	267.9	.. d
Slovenia	.. c	.. c	1.1	-	-	.. c	.. c	2.3	4.7	1.1
Spain	-	-	-	-	-	-	-	-	-	-
Sweden	1 008.3	531.9	348.3	319.8	686.2	.. d	.. d	19.2	98.0	200.4
Switzerland	1 223.5	517.5	669.6	.. d	-47.0	.. d	.. c	-497.1	316.3	485.8
Turkey	.. c	.. c	-18.0	-4.7	.. d	.. d	.. d	3 079.7	1 256.9	1 016.5
United Kingdom	-2 814.2	6 699.1	5 682.6	1 072.8	-3 584.5	7 553.0	.. d	21 733.7	4 771.6	-10 673.9
United States	-2 931.8	.. d	8 480.4	3 062.7	266.4	4 604.5	14 355.9	14 821.3	4 694.9	2 443.7
EUROPE	**5 021.6**	**26 952.3**	**30 695.5**	**41 824.6**	**10 603.4**	**9 505.3**	**9 039.0**	**35 746.8**	**16 676.5**	**3 174.7**
Bulgaria	.. c	.. c	-	.. c	1.1	.. c	.. c	.. d	5.9	4.5
Croatia	.. c	.. c	-	1.2	-1.1	.. c	.. c	23.7	-5.9	-25.7
Cyprus	.. c	.. c	240.1	.. d	.. d	.. c	.. c	-50.7	.. d	.. d
Malta	.. d	288.6	.. d	.. d	.. d	.. c	.. c	51.9	93.2	-60.5
Romania	.. d	.. d	.. d	.. d	.. d	.. d	.. c	-19.2	-31.9	-14.6
Russian Federation	.. d	.. d	.. d	113.3	109.7	.. d	.. d	.. d	234.9	-2 478.5
Ukraine	.. c	.. c	-16.9	.. d	.. c	.. c	.. c	-30.4	14.2	.. d
AFRICA	**.. c**	**.. d**	**.. d**	**.. d**	**.. d**	**.. d**	**426.8**	**.. d**	**-448.5**	**.. d**
Northern Africa	.. c	.. c	.. d	.. d	-47.0	.. d	212.3	370.9	-862.7	354.9
Algeria	.. c	.. c	.. c	.. c	.. c	.. d	.. d	110.5	.. d	.. d
Egypt	.. c	.. c	.. d	.. d	.. d	.. d	.. c	.. d	.. d	.. d
Libya	.. c	.. c	.. c	16.5	.. d	.. c	.. c	.. c	.. c	.. c
Morocco	.. c	.. c	.. d	.. c	.. c	.. d	.. d	296.5	-1 071.6	470.2
Tunisia	.. c	.. c	.. c	.. c	.. c	.. c	.. c	.. d	35.4	20.2
Other African countries	.. c	.. d	-30.4	-131.0	.. d	.. d	.. d	.. d	414.3	.. d
Nigeria	.. c	.. c	.. c	.. c	-3.4	.. c	.. c	1.1	4.7	-1.1
South Africa	.. c	.. c	.. c	.. c	.. c	.. c	.. c	156.7	85.0	48.1
AMERICA	**1 269.0**	**2 522.4**	**9 342.8**	**-2 334.5**	**-2 000.4**	**33 926.8**	**.. d**	**17 761.2**	**15 722.9**	**14 232.6**
Northern America	-2 604.5	308.5	8 528.9	3 010.7	373.9	15 013.9	14 870.1	16 992.4	1 768.0	2 815.4
Central America and Caribbean countries	.. d	2 995.7	-2 380.8	-2 038.2	-2 954.2	4 289.5	5 592.2	2 945.6	3 859.3	3 940.4
Bahamas	.. c	.. c	-15.8	-	-3.4	.. c	.. c	.. c	-	-53.7
Bermuda	.. c	.. c	.. d	.. d	2.2	.. d	.. d	.. c	.. d	.. c
Cayman Islands	.. d	.. d	-2 765.2	361.1	.. d	74.3	.. d	.. d	.. d	-25.7
Costa Rica	.. c	.. c	.. d	.. d	.. d	.. d	74.1	.. d	167.6	59.3
El Salvador	.. c	.. c	-	.. c	-	.. c	-60.8	.. d	.. d	.. d
Guatemala	.. c	.. c	-16.9	.. c	1.1	.. d	.. d	.. d	233.7	.. d
Honduras	.. c	.. c	1.1	1.2	1.1	.. c	.. c	-24.8	-5.9	29.1
Nicaragua	.. c	.. c	-	-	-	.. c	.. c	.. d	13.0	.. c
Panama	.. d	.. d	25.9	.. d	-1 710.5	.. c	.. d	266.0	597.2	-157.8
Virgin Islands, U.S.	.. c	.. c	-	-	-	.. c	.. c	-	-	-
South America	2 094.3	.. d	3 194.7	-3 308.2	579.9	14 623.4	12 134.2	-2 176.8	10 095.6	7 477.9
Argentina	.. d	801.7	92.4	3.5	19.0	.. d	.. d	1 701.0	2 648.4	960.5
Bolivia	.. c	.. c	-29.3	.. d	.. c	.. d	141.5	112.7	.. d	131.0
Brazil	330.6	-1 172.2	21.4	-3 513.5	360.5	8 139.8	3 517.6	2 132.8	5 316.9	2 158.3
Colombia	.. d	.. d	165.7	112.1	-90.7	356.1	1 375.7	1 117.1	221.9	481.4
Ecuador	.. c	.. c	.. d	.. d	.. d	.. d	.. c	154.4	110.9	545.2
Paraguay	.. c	.. c	-	.. c	.. c	.. c	.. c	.. d	-24.8	.. d
Peru	.. d	.. c	-91.3	135.7	21.3	.. c	899.0	148.8	168.8	105.2
Uruguay	-675.5	.. d	2 673.9	-129.8	287.7	.. d	.. d	2 628.8	657.4	1 053.4
Venezuela	.. d	-219.0	.. c	.. d	51.5	-232.9	.. d	-767.7	500.4	144.4

Table 1. Foreign direct investment flows by country *(cont.)*

Million US dollars

	Inward					Outward				
	2015	2016	2017	2018	2019	2015	2016	2017	2018	2019
ASIA	**2 095.4**	**.. d**	**1 704.4**	**13 996.2**	**-471.3**	**.. d**	**2 088.9**	**1 387.7**	**5 465.6**	**1 213.5**
Near and Middle East	564.6	.. d	861.2	4 396.3	-1 387.0	.. d	90.7	.. d	3 668.1	395.2
Gulf Arabian countries	531.3	.. d	853.3	4 391.6	.. d	.. c	98.4	361.9	3 334.1	372.8
Kuwait	.. c	.. c	18.0	.. c	.. c	.. c	.. c	.. d	.. d	.. d
Qatar	.. c	.. c	.. c	.. c	-264.2	.. c	.. d	25.9	53.1	-3.4
Saudi Arabia	.. c	.. c	.. d	.. d	.. d	.. c	80.7	286.3	157.0	453.4
United Arab Emirates	.. d	.. d	1 099.1	.. d	.. d	.. c	.. c	-15.8	.. c	-64.9
Other Near and Middle East	.. c	.. c	.. d	.. d	.. d	.. c	.. c	67.6	334.0	22.4
Jordan	.. c	.. c	-	-	-	.. c	.. c	21.4	.. d	.. d
Other Asian countries	1 530.8	.. d	844.3	9 599.9	915.7	.. d	.. d	.. d	1 797.5	818.3
China	.. c	.. d	-162.3	1 552.0	106.3	.. d	.. d	.. d	.. d	138.8
Hong Kong, China	.. d	.. c	524.2	596.0	103.0	.. d	.. d	-73.3	205.4	174.6
India	100.9	.. d	24.8	51.9	.. d	.. d	.. d	502.8	479.2	389.6
Indonesia	.. c	.. c	.. c	.. c	.. c	.. c	.. c	.. d	40.1	4.5
Iran, Islamic Republic of	.. c	.. c	-	-	-	.. c	.. c	-	9.4	.. d
Malaysia	.. c	.. c	.. d	.. c	.. d	.. d	.. d	122.9	147.5	.. d
Philippines	.. c	.. c	-4.5	.. d	.. d	.. c	.. c	22.5	.. c	12.3
Singapore	.. d	.. d	1.1	2 773.5	51.5	.. c	.. d	226.6	.. d	72.8
Chinese Taipei	.. c	.. c	.. c	-	-	.. c	.. c	36.1	.. d	44.8
Thailand	.. c	.. c	-	.. c	.. d	.. c	.. c	14.7	10.6	-60.5
Viet Nam	.. c	.. c	-	-	.. d	.. c	.. c	.. d	.. d	.. d
AUSTRALIA, OCEANIA AND POLAR REGIONS	**.. c**	**.. d**	**.. d**	**.. d**	**.. d**	**87.6**	**.. d**	**563.6**	**.. d**	**621.3**
WORLD unallocated and confidential	**.. d**	**.. d**	**.. d**	**.. d**	**.. d**	**.. d**	**.. d**	**.. d**	**.. d**	**.. d**
European Union (EU28)	**3 517.5**	**26 679.2**	**29 904.2**	**42 792.4**	**10 704.1**	**5 427.6**	**7 327.2**	**32 188.0**	**14 068.2**	**2 475.1**
G20 countries excl. European Union	**.. d**	**.. d**	..	..	..	**.. d**	**.. d**	..	..	..
G20 OECD countries	**.. d**	**.. d**	..	..	..	**.. d**	**.. d**	..	..	..
G20 Non-OECD countries	**.. d**	**.. d**	..	..	..	**.. d**	**.. d**	..	..	..
MENA countries	**.. d**	**.. d**	..	..	..	**.. d**	**.. d**	..	..	..
ASEAN countries	**768.7**	**-214.5**	**95.8**	**2 568.2**	**7.8**	**.. d**	**.. d**	**405.8**	**.. d**	**36.9**

- Nil; .. Not available; c Confidential data; d Secondary Confidentiality

Note: Detailed metadata at: *http://stats.oecd.org/OECDStat_Metadata/ShowMetadata.ashx?Dataset=FDI_CTRY_IND_SUMM.*

Source: *OECD International Direct Investment Statistics (database): https://doi.org/10.1787/idi-data-en*

SPAIN

Table 2. Foreign direct investment positions by country

At year end

Million US dollars

	Inward					Outward				
	2015	2016	2017	2018	2019	2015	2016	2017	2018	2019
WORLD	**561 589.5**	**591 525.2**	**713 237.0**	**745 362.9**	**761 654.7**	**512 970.1**	**539 109.3**	**621 260.5**	**600 080.1**	**622 656.7**
OECD COUNTRIES	**486 835.1**	**534 379.7**	**639 185.7**	**665 819.8**	**686 218.8**	**391 384.9**	**401 958.5**	**466 783.4**	**442 674.6**	**458 303.8**
Australia	528.0	.. d	.. d	.. d	78.6	795.9	908.6	1 577.1	1 504.5	1 435.6
Austria	2 462.7	2 281.0	2 751.3	2 650.6	2 665.7	1 561.2	741.0	1 514.8	1 324.7	1 637.8
Belgium	12 694.6	13 765.2	14 986.8	15 960.6	17 328.7	5 065.9	4 410.2	4 725.4	4 278.7	5 109.0
Canada	.. d	1 799.3	.. d	.. d	.. d	.. d	13 896.9	.. d	.. d	.. d
Chile	.. c	182.4	159.5	105.3	164.0	24 655.4	29 054.5	22 291.9	21 549.1	21 497.4
Czech Republic	234.1	72.7	193.1	249.6	280.8	818.7	855.9	1 092.6	1 078.5	1 241.3
Denmark	2 880.8	4 629.5	5 038.4	5 372.1	5 374.1	1 693.0	1 189.0	609.3	941.2	135.9
Estonia	131.7	.. c	.. c	.. c	-	.. c	22.1	25.2	26.3	28.1
Finland	688.1	339.4	445.0	475.2	449.3	142.6	138.1	84.0	522.1	343.7
France	49 139.9	65 928.1	78 625.6	76 359.1	78 887.9	13 467.6	15 324.1	21 066.2	22 761.6	26 316.6
Germany	39 033.2	48 079.5	62 570.2	67 986.0	71 706.4	19 597.2	22 639.4	27 140.8	24 686.3	24 140.6
Greece	217.7	149.7	123.5	138.5	-208.9	869.9	809.5	782.0	912.5	551.6
Hungary	766.5	-108.6	-142.7	-57.2	-23.6	.. c	.. c	1 168.1	1 477.0	1 314.3
Iceland	139.4	41.1	26.4	28.6	33.7	.. c	6.3	6.0	8.0	6.7
Ireland	5 358.7	6 759.8	12 804.0	12 735.3	12 798.2	13 765.9	10 073.8	13 763.5	11 199.9	15 333.6
Israel	240.6	82.2	-38.4	176.3	175.2	.. c	70.6	143.9	143.1	147.2
Italy	36 819.8	34 355.4	35 009.6	40 306.8	43 161.1	9 176.9	9 426.6	12 272.7	12 261.3	13 245.3
Japan	1 934.7	2 589.9	2 886.8	7 136.5	7 310.7	389.8	358.4	389.8	470.6	515.6
Korea	706.6	696.7	826.3	780.9	1 139.1	347.3	476.4	526.5	1 881.2	1 845.7
Latvia	238.4	.. c	.. c	.. c	.. c	.. c	3.2	.. c	.. c	3.4
Lithuania	133.9	-	-	1.1	.. c	.. c	15.8	52.8	52.7	6.7
Luxembourg	74 101.3	76 991.7	98 179.4	111 008.7	116 433.4	6 378.9	7 972.0	8 193.8	9 837.4	11 014.4
Mexico	7 552.5	8 504.3	9 351.2	9 021.1	8 361.0	36 186.2	35 279.9	43 189.0	42 004.8	45 466.2
Netherlands	117 213.9	132 238.9	138 427.7	135 303.4	137 924.1	3 727.8	-2 862.9	.. d	.. d	1 636.7
New Zealand	480.1	514.4	784.4	720.2	713.3	.. c	.. d	.. d	.. d	.. c
Norway	4 641.3	4 662.2	5 738.8	6 007.6	6 260.4	2 215.6	2 430.7	3 149.4	3 220.7	3 614.9
Poland	-2 467.1	-3 247.6	-3 656.8	-419.1	-338.1	8 338.6	7 766.4	11 247.3	10 863.3	9 169.8
Portugal	11 309.7	12 930.3	15 792.8	14 856.9	18 271.2	24 051.2	24 503.0	27 681.7	23 897.4	25 115.7
Slovak Republic	.. c	-4.2	-13.2	-18.3	2.2	288.5	565.0	737.6	890.8	612.2
Slovenia	.. c	.. c	4.8	4.6	4.5	.. c	4.2	7.2	9.2	10.1
Spain	-	-	-	-	-	-	-	-	-	-
Sweden	7 139.9	10 376.3	12 843.6	13 105.1	13 964.3	1 683.2	1 165.8	1 268.9	1 268.6	1 408.7
Switzerland	19 392.5	18 397.8	21 703.0	20 233.6	20 683.0	14 706.6	14 659.0	15 217.1	12 413.6	12 329.8
Turkey	117.6	36.9	122.3	115.6	35.9	7 513.3	7 027.5	9 397.9	5 760.2	6 749.0
United Kingdom	68 239.5	69 291.7	88 695.1	89 547.7	87 110.8	96 595.5	91 625.4	124 631.8	118 630.6	111 942.3
United States	22 885.1	21 633.8	32 705.7	33 922.6	33 327.3	65 670.1	77 593.5	101 573.5	99 587.8	101 603.0
EUROPE	**463 316.3**	**509 813.4**	**604 639.0**	**627 206.3**	**649 327.1**	**253 675.6**	**249 828.2**	**287 172.0**	**269 725.2**	**281 324.4**
Bulgaria	.. c	.. c	.. c	.. c	4.5	333.2	407.9	705.2	690.4	679.6
Croatia	.. c	9.5	.. c	.. c	4.5	.. c	109.6	154.7	146.6	212.3
Cyprus	305.9	113.8	1 081.8	1 080.8	1 208.7	862.3	577.6	665.6	482.0	435.9
Malta	1 455.6	1 546.3	1 091.4	1 248.0	1 279.5	827.4	480.7	468.9	548.4	1 025.6
Romania	-189.4	-426.9	.. c	.. c	-257.2	1 156.2	1 138.4	1 212.5	1 071.7	1 458.1
Russian Federation	6 848.1	2 616.2	3 362.9	3 497.8	3 678.9	687.0	952.9	1 399.6	1 020.2	833.5
Ukraine	.. c	-266.7	-321.4	-389.3	-408.9	.. c	71.7	67.2	80.1	56.2
AFRICA	**1 759.4**	**1 147.9**	**1 081.8**	**.. d**	**.. d**	**6 124.1**	**5 600.3**	**6 823.0**	**6 763.2**	**7 175.9**
Northern Africa	1 333.7	741.0	813.1	688.1	620.1	4 377.8	3 657.6	4 522.7	4 718.3	4 991.0
Algeria	555.3	.. c	.. c	.. c	.. c	374.5	247.7	377.8	761.4	651.5
Egypt	.. c	-	-	.. c	.. d	1 679.9	845.4	.. d	.. d	.. d
Libya	.. c	.. c	.. c	.. c	.. c	.. c	-26.4	.. c	.. c	.. c
Morocco	236.3	27.4	19.2	-5.7	-40.4	2 182.9	2 410.7	2 903.6	2 458.2	2 817.3
Tunisia	.. c	.. c	.. c	63.0	.. c	.. d	179.2	.. d	.. d	.. d
Other African countries	425.7	406.9	268.7	.. d	.. d	1 746.3	1 942.7	2 300.3	2 044.9	2 184.9
Nigeria	.. c	.. c	.. c	.. c	.. c	.. c	-	-	24.0	.. c
South Africa	.. c	13.7	.. c	-9.2	-9.0	892.8	1 078.3	1 274.9	1 198.8	1 235.7
AMERICA	**58 386.5**	**61 412.5**	**84 383.5**	**81 314.4**	**75 668.4**	**240 939.6**	**271 534.7**	**312 293.1**	**303 122.3**	**312 837.6**
Northern America	25 010.3	23 433.1	34 920.8	35 986.9	35 461.7	80 902.6	91 489.4	118 384.5	111 276.6	113 735.1
Central America and Caribbean countries	13 585.2	16 154.7	18 656.8	18 302.0	16 617.6	47 525.3	47 667.3	56 917.7	54 704.6	60 945.9
Bahamas	.. c	340.5	361.0	243.9	234.8	.. c	47.4	84.0	71.0	16.9
Bermuda	.. c	1.1	2.4	4.6	6.7	.. c	.. c	.. c	.. c	.. c
Cayman Islands	254.8	140.2	171.5	583.9	466.2	1 686.4	1 640.1	3 042.7	1 444.9	1 495.2
Costa Rica	319.0	207.7	235.1	163.7	164.0	1 219.4	1 718.1	1 912.9	1 825.1	1 914.2
El Salvador	.. c	13.7	14.4	-22.9	-22.5	766.5	734.7	704.0	535.8	693.1
Guatemala	.. c	34.8	20.4	19.5	20.2	575.9	788.4	1 140.6	978.9	1 071.7
Honduras	.. c	7.4	9.6	10.3	12.4	142.6	145.5	110.3	107.6	135.9
Nicaragua	.. c	.. c	.. c	11.5	11.2	360.4	227.7	214.7	204.9	123.6
Panama	1 172.6	1 613.8	2 143.2	3 180.7	3 163.3	2 335.3	2 686.8	2 303.9	2 793.7	3 984.5
Virgin Islands, U.S.	.. c	-	-	-	-	.. c	-	-	-	-
South America	19 791.0	21 824.6	30 805.9	27 026.6	23 589.1	112 511.7	132 378.0	136 990.9	137 141.1	138 156.6
Argentina	521.5	316.2	898.3	1 044.2	-697.6	18 258.0	17 112.9	21 821.8	24 868.3	17 330.9
Bolivia	.. c	14.8	.. c	.. c	.. c	1 993.5	2 052.3	2 236.7	2 439.9	2 582.6
Brazil	6 607.5	6 447.8	8 641.2	5 262.2	5 338.1	43 924.9	58 125.9	60 858.7	60 304.6	66 130.1
Colombia	3 571.0	3 476.3	4 250.4	4 064.6	2 364.6	6 402.8	6 965.3	8 522.4	7 775.4	8 407.1
Ecuador	.. c	88.5	121.1	104.2	134.8	3 810.6	4 031.8	4 219.2	4 518.0	4 864.1
Paraguay	.. c	-	-	.. c	-	484.5	638.8	617.7	466.0	438.1
Peru	512.8	533.4	526.5	613.7	627.9	4 739.2	4 648.5	5 341.8	4 244.3	5 007.9
Uruguay	6 783.9	6 907.3	11 871.0	11 258.3	11 275.0	4 943.9	5 138.6	7 415.4	6 936.1	7 656.7
Venezuela	1 659.2	3 853.7	4 317.6	4 577.5	4 505.7	3 224.8	4 546.2	3 582.4	3 905.4	4 067.6

Table 2. Foreign direct investment positions by country *(cont.)*

At year end

Million US dollars

	Inward					Outward				
	2015	2016	2017	2018	2019	2015	2016	2017	2018	2019
ASIA	**12 938.5**	**11 526.3**	**14 281.6**	**27 526.9**	**27 393.8**	**11 409.9**	**11 204.8**	**13 364.1**	**19 002.7**	**19 359.7**
Near and Middle East	7 053.9	5 275.6	5 843.1	10 581.6	9 396.8	1 555.8	1 484.1	1 918.9	5 436.2	5 574.0
Gulf Arabian countries	6 545.5	5 138.6	5 817.9	10 343.5	9 153.0	1 487.2	1 397.7	1 699.4	5 262.2	5 381.9
Kuwait	766.5	.. c	.. c	.. c	.. c	133.9	51.7	135.5	258.8	244.9
Qatar	509.5	11.6	20.4	.. c	.. c	237.3	140.2	117.5	178.6	173.0
Saudi Arabia	301.6	17.9	-18.0	-9.2	-58.4	810.0	796.9	1 008.6	1 088.8	1 344.6
United Arab Emirates	4 596.6	4 106.7	5 004.8	6 236.5	5 304.4	292.9	254.0	244.7	.. c	3 481.2
Other Near and Middle East	508.4	137.0	25.2	237.0	242.6	.. c	86.4	218.3	174.0	192.1
Jordan	.. c	-	-	-	-	.. c	-16.9	3.6	1.1	7.9
Other Asian countries	5 884.6	6 250.7	8 438.5	16 946.4	17 997.1	9 854.1	9 720.7	11 446.4	13 565.4	13 785.7
China	430.0	929.7	1 387.6	2 839.5	2 900.5	2 942.8	3 068.4	3 548.8	3 553.9	3 630.6
Hong Kong, China	804.6	866.4	1 253.3	1 892.6	2 071.4	2 112.1	2 308.4	2 610.9	2 285.3	1 965.9
India	.. c	14.8	50.4	121.4	160.6	2 212.3	1 361.9	1 775.0	2 920.8	2 973.5
Indonesia	.. c	.. c	.. c	.. c	.. c	.. c	42.2	105.5	83.6	89.9
Iran, Islamic Republic of	.. c	-1.1	-1.2	18.3	18.0	.. c	10.5	10.8	18.3	16.9
Malaysia	.. c	-26.4	287.8	246.2	105.6	975.5	1 037.2	1 156.2	1 268.6	1 275.0
Philippines	.. c	17.9	20.4	27.5	30.3	.. c	.. c	470.1	104.2	120.2
Singapore	1 834.5	1 315.5	1 854.2	3 950.1	4 239.5	186.2	413.2	593.7	673.2	747.0
Chinese Taipei	.. c	.. c	.. c	-	-	.. c	25.3	60.0	65.3	132.6
Thailand	.. c	10.5	.. c	.. c	.. c	.. c	84.3	110.3	119.1	381.9
Viet Nam	.. c	-	.. c	2.3	-	.. c	12.6	12.0	26.3	30.3
AUSTRALIA, OCEANIA AND POLAR REGIONS	**1 130.1**	**.. d**	**.. d**	**.. d**	**.. d**	**803.5**	**.. d**	**.. d**	**.. d**	**.. d**
WORLD unallocated and confidential	**298.3**	**.. d**	**.. d**	**.. d**	**.. d**	**17.4**	**.. d**	**.. d**	**.. d**	**.. d**
European Union (EU28)	**428 099.1**	**482 670.0**	**572 229.6**	**595 745.4**	**617 192.8**	**226 789.3**	**222 891.3**	**255 730.4**	**245 335.5**	**254 128.3**
G20 countries excl. European Union	**.. d**	**..**	**..**	**..**	**..**	**.. d**	**..**	**..**	**..**	**..**
G20 OECD countries	**.. d**	**..**	**..**	**..**	**..**	**.. d**	**..**	**..**	**..**	**..**
G20 Non-OECD countries	**.. d**	**..**	**..**	**..**	**..**	**.. d**	**..**	**..**	**..**	**..**
MENA countries	**.. d**	**..**	**..**	**..**	**..**	**.. d**	**..**	**..**	**..**	**..**
ASEAN countries	**1 787.7**	**1 155.3**	**2 038.9**	**4 147.0**	**4 386.7**	**1 762.7**	**2 039.6**	**2 449.0**	**2 275.0**	**2 645.5**

- Nil; .. Not available; c Confidential data; d Secondary Confidentiality

Note: Detailed metadata at: *http://stats.oecd.org/OECDStat_Metadata/ShowMetadata.ashx?Dataset=FDI_CTRY_IND_SUMM.*

Source: *OECD International Direct Investment Statistics (database): https://doi.org/10.1787/idi-data-en*

SPAIN

Table 3. Foreign direct investment income by country

Million US dollars

	Inward					Outward				
	2015	2016	2017	2018	2019	2015	2016	2017	2018	2019
WORLD	**22 030.0**	**23 652.5**	**28 808.5**	**31 280.5**	**26 860.0**	**31 693.8**	**33 708.9**	**36 231.5**	**41 981.6**	**35 977.8**
OECD COUNTRIES	**20 645.6**	**22 342.1**	**26 277.8**	**28 764.3**	**24 858.4**	**22 210.8**	**22 331.1**	**26 904.5**	**30 182.9**	**26 765.9**
Australia	.. c	.. c	-	-	.. d	.. c	.. d	94.7	69.6	80.6
Austria	.. d	.. d	154.4	205.4	189.2	.. d	.. d	.. d	.. d	.. d
Belgium	.. d	.. d	.. d	.. d	281.0	153.1	.. d	299.9	501.6	350.4
Canada	.. d	.. c	.. d	212.4	104.1	.. d	.. d	295.3	186.5	326.9
Chile	.. c	.. c	1.1	20.1	11.2	.. d	.. d	1 370.8	1 411.5	.. d
Czech Republic	.. c	.. c	.. d	.. d	.. d	.. d	.. d	115.0	76.7	101.9
Denmark	.. d	.. d	191.6	177.0	159.0	.. d	.. d	.. d	.. d	.. d
Estonia	.. c	.. c	.. c	.. c	.. c	.. c	.. c	2.3	.. c	.. c
Finland	.. c	.. d	.. d	.. d	.. d	.. c	.. c	7.9	13.0	9.0
France	.. d	.. d	4 470.7	5 226.0	4 345.7	609.0	.. d	1 262.5	1 452.9	1 162.0
Germany	2 318.4	.. d	2 500.3	3 708.3	2 828.8	.. d	.. d	378.8	862.7	649.3
Greece	.. c	.. c	.. d	.. d	.. d	.. c	.. d	.. d	60.2	61.6
Hungary	.. d	.. c	.. d	-13.0	3.4	.. d	.. c	233.3	158.1	173.5
Iceland	.. c	.. c	.. c	5.9	5.6	.. c	.. c	-	-	-
Ireland	.. d	.. d	250.3	289.2	245.2	597.9	549.6	437.4	22.4	325.8
Israel	.. c	.. c	-	.. d	.. d	.. c	.. c	.. d	14.2	13.4
Italy	.. d	.. d	2 475.5	1 969.8	1 843.7	.. d	.. d	804.9	898.1	760.1
Japan	.. d	.. d	195.0	.. d	.. d	.. c	.. c	-6.8	13.0	9.0
Korea	.. c	.. c	.. d	.. d	.. d	.. c	.. c	.. d	.. d	.. d
Latvia	.. c	.. c	.. c	.. c	-	.. c	.. c	.. c	.. c	.. c
Lithuania	.. c	.. c	.. c	-	.. c	.. c	.. c	.. d	-	-
Luxembourg	1 843.6	723.2	3 287.1	2 994.2	2 816.5	-118.7	.. c	452.0	374.1	359.3
Mexico	.. c	.. d	112.7	292.7	133.2	.. d	.. d	5 286.9	6 289.4	5 935.3
Netherlands	.. d	.. d	5 516.9	5 948.3	4 967.0	1 913.5	990.8	1 321.2	1 681.8	2 013.9
New Zealand	.. c	.. c	24.8	-47.2	3.4	.. c	.. c	.. d	.. d	5.6
Norway	.. d	.. d	.. d	54.3	.. d	.. d	.. d	444.1	483.9	.. d
Poland	.. d	.. d	-184.9	-144.0	-22.4	.. d	.. d	541.1	663.3	481.4
Portugal	.. c	.. d	127.4	-4.7	106.3	.. d	.. d	1 916.4	2 597.7	2 027.3
Slovak Republic	.. c	.. c	.. c	.. c	.. c	.. c	56.4	75.5	.. d	.. d
Slovenia	.. c	.. c	.. c	-	-	.. c	.. c	.. c	1.2	1.1
Spain	-	-	-	-	-	-	-	-	-	-
Sweden	.. d	.. d	269.4	273.8	262.0	.. d	.. d	172.5	374.1	.. d
Switzerland	.. d	.. d	1 586.1	1 683.0	1 443.0	.. d	.. d	360.7	479.2	341.4
Turkey	.. c	.. c	12.4	-18.9	-5.6	.. d	.. d	.. d	1 531.9	1 119.4
United Kingdom	2 948.4	.. d	3 043.6	2 869.1	2 906.1	.. d	4 732.9	7 286.7	7 926.4	6 123.4
United States	.. d	.. d	.. d	2 225.9	.. d	1 403.2	.. d	2 225.2	1 912.0	2 007.2
EUROPE	**19 446.5**	**20 403.6**	**24 078.5**	**25 810.2**	**22 507.6**	**15 306.7**	**14 131.4**	**18 237.0**	**21 097.6**	**17 591.0**
Bulgaria	.. c	.. c	-	-	-	.. c	.. c	.. d	.. d	26.9
Croatia	.. c	.. c	-	-	.. c	.. c	.. c	.. d	5.9	9.0
Cyprus	.. c	.. c	-12.4	.. d	-72.8	.. c	.. c	75.5	-14.2	-36.9
Malta	.. c	.. c	.. d	151.1	53.7	.. c	.. c	20.3	16.5	17.9
Romania	.. c	.. c	.. d	7.1	.. d	.. c	.. d	.. d	.. d	.. d
Russian Federation	.. c	.. c	.. d	.. d	17.9	.. c	.. d	202.9	434.3	241.8
Ukraine	.. c	.. c	.. d	.. d	.. d	.. c	.. c	27.1	28.3	26.9
AFRICA	**.. d**	**.. d**	**96.9**	**145.2**	**106.3**	**.. d**	**.. d**	**654.9**	**.. d**	**.. d**
Northern Africa	.. d	.. d	86.8	93.2	.. d	.. d	.. d	.. d	495.7	347.0
Algeria	.. d	.. c	.. d	.. c	50.4	.. c	.. c	-1.1	.. d	.. d
Egypt	.. c	.. c	-	.. d	.. d	.. c	.. c	.. d	.. d	.. d
Libya	.. c	.. c	.. c	.. c	.. c	.. c	.. c	.. c	.. c	.. c
Morocco	.. c	.. c	.. d	.. d	12.3	.. d	.. d	392.3	180.6	181.4
Tunisia	.. c	.. c	.. c	.. c	.. c	.. c	.. c	23.7	30.7	21.3
Other African countries	.. c	.. c	9.0	51.9	.. d	.. c	.. d	.. d	.. d	.. d
Nigeria	.. c	.. c	.. c	-	.. c	.. c	.. c	-	.. c	.. c
South Africa	.. c	.. c	-	23.6	.. c	.. c	.. d	71.0	61.4	69.4
AMERICA	**1 884.6**	**2 119.9**	**3 032.4**	**3 563.1**	**2 881.5**	**15 937.9**	**17 964.2**	**16 517.9**	**19 057.0**	**16 913.7**
Northern America	.. d	.. d	1 792.4	2 438.3	.. d	2 589.0	.. d	2 520.6	2 099.6	2 334.0
Central America and Caribbean countries	-84.3	.. d	179.2	365.9	225.0	.. d	.. d	5 950.9	7 147.4	6 852.1
Bahamas	.. c	.. c	-7.9	-1.2	-4.5	.. c	.. c	-	.. d	1.1
Bermuda	.. c	.. c	.. c	-	-	.. c	.. c	.. c	.. c	.. c
Cayman Islands	.. c	.. c	.. d	-7.1	.. d	.. c	.. d	-66.5	263.2	103.0
Costa Rica	.. c	.. c	.. d	.. d	-	.. d	.. d	.. d	.. d	107.5
El Salvador	.. c	.. c	-	-	-	.. d	.. d	.. d	.. d	.. d
Guatemala	.. c	.. c	2.3	-	1.1	.. d	.. c	83.4	.. d	97.4
Honduras	.. c	.. c	.. c	.. c	.. c	.. c	.. c	1.1	3.5	4.5
Nicaragua	.. c	.. c	-	-	-	.. c	.. c	.. d	.. d	29.1
Panama	.. d	.. d	38.3	.. d	.. d	.. d	.. d	.. d	.. d	277.6
Virgin Islands, U.S.	.. c	.. c	-	-	-	.. c	.. c	-	-	-
South America	748.8	188.0	1 058.5	757.7	704.1	.. d	.. d	8 046.4	9 810.0	7 727.5
Argentina	.. c	.. c	81.2	69.6	.. d	.. d	.. d	2 500.3	2 778.2	1 082.5
Bolivia	.. c	.. c	-	-	-	.. d	.. c	.. d	66.1	72.8
Brazil	.. c	.. c	-122.9	70.8	28.0	.. d	.. d	2 325.6	3 704.7	3 460.2
Colombia	-56.6	-108.4	.. d	-323.4	-125.4	.. d	.. d	414.8	.. d	.. d
Ecuador	.. c	.. c	-3.4	.. c	.. c	.. d	.. d	174.7	237.2	172.4
Paraguay	.. c	.. c	-	-	-	.. d	.. d	138.7	149.9	114.2
Peru	.. c	.. c	23.7	.. d	19.0	.. d	.. d	193.9	267.9	343.7
Uruguay	.. d	.. d	667.3	591.3	581.0	.. d	.. c	.. d	593.7	445.5
Venezuela	.. c	.. c	.. c	.. c	.. c	.. c	.. d	289.7	220.7	.. d

Table 3. Foreign direct investment income by country *(cont.)*

Million US dollars

	Inward					Outward				
	2015	2016	2017	2018	2019	2015	2016	2017	2018	2019
ASIA	**.. d**	**.. d**	**1 565.8**	**1 795.1**	**1 347.8**	**.. d**	**.. d**	**712.4**	**1 123.6**	**930.3**
Near and Middle East	.. d	.. d	1 311.0	1 347.8	1 016.5	.. c	.. c	58.6	120.4	91.8
Gulf Arabian countries	.. d	.. d	.. d	1 340.7	.. d	.. c	.. c	38.3	103.9	75.0
Kuwait	.. c	.. c	21.4	.. c	.. c	.. c	.. c	1.1	-7.1	-4.5
Qatar	.. c	.. c	.. c	157.0	137.7	.. c	.. c	.. d	.. d	.. d
Saudi Arabia	.. c	.. c	-13.5	-15.3	-6.7	.. c	.. d	21.4	40.1	61.6
United Arab Emirates	.. c	.. c	.. c	.. c	.. c	.. c	.. c	.. d	.. d	.. d
Other Near and Middle East	.. c	.. c	.. d	.. d	.. d	.. c	.. c	.. d	15.3	17.9
Jordan	.. c	.. c	-	-	2.2	.. c	.. c	12.4	-1.2	4.5
Other Asian countries	.. d	.. d	252.5	443.8	330.2	.. d	.. d	653.8	1 004.4	838.5
China	.. c	.. c	.. d	.. d	36.9	.. c	.. d	.. d	325.7	.. d
Hong Kong, China	.. c	.. c	.. d	.. d	.. d	.. d	.. d	51.9	171.1	139.9
India	.. c	.. c	.. d	.. d	.. c	.. d	.. c	271.7	230.1	332.5
Indonesia	.. c	.. c	.. c	.. c	.. c	.. c	.. c	5.6	-4.7	-4.5
Iran, Islamic Republic of	.. c	.. c	-	-	-	.. c	.. c	.. c	.. c	.. c
Malaysia	.. c	.. c	.. d	.. c	.. c	.. d	.. c	.. d	.. d	.. d
Philippines	.. c	.. c	-	2.4	.. c	.. c	.. c	.. d	.. d	.. d
Singapore	.. c	.. c	37.2	175.9	.. d	.. c	.. c	-62.0	.. d	-20.2
Chinese Taipei	.. c	.. c	-	-	-	.. c	.. c	3.4	-11.8	.. c
Thailand	.. c	.. c	-	.. d	.. d	.. c	.. c	.. d	10.6	.. d
Viet Nam	.. c	.. c	-	-	-	.. c	.. c	2.3	-	2.2
AUSTRALIA, OCEANIA AND POLAR REGIONS	**.. c**	**.. c**	**.. d**	**.. d**	**5.6**	**.. c**	**.. d**	**.. d**	**.. d**	**96.3**
WORLD unallocated and confidential	**.. d**	**.. d**	**.. d**	**.. d**	**11.2**	**- d**	**.. d**	**.. d**	**.. d**	**- d**
European Union (EU28)	**17 997.8**	**19 122.0**	**22 419.1**	**24 050.5**	**21 051.2**	**13 038.3**	**11 260.6**	**15 395.1**	**17 849.6**	**15 136.0**
G20 countries excl. European Union	**.. d**	**.. d**	**..**	**..**	**..**	**.. d**	**.. d**	**..**	**..**	**..**
G20 OECD countries	**.. d**	**.. d**	**..**	**..**	**..**	**.. d**	**.. d**	**..**	**..**	**..**
G20 Non-OECD countries	**.. d**	**.. d**	**..**	**..**	**..**	**.. d**	**.. d**	**..**	**..**	**..**
MENA countries	**.. d**	**.. d**	**..**	**..**	**..**	**.. d**	**.. d**	**..**	**..**	**..**
ASEAN countries	**.. c**	**.. c**	**.. d**	**.. d**	**26.9**	**.. d**	**.. c**	**-15.8**	**.. d**	**77.2**

- Nil; .. Not available; c Confidential data; d Secondary Confidentiality

Note: Detailed metadata at: *http://stats.oecd.org/OECDStat_Metadata/ShowMetadata.ashx?Dataset=FDI_CTRY_IND_SUMM.*

Source: *OECD International Direct Investment Statistics (database): https://doi.org/10.1787/idi-data-en*

SPAIN

Table 4. Foreign direct investment flows by industrial sector

Million US dollars

	Inward					Outward				
	2015	2016	2017	2018	2019	2015	2016	2017	2018	2019
All FDI activities	**8 556.9**	**31 538.2**	**41 876.9**	**53 461.6**	**8 514.5**	**41 916.8**	**43 902.5**	**55 926.1**	**37 710.4**	**19 670.9**
Agriculture, forestry and fishing	**68.8**	**.. c**	**54.1**	**37.8**	**..**	**.. c**	**.. c**	**47.3**	**23.6**	**..**
Mining and quarrying	**206.3**	**-358.3**	**-1 484.6**	**.. d**	**..**	**10 266.2**	**266.5**	**1 907.3**	**296.2**	**..**
Extraction activities	69.9	.. c	-178.1	688.1	..	10 163.1	726.5	2 012.2	.. d	..
Manufacturing	**746.5**	**-2 464.9**	**9 005.7**	**5 858.6**	**..**	**3 988.9**	**-748.6**	**-396.8**	**-1 704.2**	**..**
of which:										
Food products, beverages and tobacco	807.5	-1 177.7	-705.7	-385.9	..	1 219.1	633.6	-331.4	-585.4	..
Textiles, wood and paper products; printing	-424.8	295.3	110.5	192.4	..	-114.3	231.1	-6.8	-2.4	..
Chemical, rubber, plastic, non-metallic mineral products	731.0	1 594.6	271.7	4 628.8	..	814.2	1 200.9	-1 743.9	-1 921.4	..
Metal and machinery products, except electrical equipment	-619.0	-3 493.3	-2 699.8	-2 386.4	..	414.9	-705.5	-1 783.3	-2 076.0	..
Motor vehicles, trailers, semi-trailers, other transport equipment	-970.6	-92.9	2 455.2	4 369.2	..	1 251.2	-2 930.4	1 963.7	3 139.4	..
Other manufacturing	1 223.5	409.2	9 573.9	-558.2	..	402.7	821.6	1 504.9	-258.5	..
Electricity, gas, steam and air conditioning supply	**-4 239.6**	**832.7**	**-11 812.6**	**-4 643.0**	**..**	**303.9**	**368.2**	**-7 827.8**	**-1 049.2**	**..**
Water supply; sewerage, waste management and remediation activities	**519.1**	**.. c**	**-149.9**	**105.0**	**..**	**.. c**	**.. c**	**304.4**	**-86.2**	**..**
Construction	**2 132.0**	**295.3**	**196.1**	**2 299.1**	**..**	**2 128.7**	**1 733.9**	**2 815.9**	**1 175.5**	**..**
Services	**6 988.4**	**29 775.5**	**41 418.1**	**48 741.9**	**..**	**26 117.6**	**42 472.6**	**58 866.0**	**38 911.8**	**..**
Wholesale and retail trade; repair of motor vehicles and motorcycles	2 686.6	13 212.4	-7 817.6	3 353.0	..	2 208.5	10 753.1	6 029.8	-1 953.3	..
Transportation and storage	2 553.5	2 358.7	661.7	951.3	..	5 690.5	4 328.2	5 386.1	2 480.8	..
Accommodation and food service activities	640.0	-1 012.9	-258.1	2 934.0	..	157.5	564.0	368.6	1 321.8	..
Information and communication	747.6	1 185.4	2 152.0	2 530.4	..	6 185.2	240.0	1 467.7	1 416.3	..
Financial and insurance activities	-5 765.9	9 786.6	40 749.6	30 799.0	..	9 843.6	21 005.2	41 034.8	20 018.9	..
Activities of holding companies	-5 101.5	10 160.3	42 316.5	27 599.4	..	-6 806.4	12 830.9	31 249.0	7 479.1	..
Real estate activities	3 737.1	2 976.9	215.3	3 322.3	..	1 152.5	2 537.9	-927.7	2 353.4	..
Professional, scientific and technical activities	1 315.6	429.1	3 013.2	2 287.3	..	2 208.5	3 624.9	5 389.5	12 460.8	..
Administrative and support service activities	1 282.3	230.0	1 667.2	2 347.5	..	-1 289.0	-776.3	-53.0	217.2	..
Public administration; activities of households and of extraterritorial organisations	.. c	.. c	-6.8	-1.2	..	.. c	.. c	-	-	..
Education	.. c	.. c	-219.8	29.5	..	.. c	.. c	30.4	80.3	..
Human health and social work activities	74.3	.. c	157.8	214.8	..	96.5	.. c	11.3	186.5	..
Arts, entertainment and recreation	164.2	433.5	945.8	-59.0	..	.. c	-183.6	-	87.3	..
Other services	109.8	.. c	160.1	31.9	..	-118.7	164.8	126.3	240.8	..
Not allocated and confidential	**..**	**..**	**2 182.4**	**.. d**	**8 514.5**	**..**	**..**	**196.1**	**.. d**	**19 670.9**
Private real estate activities	**..**	**..**	**2 467.6**	**2 086.6**	**..**	**..**	**..**	**13.5**	**.. d**	**..**

- Nil; .. Not available; c Confidential data; d Secondary Confidentiality

Note: Detailed metadata at: *http://stats.oecd.org/OECDStat_Metadata/ShowMetadata.ashx?Dataset=FDI_CTRY_IND_SUMM.*

Source: *OECD International Direct Investment Statistics (database)*: *https://doi.org/10.1787/idi-data-en*

Table 5. Foreign direct investment positions by industrial sector
At year end

Million US dollars

	Inward					Outward				
	2015	2016	2017	2018	2019	2015	2016	2017	2018	2019
All FDI activities	561 589.5	591 525.2	713 237.0	745 362.9	761 654.7	512 970.1	539 109.3	621 260.5	600 080.1	622 656.7
Agriculture, forestry and fishing	1 027.8	1 190.1	1 501.6	1 522.8	..	396.3	450.1	485.7	577.1	..
Mining and quarrying	6 542.2	7 032.8	6 320.5	4 836.3	..	15 517.7	11 387.2	15 194.3	6 415.2	..
Extraction activities	557.4	1 106.8	1 162.1	1 167.9	..	12 853.6	9 370.7	13 223.8	5 107.6	..
Manufacturing	122 152.4	90 732.6	113 291.0	108 632.9	..	94 196.0	68 314.5	79 196.5	73 543.6	..
of which:										
Food products, beverages and tobacco	21 696.2	18 247.1	19 847.7	18 639.8	..	11 018.0	9 002.8	9 889.7	9 064.6	..
Textiles, wood and paper products; printing	3 391.4	3 715.6	3 723.9	3 574.5	..	2 620.6	3 052.6	3 490.0	3 294.0	..
Chemical, rubber, plastic, non-metallic mineral products	29 817.1	30 816.9	34 497.5	35 953.7	..	24 003.3	25 072.2	25 534.9	21 801.0	..
Metal and machinery products, except electrical equipment	23 859.6	19 110.4	22 728.5	18 709.6	..	17 482.9	16 344.5	16 038.6	12 499.4	..
Motor vehicles, trailers, semi-trailers, other transport equipment	11 835.6	8 024.7	13 416.9	14 202.0	..	4 212.3	6 143.1	10 308.2	12 339.1	..
Other manufacturing	31 553.6	10 816.9	19 075.3	17 553.2	..	34 857.9	8 698.2	13 935.0	14 544.3	..
Electricity, gas, steam and air conditioning supply	58 351.7	55 279.9	53 462.5	50 967.5	..	34 352.7	31 150.0	26 533.9	22 031.1	..
Water supply; sewerage, waste management and remediation activities	1 473.1	2 261.0	2 651.7	.. c	..	1 845.4	1 167.9	1 476.4	701.9	..
Construction	10 317.9	11 052.0	14 134.1	15 366.4	..	21 097.4	27 277.3	31 302.5	27 966.6	..
Services	225 635.3	285 978.7	349 823.7	387 254.4	..	316 141.5	373 591.2	436 980.1	439 338.2	..
Wholesale and retail trade; repair of motor vehicles and motorcycles	37 812.7	53 550.1	54 090.9	55 652.6	..	30 121.9	37 303.7	42 500.6	45 131.7	..
Transportation and storage	10 135.0	13 088.4	18 738.3	17 260.1	..	9 750.7	11 492.6	16 947.7	14 736.7	..
Accommodation and food service activities	3 985.8	4 572.6	5 853.9	7 463.9	..	5 788.8	5 440.1	6 936.9	7 271.6	..
Information and communication	29 326.1	28 694.0	32 386.7	30 572.5	..	49 477.4	50 034.8	56 653.9	52 239.5	..
Financial and insurance activities	80 270.0	115 759.5	148 885.8	179 729.8	..	194 900.4	233 764.1	276 598.7	266 789.6	..
Activities of holding companies	31 645.1	69 739.6	99 063.3	129 323.3	..	29 771.4	70 967.6	80 557.7	87 981.5	..
Real estate activities	21 436.0	25 252.5	29 990.4	32 870.4	..	9 325.0	13 213.9	13 867.8	8 961.5	..
Professional, scientific and technical activities	17 907.5	18 830.0	25 588.9	27 663.2	..	7 587.4	17 165.6	18 330.5	36 994.5	..
Administrative and support service activities	20 765.4	21 109.9	27 140.8	28 920.3	..	7 200.9	3 737.7	3 280.2	3 647.8	..
Public administration; activities of households and of extraterritorial organisations	.. c	45.3	22.8	20.6	..	.. c	-	-	-	..
Education	.. c	.. c	.. c	.. c	..	.. c	.. c	.. c	.. c	..
Human health and social work activities	636.9	703.1	1 235.3	1 439.2	..	153.5	.. c	195.5	416.8	..
Arts, entertainment and recreation	1 935.8	2 044.9	2 989.9	2 786.8	..	-145.9	-431.1	-467.7	626.3	..
Other services	387.6	.. d	621.3	593.1	..	1 083.3	878.0	1 246.1	1 188.5	..
Not allocated and confidential		4 484.0	9 798.5	.. c	761 654.7		4 640.0	6 667.1	6 970.5	622 656.7
Private real estate activities	..	133 514.3	162 253.5	165 512.9	..	..	21 131.0	23 424.1	22 536.1	..

- Nil; .. Not available; c Confidential data; d Secondary Confidentiality

Note: Detailed metadata at: *http://stats.oecd.org/OECDStat_Metadata/ShowMetadata.ashx?Dataset=FDI_CTRY_IND_SUMM.*

Source: *OECD International Direct Investment Statistics (database): https://doi.org/10.1787/idi-data-en*

SPAIN

Table 6. Foreign direct investment income by industrial sector

Million US dollars

	Inward					Outward				
	2015	2016	2017	2018	2019	2015	2016	2017	2018	2019
All FDI activities	**22 030.0**	**23 652.5**	**28 808.5**	**31 280.5**	**26 860.0**	**31 693.8**	**33 708.9**	**36 231.5**	**41 981.6**	**35 977.8**
Agriculture, forestry and fishing	**.. c**	**.. c**	**37.2**	**30.7**	..	**.. c**	**.. c**	**28.2**	**38.9**	..
Mining and quarrying	**246.3**	**.. c**	**376.5**	**159.3**	..	**881.9**	**204.6**	**373.1**	**612.5**	..
Extraction activities	73.2	65.2	23.7	73.2	..	732.1	.. c	86.8	499.2	..
Manufacturing	**6 403.8**	**7 193.4**	**8 589.8**	**9 524.4**	..	**2 636.7**	**3 889.2**	**3 271.3**	**5 036.0**	..
of which:										
Food products, beverages and tobacco	938.4	1 038.4	892.8	542.9	..	828.6	498.7	509.5	404.8	..
Textiles, wood and paper products; printing	.. c	338.4	272.8	403.6	..	56.6	200.2	220.9	297.4	..
Chemical, rubber, plastic, non-metallic mineral products	2 896.3	3 777.5	3 814.7	4 902.6	..	982.8	1 353.5	893.9	1 857.7	..
Metal and machinery products, except electrical equipment	.. d	-299.7	1 227.6	1 463.5	..	881.9	731.0	676.4	1 157.8	..
Motor vehicles, trailers, semi-trailers, other transport equipment	1 610.6	1 639.9	1 510.5	1 624.0	..	-280.6	434.6	92.4	492.2	..
Other manufacturing	471.4	697.8	871.4	585.4	..	166.4	671.2	878.1	826.2	..
Electricity, gas, steam and air conditioning supply	**1 105.9**	**1 967.3**	**2 414.6**	**1 878.9**	..	**1 426.5**	**1 954.0**	**1 649.2**	**1 266.4**	..
Water supply; sewerage, waste management and remediation activities	**.. c**	**.. c**	**48.5**	**55.5**	..	**267.3**	**257.7**	**277.3**	**30.7**	..
Construction	**97.6**	**.. c**	**120.6**	**465.0**	..	**259.6**	**-65.2**	**860.1**	**1 046.9**	..
Services	**11 828.1**	**12 222.7**	**15 665.7**	**17 392.9**	..	**25 449.8**	**27 612.5**	**29 403.7**	**33 556.0**	..
Wholesale and retail trade; repair of motor vehicles and motorcycles	2 728.8	3 728.9	3 357.0	5 392.4	..	2 538.0	3 333.0	4 259.9	4 048.2	..
Transportation and storage	406.0	442.3	794.7	820.3	..	2 002.2	1 433.2	3 313.0	4 242.9	..
Accommodation and food service activities	343.9	179.1	554.6	622.0	..	429.3	399.2	471.2	635.0	..
Information and communication	816.4	1 112.5	1 122.8	1 003.2	..	2 086.5	3 974.3	1 926.5	2 073.6	..
Financial and insurance activities	5 646.1	4 803.7	6 875.2	6 102.9	..	18 234.1	16 065.5	17 044.3	20 068.5	..
Activities of holding companies	2 021.1	2 276.9	3 979.3	2 790.0	..	2 995.0	3 442.4	2 866.6	2 607.1	..
Real estate activities	438.2	679.0	1 021.3	1 229.8	..	196.3	289.7	363.0	192.4	..
Professional, scientific and technical activities	342.8	253.2	825.2	999.6	..	-605.7	1 683.1	1 792.4	1 836.4	..
Administrative and support service activities	1 074.9	948.8	873.6	1 018.5	..	582.4	384.8	287.5	322.2	..
Public administration; activities of households and of extraterritorial organisations	.. c	.. c	.. d	-	..	.. c	.. c	-	-	..
Education	.. c	.. c	29.3	20.1	..	.. c	.. c	-85.7	.. c	..
Human health and social work activities	.. c	.. c	53.0	60.2	..	.. c	.. c	2.3	11.8	..
Arts, entertainment and recreation	.. c	.. c	4.5	-2.4	..	-63.2	-73.0	-38.3	-31.9	..
Other services	.. c	.. c	154.4	125.1	..	.. c	.. c	.. d	121.6	..
Not allocated and confidential	..	..	**71.0**	**153.4**	**26 860.0**	..	..	**163.5**	**146.3**	**35 977.8**
Private real estate activities	..	..	**1 484.6**	**1 620.4**	..	..	..	**205.2**	**247.8**	..

- Nil; .. Not available; c Confidential data; d Secondary Confidentiality

Note: Detailed metadata at: *http://stats.oecd.org/OECDStat_Metadata/ShowMetadata.ashx?Dataset=FDI_CTRY_IND_SUMM.*

Source: *OECD International Direct Investment Statistics (database): https://doi.org/10.1787/idi-data-en*

SWEDEN

Table 1. Foreign direct investment flows by country

Million US dollars

	Inward					Outward				
	2015	2016	2017	2018	2019	2015	2016	2017	2018	2019
WORLD	**8 449.5**	**19 153.0**	**15 903.5**	**4 217.6**	**11 732.8**	**13 045.0**	**4 702.5**	**27 367.5**	**17 838.8**	**15 522.5**
OECD COUNTRIES	..	..	..	**5 156.1**	**9 428.1**	..	..	..	**14 231.0**	**11 565.2**
Australia	.. c	.. c	-29.8	-177.3	24.3	44.1	112.0	-	242.2	116.3
Austria	117.6	20.7	758.2	144.8	164.2	48.5	76.2	183.5	76.2	42.4
Belgium	-627.0	401.3	-394.8	-17.0	794.1	-3 365.3	4 275.2	-13 935.9	-6 860.9	1 503.5
Canada	4 214.7	104.7	-72.1	-11.2	366.8	376.8	1 241.7	966.8	-44.1	545.6
Chile	.. c	.. c	-	.. c	.. c	-203.9	-24.3	145.1	-3.7	429.7
Czech Republic	23.7	1.4	2.8	-18.2	8.9	13.6	1 781.1	-111.3	32.3	262.5
Denmark	-31.1	809.2	1 585.4	3 172.6	-78.4	1 608.1	-191.2	1 118.9	2 333.4	1 118.1
Estonia	2.3	13.2	19.3	7.2	63.7	-219.0	265.5	709.3	238.9	456.4
Finland	-4 317.6	1 149.9	301.9	1 693.4	874.5	1 993.9	2 433.2	-900.0	885.1	-341.3
France	87.8	112.3	2 543.6	326.8	-365.6	311.9	1 202.7	384.5	1 072.2	-65.9
Germany	5 579.1	-424.1	-266.1	754.6	1 307.2	1 547.3	249.6	9 190.6	-6 381.1	1 126.2
Greece	-	.. c	-	-	.. c	3.3	-13.8	6.2	4.9	3.5
Hungary	.. c	.. c	1.2	-3.3	.. c	87.4	113.2	-10.1	-70.3	101.0
Iceland	-18.5	-55.5	-3.0	-7.6	-	0.1	-0.6	-5.7	15.1	11.7
Ireland	704.1	-3 636.1	2 461.0	1 986.0	1 453.6	359.1	670.6	3 269.0	11 414.1	-1 195.6
Israel	.. c	6.4	4.8	-	6.7	18.7	40.1	17.4	74.1	475.8
Italy	97.3	62.1	94.1	.. c	190.5	140.0	-2 255.5	651.5	1 838.4	-27.4
Japan	.. c	352.4	920.2	1 072.1	132.4	342.9	231.6	214.7	379.7	-162.2
Korea	.. c	.. c	42.7	32.1	76.7	-27.4	158.6	-258.6	-235.9	297.5
Latvia	-1.2	-7.9	.. c	-5.3	-89.4	23.1	-424.1	841.6	143.7	-294.6
Lithuania	-18.9	3.3	.. c	.. c	14.2	-308.9	-371.1	1 159.8	392.3	-575.8
Luxembourg	7 585.2	164.0	-310.4	-3 692.6	2 336.8	837.9	-6 890.9	-3 792.7	807.8	-2 534.2
Mexico	.. c	.. c	-7.5	26.1	62.6	97.8	1 681.1	-1 419.1	-432.8	123.9
Netherlands	-6 221.5	9 550.5	-1 426.3	-4 008.8	-794.1	-1 665.7	-5 138.8	15 380.3	-5 988.6	2 453.5
New Zealand	.. c	.. c	-	0.2	.. c	24.0	3.6	28.0	17.7	54.7
Norway	1 143.4	-1 095.0	1 773.6	-149.4	-1 533.3	2 405.9	1 644.1	4 665.1	4 604.9	2 540.4
Poland	.. c	.. c	760.7	60.3	1 126.7	-657.9	1 196.4	440.3	-316.4	-7.3
Portugal	-0.7	.. c	.. c	.. c	-81.2	132.9	119.3	119.2	103.2	54.0
Slovak Republic	-1.7	3.9	.. c	-15.3	3.3	-21.5	324.8	205.1	-59.3	-63.6
Slovenia	.. c	.. c	.. c	.. c	.. c	31.4	49.7	41.3	41.2	59.6
Spain	-16.6	37.2	-99.8	16.7	58.4	-92.3	814.9	1 406.9	136.4	568.4
Sweden	-	-	-	-	-	-	-	-	-	-
Switzerland	549.6	364.9	3 199.6	-251.7	2 102.1	1 246.7	1 465.1	611.2	232.8	468.0
Turkey	3.3	1.9	1.6	-4.1	19.2	67.6	59.5	137.4	64.6	141.6
United Kingdom	3 589.1	3 813.2	6 012.6	914.0	2 073.3	-1 632.0	-514.0	-378.7	4 584.0	1 676.5
United States	2 109.3	6 011.7	-3 668.3	2 373.3	-1 093.4	4 827.3	238.5	2 721.0	4 889.1	2 202.1
EUROPE	**8 240.4**	**11 686.2**	**16 630.9**	**-57.0**	**9 707.0**	**3 404.1**	**1 265.0**	**23 557.6**	**10 245.4**	**7 320.0**
Bulgaria	-	.. c	.. c	.. c	.. c	84.8	106.0	47.9	96.0	-181.1
Croatia	.. c	.. c	.. c	.. c	.. c	21.8	-58.9	50.8	31.1	47.0
Cyprus	-366.5	425.8	-480.8	.. c	-135.2	-148.5	.. c	-19.9	79.5	125.3
Malta	35.7	-98.4	.. c	109.4	20.2	20.6	-313.4	960.2	487.2	63.8
Romania	-	.. c	-	.. c	.. c	29.4	145.4	34.5	38.7	90.1
Russian Federation	1.3	11.0	3.4	-19.2	28.9	-11.9	115.6	834.6	673.0	-255.7
Ukraine	.. c	0.5	.. c	.. c	.. c	24.2	101.4	31.2	104.5	89.3
AFRICA	**.. c**	**.. c**	**5.9**	**2.6**	**.. c**	**1 849.4**	**-445.9**	**28.5**	**413.6**	**454.8**
Northern Africa	.. c	.. c	1.4	-2.5	-0.4	-180.2	-53.6	-20.5	26.5	21.4
Algeria	.. c	.. c	-	-	-	7.5	-14.5	-2.5	12.8	-16.8
Egypt	0.2	-1.3	1.4	-0.1	0.5	-30.4	.. c	.. c	23.7	5.3
Libya	-	-	-	-2.5	-	-	-	-	4.6	-
Morocco	-	-	0.1	-	-1.0	-164.1	7.6	-0.9	-17.5	29.8
Tunisia	-	-	-	-	-	6.8	.. c	0.1	2.9	3.1
Other African countries	.. c	.. c	4.4	5.2	.. c	2 029.5	-392.2	49.0	387.1	433.5
Nigeria	0.7	1.5	0.5	-2.8	6.7	3.0	.. c	-7.6	24.4	21.7
South Africa	.. c	.. c	-0.8	7.9	.. c	130.5	94.7	400.4	184.3	276.9
AMERICA	**-3 922.3**	**6 334.5**	**-7 382.9**	**2 085.4**	**787.9**	**5 506.0**	**3 530.6**	**2 614.7**	**5 761.0**	**4 072.5**
Northern America	6 324.0	6 116.4	-3 740.4	2 362.1	-726.6	5 205.2	1 478.1	3 687.5	4 848.6	2 704.2
Central America and Caribbean countries	-9 528.1	421.1	.. c	-234.4	1 495.8	26.5	1 682.8	-1 424.4	-256.8	49.8
Bahamas	-	-0.5	-1.6	-	-	1.7	-	-0.8	0.8	4.3
Bermuda	.. c	.. c	59.7	9.0	.. c	-22.5	-3.6	26.0	.. c	34.8
Cayman Islands	.. c	.. c	.. c	.. c	-9.6	-18.9	2.5	-31.6	27.8	-170.8
Costa Rica	-	-	-	-	-	.. c	2.7	-15.2	.. c	-0.8
El Salvador	-	-	-	-	.. c	.. c	.. c	.. c	.. c	.. c
Guatemala	-	-	-	-	-	.. c	4.6	-2.8	.. c	-4.8
Honduras	-	-	-	-	-	.. c	.. c	.. c	.. c	1.6
Nicaragua	-	-	-	-	-	.. c	-	-	-	-
Panama	-	-	-	-	.. c	9.4	8.4	4.6	.. c	2.1
Virgin Islands, U.S.	-	-	-	-	-	-	-	.. c	-	-
South America	.. c	.. c	2.7	.. c	18.8	274.4	369.8	351.7	1 169.2	1 318.4
Argentina	.. c	.. c	-	-	.. c	126.8	136.3	180.4	245.6	76.9
Bolivia	-	-	-	-	.. c	19.5	-111.6	-172.1	253.0	-99.5
Brazil	.. c	.. c	2.7	11.2	73.2	171.0	222.3	94.4	591.0	810.9
Colombia	.. c	.. c	-	-	.. c	36.7	38.8	53.8	-8.9	27.6
Ecuador	.. c	.. c	-	-	-	7.9	-	4.4	0.1	5.0
Paraguay	-	-	-	-	-	-1.5	-0.1	-1.1	.. c	.. c
Peru	.. c	.. c	-	-	.. c	80.1	105.7	42.2	60.2	75.0
Uruguay	.. c	.. c	-	.. c	.. c	2.6	13.8	-0.9	14.8	-13.5
Venezuela	.. c	.. c	-	-	0.6	35.4	-14.5	5.4	17.4	3.1

Table 1. Foreign direct investment flows by country *(cont.)*

Million US dollars

	Inward					Outward				
	2015	2016	2017	2018	2019	2015	2016	2017	2018	2019
ASIA	**3 921.7**	**1 765.9**	**6 680.7**	**2 363.9**	**1 303.0**	**2 220.1**	**243.7**	**1 145.1**	**1 158.9**	**3 504.2**
Near and Middle East	-48.3	.. c	.. c	.. c	-10.9	79.2	112.8	16.5	119.4	519.1
Gulf Arabian countries	-47.5	.. c	.. c	.. c	-17.4	3.6	75.0	4.4	43.0	17.3
Kuwait	-	-	-	-	-	2.0	0.7	0.5	1.4	.. c
Qatar	-	-	-	-	3.2	-	-0.2	-0.2	-1.2	-14.0
Saudi Arabia	-52.0	.. c	.. c	.. c	.. c	-36.4	19.4	8.2	-23.9	20.2
United Arab Emirates	3.7	-1.2	0.1	-0.3	5.1	47.2	56.2	-6.2	53.7	-4.8
Other Near and Middle East	.. c	.. c	4.8	-	6.7	75.6	37.6	12.1	76.4	501.7
Jordan	-	-	-	-	-	6.3	0.2	0.4	0.1	0.1
Other Asian countries	3 970.0	1 930.0	6 780.3	2 456.6	1 313.9	2 140.9	131.0	1 128.6	1 039.4	2 985.1
China	865.7	1 473.1	5 375.9	1 667.4	1 202.8	1 934.4	711.2	671.7	-26.4	593.4
Hong Kong, China	.. c	.. c	26.3	-291.4	-163.1	-122.4	-864.0	343.4	210.6	2 158.7
India	2.6	-0.1	16.8	0.2	11.0	-501.8	350.5	568.0	390.1	245.8
Indonesia	.. c	.. c	-	-	.. c	-53.1	33.7	7.6	36.5	53.3
Iran, Islamic Republic of	-0.6	-	-	1.8	-	.. c	.. c	.. c	-86.6	22.4
Malaysia	.. c	6.1	31.2	-12.0	19.6	77.1	96.8	34.4	24.9	3.0
Philippines	.. c	.. c	-	-	.. c	60.6	77.7	-44.1	-67.3	20.7
Singapore	-65.5	.. c	.. c	-11.9	50.7	76.8	-113.7	-583.8	126.1	-81.7
Chinese Taipei	1.1	-1.9	0.2	0.7	0.5	88.7	-0.6	-19.2	-11.7	44.1
Thailand	.. c	.. c	0.5	-	.. c	79.1	52.4	55.8	131.9	-55.0
Viet Nam	-1.5	3.6	1.1	-1.2	3.0	14.0	5.0	9.5	18.6	19.4
AUSTRALIA, OCEANIA AND POLAR REGIONS	**.. c**	**.. c**	**-29.8**	**-177.1**	**20.9**	**65.5**	**115.6**	**28.0**	**259.9**	**171.1**
WORLD unallocated and confidential	**.. d**	**.. d**	**-1.2**	**-0.2**	**.. d**	**-0.1**	**-6.5**	**-6.4**	**-**	**-0.1**
European Union (EU28)	**7 425.1**	**12 615.1**	**11 714.9**	**303.1**	**9 178.1**	**-505.5**	**-2 454.3**	**17 024.9**	**5 211.8**	**4 213.2**
G20 countries excl. European Union	**17 776.3**	**11 198.5**	**10 864.9**	**7 669.5**	**4 000.4**	**7 855.8**	**4 089.5**	**14 975.2**	**8 046.5**	**7 796.1**
G20 OECD countries	**17 558.6**	**9 472.4**	**5 571.1**	**6 094.5**	**2 793.9**	**6 096.1**	**2 405.9**	**12 209.9**	**5 976.1**	**5 974.4**
G20 Non-OECD countries	**217.7**	**1 725.9**	**5 293.8**	**1 575.0**	**1 206.4**	**1 759.7**	**1 683.6**	**2 765.3**	**2 070.2**	**1 821.7**
MENA countries	**-46.7**	**.. c**	**.. c**	**.. c**	**-17.9**	**-178.8**	**17.2**	**-23.4**	**67.1**	**59.9**
ASEAN countries	**.. c**	**.. c**	**.. c**	**-25.1**	**53.9**	**265.1**	**167.5**	**-525.2**	**298.7**	**-40.9**

- Nil; .. Not available; c Confidential data; d Secondary Confidentiality

Note: Detailed metadata at: *http://stats.oecd.org/OECDStat_Metadata/ShowMetadata.ashx?Dataset=FDI_CTRY_IND_SUMM.*

Source: *OECD International Direct Investment Statistics (database): https://doi.org/10.1787/idi-data-en*

SWEDEN

Table 2. Foreign direct investment positions by country

At year end

Million US dollars

	Inward					Outward				
	2015	2016	2017	2018	2019	2015	2016	2017	2018	2019
WORLD	**317 407.1**	**317 160.8**	**367 705.7**	**340 572.9**	**340 853.4**	**355 227.1**	**355 800.8**	**386 531.1**	**395 702.4**	**410 493.0**
OECD COUNTRIES	..	..	..	**318 031.9**	**317 003.5**	..	..	..	**342 783.5**	**352 320.2**
Australia	967.0	334.6	225.1	202.4	932.2	2 350.8	2 190.7	2 864.8	2 648.0	3 106.5
Austria	2 256.5	2 668.0	2 866.8	2 568.7	2 407.8	3 191.9	1 329.1	1 891.1	1 102.0	1 383.0
Belgium	1 213.9	1 976.7	4 714.5	1 027.0	1 316.6	12 966.2	18 130.1	-707.6	1 384.3	1 925.6
Canada	3 566.6	2 403.1	1 786.9	1 835.9	1 857.7	3 053.9	3 702.9	4 883.4	5 070.1	5 502.7
Chile	.. c	.. c	.. c	.. c	.. c	1 442.9	1 320.0	1 547.1	1 546.8	1 749.4
Czech Republic	183.3	61.5	48.0	68.7	120.1	1 047.3	2 206.2	3 373.3	3 035.2	3 229.9
Denmark	25 593.8	23 463.7	24 358.1	25 320.9	25 065.4	19 869.6	21 135.7	21 306.4	23 952.1	26 318.9
Estonia	393.2	101.9	29.5	156.1	156.9	4 403.6	4 280.4	5 538.5	5 619.0	4 854.9
Finland	28 602.7	28 031.2	32 591.1	28 999.1	27 130.3	34 445.7	38 931.8	27 011.7	26 019.2	27 428.4
France	5 490.4	4 734.2	6 956.5	7 946.0	8 377.7	7 160.8	7 608.5	9 168.1	9 046.9	9 571.5
Germany	30 921.2	30 561.2	35 412.3	30 786.8	30 466.7	17 635.9	10 989.6	21 151.1	20 294.7	18 760.6
Greece	.. c	.. c	.. c	-2.6	.. c	131.9	175.7	182.5	133.7	132.8
Hungary	-60.8	41.3	30.5	34.4	370.9	616.9	595.2	687.0	368.7	420.7
Iceland	.. c	.. c	.. c	.. c	.. c	.. c	37.3	88.8	259.9	276.4
Ireland	3 554.4	-1 888.2	1 212.5	4 761.1	8 241.5	1 882.6	2 211.1	11 977.6	10 682.8	11 586.0
Israel	.. c	.. c	.. c	.. c	.. c	1 015.4	654.8	523.1	434.1	756.6
Italy	842.0	966.4	1 130.0	1 553.6	2 335.6	6 843.8	5 694.5	7 472.1	8 369.4	8 032.3
Japan	3 040.8	2 991.3	4 590.9	5 133.1	4 354.4	3 054.8	3 414.1	3 671.1	3 909.6	3 802.8
Korea	113.7	187.7	.. c	.. c	.. c	2 503.8	2 566.0	2 525.0	2 689.9	2 883.3
Latvia	.. c	89.6	11.8	26.6	23.9	2 792.3	2 221.0	3 358.9	3 167.8	2 925.1
Lithuania	45.0	19.0	10.7	491.8	376.9	3 163.0	2 484.3	4 324.6	4 446.1	3 268.7
Luxembourg	49 006.1	46 425.5	52 702.0	42 240.1	45 814.6	24 887.7	18 691.7	15 251.5	13 551.7	11 425.3
Mexico	.. c	.. c	143.8	.. c	.. c	1 771.0	3 467.6	1 624.0	1 291.1	1 381.9
Netherlands	51 513.0	56 945.3	59 077.7	59 052.9	51 701.4	22 604.1	21 408.5	34 453.1	35 765.7	42 056.5
New Zealand	.. c	.. c	.. c	.. c	.. c	136.1	130.9	189.6	175.1	241.2
Norway	22 318.5	25 059.4	28 045.9	27 616.0	29 050.1	27 778.4	31 239.8	28 314.6	27 366.4	30 179.4
Poland	-6 061.2	-3 138.9	-2 827.9	-4 399.3	-3 709.2	5 759.1	6 247.4	8 396.7	6 905.5	6 144.3
Portugal	.. c	.. c	.. c	-24.3	-75.2	1 307.7	1 325.2	1 608.2	1 548.1	1 383.5
Slovak Republic	48.6	47.2	29.5	35.5	33.1	113.6	280.0	953.9	821.7	681.9
Slovenia	-	.. c	.. c	.. c	.. c	58.8	189.9	226.0	254.2	195.0
Spain	1 301.7	1 681.5	1 784.0	1 571.6	677.4	9 660.6	10 563.8	13 932.1	14 974.8	15 930.8
Sweden	-	-	-	-	-	-	-	-	-	-
Switzerland	9 962.0	8 140.0	8 797.4	7 509.7	8 306.0	9 610.9	10 130.4	11 839.4	11 076.0	10 729.0
Turkey	-20.4	-7.6	-6.5	2.8	127.4	1 225.5	1 131.2	1 630.1	1 364.2	1 601.5
United Kingdom	40 672.7	37 130.2	50 735.7	48 107.8	47 966.7	22 791.3	20 680.1	24 270.7	29 513.3	29 872.0
United States	20 357.0	29 357.0	29 039.8	24 970.7	22 894.1	52 063.3	49 637.2	54 004.4	63 995.8	62 582.0
EUROPE	**277 701.0**	**272 543.1**	**319 233.9**	**296 264.8**	**296 355.4**	**259 335.3**	**258 545.3**	**280 081.9**	**281 449.4**	**291 759.3**
Bulgaria	-	.. c	.. c	.. c	.. c	269.1	369.0	373.7	561.2	372.4
Croatia	-	-	.. c	.. c	.. c	369.5	336.9	392.9	627.2	557.2
Cyprus	6 609.2	6 509.0	8 470.4	.. c	6 161.3	1 127.0	1 543.0	1 505.4	1 501.0	879.4
Malta	656.8	285.5	514.1	607.7	964.1	619.8	762.4	1 573.5	1 339.4	2 767.4
Romania	.. c	.. c	.. c	.. c	.. c	560.1	662.6	756.9	619.7	831.1
Russian Federation	115.9	188.8	70.4	62.1	148.6	5 663.6	6 596.7	7 401.4	6 145.7	6 043.6
Ukraine	-	-	-	.. c	-	123.7	137.3	216.5	352.2	539.3
AFRICA	**166.2**	**97.8**	**32.7**	**96.5**	**-3.3**	**4 195.1**	**4 336.9**	**4 536.7**	**4 358.5**	**4 511.3**
Northern Africa	16.5	-24.9	.. c	35.1	.. c	989.1	697.2	546.8	355.2	407.1
Algeria	-26.2	-	-	-	-	125.3	.. c	.. c	.. c	.. c
Egypt	-32.7	-24.8	.. c	-	-	387.8	246.9	.. c	.. c	.. c
Libya	-	-	-	35.1	-	-	-	-	-49.1	-
Morocco	.. c	.. c	.. c	-	.. c	417.5	383.5	.. c	244.0	236.1
Tunisia	-	-	-	-	-	.. c	.. c	.. c	.. c	.. c
Other African countries	149.7	122.8	33.3	61.4	-11.9	3 206.0	3 639.7	3 989.9	4 003.3	4 104.2
Nigeria	40.3	87.0	-	92.7	.. c	94.7	34.8	.. c	-5.4	.. c
South Africa	.. c	.. c	-18.6	-19.3	.. c	747.7	1 122.1	1 696.4	1 613.5	1 721.3
AMERICA	**28 803.2**	**34 778.9**	**32 794.0**	**28 575.1**	**28 210.9**	**66 073.0**	**65 408.5**	**69 980.8**	**79 604.9**	**79 712.5**
Northern America	23 923.6	31 760.1	30 826.8	26 806.7	24 751.8	55 137.0	53 357.0	58 964.3	69 142.6	68 119.1
Central America and Caribbean countries	4 384.5	2 821.7	1 679.0	1 650.9	3 355.2	2 377.5	4 115.8	2 253.4	1 529.4	2 185.0
Bahamas	.. c	.. c	.. c	.. c	-	.. c	.. c	.. c	.. c	.. c
Bermuda	.. c	.. c	.. c	580.9	380.2	309.1	.. c	.. c	-87.0	388.3
Cayman Islands	2 116.7	2 094.7	946.8	353.9	311.3	34.4	143.3	95.8	86.5	41.2
Costa Rica	-	-	-	-	-	.. c	11.0	-4.1	-5.0	2.0
El Salvador	-	-	.. c	-	-	.. c	.. c	.. c	.. c	12.3
Guatemala	-	-	-	-	-	.. c	.. c	.. c	.. c	.. c
Honduras	-	-	-	-	-	.. c	.. c	.. c	.. c	.. c
Nicaragua	-	-	-	-	-	-	-	-	-	-
Panama	-	-	-	-	.. c	53.8	75.4	.. c	7.9	7.4
Virgin Islands, U.S.	-	-	-	-	-	-	.. c	.. c	.. c	.. c
South America	.. c	197.2	288.3	.. c	.. c	8 558.5	7 935.7	8 762.9	8 932.8	9 408.3
Argentina	.. c	.. c	.. c	.. c	-	461.0	451.1	577.9	570.1	558.9
Bolivia	-	-	-	-	-	1 700.0	.. c	.. c	.. c	.. c
Brazil	.. c	.. c	.. c	.. c	.. c	3 977.2	4 280.6	4 608.8	4 545.9	4 772.6
Colombia	.. c	-	-	-	-	298.1	229.2	288.7	240.1	247.7
Ecuador	.. c	-	-	-	-	115.2	.. c	84.2	.. c	120.5
Paraguay	-	-	-	-	-	24.9	.. c	.. c	.. c	.. c
Peru	.. c	-	-	-	-	372.0	377.6	440.8	447.0	599.4
Uruguay	.. c	-	-	-	.. c	77.5	91.0	77.4	77.5	68.3
Venezuela	.. c	-	.. c	.. c	.. c	89.8	116.4	50.2	.. c	.. c

SWEDEN

Table 2. Foreign direct investment positions by country *(cont.)*

At year end

Million US dollars

	Inward					Outward				
	2015	2016	2017	2018	2019	2015	2016	2017	2018	2019
ASIA	**9 540.7**	**9 267.7**	**15 246.5**	**15 280.7**	**15 209.7**	**23 134.4**	**25 188.6**	**28 877.3**	**27 466.6**	**31 162.2**
Near and Middle East	920.8	336.1	.. c	.. c	236.3	1 675.4	1 190.7	1 002.8	1 029.1	1 503.2
Gulf Arabian countries	.. c	.. c	.. c	.. c	97.3	576.1	512.3	465.3	583.4	729.3
Kuwait	-	-	-	-	-	.. c	.. c	.. c	.. c	.. c
Qatar	-	-	-	-	-24.3	.. c	.. c	.. c	.. c	103.8
Saudi Arabia	.. c	.. c	.. c	.. c	.. c	161.8	145.7	170.7	157.2	64.2
United Arab Emirates	-41.1	-24.3	.. c	.. c	-37.1	308.1	284.3	228.7	354.7	480.0
Other Near and Middle East	.. c	.. c	.. c	.. c	.. c	1 099.3	678.3	537.5	445.6	773.9
Jordan	-	-	-	-	-	.. c	.. c	.. c	.. c	.. c
Other Asian countries	8 619.9	8 931.6	14 821.0	15 117.8	14 973.4	21 459.0	23 997.9	27 874.5	26 437.6	29 659.0
China	.. c	.. c	.. c	8 666.7	9 448.9	8 170.3	10 669.4	13 182.6	11 208.5	12 721.5
Hong Kong, China	29.7	.. c	564.0	392.4	227.0	1 414.2	508.8	511.3	1 121.5	2 850.9
India	147.6	102.3	104.7	-7.6	10.8	1 739.2	2 261.8	2 909.6	2 619.6	2 792.9
Indonesia	.. c	-	.. c	.. c	.. c	119.8	267.4	305.3	265.7	313.5
Iran, Islamic Republic of	.. c	-	-	.. c	.. c	.. c	.. c	.. c	.. c	.. c
Malaysia	-	.. c	.. c	-9.8	-1.7	898.0	715.7	858.1	750.8	724.0
Philippines	-9.2	.. c	.. c	.. c	.. c	370.7	359.8	296.3	151.3	156.0
Singapore	725.3	267.8	18.8	.. c	.. c	1 336.5	1 082.1	725.6	711.6	940.5
Chinese Taipei	31.9	29.1	24.6	.. c	34.7	370.9	204.8	239.9	335.7	262.2
Thailand	-1.5	.. c	-21.8	-	-	1 370.0	1 414.7	1 888.4	1 820.0	1 843.1
Viet Nam	34.6	42.3	38.0	49.8	59.6	2.6	-5.2	0.9	7.1	20.8
AUSTRALIA, OCEANIA AND POLAR REGIONS	**1 048.1**	**334.5**	**222.7**	**192.6**	**917.9**	**2 489.3**	**2 321.5**	**3 054.3**	**2 823.0**	**3 347.7**
WORLD unallocated and confidential	**147.9**	**138.9**	**175.9**	**163.2**	**162.7**	**-**	**-**	**0.1**	**0.1**	**0.1**
European Union (EU28)	**244 085.4**	**238 108.8**	**281 411.4**	**259 464.4**	**257 304.9**	**213 776.7**	**208 391.0**	**229 483.7**	**234 315.3**	**241 930.7**
G20 countries excl. European Union	**112 774.5**	**114 665.0**	**140 032.0**	**129 912.8**	**129 718.2**	**141 495.6**	**136 877.1**	**164 117.4**	**175 319.2**	**176 085.5**
G20 OECD countries	**107 339.7**	**108 767.6**	**130 295.7**	**120 980.3**	**119 912.8**	**120 455.1**	**111 082.3**	**133 264.9**	**148 192.8**	**147 097.0**
G20 Non-OECD countries	**5 434.8**	**5 897.4**	**9 736.4**	**8 932.5**	**9 805.4**	**21 040.5**	**25 794.8**	**30 852.6**	**27 126.5**	**28 988.5**
MENA countries	**905.8**	**.. c**	**.. c**	**188.8**	**105.9**	**1 640.5**	**1 224.1**	**1 003.0**	**921.4**	**1 141.5**
ASEAN countries	**700.3**	**356.2**	**96.1**	**649.4**	**597.2**	**4 146.1**	**3 894.9**	**4 125.4**	**3 847.4**	**4 030.0**

- Nil; .. Not available; c Confidential data

Note: Detailed metadata at: *http://stats.oecd.org/OECDStat_Metadata/ShowMetadata.ashx?Dataset=FDI_CTRY_IND_SUMM.*

Source: OECD *International Direct Investment Statistics (database): https://doi.org/10.1787/idi-data-en*

SWEDEN

Table 3. Foreign direct investment income by country

Million US dollars

	Inward					Outward				
	2015	2016	2017	2018	2019	2015	2016	2017	2018	2019
WORLD	**22 052.7**	**21 835.7**	**22 165.9**	**25 395.8**	**23 836.2**	**26 829.6**	**25 633.3**	**30 743.7**	**34 932.8**	**34 742.4**
OECD COUNTRIES	..	..	..	**23 318.8**	**21 964.8**	..	..	..	**28 654.6**	**28 693.4**
Australia	-0.8	-0.9	-5.4	-7.5	47.9	194.4	207.7	248.9	132.1	315.3
Austria	244.0	236.4	250.3	326.3	251.1	323.9	155.6	217.7	206.7	170.4
Belgium	75.6	309.1	246.3	-6.9	105.0	500.0	933.8	1 091.5	1 359.3	1 267.7
Canada	250.0	200.5	549.6	152.2	204.2	444.4	367.6	276.8	208.6	447.8
Chile	8.3	.. c	.. c	5.4	0.7	-112.0	149.4	150.7	80.0	417.6
Czech Republic	22.9	0.5	-	0.2	-5.5	196.2	242.5	302.9	217.6	302.0
Denmark	875.5	1 582.7	1 378.6	1 515.8	1 286.0	1 689.5	1 690.3	1 680.1	1 701.1	1 360.0
Estonia	1.1	7.7	17.4	11.0	59.0	342.5	462.9	486.6	540.0	450.2
Finland	2 125.6	2 020.3	1 916.9	3 355.0	3 551.5	1 886.3	2 512.1	4 206.3	3 731.4	2 944.1
France	179.6	526.0	624.9	412.5	390.0	430.0	526.7	1 077.7	1 006.9	667.1
Germany	2 270.7	1 546.1	1 930.7	1 997.3	2 846.1	2 695.2	220.0	1 231.9	1 675.1	567.5
Greece	-	-	-	-	.. c	10.8	14.0	12.8	17.5	29.1
Hungary	.. c	.. c	.. c	.. c	10.9	50.3	41.6	93.5	77.7	49.5
Iceland	-17.8	-55.5	-3.0	-7.6	-	0.8	0.6	-7.6	15.5	6.0
Ireland	226.4	-3.7	184.9	112.8	-174.0	141.6	199.4	296.4	431.2	474.1
Israel	-0.8	6.4	4.8	-	6.7	12.2	27.3	38.5	119.0	-15.0
Italy	101.6	109.3	115.4	-58.7	161.4	417.7	327.4	435.4	310.6	432.4
Japan	521.3	511.7	456.9	535.2	214.0	92.5	425.4	277.5	209.1	149.1
Korea	19.1	14.0	41.3	35.4	69.0	133.9	124.4	408.9	305.6	450.0
Latvia	-	-9.5	.. c	-	-10.4	289.5	308.4	463.7	429.7	325.6
Lithuania	-20.0	-	.. c	12.3	4.0	225.3	332.6	470.6	542.2	426.5
Luxembourg	907.1	959.3	1 317.3	2 215.1	1 641.2	408.6	1 145.9	636.8	135.6	265.9
Mexico	.. c	.. c	-5.9	21.4	17.7	194.9	158.6	213.1	230.3	152.1
Netherlands	3 593.8	3 539.6	4 450.9	3 548.3	2 966.4	2 381.7	2 361.8	2 512.0	3 484.8	4 761.8
New Zealand	.. c	.. c	.. c	0.2	.. c	17.7	18.2	16.3	13.0	11.1
Norway	1 824.2	1 623.4	1 465.7	1 625.4	1 407.0	2 178.6	3 297.4	3 207.4	3 722.3	3 383.0
Poland	18.9	-65.2	-25.2	-51.4	-216.2	430.9	462.3	267.8	332.9	370.4
Portugal	-	.. c	-	-	16.0	134.4	86.5	101.8	172.1	116.5
Slovak Republic	-	-	-	-	-	32.0	27.2	35.8	29.3	31.9
Slovenia	-	-	-	-	-	13.8	3.5	9.4	23.0	34.8
Spain	234.7	249.3	86.2	320.8	233.8	608.1	558.9	522.6	763.6	397.4
Sweden	-	-	-	-	-	-	-	-	-	-
Switzerland	1 169.7	811.5	802.4	1 005.0	715.3	1 240.2	1 701.0	1 137.7	1 213.2	1 431.6
Turkey	-	-	-	-	0.1	54.6	55.7	91.4	83.2	61.1
United Kingdom	4 957.0	3 934.0	2 963.6	4 156.2	4 209.6	1 391.9	259.7	296.4	2 179.0	1 924.2
United States	1 081.8	2 033.1	1 300.6	2 086.9	1 956.9	3 891.9	2 572.1	3 282.6	2 956.0	4 514.5
EUROPE	**19 125.4**	**17 594.6**	**18 078.5**	**20 937.9**	**19 621.3**	**19 032.3**	**19 026.2**	**22 209.7**	**25 891.3**	**23 633.1**
Bulgaria	-	-	-	-	-	31.1	51.7	48.0	41.3	40.3
Croatia	-	.. c	-	-	.. c	17.7	18.9	9.6	46.6	24.6
Cyprus	52.6	78.4	205.1	202.6	121.1	3.7	78.4	89.6	117.9	74.5
Malta	235.3	103.0	80.6	219.1	20.6	123.5	156.4	181.0	196.7	236.0
Romania	-	.. c	.. c	.. c	.. c	53.1	34.7	32.9	71.8	55.5
Russian Federation	-	-1.2	-	-	1.8	367.2	511.3	763.5	807.2	765.6
Ukraine	-	-	-	-	-	33.8	85.2	32.8	91.4	71.5
AFRICA	**.. c**	**-3.3**	**4.8**	**.. c**	**.. c**	**-61.9**	**242.5**	**231.3**	**345.6**	**325.6**
Northern Africa	-	-	-	-	-	-141.1	49.9	14.7	19.1	44.4
Algeria	-	-	-	-	-	20.2	4.2	-2.5	12.8	4.4
Egypt	-	-	-	-	-	-12.0	28.2	3.0	11.9	7.8
Libya	-	-	-	-	-	-	-	-	-	-
Morocco	-	-	-	-	-	-155.8	14.7	14.0	-8.5	29.1
Tunisia	-	-	-	-	-	6.5	2.8	0.1	2.9	3.1
Other African countries	.. c	-3.3	4.8	.. c	.. c	79.0	192.6	216.5	326.3	281.2
Nigeria	-	-	-	-	.. c	4.2	-0.5	-7.0	19.3	28.9
South Africa	.. c	.. c	-	-	.. c	66.9	91.9	99.7	160.4	149.2
AMERICA	**1 574.4**	**2 579.9**	**1 860.5**	**2 251.5**	**1 921.0**	**5 087.5**	**3 791.2**	**4 671.5**	**4 728.6**	**6 577.7**
Northern America	1 331.8	2 233.6	1 850.0	2 239.3	2 161.1	4 338.0	2 941.5	3 559.1	3 168.2	4 960.3
Central America and Caribbean countries	274.5	371.2	5.3	-5.4	-270.1	218.9	209.3	288.1	326.6	211.6
Bahamas	-	-0.5	-1.6	-	-	1.7	-	0.5	0.8	4.3
Bermuda	19.7	29.7	54.4	67.7	33.1	-21.2	14.5	21.9	10.8	29.0
Cayman Islands	238.3	288.7	24.5	3.3	9.4	32.7	32.1	18.7	74.1	21.7
Costa Rica	-	-	-	-	-	1.9	-14.6	4.4	-3.7	-1.7
El Salvador	-	-	-	-	.. c	1.4	1.1	0.8	1.5	-0.1
Guatemala	-	-	-	-	-	0.8	-7.9	14.3	-7.0	-4.8
Honduras	-	-	-	-	-	0.2	0.9	0.2	0.7	1.6
Nicaragua	-	-	-	-	-	-	-	-	-	-
Panama	-	-	-	-	.. c	14.5	7.1	4.8	-	0.4
Virgin Islands, U.S.	-	-	-	-	-	-	-	-	-	-
South America	-31.9	-24.9	5.1	17.6	30.1	530.8	640.3	824.3	1 233.8	1 405.9
Argentina	.. c	.. c	-	-	.. c	154.6	180.0	184.0	170.8	137.1
Bolivia	-	-	-	-	.. c	270.5	204.2	218.1	452.8	221.2
Brazil	.. c	-20.9	4.7	12.1	28.7	57.2	7.6	200.0	462.1	526.4
Colombia	.. c	.. c	-	-	.. c	27.9	11.7	-0.4	9.2	24.1
Ecuador	.. c	.. c	-	-	-	5.2	-0.6	4.1	3.3	4.4
Paraguay	-	-	-	-	-	-0.1	-1.2	-1.4	-1.2	0.7
Peru	.. c	.. c	.. c	.. c	.. c	79.8	79.1	40.7	40.3	55.4
Uruguay	.. c	.. c	-	-	.. c	11.6	25.8	22.5	-0.7	15.7
Venezuela	0.9	.. c	-	-	0.6	36.1	-15.8	6.0	17.4	3.1

Table 3. Foreign direct investment income by country *(cont.)*

Million US dollars

	Inward					Outward				
	2015	2016	2017	2018	2019	2015	2016	2017	2018	2019
ASIA	**1 359.9**	**1 664.1**	**2 226.9**	**2 213.0**	**2 256.9**	**2 560.9**	**2 347.5**	**3 366.1**	**3 822.4**	**3 879.7**
Near and Middle East	61.0	24.3	19.0	.. c	15.4	113.9	107.9	76.8	196.0	50.0
Gulf Arabian countries	61.8	.. c	.. c	.. c	.. c	80.3	66.4	37.8	69.8	60.0
Kuwait	-	-	-	-	-	2.0	2.0	1.2	1.4	0.8
Qatar	-	-	-	-	-	-	-0.2	-0.2	-1.2	-1.4
Saudi Arabia	61.8	.. c	.. c	.. c	.. c	15.9	17.3	11.2	14.6	18.2
United Arab Emirates	.. c	-	-	.. c	-	35.6	33.5	15.2	42.6	19.6
Other Near and Middle East	-0.8	6.7	4.8	-	6.7	33.5	41.5	38.8	126.1	-9.9
Jordan	-	-	-	-	-	6.3	0.2	0.4	0.1	0.1
Other Asian countries	1 298.9	1 639.8	2 207.9	2 202.7	2 241.5	2 447.1	2 239.6	3 289.5	3 626.4	3 829.7
China	860.9	1 081.6	1 629.8	1 613.5	1 936.4	1 029.5	821.9	1 585.0	1 425.4	1 718.4
Hong Kong, China	-5.9	-8.8	26.6	7.2	-2.2	388.1	229.9	182.9	668.0	638.1
India	-1.3	1.1	14.6	1.6	1.5	163.1	247.5	474.1	401.6	297.7
Indonesia	.. c	.. c	.. c	.. c	.. c	-2.4	24.9	16.7	33.9	16.7
Iran, Islamic Republic of	-	-	-	-	-	18.0	15.3	-16.7	-69.5	22.4
Malaysia	.. c	7.0	35.2	-12.0	3.2	115.2	65.1	75.6	80.5	95.2
Philippines	.. c	.. c	.. c	.. c	.. c	20.4	36.6	22.2	21.4	16.8
Singapore	-87.9	26.1	4.1	21.5	20.7	132.2	3.4	-86.8	91.6	106.8
Chinese Taipei	.. c	.. c	-	.. c	.. c	39.6	32.7	62.0	89.8	66.4
Thailand	.. c	.. c	.. c	.. c	.. c	98.0	99.5	154.3	164.0	149.1
Viet Nam	-	-	-	-	-	17.0	18.8	13.8	21.2	13.6
AUSTRALIA, OCEANIA AND POLAR REGIONS	**1.1**	**-0.2**	**-5.4**	**-7.2**	**47.5**	**210.8**	**225.9**	**265.1**	**145.1**	**326.4**
WORLD unallocated and confidential	**.. d**	**0.6**	**0.6**	**.. d**	**.. d**	**-**	**-**	**-**	**-0.1**	**-**
European Union (EU28)	**16 104.1**	**15 127.8**	**15 749.7**	**18 294.1**	**17 472.8**	**14 873.6**	**13 260.6**	**16 861.9**	**19 896.0**	**17 853.7**
G20 countries excl. European Union	**10 252.2**	**9 943.6**	**9 635.1**	**10 968.8**	**12 086.1**	**11 793.6**	**7 147.3**	**11 174.7**	**12 772.3**	**13 310.4**
G20 OECD countries	**9 380.9**	**8 875.1**	**7 971.7**	**9 331.0**	**10 116.8**	**9 941.8**	**5 245.0**	**7 840.4**	**9 296.2**	**9 681.2**
G20 Non-OECD countries	**871.2**	**1 068.3**	**1 663.4**	**1 637.8**	**1 969.4**	**1 851.9**	**1 902.3**	**3 334.3**	**3 476.0**	**3 629.3**
MENA countries	**61.8**	**.. c**	**.. c**	**.. c**	**.. c**	**-51.1**	**116.1**	**48.0**	**85.5**	**108.2**
ASEAN countries	**-95.0**	**29.5**	**39.4**	**9.7**	**23.2**	**391.5**	**261.4**	**198.0**	**458.1**	**397.6**

- Nil; .. Not available; c Confidential data; d Secondary Confidentiality

Note: Detailed metadata at: *http://stats.oecd.org/OECDStat_Metadata/ShowMetadata.ashx?Dataset=FDI_CTRY_IND_SUMM.*

Source: *OECD International Direct Investment Statistics (database): https://doi.org/10.1787/idi-data-en*

SWEDEN

Table 4. Foreign direct investment flows by industrial sector

Million US dollars

	Inward					Outward				
	2015	2016	2017	2018	2019	2015	2016	2017	2018	2019
All FDI activities	**8 449.5**	**19 153.0**	**15 903.5**	**4 217.6**	**11 732.8**	**13 045.0**	**4 702.5**	**27 367.5**	**17 838.8**	**15 522.5**
Agriculture, forestry and fishing	**29.3**	**30.3**	**3.7**	**2.8**	**33.9**	**3.8**	**-0.5**	**5.4**	**8.4**	**-1.0**
Mining and quarrying	**25.2**	**1 394.1**	**412.2**	**684.1**	**-1 436.8**	**-434.0**	**1 562.7**	**544.3**	**177.0**	**704.6**
Extraction activities	21.1	1 372.6	398.4	687.9	.. c	-458.3	779.8	311.0	-18.0	430.6
Manufacturing	**6 731.6**	**818.0**	**5 787.8**	**6 469.3**	**4 363.1**	**6 724.0**	**4 417.3**	**13 202.3**	**15 671.7**	**7 481.8**
of which:										
Food products, beverages and tobacco	-709.5	-128.8	441.6	756.2	476.8	-168.7	.. c	679.7	476.6	-297.0
Textiles, wood and paper products; printing	-498.3	-68.5	-504.6	245.1	1 656.4	-451.8	321.4	.. c	.. c	.. c
Chemical, rubber, plastic, non-metallic mineral products	2 659.8	511.9	1 995.3	-375.2	549.8	-597.4	-338.5	2 140.5	409.0	818.1
Metal and machinery products, except electrical equipment	-217.1	422.7	1 575.3	3 747.8	241.8	-122.3	323.6	5 261.6	11 431.9	1 469.1
Motor vehicles, trailers, semi-trailers, other transport equipment	4 325.9	397.0	-115.1	2 333.3	793.3	4 661.4	4 414.5	1 084.1	3 021.7	4 588.9
Other manufacturing	.. c	-316.3	2 395.3	-237.7	645.0	3 402.9	660.3	-912.5	-205.2	918.8
Electricity, gas, steam and air conditioning supply	**-3 793.2**	**105.4**	**-2 095.1**	**-667.7**	**459.6**	**.. c**	**.. c**	**.. c**	**.. c**	**.. c**
Water supply; sewerage, waste management and remediation activities	**65.0**	**-23.3**	**15.2**	**33.6**	**-7.4**	**-31.0**	**-134.6**	**76.4**	**46.7**	**-147.1**
Construction	**-531.0**	**370.6**	**134.0**	**-205.3**	**260.5**	**.. c**	**-13.9**	**.. c**	**75.5**	**.. c**
Services	**3 793.7**	**16 489.8**	**10 020.7**	**2 285.4**	**3 613.5**	**6 727.8**	**-2 342.7**	**12 259.5**	**2 174.1**	**7 692.6**
Wholesale and retail trade; repair of motor vehicles and motorcycles	2 102.1	15 379.3	4 397.4	-3 378.1	1 333.5	-877.2	-2 116.4	2 146.3	-1 262.9	2 553.0
Transportation and storage	539.1	285.2	38.8	464.1	-267.2	865.3	-168.5	-1 200.9	394.5	-297.0
Accommodation and food service activities	-30.8	-254.5	105.5	10.5	-16.8	178.4	476.8	74.4	14.5	8.9
Information and communication	-109.3	-1 050.5	-612.4	-864.9	699.5	309.3	-1 722.4	-412.0	852.3	1 118.5
Financial and insurance activities	-1 208.0	3 348.7	2 399.3	-76.3	-241.8	2 556.0	-656.6	721.2	-2 262.6	844.3
Activities of holding companies	-123.0	3 648.7	-94.3	-1 446.3	-188.9	.. c	1 081.5	-31.2	-2 795.8	325.8
Real estate activities	-409.2	-1 200.0	-956.6	972.2	500.6	785.2	288.0	2 243.6	1 638.4	-121.7
Professional, scientific and technical activities	3 052.6	-498.7	1 992.3	2 353.7	1 477.7	2 087.6	59.0	2 795.1	790.3	2 850.3
Administrative and support service activities	-91.8	573.7	2 748.2	1 791.4	40.5	455.2	1 345.6	5 377.8	1 775.8	925.7
Public administration; activities of households and of extraterritorial organisations	-	-	-	-	-	-	78.2	527.7	98.2	58.6
Education	-2.0	0.2	8.4	8.5	0.1	-	0.6	5.3	18.9	9.8
Human health and social work activities	.. c	-119.2	-107.9	.. c	.. c	.. c	80.6	156.9	131.8	-263.9
Arts, entertainment and recreation	-8.7	-9.4	-7.4	24.2	-8.5	80.0	-50.6	22.1	25.7	45.2
Other services	-28.5	35.3	15.1	2.0	-14.8	-0.1	43.0	-198.0	-40.4	-39.1
Not allocated and confidential	**1 986.3**	**-149.8**	**1 521.2**	**-4 701.2**	**4 228.7**	**.. c**	**.. c**	**.. c**	**.. c**	**.. c**
Private real estate activities	**142.6**	**117.9**	**103.8**	**316.7**	**217.6**	**633.7**	**-54.9**	**.. c**	**127.7**	**-343.8**

- Nil; c Confidential data

Note: Detailed metadata at: *http://stats.oecd.org/OECDStat_Metadata/ShowMetadata.ashx?Dataset=FDI_CTRY_IND_SUMM.*

Source: *OECD International Direct Investment Statistics (database): https://doi.org/10.1787/idi-data-en*

SWEDEN

Table 5. Foreign direct investment positions by industrial sector
At year end

Million US dollars

	Inward					Outward				
	2015	2016	2017	2018	2019	2015	2016	2017	2018	2019
All FDI activities	**317 407.1**	**317 160.8**	**367 705.7**	**340 572.9**	**340 853.4**	**355 227.1**	**355 800.8**	**386 531.1**	**395 702.4**	**410 493.0**
Agriculture, forestry and fishing	**401.5**	**87.0**	**27.2**	**.. c**	**.. c**	**-232.9**	**315.9**	**267.3**	**476.5**	**59.9**
Mining and quarrying	**1 677.2**	**1 400.2**	**1 696.9**	**1 577.9**	**1 205.8**	**2 369.4**	**3 560.5**	**3 596.7**	**3 953.5**	**4 963.1**
Extraction activities	.. c	959.3	.. c	1 236.0	698.3	.. c	.. c	.. c	1 608.6	.. c
Manufacturing	**137 035.4**	**126 855.4**	**143 295.8**	**132 534.2**	**129 793.0**	**152 650.5**	**143 849.8**	**159 329.1**	**166 549.3**	**166 875.6**
of which:										
Food products, beverages and tobacco	23 432.1	22 480.4	23 642.7	21 672.8	22 655.6	6 604.6	4 965.9	4 359.0	4 868.0	4 925.6
Textiles, wood and paper products; printing	15 360.4	14 300.8	15 442.4	14 368.3	16 756.0	11 848.0	11 869.2	.. c	.. c	.. c
Chemical, rubber, plastic, non-metallic mineral products	51 258.6	46 418.3	53 826.8	51 619.3	50 993.7	37 211.8	35 800.1	43 214.8	43 581.2	41 267.6
Metal and machinery products, except electrical equipment	13 066.9	13 125.1	16 100.0	16 179.1	14 353.7	55 824.9	46 384.3	47 357.7	50 055.9	50 464.2
Motor vehicles, trailers, semi-trailers, other transport equipment	21 588.5	20 459.8	21 700.8	19 201.3	18 467.6	32 984.9	35 884.1	38 412.3	40 956.3	44 724.4
Other manufacturing	12 328.9	10 071.0	12 583.1	9 493.4	6 566.3	8 176.2	8 946.2	10 120.2	12 429.3	10 079.1
Electricity, gas, steam and air conditioning supply	**24 155.9**	**22 630.4**	**24 152.0**	**20 934.4**	**21 797.6**	**.. c**	**.. c**	**.. c**	**.. c**	**.. c**
Water supply; sewerage, waste management and remediation activities	**601.8**	**768.6**	**875.2**	**855.3**	**1 122.6**	**550.4**	**586.7**	**664.7**	**674.7**	**592.2**
Construction	**1 947.3**	**1 823.4**	**2 306.9**	**1 372.1**	**1 178.8**	**4 508.9**	**3 772.2**	**4 089.2**	**4 651.4**	**5 263.8**
Services	**134 601.5**	**145 536.8**	**171 678.9**	**156 449.2**	**153 119.5**	**158 311.9**	**168 696.7**	**176 821.9**	**174 720.9**	**185 713.0**
Wholesale and retail trade; repair of motor vehicles and motorcycles	30 055.8	34 316.8	45 380.8	40 880.5	39 099.7	36 019.7	36 711.7	42 604.2	39 754.1	43 354.9
Transportation and storage	4 972.4	3 500.7	4 980.3	6 322.2	5 698.1	6 226.7	6 627.9	6 245.4	6 003.9	7 912.3
Accommodation and food service activities	1 114.6	897.5	1 697.2	529.7	188.2	578.4	2 402.6	585.2	.. c	.. c
Information and communication	14 436.0	13 554.8	15 140.6	13 435.9	11 742.8	14 139.7	17 386.6	23 408.4	28 671.1	23 442.7
Financial and insurance activities	46 374.2	59 826.0	63 977.0	57 970.7	58 731.2	72 985.7	74 760.7	57 176.2	45 318.6	48 258.4
Activities of holding companies	16 455.1	24 801.6	23 556.7	22 962.1	25 140.2	7 050.0	7 495.9	9 367.6	11 907.7	12 461.8
Real estate activities	18 024.1	17 034.6	19 253.7	17 178.4	20 150.3	8 482.5	11 045.6	16 808.1	18 596.6	25 565.0
Professional, scientific and technical activities	14 675.1	10 890.4	12 126.3	13 799.3	12 858.6	10 991.4	8 528.9	13 016.7	16 310.3	15 798.2
Administrative and support service activities	4 296.7	4 791.9	8 348.4	4 625.6	3 940.2	7 981.5	8 803.3	12 815.8	13 904.8	13 933.6
Public administration; activities of households and of extraterritorial organisations	-	-	-	-	.. c	-	.. c	.. c	2 163.8	.. c
Education	.. c	.. c	.. c	139.3	.. c	-	.. c	.. c	.. c	.. c
Human health and social work activities	318.3	282.4	.. c	1 095.3	.. c	.. c	1 162.3	2 479.9	2 760.4	2 565.8
Arts, entertainment and recreation	.. c	.. c	.. c	447.3	376.9	.. c	556.7	588.5	.. c	237.3
Other services	.. c	233.7	214.5	25.0	.. c	.. c	.. c	.. c	.. c	.. c
Not allocated and confidential	**3 961.8**	**5 438.7**	**8 549.5**	**.. c**	**.. c**	**.. c**	**.. c**	**.. c**	**.. c**	**.. c**
Private real estate activities	**13 024.7**	**12 620.3**	**15 123.3**	**14 196.1**	**14 454.6**	**20 437.3**	**20 236.9**	**25 655.1**	**24 175.2**	**24 655.2**

- Nil; c Confidential data

Note: Detailed metadata at: *http://stats.oecd.org/OECDStat_Metadata/ShowMetadata.ashx?Dataset=FDI_CTRY_IND_SUMM.*

Source: *OECD International Direct Investment Statistics (database): https://doi.org/10.1787/idi-data-en*

SWEDEN

Table 6. Foreign direct investment income by industrial sector

Million US dollars

	Inward					Outward				
	2015	2016	2017	2018	2019	2015	2016	2017	2018	2019
All FDI activities	**22 052.7**	**21 835.7**	**22 165.9**	**25 395.8**	**23 836.2**	**26 829.6**	**25 633.3**	**30 743.7**	**34 932.8**	**34 742.4**
Agriculture, forestry and fishing	**35.8**	**30.3**	**3.7**	**2.8**	**38.4**	**5.2**	**-0.5**	**5.4**	**8.9**	**-0.5**
Mining and quarrying	**64.7**	**363.0**	**463.6**	**329.6**	**-0.2**	**-28.6**	**554.5**	**659.9**	**476.0**	**760.7**
Extraction activities	21.1	310.1	436.1	333.4	0.6	-262.9	297.0	304.9	140.6	533.8
Manufacturing	**10 519.3**	**11 210.4**	**11 192.6**	**13 351.1**	**12 647.9**	**13 087.1**	**11 593.5**	**14 395.6**	**17 699.9**	**17 673.3**
of which:										
Food products, beverages and tobacco	304.4	962.3	661.9	1 129.1	1 300.5	495.3	1 325.8	832.9	814.3	745.2
Textiles, wood and paper products; printing	350.8	149.1	498.1	569.9	679.8	1 221.3	663.6	1 388.8	985.7	1 254.6
Chemical, rubber, plastic, non-metallic mineral products	5 040.4	5 323.7	4 225.3	5 868.4	5 138.2	1 124.2	159.3	1 425.8	2 348.0	3 021.8
Metal and machinery products, except electrical equipment	1 468.6	1 113.4	1 714.1	1 351.6	1 167.3	6 847.2	5 249.6	6 131.4	7 485.4	6 782.6
Motor vehicles, trailers, semi-trailers, other transport equipment	2 286.8	2 822.4	3 255.9	3 320.9	3 591.9	1 715.0	2 516.2	3 852.8	4 691.8	4 911.5
Other manufacturing	1 068.4	839.5	837.4	1 111.1	770.2	1 684.2	1 679.2	763.9	1 374.6	957.4
Electricity, gas, steam and air conditioning supply	**870.9**	**186.9**	**204.4**	**708.0**	**1 208.7**	**734.3**	**108.5**	**596.2**	**361.4**	**94.4**
Water supply; sewerage, waste management and remediation activities	**65.0**	**3.0**	**15.2**	**34.2**	**22.0**	**-21.6**	**-32.8**	**77.8**	**60.6**	**9.6**
Construction	**-58.0**	**162.6**	**458.5**	**115.2**	**113.3**	**404.8**	**198.8**	**-59.9**	**115.3**	**325.9**
Services	**10 079.8**	**9 764.4**	**9 519.5**	**10 208.5**	**8 723.8**	**11 961.5**	**12 640.6**	**14 402.8**	**15 529.6**	**15 140.0**
Wholesale and retail trade; repair of motor vehicles and motorcycles	2 564.7	3 090.3	3 042.5	2 756.6	2 529.8	2 908.9	3 394.6	4 078.3	4 252.6	4 877.2
Transportation and storage	559.8	339.0	207.3	-138.2	155.0	278.3	-20.9	57.4	-439.9	-40.0
Accommodation and food service activities	131.7	37.7	132.1	60.3	-16.8	191.1	126.3	99.9	18.1	8.9
Information and communication	1 183.8	1 209.5	703.1	1 576.9	1 104.3	1 535.8	1 874.8	2 300.7	3 107.3	2 391.2
Financial and insurance activities	3 680.7	3 218.3	3 142.4	3 914.3	3 363.4	4 438.6	4 242.3	5 120.0	4 584.6	4 713.8
Activities of holding companies	1 192.6	642.4	264.0	390.2	554.4	172.6	314.1	197.8	295.3	465.5
Real estate activities	568.1	310.5	537.1	186.2	277.1	653.6	245.1	167.1	366.2	411.4
Professional, scientific and technical activities	1 018.1	1 119.1	1 219.8	1 330.2	777.1	980.6	1 283.8	941.5	1 630.1	808.4
Administrative and support service activities	421.6	484.0	541.5	446.1	498.5	828.4	1 114.2	1 201.0	1 682.9	1 627.3
Public administration; activities of households and of extraterritorial organisations	-	-	-	-	-	-	78.2	170.7	144.5	60.2
Education	-2.0	0.2	8.4	8.5	0.1	-	0.6	5.3	18.9	9.8
Human health and social work activities	-9.6	-77.0	-27.3	41.4	58.5	17.2	89.3	79.8	-18.8	189.6
Arts, entertainment and recreation	-8.7	-9.4	-7.4	24.2	-8.5	129.0	138.3	119.8	147.5	54.1
Other services	-28.5	42.0	19.8	2.0	-14.8	-0.1	74.2	61.7	35.8	28.1
Not allocated and confidential	**444.8**	**1.5**	**110.3**	**435.1**	**576.7**	**577.3**	**426.5**	**428.7**	**491.2**	**528.3**
Private real estate activities	**30.5**	**113.6**	**198.1**	**211.5**	**505.8**	**109.6**	**144.2**	**237.2**	**189.9**	**210.7**

- Nil

Note: Detailed metadata at: *http://stats.oecd.org/OECDStat_Metadata/ShowMetadata.ashx?Dataset=FDI_CTRY_IND_SUMM.*

Source: *OECD International Direct Investment Statistics (database): https://doi.org/10.1787/idi-data-en*

SWITZERLAND

Table 1. Foreign direct investment flows by country

Million US dollars

	Inward					Outward				
	2015	2016	2017	2018	2019	2015	2016	2017	2018	2019
WORLD	**84 326.6**	**150 511.7**	**110 721.9**	**-68 312.2**	**-79 075.3**	**91 550.9**	**166 901.4**	**19 522.2**	**43 490.7**	**-43 721.5**
OECD COUNTRIES	**65 220.3**	**143 363.7**	**63 589.3**	**-43 939.9**	**-90 378.1**	**91 331.5**	**190 460.6**	**-34 315.6**	**14 459.3**	**-31 564.5**
Australia	.. c	.. c	.. c	.. c	.. c	6 979.9	-489.1	-1 952.5	-8 743.6	-920.1
Austria	-78.7	10 231.0	-1 124.1	3 540.1	77.7	76.9	248.7	-280.7	-214.7	1 785.4
Belgium	1 662.6	-1 125.3	-1 201.2	-548.3	12 537.6	3 207.4	-1 647.8	-4 342.3	-3 252.1	5 074.2
Canada	259.3	-137.6	2 989.8	50.7	-1 835.9	-2 122.9	-3 334.5	534.1	-6 877.1	8 427.5
Chile	.. c	.. c	.. c	.. c	.. c	-3 419.0	-467.5	-47.4	3 688.7	294.9
Czech Republic	.. c	.. c	.. c	.. c	.. c	-611.7	-840.6	429.7	-3.4	-342.6
Denmark	-2 869.0	-373.1	1 515.9	244.9	-15 804.4	-277.7	-413.6	133.0	139.7	-105.1
Estonia	.. c	.. c	.. c	.. c	.. c	-100.1	354.6	-328.1	18.9	44.3
Finland	.. c	.. c	.. c	.. c	.. c	-38.0	171.9	-432.8	180.3	154.0
France	120.5	-2 933.5	528.9	10 624.7	1 798.1	23 294.8	2 932.7	-934.3	9 228.1	4 039.7
Germany	889.7	2 354.8	1 368.7	-7 477.8	503.0	1 989.7	7 342.8	5 746.7	11 060.0	5 187.4
Greece	.. c	.. c	.. c	.. c	.. c	5.7	-382.7	187.5	-47.3	-52.5
Hungary	1 980.5	4 529.9	2 553.2	-2 321.2	-1 077.3	327.0	4 048.3	392.6	385.3	20 559.2
Iceland	.. c	.. c	.. c	.. c	.. c	.. c	.. c	.. c	.. c	.. c
Ireland	13 893.8	25 811.9	11 032.5	19 151.5	-58 104.8	39 414.5	36 712.1	-42 891.7	6 042.8	-35 555.8
Israel	51.3	-200.0	-177.3	-26.1	50.3	163.7	917.6	-152.8	39.8	-369.4
Italy	425.1	535.4	25.7	-1 400.9	235.9	-513.0	819.8	587.5	1 309.1	2 101.5
Japan	543.1	-441.9	-1 935.9	-656.7	17 429.2	262.6	2 281.6	4 507.7	2 413.4	685.5
Korea	.. c	.. c	.. c	.. c	.. c	255.5	-835.2	304.3	5.4	65.7
Latvia	.. c	.. c	.. c	.. c	.. c	0.7	4.1	96.2	37.5	45.4
Lithuania	.. c	.. c	.. c	.. c	.. c	-5.9	-0.4	-19.2	75.9	181.1
Luxembourg	7 346.5	33 881.6	42 788.2	-30 371.9	-4 824.8	9 652.7	26 771.8	-6 200.7	-3 267.2	-44 282.7
Mexico	.. c	.. c	.. c	.. c	.. c	145.0	614.2	484.3	777.4	751.4
Netherlands	37 266.1	51 810.0	46 940.9	-46 736.3	-6 211.9	14 872.9	36 253.8	7 254.2	548.3	-7 184.4
New Zealand	.. c	.. c	.. c	.. c	.. c	28.3	38.1	-18.9	41.1	122.7
Norway	.. c	.. c	.. c	.. c	.. c	-236.1	2 357.4	-364.8	-289.9	-2 546.0
Poland	.. c	.. c	.. c	.. c	.. c	-394.6	356.8	591.3	528.1	523.9
Portugal	.. c	.. c	.. c	.. c	.. c	312.7	54.6	183.5	-6.0	-38.7
Slovak Republic	.. c	.. c	.. c	.. c	.. c	107.5	69.5	267.6	205.1	15.4
Slovenia	.. c	.. c	.. c	.. c	.. c	.. c	.. c	.. c	.. c	.. c
Spain	134.5	-563.5	-53.1	-248.0	-632.0	-309.7	-225.4	330.1	1 142.2	1 528.6
Sweden	2 087.1	-103.7	800.5	587.4	299.4	-477.4	-1 013.6	1 073.3	148.2	-429.2
Switzerland	-	-	-	-	-	-	-	-	-	-
Turkey	.. c	.. c	.. c	.. c	.. c	421.1	394.6	221.2	218.7	17.7
United Kingdom	14 326.0	6 064.1	-26 403.8	39 658.9	-7 071.6	-13 436.7	13 525.9	-14 770.5	12 738.6	6 206.2
United States	-2 717.0	14 077.8	-16 655.4	-28 323.3	-28 412.1	17 391.5	63 742.3	15 167.0	-13 872.4	2 329.5
EUROPE	**70 206.8**	**135 481.5**	**86 963.6**	**10 790.2**	**-85 272.3**	**72 321.6**	**132 131.9**	**11 308.5**	**38 784.4**	**-36 483.9**
Bulgaria	.. c	.. c	.. c	.. c	.. c	22.5	-15.4	36.9	-25.4	35.0
Croatia	.. c	.. c	.. c	.. c	.. c	-3.2	17.6	56.5	-6.4	72.4
Cyprus	-1 920.1	-487.9	1 298.6	-619.3	1 155.1	-777.4	-1 387.2	53 018.2	-501.0	-28.2
Malta	.. c	.. c	.. c	.. c	.. c	.. c	.. c	.. c	.. c	.. c
Romania	.. c	.. c	.. c	.. c	.. c	-127.9	-56.2	393.3	214.5	509.1
Russian Federation	.. c	.. c	.. c	.. c	.. c	295.8	1 068.9	4 602.2	2 664.1	4 176.3
Ukraine	.. c	.. c	.. c	.. c	.. c	-133.3	-38.2	756.1	615.8	714.4
AFRICA	**.. c**	**.. c**	**.. c**	**.. c**	**.. c**	**3 142.1**	**359.0**	**-1 402.0**	**-633.0**	**3 198.9**
Northern Africa	.. c	.. c	.. c	.. c	.. c	555.6	-705.5	-98.6	-31.3	70.3
Algeria	.. c	.. c	.. c	.. c	.. c	.. c	.. c	.. c	.. c	.. c
Egypt	.. c	.. c	.. c	.. c	.. c	522.0	-415.5	-113.3	-72.0	78.9
Libya	.. c	.. c	.. c	.. c	.. c	.. c	.. c	.. c	.. c	.. c
Morocco	.. c	.. c	.. c	.. c	.. c	25.5	-333.4	-14.4	23.2	-14.9
Tunisia	.. c	.. c	.. c	.. c	.. c	-15.2	2.4	12.7	15.4	22.1
Other African countries	.. c	.. c	.. c	.. c	.. c	2 586.5	1 064.5	-1 303.4	-601.7	3 128.6
Nigeria	.. c	.. c	.. c	.. c	.. c	244.6	162.8	35.0	-2.9	35.7
South Africa	.. c	.. c	.. c	.. c	.. c	-215.8	861.8	-74.9	-365.7	2 304.8
AMERICA	**18 220.1**	**13 913.0**	**23 655.0**	**-79 849.8**	**-15 752.4**	**3 836.1**	**36 989.7**	**2 890.2**	**8 197.2**	**-561.5**
Northern America	-2 457.7	13 940.2	-13 665.6	-28 272.4	-30 248.0	15 268.6	60 407.8	15 701.0	-20 749.4	10 757.0
Central America and Caribbean countries	.. c	.. c	.. c	.. c	.. c	-6 930.2	-23 435.4	-13 513.4	19 634.6	-10 038.3
Bahamas	.. c	.. c	.. c	.. c	.. c	.. c	.. c	.. c	.. c	.. c
Bermuda	.. c	.. c	.. c	.. c	.. c	-27 182.0	-2 440.6	-15 192.1	23 783.1	-20 974.5
Cayman Islands	.. c	.. c	.. c	.. c	.. c	.. c	.. c	.. c	.. c	.. c
Costa Rica	.. c	.. c	.. c	.. c	.. c	93.2	79.0	154.5	154.8	286.5
El Salvador	.. c	.. c	.. c	.. c	.. c	.. c	.. c	.. c	.. c	.. c
Guatemala	.. c	.. c	.. c	.. c	.. c	2.9	17.6	-59.3	1.0	75.0
Honduras	.. c	.. c	.. c	.. c	.. c	.. c	.. c	.. c	.. c	.. c
Nicaragua	.. c	.. c	.. c	.. c	.. c	.. c	.. c	.. c	.. c	.. c
Panama	.. c	.. c	.. c	.. c	.. c	-2 160.5	-3 795.0	4 031.1	-221.9	74.0
Virgin Islands, U.S.	.. c	.. c	.. c	.. c	.. c	.. c	.. c	.. c	.. c	.. c
South America	.. c	.. c	.. c	.. c	.. c	-4 502.3	17.3	702.6	9 312.0	-1 280.2
Argentina	.. c	.. c	.. c	.. c	.. c	34.1	-514.5	51.2	865.0	-103.3
Bolivia	.. c	.. c	.. c	.. c	.. c	2.6	-15.6	11.5	8.0	1.1
Brazil	.. c	.. c	.. c	.. c	.. c	-1 108.0	59.4	-184.8	1 251.9	760.0
Colombia	.. c	.. c	.. c	.. c	.. c	28.5	11.0	301.7	3 544.2	612.5
Ecuador	.. c	.. c	.. c	.. c	.. c	33.9	-15.2	37.0	81.7	0.5
Paraguay	.. c	.. c	.. c	.. c	.. c	.. c	.. c	.. c	.. c	.. c
Peru	.. c	.. c	.. c	.. c	.. c	109.0	-1.3	314.9	-217.6	-3 069.5
Uruguay	.. c	.. c	.. c	.. c	.. c	37.1	660.7	62.8	138.0	21.5
Venezuela	.. c	.. c	.. c	.. c	.. c	-219.2	297.5	140.2	-38.7	179.8

Table 1. Foreign direct investment flows by country *(cont.)*

Million US dollars

	Inward					Outward				
	2015	2016	2017	2018	2019	2015	2016	2017	2018	2019
ASIA	**.. c**	**.. c**	**.. c**	**.. c**	**.. c**	**4 858.3**	**-2 927.7**	**9 018.4**	**7 083.9**	**-7 871.2**
Near and Middle East	.. c	.. c	.. c	.. c	.. c	68.9	-3 273.7	-608.0	-2 818.8	-9 206.8
Gulf Arabian countries	.. c	.. c	.. c	.. c	.. c	.. c	.. c	.. c	.. c	.. c
Kuwait	.. c	.. c	.. c	.. c	.. c	.. c	.. c	.. c	.. c	.. c
Qatar	.. c	.. c	.. c	.. c	.. c	5.7	-3.1	4.7	0.2	4.5
Saudi Arabia	.. c	.. c	.. c	.. c	.. c	-1.9	93.9	90.7	194.0	930.9
United Arab Emirates	.. c	.. c	.. c	.. c	.. c	44.8	-3 869.3	-530.7	-3 397.1	-9 276.7
Other Near and Middle East	.. c	.. c	.. c	.. c	.. c	.. c	.. c	.. c	.. c	.. c
Jordan	.. c	.. c	.. c	.. c	.. c	-41.0	25.3	33.6	-3.5	25.2
Other Asian countries	.. c	.. c	.. c	.. c	.. c	4 789.4	346.0	9 626.4	9 902.6	1 335.6
China	.. c	.. c	.. c	.. c	.. c	1 540.7	1 505.1	3 216.3	3 182.0	1 559.6
Hong Kong, China	.. c	.. c	.. c	.. c	.. c	599.5	-489.8	499.6	-286.7	-272.2
India	.. c	.. c	.. c	.. c	.. c	805.8	164.6	1 050.6	895.8	107.8
Indonesia	.. c	.. c	.. c	.. c	.. c	107.7	277.8	84.3	33.4	537.7
Iran, Islamic Republic of	.. c	.. c	.. c	.. c	.. c	.. c	.. c	.. c	.. c	.. c
Malaysia	.. c	.. c	.. c	.. c	.. c	40.1	162.4	618.5	-2 812.7	3 344.8
Philippines	.. c	.. c	.. c	.. c	.. c	467.7	-18.1	770.3	-184.5	204.5
Singapore	.. c	.. c	.. c	.. c	.. c	450.2	-2 517.6	-1 395.0	6 567.2	-4 896.8
Chinese Taipei	.. c	.. c	.. c	.. c	.. c	239.6	120.2	202.2	115.7	170.3
Thailand	.. c	.. c	.. c	.. c	.. c	141.9	-38.1	143.3	114.5	243.2
Viet Nam	.. c	.. c	.. c	.. c	.. c	79.7	83.9	73.2	-7.5	86.2
AUSTRALIA, OCEANIA AND POLAR REGIONS	**.. c**	**.. c**	**.. c**	**.. c**	**.. c**	**7 101.8**	**-429.4**	**-1 874.1**	**-8 783.9**	**-685.5**
WORLD unallocated and confidential	**-4 694.8**	**1 759.1**	**2 216.5**	**1 430.3**	**4 469.9**	**291.1**	**778.0**	**-418.7**	**-1 157.8**	**-1 318.4**
European Union (EU28)	**74 481.3**	**132 645.9**	**77 928.3**	**-16 608.7**	**-76 853.2**	**76 206.0**	**123 925.5**	**901.4**	**36 549.2**	**-39 717.7**
G20 countries excl. European Union	**12 162.1**	**19 416.5**	**-34 489.4**	**8 731.6**	**-16 034.8**	**36 125.8**	**90 511.9**	**18 731.1**	**16 978.1**	**39 165.7**
G20 OECD countries	**.. c**	**.. c**	**.. c**	**.. c**	**.. c**	**34 667.4**	**86 994.9**	**9 895.5**	**8 257.5**	**28 891.9**
G20 Non-OECD countries	**.. c**	**.. c**	**.. c**	**.. c**	**.. c**	**1 458.4**	**3 517.0**	**8 835.6**	**8 720.6**	**10 273.8**
MENA countries	**.. c**	**.. c**	**.. c**	**.. c**	**.. c**	**529.2**	**-4 908.5**	**-549.3**	**-2 883.2**	**-8 777.3**
ASEAN countries	**.. c**	**.. c**	**.. c**	**.. c**	**.. c**	**1 277.5**	**-2 059.1**	**295.1**	**3 779.8**	**-537.0**

- Nil; c Confidential data

Note: Detailed metadata at: *http://stats.oecd.org/OECDStat_Metadata/ShowMetadata.ashx?Dataset=FDI_CTRY_IND_SUMM.*

Source: *OECD International Direct Investment Statistics (database): https://doi.org/10.1787/idi-data-en*

Table 2. Foreign direct investment positions by country
At year end

Million US dollars

	Inward					Outward				
	2015	2016	2017	2018	2019	2015	2016	2017	2018	2019
WORLD	**982 396.2**	**1 280 154.4**	**1 427 238.9**	**1 418 473.0**	**1 453 897.1**	**1 137 305.1**	**1 337 936.8**	**1 423 980.0**	**1 488 344.5**	**1 499 134.5**
OECD COUNTRIES	**781 032.0**	**1 131 402.5**	**1 242 931.5**	**1 215 400.6**	**1 230 104.6**	**838 339.4**	**1 049 435.4**	**1 080 192.3**	**1 121 083.4**	**1 124 680.4**
Australia	3 502.7	1 940.5	2 079.6	2 441.2	2 278.9	17 502.0	16 737.3	15 604.5	6 592.4	6 105.1
Austria	7 755.5	7 194.3	8 849.3	10 470.8	10 672.7	7 830.0	8 578.4	10 077.8	9 695.9	10 649.0
Belgium	7 053.7	5 524.9	4 921.4	3 675.4	17 014.1	14 922.8	15 311.7	13 573.5	8 585.1	12 648.5
Canada	38 515.4	34 915.7	37 968.4	30 544.0	35 297.2	44 531.0	43 371.2	37 232.3	28 304.5	36 407.2
Chile	.. c	.. c	.. c	.. c	.. c	-1 529.8	-2 056.7	-2 018.7	1 828.3	1 880.9
Czech Republic	.. c	.. c	.. c	.. c	.. c	3 936.5	2 964.7	3 660.6	3 794.7	3 419.3
Denmark	3 202.6	2 447.4	4 075.3	4 337.8	5 350.0	1 712.7	1 547.2	1 671.1	1 588.7	1 409.7
Estonia	.. c	.. c	.. c	.. c	.. c	48.6	418.6	114.0	157.5	174.9
Finland	.. c	.. c	.. c	.. c	.. c	575.3	776.1	550.5	946.9	1 110.4
France	43 161.5	38 499.6	44 185.0	51 045.4	60 389.4	56 590.0	58 600.3	60 706.3	63 887.7	65 961.6
Germany	32 442.7	30 038.3	44 849.7	41 298.9	53 438.5	37 591.8	40 465.5	48 313.5	59 647.3	64 904.7
Greece	.. c	.. c	.. c	.. c	.. c	1 493.0	1 124.3	1 455.5	1 365.0	1 246.5
Hungary	677.5	1 029.8	2 158.6	1 219.9	871.5	1 974.4	5 485.3	5 934.5	5 731.3	26 897.6
Iceland	.. c	.. c	.. c	.. c	.. c	.. c	.. c	.. c	.. c	.. c
Ireland	108 101.8	116 412.3	118 166.4	155 095.5	83 597.3	69 336.8	134 711.8	102 440.5	118 937.1	83 227.1
Israel	1 560.9	1 911.8	1 628.2	1 721.2	1 633.1	1 171.8	1 504.9	1 566.0	1 516.9	1 141.5
Italy	6 013.1	6 456.2	6 565.9	3 974.5	3 794.4	15 748.7	15 681.2	18 169.7	18 220.5	21 799.5
Japan	11 113.6	24 229.3	26 166.9	28 013.0	39 411.5	9 276.9	11 380.0	14 526.4	16 913.6	18 841.0
Korea	.. c	.. c	.. c	.. c	.. c	4 358.0	3 308.1	3 951.0	3 909.0	3 666.3
Latvia	.. c	.. c	.. c	.. c	.. c	33.7	39.2	141.4	170.0	211.5
Lithuania	.. c	.. c	.. c	.. c	.. c	295.6	392.6	397.6	468.7	677.8
Luxembourg	25 940.6	25 780.5	22 990.2	15 224.4	5 834.0	155 061.2	193 803.6	195 540.2	193 568.3	152 908.3
Mexico	12 916.4	12 901.1	12 632.0	11 259.8	11 651.6	6 400.7	4 575.7	4 862.5	5 536.4	6 103.8
Netherlands	72 628.9	75 748.2	70 600.8	56 147.3	61 341.1	108 136.8	141 337.6	160 520.9	154 576.1	180 104.1
New Zealand	.. c	.. c	.. c	.. c	.. c	421.9	604.3	392.5	379.3	559.0
Norway	.. c	.. c	.. c	.. c	.. c	1 798.4	4 830.8	4 441.0	4 605.8	1 662.1
Poland	.. c	.. c	.. c	.. c	.. c	4 948.0	5 091.2	6 410.7	6 629.9	5 870.9
Portugal	.. c	.. c	.. c	.. c	.. c	1 085.9	832.9	997.9	945.5	859.4
Slovak Republic	.. c	.. c	.. c	.. c	.. c	538.9	519.8	818.1	944.0	951.1
Slovenia	.. c	.. c	.. c	.. c	.. c	.. c	.. c	.. c	.. c	.. c
Spain	6 446.0	5 999.5	6 713.0	7 173.4	6 380.2	8 863.6	9 043.2	9 938.6	10 957.5	11 755.4
Sweden	10 303.6	10 116.7	12 231.3	12 743.2	12 698.2	7 584.6	6 218.9	7 754.5	8 445.4	8 044.3
Switzerland	.. c	.. c	.. c	.. c	.. c	-	-	-	-	-
Turkey	.. c	.. c	.. c	.. c	.. c	2 381.8	2 392.0	2 388.5	2 308.6	2 247.6
United Kingdom	34 199.7	53 643.6	73 160.8	75 065.7	70 381.7	46 653.5	55 003.5	54 249.7	81 712.6	81 200.6
United States	414 509.9	638 762.4	702 858.8	644 310.2	672 642.0	206 931.4	263 399.6	292 362.9	296 363.5	308 117.6
EUROPE	**405 979.4**	**464 759.6**	**509 697.5**	**567 983.9**	**535 031.3**	**585 542.9**	**756 982.6**	**813 182.2**	**860 649.3**	**856 356.2**
Bulgaria	.. c	.. c	.. c	.. c	.. c	312.1	280.2	338.7	243.0	330.9
Croatia	.. c	.. c	.. c	.. c	.. c	340.9	363.4	443.6	426.2	523.8
Cyprus	.. c	.. c	.. c	.. c	.. c	2 706.9	8 522.8	46 630.3	47 111.6	51 566.1
Malta	.. c	.. c	.. c	.. c	.. c	.. c	.. c	.. c	.. c	.. c
Romania	.. c	.. c	.. c	.. c	.. c	2 152.7	2 054.4	2 625.7	2 509.0	2 761.2
Russian Federation	5 486.0	21 016.8	28 394.1	18 895.9	17 101.5	8 173.8	17 512.2	21 932.5	23 300.1	29 820.0
Ukraine	.. c	.. c	.. c	.. c	.. c	407.2	589.7	1 522.0	2 022.3	2 988.1
AFRICA	**.. c**	**.. c**	**.. c**	**.. c**	**.. c**	**13 205.1**	**13 360.5**	**12 099.3**	**11 663.0**	**14 693.1**
Northern Africa	.. c	.. c	.. c	.. c	.. c	2 507.0	1 520.0	1 475.9	1 449.0	1 541.1
Algeria	.. c	.. c	.. c	.. c	.. c	.. c	.. c	.. c	.. c	.. c
Egypt	.. c	.. c	.. c	.. c	.. c	1 796.4	849.8	749.7	768.2	916.0
Libya	.. c	.. c	.. c	.. c	.. c	.. c	.. c	.. c	.. c	.. c
Morocco	.. c	.. c	.. c	.. c	.. c	613.9	405.7	429.0	478.9	430.5
Tunisia	.. c	.. c	.. c	.. c	.. c	44.5	34.7	41.0	47.1	51.6
Other African countries	.. c	.. c	.. c	.. c	.. c	10 698.1	11 840.5	10 623.4	10 214.0	13 152.0
Nigeria	.. c	.. c	.. c	.. c	.. c	602.7	478.5	448.9	437.6	412.6
South Africa	.. c	.. c	.. c	.. c	.. c	2 036.8	2 519.6	2 423.9	2 506.4	4 919.6
AMERICA	**516 652.3**	**740 323.0**	**825 895.7**	**757 195.4**	**806 612.2**	**415 459.8**	**443 434.3**	**464 094.8**	**486 330.6**	**498 611.0**
Northern America	453 025.3	673 678.1	740 827.0	674 854.2	707 939.2	251 462.4	306 770.8	329 595.2	324 668.0	344 524.8
Central America and Caribbean countries	.. c	.. c	.. c	.. c	.. c	147 177.8	119 505.5	115 931.3	136 518.6	130 699.2
Bahamas	.. c	.. c	.. c	.. c	.. c	.. c	.. c	.. c	.. c	.. c
Bermuda	.. c	.. c	.. c	.. c	.. c	46 991.2	42 172.9	46 895.4	74 654.9	48 030.1
Cayman Islands	.. c	.. c	.. c	.. c	.. c	.. c	.. c	.. c	.. c	.. c
Costa Rica	.. c	.. c	.. c	.. c	.. c	639.5	770.4	927.1	1 061.9	1 329.1
El Salvador	.. c	.. c	.. c	.. c	.. c	.. c	.. c	.. c	.. c	.. c
Guatemala	.. c	.. c	.. c	.. c	.. c	195.6	181.9	167.3	182.0	235.6
Honduras	.. c	.. c	.. c	.. c	.. c	.. c	.. c	.. c	.. c	.. c
Nicaragua	.. c	.. c	.. c	.. c	.. c	.. c	.. c	.. c	.. c	.. c
Panama	.. c	.. c	.. c	.. c	.. c	3 036.1	260.1	4 017.1	3 331.8	3 366.9
Virgin Islands, U.S.	.. c	.. c	.. c	.. c	.. c	.. c	.. c	.. c	.. c	.. c
South America	.. c	.. c	.. c	.. c	.. c	16 819.5	17 158.0	18 568.3	25 144.0	23 387.0
Argentina	.. c	.. c	.. c	.. c	.. c	4 716.7	3 993.5	3 955.1	3 066.6	3 166.9
Bolivia	.. c	.. c	.. c	.. c	.. c	72.9	58.1	69.2	75.1	76.0
Brazil	.. c	.. c	.. c	.. c	.. c	8 919.3	10 430.1	10 712.5	10 433.1	10 897.3
Colombia	.. c	.. c	.. c	.. c	.. c	624.9	662.9	1 010.3	4 548.5	5 112.8
Ecuador	.. c	.. c	.. c	.. c	.. c	254.4	214.4	240.1	325.5	290.4
Paraguay	.. c	.. c	.. c	.. c	.. c	.. c	.. c	.. c	.. c	.. c
Peru	.. c	.. c	.. c	.. c	.. c	660.2	655.5	329.8	24.2	-2 905.1
Uruguay	.. c	.. c	.. c	.. c	.. c	1 803.3	2 239.2	2 305.2	2 523.1	2 533.8
Venezuela	.. c	.. c	.. c	.. c	.. c	1 197.3	856.4	1 772.9	2 136.9	2 130.8

Table 2. Foreign direct investment positions by country *(cont.)*

At year end

Million US dollars

	Inward					Outward				
	2015	2016	2017	2018	2019	2015	2016	2017	2018	2019
ASIA	**.. c**	**.. c**	**.. c**	**.. c**	**.. c**	**102 218.6**	**103 408.4**	**113 987.4**	**117 232.7**	**115 997.1**
Near and Middle East	.. c	.. c	.. c	.. c	.. c	25 244.7	23 528.4	23 535.9	20 747.1	16 812.1
Gulf Arabian countries	.. c	.. c	.. c	.. c	.. c	.. c	.. c	.. c	.. c	.. c
Kuwait	.. c	.. c	.. c	.. c	.. c	.. c	.. c	.. c	.. c	.. c
Qatar	.. c	.. c	.. c	.. c	.. c	46.4	58.6	60.3	162.4	165.2
Saudi Arabia	.. c	.. c	.. c	.. c	.. c	943.2	900.0	983.0	1 135.1	1 986.6
United Arab Emirates	1 768.0	837.9	793.8	739.5	2 250.3	20 908.9	18 484.5	18 255.6	14 897.9	10 707.8
Other Near and Middle East	.. c	.. c	.. c	.. c	.. c	.. c	.. c	.. c	.. c	.. c
Jordan	.. c	.. c	.. c	.. c	.. c	227.5	240.9	283.1	263.9	277.4
Other Asian countries	.. c	.. c	.. c	.. c	.. c	76 973.8	79 880.1	90 451.4	96 485.6	99 185.0
China	.. c	7 228.0	17 357.5	17 092.9	15 368.0	19 864.2	19 644.5	22 690.5	22 628.5	23 244.7
Hong Kong, China	.. c	.. c	.. c	.. c	.. c	6 206.9	5 876.9	7 592.1	7 057.3	7 364.6
India	1 597.2	1 881.8	1 856.2	2 338.3	2 576.3	4 939.1	4 788.8	6 281.4	6 742.8	6 795.2
Indonesia	.. c	.. c	.. c	.. c	.. c	1 150.6	1 415.9	1 529.4	1 527.7	1 747.1
Iran, Islamic Republic of	.. c	.. c	.. c	.. c	.. c	.. c	.. c	.. c	.. c	.. c
Malaysia	.. c	.. c	.. c	.. c	.. c	3 999.8	5 921.5	6 211.2	2 998.3	6 074.6
Philippines	.. c	.. c	.. c	.. c	.. c	1 414.4	1 427.3	2 201.0	1 886.5	2 248.8
Singapore	.. c	.. c	.. c	.. c	.. c	17 776.1	18 331.3	17 661.1	25 363.3	21 526.0
Chinese Taipei	.. c	.. c	.. c	.. c	.. c	1 766.3	1 818.4	1 930.5	1 830.6	1 915.4
Thailand	.. c	.. c	.. c	.. c	.. c	2 503.2	2 465.7	2 710.5	3 030.8	3 272.1
Viet Nam	.. c	.. c	.. c	.. c	.. c	630.3	649.3	727.6	715.4	1 037.9
AUSTRALIA, OCEANIA AND POLAR REGIONS	**.. c**	**.. c**	**.. c**	**.. c**	**.. c**	**18 047.2**	**17 449.2**	**16 191.5**	**7 082.3**	**6 882.2**
WORLD unallocated and confidential	**40 222.1**	**37 042.6**	**41 763.6**	**40 947.5**	**48 735.7**	**2 831.5**	**3 301.8**	**4 424.9**	**5 386.7**	**6 595.0**
European Union (EU28)	**357 873.6**	**380 781.4**	**424 235.5**	**444 122.5**	**400 442.4**	**552 066.1**	**710 886.2**	**755 746.2**	**803 396.7**	**793 295.1**
G20 countries excl. European Union	**639 909.5**	**902 321.1**	**1 021 827.4**	**951 052.3**	**1 007 982.4**	**498 709.5**	**576 118.8**	**622 875.5**	**654 736.3**	**697 932.2**
G20 OECD countries	**.. c**	**.. c**	**.. c**	**.. c**	**.. c**	**447 965.9**	**514 914.3**	**552 367.2**	**583 396.2**	**615 354.8**
G20 Non-OECD countries	**.. c**	**.. c**	**.. c**	**.. c**	**.. c**	**50 743.6**	**61 204.5**	**70 508.2**	**71 340.2**	**82 577.4**
MENA countries	**.. c**	**.. c**	**.. c**	**.. c**	**.. c**	**26 572.0**	**23 526.7**	**23 433.5**	**20 671.9**	**17 193.2**
ASEAN countries	**.. c**	**.. c**	**.. c**	**.. c**	**.. c**	**27 545.4**	**30 238.5**	**31 121.0**	**35 664.1**	**35 996.3**

- Nil; c Confidential data

Note: Inward FDI positions are allocated according to the ultimate investing country. Detailed metadata at: *http://stats.oecd.org/OECDStat_Metadata/ShowMetadata.ashx?Dataset=FDI_CTRY_IND_SUMM*.

Source: *OECD International Direct Investment Statistics (database): https://doi.org/10.1787/idi-data-en*

SWITZERLAND

Table 3. Foreign direct investment income by country

Million US dollars

	Inward					Outward				
	2015	2016	2017	2018	2019	2015	2016	2017	2018	2019
WORLD	**61 254.5**	**72 638.1**	**96 040.6**	**119 224.7**	**98 933.0**	**85 935.5**	**86 093.6**	**100 161.7**	**104 657.5**	**91 709.3**
OECD COUNTRIES	**.. c**	**61 032.6**	**79 678.6**	**109 025.0**	**88 931.8**	**.. c**	**58 154.0**	**68 055.0**	**69 474.2**	**65 281.5**
Australia	.. c	.. c	.. c	.. c	.. c	-837.8	552.2	733.5	874.8	1 308.0
Austria	-1 680.4	2 021.9	-2 714.7	2 816.4	487.5	1 263.1	1 267.8	1 119.0	1 133.3	2 116.4
Belgium	931.7	-20.3	55.8	-24.3	101.4	-994.5	-229.2	638.1	1 193.5	749.6
Canada	-4.5	-2.4	-21.7	-20.1	-13.3	-935.4	-1 648.3	892.6	-533.5	-1 586.8
Chile	.. c	.. c	.. c	.. c	.. c	165.5	34.7	117.6	138.3	131.2
Czech Republic	.. c	.. c	.. c	.. c	.. c	401.5	358.4	421.0	284.3	110.7
Denmark	1 376.9	1 824.5	1 594.4	1 163.8	3 021.1	117.8	80.1	87.4	95.9	142.2
Estonia	.. c	.. c	.. c	.. c	.. c	1.5	4.1	4.6	17.2	17.6
Finland	.. c	.. c	.. c	.. c	.. c	133.7	209.7	223.9	233.2	183.4
France	3 338.5	4 344.6	5 267.5	3 878.4	3 184.3	4 988.7	3 746.8	2 868.8	4 944.0	4 009.0
Germany	2 757.0	3 149.8	3 505.9	2 649.0	3 454.1	4 200.1	6 194.9	5 495.9	4 855.4	5 469.1
Greece	.. c	.. c	.. c	.. c	.. c	108.2	-59.8	74.4	147.4	123.9
Hungary	1 270.3	1 391.3	1 357.1	844.3	1 168.7	261.4	640.9	643.6	485.6	251.3
Iceland	.. c	.. c	.. c	.. c	.. c	.. c	.. c	.. c	.. c	.. c
Ireland	-2 336.5	-1 755.0	-2 331.5	10 463.0	4 668.9	1 534.3	4 165.8	788.6	-3 843.9	752.4
Israel	33.9	-124.1	-173.8	-303.2	-126.8	138.8	138.3	125.4	123.0	140.1
Italy	195.9	210.6	39.2	306.0	151.0	337.3	948.9	1 378.9	1 629.4	1 786.4
Japan	155.9	113.6	-194.8	-40.3	40.1	1 272.2	1 619.7	1 892.8	1 661.7	2 290.0
Korea	.. c	.. c	.. c	.. c	.. c	566.6	407.2	176.1	279.7	341.1
Latvia	.. c	.. c	.. c	.. c	.. c	5.5	5.1	8.4	10.6	15.3
Lithuania	.. c	.. c	.. c	.. c	.. c	11.5	13.0	19.9	72.8	45.7
Luxembourg	12 286.9	6 978.0	32 235.3	32 691.5	26 171.4	6 012.7	4 485.4	2 718.4	8 468.7	4 501.7
Mexico	.. c	.. c	.. c	.. c	.. c	537.2	542.9	514.4	632.8	540.3
Netherlands	18 510.4	26 819.5	38 076.6	38 195.1	37 126.5	11 041.2	11 879.3	20 347.8	14 915.2	12 535.8
New Zealand	.. c	.. c	.. c	.. c	.. c	67.3	64.8	65.9	75.2	94.0
Norway	.. c	.. c	.. c	.. c	.. c	206.5	36.3	93.5	116.2	140.6
Poland	.. c	.. c	.. c	.. c	.. c	426.2	487.5	431.6	617.7	524.6
Portugal	.. c	.. c	.. c	.. c	.. c	264.0	34.0	110.7	75.3	107.9
Slovak Republic	.. c	.. c	.. c	.. c	.. c	46.3	40.2	44.5	92.7	63.5
Slovenia	.. c	.. c	.. c	.. c	.. c	.. c	.. c	.. c	.. c	.. c
Spain	189.2	30.2	-159.6	-71.7	-0.3	912.7	1 345.8	1 207.4	1 444.7	1 967.9
Sweden	717.0	722.9	1 367.3	689.6	756.6	528.3	448.2	1 503.7	1 306.4	1 627.8
Switzerland	-	-	-	-	-	-	-	-	-	-
Turkey	.. c	.. c	.. c	.. c	.. c	287.4	274.9	257.8	141.3	197.4
United Kingdom	3 089.0	2 824.2	3 238.6	7 538.1	4 375.9	3 089.9	967.5	1 928.3	2 233.6	2 347.6
United States	14 302.2	12 586.0	-1 518.9	8 201.5	4 370.9	20 643.9	19 085.6	21 036.6	25 416.6	22 151.3
EUROPE	**37 671.0**	**47 296.7**	**86 402.8**	**102 247.4**	**88 126.8**	**35 157.5**	**42 502.2**	**53 996.4**	**54 583.9**	**45 230.9**
Bulgaria	.. c	.. c	.. c	.. c	.. c	37.5	59.7	50.1	39.8	68.1
Croatia	.. c	.. c	.. c	.. c	.. c	21.9	33.5	42.3	55.5	62.9
Cyprus	-1 275.5	-21.0	309.2	9.8	1 460.6	-1 239.6	135.5	10 194.0	10 919.4	384.5
Malta	.. c	.. c	.. c	.. c	.. c	.. c	.. c	.. c	.. c	.. c
Romania	.. c	.. c	.. c	.. c	.. c	62.3	72.0	70.6	207.2	138.1
Russian Federation	.. c	.. c	.. c	.. c	.. c	-6.1	899.3	-10.5	2 113.7	3 055.2
Ukraine	.. c	.. c	.. c	.. c	.. c	-118.9	-14.7	253.8	486.1	459.5
AFRICA	**.. c**	**.. c**	**.. c**	**.. c**	**.. c**	**384.2**	**166.5**	**365.1**	**93.3**	**404.6**
Northern Africa	.. c	.. c	.. c	.. c	.. c	195.3	-128.5	68.5	74.8	124.3
Algeria	.. c	.. c	.. c	.. c	.. c	.. c	.. c	.. c	.. c	.. c
Egypt	.. c	.. c	.. c	.. c	.. c	160.8	-152.9	22.5	41.4	137.3
Libya	..	..	..	..	..	.. c	.. c	.. c	.. c	.. c
Morocco	.. c	.. c	.. c	.. c	.. c	37.9	14.2	23.4	5.0	-35.4
Tunisia	.. c	.. c	.. c	.. c	.. c	-1.5	2.3	7.1	13.6	13.9
Other African countries	.. c	.. c	.. c	.. c	.. c	188.9	295.0	296.6	18.5	280.4
Nigeria	.. c	.. c	.. c	.. c	.. c	-4.6	58.4	65.5	152.8	87.6
South Africa	.. c	.. c	.. c	.. c	.. c	-127.0	-71.5	-42.2	-439.6	-15.2
AMERICA	**23 070.2**	**25 406.0**	**9 612.6**	**16 256.3**	**10 952.5**	**33 932.9**	**26 827.9**	**28 031.0**	**29 427.6**	**24 715.7**
Northern America	14 297.7	12 583.6	-1 540.6	8 181.4	4 357.6	19 708.5	17 437.3	21 929.2	24 883.1	20 564.5
Central America and Caribbean countries	.. c	.. c	.. c	.. c	.. c	14 935.9	7 703.5	5 458.1	2 984.0	3 658.2
Bahamas	.. c	.. c	.. c	.. c	.. c	.. c	.. c	.. c	.. c	.. c
Bermuda	.. c	.. c	.. c	.. c	.. c	7 111.9	5 009.9	4 297.2	2 497.4	5 826.2
Cayman Islands	.. c	.. c	.. c	.. c	.. c	.. c	.. c	.. c	.. c	.. c
Costa Rica	.. c	.. c	.. c	.. c	.. c	89.0	127.2	165.3	188.2	157.1
El Salvador	.. c	.. c	.. c	.. c	.. c	.. c	.. c	.. c	.. c	.. c
Guatemala	.. c	.. c	.. c	.. c	.. c	21.7	10.3	18.7	32.1	26.8
Honduras	.. c	.. c	.. c	.. c	.. c	.. c	.. c	.. c	.. c	.. c
Nicaragua	.. c	.. c	.. c	.. c	.. c	.. c	.. c	.. c	.. c	.. c
Panama	.. c	.. c	.. c	.. c	.. c	417.2	344.9	566.5	422.0	257.3
Virgin Islands, U.S.	.. c	.. c	.. c	.. c	.. c	.. c	.. c	.. c	.. c	.. c
South America	.. c	.. c	.. c	.. c	.. c	-711.5	1 687.2	643.7	1 560.5	492.9
Argentina	.. c	.. c	.. c	.. c	.. c	-312.2	175.6	181.1	715.1	-87.4
Bolivia	.. c	.. c	.. c	.. c	.. c	2.9	5.0	5.7	7.7	1.0
Brazil	.. c	.. c	.. c	.. c	.. c	-635.8	280.0	-36.8	573.3	596.0
Colombia	.. c	.. c	.. c	.. c	.. c	69.3	91.7	78.3	70.5	68.3
Ecuador	.. c	.. c	.. c	.. c	.. c	50.1	34.8	49.8	55.1	26.1
Paraguay	.. c	.. c	.. c	.. c	.. c	.. c	.. c	.. c	.. c	.. c
Peru	.. c	.. c	.. c	.. c	.. c	110.2	83.2	36.8	49.9	-110.7
Uruguay	.. c	.. c	.. c	.. c	.. c	338.9	478.3	152.8	151.6	114.7
Venezuela	.. c	.. c	.. c	.. c	.. c	-499.2	494.4	49.6	-212.7	-266.8

Table 3. Foreign direct investment income by country *(cont.)*

Million US dollars

	Inward					Outward				
	2015	2016	2017	2018	2019	2015	2016	2017	2018	2019
ASIA	**.. c**	**.. c**	**.. c**	**.. c**	**.. c**	**17 220.6**	**15 965.0**	**16 955.1**	**19 617.7**	**19 938.8**
Near and Middle East	.. c	.. c	.. c	.. c	.. c	3 999.0	3 121.3	2 687.5	1 228.6	-2 433.4
Gulf Arabian countries	.. c	.. c	.. c	.. c	.. c	.. c	.. c	.. c	.. c	.. c
Kuwait	.. c	.. c	.. c	.. c	.. c	.. c	.. c	.. c	.. c	.. c
Qatar	.. c	.. c	.. c	.. c	.. c	10.9	10.6	14.7	18.6	17.5
Saudi Arabia	.. c	.. c	.. c	.. c	.. c	-6.1	101.3	90.4	33.1	26.6
United Arab Emirates	.. c	.. c	.. c	.. c	.. c	3 532.5	2 674.8	2 124.3	838.8	-2 944.3
Other Near and Middle East	.. c	.. c	.. c	.. c	.. c	.. c	.. c	.. c	.. c	.. c
Jordan	.. c	.. c	.. c	.. c	.. c	42.6	43.4	46.9	44.7	23.1
Other Asian countries	.. c	.. c	.. c	.. c	.. c	13 221.6	12 843.6	14 267.6	18 389.2	22 372.2
China	.. c	.. c	.. c	.. c	.. c	2 555.4	2 327.0	2 385.2	3 490.4	2 720.7
Hong Kong, China	.. c	.. c	.. c	.. c	.. c	2 259.5	1 052.8	1 935.9	2 104.0	1 890.0
India	.. c	.. c	.. c	.. c	.. c	289.6	359.5	778.1	694.9	539.2
Indonesia	.. c	.. c	.. c	.. c	.. c	103.1	193.8	215.5	194.2	217.1
Iran, Islamic Republic of	..	..	..	..	..	.. c	.. c	.. c	.. c	.. c
Malaysia	.. c	.. c	.. c	.. c	.. c	439.1	435.2	-33.2	699.7	626.5
Philippines	.. c	.. c	.. c	.. c	.. c	432.8	499.4	498.7	522.8	463.9
Singapore	.. c	.. c	.. c	.. c	.. c	3 750.8	4 407.2	4 868.5	7 411.6	11 998.8
Chinese Taipei	.. c	.. c	.. c	.. c	.. c	478.1	423.6	463.3	451.5	396.4
Thailand	.. c	.. c	.. c	.. c	.. c	477.1	449.5	536.9	464.9	504.5
Viet Nam	.. c	.. c	.. c	.. c	.. c	120.5	166.0	174.2	198.1	197.0
AUSTRALIA, OCEANIA AND POLAR REGIONS	**.. c**	**.. c**	**.. c**	**.. c**	**.. c**	**-759.9**	**631.9**	**814.0**	**934.9**	**1 419.3**
WORLD unallocated and confidential	**323.5**	**-54.0**	**393.7**	**1 064.6**	**-59.5**	**0.1**	**0.0**	**0.1**	**0.0**	**0.0**
European Union (EU28)	**39 473.2**	**48 590.8**	**81 938.2**	**101 248.2**	**.. c**	**33 753.4**	**37 466.2**	**52 588.8**	**51 828.0**	**.. c**
G20 countries excl. European Union	**22 861.0**	**22 939.3**	**9 347.5**	**22 529.5**	**15 818.7**	**36 010.9**	**36 957.5**	**40 736.5**	**49 510.7**	**45 905.6**
G20 OECD countries	**.. c**	**.. c**	**.. c**	**.. c**	**.. c**	**34 150.0**	**32 692.3**	**37 175.8**	**42 135.7**	**38 853.4**
G20 Non-OECD countries	**.. c**	**.. c**	**.. c**	**.. c**	**.. c**	**1 860.9**	**4 265.2**	**3 560.7**	**7 375.0**	**7 052.2**
MENA countries	**.. c**	**.. c**	**.. c**	**.. c**	**.. c**	**4 054.0**	**2 854.4**	**2 629.3**	**1 177.6**	**-2 452.0**
ASEAN countries	**.. c**	**.. c**	**.. c**	**.. c**	**.. c**	**5 334.3**	**6 158.4**	**6 273.7**	**9 501.9**	**14 023.6**

- Nil; .. Not available; c Confidential data

Note: Detailed metadata at: *http://stats.oecd.org/OECDStat_Metadata/ShowMetadata.ashx?Dataset=FDI_CTRY_IND_SUMM.*

Source: *OECD International Direct Investment Statistics (database): https://doi.org/10.1787/idi-data-en*

SWITZERLAND

Table 4. Foreign direct investment flows by industrial sector

Million US dollars

	Inward					Outward				
	2015	2016	2017	2018	2019	2015	2016	2017	2018	2019
All FDI activities	**84 326.6**	**150 511.7**	**110 721.9**	**-68 312.2**	**-79 075.3**	**91 550.9**	**166 901.4**	**19 522.2**	**43 490.7**	**-43 721.5**
Agriculture, forestry and fishing	..	..	..	..	..	**.. c**	**.. c**	**.. c**	**.. c**	**.. c**
Mining and quarrying	**.. c**	**.. c**	**.. c**	**.. c**	**.. c**	**.. c**	**.. c**	**.. c**	**.. c**	**.. c**
Extraction activities	.. c	.. c	.. c	.. c	.. c	.. c	.. c	.. c	.. c	.. c
Manufacturing	**13 327.3**	**5 158.7**	**58 362.2**	**-24 272.7**	**3 355.9**	**8 520.6**	**30 638.9**	**-8 446.9**	**14 003.6**	**13 877.4**
of which:										
Food products, beverages and tobacco	.. c	.. c	.. c	.. c	.. c	.. c	.. c	.. c	.. c	.. c
Textiles, wood and paper products; printing	.. c	.. c	.. c	.. c	.. c	.. c	.. c	.. c	.. c	.. c
Chemical, rubber, plastic, non-metallic mineral products	.. c	.. c	.. c	.. c	.. c	.. c	.. c	.. c	.. c	.. c
Metal and machinery products, except electrical equipment	.. c	.. c	.. c	.. c	.. c	.. c	.. c	.. c	.. c	.. c
Motor vehicles, trailers, semi-trailers, other transport equipment	.. c	.. c	.. c	.. c	.. c	.. c	.. c	.. c	.. c	.. c
Other manufacturing	.. c	.. c	.. c	.. c	.. c	.. c	.. c	.. c	.. c	.. c
Electricity, gas, steam and air conditioning supply	**.. c**	**.. c**	**.. c**	**.. c**	**.. c**	**.. c**	**.. c**	**.. c**	**.. c**	**.. c**
Water supply; sewerage, waste management and remediation activities	**.. c**	**.. c**	**.. c**	**.. c**	**.. c**	..	..	..	..	..
Construction	**.. c**	**.. c**	**.. c**	**.. c**	**.. c**	**.. c**	**.. c**	**.. c**	**.. c**	**.. c**
Services	**70 531.7**	**144 344.4**	**50 951.9**	**-43 027.9**	**-81 885.3**	**78 065.5**	**136 770.9**	**28 039.8**	**29 895.7**	**-53 273.9**
Wholesale and retail trade; repair of motor vehicles and motorcycles	4 015.9	11 478.5	11 863.0	16 869.9	-25 088.1	23 526.8	14 484.4	-7 529.6	31 463.0	-27 299.9
Transportation and storage	140.6	771.7	1 500.9	313.4	3 976.2	872.6	1 248.7	3 850.0	3 945.5	1 751.1
Accommodation and food service activities	-184.8	34.2	-273.9	-33.9	301.5	205.2	-134.6	85.9	-48.6	169.6
Information and communication	792.3	245.7	-703.9	-687.8	7 332.5	2 831.9	-218.5	-1 066.4	-95.7	-636.5
Financial and insurance activities	18 121.8	108 002.5	63 706.5	-54 411.3	-33 011.5	24 214.3	108 806.2	52 996.6	8 901.4	2 968.5
Activities of holding companies	312.8	92 744.7	60 178.4	205.1	-28 425.8	3 909.2	78 527.4	54 328.0	6 590.8	-16 984.3
Real estate activities	.. c	.. c	.. c	.. c	.. c	.. c	.. c	.. c	.. c	.. c
Professional, scientific and technical activities	30 995.0	19 291.4	-24 741.2	2 026.6	-34 544.6	26 892.9	7 255.3	-19 654.4	-11 898.7	-31 297.1
Administrative and support service activities	.. c	.. c	.. c	.. c	.. c	.. c	.. c	.. c	.. c	.. c
Public administration; activities of households and of extraterritorial organisations	..	..	..	..	..	..	..	..	..	..
Education	.. c	.. c	.. c	.. c	.. c	..	..	..	..	..
Human health and social work activities	.. c	.. c	.. c	.. c	.. c	.. c	.. c	.. c	.. c	.. c
Arts, entertainment and recreation	.. c	.. c	.. c	.. c	.. c	.. c	.. c	.. c	.. c	.. c
Other services	.. c	.. c	.. c	.. c	.. c	.. c	.. c	.. c	.. c	.. c
Not allocated and confidential	**.. c**	**.. c**	**.. c**	**.. c**	**.. c**	**.. c**	**.. c**	**.. c**	**.. c**	**.. c**
Private real estate activities	**455.8**	**271.6**	**51.7**	**53.7**	**167.6**	**291.1**	**778.2**	**-419.3**	**-1 157.8**	**-1 318.4**

.. Not available; c Confidential data

Note: Detailed metadata at: *http://stats.oecd.org/OECDStat_Metadata/ShowMetadata.ashx?Dataset=FDI_CTRY_IND_SUMM.*

Source: *OECD International Direct Investment Statistics (database): https://doi.org/10.1787/idi-data-en*

Table 5. Foreign direct investment positions by industrial sector

At year end

Million US dollars

	Inward					Outward				
	2015	2016	2017	2018	2019	2015	2016	2017	2018	2019
All FDI activities	**982 396.2**	**1 280 154.4**	**1 427 238.9**	**1 418 473.0**	**1 453 897.1**	**1 137 305.1**	**1 337 936.8**	**1 423 980.0**	**1 488 344.5**	**1 499 134.5**
Agriculture, forestry and fishing	..	..	..	..	..	..	..	..	**.. c**	**.. c**
Mining and quarrying	**.. c**	**.. c**	**.. c**	**.. c**	**.. c**	**.. c**	**.. c**	**.. c**	**.. c**	**.. c**
Extraction activities	.. c	.. c	.. c	.. c	.. c	.. c	.. c	.. c	.. c	.. c
Manufacturing	**122 731.0**	**131 967.4**	**171 359.0**	**175 555.9**	**186 171.5**	**393 387.2**	**402 990.1**	**419 129.1**	**440 984.2**	**459 736.0**
of which:										
Food products, beverages and tobacco	.. c	.. c	.. c	.. c	.. c	.. c	.. c	.. c	.. c	.. c
Textiles, wood and paper products; printing	.. c	.. c	.. c	.. c	.. c	.. c	.. c	.. c	.. c	.. c
Chemical, rubber, plastic, non-metallic mineral products	.. c	.. c	.. c	.. c	.. c	.. c	.. c	.. c	.. c	.. c
Metal and machinery products, except electrical equipment	.. c	.. c	.. c	.. c	.. c	.. c	.. c	.. c	.. c	.. c
Motor vehicles, trailers, semi-trailers, other transport equipment	.. c	.. c	.. c	.. c	.. c	.. c	.. c	.. c	.. c	.. c
Other manufacturing	.. c	.. c	.. c	.. c	.. c	.. c	.. c	.. c	.. c	.. c
Electricity, gas, steam and air conditioning supply	**.. c**	**.. c**	**.. c**	**.. c**	**.. c**	**.. c**	**.. c**	**.. c**	**.. c**	**.. c**
Water supply; sewerage, waste management and remediation activities	**.. c**	**.. c**	**.. c**	**.. c**	**.. c**	**.. c**	**.. c**	**.. c**	**.. c**	**.. c**
Construction	**.. c**	**.. c**	**.. c**	**.. c**	**.. c**	**.. c**	**.. c**	**.. c**	**.. c**	**.. c**
Services	**817 659.8**	**1 106 268.5**	**1 210 521.1**	**1 199 404.4**	**1 225 141.2**	**725 731.6**	**917 051.8**	**983 637.9**	**1 025 550.0**	**1 020 265.9**
Wholesale and retail trade; repair of motor vehicles and motorcycles	158 848.0	174 365.0	194 313.2	209 547.1	242 808.2	128 466.2	143 948.2	139 158.5	158 006.1	171 213.7
Transportation and storage	7 525.0	8 466.5	10 437.7	12 654.1	17 406.3	19 986.6	20 104.8	24 219.4	31 416.1	33 329.9
Accommodation and food service activities	2 803.9	2 859.0	2 943.4	2 877.1	3 197.4	1 240.6	996.8	1 195.0	1 222.6	1 284.7
Information and communication	16 145.2	15 596.9	14 574.4	14 317.5	17 894.1	10 396.5	9 368.5	10 383.8	10 483.2	10 020.8
Financial and insurance activities	400 778.8	610 588.0	704 144.6	694 259.1	688 339.9	383 584.1	521 794.5	586 425.5	607 423.1	620 589.0
Activities of holding companies	185 639.3	342 544.4	418 871.1	444 856.1	447 187.0	197 926.5	302 945.1	359 987.4	387 447.9	383 131.1
Real estate activities	.. c	.. c	.. c	.. c	.. c	.. c	.. c	.. c	.. c	.. c
Professional, scientific and technical activities	208 080.8	261 745.9	251 913.3	242 951.3	233 200.0	171 873.9	204 537.0	206 752.4	202 516.4	168 182.2
Administrative and support service activities	.. c	.. c	.. c	.. c	.. c	.. c	.. c	.. c	.. c	.. c
Public administration; activities of households and of extraterritorial organisations	.. c	.. c	.. c	.. c	.. c	.. c	.. c	.. c	.. c	.. c
Education	.. c	.. c	.. c	.. c	.. c	.. c	.. c	.. c	.. c	.. c
Human health and social work activities	.. c	.. c	.. c	.. c	.. c	.. c	.. c	.. c	.. c	.. c
Arts, entertainment and recreation	.. c	.. c	.. c	.. c	.. c	.. c	.. c	.. c	.. c	.. c
Other services	.. c	.. c	.. c	.. c	.. c	.. c	.. c	.. c	.. c	.. c
Not allocated and confidential	**.. c**	**.. c**	**.. c**	**.. c**	**.. c**	**.. c**	**.. c**	**.. c**	**.. c**	**.. c**
Private real estate activities	**37 822.5**	**37 130.3**	**38 800.6**	**38 485.3**	**39 285.5**	**2 831.5**	**3 302.1**	**4 424.9**	**5 386.7**	**6 595.0**

.. Not available; c Confidential data

Note: Detailed metadata at: *http://stats.oecd.org/OECDStat_Metadata/ShowMetadata.ashx?Dataset=FDI_CTRY_IND_SUMM.*

Source: *OECD International Direct Investment Statistics (database): https://doi.org/10.1787/idi-data-en*

SWITZERLAND

Table 6. Foreign direct investment income by industrial sector

Million US dollars

	Inward					Outward				
	2015	2016	2017	2018	2019	2015	2016	2017	2018	2019
All FDI activities	**61 254.5**	**72 638.1**	**96 040.6**	**119 224.7**	**98 933.0**	**85 935.5**	**86 093.6**	**100 161.7**	**104 657.5**	**91 709.3**
Agriculture, forestry and fishing	..	..	..	..	..	.. c	.. c	.. c	.. c	.. c
Mining and quarrying	.. c	.. c	.. c	.. c	.. c	.. c	.. c	.. c	.. c	.. c
Extraction activities	.. c	.. c	.. c	.. c	.. c	.. c	.. c	.. c	.. c	.. c
Manufacturing	**15 251.8**	**14 936.6**	**16 472.6**	**19 371.8**	**17 681.9**	**45 452.7**	**37 184.4**	**37 262.8**	**47 031.1**	**41 165.2**
of which:										
Food products, beverages and tobacco	.. c	.. c	.. c	.. c	.. c	.. c	.. c	.. c	.. c	.. c
Textiles, wood and paper products; printing	.. c	.. c	.. c	.. c	.. c	.. c	.. c	.. c	.. c	.. c
Chemical, rubber, plastic, non-metallic mineral products	.. c	.. c	.. c	.. c	.. c	.. c	.. c	.. c	.. c	.. c
Metal and machinery products, except electrical equipment	.. c	.. c	.. c	.. c	.. c	.. c	.. c	.. c	.. c	.. c
Motor vehicles, trailers, semi-trailers, other transport equipment	.. c	.. c	.. c	.. c	.. c	.. c	.. c	.. c	.. c	.. c
Other manufacturing	.. c	.. c	.. c	.. c	.. c	.. c	.. c	.. c	.. c	.. c
Electricity, gas, steam and air conditioning supply	.. c	.. c	.. c	.. c	.. c	.. c	.. c	.. c	.. c	.. c
Water supply; sewerage, waste management and remediation activities	.. c	.. c	.. c	.. c	.. c	..	..	..	..	..
Construction	.. c	.. c	.. c	.. c	.. c	.. c	.. c	.. c	.. c	.. c
Services	**46 037.3**	**57 447.7**	**79 364.3**	**99 719.7**	**81 157.4**	**40 434.5**	**49 055.1**	**62 307.6**	**56 596.0**	**49 910.5**
Wholesale and retail trade; repair of motor vehicles and motorcycles	13 440.7	15 466.8	28 346.3	24 216.6	23 080.3	4 415.5	9 711.5	7 564.0	5 664.8	9 676.3
Transportation and storage	628.6	1 042.2	1 217.1	1 394.7	2 537.3	1 450.7	1 483.9	2 114.1	1 726.4	1 220.7
Accommodation and food service activities	-47.7	165.1	72.5	46.5	-86.4	130.8	-146.7	80.5	69.6	87.0
Information and communication	3 149.1	3 339.2	3 541.7	2 159.4	8 075.4	213.2	179.4	621.1	184.0	-183.2
Financial and insurance activities	18 216.0	20 956.7	38 896.0	37 098.0	24 192.9	22 943.0	21 030.4	31 924.6	32 305.2	30 325.3
Activities of holding companies	5 617.3	1 581.5	17 970.8	24 080.5	11 096.0	11 452.4	7 015.3	21 729.3	18 089.9	13 516.3
Real estate activities	.. c	.. c	.. c	.. c	.. c	.. c	.. c	.. c	.. c	.. c
Professional, scientific and technical activities	10 437.0	16 045.8	11 096.0	36 410.2	22 841.5	10 874.2	15 300.5	18 488.1	15 942.9	7 464.6
Administrative and support service activities	.. c	.. c	.. c	.. c	.. c	.. c	.. c	.. c	.. c	.. c
Public administration; activities of households and of extraterritorial organisations	..	..	..	..	..	..	..	..	..	..
Education	.. c	.. c	.. c	.. c	.. c	..	..	..	..	..
Human health and social work activities	.. c	.. c	.. c	.. c	.. c	.. c	.. c	.. c	.. c	.. c
Arts, entertainment and recreation	.. c	.. c	.. c	.. c	.. c	.. c	.. c	.. c	.. c	.. c
Other services	.. c	.. c	.. c	.. c	.. c	.. c	.. c	.. c	.. c	.. c
Not allocated and confidential	.. c	.. c	.. c	.. c	.. c	.. c	.. c	.. c	.. c	.. c
Private real estate activities	..	..	..	..	..	..	..	..	..	..

.. Not available; c Confidential data

Note: Detailed metadata at: *http://stats.oecd.org/OECDStat_Metadata/ShowMetadata.ashx?Dataset=FDI_CTRY_IND_SUMM.*

Source: *OECD International Direct Investment Statistics (database): https://doi.org/10.1787/idi-data-en*

TURKEY

Table 1. Foreign direct investment flows by country

Million US dollars

	Inward					Outward				
	2015	2016	2017	2018	2019	2015	2016	2017	2018	2019
WORLD	**18 916.2**	**13 719.1**	**11 033.2**	**12 988.0**	**8 799.2**	**4 900.6**	**2 891.6**	**2 622.9**	**3 607.0**	**2 938.0**
OECD COUNTRIES	**11 504.5**	**6 939.7**	**4 192.7**	**5 671.3**	**2 480.5**	**3 965.4**	**2 180.2**	**1 908.1**	**3 205.8**	**2 322.9**
Australia	4.0	28.1	462.7	48.0	12.1	0.1	1.2	1.6	0.9	-0.5
Austria	84.0	364.4	-1 152.9	454.7	9.2	44.0	3.0	10.4	38.6	59.8
Belgium	856.2	406.7	213.9	142.6	-12.5	-102.4	2.8	11.2	19.8	39.1
Canada	33.1	117.9	41.7	33.6	37.1	15.6	12.9	12.8	10.4	10.3
Chile	-	5.6	1.9	-	-	-	0.1	0.1	-	4.4
Czech Republic	2.4	1.9	65.7	13.7	12.7	0.9	0.4	5.3	0.3	-0.4
Denmark	43.6	63.6	31.0	218.3	22.0	0.9	1.8	0.7	0.4	0.6
Estonia	1.0	3.0	-	1.0	1.1	0.2	0.0	0.7	1.0	0.8
Finland	7.2	8.9	12.9	11.6	13.1	0.1	0.4	3.6	4.3	47.2
France	172.8	-123.9	396.7	451.5	77.0	17.4	28.8	28.9	26.3	19.1
Germany	654.5	644.7	374.6	232.6	-44.9	220.5	13.3	178.0	52.3	322.9
Greece	51.1	7.0	1.3	20.1	10.1	0.8	2.4	19.0	21.5	11.0
Hungary	-0.1	3.9	1.1	1.2	2.2	3.5	5.9	15.2	-14.6	11.3
Iceland	-	-	-	-	-1.0	-	-	-	-	-
Ireland	144.5	300.1	44.4	-168.3	189.2	0.1	-0.4	-0.9	0.9	0.5
Israel	13.7	5.2	3.2	36.7	36.2	2.6	1.0	1.2	6.6	4.4
Italy	242.8	209.0	43.6	389.4	69.6	21.9	30.7	31.5	46.1	44.8
Japan	315.3	460.9	184.3	147.5	255.1	0.0	3.6	0.8	0.1	-0.5
Korea	59.1	132.5	34.2	191.9	56.4	32.5	15.7	0.3	-7.5	0.4
Latvia	1.0	3.2	0.0	1.2	2.4	2.6	1.2	8.6	0.9	1.2
Lithuania	1.0	1.0	1.0	1.0	1.1	0.4	-	0.1	1.1	0.7
Luxembourg	2 376.7	506.5	-265.9	443.3	-5.8	136.9	57.8	-389.4	42.7	17.6
Mexico	-	-	-	-	1.1	0.0	1.1	4.1	3.9	3.5
Netherlands	1 625.8	1 634.9	1 647.9	1 132.0	64.2	1 507.0	716.2	697.8	1 664.7	679.2
New Zealand	-	-	4.8	2.0	2.0	-	0.1	-	0.2	0.1
Norway	49.8	10.9	61.8	224.7	20.8	89.0	-4.0	0.9	0.4	-0.6
Poland	-3.0	1.5	8.0	7.9	6.9	1.6	1.5	3.0	6.8	2.2
Portugal	4.0	-0.5	1.1	1.3	0.7	0.2	2.3	49.5	13.8	4.8
Slovak Republic	6.4	1.6	2.0	1.0	4.9	0.0	0.2	-1.2	1.0	1.1
Slovenia	1.3	0.0	6.6	-	0.2	0.0	1.0	11.8	2.3	12.3
Spain	2 338.4	293.8	1 403.2	219.4	293.8	3.8	6.6	9.6	21.1	36.4
Sweden	50.9	44.7	42.7	87.6	9.0	0.4	49.0	38.9	16.4	6.5
Switzerland	192.7	343.9	11.6	145.5	320.4	11.5	54.7	23.2	107.0	99.0
Turkey	-	-	-	-	-	-	-	-	-	-
United Kingdom	598.0	952.5	275.1	680.6	664.7	621.7	337.8	334.9	340.6	288.7
United States	1 578.2	507.6	233.7	498.0	349.5	1 334.5	831.0	796.2	775.4	595.3
EUROPE	**12 054.5**	**8 535.1**	**6 353.3**	**7 124.4**	**3 429.2**	**3 009.4**	**1 473.8**	**1 175.9**	**2 616.7**	**1 983.3**
Bulgaria	16.4	13.2	4.8	21.5	10.8	31.8	4.1	43.7	8.9	25.6
Croatia	0.4	0.2	0.9	-	1.0	36.8	14.3	2.7	0.7	4.5
Cyprus	13.5	5.3	-	-	-	-	-	-	-0.8	-
Malta	3.7	-39.7	0.9	21.1	0.9	80.4	19.8	15.6	30.9	15.3
Romania	3.3	4.0	1.0	7.1	3.6	27.6	53.1	12.3	21.8	24.8
Russian Federation	902.3	788.1	44.9	113.7	103.8	65.5	-59.2	30.9	20.1	97.6
Ukraine	49.0	35.1	18.0	53.5	33.5	13.0	12.2	-55.0	23.7	26.3
AFRICA	**144.5**	**86.2**	**124.2**	**239.2**	**403.1**	**34.5**	**91.1**	**105.2**	**64.6**	**43.8**
Northern Africa	128.0	72.4	59.4	188.8	297.0	14.2	60.6	78.3	44.6	18.2
Algeria	7.0	10.0	6.0	37.0	50.0	3.5	26.0	39.2	11.1	9.3
Egypt	35.0	36.0	32.2	71.8	99.0	7.4	24.9	30.8	3.8	7.4
Libya	82.0	22.6	20.0	66.0	124.0	0.1	-	-	0.4	0.4
Morocco	1.0	1.0	1.4	7.0	13.0	1.0	9.4	7.4	28.9	1.0
Tunisia	3.0	2.8	-0.2	7.0	11.0	2.2	0.4	1.0	0.5	0.2
Other African countries	16.5	13.8	64.9	50.5	106.0	20.4	30.4	26.9	20.0	25.5
Nigeria	-	-2.0	-	1.0	2.0	0.2	11.0	1.8	-	0.0
South Africa	-1.5	0.0	1.0	3.8	11.8	8.8	0.0	0.1	7.0	5.6
AMERICA	**1 626.3**	**644.2**	**340.7**	**618.0**	**532.8**	**1 338.7**	**870.8**	**821.7**	**806.7**	**634.5**
Northern America	1 611.3	625.6	275.4	531.6	386.6	1 350.0	843.9	809.0	785.8	605.6
Central America and Caribbean countries	9.0	13.3	62.3	79.5	149.8	-12.8	8.8	7.6	7.3	4.6
Bahamas	1.0	-	-	-	0.0	-	-	-	-	-
Bermuda	-	-	-	-	1.0	-8.8	7.0	-	-	-
Cayman Islands	3.7	0.2	1.3	-	0.1	-	-	2.7	-	-
Costa Rica	-	-	-	-	-	-	-	-	-	-
El Salvador	0.1	-	-	-	-	-	-	-	-	-
Guatemala	-	-	-	-	-	-	-	-	1.2	-0.2
Honduras	-	-	-	-	-	-	-	-	-	-
Nicaragua	-	-	-	-	-	-	-	-	-	-
Panama	0.2	0.1	1.3	2.1	-	-	-	-	0.2	-
Virgin Islands, U.S.	-	-	7.0	0.3	1.5	-	0.3	-	-	-
South America	6.1	5.3	2.9	7.0	-3.5	1.5	18.0	5.1	13.5	24.3
Argentina	-	-	1.0	-	1.0	-	-	-	-	-
Bolivia	-	-	-	-	-	-	-	-	-	-
Brazil	6.1	-0.3	-	1.0	-4.5	1.2	0.1	0.8	1.1	3.9
Colombia	-	-	-	-	-	0.2	17.9	2.2	9.9	5.4
Ecuador	-	-	-	-	-	-	-	2.0	2.5	-
Paraguay	-	-	-	-	-	-	-	-	-	-
Peru	-	-	-	-	-	-	-	0.0	0.1	10.5
Uruguay	-	-	-	-	-	-	-	-	-	-
Venezuela	-	-	-	6.0	-	-	-	-	-	-

Table 1. Foreign direct investment flows by country *(cont.)*

Million US dollars

	Inward					Outward				
	2015	2016	2017	2018	2019	2015	2016	2017	2018	2019
ASIA	**5 086.8**	**4 425.7**	**3 747.5**	**4 956.4**	**4 415.8**	**518.0**	**454.6**	**518.5**	**117.9**	**276.8**
Near and Middle East	3 582.2	3 257.0	3 087.5	3 234.8	2 867.2	414.2	313.6	402.8	27.6	164.5
Gulf Arabian countries	2 059.7	1 499.3	1 244.1	1 947.3	1 673.7	115.2	72.0	125.4	-14.2	29.4
Kuwait	246.2	258.2	197.7	343.0	167.2	43.5	-1.6	-0.1	-0.2	1.0
Qatar	427.2	462.9	164.3	588.1	679.0	14.7	-4.7	-0.3	-3.0	0.0
Saudi Arabia	554.3	372.3	525.2	432.4	253.5	2.8	0.3	5.3	-4.0	-0.4
United Arab Emirates	362.6	291.3	135.1	134.1	12.7	23.6	38.8	52.6	-15.2	26.3
Other Near and Middle East	1 522.5	1 757.7	1 843.5	1 287.5	1 193.5	299.0	241.6	277.5	41.8	135.1
Jordan	28.4	39.3	37.1	138.9	172.2	2.3	-0.1	1.2	-0.3	0.2
Other Asian countries	1 504.6	1 168.7	660.0	1 721.6	1 548.6	103.7	141.0	115.7	90.3	112.4
China	521.4	346.1	146.9	81.2	105.6	21.3	33.0	10.3	26.9	3.2
Hong Kong, China	29.8	-53.0	17.2	178.5	193.0	20.6	0.3	0.1	0.8	-0.2
India	2.4	-1.4	9.2	30.4	15.1	18.2	1.0	5.9	6.7	-8.7
Indonesia	1.0	-5.4	1.0	1.0	1.0	0.5	5.1	0.0	9.2	0.2
Iran, Islamic Republic of	95.4	95.2	55.0	425.4	518.0	0.1	0.1	-4.0	2.2	-
Malaysia	317.5	13.1	33.9	2.4	4.5	0.2	0.1	6.9	5.7	2.0
Philippines	-	-	-	0.0	1.0	0.0	-	-	0.1	0.6
Singapore	12.1	32.5	21.8	10.8	21.0	0.1	0.3	1.6	2.3	-0.2
Chinese Taipei	0.6	0.9	6.2	247.5	32.2	0.4	0.4	0.1	0.3	0.2
Thailand	0.1	-6.4	54.1	68.5	0.2	4.4	0.5	0.4	0.9	0.4
Viet Nam	-	0.4	-	-	-	0.1	20.4	1.3	2.9	1.0
AUSTRALIA, OCEANIA AND POLAR REGIONS	**4.0**	**28.1**	**467.4**	**50.0**	**18.3**	**0.1**	**1.4**	**1.6**	**1.2**	**-0.4**
WORLD unallocated and confidential	**0.0**	**0.0**	**0.0**	**0.0**	**0.0**	**0.0**	**0.0**	**0.0**	**0.0**	**0.0**
European Union (EU28)	**9 297.8**	**5 311.2**	**3 161.4**	**4 393.2**	**1 407.0**	**2 659.1**	**1 354.0**	**1 141.2**	**2 369.8**	**1 677.2**
G20 countries excl. European Union	**5 643.8**	**4 428.6**	**2 775.7**	**3 336.5**	**1 964.9**	**2 382.5**	**1 256.5**	**1 442.4**	**1 315.3**	**1 385.2**
G20 OECD countries	**3 657.9**	**2 929.2**	**2 046.6**	**2 673.0**	**1 477.7**	**2 264.2**	**1 276.2**	**1 389.1**	**1 248.5**	**1 283.9**
G20 Non-OECD countries	**1 985.9**	**1 499.5**	**729.1**	**663.6**	**487.2**	**118.3**	**-19.8**	**53.3**	**66.8**	**101.4**
MENA countries	**2 257.5**	**1 761.0**	**1 379.3**	**2 386.2**	**2 343.7**	**131.6**	**132.8**	**205.6**	**31.3**	**46.9**
ASEAN countries	**330.7**	**34.2**	**110.8**	**82.7**	**27.7**	**5.3**	**26.4**	**10.1**	**21.1**	**3.9**

- Nil

Note: Detailed metadata at: *http://stats.oecd.org/OECDStat_Metadata/ShowMetadata.ashx?Dataset=FDI_CTRY_IND_SUMM.*

Source: *OECD International Direct Investment Statistics (database): https://doi.org/10.1787/idi-data-en*

TURKEY

Table 2. Foreign direct investment positions by country

At year end

Million US dollars

	Inward					Outward				
	2015	2016	2017	2018	2019	2015	2016	2017	2018	2019
WORLD	..	**148 428.2**	**196 877.4**	**145 554.6**	**161 650.1**	**35 615.0**	**38 368.6**	**45 583.4**	**44 496.6**	**48 979.4**
OECD COUNTRIES	..	**113 130.5**	**149 856.0**	**105 187.4**	**110 415.2**	**19 879.9**	**22 665.3**	**26 993.5**	**29 563.3**	**32 232.2**
Australia	..	69.3	27.4	13.0	9.6	2.7	-2.8	-7.5	-12.1	-17.0
Austria	..	9 231.8	4 198.1	1 942.1	2 359.8	1 206.5	1 251.5	1 831.6	1 916.5	2 026.1
Belgium	..	3 191.7	3 367.1	2 484.5	2 792.2	130.3	213.7	205.9	353.5	696.5
Canada	..	879.7	1 687.2	1 369.4	1 295.8	18.0	18.5	20.6	15.5	13.8
Chile	..	11.8	..	..	..	6.8	7.1	8.1	-	8.0
Czech Republic	..	151.0	626.2	171.0	316.6	-	-0.2	-0.1	-0.8	-0.9
Denmark	..	541.8	896.2	695.7	694.7	0.0	0.0	-0.2	0.1	0.0
Estonia	..	0.2	0.3	..	..	0.4	-	-	-	-
Finland	..	2 440.4	2 375.3	1 358.9	1 352.7	0.3	0.4	1.8	2.7	18.6
France	..	6 174.8	8 571.0	4 658.7	5 972.7	60.7	106.6	137.4	98.4	187.6
Germany	..	15 383.4	20 431.9	13 310.3	15 989.1	1 216.7	1 356.5	1 777.8	1 729.8	1 769.8
Greece	..	152.9	180.7	77.3	77.5	24.3	26.3	42.0	41.3	50.5
Hungary	..	29.6	11.2	..	..	19.1	26.9	25.5	-0.2	26.8
Iceland	..	..	..	..	..	-	-	-	-	-
Ireland	..	728.4	788.3	752.1	920.6	598.5	647.7	659.0	584.7	543.1
Israel	..	944.0	1 262.3	881.3	1 026.8	203.9	114.1	124.5	143.4	142.2
Italy	..	4 207.3	5 117.2	2 783.1	3 418.0	117.8	144.4	155.3	140.1	172.1
Japan	..	3 041.5	5 252.1	2 695.4	3 383.6	0.1	0.2	0.6	2.3	3.4
Korea	..	1 796.3	2 323.5	1 908.0	2 210.7	4.0	6.7	0.6	2.2	18.0
Latvia	..	..	..	..	..	23.0	4.8	-12.9	-15.1	-17.2
Lithuania	..	0.6	..	..	..	-	-	-	-	15.6
Luxembourg	..	9 110.5	13 148.3	6 177.5	7 898.6	988.9	1 846.6	511.2	534.7	636.7
Mexico	..	..	..	..	..	-0.7	-8.0	7.9	-8.5	15.3
Netherlands	..	22 320.4	35 194.3	35 908.8	29 353.3	11 726.5	13 020.1	15 036.7	17 574.8	18 233.0
New Zealand	..	1.9	4.5	..	..	2.5	1.5	1.9	2.1	2.2
Norway	..	788.9	845.7	396.2	530.5	-0.3	-	-	-	0.1
Poland	..	29.7	47.7	..	..	8.1	37.3	74.9	52.6	83.0
Portugal	..	39.4	45.5	..	..	4.8	5.3	6.3	13.7	16.8
Slovak Republic	..	..	27.3	21.5	41.7	-0.2	-0.2	-2.2	-2.7	14.5
Slovenia	..	0.7	..	..	..	0.5	-0.1	1.6	12.4	20.4
Spain	..	7 448.1	10 618.3	5 741.0	7 047.5	175.1	273.4	250.7	205.9	74.9
Sweden	..	460.6	472.8	360.6	1 204.4	8.0	4.1	52.2	42.3	89.2
Switzerland	..	5 046.1	7 078.4	5 624.1	6 138.3	161.9	165.6	184.8	205.4	291.1
Turkey	..	91.1	..	..	..	-	-	-	-	-
United Kingdom	..	12 756.6	16 265.9	10 228.6	11 607.3	1 626.9	1 570.9	3 890.6	4 113.0	3 650.0
United States	..	6 058.8	8 814.8	5 432.8	4 464.3	1 567.9	1 826.6	2 007.0	1 815.1	3 448.2
EUROPE	..	**111 203.1**	**143 664.1**	**109 096.7**	**103 722.5**	**25 793.9**	**29 278.9**	**35 741.9**	**36 685.3**	**37 476.9**
Bulgaria	..	5.0	2.0	3.8	3.2	141.7	267.5	291.9	291.6	248.3
Croatia	..	0.0	0.0	..	..	153.6	157.2	139.8	157.3	209.4
Cyprus	..	..	..	..	..	-	-	-	-	-
Malta	..	132.8	107.2	27.3	27.0	1 646.5	1 754.4	2 050.6	1 760.4	1 898.0
Romania	..	1.0	..	..	0.1	107.5	219.3	255.4	330.8	313.0
Russian Federation	..	10 415.2	12 732.4	16 048.6	5 513.3	594.1	467.5	428.7	694.5	863.3
Ukraine	..	7.5	..	..	..	59.1	124.7	115.3	176.7	263.2
AFRICA	..	**122.8**	**147.2**	**94.6**	**139.7**	**966.6**	**1 258.8**	**1 568.7**	**1 265.8**	**1 899.6**
Northern Africa	..	102.9	..	..	..	633.7	1 141.9	1 371.0	1 110.0	1 462.2
Algeria	..	..	..	..	..	181.1	632.3	1 174.1	908.2	1 238.3
Egypt	..	2.4	..	..	..	245.0	195.0	204.5	245.4	208.3
Libya	..	98.9	..	..	..	123.2	16.7	-119.4	-160.9	-113.4
Morocco	..	1.6	..	..	..	33.5	247.9	72.3	88.5	106.2
Tunisia	..	0.0	..	..	..	50.9	50.1	39.4	28.8	22.8
Other African countries	..	19.9	13.1	5.7	4.8	332.9	116.9	197.7	155.8	437.4
Nigeria	..	..	..	..	..	70.9	64.9	80.3	23.2	22.5
South Africa	..	2.2	..	..	..	3.0	7.8	14.8	8.3	9.3
AMERICA	..	**8 356.1**	**12 709.9**	**8 201.0**	**7 288.7**	**3 052.4**	**2 868.3**	**3 322.3**	**2 240.2**	**4 197.9**
Northern America	..	6 938.5	10 502.0	6 802.2	5 760.2	1 585.9	1 845.1	2 027.5	1 830.6	3 462.0
Central America and Caribbean countries	..	1 188.5	1 931.7	1 398.8	1 528.5	1 415.6	966.4	1 237.4	370.0	653.2
Bahamas	..	4.6	138.7	112.5	121.4	2.6	2.6	2.6	2.6	2.6
Bermuda	..	50.5	..	..	..	1.9	3.7	7.8	7.4	7.0
Cayman Islands	..	255.5	421.3	503.7	553.0	706.2	831.7	1 055.8	540.8	509.7
Costa Rica	..	..	..	..	..	-	-	-	-	-
El Salvador	..	..	..	..	..	-	-	-	-	-
Guatemala	..	..	..	..	..	-	-	-	-	-
Honduras	..	..	..	..	..	-	-	-	-	-
Nicaragua	..	..	..	..	..	-	-	-	-	-
Panama	..	740.2	847.9	543.9	521.7	394.7	34.9	41.2	-261.5	3.9
Virgin Islands, U.S.	..	-	7.0	..	..	-	-	-	-	-
South America	..	229.1	..	..	..	51.0	56.8	57.4	39.6	82.7
Argentina	..	..	..	..	..	-	-	-	-	-
Bolivia	..	..	..	..	..	-	-	-	-	-
Brazil	..	217.3	..	..	..	16.6	-0.1	-0.6	-0.5	34.8
Colombia	..	..	..	..	..	27.6	47.4	49.9	40.0	40.0
Ecuador	..	..	..	..	..	-	2.3	-	-	-
Paraguay	..	..	..	..	..	-	-	-	-	-
Peru	..	..	..	..	..	-	-	-	0.1	-0.1
Uruguay	..	..	..	..	..	-	-	-	-	-
Venezuela	..	..	..	..	..	-	-	-	-	-

Table 2. Foreign direct investment positions by country (*cont.*)

At year end

Million US dollars

	Inward					Outward				
	2015	2016	2017	2018	2019	2015	2016	2017	2018	2019
ASIA	..	**28 675.2**	**40 324.4**	**28 147.6**	**50 484.7**	**5 530.4**	**4 767.0**	**4 819.3**	**4 367.3**	**5 427.4**
Near and Middle East	..	21 226.3	27 940.2	20 352.7	41 281.9	3 359.5	2 526.8	2 467.3	2 622.6	2 502.9
Gulf Arabian countries	..	12 485.6	14 495.1	10 963.6	31 654.6	1 284.6	1 048.4	1 400.0	1 502.7	1 564.6
Kuwait	..	1 056.4	1 272.8	1 081.2	1 494.3	0.9	7.2	8.5	-83.0	-105.1
Qatar	..	4 940.6	..	..	..	43.5	110.0	-251.9	102.2	104.4
Saudi Arabia	..	3 888.3	..	..	..	95.2	-0.8	-49.7	-47.4	-59.9
United Arab Emirates	..	1 493.2	1 743.9	1 020.6	4 523.3	267.4	552.6	907.6	935.4	755.3
Other Near and Middle East	..	8 740.7	13 445.1	9 389.1	9 627.3	2 074.9	1 478.3	1 067.3	1 119.9	938.3
Jordan	..	70.4	83.5	21.4	11.4	15.2	22.6	13.7	13.2	16.7
Other Asian countries	..	7 448.9	12 384.2	7 794.9	9 202.8	2 170.9	2 240.3	2 352.0	1 744.7	2 924.4
China	..	492.4	1 566.8	1 155.0	1 244.0	143.6	181.1	260.9	190.8	60.6
Hong Kong, China	..	57.0	69.4	68.6	222.0	0.6	0.1	10.5	21.5	17.9
India	..	65.6	143.2	143.3	126.7	130.4	111.9	124.0	200.9	152.4
Indonesia	..	0.6	..	..	..	111.2	-48.2	-54.2	-49.0	138.7
Iran, Islamic Republic of	..	176.0	..	..	..	503.0	408.2	394.2	387.3	323.6
Malaysia	..	951.2	1 462.6	641.7	744.8	145.8	142.6	193.6	186.9	201.3
Philippines	..	..	..	..	..	0.4	-0.7	-0.6	-1.0	-1.1
Singapore	..	193.5	274.2	213.4	335.4	18.8	17.5	24.4	32.5	11.6
Chinese Taipei	..	14.5	..	..	..	0.1	0.2	0.3	0.1	0.2
Thailand	..	493.7	..	..	..	128.6	104.0	91.6	128.9	120.3
Viet Nam	..	..	..	..	..	-	-	0.2	-	2.7
AUSTRALIA, OCEANIA AND POLAR REGIONS	..	**71.1**	**31.9**	**14.7**	**14.5**	**271.6**	**195.5**	**131.3**	**-61.9**	**-22.4**
WORLD unallocated and confidential	..	**0.0**	**0.0**	**0.0**	**0.0**	**-**	**-**	**0.0**	**0.0**	**0.0**
European Union (EU28)	..	**94 540.5**	**122 500.4**	**86 745.2**	**91 119.7**	**19 985.4**	**22 934.2**	**27 382.6**	**29 938.0**	**30 975.5**
G20 countries excl. European Union	..	**65 540.5**	**87 550.0**	**61 900.6**	**58 689.8**	**5 708.2**	**5 738.9**	**8 714.0**	**8 893.4**	**10 460.4**
G20 OECD countries	..	**50 458.9**	**68 651.9**	**42 549.6**	**48 615.4**	**4 614.2**	**5 019.7**	**7 990.2**	**7 895.8**	**9 261.3**
G20 Non-OECD countries	..	**15 081.6**	**18 898.1**	**19 351.0**	**10 074.4**	**1 094.0**	**719.2**	**723.8**	**997.6**	**1 199.1**
MENA countries	..	**13 467.0**	**15 604.0**	**11 549.3**	**32 413.4**	**1 941.7**	**2 213.4**	**2 789.0**	**2 626.0**	**3 044.0**
ASEAN countries	..	**1 639.0**	**2 686.1**	**1 600.8**	**1 783.5**	**404.8**	**215.2**	**255.0**	**298.2**	**473.5**

- Nil; .. Not available

Note: Inward FDI positions are allocated according to the ultimate investing country. Inward FDI positions by immediate counterpart country are available for more years in the *OECD FDI database according to BMD4*. Detailed metadata at: *http://stats.oecd.org/OECDStat_Metadata/ShowMetadata.ashx?Dataset=FDI_CTRY_IND_SUMM*.

Source: *OECD International Direct Investment Statistics (database)*: *https://doi.org/10.1787/idi-data-en*

TURKEY

Table 3. Foreign direct investment income by country

Million US dollars

	Inward					Outward				
	2015	2016	2017	2018	2019	2015	2016	2017	2018	2019
WORLD	**3 554.0**	**3 137.5**	**3 280.3**	**3 194.8**	**3 237.0**	**219.3**	**201.5**	**297.4**	**956.9**	**809.5**
OECD COUNTRIES	**3 290.7**	**2 887.2**	**3 022.6**	**2 944.1**	**3 075.7**	**109.8**	**86.7**	**138.7**	**607.0**	**456.7**
Australia	0.1	0.4	0.6	0.7	0.8	-	-	0.1	0.1	0.2
Austria	61.8	88.1	9.5	9.6	33.8	4.4	-	-	1.3	0.8
Belgium	121.7	82.8	53.7	124.5	148.8	-	-	0.1	-	138.3
Canada	0.5	4.9	1.0	1.6	1.4	-	0.2	-	-	-
Chile	-	5.6	1.9	-	-	-	-	-	-	-
Czech Republic	14.4	16.5	0.0	10.4	29.6	-	-	-	0.1	-
Denmark	2.6	5.4	4.3	6.5	4.4	-	-	-	-	-
Estonia	-	-	-	0.2	-	-	-	-	-	-
Finland	461.3	12.3	1.0	55.9	5.3	-	-	-	-	-
France	154.1	178.1	208.9	213.2	195.4	-	2.0	0.2	0.1	-0.1
Germany	515.8	413.0	532.4	484.2	575.7	2.9	-2.4	10.0	18.9	7.7
Greece	61.5	0.8	8.7	14.9	13.4	-	-	-	0.0	0.7
Hungary	-	6.0	7.2	-	0.2	-0.1	-0.1	-	-	-
Iceland	-	-	0.0	-	-	-	-	-	-	-
Ireland	2.8	11.5	1.0	5.9	13.2	-	0.0	-	-	0.2
Israel	7.6	9.8	5.7	15.9	0.0	-	-	-	-	0.6
Italy	76.4	75.3	62.8	69.0	93.6	0.1	-	-	2.0	0.1
Japan	45.9	148.0	13.0	39.2	39.4	-	2.6	-	-	-
Korea	12.6	20.8	34.5	37.5	65.8	-	-	4.4	-	-
Latvia	-	-	-	-	-	-	2.6	3.3	4.7	1.4
Lithuania	-	-	-	-	0.5	-	-	-	-	-
Luxembourg	94.0	90.2	242.2	310.6	335.9	20.7	0.1	13.0	23.7	10.0
Mexico	-	-	-	-	-	-	-	-	-	-
Netherlands	419.5	486.1	408.3	501.9	495.6	57.0	46.2	92.4	530.7	109.9
New Zealand	-	-	-	-	-	-	-	-	-	-
Norway	7.3	18.1	20.3	2.3	5.8	-	0.0	-	-	0.8
Poland	-	0.0	0.6	2.9	3.0	-	0.4	0.7	0.5	0.5
Portugal	6.5	7.3	5.1	4.2	-	-	-	-	-	-
Slovak Republic	14.1	18.8	13.9	1.3	0.6	-	0.0	-	-	1.5
Slovenia	-	-	-	-	-	-	-	-	-	-
Spain	185.3	211.9	127.9	195.3	174.5	-	-	0.0	11.3	6.0
Sweden	6.0	5.8	197.7	43.5	39.9	-	0.0	-	-	0.1
Switzerland	154.6	251.6	335.4	239.2	223.6	0.0	0.5	4.6	6.9	104.6
Turkey	-	-	-	-	-	-	-	-	-	-
United Kingdom	481.1	618.3	622.8	472.5	456.5	9.8	24.1	-0.1	2.6	45.5
United States	383.4	100.3	102.2	81.2	118.9	15.0	10.6	10.0	4.4	28.1
EUROPE	**3 004.6**	**2 614.5**	**2 867.3**	**2 776.8**	**2 854.3**	**99.8**	**77.9**	**143.1**	**697.3**	**500.3**
Bulgaria	0.1	0.6	0.1	1.1	0.3	0.3	0.1	0.4	8.3	3.4
Croatia	1.1	-	-	-	-	-	-	-	-	-
Cyprus	-	-	-	-	-	-	-	-	-	-
Malta	1.3	11.1	0.1	0.1	1.7	-	0.7	9.7	31.7	15.5
Romania	0.1	0.0	-	-	0.7	0.1	-	-	0.2	0.2
Russian Federation	159.4	4.3	1.0	3.2	1.6	2.9	0.8	0.6	3.3	2.1
Ukraine	0.1	-	0.0	3.5	0.2	-	1.2	7.0	-	3.1
AFRICA	**1.6**	**5.5**	**0.5**	**69.5**	**1.7**	**5.1**	**3.2**	**5.5**	**3.3**	**8.3**
Northern Africa	1.6	5.5	0.5	68.7	0.4	5.0	3.1	5.5	3.3	8.3
Algeria	1.5	-	0.0	68.7	-	3.9	2.5	3.8	3.0	2.6
Egypt	0.1	0.1	0.1	-	0.1	0.5	0.6	1.7	0.4	5.6
Libya	-	5.3	-	-	-	-	-	-	-	-
Morocco	-	-	0.4	-	0.4	0.6	-	0.1	-	0.0
Tunisia	-	-	-	-	-	-	-	-	-	0.2
Other African countries	-	0.0	0.1	0.8	1.3	0.1	0.1	-	-	0.0
Nigeria	-	-	-	-	0.5	-	-	-	-	0.0
South Africa	-	-	-	0.8	0.8	-	-	-	-	-
AMERICA	**417.6**	**114.9**	**137.7**	**128.4**	**150.9**	**14.7**	**10.6**	**9.9**	**4.4**	**28.1**
Northern America	383.9	105.1	103.2	82.8	120.2	15.0	10.7	10.0	4.4	28.1
Central America and Caribbean countries	33.7	4.2	32.6	45.6	30.7	-0.3	-0.1	-0.1	-	-
Bahamas	-	-	-	-	-	-	-	-	-	-
Bermuda	-	-	4.3	11.4	-	-0.3	-	-	-	-
Cayman Islands	3.7	4.2	-	1.0	-	-	-	-	-	-
Costa Rica	-	-	-	-	-	-	-	-	-	-
El Salvador	-	-	-	-	-	-	-	-	-	-
Guatemala	-	-	-	-	-	-	-	-	-	-
Honduras	-	-	-	-	-	-	-	-	-	-
Nicaragua	-	-	-	-	-	-	-	-	-	-
Panama	-	-	0.8	-	-	-	-	-	-	-
Virgin Islands, U.S.	-	-	-	-	-	-	-	-	-	-
South America	0.0	5.6	1.9	-	-	-	0.0	-	-	-
Argentina	-	-	-	-	-	-	-	-	-	-
Bolivia	-	-	-	-	-	-	-	-	-	-
Brazil	-	-	-	-	-	-	-	-	-	-
Colombia	-	-	-	-	-	-	0.0	-	-	-
Ecuador	-	-	-	-	-	-	-	-	-	-
Paraguay	-	-	-	-	-	-	-	-	-	-
Peru	-	-	-	-	-	-	-	-	-	-
Uruguay	0.0	-	-	-	-	-	-	-	-	-
Venezuela	-	-	-	-	-	-	-	-	-	-

Table 3. Foreign direct investment income by country *(cont.)*

Million US dollars

	Inward					Outward				
	2015	2016	2017	2018	2019	2015	2016	2017	2018	2019
ASIA	**130.1**	**372.6**	**274.2**	**219.4**	**229.3**	**99.8**	**106.2**	**138.8**	**251.9**	**272.5**
Near and Middle East	28.2	153.5	156.7	84.1	67.5	95.1	83.3	95.1	209.0	242.6
Gulf Arabian countries	17.3	128.9	144.9	67.4	64.8	78.2	82.1	93.2	195.6	229.8
Kuwait	-	52.6	57.9	54.4	51.6	-	-	0.0	-	0.0
Qatar	0.8	43.3	52.4	0.4	0.0	-	-	-	-	4.6
Saudi Arabia	-	6.6	21.3	6.9	6.3	0.1	0.5	-	10.0	1.8
United Arab Emirates	16.6	26.4	10.9	4.9	6.8	13.1	0.3	0.1	0.7	4.4
Other Near and Middle East	10.9	24.6	11.8	16.7	2.7	16.9	1.2	1.9	13.4	12.8
Jordan	1.0	-	0.1	0.0	0.2	1.3	-	0.0	-	-
Other Asian countries	101.9	219.2	117.5	135.4	161.8	4.7	22.9	43.8	42.9	29.9
China	0.2	2.6	2.4	22.1	20.3	-	0.8	18.1	0.1	0.2
Hong Kong, China	20.1	5.4	0.5	0.2	0.4	0.3	-	0.0	0.1	0.0
India	0.3	1.0	0.4	-	-	-	-	0.2	0.2	-
Indonesia	-	1.0	0.4	-	-	-	-	-	-	-
Iran, Islamic Republic of	0.4	-	-	-	-	-	-	0.2	26.0	0.2
Malaysia	9.2	8.5	4.0	5.2	-	-	-	-	0.1	0.1
Philippines	-	-	-	-	-	-	-	-	-	-
Singapore	11.8	27.5	32.2	27.7	34.3	-	2.4	0.5	-	0.0
Chinese Taipei	1.3	2.5	3.2	3.4	-	-	-	-	-	-
Thailand	-	1.0	26.7	-	-	-	-	-	-	-
Viet Nam	-	-	-	-	-	-	-	-	-	-
AUSTRALIA, OCEANIA AND POLAR REGIONS	**0.1**	**0.4**	**0.6**	**0.7**	**0.8**	**-**	**-**	**0.1**	**0.1**	**0.3**
WORLD unallocated and confidential	**-**	**0.0**	**0.0**	**0.0**	**0.0**	**0.0**	**-**	**0.0**	**0.0**	**0.0**
European Union (EU28)	**2 681.3**	**2 339.6**	**2 508.2**	**2 527.7**	**2 622.6**	**95.2**	**73.6**	**129.8**	**635.9**	**341.4**
G20 countries excl. European Union	**1 829.5**	**1 574.4**	**1 603.7**	**1 432.1**	**1 576.5**	**30.7**	**39.1**	**43.5**	**41.5**	**85.5**
G20 OECD countries	**1 669.8**	**1 558.9**	**1 578.2**	**1 399.1**	**1 547.6**	**27.8**	**37.0**	**24.6**	**28.0**	**81.4**
G20 Non-OECD countries	**159.8**	**15.4**	**25.5**	**33.1**	**28.9**	**2.9**	**2.1**	**19.0**	**13.6**	**4.1**
MENA countries	**21.4**	**137.4**	**147.4**	**136.8**	**66.7**	**96.6**	**85.3**	**98.7**	**198.9**	**238.1**
ASEAN countries	**20.9**	**37.9**	**63.2**	**32.9**	**34.3**	**-**	**2.4**	**0.5**	**0.1**	**0.1**

- Nil

Note: Detailed metadata at: *http://stats.oecd.org/OECDStat_Metadata/ShowMetadata.ashx?Dataset=FDI_CTRY_IND_SUMM.*

Source: *OECD International Direct Investment Statistics (database): https://doi.org/10.1787/idi-data-en*

TURKEY

Table 4. Foreign direct investment flows by industrial sector

Million US dollars

	Inward					Outward				
	2015	2016	2017	2018	2019	2015	2016	2017	2018	2019
All FDI activities	**18 916.2**	**13 719.1**	**11 033.2**	**12 988.0**	**8 799.2**	**4 900.6**	**2 891.6**	**2 622.9**	**3 607.0**	**2 938.0**
Agriculture, forestry and fishing	**49.8**	**41.5**	**50.5**	**91.4**	**27.4**	**9.2**	**7.2**	**20.2**	**18.3**	**11.1**
Mining and quarrying	**221.3**	**161.7**	**453.9**	**67.0**	**41.7**	**1 800.2**	**1 068.3**	**1 036.1**	**835.1**	**738.3**
Extraction activities	159.5	125.7	443.1	24.0	-20.1	1 760.5	1 074.2	994.5	819.8	724.6
Manufacturing	**4 463.6**	**2 410.2**	**1 185.4**	**2 085.6**	**1 469.9**	**819.9**	**397.7**	**361.7**	**523.3**	**626.9**
of which:										
Food products, beverages and tobacco	918.6	728.1	363.3	475.8	160.0	294.2	41.5	25.7	63.0	-4.4
Textiles, wood and paper products; printing	470.9	168.0	137.3	175.0	31.9	93.1	71.6	126.1	190.1	120.7
Chemical, rubber, plastic, non-metallic mineral products	2 059.5	273.1	423.1	524.4	987.5	36.6	54.6	72.6	37.5	91.9
Metal and machinery products, except electrical equipment	410.3	721.7	118.7	109.3	212.4	109.1	60.7	22.5	47.3	125.4
Motor vehicles, trailers, semi-trailers, other transport equipment	152.0	168.6	30.7	349.4	182.9	6.7	13.0	18.9	1.3	103.0
Other manufacturing	452.3	350.8	112.3	451.8	-104.8	280.3	156.3	95.9	184.1	190.3
Electricity, gas, steam and air conditioning supply	**1 576.2**	**629.5**	**-945.0**	**370.1**	**183.6**	**87.4**	**39.2**	**24.7**	**387.2**	**32.3**
Water supply; sewerage, waste management and remediation activities	**11.9**	**3.1**	**-5.3**	**4.0**	**2.1**	**0.2**	**0.6**	**0.7**	**0.3**	**0.1**
Construction	**39.1**	**270.7**	**567.8**	**171.6**	**431.6**	**305.0**	**39.6**	**144.5**	**67.3**	**485.3**
Services	**8 398.3**	**6 312.4**	**5 083.0**	**4 283.4**	**1 663.9**	**1 878.9**	**1 339.0**	**1 034.7**	**1 775.7**	**1 044.0**
Wholesale and retail trade; repair of motor vehicles and motorcycles	801.3	932.9	1 262.2	1 267.8	675.7	53.3	78.4	118.2	12.3	109.8
Transportation and storage	2 042.9	1 553.1	1 926.5	878.5	440.4	37.1	139.5	108.5	37.3	170.3
Accommodation and food service activities	9.5	258.2	91.2	422.0	91.0	44.1	47.9	123.7	-26.5	27.4
Information and communication	1 464.9	858.3	-173.8	203.4	181.4	647.3	84.7	38.8	16.1	-336.4
Financial and insurance activities	3 522.2	1 856.8	1 249.2	1 191.7	-0.3	647.0	481.8	-79.7	1 152.1	400.4
Activities of holding companies	205.9	126.5	-2.2	83.1	266.2	490.3	257.3	191.5	886.4	257.8
Real estate activities	190.7	367.8	178.5	77.6	152.1	378.1	367.7	567.3	430.4	320.0
Professional, scientific and technical activities	44.2	105.1	70.2	-35.1	225.3	13.5	13.9	19.0	56.8	276.3
Administrative and support service activities	218.9	149.0	323.5	54.5	-249.3	20.5	2.5	19.1	8.9	15.8
Public administration; activities of households and of extraterritorial organisations	-	0.1	0.4	2.0	-	0.0	0.1	-0.8	-	0.1
Education	0.0	-74.1	-10.8	0.6	0.1	0.7	0.6	1.5	11.0	0.7
Human health and social work activities	81.6	315.0	126.2	95.5	89.8	19.5	85.3	4.3	4.1	10.0
Arts, entertainment and recreation	1.6	16.3	9.7	19.5	3.1	0.4	-0.6	2.6	1.2	0.8
Other services	20.7	-26.0	30.2	105.3	54.6	17.6	37.1	112.3	72.0	48.9
Not allocated and confidential	**0.0**	**-**	**0.0**	**0.0**	**0.0**	**-0.3**	**0.0**	**0.3**	**0.0**	**-0.1**
Private real estate activities	**4 156.0**	**3 890.0**	**4 643.0**	**5 915.0**	**4 979.0**	..	..	..	..	..

- Nil; .. Not available

Note: Detailed metadata at: *http://stats.oecd.org/OECDStat_Metadata/ShowMetadata.ashx?Dataset=FDI_CTRY_IND_SUMM.*

Source: *OECD International Direct Investment Statistics (database): https://doi.org/10.1787/idi-data-en*

Table 5. Foreign direct investment positions by industrial sector
At year end

Million US dollars

	Inward					Outward				
	2015	2016	2017	2018	2019	2015	2016	2017	2018	2019
All FDI activities	..	**148 428.2**	**196 877.4**	**145 554.6**	**161 650.1**	**35 615.0**	**38 368.6**	**45 583.4**	**44 496.6**	**48 979.4**
Agriculture, forestry and fishing	**806.3**	**748.0**	**1 399.7**	**484.0**	**627.3**	**3.3**	**8.8**	**29.6**	**32.2**	**21.7**
Mining and quarrying	**3 135.4**	**2 690.9**	**4 770.7**	**3 427.4**	**3 271.8**	**4 630.2**	**4 202.3**	**5 296.4**	**3 577.5**	**3 181.2**
Extraction activities	1 183.2	1 091.6	2 081.3	1 443.7	1 453.3	4 470.6	4 045.2	5 137.9	3 480.7	2 937.6
Manufacturing	**52 233.5**	**45 957.9**	**61 606.8**	**34 642.2**	**38 688.6**	**5 233.4**	**4 483.8**	**4 080.1**	**4 105.7**	**4 714.5**
of which:										
Food products, beverages and tobacco	11 320.5	9 858.9	12 305.4	6 394.6	7 897.5	1 771.7	2 051.6	709.2	787.9	1 062.2
Textiles, wood and paper products; printing	952.1	992.7	1 718.3	935.2	1 446.2	1 481.9	790.2	1 021.4	973.6	1 316.5
Chemical, rubber, plastic, non-metallic mineral products	16 424.6	13 787.1	19 168.4	12 855.4	11 729.6	962.5	641.6	819.5	649.3	649.3
Metal and machinery products, except electrical equipment	4 620.7	4 948.8	6 931.8	2 505.3	3 061.8	507.1	769.6	1 345.0	1 277.1	1 304.4
Motor vehicles, trailers, semi-trailers, other transport equipment	9 254.1	8 922.2	12 504.0	6 514.3	8 381.4	95.8	121.6	101.1	140.1	221.0
Other manufacturing	9 661.5	7 448.2	8 978.8	5 437.4	6 172.2	414.5	109.2	84.0	277.8	161.1
Electricity, gas, steam and air conditioning supply	**15 558.9**	**11 829.6**	**18 971.8**	**5 709.1**	**8 684.5**	**699.5**	**468.4**	**425.8**	**305.7**	**706.2**
Water supply; sewerage, waste management and remediation activities	**63.8**	**62.6**	**53.1**	**10.3**	**10.1**	**12.8**	**10.3**	**2.4**	**2.9**	**3.2**
Construction	**1 610.9**	**1 459.9**	**903.3**	**583.5**	**651.8**	**1 005.7**	**1 085.2**	**466.7**	**333.0**	**1 377.0**
Services	**84 668.9**	**85 679.5**	**109 172.1**	**100 698.4**	**109 716.1**	**24 030.2**	**28 109.9**	**35 282.4**	**36 139.6**	**38 975.6**
Wholesale and retail trade; repair of motor vehicles and motorcycles	26 398.6	32 069.7	40 345.8	45 043.3	39 106.9	934.6	1 574.7	2 057.6	2 709.7	2 443.6
Transportation and storage	2 918.6	3 359.9	7 086.5	4 629.9	5 064.6	1 169.8	1 433.2	2 826.7	1 399.5	1 598.5
Accommodation and food service activities	511.2	455.7	943.9	459.0	799.8	188.1	411.0	338.9	204.2	247.5
Information and communication	16 036.0	12 633.9	16 122.2	8 545.5	9 704.9	2 639.1	2 510.0	1 774.9	1 086.2	1 080.2
Financial and insurance activities	33 219.9	31 950.3	37 991.0	37 883.1	51 294.1	18 598.7	21 595.0	27 650.6	29 978.4	32 531.3
Activities of holding companies	4 750.9	3 999.7	5 187.8	3 019.2	3 246.7	11 891.5	13 266.3	18 980.4	21 067.0	23 118.1
Real estate activities	1 475.2	1 354.6	2 176.9	1 644.0	1 568.8	347.7	321.9	471.1	573.9	755.5
Professional, scientific and technical activities	305.9	315.8	686.3	314.9	330.4	46.1	45.4	53.6	6.3	39.0
Administrative and support service activities	1 859.6	1 569.8	2 103.3	1 464.3	1 150.1	13.3	60.4	12.2	27.9	27.3
Public administration; activities of households and of extraterritorial organisations	-	0.0	0.4	0.4	0.4	-	-	-0.8	-0.8	-0.8
Education	60.9	11.6	13.6	6.8	7.0	6.0	5.6	4.8	2.5	-5.6
Human health and social work activities	1 049.4	759.7	651.9	298.4	292.9	8.8	80.5	35.9	73.8	98.5
Arts, entertainment and recreation	112.3	572.4	129.1	74.7	59.6	2.4	24.6	26.2	59.8	47.6
Other services	721.4	626.2	921.2	334.0	336.6	75.7	47.6	30.6	18.1	113.0
Not allocated and confidential	**-0.1**	**-0.1**	**-0.1**	**-0.1**	**-0.1**	-	-	**0.0**	**0.0**	**0.0**
Private real estate activities	..	..	..	..	..	..	..	..	..	..

- Nil; .. Not available

Note: Detailed metadata at: *http://stats.oecd.org/OECDStat_Metadata/ShowMetadata.ashx?Dataset=FDI_CTRY_IND_SUMM.*

Source: *OECD International Direct Investment Statistics (database): https://doi.org/10.1787/idi-data-en*

Table 6. Foreign direct investment income by industrial sector

Million US dollars

	Inward					Outward				
	2015	2016	2017	2018	2019	2015	2016	2017	2018	2019
All FDI activities	**3 554.0**	**3 137.5**	**3 280.3**	**3 194.8**	**3 237.0**	**219.3**	**201.5**	**297.4**	**956.9**	**809.5**
Agriculture, forestry and fishing	**0.3**	**22.9**	**12.7**	**13.3**	**3.6**	**0.2**	**0.2**	**-**	**0.1**	**0.6**
Mining and quarrying	**198.2**	**116.6**	**240.2**	**75.0**	**249.3**	**1.1**	**0.1**	**0.3**	**1.5**	**2.5**
Extraction activities	61.2	46.0	115.2	56.3	80.8	-	-	-	-	-
Manufacturing	**1 222.1**	**1 369.8**	**1 288.3**	**1 140.6**	**1 321.4**	**40.8**	**70.2**	**122.9**	**292.3**	**262.2**
of which:										
Food products, beverages and tobacco	391.3	496.8	483.4	337.9	275.0	-	13.3	23.6	24.4	171.9
Textiles, wood and paper products; printing	59.5	28.4	59.8	67.6	47.9	1.2	3.5	5.0	21.8	0.7
Chemical, rubber, plastic, non-metallic mineral products	147.6	350.2	196.2	168.4	177.9	21.9	29.3	34.4	30.7	32.7
Metal and machinery products, except electrical equipment	52.4	169.2	169.0	149.5	149.5	3.1	15.2	15.1	25.9	41.5
Motor vehicles, trailers, semi-trailers, other transport equipment	343.0	193.1	141.2	192.4	355.1	-	1.0	0.5	-	0.1
Other manufacturing	228.3	132.1	238.8	224.9	315.9	14.6	7.9	44.3	189.5	15.2
Electricity, gas, steam and air conditioning supply	**153.8**	**133.4**	**88.7**	**121.8**	**88.2**	**0.5**	**1.5**	**0.1**	**20.3**	**13.1**
Water supply; sewerage, waste management and remediation activities	**-**	**0.2**	**1.2**	**0.0**	**0.4**	**-**	**-**	**-**	**-**	**-**
Construction	**42.1**	**27.4**	**41.4**	**51.1**	**49.1**	**22.9**	**1.2**	**18.0**	**28.9**	**26.2**
Services	**1 937.6**	**1 467.1**	**1 607.9**	**1 793.0**	**1 525.0**	**153.8**	**128.3**	**157.2**	**613.8**	**504.9**
Wholesale and retail trade; repair of motor vehicles and motorcycles	410.1	517.0	456.0	364.8	264.1	3.6	4.5	5.2	14.9	34.7
Transportation and storage	193.0	313.2	193.5	358.0	469.3	4.8	0.1	4.9	11.2	7.2
Accommodation and food service activities	8.7	27.1	23.9	132.9	34.5	-	0.4	4.0	9.0	9.2
Information and communication	649.3	44.1	462.2	296.4	277.6	-0.3	-0.2	19.3	2.2	4.5
Financial and insurance activities	520.4	319.4	308.3	488.4	307.6	118.2	121.2	104.3	519.1	406.1
Activities of holding companies	14.5	18.1	9.7	56.3	60.8	26.9	3.4	2.1	261.1	110.7
Real estate activities	17.2	35.9	13.0	19.5	25.2	-	-0.1	3.4	1.2	14.5
Professional, scientific and technical activities	37.5	123.0	62.5	25.4	43.2	1.1	0.4	4.8	4.6	4.4
Administrative and support service activities	29.5	35.4	20.8	34.9	45.7	-	0.7	9.9	1.1	0.1
Public administration; activities of households and of extraterritorial organisations	-	-	-	0.0	-	-	-	-	-	-
Education	0.1	0.0	0.0	0.4	0.6	-	0.1	0.0	-	-
Human health and social work activities	34.5	28.1	7.1	4.9	4.1	23.7	-	0.4	45.1	2.9
Arts, entertainment and recreation	18.1	7.2	5.0	6.4	25.2	-	0.4	-	3.1	-
Other services	19.3	16.7	55.6	61.0	28.0	2.6	0.9	1.1	2.4	21.4
Not allocated and confidential	**0.0**	**0.0**	**0.0**	**0.0**	**0.0**	**0.0**	**0.0**	**-1.0**	**0.0**	**0.0**
Private real estate activities	..	..	..	..	..	..	..	..	..	..

- Nil; .. Not available

Note: Detailed metadata at: *http://stats.oecd.org/OECDStat_Metadata/ShowMetadata.ashx?Dataset=FDI_CTRY_IND_SUMM.*

Source: *OECD International Direct Investment Statistics (database): https://doi.org/10.1787/idi-data-en*

UNITED KINGDOM

Table 1. Foreign direct investment flows by country

Million US dollars

	Inward					Outward				
	2015	2016	2017	2018	2019	2015	2016	2017	2018	2019
WORLD	**38 669.2**	**196 503.4**	**78 511.5**	**65 450.8**	**49 898.6**	**-65 561.5**	**-22 310.4**	**106 692.0**	**41 491.7**	**-35 355.4**
OECD COUNTRIES	**19 066.5**	**152 390.0**	**51 399.7**	**.. d**	**58 391.0**	**-65 795.3**	**.. c**	**111 666.2**	**.. d**	**-41 305.6**
Australia	1 996.9	-2 159.2	3 026.0	919.0	-4 546.9	186.4	1 215.9	-4 470.8	2 451.8	-667.1
Austria	48.9	-101.2	-10.3	16.4	-158.5	.. c	114.7	385.0	110.9	140.2
Belgium	-825.1	.. c	-2 818.7	1 191.8	1 002.9	2 459.9	.. c	.. c	.. c	.. c
Canada	5 388.8	155.2	.. d	.. d	.. d	.. c	-1 391.4	137.8	1 011.0	1 560.5
Chile	-	-1.4	12.9	-7.4	4.3	-812.8	274.0	-42.5	109.8	.. c
Czech Republic	32.1	-	-1.3	14.9	.. c	7.6	-66.1	218.9	90.3	166.6
Denmark	689.1	36.4	534.4	443.9	6 247.2	-1 222.3	1 063.4	-464.8	.. c	69.5
Estonia	-	-	-	0.8	-2.8	.. c	-112.0	43.8	124.7	31.7
Finland	103.9	-55.3	34.8	123.7	487.8	-65.7	62.1	82.4	-37.6	.. c
France	.. c	618.1	7 700.2	-656.1	8 701.6	1 657.8	697.7	-1 984.3	5 035.5	199.7
Germany	7 605.8	3 330.6	318.1	.. c	675.2	-2 397.3	-174.1	894.9	3 668.4	-1 584.6
Greece	32.1	12.1	-55.4	.. c	13.4	244.5	.. c	148.1	109.7	-69.2
Hungary	10.7	-13.5	43.8	-3.8	-0.1	-187.9	.. c	218.9	-34.5	190.8
Iceland	35.1	56.7	-23.2	10.7	.. c	-	-1.4	2.6	.. c	55.3
Ireland	1 040.5	-948.7	673.4	.. c	-42.2	-123.8	-7 641.0	13 060.8	-2 812.9	5 085.1
Israel	68.8	25.6	.. d	1 153.6	1 281.1	160.4	125.5	230.5	91.9	41.5
Italy	348.4	-755.7	1 862.0	-278.0	1 366.6	.. c	430.5	-632.2	-837.6	-2 059.9
Japan	2 624.9	2 295.5	10 144.2	461.0	-13 649.5	.. c	-27.0	.. c	344.0	-223.8
Korea	.. c	188.9	202.2	360.4	-23.1	.. c	1 654.5	.. c	526.8	.. c
Latvia	-1.5	1.4	7.7	10.1	3.3	-13.8	-20.2	-	23.1	-187.5
Lithuania	-	1.4	.. c	0.4	7.6	4.6	-44.5	9.0	-28.2	-25.6
Luxembourg	-1 298.7	29 121.5	5 499.6	.. c	8 328.3	-12 168.1	2 112.0	7 078.3	-736.5	-4 751.5
Mexico	-18.3	6.7	7.7	-9.5	.. c	1 066.5	569.5	1 129.3	1 882.8	648.2
Netherlands	-34 055.0	.. c	-2 319.1	-22 506.1	5 562.2	-10 400.3	-17 797.6	.. c	8 098.4	-19 753.7
New Zealand	29.0	55.3	-37.3	42.5	5.3	-195.6	14.8	155.8	240.4	.. c
Norway	.. c	.. c	461.0	.. c	1 235.5	1 563.0	1 376.5	.. c	-7 256.1	-966.8
Poland	29.0	-1.4	67.0	7.8	84.1	1 715.8	-151.1	378.6	471.6	495.4
Portugal	19.9	8.1	-27.0	-0.8	235.7	-516.4	-599.2	211.2	250.0	-83.4
Slovak Republic	32.1	2.7	.. c	14.1	-8.0	-18.3	-60.7	.. c	.. c	-25.2
Slovenia	-1.5	-	2.6	-1.4	-0.3	-9.2	13.5	-25.8	43.8	51.6
Spain	3 495.8	2 531.7	-797.1	5 079.3	-641.0	441.6	1 066.1	.. c	189.8	.. c
Sweden	918.3	-13.5	1 070.0	-383.6	1 404.8	728.8	3 170.0	866.6	2 033.9	-110.9
Switzerland	670.7	1 144.4	5 114.6	1 857.8	-867.4	2 021.4	-1 334.7	209.9	-3 409.9	-14 832.7
Turkey	1.5	-10.8	39.9	-85.9	-35.7	-71.8	359.0	-316.8	506.8	-91.2
United Kingdom	-	-	-	-	-	-	-	-	-	-
United States	32 258.2	25 049.9	20 392.7	53 328.1	38 509.5	-17 153.6	982.5	92 951.3	5 712.3	-8 101.3
EUROPE	**-18 800.6**	**131 993.3**	**28 489.6**	**1 108.1**	**31 452.6**	**-18 453.8**	**-34 803.0**	**13 574.6**	**3 572.8**	**-30 838.9**
Bulgaria	-3.1	-1.4	15.5	1.1	6.0	39.7	-1.4	94.0	-9.0	17.7
Croatia	.. d	-	.. c	.. d	.. d	38.2	-17.5	-32.2	.. d	-33.5
Cyprus	592.8	103.9	.. c	536.0	-699.6	38.2	.. c	-320.6	.. c	404.5
Malta	.. c	-44.5	-106.9	118.9	47.7	.. c	62.1	-1 344.3	-57.5	39.6
Romania	-	2.7	.. d	-3.9	2.4	125.3	.. c	166.1	-32.3	-27.3
Russian Federation	.. c	-64.8	-55.4	70.4	.. c	1 167.3	-583.0	-725.0	1 263.9	-16.6
Ukraine	.. c	-2.7	11.6	1.7	2.6	.. c	-545.2	-83.7	-61.7	119.1
AFRICA	**.. c**	**17.5**	**376.0**	**.. c**	**1 147.9**	**343.8**	**-8 461.5**	**.. c**	**13 328.1**	**5 114.6**
Northern Africa	22.9	5.4	2.6	3.2	.. d	-2 097.8	-1 596.5	.. c	.. c	.. d
Algeria	.. c	-	.. c	0.1	.. c	.. c	.. c	.. c	.. c	.. c
Egypt	-1.5	-	-1.3	1.2	2.2	-267.4	-399.5	.. c	.. c	-230.3
Libya	.. c	5.4	.. c	-	-	.. c	.. c	.. c	4.0	0.6
Morocco	-	-	-1.3	2.0	0.4	.. c	-141.7	.. c	25.9	-50.8
Tunisia	-	-	.. c	-	-	149.7	-5.4	-	-2.7	-1.1
Other African countries	.. c	12.1	373.4	.. c	.. d	2 441.6	-6 865.0	-5 973.5	.. d	.. d
Nigeria	.. c	56.7	.. c	24.9	.. c	.. c	746.3	330.9	-476.0	.. c
South Africa	539.3	-89.1	.. c	-341.1	.. c	1 364.4	.. c	423.6	3 333.0	-69.4
AMERICA	**42 771.6**	**28 348.2**	**28 581.0**	**60 739.8**	**28 850.3**	**-32 724.2**	**2 657.2**	**99 262.2**	**9 859.0**	**-5 397.5**
Northern America	37 647.1	25 203.8	.. d	.. d	.. d	.. d	-406.2	93 089.1	6 723.1	-6 555.7
Central America and Caribbean countries	5 129.1	3 129.6	6 847.8	-229.3	-12 819.2	2 308.6	2 086.4	5 270.4	2 029.9	238.1
Bahamas	7.6	-78.3	33.5	204.3	-502.8	.. c	93.1	.. c	-15.1	67.7
Bermuda	1 644.0	1 658.6	1 943.1	313.5	-786.9	-553.1	-547.9	-157.1	-495.7	-458.6
Cayman Islands	617.3	3 681.5	-16.7	-1 879.7	-5 921.8	3 454.5	.. c	3 427.8	.. c	848.1
Costa Rica	-	-1.4	-	-0.3	-1.3	128.3	.. c	.. c	-23.3	-1.3
El Salvador	-	-	-	-	-	-1.5	.. c	.. c	.. c	-0.9
Guatemala	111.5	44.5	158.4	15.2	-31.2	-1.5	-20.2	101.7	-7.3	.. c
Honduras	-	-	-	-	-	-7.6	-4.0	.. c	.. c	.. c
Nicaragua	-	-	-	-	-	.. c	-1.4	20.6	2.7	.. c
Panama	-6.1	-2.7	6.4	-29.8	-7.9	.. c	12.1	.. c	.. c	8.6
Virgin Islands, U.S.	.. c	2.7	.. c	9.1	.. c	-	1.4	-3.9	-0.3	2.7
South America	-3.1	14.8	.. c	.. c	.. c	.. d	978.4	902.7	1 106.0	920.2
Argentina	1.5	-	-	-0.2	125.8	693.7	.. c	.. c	284.9	.. c
Bolivia	-	-	-	-	-	-	-	1.3	1.3	1.2
Brazil	-3.1	16.2	.. c	.. c	-47.6	1 451.5	466.9	261.4	706.1	274.0
Colombia	.. c	-	.. c	0.9	-0.7	-183.3	-167.3	.. c	38.0	-73.2
Ecuador	.. c	-	.. c	-	-	6.1	.. c	18.0	.. c	16.4
Paraguay	-	-	.. c	-	.. d	.. c	2.7	1.3	.. d	-0.4
Peru	-	-	-	-0.4	-0.2	29.0	29.7	61.8	35.4	70.5
Uruguay	-	-	-	-	-	-158.9	.. c	1.3	9.3	.. c
Venezuela	-	-	-	-	-	-62.6	43.2	94.0	-74.4	-25.8

Table 1. Foreign direct investment flows by country *(cont.)*

Million US dollars

	Inward					Outward				
	2015	2016	2017	2018	2019	2015	2016	2017	2018	2019
ASIA	**12 022.9**	**37 720.6**	**19 660.1**	**2 875.3**	**-7 005.7**	**-14 866.3**	**16 969.0**	**.. c**	**11 430.0**	**-1 238.4**
Near and Middle East	.. c	.. c	891.1	1 381.6	1 850.6	.. c	.. c	.. d	3 904.4	-2 075.7
Gulf Arabian countries	.. c	.. c	844.7	205.8	557.1	.. c	.. c	1 282.5	3 657.1	-3 527.0
Kuwait	-12.2	20.2	-9.0	5.7	14.5	1.5	8.1	.. c	1.5	.. c
Qatar	6.1	4.0	16.7	.. c	.. c	51.9	33.7	.. c	25.3	.. c
Saudi Arabia	-1.5	-74.2	3.9	-4.4	86.8	718.1	653.2	696.6	424.2	-229.6
United Arab Emirates	.. c	.. c	645.1	52.5	338.1	.. c	.. c	.. c	2 597.8	-3 003.3
Other Near and Middle East	76.4	27.0	47.6	1 175.8	1 293.4	.. c	655.9	.. d	247.3	1 451.3
Jordan	.. c	-	.. d	9.1	2.0	33.6	.. c	.. c	.. c	4.7
Other Asian countries	.. d	.. d	18 769.0	1 493.7	-8 856.3	.. d	.. d	5 329.6	7 525.6	837.3
China	702.8	552.0	1 357.2	-112.0	1 032.2	-1 233.0	1 526.3	-330.9	1 999.3	-2 169.2
Hong Kong, China	1 416.3	.. c	2 724.7	1 539.7	3 069.1	5 112.3	3 859.6	2 978.4	5 396.3	-989.8
India	.. c	-792.2	1 874.8	-275.3	-26.7	994.7	.. c	-441.7	116.1	1 016.8
Indonesia	.. c	.. c	.. c	9.9	.. c	-250.6	1 081.0	-614.2	-1 002.1	408.2
Iran, Islamic Republic of	-3.1	5.4	.. c	0.3	7.8	.. c	.. c	-1.3	0.1	0.0
Malaysia	38.2	-145.7	94.0	-0.6	154.6	99.3	902.8	535.7	456.0	.. c
Philippines	.. c	2.7	23.2	2.6	7.3	-58.1	43.2	65.7	139.5	218.6
Singapore	5 735.7	5 612.7	-664.4	404.3	-114.9	4 181.8	.. c	-387.6	-2 796.2	4 117.8
Chinese Taipei	3.1	-2.7	10.3	0.3	35.8	302.5	483.1	337.4	97.5	.. c
Thailand	.. c	-4.0	38.6	.. c	92.8	-48.9	790.8	-37.3	417.0	.. c
Viet Nam	-	.. c	-	-0.2	0.6	230.7	-54.0	.. c	360.5	792.5
AUSTRALIA, OCEANIA AND POLAR REGIONS	**2 016.8**	**-1 576.2**	**1 406.1**	**962.7**	**-4 546.5**	**140.6**	**1 326.6**	**-4 567.3**	**3 301.8**	**-2 995.3**
WORLD unallocated and confidential	**111.5**	**-**	**-1.3**	**.. d**	**0.0**	**-1.5**	**1.4**	**-2 468.5**	**0.0**	**0.0**
European Union (EU28)	**-21 095.5**	**124 186.2**	**10 816.4**	**-19 687.6**	**32 770.7**	**-20 478.2**	**-30 313.1**	**19 025.2**	**4 080.6**	**-14 942.1**
G20 countries excl. European Union	**.. d**	**.. d**	**.. d**	**.. d**	**.. d**	**.. d**	**.. d**	**.. d**	**27 427.1**	**.. d**
G20 OECD countries	**.. d**	**28 719.3**	**.. d**	**.. d**	**.. d**	**.. d**	**4 317.1**	**.. d**	**20 301.7**	**.. d**
G20 Non-OECD countries	**.. d**	**.. d**	**.. d**	**.. d**	**.. d**	**4 906.0**	**.. d**	**.. d**	**7 125.3**	**.. d**
MENA countries	**.. d**	**.. d**	**.. d**	**.. d**	**.. d**	**.. d**	**.. d**	**.. d**	**.. d**	**.. d**
ASEAN countries	**5 890.0**	**5 261.8**	**23.2**	**-477.7**	**663.0**	**4 242.9**	**-1 083.7**	**-283.3**	**-2 300.3**	**5 502.4**

- Nil; .. Not available; c Confidential data; d Secondary Confidentiality

Note: Detailed metadata at: *http://stats.oecd.org/OECDStat_Metadata/ShowMetadata.ashx?Dataset=FDI_CTRY_IND_SUMM.*

Source: *OECD International Direct Investment Statistics (database): https://doi.org/10.1787/idi-data-en*

Table 2. Foreign direct investment positions by country
At year end

Million US dollars

	Inward					Outward				
	2015	2016	2017	2018	2019	2015	2016	2017	2018	2019
WORLD	**1 530 133.4**	**1 475 523.4**	**1 608 032.7**	**1 930 434.0**	**1 974 480.5**	**1 606 364.8**	**1 491 940.0**	**1 624 231.9**	**1 788 397.1**	**1 901 117.2**
OECD COUNTRIES	**1 174 173.1**	**1 199 040.5**	**1 302 699.6**	**.. d**	**1 619 943.9**	**1 132 488.1**	**1 082 914.3**	**1 228 098.9**	**.. d**	**1 434 946.1**
Australia	21 298.2	13 707.7	9 537.9	20 200.4	19 493.5	41 861.3	50 488.4	41 335.0	45 205.3	50 690.0
Austria	2 682.3	1 620.1	3 295.5	1 338.5	2 202.5	1 461.2	1 237.5	6 516.7	6 276.1	6 778.1
Belgium	31 358.9	32 478.8	21 928.1	119 796.1	121 472.3	23 441.0	18 363.9	16 087.0	19 078.8	31 328.2
Canada	25 080.0	.. d	25 777.6	.. d	.. d	25 497.9	25 920.8	30 636.4	36 465.3	.. d
Chile	.. c	64.0	177.0	.. c	45.1	1 886.5	1 504.5	1 364.7	1 414.7	1 618.3
Czech Republic	244.5	7.4	13.5	498.5	.. c	2 588.9	2 301.6	2 864.5	2 567.7	3 113.0
Denmark	9 629.5	8 335.6	9 085.3	7 467.8	8 304.3	8 965.6	8 488.1	6 949.1	7 633.4	8 511.6
Estonia	-	.. d	1.4	20.9	30.0	243.0	254.6	328.3	838.0	.. d
Finland	1 677.5	728.3	1 417.4	681.9	1 115.9	1 089.2	1 082.5	737.7	788.4	3 736.8
France	103 141.7	73 722.5	92 834.8	69 977.0	90 346.0	89 638.4	88 253.2	96 604.5	104 216.0	97 678.2
Germany	74 831.1	73 599.5	60 671.5	106 569.6	61 567.0	26 286.3	25 709.2	29 363.6	42 028.9	42 535.0
Greece	1 052.2	145.2	410.8	-1 396.9	277.2	806.2	338.3	294.6	324.8	477.6
Hungary	213.4	-20.9	258.1	14.9	13.8	1 040.3	1 322.4	1 232.3	1 308.3	2 237.8
Iceland	297.9	.. d	320.2	.. d	.. d	4.4	.. c	9.5	60.9	-131.9
Ireland	18 241.0	14 128.4	18 897.4	18 870.5	30 460.0	63 484.0	59 292.7	87 562.5	67 402.6	65 276.8
Israel	.. d	585.6	702.6	15 806.7	1 790.6	869.9	.. d	1 299.8	.. d	1 068.6
Italy	11 338.2	6 223.4	11 594.4	7 624.5	6 896.3	16 227.0	15 318.0	13 023.9	19 196.8	18 253.5
Japan	61 144.0	57 189.1	66 968.0	113 216.0	109 081.5	6 664.2	5 411.5	7 213.9	9 307.0	7 188.9
Korea	2 720.8	2 278.3	3 025.3	2 674.6	2 027.3	5 112.6	7 549.5	8 779.9	7 242.3	5 093.0
Latvia	69.7	.. d	77.0	41.3	61.2	108.2	.. d	293.2	.. d	.. c
Lithuania	1.5	3.7	1.4	25.9	45.4	77.1	52.9	64.9	60.2	461.5
Luxembourg	103 286.9	141 221.6	157 273.3	141 472.9	155 449.4	139 059.0	138 730.5	138 135.4	148 187.9	146 667.5
Mexico	90.4	137.8	143.2	.. c	.. c	10 889.2	9 244.7	12 657.7	12 179.9	15 434.2
Netherlands	216 009.2	260 914.0	298 142.1	174 662.8	188 103.1	190 733.6	174 360.9	184 431.8	203 387.7	192 069.6
New Zealand	779.5	324.8	644.5	307.8	397.2	1 590.1	1 077.6	1 189.0	1 545.0	1 612.9
Norway	6 702.7	6 562.9	8 744.8	10 364.4	11 287.8	4 976.3	8 408.2	4 988.5	2 455.1	6 825.8
Poland	429.8	147.6	237.8	249.9	907.5	8 961.2	7 620.9	9 197.4	7 926.2	9 566.7
Portugal	806.2	513.0	936.4	316.2	690.3	4 503.6	4 139.5	4 961.5	5 575.3	5 615.5
Slovak Republic	237.1	13.5	-1.4	13.3	104.3	354.2	392.4	647.2	892.1	1 121.7
Slovenia	8.9	3.7	5.4	11.0	8.3	164.5	153.8	154.0	218.5	254.6
Spain	56 827.2	37 244.4	55 279.0	63 666.0	70 704.5	66 708.7	68 820.3	85 680.3	94 009.6	95 121.9
Sweden	14 073.8	9 070.0	13 673.8	12 014.5	9 775.8	24 265.0	22 833.1	26 604.5	26 053.0	28 497.0
Switzerland	57 891.2	55 736.3	61 018.8	85 602.5	100 180.8	26 704.2	27 217.4	38 721.8	62 093.7	74 171.0
Turkey	253.4	120.6	329.7	42.7	402.5	9 506.5	9 554.7	9 256.9	7 737.7	9 377.0
United Kingdom	-	-	-	-	-	-	-	-	-	-
United States	458 850.0	379 012.2	379 278.5	528 959.2	603 643.9	351 603.4	296 443.6	358 975.8	374 599.9	466 462.0
EUROPE	**806 748.7**	**831 161.3**	**948 009.7**	**1 015 812.7**	**1 005 630.2**	**791 412.3**	**761 980.6**	**838 956.9**	**923 016.8**	**944 935.6**
Bulgaria	7.4	48.0	129.7	17.0	55.4	131.9	66.4	198.6	37.7	213.5
Croatia	-	-	-	0.2	.. d	340.8	294.0	-40.5	-8.1	427.4
Cyprus	6 157.4	5 212.2	5 080.4	9 809.2	5 374.6	770.6	3 973.4	3 026.6	.. c	6 401.6
Malta	938.1	830.4	968.8	1 345.4	1 138.0	3 236.5	.. c	1 871.4	682.0	1 059.9
Romania	13.3	7.4	8.1	3.7	7.5	1 310.0	1 216.6	824.2	586.3	724.8
Russian Federation	.. c	1 233.9	.. c	893.4	.. c	12 249.6	14 423.7	.. c	.. c	17 654.8
Ukraine	-	48.0	150.0	27.3	31.6	195.6	200.5	-448.6	-375.7	463.1
AFRICA	**3 608.5**	**2 405.0**	**4 437.2**	**2 441.0**	**4 058.9**	**57 590.4**	**55 471.8**	**44 658.8**	**49 148.6**	**43 953.6**
Northern Africa	.. c	253.4	.. c	278.1	.. c	.. c	.. c	.. c	.. c	.. c
Algeria	.. c	-	-	0.1	-	.. c	.. c	.. c	.. c	.. c
Egypt	25.2	22.1	35.1	36.9	44.9	.. c	.. c	.. c	.. c	.. c
Libya	.. c	228.8	.. c	231.1	.. c	.. c	-7.4	-8.1	.. c	-21.7
Morocco	3.0	1.2	-	10.0	5.8	244.5	251.0	344.5	324.7	.. c
Tunisia	1.5	1.2	.. c	-	-	1 132.2	9.8	-	-9.1	3.3
Other African countries	.. d	2 151.6	.. d	2 162.9	.. d	.. d	.. d	.. d	.. d	.. d
Nigeria	.. c	343.2	.. c	213.4	.. c	6 108.5	6 318.1	.. c	5 390.8	6 852.8
South Africa	2 279.2	1 283.1	2 995.5	1 238.8	1 753.6	17 138.4	16 511.3	12 221.3	14 292.8	5 820.4
AMERICA	**575 829.9**	**506 918.4**	**504 675.0**	**689 993.8**	**767 317.8**	**508 150.6**	**435 309.4**	**488 116.5**	**532 887.9**	**619 199.2**
Northern America	483 930.1	.. d	405 056.1	.. d	.. d	377 102.8	322 376.7	389 619.0	411 071.9	.. d
Central America and Caribbean countries	91 624.2	104 814.9	96 187.0	128 219.1	.. d	98 473.6	87 270.3	75 695.2	97 053.7	85 568.6
Bahamas	103.7	899.3	982.3	2 250.1	4 230.8	.. c	916.5	.. c	827.6	1 016.7
Bermuda	26 338.2	22 099.9	24 192.7	25 274.8	34 990.5	22 046.5	26 139.7	7 742.2	39 786.4	29 354.7
Cayman Islands	28 202.4	33 373.1	31 897.0	50 542.0	53 094.6	26 444.9	16 754.8	.. c	1 051.3	2 894.8
Costa Rica	-	-4.9	-	1.5	-1.2	400.1	264.5	56.7	7.5	24.3
El Salvador	-	-	-	-	-	3.0	20.9	52.7	12.9	20.6
Guatemala	2 611.1	1 269.5	3 034.7	671.6	856.7	134.9	123.0	195.9	65.2	-24.8
Honduras	-	-	-	-	-	.. d	.. c	.. c	12.5	.. c
Nicaragua	-	-	-	-	-	.. c	2.5	39.2	.. c	.. c
Panama	340.8	966.9	351.3	.. c	508.5	.. c	.. c	.. c	.. c	209.2
Virgin Islands, U.S.	.. c	11.1	.. c	0.8	-	-	1.2	-24.3	0.5	3.4
South America	277.1	.. d	3 432.0	.. d	.. d	32 574.1	25 663.7	22 802.3	24 762.2	.. d
Argentina	13.3	1.2	1.4	3.4	5.8	5 773.6	5 978.6	5 676.3	.. c	.. c
Bolivia	-	-	-	-	-	3.0	4.9	6.8	6.7	27.7
Brazil	211.9	.. c	.. c	.. c	2 183.9	23 184.6	16 604.7	14 784.5	11 636.7	18 139.2
Colombia	.. c	1.2	-	0.6	1.1	859.5	720.9	535.1	400.2	759.7
Ecuador	.. c	-	.. c	-	-	40.0	32.0	58.1	124.6	129.8
Paraguay	-	-	.. c	-	.. d	.. d	.. d	10.8	24.6	37.3
Peru	1.5	1.2	2.7	0.7	1.5	315.6	220.2	143.2	.. c	758.0
Uruguay	-	-	-	-	-	-81.5	40.6	63.5	88.6	132.5
Venezuela	-	-	-	-	-	503.9	479.8	156.7	.. c	29.4

Table 2. Foreign direct investment positions by country *(cont.)*

At year end

Million US dollars

	Inward					Outward				
	2015	2016	2017	2018	2019	2015	2016	2017	2018	2019
ASIA	**121 621.2**	**118 903.9**	**139 605.5**	**201 646.0**	**177 557.9**	**204 825.1**	**187 341.6**	**210 516.1**	**236 710.5**	**234 999.6**
Near and Middle East	9 328.7	8 028.0	9 832.5	25 456.2	13 548.3	24 358.3	29 862.2	48 280.0	43 249.6	52 961.5
Gulf Arabian countries	8 183.2	7 063.6	8 665.0	9 280.2	11 346.7	.. d	.. d	34 156.2	.. d	.. d
Kuwait	389.7	381.4	432.4	337.4	.. c	1.5	17.2	40.5	40.1	54.5
Qatar	143.7	62.7	145.9	421.1	.. c	168.9	200.5	.. c	189.3	.. c
Saudi Arabia	47.4	109.5	277.0	92.4	738.1	5 117.1	4 638.9	5 660.0	5 868.4	6 304.7
United Arab Emirates	.. c	5 274.9	6 481.6	7 052.7	7 538.6	2 347.4	6 256.6	8 308.3	16 785.1	13 854.0
Other Near and Middle East	1 147.0	963.2	1 167.4	16 176.0	2 201.6	.. c	.. c	14 123.8	.. c	.. c
Jordan	.. c	.. d	.. c	322.5	.. c	.. c	.. c	.. c	10.1	21.6
Other Asian countries	112 291.0	110 875.9	129 771.7	176 189.8	164 009.6	180 466.8	157 479.4	162 236.2	193 460.9	182 038.1
China	3 350.6	1 874.8	3 102.3	2 253.8	4 302.7	14 614.7	14 276.0	11 268.7	20 269.7	13 732.4
Hong Kong, China	16 135.2	.. c	27 569.2	29 250.7	23 526.6	81 575.3	75 429.9	.. c	91 193.6	91 132.3
India	3 916.7	1 830.5	10 772.9	14 359.9	11 828.4	17 956.4	16 223.4	17 726.0	18 597.1	20 615.1
Indonesia	.. c	.. c	-	1.2	0.7	6 779.8	7 229.7	6 170.8	5 738.8	7 806.3
Iran, Islamic Republic of	.. c	301.4	.. c	327.8	.. c	.. c	.. c	21.6	2.4	16.0
Malaysia	632.8	321.1	760.7	-307.2	968.7	4 761.4	4 215.8	4 514.3	3 680.0	4 831.1
Philippines	.. c	98.4	.. d	69.7	67.8	265.3	.. d	370.2	733.2	766.8
Singapore	22 766.7	22 418.5	12 241.6	9 959.6	10 717.1	27 709.0	13 125.8	8 882.6	14 408.0	21 205.7
Chinese Taipei	143.7	76.3	197.3	70.3	101.5	3 586.2	3 667.1	5 042.6	4 182.4	2 185.4
Thailand	206.0	152.5	471.6	.. c	860.9	2 605.2	2 973.3	2 968.5	4 409.5	3 125.4
Viet Nam	1.5	.. c	-	0.0	1.0	90.4	238.7	206.7	.. c	1 922.8
AUSTRALIA, OCEANIA AND POLAR REGIONS	**22 323.7**	**16 136.1**	**11 305.2**	**20 540.6**	**19 915.7**	**44 385.0**	**51 836.6**	**41 982.2**	**46 633.3**	**58 029.3**
WORLD unallocated and confidential	**1.5**	**-1.2**	**-**	**0.0**	**0.0**	**1.5**	**-**	**1.4**	**0.0**	**0.0**
European Union (EU28)	**653 278.0**	**666 208.6**	**752 218.6**	**735 112.8**	**756 213.3**	**675 997.3**	**647 232.1**	**717 615.2**	**763 483.5**	**769 542.4**
G20 countries excl. European Union	**.. d**	**.. d**	**.. d**	**.. d**	**.. d**	**686 101.1**	**629 779.8**	**.. d**	**.. d**	**.. d**
G20 OECD countries	**758 747.8**	**.. d**	**650 160.8**	**.. d**	**.. d**	**583 286.9**	**533 893.5**	**607 847.6**	**658 179.2**	**.. d**
G20 Non-OECD countries	**.. d**	**.. d**	**.. d**	**.. d**	**.. d**	**102 814.2**	**95 886.3**	**.. d**	**.. d**	**.. d**
MENA countries	**.. d**	**.. d**	**.. d**	**9 927.5**	**.. d**	**.. d**	**.. d**	**.. d**	**.. d**	**.. d**
ASEAN countries	**24 398.3**	**24 397.8**	**14 764.2**	**13 757.9**	**.. d**	**43 375.8**	**29 233.6**	**25 014.2**	**31 456.7**	**41 169.3**

- Nil; .. Not available; c Confidential data; d Secondary Confidentiality

Note: Detailed metadata at: *http://stats.oecd.org/OECDStat_Metadata/ShowMetadata.ashx?Dataset=FDI_CTRY_IND_SUMM.*

Source: *OECD International Direct Investment Statistics (database): https://doi.org/10.1787/idi-data-en*

UNITED KINGDOM

Table 3. Foreign direct investment income by country

Million US dollars

	Inward					Outward				
	2015	2016	2017	2018	2019	2015	2016	2017	2018	2019
WORLD	**73 579.8**	**70 274.0**	**67 481.3**	**96 922.4**	**70 636.2**	**87 384.3**	**68 005.4**	**95 923.3**	**125 459.4**	**100 945.2**
OECD COUNTRIES	**60 730.3**	**54 981.1**	**59 286.6**	**.. d**	**59 996.1**	**52 395.7**	**41 728.7**	**62 389.9**	**.. d**	**65 184.3**
Australia	-433.9	-835.4	-288.4	-267.1	-76.4	3 436.2	2 580.3	5 269.1	5 222.0	1 928.6
Austria	48.9	108.0	96.6	123.5	259.0	18.3	226.7	283.3	259.5	276.3
Belgium	2 363.6	2 807.0	2 356.4	3 719.4	1 934.7	543.9	1 944.7	1 551.6	1 907.6	2 846.9
Canada	473.6	1 503.4	-324.5	.. d	.. d	.. d	2 603.2	.. d	1 867.2	2 105.8
Chile	3.1	6.7	5.2	-1.5	3.6	136.0	183.5	445.5	280.2	-10.8
Czech Republic	12.2	-	-1.3	0.2	20.8	203.2	117.4	39.9	255.1	252.2
Denmark	944.2	1 013.5	149.4	804.3	841.9	403.4	782.7	1 201.4	506.9	621.4
Estonia	-	-	-	0.7	4.8	16.8	1.4	3.9	24.4	39.3
Finland	116.1	-10.8	59.2	112.4	383.0	157.4	136.3	70.8	161.1	35.6
France	4 045.8	-156.5	1 604.4	2 275.8	1 844.0	3 916.0	3 175.4	3 847.5	3 914.7	3 043.4
Germany	6 540.9	7 066.1	3 416.2	8 791.7	3 137.6	3 703.6	2 916.3	4 402.5	4 687.8	2 295.8
Greece	81.0	64.8	28.3	104.5	31.5	3.1	32.4	70.8	101.3	59.7
Hungary	18.3	1.4	-18.0	1.0	-0.6	134.5	124.2	154.5	235.9	270.2
Iceland	.. d	.. d	.. d	.. d	22.5	-	1.4	-	.. c	.. c
Ireland	1 489.7	369.8	1 103.5	3 218.9	2 426.6	1 809.0	6 047.2	4 465.6	6 046.7	7 600.4
Israel	.. d	.. d	29.6	1 310.9	22.9	.. d	.. d	.. d	188.0	98.0
Italy	417.1	390.0	600.1	346.3	1 045.0	1 113.8	628.9	920.7	592.3	812.8
Japan	2 450.7	4 247.0	8 593.9	6 800.3	3 029.6	470.6	1 346.8	819.0	535.7	675.1
Korea	45.8	133.6	212.5	404.4	172.7	351.4	620.8	892.4	1 049.0	895.1
Latvia	4.6	1.4	.. d	.. d	9.0	.. d	.. d	.. c	.. d	.. d
Lithuania	-	1.4	.. c	1.8	11.3	19.9	6.7	15.5	16.2	-66.6
Luxembourg	1 798.3	1 638.3	2 259.9	4 456.2	4 159.0	1 680.7	.. c	3 274.5	2 179.7	95.3
Mexico	1.5	12.1	11.6	.. c	.. c	1 219.3	919.0	1 254.2	1 274.7	1 165.7
Netherlands	5 156.6	4 527.7	2 603.7	5 753.9	4 175.4	6 010.7	3 132.3	8 555.2	10 775.0	6 218.6
New Zealand	33.6	27.0	1.3	21.2	43.1	.. d	287.4	338.7	351.4	208.6
Norway	313.2	35.1	140.4	-7.3	.. c	6.1	-242.9	631.0	874.0	98.1
Poland	15.3	5.4	11.6	17.6	41.7	547.0	642.4	920.7	727.5	901.4
Portugal	186.4	129.6	47.6	28.8	44.6	74.9	4.0	172.5	234.6	369.7
Slovak Republic	10.7	-	-	0.1	10.2	65.7	41.8	81.1	60.9	121.6
Slovenia	-	-	-	-0.1	0.5	22.9	18.9	15.5	19.1	40.4
Spain	3 217.7	3 052.6	3 251.4	6 846.2	1 759.9	1 341.5	1 450.7	1 813.0	2 147.8	2 094.3
Sweden	999.2	743.6	1 220.7	798.6	880.2	3 107.7	3 263.2	1 746.1	.. c	.. c
Switzerland	2 158.9	2 731.4	5 923.3	6 541.3	5 089.1	3 749.4	3 824.6	2 472.3	4 098.4	3 484.6
Turkey	7.6	8.1	7.7	37.1	28.1	22.9	6.7	197.0	385.7	211.7
United Kingdom	-	-	-	-	-	-	-	-	-	-
United States	27 862.5	25 295.5	26 149.9	30 481.6	27 265.1	17 746.4	3 456.1	14 439.9	22 374.4	23 140.7
EUROPE	**33 566.1**	**29 561.4**	**28 839.8**	**47 740.0**	**30 611.5**	**33 760.1**	**33 303.6**	**41 867.1**	**52 586.0**	**44 293.7**
Bulgaria	-1.5	4.0	-1.3	1.5	13.6	22.9	9.4	14.2	-3.1	23.9
Croatia	-	-	.. c	0.0	0.4	47.4	36.4	-5.2	.. d	.. d
Cyprus	433.9	465.6	479.0	.. c	244.8	10.7	-29.7	.. c	.. c	.. c
Malta	3.1	33.7	142.9	93.3	89.1	.. c	202.4	-33.5	-64.2	23.0
Romania	1.5	-	.. d	0.1	-0.2	195.6	222.7	95.3	124.9	128.5
Russian Federation	.. c	-63.4	-18.0	118.9	.. c	1 816.7	1 047.2	1 035.3	.. c	.. c
Ukraine	-	5.4	5.2	0.8	1.3	-35.1	.. c	-12.9	69.0	111.3
AFRICA	**129.9**	**58.0**	**-240.8**	**-114.8**	**15.8**	**1 969.4**	**3 757.1**	**4 222.3**	**8 267.1**	**4 051.8**
Northern Africa	.. c	6.7	5.2	1.6	.. d	-554.6	.. d	.. d	.. d	.. d
Algeria	.. c	-	.. c	0.0	.. c	38.2	.. c	.. c	.. c	.. c
Egypt	1.5	2.7	1.3	0.9	1.2	33.6	-36.4	-197.0	142.6	-505.1
Libya	.. c	5.4	.. c	-	-	.. c	1.4	-	1.3	-2.2
Morocco	-	-	-	0.7	0.4	-10.7	-67.5	1.3	-6.5	-18.1
Tunisia	-	-	.. c	-	-	.. d	-1.4	-3.9	-1.3	-1.0
Other African countries	.. d	51.3	-245.9	-116.4	.. d	2 525.6	.. d	.. d	.. d	.. d
Nigeria	.. c	48.6	.. c	27.9	.. c	.. c	237.5	339.9	418.1	440.2
South Africa	79.5	-39.1	-279.4	-188.0	-104.5	2 635.6	2 261.8	2 868.9	3 607.5	677.1
AMERICA	**32 861.7**	**33 415.7**	**27 531.5**	**38 935.3**	**34 246.1**	**25 642.5**	**11 785.4**	**21 917.3**	**31 626.2**	**27 835.2**
Northern America	28 334.6	26 798.9	25 825.4	.. d	.. d	.. d	6 059.4	.. d	24 241.6	25 249.9
Central America and Caribbean countries	4 510.3	6 596.5	1 702.3	.. d	5 701.6	6 279.6	4 835.4	4 026.5	6 379.3	1 571.6
Bahamas	22.9	17.5	36.1	285.1	73.4	181.8	101.2	.. c	83.2	79.4
Bermuda	1 650.1	1 966.3	355.4	1 589.3	1 116.6	.. c	1 071.5	.. c	2 769.9	335.9
Cayman Islands	951.9	1 496.6	-21.9	1 878.1	1 655.4	2 562.3	1 504.7	1 568.4	-140.2	-381.8
Costa Rica	-	-1.4	-	-0.4	0.4	.. c	13.5	.. c	-19.6	.. c
El Salvador	-	-	-	-	-	-	-	-1.3	0.3	1.1
Guatemala	162.0	95.8	81.1	18.0	62.0	16.8	-5.4	18.0	11.4	20.2
Honduras	-	-	-	-	-	.. c	-2.7	2.6	1.8	.. c
Nicaragua	-	-	-	-	-	-6.1	-2.7	1.3	0.1	-0.1
Panama	-12.2	33.7	-25.8	-45.3	15.2	272.0	242.9	3.9	.. c	31.2
Virgin Islands, U.S.	.. c	-	.. c	8.7	.. c	-	1.4	-2.6	0.1	0.9
South America	15.3	18.9	5.2	.. c	.. c	.. d	889.3	.. d	1 005.2	1 013.7
Argentina	.. d	-	-	0.3	0.9	686.0	.. d	.. d	.. d	174.1
Bolivia	-	-	-	-	-	-	-	-	1.1	2.9
Brazil	10.7	12.1	-2.6	.. c	.. c	1 417.9	51.3	571.7	390.0	774.9
Colombia	-	-	.. c	0.4	-0.5	-27.5	1.4	9.0	67.0	17.9
Ecuador	.. c	-	.. c	-	-	6.1	5.4	5.2	0.9	2.5
Paraguay	-	-	.. c	-	-	15.3	.. d	1.3	.. d	4.6
Peru	-	-	-	-0.1	0.1	74.9	79.6	86.3	61.8	60.4
Uruguay	-	-	-	-	-	-33.6	20.2	10.3	5.1	-4.1
Venezuela	-	-	-	-	-	.. c	9.4	42.5	-88.1	.. c

Table 3. Foreign direct investment income by country *(cont.)*

Million US dollars

	Inward					Outward				
	2015	2016	2017	2018	2019	2015	2016	2017	2018	2019
ASIA	**7 417.9**	**7 450.7**	**13 230.7**	**10 611.1**	**5 795.4**	**22 071.8**	**16 130.9**	**21 202.7**	**26 546.4**	**21 880.4**
Near and Middle East	1 318.6	187.6	206.0	1 729.9	596.9	2 495.0	1 673.4	3 423.9	4 345.6	4 725.7
Gulf Arabian countries	1 277.3	161.9	172.5	400.4	566.5	.. d	1 305.0	2 428.5	3 069.4	4 015.2
Kuwait	.. c	-5.4	1.3	11.3	19.6	.. c	.. c	.. c	.. c	.. c
Qatar	6.1	1.4	-2.6	.. c	.. c	33.6	33.7	.. c	16.8	.. c
Saudi Arabia	-	-2.7	-3.9	-2.4	18.9	829.6	686.9	913.0	687.7	953.8
United Arab Emirates	1 252.9	148.4	161.0	.. c	283.8	490.5	377.9	.. c	1 683.6	737.5
Other Near and Middle East	42.8	25.6	33.5	1 329.5	30.4	.. c	368.4	995.4	1 276.2	710.4
Jordan	.. c	.. d	1.3	9.7	.. d	16.8	.. d	3.9	0.3	3.7
Other Asian countries	6 099.3	7 263.2	13 026.0	8 881.2	5 198.5	19 576.8	14 457.5	17 780.1	22 200.8	17 154.8
China	64.2	5.4	-56.7	-265.7	67.5	1 819.7	2 615.4	2 017.8	2 473.0	847.7
Hong Kong, China	2 429.3	2 129.6	.. c	1 615.4	1 771.4	7 793.7	4 365.7	8 338.9	7 429.6	6 354.3
India	226.1	558.7	2 146.5	-124.0	12.7	2 395.7	1 523.6	1 276.1	1 624.8	2 261.0
Indonesia	.. c	.. c	.. c	9.4	0.2	635.6	885.3	256.2	2 255.3	825.0
Iran, Islamic Republic of	-	1.4	.. c	1.4	10.1	.. c	.. c	-	0.1	1.2
Malaysia	30.6	-141.7	20.6	9.7	59.5	1 544.7	697.7	1 198.8	963.3	648.8
Philippines	.. c	.. d	5.2	5.4	7.5	.. d	207.8	153.2	187.9	167.1
Singapore	741.0	542.5	391.5	407.9	-15.9	1 954.2	310.4	834.4	2 185.7	2 651.6
Chinese Taipei	7.6	6.7	6.4	2.6	12.2	382.0	345.5	358.0	301.6	335.9
Thailand	.. c	8.1	6.4	6.6	36.6	310.2	276.7	381.1	398.9	105.1
Viet Nam	-	.. c	-	0.0	0.1	294.9	233.5	279.4	245.4	181.1
AUSTRALIA, OCEANIA AND POLAR REGIONS	**-395.7**	**-211.9**	**-1 880.0**	**-249.1**	**-32.6**	**3 940.4**	**3 028.3**	**6 712.6**	**6 433.8**	**2 884.0**
WORLD unallocated and confidential	**-**	**-**	**-**	**0.0**	**..**	**-**	**-**	**1.3**	**0.0**	**..**
European Union (EU28)	**27 903.7**	**22 259.1**	**19 488.8**	**38 983.1**	**23 367.7**	**25 457.6**	**26 484.5**	**34 195.2**	**39 530.9**	**31 805.8**
G20 countries excl. European Union	**.. d**	**.. d**	**.. d**	**.. d**	**.. d**	**.. d**	**.. d**	**.. d**	**.. d**	**.. d**
G20 OECD countries	**41 411.8**	**37 664.0**	**39 983.3**	**.. d**	**.. d**	**.. d**	**18 253.7**	**.. d**	**41 903.5**	**36 274.6**
G20 Non-OECD countries	**.. d**	**.. d**	**.. d**	**.. d**	**.. d**	**12 236.8**	**.. d**	**.. d**	**.. d**	**.. d**
MENA countries	**.. d**	**.. d**	**.. d**	**.. d**	**.. d**	**.. d**	**.. d**	**.. d**	**.. d**	**.. d**
ASEAN countries	**864.8**	**201.1**	**445.5**	**439.3**	**88.4**	**4 968.7**	**2 637.0**	**3 145.8**	**.. d**	**4 822.7**

- Nil; .. Not available; c Confidential data; d Secondary Confidentiality

Note: Detailed metadata at: *http://stats.oecd.org/OECDStat_Metadata/ShowMetadata.ashx?Dataset=FDI_CTRY_IND_SUMM.*

Source: *OECD International Direct Investment Statistics (database): https://doi.org/10.1787/idi-data-en*

UNITED KINGDOM

Table 4. Foreign direct investment flows by industrial sector

Million US dollars

	Inward					Outward				
	2015	2016	2017	2018	2019	2015	2016	2017	2018	2019
All FDI activities	**38 669.2**	**196 503.4**	**78 511.5**	**65 450.8**	**49 898.6**	**-65 561.5**	**-22 310.4**	**106 692.0**	**41 491.7**	**-35 355.4**
Agriculture, forestry and fishing	**.. d**	**.. d**	..	**130.2**	..	**155.8**	**.. d**	..	**.. d**	..
Mining and quarrying	**.. c**	**-5 006.7**	..	**.. c**	..	**-55 168.8**	**-10 352.2**	..	**-13 086.4**	..
Extraction activities	.. c	-5 363.0	..	.. c	..	-31 489.7	-7 040.5	..	-18 271.1	..
Manufacturing	**4 058.1**	**.. c**	..	**3 368.9**	..	**-2 756.3**	**-19 759.8**	..	**-12 568.4**	..
of which:										
Food products, beverages and tobacco	913.7	.. c	..	.. d	..	-2 273.5	.. c	..	3 274.1	..
Textiles, wood and paper products; printing	631.0	-1 206.5	..	669.5	..	297.9	676.1	..	386.4	..
Chemical, rubber, plastic, non-metallic mineral products	-753.2	4 753.0	..	2 308.1	..	621.8	-20 716.6	..	-17 124.5	..
Metal and machinery products, except electrical equipment	4 890.8	-3 666.7	..	405.6	..	-293.4	-20.2	..	-1 527.5	..
Motor vehicles, trailers, semi-trailers, other transport equipment	2 942.7	190.3	..	1 125.6	..	.. c	.. c	..	1 262.9	..
Other manufacturing	-4 568.4	.. c	..	.. c	..	.. d	-744.9	..	1 160.3	..
Electricity, gas, steam and air conditioning supply	**2 145.1**	**948.7**	..	**.. c**	..	**-499.6**	**2 480.4**	..	**2 096.0**	..
Water supply; sewerage, waste management and remediation activities	**762.4**	**155.2**	..	**-35.7**	..	**.. c**	**232.1**	..	**290.7**	..
Construction	**1 509.5**	**632.9**	..	**973.7**	..	**-32.1**	**228.1**	..	**308.9**	..
Services	**59 229.9**	**90 098.5**	..	**86 937.1**	..	**.. c**	**4 178.1**	..	**62 733.2**	..
Wholesale and retail trade; repair of motor vehicles and motorcycles	-5 778.5	-776.0	..	-738.7	..	-5 064.9	2 920.4	..	11 489.0	..
Transportation and storage	5 110.8	4 045.9	..	7 344.2	..	1 951.1	2 446.7	..	-312.4	..
Accommodation and food service activities	2 187.9	556.0	..	-4 422.2	..	4 288.8	3 863.7	..	3 311.0	..
Information and communication	11 618.0	6 530.4	..	50 533.2	..	-2 939.6	-2 383.3	..	3 872.4	..
Financial and insurance activities	33 865.5	33 583.0	..	10 691.9	..	-12 719.6	-2 970.3	..	38 088.7	..
Activities of holding companies	.. c	2 979.8	..	3 495.6	..	.. c	4 287.4	..	10 151.3	..
Real estate activities	.. c	691.0	..	1 380.9	..	2 019.9	.. c	..	-163.9	..
Professional, scientific and technical activities	11 020.6	40 257.8	..	7 963.9	..	.. c	1 052.6	..	5 146.8	..
Administrative and support service activities	-1 709.7	5 153.8	..	16 491.2	..	935.1	414.3	..	765.7	..
Public administration; activities of households and of extraterritorial organisations	.. d	-5.4	..	-0.6	..	.. c	.. c	..	-6.0	..
Education	-162.0	16.2	..	-358.1	..	.. c	577.6	..	385.4	..
Human health and social work activities	759.4	36.4	..	-1 489.9	..	59.6	.. c	..	-311.2	..
Arts, entertainment and recreation	22.9	484.5	..	-728.6	..	90.1	-17.5	..	456.2	..
Other services	13.8	-477.7	..	269.9	..	29.0	-18.9	..	11.4	..
Not allocated and confidential	**.. c**	**.. c**	**78 511.5**	**.. c**	..	**.. c**	**.. d**	**106 692.0**	**.. d**	..
Private real estate activities	-	**975.7**	..	**500.2**	..	**.. c**	**354.9**	..	**1 635.3**	..

- Nil; .. Not available; c Confidential data; d Secondary Confidentiality

Note: Detailed metadata at: *http://stats.oecd.org/OECDStat_Metadata/ShowMetadata.ashx?Dataset=FDI_CTRY_IND_SUMM.*

Source: *OECD International Direct Investment Statistics (database): https://doi.org/10.1787/idi-data-en*

UNITED KINGDOM

Table 5. Foreign direct investment positions by industrial sector

At year end

Million US dollars

	Inward					Outward				
	2015	2016	2017	2018	2019	2015	2016	2017	2018	2019
All FDI activities	**1 530 133.4**	**1 475 523.4**	**1 608 032.7**	**1 930 434.0**	**1 974 480.5**	**1 606 364.8**	**1 491 940.0**	**1 624 231.9**	**1 788 397.1**	**1 901 117.2**
Agriculture, forestry and fishing	**.. d**	**1 264.6**	..	**1 454.6**	..	**2 110.3**	**2 510.8**	..	**2 720.2**	..
Mining and quarrying	**119 963.0**	**132 329.9**	..	**79 600.3**	..	**253 109.1**	**202 806.0**	..	**182 543.9**	..
Extraction activities	118 995.3	130 880.8	..	78 890.1	..	249 428.0	212 398.8	..	178 582.0	..
Manufacturing	**276 431.5**	**334 730.0**	..	**323 151.7**	..	**278 878.2**	**258 536.1**	..	**295 432.4**	..
of which:										
Food products, beverages and tobacco	68 039.4	157 723.0	..	102 220.7	..	80 726.1	75 635.4	..	94 239.3	..
Textiles, wood and paper products; printing	11 218.1	6 014.3	..	4 970.2	..	1 132.2	3 001.6	..	3 234.9	..
Chemical, rubber, plastic, non-metallic mineral products	53 703.3	49 282.8	..	73 299.2	..	102 458.5	94 373.2	..	128 904.7	..
Metal and machinery products, except electrical equipment	68 149.1	54 824.7	..	59 513.6	..	26 689.4	22 262.3	..	26 439.1	..
Motor vehicles, trailers, semi-trailers, other transport equipment	22 302.9	18 538.6	..	39 036.6	..	21 032.9	18 020.7	..	20 014.2	..
Other manufacturing	53 020.2	48 346.7	..	44 111.5	..	46 840.5	45 243.0	..	22 600.2	..
Electricity, gas, steam and air conditioning supply	**66 665.7**	**54 853.0**	..	**60 078.9**	..	**.. c**	**.. c**	..	**23 358.1**	..
Water supply; sewerage, waste management and remediation activities	**4 198.3**	**3 333.7**	..	**5 264.0**	..	**.. c**	**1 987.9**	..	**4 801.7**	..
Construction	**11 510.1**	**11 789.9**	..	**12 460.8**	..	**2 036.2**	**1 732.1**	..	**.. c**	..
Services	**1 030 195.6**	**919 501.8**	..	**1 428 676.4**	..	**923 218.7**	**875 655.1**	..	**1 104 195.5**	..
Wholesale and retail trade; repair of motor vehicles and motorcycles	185 336.4	149 114.3	..	159 073.2	..	65 988.4	60 396.1	..	106 366.3	..
Transportation and storage	57 025.8	59 575.6	..	91 741.7	..	28 163.9	28 931.0	..	23 489.2	..
Accommodation and food service activities	28 366.9	26 292.3	..	150 487.7	..	39 589.5	34 191.2	..	41 514.7	..
Information and communication	127 621.5	98 525.0	..	178 615.1	..	163 784.8	151 643.5	..	152 071.2	..
Financial and insurance activities	477 211.0	443 907.0	..	556 534.0	..	526 796.1	518 002.2	..	641 559.4	..
Activities of holding companies	514.2	16.0	..	.. c	..	.. c	147 121.4	..	171 924.7	..
Real estate activities	8 867.8	7 582.7	..	9 964.9	..	9 930.4	12 874.9	..	13 873.5	..
Professional, scientific and technical activities	94 248.7	87 481.9	..	193 580.1	..	49 832.5	45 967.5	..	85 824.6	..
Administrative and support service activities	41 273.0	36 081.9	..	57 224.4	..	29 548.0	18 024.4	..	30 772.2	..
Public administration; activities of households and of extraterritorial organisations	3.0	1.2	..	4.4	..	.. d	.. c	..	-2 050.1	..
Education	1 892.4	2 409.9	..	3 089.9	..	.. c	5 345.1	..	1 284.0	..
Human health and social work activities	2 249.6	1 675.5	..	5 068.2	..	280.1	654.4	..	3 696.8	..
Arts, entertainment and recreation	4 813.3	5 553.0	..	20 959.9	..	3 681.1	1 614.0	..	5 490.6	..
Other services	1 286.3	1 301.5	..	2 333.1	..	238.6	.. d	..	303.2	..
Not allocated and confidential	**.. c**	**-**	**1 608 032.7**	**0.0**	..	**.. c**	**.. c**	**1 624 231.9**	**.. c**	..
Private real estate activities	**.. c**	**17 720.5**	..	**19 747.4**	..	**.. c**	**130 103.3**	..	**154 386.2**	..

- Nil; .. Not available; c Confidential data; d Secondary Confidentiality

Note: Detailed metadata at: *http://stats.oecd.org/OECDStat_Metadata/ShowMetadata.ashx?Dataset=FDI_CTRY_IND_SUMM.*

Source: *OECD International Direct Investment Statistics (database): https://doi.org/10.1787/idi-data-en*

Table 6. Foreign direct investment income by industrial sector

Million US dollars

	Inward					Outward				
	2015	2016	2017	2018	2019	2015	2016	2017	2018	2019
All FDI activities	**73 579.8**	**70 274.0**	**67 481.3**	**96 922.4**	**70 636.2**	**87 384.3**	**68 005.4**	**95 923.3**	**125 459.4**	**100 945.2**
Agriculture, forestry and fishing	**.. d**	**44.5**	..	**119.5**	..	**162.0**	**.. d**	..	**114.7**	..
Mining and quarrying	**1 943.5**	**.. c**	..	**2 384.4**	..	**342.2**	**940.6**	..	**24 738.5**	..
Extraction activities	1 922.1	.. c	..	2 356.8	..	4 837.3	-2 183.5	..	16 909.1	..
Manufacturing	**12 991.6**	**13 948.7**	..	**15 852.1**	..	**29 524.8**	**21 915.0**	..	**28 222.8**	..
of which:										
Food products, beverages and tobacco	2 866.3	2 179.5	..	3 115.2	..	9 538.6	5 726.0	..	11 141.9	..
Textiles, wood and paper products; printing	485.9	539.8	..	747.3	..	470.6	847.5	..	486.6	..
Chemical, rubber, plastic, non-metallic mineral products	3 252.9	3 040.5	..	4 327.7	..	13 214.7	10 425.1	..	9 998.8	..
Metal and machinery products, except electrical equipment	1 949.6	1 851.6	..	4 169.5	..	2 129.9	1 893.4	..	2 557.1	..
Motor vehicles, trailers, semi-trailers, other transport equipment	3 223.8	2 913.6	..	2 412.9	..	2 328.5	2 164.6	..	2 758.7	..
Other manufacturing	1 213.1	3 422.4	..	1 079.6	..	1 841.1	857.0	..	1 279.7	..
Electricity, gas, steam and air conditioning supply	**4 909.1**	**4 485.8**	..	**3 366.0**	..	**.. c**	**1 290.1**	..	**.. c**	..
Water supply; sewerage, waste management and remediation activities	**357.5**	**.. c**	..	**41.5**	..	**137.5**	**230.8**	..	**166.1**	..
Construction	**628.0**	**-570.9**	..	**722.1**	..	**201.7**	**256.4**	..	**.. c**	..
Services	**52 531.7**	**50 503.4**	..	**74 266.0**	..	**53 902.2**	**41 396.8**	..	**68 686.5**	..
Wholesale and retail trade; repair of motor vehicles and motorcycles	9 196.3	9 179.5	..	13 605.5	..	1 861.0	3 870.4	..	6 676.4	..
Transportation and storage	5 778.5	5 427.8	..	8 626.9	..	965.6	1 021.6	..	1 801.8	..
Accommodation and food service activities	698.2	.. c	..	.. c	..	7 398.0	6 897.4	..	7 991.4	..
Information and communication	7 356.8	2 956.8	..	8 050.7	..	5 398.0	4 124.2	..	4 511.4	..
Financial and insurance activities	29 288.0	28 310.4	..	35 366.2	..	30 583.7	19 581.6	..	39 138.4	..
Activities of holding companies	.. c	2 558.7	..	3 262.9	..	.. c	5 160.6	..	12 696.1	..
Real estate activities	363.6	193.0	..	157.4	..	1 081.7	689.6	..	571.5	..
Professional, scientific and technical activities	-1 469.8	4 106.6	..	6 779.5	..	3 931.2	2 522.3	..	4 807.7	..
Administrative and support service activities	1 359.8	1 336.0	..	3 808.1	..	1 323.1	1 442.6	..	1 795.5	..
Public administration; activities of households and of extraterritorial organisations	-	.. d	..	.. d	..	.. c	.. c	..	.. c	..
Education	-59.6	-64.8	..	-137.6	..	.. c	630.2	..	297.2	..
Human health and social work activities	58.1	8.1	..	-1 442.9	..	-10.7	-1.4	..	-102.5	..
Arts, entertainment and recreation	-77.9	20.2	..	666.4	..	302.5	161.9	..	406.1	..
Other services	39.7	78.3	..	-188.1	..	27.5	.. d	..	.. d	..
Not allocated and confidential	**.. c**	**.. c**	**67 481.3**	**0.0**	..	**.. c**	**.. d**	**95 923.3**	**.. c**	..
Private real estate activities	**.. c**	**147.1**	..	**170.7**	..	**.. c**	**1 662.6**	..	**1 678.0**	..

- Nil; .. Not available; c Confidential data; d Secondary Confidentiality

Note: Detailed metadata at: *http://stats.oecd.org/OECDStat_Metadata/ShowMetadata.ashx?Dataset=FDI_CTRY_IND_SUMM.*

Source: *OECD International Direct Investment Statistics (database): https://doi.org/10.1787/idi-data-en*

UNITED STATES

Table 1. Foreign direct investment flows by country

Million US dollars

	Inward					Outward				
	2015	2016	2017	2018	2019	2015	2016	2017	2018	2019
WORLD	**467 625.0**	**459 419.0**	**295 296.0**	**223 401.0**	**261 412.0**	**264 359.0**	**284 469.0**	**327 781.0**	**-194 412.0**	**93 552.0**
OECD COUNTRIES	..	..	..	..	..	**181 055.0**	..	..	..	..
Australia	10 587.0	5 660.0	-1 579.0	3 113.0	16 196.0	271.0	6 987.0	-621.0	-3 048.0	258.0
Austria	198.0	3 496.0	2 386.0	-1 570.0	1 607.0	92.0	906.0	946.0	481.0	1 009.0
Belgium	-12 327.0	186.0	-999.0	1 264.0	3 115.0	3 014.0	2 727.0	1 481.0	9 552.0	3 746.0
Canada	58 887.0	65 140.0	83 657.0	39 115.0	36 489.0	10 114.0	12 589.0	16 356.0	17 752.0	29 889.0
Chile	158.0	116.0	7.0	219.0	208.0	1 450.0	287.0	-1 546.0	689.0	-60.0
Czech Republic	30.0	-1.0	18.0	-39.0	38.0	433.0	-262.0	243.0	1 169.0	123.0
Denmark	1 013.0	3 986.0	306.0	1 892.0	2 943.0	-122.0	2 225.0	-222.0	-1 783.0	-259.0
Estonia	-	-	.. c	1.0	.. c	-2.0	-79.0	8.0	15.0	9.0
Finland	655.0	-73.0	775.0	1 556.0	361.0	-1 322.0	2 196.0	-621.0	-472.0	757.0
France	33 472.0	28 553.0	15 862.0	3 791.0	7 702.0	4 156.0	357.0	3 708.0	1 862.0	3 549.0
Germany	25 353.0	15 637.0	18 727.0	28 346.0	42 052.0	1 691.0	3 407.0	4 025.0	6 040.0	14 423.0
Greece	35.0	44.0	-32.0	-214.0	-60.0	1 054.0	40.0	80.0	112.0	-209.0
Hungary	-5 312.0	4 166.0	3 279.0	9 026.0	1 661.0	163.0	-604.0	541.0	1 382.0	-319.0
Iceland	.. c	.. c	-60.0	-38.0	.. c	131.0	.. c	67.0	.. c	9.0
Ireland	14 892.0	8 645.0	24 578.0	60 388.0	-1 816.0	69 631.0	49 963.0	47 842.0	-36 161.0	-73 956.0
Israel	952.0	90.0	-100.0	1 871.0	552.0	553.0	683.0	1 235.0	828.0	378.0
Italy	6 924.0	737.0	247.0	1 526.0	1 012.0	800.0	298.0	388.0	7 138.0	411.0
Japan	32 997.0	33 732.0	42 890.0	18 715.0	38 526.0	5 177.0	-2 911.0	9 094.0	1 919.0	6 046.0
Korea	1 302.0	3 699.0	13 348.0	1 868.0	5 339.0	2 225.0	2 022.0	668.0	-1 699.0	1 413.0
Latvia	.. c	-	-	.. c	.. c	8.0	11.0	10.0	8.0	7.0
Lithuania	.. c	.. c	.. c	.. c	.. c	-34.0	4.0	16.0	18.0	-7.0
Luxembourg	172 740.0	49 203.0	24 482.0	-119 464.0	5 578.0	-365.0	31 153.0	39 283.0	32 823.0	12 195.0
Mexico	1 116.0	2 900.0	3 191.0	-117.0	256.0	7 255.0	5 837.0	5 907.0	5 998.0	4 507.0
Netherlands	33 318.0	43 143.0	21 738.0	83 097.0	13 093.0	41 337.0	33 363.0	22 491.0	-67 749.0	5 497.0
New Zealand	-317.0	-233.0	104.0	458.0	250.0	145.0	468.0	469.0	-156.0	186.0
Norway	8 130.0	-1 097.0	1 056.0	.. c	2 070.0	-235.0	-151.0	34.0	155.0	-3 592.0
Poland	-6.0	170.0	446.0	147.0	255.0	72.0	861.0	463.0	1 832.0	-228.0
Portugal	6.0	-5.0	45.0	-128.0	43.0	15.0	402.0	120.0	216.0	-48.0
Slovak Republic	.. c	2.0	.. c	4.0	-24.0	49.0	-280.0	289.0	-8.0	90.0
Slovenia	-	.. c	.. c	8.0	-1.0	18.0	16.0	8.0	-3.0	-19.0
Spain	4 956.0	2 546.0	4 343.0	5 927.0	3 159.0	1 387.0	206.0	417.0	152.0	3 375.0
Sweden	3 685.0	4 610.0	509.0	679.0	2 801.0	50.0	1 908.0	3 141.0	6 433.0	-2 694.0
Switzerland	-5 732.0	46 595.0	-3 539.0	27 754.0	11 316.0	17 059.0	18 818.0	35 815.0	-3 972.0	13 723.0
Turkey	46.0	266.0	362.0	256.0	166.0	333.0	379.0	506.0	767.0	101.0
United Kingdom	50 294.0	88 081.0	29 235.0	3 798.0	23 234.0	14 426.0	42 027.0	24 590.0	8 151.0	32 010.0
United States	-	-	-	-	-	-	-	-	-	-
EUROPE	**338 653.0**	**.. c**	**.. c**	**.. c**	**.. c**	**.. c**	**.. c**	**.. c**	**.. c**	**.. c**
Bulgaria	.. c	-45.0	.. c	.. c	.. c	49.0	33.0	26.0	50.0	34.0
Croatia	.. c	.. c	.. c	.. c	.. c	-89.0	10.0	30.0	-12.0	14.0
Cyprus	151.0	-607.0	-1 346.0	-99.0	-222.0	-69.0	-709.0	-524.0	-346.0	-136.0
Malta	-257.0	601.0	340.0	-33.0	-43.0	61.0	-14.0	66.0	-70.0	-28.0
Romania	25.0	.. c	-48.0	-46.0	-41.0	251.0	100.0	-219.0	-111.0	77.0
Russian Federation	-376.0	102.0	-85.0	121.0	-81.0	539.0	1 470.0	-1 149.0	1 568.0	-244.0
Ukraine	.. c	-2.0	7.0	-14.0	3.0	17.0	5.0	-54.0	18.0	185.0
AFRICA	**1 853.0**	**-48.0**	**1 488.0**	**246.0**	**4 151.0**	**829.0**	**-2 660.0**	**534.0**	**-1 800.0**	**-2 395.0**
Northern Africa	.. c	.. c	.. c	.. c	.. c	176.0	-1 524.0	.. c	.. c	-5.0
Algeria	.. c	-3.0	.. c	.. c	.. c	15.0	-673.0	-105.0	-169.0	-211.0
Egypt	8.0	-39.0	99.0	-23.0	44.0	325.0	-465.0	-525.0	-517.0	152.0
Libya	.. c	.. c	.. c	.. c	-	-112.0	-332.0	.. c	.. c	59.0
Morocco	.. c	.. c	.. c	-2.0	1.0	-10.0	-74.0	-6.0	.. c	-19.0
Tunisia	1.0	-1.0	4.0	15.0	1.0	-42.0	20.0	-23.0	-7.0	14.0
Other African countries	.. c	.. c	.. c	.. c	.. c	653.0	-1 136.0	.. c	.. c	-2 390.0
Nigeria	5.0	23.0	9.0	30.0	25.0	1 094.0	-156.0	1 354.0	-291.0	974.0
South Africa	1 893.0	88.0	1 132.0	23.0	33.0	-205.0	-86.0	429.0	56.0	525.0
AMERICA	**70 515.0**	**95 795.0**	**90 674.0**	**.. c**	**.. c**	**62 030.0**	**71 334.0**	**91 495.0**	**-129 195.0**	**34 825.0**
Northern America	58 887.0	65 140.0	83 657.0	.. c	.. c	10 113.0	12 588.0	16 355.0	17 751.0	29 888.0
Central America and Caribbean countries	.. c	.. c	.. c	.. c	.. c	50 016.0	56 355.0	75 718.0	-143 213.0	-183.0
Bahamas	-128.0	-460.0	94.0	186.0	442.0	-4 178.0	1 163.0	-37.0	-11 022.0	587.0
Bermuda	-933.0	23 222.0	-1 384.0	30 358.0	21 523.0	25 106.0	32 795.0	42 588.0	-149 922.0	-32 554.0
Cayman Islands	11 574.0	3 082.0	1 667.0	4 903.0	5 647.0	20 608.0	9 497.0	24 604.0	8 688.0	21 252.0
Costa Rica	20.0	82.0	-134.0	-74.0	31.0	70.0	51.0	197.0	295.0	-108.0
El Salvador	6.0	2.0	10.0	.. c	10.0	-288.0	325.0	15.0	-41.0	550.0
Guatemala	6.0	17.0	-1.0	-8.0	17.0	-49.0	-353.0	30.0	68.0	17.0
Honduras	3.0	17.0	-26.0	-27.0	-5.0	425.0	9.0	24.0	-481.0	429.0
Nicaragua	.. c	.. c	1.0	-15.0	.. c	8.0	-35.0	-19.0	-43.0	-47.0
Panama	243.0	89.0	-317.0	323.0	129.0	-189.0	599.0	349.0	514.0	222.0
Virgin Islands, U.S.	..	..	..	..	..	..	..	..	..	..
South America	.. c	.. c	.. c	.. c	.. c	1 832.0	2 381.0	-574.0	-3 737.0	5 111.0
Argentina	-50.0	17.0	163.0	-207.0	-262.0	813.0	504.0	1 898.0	-3 792.0	1 531.0
Bolivia	.. c	.. c	.. c	.. c	.. c	14.0	95.0	61.0	36.0	81.0
Brazil	-750.0	-1 694.0	-80.0	1 666.0	2 210.0	448.0	3 336.0	2 351.0	-421.0	1 594.0
Colombia	169.0	75.0	-5.0	-14.0	38.0	770.0	-170.0	13.0	809.0	437.0
Ecuador	2.0	-5.0	31.0	7.0	9.0	-41.0	30.0	-202.0	52.0	-32.0
Paraguay	.. c	-	.. c	.. c	.. c	-9.0	.. c	.. c	.. c	.. c
Peru	-3.0	23.0	31.0	18.0	13.0	-477.0	-486.0	1 511.0	-372.0	1 705.0
Uruguay	-299.0	68.0	-194.0	457.0	141.0	9.0	-58.0	-226.0	-130.0	-13.0
Venezuela	224.0	369.0	17.0	783.0	179.0	-1 449.0	-1 295.0	-701.0	-982.0	-140.0

Table 1. Foreign direct investment flows by country *(cont.)*

Million US dollars

	Inward					Outward				
	2015	2016	2017	2018	2019	2015	2016	2017	2018	2019
ASIA	**.. c**	**.. c**	**.. c**	**.. c**	**.. c**	**.. c**	**.. c**	**.. c**	**.. c**	**.. c**
Near and Middle East	.. c	.. c	.. c	2 546.0	.. c	1 435.0	.. c	.. c	.. c	.. c
Gulf Arabian countries	.. c	569.0	.. c	867.0	.. c	973.0	.. c	.. c	.. c	.. c
Kuwait	41.0	17.0	23.0	172.0	-143.0	-56.0	18.0	.. c	101.0	-103.0
Qatar	.. c	178.0	254.0	.. c	.. c	502.0	700.0	1 237.0	.. c	99.0
Saudi Arabia	474.0	716.0	218.0	711.0	-707.0	1 322.0	744.0	519.0	225.0	-32.0
United Arab Emirates	129.0	-432.0	2 060.0	657.0	-34.0	-565.0	-2 335.0	3 386.0	952.0	-372.0
Other Near and Middle East	.. c	.. c	.. c	1 679.0	.. c	462.0	.. c	.. c	.. c	.. c
Jordan	.. c	-18.0	.. c	-197.0	.. c	11.0	.. c	.. c	-44.0	-6.0
Other Asian countries	.. c	.. c	.. c	.. c	.. c	.. c	25 299.0	.. c	.. c	.. c
China	5 127.0	18 004.0	2 746.0	1 590.0	4 260.0	6 029.0	8 468.0	7 943.0	6 228.0	7 454.0
Hong Kong, China	682.0	1 720.0	343.0	3 025.0	770.0	4 988.0	583.0	1 093.0	-819.0	2 786.0
India	298.0	-544.0	844.0	-692.0	62.0	3 820.0	4 854.0	3 623.0	704.0	3 932.0
Indonesia	173.0	-1 059.0	-234.0	26.0	49.0	176.0	-729.0	-861.0	-2 599.0	1 922.0
Iran, Islamic Republic of	-3.0	-	.. c	-	-	-	-	-	-	-
Malaysia	118.0	-172.0	-74.0	124.0	-278.0	2 054.0	-1 191.0	1 342.0	-248.0	-817.0
Philippines	145.0	-435.0	-48.0	-309.0	113.0	75.0	756.0	562.0	235.0	39.0
Singapore	2 660.0	491.0	-840.0	-61.0	2 917.0	21 390.0	10 095.0	23 369.0	-38 450.0	27 798.0
Chinese Taipei	760.0	668.0	401.0	2 451.0	577.0	751.0	548.0	680.0	214.0	276.0
Thailand	469.0	711.0	-771.0	-293.0	-186.0	200.0	1 772.0	1 041.0	1 150.0	1 186.0
Viet Nam	473.0	-1 123.0	-297.0	-61.0	-1.0	88.0	171.0	36.0	154.0	-198.0
AUSTRALIA, OCEANIA AND POLAR REGIONS	**.. c**	**.. c**	**.. c**	**.. c**	**.. c**	**620.0**	**7 570.0**	**.. c**	**.. c**	**.. c**
WORLD unallocated and confidential	**-1 035.0**	**3 033.0**	**326.0**	**4 709.0**	**319.0**	**-35.0**	**-8 062.0**	**3 265.0**	**368.0**	**-88.0**
European Union (EU28)	**329 844.0**	**253 064.0**	**144 947.0**	**79 931.0**	**106 519.0**	**136 756.0**	**170 266.0**	**148 625.0**	**-29 282.0**	**-575.0**
G20 countries excl. European Union	**227 767.0**	**260 035.0**	**210 644.0**	**103 649.0**	**176 536.0**	**59 390.0**	**89 553.0**	**79 374.0**	**46 849.0**	**109 289.0**
G20 OECD countries	**220 978.0**	**244 405.0**	**205 940.0**	**100 411.0**	**170 972.0**	**46 448.0**	**70 992.0**	**64 621.0**	**44 880.0**	**92 607.0**
G20 Non-OECD countries	**6 789.0**	**15 630.0**	**4 704.0**	**3 238.0**	**5 564.0**	**12 942.0**	**18 561.0**	**14 753.0**	**1 969.0**	**16 682.0**
MENA countries	**.. d**	**.. d**	**.. d**	**.. d**	**.. d**	**.. d**	**.. d**	**.. d**	**.. d**	**.. d**
ASEAN countries	**.. d**	**.. d**	**-2 258.0**	**.. d**	**.. d**	**23 996.0**	**.. d**	**25 503.0**	**.. d**	**.. d**

- Nil; .. Not available; c Confidential data; d Secondary Confidentiality

Note: Detailed metadata at: *http://stats.oecd.org/OECDStat_Metadata/ShowMetadata.ashx?Dataset=FDI_CTRY_IND_SUMM.*

Source: *OECD International Direct Investment Statistics (database): https://doi.org/10.1787/idi-data-en*

Table 2. Foreign direct investment positions by country

At year end

Million US dollars

	Inward					Outward				
	2015	2016	2017	2018	2019	2015	2016	2017	2018	2019
WORLD	**3 354 907.0**	**3 561 808.0**	**3 786 848.0**	**4 127 175.0**	**4 458 362.0**	**5 289 071.0**	**5 518 644.0**	**6 097 690.0**	**5 801 025.0**	**5 959 592.0**
OECD COUNTRIES	**.. d**	**..**	**..**	**..**	**..**	**.. d**	**..**	**..**	**..**	**..**
Australia	68 733.0	73 526.0	67 212.0	68 753.0	86 537.0	160 061.0	167 791.0	169 749.0	163 999.0	162 400.0
Austria	3 181.0	3 507.0	3 978.0	5 157.0	6 250.0	6 508.0	7 566.0	7 987.0	6 740.0	7 643.0
Belgium	47 192.0	76 496.0	62 529.0	65 754.0	70 073.0	48 096.0	49 692.0	53 645.0	61 271.0	63 157.0
Canada	394 814.0	422 956.0	478 986.0	533 910.0	580 752.0	361 954.0	355 394.0	371 274.0	368 498.0	402 255.0
Chile	2 394.0	2 545.0	2 445.0	3 047.0	3 431.0	28 134.0	28 141.0	25 793.0	25 986.0	25 084.0
Czech Republic	2.0	2.0	2.0	2.0	1.0	6 343.0	4 896.0	4 844.0	4 515.0	4 815.0
Denmark	14 534.0	18 375.0	19 221.0	20 302.0	23 541.0	15 794.0	16 909.0	12 107.0	9 498.0	8 992.0
Estonia	-5.0	-5.0	-5.0	-6.0	-6.0	160.0	72.0	74.0	82.0	68.0
Finland	8 750.0	8 203.0	8 816.0	9 912.0	9 947.0	1 258.0	2 538.0	2 513.0	3 268.0	3 745.0
France	255 524.0	264 026.0	283 794.0	295 395.0	310 743.0	81 274.0	72 926.0	78 632.0	68 035.0	83 826.0
Germany	356 982.0	347 963.0	387 997.0	482 608.0	521 979.0	120 519.0	129 985.0	132 595.0	137 148.0	148 259.0
Greece	978.0	1 055.0	1 226.0	1 162.0	1 122.0	1 007.0	1 017.0	1 198.0	1 399.0	938.0
Hungary	108.0	62.0	85.0	90.0	91.0	7 625.0	7 392.0	6 672.0	6 597.0	6 114.0
Iceland	.. c	.. c	72.0	.. c	.. c	.. c	.. c	.. c	.. c	824.0
Ireland	260 047.0	234 899.0	235 942.0	322 531.0	343 538.0	337 831.0	399 885.0	457 301.0	410 636.0	354 940.0
Israel	24 923.0	56 198.0	36 245.0	36 700.0	36 641.0	10 251.0	11 615.0	28 160.0	27 715.0	28 543.0
Italy	34 425.0	34 583.0	35 762.0	38 625.0	43 660.0	30 869.0	30 573.0	27 617.0	33 080.0	34 900.0
Japan	404 081.0	431 555.0	484 696.0	499 088.0	644 727.0	106 932.0	124 039.0	117 134.0	113 254.0	131 793.0
Korea	37 837.0	41 129.0	53 233.0	55 843.0	61 135.0	38 608.0	39 278.0	40 237.0	39 021.0	39 105.0
Latvia	-	-	-	.. c	.. c	39.0	69.0	38.0	38.0	38.0
Lithuania	-	-	-	-	-	109.0	131.0	157.0	176.0	171.0
Luxembourg	12 728.0	28 851.0	31 321.0	26 176.0	22 760.0	599 001.0	646 508.0	703 066.0	726 121.0	766 099.0
Mexico	34 390.0	34 967.0	39 068.0	42 621.0	42 902.0	101 326.0	98 421.0	100 169.0	95 873.0	100 888.0
Netherlands	165 597.0	169 633.0	184 386.0	253 112.0	290 429.0	829 693.0	816 667.0	929 746.0	810 238.0	860 528.0
New Zealand	509.0	356.0	1 148.0	2 183.0	2 619.0	11 427.0	12 042.0	12 384.0	11 667.0	12 018.0
Norway	29 477.0	25 848.0	23 747.0	24 450.0	22 765.0	31 697.0	28 657.0	26 901.0	26 145.0	25 556.0
Poland	.. c	.. c	.. c	.. c	.. c	11 872.0	11 260.0	12 266.0	11 744.0	10 403.0
Portugal	.. c	.. c	.. c	.. c	.. c	1 971.0	2 288.0	2 372.0	2 513.0	2 425.0
Slovak Republic	-1.0	-1.0	-1.0	-1.0	4.0	987.0	783.0	1 108.0	817.0	925.0
Slovenia	2.0	2.0	1.0	1.0	-	336.0	353.0	337.0	305.0	286.0
Spain	66 106.0	70 766.0	75 990.0	81 480.0	84 338.0	36 075.0	36 651.0	35 482.0	35 425.0	40 793.0
Sweden	48 137.0	53 132.0	54 936.0	55 171.0	61 316.0	32 593.0	34 722.0	36 896.0	41 024.0	38 787.0
Switzerland	143 403.0	158 672.0	159 168.0	202 043.0	224 368.0	171 342.0	185 329.0	252 231.0	253 253.0	228 968.0
Turkey	1 969.0	2 147.0	2 187.0	2 373.0	2 346.0	3 798.0	3 726.0	4 074.0	3 903.0	3 333.0
United Kingdom	558 931.0	587 407.0	587 618.0	527 839.0	446 179.0	632 327.0	747 425.0	815 059.0	796 564.0	851 414.0
United States	83 796.0	70 891.0	78 061.0	75 733.0	84 119.0	-	-	-	-	-
EUROPE	**2 023 546.0**	**2 099 970.0**	**2 173 102.0**	**2 434 284.0**	**2 505 977.0**	**.. c**	**.. c**	**.. c**	**.. c**	**.. c**
Bulgaria	.. c	5.0	.. c	.. c	.. c	684.0	691.0	639.0	719.0	756.0
Croatia	4.0	4.0	4.0	4.0	4.0	180.0	197.0	225.0	209.0	184.0
Cyprus	.. c	.. c	102.0	114.0	-117.0	2 583.0	4 903.0	4 340.0	5 004.0	4 853.0
Malta	7.0	8.0	11.0	55.0	51.0	504.0	547.0	597.0	626.0	579.0
Romania	1.0	-	-	-	-	3 774.0	3 956.0	3 761.0	3 490.0	3 466.0
Russian Federation	4 111.0	4 265.0	4 053.0	3 748.0	3 661.0	10 259.0	14 357.0	13 786.0	14 071.0	14 439.0
Ukraine	3.0	3.0	2.0	4.0	6.0	498.0	484.0	402.0	532.0	596.0
AFRICA	**4 470.0**	**4 484.0**	**5 705.0**	**5 925.0**	**6 014.0**	**52 004.0**	**49 926.0**	**50 403.0**	**44 378.0**	**43 193.0**
Northern Africa	-32.0	.. c	.. c	.. c	.. c	19 376.0	15 176.0	15 160.0	15 325.0	15 383.0
Algeria	-	-	-	-	-	2 698.0	2 697.0	2 567.0	2 978.0	2 749.0
Egypt	-16.0	-6.0	49.0	41.0	17.0	14 068.0	10 545.0	11 095.0	10 781.0	11 000.0
Libya	5.0	.. c	.. c	.. c	.. c	1 820.0	1 173.0	761.0	854.0	908.0
Morocco	-21.0	-21.0	-21.0	-22.0	-22.0	493.0	423.0	423.0	410.0	406.0
Tunisia	-	-	-	-	-	297.0	338.0	314.0	302.0	320.0
Other African countries	4 502.0	.. c	.. c	.. c	.. c	32 628.0	34 750.0	35 243.0	29 053.0	27 810.0
Nigeria	.. c	.. c	.. c	.. c	.. c	5 872.0	4 252.0	4 844.0	4 501.0	5 469.0
South Africa	3 934.0	3 880.0	4 960.0	5 151.0	5 179.0	6 926.0	7 398.0	8 058.0	7 313.0	7 812.0
AMERICA	**638 071.0**	**638 554.0**	**728 867.0**	**814 569.0**	**892 560.0**	**1 264 600.0**	**1 248 956.0**	**1 380 019.0**	**1 317 291.0**	**1 314 128.0**
Northern America	478 615.0	493 850.0	557 047.0	609 641.0	664 866.0	361 958.0	355 398.0	371 278.0	368 502.0	402 259.0
Central America and Caribbean countries	.. c	101 115.0	111 288.0	.. c	165 834.0	770 364.0	758 558.0	867 623.0	809 533.0	767 074.0
Bahamas	123.0	159.0	155.0	.. c	278.0	22 737.0	20 191.0	18 524.0	17 330.0	17 609.0
Bermuda	30 555.0	36 191.0	34 848.0	60 785.0	77 140.0	303 244.0	311 363.0	401 435.0	333 843.0	262 418.0
Cayman Islands	11 559.0	.. c	.. c	21 865.0	24 630.0	303 438.0	282 111.0	286 601.0	282 937.0	300 505.0
Costa Rica	.. c	.. c	.. c	79.0	77.0	1 642.0	1 335.0	1 546.0	1 597.0	1 521.0
El Salvador	.. c	.. c	.. c	.. c	.. c	2 576.0	2 777.0	2 754.0	2 830.0	3 380.0
Guatemala	15.0	15.0	15.0	15.0	15.0	1 098.0	737.0	748.0	733.0	746.0
Honduras	2.0	2.0	2.0	2.0	2.0	1 274.0	1 283.0	1 330.0	850.0	1 281.0
Nicaragua	.. c	.. c	.. c	.. c	.. c	256.0	216.0	189.0	138.0	82.0
Panama	658.0	728.0	749.0	823.0	899.0	4 447.0	4 472.0	4 821.0	5 075.0	5 272.0
Virgin Islands, U.S.	..	..	..	..	..	..	..	..	..	..
South America	.. c	43 589.0	60 532.0	.. c	61 860.0	131 775.0	134 485.0	140 609.0	138 740.0	144 266.0
Argentina	5 134.0	4 936.0	4 600.0	5 094.0	5 378.0	14 624.0	14 273.0	15 219.0	9 522.0	10 698.0
Bolivia	9.0	9.0	9.0	9.0	9.0	481.0	454.0	505.0	486.0	556.0
Brazil	43 662.0	31 266.0	48 482.0	45 010.0	45 273.0	56 847.0	67 922.0	77 486.0	79 032.0	81 731.0
Colombia	2 443.0	2 428.0	2 577.0	3 233.0	4 080.0	7 750.0	7 884.0	7 669.0	8 055.0	8 264.0
Ecuador	-23.0	-27.0	-27.0	-7.0	10.0	913.0	981.0	715.0	722.0	619.0
Paraguay	-	-	-	-	-	.. c	189.0	168.0	163.0	45.0
Peru	240.0	246.0	257.0	276.0	298.0	7 573.0	4 541.0	5 700.0	5 765.0	7 470.0
Uruguay	326.0	354.0	368.0	383.0	391.0	2 239.0	2 149.0	1 087.0	1 080.0	999.0
Venezuela	4 558.0	1 830.0	1 819.0	1 825.0	1 864.0	9 825.0	5 113.0	3 174.0	2 185.0	2 228.0

Table 2. Foreign direct investment positions by country *(cont.)*
At year end

Million US dollars

	Inward					Outward				
	2015	2016	2017	2018	2019	2015	2016	2017	2018	2019
ASIA	**.. c**	**.. c**	**.. c**	**.. c**	**.. c**	**.. c**	**.. c**	**.. c**	**.. c**	**.. c**
Near and Middle East	65 601.0	99 663.0	83 647.0	84 197.0	83 836.0	.. c	.. c	.. c	.. c	.. c
Gulf Arabian countries	40 412.0	43 108.0	46 980.0	.. c	.. c	.. c	.. c	.. c	.. c	46 074.0
Kuwait	808.0	1 704.0	1 739.0	1 913.0	1 820.0	342.0	345.0	407.0	499.0	398.0
Qatar	2 784.0	2 988.0	3 080.0	2 477.0	3 363.0	7 252.0	7 992.0	13 008.0	14 151.0	14 198.0
Saudi Arabia	11 497.0	12 953.0	14 980.0	14 697.0	13 242.0	10 025.0	10 164.0	10 702.0	10 884.0	10 826.0
United Arab Emirates	24 978.0	24 904.0	26 809.0	27 539.0	27 633.0	16 205.0	13 699.0	16 881.0	17 437.0	17 153.0
Other Near and Middle East	25 189.0	56 555.0	36 667.0	.. c	.. c	.. c	.. c	.. c	.. c	.. c
Jordan	.. c	.. c	.. c	.. c	.. c	224.0	199.0	220.0	180.0	179.0
Other Asian countries	.. c	.. c	.. c	.. c	.. c	.. c	.. c	.. c	.. c	.. c
China	33 050.0	54 393.0	54 710.0	55 489.0	59 043.0	92 150.0	97 458.0	105 146.0	109 332.0	116 203.0
Hong Kong, China	14 567.0	15 167.0	15 242.0	16 908.0	17 594.0	69 367.0	69 287.0	79 048.0	79 797.0	81 883.0
India	11 647.0	8 445.0	9 476.0	10 212.0	16 693.0	35 361.0	40 121.0	45 160.0	42 444.0	45 883.0
Indonesia	504.0	516.0	576.0	690.0	710.0	15 717.0	15 049.0	13 866.0	10 240.0	12 151.0
Iran, Islamic Republic of	1.0	1.0	1.0	1.0	1.0	2.0	2.0	2.0	2.0	2.0
Malaysia	1 307.0	1 483.0	1 466.0	2 442.0	1 050.0	15 765.0	10 069.0	11 767.0	10 867.0	10 849.0
Philippines	856.0	890.0	971.0	1 103.0	320.0	5 992.0	6 412.0	6 926.0	6 922.0	6 940.0
Singapore	38 573.0	77 885.0	92 355.0	58 399.0	60 138.0	253 277.0	243 165.0	293 452.0	254 670.0	287 951.0
Chinese Taipei	10 249.0	10 867.0	11 516.0	14 176.0	16 183.0	15 295.0	15 510.0	16 484.0	16 562.0	17 353.0
Thailand	514.0	2 132.0	2 145.0	2 052.0	1 684.0	17 942.0	18 386.0	15 578.0	16 952.0	17 738.0
Viet Nam	11.0	11.0	12.0	10.0	11.0	1 816.0	2 433.0	2 461.0	2 849.0	2 615.0
AUSTRALIA, OCEANIA AND POLAR REGIONS	**.. c**	**.. c**	**.. c**	**.. c**	**.. c**	**.. c**	**.. c**	**.. c**	**.. c**	**.. c**
WORLD unallocated and confidential	**689.0**	**771.0**	**753.0**	**776.0**	**712.0**	**20 854.0**	**20 749.0**	**25 553.0**	**23 103.0**	**23 294.0**
European Union (EU28)	**1 838 900.0**	**1 902 778.0**	**1 978 285.0**	**2 190 367.0**	**2 241 286.0**	**2 810 011.0**	**3 030 601.0**	**3 331 275.0**	**3 177 281.0**	**3 299 103.0**
G20 countries excl. European Union	**2 345 021.0**	..	..	..	..	**1 879 577.0**	**2 036 300.0**	**2 145 963.0**	**2 102 213.0**	**2 257 916.0**
G20 OECD countries	**2 231 482.0**	..	..	..	..	**1 637 668.0**	**1 769 558.0**	**1 856 540.0**	**1 819 375.0**	**1 958 173.0**
G20 Non-OECD countries	**113 539.0**	..	..	..	..	**241 909.0**	**266 742.0**	**289 423.0**	**282 838.0**	**299 743.0**
MENA countries	**.. d**	..	..	..	..	**.. d**	**.. d**	**.. d**	**.. d**	**.. d**
ASEAN countries	**.. d**	..	..	..	..	**310 640.0**	**295 689.0**	**344 239.0**	**.. d**	**.. d**

- Nil; .. Not available; c Confidential data; d Secondary Confidentiality

Note: Inward FDI positions are allocated according to the ultimate investing country. Detailed metadata at: *http://stats.oecd.org/OECDStat_Metadata/ShowMetadata.ashx?Dataset=FDI_CTRY_IND_SUMM.*

Source: *OECD International Direct Investment Statistics (database): https://doi.org/10.1787/idi-data-en*

UNITED STATES

Table 3. Foreign direct investment income by country

Million US dollars

	Inward					Outward				
	2015	2016	2017	2018	2019	2015	2016	2017	2018	2019
WORLD	**149 926.0**	**141 603.0**	**174 241.0**	**206 522.0**	**208 140.0**	**433 333.0**	**430 948.0**	**518 653.0**	**543 960.0**	**532 724.0**
OECD COUNTRIES	..	..	..	..	..	**300 546.0**	..	..	..	..
Australia	1 221.0	477.0	295.0	4 381.0	3 448.0	8 743.0	6 123.0	8 025.0	10 362.0	9 256.0
Austria	509.0	569.0	855.0	1 171.0	971.0	172.0	391.0	346.0	676.0	818.0
Belgium	2 616.0	2 919.0	2 629.0	1 993.0	3 605.0	3 244.0	4 558.0	6 018.0	6 241.0	6 591.0
Canada	14 732.0	13 954.0	22 463.0	26 454.0	29 727.0	21 096.0	18 326.0	24 917.0	30 000.0	25 885.0
Chile	69.0	120.0	15.0	201.0	217.0	2 091.0	1 664.0	2 069.0	2 646.0	2 136.0
Czech Republic	-	1.0	.. c	.. c	.. c	596.0	611.0	515.0	388.0	421.0
Denmark	1 051.0	1 093.0	1 233.0	1 614.0	1 679.0	668.0	658.0	451.0	-1.0	501.0
Estonia	-	-	-	-	-	2.0	3.0	9.0	15.0	10.0
Finland	398.0	472.0	323.0	806.0	1 042.0	109.0	47.0	85.0	133.0	123.0
France	15 808.0	12 751.0	11 170.0	12 061.0	10 671.0	1 445.0	2 716.0	3 202.0	1 792.0	3 056.0
Germany	12 872.0	12 397.0	19 877.0	24 465.0	24 149.0	6 322.0	4 805.0	6 649.0	6 868.0	6 147.0
Greece	.. c	.. c	.. c	.. c	.. c	19.0	125.0	134.0	234.0	134.0
Hungary	445.0	.. c	.. c	.. c	1 980.0	591.0	447.0	532.0	543.0	388.0
Iceland	.. c	268.0	292.0	.. c	.. c	43.0	47.0	74.0	84.0	37.0
Ireland	9 772.0	7 153.0	8 599.0	9 160.0	8 787.0	56 589.0	54 310.0	62 276.0	57 701.0	63 314.0
Israel	-845.0	229.0	322.0	197.0	22.0	260.0	837.0	814.0	851.0	1 029.0
Italy	516.0	550.0	637.0	1 341.0	933.0	1 622.0	1 620.0	1 521.0	1 416.0	1 632.0
Japan	17 789.0	18 107.0	25 977.0	24 392.0	26 904.0	12 365.0	12 872.0	12 456.0	12 510.0	12 166.0
Korea	1 948.0	1 086.0	1 629.0	1 614.0	2 175.0	2 867.0	2 638.0	1 924.0	2 781.0	2 598.0
Latvia	-	-	-	1.0	1.0	8.0	11.0	10.0	8.0	7.0
Lithuania	-	-	-	-	-	-	-1.0	3.0	-1.0	5.0
Luxembourg	8 264.0	11 347.0	16 387.0	16 653.0	13 223.0	28 340.0	35 403.0	42 422.0	42 346.0	39 801.0
Mexico	1 352.0	1 372.0	1 255.0	1 414.0	1 625.0	7 351.0	6 846.0	8 733.0	8 600.0	7 357.0
Netherlands	16 069.0	11 849.0	12 070.0	19 582.0	16 513.0	70 573.0	70 098.0	79 489.0	72 504.0	83 975.0
New Zealand	-64.0	-122.0	38.0	377.0	330.0	537.0	504.0	881.0	486.0	633.0
Norway	71.0	-254.0	471.0	2 222.0	1 153.0	1 750.0	815.0	1 619.0	1 371.0	1 559.0
Poland	22.0	.. c	.. c	.. c	.. c	601.0	1 189.0	869.0	1 464.0	1 116.0
Portugal	10.0	-2.0	18.0	-47.0	.. c	207.0	167.0	190.0	146.0	171.0
Slovak Republic	-	-	-	1.0	-	37.0	-21.0	-1.0	30.0	20.0
Slovenia	-	-	-	-	-	22.0	21.0	12.0	13.0	2.0
Spain	2 105.0	1 507.0	2 037.0	3 158.0	2 960.0	3 088.0	1 864.0	2 936.0	2 854.0	3 529.0
Sweden	3 278.0	3 292.0	3 087.0	3 387.0	3 379.0	809.0	1 841.0	3 043.0	961.0	835.0
Switzerland	19 588.0	18 291.0	14 514.0	20 449.0	19 735.0	28 953.0	29 971.0	29 532.0	31 029.0	23 130.0
Turkey	.. c	115.0	69.0	.. c	128.0	412.0	260.0	622.0	605.0	451.0
United Kingdom	8 942.0	14 621.0	22 873.0	17 291.0	21 945.0	39 022.0	39 967.0	46 875.0	50 661.0	57 329.0
United States	-	-	-	-	-	-	-	-	-	-
EUROPE	**103 476.0**	**98 557.0**	**116 759.0**	**135 354.0**	**130 748.0**	**243 582.0**	**.. c**	**.. c**	**.. c**	**.. c**
Bulgaria	2.0	3.0	-1.0	7.0	5.0	71.0	58.0	41.0	50.0	48.0
Croatia	-	-	-	-	-	-2.0	10.0	11.0	11.0	12.0
Cyprus	94.0	125.0	-16.0	-94.0	-55.0	103.0	172.0	297.0	264.0	360.0
Malta	.. c	.. c	.. c	.. c	57.0	44.0	45.0	46.0	80.0	190.0
Romania	-	-	-	-	-	-60.0	24.0	169.0	219.0	387.0
Russian Federation	-286.0	-36.0	216.0	290.0	46.0	630.0	907.0	1 096.0	1 305.0	1 396.0
Ukraine	-	-	-	-	-	42.0	39.0	89.0	107.0	501.0
AFRICA	**189.0**	**4.0**	**160.0**	**232.0**	**323.0**	**2 915.0**	**2 040.0**	**2 485.0**	**3 121.0**	**3 697.0**
Northern Africa	3.0	.. c	.. c	.. c	-20.0	569.0	266.0	.. c	1 628.0	1 413.0
Algeria	-	-	-	-	-	477.0	254.0	391.0	436.0	488.0
Egypt	3.0	.. c	.. c	.. c	-20.0	105.0	180.0	581.0	1 104.0	817.0
Libya	-	-	-	-	-	-27.0	-139.0	.. c	77.0	59.0
Morocco	-	-	-	-	-	15.0	-43.0	1.0	-5.0	18.0
Tunisia	-	-	-	-	-	-1.0	14.0	16.0	16.0	31.0
Other African countries	186.0	.. c	.. c	.. c	343.0	2 346.0	1 774.0	.. c	1 493.0	2 284.0
Nigeria	.. c	.. c	8.0	.. c	.. c	1 120.0	693.0	523.0	244.0	734.0
South Africa	.. c	17.0	-36.0	68.0	250.0	420.0	288.0	596.0	315.0	580.0
AMERICA	**23 292.0**	**20 658.0**	**25 338.0**	**34 615.0**	**38 510.0**	**103 307.0**	**102 227.0**	**127 557.0**	**135 026.0**	**123 996.0**
Northern America	14 732.0	13 954.0	22 463.0	26 454.0	29 727.0	21 095.0	18 325.0	24 916.0	29 999.0	25 884.0
Central America and Caribbean countries	7 648.0	.. c	2 290.0	7 004.0	.. c	75 015.0	78 687.0	93 038.0	95 371.0	88 637.0
Bahamas	66.0	-32.0	-33.0	11.0	27.0	2 818.0	708.0	1 323.0	4 130.0	3 648.0
Bermuda	2 718.0	989.0	801.0	2 443.0	2 830.0	38 357.0	43 030.0	48 188.0	44 110.0	38 833.0
Cayman Islands	3 143.0	3 727.0	-64.0	2 475.0	2 519.0	23 664.0	25 413.0	31 880.0	33 277.0	33 504.0
Costa Rica	1.0	-1.0	1.0	-3.0	3.0	174.0	125.0	129.0	150.0	234.0
El Salvador	-	-	-	-	-	38.0	600.0	317.0	364.0	379.0
Guatemala	-	-	-	-	-	31.0	10.0	75.0	48.0	61.0
Honduras	-	-	-	-	-	61.0	114.0	74.0	67.0	290.0
Nicaragua	-	-	-	-	-	-9.0	-23.0	-18.0	-24.0	-27.0
Panama	301.0	117.0	16.0	135.0	139.0	308.0	475.0	605.0	607.0	715.0
Virgin Islands, U.S.	..	..	..	..	..	..	..	..	..	..
South America	912.0	.. c	584.0	1 156.0	.. c	7 189.0	5 205.0	9 606.0	9 649.0	9 464.0
Argentina	-88.0	-71.0	.. c	16.0	-16.0	1 451.0	1 698.0	1 811.0	1 126.0	748.0
Bolivia	-	-	-	-	-	39.0	108.0	84.0	70.0	78.0
Brazil	12.0	213.0	193.0	159.0	526.0	2 068.0	1 557.0	3 338.0	3 478.0	4 208.0
Colombia	19.0	21.0	23.0	25.0	26.0	286.0	404.0	831.0	1 124.0	1 025.0
Ecuador	1.0	.. c	3.0	7.0	8.0	99.0	147.0	127.0	-54.0	147.0
Paraguay	-	-	-	-	-	9.0	21.0	.. c	15.0	81.0
Peru	.. c	.. c	.. c	.. c	.. c	151.0	296.0	1 092.0	664.0	1 048.0
Uruguay	67.0	36.0	16.0	16.0	13.0	8.0	-54.0	111.0	124.0	75.0
Venezuela	.. c	73.0	281.0	.. c	.. c	1 094.0	-592.0	-225.0	61.0	-349.0

Table 3. Foreign direct investment income by country *(cont.)*

Million US dollars

	Inward					Outward				
	2015	2016	2017	2018	2019	2015	2016	2017	2018	2019
ASIA	**.. c**	**20 177.0**	**.. c**	**.. c**	**.. c**	**73 941.0**	**.. c**	**.. c**	**.. c**	**.. c**
Near and Middle East	-244.0	1 154.0	1 360.0	.. c	.. c	9 343.0	.. c	.. c	.. c	.. c
Gulf Arabian countries	604.0	928.0	1 042.0	.. c	.. c	8 906.0	..	8 174.0	9 340.0	.. c
Kuwait	66.0	30.0	34.0	24.0	-122.0	40.0	69.0	57.0	77.0	46.0
Qatar	.. c	.. c	.. c	.. c	.. c	6 210.0	3 343.0	5 475.0	6 904.0	4 488.0
Saudi Arabia	.. c	.. c	.. c	.. c	48.0	1 355.0	1 097.0	1 165.0	952.0	856.0
United Arab Emirates	197.0	232.0	152.0	20.0	146.0	1 809.0	1 375.0	1 597.0	1 429.0	1 557.0
Other Near and Middle East	-848.0	226.0	318.0	.. c	.. c	437.0	.. c	.. c	.. c	.. c
Jordan	-4.0	-4.0	-5.0	.. c	.. c	24.0	.. c	35.0	1.0	.. c
Other Asian countries	.. c	19 023.0	.. c	.. c	.. c	64 598.0	.. c	.. c	.. c	90 398.0
China	683.0	-745.0	321.0	1 170.0	958.0	10 674.0	12 330.0	13 634.0	13 309.0	11 852.0
Hong Kong, China	-284.0	-202.0	-662.0	464.0	296.0	5 663.0	4 763.0	7 158.0	9 655.0	9 099.0
India	477.0	120.0	199.0	210.0	-140.0	3 110.0	4 094.0	4 351.0	3 895.0	4 693.0
Indonesia	20.0	29.0	.. c	27.0	36.0	989.0	1 031.0	1 542.0	3 127.0	2 302.0
Iran, Islamic Republic of	-	-	-	-	-	-	-	-	-	-
Malaysia	-	4.0	1.0	21.0	-37.0	1 539.0	862.0	1 349.0	1 636.0	1 427.0
Philippines	.. c	2.0	2.0	3.0	2.0	435.0	815.0	855.0	535.0	756.0
Singapore	831.0	166.0	162.0	727.0	724.0	22 937.0	23 810.0	29 955.0	44 574.0	39 982.0
Chinese Taipei	554.0	381.0	622.0	736.0	493.0	1 177.0	1 343.0	1 416.0	1 448.0	1 126.0
Thailand	18.0	89.0	-3.0	-56.0	15.0	1 315.0	1 657.0	2 136.0	1 555.0	1 358.0
Viet Nam	-	-	-	-1.0	1.0	79.0	136.0	77.0	161.0	169.0
AUSTRALIA, OCEANIA AND POLAR REGIONS	**.. c**	**405.0**	**.. c**	**.. c**	**.. c**	**9 587.0**	**..**	**..**	**10 923.0**	**10 075.0**
WORLD unallocated and confidential	**2.0**	**1 802.0**	**2 058.0**	**2 034.0**	**3 244.0**	**1.0**	**-7 794.0**	**-8 029.0**	**-7 105.0**	**6.0**
European Union (EU28)	**82 831.0**	**81 615.0**	**102 630.0**	**113 176.0**	**112 267.0**	**214 242.0**	**221 139.0**	**258 148.0**	**247 618.0**	**270 923.0**
G20 countries excl. European Union	**.. d**	**.. d**	**.. d**	**.. d**	**123 413.0**	**121 942.0**	**119 175.0**	**142 457.0**	**153 102.0**	**152 512.0**
G20 OECD countries	**.. d**	**75 430.0**	**106 245.0**	**.. d**	**121 705.0**	**101 245.0**	**96 173.0**	**114 924.0**	**125 595.0**	**125 877.0**
G20 Non-OECD countries	**.. d**	**.. d**	**.. d**	**.. d**	**1 708.0**	**20 697.0**	**23 002.0**	**27 533.0**	**27 507.0**	**26 635.0**
MENA countries	**..**	**.. d**	**.. d**	**.. d**	**.. d**	**.. d**	**.. d**	**.. d**	**.. d**	**.. d**
ASEAN countries	**..**	**290.0**	**.. d**	**.. d**	**.. d**	**27 306.0**	**28 323.0**	**35 923.0**	**.. d**	**.. d**

- Nil; .. Not available; c Confidential data; d Secondary Confidentiality

Note: Detailed metadata at: *http://stats.oecd.org/OECDStat_Metadata/ShowMetadata.ashx?Dataset=FDI_CTRY_IND_SUMM.*

Source: *OECD International Direct Investment Statistics (database): https://doi.org/10.1787/idi-data-en*

UNITED STATES

Table 4. Foreign direct investment flows by industrial sector

Million US dollars

	Inward					Outward				
	2015	2016	2017	2018	2019	2015	2016	2017	2018	2019
All FDI activities	**467 625.0**	**459 419.0**	**295 296.0**	**223 401.0**	**261 412.0**	**264 359.0**	**284 469.0**	**327 781.0**	**-194 412.0**	**93 552.0**
Agriculture, forestry and fishing	**152.0**	**-249.0**	**407.0**	**831.0**	**454.0**	**172.0**	**202.0**	**-79.0**	**201.0**	**-1 204.0**
Mining and quarrying	**3 350.0**	**19 935.0**	**6 307.0**	**1 172.0**	**6 520.0**	**416.0**	**-5 073.0**	**-11 233.0**	**-3 756.0**	**-2 807.0**
Extraction activities	4 903.0	19 755.0	4 829.0	-2 527.0	6 096.0	-1 390.0	-3 478.0	-11 059.0	-3 830.0	-7 465.0
Manufacturing	**230 981.0**	**200 578.0**	**135 716.0**	**169 976.0**	**94 944.0**	**43 502.0**	**57 908.0**	**82 886.0**	**46 199.0**	**63 370.0**
of which:										
Food products, beverages and tobacco	15 928.0	24 265.0	26 663.0	35 328.0	6 729.0	5 947.0	4 722.0	9 499.0	4 937.0	4 819.0
Textiles, wood and paper products; printing	666.0	2 056.0	3 268.0	3 578.0	-290.0	470.0	969.0	2 049.0	2 411.0	1 668.0
Chemical, rubber, plastic, non-metallic mineral products	164 986.0	117 197.0	67 754.0	96 595.0	56 033.0	9 024.0	.. c	.. c	.. c	.. c
Metal and machinery products, except electrical equipment	22 071.0	32 684.0	28 920.0	20 126.0	17 668.0	14 926.0	23 406.0	43 940.0	20 479.0	17 013.0
Motor vehicles, trailers, semi-trailers, other transport equipment	21 511.0	23 903.0	8 101.0	13 309.0	15 355.0	11 282.0	7 697.0	7 995.0	5 701.0	4 777.0
Other manufacturing	5 820.0	473.0	1 011.0	1 042.0	-549.0	1 853.0	.. c	.. c	.. c	.. c
Electricity, gas, steam and air conditioning supply	**.. c**	**.. c**	**.. c**	**.. c**	**14 447.0**	**1 140.0**	**1 558.0**	**153.0**	**-1 647.0**	**593.0**
Water supply; sewerage, waste management and remediation activities	**.. c**	**.. c**	**.. c**	**.. c**	**228.0**	**-29.0**	**-124.0**	**51.0**	**-55.0**	**-401.0**
Construction	**2 563.0**	**-72.0**	**1 434.0**	**-722.0**	**12 227.0**	**174.0**	**1 008.0**	**-368.0**	**-985.0**	**-274.0**
Services	**231 243.0**	**.. c**	**145 045.0**	**43 720.0**	**132 593.0**	**218 985.0**	**228 990.0**	**256 370.0**	**-234 367.0**	**34 274.0**
Wholesale and retail trade; repair of motor vehicles and motorcycles	30 558.0	33 885.0	69 351.0	53 806.0	38 467.0	11 678.0	20 291.0	12 133.0	-15 134.0	23 357.0
Transportation and storage	7 609.0	14 495.0	8 533.0	-3 538.0	6 757.0	3 021.0	3 539.0	3 560.0	-2 257.0	1 557.0
Accommodation and food service activities	2 174.0	1 889.0	12 122.0	992.0	2 630.0	774.0	1 295.0	246.0	4 439.0	5 748.0
Information and communication	8 810.0	19 035.0	-10 934.0	5 068.0	8 262.0	13 488.0	21 466.0	16 316.0	52 178.0	2 716.0
Financial and insurance activities	152 978.0	.. c	29 587.0	44 051.0	48 169.0	168 550.0	151 306.0	201 972.0	-297 377.0	-23 325.0
Activities of holding companies	86 662.0	.. c	-1 485.0	6 189.0	19 440.0	159 366.0	137 866.0	169 491.0	-370 879.0	-29 444.0
Real estate activities	5 618.0	13 110.0	9 657.0	30 404.0	8 597.0	1 670.0	402.0	4 219.0	-19.0	-2 944.0
Professional, scientific and technical activities	22 593.0	.. c	13 021.0	-97 747.0	16 553.0	7 065.0	14 473.0	-2 580.0	14 395.0	4 912.0
Administrative and support service activities	-2 457.0	.. c	13 122.0	2 884.0	2 392.0	11 991.0	14 178.0	11 436.0	7 323.0	21 138.0
Public administration; activities of households and of extraterritorial organisations	..	..	..	..	..	..	..	..	..	..
Education	914.0	1 533.0	-948.0	-261.0	-56.0	311.0	-281.0	362.0	476.0	-115.0
Human health and social work activities	548.0	3 334.0	1 458.0	109.0	2 800.0	662.0	284.0	-958.0	283.0	173.0
Arts, entertainment and recreation	893.0	304.0	460.0	7 303.0	-1 981.0	-1 034.0	1 414.0	7 782.0	135.0	604.0
Other services	1 005.0	1 928.0	-384.0	649.0	3.0	809.0	623.0	1 882.0	1 191.0	453.0
Not allocated and confidential	**-3 700.0**	**65 383.0**	**6 387.0**	**8 424.0**	**-1.0**	**-1.0**	**-**	**1.0**	**-2.0**	**1.0**
Private real estate activities	..	..	..	..	..	..	..	..	..	..

- Nil; .. Not available; c Confidential data

Note: Detailed metadata at: *http://stats.oecd.org/OECDStat_Metadata/ShowMetadata.ashx?Dataset=FDI_CTRY_IND_SUMM.*

Source: *OECD International Direct Investment Statistics (database): https://doi.org/10.1787/idi-data-en*

Table 5. Foreign direct investment positions by industrial sector

At year end

Million US dollars

	Inward					Outward				
	2015	2016	2017	2018	2019	2015	2016	2017	2018	2019
All FDI activities	**3 354 907.0**	**3 561 808.0**	**3 786 848.0**	**4 127 175.0**	**4 458 362.0**	**5 289 071.0**	**5 518 644.0**	**6 097 690.0**	**5 801 025.0**	**5 959 592.0**
Agriculture, forestry and fishing	**4 519.0**	**3 767.0**	**4 139.0**	**5 157.0**	**5 685.0**	**6 800.0**	**6 161.0**	**5 289.0**	**5 938.0**	**5 823.0**
Mining and quarrying	**117 142.0**	**93 054.0**	**99 772.0**	**107 202.0**	**113 224.0**	**180 418.0**	**163 529.0**	**162 908.0**	**155 221.0**	**154 267.0**
Extraction activities	83 594.0	68 070.0	72 693.0	69 270.0	75 392.0	133 823.0	124 240.0	124 952.0	120 252.0	115 647.0
Manufacturing	**1 359 812.0**	**1 476 461.0**	**1 482 932.0**	**1 664 397.0**	**1 785 688.0**	**693 847.0**	**687 625.0**	**806 448.0**	**773 622.0**	**903 664.0**
of which:										
Food products, beverages and tobacco	153 111.0	132 788.0	173 145.0	202 786.0	210 010.0	115 332.0	107 656.0	139 566.0	124 572.0	127 818.0
Textiles, wood and paper products; printing	18 105.0	20 851.0	21 394.0	24 021.0	25 949.0	20 834.0	19 213.0	20 409.0	21 268.0	22 829.0
Chemical, rubber, plastic, non-metallic mineral products	708 611.0	847 652.0	784 704.0	856 121.0	.. c	204 271.0	.. c	.. c	.. c	.. c
Metal and machinery products, except electrical equipment	277 034.0	325 841.0	364 223.0	412 360.0	435 786.0	260 665.0	252 649.0	327 841.0	310 473.0	356 778.0
Motor vehicles, trailers, semi-trailers, other transport equipment	131 842.0	137 494.0	126 385.0	154 973.0	178 914.0	62 087.0	75 646.0	87 292.0	83 105.0	87 454.0
Other manufacturing	71 109.0	11 836.0	13 083.0	14 136.0	.. c	30 659.0	.. c	.. c	.. c	.. c
Electricity, gas, steam and air conditioning supply	**.. c**	**.. c**	**.. c**	**.. c**	**.. c**	**16 274.0**	**15 839.0**	**21 102.0**	**13 394.0**	**13 601.0**
Water supply; sewerage, waste management and remediation activities	**.. c**	**.. c**	**.. c**	**.. c**	**.. c**	**1 251.0**	**746.0**	**908.0**	**936.0**	**1 204.0**
Construction	**23 178.0**	**25 807.0**	**28 903.0**	**27 684.0**	**39 717.0**	**4 075.0**	**6 477.0**	**6 444.0**	**5 616.0**	**5 395.0**
Services	**1 785 372.0**	**1 881 025.0**	**.. c**	**2 220 371.0**	**2 394 903.0**	**4 386 407.0**	**4 638 266.0**	**5 094 592.0**	**4 846 300.0**	**4 875 639.0**
Wholesale and retail trade; repair of motor vehicles and motorcycles	434 145.0	435 451.0	537 472.0	583 520.0	623 924.0	291 265.0	297 274.0	324 223.0	290 076.0	305 397.0
Transportation and storage	70 394.0	85 969.0	91 683.0	136 262.0	144 333.0	33 911.0	37 566.0	39 441.0	35 874.0	37 321.0
Accommodation and food service activities	17 766.0	22 388.0	36 083.0	53 467.0	57 760.0	18 671.0	25 067.0	25 048.0	38 859.0	50 127.0
Information and communication	168 281.0	171 474.0	170 487.0	181 791.0	185 371.0	198 689.0	218 343.0	240 143.0	292 184.0	284 224.0
Financial and insurance activities	806 094.0	822 612.0	.. c	859 599.0	947 219.0	3 516 420.0	3 694 843.0	4 074 718.0	3 796 468.0	3 771 362.0
Activities of holding companies	168 184.0	183 030.0	.. c	163 344.0	183 875.0	2 678 541.0	2 869 915.0	3 169 493.0	2 836 297.0	2 788 913.0
Real estate activities	52 755.0	74 839.0	80 041.0	112 993.0	123 135.0	39 505.0	40 719.0	43 810.0	42 651.0	40 370.0
Professional, scientific and technical activities	165 832.0	190 599.0	.. c	190 922.0	208 099.0	125 583.0	147 181.0	147 331.0	157 317.0	170 183.0
Administrative and support service activities	49 615.0	53 928.0	70 573.0	69 433.0	71 354.0	132 847.0	136 518.0	150 384.0	143 110.0	164 460.0
Public administration; activities of households and of extraterritorial organisations	..	..	..	..	..	..	..	..	..	..
Education	3 655.0	5 042.0	4 048.0	3 828.0	4 029.0	2 650.0	2 426.0	2 601.0	2 651.0	2 373.0
Human health and social work activities	9 697.0	12 181.0	13 093.0	13 954.0	16 889.0	7 841.0	8 251.0	6 236.0	6 319.0	6 608.0
Arts, entertainment and recreation	3 241.0	3 371.0	3 756.0	11 056.0	9 013.0	10 799.0	9 831.0	19 607.0	19 267.0	19 853.0
Other services	3 897.0	3 171.0	2 882.0	3 546.0	3 777.0	8 226.0	20 247.0	21 050.0	21 524.0	23 361.0
Not allocated and confidential	**66 389.0**	**81 694.0**	**607 700.0**	**102 364.0**	**111 817.0**	**12 838.0**	**1.0**	**-1.0**	**-2.0**	**-1.0**
Private real estate activities	..	..	..	..	..	..	..	..	..	..

.. Not available; c Confidential data

Note: Detailed metadata at: *http://stats.oecd.org/OECDStat_Metadata/ShowMetadata.ashx?Dataset=FDI_CTRY_IND_SUMM.*

Source: *OECD International Direct Investment Statistics (database): https://doi.org/10.1787/idi-data-en*

Table 6. Foreign direct investment income by industrial sector

Million US dollars

	Inward					Outward				
	2015	2016	2017	2018	2019	2015	2016	2017	2018	2019
All FDI activities	**149 926.0**	**141 603.0**	**174 241.0**	**206 522.0**	**208 140.0**	**433 333.0**	**430 948.0**	**518 653.0**	**543 960.0**	**532 724.0**
Agriculture, forestry and fishing	**65.0**	**252.0**	**137.0**	**170.0**	**94.0**	**290.0**	**535.0**	**346.0**	**66.0**	**741.0**
Mining and quarrying	**-518.0**	**-2 289.0**	**-35.0**	**3 122.0**	**2 320.0**	**3 541.0**	**2 552.0**	**11 495.0**	**16 815.0**	**12 934.0**
Extraction activities	-1 130.0	-3 491.0	-1 680.0	1 708.0	821.0	1 143.0	-248.0	5 756.0	9 580.0	6 569.0
Manufacturing	**64 636.0**	**66 812.0**	**89 199.0**	**90 215.0**	**83 344.0**	**67 102.0**	**72 843.0**	**89 883.0**	**85 780.0**	**80 986.0**
of which:										
Food products, beverages and tobacco	5 461.0	7 885.0	11 164.0	10 168.0	11 265.0	7 840.0	6 761.0	10 006.0	8 742.0	8 676.0
Textiles, wood and paper products; printing	923.0	1 252.0	1 880.0	1 855.0	1 396.0	1 688.0	1 896.0	2 211.0	2 282.0	1 665.0
Chemical, rubber, plastic, non-metallic mineral products	35 449.0	29 525.0	48 747.0	42 024.0	37 004.0	22 245.0	28 543.0	30 537.0	29 956.0	30 442.0
Metal and machinery products, except electrical equipment	11 110.0	18 100.0	16 123.0	24 676.0	19 510.0	22 430.0	26 595.0	35 822.0	33 199.0	31 005.0
Motor vehicles, trailers, semi-trailers, other transport equipment	8 803.0	8 888.0	10 390.0	10 648.0	13 399.0	10 632.0	8 167.0	9 700.0	10 672.0	8 105.0
Other manufacturing	2 889.0	1 161.0	893.0	843.0	770.0	2 266.0	882.0	1 607.0	928.0	1 092.0
Electricity, gas, steam and air conditioning supply	**.. c**	**.. c**	**1 822.0**	**3 600.0**	**4 473.0**	**1 980.0**	**2 128.0**	**1 505.0**	**.. c**	**960.0**
Water supply; sewerage, waste management and remediation activities	**.. c**	**.. c**	**407.0**	**428.0**	**604.0**	**28.0**	**44.0**	**50.0**	**.. c**	**92.0**
Construction	**1 458.0**	**918.0**	**-437.0**	**-709.0**	**382.0**	**823.0**	**264.0**	**-35.0**	**-261.0**	**18.0**
Services	**82 089.0**	**.. c**	**83 150.0**	**109 695.0**	**116 921.0**	**359 568.0**	**352 583.0**	**415 410.0**	**440 461.0**	**436 992.0**
Wholesale and retail trade; repair of motor vehicles and motorcycles	23 551.0	14 403.0	21 959.0	33 363.0	31 706.0	24 803.0	27 382.0	27 137.0	33 715.0	34 236.0
Transportation and storage	3 793.0	3 218.0	4 719.0	7 253.0	8 086.0	3 580.0	4 334.0	4 249.0	3 495.0	4 229.0
Accommodation and food service activities	987.0	1 510.0	1 801.0	2 016.0	2 868.0	2 627.0	2 687.0	3 464.0	3 878.0	3 722.0
Information and communication	2 611.0	2 119.0	3 719.0	6 754.0	8 016.0	14 756.0	17 128.0	15 043.0	20 330.0	17 493.0
Financial and insurance activities	38 939.0	40 281.0	36 990.0	47 222.0	51 967.0	280 867.0	266 748.0	325 615.0	347 047.0	334 360.0
Activities of holding companies	7 383.0	7 661.0	9 196.0	11 952.0	10 708.0	231 586.0	220 726.0	274 381.0	284 092.0	273 661.0
Real estate activities	1 546.0	3 630.0	2 450.0	1 829.0	3 538.0	508.0	1 386.0	2 446.0	1 696.0	1 356.0
Professional, scientific and technical activities	5 602.0	2 892.0	5 096.0	4 789.0	4 773.0	12 830.0	12 038.0	12 491.0	11 117.0	17 160.0
Administrative and support service activities	4 427.0	.. c	5 637.0	5 079.0	5 231.0	17 861.0	18 668.0	21 904.0	16 000.0	21 008.0
Public administration; activities of households and of extraterritorial organisations	..	..	..	..	..	..	..	..	..	..
Education	-141.0	-174.0	-353.0	-290.0	-112.0	260.0	236.0	195.0	591.0	730.0
Human health and social work activities	754.0	829.0	885.0	842.0	599.0	215.0	150.0	197.0	206.0	221.0
Arts, entertainment and recreation	-41.0	-140.0	138.0	620.0	265.0	375.0	724.0	1 095.0	1 056.0	1 322.0
Other services	61.0	-80.0	109.0	218.0	-16.0	886.0	1 102.0	1 574.0	1 330.0	1 155.0
Not allocated and confidential	**2 261.0**	**4 586.0**	**-2.0**	**1.0**	**2.0**	**1 417.0**	**-1.0**	**-1.0**	**1 099.0**	**1.0**
Private real estate activities	..	..	..	..	..	..	..	..	..	..

.. Not available; c Confidential data

Note: Detailed metadata at: *http://stats.oecd.org/OECDStat_Metadata/ShowMetadata.ashx?Dataset=FDI_CTRY_IND_SUMM.*

Source: *OECD International Direct Investment Statistics (database): https://doi.org/10.1787/idi-data-en*

www.ingramcontent.com/pod-product-compliance
Lightning Source LLC
Chambersburg PA
CBHW061159240926
51846CB00006B/1061
9789264282889